Economics

Second Edition

MARTIN BRONFENBRENNER

Aoyama Gakuin University, Japan
Professor Emeritus, Duke University

WERNER SICHEL

Western Michigan University

WAYLAND GARDNER

Western Michigan University

Houghton Mifflin Company   Boston
Dallas   Geneva, Illinois   Lawrenceville, New Jersey
Palo Alto

We gratefully acknowledge the following sources for providing photographs used in this book: The Bettmann Archive, pp. 150, 212, 213, 647, 825. Bettmann News Photos, p. 782 (UPI photo). Brown Bros., pp. 86, 87 right, 824. Culver Pictures, Inc., p. 87 left. Milton Friedman, p. 270 (photo by Bachrach Photographers). Historical Pictures Service, Inc., pp. 390, 479. NYT Pictures, p. 570 (photos by Peter Freed). Presidential Airways, p. 784. Sygma, p. 648 (photo by Atlan). Wide World Photos, pp. 329, 331, 394. Wilmington Sales, Inc., p. 569.

Cover photograph by Michel Tcherevkoff.

Printed in the U.S.A.

Library of Congress Catalog Card Number: 86-80545

ISBN 0-395-35644-X

BCDEFGHIJ-RM-8987

To our colleagues everywhere who helped make the first edition of this book a great success so that we have the opportunity to offer this substantially improved second edition.

MB   WS   WG

Preface

From the beginning, our goal has been to write a text which would answer the needs of students and instructors concerning the well-established as well as the controversial topics in economics. To accomplish this goal, we believe that a beginning text should be (1) open-minded and searching for the best in all schools of thought where there is disagreement, (2) thorough and realistic in presenting material that is generally accepted, and (3) flexible and oriented to a broad view in matters like international trade, economic development, and comparative economic systems.

We have built these characteristics into our book. We believe that they make it an appropriate text for the late nineteen eighties. We also believe that they form the basis for the kind of "economic literacy" which sees the *applicability* of economic principles beyond the specific applications in any one topic or any one period of time.

NEW FEATURES IN THE SECOND EDITION

We have benefited greatly from suggestions offered by users of our first edition and have incorporated many of these ideas into our second edition. The following is a check-list of the more important new features in our second edition.

- Shortened and restructured introductory section.

- Improved sequence of macroeconomics material.
- Revised and simplified presentation of the Keynesian model.
- Strengthened treatment of monetary economics.
- Improved coverage of aggregate demand and aggregate supply.
- Greater integration of expectations theories.
- More applications of microeconomic concepts and tools.
- Broadened discussion of the "fourth merger wave."
- Up–to–date analysis of OPEC.
- New chapter on Government and Taxation.
- Expanded analysis of the shifting U.S. international trade position.
- New discussion of farm debt problems and U.S. farm programs.
- New material on China's economy under Deng Xiaoping.
- Several new and revised essays.
- Integrated study guide and testbank.
- New computerized ancillaries.

ORGANIZATION

Introductory Chapters

The first five chapters provide the basic groundwork for all that is to come. In the first chapter, we present a broad overview of economics. It goes beyond explaining what microeconomics and macroeconomics are about, and considers alternative economic systems and several criteria for judging them. Chapter 2 introduces the "actors on the economic stage"—households, business firms, governments, and the rest of the world. This is a new chapter in the second edition, consisting of selected materials from two chapters of the introductory section of the first edition plus information about the stock market, which was not included in the first edition. The remaining three chapters of the introductory section outline the methodology of economics, present scarcity as *the* economic problem, and introduce the basic concepts of supply and demand. From Chapter 5, which outlines supply and demand (including aggregate supply and demand), students can proceed easily to either the macroeconomics or the microeconomics section of the book.

Macroeconomics

In our second edition, macroeconomics is covered in four parts, each consisting of three chapters. The first part provides basic definitions and measurements (unemployment, inflation, index numbers, national income accounting, and the circular flow) that students need as a foundation for the theories that follow. The material on unemployment and inflation, which leads off the macroeconomics section, appeared as Chapter 15 in the first edition.

The Keynesian approach to the determination of output and employment is presented in the second part of the macroeconomics material—Chapters 9, 10, and 11. In our second edition, we have simplified these models by using the concept of autonomous consumption expenditure and by assuming a lump-sum net tax rather than the 20 percent income tax assumed in the first edition. This has enabled us to reduce the number of charts and graphs needed to present the basic Keynesian model. As in our first edition, exports, imports, and government purchases are part of the expenditures model from the very start of the exposition. They are not "add-ons," as in some texts.

Monetary economics and monetarism are presented in the third part of the macroeconomics material—Chapters 12, 13, and 14. In describing money (Chapter 12), we have added the concept of money as "a standard for deferred payments" and, in discussing monetary control institutions (Chapter 13), we have updated the material to include information about the *Garn-St. Germaine Depository Institutions Act.* We have strengthened the chapter on monetarism (Chapter 14) by (a) adding material on the "direct" mechanism for transmitting the effects of monetary actions, (b) by adding a discussion of inflationary expectations, and (c) by moving the discussion of the loanable funds market to the end of the chapter, to distinguish it more clearly from the money market and to provide a stronger presentation of modern monetarism.

Aggregate demand and aggregate supply, which are introduced in the introductory section (Chapter 5) are developed fully in Chapter 15—the lead-off chapter of the fourth part of the macroeconomics material. New in our second edition are (a) a simple graphic derivation of the aggregate-demand curve, connecting this concept with both Keynesian and monetarist models, and (b) a wage-cost-lag theory of the aggregate-supply curve to go along with the money-illusion theory of the first edition. The aggregate demand and aggregate supply presentation is thus substantially strengthened in our second edition. In Chapter 16, on demand-side macroeconomic policies, we offer new graphs to illustrate differing views about the demand-for-money curve and in Chapter 17, on supply-side policies, we have (a) enhanced our discussion of inflationary expectations theories and (b) provided a graph applying aggregate demand and aggregate supply reasoning to wage and price controls. As before, our presentations are designed to be analytical rather than political.

International Macroeconomics and Economic Development

The international aspects of economics are becoming much more important to Americans. Part

Six of our second edition begins with international macroeconomics (Chapter 18), in which we explain exchange rates and balance of payments accounting. Our second edition includes (a) a revised and simplified format for the U.S. International Accounts and (b) an expanded discussion of the U.S. balance of payments situation in the mid-1980s.

Economic growth and development (Chapter 19) are given careful economic analysis, but are also recognized as highly sensitive issues of political economy. Along with the theories of development we also offer theories of underdevelopment, presenting the views of many who claim to speak for the billions of people who live in Third World countries. Our discussion of a New International Economic Order (NIEO) in Chapter 20 is tuned to the demands of Third World leaders and the responses from the developed countries.

Microeconomics

We believe that students today should be given a solid, no-nonsense understanding of microeconomics. We begin by laying the foundations of microeconomics in Part Seven, where we analyze the behavior of consumers and firms. The discussion of consumer choice (Chapter 21) leads logically to an analysis of market demand and elasticity of demand (Chapter 22). Then, after discussing business firm choice (Chapter 23), we analyze market supply and elasticity of supply (Chapter 24).

Our application of microeconomic principles to market structures and economic performance (Part Eight) is fuller than in many texts. The basic market structures of pure competition, pure monopoly, monopolistic competition, and oligopoly are examined in Chapters 25 through 27. Then, in Chapter 28, we place strong emphasis on oligopoly and "real world" issues concerning industrial organization.

Resource markets are explained in Part Nine. The basic principles that surround all the resource markets are examined in Chapter 29, then applied specifically to labor in Chapter 30, and to capital in Chapter 31, where we have rewritten and

simplified the section on the investment demand for loanable funds. Included in Chapter 30 is a brief history of American labor unions and an analysis of how union and government policies affect wage rates.

In our second edition, we have gathered together six chapters designed to give students interesting and useful opportunities to apply basic tools and concepts of microeconomics. Chapter 32 (Government and Taxation) is a new chapter. It includes public choice models, benefit-cost analysis, the U.S. budget process, analysis of tax shifting, the economic effects of the major taxes used in the United States, and discussions of alternatives such as the "flat tax" and the Gram-Rudman-Hollings approach to controlling deficits.

Other chapters in the applied microeconomics section are Chapter 33 (Poverty and Income Distribution) which includes a new note on comparable worth, Chapter 34 (Government Antitrust and Regulation Policy) which includes a new discussion of OPEC and the world petroleum market, Chapter 35 (International Microeconomics: Free Trade versus Protection) which has a new section on the changing U.S. trade position in the 1980s, Chapter 36 (Agriculture, Food, and Hunger), which includes new material on the farm debt problem and U.S. farm programs, and Chapter 37 (Natural Resources and the Environment) which has been substantially revised from its counterpart chapter in the first edition.

Comparative Economic Systems

In Part Eleven we compare systems in the context of "more planning or less?" (Chapter 38), because all modern economies employ some planning. After exploring a few basic ideas from Marxian economics, we examine planning systems and welfare state systems actually operating in the world today. We observe that a strong ideology is no protection against errors of judgment and that no system has all the answers, whether it is "Japan, Incorporated," Soviet socialism, workers' self-management in Yugoslavia, or modern American capitalism. New material has been added on China's economy under Deng Xiaoping.

We close with a discussion of radical economics (Chapter 39). Here we examine radical movements, of both the left and the right, and include a list of questions designed to help the student discover whether he or she is in fact a radical.

Topical Essays

At the end of each part, we present an original essay, adding a special dimension to the subjects just studied. Some of these essays provide a broader perspective to the topics just examined— "Classical Economics: The Dismal Science?" and "Neoclassical Economics: The Complacent Science." Some discuss the contributions of famous economists—"John Maynard Keynes and the Great Depression"; "Friedman and Monetarism: Do Not Confuse Them!"; and "From Karl Marx to the New Left." Still others provide historical flavor or extensions of the materials covered—"Macroeconomic Policy: From the New Frontier to Supply Side"; "Japan's Economic Miracles and the International Economy." Four essays are entirely new for the second edition: "Headaches in the Economics of Inflation"; "Living With Oligopoly"; "A Real Threat to the Labor Movement?"; and "The Deregulation Movement."

We put these essays at the end of parts rather than in boxes inside chapters so as not to interrupt the reader's concentration on the text material itself. The text is complete without them. However, the essays help to tie some ideas together and to place them more clearly in their historical context.

Sequence Alternatives

MACRO-MICRO SEQUENCE In this book, macroeconomics appears before microeconomics because this is the sequence used most often in two-semester principles of economics programs. However, we have planned the book to serve equally well with a micro-first sequence. Chapters 1 through 5 come at the start of the first semester under either sequence. In a micro-first sequence,

these chapters are followed by the micro material beginning with Chapter 21. The chapters on comparative economic systems (Chapters 38 and 39) can be included in either the macro or the micro semester of a two-semester sequence.

INTERNATIONAL ECONOMICS We have also designed the book for maximum flexibility in presenting the chapters on international economics. Chapter 35 (International Microeconomics: Free Trade versus Protection) can be inserted immediately following Chapter 18 (International Macroeconomics: Exchange Rates and the Balance of Payments) in order to obtain a single section on international economics. Moreover, that section (consisting of Chapters 18, 19, 20, and 35) can be covered in either the macroeconomics or the microeconomics portion of a two-semester course sequence.

Built-in Learning Aids

A number of learning aids are built into this book. Each chapter starts with a preview, designed to show how that chapter fits into the pattern of the book and to give a foretaste of its contents. At the end of each chapter, there is a summary listing the main ideas in the chapter.

Also, at the end of each chapter are discussion questions relating to subjects studied in that chapter. Some provide problems or exercises to work out. Most are designed to encourage students to think beyond the basic concepts presented in the chapter and to gain added insight by applying the concept to real-world situations. Students can compose their own answers, which can provide the basis for classroom discussion.

At the back of the book, there is a glossary giving nearly 1,000 key economic terms and phrases and their definitions or descriptions. Most of these key terms are highlighted in the text itself, appearing in boldface type the first time they are used. A definition or description appears along with each boldface term in the text. But it is a good idea for readers to check the glossary whenever they come upon a word or phrase that they believe has special meaning in economics. Learning the language of economics is an important part of mastering the subject.

THE AUTHORS

Each of us has instructed thousands of students in elementary economics. We have used many different texts, and each of us has taught many parts of the subject—micro, macro, international, comparative systems, and points between and beyond. Each of us has his areas of special interest. However, the final product is far less the work of three individuals than it is the combined efforts of a team. Each chapter is the result of the cooperative efforts of all the authors. The result, we believe, is far superior to what any one of us could have accomplished alone.

ACKNOWLEDGMENTS

It is a pleasure to acknowledge the help we have received in writing this book and preparing it for publication. Martin Bronfenbrenner gratefully acknowledges the assistance provided by Faik Koray, Masato Yamazaki, and Chuck Yaros at Duke University. Werner Sichel and Wayland Gardner acknowledge help from their colleagues at Western Michigan University who generously shared their knowledge of economics and their teaching insights. Especially helpful were Sisay Asefa,

Phillip Caruso, Bassam Harik, Salim Harik, Emily Hoffman, Gangaram Kripalani, Jon Neill, Susan Pozo, Myron Ross, Raymond Zelder, and David Zinn. All three of us are grateful for the typing services of Bonnie Guminski and Becky Ryder.

Werner Sichel wishes especially to thank Peter Eckstein, his co-author of a previous book, *Basic Economic Concepts,* for his efforts on that volume, which have surely carried over and benefited this one. While Werner Sichel was very careful to use only examples and other material that he had initially contributed, he is indebted to Peter Eckstein for helping him to develop his ideas and materials for the earlier book.

All three of us acknowledge the help of students who, over the years, have plied us with questions that remained in our minds long after the answer was given. And, most importantly, each of us wants to acknowledge the help and support from family members who did without our company, sacrificed vacations, and in many ways were essential to the completion of the project. For Martin Bronfenbrenner, this means his wife Teruko; his children were old enough to escape involvement. For Werner Sichel, they are Beatrice, Linda, and Larry. For Wayland Gardner, they are Suzanne, Janet, Elaine, Edward, and James. We trust that they understand the depth of our appreciation.

We also want to thank the crew at Houghton Mifflin. Perhaps their help was "in the line of duty," but they managed to be nice people at the same time.

M.B. W.S. W.G.

Acknowledgments

Last but not least are the reviewers of the manuscript at various stages of its development. Rose Pfefferbaum provided an especially penetrating review as she studied the manuscript in preparing the study guide and test bank. Below are listed the reviewers of the first edition.

Robert E. Berry
Miami University, Ohio

Phillip Caruso
Western Michigan University

James M. Cypher
California State University, Fresno

Michael T. Doyle
University of Nebraska, Omaha

Max E. Fletcher
University of Idaho

Ann Garrison
University of Northern Colorado

Kathie Gilbert
Mississippi State University

Otis W. Gilley
University of Texas, Austin

Constantine Glezakos
California State University, Long Beach

Nicholas D. Grunt
Tarrant County Junior College

Robert E. Herman
Nassau Community College

Donald Holley
Boise State University

Jack L. Jeppesen
Cerritos College

Stanley R. Keil
Ball State University

Allan B. Mandelstamm
Virginia Polytechnic Institute & State University

Norris McClain
Old Dominion University

Joan M. McCrea
University of Texas, Arlington

R. D. Peterson
Colorado State University

Rose Pfefferbaum
Mesa Community College

John Pisciotta
University of Southern Colorado

Dean Popp
San Diego State University

John A. Powers
University of Cincinnati

Terry Riddle
Central Virginia Community College

Paul J. Schmitt
St. Clair County Community College

Carole Scott
West Georgia College

Arlene Silvers
Drexel University

M. Dudley Stewart, Jr.
Stephen F. Austin State University

Emily Sun
Manhattan College

John F. Walker
Portland State University

Jeffrey J. Wright
Bryant College

Invaluable assistance in preparing the second edition was provided by helpful comments from users of the first edition. These reviewers are listed below.

David Abel
Mankato State University

Jack Adams
University of Arkansas

Richard Agnello
University of Delaware

J. Barry
Fordham University

Philip Bartholomew
University of Michigan

Paul T. Bechtol
Ohio State University

Klaus Becker
University of Kansas

Carolyn Shaw Bell
Wellesley College

Calvin Blair
Wilson College

Paul Blume
Hanover College

Joe Brum
Fayetteville Technical Institute

E. Buchholz
Santa Monica College

J. Alvin Carter
Catawba College

Phillip Caruso
Western Michigan University

J. Cavallo
College of Mt. St. Vincent

Ming Chow
Kansas State University

K. Chu
California State Univeristy

Charles Cole
California State University

Robert Collier
Western Washington University

Michael T. Cook
William Jewell College

Eleanor Craig
University of Delaware

Peter Eelkema
University of Kansas

William Field
Depauw University

Carroll Foster
University of Michigan

R. Freed
*California State University,
Dominguez Hills*

Mark Gardner
Emory & Henry College

Douglas Gordon
Arapahoe Community College

A. Grow
Mesa Community College

George Hartley
Northwestern State University

Curtis Harvey
University of Kentucky

Frank Hefner
Washburn University

Ali Hekmat
Western Washington University

C. A. Hofmann
Idaho State University

Estelle Horowitz
Pratt Institute

Brooks Hull
University of Michigan

Paul C. Huszar
Colorado State University

Harry Hutchinson
University of Delaware

Eric Jacobson
University of Delaware

Larry Kendra
Cuyahoga Community College

Dan Knighton
Moorhead State University

A. Kohen
James Madison University

R. Kolinski
University of Michigan

B. Lanciaux
Hobart & William Smith College

John Larson
University of Oregon

Soyen Lee
Illinois Benedictine College

E. Liebhafsky
University of Houston, Clear Lake

M. London
Butte College

Allan B. Mandelstamm
*Virginia Polytechnic Institute & State
University*

Gabriel Manrique
Quincy College

Wolfgang Mayer
University of Cincinnati

Michelle McAlpin
Tufts University

Roger McCain
*City University of New York,
Brooklyn College*

Jesse Mercer
College of the Albemarle

Ellen Miller
University of North Carolina

Jack Minkoff
Pratt Institute

Eric Mitchell
University of New Hampshire

Gary Mongiovi
St. John's University

R. B. Moore
U.S. Naval Academy

W. Morrison
Mesa Community College

Joseph Murray
Community College of Philadelphia

P. J. Nickless
University of North Carolina

T. Lee Norman
Idaho State University

James O'Neill
University of Delaware

Carl D. Parker
Ft. Hayes State University

Peter Penndorf
Quinsigamond Community College

Myron Re
Gogebic Community College

Mike Reed
University of Nevada

Richard Roehl
University of Michigan

G. Roth
Hofstra University

Lars G. Sandberg
Ohio State University

William Shingleton
Ball State University

Nat Simons
Ohio State University

Gordon Skinner
University of Cincinnati

Charles Skoro
Boise State University

Russell E. Smith
Washburn University

J. Ronald Stanfield
Colorado State University

Barry Stregeusky
Ball State University

Gilbert Suzawa
University of Rhode Island

W. Swift
Hofstra University

K. Taylor
University of Southern California

Fred Tiffany
Bryn Mawr College

Tom Till
St. Andrew's Presbyterian College

Ralph Townsend
University of Maine

Harold L. Wattel
Hofstra University

Charles Weber
University of Michigan

James Wible
University of New Hampshire

William Wood
University of Virginia

The Complete Teaching/Learning System

- *Economics,* the hardcover text

- *Macroeconomics* and *Microeconomics,* paperbacks. International trade, comparative economic systems, and radical economics chapters included in both volumes.

- *Instructor's Manual,* prepared by the text authors. Provides for each chapter:

  Schematic Outlines

  Teaching Notes

  Suggested answers to all discussion questions in the text

  The Instructor's Manual also provides transparency masters for all figures and a number of tables in the text; and instructions for using the computerized Test Bank.

- *Study Guide,* by Rose Pfefferbaum, Mesa Community College. Provides for each chapter:

  Summary

  List of Objectives

  Review Terms

  New Terms

  Completion Exercises

  Problems and Applications

  True-False Questions

  Multiple-Choice Questions

  Discussion Questions

- *Test Bank,* A, B, C, by Rose Pfefferbaum, Mesa Community College. Over 3,000 items.

- *Two-Color Overhead Transparencies*

- *Quadrant I*

- *Computerized Study Guide*

- *Computerized Test Bank*

Suggested Outlines for One-Term Courses*

Chapter	Macro Emphasis	Micro Emphasis	Contemporary Problems Emphasis	Combined Macro-Micro
1. What Economics Is	■	■	■	■
2. The Actors on the Economic Stage	■	■	■	■
3. How Economists Approach Problems	■	■	■	■
4. Scarcity: The Economic Problem	■	■	■	■
5. Demand and Supply—or Supply and Demand	■	■	■	■
6. Unemployment and Inflation	■		■	■
7. National Income Accounting	■			□
8. The Circular Flow and Macroeconomic Equilibrium	■			■
9. The Keynesian Model	■			■
10. The Multiplier and Business Fluctuations	■			□
11. Fiscal Instruments	■			□
12. Money and Banks	■			□
13. The Federal Reserve System and Monetary Instruments	■			□
14. Monetary Economics and Monetarism	■			■
15. Aggregate Demand and Aggregate Supply	■		■	■
16. Macroeconomic Policy: Demand Side	■		■	■
17. Macroeconomic Policy: Supply Side	■		■	■
18. International Macroeconomics: Exchange Rates and the Balance of Payments	■	□	■	■
19. Economic Growth and Development	■		■	

*Our assumption is that each of these would be a first course in economics

Chapter	Macro Emphasis	Micro Emphasis	Contemporary Problems Emphasis	Combined Macro-Micro
20. A New International Economic Order? North-South Confrontation	□		■	
21. Consumer Choice		■		■
22. Market Demand and Elasticity		■		■
23. Business Firm Choice		■		■
24. Market Supply and Elasticity		■		■
25. Pure Competition		■		■
26. Monopoly		■		■
27. Monopolistic Competition and Oligopoly		■		■
28. Oligopoly: The Real World		■	■	
29. Resource Supply and Demand		■		□
30. Labor, Wages, and Collective Bargaining		■	■	□
31. Capital, Interest, and Investment		■	■	□
32. Government and Taxation		■	■	
33. Poverty and Income Distribution		■	■	
34. Government Antitrust and Regulation Policy		■	■	
35. International Microeconomics: Free Trade Versus Protection	□	■	■	■
36. Agriculture, Food, and Hunger		■	■	
37. Natural Resources and the Environment		■	■	
38. Comparative Economic Systems—More Planning or Less?	□	□	■	■
39. Radical Economics	□	□	■	□

■ = recommended   □ = optional

Contents in Brief

Contents

CONTENTS

V AGGREGATE DEMAND, AGGREGATE SUPPLY AND MACROECONOMIC POLICY 273

Introduction to Economics

- ■ What Economics Is
- ■ The Actors on the Economic Stage
- ■ How Economists Approach Problems
- ■ Scarcity: The Economic Problem
- ■ Demand and Supply — or Supply and Demand

1 *What Economics Is*

PREVIEW Surely you have heard at least one of the following opinions: "Economists know the price of everything and the value of nothing." "Economists have an irrational passion for dispassionate rationality." "Supply and demand—that's all there is to economics. The rest is nonsense." "If economics were a science, the economists would have all the money, and the rest of us would be broke." "Economics is about what everyone knows in language nobody understands." "Economists are a bunch of do-gooders who want to create a welfare state." "Economists are stooges and mouthpieces of Wall Street; they are for sale to the highest bidder." "If you stretched all the economists end to end, it would be a good thing, but they would reach no conclusion." Notice that some of these criticisms are inconsistent with others. Any of them may be true of one or more particular economists, but they cannot *all* be true of *all* economists (or of economics) at the same time.

This chapter gives an overview of what economics is. After some formal definitions of the subject, we consider its two main divisions, microeconomics and macroeconomics. Microeconomics focuses on individual decision makers, like consumers and business firms, whereas macroeconomics deals with the overall performance of the economy. We also examine economic growth and development, which consider how economies may change over time.

After surveying the basic content of economics, we explore how economic systems are organized to deal with economic problems. Some are organized around systems of markets; others are based on planning. Similarly, some are based on private property ownership and others have collectivist agencies that own the tools of production.

We close by listing a set of criteria that might be used to decide which type of economic system works best. We stress, however, that each person must use his or her own values in answering that sort of question. Our list can only start you thinking about this subject.

WHAT IS ECONOMICS?

Many definitions have been offered for **economics.** Most focus on either (a) the problems that economists usually deal with or (b) the methods that economists use in dealing with these problems. An example of the "problem" type of definition is the following, taken from a widely used textbook:

> Economics can be defined as the social science concerned with the problem of using or administering scarce resources (the means of producing) so as to attain the greatest or maximum fulfillment of society's unlimited wants (the goal of producing).[1]

An example of the "methods" type of definition comes from the famous economist John Maynard Keynes (1883–1946), who said,

---

1. Campbell McConnell, *Economics,* 9th ed. (New York: McGraw-Hill, 1984), p. 18.

It [economics] is a method rather than a doctrine, an apparatus of the mind, a technique of thinking which helps its possessor to draw correct conclusions.[2]

Most of the "problems" definitions, such as the first one given above, focus on situations that arise as a result of **scarcity**—defined as a situation in which the amount of something actually available would not be sufficient to satisfy the desire for it if it were provided "free of charge." Because of scarcity, people find it necessary to give up some things they enjoy so they can obtain other things they want more urgently. In other words, they make choices.

The "methods" definitions focus on how economists deal with problems rather than on the problems themselves. They see economics as a tool kit or "apparatus of the mind" that enables the economist to "draw correct conclusions" not only about subjects ordinarily considered economic but about human actions quite generally. For example, the "new home economics" of Professor Gary Becker and his disciples applies the technical apparatus of economics to the analysis of such problems as whether or not to marry, or have children, or engage in criminal activity.

Now it is time for you to make an economic decision—that is, whether or not to memorize one or more definitions of economics. Memorizing a definition will take some time, and that time could be used by you to do other things. The "problems" approach focuses on the fact that you do not have enough time to do everything that you would like to do. The "methods" approach suggests comparing the benefits of memorizing a definition with the benefits that would come from the best alternative use of your time. Memorizing can be a useful method of learning. But understanding that economics is about scarcity and practicing the processes of economic reasoning will probably do you more good than memorizing a definition. You must make your own evaluation of benefits when comparing one alternative with another. Economic training can sharpen the ability to do this, but each person's own values must be used in actual decisions.

2. J. M. Keynes, in introducing each of a series of *Cambridge Economic Handbooks* in the 1920s.

MICROECONOMICS AND MACROECONOMICS

The study of economics is generally divided into two main parts, one called microeconomics and the other called macroeconomics. These two divisions make up the main body of economic analysis. However, there are many special areas of application, such as international trade, government finance, industrial organization, and labor economics, that are important extensions of both parts of this main body.

Microeconomics: Three Basic Choices

Microeconomics focuses on the behavior of decision makers in the economy. A person in his or her role as a consumer or a worker is a decision maker. Business firms and governments are decision makers too. Microeconomics centers on how these decision makers choose among alternatives and what are the results of these choices.

Microeconomics is built around three basic types of choice that must be made in any economy: (1) What goods and services shall be produced, and how much of each per time period? (2) How shall they be produced, with what proportions of labor to machinery (including robots), or of machinery to natural resources, or of natural resources to labor—and within the work force, with what proportions of more-skilled to less-skilled workers? (3) To whom shall the final products be distributed? How much should go to the suppliers of labor, how much to the suppliers of natural resources, and how much to the suppliers of machinery and equipment? Or if we look at the distribution question through personal glasses, how much should go to the poor, how much to the middle classes, and how much to the rich? All these problems are interrelated.

WHAT TO PRODUCE Every economic system must establish some way of deciding what to produce. Each must make this decision because of scarcity.

Consider, for example, the question of what to produce with certain land resources available to an economy. Shall dairy cattle be grazed so that milk can be produced? Shall beef cattle be grazed so that meat can be produced? Shall corn be grown so that breakfast cereal (or bacon) can be produced? Shall the land be used for a baseball playing field so that recreational services can be produced? Shall a factory be built on it so that manufactured goods can be produced? Shall residential houses be built on it? The possibilities are almost unlimited, but some decision must be made.

HOW TO PRODUCE The question of how to produce is quite different from the question of what to produce. Ice cream can be made in a small shop with a hand-cranked or motor-driven ice cream maker, or it can be produced in a large automated factory in quantities large enough to serve all the people in a great city or a large region. Corn can be grown intensively, with much fertilizer and irrigation, or it can be grown extensively, with more land and less fertilizer or irrigation. Roads can be built with thousands of pick-and-shovel laborers moving soil in woven baskets, or they can be built with huge earthmoving machines and fewer workers. Every economic system must provide some method of choosing among the different available technologies of production.

FOR WHOM TO PRODUCE Microeconomic decisions must also be made about which individuals or groups of people will enjoy the goods and services that are produced. Should all persons who are part of the economy share equally in the results of its productive undertakings? Should inequality be permitted in the distribution of the finished goods and services? How much inequality can be justified? If some are to receive more than others, how shall the lucky ones be chosen? This is the "for whom" aspect of microeconomics. It often is called "distribution of income," although income should be understood as goods and services rather than money. Every economic system must establish ways of answering this question.

Macroeconomics: Analysis of Aggregate Economic Activity

Macroeconomics is the part of economic analysis that deals with aggregate, or "grand total," economic activity. The actions of the separate decision makers that are analyzed in microeconomics are added together in macroeconomics in order to focus on things that affect the economy as a whole. The two main topics of macroeconomics are inflation and unemployment, although there are important macroeconomics aspects to international trade and economic growth as well.

Inflation is a sustained increase in the general level of prices. Figure 1-1 illustrates inflation in the United States since 1960, measured by using the consumer price index (cost-of-living index). The price level today is more than three and one-half times as high as it was in 1960, which means that a dollar today buys less than 30 percent as much as one did in 1960. Inflation can put great strains on an economy and on the social arrangements supporting it.

Unemployment, the second main topic of macroeconomics, means that some people who would like to work at the going wage rates are not able to find a job. Unemployment in the United States over the past 25 years, as measured by official statistics, is shown in Figure 1-2.

Unemployment actually is a topic that fits into both macroeconomics and microeconomics—in other words, there are two general types of unemployment as far as economic analysis is concerned. Unemployment is a microeconomic matter if a person's failure to find a job can be traced to decisions about what to produce or how to produce. For example, if people decide to stop playing golf and start playing tennis, there is likely to be unemployment among people who are trained to work as golf pros and are trying to find such jobs. This would be **microeconomic unemployment** because the reason can be traced to decisions about what to produce. Similarly, if banks switch to electronic teller machines run by bank customers, people who are trained as bank tellers may fail to find jobs in that line of work. This kind of unemployment can be traced to a decision about how to produce, so it also can be

FIGURE 1-1   Inflation in the United States

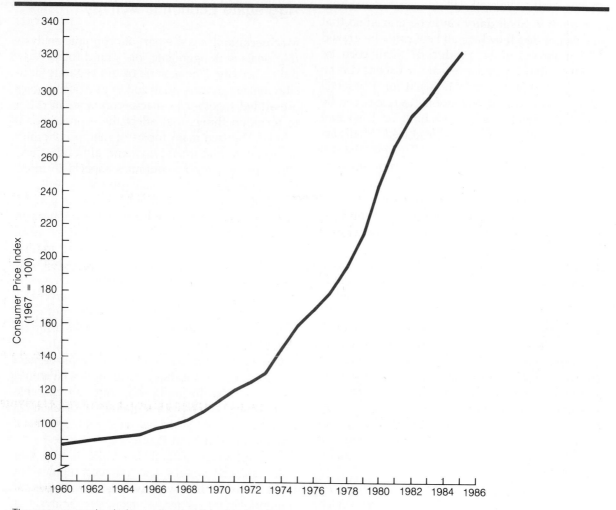

The consumer price index, or "cost-of-living" index, is one way of measuring inflation. This index has increased greatly over the past 25 years.

Source: Economic Report of the President, 1986, Table B-55.

called microeconomic unemployment. In most economies, changes are taking place almost continually in matters of what and how to produce. Therefore, some amount of microeconomic unemployment usually exists. But this unemployment will be concentrated in certain industries or areas and will be more or less short-term.

Macroeconomic unemployment is the kind that exists throughout the whole economy (or at least affects many parts of the economy at the same time) and that is not related to particular decisions about what or how to produce. Golf pros, bank tellers, tennis pros, and many others are out of work at the same time, and their job searches are

FIGURE 1-2   Unemployment in the United States

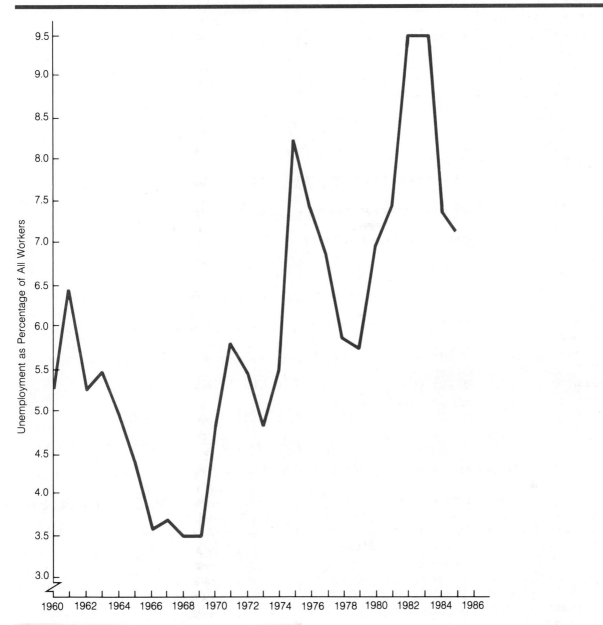

The unemployment rate is the number unemployed divided by all workers.

Source: Economic Report of the President, 1986, Table B-35.

all unsuccessful. Macroeconomic unemployment sometimes is called "cyclical" unemployment because it comes during bad times or recessions, when total unemployment rises far above the amount of normal microeconomic joblessness.

ECONOMIC GROWTH AND DEVELOPMENT

Economic growth and development are economic topics that are considered sometimes part of macroeconomics and sometimes part of microeconomics, but they could, perhaps, be considered separate branches of economics in themselves. Though related, economic growth and economic development are not the same thing.

Economic Growth: More of the Same Output

Economic growth means more output per capita of essentially the same collection of goods and services. Development, on the other hand, means "progress," usually represented by some different and presumably "better" lifestyle or collection of goods. We can illustrate the difference between them with the aid of the well-known story of Robinson Crusoe and his Man Friday, catching fish and raising vegetables on their Pacific island. Imagine a female Crusoe and a female Friday somehow added to the party, so that the Crusoes and Fridays increase and multiply. Imagine too that every Crusoe, as well as every Friday, becomes a successful practitioner of fishing, farming, boat making, or net making by the original Crusoe-Friday methods. The amount of boats and nets, total and per capita, increases steadily, along with the income to the island population. Does this fanciful tale represent economic growth? Yes, it does. After a generation or two the Crusoes and the Fridays are economically better off than before. Is it economic development? Probably not. The islanders are still consuming the same old products produced and distributed in the same old ways. All they have is more of the same, piled higher and deeper.

Economic Development: Growth Plus Progress

Economic development is growth plus other changes that are judged to constitute "progress" or to make life "better." Clearly, the concept of economic development raises many questions that involve value judgments about whether particular changes or lifestyles are good or bad. Typically, economic development includes distributional and quality-of-life considerations. A country whose measured growth is concentrated in a particular region, like the Rio de Janeiro–São Paulo area of Brazil, ranks lower in development than in growth since most Brazilians are untouched by these changes. This is the case as well when economic growth has not touched the lower half of the income distribution—so that "the figures prosper while the people suffer," to quote Premier George Papandreou of Greece.

What are some of the indexes used to measure economic development? Some that have to do with health, education, and welfare are a rising life expectancy at birth, a rising literacy rate, equalizing trends in the distributions of income and wealth, rising numbers of educational and health service personnel per thousand people, falling death and illness rates from contagious and deficiency diseases, and falling dependence on subsistence agriculture. Other kinds of indexes are the rising consumption of steel and electricity per capita, rising ratios of saving and investment to total income, and rising proportions of the representative family budget available for purchases other than food. The biases are obvious; no one index tells the whole story. Even so, it is fairly clear what all these indexes are driving at. Table 1-1 shows how some countries compare according to two indexes of development.

HOW SOCIETIES SOLVE ECONOMIC PROBLEMS

Economic systems are the combinations of institutions that different societies have developed to deal with economic problems. These systems can

TABLE 1-1   Indexes of Economic Development

Infant Mortality (selected countries, various years)[a]	Illiteracy (selected countries)[b]
0	0
Japan, Netherlands	United States, Soviet Union, Japan
10 Australia, Canada, W. Germany	5
United States, E. Germany	Thailand, Yugoslavia
20	10
	Philippines
30 Soviet Union	15
Argentina	
40	20
	Brazil
50	25
Mexico	
60	30 China
Philippines	
70	35
Brazil	
80	40 Kenya
90	45
Algeria	Iran
100	50 Algeria
110 Iran	55 Egypt
South Africa	India
120	60
India, Turkey	Mozambique
130	65
	Bangladesh
140 Tanzania	70 Pakistan
Bangladesh	
150	75 Afghanistan
160	80
170 Nigeria, Zaire	
180 Mozambique	

a. Deaths of children under one year of age per 1,000 live births in a calendar year.

b. Percentage of population fifteen years of age and over unable to read and write in any, or a specified, language. Data are for 1985 except for the United States, the Soviet Union, and Japan, which are 1980 data.

Source: Statistical Abstract of the United States, 1986, Tables 1469 and 1471; *Statistical Abstract of the United States,* 1985, Table 1480, and United Nations Educational, Scientific, and Cultural Organization, Paris, France, *Statistical Yearbook* and "Estimates and Projections of Illiteracy," CSR E-29.

generally be classified on two bases, the *mechanism* and the *ownership* bases. As we shall see, these bases are not wholly independent of each other in practice.

On the mechanism basis, we have *market* and *planning* systems. We also have *traditional* systems in parts of the world that are not highly industrialized. On the ownership basis, we have *capitalist* and *socialist* (or more accurately, *collectivist*) systems. In a **capitalist system,** most things can be owned privately. In a **collectivist system,** land and machinery are owned by collective bodies. In a **socialist system,** the particular collective body that owns land and machinery is the state. Most market economies are capitalist, and most planned economies are socialist. However, Sweden and Japan are capitalist economies with a great deal of planning, and Hungary and Yugoslavia are socialist ones with active elements of the market mechanism.

Actually, all existing economies are *mixed* and none is *pure*. But the composition of the mix varies so greatly that they can be treated as different in kind. We shall call the United States a *market capitalist economy*, despite important elements of planning and/or socialism, ranging from the defense establishment to your city's water-purification plant. And we shall call the Soviet Union a *planned socialist economy*, despite important elements of capitalism and the market mechanism, such as peasants growing and selling products from their private plots within the collective farms. We do not call the Soviet Union a communist economic system, however. A **communist** is a socialist who believes that, after a few generations of near-worldwide socialism, socialist economies will reach a state of communism where most or all important goods will become free, scarcity will have been eliminated, and economics will have no excuse for existence. The Soviet leaders profess to believe that someday the U.S.S.R. will approach a communist economy, but that this utopia has not yet been attained.

Market or Planning?

Every economic system devises, or more often inherits, *mechanisms* that it uses to make the three

FIGURE 1-3   Microeconomic Decisions in a Market Economy

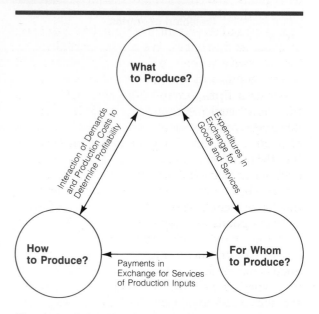

The three circles identify the three microeconomic questions that must be answered in any economic system. The double-headed arrows suggest that, in market systems, the answer to each question both requires information from and provides information for the answer to each of the other questions.

basic microeconomic decisions of *what* goods and services (and how much of each) to produce, *how* to combine inputs to produce these things, and *for whom* among the population these goods are being produced. In modern economies, these decisions are made more or less impersonally and automatically by market mechanisms, or more or less deliberately and personally by planning mechanisms, or by some combination of the two.

MARKET ECONOMIES   Figure 1-3 presents a simple picture of how these decisions are organized in a **market economy.** In this figure, each of the circles stands for one of the basic decisions that must be made in an economic system. Each of these circles is connected to each of the other circles. If we put ourselves inside the "for whom" circle, we are members of households that (under the capitalist system) own productive inputs such as labor, machinery, and natural resources and buy goods and services to consume. We are connected to the "how" circle because we provide inputs for and receive income from the production of goods and services. We are connected to the "what" circle when we spend our income and receive goods and services in exchange.

Business firms occupy both the "what" and the "how" circles. In the "what" circle, they are deciding what goods and services (and how much of each) to produce. They do this by interpreting the dollar votes that come from the "for whom" circle when households purchase goods and services and by combining this with information from the "how" circle about the costs of producing different goods and services.

In the "how" circle, firms are deciding what mixtures of productive inputs to use in producing goods and services. Information is received from the "what" circle about which goods and services are demanded and from the "for whom" circle about the costs of the different productive inputs that can be used to produce them.

Our tour of the connected circles shows that the market mechanism is actually an integrated process, not just pure chance or "jungle law."

PLANNED ECONOMIES The planning mechanism answers the same three microeconomic questions, but does so in a different way. The Soviet revolutionary leader Vladimir Ilich Lenin (1870–1924) thought this way was so simple that it could be explained in adequate detail to any semi-literate Russian worker or peasant. However, he seems to have been too optimistic.

The three microeconomic decisions for a **planned economy** are again shown by three circles in Figure 1-4. In addition, there is a fourth circle, representing the government in its planning function; in the U.S.S.R., it is an institution called Gosplan. The government (Gosplan) coordinates decisions in the three areas of microeconomics. In a pure planned system, there are no direct links between "what," "how," and "for whom." Each of the three microeconomic decisions depends upon the priorities set by government in the central circle.

Not being fools and having lived through failures, the bureaucrats of Gosplan (as well as the

FIGURE 1-4   Microeconomic Decisions in a Planned Economy

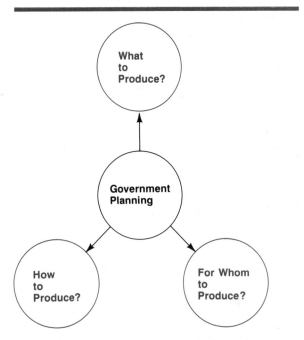

The three circles identify the three microeconomic questions that must be answered in any economic system. The single-headed arrows suggest that, in a planned economy, the answers to the three questions are worked out and coordinated through government planning in the central circle.

party politicians and military people looking over their shoulders) realize that a plan is not a magic wand. They know that the three types of decisions must be consistent with each other. Writing numbers down on paper will not produce the shoes and ships and sealing wax represented by these quantities. So the planners use elaborate statistical techniques to replace the market in integrating their several decisions. Not only is the detail of these techniques beyond the understanding of the Soviet worker or peasant whom Lenin hoped to draw into the planning process, but it is beyond the level of this book. The plans seldom work out perfectly. Neither, however, does "the obvious and simple system of natural liberty," the market mechanism as described by Adam Smith, the eighteenth-century scholar who wrote the *Wealth of Nations* and who is credited with launching the modern study of how markets operate.

TRADITIONAL ECONOMIES   It is, of course, much harder to generalize about **traditional economies,** but certain features are common to a good many of them. A great deal of property, particularly in land, is often held by a clan or tribe in common; Karl Marx spoke of this as "primitive communism." At the same time, there is much barter trade (exchanging goods for goods without the use of money) both within tribes and across tribal lines; the anthropologist Sol Tax calls this "penny capitalism." As for the major economic decisions, they are generally made by rulers (priests, kings and queens, chiefs, feudal barons, medicine men) either singly or in conference. They tend to be made on the basis of ethical ideas like "just" prices for goods and "fair" wages for labor, or the "duty" of at least the eldest child to follow the family's occupation of farming or fishing or pottery making. Rather than attempting economic planning or trusting any abstract market mechanism, primitive economies count on divine help, achieved through magic, prayers, and sacrifices, to solve any problems that may result from droughts or floods or earthquakes. The Islamic Republic of Iran under the Ayatollah Khomeini can be regarded as a revival of a traditional kind of economy. The guiding principles are religious or ethical in nature, with little concern for efficiency or progress in the modern sense.

Capitalism or Socialism?

Let us now turn to the *ownership* basis for classifying economic systems. In a *capitalist economy,* which usually relies upon the market mechanism, natural resources and machinery may be privately owned just like food, clothing, or other consumption goods. Not only is private ownership legal, either by individuals or by those "legal persons" called corporations, but it is the dominant form of ownership. In capitalist countries, people engage in the economic game routinely and automatically. They do so as decision makers, as property owners, as workers, and as consumers. The most important motives for engaging in economic activities are, of course, the increase in income and wealth and the satisfaction derived from income and wealth.

In a *collectivist economy,* natural resources and machinery are owned only by collective groups. Individuals, however, may own consumption goods privately. The main appeal of socialism and all other collectivist systems is greater equality. These systems strive for a higher standard of living for the poor and an end to poverty, at the expense of the rich rather than of the people in general. Socialists believe that property in productive inputs should belong predominantly to the political state as trustee for the community as a whole.

EVALUATING ECONOMIC SYSTEMS

When Nikita Khrushchev banged his shoe on a United Nations table in the early 1960s and roared, "We shall bury you!" we can only guess what the head of the Soviet state may have meant. The meaning for some is that Khrushchev expected a few more years of competitive coexistence—the period 1960–1980 was often mentioned—to prove the superiority of planned socialism over market capitalism. Other leaders, who favored capitalism, were making exactly the opposite forecasts for the same period, without (to our knowledge) emphasizing their arguments with their shoes. In any case, 1980 has come and gone, leaving the argument still open.

Six Criteria

What do we mean, anyhow, when we say that one economic system outperforms another? This is basically a subjective value judgment. It may be based on a great many criteria weighted in a great many different ways, not all of them conscious. We suggest here six criteria or bases of judgment, with no weighting system at all. (Other economists use somewhat different criteria, and some try to rank them by importance.) On some of our criteria, the United States performs better than the Soviet Union; on others, the Soviet Union comes out on top.

1. CURRENT STANDARD OF LIVING   Nearly all of us believe that, other things being equal, a high standard of living here and now is better than a lower one. As the famous singer Sophie Tucker put it, "I been rich and I been poor, but believe me, rich is better." It can be said, however, that even our present living standard may be too high for our own good, because some of us "dig our graves with our teeth," not to mention our lack of exercise. To quote Oliver Goldsmith's *The Deserted Village,*

Ill fares the land, to hast'ning ills a prey,
Where wealth accumulates, and men decay.

Standard of living is usually measured in terms of current income or consumption per person, but the results differ when other measures are used. Not enough attention is paid to per capita *wealth*. Also, this criterion allows an economic system to claim credit for what may be due to a favorable location, rich natural resources, or a large population of working age.

2. ECONOMIC GROWTH—FUTURE STANDARD OF LIVING   Nearly all of us believe that living standards, at least for "the poor," should improve over time, and also that overall economic growth will make this more likely to happen. People are generally happier when they expect progress than when "Tomorrow, and tomorrow, and tomorrow,/Creeps in this petty pace from day to day." The prospect of progress is also an incentive for people to put forth the extra effort to make it a reality. At the same time, there may be limits to growth set by food, energy, raw materials, pollution, and sheer physical entropy, so that the same growth that raises economic prospects for our children may only make things worse for our grandchildren.

3. EQUITY OF DISTRIBUTION   Everyone is in favor of "equity" and "fairness," but nobody knows what it consists of, or how important it is. **Equity**

may, but need not, mean "equality" in consumption, income, or wealth. Without economic incentives for risk taking and the development of their economic potentials, the gifted and talented may complain of unfair treatment. Some balance—called by economists a tradeoff—must be achieved between what socialists call the "freedom to exploit" and the ethical judgments of ordinary people who feel that some limits should be placed on inequality. Different economies have consciously or unconsciously hit upon different compromises. Socialist distributions, incidentally, are *not* automatically closer to being equal than capitalist ones. Peter J.D. Wiles, in *Distribution of Income: East and West,* for example, argues that the capitalist United Kingdom is more egalitarian in practice than either the capitalist United States or the socialist Soviet Union. The same argument might be made for capitalist Holland or the Scandinavian countries. On the other hand, he finds socialist Poland more egalitarian than Britain.[3]

Intergroup income distributions within a society are also important. Japanese critics, among others, fault the income position of blacks, Hispanics, and American Indians in the United States, charging quite reasonably that it is due to racial discrimination. But if Japan's own minorities were as large as the American ones, Japanese discrimination and racism problems would probably be about as serious as those in the United States.

4. SECURITY OF THE LIVING STANDARD   People want to be sure that they will not wake up tomorrow morning to find that their jobs have disappeared without warning in a business cycle downturn, and that they have no other way to maintain their standard of living. Neither do they want to lose their living standards more gradually but just as hopelessly because of technical changes, such as when railroad trains are replaced by trucks and airplanes, or unskilled labor is made idle by robots. This goal suggests an advantage of the large country over the small one, given the difficulties of international migration. It also suggests that an economy, particularly a small one,

3. Peter J.D. Wiles, *Distribution of Income: East and West* (Amsterdam: North Holland Publishing Co., 1974).

should not be tied to a single industry. Finally, it suggests the desirability of defenses against these cyclical and technical declines.

5. COMPATIBILITY WITH HUMAN RIGHTS Without going into detail as to precisely what human rights are or by what actions they should be protected, we may safely say that an economy that depends on conscripts and prisoners for a major part of its labor force can be faulted on these grounds. This is what Solzhenitsyn says about the Soviet Union in *The Gulag Archipelago*. So, obviously, may be faulted a slave economy like the American South for about two hundred years before the Civil War—and in some states for several generations afterwards. Both China under Mao Zedong and the Soviet Union ever since the Russian Revolution have been accused of working people to death in and out of prison camps to speed up their economic development. In the nineteenth century, similar accusations were made against the Central Pacific Railroad in the United States, where the workers concerned were Chinese contract laborers.

6. COMPATIBILITY WITH PHYSICAL AND MENTAL HEALTH A high "standard of living" is not synonymous with a high "quality of life." A particular economic system may enhance one while making the other more difficult to achieve. In the United States today, some argue that the competitive "rat race" of the capitalist struggle to get ahead drives people to mental hospitals in large numbers.[4] According to some psychologists and psychiatrists, any economy that encourages "keeping up with the Joneses" and conspicuous consumption, while making inadequate provision for the poor, is incompatible with physical and mental health. In such an economy, there are many sources of harmful stress: too heavy a

---

4. It cannot be doubted that the statistical probability of spending part of one's life in a mental institution is unusually high in the United States; it has been estimated as high as one out of eight. But this figure reflects greater availability of such institutions in the United States and also the greater life expectancy of the adult American, which increases the likelihood of senility.

workload, impossible deadlines, the loss of a job, and all sorts of financial worries. It should not be inferred, however, that similar problems are unknown in collectivist societies. Unrealistic expectations and work quotas, the possible loss of a job, and other economic ills are part of the worker's lot in the Soviet Union too.

Policy Tradeoffs

Conflicts often arise among accepted social goals, so that choices and tradeoffs are necessary at the most general policy levels. We have noted already what the late economist Arthur Okun called "the big tradeoff" between the common desire to maintain incentives for work and risk taking and the common desire to limit inequality in income and wealth. Another example is the experience of the United Nations in promoting economic growth and development between 1950 and 1970. Measured *economic growth*, our second criterion, appeared to be going quite well. In fact, the less-developed countries grew more rapidly as a group than did the more-developed (industrialized) countries, narrowing the measured gap between them. But *economic development*, which is generally defined to include most or all of our last four criteria, was disappointing. Conditions in rural areas and for the urban poor remained largely unaffected and unimproved in many countries with the highest growth rates. So development specialists, including economists, rejected as "growthmanship" the focus on measured national income and its rate of change per capita. They offered instead a plan based on providing every family in every developing country, rural as well as urban, with **basic human needs.** These needs were defined as minimal amounts of food, clothing, shelter, education, health care, and sometimes also "access" to public decision making. Only after these needs are met, runs the argument, should attention be paid to attaining economic growth. The conflict continues in the developing countries, in the aid-giving industrial countries, and in the international agencies, with no solution or compromise presently in sight.

WHY SO HARD?

Why is economics supposed to be so hard—harder for many students than history or many other social sciences? There are three reasons; if you are prepared, you will have less to worry about.

The first reason is that economics and economists are likely to challenge some of your previous half-formed ideas. You may temporarily find yourself unlearning more than you learn, or operating in a fog of confusion.

The second reason is that economics, like Switzerland, talks three languages at once. There is the language of words, which for us is English. There is the language of diagrams and graphs. And there is also the language of mathematics, which is used more and more extensively as the student goes on to advanced work. Just as the educated Swiss is translator and interpreter between and among the three languages of his or her country, the good economist should be a translator and interpreter among the three languages of this discipline. This is not, for many people, an easy task.

A third reason is that economics makes extensive use of theories and models involving more assumptions and higher levels of abstraction than many students have yet encountered. These theories and models are a fundamental part of the "methods," or "way of thinking," view of economics. Since one theory often builds on another, it is important to get a solid grasp of each one before going on to the next. So careful learning, step by step, is important in economics.

SUMMARY

1. Some definitions of economics stress subject matter—how scarcity is dealt with and how people's wants are satisfied. Another type of definition stresses the methods and techniques used by economists.

2. The two main branches of economics are microeconomics and macroeconomics. Micro-economics is the part that focuses on the behavior of decision makers who are inside or part of a larger economic system. Every economic system must provide ways of answering the microeconomic questions of what to produce, how to produce, and for whom to produce.

3. Macroeconomics is the branch of economics that deals with aggregate or "grand total" economic activity. It examines how the whole economic system operates and focuses mainly on the topics of inflation and unemployment.

4. Inflation is a sustained increase in the general price level. Unemployment may be either microeconomic or macroeconomic, depending on the reason why a person is unable to find work. Microeconomic unemployment arises because of changes in the types of goods and services produced or in the ways of producing them—the what and how decisions in microeconomics. Macroeconomic unemployment extends over the whole economy and affects many different occupations at the same time.

5. Economic growth and development are two other important economic subjects. Economic growth is a measured percentage rise each year or each decade in production, either total or per capita. Economic development means economic growth as well as some improvements in the "quality of life" and in the distribution of income.

6. Economic systems are the combinations of institutions that societies have set up to deal with economic problems. On a mechanism basis, they can be classified as market economies or planned economies. Market economies integrate the various economic questions through the institutions of free exchange in markets. Planned economies use governments and other agencies to accomplish this integration. All existing economies are mixed, with elements of both market and planning systems.

7. Economic systems can also be classified on the basis of ownership. In capitalist systems, private property rights extend from ordinary consumption goods to productive inputs. In collectivist systems, productive inputs (except for labor) are collectively owned. If the agency owning these goods is the political state or an agency of the state, we have socialism, which is the most important form of collectivism.

8. A capitalist economy is more apt to rely on the market mechanism than is a collectivist one. Collectivist (including socialist) economies are more likely to be planned than are capitalist ones. Conversely, a market economy is apt to be capitalistic, and a planned economy socialistic, but there are important exceptions to this generalization.

9. In traditional economies, custom and religion play major parts. Much property is usually held in common, and occupations tend to remain in families. There is much stress on "justice" in price and wage fixing, and often we find resort to prayer, magic, and the supernatural. In these economies, the important decisions are made by kings and queens, chiefs, priests, or feudal lords.

10. Six criteria are suggested for evaluating economic systems: (a) a high current living standard; (b) economic growth, pointing to a high future living standard; (c) "equitable" distributions of income and wealth; (d) security of the living standard against downward shocks; (e) compatibility with human rights; and (f) compatibility with physical and mental health.

DISCUSSION QUESTIONS

1. The famous economist Alfred Marshall defined economics as "a study of mankind in the ordinary business of life; it examines that part of individual and social action which is most closely connected to the attainment and with the use of the material requisites of wellbeing."[5] Is this closer to the subject-matter type of definition or the methodology type of definition? Explain your answer.

2. In market economies, the what, how, and for whom decisions are linked to one another. In fact, many events have roots in all three of these economic decisions. Consider the increase in the

quantity of computers produced in our society. Explain how the what, how, and for whom decisions each played a part in this outcome.

3. Market economies use profits and losses to stimulate the search for better production methods. What nonmoney rewards for success exist in capitalist market systems? Is the money or the honor more important for Nobel Prize winners? Is a gold watch better than money for a retirement gift?

4. Do you believe the present distribution of income in the United States is unfair or unjust in any way? If so, how should it be different? What changes would you expect in the way the economy operates if your desired reforms were actually to take place?

5. The figures in this chapter showing the relations of what, how, and for whom in market and planned economies are great simplifications of reality. Most actual systems are mixed. Explain how the U.S. economy would be better illustrated by putting a government planning circle in the center of Figure 1-3. Explain how the Soviet Union's economy would be better illustrated by adding arrows between the three outer circles in Figure 1-4.

6. The distinction between microeconomic and macroeconomic unemployment is helpful in theorizing about the economy. But the unemployed worker may not know (or really care) which has put him or her out of work. Consider an unemployed auto worker in Flint, Michigan, in the early 1980s. Remember that car sales are especially sensitive to general economic conditions and that the economy was in recession during those years. Also, the U.S. auto firms faced severe competition from imported Japanese and German automobiles. Discuss the unemployment in Flint in terms of microeconomic and macroeconomic determinants.

7. As you learned in this chapter, economic development means economic growth plus some qualitative changes in the conditions of life. Growth is a part of development. What arguments can you think of against growth itself? In your opinion, is the United States experiencing economic development today? Explain your answer.

5. Alfred Marshall, *Principles of Economics*, 8th ed. (London: Macmillan, 1920), p. 1.

8. Our list of ways to evaluate economic systems may not be the same as a list you would make. If you could add one item to the list, what would it be? Do you believe that people in China or the Soviet Union would want a different set of goals? Explain your answers.

9. President Warren Harding once said, "There is more happiness in the American small town than anywhere else on earth." Do you think he was correct then—in the 1920s? Do you think his statement is true today? Explain.

10. Do you think that human happiness has the best chance of being realized under capitalism, socialism, or a traditional economy? Explain.

2 *The Actors on the Economic Stage*

PREVIEW Understanding how an economic system works requires economists to identify the major actors on the economic stage and the roles they play in the operation of the system. We introduce them in this chapter.

We shall look first at households. In a capitalist economic system, households actually contain *two* decision-making entities—consumers and resource owners.[1] Imagine that each member of the household wears two hats, one marked "consumer" and the other marked "resource owner." As consumers, household members help to make the "what to produce" decisions in the economy. As resource owners, they are involved with both the "how" and the "for whom" decisions.

Next we will look at business firms, which are the economic units concerned with production. In the capitalist system, business firms make decisions about "how to produce" goods and services. Business firms obtain resources from households and combine them to produce goods and services. Household members place their resources in the hands of business firms because they expect to be rewarded with income. The firm, if successful, is able to make a profit from its operations.

The third major element in the economy is government. We will describe the major functions and responsibilities that economists say properly fall upon government in a market-capitalist system. These responsibilities involve (1) financing certain goods and services (which contributes to the "what to produce" decision), (2) redistributing income (which influences the "for whom" decision), and

1. See page 36–38 for a discussion of rational economic decision makers.

(3) moderating business cycles (which is a macroeconomic activity).

Households, business firms, and governments in foreign countries are the fourth major element influencing an economy. Foreigners buy goods and services produced in the United States, thus adding to the demand for U.S. resources, but foreigners also are producers of goods and services bought by Americans, thus competing with U.S. resource owners.

The interactions among the actors on the economic stage—households, business firms, government, and foreigners—will be examined in detail in later chapters.

HOUSEHOLDS

For statistical purposes, a **household** may be defined either as a family group living together or as one or more persons living together in the same dwelling unit. There are about 87 million households in the United States today. Households are made up of individuals who, in capitalist-market economic systems, are the owners of resources as well as consumers of goods and services. Each individual, of course, is the owner of his or her own labor resource. But in capitalist economic systems, nonhuman resources, too, are owned by individuals, either directly or indirectly. Land and buildings can be owned directly by individuals. Indirect ownership, on the other hand, occurs when corporations hold title to resources. This is indirect ownership by individ-

18

TABLE 2-1 Population Size and Age Distribution in the United States, 1960–2000

	1960	1970	1980	1990	2000
Population (millions)	180.7	205.1	227.7	249.7	268.0
Percentage by Age Groups (%)					
17 and under	35.7	34.1	28.0	25.8	25.1
18–44	35.0	35.7	41.2	42.9	39.1
45–64	20.0	20.5	19.6	18.6	22.7
65 and over	9.2	9.8	11.3	12.7	13.0

Note: Figures may not add to 100 percent because of rounding. Projections for 1990 and 2000 are for "middle series" estimates.

Source: Computed from *Statistical Abstract of the United States*, 1986, Tables 25 and 26.

uals, since corporations themselves are owned by shareholders, who are individuals. As resource owners, individuals receive the income generated in the production activities of the economy.

When household members spend the income they have earned as resource owners, they are functioning in their economic capacity as consumers. They are casting "dollar votes" for the goods and services that they want. In this way, they help make the "what to produce" decisions in the economy.

Population and Age Groups

The size and age distribution of the population are facts of great importance to economics because they affect production and spending. Will people, or households, demand baby food, rock concerts and sports cars, or retirement homes? What proportion of the population will be of working age, and how many nonworkers will there be for every worker? Will the typical person make decisions with the aggressiveness and flexibility of youth, or with the caution and stability of age?

Table 2-1 shows the age distribution of the United States population from 1960 to 2000, based on both actual data and estimates. The total population is expected to increase by almost 50 percent over this forty-year span. The numbers in this table show the effects of the "baby boom" of the 1950s and 1960s and of the sharp drop in

the birthrate during the 1970s. Though the percentage of the population 17 years and under declined greatly during the 1970s, it is expected to decline only moderately through the end of the century as the people born in the 1950s and 1960s produce their own children. The younger working-age group, from age 18 through 44, is expected to continue to increase during the remaining years of the 1980s but to decline thereafter. The older working-age group, from 45 through 64 years, is expected to begin its growth spurt in the decade of the 1990s. The over-65 age group probably will grow moderately through the end of the century but then experience a major expansion.

This population "ripple" may be one of the most significant economic events in the lives of college students today. Students graduating during the late 1980s will be entering a labor force that will include a much larger percentage of the population than was the case for students graduating in the 1960s and early 1970s. Competition for jobs will probably be vigorous, but living standards may be high because the percentage of nonworkers will be relatively low. These graduates will face different challenges after the year 2000, when they will be entering the 45–64 "older-worker" category. The expanding proportion of people over age 65 then will place increasing pressures on those still working, who will be expected to support a larger and larger nonworking population.

TABLE 2-2   National Income by Type of Income in the United States for Selected Years (percentage distribution)

Type of Income	1940	1950	1960	1970	1980	1985
Compensation of Employees	65.6	64.8	69.8	74.3	74.3	73.8
Proprietors' Income	15.8	16.2	12.3	9.6	8.2	7.5
Rental Income of Persons	3.4	3.2	3.6	2.2	0.3	0.4
Corporate Profits	11.1	14.6	11.6	9.0	8.0	9.3
Net Interest	4.1	1.3	2.7	4.9	9.1	8.9
Total	100.0	100.0	100.0	100.0	100.0	100.0

Note: Amounts may not add to total because of rounding.

Source: Computed from *Economic Report of the President, 1986,* Table B-23.

The political effect of the "ripple" may also be important. Many believe that people tend to be "liberal" when they are young and "conservative" when they are old. In fact, there is persuasive economic logic behind this observation, since older people have more at stake in the status quo than do younger people. The young people of the 1960s and 1970s were influential in bringing about many changes in the United States through their political activity. Civil rights, women's liberation, antiwar, and antinuclear movements relied heavily on the support of young people. As these same people grow older, they will continue to leave their mark on political history—this time as an older generation.

Sources of Income

As owners of resources, individuals are the ultimate recipients of the income generated in the economy. In the accounting system for the economy, the total of these earnings is called **national income.**

Table 2-2 shows the breakdown of the national income of the United States for selected years between 1940 and 1985. Compensation to employees was, by far, the largest component of national income. This compensation represents the return to labor resources and includes wages, salaries, and bonuses as well as the value of fringe benefits, such as health and retirement insurance paid for by employers. Part of the proprietors' income shown in the table probably also was a return to the labor resource, since it is difficult to separate labor income from other income of people who run their own businesses. The other components of national income—corporate profits, rental income of persons, and net interest—report income from nonhuman (property) resources. Altogether, property income probably amounted to less than one-fourth of the total income in the United States in 1985 and labor resources generated more than three-fourths of this income.

Table 2-2 also shows national income data for earlier years. Note that the relative importance of net interest and compensation of employees have increased significantly over the years. On the other hand, the share for proprietors' income has gone down.

Median Family Income

Table 2-3 shows the median family income in the United States for selected years from 1950 through 1984. The "median" means that half the families in the country had incomes higher than the one shown in the table for each year and that half had incomes lower than this amount. Also, the income figures in this table have been adjusted

TABLE 2-3 Median Money Income of U.S. Families in Constant (1984) Dollars for Selected Years.

Year	Median Income
1950	$14,321
1955	17,138
1960	19,711
1965	22,903
1970	26,394
1971	26,378
1972	27,599
1973	28,167
1974	27,175
1975	26,476
1976	27,293
1977	27,440
1978	28,085
1979	28,029
1980	26,500
1981	25,569
1982	25,216
1983	25,594
1984	26,433

Source: Statistical Abstract of the United States, 1986, Table 752.

so as to remove changes in the cost of living that arose from changes in the price level. All the figures in the table are in dollars of the purchasing power that prevailed in 1984. Therefore, they are useful in showing what has happened to the standard of living of U.S. families over this thirty-four-year period.

At first you may notice that the median family income was much higher in 1984 than it was in 1950—84.6 percent higher, in fact. A closer examination, however, shows that the highest median family income shown in the table is for 1973. In the twenty-three years from 1950 to 1973, the median family income in the United States almost doubled, but the median family income fell in 1974 and 1975 and in the years from 1978 through 1982. Although the median family income increased after 1982, as of 1984 it had not yet regained the level of 1973.

Economists are, of course, very interested in the forces that may cause changes in the levels of family income. Even a casual reflection on the figures in Table 2-3 suggest that the shocks to the economy that were caused by large changes in the price of crude oil in 1973 and 1978 may have been at least partly responsible for the lack of growth in U.S. median family income in the late 1970s and early 1980s.

Several words of caution are appropriate even at this early stage in our exploration of economics. Money income tells only part of the story about the economic well-being of a family. Nonmoney incomes, such as subsidized food, housing, and health care, also are important. "Do-it-yourself" home building and repair, as well as back-yard vegetable gardens, are other ways of adding to the nonmoney income of the family. Moreover, income is not the same thing as wealth. For example, families that appear poor in terms of money income may not be poor in terms of other signs of well-being, such as bank balances or property ownership.

Labor Force Participation

Since labor is the most important resource in the economy, it is interesting to know what portion of the adult population actually is working or looking for work. This is revealed in Table 2-4, which shows the U.S. **civilian labor force participation rate** between 1950 and 1985. The civilian labor force participation rate is the percentage of the civilian noninstitutional population, age 16 or older, that is either working or looking for work. The table shows that the U.S. participation rate was higher in 1985 than it was in earlier years. It is especially significant that the rate for females increased greatly over the years shown in the table. This change in the labor force participation rate for females is one of the most dramatic phenomena in recent U.S. economic history. Increased female participation accounts for the entire increase in the overall participation rate and made up for the decrease in the participation rate for males.

TABLE 2-4   Civilian Labor Force Participation Rate (percent)

Year	Total	Both sexes 16–19 years	Males 20 years and over	Females 20 years and over
1950	59.2	51.8	88.4	33.3
1960	59.4	47.5	86.0	37.6
1970	60.4	49.9	82.6	43.3
1980	63.8	56.7	79.4	51.3
1985	64.8	54.5	78.1	54.7

Note: The civilian labor force participation rate is the percentage of the civilian noninstitutional population in the group specified. Data relate to persons 16 years of age or over. A person is in the labor force if he or she is either working or looking for work. Institutionalized persons are those in prisons, mental hospitals, and so on.

Source: Economic Report of the President, 1986, Table B-34.

Uses of Income

As we have said, household members are helping make the "what to produce" decision when they purchase goods and services. Table 2-5 shows how households disposed of their income. In 1985, 78.4 percent went for consumption goods and services, 15 percent for taxes, 2.6 percent for interest payments, and 3.9 percent was saved. As you continue to study economics, you will see that each of these dispositions of household income is carefully analyzed by economists in their efforts to understand the economy. The table shows that the percentage of income used for consumption goods and services has dropped since 1950, while the percentage paid in taxes and interest has increased. Even the money that is saved plays a role in the "what to produce" decision. This happens when savings are placed in banks or other financial institutions and then borrowed by a person or a business firm that wants to buy something.

Table 2-6 gives a breakdown of the consumption expenditures of households. As you can see, housing and household operation now account for almost one-fourth of consumption expenditure while food claims less than 20 percent. The famous trio of "food, clothing, and shelter" add up to about half of all consumption. The percentages spent for food and clothing decreased significantly while the percentage spent for medical care showed a spectacular increase.

TABLE 2-5   Disposition of Personal Income in the United States for Selected Years (percentage distribution)

	1950	1960	1970	1980	1985
Personal consumption spending	84.2	80.8	76.9	76.7	78.4
Interest paid by consumers	1.0	1.7	2.0	2.1	2.6
Personal saving	5.5	5.1	6.9	6.1	3.9
Personal tax and nontax payments	9.0	12.3	14.0	15.1	15.0
Total	100.0	100.0	100.0	100.0	100.0

Note: Amounts may not add to total because of rounding and because of "transfers to foreigners" not included as a separate item in the table.

Source: Computed from Economic Report of the President, 1986, Table B-25.

TABLE 2-6 Personal Consumption Expenditures in the United States for Selected Years (percentage distribution)

	1950	1960	1970	1980	1985
Durable goods	16.0	13.2	13.4	12.6	14.0
Food	28.1	25.0	22.2	20.1	18.4
Clothing and shoes	10.2	8.2	7.5	6.3	6.0
Housing and household operation[a]	18.0	21.7	21.3	22.7	22.9
Transportation[b]	6.1	7.0	7.1	8.6	6.9
Medical care	3.6	5.0	7.2	9.5	10.9
Other	18.0	19.9	21.3	20.2	20.9
Total	100.0	100.0	100.0	100.0	100.0

a. Includes electricity, gas, fuel oil and coal and imputed rental value of owner-occupied homes.
b. Includes gasoline and oil and purchased transportation services.

Source: Computed from *Economic Report of the President, 1986,* Table B-14.

BUSINESS FIRMS

The business firm is the second actor on the economic stage to be examined in this chapter. Business firms purchase resources or resource services and combine them to produce goods and services. In this sense, business brings resource owners and consumers together and makes the "how to produce" decisions in a market economy.

Forms of Business Organization

The three basic forms of business organization are the proprietorship, the partnership, and the corporation. Each form has special features, which we shall describe briefly.

THE PROPRIETORSHIP A **proprietorship** exists simply because some person decides to start his or her own business. No legal papers have to be filled out, and no formal declaration about being in business is necessary unless there are laws that relate to the particular work to be done, such as the necessity of obtaining a license to practice medicine or permission from a health department to operate a restaurant. The owner, or proprietor,

is responsible for financing and managing the business. Assuming the risks of possible losses, the proprietor has the right to whatever profits may come after all outside debts have been paid. A large percentage of small retail stores, small farms, and small manufacturing companies in the United States are proprietorships.

THE PARTNERSHIP A **partnership** exists when two or more people agree to share the financial and managerial responsibilities of a business firm as well as its profits and losses. A partnership agreement is necessary because partners must set the terms and conditions of their participation in the business. The agreement does not have to be in writing, but experience suggests that written agreements will cause much less trouble than oral agreements. In the agreement, the partners can set up almost any methods of financing, managing, and profit sharing that they choose.

There are two very important legal requirements that apply to both proprietorships and partnerships but pose special problems for partnerships. These are unlimited liability and limited life.

Each partner must accept **unlimited liability,** or complete responsibility for all the debts of the business. The partnership agreement may specify how debts are to be paid in most cases, but if any partners fail to meet their obligations, the other partners must make sure that the partnership meets all its commitments to outsiders. Because each partner is liable for the obligations of the whole business, outsiders have extra assurance that any promises made by the partnership will be kept. Of course, before joining a partnership, individuals must be sure that they trust and share the business goals of other members of the partnership.

The partnership has a **limited life.** It lasts only as long as the partnership agreement is in force. Many events can put an end to the agreement and thus to the life of the partnership. If a partner dies or leaves the business, the other partners must make a new agreement in order to continue together in business. To add a new partner also means making a new agreement. The limited life of the partnership gives the partners the necessary flexibility to deal with changes but at the same time makes it a very fragile form of business organization.

Creating partnerships and adding partners with special talents or training can give financial power and technical specialization to a business such as a law firm or a medical practice. However, the problems connected with limited life and unlimited liability make many people hesitate to join a partnership.

THE CORPORATION A **corporation** comes into being when the government issues a charter. In the United States, corporate charters are issued by state governments. Obtaining a charter is simple and inexpensive, and the charter itself places very few restrictions on the operations of corporations. The charter authorizes the corporation to issue and sell shares of stock. The people who own these shares, the stockholders, are the owners of the corporation. Also, the charter establishes the corporation as a "legal person," separate from the "real persons" who are the owners and the managers of the corporation.

As a legal person, the corporation can enter into contracts and make commitments in its own name. Under the law, the corporation itself is responsible for these obligations. Neither the owners nor the managers are individually liable for its debts and obligations. If the corporation does well, the stockholders reap the profits, but if corporate operations are not successful, a stockholder's loss is limited to the value of the shares owned. This **limited liability** feature of corporations greatly increases their ability to accumulate large sums of money for the enterprise. Because stockholders can share the profits and face only limited liability for losses, they are generally willing to let other people carry out the day-to-day management of the corporation.

The legal person created by the corporate charter has perpetual or **unlimited life,** which means that the corporation itself does not have to be reorganized every time individual persons enter or leave the ownership or management of the corporation. This stability is attractive to shareholders, who need not fear that their wealth will be tied up in endless legal battles, as may happen in partnerships. Also, customers, banks, and other firms can enter into long-term contracts with the corporation, knowing that its existence does not hinge on the lives of mortal human beings.

Thus the corporate form of business overcomes the problems of unlimited liability and limited life to which both proprietorships and partnerships are subject. The corporate form opens up vast possibilities for business firms to bring together financial power and technical expertise. Even though U.S. proprietorships far outnumber U.S. corporations, it is no wonder that the great majority of business assets in the United States are held by corporations.

The chief disadvantage of the corporate form of business is that the net income of corporations is subject to taxation by the U.S. federal government and also by many state governments. These taxes are in addition to the individual income tax paid by stockholders on the profits they receive from corporations as dividends. Thus, corporation dividends are taxed twice, once when the money is earned by the corporation and again when it is received by the stockholder. From the point of view of the individual decision maker, taxation cancels some of the advantages of the corporate form of business.

The Stock Market

The outstanding feature of the corporate form of business is that corporations obtain funds by selling securities that convey ownership rights to the buyers of the securities. These securities are called **shares,** or **stock,** in the corporation. Those who purchase shares or stocks obtain, among other things, specified rights to vote on matters of corporate policy and in elections for the corporation's board of directors, which makes day-to-day policy decisions. Stockholders also have specified rights to receive **dividends,** which are distributions of money (or additional stock) from the corporation. However, stockholders do not necessarily receive dividends equal to all the profits of the corporation in any particular period of time. The corporation's board of directors decides how much of the profit will be paid out as dividends and how much retained to finance future corporate operations.

One of the reasons why corporations are able to obtain huge amounts of money to finance their operations is that stockholders can sell some or all of their stock whenever they want to reduce or terminate their association with the corporation. Most buying and selling of shares or stock in corporations is carried out in a **stock exchange,** where those who want to sell stock carry out transactions with those who want to buy it. There are stock exchanges in major cities all over the world and they are linked by a very effective communication network. Only those individuals or firms that are members of a stock exchange— that is, who own a "seat" on the exchange—are allowed to do business on the "floor" of the exchange. Therefore, a person who wants to buy or sell stock usually works through a **stockbroker,** who can have the transaction carried out on behalf of the buyer or seller. The broker, or brokerage firm, either owns a seat on an exchange or works through someone who does own one. The broker has the transaction carried out on a stock exchange and charges a fee or **commission** for the service. Stock exchange memberships are limited in number and are themselves bought and sold.

Figure 2-1 reproduces a portion of a newspaper report of stock market transactions on Thursday,

March 13, 1986.[2] To learn how to read the stock exchange report, look at the line reporting that day's transactions in the common stock of American Express (abbreviated AmExp). The numbers in the first two columns report the highest and lowest prices per share paid for this stock over the past 52 weeks; in this example, the highest price was $68.75 a share (68¾) and the lowest price was $40.25 a share (40¼). The first number following the name of the stock shows that the annual amount of dividend paid per share is $1.36, which is a yield of 2.0 percent (shown in the next column) on its current price. The next number, which is 19, shows the price/earnings (P-E) ratio. This means that the current price of the stock is 19 times the amount of the annual profits per share of the corporation. The last five numbers report this particular day's transactions for this stock. On that day, 5,598 "blocks" (of 100 shares each) were traded. The highest-priced block traded at $67.875 per share (67⅞), the lowest-priced block at $66.625 per share (66⅝), and the last block sold that day went at $67.625 per share (67⅝). The price in this "closing" transaction was 25 cents higher (+¼) than the price of the closing transaction on the preceding business day.

As you can see, a huge amount of information is contained in the stock exchange reports. Investors and brokerage firms study this information carefully in deciding whether and what to buy or sell. Since stock market prices reflect expectations about future profitability, they provide useful information for guiding resources among alternative uses in capitalist-market economies.

Business Accounting

Keeping records is extremely important in business operations. Thus it is not surprising that some of the earliest known writing and calculating techniques were developed to keep business records. Information provided through business records can improve management's ability to make wise decisions. It also helps others, such as

2. *The Wall Street Journal,* March 14, 1986, p. 40.

FIGURE 2-1 Newspaper Report of Stock Exchange Transactions

NEW YORK STOCK EXCHANGE COMPOSITE TRANSACTIONS

Thursday, March 13, 1986

Quotations include trades on the Midwest, Pacific, Philadelphia, Boston and Cincinnati stock exchanges and reported by the National Association of Securities Dealers and Instinet

52 Weeks High	52 Weeks Low	Stock	Div.	Yld %	P-E Ratio	Sales 100s	High	Low	Close	Net Chg.
67½	48	ACyan	1.90	2.8	25	2099	u67¾	65⅝	67¾	+2
29¾	21¾	ADT	.92	3.6	..	231	26	25½	25⅞	+ ¼
28⅛	19⅞	AEIPw	2.26	8.3	11	2271	27⅝	27	27⅛	− ½
68¾	40¼	AmExp	1.36	2.0	19	5598	67⅞	66⅝	67⅝	+ ¼
31⅛	12½	AFaml	s .40	1.4	22	688	29½	29⅛	29½	+ ¼
41⅝	27¼	AGnCp	1.12	2.7	12	2559	41½	40⅜	41¼	+ ½
21½	10¼	AGnl wt		..	..	280	20¾	20	20¾	+ ½
56¾	53	AGnl pfA	5.42e	10.	..	233	53½	53½	53½	+ ¼
82¾	55	AGn pfD	2.64	3.2	..	119	82¾	81	82¾	+1
44⅛	30	AHerit	1.20	2.9	15	3	41½	41⅛	41½	+ ⅛
13⅜	8¼	AHoist		..	..	519	9⅞	8⅝	9⅞	+1⅛
23	19¼	AHoist pf	1.95	9.0	..	779	21¾	20¾	21¾	+1¼
80	54¾	AHome	3.10	4.0	16	3580	77½	76¼	77⅛	−1¼
118⅞	80⅝	Amrtch	6.60	5.6	11	1490	u119⅜	117¼	118¼	+ ⅝
133½	69¼	AInGrp	.44	.3	25	1440	u136	131⅜	135¾	+3⅝
215	120	AIGp pf	5.85	2.7	..	6	u216	215	216	+1
28⅝	16	AMI	.72	3.4	12	3436	21½	20⅞	20⅞	− ⅝
4½	2¼	AmMot		..	..	14954	u5	4¼	5	+ ¾
26⅛	13⅞	APresd	s.50	2.4	11	4070	21	19¼	20⅞	+1⅞
13½	5	ASLFla		..	..	152	12¾	12¼	12⅜	− ⅛
20¾	12¼	ASLFl pf	2.19	11.	..	68	20½	20⅜	20⅜	.....
15⅝	9⅞	AShip	.80	7.4	8	59	10⅞	10⅝	10¾	+ ⅛
46½	26¾	AmStd	1.60	3.5	82	740	46½	45¼	46	− ¼
68¼	48⅝	AmStor	.84	1.4	15	864	60⅛	59½	60	.....
78	59½	AStr pfA	4.38	6.2	..	103	71¼	70½	70⅞	− ⅝
61½	53¼	AStr pfB	6.80	11.	..	36	60	59¼	59¼	− ¾
25⅜	19⅞	AT&T	1.20	5.2	17	15905	23⅜	22¾	23	− ⅛
48⅝	34⅞	AT&T pf	3.64	7.6	..	481	48	47⅜	47¾	− ⅛
49¼	36	AT&T pf	3.74	7.7	..	2840	49	48½	48¾	− ⅛
33	21¾	AmWtr	1.12	3.6	10	173	31¾	31⅜	31⅜	− ½
14	11	AWat pf	1.25	9.3	..	z150	13½	13⅛	13½	+ ⅜
28⅛	9¼	AmHotl		..	4	278	10¼	9⅞	10	− ⅛
74	66	ATr pr	5.64	7.7	..	42	73	72	73	+ ¼
29¼	10	ATr sc		..	..	47	u29⅝	28⅞	29⅝	+ ½
102	76¼	ATr un	5.64	5.5	..	4	102	102	102	.....
56¼	30½	Ameron	1.60	2.9	10	8	55	55	55	.....
29	16¾	AmesD	s.10	.4	23	12093	25⅜	24¼	25⅜	− ⅛
30¾	19⅞	Ametek	1	3.4	19	186	29¾	29⅛	29¾	+ ⅜
11⅝	9¾	AmevSc	1.08	9.8	..	109	11⅛	10⅞	11	− ⅛
29⅝	22	Amfac		..	318	305	28⅞	28⅜	28⅝	.....

52 Weeks High	52 Weeks Low	Stock	Div.	Yld %	P-E Ratio	Sales 100s	High	Low	Close	Net Chg.
70¼	53⅛	Amoco	3.30b	5.6	8	3874	59⅝	58¾	58¾	− ½
42½	27½	AMP	.72	1.7	41	2990	41½	40⅝	41¼	+ ⅛
16	11½	Ampco	.30	1.9	43	53	15⅞	15⅝	15⅝	− ¼
27¾	12⅝	Amrep	s	..	14	40	26¾	26¼	26½	.....
35⅝	17½	AmSth	s1.04	2.9	13	227	35⅜	34¾	35⅜	− ⅛
47¼	34⅝	Amsted	1.60	3.5	20	98	46½	46⅜	46⅜	.....
5⅛	2⅜	Anacmp		..	13	8277	u 5¼	4½	5⅛	+ ½
31	18	Anlog		..	39	429	30¼	29⅝	30	+ ¼
28½	20⅝	Anchor	1.48	5.0	128	584	u30¼	28½	29½	+1⅛
61¼	35⅝	AnClay	.33i	..	31	108	54⅝	54⅜	54⅜	.....
16½	9⅛	AndrGr	.24b	1.5	18	295	16⅛	16	16⅛	+ ⅛
29⅝	18½	Angelic	.60	2.2	15	188	28¼	27⅛	27½	−1
48	25⅜	Anheus	s.80	1.7	17	4332	u48⅜	47½	48	.....
93¾	55½	Anheu pf	3.60	3.9	..	19	93	92¾	93	− ¾
22⅞	13½	Anixtr	.28	1.2	21	411	u23½	21½	23⅜	+1
19⅛	10¼	Anthem	.04	.2	42	57	18½	18⅜	18½	.....
16⅞	11	Anthny	.44b	2.6	17	4	16⅞	16¾	16⅞	+ ⅛
13⅜	8¾	Apache	.28	3.0	25	326	9⅝	9⅜	9⅜	− ⅛
2	9-128	ApchP wt		..	..	58	3-32	5-64	11-128	....
19⅞	10⅞	ApchP un	2.10	16.	..	1001	13	12⅝	12¾	− ⅛
92½	64	ApPw pf	8.12	8.9	..	z4800	91	91	91	.....
27¼	24¼	ApPw pf	2.65	9.8	..	4	27⅛	27⅛	27⅛	− ⅛
34⅜	31	ApPw pf	4.18	12.	..	18	34	33⅞	34	+ ¼
32	28½	ApPw pf	3.80	12.	..	9	30⅞	30¾	30⅞	.....
19½	11¾	ApplMg		..	30	317	19¼	18⅛	18⅜	− ⅞
29⅞	19¼	ArchDn	.14b	.5	15	2045	29¼	28¾	29⅛	− ⅛
31½	27⅛	AriP pf	3.58	12.	..	45	30⅞	30¼	30¾	− ⅛
105	94	AriPpf	10.70	10.	..	z220	103½	102	103½	+1½
42½	18	ArkBst	.60	1.4	14	80	42⅛	41⅜	41½	− ⅞
24¼	16	Arkla	1.08	6.0	13	3258	18¼	17½	18	+ ½
15-16	1-16	ArInCp		..	..	249	15-32	13-32	7-16	+1-16
11⅞	6¾	Armco		..	17	1698	u12	11¼	12	+ ⅝
24⅞	15½	Armc pf	2.10	8.4	..	97	u25	24⅝	24⅞	+ ⅛
23½	13½	ArmsRb	.48	2.9	18	583	16¾	16½	16½	− ⅛
60⅛	30⅜	ArmWin	1.30	2.2	14	746	58⅞	58	58⅝	− ⅜
43	34¼	ArmW pf	3.75	9.0	..	z30	41½	41½	41½	−1
18	11¼	ArowE	.20	1.3	..	51	16	15¾	15¾	− ½
30¼	19¾	Artra	.22	.8	47	209	28	27½	28	+ ½
27	14¼	Aryin	s .61	2.3	12	502	u27¾	26⅝	27¼	+ ½

Source: *The Wall Street Journal*, March 14, 1986, p. 40.

stockholders, banks, and investors, to judge the profitability of the business. Economists study these records to discover trends and changes in the economy. The two basic financial statements of a company are the balance sheet and the income statement.

THE BALANCE SHEET The **balance sheet** is an accountant's report on the condition of a business firm as of the close of business on a particular date. It is like a snapshot or still photograph that shows the firm's financial condition at some instant in time. The balance sheet has three elements, called assets, liabilities, and net worth (or owners' equity). **Assets** represent all the things that the firm owns. **Liabilities** are the claims that outsiders have for payments from the firm. The amount that is left over for the owners of the firm is called **net worth.** These three elements make up the balance-sheet equation:

$$\text{assets} = \text{liabilities} + \text{net worth}$$

TABLE 2-7   Precision Printing Company, Balance Sheet, December 31, 1987

Assets		Liabilities	
Current Assets		**Current Liabilities**	
Cash	$ 30,000	Accounts Payable	$ 40,000
Inventory	210,000	Notes Payable	70,000
Fixed Assets		**Long-Term Liabilities**	
Equipment	420,000	Bonds	380,000
Buildings	160,000	Total Liabilities	$490,000
		Net Worth	
		Preferred Stock	$ 30,000
		Common Stock	220,000
		Retained Earnings	80,000
		Total Net Worth	$330,000
		Total Liabilities and	
Total Assets	$820,000	Net Worth	$820,000

Accountants make the best estimates they can of the actual values for assets and liabilities. Then, to satisfy the balance-sheet equation, the net worth of the business (the value that belongs to the owners) must be adjusted upward or downward until the equality is established. But first the accountant will need to evaluate both assets and liabilities as objectively as possible. Because legitimate accounting must stick to the facts in evaluating assets and liabilities, the value of the owners' equity (net worth) is the only item that can be adjusted to achieve the necessary balance.

A hypothetical balance sheet is illustrated in Table 2-7. Assets are listed on the left side of the account, and liabilities and net worth are listed on the right side. The total on one side must equal the total on the other side; that is, the balance sheet must "balance." Though the specific items that will be listed on a balance sheet depend on the nature of the business itself, there are some general rules or guidelines that accountants follow in presenting balance sheets. On the asset side, items are listed according to how quickly they can be converted into cash. In the illustrated balance sheet, cash itself comes first,

of course, followed by inventory (goods on hand), equipment, and buildings. The assets that ordinarily would be converted to cash in the course of a normal year's business are called current assets. Items that would not be converted to cash during a normal year's operation are called fixed or long-term assets. The order of the liabilities (on the right side of the balance sheet) follows a similar pattern. Current liabilities are obligations that normally are payable during a year's business operations. Long-term liabilities are obligations that will be payable at some more distant time.

Of special interest to the owners or potential owners of a company, of course, is the net worth section of the balance sheet. The entries in this section will vary depending on whether the firm is organized as a proprietorship, a partnership, or a corporation. The net worth section for a partnership will show the ownership interests of the different partners, and the net worth section for a corporation will show the interests of the various classes of stockholders. Also, a distinction is usually made between amounts paid in by owners and amounts of earnings that have been retained by the firm.

TABLE 2-8   Income Statement for Precision Printing Company for the Year Ended December 31, 1987

Net Sales			$380,000
Manufacturing Cost			
Materials	$ 40,000		
Labor	90,000		
Depreciation	75,000		
Subtotal		$205,000	
Plus Beginning Inventory	$245,000		
Less Closing Inventory	−210,000		
Subtotal		35,000	
Total Manufacturing Cost			240,000
Gross Profit from Sales			$140,000
Selling and Administrative Costs			40,000
Fixed Interest Charges and State and Local Taxes			15,000
Net Income Before Income Taxes			$ 85,000
Corporation Income Taxes			35,000
Net Income After Taxes			$ 50,000
Dividends Paid on Preferred Stock			2,000
Net Income After Preferred Stock Dividends			$ 48,000
Dividends Paid on Common Stock			26,000
Addition to Retained Earnings			$ 22,000

THE INCOME STATEMENT The **income statement,** or **profit and loss statement,** is an accountant's report of the operations of a business firm over some specified period of time. In a sense, it is like a movie, or part of one, because it reports the firm's activities over a finite period. It is different from the balance sheet, which, as we said, is like a still picture or snapshot and describes the condition of the firm at some fixed point in time.

Table 2-8 illustrates a hypothetical income statement. There is no balancing feature in this statement. Instead, it starts at the top with a report of the net amount of money received from sales during the time period. Then it shows how various items are subtracted from these receipts. At the bottom is the amount left over or remaining with the business. The specific items that appear on the income statement will differ greatly among firms, but certain general categories appear in almost all statements. For example, businesses usually want to separate manufacturing costs, selling and administrative costs, interest costs, and taxes. Cost-accounting and tax-accounting techniques are used to determine these various amounts. After costs and taxes have been subtracted, the statement shows the amount of income left. This is the amount available to be paid to the owners (as dividends in the corporate form of business) or to be retained for use by the company. The income statement will report the disposition that was made of these earnings.

Balance sheets and income statements can be fitted together to give a full and continuous account of the financial life of a firm. Balance sheets report the condition of a business at specific points in time, and income statements report its operations over periods of time. The difference between the balance sheet picture on one date and the balance sheet picture on another date is "explained" by the income statements that cover the period of time between the balance sheets.

GOVERNMENTS

Government is the third actor on the economic stage. The economic role of government depends a great deal upon the type of economic system in a country. For example, you learned in Chapter 1 that socialist governments own many natural and capital resources and may develop detailed plans for the economy. On the other hand, government typically plays a much smaller role in capitalist-market economies. In this chapter, we shall limit our discussion to the main functions of government in capitalist-market economies. In these economic systems, there are three basic economic responsibilities or functions of government—the allocation function, the distribution function, and the stabilization function.

The Allocation Function

The **allocation function** refers to the allocation of resources among alternative uses. Specifically, the allocation responsibility of government is to take appropriate corrective action in circumstances where private markets fail to provide the combination of goods and services desired by the people. Such market failures occur because the markets, left to themselves, produce too much of certain goods and services and not enough of others. In other words, without government action, resources would be misallocated.

There are several reasons why markets may give wrong answers to the "what to produce" question and thus misallocate resources. One is that monopolies may restrict output, thereby causing the prices of their products to rise and distorting the choices available to consumers. Allocational market failures also can arise when the production or consumption of a good or service affects people who have no way, through the markets, to influence the decision about how much of the good or service should be produced. These effects on people who are unrepresented in the market processes are called **externalities** because they are outside the scope of the market mechanism. Pollution is a common example of a harmful ("negative") externality. Smoke in the air can damage the lungs of people who have no way, through markets, to cause factories to install filters on their smokestacks. In this case, there may be overproduction of the good manufactured in the smoke-producing factory. Beneficial ("positive") externalities also can arise, as when people other than parents, students, and teachers benefit from the education of children in the community. In this situation, the market system might provide too small a quantity of education service.

National defense and other services financed entirely by government illustrate the **collective goods** area of government allocation responsibility. Collective goods are those which, by their nature, must be consumed in common by all the people in an area, that is, all must consume the same quality and quantity of the good or service.

The Distribution Function

Under the **distribution function** government has the responsibility to adjust the distribution of income among individuals. As you can see, it is a responsibility that relates directly to the "for whom" decision that must be made in every economic system. Of course, the normal operation of the market system results in some amount of inequality in the distribution of income among individuals. If the markets fail to generate the degree of inequality that is considered desirable, the government may redistribute incomes to achieve a better distribution.

There are many causes of inequality in a market-capitalist system. If the system is operating effectively, people who have great talent, are skillful, work hard, and are lucky will be rewarded with high incomes. Others can gain income if they have rich parents or obtain monopoly power. But the market system generates very little income for people who lack these advantages. Therefore, market-capitalist (as well as most collectivist-planned) economic systems are likely to generate more inequality than the people, speaking through the political system, say ought to exist. Of course, people do not agree on exactly what is a "fair" or "just" or "equitable" distribution of income, and there is no scientific way to prove that one distribution is necessarily better than another.

Nevertheless voters do let their government know what kind of distribution they want. Their instructions may be vague, since they are filtered through political candidates who may campaign on confusing and complicated sets of promises. They may often be self-serving too, since most people apparently feel that fairness means more income for themselves. But the fact is that citizens do expect their government to take steps to ensure that the distribution of income is not unreasonable. Government programs aimed, in part at least, at income redistribution include progressive income taxes, welfare programs, and a complicated set of taxes and subsidies for particular goods and services that are intended to improve the income position of certain groups. Minimum wage laws and farm subsidies illustrate this last redistributive approach.

One aspect of income distribution must be emphasized now, before you go further in your study of economics. The demand curves that you will study in this book reflect both the willingness and the ability of people to purchase goods. This ability reflects the income distribution. How much caviar and how much corn flakes we produce depends in part on the distribution of income. Demand-and-supply analysis will work equally well under any income distribution, but whether the choice of goods and services that comes out of the market process fits what you believe is right depends in part on whether you approve of the income distribution influencing demand curves throughout the economy.

The Stabilization Function

The **stabilization function,** or responsibility, of government is to achieve price stability, a high level of employment, and a reasonable rate of economic growth for the economy. It is a function that focuses heavily on macroeconomics, although microeconomic instruments also are involved. The stabilization responsibility arises because the market system of economic organization has a record of business cycles or fluctuations, bringing unemployment, inflation, or both. Before the 1930s, most economists (Karl Marx and

his followers excepted, of course) believed that fluctuations in the capitalist system were fairly minor and self-correcting so that there was no need for government to step in. But the experience of the Great Depression and the economic theories of the famous British economist, John Maynard Keynes (1883–1946), brought a great change in economic thought about this aspect of government activity. After Keynes, a whole generation of economists worked to perfect his theories about why the macroeconomy experiences fluctuations and to work out ways for the government to carry out its stabilization responsibilities. Economists today are still working on these problems.

You probably have heard about the major instruments of government stabilization policy, since they often make headlines in newspapers and television news reports. For example, government may try to control the size of the nation's money supply in the belief that the amount of money in the economy has a lot to do with inflation or other changes in the price level. Similarly, a lot of attention is paid to whether or not the government's budget is balanced because deficits are thought to stimulate the economy, whereas surpluses are thought to slow down economic activity.

How successful has the government been in actually improving the macroeconomic performance of the economy? During the 1960s, many people gave the U.S. government good marks in this area. Today, however, after the sobering experiences of the 1970s, when both inflation and unemployment reached very high levels, the high hopes of earlier days have been dampened.

THE REST OF THE WORLD

The fourth actor on the economic stage for any particular economy is "the rest of the world"— that is, the exporting, importing, and financial transactions that take place with households, business firms, and governments in other countries. In 1985, U.S. business firms sold $370.4 billion of goods and services to foreigners, which amounted to 9.3 percent of the total production in the U.S. economy. In that same year, Americans bought $444.8 billion of goods and services from foreigners, so that the United States had a trade deficit of some $74.4 billion.[3] Clearly, these transactions are important in the operation of the U.S. economy. Many American workers have jobs producing goods for export and American consumers enjoy the products that they buy from foreigners. But other American workers feel that their jobs are threatened by foreign competitors.

Table 2-9 shows that the dollar value of U.S. exports as a percent of gross national product (the value of total production) has increased substantially since World War II. This means that "the rest of the world" is much more important to the U.S. economy today than it was in earlier times. Important as "the rest of the world" is for the United States, it is much more important for many countries in the world. A country that allows relatively unrestricted trade across its borders is called an **open economy;** if such an economy is small, it is likely that transactions with foreigners will be extremely important. On the other hand, large countries that have a great variety of resources have to depend less on obtaining goods from foreigners and for them "the rest of the world" is less important. Of course, **closed economies,** which severely restrict trade across their borders, are more insulated from outside forces. China and the Soviet Union are relatively closed economies, although China is becoming more and more involved in international transactions.

Exports and imports are not the only reasons why "the rest of the world" is an important actor on a country's economic stage. Money also flows from country to country in search of the best returns in interest on bonds and bank accounts or dividends from corporate stocks. These financial or "capital account" transactions have important effects on economic conditions in the countries involved, since they influence economic growth by affecting the funds available to finance new capital goods. Business firms, governments, the United Nations, and major banking houses are active in international lending and finance.

3. *Economic Report of the President, 1986,* Table B-1.

TABLE 2-9 U.S. Exports as a Percentage of Gross National Product for Selected Years

Year	Exports as Percent of GNP
1929	6.8
1940	5.3
1945	3.5
1950	5.0
1955	5.2
1960	5.8
1965	6.1
1970	6.8
1975	10.1
1980	12.8
1985	9.3

Source: Computed from *Economic Report of the President, 1986,* Table B-1.

THE ACTORS IN ACTION

The economic actors that you have met in this chapter—households, business firms, governments, and "the rest of the world"—will appear again and again in your study of economics. In microeconomics, you will learn about decision-making criteria and processes and how the actors interact with each other. In macroeconomics, you will find that the four actors provide the organizing scheme for the model of how the macroeconomy works and how the national income accounting system keeps track of total income and production in the economy.

SUMMARY

1. To understand how economic systems operate, economists consider four actors on the economic stage—households, business firms, governments, and "the rest of the world."

2. Households are made up of individuals, who, in capitalist economic systems, are the owners of resources. As the owners of resources in capitalist systems, individuals are the ultimate recipients of the income generated by production.

3. Household members also are the ultimate consumers of the goods and services produced in an economy. When individuals spend the income earned as owners of resources, that is, when they function in their role as consumers, they are helping to make the "what to produce" decision.

4. Business firms are the decision-making units concerned with production. They purchase resources and resource services from households and combine them to produce goods and services. Thus, their role is to make the "how to produce" decisions in the economy.

5. Proprietorships, partnerships, and corporations are the three major kinds of business organizations. Corporations have become large and powerful because their charters grant limited liability and unlimited life, which allow them to accumulate large quantities of money and technical expertise.

6. Corporations obtain funds by selling shares or stock which convey to the buyer certain ownership rights in the corporation. The shareholders may receive dividends and normally vote in electing the board of directors and in deciding corporate policy.

7. The sale and purchase of corporate stock usually is carried out in stock exchanges located in major cities. An individual wishing to buy or sell stock works through a stockbroker, who carries out the transaction and charges a commission for the service. Reports of stock exchange transactions are published regularly in major newspapers.

8. Balance sheets and income statements are accounting reports about the condition and the operation, respectively, of businesses. Together these two reports give a continuing record of a company's financial life.

9. Most economists recognize three basic responsibilities or "functions" of government in capitalist-market economic systems—the allocation function, the distribution function, and the stabilization function. In its allocation function, government is viewed as correcting for market failures in deciding "what to produce." In its

distribution function, government is expected to promote a desirable distribution of income among individuals. The stabilization function involves moderating business cycles while maintaining high-level employment and stability in the general price level.

10. Households, business firms, and governments in "the rest of the world" make up the fourth actor on the economic stage of any given country. This actor has become increasingly important for the U.S. economy.

DISCUSSION QUESTIONS

1. It is often observed that, in political action dealing with legislation, consumer-interest lobbies are unable to prevail against lobbies promoting the interests of producers and resource owners. But each individual involved is a consumer as well as an owner of resources. Why, in your opinion, do people tend to place their interests as resource owners ahead of their interests as consumers?

2. The population ripple is one of the causes of problems in financing the Social Security retirement program. In view of these population changes, some experts estimate that Social Security taxes as high as 25 percent may be necessary to support the large retired population. You may be asked to pay this tax to help those ten or fifteen years older than yourself. Will you vote for such a tax on your paycheck? What effects might such a tax have on the economy?

3. Adding together the percentages in Table 2-2 for compensation of employees and proprietors' income yields a sum that is fairly constant over a forty-five-year period. But compensation has increased significantly while proprietors' income has decreased as a percentage of national income. What trends in the society might, in your opinion, tend to produce this result?

4. Although the distribution of income receives a great deal of attention in the media and in government debate, many economists believe that the distribution of wealth is equally (or perhaps more) important. Describe a set of circumstances in which a person would have low

income but a significant quantity of wealth. Describe the circumstances in which a person would have high income but little wealth.

5. Many forces have combined to increase the percentage of the female population in the labor force. Identify two such forces and explain how you believe they have led to greater female labor force participation. What changes do you expect in the future?

6. Explain how both unlimited liability and limited life can cause problems for firms organized under the proprietorship or the partnership form. Explain how the corporate form of business organization resolves these problems.

7. Suppose that you believe that the future profitability of corporation A will be better than the future profitability of corporation B, in which you now own some stock. Therefore, you sell your shares of B and purchase shares of A. How would the prices of these stocks be affected if many people behave the same as you?

8. Using the following information, construct a simple balance sheet for a business firm: accounts payable, $15,000; equipment owned, $120,000; stock outstanding, $70,000; notes payable, $40,000; cash on hand, $10,000; retained earnings, $15,000; inventory, $50,000; bonds outstanding, $100,000; buildings, $60,000. Explain how a balance sheet is different from an income statement.

9. Name the three functions of government that are described in this chapter. Which do you believe will be the most important to voters in the next election? Under which function would you place a responsibility to promote economic growth? Why?

10. The increasing importance of "the rest of the world" in the economy of the United States has been accompanied, lately, by great political pressure for laws that would restrict entry of foreign goods into the United States. Discuss how this is related to the differing interests of individuals as consumers and as resource owners.

3 *How Economists Approach Problems*

PREVIEW We human beings are curious creatures who want to know what makes things "tick." More important, we have problems to be solved. Very often we do not have enough of the things we would like to have, yet sometimes we may even have too much. These are the problems that economists try to solve, or at least try to describe clearly, using economic theories and mathematical models of functional relationships.

In this chapter we look at the methods used in economics—how economists deal with economic problems. Most of what will be described and explained applies to all fields that use scientific analysis. A few terms and concepts may be unique to economics.

We begin with a discussion of economic theory and the difficulties inherent in testing these theories. We describe how the analysis of economic theories rests on assumptions, and the role played by the central assumption of economic rationality. Then we explain how economists show the relationships among variables in terms of functions, and we give a short review of how functions are shown in graphs. Next we introduce marginal analysis and equilibrium, two very important ideas often used in economics.

The rest of the chapter points out some difficulties that often beset beginning students of economics (and sometimes careless veterans as well). One such problem is that fairly common terms may take on entirely different meanings in economics. Other difficulties lie in assuming that when one event follows another in time, there is necessarily a cause-and-effect relationship, and in assuming that what is true for a part is also going to be true for the whole. Two final problems result from not paying enough attention to time lags and to expectations.

ECONOMIC THEORY

The discipline of economics consists of a large number of theories. A reasonable, if not precise, definition of an economist is one who knows the major economic theories and is engaged in testing and modifying some of them.

A **theory** is a systematically organized body of knowledge that can be applied in a fairly wide range of circumstances. It provides a set of rules or assumptions for analyzing information, for studying cause-and-effect relationships, and for solving real-life problems by enabling us to improve our ability to predict future events. In fact, theory guides research.

Economic theories are often called models. A **model** is a formal statement of a theory—a simplified view of how some part of the economy is assumed to operate. For example, a simple model of total consumption might describe it as dependent only on current income, whereas a more sophisticated model might describe other influences, like wealth or expected future income. Economic models are often expressed mathematically, but we shall minimize our dependence on mathematics in this elementary textbook.

The study of economics is a search for relationships that occur between different economic variables. A **variable** is a quantity that can assume any of a set of values. For example, the price of a good is a variable, and the quantity of this good that is demanded is another variable. We may be interested in the relationship between them. That is, we want to know how a change in the price will affect the amount people will buy. Theory, however, is more than just a description of particular relationships. It is an effort to generalize about relationships that occur regularly, not about coincidental happenings. The observation that a certain relationship between two variables occurs very often leads to the prediction that it will occur again in the future.

The most important requirement of a theory is that it be useful. Most economists are not interested in theorizing for its own sake. They want to learn how to solve economic problems, and the answers lie in the use of present theories or of theories not yet devised.

Testing Economic Theory

Economics is a social science. In general, the social sciences are less exact than the natural or physical sciences. For this reason the social scientist must often be satisfied with predicting the direction of change rather than the amount. The natural scientist deals with molecules and cells and is concerned with people in an anatomical or physiological sense; the social scientist is interested in people's behavior. Therefore, the social scientist is not able to use the "laboratory method," or the controlled experiment, as effectively as can the natural scientist. If a chemist wants to discover the color reaction of chemical A with chemical B, he or she can place in two identical and sterile test tubes the same measured amount of chemical B and then add a certain amount of chemical A to one of the two test tubes. If the chemist now sees a color change in the test tube to which chemical A was added but observes no color change in the other test tube, the color change may clearly be attributed to the reaction between chemicals A and B. If this experiment were performed hundreds of times, we would expect the same results to occur each time.

How would a simple experiment in economics be performed? Suppose that we want to find out

by means of a controlled experiment what effect a one-shot $1,000 increase in income will have on people's spending and saving patterns. We choose 100 people for group A and another 100 people for group B. These people are not chosen at random. They are selected because they have certain similar characteristics: all have annual incomes of $25,000, all have about the same wealth, all are thirty years of age, all have three dependents, and all live in the same section of the same city. After giving $1,000 to each person in group A but nothing to the people in group B, we note the difference in spending patterns of the two groups. Let us assume we find that group A spends more than group B; specifically, that group A members spend an average of $738.50 more per person than do members of group B. How much faith do you have in this experiment? Would you expect that if the $1,000 had been given to the people in group B instead of group A, they, too, would have spent $738.50 more per person than those of group A? The chances are that the figure would be at least slightly different—perhaps quite different. Why? The reason is that we are dealing with people, who do not all behave in the same way. Though this experiment may allow us to predict that a one-shot increase in income will cause people to spend more, it does not allow us to predict confidently that they will spend 73.85 percent of their additional income.

From this example it is clear that the social scientist must make use of "experiments" that come from everyday experiences. Irrelevant variables must be filtered out by using statistical methods. How do we do this? First, we develop a theory predicting that, if one event occurs, another event will follow. Next, we devise a way of measuring exactly when and where the two events actually took place. Then we use statistical techniques to find out whether the time and place of the first event are associated, or correlated, with the time and place of the second event, as predicted by the theory. This correlation procedure can measure the probability, or likelihood, that the relationship between the two events could have arisen purely by chance. If we find the relationship too strong to be attributed to chance, the statistical technique has given us some evidence that the theory being tested has a foundation in fact or in the real world. Of course, many more tests would have to be run to convince social scientists that a theory is valid and useful. Perhaps the two events were really the common outcome of some third event. This possibility would have to be tested through the development of another theory, which, in turn, would be tested against actual experience.

Clearly, the approach to truth and understanding in economics and the other social sciences is a continuing process. New evidence may arise that casts doubt on long-established theories, and new theories can offer fresh approaches to understanding that may make older theories obsolete. But knowledge builds on knowledge, and new theories, when tested and supported by evidence, should be better than the old knowledge that is displaced. Economics is an optimistic science.

The Role of Assumptions

A theory need not fit all the facts. This statement often bothers beginning students of economics. It should not. Nor does ignoring certain real-world happenings mean that the theory is naive. Reality is often too complex to be grasped all at once. Sometimes we must simplify and isolate facts in order to see and understand relationships between particular variables. This is the role of **assumptions**—to set forth the limits of the variables in a theory and to state which of the variables are to be omitted.

An especially useful assumption in economics is expressed by the Latin phrase **ceteris paribus,** which means "other things being equal," that is, all other variables are held constant. For example, in order to analyze the effect of a change in the price of fuel oil on the quantity of fuel oil that is consumed, it may be helpful, at least initially, to disregard such other relevant variables as consumer incomes, the prices of competitive energy sources, and the severity of the weather. Thus, we might say, "When the price of a good such as fuel oil changes in one direction, the amount

consumed changes in the opposite direction, *ceteris paribus.*" This may be a valid and useful theory that can yield reliable and meaningful predictions about things or events that we may not yet have observed.

However, this simple theory may not be sufficient for predicting events in the real world. During a very mild winter or just after a big price change in a substitute fuel, we would certainly not want to predict on the assumption that these variables had not changed. Theories that take into account these important variables must be brought into the total analysis before any predictions are made and real-world policy conclusions are drawn.

Ceteris paribus is, of course, an example of only one simplifying assumption. Countless others may be made. For example, we shall next discuss "economic rationality," which assumes that people behave in a particular way. Some other frequently used assumptions are those about the level of information that people have, about the degree of competition that exists, and about the role that government does or does not play.

Economic Rationality

How would you describe human behavior in a word? Puzzling? Unpredictable? Because it is so complex, economists must make certain assumptions about the way people are likely to act. Thus, most economic theories contain a key assumption—that people act rationally. Economically rational behavior, or **economic rationality,** is any action that people take to make them better off or to prevent them from becoming worse off. The assumption of economic rationality allows economists to predict on the basis that people are motivated by self-interest. It is assumed that individuals appraise alternative courses of action and then choose that one that promises the greatest net gains.

Rational behavior need not be totally selfish. "Good things" come in many different packages. Though it is rational for Sally to prefer two new pairs of jeans to only one new pair, it may also be rational for her to prefer to buy her brother a shirt for his birthday rather than buy herself the second pair of jeans. If a rich old uncle wishes to be well remembered after he leaves this world and feels a sense of responsibility to his relatives, it is rational for him to leave $500,000 to his favorite niece. Furthermore, it is rational to give to one's favorite charity. Self-interest, then, has a broader meaning in economics than it does in common usage. People not only consider themselves better off when they add to their stock of material goods but also feel better off when they believe that they have done the right thing.

Actually, most individuals base decisions on social, political, and ethical considerations as well as on personal gain. Also, what people do may be strongly affected by habit, custom, and tradition. Every society weaves a fabric of institutions that guide economic behavior. Whether self-interest is institutionally determined or whether it is just part of human nature is a question that few economists feel qualified to explore. Instead they merely recognize that theories using this assumption have been tested time and again and found to be good predictors. Self-interest is a powerful economic insight.

In studying economic rationality, we shall examine four decision-making groups: (1) consumers; (2) business decision makers; (3) owners of capital, natural resources, and labor; and (4) government. Let us see what economic rationality means for each of these groups.

THE RATIONAL CONSUMER The rational consumer is one who seeks to gain the greatest possible satisfaction from purchases. To get the best value from income, the consumer chooses to buy a set of goods and services that is more attractive than any other set that he or she can afford. This means that the rational consumer is consistent and can calculate. If this person prefers A to B and B to C, then he or she must prefer A to C. The consumer need not be maximizing satisfaction under perfect conditions, but doing so with the limited information available at the time. Therefore the consumer who is disappointed after a purchase will buy different things on the next shopping trip because he or she now has more or better information.

THE RATIONAL BUSINESS DECISION MAKER The rational *entrepreneur*—the business decision maker—is defined as one who seeks maximum profits. Therefore, an entrepreneur will be willing to produce more goods only as long as expected additional income is greater than expected additional cost. Likewise, he or she will be willing to limit output if such action is expected to result in lowering cost more than revenue. In this way profits can be increased—or losses reduced.

THE RATIONAL OWNER OF CAPITAL, NATURAL RESOURCES, AND LABOR The rational owner of capital, natural resources, and labor tries to get the greatest possible return. In much the same way as the rational entrepreneur, the rational owner of capital (such as machines and factory buildings) seeks the maximum interest payment, the rational owner of natural resources (such as land and minerals) seeks maximum rent payment, and the rational owner of labor (the laborer) seeks the maximum wage. Suppose, for example, that someone is offered a job as a nurse at the XYZ hospital at a wage of $11.00 per hour. This person would not be a rational laborer if he or she would accept the same job for the same number of hours and under similar working conditions at the ABC hospital at a wage rate of only $10.00 per hour.

RATIONAL GOVERNMENT The groups discussed so far are all concerned primarily with maximizing their own incomes or satisfactions. Clearly, however, this is not the function that governments are supposed to perform. We shall briefly describe several approaches to the concept of rational government.

One approach is for the economist to recognize that government is made up of individuals who have their own personal motives. Here the economist tries to predict government behavior on the assumption that government workers, just like private citizens, will direct their behavior toward ends that will serve their self-interest. Specifically, government workers are expected to try to maximize their own job security, income, and glory. In the case of elected officials, job security—or being re-elected—is of major importance. This goal may lead them to advocate "popular" policies or at least to offer whatever the majority of their constituents favor. But all government workers, including those whose jobs do not depend on the voting public, are concerned with keeping their jobs, being promoted, and enjoying good working conditions. In this view, rational government action is that which brings government workers closer to these goals, however useless it may be to the public.[1]

Quite a different approach is to define rational government in terms of the functions and services that government should perform, such as the allocation, distribution, and stabilization responsibilities outlined in Chapter 2. Economists might define a rational government as one that can most accurately reflect what its citizens want government to do in these areas. Other economists define a rational government as one that will maximize social welfare (if they can define social welfare), even if the policies to be followed are not always popular. For example, suppose that a policy maker decides on the basis of a value judgment that the elderly widows of World War I veterans are more deserving of additional income than are wheat growers. Then it is rational to cut price supports for wheat and use the money to increase pensions for the widows, even though the wheat growers may represent many more votes than the widows. In this view, rational government is judged in the light of its own goals, rather than those of the majority of its citizens.

Positive and Normative Economics

Economics plays an important role in our lives. It is therefore not surprising that people have strong feelings concerning many economic issues, such as inflation, unemployment, nationalization of industry, unionization, minimum wages, energy, and environmental pollution. So that we are not misled by those who hope to have us side with them, a distinction is made between positive and normative approaches in economics.

1. In terms of maximization, it has been suggested that each government bureau or department tries to maximize its own appropriation or budget, year in and year out.

Positive economics deals with what is. It tries to be objective and to stay away from value judgments or opinions. **Normative economics** concerns itself with what ought to be. It is subjective and expresses a person's or a group's opinion. One example of positive economics would be a front-page newspaper article on the facts and figures of inflation. Another would be an article presenting various economic theories that try to explain inflation. By contrast, the same newspaper's editorial stating that inflation is the country's most serious problem and calling for certain courses of action is an example of normative economics.

One approach is not necessarily better than the other—as long as it is clear to the reader which is being employed. People can easily be fooled, however, when normative economics is disguised in positive clothes.

Of course, the positive-normative separation can become quite fuzzy when normative ideas enter the choice of subjects to be studied positively. Some suggest that for a long time black-white and male-female wage differences were not approved subjects for detailed study, because the results might provide ammunition to "radicals."

FUNCTIONAL RELATIONSHIPS

In discussing economic theory, we pointed out that economists look for relationships that occur between different economic variables. Such a relationship is often expressed in terms of a **function**—a statement of how one variable depends on other variables. For example, one variable—the weekly earnings of coal miners in West Virginia—may be a function of such variables as the number of hours worked per week and the wage rate per hour. This relationship may be written as

$$E = f(H, W)$$

where E is the weekly earnings of the coal miners, f is a symbol for function and can be read as "depends on," H is the number of hours worked per week, and W is the hourly wage rate.

Dependent and Independent Variables

When one variable is being described as a function of other variables, it is called the **dependent variable,** and the variables upon which it depends are called the **independent variables.** Thus, in our example, the dependent variable is the weekly earnings of West Virginia coal miners, and the independent variables are the number of hours that they work per week and the hourly wage rate that they receive. If we were considering another functional relationship, however, the classification of variables might change. For example, the hourly wage rate of the miners might be treated as a function of such variables as the desirability of the particular task performed on the job (that is, how clean, safe, and pleasurable it is), the number of years worked on the job, and the level of skill that the job requires. If these were the independent variables, the hourly wage rate of the miners would then be the dependent variable in this functional relationship.

Direct and Inverse Relationships

The relationship between the dependent and independent variables in a function may be either direct or inverse. A **direct relationship** is one where the dependent and the independent variables change in the same direction. The relationship $E = f(H, W)$ is a direct one between earnings and hours worked and between earnings and the wage rate. Coal miners' earnings go up when they work more hours and when their hourly wages are higher, *ceteris paribus.* Likewise, their earnings go down when they work fewer hours and when their wage rates are lower, *ceteris paribus.* An **inverse relationship** is one in which the dependent and independent variables change in opposite directions. An example is the case where we related the hourly wage rate of miners to the desirability of the task performed. This relationship may be expressed as

$$W = f(T)$$

where the symbols W and f are as before and T is the degree of desirability of the task. The more desirable the task is for the miners, the lower the wage rate would be; the less desirable they find the task, the higher the wage rate would be, other things being equal.

Graphs

Functional relationships are often expressed algebraically or geometrically. The geometrical expression, by means of graphs, is usually simpler for most students than the algebraic one. There is an old saying that "a picture is worth a thousand words." In economics that is often the case. The "thousand words," or even a hundred words, are not as easy to grasp as a simple "picture"— a graph. Learning to read graphs will help you to understand a functional relationship at a glance.

QUADRANTS AND SCALES A review of the basics of graphing will be helpful. Figure 3-1 shows the four sections, or **quadrants,** that are formed when a horizontal axis is placed on a vertical axis. The point of intersection is at zero and is called the **origin.** Each axis is marked off with numbers, or **scaled,** to show the different values for the variable being measured along that axis. In the upper right part of the graph is quadrant I, showing values that are positive on both axes. To the left, quadrant II is for values that are negative on the horizontal axis and positive on the vertical axis. Just below, quadrant III provides for values that are negative on both axes. In the lower right, quadrant IV takes care of values that are positive on the horizontal axis and negative on the vertical axis. Most graphs in this book will be in quadrant I, where both axes show positive values.

PLOTTING Recall the functional relationship $E = f(H, W)$, where coal miners' earnings are a function of the number of hours they work and of their hourly wage rate. Table 3-1 shows a hypothetical relationship between the weekly earnings of coal miners and the number of hours they work per week. The wage rate is held constant at $10 per hour.

FIGURE 3-1   Axes and Quadrants for Graphing

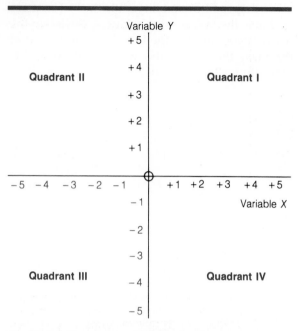

When the vertical axis is placed on the horizontal axis, four quadrants are formed. Quadrant I, where both axes show positive values, is the one most often used in this book.

In Figure 3-2 the information from Table 3-1 has been plotted on a graph. Each point is located by drawing two straight lines, called **perpendiculars,** from any of the values along the axes. For example, the perpendicular drawn at $100 of earnings meets the perpendicular drawn at 10 hours to determine point A. The information in

TABLE 3-1   Relation of Coal Miners' Earnings to Hours Worked (Hypothetical Numbers)

Coal Miners' Weekly Earnings (in dollars)	Number of Hours Worked per Week
50	5
100	10
200	20
350	35

Table 3-1 also establishes the other three points (B, C, and D in Figure 3-2). The plotted points may then be joined by drawing a line through them, and additional information can be obtained from this line. Though Table 3-1 did not contain information about coal miners' earnings when they work 15 hours or when they work 23½ hours a week, the line or curve provides good estimates of such intermediate values. Just draw a perpendicular from the horizontal axis at 23½ hours to the curve and then read off the earnings ($235) for that point on the vertical axis. The graph, then, is a quick way of summarizing information about the relationship between coal miners' earnings and the number of hours they work.

SLOPE   When dealing with functional relationships, economists are often very much interested in knowing the size of the change in one variable that is associated with a change in the other variable. The term used to express this relation is **slope.**

Slope is stated in the following form:

$$\text{slope} = \frac{\text{change in variable on vertical axis}}{\text{change in variable on horizontal axis}}$$

Slope may be either positive or negative. A direct relationship between the variables indicates a **positive slope,** and an inverse relationship a **negative slope.**

The example that was pictured in Figure 3-2 illustrated positive slope, since when a coal miner works an additional hour, earnings increase by $10, and when the miner works an hour less, earnings decrease by $10. The slope in this example is therefore 10/1 or 10. Clearly, the slope of a line depends on the scaling values that were used in constructing the graph. If earnings were scaled in pennies, the slope would be 1,000/1 or 1,000.

The case of the inverse relationship between hourly wage rates received by coal miners and the desirability of the task performed offers an example of a negative slope. This is graphed in Figure 3-3, where the curve goes down from left to right, indicating that the slope is negative. (This is in contrast to the curve in Figure 3-2,

FIGURE 3-2 **Relation of Coal Miners' Earnings to Hours Worked**

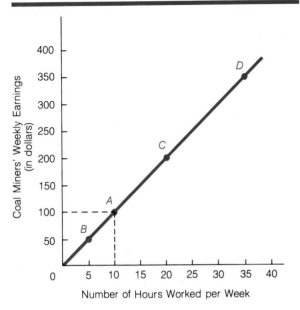

The curve pictures the function $E = f(H)$, where E is the weekly earnings of coal miners and H is the number of hours per week that they work. Their hourly wage rate is fixed at $10.

The numbers plotted from Table 3-1 establish the points B, A, C, and D. The line or curve that is drawn to join these points gives you good estimates of intermediate values.

FIGURE 3-3 **Relation of Coal Miners' Wage Rates to Desirability of Tasks**

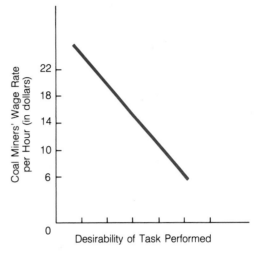

The curve pictures the function $W = f(T)$, where W is the hourly wage rate received by coal miners for performing different tasks and T is the desirability of the task performed (how clean, safe, and pleasurable it is). It shows an inverse relationship between these variables and therefore has a negative slope.

which goes up from left to right, showing that the slope is positive.)

The curves drawn in Figures 3-2 and 3-3 are straight lines and represent **linear relationships.** This means that for the range of values shown, the dependent variable is uniformly responsive to changes in the independent variable. In other words, the slope is constant throughout the length of the curve.

Many relationships between economic variables are **nonlinear,** which means that equal changes in the independent variable do not always bring about the same response in the dependent variable. Simple nonlinear curves fall into four categories, which are graphed in Figure 3-4. In describing slopes as increasing or decreasing, we use absolute values (values without reference to

sign) to avoid confusion when dealing with curves that have negative slopes. Panel (a) shows a direct relationship between the variables. However, as the independent variable increases, so does the slope of the curve. For equal increases of the independent variable, the dependent variable increases by increasing amounts. For example, the curve relating coal miners' weekly earnings to the number of hours a week that they work would have an increasing positive slope if miners received higher and higher hourly wage rates the more hours per week that they worked.

Panel (b) also shows a direct relationship between the variables, but this time, as the independent variable increases, the slope of the curve decreases. For equal increases of the independent variable, the dependent variable increases by decreasing amounts.

Panels (c) and (d) illustrate nonlinear inverse relationships. In (c), as the independent variable

FIGURE 3-4   Nonlinear Curves

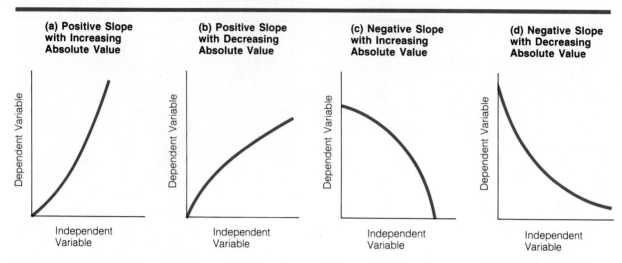

| **(a) Positive Slope with Increasing Absolute Value** | **(b) Positive Slope with Decreasing Absolute Value** | **(c) Negative Slope with Increasing Absolute Value** | **(d) Negative Slope with Decreasing Absolute Value** |

Each of the four graphs pictures a different nonlinear curve. Panels (a) and (b) show positive relationships between the variables, and panels (c) and (d) show negative relationships. In panel (a) the absolute value of the slope is increasing, in panel (b) it is decreasing, in panel (c) it is increasing, and in panel (d) it is decreasing.

increases, the dependent variable decreases at an increasing rate—the curve becomes steeper, showing that the absolute value of the slope becomes greater. In (d), as the independent variable increases, the dependent variable decreases at a decreasing rate—the curve becomes flatter, showing that the absolute value of the slope becomes smaller.[2]

In Figure 3-4, the dependent variable appears on the vertical axes and the independent variable appears on the horizontal axes of the graphs. This is convenient for our explanation of slope. In illustrating actual economic theories, the dependent variable is *not* always on the vertical axis and the independent variable is *not* always on the horizontal axis. In each economic graph, the theory itself must be consulted to determine which variable is dependent and which is independent. However, slope is always measured as the change on the vertical axis divided by the change on the horizontal axis.

MARGINAL ANALYSIS

Economists often use **marginal analysis** to predict or evaluate the outcome of economic decisions. **Marginal** means "extra" or "additional." It refers to either the last unit that has been added or the next unit that may be added. For an individual thinking about how much of a product to buy, the marginal unit is the last one bought, or the next one that might be bought. Being "on the margin" means being in the process of deciding between alternatives. The child standing in front of a candy counter with 30¢ in hand is on the margin for various kinds of candy. The youngster

2. *Percentage* changes present us with special problems in graphing. For example, a quantity rising at a constant percentage rate is rising by increasing amounts. Therefore, it would be shown in our diagrams as a curve that is concave upward. If you have studied logarithms, you will remember that a linear *logarithmic* function represents a constant *percentage* rise or fall. Curvature on a logarithmic function represents rising or falling percentage changes. The slope of a logarithmic function is therefore a percentage change.

may buy one more Hershey bar, one more roll of Lifesavers, or one more Milky Way.

Marginal analysis recognizes that economic decisions are only rarely of an all-or-nothing nature. Business firms are not usually trying to decide whether to produce or not to produce. Rather, they are more often concerned with how much of certain goods to produce this week or this year. Individuals, likewise, rarely ask whether they should purchase food, clothing, or shelter, but instead ask what combination of these things they should purchase. Should they buy a little more food and a little less clothing, or more of both at the expense of renting a somewhat less attractive apartment? Individuals also face marginal decisions in regard to the amount of work they wish to do. Students typically do not think in terms of studying versus not studying at all. Rather they decide how much time to devote to study and therefore how much to leisure activities or to outside jobs. Should a third hour be devoted to studying for an exam, or should that hour be spent resting?

Marginal Analysis in Functional Relationships

Marginal analysis can be joined with the earlier discussion of functional relationships. Economists are often concerned with how much one variable changes as another variable changes. How much will an individual miner's weekly earnings increase if the hourly wage rate increases by a certain amount? The miner may receive an increase in hourly wage rate from $10 to $12, so that the marginal change in the hourly wage rate is $2. If the miner works 40 hours a week, then the weekly earnings will increase from $400 to $480, or a marginal increase of $80.

Relationship Between Marginal, Average, and Total Amount

Many theories in economics make use of marginal, average, and total measures. Thus, it is important to recognize how they differ and how they are related. The *total* is the whole of whatever variable is being measured. What is added to the total or subtracted from it in any one step is the *marginal* amount. The *average* is the total divided by the number of units. For example, a student may have gone to the movies 25 times this year and paid $4 each time. The total amount spent on movies is $100, the average expense is $4 ($100/25), and the marginal expense is also $4 (the price of the last movie). The total amount is always the sum of all the marginal amounts—25 movies at $4 per movie add up to $100. Suppose that the student were to go once more to the movies and find that the price had suddenly increased to $5. In this case, the marginal expense (on the 26th movie) is $5, the new total expense is $105, and the new average expense is about $4.04 ($105/26 = $4.04). Note that the increased marginal expenditure caused an increase in the average expense. Whenever a marginal amount is higher than an average amount, the average amount must be increasing over that range of values. Likewise, whenever a marginal amount is below an average amount, the average amount must be decreasing. Therefore, only when the marginal amount is equal to the average amount— as in our case before the price of movies increased—is the average amount neither increasing nor decreasing. This relationship will always hold because the marginal amount causes the average amount to rise or fall or remain the same.

Marginal Cost and Marginal Benefit

Many economic theories predict by comparing **marginal cost** with **marginal benefit**. People are expected to act so as to maximize their well-being, and they will normally do so by equating their marginal cost with their marginal benefit.

The idea of equating marginal cost and marginal benefit is best explained in terms of an example. Suppose you are out hiking in the woods and come across an area where wild blueberries are growing. You reach down and pick a handful growing at your feet. Since you were hungry, the blueberries give you a good deal of benefit in return for very little cost in terms of effort. You

FIGURE 3-5 The Marginal Benefit and Marginal Cost of Picking and Eating Blueberries

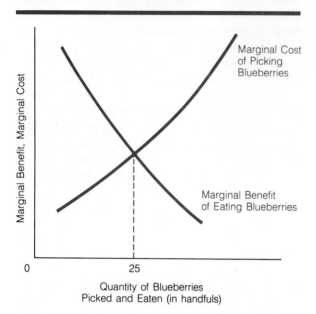

Well-being is maximized by picking and eating 25 handfuls of blueberries. If you eat any less than that amount, the marginal benefit of eating blueberries is greater than the marginal cost of picking them, and so you have not taken full advantage. Any more than 25 handfuls finds the marginal cost greater than the marginal benefit, so that well-being has been reduced.

see more berries growing nearby and walk over and pick those as well. The satisfaction of eating fresh blueberries is still well worth a little bit of extra effort. After you have spent twenty minutes or so eating blueberries, you are no longer as hungry as you were, but still you derive some satisfaction from eating additional blueberries. The longer you pick and eat, however, the harder it is to find berries that are conveniently located. Some of them are up on a hill, others are guarded by thistles, and still others are perilously close to what looks like poison ivy. So as you continue picking blueberries, the cost of picking them becomes greater, since it is harder to get to them. At the same time, the longer you continue eating blueberries, the less enjoyment the next handful provides. After half an hour or so, you reach the

point where the benefit to you from eating another handful of blueberries is just equal to the cost (in inconvenience) of picking another handful. At this point, you stop picking blueberries and continue with your hike. Any additional berries you might pick at this time would be more trouble than they would be worth. Thus, consciously or not, you used marginal analysis to reach an optimal—best—level of blueberry picking and eating. You continued up to the point at which the marginal benefit of eating blueberries was equal to the marginal cost of picking blueberries, and after that you stopped.

This example is clearly illustrated through the use of a diagram. Figure 3-5 includes a positively sloped curve, showing the marginal cost of picking blueberries, and a negatively sloped curve, showing the marginal benefit from eating blueberries. On the far left part of the diagram, the marginal benefit is far greater than the marginal cost (you're very hungry and the blueberries are very easy to reach). On the far right part, the marginal cost is much greater than the marginal benefit (your hunger is pretty well satisfied and the blueberries are quite hard to reach). Anywhere to the left of the intersection of the two curves (less than 25 handfuls of blueberries), the marginal benefit exceeds the marginal cost, and it pays to continue picking. Anywhere to the right of the intersection of the two curves (more than 25 handfuls of blueberries), the marginal cost exceeds the marginal benefit, and it is not economically rational to pick and eat blueberries. Therefore, during this particular stop on your hike you pick and eat exactly 25 handfuls of blueberries, your optimal level of blueberry picking and eating.

This simple story illustrates a technique that can be applied to a great many economic problems. When marginal benefits are high but declining and marginal costs are low but rising, it generally is true that an individual or an organization will reach an optimum point by equating marginal cost and marginal benefit. A worker may use this technique in deciding how many hours of overtime to put in. Sometimes a family uses it in deciding how big a car to buy. It can also be used by a company in deciding how much of a good to produce or how many workers to hire. And a government may use it in deciding how many tax dodgers to prosecute. Equating marginal benefit and marginal cost, then, is the basis upon which economists predict the outcomes of decisions made by individuals and organizations.

Criticism of Marginal Analysis

The marginal technique is not every economist's "cup of tea." The institutionalist school of American economists argues that economic choice can be understood only in the framework of history and contemporary economic laws, customs, and attitudes. Radical political economists take particular issue with marginalism. They argue that marginalism deliberately ignores history and present institutions and is too narrowly concerned with the mechanics of choice. Furthermore, they believe that marginalism diverts the economist's attention from other issues, such as income distribution, freedom of consumer choice, economic growth and the environment, that are of greater importance. The question is whether the usefulness of marginal analysis as a tool can be separated from normative questions about the issues themselves. The majority of American economists believe that it can, and therefore that marginalism is equally consistent with both changing institutions and constant ones.

EQUILIBRIUM

Equilibrium is a state of balance. In a state of equilibrium, forces for change within a system offset each other so that there is no net tendency for the system to change.

An example will help to make the meaning of equilibrium clearer. Imagine a line of three adjoining rooms, connected by two doors. These doors are closed. The room on the right is heated to, say, 90°. The room on the left is air-conditioned, say, at 30°. There is neither heating nor air-conditioning in the middle room. If the doors

are opened, both hot air and cold air will rush into the middle room. After a while the temperature in the middle room will reach an equilibrium position—a state of balance.

Stable and Unstable Equilibrium

Equilibrium may be stable or unstable. In our example it is likely that the temperature of the middle room will go to about 60° and stay there. This would be a **stable equilibrium**—one that tends to restore itself in the face of disturbances. For example, if a large cake of ice were placed in the middle room, it would cause the temperature to drop, say, to 50°. However, after a while the ice will melt and the temperature in the room will return to 60°—the stable equilibrium.

Unstable equilibrium may also be observed. Suppose that you are attempting to balance an egg on its end. Small shifts in direction that you make with your hand allow you to bring it to an equilibrium position and leave it there. However, one small gust of wind or a gentle push will cause it to fall over. There will be no tendency for it to bounce back up and regain its unstable (upright) equilibrium position.

Equilibrium is an important idea in economic analysis because it is a basic tool that economists use to predict future situations. Knowing the requirements for an equilibrium enables economists to identify events that might cause a change, the direction of that change, and what the new equilibrium will be. If an event upsets an existing equilibrium, economists try to find out whether a new equilibrium has been established or whether the initial equilibrium will tend to be restored. If the initial equilibrium was a stable one, economists can predict on that basis. If a new equilibrium has been established, a different set of predictions will be needed. Disturbances to equilibrium happen almost continuously, so that most of the time situations are moving from one equilibrium to another. In our earlier example involving the three adjoining rooms, the thermostats controlling the temperature in the heated room and in the air-conditioned room may be changed from time to time, altering the equilibrium temperature in the middle room. But disturbances do not make the equilibrium concept any less useful as a tool for predicting what will happen as a result of disturbances. In fact, the idea of economics as a useful guide for carrying out economic policy is based on this ability to predict consequences of disturbances. If the consequences of a certain disturbance are judged to be desirable by policy makers, the disturbance itself may be created as an instrument of policy.

Partial Equilibrium Versus General Equilibrium

Equilibrium analysis may be partial or general. **Partial equilibrium analysis** deals with the effects of some disturbance on one set of economic variables, assuming that all other variables are unaffected. **General equilibrium analysis** takes into account all the different effects related to the specific economic disturbance that is being studied.

Widely used in economics, partial equilibrium analysis can be justified by the need to simplify and handle as few variables as possible at one time. This approach is proper for a wide range of economic problems. For example, in the automobile industry—one of the largest and most influential industries in the United States—partial equilibrium analysis is appropriate in some cases, but in other cases general equilibrium analysis is necessary. A rise in the hourly wage rate for auto workers will raise the cost of producing cars. Partial equilibrium analysis would examine this immediate effect, which may be all that is of concern. However, several other effects could be examined if a general equilibrium framework were used. The increase in the income of auto workers will increase their ability to buy automobiles. But if the increase in the cost of producing automobiles leads to higher prices of automobiles, it may change the percentage of consumers' incomes spent on automobiles and therefore affect how much they buy of other goods and services. These effects could, in turn, feed back on the automobile market and thus influence the price and quantity of automobiles

sold as well. Partial equilibrium analysis does not take all these factors into account, but general equilibrium analysis tries to take account of them. In the automobile industry, where a wage hike may have a great impact on the demand for both automobiles and other goods, the use of partial equilibrium will sometimes be insufficient. However, in smaller and less economically important industries, such as those producing watchbands or golf carts, a wage hike would have fairly mild effects, and the use of partial equilibrium would usually be sufficient.

A WORD TO THE WISE . . .

So far we have described some essential tools for understanding and using economics. A few warnings are needed now to identify some of the problems that can lead to wrong conclusions.

Terms

When students enter a new field, they usually expect to encounter some unfamiliar terms. What they may not expect, however, is that familiar words can take on quite different meanings. An important example is **capital.** In everyday language, particularly in a business context, the word refers to money. A person who is thinking of starting a neighborhood restaurant may wonder how much "capital" is required to make a go of it—$150,000 or $200,000? In economics, however, *capital* refers to real goods, such as machinery and factory buildings, which are used in a production process.

A related term, **investment,** is another good example of a word that has a particular meaning in economics. In everyday language, a person is said to "invest" when he or she buys financial securities such as stocks and bonds, or real estate, or works of art. In economics, investment refers to the creation of capital. Business people invest when they purchase goods that enable them to produce yet other goods.

Cause and Effect

Mistaken causation is another danger in economic reasoning. The fact that one event precedes another does not necessarily mean that the first causes the second to occur. Just after more and more college students began to wear jeans to school, they got higher and higher grades in their courses. Would the rise in grades have occurred if jeans had not become so popular? It probably would have. There is no apparent cause-and-effect logic showing that the increased wearing of jeans led to students' higher course grades.

It has been suggested that union-imposed wage increases cause inflation and that the massive stock market crash of 1929 caused the Great Depression of the 1930s. More careful analysis leads us to regard these ideas with great skepticism. Though facts are important, they cannot be relied upon alone to explain relationships. Theory based on logical analysis must serve as the real foundation of the search for truth.

Fallacy of Composition

The **fallacy of composition** is another pitfall to watch out for in economics. We can avoid the difficulty by understanding that what is true for one part is not necessarily true for the whole. A person watching a soccer match in a crowded stadium may be better able to see an exciting play when she stands up. But if the whole crowd stands up to see the play, no one will be able to see any better than when all were seated. Similarly in economics, what is advantageous behavior for a single individual may be quite harmful if engaged in by many individuals or an entire economy. Consider a wheat farmer who produces more wheat in order to increase his income. If he were the only one, or one of a few, to do so, he might achieve his objective. But if all or most of the wheat farmers in the country increased output, the much greater amount of wheat produced would lower the price of wheat so much that each individual farmer's income might actually be reduced.

Time Lags

Yet another difficulty often faced in economics is the matter of **time lags**—the amount of time it takes for a change in an economic variable to have an effect. For example, consider the effect that a tuition increase will have on enrollment at a certain college or university. The immediate effect may be very minor, since most students will already have paid tuition for the present semester or term and are not affected until the next one begins. In the new term some students will drop out or transfer to other schools, but probably most will grudgingly pay the higher tuition rather than leave their friends, lose credits in transfer, and go through the hassle of making a move. Just the same, the effect of the tuition hike may still be substantial on new enrollment. Students who would have enrolled for the next and subsequent terms may decide that the higher tuition is too much. There are a number of time lags in this example, and the more time that passes, the greater the effect. In order to make a useful prediction about the effect on enrollment of the tuition increase, valid information about the length of the time lags must be examined.

Expectations

Often people react to *expectations,* or what they expect will happen, rather than to what actually is happening. For example, a large increase in the price of a good will usually discourage people from buying it. However, there are cases where we find the opposite result. The price rise may make people think that the price will go up even more—in other words, it changes their expectation concerning future prices. Therefore, if the good is storable, purchasers hurry to buy it in order to avoid the still higher price yet to come.

What is the explanation for the fact that at one time the price of General Motors stock goes up after the company reports higher earnings and at another time the stock price goes down after just as glowing a report? The answer may be expectations. In the first instance, the earnings increase may have been a pleasant surprise since people had expected poorer earnings. The second time, it may have been a disappointment because people expected even higher earnings. Likewise, a government action such as a tax cut may at one time cause people to spend the extra money, but at another time have no such effect. The explanation may be that in the second case the tax cut had been anticipated for months so that people were spending according to the amount of money they expected to receive long before the tax cut actually took place.

It is important to be aware of the effect that a change in a variable has on expectations. Changes in expectations depend upon a great many different variables, which extend well beyond the realm of economics and are very difficult to predict.

Pervasive Errors

The major problems of amateur economic thinking lie, we think, not so much in errors of logic as in *nonrational ways of knowing* and in *temporal limitations*.

The main nonrational ways of knowing are intuition, faith, and slogan thinking. Do you believe an economic argument or policy is right or wrong simply because it is "radical" or "progressive" or "conservative" or "reactionary" or "hard-headed" or "compassionate" or "probusiness" or "prolabor" or "socialistic" or "fascistic" or "old-fashioned" or "un-American"? (The list is endless.) If you do, you are indulging in some combination of these nonrational ways of knowing, as indeed everyone does some of the time.

One temporal limitation—a most common one among politicians—is a refusal to consider ideas or policies that are not likely to win votes in the next election—for example, the possibility that problems can ever be caused by any wage rate being too high. Another mistake—more common among professional economists—is to consider only policies that will work too slowly to help in emergencies—like doing nothing in a depression while waiting for wages and prices to fall.

SUMMARY

1. Economic theory is used for logically analyzing information, studying cause and effect, and solving real problems in economics.

2. Because economics is a social science, it must often be satisfied with predicting the direction of change instead of the exact amount of change.

3. In order to keep theories as simple as possible and to isolate extraneous, or less important, variables, economists often use assumptions such as *ceteris paribus* and economic rationality.

4. Economically rational behavior is any action that people take to make them better off or to keep them from becoming worse off. Economists predict on the basis that all economic units—consumers; businesses; owners of natural resources, capital, and labor; and government—act in a rational way.

5. Positive economics deals with what is—with facts. Normative economics concerns itself with what ought to be—with opinions. It is important to be aware of this difference.

6. Functional relationships between dependent and independent variables may be direct or inverse. Economists find it useful to present these functions by means of graphs or diagrams. On these graphs, direct relationships are shown as a positive slope, and inverse relationships are shown as a negative slope. If the slope of a curve is constant throughout its length, it will be linear (appear as a straight line), and if the slope increases or decreases, the curve will be nonlinear.

7. Marginal means extra or additional—one more or one less. Marginal analysis recognizes that most economic decisions are made "on the margin" and are not of an all-or-nothing type.

8. When the marginal cost of an activity is increasing and marginal benefit from the same activity is decreasing, a person will maximize his or her well-being gained from the activity by equating marginal cost and marginal benefit.

9. Equilibrium is a state of balance. Though the economy may only rarely be at equilibrium, this is an important concept. It allows economists to focus on the effects of particular disturbances and to predict future events.

10. It is important to watch out for several problems in the study of economics:

a. Some familiar terms such as *capital* and *investment* take on quite different meanings in economics from those in common usage.

b. The fact that one event precedes another does not necessarily indicate a cause-and-effect relationship between them.

c. What is true for a part is not necessarily true for the whole.

d. It is important to consider time lags—how long it takes for a change in an economic variable to have an effect.

e. People will often react to what they expect will happen, rather than to what is actually occurring.

DISCUSSION QUESTIONS

1. Marcia and Jim are having a discussion concerning a certain theory of inflation. Jim explains the theory, including the variables involved, the relationships among the variables, and the assumptions that the theory sets forth. Marcia responds that she considers the theory to be quite meaningless because it seems to be based on several quite unrealistic assumptions. Putting yourself in the place of Jim, how would you defend yourself?

2. Experimentation ought to be left to physical scientists. Since economics is a social science, economists should stick to describing human behavior. Do you agree? Explain.

3. Using the economist's assumption that human beings act rationally in their economic decision making, describe how:

a. a consumer will shop

b. an entrepreneur will decide what and how many inputs to use and outputs to produce

c. a worker will choose among job alternatives

4. Why is it so much more difficult to describe rational government than to describe rational consumers, entrepreneurs, and the owners of capital, natural resources, and labor?

5. Differentiate between positive and normative economics. Give three examples of positive statements and three examples of normative statements in the field of economics. Would a positively or a normatively oriented economist be of greater value to a politician?

6. How is the demand for public transportation related to the price of gas? Tell what type of variable each is and how they interact.

7. The Greasy Spoon is open daily from 4 P.M. to 4 A.M. The employees (primarily college students) may choose the number of hours they wish to work. Their daily earnings, then, depend on the number of hours worked and the hourly wage, which is $3.50. On weekends they choose to work fewer hours than on weekdays. Write the function for this relationship. Using the following information, graph the relationship and show the slope:

Daily Earnings	Hours worked
$10.50	3 (Friday)
10.50	3 (Saturday)
14.00	4 (Sunday)
17.50	5 (Monday)
21.00	6 (Tuesday)
24.50	7 (Wednesday)
28.00	8 (Thursday)

8. The Miller Brewing Company buys barley from a group of farmers in Iowa. The more Miller buys, the greater is its total expenditure on barley. However, the more Miller buys, the lower is the price per bushel that it has to pay. What is the sign of the relationship between the amount of barley purchased and the total expenditure on barley? Is this a linear relationship? Draw a graph that shows the relationship between the amount of barley purchased and the total amount paid for barley.

9. During a certain month John buys a pound of hamburger every third day (ten pounds in all). He pays $1.50 for each of the first five pounds, $1.60 for each of the next four pounds, and $1.70 for the tenth pound. Calculate John's total cost, average cost, and marginal cost for hamburger for that month.

10. Suppose that you have an economics exam

tomorrow and decide to study for it tonight. Suppose further that your negatively sloped marginal-benefit curve for studying intersects your positively sloped marginal-cost curve for studying at four hours of studying. (You may now want to draw these two curves on a set of axes, scaling marginal benefit and marginal cost along the vertical axis and the number of study hours along the horizontal axis.)

Using marginal benefit–marginal cost analysis, explain why you would not want to stop studying after only three hours.

Using marginal benefit–marginal cost analysis, explain why you would not want to study as much as five hours.

11. Why are economists so concerned with equilibrium when, in fact, it is very seldom reached?

12. Under what conditions might an economist prefer to use partial rather than general equilibrium analysis?

4 *Scarcity: The Economic Problem*

PREVIEW This chapter returns to the concept of *scarcity*, which you met earlier in the book. Most economists assume, despite the doubts of the communists, that scarcity is unavoidable and that there is no such thing as an economy of abundance. This assumption is certainly correct in the short run, though it is debatable over the longer term.

For as long as scarcity is with us, it will be the central problem of economics. All our everyday economic problems can be traced back to it. Furthermore, goods and services are scarce because they are produced by combining resources, which are themselves scarce. These resources are divided into labor, natural resources, and capital (further divided into physical and human capital), and we shall discuss each in turn. The special function of combining these resources—particularly in the production of new goods or services and in the application of new ways to produce standard goods and services, all under conditions of uncertainty—we call enterprise or entrepreneurship, an important form of the labor resource.

A major theme running through this chapter is that the existence of scarcity necessitates choice. In other words, we must answer the basic questions raised in Chapter 1: what to produce, how to produce it, and to whom it should go. Also because of scarcity we must consider opportunity cost, the idea that the real cost of something is what is given up to obtain it. Opportunity cost applies to both consumption and production decisions. The chapter is thus an introduction to the important topics of consumer choice, to the production decisions of firms, and to the concepts of supply and demand.

SCARCITY

There are many economic problems. We have them, our neighbors have them, business firms have them, and government agencies have them—not just in this country, but around the whole world. You would like to have a new car but cannot afford it. You want to go to a party on Thursday night; however, there is an economics exam Friday morning and you need time to study for it. Your family wants to live in a better house, but it costs too much. The farmer wants a new tractor, but the bank is unwilling to provide a loan. Though the Pentagon desires a new-generation bomber, Congress refuses to pass the enabling legislation. The family in rural Bangladesh wishes to have enough to eat but does not have the means to grow or buy the food. These and trillions of other economic problems are common. Though they vary greatly in type and in urgency, they are all just examples of a single problem—scarcity, *the* economic problem.

Scarcity means that the amount of something actually available is not sufficient to meet some requirement. The critical word in this definition is *requirement*, since a given amount of something may or may not constitute scarcity, depending on how this amount compares with the requirement. In the illustrations given in the preceding paragraph, the requirement appeared in such terms as "would like to have," "wishes," "wants," or "desires." The things discussed were scarce because the amount actually available was less than the amount wanted or desired. Thus, economics specifies a very distinctive meaning for the term *scarcity*. It is an important term to remember.

Scarce Goods and Services

Economists use some words in ways that differ from ordinary usage. *Scarcity* is such a word. In everyday language a good or a service is "scarce" when the demand for it is greater than the supply available. Economists agree only if the terms *demand* and *supply* are understood to refer to amounts demanded and supplied at a price of zero. (Price also does not have to take the form of money. So the "price of zero" can mean that a demander does not have to give up goods or time and that a supplier does not receive goods or anything else in the exchange.) Whenever people want more of a good or service than is available free of charge, economists refer to that good or service as scarce. Suppose that a clothing manufacturer decides to introduce a new line of designer socks and after doing some market research offers 1,000 pairs per day for sale at a price of $5 per pair. If only 400 pairs are sold per day, these socks would not be considered scarce in everyday language. However, economists would want to withhold judgment until they had information about the quantity demanded at prices below $5. If, indeed, 1,000 pairs per day are sold at $2 per pair and if consumers would buy more than 1,000 pairs at some even lower price, then economists would consider these socks to be scarce. At a price of zero, the quantity of pairs of socks demanded would far exceed the quantity offered by suppliers.

A good or service becomes scarcer over time if the difference between the quantities demanded and supplied at a price of zero increases. Similarly, a good or service becomes less scarce over time if the difference between the quantities demanded and supplied at a price of zero decreases.

Scarce Resources

Why do most goods and services command a positive price? Why are most goods and services scarce? The answer can be found by examining how goods and services are produced.

Production involves bringing together certain inputs—called **factors of production** or **resources**—to create goods and services, that is, the output. Resources are the ingredients necessary for producing goods and services. Just as you cannot bake a cake without the ingredients of flour, eggs, sugar, and so on, you cannot produce goods and services without resources. It is these resources that are scarce and, in turn, cause goods and services that are produced with them to be scarce.

It is useful to separate resources into three broad classes:

1. **Labor resources** are all kinds of human work efforts that are or can be directed at production or at enterprise, which is the organizing of production.
2. **Natural resources** are all things provided by nature that can be used in production, such as land and minerals.
3. **Capital resources** are goods or tools or skills that are produced for use in further production.

These three kinds of resources—labor, natural, and capital—are defined broadly enough to cover everything that goes into production.

LABOR RESOURCES Labor includes all forms of human work, blue-collar and white-collar alike, from the most menial and routine to the most intellectual and managerial.

It is easy to recognize the labor of the machine operator, the ditch digger, the assembly-line worker, and the fruit picker. But other types of labor are included in the concept of the labor resource. The accountant, the secretary, and the company president are all examples here. Also classified as labor are **enterprisers** or **entrepreneurs**—those who seek the best opportunities for production and take risks when making such decisions.

Enterprise differs from administrative and managerial labor in that it is less routine. The labor done by the entrepreneur is to make the basic choices and decisions within a company, particularly those decisions that involve taking chances. The entrepreneur must judge the merits of past and present ways of producing goods or services and must decide how to apply new production methods or how to produce new goods. Thus an enterpriser or entrepreneur is often an innovator, but only rarely an inventor.

The distinction between innovator and inventor is worth clarifying. It is the **inventor** who discovers or devises a new or improved process or product. The **innovator** is the one who brings the invention out of the laboratory, makes it practical, and applies it to actual production. The physicist Enrico Fermi was an inventor of the fission process of releasing atomic energy, but he was not an important innovator in either the civilian or the military applications of atomic energy. Henry Ford was the innovator who applied assembly-line techniques to automobile production, and Alfred Sloan, Jr., was the innovator who introduced the annual model change in automobile marketing. So far as we know, neither invented anything of importance. Many of us are surprised that the innovators of new products and processes so often make higher incomes and amass greater wealth than the inventors do. Both Ford and Sloan made more money from their innovations than Fermi did from his invention. (Of course, Fermi won a Nobel Prize—something that Ford and Sloan never did.)

QUANTITY AND QUALITY OF LABOR The quantity of labor available to a society is determined by the size of its population, the age distribution, and the prevailing attitudes about who should work, over what periods of their lives, and for how long each year. Countries with large populations and with small percentages of very young (below working age) and very old (above working age) people have large amounts of labor. Societies that deny work to certain groups of people or support a leisure class possess less labor. Those that offer many years of schooling to young

people and provide retirement income to older people have less labor. Finally, the amount of labor that a country has will depend on the length of the workday and the workweek, and the amount of holiday and vacation time that workers receive.

There is also a qualitative aspect of the labor resource. Certainly, production is more than simply expending energy. The workers' attitude toward the job, for example, is important to production. When that attitude is wholesome and constructive and when the workers enjoy what they are doing and take pride in the results, there will be more production from the work effort than when the attitude is negative.

COMBINATION WITH OTHER RESOURCES Because the labor resource is usually employed in combination with other resources, it is sometimes difficult in practice to recognize these resources separately. For example, the skills that people use in combination with their labor effort are a kind of capital, called **human capital.** These skills are the results of production efforts (education or training) carried out sometime in the past and used for future production. A long period of schooling, then, lowers the society's quantity of labor resource, but the lost working time is offset by the greater amount of human capital that results from the knowledge and skill gained from the education. Even the strength, health, and vigor that are displayed along with the work effort can be distinguished from the work effort itself, but it is hard to decide whether these should be considered natural resources or capital. Does health come from the "natural resource" of being born healthy or from capital that previously provided health care?

Actually, none of the resource categories can be fully understood if examined in a vacuum. The quantity and quality of natural resources and capital will affect labor's ability to produce, just as the productivity of capital depends on the quantity and quality of the labor and natural resources that can be combined with it. A worker with a bulldozer can produce more than the same worker with a shovel. Should the whole difference be attributed to the bulldozer? A bulldozer with a worker can produce a lot, but the bulldozer could produce nothing without the worker. Should the entire difference be attributed to the worker? These are matters that economic systems attempt to resolve.

NATURAL RESOURCES Natural resources are things that are provided by nature and that are used or usable in production. These "gifts of nature" include the land in its natural state, the sea, the minerals in the ground, the vegetation that grows without anyone planting it, and all the living creatures that are found in the wild.

To be usable, natural resources must often be combined with labor resources and capital resources. Crude oil in a pool deep under the surface of the earth is a natural resource, but bringing it to the surface requires labor and machines (capital). So when the crude oil becomes available for use in production, it has already been mixed with labor and capital. Land in its natural state is a pure natural resource, but land with an irrigation system or with contour plowing is more than a natural resource, since it has been combined with labor and capital.

The idea that a natural resource is something that is "usable" in production brings up still another interesting aspect of the relationships among the resources of labor, natural resources, and capital. For many hundreds of years, crude oil seeped to the surface of the earth. However, it had no value as a natural resource until knowledge and skills were developed to allow this crude oil to be used in production. Future advances in knowledge may bring to light some natural resources that exist today but are as yet unrecognized. Are natural resources being used up in production, or is the development of knowledge expanding the quantity of recognized natural resources?

CAPITAL RESOURCES Capital resources are goods, tools, and skills that are meant for use in further production. Factory buildings as well as many machines and tools are produced, not for consumers or families to enjoy, but for the entre-

preneur to combine with labor and natural resources to produce consumer goods.

Capital goods are "derived" rather than "original" resources because they are produced from other resources. They are made by people and/or other capital goods. An old-fashioned textbook definition was "Capital is wealth used to produce other wealth," and economists spoke of capital-using production as a "roundabout" way of using labor and natural resources in production. Karl Marx wrote that capital was "dead labor that, vampire-like, lives by sucking living labor." Most modern economists do not resent capital, but instead give it credit for providing billions of people with a much higher standard of living than would otherwise be possible. Public and private capital resources are used to educate and train labor. In the form of tools and human skills, capital is also used to explore for coal, iron, or oil, which increases the amount of known natural resources. Various combinations of capital resources are used to raise or maintain the fertility of farm land, as well as to produce the land in Boston's Back Bay, Tokyo's Marunouchi, or half of Holland by filling in and desalinating sea bottoms, river bottoms, or swamps.

Capital is a very important resource for production. The quantity and quality of capital in a country depend upon decisions made concerning the use of its scarce resources. The more a nation chooses to employ its resources in the production of consumer goods and services, the less will be available for the production of capital (and vice versa). Consider the case of a poor nation that is endowed with few and low-grade natural and labor resources. Its people are probably living near the subsistence level, with barely enough consumption goods and services to sustain their lives. It is unlikely that much capital would be produced under such conditions, since almost all of this country's resources would be used to produce consumer goods.

The definition of capital offered at the beginning of this section included human skills. Skill or **technological know-how** is the ability to combine resources in producing the goods and services that a society wants. It is a kind of capital because skills are developed through experience, that is, through the use of resources in some sort of an educational process. Of course, these skills can also be seen to be a part of the labor resource. Skilled labor is, after all, still labor. Both views are correct and even useful in analysis. However, we do not want to double-count. When an economy's resources are estimated, labor skills must not be counted as part of that economy's capital resources and then again as part of its labor resources.

Technological know-how is an especially important kind of capital because it helps to determine how much a society will be able to produce with its limited amounts of other resources. A society with a good stock of technological know-how will be able to produce a great many more goods and services with its resources than it could produce if it had less. No level of technological excellence will "solve" the economic problem of scarcity, but gains in "know-how" can go a long way toward easing the burden of scarcity.

Choice

The economic problem—the existence of scarcity—necessitates choice. Since we cannot all have as much of everything as we would like, choices or economic decisions have to be made. Chapter 1 introduced the three major decisions that face all societies: what to produce, how to produce, and who shall receive the finished goods and services. It also explored some of the economic arrangements that societies have made to answer these questions. Now, these three questions can be applied directly to the problems of scarcity and choice.

The question of what to produce is based on the realization that choices have to be made between alternative uses of scarce resources. How many telephones shall be produced? How much toothpaste? How many factories? How many machines? How much conservation? How much research? Clearly, the "what to produce" question not only divides resources among alternative consumer goods but also allocates resources to

the creation of capital, which will open the way for more and better consumer goods in the future.

The question of how to produce involves the choice of which resources to use in production. It is almost always possible to substitute one resource for another, such as a machine (capital) for some labor, or a more elaborate machine for two less elaborate ones. Certainly, in the case of an economy that finds itself with a large amount of labor and a small amount of capital, this question would be answered differently than it would be in an economy in the opposite situation.

The question of for whom to produce also shows the existence of scarcity in the real world. If there were enough resources for us all to have as much of everything as we wanted, there would be little need to make the hard choices of providing more to some people and less to other people. The fact that societies have to make this choice is the "bottom line" of the economic problem. Because receiving goods and services is a powerful incentive, the way goods and services are distributed has a lot to do with the labor, natural resources, and capital resources that will be available in the future.

OPPORTUNITY COST

Since resources are scarce, the decision to use them for one thing means that something else will be given up. Suppose that a company could manufacture either 100 chairs or 30 tables using the same resources. The opportunity cost of using its resources to produce 100 chairs is the benefit that could have been obtained from producing 30 tables (the best alternative) with the same resources. Thus, **opportunity cost** is the true cost of choosing one alternative over another. With limited resources, people cannot "have their cake and eat it too." Opportunity cost recognizes the fact that when resources are employed in a certain way, there is a simultaneous choice made not to use those resources in some other way. That which is given up, then, is the opportunity cost of what is actually chosen. If, instead of producing

TABLE 4-1 **Alternative Combinations of Shrimps and Scallops (Hypothetical Example)**

Combination	Number of Shrimps	Number of Scallops
1	10	0
2	9	2
3	8	4
4	7	6
5	6	8
6	5	10
7	4	12
8	3	14
9	2	16
10	1	18
11	0	20

one chair, we might have produced three dresses or five taxi rides or seven hours of leisure, the opportunity cost of one chair is whichever of these would yield the most benefit. It is certainly *not* the sum of all three.

Opportunity Cost in Consumption

Opportunity cost applies to both consumption and production. In discussing consumption, we consider how consumers spend their income, wealth, and time and how governments spend the resources that they have at their disposal.

THE INDIVIDUAL   Since people have only so much income and hold a limited amount of wealth, they are continually faced with buying decisions. When consumers decide to spend their dollars for one item, those dollars are not available to them for some other item. The opportunity cost of buying a blue sweater may be the green sweater that was therefore not bought. Taking a trip to the Caribbean might mean forgoing, or giving up, a new car.

To get a better understanding of the opportunity cost involved in consumer choice, consider the following example. Suppose that you are having dinner in a seafood restaurant and that

you select the combination shrimp and scallop plate shown on the menu for $5. This restaurant allows you to choose the particular mix of shrimps and scallops that you want. Shrimps, however, are twice as expensive (50¢ each) as scallops (25¢ each). Thus, the opportunity cost of each shrimp is two scallops, and the opportunity cost of each scallop is one-half shrimp.

Your eleven possible combinations are listed in Table 4-1 and are plotted graphically in Figure 4-1. Since shrimps are on one axis and scallops on the other, any point on the diagram represents some combination of shrimps and scallops. Your $5 plate will not allow you, however, to choose a point like X (8 shrimps plus 10 scallops). You would not want to order a combination like Z (4 shrimps plus 4 scallops), since you can have more shrimps and/or scallops for your $5. Depending upon your taste, your order might be all shrimps (point A) or all scallops (point B), but most likely it will be some combination like C (6 shrimps plus 8 scallops) because it offers some variety.

The graph in Figure 4-1 helps you to visualize opportunity cost. The slope of the line (ignoring the sign) measures opportunity cost of scallops because it shows how many shrimp must be sacrificed to obtain one more scallop. In this illustration, the curve is actually a straight line, which means that the slope is the same all along the line, because opportunity cost neither increases nor decreases from one combination on the line to another.

People also face opportunity costs in allocating their time and their effort. This choice may be between work and leisure, between one kind of work and another kind of work, or between one leisure activity and another leisure activity. If a particular Saturday night offers a college student both a party and a basketball game, and if these are the best alternatives available, the event that the student doesn't attend is the opportunity cost of the one that he or she does decide to attend. A student who decides to attend a summer session may experience three kinds of opportunity costs. The first cost is the goods and services that the student forgoes so that he or she can pay for tuition and books. A second includes the goods and services that the student could have

FIGURE 4-1 Alternative Combinations of Shrimps and Scallops (Hypothetical Example)

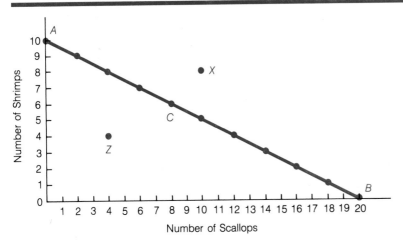

The numbers plotted from Table 4-1 establish the points along the curve *AB*. These eleven possible combinations of shrimps and scallops are available to a person ordering the $5 shrimp and scallop plate in the restaurant. The opportunity cost of each shrimp is two scallops, and the opportunity cost of each scallop is one-half shrimp.

Any combination that lies above *AB* (such as *X*) is not available on the $5 plate. Any combination that lies below *AB* (such as *Z*) is available but offers fewer shrimps and/or scallops than the restaurant is willing to provide on the $5 plate.

bought with the money he or she would have earned on a summer job. The third is the extra leisure time that the student would have enjoyed, since school is more time-consuming than a job would have been.

THE GOVERNMENT Government also is faced with opportunity costs. At first, it may seem that government is exempted because it can tax people, borrow money, or even print money if it wishes to undertake more programs. On closer examination, however, we discover that when government draws additional resources from private individuals or businesses, private goods must be foregone. This is the opportunity cost of the expanded government operation. For example, if a country became fearful of its neighbors, it might raise taxes to buy more military equipment. The opportunity cost of the defense build-up would be the private goods that the taxpayers could no longer afford to buy.

If a total dollar budget has already been set, the opportunity cost of one government program is another program that must be given up. A state legislature may have to decide between funding mass transportation or the prison system. If you are told the amount of the total budget and the prices of mass transportation and prison facilities, this opportunity-cost calculation can be illustrated just like the consumer-choice case involving shrimps and scallops.

Opportunity Cost in Production

The concept of opportunity cost can be applied to production choices in a way similar to that applied to consumption choices. Opportunity cost in production is also a **trade-off**—how much of one good or service must be given up to gain a certain quantity of another good or service. Extending opportunity cost further leads us to the

FIGURE 4-2 Production Possibilities for an Ice Cream–Sherbet Firm (Hypothetical Example)

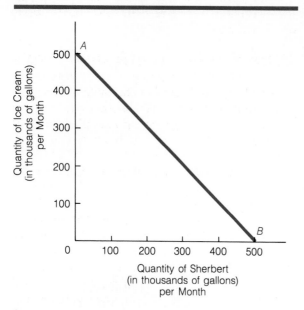

Curve *AB* is the production possibilities boundary for a hypothetical firm that has the capacity to produce 500,000 gallons of ice cream and/or sherbet per month. Its fixed supply of resources is equally well able to produce either good. The opportunity cost of a gallon of ice cream is a gallon of sherbet, and vice versa.

concept of **production possibility,** which describes the limits to the quantities of goods and services that can be produced with a given supply of resources and technological knowledge during any given time period. We shall consider production possibilities both for an individual firm and for an entire nation.

THE FIRM Suppose that a firm is set up to manufacture only two products: ice cream and sherbet. Suppose further that its factory building contains machinery that can be used equally well to produce ice cream or sherbet and that its workers can produce either of the two products equally well. The capacity of the factory building and the machinery is 500,000 gallons of ice cream and/or sherbet per month.

Figure 4-2 illustrates this case. The amount of ice cream is on one axis and the amount of sherbet is on the other. Any point on the diagram represents some combination of the production of ice cream and sherbet. If the company chooses to produce all the ice cream that it can (and therefore no sherbet), it can produce 500,000 gallons (point *A*). Alternatively, if it chooses to produce all the sherbet that it can (and therefore no ice cream), it can produce 500,000 gallons of sherbet (point *B*). All the remaining maximum production possibilities are combinations of positive amounts of both ice cream and sherbet and fall along the curve drawn between *A* and *B*. (It is actually a straight line because all the resources in this example are able to produce either good equally well.) We call *AB* a **production possibilities boundary**—a curve that represents all the alternative maximum combinations that can be produced with a given supply of resources and technological knowledge.

THE WHOLE ECONOMY Let's see how opportunity cost in production may now be applied to an entire economy. No matter what economic system prevails—whether private business firms like the ice cream–sherbet company exist or not—each nation is limited in what it can produce by its resources, including its technological know-how. Of course, the actual production possibilities of a nation are too diverse to be expressed in tabular form or to be represented in a diagram. But for illustrative purposes all the different goods and services that a nation produces can be lumped together in two categories, such as "consumption goods" and "capital goods," or "guns" and "butter," or "goods" and "services."

A PRODUCTION POSSIBILITIES SCHEDULE Table 4-2 represents a production possibilities table or schedule for the fictitious nation of Yano. All possible production has been divided into the two categories of goods and services, and there is a common unit of measure for each category. For example, a haircut may be 1 service unit, and an examination by a physician may be 30 service units. A potholder may be 1 goods unit, and a

TABLE 4-2 Production Possibilities for the Nation of Yano in 1987

Goods (in billions of units)	Services (in billions of units)
10,000	0
9,800	500
9,400	1,000
8,800	1,500
8,000	2,000
7,000	2,500
5,800	3,000
4,400	3,500
0	4,000

This table or schedule shows nine of the countless alternative combinations of goods and services that the fictitious nation of Yano is able to produce in 1987. The alternatives range from 10,000 billion units of goods plus no services to no goods plus 4,000 billion units of services. It is most likely that the people of Yano will want a mix of goods and services, and so they might choose a combination such as 8,000 billion units of goods plus 2,000 billion units of services.

pound of hamburger 5 goods units. Imagine that during a particular year (1987) Yano's production possibilities have been tabulated in this fashion. The numbers are based on the amount of resources and technological know-how available for use in Yano's production during 1987. The numbers in Table 4-2 show that there is no way for Yano to produce more than 10,000 billion units of goods or to produce more than 4,000 billion units of services. In fact, the only way to produce such a high level of either category is to produce none of the other.

Between these all-of-one-and-none-of-the-other choices are many possible combinations of goods and services for Yano to produce. The schedule gives seven examples (such as 9,800 billion units of goods plus 500 billion units of services, or 7,000 billion units of goods plus 2,500 billion units of services), but there are countless others. It follows from the data that if Yano decides, for example, to produce 2,000 billion units of services in 1987, then no more than 8,000 billion units of

goods can be produced. Alternatively, if Yano decides to produce 9,400 billion units of goods, it can produce no more than 1,000 billion units of services.

INCREASING MARGINAL OPPORTUNITY COSTS

The tradeoff between goods and services is different in different parts of the table. At the top is the combination of 10,000 billion units of goods and no services. By giving up 200 billion units of these goods, Yano can gain 500 billion units of services. Thus the opportunity cost of 500 billion units of services is 200 billion units of goods. However, Yano must give up 400 billion units of goods to get the next 500 billion units of services.[1] Note that this pattern continues. As you move down Table 4-2, larger and larger amounts of goods must be given up in order to gain additional blocks of 500 billion units of services. If you compare the last two lines in the table, you will see that the opportunity cost of the last 500 billion units of services is 4,400 billion units of goods.

Likewise, the marginal opportunity cost of goods in terms of services increases as you move up Table 4-2. Going from the combination of no goods and 4,000 billion units of services to the next higher combination, you will see that the opportunity cost of 4,400 billion units of goods is only 500 billion units of services. Finally, when you compare the top two lines in the table, you will observe that the opportunity cost of only 200 billion units of goods is 500 billion units of services.

Why should increasing marginal opportunity costs be expected? Why is it that the more goods or the more services that Yano has, the higher the opportunity cost of gaining even more units? The answer is that not all of Yano's resources are equally suited to producing both goods and services. Some are much more capable of producing goods, and others are much better at producing services. Workers skilled in performing appendectomies may be unsuited for producing cars.

1. The marginal opportunity cost of 500 billion units of services has increased from 200 billion units of goods to 400 billion units of goods.

Land that is just right for growing wheat may be a poor location for a barbershop. And a factory building designed for manufacturing steel may be poorly suited as a dental clinic.

It is reasonable to expect that, at some combination around the middle of Table 4-2, most resources are being used in the way that suits them reasonably well. Perhaps this combination would be 8,000 billion units of goods plus 2,000 billion units of services. At other combinations—either up or down the table—resources are shifted to tasks for which they are less well suited. Toward the very top of the table, only the resources best fitted to the production of services will be producing services. At the same time, it is necessary to use less-suitable resources for producing goods, making it very expensive to produce any more goods by giving up more services. Likewise, toward the very bottom of the table, only the resources best suited to the production of goods will be producing goods and those resources less capable of producing services will be doing so, making it very expensive in terms of goods forgone to produce any more services.

A PRODUCTION POSSIBILITIES BOUNDARY Just as a production possibilities boundary was drawn for the ice cream–sherbet firm in Figure 4-2, a production possibilities boundary may be drawn for the nation of Yano. Figure 4-3 plots the data from Table 4-2 on a set of axes and joins the points to obtain a production possibilities boundary. The curve is bowed out, reflecting increasing marginal opportunity costs because Yano's resources are not all equally good at producing both goods and services. In contrast, the straight-line production possibilities boundary for the ice cream–sherbet firm reflected a constant marginal opportunity cost, since all its resources were equally good at producing ice cream and sherbet.

The production possibilities boundary in Figure 4-3 represents the maximum amounts that Yano can produce in 1987. Production levels such as X (a combination of 9,500 billion units of goods plus 3,000 billion units of services) or Z (a combination of 8,500 billion units of goods plus 3,500 billion

units of services) are impossible for Yano to achieve. However, the entire shaded area is made up of combinations of goods and services that are attainable. For example, point A (a combination of 6,500 billion units of goods plus 1,500 billion units of services) is an attainable combination for Yano. But, given its resources and technological know-how, Yano can do better than point A by producing more goods, or more services, or more of both. Instead of 6,500 billion units of goods, it could produce 8,800 billion (which would place it at point B), with no reduction in the services produced. Or, instead of 1,500 billion units of services, it could produce 2,700 billion (which would place it at point C), with no reduction in the amount of goods produced. Finally, it could produce more of both and move to a point such as D (7,500 billion units of goods plus 2,250 billion units of services).

Suppose that Yano is producing at point A in Figure 4-3. What does this fact tell us about the Yano economy? One possible cause of the relatively low production indicated by point A may be that some resources are idle—that is, unemployed. For example, certain workers may not be able to find jobs, some mineral deposits may not be mined, or machines to stamp out automobile bodies may not be in operation. The other possibility that gives rise to producing below the production possibilities boundary is the inefficient use of resources. This could be due to outright waste, for example, not allowing qualified and healthy people over the age of sixty-five to hold jobs. Or it could be due to combining resources in a less than optimal way. For instance, if each individual Chevrolet fender were cut out by hand instead of stamped out by a press, the cost of production would be greatly increased. Whenever goods or services are produced at higher cost than could be achieved by using another combination of resources, production is not efficient.

Point A production, or some other point below the production possibilities boundary, is a very likely combination for Yano. In fact, Yano would be a very rare nation if it did not experience some unemployment of resources and some production inefficiencies. It is important to understand,

FIGURE 4-3   **Production Possibilities for the Nation of Yano, 1987**

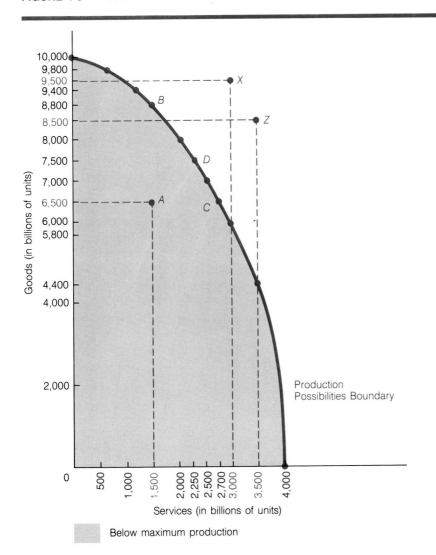

Below maximum production

The curve pictures the production possibilities boundary for the fictitious country of Yano. It is established by joining the points plotted from Table 4-2. All points on the curve (such as *B, C,* and *D*) represent alternative maximum combinations of goods and/or services that Yano can produce in 1987.

Any combinations that lie above the curve (such as *X* and *Z*) are not attainable. Any combinations that lie in the shaded area below the curve (such as *A*) are attainable, but indicate some level of unemployment of resources and/or inefficient use of resources.

however, that a country producing below its production possibilities boundary can increase output without an expansion of its resource base or technological knowledge, both of which take time to achieve. In Yano's case, the nation could produce more goods or more services, or more of both, with its present resources and know-how.[2] But if Yano were producing on its production possibilities boundary, it could increase its production of goods at this time only by decreasing its production of services. Alternatively, Yano could increase its production of services only by decreasing its production of goods.

SHIFTS IN PRODUCTION POSSIBILITIES BOUNDA-RIES What might the production possibilities boundary for Yano be expected to look like in 1992? Since the 1987 boundary was limited by Yano's resource base and technological knowl-edge, it would be very surprising if the boundary had not shifted by 1992. Figure 4-4 illustrates an outward shift. The 1992 production possibilities boundary is everywhere above the 1987 boundary because Yano has increased its resources and/or technology related to both goods and services during those five years. Resources may have increased because the population has grown (more working-age people), the amount of capital has increased, or more new natural resources have been discovered than have been used up. Prob-ably the technological knowledge or the "state of the art" in many industries has also improved, so that by 1992 more goods and services could be produced even with no additional resources.

Figure 4-4 shows the output points B, D, and C—maximum output combinations in 1987—to be less than maximum output combinations in 1992. Point Z, which was impossible to reach in 1987, is on the new production possibilities boundary and therefore attainable in 1992. But point X, which was impossible to reach in 1987, is still unattainable, though not by nearly so much.

2. Such improvement may be made through better manage-ment by Yano's private businesses and through more enlight-ened policy by the government of Yano.

FIGURE 4-4   Shift of Production Possibilities Boundary for the Nation of Yano, 1987 to 1992

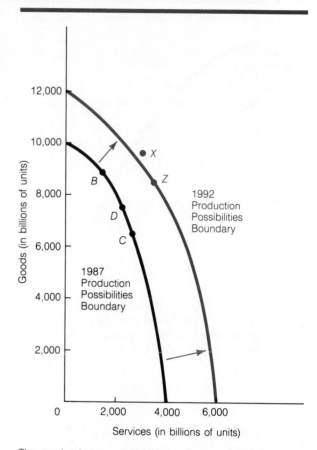

The production possibilities boundary of Yano has shifted outward over the period 1987 to 1992. In 1992 Yano can produce greater amounts of goods and services than it could in 1987.

Alternative shifts are shown in Figure 4-5. Panel (a) shows a situation in which the 1992 production possibilities boundary has expanded for goods, but not for services. This might have been the result of a gain in some resources or in techno-logical knowledge that can only produce goods. In 1992 Yano can produce as much as 2,000 billion additional units of goods, but still no more than 4,000 billion units of services. Note, however, that in 1992 compared with 1987, with the excep-tion of the "all-services" output choice, Yano is

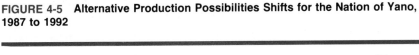

FIGURE 4-5   Alternative Production Possibilities Shifts for the Nation of Yano, 1987 to 1992

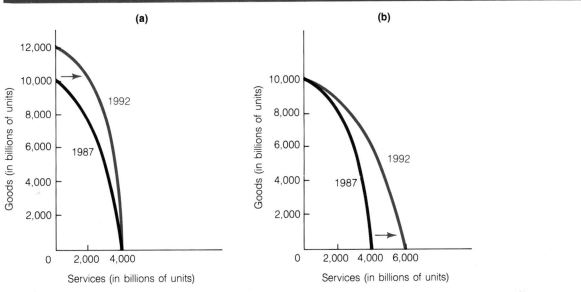

Both panels show outward shifts of Yano's production possibilities boundary over the period 1987 to 1992. Panel (a) pictures the special case where the expansion has taken place only for goods, and panel (b) shows the special case where the expansion has taken place only for services.

able to produce combinations of output with more goods and the same amount of services, with more services and the same amount of goods, or with more goods and more services.

Panel (b) shows an alternative situation—the production possibilities boundary has expanded for services, but not for goods. This might have occurred because of a gain in resources or in technological knowledge that can only produce services.

Production possibilities boundaries are expected to shift outward over time, but there is no guarantee that they will. They could remain the same or actually shift inward. Population—especially of working age—could drop. A decrease in capital goods could take place if saving and investment do not keep up with the replacement of capital goods as they wear out. And natural resources may be used up faster than new discoveries are made.

SUMMARY

1. Scarcity refers to the limitations on obtaining all the goods and services that people want. Scarcity is considered *the* economic problem since it gives rise to the trillions of economic problems experienced by people everywhere. Most economists believe that scarcity of the goods and services that people want is unavoidable.

2. Goods and services are considered scarce whenever people want more of a good or service than is available to them at a price of zero. They are scarce because the ingredients necessary to produce them, called resources or factors of production, are scarce.

3. Resources or factors of production are divided into three broad categories: (a) labor resources, (b) natural resources, and (c) capital resources. On closer examination, it becomes clear that the productive ability of any one of these resources depends very much on the quantity and quality of the other resources.

4. Whenever resources are scarce, the decision to produce or consume something involves an opportunity cost. Opportunity cost—that which is given up—can be seen as the true cost of choosing a particular alternative.

5. People face an opportunity cost in allocating their limited incomes as well as their time and effort. Government, too, must make choices; the opportunity cost of certain programs may be other programs, or it may be private sector spending.

6. Opportunity cost in production may be applied to a single firm or to an entire economy. In both cases it can be incorporated into a production possibilities boundary—a curve that shows all the alternative maximum combinations that can be produced with a given supply of resources and technological knowledge.

7. Production possibilities are expected to reflect increasing marginal opportunity costs. This means that the more units of a good or service that are produced, the higher the opportunity cost of producing even more units. The reason is that resources are generally not equally well suited for producing all kinds of goods or services.

8. A business firm or a country cannot produce amounts that are beyond its production possibilities boundary. It may, however, produce below the boundary. When it does so, it is either not using all of its resources or using them in an inefficient way.

9. Over time, production possibilities boundaries may shift outward or inward. It is more likely that the shift will be outward, reflecting an increase in resources and/or technological know-how. There will be an inward shift when fewer resources are available for production.

DISCUSSION QUESTIONS

1. Alex, who has just studied this chapter, tells his friend Beth that new cars are scarce in this country even though there are many unsold cars sitting around in new-car dealer show rooms and lots. Beth disagrees. She argues that these cars are not scarce goods, since there are plenty around waiting to be sold. Putting yourself in Alex's place, convince Beth that these cars are indeed scarce goods according to the definition of scarcity in economics.

2. Explain the relationship between the scarcity of goods and services and the factors of production or resources available in an economy.

3. The three classes of resources—labor, natural resources, and capital—are defined so broadly that all ingredients of production can be included. Classify each of the following and justify your answer:

   a. an automatic fruit picker
   b. a brain surgeon
   c. a wild horse
   d. an inventor
   e. an irrigated piece of land

4. Suppose you were the ruler of the country of Tava. Because you would like to increase the productive output of Tava, you decide to do whatever you can to increase the quantity of labor available for production. List ten different actions that you might take.

5. Joe says to Mary, "I just bought a beautiful blue cardigan sweater. It cost me $29.95." Mary responds, "It did? I thought it cost you those $29.95 slacks that you also wanted but now can't afford to buy." Who is right? Explain.

6. Government has the power to tax, borrow money, and even print money if it wishes to provide more goods and services. Therefore, government is *not* subject to opportunity cost. True or false? Explain.

7. Suppose that the nation of Doodag can produce only doods and dags and that its production possibilities schedule is the following:

Doods	Dags
0	1,000
200	800
350	600
425	400
500	200
550	0

a. Construct a graph showing Doodag's production possibilities curve.

b. Pick a point on the diagram that shows a combination of doods and dags that Doodag cannot now produce.

c. Pick another point on the diagram that shows a combination of doods and dags consistent with some idle resources.

d. Pick a third point at which no more doods can be produced, no matter how many or how few dags are being produced.

8. The production possibilities curve that you drew in the previous question was bowed out.

a. What does that tell you about the marginal opportunity cost of doods in terms of dags and dags in terms of doods?

b. Set up a new production possibilities schedule for Doodag, using output levels of doods and dags that result in a straight-line production possibilities curve.

c. What does that tell you about the marginal opportunity cost of doods in terms of dags and dags in terms of doods?

d. Set up yet another production possibilities schedule for Doodag, using output levels of doods and dags that result in a bowed-in production possibilities curve.

e. What does that tell you about the marginal opportunity cost of doods in terms of dags and dags in terms of doods?

9. What are the public policy implications for a nation that is producing on its production possibilities curve compared with those for one that is producing below (to the left of) its production possibilities curve?

10. Suppose that you know the production possibilities curve for a particular nation. What would you expect this nation's production possibilities curve to look like ten years later? Why?

11. Describe a set of specific circumstances that you believe would result in an inward (to the left) shift of a nation's production possibilities boundary.

5 Demand and Supply–or Supply and Demand

PREVIEW Ask the man or woman on the street what economics is about. The answer is apt to be either "supply and demand" or "demand and supply." If you ask a few more questions, you may hear about an "economic law" of supply and demand, which says that demand and supply determine prices and employment and the standard of living. You may also hear about the dangers that come from tampering with this "law." But if you go still further and inquire how we can tell what demand or supply *is* without already knowing the price, you can expect a blank stare, or hostility, or some less-than-flattering comment about economics and economists.

There is a problem here, which we must face at once. *Demand* and *supply* are used in two meanings. The person on the street uses them in the sense of *quantity*—amounts actually demanded or supplied, usually per week, month, or year. In this sense, the "economic law" of demand and supply means nothing more than that the amount bought must also be the amount sold. But most economists most of the time use *demand* and *supply* in the sense of a *schedule,* involving planned amounts demanded or supplied over a range of different prices. As will become clear in this chapter, no more than one point on a demand schedule, or on a demand curve graphed from a demand schedule, represents demand in the quantity sense. The same is true for supply.

This chapter introduces demand and supply in a schedule sense on three levels: (1) the individual consumer and individual firm, (2) consumers and firms in markets, and (3) aggregate demand and aggregate supply in an economy. Let us take a quick look at each.

Individual consumer demand stems from each consumer's decisions. A consumer who has the money to spend will decide just what and how much to buy. Likewise, individual firm supply stems from decisions made by each business firm. A company that can attract labor resources, natural resources, and capital will decide what and how much to offer for sale.

Market demand is the sum of all the individual consumers' demands for a particular good or service in a certain location. Market supply is the sum of all the individual firms' supplies of that good or service in that same location. The interaction of market demand and market supply determines the market price used in buying and selling.

Aggregate demand and aggregate supply, in turn, result from adding up the money values of all the different market demands and market supplies that exist in a nation or an economy. These concepts are basic tools in macroeconomic analysis of price levels, employment, and national income.

INDIVIDUAL CONSUMER DEMAND DECISIONS

Individual consumer demand refers to the quantity of a good or service that an individual consumer is willing and able to purchase at a particular moment at each possible price that might be charged for that good or service.

The term *demand* should not be confused with words such as *want, desire,* or *need.* A college student may very much want or desire to purchase an expensive sports car, but that does not constitute demand unless he or she is also able to buy it. The same college student may even be convinced that he or she really needs that sports car. But, once again, if the student cannot afford to buy the car, it is not considered demand. On the other hand, a very wealthy person may be able to afford to buy five such sports cars, but if that person decides to keep the money in the bank, there is also no demand. Demand requires both willingness and ability to buy a product.

The definition at the start of this section indicated that economists view demand "at a particular moment at each possible price." How is it possible for a consumer actually to be faced with different prices for the same good at the same time? It isn't, of course. The point is that the economist conceives of the individual's demand as his or her *plan* about how much to buy at different possible prices. The "at a particular moment" part of the definition simply means that we do not have to consider at the same time any variables other than the price and the quantity demanded of the good being studied. It is thus a simplifying assumption—a somewhat disguised use of the *ceteris paribus* assumption, which was introduced in Chapter 3.

To illustrate the relationship between price and quantity demanded by an individual consumer, let's take the case of Alex, who buys and wears jeans. Economists might express his demand function for jeans as follows:

$$QD_j^A = f(P_j), \text{ ceteris paribus}$$

In this functional relationship, QD_j^A is the quantity demanded of good j (jeans) by person A (Alex), f is the symbol for function (which may be read "depends on"), P_j is the price of jeans, and *ceteris paribus* means that all other variables are held constant. That is, we assume that there are no changes in such influential variables as Alex's tastes, his income, and the prices of other goods that he could or does buy. (Later in this chapter we shall discuss the effects of changes in these other variables.)

TABLE 5-1 Alex's Demand Schedule for Jeans, September 24, 1987

Price per Pair of Jeans (in dollars)	Quantity of Jeans Demanded (over next 12 months)
50	0
40	1
30	2
20	4
10	7

Think of Alex being interviewed as part of a market survey that seeks to discover consumers' demand for jeans at various prices. During a period of a minute or so, the interviewer may ask Alex how many pairs of jeans he would buy over the next twelve months at five different prices. The interview is not long enough for Alex's tastes to have changed, nor does Alex receive any new information about his income or the prices of other goods that he could or does buy. Thus the interview setting comes close to meeting economists' requirements for defining demand: at alternative prices, different quantities of a good are demanded, provided other influential variables are held constant.

The Demand Schedule and Curve

Information such as that obtained from interviewing Alex may be recorded in a **demand schedule**—a table showing different prices for a good and the quantity of that good demanded at each of these prices.

Table 5-1 illustrates a demand schedule that is based on the interview with Alex. His answers are not surprising, since he said that he would demand fewer pairs of jeans at higher prices and more pairs at lower prices.

The information given in the demand schedule may be plotted on a graph. It is customary in economics to put the price on the vertical axis and quantity demanded on the horizontal axis.

FIGURE 5-1   Alex's Demand for Jeans, September 24, 1987

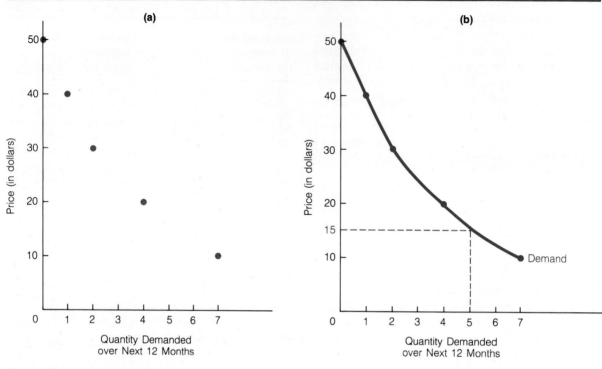

Panel (a) shows the points plotted from Table 5-1. Each point shows the quantity of jeans that Alex demands at a certain price. The information given in this graph is the same as that given in Table 5-1.

Panel (b) shows a line that joins the points in panel (a).

This is Alex's demand curve. This graph gives us much more information than panel (a) does. It adds an infinite number of price–quantity-demanded points for which there were no actual data.

Price is the independent variable, and the quantity demanded is the dependent variable. Panel (a) of Figure 5-1 includes exactly the same information as is given in the demand schedule in Table 5-1. In panel (b) of Figure 5-1, a line has been drawn through these five plotted points to join them. This line adds an infinite number of price–quantity-demanded points. For example, you can read from the graph that, at a price of $15, Alex will demand five pairs of jeans. However, since the interviewer did not ask Alex how many jeans he would demand at $15, it is only an assumption that his answer would have been five pairs. All the points along the demand curve, except those few that come from actual data, are based on the assumption that the connecting line accurately describes the consumer's demand.

Slope of the Demand Curve

A glance at the demand curve in Figure 5-1 reveals that it is negatively sloped. That is, the variables of price and quantity demanded change in opposite directions. This relationship is to be expected in just about every case. It is as true for pizzas as it is for jeans. It holds true for haircuts, physical exams, houses, cars, and so on. Why do people demand greater amounts of goods and services at lower prices and smaller amounts at higher prices? There are two reasons: the income effect and the substitution effect.

INCOME EFFECT We shall first examine the income effect. Whenever a good or a service that a person buys goes up or down in price, it will affect that person's **real income,** that is, it will affect the purchasing power of that person's money (dollar) income. If the good or service goes up in price, the person's real income will go down (other things being equal). Alternatively, if it goes down in price, the person's real income will go up. Alex is somewhat "richer" when jeans are $10 per pair than when they are $30 per pair because he can buy more with his money income. The **income effect** is the influence that a change in a person's real income (resulting from a change in the price of a good or service that this person buys) has on the quantity that this person demands of that good or service.

For a typical American family, the income effect of a change in the price of jeans would probably be trivial compared, say, to the effect of a change in the price of meat. Suppose, for example, that a family spends $100 a month on meat out of its $1,000 after-tax monthly income. Suppose further that the price of meat suddenly doubles. This decreases the family's real income by about 10 percent, the percentage of its money income that it spent on meat. The family has become poorer and must lower its consumption. It could decide to eat as much meat as it did before the price rise by spending $200 on meat instead of $100 and spending $100 less on other foods, clothing, entertainment, or anything else. More likely, however, the family will decide to buy less meat and also less of some other goods and services— all because of the drop in its real income. Thus, the income effect of the increase in the price of meat probably is that the family will demand less meat.

If, on the other hand, the price of meat had been cut in half, the family's real income would have been raised. Being richer, then, the family would be able to buy the same amount of meat as before the price decrease and have $50 left over. This $50 could be spent on any other goods and services such as beer, stereo records, and movies, but it could also be spent on meat. The drop in the price of meat raises the family's real income and probably increases the quantity of meat it will demand.

SUBSTITUTION EFFECT The second reason why the demand curve is expected to be negatively sloped is the **substitution effect.** This is the effect that a change in *relative* prices of substitute goods or services (resulting from a change in the price of a good or service) has on the quantity that a person demands of that good or service. Whenever the price of any one good or service changes while other prices stay constant, relative prices are altered. People will wish to substitute goods that became relatively cheaper for those that became relatively higher priced. At higher prices for jeans, Alex will find that other types of pants, such as cords, will be relatively cheaper. He will probably substitute some cords for some jeans. On the other hand, at lower prices for jeans, cords are relatively higher priced, and Alex will most likely buy more jeans and fewer cords. Thus, because of the substitution effect, the quantity demanded of a good will increase when its price falls and decrease when its price rises.

The discussion above has treated the income effect and the substitution effect separately; in fact, they occur together. Alex is quite typical in that a substantial rise in the price of jeans will lower his real income *and* cause him to substitute other types of pants for jeans. Thus the income effect and the substitution effect work together to explain the negative slope of the demand curve.

Changes in the Quantity Demanded and Changes in Demand

Economists usually mean something different when they talk about a "change in the quantity demanded" than when they talk about a "change in demand." The quantity demanded of a good is expected to change as the price of that good changes. A *change in the quantity demanded* is reflected in a **movement along a demand curve.** It is important to keep in mind that while this movement along the demand curve is taking

FIGURE 5-2   Alex's Demand for Jeans: Two Alternative Demand Shifts

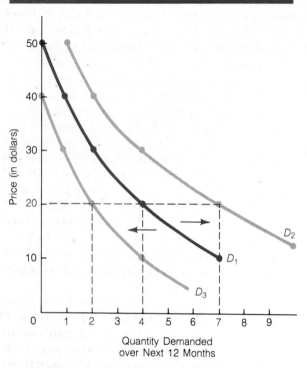

Quantity Demanded
over Next 12 Months

Curve D_1 is the original demand curve that was derived for Alex in Figure 5-1. When time is allowed to enter the model so that Alex's taste, his income, or the prices that he pays for other goods may change, his demand curve may shift to D_2 or D_3. A shift to D_2 shows that Alex will demand more jeans at any given price. A shift to D_3 shows that Alex will demand fewer jeans at any given price.

place, tastes, income, and prices of other goods are being held constant through the *ceteris paribus* assumption. As you will recall, Alex said that he would demand four pairs of jeans at a price of $20 per pair, but only two pairs at a price of $30 per pair. A glance back at panel (b) of Figure 5-1 reveals several such changes in the quantity demanded—movements from one plotted point to another along Alex's demand curve for jeans.

A "change in demand," on the other hand, is not caused by a change in the price of that good. A *change in demand* is reflected in a **shift of the demand curve**—a displacement of the entire curve

to the right or to the left. But this can happen only when the *ceteris paribus* assumption is relaxed or removed. If time is allowed to enter the model (another interview takes place at a different time), tastes, income, and prices of other goods may change. This means that at any given price of the good, either more or less may be demanded. Figure 5-2 illustrates two alternative demand shifts. Curve D_1—the original demand curve—is the same demand curve as that derived for Alex in Figure 5-1. Curve D_2 is the result of a demand shift to the right, which shows that Alex will demand more jeans at any given price. Curve D_3 is the result of a demand shift to the left, which shows that Alex will demand fewer jeans at any given price. For example, Figure 5-2 shows that Alex originally demanded four pairs of jeans at $20 a pair. When Alex demands seven pairs at $20 a pair, it shows that the demand curve has shifted to the right (to D_2). When he demands only two pairs of jeans at the same $20 price, the demand curve has shifted to the left (to D_3).

SHIFT VARIABLES   Economists use the term *shift variables* to refer to variables that cause a curve to be relocated—to "shift"—on a graph. Clearly, there can be a great many shift variables for any function or curve, since there is no limit to the number of variables that are covered by the *ceteris paribus* assumption. There are three especially important shift variables for an individual's demand curve.

An increase in a consumer's *taste* for a good or service will cause the demand curve to shift to the right, and a decrease in taste will bring about a shift to the left, other things being equal. If Alex, who has been wearing dress pants to work, suddenly decides that jeans are more comfortable and just as appropriate, his demand curve for jeans will shift to the right. On the other hand, if Alex has been wearing jeans to work and his boss "suggests" that dress pants are more correct, his demand curve for jeans will probably shift to the left.

An increase in a consumer's *income* will usually cause his or her demand curve to shift to the right, and a decrease in income usually brings about a shift to the left. Alex can afford to buy more jeans when his income is higher and fewer when it is lower. Only in rare cases will higher income cause people to demand less and lower income cause them to demand more. It is possible, however, that at very much higher income levels some people will demand fewer hamburgers since they will have switched to steak.[1]

Shifts in demand for a good also result from *price changes of other goods*, especially closely related goods. Such "other" goods may be grouped into two categories: substitutes and complements.

SUBSTITUTES **Substitutes** are goods that may be used instead of one another. Examples of good substitutes are beer and ale, Coca-Cola and Pepsi-Cola, and vinyl kitchen flooring and kitchen carpeting. An increase in the price of a substitute will cause the demand curve for the other good to shift to the right, and a decrease in the price of a substitute brings about a shift to the left. If Alex finds that jeans and cords are fairly good substitutes, and if cords go up in price, he will buy more jeans and fewer cords. In this case, Alex's *quantity demanded* for cords goes down and his *demand* for jeans goes up. Similarly, a decrease in the price of cords will cause Alex to demand fewer jeans and more cords. This time Alex's *quantity demanded* for cords goes up and his *demand* for jeans goes down.

COMPLEMENTS **Complements** are goods that are used with each other. Examples are automobiles and gasoline, ski boots and ski poles, and kites and string. Alex will demand fewer jeans if the type of belt that he wears with jeans, but not with other pants, goes up in price. That is, if the package, made up of a pair of jeans and one of these belts, has gone up in price, he will demand fewer jeans. Also, if the price of these belts decreases, Alex may demand more jeans.

When goods have several uses, they may be complementary in some cases and substitutable in others. It is then a complicated problem in economic statistics (econometrics) to discover

which relation dominates at any particular time or place. And, of course, the answer may vary from time to time or from place to place. At a time or place where soft drinks like Coca-Cola or Pepsi-Cola are never used as mixers for alcoholic drinks, soft drinks will be substitutes for alcoholic ones. At a time or place where soft drinks are used almost entirely as mixers and almost never consumed by themselves, the dominant relation will be complementary.

This discussion of complementary and substitute goods has been limited to the demand side of the market. As you will see, there are similar relationships on the supply side, and it will be useful to distinguish between the effects of complementarity and substitutability in demand (as here) and the effects of complementarity and substitutability in supply.

INDIVIDUAL FIRM SUPPLY DECISIONS

Individual firm supply refers to the amount of a good or service that an individual business firm is willing and able to sell at a particular moment at each possible price. Notice that this definition is quite similar to the one offered for demand on page 66. The only real difference is that the word *sell* is substituted for the word *purchase*.

More than just the willingness to supply a good is needed in order to supply it. A firm must be able to attract the resources or factors of production that are necessary to produce the good or service. A company that manufactures jeans may wish to produce 10,000 pairs per week, but it will not supply that many if it lacks the right machinery or enough employees to do the work.

As was true of demand, economists use the *ceteris paribus* assumption when viewing supply. Thus they avoid having to consider at the same time any variables other than the price and the quantity supplied of the good being studied.

To illustrate the functional relationship between price and quantity supplied by an individual firm, we shall use the hypothetical Cohen Clothing Corporation, which manufactures jeans, as an

---

1. When the demand for a product is negatively related to a person's income (such as the hamburgers in our example), economists refer to that product as *inferior*.

TABLE 5-2   Cohen Clothing Corporation's Supply Schedule for Jeans, September 24, 1987

Price per Pair of Jeans (in dollars)	Quantity of Jeans Supplied (over next 12 months)
50	80,000
40	70,000
30	50,000
20	30,000
10	0

example. In economics, we might express the relationship as follows:

$$QS_j^C = f(P_j), \textit{ceteris paribus}$$

Here QS_j^C is the quantity supplied of good j (jeans) by firm C (Cohen Clothing Corporation), f is the symbol for function (and may be read as "depends on"), P_j is the price of jeans, and *ceteris paribus* means that all other variables are held constant.

Specifically, *ceteris paribus* holds constant a number of influential variables. Most important among them are the prices of inputs needed for production, the state of the technology, the company's expectations about the prices of other goods that it does or could produce, and its goals. (As you will see, these are *shift variables* in respect to the firm's supply curve.)

Imagine that Mr. Cohen, the president of Cohen Clothing Corporation, is being interviewed as part of a survey trying to discover the quantity of jeans supplied by companies at various prices. During a very short interview, the interviewer may ask Mr. Cohen how many pairs of jeans his firm would supply over the next twelve months at each of five alternative prices. The interview is not long enough for Mr. Cohen's goals to change, nor does he receive any new information on the prices of inputs, the state of jean technology, or the prices of other goods that his firm is or could be producing. Thus, this interview setting, like that used in defining demand, closely

meets economists' needs for defining supply: at alternative prices, different quantities of a good are supplied, so long as other influential variables are held constant.

The Supply Schedule and Curve

Information such as that obtained from interviewing Mr. Cohen may be placed on a **supply schedule**—a table showing different prices for a good and the quantity of that good supplied at each of these prices.

Table 5-2 illustrates the supply schedule based on the interview with Mr. Cohen. Economists are not surprised to learn that his firm would supply more jeans at higher prices and fewer jeans at lower prices.

The information in the supply schedule is plotted on the graphs in Figure 5-3. As we pointed out earlier, the economist customarily places price on the vertical axis and the quantity variable—quantity supplied in this case—on the horizontal axis. Price is the independent variable, and quantity supplied is the dependent variable. Panel (a) of Figure 5-3 shows the plotted points from Table 5-2. Panel (b) of Figure 5-3 has a line drawn through the plotted points to show all the price–quantity-supplied points, whether plotted from actual interview data or only assumed, which make up the supply curve.

Slope of the Supply Curve

The supply curve in Figure 5-3 is positively sloped—the variables of price and quantity supplied change in the same direction. This relationship can be expected in just about every instance as long as we stick to the conditions existing for the interview with Mr. Cohen. Under these conditions, which hold other influential variables constant, what is true for jeans will be true for almost any good or service that a firm might produce. Why, under these circumstances, do firms supply greater amounts at higher prices and smaller amounts at lower prices? In a word,

FIGURE 5-3   Cohen Clothing Corporation's Supply of Jeans, September 24, 1987

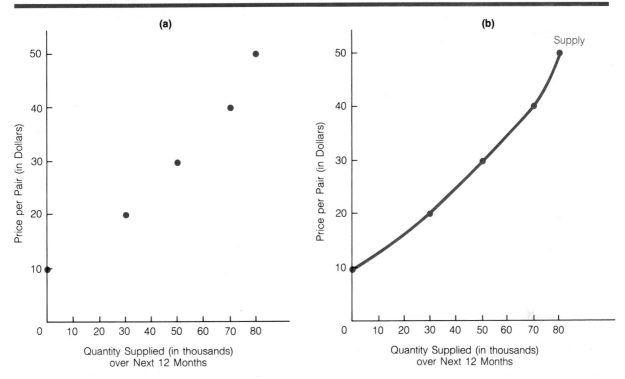

Panel (a) shows the points plotted from Table 5-2. Each point shows the quantity of jeans that the Cohen Clothing Corporation would supply at a specified price. The information given in this graph is the same as that given in Table 5-2.

Panel (b) shows a line that joins the points in panel (a). This is the Cohen Clothing Corporation's supply curve. The information given in this graph is much greater than that in panel (a). It adds an infinite number of price–quantity-supplied points for which there were no actual data.

the reason is *profit*. The supply curve for an individual firm is expected to be positively sloped because profits are an important goal for businesses. Under the *ceteris paribus* assumption used in deriving the supply curve, supplying jeans will be more profitable when their price is $30 than when their price is $20. Therefore, the company will naturally want to put more resources into the production of jeans when their price is $30 than it would when the price is only $20.

The company might find that it pays to use some of its older equipment (despite a higher production cost) to produce more jeans when their price reaches a certain higher level. It is

likely that the Cohen Clothing Corporation produces other clothing besides jeans—that it is a multiproduct firm. It may also produce shirts, skirts, and socks. If, indeed, the Cohen Clothing Corporation is a multiproduct firm, it will probably find that, at a high price of jeans, it pays to alter its product mix. Thus it will commit more of its production facilities and its employees to the production of jeans and less to the production of shirts, skirts, and socks. Taken together, these various explanations make it quite clear why firms find it profitable to supply more of a good when they can sell it at a higher price and less of a good when its price is lower.

FIGURE 5-4   Cohen Clothing Corporation's Supply of Jeans: Two Alternative Shifts

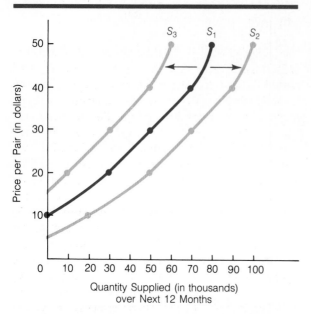

Curve S_1 is the original supply curve derived for the Cohen Clothing Corporation in Figure 5-3. When time is allowed to enter the model so that this company may experience changes in the price of inputs, technological know-how, expectations about the prices of other goods that it is or could be producing, or its goals, its supply curve may shift to S_2 or S_3. A shift to S_2 shows that the company will supply more jeans at any given price. A shift to S_3 shows that it will supply fewer jeans at any given price.

Changes in the Quantity Supplied and Changes in Supply

Now it is time to make a distinction between a "change in the quantity supplied" and a "change in supply," which is similar to the distinction made between a "change in the quantity demanded" and a "change in demand." A *change in the quantity supplied* is expected to take place as a result of a change in the price of the good (shown as a **movement along a supply curve**). A *change in supply* takes place when the variables held constant by the *ceteris paribus* assumption,

which we can call "shift variables," are allowed to change (shown as a **shift of the supply curve**).

Panel (b) of Figure 5-3 showed several changes in the quantity supplied—movements from one plotted point to another—along the Cohen Clothing Corporation's supply curve for jeans. Figure 5-4 shows changes in supply—two possible shifts of Cohen's supply curve that result from relaxing or removing the *ceteris paribus* assumption. Curve S_1, the original supply curve, is the same as that derived for the Cohen Clothing Corporation in Figure 5-3. Curve S_2, the result of a supply shift to the right, shows that the company will supply more jeans at any given price. Curve S_3, the result of a supply shift to the left, shows that the company will supply fewer jeans at any given price.

SHIFT VARIABLES AFFECTING SUPPLY CURVES
Once time is allowed to enter the case (if another interview takes place at a different time), the price of inputs, technological know-how, expectations about the prices of other goods that are or could be produced, and the seller's goals may change.

INPUT PRICES   An increase in the prices of inputs used in the production of jeans, such as higher wages to jean workers, higher prices of denim, or higher shipping charges, will cause the supply curve to shift to the left. The Cohen Clothing Corporation will find it profitable to alter its product mix away from jeans and in favor of shirts, skirts, and socks, which are now relatively more profitable. The reverse case—decreasing input prices—will cause the supply curve to shift to the right. Cohen will then use more resources to produce more jeans at each price.

TECHNOLOGICAL KNOW-HOW   An advance in technological know-how related to producing jeans, such as new and more efficient sewing machines or a better managerial technique, results in decreased costs. The Cohen Clothing Corporation would not be expected to adopt a new method of producing jeans unless it lowered costs and increased profits. In such cases, the supply curve shifts to the right.

EXPECTED PRICES OF OTHER GOODS The supply curve may also shift because of a change in the expected prices of other goods. At any given price of jeans, the Cohen Clothing Corporation will alter its product mix in favor of more jeans if it expects lower prices for shirts, skirts, and socks. Likewise, it will produce fewer jeans and more shirts, skirts, and socks if its price expectations for these other goods are raised. Hence, a firm's supply curve for one product tends to shift to the right when expected prices of its other products fall and to shift to the left when expected prices of its other products rise.

GOALS OF SELLERS Finally, supply curves shift because of changes in the goals or motives of sellers. Throughout this discussion it has been assumed that the sellers were in business to make profits. If firms did not care about profits, the theory of supply would break down, since they would just as soon sell more as less when the price is low. However, the assumption that firms prefer more rather than less profit does not mean that no other motives can play a role.

The desire to *do good* may be a strong motive. Part of Cohen's desire to sell more jeans may be that they last well and give people good value for their money. *Security*, or a concern about survival, may be another motive for firms. Perhaps the Cohen Clothing Corporation wants to sell more jeans because it expects *"bigness"* will give greater long-term security, and not because it expects larger profits. Firms may wish to avoid large risks—even if there is a chance that they will pay off handsomely—and decide not to commit themselves to produce certain goods whose prices have temporarily gone up.

Individual managers' goals—as distinct from the firm's goals—may also affect supply. The president of the Cohen Clothing Corporation may seek the *prestige* and *salary* that go with being the head of a very large firm. Thus the supply curve would shift to the right, as he would be willing to supply more at any given price. Of course, another firm's president may be motivated to act in exactly the opposite way. That president may wish to decrease the size of the firm so that he

or she can have a hand in every part of the business. In that case, the supply curve would shift to the left, as the firm would supply less at any given price.

"INCREASES" AND "DECREASES" IN SUPPLY When is a supply shift an increase in supply, and when is it a decrease? Because supply curves usually slope upward, there sometimes is confusion on this important point. (Because demand curves usually slope downward, there is no similar problem on the demand side.) To illustrate the problem, we shall return to Figure 5-4. The shift from S_1 to S_2 is an increase in supply, since for any given price, quantity supplied is greater on curve S_2 than on curve S_1. The shift from S_1 to S_3 is a decrease in supply, since for any given price, quantity supplied is less on curve S_3 than on curve S_1. The direction of the arrows tells us which is which, but notice that S_3 lies vertically *above* S_1, which lies vertically above S_2. When reading supply and demand curves, then, we should remember to concentrate on horizontal comparisons.

MARKET DEMAND AND SUPPLY

A **market** is the organized action between potential buyers (market demand) and potential sellers (market supply) that enables them to trade. In a

TABLE 5-3 Market-Demand Schedule for Jeans in Chicago, September 24, 1987

Price per Pair of Jeans (in dollars)	Quantity of Jeans Demanded (over next 12 months)
50	50,000
40	500,000
30	2,000,000
20	5,000,000
10	9,000,000

free market, demand and supply determine the terms of trade, or the price at which a purchase or sale is made.

Market demand is the sum of all of the individual consumers' demands (the information found in their demand schedules) for a particular good or service in a certain place over some period of time. Recall Alex, whose demand schedule for jeans was shown in Table 5-1. Suppose that Alex lives in Chicago and that everyone in that city also gives us his or her demand schedule for jeans. All the quantities demanded at each possible price can then be added together to determine the market demand for jeans in Chicago over the same twelve-month period. Table 5-3 presents some hypothetical numbers, and Figure 5-5 illustrates that market-demand curve.

Market supply is the sum of all of the individual firms' supplies (the information found in their

TABLE 5-4 **Market-Supply Schedule for Jeans in Chicago, September 24, 1987**

Price per Pair of Jeans (in dollars)	Quantity of Jeans Supplied (over next 12 months)
50	8,000,000
40	7,000,000
30	5,000,000
20	3,000,000
10	0

supply schedules) for a particular good or service in a certain place over some period of time. One such schedule, the Cohen Clothing Corporation's supply schedule for jeans, was given in Table 5-2. Suppose that the Cohen Clothing Corporation supplies jeans only to the Chicago area and that all the other clothing firms that also serve Chicago provide us with their Chicago supply schedules for jeans as well. The quantities supplied at each possible price can then be added up to determine the market supply for jeans in Chicago over the same twelve-month period. Table 5-4 provides some hypothetical numbers, and Figure 5-6 pictures that market-supply curve.

Equilibrium Price and Quantity

Up to this point, demand and supply have been treated separately but in a similar way. In real life, of course, demand and supply actions take place at the same time. Only when they are examined together, therefore, can it be seen how market demand and market supply determine the price of a product and the quantity that is bought and sold.

Both market demand and market supply limit the quantity of a product that is traded. The amount of a product that is sold at a certain price cannot exceed the demand for it at that price. Nor can more of a product be bought at a particular price than firms are willing to supply at that price. Therefore, the price tends to change

FIGURE 5-5 **Market Demand for Jeans in Chicago, September 24, 1987**

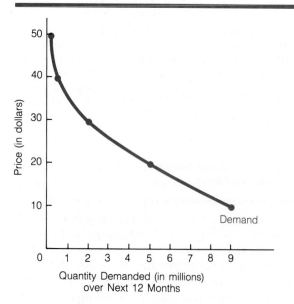

The numbers plotted from Table 5-3 establish the points along this market-demand curve. It combines all of the individual consumers' demands for jeans over the next 12 months in Chicago.

FIGURE 5-6 **Market Supply of Jeans in Chicago, September 24, 1987**

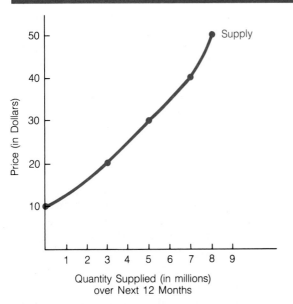

The numbers plotted from Table 5-4 establish the points along this market-supply curve. It combines all of the individual firms' supplies of jeans over the next 12 months in Chicago.

FIGURE 5-7 **Market Demand and Market Supply for Jeans in Chicago, September 24, 1987**

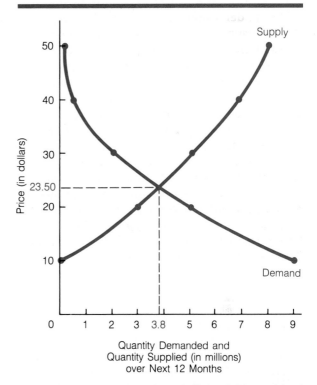

The market-demand curve shown in Figure 5-5 is combined with the market-supply curve in Figure 5-6. Their intersection marks the equilibrium price ($23.50) and equilibrium quantity (3.8 million pairs of jeans) in this market. At prices above $23.50 there is excess supply, and at prices below $23.50 there is excess demand.

whenever it does not equate the quantities of market demand and market supply.

The price that does equate quantity demanded with quantity supplied in the market is called the **equilibrium price,** and the accompanying quantity is called the **equilibrium quantity.** As you will recall, equilibrium means that a state of balance has been achieved and that there is no longer a tendency for change.

To illustrate equilibrium price and quantity, let us return to our example involving the market demand and market supply of jeans in Chicago. Figure 5-7 combines the market-demand curve shown in Figure 5-5 and the market-supply curve shown in Figure 5-6 in a single diagram. At any price above $23.50, more jeans will be supplied than are demanded. For example, Figure 5-7 shows that at a price of $30 a pair, only 2 million would be demanded but 5 million would be

offered by suppliers. (These numbers can also be taken from the market-demand and market-supply schedules shown in Tables 5-3 and 5-4.) Such **excess supply**—quantity supplied exceeding quantity demanded—will cause supplier firms to compete with one another in an attempt to sell their jeans, thereby driving down the price. Alternatively, at any price below $23.50, more jeans will be demanded than firms are willing to supply. Figure 5-7 shows, for example, that at a price of $20 per pair of jeans, 3 million would be supplied, but 5 million would be demanded. Such **excess demand**—quantity demanded exceeding quantity supplied—will cause buyers to compete with one another in an attempt to buy jeans, thereby driving up the price.

Only at a price of $23.50, where the market demand of 3.8 million jeans is exactly equal to the market supply of 3.8 million jeans, will excess demand and excess supply be eliminated. In a **free market**—one in which the forces of demand and supply have the opportunity to alter the price—a market equilibrium will tend to appear.

In real-world markets, equilibria are rather elusive—that is, they are moving targets rather than points that will be reached and then remain. Changing demand and/or supply conditions cause changes in the equilibrium price and/or quantity. In our discussion of demand shifts and supply shifts, we offered several reasons why such shifts may occur. For example, demand may shift to the right if consumers' incomes increase, if their taste for the good gets stronger, if prices of substitute goods increase, or if prices of complementary goods go down. Supply may shift as a result of changes in input costs, technological knowledge, prices of other goods that firms are or could be producing, or the motives to which sellers respond. We expect fairly frequent changes in some of these variables. Every such change will bring about a shift, except for the coincidental case in which changes exactly offset each other—as, for example, where income goes up at the same time as there is a compensating decrease in the price of a substitute good. Every shift will bring with it a new equilibrium price and/or quantity. But supply and demand curves usually shift so often that there is not enough time to adjust to any one equilibrium before a new one appears. Thus, market equilibria are seen as moving targets that may never be reached.

Market Manipulation[2]

Markets can be manipulated, or controlled, by buyers, sellers, or outsiders (regulators). These

2. The following material on market manipulation provides useful exercises with the concepts of market demand, market supply, and market equilibrium. However, instructors who wish to move more quickly to later portions of the text may skip this section and proceed directly to "Aggregate Demand and Supply" on page 81.

manipulators can try either to change the equilibrium position or to preserve a disequilibrium position. Equilibrium and disequilibrium cases should be distinguished carefully. As you know, equilibrium in a market is a state of balance between quantity demanded and quantity supplied. When the two are unequal, there is **disequilibrium.**

Buyers sometimes think that they would be better off if they forced the price of a product down by combining to purchase less of it. Likewise, sellers sometimes think they would be better off if they sold less but received a higher price for each unit. A third party, such as a public agency or a Mafia family, may feel that the public (or the agency, or the family) would be better off with some other price and output than the current market offers. Let us examine several real-world instances of market manipulation.

WARTIME PRICE CONTROLS   Under normal conditions it would be practically impossible for the final users of a consumption good like jeans in Chicago to agree among themselves (a process called *collusion*) in order to manipulate the demand for jeans. It would involve a huge number of people getting together and presenting a united front against those who broke their agreement, often called "chiselers." But consider the market for a civilian good—jeans will do—in a war economy, after productive capacity has been diverted to the production of a military good—uniforms. Look at Figure 5-8, which again shows the supply (S_1) and demand (D_1) curves found in Figure 5-7. Think of these curves as describing the prewar situation—the equilibrium quantity is 3.8 million pairs of jeans, and the equilibrium price is $23.50. Next, consider how diverting production from jeans to military uniforms will affect the supply of jeans. Because of the war, supply has fallen (shifted to the left) from S_1 to S_2 and the free-market price has risen from $23.50 to $30.

Now suppose that the government proposes to hold the price at $23.50 without restraining civilian demand in general by some means such as higher taxes. Government can try to hold the price of jeans at $23.50 by either an equilibrium or a disequilibrium method. Since the disequilib-

FIGURE 5-8 Market Manipulation: Disequilibrium Method with a Ceiling (Maximum) Price in the Market for Jeans

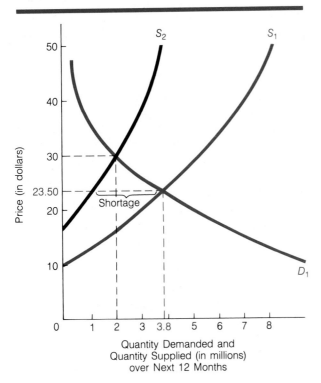

In this diagram, S_1 is the supply curve and D_1 is the demand curve before the war, when 3.8 million pairs of jeans are bought and sold at a price of $23.50. In wartime the supply falls from S_1 to S_2, which would cause the price to increase to $30 and the sales to drop to 2 million. If the government dislikes this free-market solution and decides to hold the price at $23.50 (a ceiling price), only 1.1 million pairs of jeans will be supplied, and a disequilibrium situation (a shortage of 2.7 million pairs) is created.

rium method is simpler, at least on the diagram, we will examine it first. The government may establish a **ceiling price**—a maximum price at which a product may legally be sold—at $23.50. This is called a *disequilibrium method* because, since the new supply curve (S_2) shows that only 1.1 million pairs of jeans will be supplied at $23.50, an excess demand or a **shortage** of 2.7 million pairs is created (3.8 million demanded minus 1.1 million supplied equals the 2.7 million shortage).

The legal price can be enforced reasonably well for a time, especially if the war is a popular one like World War II in the United States between 1942 and 1945. (No such method was tried during the unpopular Vietnam War.)

The *equilibrium method* of market manipulation involves shifting the demand curve, usually through "formal" rationing. (Shortages usually also give rise to "informal rationing," through individual merchants reserving supplies for their best customers, and so on.) Formal **rationing** calls for a detailed and often complicated plan involving the issuance by government of special coupons or tokens that act as a second form of money.[3] For example, it might take $23.50 plus a special ration coupon to buy a pair of jeans. If successful, a formal rationing system will cut demand. This is shown in Figure 5-9, which is identical to Figure 5-8 except that it shows a shift of the demand curve from D_1 to D_2. The new demand curve is shown to be vertical at 1.1 million pairs of jeans, since the government issues only 1.1 million ration coupons. The shortage at the $23.50 price is eliminated.

In the real world, things seldom work out quite so neatly. With either the disequilibrium or the equilibrium method, a problem arises when quantities of the goods—jeans in our example—are diverted to a "black market," in which goods are sold at illegally high prices. This makes the situation worse by shifting S_2 in the legal market further to the left and increasing the shortage at the $23.50 price. History suggests that neither a formal nor an informal rationing system can satisfy all consumers as "equitable." It also suggests that strong measures (perhaps even death for large-scale black-marketing) would be necessary to maintain an equilibrium or a disequilibrium system in the long run. In the United States, rationing and price controls practically collapsed within a year after the end of World War II.

3. Consider gasoline rationing. The plan would need to take into account many different factors. For example, some families have more cars and some more drivers than others. Some people live much closer to work than others. Access to public transportation and to car pooling also varies greatly. Some people use automobiles in their jobs more than others, especially in emergencies. And a few also use gasoline for tractors, trucks, and other vehicles.

FIGURE 5-9 Market Manipulation: Equilibrium Method with Rationing in the Market for Jeans

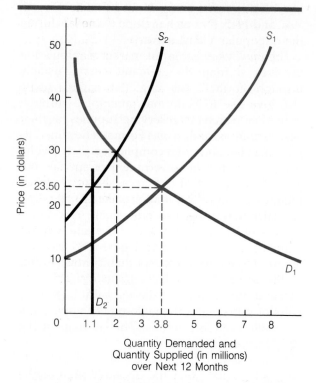

In this diagram, S_1 is the supply curve and D_1 is the demand curve before the war, when 3.8 million pairs of jeans are bought and sold at a price of $23.50. In wartime the supply falls from S_1 to S_2, which would cause the price to increase to $30 and the sales to drop to 2 million. If the government dislikes this free-market solution, it may wish to hold the $23.50 price through rationing, shown as lowering the demand to D_2. A new equilibrium situation is created as 1.1 million pairs of jeans are bought and sold at $23.50.

FARM PRICE SUPPORTS AND OPEC Manipulations that set minimum prices, or floor prices, for certain products can also be analyzed and explained with our supply and demand curves. We shall describe the American farm price supports as a case of disequilibrium and the OPEC (Organization of Petroleum Exporting Countries) system as a case of equilibrium.

Agricultural price supports have been in use in the United States for about fifty years. They are applied on a product-by-product basis. Figure

FIGURE 5-10 Market Manipulation with a Floor (Minimum) Price: Price Support in the Wheat Market

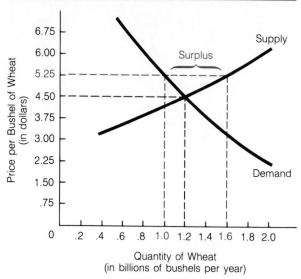

Quantity of Wheat
(in billions of bushels per year)

Pictured are the market-demand and market-supply curves for wheat. The equilibrium price is $4.50 per bushel of wheat, and the equilibrium quantity is 1.2 billion bushels per year. The government decides to impose a support price of $5.25. At this disequilibrium price, the quantity supplied is 1.6 billion bushels per year, and the quantity demanded is only 1.0 billion bushels. The result is a surplus of 0.6 billion bushels per year.

5-10 illustrates a hypothetical case involving wheat. Let's say that if a free market were allowed to determine equilibrium price and quantity, the price would settle at $4.50 a bushel, and the quantity bought and sold would be 1.2 billion bushels. If, instead, a **floor price** or **support price**—a minimum price at which a product may legally be sold—of $5.25 were established by the government, a surplus would be created. A **surplus** is the amount of excess supply that stems from a disequilibrium situation. The amount of the surplus in this example is 0.6 billion bushels. At the support price of $5.25, consumers would demand 0.2 billion bushels less and farmers would supply 0.4 billion bushels more than they would have at the free-market price of $4.50. Govern-

FIGURE 5-11   **Market Manipulation with a Floor (Minimum) Price: OPEC Price in the Crude Petroleum Market**

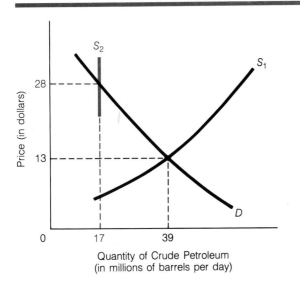

In this diagram, S_1 is the market-supply curve and D is the market-demand curve. In a free market, 39 million barrels of crude oil per day are bought and sold at $13 per barrel. When OPEC reduces the supply to 17 million barrels, as shown by the new vertical supply segment S_2, the resulting equilibrium price increases to $28 per barrel.

ment can maintain the floor price by purchasing the surplus.[4]

The OPEC experience illustrates an equilibrium variety of market manipulation aimed at achieving a higher price. Formed in 1960, OPEC became an effective international petroleum force in the early 1970s. Through market manipulation it was successful in raising the price of crude oil about fortyfold in less than a decade. Figure 5-11 is a simplified illustration of how this system operates. The market-supply and market-demand curves are labeled S_1 and D, respectively. If a free market were allowed to determine equilibrium price and quantity, the price would be $13 per

4. In practice, a system of production controls is used along with government purchase of the surplus.

barrel and the quantity bought and sold would be 39 million barrels per day. But OPEC has the authority to reduce supply to 17 million barrels per day, as shown by the vertical line labeled S_2. The new price of $28 per barrel of crude oil is an equilibrium one that leaves no surplus.

AGGREGATE DEMAND AND SUPPLY

To help you understand microeconomics, we described individual consumer demand and individual firm supply and then explained how they are added together in their respective markets to derive market demand and market supply. To offer similar help in understanding macroeconomics, we devote the last part of this chapter to **aggregate demand** and **aggregate supply**.

Graphing Aggregate Demand and Supply

In drawing a graph of the market demand for a particular good or service, it was easy to understand how the quantities demanded by individual consumers at each possible price could be summed to determine a point on the market-demand curve for that good or service. Similarly, it was easy to understand that the market-supply curve is the sum of the quantities supplied by individual firms at each possible price. But now, when we want to aggregate, or sum, the quantities demanded and supplied for all the goods and services in the economy, we encounter a new problem. Since we are dealing with many different goods and services at the same time, we must find new ways to measure prices and quantities. As you can imagine, we now must think of price as an average of all prices and we must find a common denominator that can be used to sum the quantities of many different goods and services.

Figure 5-12 presents a graph showing an aggregate-demand curve and an aggregate-supply curve. As usual, when you come upon a new type of graph, the first thing to do is to carefully

FIGURE 5-12 Aggregate Demand, Aggregate Supply, and Macroeconomic Equilibrium

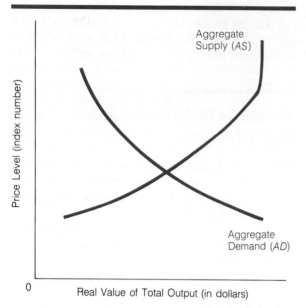

The horizontal axis shows some measure of total output (such as gross national product), which has been computed to exclude valuation changes arising from changes in the general price level during the year. The vertical axis shows various price levels, measured according to an index number (such as the consumer price index) that shows an average of prices in the economy. Macroeconomic equilibrium exists where the aggregate-demand curve and the aggregate-supply curve intersect. At the price level indicated by macroeconomic equilibrium, the quantities planned by suppliers match the quantities planned by demanders.

read the labels on each of the axes. This will tell you the variables whose relationships are being shown by the curves. Let us begin with the vertical axis. This axis shows various possible values for the **price level**, which is an average of the prices of all goods and services in the economy as represented by an index number. In other words, it is not just the price of jeans that is shown on this axis, but an average of the prices of jeans, shoes, medical examinations, and all the other goods and services that are bought and sold in the economy. The **consumer price index**, some-

times called the cost-of-living index, is the most familiar index number of this type and could be used as a measure of the price level on this graph. A rising price level is associated with **inflation** and a declining price level is associated with **deflation,** which are both extremely important concerns in macroeconomics.

Now look at the horizontal axis of the graph. Where individual and market graphs show quantities of a particular good or service, such as jeans or sweaters, aggregate-demand and aggregate-supply graphs show some measure of the total output of the economy. **Gross national product,** which is the market value of all the goods and services produced in a nation during a year, is the most familiar measure of this sort and could be used on the horizontal axis of this graph. In other words, gross national product is the market value of all the jeans produced in a year, plus the market value of all the sweaters produced that year, plus all the meals served in restaurants that year, plus the market values of all the other goods and services produced that year. Notice, however, that the label on the horizontal axis in Figure 5-12 contains the term "real value." A **real value** is one that does not include any inflation or deflation components. In other words, real increases must consist entirely of more output, without any valuation (price) writeups reflecting increases in the general price level (inflation) that took place that year. Similarly, real decreases must be reductions in actual output, without valuation (price) writedowns for decreases in the general price level (deflation) that year.

Movements to the left or the right along the horizontal axis of the aggregate-demand and aggregate-supply graph are very important in macroeconomics. Moving to the left along this axis usually means a lower standard of living and increasing unemployment (a recession and "hard times"), whereas moving to the right usually means a higher standard of living and less unemployment (if the movement stays ahead of the number of people who want to work). Together, the two axes of the aggregate-demand and aggregate-supply graph show the major concerns of macroeconomics—inflation and employment.

Macroeconomic Equilibrium

Just how the shapes and locations of the aggregate-demand (AD) and aggregate-supply (AS) curves are determined is a major part of the study of macroeconomics. At this stage in your study of economics, it is enough to know that the intersection of these curves identifies a situation known as **macroeconomic equilibrium,** where the indicated price level brings the plans of suppliers into balance with the plans of demanders in the economy. In other words, at this price level, suppliers are willing and able to provide a quantity of goods and services that is exactly equal to the quantity that demanders (households, business firms, government, and "the rest of the world") are willing and able to buy. As you know, in economics "equilibrium" means a state of balance among opposing forces such that there is no tendency for change.

By looking at Figure 5-12, you can easily see how shifts of the curves can lead to expansions or contractions of the economy (along the horizontal axis) and to inflations and deflations of the price level (along the vertical axis). For example, shifting the aggregate-demand curve to the right, other things being equal, can bring inflation, increasing output, and rising employment. On the other hand, shifting the aggregate-demand curve to the left can bring the opposite combination—deflation, decreasing output, and rising unemployment.

DEMAND-SIDE ECONOMICS Shifts in the aggregate-demand curve are the focus of **demand-side economics.** In this area of study, economists examine the forces that can cause shifts in the aggregate-demand curve and try to develop policy instruments that can bring desired shifts of this curve. The importance of demand-side economics is well illustrated by the Great Depression that hit the United States and most of the industrialized world during the 1930s. Most economists believe that the Great Depression was caused by leftward shifts of the aggregate-demand curve, triggered by the stock market crash of 1929 and by bank failures in the early 1930s.

SUPPLY-SIDE ECONOMICS Shifts of the aggregate-supply curve are in the domain of **supply-side economics.** Other things being equal, shifts of the aggregate-supply curve to the right can bring deflation, increasing output, and rising employment, whereas shifts to the left can bring the opposite—inflation, decreasing output, and falling employment, a combination known as **stagflation.** Stagflation and supply-side economics made the headlines in the 1970s when the Organization of Petroleum Exporting Countries (OPEC) reduced production of crude oil. This shifted the aggregate-supply curve to the left in many countries and caused stagflation. The main theme of supply-side economics is finding ways to shift the aggregate-supply curve to the right. Supply-side economic ideas played an important part in President Reagan's election campaigns in 1980 and 1984.

WHICH SEQUENCE: MACRO-MICRO OR MICRO-MACRO?

You may study macroeconomics before you study microeconomics, or you may study microeconomics first and then study macroeconomics. The sequence depends in part on the plans made by your own college or university. Whichever sequence you use, it is important to remember that each is simply a portion of the total subject of economics and that knowledge about one part is helpful in understanding the other part. The concepts of supply and demand and equilibrium are basic in both parts, and understanding these concepts is the key to mastery of the subject.

SUMMARY

1. The economic meaning of *demand* is that a consumer is both willing and able to purchase a good or a service, and not that he or she merely wants, desires, or needs that good or service. Likewise, the term *supply* means that a firm is both willing and able to produce a good or a service.

2. Individual consumer demand and individual firm supply are defined at a particular moment in time. This method of definition holds all variables constant except for the quantity and price of the good or service being studied. The functional relationships of demand and supply relate the respective quantities to the respective prices, while all other variables are held constant.

3. Demand curves have negative slopes, which means that the variables of price and quantity demanded change in opposite directions. The first reason for this relationship is the income effect, or the effect that a change in a person's real income (brought on by a change in the price of a good) has on the quantity that he or she demands of that good. The second is the substitution effect, or the effect that a change in relative prices of substitute goods (brought on by a change in the price of a good) has on the quantity demanded of that good.

4. Supply curves have positive slopes, which means that the variables of price and quantity supplied change in the same direction. The reason is that firms find it profitable to commit more resources to the production of a good or a service when its price is higher and less when its price is lower, other things being equal.

5. Changes in the quantity demanded and in the quantity supplied are reflected as movements along their respective curves, whereas changes in demand and supply are reflected as shifts of the curves. A movement along a curve is caused by a change in the price of the good or service being studied. A shift of a curve occurs when the *ceteris paribus* assumption is relaxed. Demand curves shift when tastes, income, or prices of other goods change. Supply curves shift when input prices, technological know-how, expectations about the prices of other goods that the firm is or could be producing, or a seller's goals change.

6. Market demand and market supply are derived by adding up, at each possible price, individual consumer demands and individual firm supplies of a particular good or service in a certain place.

7. When market supply is greater than market demand, there is excess supply, causing supplier firms to compete with one another and thereby driving down the price. When market demand is greater than market supply, there is excess demand, causing buyers to compete with one another and thus driving up the price. In a market, when quantity demanded is equal to quantity supplied, there is a state of balance—the equilibrium price and the equilibrium quantity have been reached.

8. Markets are sometimes manipulated by buyers or by sellers. This manipulation may result from a collusive agreement. Buyers may shift the market-demand curve to the left, thereby achieving a lower equilibrium price. Sellers may shift the market-supply curve to the left, thereby achieving a higher equilibrium price.

9. Disequilibrium in a market is the condition in which quantity demanded is not equal to quantity supplied. It may arise as a temporary situation, or it may be maintained by government action. Government may impose a higher-than-equilibrium price, which will be marked by excess supply, or a surplus. Or the government may impose a lower-than-equilibrium price, which will be marked by excess demand, or a shortage.

10. Aggregate demand and aggregate supply are concepts that are used to analyze major macroeconomic questions about inflation and unemployment. The aggregate-demand curve shows the different quantities of goods and services that would be demanded in the total economy at different price levels, other things being equal. The aggregate-supply curve shows the different quantities of goods and services that would be supplied in the economy at different price levels, other things being equal. Macroeconomic equilibrium is indicated by the intersection of these curves. At this price level, the aggregate quantity demanded equals the aggregate quantity supplied.

DISCUSSION QUESTIONS

1. Dave says, "I need three pairs of shoes this year." Will this information help you in con-

structing Dave's demand curve for shoes? Explain your answer.

2. Carefully describe what is meant by an income effect and a substitution effect. Then explain how the income effect and the substitution effect of a price change normally cause the demand curve for a good or service to be negatively sloped.

3. Construct a graph showing a demand curve for automobiles as you would expect it to look. On this diagram show a "change in the quantity demanded" and a "change in demand" that exactly compensate for each other. (The quantity of automobiles shown on the horizontal axis should be the same before and after these two changes occur.) What do you suppose happened to bring about these two changes?

4. Give five examples of pairs of goods and/or services that are viewed as substitutes by some consumers and as complements by others. For each pair, tell what conditions cause them to be both substitutes and complements.

5. A company's supply curve for micro-computers has shifted to the right. Give four reasons why this may have occurred.

6. Becky Ryder buys one pound of Jarlsberg cheese for $5.60, but when the price rises to $6.00, she buys only three-fourths of a pound. Draw a demand curve that shows her purchases. Is this a shift or a movement along a curve? Becky's favorite cheese is Brie, the price of which has just dropped to $4.00 a pound. Show the effect of this

change on her demand curve for Jarlsberg. Is this a shift or a movement along a curve?

7. If faced with a serious excess supply in a particular market, what would you advise the government to do? Explain the basis for your recommendation.

8. During an emergency period a government may impose a ceiling price on a certain good in order to slow down the flow of an important resource into that good. This ceiling price may go along with either an equilibrium or a disequilibrium situation. How might the government bring about each of these situations? Why might it choose one over the other?

9. In New York City certain apartments have been "rent controlled" for the last several decades. (Rent control is a form of ceiling price.) How does this help you to explain each of the following?

    a. Poor maintenance of these apartment houses
    b. Apartment shortages
    c. Well-to-do rental agents (often superintendents)

10. What is the label on the vertical axis of an aggregate-demand-and-supply graph? Why must it be different from the label for this axis on a graph of a market for a specific product? What is the label on the horizontal axis of an aggregate-demand-and-supply graph? Why must these values be calculated at one particular price level?

Classical Economics: The Dismal Science?

Two unflattering terms, "dismal science" and "pig philosophy," were attached to political economy, as economics was called, in mid-Victorian Britain. They both come from the pen of the great Scottish historian and social critic Thomas Carlyle (1795–1881). The term "dismal science" has survived, though "pig philosophy" has not. Which economic doctrines of Carlyle's day inspired the term "dismal science"?

Adam Smith, who died before Carlyle was born, could hardly be called a dismal scientist, for his doctrine was quite upbeat. In an essay on development, written in 1755, Smith said,

Adam Smith (1723–1790)

Little else is requisite, to carry a state to the highest level of opulence from the lowest barbarism, but peace, easy taxes, and a tolerable administration of justice, all the rest being brought about by the natural course of things.

Five Dismal Ideas

It was with the two following generations of economists, writing under the influence of the French Revolution, the Napoleonic Wars, and the Industrial Revolution, that the "dismal" ideas—some indeed implied by other passages in Smith's work—achieved their prominence. We stress five of these doctrines:

1. The Malthusian principle of population
2. The subsistence theory of wages
3. The principle of diminishing returns (to both labor and capital)
4. The tendency of profits to a minimum
5. Economic stagnation in the stationary state

The first of these ideas is due primarily to Thomas Robert Malthus (1766–1834) and the others mainly to David Ricardo (1772–1823). These doctrines are all related to each other in what is called "the English classical system." Even though they refer only to a pure market economy, their proponents are sure that no other economic organization can do better than what Adam Smith described as "the obvious and simple system of natural liberty."

The first two doctrines (of the above five) are dismal in their implication that the ordinary worker gains little or nothing from economic progress. The second pair imply that the ordinary capitalist may also lose as capital is accumulated in a growing economy, so that the major beneficiary of economic growth is a passive and unproductive class of landowners. The fifth and last of these ideas predicts that economic progress itself will be short lived, and will eventually peter out in a dull and gloomy stagnation.

David Ricardo (1772–1823)

Thomas Robert Malthus (1766–1834)

It is interesting to note, however, that the most popular "classical" economics textbook, John Stuart Mill's *Principles of Political Economy* (1848), was far from dismal as to either the future of the working class or the nature of the stationary state. Mill thought wages might rise gradually to meet the basic needs of the workers. And he imagined the stationary state as a pleasant period of economic inactivity, when people might turn their attention from money grubbing and materialism to plain living, high thinking, and the higher culture generally.

But let us return to the five dismal ideas themselves.

MALTHUSIAN PRINCIPLE OF POPULATION Malthus believed he observed, mainly from what happened in the American colonies, a natural tendency for population to grow faster than the means of subsistence (the food supply). As the population grew at a geometric rate (2, 4, 8, . . .), the food supply would rise only at an arithmetical one (1, 2, 3, 4, . . .). Only the "positive checks" of famine, war, and disease would hold the population within bounds, unless of course human nature could be changed to accept such "preventive checks" as later marriage and sexual continence within marriage.[1]

---

1. Malthus, an ordained clergyman of the Church of England, regarded contraception, abortion, infanticide, and homosexuality as forms of "vice," and did not include them in his "preventive checks."

SUBSISTENCE THEORY OF WAGES From Malthusian demography to a subsistence theory of wages is only a short step. If wage rates, set by supply and demand, remain higher than the workers' customary level of subsistence, workers will marry earlier and more of their children will live, until the rising supply of workers pushes wage rates down again. On the other hand, if wage rates fall below the subsistence level, later marriage, infant mortality, and emigration will after a time lower the supply of workers and raise wages again. There is a complication, however, because the classical economists all knew that English wages and subsistence levels were higher than those of Ireland or of Continental Europe. They reasoned that this could happen if wages remained high or low for long enough to improve or lower workers' level of living in general—raising the staple diet from potatoes to wheat, or lowering it from wheat to potatoes. But this important complication was often overlooked in the simpler statements of classical wage theory.

PRINCIPLE OF DIMINISHING RETURNS "With every mouth," said Benjamin Franklin, "God sends a pair of hands." And so, especially if more machinery is accumulated along with the extra hands, why should food ever run short? Because, according to the dismal scientists, the principle of diminishing returns is operating. The extra hands, even with extra equipment, yield lesser amounts of additional output from a constant stock of agricultural land and other natural resources. It follows, then, that a doubling of the population, even if accompanied by a doubling of the capital supply, does not double the total output. For this reason, output per person falls off. (This argument ignores any qualitative improvements in either physical or human capital—as when a tractor replaces a team of oxen or a literate peasant steps into the shoes of his or her illiterate parent.)

TENDENCY OF PROFITS TO A MINIMUM Classical economists used the term "profits" to refer to the returns to capital. As physical capital in particular is accumulated and becomes subject to diminishing returns, new investment will only be demanded at a real rate of interest that tends to fall over time.[2] And as the return on their savings falls, capitalists will save less. These processes of falling real interest rates and falling saving rates will continue until the rate of return to capital is so low, and capitalists' savings are so small, that there is no longer any net increase in the capital stock. In other words, capitalists' savings will just balance the depreciation and obsolescence of the existing stock.

ECONOMIC STAGNATION With wages approximately constant and return on capital falling to a minimum, which some economists suspect is near zero, the principal gainer from economic progress becomes the landlord. Landlords win out because both increasing population and increasing capital raise the demand for land, both good and bad. Much land that is infertile or remote and that commands no rent in "the early and rude state of society" comes to earn substantial rent as society grows—in the American case as the frontier moved west. The gain comes with minimum effort on the part of the landowning family, which may be descended from a successful capitalist of a few generations back.

Are the Ideas Still Alive Today?

Some combination of the five gloomy ideas that gave economics the name of "the dismal science" has outlived the English classical school itself. The depressing ideas live on today in such statements as "American agriculture is a losing proposition, subsidized by returns from land speculation," and in assurances that no other system could do better than the free market.[3] Perhaps the name itself persists also because so many students are required to take economics when they would rather study an easier or more immediately appealing subject.

Strange as it may seem, there are more than a few economists today who, calling themselves "new-classicals" or "neo-Ricardians," propose to bring back these dismal ideas about the working of a market economy. They would substitute the gloomy ideas for the pleasanter "neoclassical" ideas that succeeded them and to some extent de-dismalized the subject!

2. A real rate of interest is one that has been adjusted to correct for inflation.

3. The argument here is that every individual is a better judge of his or her own interest than is any government bureau, and that every individual will work harder in his or her own interest than in carrying out the orders of superiors.

II The Macroeconomy

- Unemployment and Inflation
- National Income Accounting
- The Circular Flow and Macroeconomic Equilibrium

6 *Unemployment and Inflation*

PREVIEW We now begin our study of macroeconomics—the part of economics that is concerned with aggregate or "grand total" economic activity.[1] Often it is subtitled "the theory of income, employment, and price levels" because it tries to explain why inflation and unemployment occur and how total income for a nation reaches a certain level.

The macroeconomic problems of inflation and unemployment are among the most pressing of our time. If allowed to go too far, either can disrupt an economy and a society. They can bring down governments and even lead to revolutions. Dealing with these problems is one of the "stabilization" responsibilities of government described in Chapter 2.

The first part of this chapter deals with unemployment. Economists have a well-defined concept of unemployment, but great difficulty arises in finding ways of measuring the actual amount of unemployment in the economy. After learning about the economists' concept of unemployment and the measuring instruments they use, we will briefly note how unemployment affects different groups in the society.

The second part of the chapter presents similar information about inflation, explaining the economists' concept of inflation and the index numbers used to measure it. The effects of inflation on economic, social, and political life are profound. The choices made by all the actors on the economic stage are altered by inflation and by expectations of future inflation. At the same time, social and political problems arise because inflation redistributes income and wealth in ways that many people believe to be unfair.

Understanding the economic concepts of unemployment and inflation is the first step in studying macroeconomics. After you complete this chapter, we will examine the forces that cause these problems and the instruments of social policy that can be used to deal with them.

HISTORICAL PERSPECTIVE

The performance of the aggregate economy has been an important concern for many centuries. When modern nations were being formed in Europe in the 1500s and 1600s, the focus was on ways to increase the power and security of the state. Great wealth was required for a nation or its ruler to hire an army or support a navy. So there developed an early branch of macroeconomics called **bullionism,** which was concerned with how to accumulate treasure. In due time, this interest evolved into a school of thought called **mercantilism,** which paid particular attention to regulating trade—especially foreign trade—in order to make the nation strong. The mercantilists, arguing that government regulation was needed to maintain an orderly economy, rose to positions of great power in France and England in the eighteenth century. Consequently, England's treatment of her North American colonies reflected mercantilist thinking.

1. See Chapter 1, pages 5–8.

Modern-day macroeconomics is still concerned about the total performance of the economy, but the specific concerns of unemployment and inflation now claim center stage, as industrialized economies experience the ups and downs of economic activity known as **business cycles.** In the mid-nineteenth century, Karl Marx, the intellectual father of communism, contended that business cycles were inherent in capitalist economic systems. His theories stated that periodic downturns in economic activity (recessions) would inevitably get worse and worse and that the number of people unemployed would continue to increase until workers rose up and overthrew the capitalist system.[2]

Interest in macroeconomics soared when the **Great Depression** hit the United States and most industrialized countries in the world in the 1930s. Unemployment reached unprecedented levels and many people concluded that Marx's prediction was proving to be accurate. Non-Marxist economists tried desperately to resolve the problem of persistent unemployment. In the midst of these troubled times, a prominent British economist, John Maynard Keynes (pronounced "cains"), presented a theory explaining the causes of unemployment in capitalist economies and suggesting policy measures that could be taken to ease the problem.[3]

The **Keynesian theory** dominated non-Marxist macroeconomic thinking until the 1970s, when a situation arose that defied solution by the then well established theory. Most major industrial countries found themselves experiencing rising unemployment and rising price levels (inflation) at the same time—a combination that fell outside the standard Keynesian framework. Inflation, of course, was nothing new. Most major wars had been accompanied by rising price levels. But wartime inflations had gone along with low levels of unemployment and inflation usually stopped or slowed down when the wars ended. But, in the 1970s, price levels rose substantially and persistently in peacetime while unemployment

2. For further explanation of Marx's theories, see Chapters 10 and 39.

3. Keynes's theory will be explained in Part III.

also was going up. Again economists searched for solutions.

Today, in the 1980s, inflation has moderated substantially, and unemployment, although still higher than many would like, is at least not as severe as in the previous decade. Some new theories have been developed and some old ones have been revised and updated. Economists are once again hopeful that their understanding is good enough to enable them to offer constructive advice for establishing economic policy.

We can be reasonably sure, however, that the definitive theory of macroeconomics has not yet been devised. As societies and economies evolve, new situations are likely to arise, bringing new problems and new challenges. In preparing for these problems and challenges, it is best to start with a sound understanding of the present theories and a mind that is open to recognize their weaknesses and alert to the possibilities of new and better models.

UNEMPLOYMENT

Earlier in the book you encountered some introductory definitions and classifications of unemployment. You may remember from Chapter 1 that a person is considered unemployed if he or she does not have a job and is actively trying to find one. That is an "official" definition of unemployment, used by the government in estimating the number of people who are out of work. You also learned that the character of unemployment depends on the reason why the unemployed person is not able to find a job. This is an economic meaning of unemployment. If the job search is unsuccessful because changes have taken place in *what* goods and services are demanded in the economy or in *how* goods and services are produced, the unemployment is microeconomic, and remedies should be sought in retraining and/or relocating the person so that he or she will be able to find a new job. But if the job search fails for reasons that cannot be traced to microeconomic choices in the economy, the unemployment may be macroeconomic in character. In this case, unemployment is widespread or general throughout the economy and affects people with many different levels of skill and in many different lines of work.

Now it is time to explore the subject in greater depth. We shall begin by considering the economic concept of unemployment. Then we move on to the measurement of unemployment and the different varieties of unemployment.

The Economic Concept of Unemployment

In economics, **unemployment** means that a person is spending more time for leisure than desired and less time for wage earning than desired *at the going wage rate.* This definition may sound more microeconomic than macroeconomic, but of course the same definition should apply in both areas of our discipline. To understand unemployment, we must begin by examining the microeconomics of wage rates and hours worked. We shall use the demand and supply concepts that you learned in Chapter 5 and apply them to labor.[4]

THE SUPPLY OF LABOR Figure 6-1 shows a supply curve for labor—the key to understanding the economic concept of unemployment. On the vertical axis are different possible wage rates, which we specify here to be **real wage rates**— that is, wage rates expressed in terms of the goods and services that can be purchased rather than in terms of some specific number of dollars. It is very important to remember this distinction between a "real" wage rate and a **nominal wage rate,** which is simply the amount of money a worker receives per hour (or other time unit) of work. Inflation can change the real (purchasing-power) value of wages expressed in nominal dollar amounts. But we define the wage rates on the vertical axis of Figure 6-1 to be free of inflation effects, that is, as if there was no inflation. We use the real wage because we want to understand

4. A more detailed treatment of labor and wages is presented in microeconomics.

FIGURE 6-1   **The Labor-Supply Curve and the Concept of Unemployment**

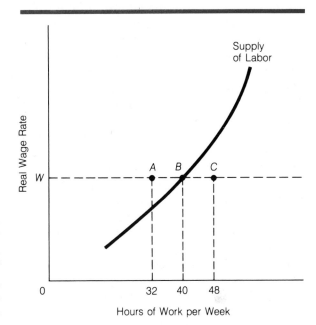

The labor-supply curve shows the number of hours per week that a person would like to work at various possible wage rates. When the wage rate is W, a person is underemployed if he or she is working 32 hours per week (point A), fully employed if working 40 hours per week (point B), and overemployed if working 48 hours per week (point C).

the behavior of workers and employers and because we believe that they use the real wage rate, or what they believe is the real wage rate, in making work decisions.

The horizontal axis shows quantities of work that will be supplied. The labor-supply curve shows the willingness of people to exchange their leisure time for income. When a person is working, he or she is exchanging leisure time for wage income. The supply curve slopes upward to the right (a positive slope), suggesting that people are willing to give up more of their leisure time when real wage rates are high than when real wage rates are low, other things being equal.

The wage rate often is thought of as the opportunity cost of leisure time. In other words, when you take time off to enjoy leisure, you are giving up the wage that you otherwise would have earned during this time. Thus, the wage is the opportunity cost of the leisure. At low wage rates, leisure is very inexpensive, and people will use a lot of their time for it. But as the wage rate rises, the tradeoff turns more and more away from leisure and in favor of the wage that working will bring. This is another way of saying that the supply of labor is positively related to the wage rate.[5]

Before you go on, take a moment to think through this concept of the individual's labor-supply curve. Be sure you understand the reasoning that lies behind the idea that people want to work more hours when the real wage rate is high than when it is low. Of course, we realize that low-wage earners sometimes work more hours per week than high-wage earners, but since that proposition compares different people, it does not match the specifications of our graph in Figure 6-1. Also, we realize that, when a worker experiences a wage cut, his or her first reaction may be to take a second job and to work more hours each week. But, given more time to adjust, he or she is likely to switch to a different job and get back on the type of supply curve shown in our graph. You will stay on the right track in your economic thinking if you see the labor-supply curve as having a positive slope and showing a tradeoff of the worker's time between leisure and the wage that can be gotten from working.

UNDEREMPLOYMENT AND OVEREMPLOYMENT
In Figure 6-1, W is the wage rate that has been determined by the market supply and market demand for the kind of work done by the individual whose supply curve is shown. (Remember from Chapter 5 that a "market" involves many suppliers and demanders for a particular good or service.) If the person whose labor-supply curve is shown is working 40 hours per week at this wage rate (point B in Figure 6-1), he or she is fully employed—working exactly the desired

number of hours per week. But if that person is working only 32 hours per week (point A), he or she is underemployed—working fewer hours per week than desired at that wage rate.[6] At point C, the person is overemployed, since, at 48 hours of work per week, he or she is giving up more hours of leisure than desired at that wage rate.

UNEMPLOYMENT IN A LABOR MARKET The preceding exercise explained overemployment, full employment, and underemployment from the perspective of an individual worker. Let us now broaden the scope to consider all the workers in an economy.

Figure 6-2 represents a labor market for an entire economy. The supply curve is the aggregate, or sum, of the quantities of labor supplied by the individuals who make up this economy. The demand curve represents the aggregate, or sum, of the quantities of labor demanded by all the firms in the economy. As explained in microeconomics, this demand depends in large part on the demand for final goods and services sold by firms and on the productivity of labor in producing them.

The intersection of the demand curve D_1 and supply curve S at point A in Figure 6-2 identifies the particular real wage rate that balances the quantity of labor supplied with the quantity demanded. This is an equilibrium real wage rate. At this equilibrium real wage of W_1, quantity Q_1 of labor is supplied and demanded. The economy is at "full employment," if we assume that each individual in the economy also is on his or her individual labor-supply curve. (We will see shortly, however, that some workers will usually be between jobs so that official statistics will show some unemployment.)

Underemployment or overemployment can arise in this market if there is a shift of one or the other (or both) of these curves and if there is a time lag in the adjustment to the new equilibrium. This is illustrated in Figure 6-2, where we show a leftward shift in the labor-demand curve from D_1 to D_2. Many economists believe that this sort

---

5. In microeconomics you learn that some part of the individual's labor-supply curve may have a negative slope. In dealing with macroeconomics and aggregate data, we can ignore this possibility.

6. Underemployment can also mean working at a job that does not utilize all of the skill and training that the worker possesses.

FIGURE 6-2 Unemployment as Disequilibrium in the Labor Market

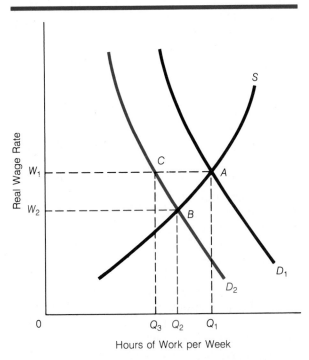

Equilibrium may exist at point A with wage rate W_1 and Q_1 hours of work per week demanded and supplied. If the demand curve shifts from D_1 to D_2, the new equilibrium is at point B with wage rate W_2 and Q_2 hours of work demanded and supplied per week. Point C illustrates a case of disequilibrium with unemployment, represented by Q_1 minus Q_3 hours of work per week.

of demand shift may be what causes the economy to go into recession. In Figure 6-2, the new equilibrium, after the demand shift, is at B, with the real wage rate W_2 and Q_2 hours of labor demanded and supplied per week. There would be fewer hours worked per week than at the original equilibrium, but this would not mean that there was more unemployment—only that people had reached a new balance between the hours of leisure time and wages from working.

Unemployment can arise, however, in the adjustment from one equilibrium to the next. If workers refuse to accept the wage cut from W_1 to W_2, or if they do not believe that the equilibrium wage rate actually has changed, Q_1 hours of labor

may still be offered when only Q_3 hours are demanded at the W_1 wage rate, as shown by point C in Figure 6-2. The excess quantity supplied, Q_1 minus Q_3, represents unemployment.

Before the Great Depression, most non-Marxist economists believed that shifts in labor market demand and/or supply would be moderate and that adjustments to new equilibrium conditions would take place smoothly and without undue delay. They believed that disequilibrium conditions would exist only for short periods of time. The experience of the Great Depression caused many economists to abandon that comfortable view.

Now that you understand the economists' concept of unemployment, you are ready to learn how it is actually measured. In the next section, you will discover why it is so hard to devise measurements that correspond to the economists' concept of unemployment.

Measuring Unemployment

Since economists define unemployment by comparing actual work time with a person's desired work time, many difficulties arise in finding a measuring system consistent with the theory. Take, for example, the forty-hour workweek, which is more or less standard in the United States today. At the current wage rate, do you feel that this workweek provides the best combination of leisure time and money income? You may know some people who prefer part-time work (less than forty hours a week) and others who want to work overtime or hold two jobs at the same time (moonlighters). If all these people actually work forty hours a week, economists would call the first group "overemployed" and the second "underemployed." This may sound like a strange conclusion, but thinking about it will help you understand the economists' concept of unemployment and will suggest some of the problems in measuring actual unemployment.

In official U.S. government statistics, each of the people in the preceding example is called "employed." Thus it is clear that the official statistics are only an approximate measure of unemployment, in the economists' view. But since decisions that affect all of us are based on official statistics, they are very important in policy making.

THE CIVILIAN UNEMPLOYMENT RATE The published **civilian unemployment rate** is the percentage of the civilian labor force that is unemployed. The **civilian labor force** consists of the civilian noninstitutional population, age sixteen and over, who are willing and able to work. The civilian unemployment rate is calculated by dividing the number of unemployed people by the number of people in the civilian labor force. In other words,

$$\frac{\text{civilian}}{\text{unemployment rate}} = \frac{\text{unemployed persons}}{\text{civilian labor force}}$$

Therefore, if there were 8.5 million people unemployed and if the civilian labor force totalled 120 million people, this formula would give a civilian unemployment rate of 0.071. It is customary, however, to move the decimal point two places to the right by multiplying by 100, so as to give the rate as a percentage. The published civilian unemployment rate in our illustration would now be 7.1 percent.

In the United States, the civilian unemployment rate is computed monthly by the Bureau of Labor Statistics of the Department of Labor. First, a representative sample of people is selected for interview. The interviewer asks whether the person is currently working for pay or has been employed during the past two weeks. Part-time work on a regular basis is counted. A person who works as little as one hour a week for pay is classified as employed. If a person is not working, the interviewer asks whether he or she is searching for work. If the answer is "yes," the person is classified as unemployed.

The question about the job search is important because it helps establish the size of the civilian labor force, which is the denominator of the fraction used in computing the civilian unemployment rate. A person who is neither holding a job nor searching for one is not part of the civilian labor force according to the official statistics. In this group are retired people as well as students, homemakers, and others who have chosen nonmarket activities. Some may be **discouraged workers**—labor force dropouts who have stopped searching for work because they believe there is little chance of ever finding a job. Others may claim to be looking for work but really are not because they prefer unemployment compensation to the best job they expect to find.

Certain other groups are excluded from the civilian labor force as well. The rules exclude people in institutional care facilities, such as prisons and mental hospitals, and persons under sixteen years of age. Drawing the line at the sixteenth birthday may be somewhat arbitrary, but you will agree that some cutoff is needed for a meaningful definition of the civilian labor force. There are proposals to raise the cutoff line to seventeen or eighteen. If these changes were made, they would lead to important changes in the civilian unemployment rate because sixteen- and seventeen-year-old job seekers, who are often high school dropouts, have great difficulty in finding work. Not counting people in this age group would lower the official civilian unemployment rate. On the other hand, including the "discouraged worker" would raise the rate.

THE UNEMPLOYMENT RECORD The top line in Figure 6-3 shows the official civilian unemployment rate for the United States from 1970 through 1985. The lowest rate during this period was 4.8 percent. This point was reached in 1970 and again in 1973. The highest rate for any full year during the period was 9.5 percent reached in both 1982 and 1983. Compared with the 1950s and 1960s, unemployment was relatively high all through the 1970s and early 1980s. In the 1950s, annual civilian unemployment rates averaged 4.5 percent and never exceeded 6.8 percent. In the 1960s, civilian unemployment rates averaged 4.8 percent and never exceeded 6.7 percent. For 1933, during the Great Depression, measured civilian unemployment was 24.9 percent. For 1944, during World War II, it was 1.2 percent.

Types of Unemployment

In Chapter 1 you learned to classify unemployment as either microeconomic or macroeconomic.

FIGURE 6-3   **Unemployment in the United States, 1970 through 1985**

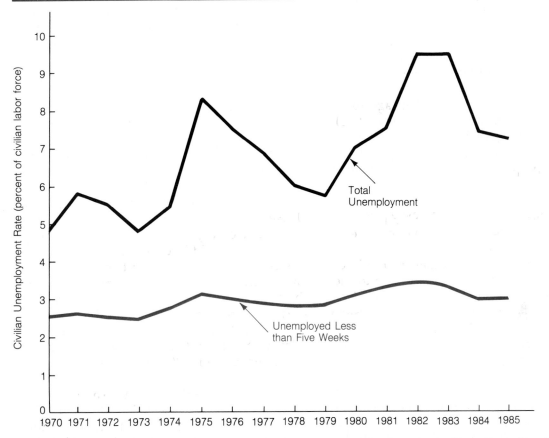

The black line illustrates annual civilian unemployment rates in the United States from 1970 through 1985. The colored line shows annual data for the percentage of the civilian labor force that had been unemployed for less than five weeks. It attempts to illustrate frictional unemployment.

Source: *Economic Report of the President, 1986*, Tables B-31 and B-33.

Now it is time to refine the classification still further. In common usage, economists generally classify unemployment as seasonal, frictional, structural, or cyclical.

SEASONAL UNEMPLOYMENT **Seasonal unemployment** arises because some occupations require workers only during part of each year. Many seasonal occupations, such as picking and processing fruits and vegetables, depend on the growing seasons for various crops. Some, like tourism and resorts, depend on annual climatic conditions. Some, like the Post Office or retail sales, arise from the Christmas rush or other special annual events. People who work in occupations such as these often are unemployed part of the time each year.

Seasonal unemployment explains why some people have low money incomes, but for others it is an opportunity to earn extra income. Because this type of unemployment follows a pattern that is more or less regular each year, it can be predicted with reasonable accuracy. To avoid confusion, most published statistics on unemployment are "seasonally adjusted," meaning that the seasonal component has been smoothed out or averaged so that direct month-to-month and year-to-year comparisons can be made for other types of unemployment.

FRICTIONAL UNEMPLOYMENT Frictional unemployment arises because it takes time to move from one job to another. Because people do not have perfect information about alternative jobs, they must take time to search and to make decisions among jobs. They may need to learn a new skill as they move from their old jobs to ones that pay better or that they expect to like better. Delays arise, too, in gaining entry to a new line of work. All of these facts of life suggest that some frictional unemployment will always exist in a society in which people are free to move from place to place and job to job.

Barriers to the freedom of movement that increase frictional unemployment are of course not desirable. Some barriers are particularly unfair to groups or individuals, such as discrimination based on age, race, or sex, unnecessary apprenticeship requirements, or union membership limitations. However, frictional unemployment is not considered a serious problem in itself. Continuous movement among jobs and locations is the way in which an economy refines and tunes its operations to the preferences of people.

Actual measurements of frictional unemployment are not exact. One way to estimate its size is to look at very short-term unemployment. Looking back to Figure 6-3, we see a line for the percentage of the civilian labor force for whom the current spell of unemployment had lasted less than five weeks. This percentage changed only a little each year (though it increased slightly over this period). It is like a "background noise" regularly picked up by government unemployment statistics.[7]

7. Many labor economists prefer to estimate frictional unemployment by using the percentage unemployed for up to fourteen weeks. For this reason, our line in Figure 6-3 may understate the amount of frictional unemployment, but it illustrates the idea that frictional unemployment almost always exists in the economy.

Figure 6-4 shows another way to distinguish frictional from other kinds of unemployment. On this chart, the colored line shows the civilian unemployment rate for people who left their last job voluntarily and people who were entering the civilian labor force, either for the first time or after being out of the civilian labor force for a while. This line appears quite similar to the line in Figure 6-3 for people out of work for less than five weeks.

Even though these illustrations of frictional unemployment are helpful, a precise measure of this kind of joblessness is impossible. The barriers to movement between jobs that lead to frictional unemployment are hard to separate from the more serious problems that define structural unemployment.

STRUCTURAL UNEMPLOYMENT Structural unemployment involves a mismatch between worker qualifications and job requirements. It often arises when changes take place in production methods (how to produce) and in the types of goods and services produced (what to produce). It corresponds to our definition of microeconomic unemployment. As we noted in Chapter 1, new automatic banking machines may mean unemployment for bank tellers and bookkeepers, and a switch in consumer preference from golf to tennis might mean unemployment for golf pros and golf-ball makers. Structural unemployment also comes from job discrimination and other barriers in the job market.

Structural unemployment is more serious than frictional unemployment because workers are not leaving their old jobs voluntarily in order to search for better ones. Their old jobs have disappeared owing to circumstances beyond their control, so they are forced to retrain themselves and move their families to wherever new jobs are opening up. Moreover, the new job often will not pay as well as the old one, and some time may pass before the worker recognizes the reality of his or her lower real wage and living standard. This can cause delay in accepting the new job.

Dealing with structural unemployment requires programs that not only retrain people but also help them discover and move to where new jobs

FIGURE 6-4   Reasons for Unemployment in the United States, 1970 through 1985

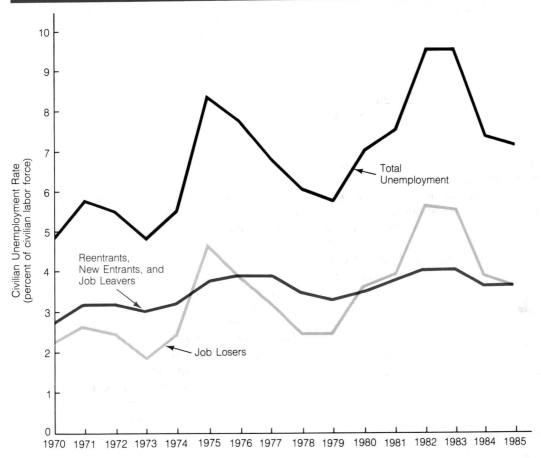

The unemployment rate for people who lost their last job follows a pattern similar to the total civilian unemployment rate. On the other hand, the colored line shows the un- employment rate for people who left their last job voluntarily or who were entering or re-entering the civilian labor force. It may be used as an estimate of frictional unemployment.

Source: Economic Report of the President, 1986, Tables B-31 and B-35.

are available. However, it is hard to design and operate these retraining and relocation programs. An approach that sometimes succeeds is on-the-job training, in which employers receive govern- ment subsidies to help pay the workers who are being trained for new jobs. Another program provides tuition aid to persons who enroll in training schools, colleges, and universities. There are also training programs operated directly by the government. Since structural unemployment crops up in an ever-changing group of trades and industries, no single program will be right for all people and all times.

Probably some structural unemployment is al- ways present because workers cannot keep up with the constant changes in the economy. For this reason, some part of the measured unem- ployment rate can usually be attributed to this "normal" state of affairs. But the amount of structural unemployment may rise when changes in the economy come rapidly. The great increase in the relative price of energy during the 1970s brought a rise in structural unemployment for people working in gas stations and resort hotels as the economy adapted to the new set of relative prices.

Measurement is further complicated because no clear line can be drawn between structural unemployment and cyclical unemployment. Recessions may bring an end to businesses that have already been weakened by changes in the economy, and expansionary times often speed the introduction of new products and technologies. For this reason, structural unemployment moves up and down along with cyclical unemployment. The statistics are not able to separate the two completely.

CYCLICAL (MACROECONOMIC) UNEMPLOYMENT

Cyclical (macroeconomic) unemployment is called cyclical because the historical record shows alternating ups and downs, and it is called macroeconomic because it affects the whole economy rather than particular industries. There are simply not enough job openings for all the people qualified to fill them. Some economists measure fluctuations in cyclical unemployment by using statistics on the average length of unemployment or on the percentage of the civilian labor force that has been out of work for more than fourteen weeks. But the actual amount of cyclical unemployment cannot be measured precisely. In 1933 and in other depression years, there surely was joblessness that could not be classed as frictional or structural. On the other hand, cyclical unemployment was probably absent in 1944 when total unemployment was only 1.2 percent of the civilian labor force.

The Incidence of Unemployment

Figure 6-5 shows unemployment rates for different groups within the civilian labor force from 1970 through 1985. Several important aspects of unemployment are shown in this figure. Note first that unemployment rates are higher for blacks and for young people than for adult whites.

Also, unemployment rates have usually been higher for women than for men in both racial groups, though there is a tendency for male unemployment to exceed female unemployment during peak unemployment periods. Unemployment rates for young people, age sixteen through nineteen, are much higher than for any of the other groups shown in the chart. This chart does not show male–female or racial distinctions within the sixteen- to nineteen-year-old group, but important differences do exist. Unemployment rates are more than twice as high for black and minority-group teenagers as for whites in this age group. Within each racial group, however, there is little difference between teenage male and female unemployment rates. These facts show that unemployment does not affect different groups in the society equally. Some are much more vulnerable to unemployment than others.

There is also another message in the data shown in Figure 6-5. All the lines move up and down together. This fact suggests that all groups share a common experience of fluctuating good and bad times. The range between peaks and troughs is greater for sixteen- to nineteen-year-olds and for black males than it is for others, so these people gain more from prosperity and lose more from recession than others do. But effective policies on unemployment are important to all segments of the labor force.

The Social Consequences of Unemployment

Unemployment is more than a statistic and more than just a topic in economic theory. Anyone who has lost his or her job or has been laid off recognizes the shock, the frustrations, and the fears of unemployment. Few events in life are more devastating both to individuals and to families. For the society as a whole, unemployment is a loss of production that can never be replaced. No factor of production is more perishable than labor. It cannot be saved and used later. If it is not used when it is available, it is lost forever. Thus, unemployment means a permanently lower standard of living for the whole society. To the

FIGURE 6-5   **The Incidence of Unemployment in the United States, 1970 through 1985**

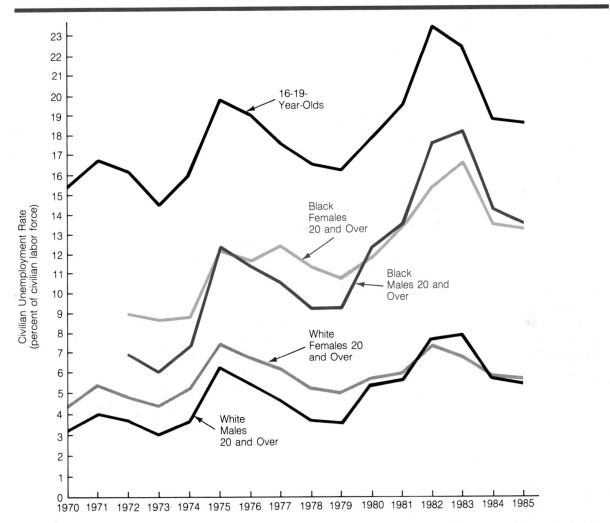

Unemployment rates are higher for some groups than for others. Teenage workers have the highest unemployment rate and blacks have higher unemployment rates than whites.

Source: Economic Report of the President, 1986, Tables B-35 and B-38.

extent that the leisure time from unemployment is not put to constructive use, both present and future production possibilities are diminished.

Unemployment also can damage the social and political structure of a society. The destabilizing effects of widespread unemployment are well documented. During the Great Depression of the 1930s, unemployment contributed to the overthrow of democratic processes and the rise of Hitler in Germany. In 1932, an "army of bonus marchers" descended on Washington, D.C., demanding jobs and more help from the U.S. government. Army tanks and troops were used to disperse these marchers. Also during this period, unemployed French workers staged riots in Paris.

An especially moving description of the personal and social consequences of unemployment is contained in the following quotation from *The Great Depression:*

Finally, of course, you joined the breadlines and your family went on relief. They might barely survive on the three or four dollars a week that local relief agencies could afford. Or they might break up. You might go to the local poorhouse, your children to an orphanage. Or the family might scatter to stay with more fortunate relatives in the country, where food, at least, could be grown for consumption. If your children were over the age of eight or nine, they might start wandering over the countryside, looking for handouts at farmhouse doors. In the end, it would seem to you that you had never known any other life than that of a beggar. Even humiliation would be too exhausting an emotion for you; only numb hopelessness and sick despair could find room in your emaciated body. And you wondered what you'd done wrong. You wracked your brain to find out where you'd made a false turn, what sin you'd committed to earn so terrible a punishment. But if you looked around and saw the thousands and thousands of others just like yourself, you began to wonder if perhaps there wasn't something wrong with the system itself that had brought about this national catastrophe. Maybe capitalism was at fault, maybe democracy. You didn't make up your mind about that right away, but you were wondering.[8]

Even though unemployment is still a serious problem, comparisons with the 1930s are difficult for several reasons. Many economists believe that a given unemployment rate causes less hardship today than it did then because of government aid. In the 1930s unemployment compensation was almost unknown, whereas today most employed persons are covered by this insurance. Under this system, both the worker and the employer pay money into an insurance trust fund as long as the worker is employed. The amounts paid in are based on a percentage of the worker's wage. Then, if the worker loses his or her job, benefit checks equal to a significant fraction of the old wage rate will be received, at least for a

8. Robert Goldston, *The Great Depression* (New York: Bobbs-Merrill, 1968), pp. 48–49.

period of time. In addition, today there are many welfare programs that help the unemployed after their unemployment insurance benefits run out. To a large extent, it was the suffering of the 1930s that brought the introduction of many of these programs.

Another important difference between now and the Great Depression years is the increase in the number of women in the labor force. During the 1930s, few women worked outside the home, so when a man lost his job, there were usually devastating economic effects on the family and psychological effects on the family "breadwinner." Today, with a second income often available to the family, unemployment is less damaging.

The Employment Rate

The civilian unemployment rate that you have just studied is the most widely used statistic for showing how the economy is functioning with respect to labor, but it is not the only statistic that is useful for this purpose. Economists also use the **civilian employment rate.** This is calculated by dividing the number of civilians who have jobs by the total civilian noninstitutional population of the country. In other words,

$$\frac{\text{civilian}}{\text{employment rate}} = \frac{\text{employed persons (civilian)}}{\text{civilian noninstitutional population}}$$

Therefore, if there were 111.5 million civilians with jobs out of a civilian noninstitutional population of 198 million, the civilian employment rate would be 0.563, according to this formula. As with the civilian unemployment rate, however, it is customary to express it as a percentage by multiplying by 100, so that the published civilian employment rate in our illustration would be 56.3 percent.

There are important differences between the employment rate and the unemployment rate. First, the numerator of the fraction records the number of people who have a job rather than the number who do not have a job and are trying to find one. This is less ambiguous than the number

FIGURE 6-6   The Civilian Employment Rate, Civilian Unemployment Rate, and Civilian Labor Force Participation Rate in the United States, 1970 through 1985

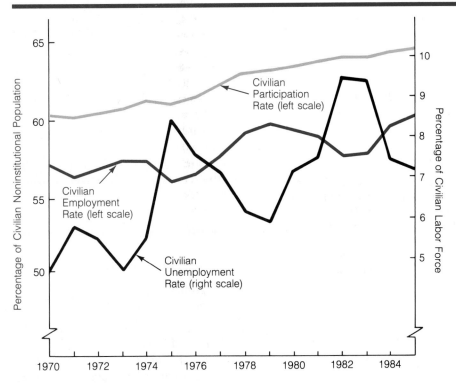

The civilian labor force participation rate is the percentage of the civilian noninstitutional population that is in the civilian labor force. The civilian employment rate is the percentage of the civilian noninstitutional population that is working.

The civilian unemployment rate is the percentage of the civilian labor force that is not working but is trying to find work.

Source: Economic Report of the President, 1986, Tables B-34 and B-35.

unemployed because it does not raise the question of whether the person is trying to find work. However, distinctions between part-time, full-time, and overtime work (or holding two jobs) are still ignored. The denominator of the fraction is the total civilian noninstitutional population. It is not the same as the civilian labor force because it includes people who are not looking for work, young people, and retirees.

Figure 6-6 compares the civilian employment rate with the civilian unemployment rate in the United States between 1970 and 1985. Note that the employment rate tended to go up when the

unemployment rate went down, and vice versa. Each of these statistics gives some indication of general economic conditions. However, fluctuations in the employment rate are less extreme because this rate is calculated from a larger base number—the total civilian noninstitutional population, instead of the civilian labor force. Note especially that the employment rate showed a general upward trend over the time period and that the unemployment rate also tended upward. How is it possible that both employment and unemployment could increase at the same time? We answer this question next.

The Civilian Labor Force Participation Rate

The **civilian labor force participation rate** is the number of persons in the civilian labor force divided by the civilian noninstitutional population, that is

$$\frac{\text{civilian labor force}}{\text{participation rate}} = \frac{\text{civilian labor force}}{\text{civilian noninstitutional population}}$$

Using the same numbers as before, if the civilian labor force totalled 120 million people and if the civilian noninstitutional population was 198 million, the participation rate would be 0.606. Again, it is customary to express it as a percentage by multiplying by 100, so that this participation rate would be published as 60.6 percent.

Changes in the participation rate help explain how both employment and unemployment rates can increase at the same time. Both can increase if the participation rate is rising. Women increased their participation rate greatly between 1960 and 1985. At the same time, men's participation fell. In total, the civilian labor force participation rate in the United States went from 59.4 percent in 1960 to 64.8 percent in 1985.[9]

Some economists reason that the increase in the participation rate was a cause of the increase in the unemployment rate over that period. They suggest that people newly entering the labor force have a harder time finding work than people who have been in the labor force for some time. Others suggest that the participation rate increased because registering for work at an employment office became a requirement for certain welfare programs during that time. This could also cause measured unemployment to increase.

The "baby boom" (or unusually high birthrate) in the United States between 1946 and 1962 was another factor that raised the civilian labor force participation rate during the 1970s and 1980s. During this period the percentage of the population in its "working years" was unusually high. Many economists believe that the U.S. economy

did well in providing jobs for this large increase in the civilian labor force, especially in view of the structural unemployment shocks that came from large increases in energy prices.

In some respects, the problems of employment and unemployment in the United States may be different in the closing years of the century. In the 1980s and 1990s, the baby boom people will have become experienced workers. Though female participation may continue to rise, it probably will not repeat the huge increase that it had between 1960 and 1985. As the population ages, the problems of the elderly may intensify toward the end of the century, with fewer workers supporting each retiree.

INFLATION

Inflation is a significant and sustained increase in the general price level. We will start our study of inflation by learning about index numbers and how they are used to compare different prices. Then we examine two methods of applying the index-number technique to the average of all prices in the economy. These will give us actual measurements of the changes in the general price level that occur with inflation and deflation. We will look at the record of price-level changes in the United States. Finally, we will consider some of the economic and social consequences of inflation.

Price-Index Numbers

Statisticians, economists, and others use index numbers as a method of comparing one value with another. We can define an **index number** as a way of stating a value by expressing it in terms of some other reference or "base" value, which is set to equal 100. For example, if the number 25 were the base value set equal to 100, the number 20 would have an index number value of 80, because $^{20}/_{25}$ equals $^{80}/_{100}$.

Since an index number expresses values in terms of some reference point, the first step is to

---

9. *Economic Report of the President, 1986*, Tables B-34 and B-35.

select this reference point. To apply the index-number method to prices, the prices that prevailed in some specified year are chosen as the base or reference point for constructing the index. Then the prices prevailing in other years are expressed in relation to these base-year prices. For example, if the price of apples increases from $.50 a pound to $.60 a pound and then to $1.00 a pound, and if we select the $.50 price as the base, we can construct price-index numbers for apples by dividing each year's apple price by the base-year apple price, as follows.

Reporting Period	Current Apple Price ($)	Base-Period Apple Price ($)	Index Number
1	0.50	0.50	1.00
2	0.60	0.50	1.20
3	1.00	0.50	2.00

As you can see, the index numbers provide a standardized system for measuring the change that has taken place in apple prices. In our illustration, in reporting period 2, the price of apples was 20 percent above the base-period price, as shown by the 1.20 value of the index number. In reporting period 3, the apple price was twice what it was in the base period and the index number was 2.0. Also, by dividing a particular price by its index-number value, we can calculate the base-period equivalent of that price. For example, the period-3 apple price ($1.00)

divided by the period-3 index number (2.00) equals the base-year apple price ($0.50). Similarly, base-year prices can be adjusted to their equivalents in other years by multiplying the base-year figure by the index number for the desired year. Or the prices in any pair of years can be compared by using the ratio of the index numbers.

It is common practice to move the decimal point two places to the right in published price-index numbers so that the index number for the base period is 100. Thus, our basic formula for a price-index number is

$$\frac{\text{current price}}{\text{base-period price}} \times 100 = \text{index number}$$

With this system, the published index number for period 3 in our illustration would be calculated as

$$\frac{1.00}{0.50} \times 100 = 200$$

Now that you know what a price-index number is and how it can be used, we must proceed to the next step in computing a measure of the general price level—calculating an average of all the prices in the economy. Two different systems are widely used to compute these averages. One is used with the gross national product (GNP) and the other is used in estimating the cost of living with the consumer price index.

TABLE 6-1 Computing a Price Deflator

Item	Current-Year Quantity	Current-Year Price	Current-Year Value	Base-Year Price	Base-Year Equivalent Value
Apples	100 lbs.	$1.00	$100.00	$0.60	$ 60.00
Oranges	75	1.50	112.50	0.90	67.50
Bananas	50	0.75	37.50	0.80	40.00
GNP			$250.00		$167.50

Values for goods in the current year are compared with the amounts that would have been needed to purchase the same goods at the base-year prices. The deflator index number is equal to 100 times current-year GNP divided by base-year equivalent GNP or ($250.00/$167.50) × 100 = 149.25.

FIGURE 6-7   U.S. GNP in Current and in Constant (1982) Dollars, 1960–1985

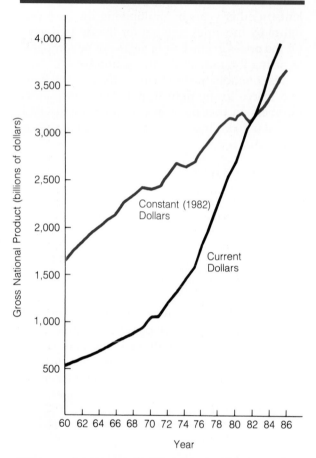

Because of increases in the general price level, GNP measured in current dollars increased faster than GNP measured in constant dollars. Because it has been adjusted for changes in the general price level, constant-dollar GNP is a measure of real GNP.

The Implicit Price Deflator for GNP

We will study the **gross national product** in detail in Chapter 7. For now, all you need to know is that GNP is a measure of the value of total production in the U.S. economy in a year. The U.S. Department of Commerce estimates total production in the economy and evaluates this production at the prices that actually prevailed

during the year in question. This is GNP in **current dollars** or in what are called **nominal values.** With this information about GNP, we can proceed to see how a price-index-number system for the total economy can be constructed.

Table 6-1 illustrates one method by which the index-number system can be applied to a whole collection of goods and services, such as is represented by the nation's GNP. In this very simple illustration, we assume that the entire GNP consists of the stated quantities of apples, oranges, and bananas, valued at the prices indicated for the current year. As you can see, the nominal, or current-dollar, value of the GNP would be $250.00. But if these quantities had been valued in the prices that prevailed in the year chosen as the base year, the GNP would have been only $167.50. With this information, we can calculate an index number to compare the average of prices in these two years. We simply apply the basic price-index-number formula to these two GNP values as follows:

$$\frac{\text{current-year value GNP}}{\text{base-year value GNP}} \times 100 = \text{index number}$$

which is equal to

$$\frac{\$250.00}{\$167.50} \times 100 = 149.25$$

The index number of 149.25 is called the **implicit price deflator for GNP.** By dividing the current or nominal value GNP by this deflator, we can find the amount of money that would have been needed to purchase the same goods at the prices that prevailed in the base year.

Table 6-2 shows the results of applying this deflation procedure to the U.S. GNP from 1960 through 1985. In this table, 1982 is the base year (that is, the 1982 prices are the common denominator). So current-dollar GNP for 1982 is exactly the same as the constant-dollar (1982) GNP, and the implicit price deflator for 1982 is 100.0. The current-dollar columns show nominal values and the constant-dollar (1982) columns show **real values,** that is, values adjusted for changes in the general price level. Note how much the real

TABLE 6-2   U.S. GNP in Current and Constant (1982) Dollars, 1960–1985

Year	Current Dollars			Constant (1982) Dollars	
	GNP ($ Billions)	% change	Deflator	GNP ($ Billions)	% change
1960	515.3	3.9	30.9	1,665.3	2.2
1961	533.8	3.6	31.2	1,708.7	2.6
1962	574.6	7.6	31.9	1,799.4	5.3
1963	606.9	5.6	32.4	1,873.3	4.1
1964	649.8	7.1	32.9	1,973.3	5.3
1965	705.1	8.5	33.8	2,087.6	5.8
1966	772.0	9.5	35.0	2,208.3	5.8
1967	816.4	5.8	35.9	2,271.4	2.9
1968	892.7	9.3	37.7	2,365.6	4.1
1969	963.9	8.0	39.8	2,423.3	2.4
1970	1,015.5	5.4	42.0	2,416.2	−0.3
1971	1,102.7	8.6	44.4	2,484.8	2.8
1972	1,212.8	10.0	46.5	2,608.5	5.0
1973	1,359.3	12.1	49.5	2,744.1	5.2
1974	1,472.8	8.3	54.0	2,729.3	−0.5
1975	1,598.4	8.5	59.3	2,695.0	−1.3
1976	1,782.8	11.5	63.1	2,826.7	4.9
1977	1,990.5	11.7	67.1	2,958.6	4.7
1978	2,249.7	13.0	72.2	3,115.2	5.3
1979	2,508.2	11.5	78.6	3,192.4	2.5
1980	2,732.0	8.9	85.7	3,187.1	−0.2
1981	3,052.6	11.7	94.0	3,248.8	1.9
1982	3,166.0	3.7	100.0	3,166.0	−2.5
1983	3,401.6	7.4	103.8	3,277.7	3.5
1984	3,774.7	11.0	108.1	3,492.0	6.5
1985ᵖ	3,992.5	5.8	111.7	3,573.5	2.3

Current values have been adjusted to their equivalent in prices that prevailed in 1982. Growth rates are shown as the percentage change from the preceding year.

p.   Preliminary Figures.

Source: Economic Report of the President, 1986, Tables B-1, B-2, and B-3.

economic growth rates (measured as the percentage change in GNP from the preceding year) differ from the growth rates measured in nominal values. (This difference is illustrated in Figure 6-7.) In real terms, economic growth was negative in five years (1970, 1974, 1975, 1980, and 1982) and reached a high point of 5.8 percent in two years (1965 and 1966). We discuss economic growth more thoroughly later in the book.

The Consumer Price Index

We will now examine a second method of applying the index-number system to the prices of a whole collection of goods and services. The **consumer price index (CPI),** often called the "cost-of-living index," is an index number used to measure changes in the cost of purchasing a specific group, or "market basket," of consumer

TABLE 6-3 **Computing a Consumer Price Index**

Item	Market-Basket Quantity	Base-Year Price	Base-Year Cost	Current-Year Price	Current-Year Cost
Hamburger	100 lbs.	$0.80	$ 80.00	$1.80	$ 180.00
Gasoline	500 gals.	0.40	200.00	1.60	800.00
Movies	40 shows	3.00	120.00	3.50	140.00
Total			$400.00		$1,120.00

The index number is based on the cost of certain amounts of goods and services in the base year. The cost of purchasing this same "market basket" of goods is calculated both in base-year prices and in current-year prices.

The index number is the ratio of current-year cost to base-year cost, multiplied by 100, that is, ($1,120/$400) × 100 = 280.

goods and services. This collection of consumer goods and services is determined from studying actual purchases by families chosen because they represent important types of spending units in the economy. The Department of Commerce calculates the consumer price index based on purchases by all urban consumers.

The computation method for the CPI differs importantly from the one used for the GNP deflator because the collection of goods and services on which the CPI is based does not change from year to year. Table 6-3 shows how to calculate a consumer price-index number. We assume here that the selected market basket consists of 100 pounds of hamburger, 500 gallons of gasoline, and 40 movie tickets a year. In the prices of the base year, this market basket of goods and services cost $400.00. In a later year, the prices of these goods and services had changed, and the cost of purchasing the market basket was $1,120.00. To calculate the index number, you divide the current-year cost of the market basket by the base-year cost of the same collection of goods and services and then multiply the result by 100, as follows: ($1,120/$400) × 100 = 280. In this case, the index number is 280, meaning that the cost of the market basket in the current year was 2.8 times its cost in the base year. Thus, the "cost of living" had increased 180 percent.

Table 6-4 shows the consumer price index for the years 1960 through 1985. The base year used

here is 1967. Also shown in the table and in Figure 6-8 is the purchasing power of the dollar according to this index. The estimated **purchasing power of the dollar** for consumer goods is the reciprocal of the index number (1/CPI). From this table, note that the CPI more than tripled between 1967 and 1985, so that a dollar purchased less than one third as much in 1985 as it did in 1967.

BIASES THAT OVERSTATE INFLATION As a measure of the "cost of living," the consumer price index suffers from several biases. Sometimes it overstates the impact of inflation on the cost of living. There also are circumstances in which the official consumer price index understates the impact of inflation. It is important to understand the nature and sources of these biases, because the CPI often is built into labor-management contracts and into government transfer payment programs (such as Social Security) as a cost-of-living-adjustment escalator clause. Under these arrangements, wage rates or benefit levels change automatically when the CPI changes. Biases in the CPI will therefore lead to incorrect adjustments in wage rates and transfer payments.

BUYER-RESPONSE BIAS The **buyer-response bias** arises because the CPI fails to recognize that consumer buying patterns respond to changes in *relative* prices. For example, consider the index number calculated in Table 6-3. The price of

TABLE 6-4 The Consumer Price Index and the Purchasing Power of the Consumer Dollar (1967 = 100)

Year	Consumer Price Index	Purchasing Power of the Dollar
1960	88.7	1.127
1961	89.6	1.116
1962	90.6	1.104
1963	91.7	1.091
1964	92.9	1.076
1965	94.5	1.058
1966	97.2	1.029
1967	100.0	1.000
1968	104.2	.960
1969	109.8	.911
1970	116.3	.860
1971	121.3	.824
1972	125.3	.798
1973	133.1	.752
1974	147.7	.678
1975	161.2	.621
1976	170.5	.587
1977	181.5	.551
1978	195.4	.512
1979	217.4	.460
1980	246.8	.405
1981	272.4	.367
1982	289.1	.345
1983	298.4	.335
1984	311.1	.321
1985	322.2	.310

The consumer price index shows the cost of purchasing a "market basket" of goods, which represents actual purchases by families. The base year for this series is 1967. The purchasing power of the consumer dollar is computed as the reciprocal of the CPI—that is, I/CPI.

Source: Economic Report of the President, 1986, Table B-55.

gasoline increased very substantially relative to the prices of the other goods and services. In the base year, a gallon of gasoline cost half as much as a pound of hamburger and less than one-seventh as much as a movie ticket. But in the "current" year, a gallon of gasoline cost almost as much as a whole pound of hamburger and was almost half the cost of a movie ticket. The CPI implies that people buy the same quantities of gasoline, hamburger, and movie tickets after the change in relative prices as they did before. Actually, when gasoline becomes more expensive in relation to other goods and services, it is likely that some consumers will switch some of their buying from gasoline to other things. People will go to the movies instead of driving to the Rockies. The CPI does not recognize how important these possible switches really are. Since consumers probably do change their buying habits quite a bit to escape the higher prices, the CPI tends to overstate the rise in the cost of living. So we may say that the CPI shows the change in the cost of the base-year "way of living" but that most families probably don't live that way any more.

QUALITY BIAS Both the implicit price deflator and the consumer price index imply that the quality of goods and services stays the same over the years. However, this is surely not the case. In fact, there is a **quality bias.** Because new products are invented and improvements are made in existing products, the goods produced in the current year are generally of higher quality, per dollar of constant value, than were their counterparts in the base year. If quality is generally improving, the "cost of living" has not risen as much as the CPI implies. People are living "better" because products have improved. Similarly, real GNP has probably risen more than is implied by the price-deflated values of GNP.

Students often find it hard to believe that quality is generally improving, when we all know of cases where it seems to be getting worse. Ask yourself, however, what would probably happen if someone invented a new type of television set that was inferior in picture quality to those already on the market. Would anyone buy it? That would depend on its relative price. If its price were equal to (or higher than) the price of the earlier model, the new set would not survive in a competitive market. The market would "weed out" such products and would assure that product quality, adjusted for price changes, would not go down. To test whether quality has actually gone up, you might think about exchanging today's television set for the equivalent model of five or ten years

FIGURE 6-8   **Purchasing Power of the Dollar (1967 = 100)**

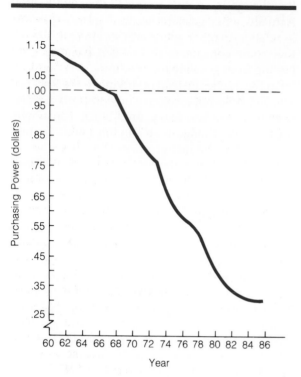

The purchasing power of the dollar is computed as the reciprocal of the consumer price index, that is, as I/CPI. With 1967 as the base year, the purchasing power of a dollar fell from $1.12 in 1960 to 31.0 cents in 1985. Thus, in terms of the goods and services included in the market basket used to compute the cost-of-living index, a dollar in 1985 purchased less than one-third as much as a dollar in 1960.

ago, assuming, of course, that the old-style set was new and unused. If the exchange were even, with no money changing hands, would you be willing to make the exchange? If the answer is "no," then quality has probably gone up.

The hypothetical exchange of today's product for the product of past times illustrates a problem we have in comparing quality over time. Often it is not possible to find a truly equivalent product. For example, automobiles today offer poorer "performance" (that is, acceleration) than did those

of fifteen to twenty years ago, but they also create less air pollution. So one kind of quality has been exchanged for another kind of quality. Of course, it is still technically possible to produce the old-style cars. The fact that we choose (in this case through various government regulations) not to produce them is some indication that we prefer the new-style car to the old-style car. In this sense, "quality" is higher.

BIASES THAT UNDERSTATE INFLATION   In some cases the CPI will fail to reveal the full impact of price increases on the actual cost of living. For example, if official price controls are in effect (along with the predictable shortages), consumers may buy products at higher prices in "black markets," and the CPI at official prices will understate the actual cost of living. Moreover, the quality of goods and services may decline in these circumstances. Also, the CPI may understate inflation for important groups in the population who spend unusually large portions of their incomes for the goods and services that have increased most in price. For example, during the 1970s and into the 1980s, the prices of "necessities"—food, housing, medical care, and fuel—increased much faster than did the CPI as a whole. Low income families, which tend to spend much of their income on these goods and services, found that the official CPI understated the actual increase in their cost of living.

Special-Purpose Index Numbers

Index numbers can be used for many purposes other than measuring changes in the cost of living or in real GNP. Dozens of special-purpose index numbers are published monthly in the *Survey of Current Business*.[10] Indexes of producer prices for farm products, chemicals, fuels, and so forth, are

10. Price indexes and deflators for many components of national income and product and for many different industrial inputs and outputs are published regularly in the *Survey of Current Business*. Cost-of-living index numbers for different cities and countries are published every year in almanacs and in *The Statistical Abstract of the United States*.

computed regularly. These are widely used to predict future changes in consumer prices, since price changes at the producer's level will probably be passed on soon to the consumer. Price-index numbers and deflators also are regularly published for many specific producer goods, such as agricultural chemicals, lumber, iron, and steel. These data are useful in anticipating changes in relative prices for food, housing, automobiles, and so forth. Still another special-purpose index number is maintained for purchases by governments. This index can be used to translate government budget figures from nominal to real values in order to compare real budget amounts for different time periods. Over the past decade, the prices for goods and services purchased by governments have risen more rapidly than the general price level.

Index numbers and deflators must be used carefully. The prices of goods that some consumers buy may not change in the same way as prices for goods that other consumers buy. There are at least two reasons for this difference. First, prices themselves are not the same at all locations. For example, prices may be higher in urban areas than in rural areas. Second, different people (old and young, rich and poor) buy different goods and so will face different situations when prices change. Therefore, those who use price indexes should be sure that both the price data and their choice of goods are suited to the way in which they are using the index.

Inflation in the United States

Figure 6-9 shows recent U.S. price level history. Panel (a) shows the GNP deflator for 1960 through 1985, and panel (b) shows the **inflation rate.** The inflation rate is the rate of change in whatever index number has been selected for measuring the price level. For example, the GNP deflator (1982 = 100) was 111.7 for 1985 and 108.1 for 1984, which means that the price level in the United States increased by 3.3 percent during 1985 (111.7/108.1 = 1.033). The rate of inflation was 3.3 percent.

Panel (b) in Figure 6-9 provides the clearest picture of inflation in the United States over those years. In the first half of the 1960s, the inflation rate hovered around 1½ percent a year. This was called inflation at the time, since it was a sustained increase in the general price level, but might not now be called inflation as compared with other periods. As noted earlier, price-level increases in this modest range can quite possibly be offset against normal increases in the quality of the goods and services that make up the GNP.

Inflation clearly existed after 1965. If we accept the early 1960s as a benchmark, or point of reference, the years after 1965 brought the longest period of sustained significant price-level increases in the nation's history. The rate of increase in the price level remained above the benchmark throughout the entire period, and the 1985 price level was 3.3 times the 1965 price level (111.7/33.8 = 3.3). Prices had more than tripled. For comparison, the inflationary period in the United States from 1940 through 1948, during and after World War II, lasted for nine years, and the price level did not even double (52.98/29.06 = 1.82). The annual rate of price-level increase was 15.7 percent in 1946 and 12.9 percent in 1947.[11]

Figure 6-9(b) also shows that the rate of inflation decreased greatly after 1981. Economists use the term **disinflation** to refer to a falling inflation rate. During periods of disinflation, the price level is still rising and inflation is taking place, but the rate of increase in the price level is becoming less and less. As we go further into the study of macroeconomics, we will see that the inflation rate is an important consideration in many of the plans and commitments of the various actors on the economic stage. Households must decide how much they can afford to borrow to buy a home. Business firms must plan for new buildings and equipment. Governments plan future expenditures and tax collections. When the inflation rate changes abruptly, many plans go wrong, bringing

---

11. We have used the GNP deflator to measure inflation rather than the more familiar consumer price index because we believe that the "market basket" method used for the CPI tends to exaggerate the rate of inflation.

FIGURE 6-9 General Price-Level Changes in the United States, 1960 through 1985

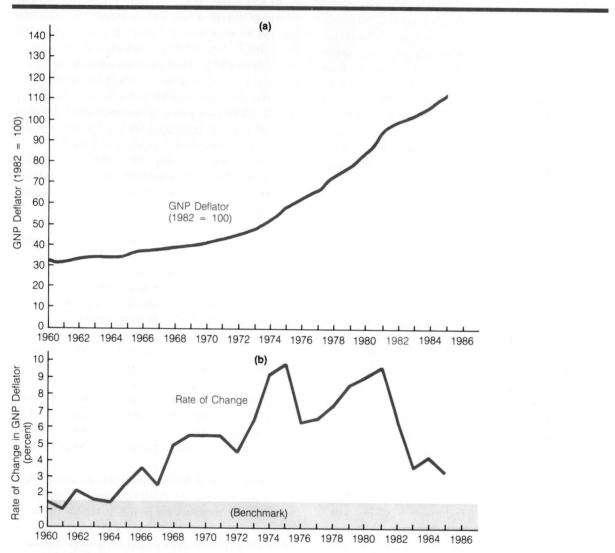

Panel (a) shows the general price level as measured by the GNP deflator (1982 = 100). Panel (b) shows the rate of change in the price level for each year. This rate is computed by dividing each year's GNP deflator by the deflator for the preceding year, subtracting 1.0, and multiplying by 100. The benchmark is the average annual rate of increase in the price level for the years 1960 through 1964.

Source: Economic Report of the President, 1986, Table B-3.

hardship for some and unexpected prosperity for others.

The Consequences of Inflation

It is important to understand that there is nothing sacred about any particular price level. The price level in 1987 is no better or worse than the price level in 1977 or 1967. An economy can function satisfactorily at any price level. Even changes in the price level can take place without seriously upsetting an economic system, if these changes are small and do not fall into a pattern of sustained increases or decreases. But inflation, as a sustained and significant increase in the general price level, does cause serious economic, social, and political problems.

DECISION-MAKING ERRORS From the point of view of economic analysis, the most serious consequences of inflation arise when a price-level-change factor has to be included in most of the day-to-day decisions that guide the operation of the economy. This would mean that labor must predict the inflation rate when it bargains for wages. When business plans new investments and estimates depreciation allowances, it must also predict the inflation rate. Individuals must consider inflation in deciding about consumption spending and saving. To estimate the costs of services and the amount of money that will be collected from the tax system, government must also take inflation into account. In other words, inflation affects the behavior of each of the major actors on the economic stage. For each of these groups, inflation or the possibility of coming inflation adds a complicating factor. More mistakes are likely to be made in inflationary situations than would be made in a period of price stability. The economy will run less efficiently.

REDISTRIBUTION OF WEALTH Changing price levels redistribute wealth by changing the real purchasing power of the monetary unit—the dollar in the United States, the yen in Japan, the mark in Germany. Wealth that is held in cash, savings accounts, bonds, insurance policies, and other forms of "paper wealth" specified in dollar amounts will drop in real value when the price level rises and will rise in real value when the price level falls. If their holders did not expect the inflation and insist on adjustments such as a lower purchase price or a higher interest rate, they will be victims of inflation. Their wealth will be redistributed to those who transferred the cash or who sold the paper wealth to them or who made better decisions about inflation. The winners from inflation may have been wiser and anticipated that inflation was coming. Perhaps they borrowed money to purchase land, or jewelry, or goods whose nominal values would increase along with the inflation. As often as not, however, their gains may have been "just luck."

Luck may be randomly distributed, but this cannot be said for knowledge or for the possession of the kinds of wealth that are most vulnerable to inflation. Inflation tends to be especially damaging to the middle-income groups in a society. These people are likely to have a large portion of their wealth in savings accounts and insurance policies, which are most vulnerable to inflation. Unexpected inflation can drain wealth from this group. Since the middle-income group generally has a moderating and stabilizing effect on the social and political system, its loss of wealth can lead to radical shifts in political positions, either to the left or to the right. After World War I, radicalized middle classes showed a greater tendency to move to the right than to the left.

Even though redistribution of wealth due to past inflation is "water over the dam," it may leave its mark on the society's future. Groups that have been hurt by past inflations may become alienated and cynical about the social, political, and economic system. In other words, they may show less concern for others in matters of income redistribution and welfare, and they may adopt lifestyles keyed to enjoyment of the present rather than to saving or preparing for the future.

POLITICAL INSTABILITY History offers many examples of political changes both from sustained periods of rising prices (inflations) and from sustained periods of falling prices (deflations). In Europe, price levels rose in the 1500s and 1600s after the Spanish discovered the gold and silver mines of Mexico and South America and began taking their riches back home. Feudal lords who had converted the obligations of their serfs from services to fixed money rents grew poorer as prices rose. For support they turned to the rising group of national monarchs who could collect money from growing trade and business activities. These events hastened the decline of feudalism and the rise of nation-states in Europe.

In the United States, price levels dropped greatly from the end of the Civil War until the close of the 1800s. Farmers and small business people who depended on debt financing were hurt as prices fell and they had to repay loans in money of a higher value than the money they had borrowed. The resulting political agitation led to many reform programs that had lasting effects on government in the United States.[12] Resentment against big business and banking, believed to be gainers from the falling price level, was widespread around the turn of the century and still colors political and economic thought in the United States.

In Germany after World War I, inflation wiped out the savings of many middle-income people. The resulting frustrations provided a fertile seedbed for the rise of Hitler's National Socialist (actually fascist) Party. The following is quoted from the reminiscences of a German woman about her experiences in 1923:

". . . workers had discovered the 'trick of inflation,' which was to figure the value of money in gold. Time and again the workers struck for the 'adjustment of their wages.' After their strikes, their wages had been adjusted—to the actual price increases. But the price increases went on and so the workers had to strike again for new adjustments. What they asked for now was wages paid daily.

"While this struggle went on, chaos increased. The Middle Ages came back. Communities printed their own money, based on goods, on a certain amount of

potatoes, of rye, for instance. Shoe factories paid their workers in bonds for shoes which they could exchange at the bakery for bread or the meat market for meat.

"At this stage, the Communists believed that their time had come. They attempted an uprising. . . ."[13]

In the United States during the 1970s, inflation and slower economic growth led to a "taxpayers' revolt," which forced changes in the government. Taxpayer frustration contributed to the defeat of President Carter in 1980 and to the combination of tax-rate cuts and cuts in certain government programs during the Reagan administrations.

SUMMARY

1. Macroeconomics has been an important concern for a long time. From the sixteenth through the eighteenth century, the focus was on how to make the nation strong. Bullionist and mercantilist ideas were prominent. In the nineteenth and twentieth centuries, the focus has been on business cycles, unemployment, and inflation. Many people believed that the Great Depression of the 1930s confirmed Karl Marx's prediction that unemployment would bring about the fall of capitalism. However, the theories of John Maynard Keynes suggested policies that could fight unemployment and preserve capitalism.

2. The economic concept of unemployment is that people are consuming unwanted quantities of leisure time and devoting less time to wage earning than desired at the going wage rate. The labor-supply curve, which shows people's willingness to exchange leisure for money, is a key to understanding this concept of unemployment. People are unemployed or underemployed if they are operating under a wage and hour combination to the left of their supply curve.

3. Full employment exists when everyone is operating on his or her labor-supply curve. Unemployment can arise during the time required for the economy to adjust from one equilibrium

12. Douglass C. North, *Structure and Change in Economic History* (New York: W. W. Norton & Co., 1982).

13. Pearl S. Buck, *How It Happens*, as cited in Fritz K. Ringer (ed.), *The German Inflation of 1923* (New York: Oxford University Press, 1969), pp. 144–145.

situation to another. The experience of the Great Depression suggested to economists that they may have seriously underestimated the hardships and social and political problems that result from such unemployment.

4. The civilian unemployment rate is the percentage of the civilian labor force that is out of work. Included in the civilian labor force are only those who are either working or looking for work and who are over sixteen years of age. Not included are retirees, persons in institutions, and people under age sixteen. A person is counted as employed even if working only part-time if the work is on a regular basis.

5. Seasonal unemployment is joblessness that arises because the person is engaged in an occupation that does not require workers all year round. For some, this is a cause of low income. For others, it is a source of extra income. In most published statistics, seasonal unemployment is averaged out to avoid confusion in comparing month-to-month or year-to-year changes in unemployment.

6. Frictional unemployment is joblessness that arises because of the time needed to move from one job to another. Some amount of this kind of unemployment is always present in an economy where people are free to move from one job to another. It is not considered a serious problem for an economy.

7. Structural unemployment arises when changes take place in production methods and in the kinds of goods and services produced in the economy. People must be retrained and relocated to match the requirements of different jobs. Training programs are helpful in dealing with structural unemployment. Because no clear line can be drawn between structural unemployment and cyclical (macroeconomic) unemployment, no precise measurement is possible.

8. Cyclical (macroeconomic) unemployment affects most parts of the economy at the same time and arises because jobs are not available for all who want to work at the going wage rate. Though the actual amount of cyclical unemployment cannot be measured exactly, it can clearly cause serious problems for an economy.

9. Unemployment rates are higher for some groups in the civilian labor force than for others. Blacks and other minority groups experience a higher unemployment rate than whites, and teenagers have especially high unemployment rates.

10. The civilian employment rate is the percentage of the civilian noninstitutional population that is actually working. During the 1970s, the U.S. civilian employment rate increased at the same time that the civilian unemployment rate increased. This was possible because the civilian labor force participation rate (the civilian labor force as a percentage of the civilian noninstitutional population) also was increasing.

11. Inflation is a sustained and significant increase in the general price level. The rate of inflation is the percentage change, from one year to the next, in whatever index number is chosen to measure the price level.

12. The implicit price deflator for the gross national product (GNP) shows the ratio between GNP measured at current prices and the amount that would have been required to purchase the same goods in a base year. It is used to convert GNP in "nominal" values to GNP in "real" values. In the United States the GNP deflator in 1985 was 3.3 times its level in 1965. This was the longest period of serious inflation in the nation's history.

13. The consumer price index is used to compare the cost of a selected "market basket" of goods and services in the current year with the cost of the same market basket of goods in the base year. It is often called the "cost-of-living" index. However, it may overstate the increase in the cost of living because it fails to recognize quality improvements and changes in the composition of family purchases. Similarly, it may understate inflation in the cost of living if prices of "necessities" increase more than the cost of other goods and services.

14. Index numbers are used for many purposes in economic statistics. For example, index numbers for producers' goods help to predict future changes in the prices of goods and services to consumers.

15. Inflation has serious economic effects because

a price-level-change factor must be included in decisions that guide the operation of the economy. To many of these decisions, inflation adds uncertainty and can cause the economy to operate less efficiently.

16. History suggests that the social and political consequences of inflation can be serious. Some of these problems arise because inflation redistributes wealth and tends to impoverish the middle-income groups that contribute stability and moderation to the social and political order. Furthermore, inflation can cause people to become cynical and alienated in their relations with others in the society.

DISCUSSION QUESTIONS

1. Review the concepts of "what, how, and for whom" that you studied in Chapter 1. Which of these are responsible for microeconomic unemployment and which for macroeconomic unemployment? Explain.

2. Construct a supply curve for labor, using the real wage rate on the vertical axis and the hours of work supplied per week on the horizontal axis. With reference to this graph, explain the economic concepts of underemployment and overemployment. Why can unemployment not be measured (to the economist's satisfaction) unless the wage rate is specified?

3. Suppose you are working a forty-hour week and receiving the going wage rate for that kind of work. Are you "employed" in terms of official statistics? If you would prefer to work only thirty-two hours at this wage rate, are you, in the economist's theoretical view, overemployed, underemployed, or fully employed? Explain your reasoning.

4. Explain how each of the following is counted in computing the official civilian unemployment rate: a full-time student who has no paying job, a person working regularly but only part-time, a retired person, a fifteen-year-old with a paper route, a person in military service, a person who is out of a job and has given up looking for another because no jobs appear to be available.

5. Explain the difference between seasonal and frictional unemployment. Discuss whether seasonal unemployment is a problem in the economy. Why is seasonal unemployment usually removed (by a statistical adjustment) from most published unemployment statistics? Why is frictional unemployment usually not considered to be a serious problem in the United States? On the other hand, describe two causes of frictional unemployment that you believe are damaging to the economy. Explain your reasons for finding them damaging.

6. Why is structural unemployment likely to be higher during periods when rapid technological change is taking place in the economy? Do you believe that government help should be given to people who are unemployed because of structural changes in the economy? If so, what type of help should be given? Explain the basis for your answer.

7. "Although unemployment still is a serious economic problem, the human and the social consequences of unemployment are less today than they were in the Great Depression." Do you believe that this is a correct statement? Explain your answer. What are some changes since the Great Depression that have affected the human and social aspects of unemployment?

8. From memory, write down the formulas for computing the civilian unemployment rate, the civilian employment rate, and the civilian labor force participation rate. Check to be sure you have them right. Explain how both the unemployment rate and the employment rate can increase at the same time. Explain how the participation rate is involved in this situation. Do you believe that the civilian labor force participation rate will grow or decrease over your lifetime? Does it matter?

9. Index numbers are illustrated in this chapter with a set of prices for apples. But the index-number principle appears in many places, such as the use of IQ values for comparing intellectual capabilities. Describe three other examples of the use of the index-number principle of stating one value by reference to some other "standard" value. (Hint: consider baseball players.)

10. In Table 6-2, the base year is 1982, and all the numbers in the constant-dollar column are expressed in terms of 1982 dollars. How could we adjust the numbers in this column to express them in dollars valued for some other base year, say, 1977? There is a simple method for doing this.

11. The CPI is based on a selection of commodities purchased by urban households and the prices paid by them. If you live in a nonurban area, discuss how your selection of commodities and the prices you pay may differ from those used in the CPI. Would you gain or lose if the CPI were used to adjust your wage rate for inflation? Explain.

12. Try this exercise about the quality bias in index numbers. Think of a product that you believe has gone down in quality over the past ten years. Use the CPI (or some other) index number to find out whether the product has increased or decreased in price after the inflation effect has been removed. If its real price has fallen, lower quality may have been exchanged for lower price. If its real price has risen, you may have a genuine case of falling quality. Try to explain why this has happened.

13. From the *Survey of Current Business* or the *Economic Report of the President* or from recent issues of news magazines, look up the GNP deflator or the consumer price index for last year and for the year before. From these data, calculate the rate of inflation for that year. How does this rate compare with those shown in Figure 6-9? How can it be that the price level itself may not matter but that changes in the price level can cause problems in the economy? Discuss.

7 *National Income Accounting*

PREVIEW The unemployment rate and the inflation rate that you studied in the last chapter are not the only performance measures that are useful in understanding the macroeconomy. Since macroeconomics is concerned with aggregate or "grand total" economic activity, it is also helpful to have a way to measure total production and income in the economy.[1]

In this chapter, we explore the system of national income and product accounting that is used to measure the overall performance of the U.S. economy. This system is made up of five different measures of economic activity, each used for its own purpose. The best known is called the gross national product, which measures the market value of all the goods and services produced in the economy in a given year. The other measures break down this grand total to focus on particular parts that are useful in understanding how the economy works.

We also describe some of the shortcomings of the American national accounting system. For example, it does not count the work that people do at home, such as caring for their children and keeping house. Nor does it take into account the "underground" trading of goods and services, which is not reported for tax purposes. In other areas, it may overstate income by counting intermediate products as final products.

Of course, no accounting system can be perfect in the sense that it provides all the information that anyone might want about the economy. What matters is that there is a consistent set of definitions and measures to help economists in their efforts to understand how the economy operates and what it is likely to do in the future.

1. See Chapter 1, pages 5–8.

NATIONAL INCOME AND PRODUCT ACCOUNTS

Table 7-1 presents the essentials of the U.S. national income and product accounts for the calendar year 1985. This accounting system was developed during the 1920s at a private research agency, the National Bureau of Economic Research. One of its principal developers, Simon Kuznets, later received a Nobel Prize in Economics for his work. Today, the tasks of refining and publishing the national income and product accounts are carried out by the Department of Commerce. We shall begin our examination of this accounting system with a quick overview of the different parts of the accounts to show how the system is organized. Then we shall take a closer look at each of its major sections.

As you can see from Table 7-1, there are three major sections of the accounting system: the national product section, the national income section, and the personal income section. The *national product* section, on the left in the table, shows the value of total production in the economy, as measured by the total amount of money spent for all goods and services produced in the economy during a given year. The best-known entry in this section is for the gross national product, which we shall discuss in detail later. The other entries in this section are needed, as we shall see, to secure a balance with the total in the national income section of the accounts.

The *national income* section, on the right in Table 7-1, shows the total amount earned by owners of resources used in producing goods and services during the same year.[2] The relation between the national income section and the national product section shows the kind of double-entry book-keeping used in the national accounts. The idea behind this double-entry system is that the amount spent for goods and services (national product) should equal the amount earned by owners of the resources used in producing these goods and services (national income).

There are some complications in making the double-entry system actually work in the national accounting system. Some of these are resolved through the specific entries in the lower portion of the national product section in Table 7-1. These adjustments (capital consumption allowance, indirect business taxes and subsidies, and statistical discrepancy) will be explained later.

The third major part of the national accounting system is the *personal income* section, at the bottom in Table 7-1. This section breaks down the total national income into special categories that are useful in economic forecasting.

The National Product Section

The national product section measures production by recording money spent to buy the goods and services that were produced during the year. In other words, it is the "value" of production that is recorded. This "value" is determined by the amount of money that purchasers spent to acquire these goods and services.

GROSS NATIONAL PRODUCT In the national product section, spending is divided into four categories: consumption, investment, government, and net exports. In general, *consumption*

spending refers to goods and services that were purchased by households, including durable goods such as autos and appliances. *Investment spending* includes purchases of buildings and equipment for use in future production and net additions to a company's supplies of raw materials, goods in process, and unsold final products. (It does not refer to purchases of stocks and bonds, which are titles to investment goods already in existence or claims against them. Such purchases, of course, are what the person in the street means by investment.) The investment category also includes purchases of new residential structures. Included in *government spending* are purchases of goods and services by federal, state, and local governments, as well as by public companies like the postal service.[3] It does not include cash **transfer payments,** which is money paid to people even though these people did not provide a good or service to earn this money during the accounting period. Welfare, Social Security, and veterans' benefit checks are examples of cash transfer payments. They are not counted in the government purchases category of the national product section but are counted in the consumption section when the recipients spend the money received from the government. Government also can transfer actual goods and services, such as food or hospital care, directly to individual recipients. Since the government must purchase these goods and services, their value is counted in the government entry in the accounts.

Net exports represent the value of American goods and services purchased by foreigners less the value of foreign goods and services purchased by Americans. Often it is a negative quantity. That is, the value of U.S. exports may be less than the value of imports from other countries. The **gross national product (GNP),** perhaps the most familiar measure of aggregate economic activity, is the total of all purchases—by consumers, by investors, by governments, and (net)

2. It is interesting to note that the United States includes all services performed by lawyers, doctors, barbers, civil servants, etc., as part of its national income and product. Marxist countries, particularly the Soviet Union and the People's Republic of China, include services only insofar as they contribute directly to the production of *physical* goods.

3. The United States treats all government purchases as public consumption; there is no separate "public investment" account. In the United Nations system, however, this distinction is made and investment has a public component. An example of public investment would be highway construction.

TABLE 7-1   National Income and Product in the United States, 1985 (billions of dollars)

National Product Section		National Income Section	
Consumption spending	$2,581.9	Compensation of employees	$2,372.7
Investment spending	670.4		
Government spending on goods and services	814.6	Proprietors' income	242.4
Net exports	− 74.4	Rental income of persons	14.0
Gross national product	$3,992.5		
Capital consumption allowance (subtract)	− 438.2	Corporate profits	299.0
Net national product	$3,554.3		
Indirect business taxes and subsidies	− 337.9	Net interest	287.7
Statistical discrepancy	− .7		
National income	$3,215.6	National income	$3,215.6

Personal Income Section	
National income (from above)	$3,215.6
Earnings not received (subtract)	− 575.0
Receipts not earned (add)	+ 653.5
Personal income	$3,294.2
Personal tax and nontax payments (subtract)	− 493.1
Disposable personal income	$2,801.1
Disposition:	
Personal consumption	2,581.9
Personal saving	129.7
Interest paid to business	87.4
Transfers to foreigners	2.1
	$2,801.1

The national product section records amounts spent to purchase goods and services produced during the year. The national income section records amounts earned by owners of resources used in producing goods and services. This is a double-entry bookkeeping system, and the same total appears at the bottom of each section. The personal income section records certain additions and subtractions that are necessary to show amounts actually received by people and available to use for consumption and saving.

Note: Items may not add to total because of rounding.

Source: Economic Report of the President, 1986, Tables B-1, B-21, B-22, B-23, B-25.

TABLE 7-2 Value Added and Final Sales

	Sales Value	Cost of Intermediate Goods		Value Added
Farmer sells wheat	.15	− .00	=	.15
Miller sells flour	.35	− .15	=	.20
Baker sells bread (wholesale)	.60	− .35	=	.25
Grocer sells bread (retail)	.70	− .60	=	.10
Totals	$1.80	− 1.10	=	$.70

The sales value of the final product (bread at retail) is equal to the sum of the values added by the firms that have processed raw materials and intermediate goods into this final product.

by foreigners—of currently produced goods and services.

In all of these estimates, only spending for *currently produced* goods and services is recorded. Spending for previously produced goods, such as old houses or used cars, is not recorded at all. Such goods were not part of the production of the year for which the estimate is made. In these cases, only the value of the services of the realtor or the used-car salesperson—that is, their commissions—is included as part of current national production.

It is important to avoid counting items of current production more than once, since such multiple-counting would overstate the true volume of production in the economy. The goal is to record the value of a currently produced item only at its final sale in the accounting period. For most goods and services, the sale to the consumer is the final sale, but for some the final sale is to the inventory of a business firm. To record these items, net inventory change (inventory at the end of the year minus inventory at the start of the year) is counted as investment in the national accounts. A rise in inventory value is a positive entry and a fall in inventory value is a negative entry.

The actual calculation of GNP and its component is done by the U.S. Department of Commerce with information from tax returns, surveys, and other data sources. Their results are estimates rather than exact figures, since it is not possible actually to record each of the billions of final-sales transactions that occur in the economy each year. The procedures used estimate the value of the goods and services sold by firms and then subtract an estimate of the value of the inputs or "intermediate goods" that firms purchase from each other. What remains is an estimate of the total **value added** by firms and reflects the production from resources employed directly by them. The value-added method estimates the value of current production, avoids multiple-counting, and gives the same results as a summation of final sales.

Table 7-2 illustrates how the two methods give the same answer. As shown in the sales-value column, a loaf of bread sells for 70 cents at retail. In the value-added method, shown in the value-added column, the contributions from all the resource owners who helped to produce the bread also add up to 70 cents. For simplicity, we have assumed that the farmer does not purchase any intermediate goods, such as seed or fertilizer. We avoid double-counting because we do not count any of the payments made for intermediate goods. As you will see, the U.S. system is not entirely successful in excluding payments for intermediate goods. Many countries, including the Soviet Union, use a measure called **value of output,** which makes no attempt to avoid double-counting. Thus, it is even "grosser" than the GNP.

NET NATIONAL PRODUCT The only difference between the gross and the net national product is the treatment of depreciation and obsolescence.

Some of the new buildings and equipment included as investment under GNP were needed to replace buildings and equipment that had worn out, become obsolete, or suffered accidental damage during the year. We say that some capital goods (production equipment) were "consumed" in the process of producing other goods. Therefore, a **capital consumption allowance** is estimated and subtracted from the gross national product to obtain a figure for the **net national product (NNP).** In other words, GNP is gross of capital consumption allowances, whereas NNP is net of them. (It is a good idea, when using the terms "gross" and "net" in economics, to be able to answer the question "gross (or net) of *what?*")

Since the capital consumption allowance relates to buildings and equipment, it is really an adjustment to the investment component of GNP. This means that the only difference between GNP and NNP is the difference between investment before the subtraction of the capital consumption allowance ("gross" investment) and investment after this subtraction ("net" investment). So we may write

$$GNP = C + I_g + G + X - Im$$

and

$$NNP = C + I_n + G + X - Im$$

where C is consumption, I_g is gross investment, I_n is net investment, G is government purchases, X is exports, Im is imports, GNP is gross national product, and NNP is net national product. Expressing net exports as $X - Im$ will be useful later when we explain what determines these amounts. It will be helpful to remember the equations given above. As we will see, many modern macroeconomic theories are built around the summation of consumption, investment, government purchases, and net exports.

Net national product is a figure that estimates the actual (net) gain from all production during the year. So it would be equal to the total income earned by all persons and companies engaged in production, except for two problems that arise in our double-entry accounting system.

SUBSIDIES AND INDIRECT BUSINESS TAXES In the double-entry system, the national product section is computed at market prices, which are higher because of taxes on these products and lower because of subsidies given to them. But the national income section is computed according to the earnings of the factors of production and adds up to an estimate of what the market prices would have been without any sales taxes, excise taxes, property taxes, or subsidies. Therefore, a major adjustment is needed in the national product section to remove the tax and subsidy components of market prices. This is the *indirect business taxes and subsidies* entry in Table 7-1.

A handy way to understand the necessity of this adjustment for indirect taxes and subsidies is as follows. Think about the federal tax on gasoline, which increases the price that you pay for gasoline at the pump. The tax part of this price is counted (along with your purchase of gasoline) as a consumption purchase (C) in estimating gross and net national product. The tax money is used by the government to pay for construction and repair of the highway system, and this spending is counted as part of the government purchases (G) component of GNP and NNP. In other words, the tax money is counted twice in the national product calculations of the accounting system. But the tax money finances only one income to factors of production, since it pays only the resources used in the work on the highways. Therefore, the indirect tax must be subtracted to remove the double-counting and to secure a balance with the earnings reported in the national income section of the accounts. Government subsidies to business work the other way—they reduce the prices paid for final goods, but do finance the earnings of factors of production. Therefore, these subsidies are an added item in the adjustments section.

STATISTICAL DISCREPANCY The *statistical discrepancy* is a different kind of adjustment. In figuring both national product and national income, estimating procedures are used rather than full and complete tabulations of all production and all incomes. National product is estimated separately from national income. The statistical discrepancy simply reports the extent to which the two estimates were not equal to each other, or the difference between them. Because the national income estimates are usually more accurate than the national product estimates, the statistical discrepancy entry is placed in the national product section.

The National Income Section

National income (NI) is the total amount that is earned in producing the national product. The five parts of national income are listed in Table 7-1. They are compensation of employees, proprietors' income, rental income of persons, corporate profits, and net interest. *Compensation of employees* covers both money wages and the amounts that are spent by employers for such things as Social Security and fringe benefits (paid vacation, sick and holiday pay, and so on). *Proprietors' income* records the incomes of all unincorporated businesses and in fact combines profits, rental income, and the labor income of the partners and proprietors in these businesses. The rents received on properties owned by businesses are included in the income or profit for these businesses, so that only the *rental income of persons* is stated as a separate item in the accounts. Capital consumption allowances are subtracted in calculating the rental income of persons and the incomes of proprietorships, partnerships, and corporations. Inventory-value adjustments are made for price-level changes that occurred during the year. *Corporate profits* are before the payment of dividends. *Net interest* is the total interest income of persons, minus interest paid by consumers to businesses and net interest paid by government, which are considered transfer payments (and not production) in the accounting system. Adding these five components together gives the amount of national income, which is equal to the net national product after the adjustments noted earlier (indirect business taxes and subsidies, statistical discrepancy) have been made.

A half-whimsical illustration of all this is as follows. Consider a super-stereo sound system selling for $3,992—an amount just about one-billionth of the 1985 GNP. You buy it. Where does your money go? Part ($438) goes into a fund to replace machines that were worn out in producing this glorious stereo system, and part ($338) goes for sales, excise, and property taxes (net of subsidies). The remainder ($3,216) is the total earned by the people who worked to produce the stereo or who owned other than labor resources that were used in its production. Most ($2,373) goes to workers, salaried managers, etc. Smaller amounts go to others in the production process—$242 as profits to proprietors or partners (perhaps subcontractors for component parts of the stereo), $14 to pay rent for land under some factory building, $299 as profits to the corporation that was the prime producer of the stereo, and $288 as interest to people who loaned money to the prime-producing company or to the subcontractors. You enjoy listening to the stereo. Other people enjoy having the money you spent. The next step is to see what they do with it.

The Personal Income Section

The personal income section of the accounting system starts with the amount of national income. It then shows amounts that must be added or subtracted in order to arrive at the amount of money that was actually available to people for spending and saving decisions.[4] Two steps are used in this process. The first reports personal income and the second reports disposable personal income.

PERSONAL INCOME The adjustment process begins by recognizing that some of the money that was earned in a given year was not actually received by the people who earned it. In Table 7-1, this is called *earnings not received*. The biggest part of the earnings not received is contributions for social insurance, or Social Security taxes. This category also includes corporate profits that were not paid out in dividends. The gap between

---

4. "People" refers primarily to households, but nonprofit institutions are also included.

profits and dividends includes both corporate income taxes paid to the government and earnings retained for reinvestment by the corporation. All these items are subtracted from national income as "earnings not received."

Receipts not earned is a companion item to earnings not received. In other words, some money that people received during a year was not earned by them in that year. The largest item under this heading is government transfer payments, which include Social Security benefits and welfare checks. It also includes interest that the government pays to people (as for savings bonds). Interest that consumers pay to businesses (as on installment purchases or loans) is a negative entry in receipts not earned. Adjusting national income by adding receipts not earned and by subtracting earnings not received, we derive the amount of **personal income (PI)**.

DISPOSABLE PERSONAL INCOME   The last step in the adjustment process recognizes that people have certain obligations that must be subtracted from personal income to discover how much income is left for spending or saving. We subtract payments of *personal taxes* (individual income, estate, and inheritance taxes) and then certain other small *nontax items,* such as traffic fines, penalties, and charges for government services. The amount that remains after these obligations are subtracted is called **disposable personal income (DPI)**.

Finally, the accounting system reports on the disposition of DPI—how disposable personal income was actually used in a given year. It comes as no surprise that *personal consumption* spending claims most of disposable personal income. *Personal saving* is another very important item here. Finally, personal transfer payments, including *interest paid to businesses* and *transfers to foreigners,* must also be recorded in accounting for disposable personal income.

Why Five Series?

The accounting system gives us five data series to estimate the volume of economic activity. In their usual order of size, these are GNP, NNP,

NI, PI, and DPI. Just what, you may ask, *is* the national income or product anyway? Why bother with five separate series? What kind of dodgeball game are the statisticians playing with us?

Economists believe that the five series, even though they are correlated closely with one another, have different meanings and can be used for different purposes. Of the five series, gross national product is the most closely related to measured *employment* and *unemployment*. Net national product, which is GNP minus capital consumption allowances, comes close to defining the economist's all-purpose symbol Y as a measure of national income and product. When stated on a per capita basis, national income is a rough but useful measure of *long-run economic welfare,* though the whole welfare idea is really much more complicated than this estimate. Personal income, on the other hand, is often used as a rough measure of *short-run economic welfare.* In the short run, it is a gain for persons to have their incomes raised when transfer payments increase or business maintains dividend rates even when profits fall. However, the long-run effects may be unfavorable if savings are neglected or debts pile up. Finally, disposable personal income is closely connected to *consumption expenditures,* which play an important part in macroeconomic theories.

The public has not objected to the duplication and "mystification" involved in having five national series to deal with all at once. On the contrary, private bodies have gone beyond the government and have come up with new estimates of their own. Some private economic and statistical consulting firms deduct "necessary consumption" (defined in different ways) from DPI to obtain what they call "discretionary" or "supernumerary" income, which they say is correlated closely with consumption spending for durable goods such as stoves, radios, and washing machines. Another innovation is "final buying income," which eliminates rises and falls in inventories—stocks of unsold goods either finished or in the process of production. Because "final buying income" smooths out a good part of the short-term business cycles in economic activity, administration politicians are especially fond of it when recessions seem to be getting under way.

SHORTCOMINGS OF THE SYSTEM

No social accounting system is perfect for all purposes. It may omit production and income that some people think should be counted. To this extent, it understates actual income and production. For example, Americans criticize the Soviet system for omitting services, except those directly related to the production of goods. Or the system may include certain items that some people think should not be counted at all. To this extent, the system overstates national income and product. The Soviets criticize the American system for including meaningless and artificial consumer frills as items of national income. We shall mention some of the more controversial points in the American system.

"Do-It-Yourself" Production

"Do-it-yourself" production is not counted in the national income accounting system, except for estimates of farmers' home-produced food and the imputed rent on owner-occupied housing (what the cost would be to a nonowner). The problem is that it is impossible to estimate the value of most "do-it-yourself" production with much accuracy.

Housekeeping and child-rearing illustrate the importance of do-it-yourself production and the seriousness of its omission from the national accounts. If both husband and wife are employed in wage-paying jobs, both of their earnings will be recorded as part of the national income. If they hire help with housekeeping and child-rearing (domestic servants, baby sitters, nursery schools, TV dinners), the earnings of those who produce these goods and services will also be counted. If one spouse chooses to be a housewife or househusband, the value of these services is not included. The national income declines not only by the wages of the one who keeps house but also by those of the housekeeper or baby sitter who is not hired. There is an old saw in national income statistics: "When you marry your cook, you lower the national income of the country."

Important as do-it-yourself production is in the United States, it is much more important in less-developed countries (LDCs). Thus, the comparison between income per head in the United States, or in any other more-developed country (MDC), and income per head in the typical LDC is apt to be biased and misleading. The MDC standard of living is not as much higher than the LDC standard of living as the national income figures would suggest. And by the same token, the present U.S. standard of living is probably not so much higher than the standard of living in pioneer days, when women made the family's clothes and families built their own cabins. Their replacement by frame houses built by specialized building contractors and hired labor represented a smaller rise in the true national income than in the recorded one.

The Underground Economy

Allied to the do-it-yourself economy is the **underground economy**. Much income and production is not included in the national accounts because no records are kept of transactions that take place in terms of **barter** (direct exchange of one good or service for another), or even in terms of cash transfers between unlicensed business units. Rough estimates can be made of the volume of such unrecorded transactions if conditions are stable. But in periods of rapid change, serious errors in the estimate are likely. Some have estimated that the underground economy amounts to over 20 percent of the measured American GNP.

In the United States as well as in many other countries, both capitalist and socialist, there seems to be a movement away from recorded market transactions toward unrecorded barter deals and other nonmarket and off-the-books transactions. Thus we have come to speak of an "underground," "parallel," "second," or "black" economy.

Services are generally better fitted to the underground economy than is the production of physical goods. A house painter may paint a house for his garage proprietor neighbor in exchange for an engine overhaul, an auto paint job, and body work done by the neighbor. A lawyer may draw up a will or a contract in exchange for carpentry or cabinet work in her home. The tax laws are quite clear: all such earnings should be reported at their money values. But when they are not in fact reported, the national accounts may underestimate the national income at the same time that taxes are evaded.

Other motives besides tax evasion inspire the underground economy, but it is not clear that their strength is increasing over time. Sometimes people wish to evade certification and licensing rules, as when bureaucrats or law clerks sell advice on legal matters without a license to practice law. Others want to get around certain trade-union rules, as when union plumbers work on their own below the union scale, or do the electrical or painting or carpentry work associated with a plumbing job. At times the motive is to evade labor and welfare laws. So an "unemployed" worker will operate his or her own business while continuing to receive unemployment benefits and/or welfare payments. (In Italy, the term *lavoro nero*, or "black labor," refers not to the labor of blacks but to work done below the minimum wage and without deductions for social security.) Also, workers who use their employers' tools, truck, or premises for work on their own during or after working hours will, of course, not report income received from the job. Nor will those involved in criminal activities like prostitution, gambling, and the narcotics trade report their profits.

Intermediate Products

An **intermediate product,** such as a ton of steel girders, is something that is produced as an input to further production. The national accounts, by using the "value-added" system, try to avoid the double-counting that would result if they included both the intermediate products used in producing a good or service *and* the final good or service as well. (If the accounts were to include a gross "value of output" series, as the Soviet ones do, there would be no problem.)

The distinction between intermediate products and final products, however, is often hard to

apply in practice. Consider gasoline that a suburbanite buys and uses mainly for commuting to and from a job in the city. Is this gasoline a final product (a consumption good) or an intermediate product (an input to the production generated at the city job)? Or should it be an intermediate good on the morning trip to the job but a final good on the way from the job to home "consumption"? Would the problem be different if the commuter took a train or bus instead of his or her own car? What if the employer were to provide a special bus?

The problem is that many goods and services are used both for consumption and for further production. The two sorts of uses are separated in the accounts by a set of rules of thumb, which probably lead on balance to an overestimate of the national income.

Relations with the Environment

The relations between people and their environment give rise to more problems in social accounting. To understand the problem, consider the following illustration.

To control or modify my immediate small environment, I purchase a furnace, fuel, insulation, sweaters, and gloves in the winter. In the summer, I buy air-conditioning equipment, fuel, fans, bathing suits, and sunglasses. Producing these things generates income, which is recorded in the national income and product accounts, even though we may think they are overcoming "bads" rather than providing "goods" in themselves.

Complications for the accounting system arise when we recognize that millions of other people also are doing the same things that I am doing. On this large scale, human behavior burdens the ecosystem, making the air around us less pure than it once was. So I equip my heating and cooling systems with filters to keep out the polluted air, after doing my share to cause the pollution. Should the production of these filters be counted as part of the GNP, without offsetting (or negative) entries somewhere in the accounts to record the environmental damage that made the filters necessary? The accounts do record the filters, but they use no negative entry to record the harm done. For this reason, the accounting system may overstate the actual amount of income and production, if we mean by "income and production" truly positive contributions to welfare and living standards.

The problem has many illustrations in the U.S. economy. In addition to air purification filters, there are devices to lessen automobile emissions, to dispose of radioactive wastes, and to purify drinking water. Should the treatment of lung cancer be a positive entry in the accounts if the air pollution that helps to cause the cancer is not a negative entry?

The problem of environmental degradation has applications in the economies of many LDCs as well, since primitive farming methods can harm the environment. The "slash-and-burn" technique, which calls for cutting and burning trees to clear land, leads to soil erosion, floods, and fouled water supplies. There is no negative entry in the accounts to record the reduced value of the environment.

Consider the opposite case, too, when nature destroys the works of human beings. The capital consumption allowance, with which you are familiar, includes certain estimates of the results of nature's violent side. But the capital consumption allowance for nature's violence is spread evenly over the years, while the violence itself is not. How, then, would national income be affected if we suffered a major disaster like the destruction of Pompeii and Herculaneum by volcanic eruption, or of Tokyo and Yokohama by earthquake and fire? Such a disaster would result in an increase in national income, as people would earn incomes repairing the damage caused by nature and replacing what was beyond repair.

War and Violence

Preparing for war and waging war are recorded as parts of national income and production. People earn incomes for producing weapons of destruction and for serving in the armed forces. In fact, durable military goods like tanks are treated as consumption goods like loaves of bread rather than as investment goods like farm tractors. So total tank production is included in NNP as well as in GNP, even when the new tanks simply replace older ones, which wear out or become obsolete. (Loaves of bread are treated in this way for obvious reasons, but tractors are subject to capital consumption allowances.)

The issues involved in national accounting for war goods are both subtle and controversial. Does production of hydrogen bombs deter war in the same way that riot police on duty at sports events deter rioting? If so, bomb production and riot-police training are legitimate entries in the social accounts, like the production of dikes as insurance against flood damage. But if bombs invite wars and police incite riots,[5] a case can be made to exclude these activities from production and income. (Criminal activity is not counted as part of national income, though crime prevention is counted.)

Usefulness of the Accounts

As you can see, no accounting system provides completely acceptable measures of production or income in terms of welfare and living standards. Over the years, many ideas have been offered for making the system a better measure of "genuine" production in the sense of contributions to the standard of living. In the early 1970s, experimental systems called the measure of economic welfare (MEW) and net national welfare (NNW) were worked out for the United States and Japan, respectively. They attempted to subtract estimated environmental damage and wartime destruction. Though they have been compared and criticized, they have not been continued on a permanent basis by any government.

The faults in our own and other national accounting systems, however, should not dim their usefulness. As a tool for the study of macroeconomics, the system offers information on changes in the volume of economic activity over time.

---

5. Consider the remark by the late Richard J. Daley, long-time Mayor of Chicago: "The police are not there to create disorder. They are there to preserve disorder."

Changes over time are very important to the understanding of how an economy operates in the aggregate (macro) sense. Macroeconomics studies both the short-term changes and the long-term growth trends in the aggregate performance of an economy. When we focus on movements of uniformly defined measures over time, many of the problems concerning the absolute values used in the accounting system disappear. For example, the difference between one year and the next may be measured with reasonable accuracy even by questionable methods when the same rules for measurement have been used for each year.

SUMMARY

1. Measuring the amount of economic activity is an important first step in understanding short- and long-term changes in the economy.
2. The national income and product system has three main parts, one for measuring current production, one for measuring current income earned, and one for measuring amounts received as personal income.
3. Gross national product is broken down into different kinds of spending: consumption, investment, government purchases, and net exports. It records only currently produced goods and services.
4. Net national product is smaller than gross national product by the amount of the capital consumption allowance, which takes into account the depreciation of capital goods. After certain adjustments are made, NNP becomes equal to national income.
5. National income records the total earnings of factors of production during the accounting year. It is broken down into compensation of employees, proprietors' income, rental income of persons, corporate profits, and net interest. National income is equal to net national product after adjustments have been made for indirect business taxes, subsidies, and the statistical discrepancy.
6. Personal income is the sum that remains after "earnings not received" have been subtracted

and "receipts not earned" have been added to national income. When personal tax and nontax payments have been subtracted from personal income, the amount left is called disposable personal income.
7. Attempts to explain national income and product in terms of human welfare face difficulties because of such matters as "do-it-yourself" production, the underground economy, intermediate goods and services, cleaning up the environment, and producing goods for war.
8. Even though there is disagreement about how the national income and product accounting system should record certain activities, the system still is very useful for understanding the economy and making predictions. This is because changes in national production may be reliably reported if the same accounting methods are used consistently throughout the period.

DISCUSSION QUESTIONS

1. Name the three major parts of the national income and product accounting system. Which two are related through a double-entry bookkeeping system? Explain the adjustments that must be made to assure that these two sections balance with each other.
2. Suppose that the values added in producing a pair of shoes are $14 by the cattle raiser, $7 by the processing plant and tannery, $12 by the shoe manufacturer, $2 by the truck lines, and $11 by the retailer. Assuming no intermediate goods were purchased by the cattle raiser, what would the shoes sell for as a final product? How much double counting would arise if intermediate goods were not excluded in evaluating this product?
3. List the five major components in the national income section of the U.S. income and product accounts. In which entry would you record fringe benefits received by workers? Where would you put the rent payment for land owned by a corporation? Where would you record interest on the national debt?
4. Suppose that national income is $100 billion. Calculate the amount of personal income if Social

Security taxes are $10 billion, undistributed corporate profits are $1 billion, Social Security benefit checks are $11 billion, corporation profits taxes are $2 billion, government transfer payments are $2 billion, and interest on government bonds and consumer credit is $1 billion. (Assume that these are all the entries that are needed in this section.)

5. A good way to summarize the national income and product accounting system is to list the "big five" entries in the system and to explain how each differs from those closest to it. Try this exercise. Then note for each entry the particular use that economists make of it.

6. The national income and product accounting system uses estimates of the rental value of owner-occupied homes but does not use estimates of the wage value of do-it-yourself housekeeping services. Why are estimates used in the one case and not in the other? List three other types of do-it-yourself income that are not included in the national income and product statistics.

7. The chapter discusses how gasoline cannot be easily classified as either a final good or an intermediate good. Identify two other products that in some uses are intermediate products and in other uses are final products. How do you believe these items should be treated in the accounting system?

8. Many states have bottle deposit laws that encourage people to return empty beer and soft-drink containers to the store to recover their deposit. The store must hire people to handle this transaction and to return the empties to the bottler. Should the wages of these workers be counted as part of national income? What difference, if any, do you see between producing a "good" and preventing a "bad"?

8 The Circular Flow and Macroeconomic Equilibrium

PREVIEW The **circular-flow model** is an illustration that will help you to visualize the macroeconomic functioning of an economy. The model shows the relationships among several components of the national income and product accounts that you studied in Chapter 7—national product, national income, consumption spending, investment spending, government purchases, and net exports.

The key idea in the circular-flow model is that every dollar spent to buy goods and services becomes income to someone else. In the circular-flow diagram, this equality is pictured as money flowing around a closed circle. In one part of the circle the money flow is spending to purchase goods (national product), and in the other part of the circle it is income (national income). This is the same idea that produced the equality between the bottom lines of the national product section and the national income section of the accounts discussed in Chapter 7.

We begin with a simplified illustration of the circular flow that assumes all income is spent for consumption purchases. This simple model then is expanded to show several different uses for funds—saving and investment, taxes and government purchases, and imports and exports. In the next step, we show how imbalances or tendencies for disequilibrium may arise in these various spending patterns. Finally, we combine all the different spending patterns and examine equilibrium and disequilibrium in the entire circular-flow model.

The circular-flow model offers a framework that will help you to understand the macroeconomic models and theories presented later in the book.

A "CONSUMPTION ONLY" CIRCULAR FLOW

A very simple picture of the circular flow is presented in Figure 8-1. All the households in the economy are represented by the box on the left side of the figure. Inside this box, the functions of households as consumers and resource owners are noted. All the firms in the economy are represented by the box on the right side of the figure. The functions of businesses as producers and resource buyers are noted inside this box. The oval on the left side of the circle represents the concept of national income and the oval on the right side represents the concept of national product, as described in Chapter 7.

The circular flow itself is shown by the arrows going in a clockwise direction from households through national product to firms and from firms across the bottom part of the circle through national income to households. This circular flow line shows the flow of money. The flow across the bottom of the figure represents payments by businesses to households to buy the resources used in production. These payments consist of wages, salaries, rents, interest, and profits—the same flows that add up to national income in the accounting system. In the official accounts themselves, they are listed as compensation of employees, proprietors' income, rental income of persons, corporate profits, and net interest. National income appears in the oval on the left side of the figure to show that these money flows together make up national income in the accounts. These payments go to hire the factors of production—natural resources, labor, and capital. Because the business owners are themselves members of households, profits are also included in this flow (as they are in the accounting system).

In the upper half of Figure 8-1, the flow runs from households to the national-product oval and then to firms. This flow represents the uses of funds by households. Payments are made when households, as consumers, buy goods and services from businesses. This simplified circular flow assumes that *all* the income received by households (the whole national income) is spent on consumer goods and services and that none is saved or used for any other purpose. Therefore, in this special and unrealistic case, the total of consumption expenditure would be equal to national product. The money received by business firms exactly covers the amounts that have been paid out to hire resources, including profits to the owners of the firms.

THE CONCEPT OF MACROECONOMIC EQUILIBRIUM

Even though this special case is highly simplified and unrealistic, it is a good way to begin our study of the idea of equilibrium in the circular flow of national income and product. As you may remember, **equilibrium** is a state of balance among opposing forces such that there is no tendency for change.[1] In our consumption-only circular flow, we have assumed that *all* income received by the households is spent to buy consumption goods from the firms. Therefore, if households receive $100 of national income, firms will receive $100 from consumption expenditure, which will pay them in full for the money they spend in producing these goods and will include their

1. The concept of equilibrium was presented in Chapter 3.

profit as well. Since receipts are equal to expenditures for the firms and for the households, there is nothing in this circular flow that should cause the firms or households either to increase or to decrease their activity in the coming time period. We expect the volume of dollar flow to be the same in the next turn around the circle as it was in the turn just completed. This is a state of equilibrium.

The consumption-only circular-flow model is useful to introduce the idea of the circular flow and to begin our study of macroeconomic equilibrium. But it is very unrealistic to assume that all income received by households is spent on consumer goods and services. Some money will be saved, some will be used to pay taxes, and some may be spent to purchase goods or services from foreigners. These alternatives not only make the circular-flow model more complex but also open up the possibility of disequilibrum. **Disequilibrium** means that opposing forces are *not* in balance, so that there *is* some tendency for change to take place. To understand the possibility of disequilibrium, we must proceed to a more complete illustration of the circular flow.

CIRCULAR FLOW WITH FINANCIAL MARKETS, GOVERNMENT, AND FOREIGN MARKETS

Figure 8-2 illustrates a circular-flow model that offers households four different ways to use their money. No longer does the model leave households no alternative but to spend 100 percent of their income on the purchase of consumption goods. In this model, households may (1) spend money for consumption goods and services, (2) save some of their income, (3) pay taxes, or (4) purchase goods and services from foreigners. Funds flow through four alternative channels as households divide their income among these four uses.

Before we examine each of these uses of funds in more detail, let us briefly trace each of the four flows in Figure 8-2. Consumption spending flows

FIGURE 8-1 A "Consumption Only" Circular Flow

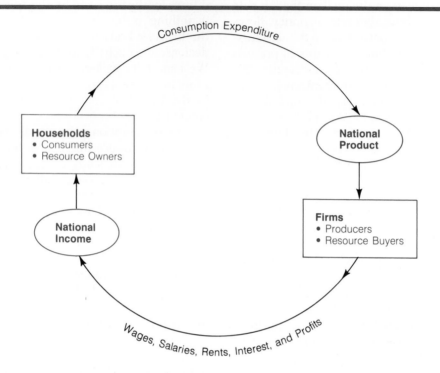

Firms, represented in the right-hand box, purchase resources to produce goods and services. The lower half of the circle represents money paid to the owners of these resources. It is the national income. Households, in the left-hand box, purchase consumption goods and services from the firms. The upper half of the circle represents money paid by households to buy consumer goods and services. This is a simplified model because it assumes that all national income is used to purchase consumer goods and services—that none is saved or used for any other purpose. All of the national product consists of consumer goods and services.

directly to the firms, as illustrated earlier. Saving flows to the financial markets—that is, to banks, stock markets, insurance companies, and similar financial institutions. From there, these funds emerge as investment spending, which goes toward purchasing part of the national product and flows on to the firms.

The next stream of money emerging from the household box is net taxes. Net taxes equal the total tax paid to government minus the amounts received back from government in the form of cash payments, such as welfare, Social Security, or veterans' benefit checks. These are called *transfer payments*. The money paid as net tax to government emerges from the government box as government purchases, which buy part of the national product and flow on to the firms.

Household spending for goods and services from foreign countries—that is, imports—flows to foreign markets, and these funds are used by foreigners to buy American goods and services that are exported. Exports are, of course, part of the national product. Note that these four flows correspond to the four components of national product in the accounting system, just as the flow in the bottom part of Figure 8-2 (which is the same as Figure 8-1) includes the components of national income.

We shall take a closer look at the saving, taxes, and import-export flows in the following sections.

FIGURE 8-2   Circular Flow with Financial Markets, Government, and Foreign Markets

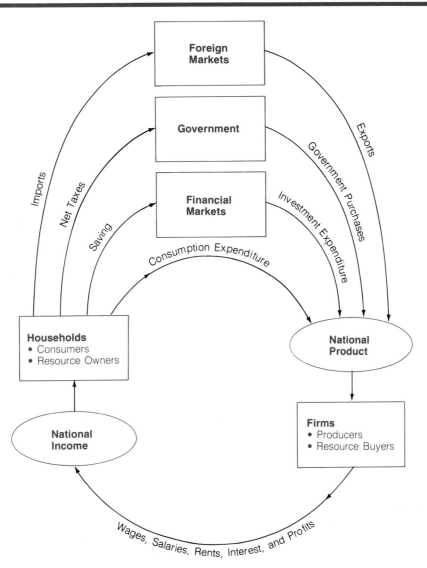

Households may divide their income among consumption, saving, net taxes, and imports. Financial markets, government, and foreign markets act as intermediaries and determine the investment, government, and export expenditures. Along with consumption, these expenditures purchase national product and provide funds to firms. Funds then flow from firms to households as wages, salaries, rents, interest, and profits.

Saving and Investment

Saving occurs when households decide not to use all of their disposable personal income (DPI) to purchase consumption goods and services. By saving, households can increase their wealth. In addition to saving out of disposable personal income, the household saving shown in the circular flow includes an indirect form of saving that takes place when businesses retain earnings instead of paying dividends. The households, as stockholders, are the owners of the corporations and are entitled to all earnings (profits) from these businesses. These earnings may be paid to the stockholders in the form of dividends, or they may be kept by the corporation and reinvested on behalf of the stockholders. In our formulation of the circular flow, undistributed profits are part of the profits shown in the bottom of the circular-flow diagram and are treated as saving by households in the top part of the circle. So we define **saving** as the part of disposable personal income that is not spent on consumption plus the part of corporate after-tax earnings that are not paid out as dividends.

Sometimes businesses are said to be "saving" when they put money into depreciation reserves to replace equipment that is expected to wear out in the future. If we think of the national product shown in Figure 8-2 as net national product, our system agrees quite well with the accounting system. Money put into depreciation reserves is *not* part of net national product, since profits are figured net of depreciation. For this reason, we do not include depreciation "saving" as part of the saving stream in our illustration. Likewise, investment spending to replace worn-out equipment is *not* part of net national product. Of course, investment to replace worn-out equipment is part of gross national product. If we wanted to deal with gross national product, we would have to treat depreciation allowances as part of saving.

FINANCIAL MARKETS As shown in Figure 8-2, the money that has been saved flows into financial markets. Remember that a market is the organized interaction of buyers and sellers that enables them to trade. It follows, then, that **financial markets**

involve the trading of financial assets between buyers and sellers. Banks, savings and loan associations, and credit unions are well-known participants in financial markets, as are stock and bond brokerage firms. Insurance companies also play an important part in financial markets, since many insurance policies have savings features and since insurance companies hold large amounts of money to pay future debts and can lend out these funds.

The function of the financial markets is to bring savers and investors together. Saving enters the financial markets and is invested when businesses borrow these funds to buy inventory and new production equipment. This investment spending goes toward purchasing part of the national product. As noted earlier, our simple circular flow describes net national product. So only *additions* to the stock of capital are being financed through these markets. If we had used a more complicated model, we could show gross national product and include a flow of depreciation "saving" from the businesses to the financial markets.[2]

CONDITIONS LEADING TO DISEQUILIBRIUM To repeat, equilibrium is a state of balance among opposing forces such that there is no tendency for change. *Dis*equilibrium, on the other hand, is a state of *im*balance among opposing forces such that there *is* a tendency for change. Disequilibrium conditions may arise in the financial path, the government path, or in the foreign path of the circular flow. We shall deal first with the financial path.

To recognize the condition of disequilibrium, we must distinguish between the spending and saving that households plan to do and the spending and saving that they actually carry out. That is, we must distinguish between plans and accomplishments or, in more technical language, between an *ex ante* view and an *ex post* view of their activity. For example, a family may have *ex ante* plans to save $25 a month, but their *ex post* accomplishment may be only $15 saved. Likewise, we must distinguish between the investment that firms plan to carry out and the investment that

2. Financial markets are described further in Chapter 12.

they actually do carry out. The distinction between *planned* saving or investment and *actual* saving or investment is extremely important in macroeconomic theory. This is because *unplanned* saving or investment takes place when the actual amount does not match the planned amount. Unplanned elements of actual saving and/or investment give rise to disequilibrium conditions.

In the saving–financial markets–investment path of the circular flow, a disequilibrium condition may arise if the amount of *planned* saving does not equal the amount of *planned* investment. Planned saving may exceed planned investment or vice versa. Let us trace, in a simple way, some possible causes and consequences of each of these cases.

MORE PLANNED SAVING THAN PLANNED INVEST-MENT If planned saving exceeds planned investment, households are putting more money into the financial markets than firms plan to take out of those markets to finance investments. As you will learn in the next chapter, this situation might bring a drop in interest rates, which in turn might make people plan to save less and businesses to invest more money, thereby correcting the imbalance. But if this fails to happen, households will be putting more money into the financial markets than firms are taking out. Funds accumulate in financial institutions and do not continue around the circular flow. If other things remain unchanged, firms will not receive enough funds to match the amount that they plan to pay out in wages, salaries, rents, interest, and profits. In other words, businesses will not receive enough money to enable them to continue their planned dollar volume of production.

Why might the plans of firms not match the plans of households? Perhaps the firms made plans based on wrong forecasts—expecting that the households would consume more and save less than they actually planned to do. Or households may have changed their saving and spending plans after firms had already made commitments for production. Whatever the reason, some of the goods and services that firms had planned to produce and sell cannot be sold at the prices that the firms had expected and planned when

they hired and paid the factors of production. As a result, the firms have unwanted or unplanned inventories (goods on hand). This is a disequilibrium condition that generates tendencies for change. So firms will probably do two things:

1. Firms will borrow money in the financial markets to "invest" in this inventory. Actually, this will happen almost automatically as sales fall short of expectations and fail to provide funds that firms need to meet their obligations. The accounting system does not distinguish between this unplanned inventory investment and the amount that firms actually planned to invest. The accounting system sees only the actual saving and the actual investment—it sees only the *ex post* situation. Saving (S) and investment (I) are defined to be equal to each other. In this *ex post* view, $S = I$ is an **identity**.

2. The second part of the firms' response to the accumulation of unplanned inventories is to set up a new and different plan for the next round of production and sales. This new plan is the "change" in our definition of disequilibrium. When sales are less than planned or expected, economic theory predicts that firms will lower their production plans for the next round or time period and/or will lower the prices that they plan to ask for their goods. This lowering of production and/or prices will result in changes in the national income part of the circular flow. Wages, salaries, rents, interest, and profits (in some combination) will absorb these cutbacks. National income will fall, often triggering, in turn, a drop in consumption, saving, net taxes, and imports (in some combination) in the next round of the circular flow. These second-round effects will be explained in Chapter 9.

MORE PLANNED INVESTMENT THAN PLANNED SAVING Let us briefly track the opposite type of disequilibrium arising in the saving and investment pathway of the circular flow. Since households and firms are separate decision-making units in a capitalist-market economy, it is quite possible that planned investment may exceed planned saving. Perhaps business optimism has boosted investment plans to levels that exceed household planned saving. Or it may be that households are planning to spend more and save less than business firms expected. Whatever the reason, firms may plan to draw more funds out of financial markets than households plan to put into these markets. In some cases, pressure may develop for interest rates to move upward to increase planned saving and decrease planned investment. But if these changes fail to balance the plans, funds that previously were idle (reserves) in the financial markets may be "put into circulation" in the circular flow.

This situation is the opposite of the one we just described. Rather than a cash-flow problem, the firms will have plenty of funds because they have sold more of their inventories than they had planned. That is, they will have made an unplanned **disinvestment** in inventory. Again, it is helpful to consider what the companies may do in the face of this disequilibrium situation.

1. On the purely financial and accounting side, the response is almost automatic. The disinvestment in inventory means that the firms need less financing to carry inventory and to meet other obligations. Borrowing declines, and again the national accounts, which record only *ex post* actualities and not *ex ante* plans, fail to reveal any imbalance. Some of the planned investment in inventory is simply not carried out in the current accounting period. Also, there may be some unplanned saving by households, if they cannot buy what they planned because inventories are down and some things are "sold out." Unplanned saving is included in the accounts, and saving will be equal to investment (*ex post*) as an identity. Again, the accounts do not reveal disequilibrium.
2. The disequilibrium will lead to changes, however, because firms will change their production and pricing plans for the next round of the circular flow. Production may be increased to replace inventory and to meet higher demand, and prices may be increased as well. These changes will increase the amounts of wages, salaries, rents, interest, and profits in the national income part of the circular flow in the next accounting period, and households will have more money to use.

In our journey through the financial-markets path of the circular flow, we have emphasized

the ideas of equilibrium and disequilibrium. With a better understanding of these concepts, let us move on to the government and the foreign-markets paths.

Taxes and Government Purchases

In our circular-flow model (Figure 8-2), net taxes are another way in which households use their income. As we use the term here, **net taxes** means the total amount of personal and business taxes paid minus transfer payments from the government. As you remember, a **transfer payment** is a payment of money that is not compensation for any service rendered or product sold during the present accounting period. Included in government transfer payments are Social Security benefits, unemployment compensation, worker's compensation, welfare payments, veterans' benefits, and so on. Sometimes government transfer payments are called "negative taxes." In this sense, our term of "net taxes" is easy to understand. It is total taxes minus government transfer payments.[3]

GOVERNMENT IN THE CIRCULAR FLOW   The government box in the circular-flow diagram represents budgetary decisions by federal, state, and local governments. As net tax collections flow into the box, the government decides how to spend these funds on currently produced goods and services. The flow of funds that emerges from this box represents these purchases. It is important to note that this amount is not the total

---

3. The concept of net tax does not appear explicitly in the national accounting system that you studied in Chapter 7. Total taxes included "personal tax payments" and the part of "earnings not received" that reports corporate profits taxes and contributions for social insurance. When we subtract "receipts not earned" (which are mostly government transfer payments) from total taxes, we are left with net taxes. However, if you are an accounting student, you may want to take another look at the procedure that subtracts indirect business taxes from net national product in order to arrive at a figure equal to national income. If indirect business taxes were included in the net tax flow, recorded consumption spending would have to be reduced to an amount net of these taxes.

budget expenditure of government, which includes transfer payments as well as purchases of goods and services. However, our circular-flow system is quite consistent with government budgets, since in calculating the net tax stream that enters the government box, government transfer payments are treated as "negative taxes" and subtracted from total taxes. Although transfer payments are not government purchases of currently produced goods and services, the households that receive these transfers use the money for consumption, saving, tax payments, or imports. In this way, the money is recorded in the accounting system and recognized in the circular flow.

THE POSSIBILITY OF DISEQUILIBRIUM The government box is another place in the circular flow where disequilibrium may arise. In terms of our simple model, the amount of money flowing into the government box as net taxes may not be equal to the amount that flows out of that box as government purchases. If net taxes exceed government purchases, the government budget has a "surplus" as far as the income and product accounts are concerned. If funds are allowed to accumulate in the government box, the flow of funds to firms will be reduced. This reduced flow of funds leads to unplanned inventory accumulation and to a lower national income in future rounds of the circular flow. On the other hand, if government purchases exceed net taxes, the budget (in income and product terms) has a "deficit." In this case, government may create spending power or put some previously idle funds to use. The methods of creating spending power will be explained in Chapter 13. With more government purchases, business inventories may be used up, so that there will be an expansion of national income in the next round.

When we discussed disequilibrium conditions in the financial-markets path of the circular flow, we noted the difference between planned (*ex ante*) amounts and actual (*ex post*) amounts. Similar terms can be used to describe the government path, but there are important differences in the causes of imbalance. Governments have legal control over both taxation and purchases, so that an imbalance between planned taxes and planned purchases cannot be blamed on different actions by separate and independent decision makers.[4] In the planning (*ex ante*) sense, the government can decide if it wants the budget to be in balance, or have a deficit or a surplus. In other words, government may create disequilibrium intentionally if the alternative economic situation is judged to be unsatisfactory. For example, in 1964 President Johnson carried through President Kennedy's plan for an intentional budget deficit achieved through a tax cut. The aim was to increase total spending and thereby to reduce unemployment and raise the rate of economic growth. As you will see in Chapter 11, the power to control the flow of funds through the government part of the circular flow is an important tool of economic policy.

Sometimes the actually achieved or *ex post* budgetary balance, deficit, or surplus does not match the plans of the government. In other words, the economy may not perform as government planners had expected. Tax collections or government spending may fall below or rise above expectations, and disequilibrium conditions may originate in the government from miscalculations as well as from purposeful policy plans.

Imports and Exports

The remaining path in the circular-flow model involves spending by households on imports and spending by foreigners on exported goods and services. Let's assume that the figure describes the U.S. economy. Dollars from American households flow into the foreign-markets box and emerge when foreigners buy currently produced American goods and services. These dollars purchase some of the national product of the U.S. economy.

The national income and product accounts (as shown in Chapter 7) do not present separate figures for exports and imports. All that system

---

4. However, you may believe, as some do, that government's right hand does not know or cannot control what its left hand is doing.

shows is an entry for "net exports" in the national product section. The reason for doing so is that purchases by Americans from foreigners (imports) have already been included in the figures for consumption, investment, and government purchases. Since the consumption, investment, and government purchases entries already include purchases from foreigners, all that is needed in the accounting system is a figure for "net exports" to record the difference between total exports and the imports already counted in the other spending flows. Of course, net exports may be negative. In the circular-flow diagram, we show a separate imports–foreign markets–exports channel because disequilibrium conditions can arise in this path of the circular flow.

The causes of disequilibrium in the foreign-trade path of the circular flow are similar in several ways to those in the financial-markets path. Again, plans are made by separate and independent decision makers—U.S. importers, foreign purchasers of U.S. goods, and the U.S. firms that produce these goods. Sometimes the plans that American companies make for production and sales do not agree with the plans that Americans make about buying foreign (rather than home-produced) goods or with the plans that foreigners make about buying American goods. U.S. auto makers may misjudge the number of Japanese cars that Americans will buy, or U.S. food or lumber producers may misjudge Japanese demand for these goods. For this reason, purchases by foreigners may not match the planned export sales of U.S. companies. This difference leads to a disequilibrium condition—either more or less inventory than was planned. In the next round of production, plans for production, employment, and pricing will be changed.

As before, the actual export sales reported in the accounts will fail to reveal the disequilibrium condition. Unplanned inventory will be included as "investment," and the identity between actual (*ex post*) saving and investment will remain. The parallel with the saving–investment path is even further illustrated by the fact that foreign exchange rates, such as the number of Japanese yen you need to exchange for an American dollar, play a part in foreign trade like the part that

interest rates play in the financial markets. Whether these rates are flexible enough to assure prompt adjustments to changing times is an important question. Foreign exchange rates and the balance of payments accounting system will be explained in Chapter 18.

THE KEY POSITION OF FINANCIAL MARKETS

So far, we have examined each of the four paths at the top (national product side) of the circular-flow diagram. We saw that disequilibrium conditions can arise in several ways. Planned saving may not equal planned investment, net taxes may not equal government purchases, and imports may not equal exports. In each case, however, we stopped short of saying that disequilibrium in the entire circular flow would actually result. We did not make this statement because an imbalance in one path may counteract an imbalance in another path. We shall now examine the key role of financial markets in linking together the different pathways of the circular flow. We have already seen how these markets provide a connection between saving and investment. Now we will see how the financial markets are linked to the government path and to the foreign-markets path of the circular flow.

Financial Markets and Government

What happens when the government budget does not balance? When there is an imbalance in the government budget (as defined for the circular flow and the national income and product accounts), funds will flow between the government box and the financial markets box in our circular-flow diagram. Figure 8-3 illustrates the two kinds of flows that can arise. The dashed arrows on the left side of the figure show what happens if there is a surplus in the government budget. Some of the net tax money received by the government flows to the financial-markets box to increase government deposit balances or to reduce the

FIGURE 8-3 Government Surpluses and Deficits and the Financial Markets

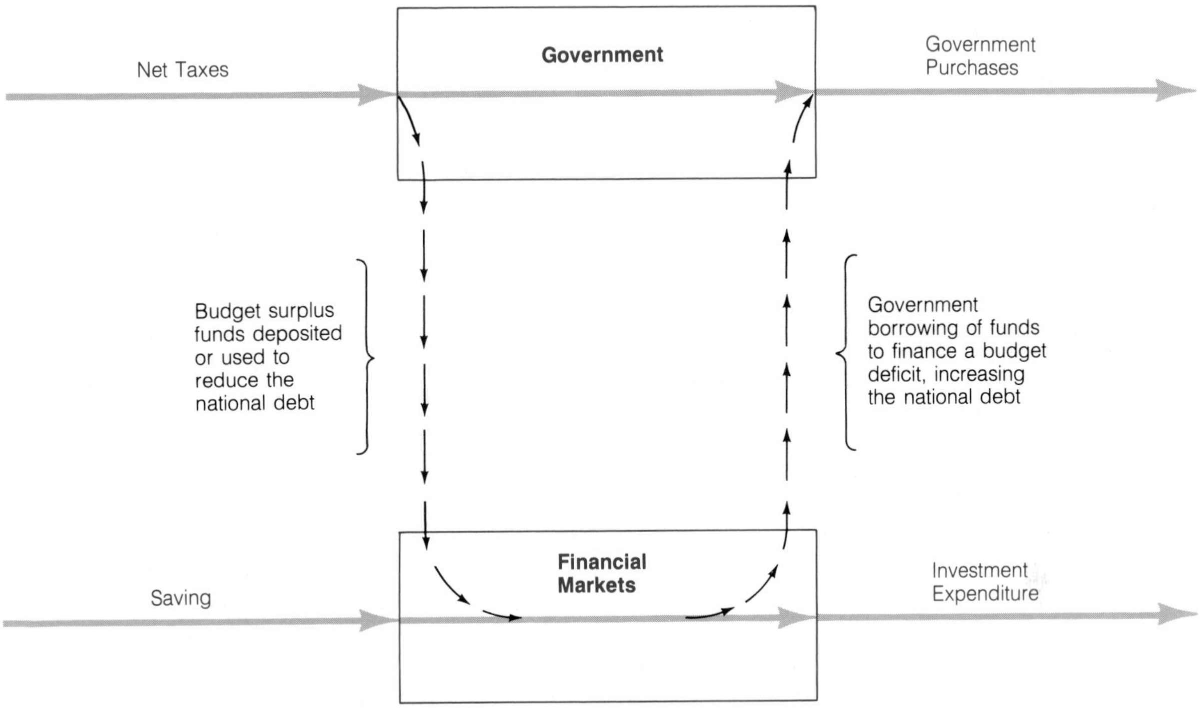

The dashed arrows on the left illustrate the flow of funds that arises when there is a surplus in the government's budget. These surplus funds are deposited in financial institutions or used to retire national debt securities. The dashed arrows on the right illustrate the flow of funds that arises when there is a deficit in the government's budget. The government borrows funds in the financial markets to finance the deficit.

national debt by buying back some outstanding government bonds. These funds then join the flow of saving from households and move on to finance investment expenditure. In this way, a surplus in the government budget could counteract an imbalance of insufficient saving in the saving–investment path of the circular flow.

The dashed arrows on the right-hand side of Figure 8-3 show what happens when there is a deficit in the government income and product budget. Funds flow from the financial-markets box to the government box as the government reduces its deposit balances in financial institutions or borrows money, either directly from institutions or by selling securities and increasing the national debt. In this process, some money

saved by households is used to finance the government deficit and is not available for financing investment. This consequence of government budget deficits is referred to as **crowding out** and has been the focus of much controversy in recent years, since it may lead to higher interest rates, reductions in investment, and a slower rate of economic growth.

Financial Markets and Foreign Markets

The U.S. financial markets also are connected to foreign markets in the circular-flow system. This linkage is illustrated in Figure 8-4. The dashed

FIGURE 8-4   Foreign Market Imbalances and U.S. Financial Markets

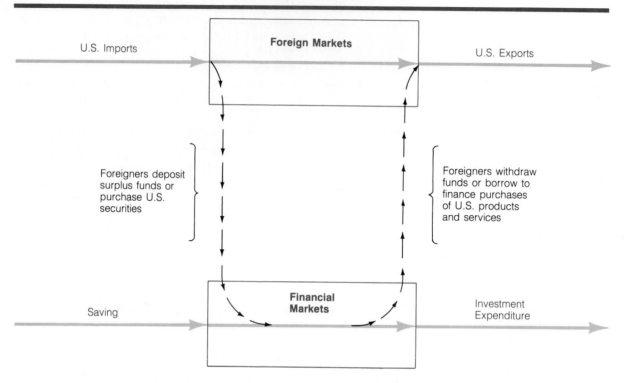

The dashed arrows on the left illustrate the flow of funds that arises when foreigners receive funds from sales to Americans and then deposit these funds in U.S. financial institutions or purchase securities in the United States. The dashed arrows on the right side illustrate the flow of funds when foreigners borrow in U.S. financial markets to pay for goods and services purchased from American firms.

arrows on the left side of this figure show that foreigners may send some of the dollars that they receive from U.S. households to U.S. financial markets, where they can purchase U.S. stocks and bonds to earn dividends and interest. These foreign funds then finance investment in the United States instead of being used to purchase U.S. exports. This route for funds has been heavily used in recent years because of relatively high interest rates in the United States and because economic prosperity has made investment in the United States potentially more profitable than investment elsewhere in the world. As you can see, this flow can work to counteract crowding out from a government budget deficit.

The right-hand side of Figure 8-4 illustrates how dollars can flow from U.S. financial markets into the foreign-markets box. This happens when the money received by foreigners from selling goods and services to Americans (U.S. imports) is not enough to pay for all the purchases that foreigners make from Americans (U.S. exports). In this situation, the foreigners borrow dollars in the U.S. financial markets and use the money to pay for their extra purchases from U.S. firms. This means that some of the money saved by U.S. households is used by foreigners to buy U.S. exports. Again, an imbalance in one path of the circular flow can offset an imbalance in another path.

EQUILIBRIUM AND DISEQUILIBRIUM IN THE WHOLE ECONOMY

The equilibrium conditions for the economy as a whole differ from those that applied in each separate path of the circular flow only in that we must combine all four expenditure paths together and compare *total* planned expenditure with the value of goods and services that firms plan to produce and sell. Companies plan to sell certain amounts of goods and services at set prices. In order to make these goods and services available, they plan to purchase and pay the factors of production. If total planned expenditure is equal to the value of goods and services that companies plan to sell, then equilibrium conditions exist in the circular flow. There is a balance of opposing forces and no tendency for change. No force is generated that would tend to bring a change in either production or total planned expenditure in the next round of the circle.

If we let Y^* represent the equilibrium level of national income, macroeconomic equilibrium in an economy exists when

$$Y^* = C + I + G + X - Im$$

provided that the values for consumption (C), investment (I), government purchases (G), exports (X), and imports (Im) all represent *planned* purchases. This is one of the basic equations of macroeconomics and will be used many times in the chapters ahead. Study it carefully to be sure that you understand its meaning.

Disequilibrium Conditions

Disequilibrium conditions arise when total planned expenditure ($C + I + G + X - Im$) is not equal to planned production, that is, when it is not equal to Y^*. In this situation, firms do not sell the quantities of goods and services that they planned to sell at the prices they had expected.

Such conditions certainly can arise. In a market-capitalist system, consumers, investors, government, and foreigners are separate decision-making units and may therefore make plans that are not consistent with one another.[5] For businesses to anticipate the plans of these groups accurately is a challenging task, and mistakes can easily be made even by experienced business planners.

EXPANSIONARY DISEQUILIBRIUM   Suppose that the sum total of planned expenditure is greater than the total value of goods that firms expect to sell. What will happen? Will there be shortages? Maybe. Buyers' plans may not be fulfilled, and they may purchase less than intended. Will inventories of goods fall below planned levels? Almost certainly. Firms will have sold more than they planned to sell. Does this situation involve an imbalance of forces so that there is a tendency for change? Yes. We can predict that companies will change their behavior in the next round of the circle. In order to build up their inventories, firms will probably expand production, and increases in factor payments (national income) will occur. Asking prices also may be raised to maximize profits, to keep inventories from decreasing too quickly, or to cover any increased costs incurred in raising output. This disequilibrium situation will probably trigger an expansion of the economy.

CONTRACTIONARY DISEQUILIBRIUM   A contractionary disequilibrium is also easy to imagine. If total planned expenditure is less than production, inventories will rise above the level planned by the firms. This imbalance will generate pressure for firms to reduce production in the next round and to lower prices to speed the reduction of unplanned inventory and to keep losses as small as possible. Factor payments and national income will fall. Most likely, this disequilibrium will trigger a contraction of the economy.

---

5. Since socialist planning does not work perfectly, disequilibrium can exist in that system too, but the processes of adjustment are different.

Is Equilibrium Desirable?

Neither equilibrium nor disequilibrium is desirable or undesirable in itself. Desirability depends on the situations that prevail in the economy at the time. For example, an equilibrium may be quite undesirable if it involves too much unemployment. An expansionary disequilibrium could be desirable if it would reduce the amount of unemployment. On the other hand, an expansionary disequilibrium could be quite undesirable if it would bring high inflation. Conversely, in inflationary times, a contractionary disequilibrium could be desirable if it would help lower inflation.

At this point in your study of macroeconomics, the important point is to recognize that equilibrium and disequilibrium are theoretical concepts that help economists predict coming situations in the economy and devise ways to deal with them. Equilibrium defines the situation *toward which* the economy will move if no new policy actions are undertaken. Economists therefore estimate and describe the nature of this equilibrium situation. If policy makers believe that the equilibrium situation would be unsatisfactory, economists suggest ways to create a disequilibrium that will improve the economy. Later chapters will explain in more detail how economists apply these ideas.

LEAKAGES AND INJECTIONS

The idea of leakages and injections provides another way of understanding equilibrium and disequilibrium in the circular flow. Both of these concepts are defined rather narrowly in terms of the circular-flow model itself. **Leakages** are all uses of funds that take them out of the direct consumption expenditure flow. In our model, saving, net taxes, and import expenditure are leakages. **Injections** are all expenditures on currently produced goods and services except those for domestic consumption. So investment, government purchases, and exports are injections. This explanation of equilibrium separates exports from imports and does not use the "net export"

concept from the national income accounts. Therefore, our listing of injections can include only the domestic portion of consumption, planned investment, and government purchases. We can show the relationship of injections and leakages by expressing our circular-flow model as follows:

$$C_d + I_d + G_d + X = C_d + S + T_n + Im$$

In this equation, C_d is planned domestic consumption spending, I_d is planned domestic investment, G_d is government domestic purchases (not including transfers), X is exports, S is saving, T_n is net tax payments, and Im is import spending. The left side of the equation shows all the flows that go into the national-product oval in the circular-flow diagram. The sum of these flows is the national product. On the right side of the equation are all the flows that come out of the households box. Together these flows account for all the national income in the economy. We show leakages and injections by canceling, or crossing out, domestic consumption expenditure (C_d) from each side of the equation. Then, the $I_d + G_d + X$ that remain on the left side are the injections. The $S + T_n + Im$ that remain on the right side are the leakages in the circular flow.

Equilibrium Between Leakages and Injections

Equilibrium in the circular flow exists when planned injections are equal to planned leakages. This means that the volume of funds that households plan to "leak" out of the direct domestic consumption purchases is exactly matched by the volume of funds that investors, governments, and foreigners plan to "inject" into the national product through their spending on goods and services produced in the economy. In equilibrium, the amount of money that firms receive from sales of goods is exactly equal to the amount that firms have paid or plan to pay in factor payments to households. So firms have no cash-flow problems, and inventories are at exactly the levels that were planned. There is no force generated that will cause firms to change their production or pricing plans for the next round of the circular flow. No funds have accumulated in the financial-markets, government, or foreign-markets boxes, nor have any previously accumulated funds been drawn out of these areas and put into circulation.

Note, however, that an exact balance in each separate path or flow is *not* necessary. Imports need not equal exports, net taxes need not equal government domestic purchases, and planned saving need not equal planned domestic investment expenditure. A net balance between the two groups is sufficient. Suppose that the dollar amounts were as follows:

Domestic investment spending	$ 30
Government domestic purchases	50
Exports	20
Total injections	$100
Saving	$ 25
Net taxes	40
Imports	35
Total leakages	$100

This situation illustrates equilibrium if all the activities take place as planned by their initiators, and if all parties are willing to continue the same behavior in the next time period. As shown above, planned domestic investment is greater than planned saving and government domestic purchases are greater than net taxes. But these net injections are balanced by a leakage in the foreign-markets sector, where imports exceed exports. If the connection from the foreign-markets box to the financial-markets box operates satisfactorily, the extra money that is flowing to the foreign markets will finance the additional investment and the government deficit. This rather dramatic or extreme illustration underlines the importance of the connections between the boxes in the circular-flow model.

Disequilibrium Between Leakages and Injections

We can illustrate disequilibrium in terms of leakages and injections by simply changing one of the values in our numerical illustration. Suppose that planned purchases by foreigners (U.S. exports) increase to $25, while all other entries remain unchanged. Now, as you can see, the total of injections will exceed the total of leakages by $5:

Domestic investment spending	$ 30
Government domestic spending	50
Exports	25
Total injections	$105
Saving	$ 25
Net taxes	40
Imports	35
Total leakages	$100

This net increase in planned purchases causes more of the firms' inventories to be sold than was planned and encourages companies to raise prices and/or production in the next time period. So an expansion in the economy will tend to occur, triggered, in this case, by an expansion of purchases by foreigners. If, on the other hand, total leakages were greater than total injections, the disequilibrium would cause a contraction in the economy. In that case, the net leakage would cause inventories to increase to unplanned levels and lead to the lowering of prices and/or production in the next round of the circular flow.

The leakage-injection explanation of equilibrium and disequilibrium gives the same answers and is analytically identical to the total-planned-expenditure explanation developed earlier in the chapter. The terms in the different equations are simply rearranged to suit the preferences of different economists. Learning both approaches is a good way to reinforce your understanding of macroeconomic equilibrium and disequilibrium.

SUMMARY

1. The circular-flow model is a simplified picture of the aggregate economy. It is an aid to understanding macroeconomics and prepares the way for more detailed analysis.
2. The circular-flow model is built on the idea of equality between national product and national income. Flows shown in the model can be related

PART II THE MACROECONOMY

to various amounts reported in the accounting system.

3. Equilibrium in the aggregate economy means a balance among opposing forces such that there is no tendency for change. Equilibrium conditions exist if total planned expenditure equals the value of goods and services that firms plan to sell.

4. Disequilibrium conditions can arise from inequalities between planned saving and planned investment, between net taxes and government purchases, and between imports and exports. However, disequilibrium in the whole circular flow is an inequality between production and total planned expenditure.

5. Sometimes disequilibrium leads to an expansion of the economy. In such a case, total planned expenditure is greater than production. Total injections are greater than total leakages. Inventories of goods and services become smaller than had been planned. When this happens, businesses increase production and/or prices in the next time period.

6. In other cases, disequilibrium may lead to a contracting economy. Here total planned expenditure is less than production. Total leakages are greater than total injections. Unsold inventories rise to higher levels, and production and/or prices are expected to be lower in the next time period.

7. The financial markets are connected directly to governments and to foreign markets. For this reason, disequilibrium conditions arising in one part of the economy may spread to other parts or may be counteracted by what happens in other parts.

DISCUSSION QUESTIONS

1. State in your own words the meaning of macroeconomic equilibrium. Then check your definition with the one given in this chapter. Review your understanding of why economists place great emphasis on the concept of equilibrium in both macroeconomics and microeconomics. Is disequilibrium undesirable? Explain.

2. Without looking at Figure 8-2, construct the circular-flow diagram showing the four streams

of the household uses of funds. Compare your work with Figure 8-2 to be sure you have it right. Why was equilibrium assured in the "consumption-only" version of the circular flow but not in the version that shows all four streams?

3. The discussion of disequilibrium in the saving–investment path of the circular flow is your first plunge into macroeconomic theory. Be sure you understand it completely. Why might *planned* saving differ from *planned* investment? How can this difference lead to a change in the flow of national income in the next round of the circle? Why do business inventories play such an important part in the equilibrium model?

4. Why do the national income and product accounts fail to reveal disequilibrium conditions in the saving–investment path of the circular flow?

5. Net taxes differ from total tax collections by government. Explain why. Government purchases differ from the total budget expenditure of government. Explain why. How do transfer payments provide the key to these differences? How do transfers enter into the circular-flow picture?

6. Since government has the power to control both its inflows and its outflows, why should a disequilibrium condition ever arise in the net tax–government purchases flow? Is government's control complete? Explain.

7. Carefully explain why a connection exists in the circular flow between the financial-markets box and the government box. Describe the activity that takes place through this connection when there is a deficit in the government budget. Describe the activity when there is a budget surplus.

8. Although you will study international trade in more detail later, it is helpful to recognize its importance here in the context of the circular flow. What happens to funds in the foreign-markets box and in the connection to U.S. financial markets when U.S. imports exceed U.S. exports? What happens when exports exceed imports?

9. Suppose that planned investment exceeds planned saving and that exports exceed imports. Does this mean there is disequilibrium in the total

144

circular flow? Explain. How might the net tax–government purchases flow enter into your explanation? What would happen in this situation if planned government purchases exceeded net taxes? Explain.

10. Without looking back in the chapter, write the leakages-and-injections equation for equilib-rium in the circular flow. Now check to make sure you have it right. Next, explain each of the entries in the equation. Make up a set of values for these items. Do your values indicate equilibrium or disequilibrium? If they show disequilibrium, will it tend to expand or to contract the economy? Why?

Headaches in the Economics of Inflation

The purpose of this essay is to encourage you, even this early in your study of economics, to think independently about some of the hard problems of inflation. Some of these problems are:

1. *When* is inflation? (supply shocks and monetary aftermaths)
2. *When* is inflation? (rationing, controls, and "suppressed inflation")
3. Do budget deficits cause inflation?
4. Does inflation keep interest rates down?
5. Does inflation break the "death grip" of past debts?
6. Would a restored gold standard solve the inflation problem?
7. Inflation, democracy, and the separation of powers.
8. Is inflation, after all, inevitable?

When Is Inflation? (Supply Shocks and Monetary Aftermaths)

We know from the history of supply shocks, notably the two OPEC oil shocks of the 1970s, that supply shocks run up the prices of a few key commodities, that monetary systems "accommodate" by increased money supplies, and that inflation spreads to the entire economy. But should we date the inflation from the supply shock or from the monetary accommodation? Did OPEC cause inflation or did the oil consumers bring it on themselves?

This is more than a terminological quibble. To see this, imagine a monetary system that did not (or could not) increase the money supply to accommodate to an oil shock. What would happen? In the short run, the result would surely be recession and inflation. The prices of crude oil and oil-intensive commodities like petro-chemicals would rise. No other price would fall. The measured price level would rise. There would be a money shortage with tight credit and high interest rates. There would surely be political-economic pressure to change the monetary system and accommodate the new and higher price level.

But if the authorities could resist this pressure, the non-oil commodity prices (and wages) would eventually fall. The price level would return to approximately its preshock level.[1] The permanent change would be confined to *relative* prices—those of oil and oil-intensive commodities would rise relative to the general price level, and the prices of non-oil commodities would fall.

This counterfactual scenario is not a policy prescription. (In America, the slowness and reluctance of monetary accommodation to the first oil shock is blamed for a recession in 1974–1975 and the failure of President Gerald Ford's bid for re-election in 1976.) It indicates only why many, if not most, economists date supply-shock inflations not from the shocks themselves but from the monetary accommodations to them.

When Is Inflation? (Rationing and Controls)

Imagine now a popular war, either a resistance to foreign aggression (as in World War II) or a "War on Poverty" at home, financed by monetary expansion. There are popular and well-enforced systems of price controls, wage and profit-margin controls, rationing and allocations, "incomes policies," or whatever one chooses to call them.[2] The measured price level does not rise. There is no measured inflation. People merely accumulate "undesired" hoards of cash, bank deposits, or government securities. These situations are called "suppressed" or "repressed" inflation, in contrast to the "open" inflation reflected in published price statistics.

---

1. If some international "monetary base" like the world gold supply were redistributed in favor of the OPEC countries, the price level of the non-oil countries would have to fall and OPEC policies would have brought on world *deflation!*

2. Alternatively, these controls could be enforced harshly by an authoritarian government, perhaps with death penalties for "economic crimes" like large-scale black-marketing.

The scenario continues. The war is won, or at any rate ended. The controls are lifted, or enforcement is curtailed. The price level rises. The suppressed inflation comes out of the closet and there is open inflation. Many economists (although not the general public) would include "suppressed inflation" as a form of inflation and date the inflation from the original resort to controls.

In a famous pamphlet called *How to Pay for the War,* Lord Keynes, the most famous economist of the twentieth century, anticipated in 1939 that the wartime expansion might be followed by a resumption of the Great Depression of the 1930s, which could itself be relieved (without inflation) by postwar spending of the balances accumulated in wartime. Had he been right, we might speak of suppressed inflation being followed by suppressed deflation or disinflation. But he was wrong, and no appropriate terminology ever developed.

Budget Deficits and Inflation

A budget deficit must be financed, but the financing need not be inflationary. Whether it is inflationary or not is a matter of political-economic decision.

The inflationary case is simple. The deficit is financed by monetary expansion, either openly (the printing press) or covertly (a central bank creating reserves that are used by commercial banks to create credits that are used to buy government securities). The inflation will originate not with the deficit, but with its financing method.

But a deficit need not be inflationary. There are at least two alternative financing methods that do not have inflationary consequences, either singly or in combination. The more common of these, and the more consistent with the market economy, is the sale of securities to the general public without the accompaniment of expanded bank reserves. The problems here are high interest rates, both real and nominal, and the "crowding out" of some private investment (or consumer credit). These effects may be exported by attracting capital from abroad and keeping at home domestic capital that might otherwise go abroad. In this case, foreign interest rates come under upward pressure and overseas investors are crowded out.

A less common form of noninflationary finance is the official or unofficial requirement that financial institutions—banks, savings and loan associations, insurance companies, investment houses—purchase the govern-

ment's debt at below-market interest rates. This method, in (Japanese) practice,[3] produces a credit squeeze on small business and agriculture, which are forced to save more, and in some cases to borrow at unrecorded and usurious interest rates from the criminal underworld.

Inflation and Interest Rates

We have mentioned that noninflationary financing methods raise interest rates. By the same token, the "easy money" of inflationary finance might be expected to lower them—whether the expansion is directed at financing a government deficit, business investment, or consumer credit. Yet we also know that in rapid inflation, long-term credit (if available at all!) commands astronomical interest rates. (The American prime rate reached over 20 percent in the Carter inflation of the late 1970s, and home mortgage rates went to about 17 percent.) How can we explain this paradox?

Economists' explanations involve the distinction between real and nominal interest rates, and also a "snapback" theory of the nominal rate.

The nominal rate of interest (i) is the rate directly observed in the marketplace. Let it be the sum of two elements: the real annual rate (r) that would prevail in a regime of long-term price-level stability and an added compensation (j) to the lender for the inflation rate expected during the year. (The money that is lent has higher purchasing power than that which is received in return.) In the simplest algebraic terms, we have

$$i = r + j$$

where j is zero in a stable-price regime and negative in a deflationary one.[4]

---

3. The method is more effective in Japan than elsewhere because a principal Japanese savings institution is a postal savings system whose investments are limited to public securities.

4. More precisely, we compute the total real return $(1 + r)$ as follows:

$$(1 + r) = (1 + i)(1 - j) = 1 + i - j - ij$$

so that, solving for (i):

$$i = \frac{r + j}{1 - j}$$

The $(1 - j)$ term may be important when (j) is large.

The snapback theory says that, at least in the early stage of an accelerating inflation, the expected inflation rate (j) lags behind the actual rate and is "too low." Monetary expansion can temporarily lower both (r) and (j), only to have them rise again, usually above their initial values, when "the market" (borrowers along with lenders) realizes what is going on.

The Dead Hand of the Creditor Class

A dollar invested at 6 percent compounded interest will grow according to the table below, with the end-value depending on the time period and the frequency of compounding.

According to this table, a dollar invested at the time of the Prophet Mohammed (let alone Jesus, Moses, the Buddha, or Adam and Eve) could now buy the entire real and personal wealth of "Spaceship Earth"! This is an extreme case of what has been called the dead hand of the creditor, rentier, or coupon-clipping class. Why do not people take more advantage of the vast economic bonanzas indicated by our little table? (A pocket calculator would suffice to flesh it out much further.) An obvious reason is the length of human life. The Biblical patriarch Methuselah of the Book of Genesis and the immortal Struldbruggs of *Gulliver's Travels* would surely have been more impressed than ourselves by such a table. In addition, preferences that various interest theorists have called time preference, agio, impatience, etc., have kept saving rates down.

One cannot help feeling, however, that fear of and experience with inflation, are important factors that have kept the creditor class small—and the dead hand of its power normally weak. The early Soviet economist Yevgeny Preobrazhensky compared the printing press of "War Communism" (1917–1918) to machine guns mowing down the coupon-clippers of the leisure or rentier class, by expropriating their wealth and incomes and forcing them to go to work. Nearly seventy years later, Northwestern University economist Robert Eisner suggested that in thinking about American budget deficits one should also consider the effect of inflationary financing on the real value of the national debt (and the economic power of individual and institutional bondholders).

Back to Gold?

The standard yardstick or meterstick itself has length. The standard pound weight or kilogram weight itself has weight. But what about the unit of monetary value? Should it not itself have value apart from its monetary use—as a dollar bill, for example, does not?

Such analogical thinking has been strong throughout the ages. The monetary reformer Irving Fisher warned in his *Purchasing Power of Money* that experiments with no-value "fiat" money always ended in runaway inflation. (The same argument also applied to paper money based on land values or tobacco or coonskins. As prices rose the prices of land or tobacco or coonskins rose too, offering bases for further monetary issues, and so proceeded *ad infinitum*.)

"Commodity" or "full-bodied" money has come to mean gold, or paper fully convertible with gold at some fixed price, because of its durability, uniformity, portability, and the limitation of its supply. The main thing wrong with the wampum of the American Indians was the ease with which enterprising British and Dutch colonists could augment its supply by counterfeiting. All over the world, the major defect of cattle, goats, and other livestock—our words "pecuniary," "impecunious," and "peculation" derive from the Latin word for cattle, presumably the exchange medium of the Romans' pre-

Time Period	Annual Compounding	Semi-annual Compounding	Continuous Compounding
10 years	1.791	1.806	1.822
20 years	3.207	3.262	3.320
50 years	18.420	19.219	20.086
2000 years	4.090×10^{50}	2.233×10^{51}	1.304×10^{52}

historic ancestors—was the lack of uniformity. Smart tradesmen try to palm off inferior specimens as standard "money," while retaining superior ones for food, hides, wool, breeding, etc.

In major inflations, a popular sport is to compute prices in terms of gold (or some foreign money convertible into gold). The arithmetic is simple. For example:

$$\frac{\text{"gold" price of a}}{\text{pound of fish}} = \frac{\text{paper price of a pound of fish}}{\text{paper price of an ounce of gold}}$$

During the period 1864–1879, during and after the American Civil War, such computation was unnecessary, as prices were quoted in both gold and "greenbacks." Much of the painful deflation of the 1870s was confined to greenback prices. As the probability of "resumption" (convertibility) increased; gold prices were largely immune to this deflation. During inflationary times, it is not unusual to find that the gold prices of many commodities have not risen above their preinflationary values. In many cases they will have fallen, as gold is a favorite inflation hedge. This naturally adds to the nostalgia or mystique of the gold standard.

It is sometimes inferred that a system that uses gold as money would not have inflation. In actual history, however, inflation has by no means been eliminated under gold standards (or other metallic standards). Counterfeiting, usually involving adulteration with heavy base metals (most often lead), was one inflation cause. It was engaged in by chancellors of the exchequer as well as by ordinary citizens and by alchemists professing to transmute lead into gold. (Had transmutation been successful, it could have been the end of the gold standard.) More common devices were "clipping" and "sweating"; the first involved shaving the edge off a coin's circumference, the second, shaking coins together vigorously to reduce their weight and give off gold dust, which constituted the revenue of the operation. If you look at contemporary American coins, you will see that the quarter and dime have milled edges (defenses against clipping) while the nickel and penny do not. Presumably it was decided at some past time that it was worth protecting the first two against clipping, but that nobody would bother to clip nickels or pennies. As defenses against sweating, pure gold and silver were replaced by alloys that were harder and more resistant to sweating. The two main sources of "gold inflation" have been:

1. Increases in the gold stocks of the Western world, either through conquest, as in Mexico and Peru, or through discovery, as in California, Australia, the Yukon, and the Transvaal.
2. Economies in the use of gold, through technological improvements in financing and banking. These permitted gold reserves to be reduced and increased the rapidity with which money could circulate. The use of bank checks and credit cards are examples.

The world's most massive gold inflation followed the conquest of Mexico and Peru by Spain in the sixteenth and seventeenth centuries. It was slow by contemporary standards—2 or 3 percent per year on average—but long-continued. It might have been much greater than it was but for (a) the European recovery after the Black Death and (b) the European taste for such luxuries as tea, coffee, sugar, spices, silk, porcelain, and cotton textiles. The Black Death (a succession of epidemics of bubonic plague during the fourteenth century) reduced the population of Western Europe by a quarter or a third, raising real wages as a result. Subsequent increases in the population and labor force seem to have kept wages down and thus reduced the inflation rate during the period of the gold inflow. At the same time, the European taste for Oriental luxuries, probably traceable to the earlier Crusades, caused a movement of monetary gold to India and China, where much of it was hoarded in nonmonetary forms like jewelry and ornamentation, thus disappearing from the money supply.

Inflation and Liberal Democracy

The political economy of inflation can be separated from the pure economics of the subject. Its basic questions are: Why do governments insist, despite the advice of financial experts, both on large-scale deficit financing and on financing their deficits increasingly by monetary expansion? If they know what to do, why don't they—why can't they—do it?

Historically, much of the blame has been put on democratic institutions, particularly on the extension of the suffrage to the propertyless, the debtors, and the recipients of public largesse. Mark Twain's recipe for political success in America was never voting for a tax or against an appropriation. (He might have added, never voting for tight money or against low interest rates.) This is supposedly an aspect of what some pessimistic political scientists have called "the increasing ungovernability" of populations under democratic regimes. It is supported by the success of armies of occupation in checking postwar inflations in the late 1940s, either by imposing financial stringency themselves (as in Japan) or by shielding disinflationary politicians from political reprisals (as in West Germany).

At first glance, of course, such pessimism makes little historical sense. The rise of parliamentary democracy in Western Europe and North America may be said to cover the century and a quarter between the French Revolution and World War I. But the great inflation of the recent past began a generation later, with the persistence of the "wartime" inflation of World War II into the peacetime generation that has followed it. (Mark Twain's denunciations of American congressmen and state legislators, for example, date from *deflationary* periods.)

There is, however, a pessimistic explanation of the delay. The rise of democracy was accompanied by what has been called a religion, or perhaps a superstition, of "sound money" backed primarily by gold and secondarily by silver. Inflationist movements—in America, the Greenbackers and the Populists—were reactions to deflations allegedly engineered on Wall Street. They faded as the deflation was reversed. As late as 1932, Franklin D. Roosevelt devoted an entire radio address to denying vile rumors that he was an enemy of the gold standard or that his election would endanger sound money. But within a year both Roosevelt and the American people had changed their minds. (The British, possibly influenced by Keynes, had already changed theirs!) The "religion of money" was no more. With the continued populist democracy of America and Europe, inflation followed from the resulting iconoclasm, godlessness, or agnosticism.

Another political economy argument, leading to similar conclusions, is about the separation of governmental powers into the executive (and administrative), the legislative, and the judicial branches. This application of eighteenth-century liberal political thought—Locke in England, Montesquieu in France, the American *Federalist* papers—allocated "the power of the purse" (increasing basic fiscal and financial control) to the legislative branch, Parliament or Congress. This was a natural reaction to the expensive dynastic warfare and courtly luxuries of such absolute monarchs as Louis XIV of

Mineworkers with gold bullion

France and Frederick the Great of Prussia. But after "one man (or woman), one vote" and the passing of the gold standard, a mixed bag of compassion, the pork barrel, log-rolling, and the welfare state supplemented (but did not replace) warfare and bureaucratic prerequisites as sources of public deficits and inflationary financing. It now has led to calls for the curtailment of legislative fiscal and financial powers.

Specimen proposals are easy to find: increased independence and de-politicizing of central banks; the "monetary rule" proposals of Milton Friedman and other monetarist economists to forestall excessive money creation; an "item veto" for the executive on appropriation bills—already in force in many American states; authorization of "impoundment powers" for the executive to interpret some or all appropriations as *permissions* rather than *requirements* to spend money.[5] In 1985 the U.S. Congress enacted the Gramm-Rudman Act to force

5. Impoundment powers were assumed in a small way by President Nixon in 1973–1974, without Congressional sanction. This action was promptly ruled *unconstitutional*.

automatic cuts in certain expenditure categories when budgetary deficits threatened, while exempting other categories. All these can be looked on as anti-inflationary measures or proposals.

Is Inflation Inevitable?

The secular trend of the price level has undoubtedly been upward. The imaginary dollar invested (in our little table) two thousand years ago would actually be worth not 1.304×10^{52} or 4.090×10^{50} or even \$1 today. Inflation (and war), like "drink and the devil" in *Treasure Island,* would have "done for the rest" meaning the whole thing. (The value today would almost certainly be zero anywhere in the world!)

This historical record has convinced many economists that inflation control is a lost cause, or at least, that any effective cure is necessarily worse than the disease. In this view it is enough to prevent run-away inflation.

But let us take a closer look at this strange eventful history of inflation. A long series of price indices for southern England from 1300 to the 1980s has been compiled by Ivor Pearce of the University of Southampton. He concluded that for the first five hundred years and more the level of prices showed no upward trend.[6] There were ups and downs, sometimes quite violent, but the recent U.S. experience of the doubling of prices in four to six years has only one precedent. This was a single great orgy towards the end of Henry VIII's reign. (Henry's experiments in monetary economics seem to have been no more successful than his better-known experiments in serial polygamy and domestic discipline.)

From this section and the last, it is hard to avoid the conclusion that some combination of political democracy (including frequent elections), the current model of the separation of powers, and the abandonment of the old-time "religion of money" for the contemporary religion of the welfare–warfare state has made inflation endemic, with occasional epidemics checked but never reversed.

6. Similarly, Sherman Maisel of the University of California at Berkeley has estimated that the 1939 level of wholesale prices in the United States was approximately the same as that at the close of the American Revolution in 1780.

III *Keynesian Economics and Fiscal Policy*

- The Keynesian Model
- The Multiplier and Business Fluctuations
- Fiscal Instruments

9 *The Keynesian Model*

PREVIEW Chapter 8 ended with the statement that neither equilibrium nor disequilibrium in itself is desirable or undesirable in the macroeconomy. They are simply useful economic concepts for economists to use in predicting future economic conditions. Now we will start our examination of how these equilibrium concepts can be used. In this chapter we look at the Keynesian school of thought, which provides a "demand-side" approach to macroeconomics. Later in the book, we will look at the monetarist and the supply-side approaches to these questions.

We begin this chapter by distinguishing demand-side from supply-side economics and by providing a brief sketch of the historical relationships between these approaches. With this background, we proceed to explain the Keynesian model of the macroeconomy. The model uses the four expenditure pathways (consumption, saving and investment, net taxes and government purchases, and imports and exports) that you studied in Chapter 8. We will show how the Keynesian approach develops the concept of total planned expenditure to predict the equilibrium level of national income and product for the economy.

Theories about what determines the equilibrium level of national income and product have been among the "hottest" topics in economics for a long time. Because the matter is not yet settled, it promises to stir up a great deal of debate in the future as well. No particular theory is likely to provide the last word on these matters. However, the Keynesian model has played a dominant role in macroeconomic thinking for the last half-century. It should be a basic component of your understanding of macroeconomics.

KEYNES AND NEOCLASSICAL ECONOMICS

The economic model presented in this chapter is, at its origin, the work of John Maynard Keynes, a British economist who was born in 1883 and died in 1946. He was a highly trained economist whose father, John Neville Keynes, was also a prominent economist. J. M. Keynes first came to widespread public notice when, as an adviser with the British delegation to the Versailles peace conference at the end of World War I, he predicted dire economic consequences from the reparations payments demanded of defeated Germany. He resigned from the peace delegation and wrote a book, *The Economic Consequences of the Peace*, which asserted that the economic terms of the peace treaty would damage the economies of Germany and other European countries and could lead to another war.

Keynes's major contribution to economic theory, however, came in his book *The General Theory of Employment, Interest, and Money*, which was published in 1936. In this book, he presented a theory suggesting that the equilibrium level of national income and product is determined primarily by the volume of expenditures planned by the various purchasing groups—consumers (households), investors (business firms), governments, and foreigners. His theory is called "demand-side" because it emphasizes the role of demand and leaves only a secondary role to suppliers and their ability to keep up with the demands of buyers.

Neoclassical Economics and Say's Identity

At the time that Keynes wrote the *General Theory*, most non-Marxist economists were of the neoclassical school of economic thought, which was and still is one of the mainstream approaches to macroeconomics. (You will learn more about this school of thought when you study monetarist and supply-side economics.) **Neoclassical economics** places great emphasis on the role of suppliers in determining macroeconomic equilibrium. During the Great Depression, when Keynes was writing his famous book, unemployment was very high and a great deal of attention focused on one particular proposition associated with the neoclassical approach.

This proposition, known as **Say's Identity,** is named after Jean Baptiste Say (1767–1832), a French economist whose *Treatise on Political Economy* appeared in 1803. The idea behind Say's Identity is that "supply creates its own demand." To understand this proposition, think back to the lower half of our circular-flow diagram—the flow made up of all wages, salaries, rents, interest, and profits in the economy.[1] According to Say's Identity, the sum of all these payments must, by definition, provide enough purchasing power to allow the households to pay for all the goods and services produced at whatever price level was in effect when they were produced. This balance would be true at any given price level.

Of course, neoclassical economists recognized that households would use some of their income for purposes other than consumption and that the proportion so diverted might change from time to time. But they argued that prices, wage rates, and interest rates would move up or down in accordance with market forces so that all funds would complete the circle. For example, if house-

holds spent less on consumption, the prices of goods would fall, so that unsold goods would not accumulate. At the same time, the additional money flowing through the saving, net tax, or import stream would automatically lead to responses that would ensure that these funds also would complete the circle. Greater saving would lower interest rates in the financial markets, so that businesses would plan to spend more on investment and households would plan to save less. Increased funds in the foreign markets would drive up the relative price of foreign goods, so that there would be fewer imports and more exports. Government budgets, which were expected to balance, would not keep the money from completing the circle. Of course, because of time lags in price changes and in responding to them, there could be temporary changes in economic activity. However, these time lags would be relatively short, so that problems would soon disappear.

Equilibrium at Full Employment

A very important conclusion of the neoclassical theory was that if the adjustment mechanisms worked effectively, full employment would be the normal equilibrium condition in an economy. Flexible wage rates were the basis for this conclusion. If people lost their jobs, they would offer to work for wages a little below the rate currently being paid. They would surely find work, since the wages paid would (by Say's Identity) be just enough to ensure demand for their goods or services at the lower price level that would result. The only people who could remain unemployed would be those refusing to work for a wage that matched the value of the goods that they could produce.[2] Neoclassical theory did not say that there would always be full employment. But the

---

1. See page 133 of Chapter 8.

2. This wage theory led to several doctrines with powerful social and political overtones. The so-called "iron law of wages" suggested that if population growth followed its "natural" course, wages would move toward subsistence levels. From ideas such as this, economics earned the "dismal science" label.

long-run tendency was for equilibrium to exist at full-employment levels of economic activity.

Keynes and Keynesian Economics

The Great Depression of the 1930s strained the neoclassical full-employment doctrine beyond acceptable limits. Debate still rages among economists about what caused unemployment to be so severe and to last so long during that period. Did the adjustment mechanisms of the neoclassical model no longer work? Had they ever really been effective? Some believe that these adjustment forces were simply too weak to cope with the particular problems of the time. Others feel that mistaken government policies interfered with the prompt operation of the neoclassical adjustment process. Had the evolution of big business and big labor prevented the changes in prices and wages needed to sustain full employment? Were Karl Marx's predictions about the collapse of capitalism proving to be correct? Keynes developed his theory because the neoclassical theories failed to explain persistent unemployment to his satisfaction. His basic model, as elaborated by later "Keynesian" economists, still is a major element in macroeconomic thinking, even though it has come under rather strong criticism in the 1970s and 1980s.

Keynesian economics challenges the neoclassical argument that changes in product prices, wage rates, and interest rates will accomplish the tasks assigned to them by the neoclassical economists. The challenge is two-pronged. First of all, prices, wage rates, and interest rates may in fact not change, or at least they may not change as quickly as the neoclassical economists believed. This argument is based on the view that modern economies do not follow competitive pricing practices. Businesses are not strongly pushed by their rivals to lower prices when sales volume drops, preferring to lay off workers while unplanned inventory is used up. Powerful labor unions are not willing to lower wage rates even when unemployment is widespread. The second Keynesian challenge is that changes in prices and wage

rates, when and if they do come, may not restore full employment. An economy that relies on the use of money might operate below its capacity indefinitely if no one could obtain the money needed to launch an expansion.

The genius of Keynes, however, was not that he raised important questions but that he offered a new theory to explain how the level of national income and product was determined. His new explanations, based on a study of consumer behavior, were eagerly accepted by those who were unhappy with the neoclassical theories. Today economists are again in a questioning mood, much as they were in the 1930s. The Keynesian prescriptions, which involve government spending to boost the economy, were energetically applied most of the time during the 1960s and 1970s, but still failed to yield satisfactory results. Unemployment and inflation occurred at the same time. It appeared that Keynesian analysis could not explain the resulting "stagflation," and Keynesian policy could not cure it.

This short historical summary gives you some background, or a frame of reference, for our study of the Keynesian theory of macroeconomic equilibrium. Looking next at each of the expenditure streams of the circular flow, we shall explore the basic Keynesian explanation for the equilibrium level of national income and product.

PLANNED CONSUMPTION EXPENDITURE

The behavior of consumers is at the heart of the Keynesian model of the macroeconomy. As you remember from the national income and product accounts in Chapter 7, consumption expenditure amounts to a large part of national income. It is clear, therefore, that relatively small changes in consumer spending can cause large proportional changes in the funds flowing through the other pathways of the circular flow. If households decide to spend a larger part of their income for consumption goods and services, the proportional impact of this change on the other pathways can be great. It is no surprise that Keynes focused great attention on consumption spending.

The Consumption Function

The key idea in Keynes's theory of consumer behavior is the **consumption function,** which is the relationship between the amount that households plan to spend to buy consumption goods and services and the level of disposable personal income. More specifically, economists say that the amount of planned consumption purchases (C) *depends on* the amount of disposable personal income (DPI). Thus, the consumption function can be written

$$C = f(\text{DPI})$$

For economists using the Keynesian system, the task is to determine precisely the nature of this relationship.

To illustrate how the Keynesian model works, let us specify some values for the consumption function equation and trace through the model. For example, suppose that the consumption function is

$$C = 100 + 0.75(\text{DPI})$$

where C is the annual dollar flow for planned consumption purchases and DPI is disposable personal income. We will assume that there is no inflation either taking place or expected, so that the consumption behavior of households is not distorted by misunderstandings (illusions) about real incomes or about the real prices of the things they buy. With these assumptions, we can state that the values for planned consumption expenditure and disposable personal income are *real* values. The importance of these assumptions will be clear later in the book, when we study the theory of inflationary expectations.

Table 9-1 illustrates how the consumption function in our example provides a set of planned consumption and disposable personal income combinations for an economy. Reading the table, we see that if disposable personal income is zero,

planned consumption expenditure is $100 billion. On the assumption that saving is the only alternative use of disposable personal income, it follows that households are obtaining the funds for their consumption purchases by reducing their savings accounts. So, when disposable personal income is zero, planned saving is −$100 billion.

If disposable personal income rises to $100 billion, the second term in our consumption function shows that planned consumption expenditure will rise by $75 billion to a total of $175 billion. But even at this higher level of income, households must fund part of their planned consumption spending from past saving. According to our consumption function, planned consumption expenditure will equal disposable personal income when DPI has reached $400 billion a year. If DPI is higher than $400 billion, planned consumption can be funded entirely from current income and there will be positive amounts of planned saving.

The Marginal Propensities to Consume and Save

The Keynesian theory has special names for the two numerical values that appear in the consumption function equation. The first value (the 100 in our illustration) is called **autonomous consumption expenditure,** meaning that this amount of planned consumption expenditure (C) is independent of the level of disposable personal income (DPI). The amount of autonomous consumption expenditure is determined by variables not included in the equation.

The second value in the equation (the 0.75 in our illustration) is called the **marginal propensity to consume (*MPC*)** because it shows how much planned consumption expenditure will change as a percentage of any change in the level of disposable personal income. In our equation, when disposable personal income increases by $100 billion, planned consumption expenditure increases by $75 billion, that is, by 75 percent of the change in DPI. Of course, the marginal propensity to consume (*MPC*) works in the opposite direction as well—when disposable personal in-

TABLE 9-1 Planned Consumption Expenditure and Planned Saving Related to Disposable Personal Income (in billions of dollars)

Disposable Personal Income (DPI)	Planned Consumption Expenditure (C)	MPC	Planned Saving (S)	MPS
$ 0	$100		$ – 100	
		0.75		0.25
100	175		– 75	
		0.75		0.25
200	250		– 50	
		0.75		0.25
300	325		– 25	
		0.75		0.25
400	400		0	
		0.75		0.25
500	475		25	
		0.75		0.25
600	550		50	
		0.75		0.25
700	625		75	
		0.75		0.25
800	700		100	
		0.75		0.25
900	775		125	
		0.75		0.25
1,000	850		150	

These hypothetical schedules show planned consumption spending and planned saving at different levels of disposable personal income. The illustrated intervals of DPI are $100 billion. Over each interval, planned consumption spending increases by $75 billion and planned saving increases by $25 billion. Therefore, $MPC = 0.75$ and $MPS = 0.25$.

come falls by $100 billion, planned consumption expenditure will fall by $75 billion. Thus, on the basis of the consumption function in our example, the marginal propensity to consume value in Table 9-1 is calculated as follows:

$$MPC = \frac{\text{change in planned consumption}}{\text{change in disposable personal income}}$$

$$= \frac{\$75 \text{ billion}}{\$100 \text{ billion}} = 0.75$$

In the Keynesian theory, the companion to the marginal propensity to consume is the **marginal propensity to save (MPS),** which is the change

in planned saving expressed as a percentage of the accompanying change in disposable personal income. If we assume that consumption and saving are the only uses for disposable personal income, the marginal propensity to save value in Table 9-1 is calculated as follows:

$$MPS = \frac{\text{change in planned saving}}{\text{change in disposable personal income}}$$

$$= \frac{\$25 \text{ billion}}{\$100 \text{ billion}} = 0.25$$

We have set up the illustration in Table 9-1 so that MPC is 0.75 and MPS is 0.25 throughout the

FIGURE 9-1   Consumption Function and Saving Function Based on Disposable Personal Income

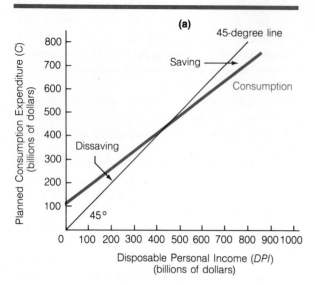

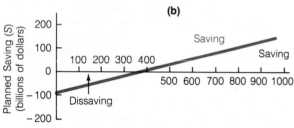

Panel (a) illustrates a consumption function with *MPC* = 0.75 and a breakeven income level of $400 billion. Panel (b) illustrates a saving function with *MPS* = 0.25 and a breakeven income level of $400 billion.

whole range of incomes shown. It is not essential to the theory that these values be constant over the whole range of incomes, but this is a reasonable assumption for an introductory explanation of the Keynesian model.

The Keynesian-Cross Graph

Figure 9-1a illustrates the consumption function on a Keynesian-cross graph.[3] Instead of price and

quantity on the axes, the **Keynesian cross** measures dollar quantities on each of its axes. The vertical axis measures dollars of planned consumption spending, and the horizontal axis measures dollars of disposable personal income. When disposable personal income is zero (at the origin of the graph), planned consumption spending is $100 billion (on the vertical axis), and when disposable personal income is $100 billion, planned consumption is $175 billion, and so on. The slope of the consumption function line (in Figure 9-1a) shows the marginal propensity to consume. (See Chapter 3 for measuring slope.) The slope here is 0.75 over the whole range of the consumption function. For this reason, a straight line describes the functional relationship.

On this graph, we also have drawn a straight line from the origin at a 45-degree angle. This **45-degree line** is very helpful because if the units of measure are the same on both axes, the line will connect all points at which the value on one axis is equal to the value on the other axis. The 45-degree line is helpful in another way as well. The vertical distance to the 45-degree line from any specified point on the horizontal axis is equal to the horizontal distance from the origin of the graph to that same point on the horizontal axis. So values measured horizontally from the origin can also be measured vertically by referring to the 45-degree line. In effect, both variables can be compared in the same vertical dimension on the graph. The geometry of isosceles right triangles explains why this is so.

In Figure 9-1a the consumption function crosses this 45-degree line at a DPI amount of $400 billion. This is the **breakeven point,** since there is neither planned saving nor planned **dissaving** (negative saving, or financing current consumption by drawing on past savings) at this income level. With the 45-degree line, we can show planned saving and dissaving on the same graph with the consumption function. The wedge-shaped gap between the consumption function and the

3. The Keynesian-cross graph should be distinguished from the supply-and-demand graph of Chapter 5. That graph is often called a Marshallian cross, after the great English neoclassical economist Alfred Marshall (1842–1924).

45-degree line, to the left of the intersection point (where the lines cross), shows planned dissaving. The wedge-shaped gap to the right of the intersection shows positive planned saving.

Figure 9-1b illustrates the saving function, drawn from the same hypothetical data. When disposable personal income is zero, planned saving is − $100 billion (dissaving). The slope of the saving function shows the marginal propensity to save (equal to 0.25 in this figure), and the planned amount saved is zero at an income of $400 billion, which is the breakeven point.

SHORT-RUN AND LONG-RUN CONSUMPTION FUNCTIONS

In explaining the consumption function, we have assumed that a change in real disposable personal income will lead to a change in planned consumption expenditure. That is, we have theorized that planned consumption expenditure will *respond to* changes in real DPI. How much response time should be allowed? Clearly, time is an important variable. If very little time is allowed, a change in DPI will bring very little change in planned consumption, the MPC will be very small, and the consumption function will have only a little slope. In this case, we shall have a **short-run consumption function.** A longer response time will permit a more complete response to the change in real DPI and a higher MPC until we reach a **long-run consumption function,** which allows enough time for all potential response to be realized. The long-run consumption function will be steeper.

It is clear that time is important for economists who use the Keynesian concepts for making forecasts or for prescribing economic policies. With enough time to adapt lifestyles to changing levels of real DPI, it appears that, in the aggregate, Americans choose to spend about 90 to 95 percent of their disposable personal income for consumption. Thus, the long-run marginal propensity to consume appears to be between 90 and 95 percent. However, in the Keynesian approach, unemployment and inflation are seen as problems that can be treated with short-run remedies. Although this idea is frequently challenged, we shall, in our exposition of the basic Keynesian theory, use the idea of the short-run consumption function.

THE PERMANENT INCOME HYPOTHESIS

The **permanent income hypothesis** is a statement about household consumption and saving behavior that is related to short-run and long-run perceptions of real income. According to this hypothesis, a household plans to spend for consumption a fixed proportion of the disposable personal income that it believes to be its "permanent," or long-run, income level. Changes in planned consumption spending are responses to changes in the perceived level of permanent income. A corollary of this idea is that income that is perceived as temporary or "transitory" is saved. The permanent income hypothesis places great emphasis on whether households see changes in DPI as permanent or transitory.

How does the permanent income hypothesis fit with our distinction between short- and long-run consumption functions? As real disposable personal income increases, households at first respond as if they believe that the increase is transitory. So, in the short run, the MPC is low and the MPS is high. However, as time passes, a greater part of the increased income flow is perceived to be permanent. The MPC rises and MPS falls. In the long run, the consumption function reflects basic attitudes about spending and thrift that are deeply embedded in the society itself.

Even though we shall be using short-run perspectives in explaining the Keynesian model for equilibrium national income, the permanent income hypothesis is a useful reminder that "perceptions" and "consumer psychology" are important in economics. For example, the question of whether a reduction in taxes would significantly increase consumer spending may depend on whether consumers expect that the reduction will be permanent or whether they expect that it will be only temporary. So changes in the basic tax structure would be more likely to affect the economy than a one-year cut or hike in taxes.

Taxes and the Consumption Function

The consumption and saving functions illustrated in Table 9-1 and Figure 9-1 were calculated on

TABLE 9-2 Planned Consumption and Saving Schedules Related to National Income and Product (in billions of dollars)

National Income and Product (Y)	− Net Tax	= Disposable Personal Income (DPI)	Planned Consumption Expenditure (C)	MPC	Planned Saving (S)	MPS
$ 100	$100	$ 0	$100		$ − 100	
				0.75		0.25
200	100	100	175		− 75	
				0.75		0.25
300	100	200	250		− 50	
				0.75		0.25
400	100	300	325		− 25	
				0.75		0.25
500	100	400	400		0	
				0.75		0.25
600	100	500	475		25	
				0.75		0.25
700	100	600	550		50	
				0.75		0.25
800	100	700	625		75	
				0.75		0.25
900	100	800	700		100	
				0.75		0.25
1,000	100	900	775		125	
				0.75		0.25
1,100	100	1,000	850		150	

All of the columns except those in the box at the left side are the same as in Table 9-1. The box at the left shows an amount of net tax ($100 billion) that does not change as a result of changes in the level of national income and product. Therefore, national income and product is uniformly $100 billion larger than disposable personal income.

---

the basis of disposable personal income. However, the concepts of net national product (NNP) and national income (NI), which you studied in Chapter 7, are more directly related to the macroeconomic problems of inflation and unemployment than is disposable personal income (DPI). Therefore, it will be helpful to adjust our consumption function so that it is based on national income and product rather than on disposable personal income. To make this adjustment, recall two points from the explanation of the national income and product accounts in Chapter 7. First, remember that national income and net national product are equal to each other conceptually,

even though the accounting system shows a difference due to indirect business taxes and subsidies and the statistical discrepancy. In explaining the Keynesian theory, we will ignore these differences and treat NNP and NI as identical. We will refer simply to national income or to national income and product and use the symbol Y to denote this value. Second, remember that taxes and transfer payments account for the difference between national income (Y) and disposable personal income (DPI). If we lump these items together in the concept of "net taxes" (as the term was used in the circular-flow model in Chapter 8), we can simply add an estimate of net taxes to our assumed value for disposable personal income to arrive at an estimate of national income and product.

In the United States, many different types of taxes are used—mainly individual income taxes, corporation income taxes, sales taxes, and property taxes. The combined effect of all these taxes may be roughly equivalent to a flat rate tax on all income. However, calculating net tax as a percentage of income adds complications that are not necessary in an elementary explanation of the Keynesian model. Therefore, in adjusting our consumption function from a disposable personal income base to a national income and product base, we will assume that the government collects a "lump-sum tax" of $100 billion, regardless of the level of national income and product.

Table 9-2 illustrates how the $100 billion lump-sum tax enables us to change the consumption function shown in Table 9-1 from a disposable personal income base to a national income and product base. Notice that all the columns except those in the box on the left side of the table are the same as in Table 9-1. The numbers in the box show that national income and product (Y) is higher than disposable personal income (DPI) by the amount of net tax, which we have assumed to be $100 billion at every level of national income and product.

Figure 9-2 illustrates our consumption and saving functions based on national income and product when the net tax is $100 billion, regardless of the level of national income and product. Note that the horizontal axis on each of the graphs in this figure is national income and product, which is a measure of macroeconomic activity that is more useful than disposable personal income in analyzing unemployment and inflation.

Because we have assumed that the amount of net tax is unchanged by the level of national income and product, the consumption function line in panel (a) and the saving function line in panel (b) have the same slopes as they did in Figure 9-1. The only difference is that these lines are located farther to the right by $100 billion (the amount of net taxes), since any given amount of planned consumption expenditure corresponds with a level of national income and product that

FIGURE 9-2 Consumption Function and Saving Function Related to National Income and Product

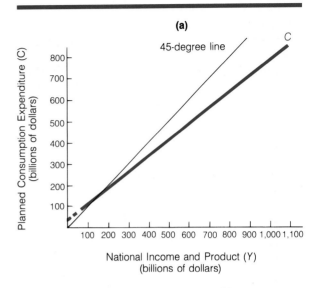

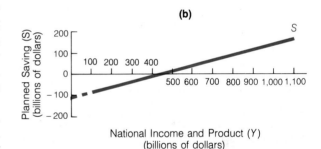

These graphs plot the data in Table 9-2 relating planned consumption expenditure and planned saving to national income and product. The consumption function, in panel (a), and the saving function, in panel (b), have the same slopes as in Figure 9-1, when they were plotted in relation to disposable personal income, because the difference between disposable personal income and national income is the amount of net tax, which is assumed to be $100 billion regardless of the level of national income and product. (The dashed segments of these plotted functions extend them to values not shown in Table 9-2.)

is $100 billion greater than the equivalent level of disposable personal income.

The graphs in Figure 9-2, with national income and product on their horizontal axes, will be used in the balance of our explanation of the Keynesian model. The reason for this is that the national income and product base provides a foundation that can be used to illustrate not only consumption expenditure, but also spending in the investment, government purchases, and net export pathways of the circular flow.

Shifting the Consumption Function

The level of income is not the only determinant of planned consumption and saving. Clearly, there are many other factors that influence these amounts. For example, if households are stocking up on durable goods (cars, appliances, and the like) after a period of shortages or hard times, planned consumption may be an especially large fraction of income. Also when financial wealth increases because of a rise in stock market prices, planned consumption may claim a higher fraction of income simply because households feel that they need not set aside as much of their current income as insurance against future financial problems. Expectations play an important role, too. When the outlook is promising, households may spend their incomes more freely than when they are fearful of bad times to come.

The list of nonincome variables that may influence planned consumption expenditure is very long. In the next chapter, we shall consider these matters in greater detail. For the moment, however, it is helpful to note that changes in these variables, indeed changes in *any* variable other than real national income and product, may cause *shifts* in the consumption function as illustrated in the Keynesian-cross graph. In Figure 9-2a, planned consumption expenditure (C) is the dependent variable and national income and product (Y) is the independent variable. Changes in the national income and product will cause *movements along* the consumption function line. But the consequences of changes in any other variable

will be represented by a relocation or *shift* of the line itself. Thus, all nonincome variables are shift variables in the Keynesian-cross graph. Shift variables will be emphasized in the next chapter.

PLANNED INVESTMENT EXPENDITURE

We proceed now to the saving–financial markets–investment pathway of the circular flow. Planned investment is very important in the Keynesian theory of national income determination. Planned investment expenditure is the amount of money that business firms intend to spend on new capital goods, such as machines, tools, and buildings, and to finance the inventories that they plan to have on hand.[4] The historical record suggests that planned investment probably is the most volatile or changeable component of total planned expenditure. We shall examine how the rate of interest influences planned investment spending and then we will note other influential variables. Finally, we will explain how planned investment expenditure is handled in the Keynesian model.

Planned Investment and the Rate of Interest

In a market-capitalist system, investment is made by firms for the purpose of earning profits. For each potential investment project, a business firm makes an estimate of the amount of money needed to obtain the capital good and the amount of income that it will generate. For example, suppose that a machine can be acquired for $1,000,

---

4. Our circular flow uses national income in its lower loop and net national product in its upper loop. Therefore, net investment expenditure is used rather than gross investment expenditure. This means that we do not include capital goods purchased as replacements for worn-out equipment. An explanation based on gross national product would, of course, include expenditures for replacing capital goods.

and that the firm's production cost will be $100 less per year using this machine than using the existing method of production. That is, it will reduce the firm's cost by $100 each year. If we assume, for simplicity, that the machine does not wear out and does not need repairs or maintenance, we can say that the rate of return on this investment is 10 percent. Should this investment project be carried out? Is it worthwhile for the firm to use its resources to acquire this machine? The answer will depend on the rate of return that this firm can realize from alternative uses of its resources.

The rate of interest prevailing in the financial markets is a measure of the rate of return that can be realized from alternative uses of funds. Therefore, the rate of interest plays a key role in the decision about whether the new machine should be acquired. If the rate of interest is, say, 8 percent, the company in the example just given could borrow $1,000 to acquire the machine and would pay $80 each year in interest to the lender. After the interest is paid, the firm would have $20 more profit each year because of the $100 cut in production cost. If the firm feels sure of this estimate, it will make the investment. If the interest rate had been 12 percent, so that annual interest payments would have been $120, the firm would not make the investment. Profits would be $20 less with the machine than without it.

Let us see how this illustration can be expanded to show a demand curve for planned investment for the whole economy. Instead of just one project with a rate of return of 10 percent, suppose that there are thousands of investment projects, some with rates of return greater than 10 percent and some with rates below 10 percent. Table 9-3 and Figure 9-3 show how these thousands of possible investment projects can be displayed as a planned-investment-demand curve. In this hypothetical illustration, $10 billion of possible investments are expected to yield rates of return of more than 14 percent. If the interest rate were 14 percent, all of these projects could be carried out profitably, and the amount of planned investment would be $10 billion (point A in Figure 9-3). An additional $2 billion of potential investment has an expected

TABLE 9-3 Demand Schedule for Planned Investment

Rate of Interest (percent)	Planned Investment (billions of dollars)
14	$10
12	12
10	17
8	25
6	35
4	48
2	70

Planned investment will be undertaken when the rate of return from the investment is expected to be greater than the rate of interest. In this hypothetical illustration, the planned-investment column shows the amount of investment that is expected to have a rate of return greater than the interest rate shown.

rate of return between 12 and 14 percent. If the interest rate were 12 percent, all of these projects plus the $10 billion of investment yielding more than 14 percent, would be undertaken, so that total planned investment expenditure would be $12 billion. (See point B in Figure 9-3.) The demand curve for planned investment suggests that the rate of interest is one of the determinants of the volume of planned investment.

Other Determinants of Planned Investment

The illustration in Table 9-3 and Figure 9-3 suggests that the rate of interest determines the volume of planned investment, *ceteris paribus,* that is, given the *location* of the planned-investment-demand curve. However, the location of this curve depends on many other factors, which can also be important in determining the volume of planned investment. These other factors receive great emphasis in the Keynesian theory. Let us look at a few of them. *Expected business conditions* can be significant. If firms expect sales

FIGURE 9-3   Demand Curve for Planned Investment

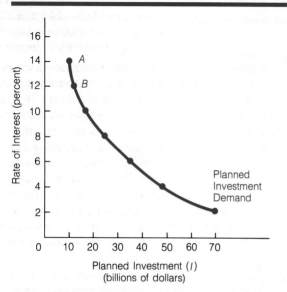

Firms will undertake planned investment if they expect the rate of return to be greater than the rate of interest. At lower rates of interest, other things being equal, more planned investment will be undertaken.

to increase, the expected rate of return on investments will probably be higher than if they expect sales to drop. The curve will shift to the right as optimism rises and to the left as pessimism grows. When a firm expects changes in the *cost of operating* some of its machines or equipment, the expected rates of return for different investment projects will be rearranged, and may cause the curve to shift. *Government policies* relating to taxation or regulation may be important. For example, if the president announces a major tax cut, the curve for planned-investment demand may shift to the right. On the other hand, laws calling for strict regulation of a major industry may shift the curve to the left. Also of great importance to the location of the planned-investment-demand curve are *technological changes*. A fast rate of technological change may offer substantial profit possibilities and shift the curve to the right, whereas a slowing rate of technological change may move the curve to the left.

Planned Investment in the Keynesian Model

How shall planned investment expenditure be built into the Keynesian model? In building planned consumption into the model, the key proposition was the consumption function, which showed a relation between planned consumption expenditure and disposable personal income. What relationship exists between planned investment and national income and product? It is most likely that planned investment expenditure also has some positive relation to the level of national income and product. However, building such a relationship into an elementary explanation of the Keynesian system adds unnecessary complications. In our explanation, we will assume that planned investment expenditure is $35 billion regardless of the level of national income and product. In other words, we assume a planned investment function of

$$I = \$35 \text{ billion}$$

This states that planned investment expenditure is determined entirely by autonomous variables, that is, by variables other than the level of national income and product.

The Keynesian approach to macroeconomic equilibrium emphasizes the importance of non-income variables in determining the volume of planned investment expenditure. The interest rate is very important, as are such other variables as expectations about future business conditions, costs of operating capital goods, government policies, technological changes, and so on. They are built into the Keynesian model as autonomous variables, that is, as changes in planned investment that are not caused by changes in the level of national income and product.

GOVERNMENT PURCHASES

Fitting government purchases into the Keynesian model raises many of the same questions considered in our explanation of planned investment expenditure. Once again it is customary and convenient to assume a government-purchases function in which the amount of these purchases is independent of the level of national income and product. We will assume a government-purchases function of

$$G = \$100 \text{ billion}$$

As with our assumed investment function, it probably is unrealistic to assume that the annual volume of government purchases is unrelated to the level of national income and product. In practice, government purchases probably are positively related to the level of national income and product. Nevertheless, in this introduction to the Keynesian system, we will assume that government purchases do not vary as a direct result of changes in the level of national income and product.

There are, of course, many nonincome variables that can influence the volume of government purchases and that are very important in the Keynesian system. These include government policies, domestic and world conditions, the attitudes of voters and taxpayers, and so on. In the Keynesian approach, the policy position taken by the government to deal with the macroeconomic problem of unemployment is especially important. As you recall, the neoclassical approach argued against active government intervention in the economy. Keynes, on the other hand, suggested that government should take forceful action to bring the economy out of the Great Depression.

IMPORTS AND EXPORTS

The import-export path in the circular flow remains to be studied. Again, building this pathway into the Keynesian model raises the question of how the volume of imports and exports (or "net exports") will respond to changes in the level of national income and product.

American purchases from foreigners (imports), like purchases of domestic goods, can be expected

to increase as income rises. The reasoning is the same as that offered for private planned consumption and for government purchases. Imported goods are probably "normal" in their relation to income. However, purchases by foreigners from Americans (exports) are less likely to show a predictable response to changes in the U.S. national income and product. Instead, they respond to income changes in the foreign countries themselves, or to changes in foreign exchange rates (which we cover in Chapter 18).

When we combine imports and exports to arrive at a relationship between "net exports" and national income and product, the normal goods assumption suggests that net exports are a declining function of national income and product. That is, net exports grow smaller as national income and product rises, because *gross* exports will remain the same while *gross* imports grow larger as U.S. national income rises. Americans *will* be buying more from foreign countries, but foreigners will *not* necessarily be buying more from the United States.

In our explanation of the Keynesian model, we assume a net export function of

$$X - Im = \$15 \text{ billion}$$

meaning we assume that the net amount of purchases by foreigners is unrelated to the level of U.S. national income and product and that changes in this amount are determined by autonomous variables. This is the same approach that we have used for incorporating planned investment and government purchases into the Keynesian system. Although reality suggests a more complicated functional relationship, these complications can be left to more advanced courses in economics.

Graphic Illustration of Planned Investment Expenditure, Government Purchases, and Net Exports

Figure 9-4 presents a graph illustrating the assumptions we have made about planned investment expenditure, government purchases, and

FIGURE 9-4 **Planned Investment Expenditure, Government Purchases, and Net Exports**

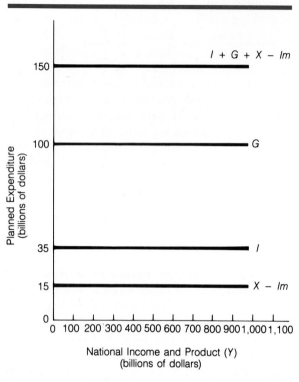

Each of these streams of planned expenditure is assumed to be unchanged by the level of national income and product. Net exports are assumed to be $15 billion per year, planned investment expenditure is assumed to be $35 billion per year, and government purchases are assumed to be $100 billion per year. When these three spending streams are added together, they constitute the curve labeled $I + G + X - Im$, at $150 billion a year. (Since the scaling is not the same on the two axes, we do not construct a 45-degree line on this graph.)

net exports. The horizontal axis shows the level of national income and product (Y). Planned expenditure is measured on the vertical axis. The bottom horizontal line labeled $X - Im$ shows that net exports are assumed to be $15 billion a year regardless of the level of national income and product. The next higher horizontal line is labeled I and shows that planned investment expenditure is assumed to be $35 billion a year. The next higher line (G) shows government purchases at $100 billion a year. The top line shows the com-

bined total of planned investment expenditure (I), government purchases (G), and net exports ($X - Im$), and is labeled $I + G + X - Im$.

In order to make the graph easier to read, we have used a larger scale on the vertical axis than on the horizontal axis. Because of the different scaling on the two axes, we do not draw a 45-degree line on this graph. Illustrating planned investment expenditure, government purchases, and net exports graphically and showing how they can be added together lays the foundation for the next step in the Keynesian model—the determination of macroeconomic equilibrium by the total-planned-expenditure method.

EQUILIBRIUM NATIONAL INCOME

So far, we have studied the four spending streams that make up total planned expenditure. We have given them numerical values so that we can show a functional relationship between national income and product and total planned expenditure. In doing so, we shall, in turn, discover the equilibrium level for national income and product according to the Keynesian model.

Table 9-4 brings together all four components of planned expenditure. The columns for national income and product and for planned consumption expenditure are the same as those in Table 9-2. The next three columns—planned investment, government purchases, and net exports—illustrate our assumptions that these spending streams are not altered, in the short run, by changes in national income and product. We assume $35 billion of planned investment, $100 billion of government purchases, and $15 billion of net exports regardless of the level of national income and product. The last column in Table 9-4 shows the total planned expenditure corresponding to each level of national income and product, that is, $C + I + G + X - Im$. Some economists devote a great deal of effort to finding accurate values based on experience for these relationships. However, simply for introducing you to the theory, these hypothetical numbers are convenient.

TABLE 9-4 Total Planned Expenditure (in billions of dollars)

(1) National Income and Product (Y)	(2) Planned Consumption Expenditure (C)	(3) Planned Investment Expenditure (I)	(4) Government Purchases (G)	(5) Net Exports (X − Im)	(6) Total Planned Expenditure (C + I + G + X − Im)
$ 100	$100	$35	$100	$15	$ 250
200	175	35	100	15	325
300	250	35	100	15	400
400	325	35	100	15	475
500	400	35	100	15	550
600	475	35	100	15	625
700	550	35	100	15	700
800	625	35	100	15	775
900	700	35	100	15	850
1,000	775	35	100	15	925
1,100	850	35	100	15	1,000

Columns 1 and 2 repeat data from Table 9-2. Columns 3, 4, and 5 illustrate our assumptions that the planned investment, government purchases, and net export spending streams are not altered, in the short run, by changes in national income. Column 6 shows the total of columns 2 through 5. Equilibrium exists when total planned expenditure equals national income and product ($700 billion).

Total-Planned-Expenditure Method

From the values in Table 9-4, you can see that the conditions for equilibrium exist when national income and product is $700 billion. For income levels of *less* than $700 billion, total planned expenditure is greater than production, so that inventories go down. As you learned from the circular flow, this is a case in which pressures arise for greater production and/or higher prices in the next production period. On the other hand, for all income levels *greater* than $700 billion, total planned expenditure is less than production. So unplanned inventory piles up, and there are pressures to lower production and/or prices in the next period. Only at a national income and product level of $700 billion are production and total planned expenditure equal. Here we have the condition for equilibrium national income and product. If we let the symbol Y^* represent the equilibrium level of national income and product, we can state this equilibrium condition as

$$Y^* = C + I + G + X - Im$$

This equation states that the equilibrium level of national income and product is determined by total planned expenditure.

Figure 9-5 shows this relationship as a Keynesian cross. National income and product appears on the horizontal axis and planned expenditure on the vertical axis. The consumption-function line (C) is the same as in Figure 9-2. Total planned expenditure is represented by the line labeled $C + I + G + X - Im$. This line lies above the consumption-function line by the amount of the other expenditure streams—planned investment (I), government purchases (G), and net exports (X − Im). The total-planned-expenditure line $(C + I + G + X - Im)$ is parallel with the consumption-function line because we have assumed that each expenditure stream other than planned consumption is independent of the level of national income and product, that is, each is assumed to be autonomous.

The total-planned-expenditure line $(C + I + G + X - Im)$ crosses the 45-degree line at the $700 billion level of national income and product. This intersection point identifies the equilibrium

FIGURE 9-5   Macroeconomic Equilibrium Illustrated on a Keynesian-Cross Graph

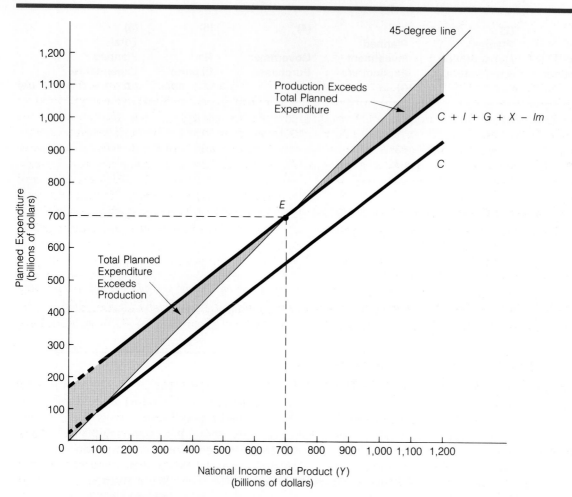

Planned consumption expenditure (C) is the same as in Figure 9-2. Planned investment expenditure (I), government purchases (G), and net exports (X − Im) are the same as in Figure 9-4, but here they are added on top of the planned-consumption-expenditure line to show the total-planned-expenditure line C + I + G + X − Im. Macroeconomic equilibrium is at E, where total planned expenditure of $700 billion equals national income and product of $700 billion. At lower levels of national income and product, total planned expenditure exceeds production and inventories are drawn down, generating pressures for expansion. At national income and product levels above $700 billion, production exceeds total planned expenditure so that excess inventories accumulate, generating pressures for contraction of the economy. (The dashed lines extend to include data not shown in tables.)

condition (E). To the left of this intersection, total planned expenditure is greater than production, as shown by the colored space between the $C + I + G + X - Im$ line and the 45-degree line. So inventories are driven down, and pressures for expansion are generated. To the right of the intersection point, total planned expenditure is less than production. Unplanned inventory begins to pile up, and there are pressures to lower production and/or prices in the next period. Only at a national income and product level of $700 billion is there a balance among the opposing forces such that there is no tendency for change—that is, equilibrium.

It is important to remember that, in the Keynesian model, equilibrium is not necessarily a "good" situation for the economy. Serious unemployment may exist, or the economy may be plagued by persistent inflation. All we are saying here is that the economy will tend to move toward its equilibrium situation. Whether that situation is good or bad and whether something should be done to change the equilibrium point are matters of public policy.

Leakage-and-Injection Method

The Keynesian approach can also explain the equilibrium level of national income and product by using the concepts of **leakages** and **injections** that were described in Chapter 8. As you remember, leakages are household uses of funds for other than consumption purchases. That is, leakages consist of saving (S), net taxes (T_n), and imports (Im). Injections are planned expenditures other than consumption purchases, that is, planned investment, government purchases, and exports. Because imports are separated from exports in this analysis, investment and government purchases include only purchases of domestic (home) outputs. Thus, our notation for injections is that government purchases are G_d and planned investment expenditure is I_d. With these definitions,

TABLE 9-5   Injections and Leakages (in billions of dollars)

National Income and Product (Y)	Injections					Leakages				
	I_d	+ G_d	+ X	= Total		S	+ T_n	+ Im	= Total
$ 100	$35	$100	$25	160		$-100	$100	$10	$ 10
200	35	100	25	160		- 75	100	10	35
300	35	100	25	160		- 50	100	10	60
400	35	100	25	160		- 25	100	10	85
500	35	100	25	160		0	100	10	110
600	35	100	25	160		25	100	10	135
700	35	100	25	160		50	100	10	160
800	35	100	25	160		75	100	10	185
900	35	100	25	160		100	100	10	210
1,000	35	100	25	160		125	100	10	235
1,100	35	100	25	160		150	100	10	260

The hypothetical values for planned domestic investment (I_d) and government domestic purchases (G_d) are taken from Table 9-4. Exports (X) are assumed to be constant at $25 billion. Values for planned saving (S) and net taxes (T_n) are taken directly from Table 9-2. Imports (Im) are assumed to be constant at $10 billion. Equilibrium exists when total injections equal total leakages so that they offset each other. Notice that equilibrium does not require a balance in each separate stream of the circular flow. In this illustration, planned saving exceeds planned domestic investment at equilibrium, but there is an excess of exports over imports.

macroeconomic equilibrium exists when planned injections equal planned leakages, that is, when

$$I_d + G_d + X = S + T_n + Im$$

Table 9-5 provides hypothetical values for injections and leakages related to various levels of national income and product. We have used the same values that were used to explain the total-planned-expenditure method. This means that we assume that the investment and government purchases discussed there were all from domestic producers and that all imports were household purchases of consumption goods and services.

In Table 9-5, the injections columns for planned domestic investment (I_d) and for government domestic purchases (G_d) are taken directly from Table 9-4. For the other injection, exports (X), we use a constant value of $25 billion. In the leakages section, the numbers for planned saving and net taxes are taken directly from Table 9-2, which showed our saving function and net taxes equal to $100. For imports (Im), we use a constant $10 billion in our example. We realize that it is unrealistic to assume that changes in national income do not change imports, but we make this assumption to simplify our explanation of the Keynesian system. Of course, exports of $25 billion minus imports of $10 billion equal our net export figure of $15 billion.

Macroeconomic equilibrium exists when total leakages equal total injections, so that they offset each other. This occurs when they are both equal to $160 billion, when national income and product is $700 billion. This equilibrium point is shown at E in Figure 9-6, where the lines for injections $(I_d + G_d + X)$ and leakages $(S + T_n + Im)$ cross. At national income and product levels of less than $700 billion, total injections are greater than total leakages. So inventories are driven down below the desired levels, and there are pressures to raise production and/or prices in the next period. But when national income and product levels are higher than $700 billion, total leakages are greater than total injections, inventories become larger than desired, and pressures grow to lower production and/or prices. Note, however, that it is not necessary to have a balance in each

separate stream of the circular flow. In our illustration of equilibrium, saving exceeds domestic investment, but exports exceed imports.

You should be warned of possible confusion in comparing the injection–leakage approach with the planned-expenditure approach. The problem arises because of the different ways of treating imports. Using the injection–leakage approach, we record imports as a leakage and exports as an injection. However, when we use the planned-expenditure approach, we combine the two as "net exports." In terms of our graphs, the wedges shown for total planned expenditure in Figure 9-4 are *not* the same as the wedges for injections and leakages in Figure 9-5. Since we believe it is easier to understand and more directly related to policy making, we shall depend mainly on the total-planned-expenditure method rather than on injections and leakages.

KEYNESIAN VERSUS NEOCLASSICAL EQUILIBRIUM

The idea of equilibrium national income and product is at the heart of both the neoclassical and the Keynesian theories. Each of them views equilibrium as a state of balance among opposing forces such that there is no tendency for change. Also, both suggest that the economy will tend to move toward a state of equilibrium from any nonequilibrium situation. In terms of the Keynesian theory, inventories that are too large or too small lead to the responses that push the economy in the direction of equilibrium. In the neoclassical view, disequilibrium conditions lead to changes in wage rates, prices of goods, interest rates, and foreign exchange rates, and these changes move the economy back toward a state of equilibrium.

The main difference between the Keynesian and the neoclassical view is the latter's prediction that, in the long run, equilibrium will exist at full-employment levels, whereas the Keynesian theory offers no such prediction. In the Keynesian view, spending propensities are related to the level of national income itself, and the equilibrium

FIGURE 9-6   **Macroeconomic Equilibrium Illustrated on a Leakages-and-Injections Graph**

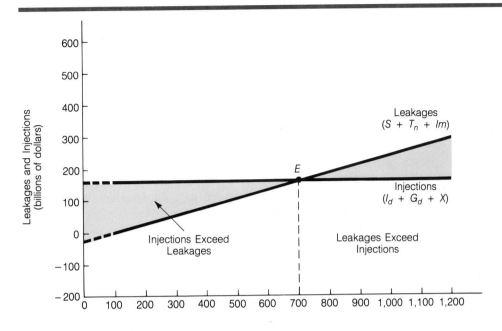

National Income and Product (Y)
(billions of dollars)

Values from Table 9-5 are plotted on this graph. The injections line $(I_d + G_d + X)$ is horizontal, reflecting the assumption that none of these values changes because of a change in national income and product. The leakage line $(S + T_n + Im)$ has a positive slope equal to the marginal propensity to save, since net taxes (T_n) and imports (Im) are assumed to be unchanged by changes in the level of national income and product. Equilibrium is at E, where injections are equal to leakages, and national income and product is $700 billion. To the left of E, injections exceed leakages, reducing inventories below desired levels and generating pressures for expansion of the economy. To the right of E, leakages exceed injections so that inventories become larger than desired, generating pressures for contraction of the economy. (The dashed lines extend to include data not shown in Table 9-5.)

level of national income and product need not correspond to full employment.

Keynes offered a theory that seemed to explain why very high rates of unemployment could last so long during the Great Depression. He also suggested ways in which the equilibrium level could be changed to match policy goals. So it is not surprising that many economists and political activists eagerly accepted Keynes's ideas. In the chapters to come, you will learn more about the Keynesian theory of how equilibrium levels of national income and product can be changed and about the role of government in these changes.

SUMMARY

1. The Keynesian approach to macroeconomic equilibrium was presented by the British economist, John Maynard Keynes, in his book, *The General Theory of Employment, Interest, and Money,* which appeared in 1936.

2. Prior to the theory of Keynes, the neoclassical school of economic thought offered the theory that flexibility of prices, wage rates, and interest rates by responding to changes in supply and/or demand would assure that the economy would move toward macroeconomic equilibrium at full employment and that periods of severe macro-economic unemployment would be brief.

3. Say's Identity, which asserts that supply creates its own demand at any given price level, is a view commonly associated with the neoclassical approach to macroeconomic equilibrium.

4. The Keynesian theory uses the concept of the consumption function, which is a relationship between the level of disposable personal income and the amount of planned consumption expenditure in the economy. The marginal propensity to consume (MPC) expresses a relationship between changes in the level of disposable personal income and changes in the amount of planned consumption expenditure. Autonomous consumption expenditure is the amount of planned consumption spending that would take place if disposable personal income were zero.

5. The value of the marginal propensity to consume is smaller if only a little time is allowed for households to respond to income changes than when more time is allowed. The permanent income hypothesis states that people save increments to their income that they believe to be temporary or "transitory." As more time passes after a change in level of income, a larger part of the change is seen as "permanent" and available for expenditure on consumption.

6. Saving is also a function of disposable personal income. The marginal propensity to save (MPS) is the relation between changes in disposable personal income and changes in planned saving.

7. The Keynesian cross is a graph that displays income on its horizontal axis and planned expenditure on its vertical axis. A 45-degree reference line is drawn from the origin of the Keynesian-cross graph.

8. Adjustments for taxes allow consumption and saving functions to be calculated on a basis of national income and product rather than on a basis of disposable personal income.

9. Planned investment expenditure is an important component of the Keynesian theory. The rate of interest is a determinant of planned investment expenditure, as are also various considerations that affect business expectations about the profitability of investments. Government purchases and net exports also are important components of the Keynesian "demand-side" theory.

10. Total planned expenditure combines all streams of planned spending. Macroeconomic equilibrium exists when total planned expenditure equals national income and product, as indicated by the equation $Y^* = C + I + G + X - Im$. According to the Keynesian theory, this equilibrium need not correspond with full employment.

11. If national income and product is greater than total planned expenditure, inventories become larger than desired by business firms, leading them to reduce prices and/or output, thus lowering the level of national income and product. If national income and product is less than total planned expenditure, inventories will fall below the levels desired by business firms, leading them to increase prices and/or output, thus causing national income and product to rise.

12. The leakage-and-injection method is an alternative way of explaining the Keynesian theory. Injections are planned expenditures other than consumption and leakages are household uses of funds other than for the purchase of domestically produced consumption goods and services. Macroeconomic equilibrium exists when total planned leakages and total planned injections are equal.

DISCUSSION QUESTIONS

1. Explain how Say's Identity provides a basis for arguing that an economy will naturally tend to operate at full employment. If planned saving temporarily exceeds planned investment, how, according to the neoclassical theory, would interest rates change? What would be the effect of this change? What is the macroeconomic role of the government budget in the neoclassical theory?

2. Keynes challenged the neoclassical macroeconomic theory by claiming that prices, wage rates, and interest rates actually do not change as quickly as the neoclassical economists believed. Describe one current government policy or program that relates to these adjustments. Does this policy or program strengthen or weaken the neoclassical adjustment mechanism?

3. If planned consumption spending increases by $80 billion whenever disposable personal income increases by $100 billion, what is the value of the marginal propensity to consume? What is the value of the marginal propensity to save? Given these values, what will be the breakeven level of disposable personal income if planned consumption spending is $50 billion when disposable personal income is zero?

4. If real disposable personal income in the United States goes up by $100 billion and enough time passes so that the long-run consumption function can be effective, by about how much would planned consumption spending increase? How would this increase differ if a much shorter time period were being used? Explain the reasons for your answer.

5. According to the permanent income hypothesis, what do people do with an increase in income that they view as only temporary? If you were to win a large amount of money in a lottery, how much of your winnings would go to a higher day-to-day level of living and how much would go into your savings account or to purchase something special that you had wanted for a long time? How much of that something special would be used up during the first year?

6. Without looking at Figure 9-3, draw the demand curve for planned investment, carefully labeling the variables shown on each axis. Now compare your graph with Figure 9-3 to be sure you have it right. How does the rate of return on a particular investment project determine its position along this demand curve? Name one change that would shift this curve to the left and one that would shift it to the right.

7. The assumption that in the short run government purchases do not change in response to changes in national income and product is useful to simplify the presentation of the Keynesian theory. However, the assumption does allow government purchases to change in response to policy actions. Explain whether this change should be shown as a shift or as a movement along a government-purchases curve graphed on a Keynesian-cross diagram.

8. In this chapter, total planned expenditure was $175 billion when national income was zero and the marginal propensity to consume was 0.75. Under these conditions, equilibrium national income and product would be $700 billion. If equilibrium national income and product is Y^*, we can say that $Y^* = 175 + 0.75Y^*$. Solve this equation for Y^* to assure yourself that it works. Then test your understanding by assuming that the marginal propensity to consume is 0.80. What would the equilibrium national income and product be in that case?

9. The Keynesian equilibrium described at the end of this chapter differs sharply from the neoclassical theory on the matter of unemployment. Explain the nature of this difference. Why was this difference important in the economic and political climate of the Great Depression?

10 *The Multiplier and Business Fluctuations*

PREVIEW   What good is all this analysis? Can it tell us anything about what caused the Great Crash of 1929 or about the possibility of it happening again? These are the questions that this chapter tries to answer. We begin with a description of how the basic Keynesian theory helps us to understand the "ups and downs" that characterize the performance of modern industrial economies. The concept of equilibrium that you studied in the last chapter is applied to explain these fluctuations. The key idea is that the equilibrium level of national income and product may change from time to time as a result of changes in the volume of planned expenditure. We begin by examining the theory—how changes in planned expenditure change the equilibrium level of national income and product and how the economy responds to these changes. In this part of the chapter, we are especially interested in the *multiplier* effect that is involved in the response process. The multiplier is a very useful tool in understanding business cycles and fluctuations.

Many events or circumstances can change the level of planned expenditure. Is there reason to expect that these events will occur regularly enough for business *cycles* to appear? Are there certain dynamic properties in the functioning of the economy that give a regularity to cyclical patterns? In the second part of the chapter, we try to answer these questions. We present the historical record and then explore the anatomy of business cycles. By using a simple model that combines the multiplier and the *accelerator* effects, we can explain, in part, the cumulative phases and the turning points of business cycles.

Finally, we note the human, social, and political aspects of economic fluctuations and cycles. Do cycles cause hardships that are serious enough to justify the policies used to moderate them? Are the fluctuations connected closely with innovations and "progress" in market-capitalist economic systems? Are these fluctuations a sign that the capitalist system will collapse as Marx predicted? Are they becoming worse? These questions and our analysis in this chapter pave the way for the next chapter, which looks at some of the instruments that governments can use to influence economic fluctuations.

THE MULTIPLIER

The **multiplier** plays an important role in the Keynesian explanation of economic fluctuations. Its basic idea is that a relatively small change in one part of the economy can lead to a great change in the total national income and product. In other words, the small change is multiplied in producing the large change.

To develop the multiplier theory, we must return to the idea of the total-planned-expenditure ($C + I + G + X - Im$) schedule presented in Chapter 9. Table 9-4 and Figure 9-5 showed how total planned expenditure is related to the level of national income and product. In our discussion, we emphasized that many variables influence each component—planned consumption spending, planned investment, government purchases, and net exports. But the only variable that we changed was the level of national income and product itself. The other variables were frozen by a *ceteris paribus* assumption. With all other variables held constant, we examined the marginal propensities to consume and to save. We showed that macroeconomic equilibrium would exist when total planned expenditure was equal to national income and product.

Now it is time to unfreeze the other variables, that is, to allow changes in variables other than national income and product. Our methodology tells us that we shall now be looking at *shifts* in the $C + I + G + X - Im$ curve rather than at movements along that curve.

Shifting Total Planned Expenditure

It helps to know some of the variables that economists think are important in explaining fluctuations. Therefore, we begin our analysis with a brief review of some nonincome variables that can influence planned expenditure. A change in any of these variables may *shift* the $C + I + G + X - Im$ curve.

Some of the nonincome variables that can influence planned consumption expenditure are household stocks of durable goods already owned, real financial wealth such as stocks, bonds, and savings accounts, and expectations about whether good or bad times are in store.

Economists predict that planned investment expenditure by firms will be influenced by the rate of interest and by all the forces that bear upon estimates of the rate of return that will come from investment projects. Among these variables are anticipated business conditions, expected changes in operating costs (especially wages), anticipated changes in taxes and government regulations, new technologies, and a host of other matters.

The government-purchases component can rise or fall when government policies change. Changes in planned expenditure initiated by government will be the focus of Chapter 11.

Finally, the net-export component of planned expenditure may change because of changes in the relative prices of foreign goods and in foreign exchange rates. It may also be affected by changes in economic conditions in the foreign countries themselves.

Changing Equilibrium

Let us assume that one of the nonincome variables changes and brings about a shift in the $C + I + G + X - Im$ curve. How will this shift affect the equilibrium level of national income and product?

Suppose that someone discovers a new process to lower the cost of extracting fuel from a type of rock called oil shale. Let us imagine that this discovery convinces business firms to increase the flow of planned investment expenditure by $50 billion each year at all levels of national income and product. We realize that this is an extremely large increase compared with the other values in our hypothetical illustration. The large size will make it easier to show changes in graphic form. Because the discovery gives business people great hopes for profits, the demand curve for planned investment spending, such as the curve in Figure 9-3 on page 166, shifts to the right by $50 billion. At any specified rate of interest, planned investment is $50 billion greater than it was before the change in business outlook brought about by the discovery. To keep things simple, we assume that this is the only change that takes place.[1] Let us see how this change alters the equilibrium level of national income and product according to the theory presented in Chapter 9.

In Table 10-1, we reproduce Table 9-4 but increase every entry in the planned-investment-expenditure column by $50 billion, since we

1. Of course, we realize that a rise in the demand for investments may change the rate of interest and that many other related changes will take place. If we were presenting a *general equilibrium* model, we could not allow ourselves the simplifying assumption that planned investment is the only thing that changes. However, at this stage, we shall use *partial* analysis for simplicity.

TABLE 10-1 Increased Planned Expenditure and Equilibrium National Income and Product (in billions of dollars)

(1) National Income and Product (Y)	(2) Planned Consumption Expenditure (C)	(3) Planned Investment Expenditure (I)		(4) Government Purchases (G)	(5) Net Exports (X − Im)	(6) Total Planned Expenditure (C + I + G + X − Im)	
		Original	New			Original	New
$ 100	$100	$35	→ $85	$100	$15	$ 250	→ $ 300
200	175	35	→ 85	100	15	325	→ 375
300	250	35	→ 85	100	15	400	→ 450
400	325	35	→ 85	100	15	475	→ 525
500	400	35	→ 85	100	15	550	→ 600
600	475	35	→ 85	100	15	625	→ 675
700	550	35	→ 85	100	15	700	→ 750
800	625	35	→ 85	100	15	775	→ 825
900	700	35	→ 85	100	15	850	→ 900
1,000	775	35	→ 85	100	15	925	→ 975
1,100	850	35	→ 85	100	15	1,000	→ 1,050

At the original level of total planned expenditure, equilibrium occurs when both total planned expenditure and national income and product are $700 billion. A $50 billion increase in planned investment increases total planned expenditure by $50 billion at all levels of national income and product.

The new equilibrium is at a national income and product of $900 billion. Thus, a $50 billion increase in planned expenditure increases equilibrium national income and product by $200 billion in this illustration.

assume that, for every level of national income and product, every year planned investment will be $50 billion greater than before the new production process began. Of course, we must also increase every entry for total planned expenditure by $50 billion. From this table we note that the conditions for macroeconomic equilibrium, which require an equality between total planned expenditure and national income and product, now exist when national income and product is $900 billion. The equilibrium level of national income and product has increased from $700 billion to $900 billion.

The same information is presented in Figure 10-1, which illustrates the upward shift of the $C + I + G + X − Im$ curve on a Keynesian-cross diagram. The $C + I_1 + G + X − Im$ line shows total planned expenditure before the assumed increase in planned investment, and the

$C + I_2 + G + X − Im$ line shows total planned expenditure after this increase. The conditions for equilibrium exist where the total-planned-expenditure curve crosses the 45-degree line. Before the rise in planned expenditure, this happened at a national income and product of $700 billion. After the rise, the intersection is at national income and product of $900 billion.

The Simple Multiplier

This simple case gives us our first experience with an interesting effect that occurs when some nonincome variable changes planned expenditure. Note that the upward shift of the $C + I + G + X − Im$ curve in Figure 10-1 was $50 billion but the equilibrium level of national income and product rose by $200 billion—four

FIGURE 10-1   Shifting the Total-Planned-Expenditure Curve Produces a Change in the Equilibrium Level of National Income and Product

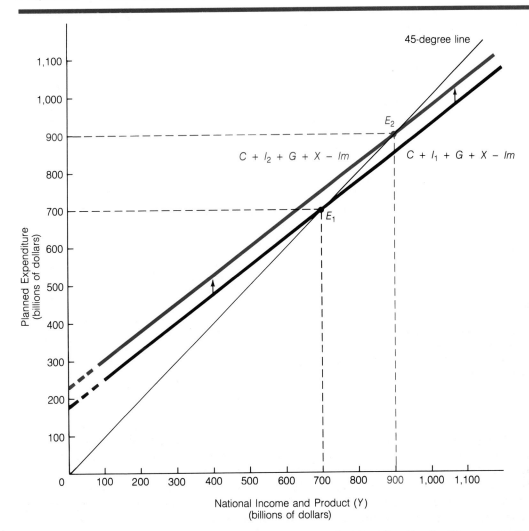

The original level of total planned expenditure is $C + I_1 + G + X - Im$. The original equilibrium exists where this curve crosses the 45-degree line at E_1, with national income and product of $700 billion. An increase in planned investment shifts the total-planned-expenditure curve to $C + I_2 + G + X - Im$. The new equilibrium is at E_2, with national income and product of $900 billion. Thus, a $50 billion increase in planned expenditure results in a $200 billion increase in equilibrium national income and product.

TABLE 10-2 The Multiplier (in billions of dollars)

Time Period ("round")	Addition to Flow of National Income and Product	Induced Planned Expenditure	Cumulative Addition to National Income and Product Flow
1	$ 50	$ 37.5	$ 50
2	37.5	28.1	87.5
3	28.1	21.1	115.6
4	21.1	15.8	136.7
5	15.8	11.9	152.5
•	↓	↓	
•	(total of $47.5)	(total of $35.6)	(total of $47.5)
•	↓	↓	
nth			200.0
Sum total	$200.0	$150.0	—

We assume a $50 billion increase in planned expenditure caused by a change in some nonincome variable. This results in a $50 billion increase in the flow of national income and product in round 1. This added income *induces*, or brings about, a $37.5 billion increase in planned expenditure, which in round 2 generates a further increase in the flow of income and product. The process repeats itself. When induced planned spending is 0.75 of the national income and product change that caused it, the multiplier value will be 4. In the *n*th round (or limit), the income and product flows will have expanded by $200 billion as a result of an initial shift of $50 billion.

times as much as the increase in planned spending that brought it about. The ratio of the change in the equilibrium national income and product to the change in total planned expenditure is called the **multiplier.** The multiplier implies that the average dollar of the initiating change in planned spending is multiplied several times (in this case, four times) in the process of reaching the new equilibrium level. To find the value or size of this multiplier factor, we divide the change in the equilibrium level of national income and product by the initiating change in planned expenditure. In our illustration, dividing $200 billion by $50 billion, we get a multiplier of 4. However, measuring the size of the multiplier in this way is "after the fact" and of little use in forecasting changes in equilibrium national income and product. Let us see, then, how the multiplier comes about and what determines its size.

INDUCED PLANNED EXPENDITURE In our illustration, we assumed that firms became more optimistic about future profits from new investments and decided to increase planned investment spending by $50 billion per year. We shall

assume that money to finance this new investment is available to companies without taking funds away from other planned expenditure.[2]

The multiplier process is illustrated in Table 10-2. The initiating increase in planned investment expenditure takes place in round 1. At that time, money is paid to workers and the owners of other resources that are employed in producing the machinery and equipment involved in the new shale investment. A $50 billion per year addition to the flow of income starts during this time period. But this is not the final result of the increased rate of planned expenditure. The people who receive the additional $50 billion of income will spend some of it to buy things they want and save some of it. Our assumption about marginal propensities (see Chapter 9) was that 75 cents of each additional national income dollar would move around the circular flow as planned expenditure *induced*, or caused, by the increase

2. We shall have more to say about this assumption when we describe how the banking system operates and how the stock of money in the economy changes, in Chapters 12, 13, and 14.

in income. The planned expenditure induced in round 1 is \$37.5 billion (\$50 billion × 0.75). This induced expenditure brings about new production and income in round 2. The expenditure of \$37.5 billion provides income for the resources used in producing these goods and services. During round 2, the flow of income and production includes both the \$50 billion flow per period that started in round 1 and the \$37.5 billion flow that started in round 2. So income and production flow at the rate of \$87.5 billion more than before the multiplier process started, as shown in the "cumulative addition" column. But the expansion has not ended. Equilibrium has not yet been reached in the circular flow.

The multiplier process continues in round after round. Each time, the flow of income and production increases (in our illustration) by an amount equal to 75 percent of the increase experienced in the preceding round—\$37.5 billion in round 2, \$28.1 billion in round 3, \$21.1 billion in round 4, and so on. The flow of national income and product is larger than its premultiplier level by \$50 billion in round 1, \$87.5 billion in round 2, \$115.6 billion in round 3, \$136.7 billion in round 4, and so on.

With each round of the multiplier process, the addition to national income and product becomes smaller. Mathematically, a progression of this kind approaches a limit. In this case, the total additions to the flow of income and production (the sum of the numbers in the second column in Table 10-2) will approach \$200 billion. This total is made up of the initiating \$50 billion increase in planned expenditure plus \$150 billion in planned-expenditure increases induced by the expanded production and income (the sum of the numbers in the third column of Table 10-2). In the right-hand column, the entry for the cumulative addition to the flow of national income and product in the nth round (the limit) is \$200 billion. Equilibrium will be reached when the flow of national income and product is \$200 billion a year greater than it was before the upward shift in planned expenditure. At that point, the multiplier process has run its course.

There is a time dimension in the operation of the multiplier. First of all, a certain amount of time will pass before the increased rate of spending will bring about increases in incomes. Second, it will take time for these increases in incomes to induce still further increases in spending. It may be roughly accurate to assume that about three months are needed for each complete circuit of the circular flow or for each round of the multiplier process. In one year, then, about four rounds might be completed. In our example, these first four rounds would expand the flow of national income and product from \$700 billion to \$836.7 billion. Though the whole multiplier effect is never fully realized, a great part of it comes fairly early in the process.

The multiplier may operate in either an upward or a downward direction. The preceding example showed how an increase in planned expenditure would increase equilibrium national income and product. But, in a similar way, when the business outlook is gloomy, the multiplier may have a cumulative downward effect on the economy.

A SHORT-CUT CALCULATION OF THE MULTIPLIER
The expansion process shown in Table 10-2 involves a numerical process that is familiar to mathematicians. It is a geometric progression in which each number in a series is a constant proportion of the number before it. In this case, each addition to national income and product is 75 percent of the preceding one. If we let 1 represent the first value in the series, we can write a generalized description of the process as follows:

$$1 + (0.75) + (0.75)(0.75) + (0.75)(0.75)(0.75) +$$

and on and on

Or we can write it in a more usual way:

$$1 + (0.75) + (0.75)^2 + (0.75)^3 + \cdots + (0.75)^n$$

where n is the final round, or nth round, of the process. Mathematicians demonstrate that the sum of this series of increases will approach a predictable limit. In our illustration, this sum of increases approaches a value of

$$\frac{1}{1-0.75} \quad \text{or} \quad \frac{1}{0.25} \quad \text{or} \quad 4$$

In Table 10-2, we started with a $50 billion increase in planned expenditure, which resulted in a $200 billion increase in the equilibrium level of national income and product. The multiplier had a value of 4.

We may now give the multiplier a still more general form by recognizing that the value (0.75) in the case just given was the value of the slope of the $C + I + G + X - Im$ line—the amounts of total planned expenditure that were induced by changes in national income and product, divided by the change in national income and product. You encountered the same idea in Chapter 9, when we discussed the marginal propensity to consume. In that discussion, it was easy to understand how an increase in income could induce households to raise planned consumption expenditure. Now we simply apply this concept to total planned expenditure for the whole economy. If we assume that net taxes and all the other expenditure streams (planned investment, government purchases, and net exports) are not altered by changes in national income and product, we can put MPC into our multiplier calculation in place of the 0.75 value used in Table 10-2.[3] We can then say that the value of the multiplier will be

$$\frac{1}{1 - MPC}$$

If the MPC is 0.75 (as in our case), the multiplier will have a value of 4. So a $50 billion initial rise in total planned expenditure leads eventually to a $200 billion rise in national income and product.

---

3. A more realistic model of equilibrium and of the multiplier could not make the assumption that the marginal propensities for net taxes, planned investment, government purchases, and net exports all are zero. Instead, it would have to recognize that changes in national income and product induce changes in each of these streams, just as our model has recognized that planned consumption spending is induced by income changes. The marginal propensities for planned investment and for government purchases probably would be positive, but the marginal propensity for net exports probably would be negative. In the more realistic model, the multiplier would be based on the increase in total planned expenditure that is induced by changes in national income and product.

If the MPC were 0.60, the multiplier would have a value of 2½. In this case, a $50 billion initial increase in planned expenditure would result in a $125 billion change in the level of equilibrium national income and product. If the MPC were 0.8, the multiplier would have a value of 5, and so forth.

The equation given above for the multiplier can also be expressed by using the marginal propensity to save (MPS) in place of the marginal propensity to consume (MPC). If we assume that consumption and saving account for all disposable personal income, it follows that $MPS = 1 - MPC$. By substituting in the multiplier formula given above, we find that it also can be stated as

$$\frac{1}{MPS}$$

With our value for MPS of 0.25, this formula also gives a multiplier value of 4, since $1/0.25 = 4$.

A SUMMARY OF THE MULTIPLIER The multiplier is not a complicated concept, but is an important one for understanding changes in the equilibrium level of national income and product. In this process, a basic distinction is made between the change that *initiates* the process (the shift in the $C + I + G + X - Im$ curve) and the responses that are *induced* by the resulting income changes (movements along the relocated curve). The multiplier is a process that is launched by some externally caused change in planned expenditure. Feeding upon itself, it generates increases in income and product and finally dwindles to insignificance.

Figure 10-2 is a graphic illustration of the multiplier process. It is an enlargement of the part of Figure 10-1 that showed the area between the original equilibrium of $700 billion ($E_1$) and the new equilibrium of $900 billion ($E_2$). The process begins with an upward shift of the total-planned-expenditure curve, which we assumed to be $50 billion. In the figure, this is the distance from *a* to *b*. This spending generates an equal amount of national income and product ($50 billion), shown by the distance from *b* to *c*. The

FIGURE 10-2 The Multiplier Process

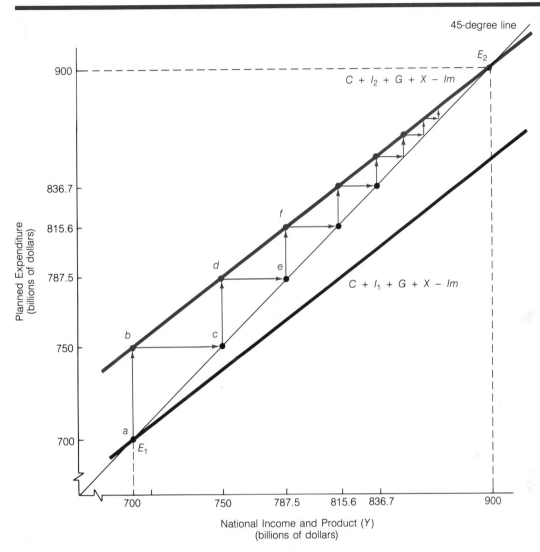

The initial equilibrium is at point E_1, with national income and product and total planned expenditure balanced at $700 billion. A $50 billion increase in planned expenditure shifts the $C + I_1 + G + X - Im$ curve upward to $C + I_2 + G + X - Im$. Planned expenditure increases from a to b and generates increased national income and product from b to c. This increase in income induces a $37.5 billion increase in planned expenditure, from c to d, which, in turn, generates increased national income and product from d to e. This process continues until the multiplier exhausts itself at the new equilibrium E_2.

FIGURE 10-3   **Phases of a Business Fluctuation**

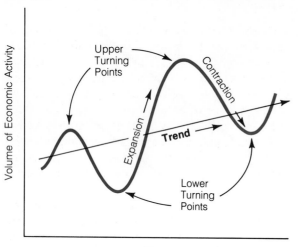

The vertical axis records some measure of the volume of economic activity. Time is recorded on the horizontal axis. Each fluctuation consists of an expansion phase and a contraction phase, an upper turning point and a lower turning point. The period or length of a fluctuation is measured from one upper turning point to the next or from one lower turning point to the next.

increase in national income and product *induces* a $37.5 billion increase in planned expenditure, shown by the distance from *c* to *d*. Then this increase generates additional income and product of $37.5 billion, shown as the distance from *d* to *e*. The multiplier process repeats itself in smaller and smaller steps, which dwindle to insignificance as the new equilibrium national income and product of $900 billion ($E_2$) is approached.

The multiplier provides information for people who are trying to manage the performance of the economy by manipulating various government programs and for people who criticize the activities of these managers. From either point of view, the multiplier implies that the end result (income, jobs, and perhaps price changes) is some multiple of the initiating change in planned spending. Since the multiplier itself is not as exact as our example has made it seem, it is not likely

that economic forecasts will be "on the nose" or that government attempts to influence national income and product will do just what is desired. The marginal propensities that determine the size of the multiplier are strongly influenced by the mood and expectations of households, businesses, and foreign customers.

Nevertheless, the multiplier helps explain why apparently minor shifts in planned spending can, if they last long enough, have major effects on the economy. Sometimes these shifts cause fluctuations in the economy, which we shall discuss in the next few pages.

BUSINESS CYCLES AND FLUCTUATIONS

Business cycles are expansions and contractions in the volume of economic activity that alternate with some regularity. Sometimes they are compared to radio waves or to the wavy lines used to describe electric current, though these descriptions greatly exaggerate the degree of regularity involved. For a long time, economists, statisticians, and business people have tried to identify business cycles accurately, hoping to discover the key variables that will yield reliable forecasts of coming changes in economic activity. Fortunes can be made with accurate economic forecasts. However, the fact is that great irregularity appears both in the size of the expansions and contractions and in their length or frequency. Some expansions are large and some are small. The same is true of the contractions. Though some expansions and contractions run for long periods of time, others are very short-lived. These facts suggest that **fluctuations** may be a better term than **cycles,** since the second term implies more regularity than really exists. There is evidence of some regularity but also of much irregularity.

Phases of Business Fluctuations

The phases of a business fluctuation are shown in Figure 10-3. Note that a fluctuation has an "upper" and a "lower" turning point as well as two cumulative phases: an "expansion" phase and a "contraction" phase. An **expansion phase** is a time of more or less continuing increases in economic activity, and a **contraction phase** is a time of fairly continuous decreases. The length of a fluctuation is measured from one upper turning point to the next one. Fluctuations vary in length and precise measurements are often difficult.

Measuring the amplitude, or size, of fluctuations poses additional problems. The expansion phase need not equal the contraction phase either in amplitude or in the length of the time period. Long and large expansion phases may be followed by brief and small contraction phases, and vice versa. The trend line shows the long-term growth path of the economy. Some fluctuations may be entirely below the trend line. In other words, the upper turning point may occur before the economy has achieved anything approaching a full recovery. Other fluctuations may be entirely or largely above the trend line.

The Historical Record

Figure 10-4 will give you a picture of business fluctuations in the United States from 1881 to 1984. Even a quick glance reveals both regularity and irregularity in this history. Also obvious are the interest and imagination that have been lavished on business-cycle research. Prosperous times have been given pleasant names, such as Railroad Prosperity, Corporate Prosperity, or even the exciting New Era Prosperity. Depressed periods have received less-happy labels, such as Primary Postwar Depression or Secondary Postwar Depression, though some taste for the dramatic is revealed in the Rich Man's Panic. How do economists measure these fluctuations, and what kind of pattern is typical of the business "cycle" in the U.S. economy?

MEASURING CYCLES Index numbers are used in measuring business cycles. You have already learned, in Chapter 6, how index numbers are constructed and that index numbers can be de-

veloped for prices, production, and many other kinds of data. Let us trace the steps that are taken in statistically identifying business cycles.

1. A series of index numbers (or a composite of several series) showing GNP, industrial production, or some other measure of economic activity is selected. This is an important step because different data series perform differently in relation to the economy as a whole. Some, like stock market prices or the average hours worked a week, tend to *lead*, or anticipate, changes in the total economy. Others, like wage rates, may *lag* behind changes in the volume of total economic activity.

2. Regular "seasonal" variations are removed from the selected index-number series. These are variations that can be traced to growing seasons, holiday shopping patterns, the school year, and so on.

3. Next, the adjusted series of index numbers is plotted on a time-series graph, such as the one in Figure 10-3. Then the analyst tries to discover and describe any regular patterns shown by the data. First, the analyst will look for any *trend* or long-term direction of change that is shown by the series of index numbers. Does the economy seem to be expanding over time? Is it expanding at a constant rate, an increasing rate, or a decreasing rate? Is the economy contracting over time? Once the trend has been identified, a trend line is drawn through the plotted data to show the long-run tendency in the economy. In the illustration of a business fluctuation in Figure 10-3, the trend line is the upward-sloping straight line.

4. After the trend line has been drawn, regular patterns in the plotted data can be described as variations around this trend. These variations are the movements that are usually called business cycles.

5. The final step is to analyze business cycles—to develop theories about the causes of patterns or regularities in the volume of economic activity. This is an important part of the task because simply viewing the future as an extension of recent events will fail to predict changes or turning points that are especially important for government and business decisions.

FIGURE 10-4   Historical Record of Fluctuations

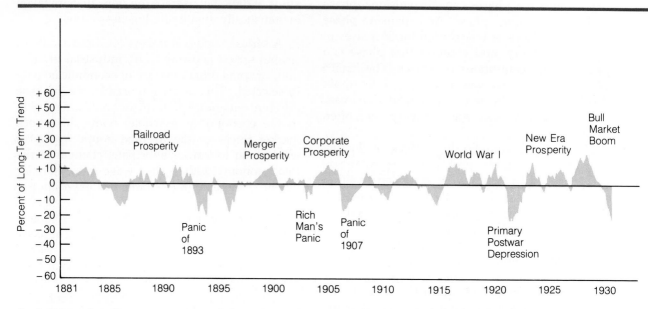

An index number for some measure of the volume of economic activity is plotted on the vertical axis, with time as the variable on the horizontal axis. In this graph, the vertical axis measures the fluctuations around an estimated long-run trend of change in the volume of economic activity. The variations around the trend are called fluctuations or business cycles.

Source: The AmeriTrust Company, Cleveland, Ohio. Reproduced by permission.

CYCLE PATTERNS   Analysts believe that they have identified several clear cyclical patterns for the U.S. economy. These are distinguished from one another by their length, by their causes, and by their names—since each has been named for the economist who is credited with discovering and explaining the particular pattern.

The shortest one, named the **Kitchin cycle,** has a length of some three to five years between upper turning points. Because it is believed to be connected with the alternate buildup and depletion of business inventories, it is sometimes called the **inventory cycle.** Inventories are a volatile part of planned expenditure.

Next in length is the **Juglar cycle,** which has a period of some 7 to 10 years. Though this is a major pattern in U.S. economic history, economists have not agreed on any specific cause for it. The Great Depression of the 1930s came be-tween the upper turning points on either side of one of these cycles. Economists still debate why planned expenditure dropped so seriously during this period.

The statistical record reveals a cycle that appears to last between 15 and 25 years and to run from the construction of buildings and transportation facilities until the time when they wear out and must be replaced. This is called the **building,** (or **Kuznets**) **cycle.** Since its length corresponds roughly to the length of a generation, one theory is that it may be related to population waves set in motion by birthrate changes following wars.

Finally, some theories assume a long wave, or **Kondratieff cycle,** of economic activity with a length of 30 to 50 years. Reliable records have not been kept over a long enough time for economists to agree on these very long cycles. Some theories suggest that they may be associated

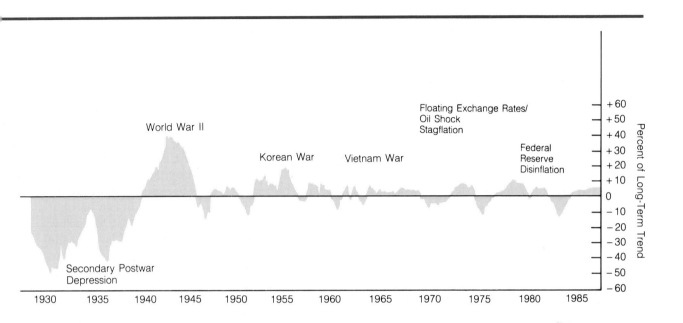

with major technological innovations, such as railroads and automobiles. Technological changes can shift planned expenditure.

All of these cycles (Kitchin, Juglar, Kuznets, and Kondratieff) are occurring at the same time and interact with one another. The shorter cycles that come during the expansion phases of the long cycles display long and vigorous expansion phases of their own with short and mild contraction phases. The short cycles that occur during the contraction phases of long cycles show the opposite pattern.

A Simple Theory of Cycles

The economic models that you studied in Chapters 8 and 9 can be combined with the multiplier to produce a simple theory of business cycles.

Let us begin by explaining the cumulative phases of cycles. Then we shall examine turning points, which play a very important part in economic forecasting.

THE CUMULATIVE PHASES The cumulative phases of the business cycle may be set in motion by changes in the flow of planned expenditure. These changes may arise in any of the spending components: planned consumption, planned investment, government purchases, or net exports. Perhaps an especially appealing line of new model automobiles causes a rise in both planned consumption and planned investment. An upward shift in planned spending will tend to set off an expansion phase in the cycle, and a downward shift will tend to trigger a contraction phase. Later we shall take a closer look at these shifts when we study the turning points of business cycles.

For the moment, we shall focus on the cumulative processes of expansion and contraction that follow an initiating shift in planned spending.

You already know about one force, the multiplier, that tends to give a cumulative character to the expansions and contractions of the economy. The new income generated by the initiating change in planned spending leads to more increases in the rate of planned spending so that the expansion feeds on itself for some period of time. In the contraction phase of the cycle, the multiplier operates in the downward direction. That is, downward shifts in spending lead to reductions in income. These income declines, in turn, cause further drops in planned spending. So the multiplier gives a cumulative character and a time dimension to both expansion and contraction phases of business cycles.

In some cycles, there are other forces that add to the cumulative character of expansion or contraction phases. These are closely related to the multiplier, but are also different from it. The multiplier, as you may remember, involves *movements along* the $C + I + G + X - Im$ curve after a shift in that curve has caused a disequilibrium situation. However, during the cumulative phase of a cycle, there may be more *shifts* of the curve which are caused by the mood of the expansion or the contraction itself. Psychological theories of business cycles place much emphasis on the great hopes generated by the very fact that an expansion is under way. These changes in expectations can shift planned-spending curves upward and add fuel to the expansion. Conversely, the pessimistic mood of the contraction phase of a cycle may discourage planned spending and cause downward shifts, which will make the contraction still worse and longer-lasting. These psychological "add-ons" are hard to predict and, by their very nature, are unreliable, but it does appear that some cumulative phases of cycles are swept along by this extra dimension. In his 1933 inaugural speech, early in the Great Depression, President Franklin D. Roosevelt said, "The only thing we have to fear is fear itself—nameless, unreasoning, unjustifiable terror—that paralyzes needed effort . . ." Later in his administration,

efforts were made to "prime the pump." That is, temporary increases in government spending were expected to start a multiplier effect. The hope was that private investors would gain confidence once more so that private investment would take over and then the government spending could be ended. As it happened, the response of private investors was insufficient.

TURNING POINTS   Turning points are the most crucial and worst-handled aspects of business-cycle theory and forecasting. However, the forecasting of turning points is especially important. As in weather forecasting, a person can be right most of the time by forecasting that tomorrow will be like today. But this method ignores the basic reason for forecasting. Anticipating changes in direction for the economy is fundamental to business and government decisions.

UPPER TURNING POINTS   Let us look at the upper **turning point** of the cycle first. Why can't the expansion continue? The main reason is that expansion in the "cycle" means a rate of increase in output and employment that is greater than the long-run trend of growth of the economy itself. In other words, an upper turning point may be reached simply because the expansion has bumped into "capacity," or resource limits. During the expansion, the use of natural resources, labor, and capital has been rising. New capital goods can still be produced, but labor and natural resources are limited. At some point, shortages or bottlenecks in these inputs will bring a slowdown in the expansion of total output.

The slowing down in the *rate* of economic expansion can lead to an *absolute* contraction in production and employment in industries that produce machines and other capital goods. This is called an **accelerator effect.** In capital goods industries, production schedules have been geared to provide equipment for the expanding economy and to replace machines that wear out. The slackening of the cycle's expansion brings an absolute drop in demand for new capital goods. So capital goods producers cut down production schedules and lay off some workers. This decline is a key factor in turning the cycle into a contraction phase. The reduced demand for resources by the capital goods industries starts a multiplier process in a downward direction. Lower income in the capital goods industries leads to decreases in planned consumption, which bring reductions in output elsewhere in the economy and further cuts in planned spending. The economy will turn around at the top of the cycle and move into the contraction phase.

Nearly all expansions "top out," or reach their upper turning points, long before actual capacity has been reached. Why? Part of the answer is that bottlenecks may arise in some sectors of the economy while idle capacity still exists in other sectors. Resources are not fully interchangeable. For this reason, the pattern of the cycle may depend on which industries or parts of the economy are leading the expansion. Sometimes external events, such as the "oil shock" following the embargo by OPEC (Organization of Petroleum Exporting Countries) in 1973, can bring an end to expansion. At other times, the ending of a war may put a stop to spending on the war-related components of planned expenditure. Upper turning points also may be triggered by subtle changes in business psychology, by decreases in demand from foreign customers, or by disappointing outcomes from business ventures that were begun in the enthusiasm of the expansion.

One of the aims of business-cycle policy is to moderate the cycle's expansion rate to bring it into line with the trend of the expansion of the economy's capacity. If the two rates could be brought together, expansion might continue as long as no external shocks occurred. Unfortunately, bringing the two expansion rates together is even harder than linking up two spacecraft in flight. In short, the idea that the economy might be sustained for very long at a high rate of economic activity implies a delicate balancing of many forces.

Those who favor planning contend that planned economies can control business cycles because decision making is more highly concentrated in a central planning agency, and also because they can cut themselves off from changes elsewhere in the world. Even if these claims could be proved, there may be a tradeoff between the slope of the trend line and fluctuations around it. Planned economies may sacrifice some growth in favor of greater stability.

LOWER TURNING POINTS What about the "bottoming out" of the economy after a contraction phase of a cycle? Why doesn't the contraction in the flow of income and production continue indefinitely? Part of the explanation is that there is a "floor," which at some point will end the decline in planned expenditure. Some consumption spending is needed simply for survival. Households will borrow money, sell assets, or dip into savings to pay for this minimum. Even though net investment has been negative in severe contractions, gross investment (except for inventory) cannot be negative. Government purchases will not fall to zero and, in fact, may be made specifically to reverse the direction of the economy. Because imports will fall and foreign customers will still buy some goods, net exports may grow. So even in the worst possible contraction, an eventual bottoming out of the decline in planned expenditure can be expected.

How far will the economy decline before it levels off? As we shall see later in the book, a major thrust of Keynesian economics is that the worst-case scenario need not be played out in the contraction phase of the business cycle. In other words, the experience of the 1930s Great Depression need not be repeated. According to the Keynesian theory, government actions can prevent the economy from falling all the way to the floor level of economic activity. We shall have more to say on these matters in the next chapter (on fiscal instruments), and in Chapter 13 (on monetary instruments).

The **lower turning point** of a cycle requires not only the leveling off of a contraction but also the upturn into the expansion phase of a new cycle. Once again, the accelerator concept can help us understand how the economy operates. As the economy experiences the contraction of business activity, idle capacity has been increasing. Labor, capital, and natural resources are not being fully used. According to the accelerator concept, the capital equipment part of these resources helps to bring the upturn, just as it helped to bring the downturn earlier in the cycle. Some machines and equipment will wear out even at the relatively low rates of use that characterize the economy during the contraction and bottoming out of the cycle. At first, idle machines can be put into service when other machines wear out. But at some point, the reserves of idle machinery will be gone, and some expansion of capital equipment production will be needed to meet the demand for replacement. This rise in capital equipment production starts a new expansion of the economy. Rising output, employment, and income in these industries will lead to increases in planned expenditure, start an upward multiplier, and the economy will be back on the expansion path of a new cycle of business activity.

Must the timing of the upturn wait until all reserves of capital equipment have been used up? Not necessarily. The upturn may come from a particularly successful innovation, which can create investor optimism in some important line of business and shift planned expenditure. Foreign demand may rise, or government spending may stimulate the economy. With the start of World War II in 1939, increases in planned spending helped the country recover from the Great Depression. The point is that the exact timing of the upturn may depend on particular events. But reliable forecasting of such events is almost impossible.

BUSINESS CYCLE DOCTRINES

Keynesian economics was born out of the hardship and suffering of the Great Depression. Our description of cumulative phases and turning points of cycles is a theory based on the Keynesian concepts. However, more fundamental "causes" of business fluctuations have been sought over the years by many scholars, business people, and reformers. Some have prophesied far-reaching consequences from cycles. We shall describe two theories that, we think, deserve attention.

Karl Marx and Business Cycles

Business-cycle theory plays an important part in the teachings of Karl Marx, who believed in the inevitable collapse of capitalism and rise of socialism. According to Marx, capitalists have an insatiable drive to make money and to invest it in machinery and equipment to expand production capacity. Indeed, the capitalist is a necessary part of the evolution from a simple agricultural economy to an industrial economy. The capitalist's profits, which come from the exploitation of workers, according to Marx, pay for these machines. The "contradiction" in capitalism is that these machines reduce the chances to exploit current labor and so lower the rate of profit—driving the capitalist to more frantic efforts at exploitation and capital accumulation.

The falling rate of profit that comes from the capitalist's drive to accumulate is very important to Marx's theory. Capitalists use machines to gain the capacity to produce more goods and services than the workers, with their low incomes, are able to buy. Because there is not enough demand to buy the output of the added capital capacity, the economy contracts and a depression follows. The depression does not end until the excess capacity has been worn out. Then the process starts all over again. Marx believed that depressions would become worse and worse and would in time cause the overthrow of the capitalist system by the ever-growing and ever more exploited working class. In the 1930s, many people saw the Great Depression as the fulfillment of Marx's prophecies. They also saw the Keynesian prescriptions for moderating recessions as a way to preserve the basic elements of the capitalist system.

Joseph Schumpeter and Innovations

Joseph Schumpeter (1883–1950) offered an explanation of business cycles based on the timing of major innovations in a capitalist system. Under this system, great, though temporary, rewards often come to the successful innovator. Major breakthroughs, such as railroads, automobiles, and electricity, bring bursts of expanding economic activity. Eventually these booms run their course and give way to relative declines in business activity as the economy waits for the next burst of innovation. "Long waves" or cycles of economic activity may be traced (after the fact) to major innovations. Shorter cycles, such as those described earlier in this chapter, may occur along with these longer waves.

Schumpeter also predicted that capitalism would someday be replaced by a different economic system. In Schumpeter's model, business cycles were simply part of the capitalist system and could not be eliminated, but cycles themselves would not be the reason or occasion (as in Marx) for replacing that system. Instead, the very success of capitalist innovation in raising living standards and in generating wealth would help to draw attention away from production itself and toward matters of distribution of income and welfare and toward less purely "economic" values. So, in Schumpeter's view, capitalism's success in solving economic problems would someday lead to its replacement by planning, by socialism, and, he feared, by a dictatorship. He did not want to live under such a regime.

THE GREAT DEPRESSION AND THE HUNGRY THIRTIES

Let us look at the Great Depression and the Hungry Thirties and see how the Keynesian model can help to explain what happened. Three sets of questions come up in connection with this important period in U.S. history: (1) What were the weaknesses of the great boom of the 1920s, and why did the stock market crash on "Black Thursday" (October 24, 1929)? (2) Why did the collapse of "paper values" on the Stock Exchange spread to the real economy, and why couldn't the Hoover administration prevent this spread? (3) Why was recovery delayed so long, and why was there a "secondary depression" in 1937–1938 before the country could recover from the primary depression?

Prosperity and the Crash

The great boom of the 1920s was *not* inflationary in the usual sense of the term. Nearly half of the World War I inflation had been squeezed out of the American economy by the short and sharp (but painful) postwar depression of 1920–1922. For the rest of the decade, American prices and wage rates held steady and prosperity continued, in contrast to the violent inflation in much of Europe and the depression in Britain and Japan. There was a rise of profits in total amount but apparently not per unit of output. This rise was connected with higher productivity. Both actual profit increases and expected future ones were reflected in stock prices on Wall Street.

The boom featured bursts of increased investment in a few industries, which set off multiplier effects of the sort we have studied. The most important of the growing industries may have been urban housing. Because of the war, the building of apartment houses had slowed down. But now people were moving to the cities and needed a place to live. Of all the growth industries, however, the most spectacular were automobiles and radios. The automobile took over a mass market, and the radio was a completely new industry. Other electrical appliances such as vacuum cleaners, refrigerators, water heaters, and washing machines also began to replace the housemaid—though not the housewife. Another growing "industry" was installment credit, which allowed people to buy durable consumption goods, including automobiles, radios, and appliances, before they saved the money to pay for them. A major weak spot in the economy, however, was agriculture. Farmers, who had not recovered completely from the 1920–1922 depression, had expanded their production during the war and contracted debts at wartime prices. Another problem area was export trade. European production had recovered from the war. So the "rest of the world" was not a good market for American goods except where American loans helped countries pay for these goods.

But why was there a crash? Most theories of the crash are not mutually exclusive; that is to say, they can be combined. Here are a few.

1. Multiplier and accelerator effects Multiplier and accelerator effects arose from the slowdowns in the leading industries of the boom. The slowdown was especially marked in housing, because the urban apartment shortage was largely overcome by 1927.

2. Agricultural fundamentalism According to this view, the American economy failed mainly because agricultural purchasing power was not able to absorb the increasing output of urban goods.

3. International fundamentalism U.S. prosperity was not enough of a "locomotive" to provide support for the world economy. Instead, worldwide difficulties eventually spread to the United States. When optimistic U.S. loans to Europe and Latin America proved difficult to repay or service, the volume of lending was cut back, and American export trade suffered accordingly.

4. Maldistribution The income distribution of the 1920s seems to have shifted against labor, as wage rates failed to keep pace with average labor productivity. (Employment, however, increased during the 1920s, and payrolls increased along with it.)

5. Overspeculation At times, income is shifted from purchasing the current output of consumption and investment goods to purchasing assets not currently produced—real estate, art works, antiques, or shares of stock. In such a case, there is a decline in expenditure on current output, which sets off multiplier effects in a downward direction. The effect on income is no different from an attempt to hoard cash.

For whatever reason or reasons, we now believe that unemployment had actually started to rise, and planned investment spending to fall, by the middle of 1929. In fact, the stock market itself had experienced several sharp price drops in the two to three months before "Black Thursday."

The Hoover Administration

President Herbert Hoover believed that the collapse of stock prices had done nothing at all to the real economy. He therefore saw no reason why prosperity should not continue at a lower level of stock prices. But, as we have noted, planned consumption seems to depend on wealth as well as on income, and consumers' wealth had been cut by the crash. Also, planned investment is sensitive to expectations of future profits. After "Black Thursday," these expectations were revised sharply downward. The real effects of the crash soon appeared in the Northeast, though it took some years before the unemployment, bread lines, and shantytowns ("Hoovervilles") spread through the rest of the country.

The administration devised two sets of policies to deal with the gathering depression, in addition to repeated assurances that prosperity was "just around the corner."[4] Hoover's own policy was to try to balance the budget. Because tax yields had fallen, the administration's response was to raise tax rates and cut public expenditure. This move later proved to be a mistake. Also, Hoover had no sympathy for wage- and price-cutting. So one White House conference after another urged business leaders *not* to cut wages and *not* to cut prices. (Indeed, they seem to have cut output and employment first, though wage rates and price levels did begin to fall by the end of 1930.)

The administration, however, had another economic spokesman. He was Andrew W. Mellon, then hailed as "our greatest Secretary of the Treasury since Alexander Hamilton." Secretary Mellon was a deflationist. In the neoclassical tradition, he saw the Depression as due to the failure of prices and wages, both in the United States and abroad, to fall to their natural, normal, or prewar levels. Mellon wanted to "liquidate" labor (wage rates), stocks (security prices), and agriculture (farm prices). He opposed any expansionary action until price and wage levels should have returned to about the 1913–1914 level. Mellon was especially opposed to monetary expansion. In fact, the U.S. money supply fell by between a quarter and a third over a four-year period.

---

4. Prosperity *did* appear to be just around the corner every spring! But with summer and fall came bumper farm crops, collapses in farm prices, and failures of small-town banks with assets "frozen" in farm mortgages and other forms of agricultural credit.

The New Deal

President Franklin Roosevelt was elected to his first term in November 1932 and began his "New Deal" administration in March 1933. The **New Deal** involved three sets of economic policies. One was to increase prices, especially farm prices, in advance of production costs. A second policy was to increase wage rates, ahead of prices. The third was general "reform," aiming at redistribution of income and wealth, "self-government in business," breakup of monopolies, strengthening of farm and labor organizations, and expanding the role of government in what we now call a "welfare state," with only secondary concern for recovery. However, it is quite untrue to call President Roosevelt a socialist. Like Keynes,[5] he thought in terms of a more friendly and compassionate capitalism "with a human face."

Despite many policy changes within the administration, and despite strong opposition from the outside, on both right and left, recovery proceeded quite well through 1936. By the standards of later years, both budget deficits and monetary expansion were small and hesitant. Perhaps for this reason, private sector recovery was slow and hesitant too. Planned-expenditure increase was limited largely to consumption, since investment was held back by the excess capacity left over from the earlier boom.

The most disappointing event during the New Deal economic administration was a severe "secondary depression" in 1937–1938. This downturn began while recovery was incomplete and unemployment still high, and its effects dragged on until World War II was already under way. Because of this secondary depression, many people concluded that a failing New Deal had been "rescued" only by a major war. It also encouraged the belief that America was now a "mature econ-

omy" in danger of peacetime stagnation unless supported by public spending—in other words, "capitalism in the oxygen tent."

For these reasons, we shall look at the causes of the secondary depression in some detail.

PUMP-PRIMING The early New Deal had placed its trust in a process called **pump-priming.** Instead of working through several rounds of induced spending (like the multiplier), pump-priming was supposed to encourage *investment* and *shift* the planned-investment curve. In the recovery atmosphere created by government spending, it was supposedly safer to invest private capital as well. Once private investment had taken over, public spending could then be ended. It would not have to be continued, as it would under the multiplier theory. Perhaps mainly because the New Deal was seen as "antibusiness" by potential investors, the Roosevelt pump-priming did not achieve its goal.

SOCIAL SECURITY TAXES The pump-priming theory received an accidental test in 1936–1937. In 1936, the deficit was larger than planned because a promised bonus for World War I veterans was made payable immediately (over a Roosevelt veto). Then, in 1937, the Social Security system went into operation. Taxes were collected and a surplus accumulated, with few persons eligible for benefits in the first year. The federal budget deficit was cut sharply; it may even have gone into surplus for a few months. The sudden change increased leakages more than injections and turned out to be one cause of the downturn.

FEAR OF INFLATION Trade unions had won higher pay through several large strikes in early 1937, those in the steel and auto industries being most important. The Wagner-Connery Act, a pro-union revision of the law governing industrial disputes, was upheld by the Supreme Court in the Jones & Laughlin case. Even though unemployment continued, wage gains were passed on to the consumer in higher prices. These high prices revived the fear of general inflation. Responding to this fear, the Federal Reserve Board tightened the money supply. Interest rates rose and the

---

5. Lord Keynes's personal influence on New Deal economics was not really great. Praising many aspects of the New Deal in the British press, he wished it might go further faster. In a visit to the United States, he had at least one interview with President Roosevelt, but impressed him more as a mathematician than as an economist. By 1938–1939, however, his American converts and their students (mainly at Harvard) were spreading Keynesian ideas in Washington.

monetary growth rate fell at just the wrong time from the recovery point of view. How these things might bring recession will be explained in Chapter 14.

THE ROLE OF CORPORATE TAXES The U.S. tax system had exempted dividends from the *individual* income tax in order not to double-tax corporate profits. During the early years of the Depression, the exemption was repealed. In 1936, however, an attempt was made to eliminate the resulting double taxation by allowing corporations to deduct dividends paid when computing their taxable income. This transformed the corporation income tax into an undistributed profits tax. But this new tax, despite its high rates, was not expected to yield as much Treasury revenue as had the corporate income tax. The Treasury wanted the loss made up. Because of congressional confusion, corporations turned out to be saddled with *both* the corporate income tax and the undistributed profits tax. The result was a drop in planned private investment—at the wrong time again!

It seems difficult and unfair to argue from this record that the New Deal, especially a New Deal seen as less antibusiness than during the first two Roosevelt administrations, would have continued a below-par batting average against depressions.

SUMMARY

1. The multiplier process is started by a shift in the $C + I + G + X - Im$ curve, that is, by a change in some nonincome determinant of planned spending. This change alters the flow of planned spending and changes the equilibrium level of national income and product.

2. The multiplier shows the size of the change in the equilibrium level of national income and product as a factor or multiple of the shift in total planned expenditure that launched the process. Equilibrium national income and product changes by several times as much as the initial spending change because further expenditure changes are *induced* by the income changes themselves.

3. The value of the multiplier is determined by the propensity of income changes to *induce* changes in planned expenditure. If we assume zero marginal propensities for planned investment, government purchases, and net exports, the value of the multiplier is $1/(1 - MPC)$ with MPC based on national income and product.

4. The multiplier operates through successive "rounds" of the circular flow. Time is needed for these rounds of activity to take place. The full multiplier effect is never realized, but most of its potential will be felt within a year or two following the shift in total planned expenditure.

5. Business fluctuations are alternating expansions and contractions in the volume of economic activity. History has revealed some regularity in these ups and downs, inviting the use of the term *business cycles*. But because there is much irregularity, as well, the term *fluctuations* may be closer to the facts.

6. A business fluctuation has two cumulative phases (expansion and contraction) and two turning points (upper and lower). The length of the fluctuation is measured from one upper turning point to the next one or from one lower turning point to the next one.

7. The cumulative nature of expansion and contraction phases of the business fluctuation reflects the time dimension of the multiplier process, the reinforcing shifts in planned expenditures that arise from the psychological atmosphere of prosperity or recession, and perhaps an accelerator effect (upward or downward) associated with the wearing out of capital goods and their need to be replaced.

8. Upper turning points occur because a slowing in the rate of expansion may bring about absolute declines in capital goods industries (an acceleration effect), which start a downward multiplier. A slowing of the expansion may arise because of bottlenecks in available resources or from any of a number of other restraints on the economy.

9. Lower turning points involve a bottoming out from the contraction of the economy and then the beginning of the expansion phase of a new fluctuation. Some minimum or floor level of spending may stop the contraction of the economy. Sometimes government programs will be used for the same purpose. Capital goods industries may expand as replacement demand grows. Innovations may also lead to a new expansion.

10. Many scholars, business people, and reformers have offered theories of business fluctuations that trace their source to the basic characteristics of capitalism. Among them are Karl Marx's theory that fluctuations are a sign of capitalism's self-destructive "contradictions" and Joseph Schumpeter's theory that fluctuations reflect capitalism's success in bringing about innovation and raising standards of living.

11. The Great Depression of the 1930s had a major impact on economic thinking. In fact, the acceptance of Keynesian economic theories grew out of the depression experience. These theories help explain why the stock market crashed in 1929, why there was a secondary recession in 1937–1938, and why recovery took so long.

DISCUSSION QUESTIONS

1. Suppose that a new and much better type of home computer is developed. Would this development shift the planned-investment curve on a Keynesian-cross diagram? If so, in which direction? Explain. Might the development of this product shift any of the other components of total planned expenditure? Which one(s)? Why?

2. This chapter illustrated a multiplier started by a change in planned investment. Could the process be started by a shift in some other component of total planned expenditure? Why or why not? What would the value of the multiplier be if the *MPC* were 0.9, based on national income and product? Would stable economic conditions exist if the *MPC* were greater than 1.0? Explain.

3. Without looking at Figure 10-2, draw an illustration of the multiplier process on a Keynesian-cross diagram. Be sure to label all axes and lines. Check your illustration with Figure 10-2 to be sure you have it right. How would your illustration be different if the *MPC* were smaller? If it were larger?

4. The multiplier illustration in this chapter is based on the assumption of a permanent increase in the annual flow of some spending stream.

How would the multiplier be different if the initiating change were only a one-shot expenditure, which was not repeated in the next time period? Explain.

5. Explain the difference between the term *cycles* and the term *fluctuations* as applied to periodic changes in the volume of economic activity. Why is there some validity to each term? Why does neither tell the whole story?

6. What are the two phases of a business cycle? How is the length or duration of a cycle measured? Why is the general trend of the economy a factor in identifying cycles?

7. Write down the names that have been given to the four major business-cycle patterns described in this chapter. After each, note its usual length and some of the causes that have been suggested for it. At what stage in each of these cycles do you believe the economy is operating at the present time? Discuss.

8. Explain how the multiplier process helps to explain the cumulative phases of business fluctuations. How do psychological theories add further dimensions to these phases? Why are announcements from the Department of Commerce almost always optimistic?

9. Explain the concept of bottlenecks and how it helps in understanding upper turning points of business fluctuations. How does the accelerator effect operate when the rate of expansion in the economy slackens?

10. Do planned economies do a better job of controlling fluctuations than the free market does? What are some of the arguments supporting your view? Do these planned economies pay any price for a smoother pattern?

11. What are some of the variables that place a floor or lower limit on a downswing of economic activity? Does the economy have to go all the way to the floor before it can start to recover? How does the accelerator process help us to understand the reasons for an eventual upturn in economic activity?

12. This chapter mentions housing, appliances, agriculture, and foreign trade as being among the important influences on the economy during the 1920s. In what way did each of these factors contribute to the stock market crash in 1929?

13. Both Karl Marx and Joseph Schumpeter placed great emphasis on business fluctuations. However, one saw them as signs of health and the other saw them as signs of sickness in capitalist economies. Explain their points of view. Both saw capitalism giving way to socialism, but for different reasons and by different processes. Explain.

14. What differences of opinion existed between President Hoover and Secretary of the Treasury Mellon about changes in wages and prices during the Great Depression? You will study more about these matters later, but it is not too early to note a connection between Mellon's views and those of the neoclassical economists. What is this connection?

15. List the three main thrusts of President Roosevelt's early New Deal economic policies. Do you think that Andrew Mellon was happy with these policies? Ex-President Hoover? Lord Keynes? Discuss these contrasting views.

16. Explain what was intended by the pump-priming action of the 1930s. Relate this explanation to your answer to question 4. Would pump-priming involve a shift or a movement along the $C + I + G + X - Im$ curve on a Keynesian-cross diagram? Explain.

11 *Fiscal Instruments*

PREVIEW According to the Keynesian system, what tools can the government use to deal with inflation, unemployment, and fluctuations? What can it do to prevent or to control these problems? In this chapter we begin our study of the instruments or tools that a government can use to influence the aggregate performance of the economy. Here we consider only the fiscal instruments, which make use of the taxing and spending powers of the government and which affect the government's budget. We base our explanations mostly on Keynesian economic models. In Part IV we shall examine the government's monetary instruments, which use the power to control banks and the money supply. In later chapters we shall examine supply-side instruments.

We begin by discussing the target levels of national income and product. These are the levels that are thought to have the most desirable effects on employment, prices, and growth rates, as well as on other elements of the national economy. Congress, the president, and the officials appointed to direct the banking system all take part in setting these targets. In this chapter, we simply outline the concept of national income and product targets.

Next we describe gaps between the target level and the level that will prevail if the government takes no special action. An expansionary gap means that, if left to itself, the economy will expand beyond the target. A contractionary gap means that, if the economy is left to itself, national income and product will be less than the target.

In the third part of the chapter, we describe the fiscal instruments that the government can use to move the economy to the target level of national income and product. These instruments include changes in planned government purchases, changes in planned tax collections, and changes in both at the same time. We show how the multiplier process operates in response to the use of the different fiscal instruments. We also describe how certain government programs work automatically to stabilize the economy.

The subject of the last part of the chapter is the national debt. This is important here because many fiscal instruments will cause a deficit or a surplus in the government budget. A deficit or a surplus changes the size of the national debt.

TARGET LEVELS OF NATIONAL INCOME AND PRODUCT

The **target level of national income and product** is the level that has been chosen as a goal for macroeconomic policy. The government may set a numerical target not only for real production but for the inflation rate as well. The idea of a target is easy to understand for planned economies, where some central planning agency is responsible for coordinating economic activity. Under such systems, five-year plans (and interim one-year plans) are formally adopted and widely publicized. In market-oriented and largely unplanned economies, target levels for national income and product are also appropriate and important. However, their adoption is less formal and the need for them is less clear. As will be noted in more detail later, the Employment Act of 1946 and the Humphrey-Hawkins Act (1978) are examples of official target setting in the United States.

The Need for a Target

The continuing use of target national income and product levels in our market economy reflects a major difference between the neoclassical ideas that dominated economic thinking before the Great Depression and the Keynesian ideas of the last fifty years. In the neoclassical view, no targets were needed, and it was felt that their use would do more harm than good. In the Keynesian view, however, targeting is necessary in order to avoid equilibrium at levels below (or above) high or "full" employment. If government action is accepted as influential and constructive in reaching continued high employment without inflation, or in speeding up this process, some goals should be set. When these goals are put in the form of national income and product levels, we speak of these levels as "targets."

Setting the Target

In the United States, targets for national income and product are set to achieve high-level employment and reasonable price stability. They emerge as part of the budget-making process. The president and his economic advisers have certain ideas about appropriate targets and build these into the budget that is proposed to Congress. Congressional committees add their views as the budget makes its way into law.

Setting the appropriate target focuses mainly on the production or supply side of the economy. Employment goals can be set to lower or eliminate macroeconomic unemployment, recognizing that some frictional and structural (microeconomic) unemployment will continue to be present. Once an employment target is set, information on productivity (output per hour of work) can be used to extend the employment target into a target for national income and product. Produc-

tivity itself depends on the amount and quality of capital goods and on incentives and production methods used in the economy. Important social and political questions also are involved. Should the standard workweek be thirty-five hours or forty hours? Should Social Security benefits begin at age 62, 65, or 68? Should retirees be allowed to work and still collect benefits? Even with well-defined answers to these questions, the appropriate target may be hard to specify.

CONTRACTIONARY AND EXPANSIONARY GAPS

Contractionary or expansionary gaps exist when forecasts indicate that the performance of the economy will not match the target or desired level of national income and product. In other words, economists predict the volume of total planned expenditure and the corresponding equilibrium level of national income and product for some coming time period on the assumption that present economic programs remain in effect. Then they compare their forecasts with the target levels that have been set by policy makers to find out whether the economy will hit the target or whether a contractionary or an expansionary gap will exist. A **contractionary gap** exists if the predicted equilibrium level of national income and product is less than the target. An **expansionary gap** exists if the predicted equilibrium level of national income and product exceeds the target.

Contractionary Gaps

When a contractionary gap exists, economists expect macroeconomic unemployment and idle production capacity in the economy. Figure 11-1 pictures such a gap. The $C + I + G + X - Im$ curve represents the volume of total planned expenditure that is expected if there are no changes in existing programs. So the equilibrium condition will be at point a, where this curve crosses the 45-degree line. The equilibrium level of national income and product is Y^*, but the target level is

Y_T. Because the equilibrium is less than the target, there is a contractionary gap. The implication is that, if left alone, the economy will operate below the desired level, Y_T, that macroeconomic unemployment will exist, and that production of some goods and services will be lost. The size of this loss is equal to $Y_T - Y^*$. From the Keynesian demand-side perspective, the contractionary gap is the extent to which total planned expenditure falls short of the target level of national income and product. In Figure 11-1 this is shown by the distance from point b to point c.

As we have said, Keynesian economic theory grew out of efforts to deal with the problem of unemployment in the 1930s. The basic Keynesian

FIGURE 11-1   A Contractionary Gap

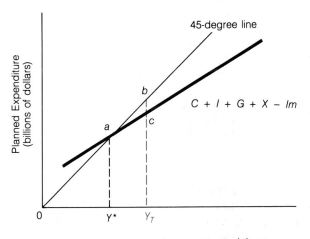

National Income and Product (Y)
(billions of dollars)

The $C + I + G + X - Im$ curve represents the levels of total planned expenditure that are forecast for various levels of national income and product on the assumption that present economic programs remain in effect. Macroeconomic equilibrium is at Y^*, as indicated by the intersection of the total-planned-expenditure curve and the 45-degree line at point a. If the target level of national income and product is Y_T, the amount of lost national income and product is indicated by $Y_T - Y^*$. From the Keynesian demand-side perspective, total planned expenditure is less than the target level of national income and product by the distance from point b to point c.

FIGURE 11-2   Closing a Contractionary Gap

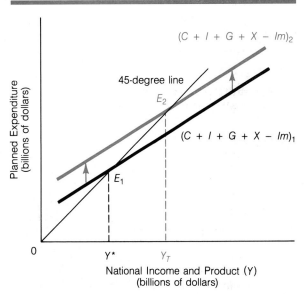

National Income and Product (Y)
(billions of dollars)

The predicted equilibrium for the economy is Y^*, where the total-planned-expenditure curve $(C + I + G + X - Im)_1$ intersects the 45-degree line at E_1. The target level of national income and product is Y_T. The contractionary gap can be closed by shifting the total-planned-expenditure curve upward to $(C + I + G + X - Im)_2$. After this shift, equilibrium is indicated by the intersection of $(C + I + G + X - Im)_2$ with the 45-degree line at E_2, and the contractionary gap has been closed.

remedy for this problem is illustrated in Figure 11-2, which shows a predicted macroeconomic equilibrium level of Y^* and a target level of Y_T, so that a contractionary gap exists. The Keynesian model indicates that this contractionary gap can be closed by shifting the total-planned-expenditure curve upward, from $(C + I + G + X - Im)_1$ to $(C + I + G + X - Im)_2$. Equilibrium will move from E_1 to E_2 and the equilibrium level of national income and product will match the target level. This is a demand-side approach to macroeconomic policy. An upward shift of the curve will move the intersection point upward along the 45-degree line. The right amount of new planned spending, together with the multiplier effect, will close the contractionary gap.

FIGURE 11-3 **An Expansionary Gap**

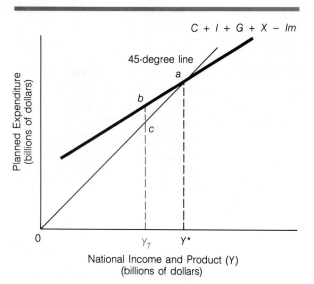

The $C + I + G + X - Im$ curve represents the levels of total planned expenditure that are forecast for various levels of national income and product on the assumption that present economic programs remain in effect. Macroeconomic equilibrium is at Y^*, as indicated by the intersection of the total-planned-expenditure curve and the 45-degree line at point a. At the target level of national income and product of Y_T, there is an excessive amount of planned expenditure, indicated by the distance from b to c. This extra expenditure may generate inflationary pressures.

Expansionary Gaps

Expansionary gaps are generally associated with shortages and inflationary pressures on the economy. Figure 11-3 pictures this situation. Here the predicted level of economic activity, Y^*, is greater than the target, Y_T. If the target has been set at "full employment" or "capacity" production, the expansionary gap means that planned spending will be greater than production as measured at the existing price level. The distance between points b and c in Figure 11-3 is a measure of inflationary pressure.

In the Keynesian demand-side approach, closing an expansionary gap calls for a downward shift in the total-planned-expenditure curve. This

is illustrated in Figure 11-4. The inflationary pressures being generated at equilibrium E_1 can be relieved by shifting the total-planned-expenditure curve downward, from $(C + I + G + X - Im)_1$ to $(C + I + G + X - Im)_2$. This will move the equilibrium from point E_1 to point E_2, so that macroeconomic equilibrium will correspond with the target level of national income and product.

Although the Keynesian model for dealing with an expansionary gap is clear, it is important to note at this point that the demand-side approach proved difficult to apply to the inflationary situations that arose in the 1970s. Many of the causes of the inflationary pressures of the 1970s can, indeed, be traced to increases in total planned

FIGURE 11-4 **Closing an Expansionary Gap**

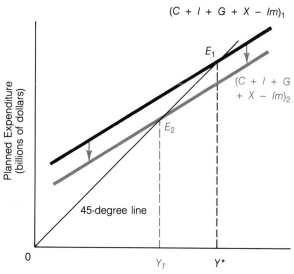

National Income and Product (Y)
(billions of dollars)

The predicted equilibrium for the economy is Y^*, where the total-planned-expenditure curve $(C + I + G + X - Im)_1$ intersects the 45-degree line at E_1. The target level of national income and product is Y_T. The expansionary gap can be closed by shifting the total-planned-expenditure curve downward to $(C + I + G + X - Im)_2$. After this shift, equilibrium is indicated by the intersection of $(C + I + G + X - Im)_2$ with the 45-degree line at E_2, and the expansionary gap has been closed.

expenditures, but there were forces at work on the supply side of the economy as well. Serious cutbacks in production took place owing to restrictions on the supply of petroleum imposed by the Organization of Petroleum Exporting Countries (OPEC). Also, certain supply-side effects arose as delayed reactions to price-level increases that had taken place during the 1960s. We will not interrupt our explanation of the Keynesian system to go into detail about these supply-side aspects of macroeconomic equilibrium. But we will consider them carefully later when we examine the aggregate-demand and aggregate-supply models of the economy in Chapter 15.

At this point it is important to go ahead to an explanation of the instruments that the Keynesian approach indicates may be used to bring about desired shifts in the total-planned-expenditure curve. We will begin by looking at **fiscal instruments,** which are those that involve taxing and spending and operate through the government budget. Then, in Chapters 12, 13, and 14, we will examine **monetary instruments,** which involve changes in the money supply and operate through the banking system.

CHANGING GOVERNMENT PURCHASES

Change in the annual flow of government purchases of goods and services is a basic demand-side fiscal instrument. As you remember from the circular-flow model in Chapter 8 and the equilibrium model in Chapter 9, government purchases are the G component of total planned expenditure. We count all government purchases of currently produced goods and services in the economy. However, we do not count transfer payments, such as veterans', welfare, or Social Security benefits. We treat these payments as negative taxes in calculating "net taxes" in the circular flow.

To begin our study of the government-purchases instrument, we again place all other variables in the deepfreeze by assuming other things unchanged. In describing the effects of changes

in the yearly volume of government purchases, we shall assume that no changes are made in the tax laws and that interest rates and the availability of money for private investment are not affected by the change in government purchases. These assumptions are very important here, even though quite unrealistic. After explaining the basic operation of the government-purchases instrument, we shall see what changes are needed when we remove some of these simplifying assumptions.

In the Keynesian approach to macroeconomic policy, the basic purpose of changing the amount of government purchases is to shift the total-planned-expenditure curve and thereby to deal with contractionary or expansionary gaps. Increases in the volume of government purchases (G) will, other things being equal, shift the $C + I + G + X - Im$ curve upward and help to close a contractionary gap, as was illustrated in Figure 11-2. Conversely, decreases in the volume of government purchases will, other things being equal, shift the $C + I + G + X - Im$ curve downward, helping to close an expansionary gap, as was illustrated in Figure 11-4.

In each of these types of change, the multiplier operates just as described in Chapter 10. For example, if the MPC is 0.75, a $50 billion increase in the annual volume of government purchases will lead eventually to a $200 billion increase in the equilibrium level of national income and product. The multiplier will have a value of 4. Similarly, a $50 billion decrease will lead to a $200 billion decrease in this equilibrium level. The change in government purchases shifts the $C + I + G + X - Im$ curve, which then intersects the 45-degree line on a Keynesian-cross graph at a different equilibrium level of national income and product.

Displacement Effects

Of course, this fiscal-instrument process does not always operate as smoothly in real life as in our hypothetical cases. Sometimes a **displacement effect** will arise when a change in one component of total planned expenditure causes an opposite change in some other component. The possibility of displacement effects is an important limitation on the effectiveness of the government-purchases instrument.

Suppose that the expanded flow of goods and services provided by government is a substitute for things that households ordinarily buy with their own money. What would happen if government expanded its purchases of medical services and delivered these services free to the public? Wouldn't household spending on health care go down as the government's spending on these services went up? Then wouldn't the change in household spending offset, to some degree, the change in government purchases? If the goods and services involved in the increased government purchases are substitutes for things that consumers are already buying, then a downward shift in the consumption function (consumer purchases) may partly or fully offset the increase in government purchases. In such a case, the $C + I + G + X - Im$ curve will not shift by the full amount of the change in government purchases.

What happens when government decreases its purchases in order to close an expansionary gap? If consumers purchase more to make up for the things that are no longer provided by government, the shift in the $C + I + G + X - Im$ curve will again be less than the change in government purchases, and the government's fiscal action will be less effective in closing the gap.

CHANGES IN TAXES

Changing the amount of taxes collected is another fiscal instrument in government's macroeconomic tool kit. Changing tax collections, like changing the amount of government purchases, can shift the total-planned-expenditure curve and change the equilibrium level of national income and product. Let us examine how these changes operate in the Keynesian model.

Tax Increases

Let us consider what happens when the government increases the amount of net tax that it

collects, while keeping government purchases unchanged. In terms of the circular-flow model, an increase in net tax forces households to reduce the amounts that they plan to use for other purposes. Since we have assumed that imports are not related to the level of disposable personal income, households must obtain the tax money by reducing planned consumption or planned saving or some combination of the two. Let us first consider two extremes of possible household reaction to a tax increase and then look at a more realistic response.

If *none* of the added tax money were obtained through reductions in planned consumption and all came from reductions in planned saving, there would be no shift of the $C + I + G + X - Im$ curve if we assume that planned investment (I), government purchases (G), and net exports ($X - Im$) are unchanged. The tax increase would be completely ineffective in changing the equilibrium level of national income and product.

If *all* of the increase in net tax were taken from planned consumption expenditure, the $C + I + G + X - Im$ curve would shift downward by the full amount of the added tax, again assuming that the other spending streams remain unchanged. Since the total-planned-expenditure curve would shift by the full amount of the tax change, the multiplier effect of the tax change would be just as large as the multiplier effect of changes in government purchases, as explained earlier.

But neither of these cases is likely to fit the real world. In practice, the outcome of a change in net tax is likely to lie somewhere between these extremes. In the Keynesian model, the marginal propensities to consume and to save indicate how households will respond to changes in net taxes. For example, if the MPC is 0.75 and the MPS is 0.25, a \$50 billion tax increase will cut planned consumption expenditure by \$37.5 billion and planned saving by \$12.5 billion. If the other spending streams continue as before, the total-planned-expenditure curve will shift downward by \$37.5 billion. Since the simple multiplier $[1/(1 - MPC)$ or $1/MPS]$ would have a value of 4, this shift would lower the equilibrium level of national income and product by \$150 billion (\$37.5 $\times$ 4).

Tax Decreases

In the Keynesian model, a tax decrease is a fiscal instrument that can be used to shift the total-planned-expenditure curve upward, raising the equilibrium level of national income and product and helping to close a contractionary gap. In other words, tax decreases operate in the same manner, but in the opposite direction, as tax increases.

When net taxes are cut, households have additional money that can be used to increase planned consumption expenditure, planned saving, or some combination of the two. The power or multiplier effect of a tax cut depends on how much of the tax-cut money is used to increase the level of planned consumption expenditure. In the Keynesian model, the marginal propensity to consume (MPC) gives an answer to this question. If the marginal propensity to consume is 0.75, a $50 billion cut in net taxes will lead to a $37.5 billion increase in planned consumption expenditure. The total-planned-expenditure curve will shift upward by this amount. Since the multiplier would again have a value of 4, the equilibrium level of national income and product would rise by $150 billion ($37.5 × 4). The logic is simply that some of the expansionary power of the tax cut is lost because households use some of the money to increase planned saving. The total-planned-expenditure curve does not shift by the total amount of the net tax change.

The Tax-Change Multiplier

In the Keynesian system, the power of changes in net taxes to change the equilibrium level of national income and product can be summarized in the concept of a **tax-change multiplier,** which is equal to the change in equilibrium national income and product divided by the change in net taxes that causes it. If we use a triangle (Δ) to mean "the change in," the tax-change multiplier is $\Delta Y^*/\Delta T_n$. In the illustrations given above, the tax-change multiplier had a value of -3, since equilibrium national income and product changed by $150 billion (in the opposite direction) as a result of a change in net taxes of $50 billion. We

observe that the tax-change multiplier is smaller, by one unit in absolute terms, than the multiplier for investment changes or changes in government purchases.

The proposition that the tax-change multiplier value is (in absolute terms) smaller by one than the investment or government-purchases multiplier can be illustrated by a series of equations. We start with the multiplier that applies to changes in planned consumption expenditure, with ΔY^* representing a change in the equilibrium level of national income and product and ΔC representing an autonomous change in planned consumption expenditure. The regular multiplier calculation gives us

$$\Delta Y^* = \Delta C(1/MPS)$$

Next, we assume that a change in net tax affects planned consumption as follows:

$$\Delta C = \Delta T_n(MPC)$$

where ΔT_n represents a tax cut. By substituting the second equation into the first equation, we have

$$\Delta Y^* = \Delta T_n(MPC)(1/MPS)$$

In this equation, we see that the tax-change multiplier is represented by $(MPC)(1/MPS)$. If we let K_{T_n} represent the tax-change multiplier, it can be written as

$$K_{T_n} = (MPC)(1/MPS) = MPC/MPS$$

But we know that $MPS = 1 - MPC$. Therefore, we can express the tax-change multiplier (K_{T_n}) as

$$K_{T_n} = MPC/(1 - MPC)$$

which reduces to

$$K_{T_n} = [1/(1 - MPC)] - 1$$

Since the term in the brackets $[1/(1 - MPC)]$ is the regular multiplier, the -1 in the equation indicates that the tax-change multiplier is smaller, by one, than the regular multiplier.[1]

POLICY APPLICATIONS

When Keynes presented his model, the obvious policy application was closing the contractionary gap that existed during the Great Depression. But the model of planned expenditures and multipliers offers many additional applications in the making of macroeconomic policy. We shall briefly note a few of these.

The Balanced-Budget Multiplier

In practice, it is unlikely that either the government-purchases or the tax-change instrument would be used by itself in closing a contractionary or expansionary gap. Usually, these instruments are combined (along with other instruments) so that several policy goals can be pursued at the same time. For example, in an attempt to fight inflation, the Reagan administration combined cuts in government nonmilitary purchases with tax cuts inspired by supply-side arguments. In that case, policy goals were not only to close the expansionary gap but also to strengthen national defense, reduce the size of government, and increase the rate of economic growth. Similarly, contractionary gaps might be closed primarily with increases in government purchases if policy goals called for more public services, or with tax cuts if the goals called for more private services. The choice or the mixture of the two instruments would depend on how policy makers wanted to divide the hoped-for expansion of the economy.

Could the government-purchases and the tax-change instruments be used together so as to keep the government's budget in balance? Yes.

For example, a contractionary gap could be closed with just the right combination of increases in both government purchases and tax collections to maintain a balanced budget. The combination would be modestly expansionary. This is because the upward shift of the $C + I + G + X - Im$ curve that comes from $50 billion of added government purchases, for example, is greater than the downward shift that comes from a $50 billion addition to tax collections each year. With an MPC of 0.75, this downward shift would be only $37.5 billion (75 percent of $50 billion), leaving a $12.5 billion net upward shift in the curve. If the multiplier factor is 4, this $12.5 billion shift would bring a $50 billion rise in the equilibrium level of national income and product. This gives us what is sometimes called the **balanced-budget multiplier,** with a value of 1 or unity (the change in equilibrium national income and product is the same as the change in the size of the budget).

Balanced changes in government purchases and tax collections could also close an expansionary gap. In this case, both government purchases and tax collections would be cut. Supply-siders feel that the effects on production and work incentives add to the appeal of this way of closing expansionary gaps.

Combining the government-purchases multiplier with the tax-change multiplier gives a numerical value for the balanced-budget multiplier that is equal to the arithmetic difference between the two. If the government-purchases multiplier is 4 and the tax-change multiplier is -3, then the balanced-budget multiplier is 1. If the MPC were 0.80, so that the government-purchases multiplier would be 5, the tax-change multiplier would be -4, so that the balanced-budget multiplier would still be 1. In this way, the balanced-budget multiplier is always 1, regardless of the size of the MPC. Of course, the actual value of these multipliers goes back to the questions of where households will cut back if taxes are increased or what they will do with the extra money if taxes are cut.

As a tool for closing expansionary or contractionary gaps, balanced changes in government purchases and tax collections make the balanced budget the determining consideration in the choice of fiscal instruments. However, other goals may

---

1. A demonstration of the last step is as follows:

$$K_{T_n} = MPC/(1 - MPC)$$
$$= [1 - (1 - MPC)]/(1 - MPC)$$
$$= [1/(1 - MPC)] - (1 - MPC)/(1 - MPC)$$
$$= [1/(1 - MPC)] - 1$$

be more important. Also, the great changes in the size of government required by the balanced-budget system could easily make the package less attractive.

Automatic or Built-in Stabilizers

Automatic or **built-in stabilizers** are specific provisions in the tax and spending laws that work automatically to moderate economic fluctuations. Progressive income taxes are one of these stabilizers. When national income rises, taxpayers on the average move into higher tax-rate brackets and pay more taxes in proportion to their income. Other things being equal, the increase in taxes leaves less of the households' additional income to use for consumption spending and puts a downward pressure on the $C + I + G + X - Im$ curve, limiting the expansion of national income and product. In times of inflation, this same "tax-bracket push" puts people into higher brackets even though they are no better off in real terms. "Indexing" income taxes by automatically lowering tax rates or widening tax brackets in step with inflation reduces the automatic stabilization effect of progressive taxes in inflationary times. Of course, the stabilization effect itself assumes that the government does not spend the extra tax money collected.

The built-in stabilizing effect of progressive tax rates can also be explained as a change in the power of the multiplier factor. In Chapter 9, our discussion of taxes and the marginal propensity to consume used a lump-sum tax. This tax produced a straight-line consumption function, with a constant marginal propensity to consume based on national income and product. With progressive income tax rates, the total-planned-expenditure curve would become flatter and flatter as national income and product rose—and the multiplier effect would become smaller as well.

Individual income taxes are not the only built-in stabilizer that operates from the tax side of the budget. Corporation profits fluctuate disproportionately with the total economy so that tax collections based on these profits are unusually high in good times and unusually low in bad times. For this reason, they have an automatic

stabilizing effect. Social Security taxes and unemployment taxes also behave in this way.

Automatic stabilizers can also be built into the expenditure side of the government budget. But since most of these government expenditures are for transfer payments, rather than for goods and services, we would call them changes in net taxes. Welfare, unemployment, and Social Security expenditures all tend to rise during a recession at the same time that payments into these funds become less. This combination of more benefit checks and fewer tax payments helps support consumer spending and helps to close the contractionary gap. We have the opposite pattern during inflationary times, when expansionary gaps are moderated.

The existence of automatic stabilizers has led some economists to propose a policy called the **full-employment balanced budget.** Under this plan, the amount of government purchases and transfer payments would be based on how much the country would need and want, and could afford, when the economy was operating at "full employment." Tax rates would be set to balance this amount of spending when there was "full employment." During economic contractions, the automatic stabilizers would lower net taxes. During an expansion, the automatic stabilizers would raise net taxes. No legislative action is needed under this plan, since economic fluctuations are automatically moderated.

Automatic stabilizers have not been powerful enough to stop all fluctuations in the economy. Other policy matters put a limit on how progressive the tax rates can be, as well as on the level of corporation profit taxes and the size of transfer payments. So there is a ceiling on the amount of automatic stabilization that can be built into the fiscal system.

Influencing Economic Behavior Through Fiscal Instruments

So far we have looked only at the financial aspect of fiscal instruments. But the tax and expenditure system is also one of the most powerful instruments available to influence the economic behavior of important actors on the economic stage.

Changing these behaviors may change planned expenditure and the performance of the economy. To illustrate the importance of these fiscal instruments, we shall briefly note how depreciation allowances and capital gains taxes can affect planned investment expenditure.

Depreciation is the decline in the market value of a machine as it wears out or becomes obsolete. On income tax returns, it is a deductible cost of doing business. The tax laws specify how quickly or how early in the life of a machine these deductions can be taken. Quicker deduction means less tax payment and encourages businesses to invest in machines and equipment. Changing the schedules or timetables for depreciation is one of the favorite fiscal instruments for changing planned investment expenditure.

A **capital gain (or loss)** is the change in the market value of an asset that takes place while it is owned by the taxpayer. Many people buy stocks, hoping that the company will prosper and that the market value of the stock will rise, providing a capital gain. In a capitalist system, this is an important means of channeling resources into promising growth industries. In the United States, capital gains are taxable as income, though at a lower rate than ordinary income. Lowering tax rates on capital gains still further could increase the flow of funds into growth industries, and raising these rates could diminish this flow. So changing the capital gains tax rates is another fiscal instrument for influencing planned investment expenditure.

The list of the regulatory features of tax and expenditure laws could go on and on. There have even been proposals for using taxes to reward or punish people and companies for cooperating or not cooperating with nonfiscal regulations, such as wage and price controls.

DEFICITS AND THE NATIONAL DEBT

In explaining the Keynesian system for using fiscal instruments, we have not yet drawn attention to the fact that applying these instruments according to the Keynesian model often will involve deficits or surpluses in the government budget. However, a brief recap of the use of these instruments will show that budget imbalances are almost certain to arise. For example, in explaining the government-purchases instrument, we assumed that there was no change in tax laws. Therefore, given the lump-sum tax specified in Chapter 9, the government would continue to collect the same amount of net tax. If the government increased its purchases in order to close a contractionary gap, the increase in the flow of government purchases would move the government budget toward a deficit. Similarly, if government purchases were reduced in an effort to close an expansionary gap, the government's budget would move toward surplus.

These same conclusions about budget deficits and surpluses would hold even under more realistic assumptions about tax rates. For example, if the government used a percentage income tax of 20 percent, a $50 billion increase in government purchases would add only $10 billion to government tax collections in the first round of the circular flow. Of course, annual tax collections would grow in future time periods, but, since the government would also continue its higher level of purchases, it would be a long time before a budget balance could be restored.[2]

It is even more obvious that the government's budget would move toward deficit or surplus with the use of the tax-change instrument. If government purchases remain unchanged while net taxes are reduced, the budget will move toward deficit. If net taxes are increased in an effort to close an expansionary gap, the budget will move toward surplus.

The Problem of Crowding Out

As you remember from the circular-flow model in Chapter 8, budget deficits and surpluses acti-

---

2. You may wish to use the "Cumulative Additions to National Income and Product Flow" column in Table 10-2 to estimate when the government budget would regain a balance if a percentage income tax were used.

vate the connections between the government box and the financial-markets box. A government deficit takes money out of the financial markets—money that might otherwise flow on as planned investment in the circular flow. This is called **crowding out**. It means that some private investment expenditure could be replaced ("crowded out") by government purchases. The reverse situation exists when the government's budget moves to surplus. Surplus funds are channeled to the financial markets and flow onward as increases in planned investment expenditure.

The process by which crowding out takes place is quite simple. The government sells bonds to finance its budget deficit. These bond sales increase the demand for money available for borrowing in the financial markets. Other things being equal, this increase in demand for loans will drive interest rates upward. These higher interest rates mean that some private investment projects, which would have appeared profitable at the lower interest rates, will no longer appear to be so. These private investments are crowded out by the budget deficit.

In our explanation of the Keynesian use of fiscal instruments, we ignored the possibility that government deficits or surpluses might change the volume of planned investment expenditure. Specifically, we assumed that interest rates and the availability of funds in the financial markets were unaffected by government deficits and surpluses. Although this may be the case in periods of extreme depression (as when Keynes wrote in the 1930s), it is not likely to be true in more normal times. If crowding out does take place, fiscal instruments that move the government budget toward a deficit will not be as effective in closing a contractionary gap as our simple model indicates. Similarly, fiscal instruments that move the budget toward a surplus will be less effective in closing an expansionary gap than the simple model indicates. Although fiscal instruments may still have significant effects, the connection between the government budget and the financial markets clearly shows that we must not make any final judgment about them until we have studied the operation of financial markets and government's monetary instruments in Part IV.

How National Debt Is Created

We have already briefly described the mechanics of debt creation. When a deficit arises in the U.S. government budget, the Treasury Department, which is responsible for financing government operations, issues bonds and other securities and offers them for sale in the securities markets. Private persons, banks, insurance companies, business firms, and others purchase these securities just as they might buy other kinds of securities.[3] The Treasury uses the money received from sales to finance the deficit in the government budget. This is the money flow between the financial markets and the government pictured in the circular flow.

It is not true that the government literally "prints money" to cover its deficits as is sometimes alleged. In the past, as during the "Greenback Era" of the Civil War, currency was issued directly by the Treasury Department, but this is not the case today. The currency now in circulation is issued by the Federal Reserve Banks. In Chapters 12 and 13, we shall explain how money is created.

How Large Is the National Debt?

The national debt has not always been very large in the United States. In the 1830s, the debt had been completely eliminated, and excess federal revenues were turned over to the states. In 1917, before the United States entered World War I, the debt was $12.36 per capita. Today the debt is nearly $2 trillion, around $7,600 for every man, woman, and child in the country. Even when inflation and the vast growth in the economy are allowed for, it is evident that the national debt has increased significantly.

Table 11-1 shows the dollar amount of the interest-bearing public debt from 1967 through 1985. These amounts include almost all of the debt—non-interest-bearing debt consisting mostly

---

3. Some national debt securities are issued to agencies of the federal government itself. These are "special issues" and are not bought and sold in the open market.

TABLE 11-1   The National Debt, 1967–1985

End of Year	Interest-Bearing Public Debt (billions of dollars)	Percentage of GNP
1967	322.3	39.5
1968	344.4	38.6
1969	351.7	36.5
1970	369.0	36.3
1971	396.3	35.9
1972	425.4	35.1
1973	456.4	33.6
1974	473.2	32.1
1975	532.1	33.3
1976	619.3	34.7
1977	697.6	35.0
1978	767.0	34.1
1979	819.0	32.7
1980	906.4	33.2
1981	996.5	32.6
1982	1,140.9	36.0
1983	1,375.8	40.4
1984	1,559.6	41.3
1985	1,821.0	45.6

The total interest-bearing public debt grew consistently between 1967 and 1985. When these amounts are expressed as a percentage of GNP, the percentage declined through 1974, fluctuated within fairly narrow bounds through 1981, and then increased significantly.

Source: Economic Report of the President, 1986, Tables B-1 and B-81.

of bonds that have already matured but have not been cashed in. In dollar amount, the debt grew continuously during these years. The dollar amount of public debt is a simple (and simplistic) way of stating the size of the debt. It is a monument to net budget deficits accumulated over the years.

Quite a different picture appears, however, when the debt is expressed as a percentage of GNP. As shown in Table 11-1, this percentage went down until 1974, fluctuated within fairly narrow bounds through 1981, and then increased significantly. Expressing the debt as a percentage of GNP is better than focusing entirely on the dollar amount because a large economy probably can support a larger debt than a small economy,

other things being equal. But recording debt as a percentage of GNP also brings price-level changes into the calculation, since GNP is expressed in current dollars. When we bring price-level changes into our measurement of the debt, we run into great controversy. When inflation happens, the GNP (in current dollars) goes up. But the face value of bonds that were bought before the inflation will not increase in dollar value along with the inflation, unless they have been indexed to change in face value automatically with changes in the price level. Since U.S. bonds are not indexed, inflation automatically reduces the national debt as a percentage of GNP. In fact, some people believe that inflation amounts to partial default on the debt.

Can Debt Lead to National Bankruptcy?

Bankruptcy is a legal concept used to indicate a state of insolvency—of being unable to repay creditors. Could the national debt ever become so large that the federal government would become bankrupt? The standard answer to this question is that it depends on the taxing power of the government, the strength of the economy, and the wealth of the citizens. If the government is firmly established, if the economy is strong, and if valuable properties exist in the country, bankruptcy is unlikely. Certainly, the U.S. government is not likely to become bankrupt.

But governments that have borrowed heavily sometimes repudiate their debts or try to renegotiate their obligations. Also, when one government is replaced by another (as by revolution), the debts of the fallen government may or may not be assumed by the new government. Even the assumption of colonial debts by the new United States government was a controversial action. Several states refused to pay their debts for construction of canals and roadways in the 1830s, and the U.S. government repudiated the Confederate debt after the Civil War. After the 1917 revolution, the Soviets refused to pay the czarist debts. What about deliberate inflation as a means of eliminating the debt in real terms? In a sense, this would be another kind of repudiation, since debts would be paid back in money that was less valuable than the money originally borrowed.

Do Deficits Burden Future Generations?

In private finance and for state and local governments, debt financing is a way to postpone final payment for a good or service. Money is borrowed and used to purchase something. The borrower uses the money to acquire an asset and also has a liability—the obligation to pay off the loan. The burden of payment is put off while funds are "rented" and interest is paid. A future generation becomes involved because the heirs of a debtor inherit whatever remains of the good or service purchased with the borrowed money, and they inherit less of something else, since the debt will have to be paid off when the estate is settled. The debt itself (the "less of something else") is a burden. In this illustration, it is not obvious that the future generation is, on balance, worse off or better off, since this depends on the value of the good or service that was bought with the borrowed money.

What about the debt of the national government? Reasoning by analogy is, we agree, a dangerous procedure. However, analogy may point to some important issues. For example, if we consider only the debt and ignore whatever benefits may have been gained in exchange, it is easy to conclude that debt is a burden to future generations. The government of the future generation must pay interest on a debt that would not exist if the transaction had not been carried out or if the government service had been financed through taxes. But this just introduces the main question.

If we consider both sides of the matter and penetrate the "money veil" to examine real goods and services and real resources, the question becomes very complex. U.S. government debt is not incurred on a project-by-project basis. For this reason, it is not possible to point to any specific government goods and services as being debt financed. Nor can the opportunity cost (the private goods and services that were given up in exchange) be clearly identified. In our circular-flow figure, the connections between the government box and the financial-markets box suggest that government debt financing may be at the expense of private capital goods investments (machines and equipment) that could have raised both productivity and the living standard of future generations. This may be as close as we can come to finding the opportunity cost to the future generation.

But we must record some reservations even here. A depression-period argument points out that the resources used by the debt-financed government operations might otherwise have been idle, so that there might have been no real burden to the future. When there is no depression, debt financing may be at the expense of private investment. But tax financing can also impinge on investment spending, though perhaps not quite so much.

Thus we cannot accept a strict "yes" or "no" answer to the question of whether debt financing is a burden to future generations. The answer most likely is "yes" in some cases, and "no" in others. Much depends on the wisdom of political decision makers and on the time horizons and incentive systems operating in the political processes. If political decisions are dominated by short-run considerations and if public money is spent foolishly, debt financing may, on balance, result in a net burden on future generations.

SUMMARY

1. Fiscal instruments are those that are available to the government through its taxing and spending powers. The monetary instruments are those that operate through the government's power to control banks and the money supply.
2. The target level of national income and product is chosen as a goal of macroeconomic policy. Choosing a target for national income and product involves value judgments and tradeoffs among different goals.

3. A contractionary or an expansionary gap is the difference between the chosen target and the equilibrium level of national income and product that is expected if no new initiatives are taken. A contractionary gap means that equilibrium will be below the target, and an expansionary gap means that equilibrium will be above the target.

4. Changing the yearly flow of government purchases of goods and services is a fiscal instrument that can shift the total-planned-expenditure curve up or down and so change the equilibrium level of national income and product. This tool becomes less effective if other components of total planned expenditure, such as household purchases, are displaced by a change in government purchases.

5. Changing the yearly flow of tax collections is another fiscal tool that can shift the total-planned-expenditure curve. Part of the change in net tax results in a change in consumption expenditure. The rest affects financial markets through changes in planned saving.

6. In our elementary Keynesian model, changes in government purchases have the same multiplier value as changes in planned investment expenditure. But, tax changes have a multiplier value that is smaller because some of the tax change goes into or comes out of planned saving. Combining changes in government purchases with changes in net tax results in a balanced-budget multiplier with a value of 1.

7. Automatic or built-in stabilizers are provisions in the tax and spending laws, such as progressive income taxes, corporation profit taxes, and transfer payment systems, that work automatically to moderate economic fluctuations. The "full-employment balanced budget" is a policy that relies on built-in stabilizers.

8. Fiscal instruments can be used to regulate the economy by changing specific rules in the tax law. The tax treatment of capital gains and the allowances for depreciation are examples of the regulatory aspects of fiscal tools.

9. Movements toward deficit or surplus in the government budget typically arise from the use of fiscal instruments in the Keynesian model. Deficits extract money from financial markets, and surpluses put money into these markets.

Thus, deficit financing may "crowd out" private investments and budget surpluses may lead to increases in private planned investment.

10. The U.S. national debt has grown continually in dollar amount. Debt as a percentage of GNP has increased significantly in recent years. The debt comes into being when the Treasury sells bonds to finance a budget deficit.

11. Bankruptcy is a state of insolvency—of not being able to repay creditors. The strength of the government, its taxing power, the size of the economy, and the wealth of the citizens suggest that debt is not likely to mean bankruptcy for the U.S. government.

12. The effect of deficit financing on future generations depends on decisions made at the time when the debt is incurred. In some cases, deficit financing will be a burden on future generations, but in other cases, it will not be a real burden.

DISCUSSION QUESTIONS

1. Why was the setting of target levels for national income and product considered unnecessary and inappropriate in the neoclassical theory but important and necessary in the Keynesian theory?

2. Without looking at Figures 11-1 and 11-3, draw the Keynesian-cross diagrams that illustrate a contractionary gap and an expansionary gap. Then check to make sure you have them right. What is the standard Keynesian strategy for dealing with a contractionary gap?

3. How large a contractionary gap would be closed by a $100 billion change in the annual amount of government purchases if the MPC is 0.80 and if other variables are held constant? Explain how you got your answer. If displacement effects are present, should your answer be larger or smaller? Explain.

4. If the MPC is 0.80, you know that the multiplier for government purchases is 5. What would the numerical value of the multiplier be for a tax cut, given this MPC? Explain why it would be different.

5. The choice between changes in government purchases and changes in tax collections involves microeconomic questions about the mix between

public and private goods in the economy. How does this factor influence your preference between them as macroeconomic instruments? Do you have a different preference between purchases changes and tax changes when promoting economic expansion than when promoting economic restraint? Explain.

6. By combining the purchases multiplier and the tax-change multiplier, explain why the balanced-budget multiplier always has a value of 1. Compare the advantages and disadvantages of making the balanced budget a basic guideline for macroeconomic policy.

7. Explain why progressive taxes, corporation taxes, and transfer payments automatically tend to stabilize the economy. Under a progressive tax system, would a 10 percent change in national income and product bring about a change in tax collections of 10 percent, or more, or less? How does the answer to this question help you to understand the automatic stabilizers in the government budget? Explain. How would the full-employment balanced-budget policy operate?

8. Why is it overly simple to express the size of the national debt in total dollar figures? Why is it better to express its size as a percentage of GNP? But why does the latter method run into trouble when the economy has experienced inflation?

9. If the government borrowed a million dollars, used the money to construct a highway, and paid off the debt (with interest) through taxes on people using the highway, would the debt have been a burden on the future generation? Explain your answer. Much of the U.S. debt arose in World War II. Do you suppose that the war would have been lost if taxation had been used instead of borrowing? If so, is today's generation burdened in net effect by this debt? Explain.

John Maynard Keynes and the Great Depression

The Great Depression of the 1930s, which began much earlier in Great Britain than in the United States, was no ordinary business cycle downturn. It was the worst such depression of at least the preceding half century. In most countries complete recovery came only after the start of World War II. The depression itself confounded many mainstream economists, particularly in the United States, who believed or hoped in 1929 that they had entered a depression-proof "New Era."[1]

1. Most cyclical booms had been accompanied by substantial price inflation. What was "different" about the 1920s boom was precisely its accompaniment by price-level stability, which led most economists to assume that prosperity might continue indefinitely.

Depression soup kitchen

Causes and Cures

When the Wall Street stock market crash of October 1929 was followed by depression, and when the depression showed signs of hanging on, many suggestions were made to bring about recovery. These suggestions ranged from doing nothing at all to what would later be called "voodoo economics." They also included business-dominated "economic plans." It is certainly not true that nobody had any ideas about the causes and cure of the Great Depression. The problem was rather that so few of the would-be saviors were able to convince anyone else that they knew what they were talking about.

Some of the more or less seriously considered ideas about depression control, dating from the early 1930s, are listed below. Their order is largely arbitrary:

1. Prosperity was "just around the corner," since the country's physical plant had not been damaged. Nothing need be done but wait patiently for prosperity to return.

2. The depression was the punishment by the Almighty for the sins of "flaming youth" during the "jazz age." The remedies were moral reform and prayers to the Almighty for forgiveness.

3. The depression had been foisted on the people by certain other wicked people, such as "the international bankers" or "the elders of Zion." The economic power of such groups should be broken, and all would be well.

4. Capitalism should be scrapped in favor of a system close to Soviet communism, since the U.S.S.R. had been able to maintain full employment.

5. A national plan should be devised primarily by the leaders of big business, with the government in a secondary role, to eliminate overproduction and assure profitable prices for output.

6. The supply of money and credit should be increased, as by going off the gold standard, raising the price of gold, or printing inconvertible paper money. This action would "reflate" the levels of prices, wages, and profits. A more extreme form of this proposal would introduce an entirely new monetary system based on an hour of labor or an erg (small unit) of physical energy.

7. Unemployment should be exported abroad, primarily by raising tariffs and otherwise decreasing imports, and secondarily by subsidizing exports of goods and services.

8. Unemployment should be reduced by keeping the young, the elderly, and married women out of the labor force and reserving jobs for heads of families.

John Maynard Keynes

9. Idle plants should be taken over and run by unemployed workers at minimum cost, with the products distributed as far as possible to the poor and the unemployed.

10. Income and wealth should be redistributed by taxation or confiscation from the rich to the poor (or from property to labor income) so as to increase purchasing power.

11. The government budget should be balanced as an aid to business confidence, preferably by cutting public expenditures but if necessary also by raising taxes.

12. The cause of the depression was that prices and wages had not yet fallen to their "natural" (pre-1914) levels. The cure for the depression was therefore to force them down by drastic deflation or "liquidation."

13. The government budget should be unbalanced deliberately to increase spending for public projects to employ the unemployed. These projects should be mainly in public works and construction, civil or military. The resulting deficit should be financed either by selling public securities or by expanding the money supply as in 6 above.

Keynes and His *General Theory*

The contribution of John Maynard Keynes, later Lord Keynes (1883–1946), was to formalize, more fully and effectively than anyone else, the approach we have numbered 13. Indeed, this was the method that was used a decade later to ward off any renewed depression after World War II. However, many of the individual building blocks of Keynes's *General Theory*—particularly the consumption function and the multiplier—had already been devised by less well known members of the "economic underworld" years before the *General Theory* itself appeared in 1936. Also, some policies now called "Keynesian" had already been advocated and even enacted before 1936 in Britain, in Sweden, and in the United States under the New Deal.[2] On a larger scale and for military purposes, they had also been adopted by Nazi Germany and expansionist Japan as the "economics of rearmament."

An Economic Heretic

Who was this man, and how did he become so influential? The son of a well-known Cambridge University economist, Keynes received the best conventional education of his day. However, he was to become best known as an economic heretic.

As a young man, he wrote widely on both economic theory and policy for the intelligent general reader as well as for the scholarly professional. He also taught at Cambridge University and achieved early prominence in the British Civil Service. In the world of economics he was noted for changing or at least modifying his views to suit changing conditions, and for placing small value on consistency over time. His most famous early work was *The Economic Consequences of the Peace* (1920), in which he concluded that the excessive burden of German monetary reparations would, if enforced, prevent the recovery of Germany and all of Europe after World War I. Many of Keynes's writings after 1920 were on monetary policy. In a period of low gold production, he was a leader among those economists who felt that the traditional gold standard (with circulating currency convertible to a fixed amount of gold) was a deflationary drag on the domestic economy.

The *General Theory* broke even more sharply with generally accepted ideas, as you know, by attacking Say's Identity and calling for budgetary deficits to counter depression conditions.

Keynesian and Post-Keynesian Economics

Keynes viewed his doctrines as a general theory, which is to say, as something more than "depression economics." He applied the same system to check inflation, when it threatened to become a problem during World War II, mainly by raising taxes.[3]

After the war, organized labor, business, and agriculture in Britain and elsewhere used the Keynesian doctrine as a means of guaranteeing "full employment and full production at whatever cost" despite inflationary wage, price, and profit increases. Keynes responded by turning his back on his own disciples, speaking of "modern stuff gone silly and sour." Not long afterward, in April 1946, he died.

Today the self-styled "post-Keynesians" are still important at Cambridge University and elsewhere. They go beyond Keynes and "generalize the *General Theory*" in ways that Keynes himself might not have welcomed. They support wage controls, price controls, and capital rationing as necessary features of the peacetime high-employment economy, in the interests of inflation control, income redistribution, and accelerated economic growth. Occasionally they even claim that Keynes "never really understood the *General Theory*." What they mean is that in his haste to publish a tract for his time he never developed what the post-Keynesians consider to be its full implications in a world of imperfect competition, simultaneous inflation and unemployment, and maldistribution that aims at high growth as well as full employment. What Keynes would himself have said of all these ideas we cannot guess.

2. Keynes came to the United States, met President Franklin Roosevelt, and tried unsuccessfully to persuade Roosevelt to increase sharply the volume of New Deal spending and the size of the government budget deficits. Roosevelt apparently distrusted Keynes, believing him to be "more mathematician than economist."

3. Foreseeing postwar depression, however, Keynes proposed to "sweeten" wartime taxes by making them compulsory loans, to be repaid when depression conditions returned.

IV Money, Banking, and Monetary Policy

- Money and Banks
- The Federal Reserve System and Monetary Instruments
- Monetary Economics and Monetarism

12 Money and Banks

PREVIEW You may have some coins and some currency in your pocket or wallet at this moment. Perhaps you examined this money and discovered the year that the coin was minted (manufactured) and even the location of the mint itself. Did you notice that the currency is a Federal Reserve Note? Was it issued by a bank in Boston, or Chicago, or San Francisco, or Dallas, or somewhere else? These bits of information may satisfy your curiosity, as long as you are sure that the coins and currency will buy your lunch or a ticket to the movie this evening. But economists want to know a lot more about what money is and what it does in the economy.

With this chapter you begin your study of the role of money in the flow of economic activity and in the determination of equilibrium national income and product. We devote three chapters to this important topic. This chapter examines the nature of money itself and how the banking system is able to expand and contract the amount of money in an economy. Chapter 13 explains how the Federal Reserve System (the "central" bank in the United States) regulates banks and controls the money supply. The final chapter in the trio, Chapter 14, develops the economic theory of how money may affect the equilibrium level of national income and product, both in real terms and in terms of inflation or deflation of the price level. Just as you learned about "fiscal" instruments and theory in Part III, you will come to understand "monetary" instruments and theory in Chapters 13 and 14. At that point, you should be ready to go on in Part V to explore aggregate demand and aggregate supply.

This chapter, on money and banks, starts with a brief discussion of the importance of money in the economy and why economists must understand money. After explaining the functions of money, we describe the things that actually serve as money in the United States.

In order to understand money, you will need to understand banks and how they operate. The second half of the chapter describes how banks are organized as profit-seeking institutions that are usually able to operate successfully on partial reserves. That is, the banks' obligations to depositors can be greatly in excess of their cash and readily available assets. You will learn how banks influence the money supply in the economy as a by-product of their partial reserve operation. To meet certain needs, the banking system can expand and contract the money supply.

MONEY

The economics that you have already learned will give you some clues about the importance of money. Business firms and governments keep track of their economic activities with accounts recorded in money amounts. In a similar way, the national income accounting system measures the volume of economic activity in money. Recall that our theory of the circular flow too was explained in money terms. We imagined money "flowing" around the circle and through the various boxes that represented decision makers in the economy. When this flow was accelerated or interrupted, possibilities for disequilibrium appeared. You learned that changing the flow of money can change the equilibrium level of national income and product as measured in dollar terms. Now what would happen if the quantity of money itself were expanded or contracted? Could such expansions and contractions in the quantity of money reinforce accelerations or interruptions in the flow? Or could they counteract these changes? Could such changes make any real difference in production, jobs, and living standards? Or could they simply change the price level and bring us inflation or deflation but leave real production unchanged? Can changes in the money supply be controlled so that money could be used as an instrument of policy?

Economists find that the answer to each of these questions is "yes." The speed or velocity of the circulation of money through the economy does change from time to time. It is also true that the amount of money itself changes, often in ways that reinforce changes in the velocity of its circulation. The resulting changes in the quantity and velocity of money can bring further changes, not only in the real volume of production and jobs but also in the general price level. We shall consider these questions in detail in Chapter 14. However, before we can do that, it is important to understand what money is and what determines the amount of money in the economy.

The Functions of Money

Before you can understand what money is in terms of economics, you need to know the functions of money. The reason for this "function first" approach is that, in various times and places, many different things have served as money. For certain people, seashells or distinctively colored or shaped stones have been money. For others, cigarettes or the bark from particular trees have served as money. Livestock or even human slaves have been "money." Today, specially printed pieces of paper or specially minted pieces of metal (and other things as well, as you will see) serve as money. So it is clear that economists cannot define money in terms of its composition. Instead, they first specify certain "functions of money" and then define money

itself as that which is generally used in carrying out these functions. If this way of describing money seems a little backwards at first, remember that you cannot define a "split end" or a "defensive linebacker" without first specifying their functions in the game of football. The position itself is defined by the functions it fills. In economics, we usually list four functions of money: medium of exchange, unit of account, store of purchasing power, and standard for deferred payment.

MEDIUM OF EXCHANGE The easiest way to understand the **medium of exchange** function of money is to compare a direct or **barter** exchange in which one item is traded directly for another with an exchange that takes place through an intermediate transaction, that is, through the "medium" of money. Consider the teacher–student exchange, for example. The famous painter and recorder of birds and animals, John James Audubon, agreed to tutor the children of a Mississippi family in exchange for room and board and half days free to roam the plantation and paint. This was a barter exchange. As you can see, there was no "medium" or intermediate step. It was a unique transaction because it required a specific combination of wants: Audubon wanted to be supported while painting, and the family wanted instruction for its children. These special conditions lasted for only one year. Then Audubon moved on. Today, the typical teacher–student exchange takes place through the medium of money. Instead of providing the teacher with room and board, students pay tuition in money. The teacher receives money, which he or she can use to pay for room and board, among other things.

Using money as a medium of exchange greatly extends the range of feasible exchanges. No longer do people need to match their specific wants with those of other people. The medium of exchange lubricates the economic machinery. Whenever the medium of exchange is eliminated, as has sometimes happened because of war or runaway inflation, the living standard falls rapidly as the system reverts to barter exchange. We can now offer a partial definition of money: money is whatever is generally accepted as a medium of exchange, that is, as something used for the intermediate step in exchange.

The medium of exchange function is basic to the economist's definition of money. The other functions that we shall explain are closely related to this one, but they are to some degree subsidiary to it. That is, if something is not customarily used as a medium of exchange, it is not likely to be accepted for the other functions.

UNIT OF ACCOUNT   The **unit of account** function of money is the "common denominator" function—a way of comparing the values of different items. It is simply easier to remember, for example, that a loaf of bread costs $0.80 or that a gallon of milk costs $2.40 than it is to remember that one gallon equals three loaves. Without the unit of account function of money, people would have to remember millions of continually changing exchange ratios, one for each pair of commodities. A common denominator or unit of account simplifies things by selecting one item, *money*, and expressing all other values in terms of that one item.

It is almost inevitable that the item that has been accepted as the medium of exchange will also be selected as the unit of account. The unit of account function is virtually a by-product of the medium of exchange function.

What happens when the two functions are different? If you travel in France, you expect price tags to be in francs. If you are carrying francs and have gotten used to them, there is no problem. But if you are accustomed to thinking in dollars, the mental gymnastics of converting from one unit to the other can be troublesome, especially if prices are subject to bargaining. You may have the same type of problem in converting from yards to meters, or from gallons to liters, or from semesters to quarters. Conversion itself is the problem. When the same money is used for both a unit of account and a medium of exchange, no conversion is needed.

STORE OF PURCHASING POWER   The third commonly listed function of money is the **store of purchasing power** function. This simply means

that people who have units of the medium of exchange want to have the option of saving some for use at some later time. Surely a medium of exchange that was good "today only" would be less than ideal for most people. Each day people who wished to save would want to exchange some of today's money for money stamped with tomorrow's (or some later) date. Even though we could expect special moneychangers to set up shop soon to help people manage their money over time, the whole process of dated money would be quite a waste of time and talent. Up to a point at least, what is used as the medium of exchange and the unit of account will probably be used as a store of purchasing power as well.

The store of purchasing power function adds a time dimension to the unit of account function of money. No longer is money comparable to yards and meters or to liters and gallons. In these physical measures, we expect tomorrow's liter to contain as much liquid as today's liter and tomorrow's meter to be the same as today's. Inflation and deflation don't affect these measures. Printing more meter sticks does not threaten the size of the meter. But money is different. Price levels do change (as we noted in discussing index numbers in Chapter 6), and when this happens, we move part way back to having dated money—"today's money" can be different from "tomorrow's money." In inflationary times, holding money until tomorrow means converting it automatically into "tomorrow's money," which is less valuable. Thus, inflation threatens the store of purchasing power function of money. Because people become less and less willing to hold it for this purpose, moneychangers, banks, and dealers in money substitutes (such as securities, gold, and jewels) do big business. Also, as you will see, interest rates may be pushed up as people insist on extra compensation for holding notes, bonds, and other IOUs that have fixed dollar amounts.

STANDARD FOR DEFERRED PAYMENT   The fourth function that people expect of their money is that it should serve as a **standard for deferred payment.** When people make an agreement that involves payments to be made at some time in the future, it is convenient to have some standard way to specify the amount of such payment. Of course, whatever is used as a medium of exchange and a unit of account is most likely to be used as the standard of deferred payment as well. A substantial portion of the transactions that take place in a modern economy involve contracts that extend over a period of time.

Changing price levels bring up some of the same problems for money as a standard for deferred payment as they did for money as a store of purchasing power. Inflation means that the money value of the deferred payment will overstate its future purchasing power equivalent measured at today's prices. Conversely, deflation means that the money value of the deferred payment will understate its future purchasing power equivalent in terms of today's prices. Of course, if the parties to the contract expect prices to change during the term of the agreement, their expectations can be built into the deferred payment amounts that are written into the contract.

What Is Money?

Having described the basic functions that money is expected to perform, we can now define **money** as *anything that is generally accepted in an economy as a medium of exchange, a unit of account, a store of purchasing power, and a standard for deferred payment.* A careful look at this definition, however, reveals that we still have to deal with some obscure concepts. The word *anything* places no limit on the composition of money. As you will see, money may be metal, paper, entries in an account book, or even electronic impulses on magnetic tape. Also, the term *generally accepted* is difficult to pin down. *Accepted* means that people routinely use the substance in exchanges, but, as we shall explain shortly, acceptance must sometimes be enforced by law. How general must acceptance be in order for something to be money? Again, the definition is loose. Actual measurements of the money supply will require more refinements. In the United States today, coins, currency, and checking account balances are the basic forms of money. Let us take a brief look at each of these forms.

COINS The medium of exchange function goes a long way toward helping us understand why coins are a component of most money systems. People want a form of money that is durable, portable, and uniform because they want to carry money with them to make "convenience transactions," such as operating automatic vending machines. The absence of many of these characteristics helps explain why livestock, slaves, wampum, and tree bark did not fare well as money. But because cigarettes came quite close to having these qualities, they served reasonably well as money in prisoner-of-war camps during World War II. Of course, convenience, durability, portability, and uniformity do not guarantee success as money. The Susan B. Anthony dollar coin still does not circulate well in the United States, perhaps because people fear it will be mistaken for a twenty-five-cent piece.

The uniformity feature is especially important in making coins generally accepted. Long ago, gold dust or nuggets in a pouch had to be weighed when a transaction was made. But by minting the gold into a coin, it was possible to achieve uniformity. Sometimes, in an effort to gain a certain edge in the transaction, people would rub or chip away some of the coin. Though even kings and princes did this, they soon found that the official mint itself was the best place to cheat on the money system. To make more money with a given amount of gold, they could add base (less-valuable) metal before the coins were minted. This practice led to one of the earliest economic theories about money, called **Gresham's Law,** which states that base money always drives the dear (more-valuable) money out of circulation. Of two coins with the same face value, the one containing base metal circulates, while the one containing dear metal is hoarded or perhaps melted down to recover the metal. This law still operates today, it seems. The real silver coins in the United States are almost all in hoards or have been melted down.

CURRENCY Printed paper money is easy to carry, reasonably durable, and can be printed in whatever denominations are wanted and even in different colors to aid in recognition. Clipping and rubbing won't erode the value of the paper money. For larger transactions, paper money clearly has advantages over coin. In fact, paper currency evolved from coins and precious metal partly because of its extra convenience. Coins or, more likely, gold would be deposited with a bank or other institution of recognized reliability in exchange for deposit receipts, that is, for promises to return the coins or the gold when the receipt was presented. The certificate might read "Pay to the bearer on demand the sum of _____." This warehouse receipt payable to the bearer was, in fact, paper currency and was called a **bank note** when it was issued by a bank. Its acceptability depended on the integrity of the issuing bank or commercial establishment since it was backed by a promise to exchange coin or precious metal for the certificate.

The early days of paper money were confusing times because many different institutions would issue these notes and some were more reliable than others. People could never be sure that their notes were really worth the amount printed on them. The reason for this confusion was that banks and others who issued notes had discovered that, in normal times, new deposits of gold or coins would just about balance withdrawals of these precious metals. So why not issue a few extra notes and lend them, charging interest, to people who want to borrow? As you will see, this was the beginning of modern partial reserve banking. However, our immediate point is that some banks would push their luck in issuing bank notes, and a bank failure would occur, shaking confidence in all bank notes, even those from banks that were not overextended. U.S. history is filled with accounts of bank panics triggered by the inability of some banks to redeem their notes. In an attempt to reduce this danger, a system of national banks was set up in 1863 to issue paper currency, and a tax was imposed on the circulation of bank notes issued by banks chartered by states.

The history of government-sponsored currency is at least as fascinating as that of private bank notes. Governments also can yield to the temptation to issue too much currency. Government currency has often been issued without any (or very much) "backing" with precious metal. The official U.S. currency today, called the Federal Reserve Note, is not backed by any promise to exchange it for gold or silver or anything else. However, the particular advantage of government-issued currency is that an official government decree, or "fiat," usually states that the currency is **legal tender.** Your Federal Reserve Note, for example, bears the statement "This note is legal tender for all debts, public and private." This means that a person who is offered this currency but refuses to accept it in settling a debt cannot continue to collect interest on the debt or go to court to claim that the debtor had refused to pay. This goes a long way toward making the official currency generally acceptable, but it does not guarantee this result. In times of actual or prospective inflation, private contractors may try to force payment in real goods or precious metal rather than legal tender money. So even legal tender money can become worthless if people refuse to exchange goods and services for it. During the American Revolution, General Washington's troops at Valley Forge often went cold and hungry because of the difficulties the Continental Army had in buying supplies with continental currency. Similarly, during the Civil War, foreign money and gold became the most valuable part of the Confederacy's treasury. One of the last acts of the Confederacy was the attempt to get its gold and foreign money to Cuba for safekeeping.

CHECKING ACCOUNT (DEMAND DEPOSIT) BALANCES In the United States today, checking account balances, or demand deposits, also serve as money. Although personal checks are not always accepted, the overwhelming portion of all transactions today are paid by check. Note, however, that our description of this money refers to the balances in checking accounts, not to the checks themselves. Under this definition, checks

FIGURE 12-1   Official Measures of the U.S. Money Supply, November 1985 (in billions of dollars)

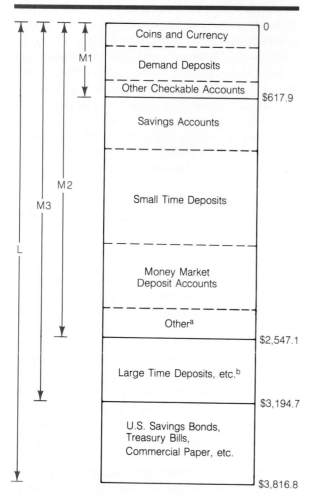

At the top of the money column are the most liquid or spendable types of money. The most widely used measure of the money supply (M1) includes coins, currency, demand deposits, and other checkable accounts. More inclusive measures of the money supply extend further down the column. Cumulative totals at the right show the larger and larger size of the money supply as more inclusive definitions are used.

a. Overnight repurchase agreements, Eurodollars, money market mutual fund shares.

b. Term repurchase agreements, term Eurodollars, institution-only money market mutual fund balances.

Source: Economic Report of the President, 1986, Tables B-64 and B-65.

that are not backed by sufficient balances are not money.

Checking account balances come into being partly as a result of deposits of coins or currency but mostly as a result of loans made by banks. When a person borrows from a bank, he or she may ask for and receive currency and coin, but most likely both the borrower and the banker will prefer the simple procedure of adding the borrowed sum to the balance in the borrower's checking account. Through this simple operation, the borrower's promise to repay the loan (the borrower's debt) is "monetized." That is, it becomes actual money. For this reason, many people say that most of our money supply is simply "monetized debt." In the context of U.S. history, it is interesting that checking account money expanded as bank note currency was eliminated. When taxes were imposed on the bank notes, bank lending switched to checking account balances. Checks replaced the bank notes and had the extra convenience of being written for the exact amount needed to discharge an obligation. Instead of promises to pay issued by the bank, a check is a payment order to the bank signed by the person or business with rights to the checking account. Bad checks are written, but they do not compromise the bank itself or invite a bank panic.

The U.S. Money Supply

The U.S. money supply as it exists today is illustrated in Figure 12-1. As you might expect from the phrase "anything that is generally accepted" in our definition of money, the actual measurement of the money supply can be somewhat complicated. Moreover, the things that are money may change from time to time as new technologies bring better ways to carry out exchanges. Four different measures of the money supply are illustrated. These are alternative definitions that are used in measuring the actual U.S. money supply. The definitions have been established by the Federal Reserve Board, which we describe in Chapter 13. In Figure 12-1, we encounter broader and broader definitions of money as we move down the column.

M1 Coins and currency are listed at the very top of the money column in Figure 12-1 because these items are extremely liquid—that is, they are easily used as a medium of exchange. Next in line come demand deposits (checking account balances), which are also very liquid. Next in order of liquidity are other checkable accounts such as NOW (negotiable orders of withdrawal) accounts, ATS (automatic transfer service) accounts, share draft accounts in credit unions, and other accounts that offer check-writing services. Such checkable accounts expanded rapidly during the 1970s. Their advantage is that interest is earned during the period before checks are written against the account. Thus, when these new systems were offered, some money came to them from demand deposit accounts, which were not allowed to earn interest, and some came from regular savings accounts, which earned interest but did not provide check-writing services. The **MI money supply concept** is the one that is used most by economists and is the one we refer to when we discuss the money supply in later chapters. In November 1985, there was $617.9 billion of this money.

M2, M3, and L As we proceed down the money supply column in Figure 12-1, we encounter assets that are less and less liquid. Small time deposits (such as certificates of deposit), money market deposit accounts, and savings accounts are not spendable in their present form, but can usually be exchanged for directly spendable forms without much delay or cost. A bit less liquid are "other" types of assets such as repurchase agreements (RPs) and money market mutual funds—arrangements with banks or with securities dealers that give the owner the chance to convert back to spendable money without great delay or cost. Also included in this "other" category are Eurodollars, which are deposits by European banks in American banks or in European branches of American banks. Even though they appear in the accounts of American banks, the lending business on these accounts is done mainly in Europe. The **M2 money supply concept** consists of M1 plus these less liquid accounts. The **M3 money supply concept** includes large time deposits, fairly long-term repurchase agreements,

and certain other assets, all of which are somewhat harder to convert into spendable money. Finally, money watchers also keep track of U.S. Savings Bonds, several relatively liquid kinds of U.S. government securities, payment promises by large corporations, and other items that are potentially convertible into spendable money. The **L money supply** is M3 plus these forms of wealth, which are sometimes called **near money.**

Some observers contend that economists, bankers, government officials, and other money watchers have gone too far in developing so many different measures of the money supply. They argue that confusion results from such a variety of money measures. Of course, the problem is that there are many ways of holding wealth and that very gradual changes in liquidity occur as assets are moved from one form to another. Sometimes the rate of change in the money supply according to one measure is different from its rate of change according to another measure. Therefore, when economists use money supply changes to make predictions about the economy, it may make a difference which measure they use. Usually there is a tradeoff between liquidity, which has its advantages, and interest earnings, which are desired for obvious reasons. The many asset forms simply give people a large number of options. In fact, the liquidity column could be extended still farther into such other near monies or money substitutes as jewelry, stamp collections, and works of art. Even credit cards have some moneylike features, though they simply give a person an easy way to borrow money.

BANKS AND DEPOSIT EXPANSION

Now that you know what money does and what the money supply is, we can consider the important matter of what determines the actual size of the money supply in the United States. The first step is to understand how banks are able to expand and contract the money supply. Then, in the next chapter, you will learn how government authorities can control these aspects of banking and thereby regulate the money supply itself.

How Banks Are Organized

Banks are profit-seeking business enterprises. With money from depositors and shareholders, banks earn income by lending money and by purchasing and holding interest-bearing securities. Some of the money that they obtain is used to pay interest to depositors. Some is used for other expenses, such as wages for employees. What is left is profit that may be paid to shareholders, just as in nonfinancial corporations.

In many ways, starting a new bank is similar to starting any new business. But what makes starting a bank somewhat different is that state and federal laws require that a charter must be obtained before the bank can do any business. The **bank charter** is the legal authority to engage in banking, much as the corporate charter is the legal authority to do business as a corporation or a medical license is the legal authority to practice medicine.

In the United States, bank charters are issued both by the federal government and by state governments. Often, the name of the bank will tell where its charter came from. The First National Bank has a federal charter, and the Home Town State Bank has a state charter. Although federal and state charters have similar provisions specifying permissible operations, state charters are frequently more generous. Federal charters require membership in the Federal Reserve System (which we describe in the next chapter). Along with general legislation, the charter sets the rules that the bank must follow in doing business. Violating these rules may mean the withdrawal of the charter and the end of business for the bank. Once the charter is in hand, the bank can sell stock and gather the money needed to launch its operations.

PARTIAL OR FRACTIONAL RESERVES A key idea in understanding the operation of banks is the concept of partial or fractional reserves. In their simplest form, **partial or fractional reserves** mean that the amount of cash or immediately available funds on hand is less than the total of the bank's obligations to all the people who have deposited money in the bank. If all depositors appeared at the same time and wanted their money, the bank would not be able to keep its promise of repayment. This would be a **run on the bank** and could be disastrous for the depositors, for the banker, and for the businesses planning to borrow from the bank.

But all banks operate on a partial reserve basis and run some risk of this disaster. Why do they do this? Why are depositors willing to place their money in banks? The answers to these questions are not as difficult as you might imagine. Bankers engage in partial reserve operations because it is profitable to do so. Depositors place their funds in these banks because they can receive low-cost checking and other services and can earn interest on their deposits. To understand how this system works, let's view it through the eyes of the banker. If a wide variety of depositors can be persuaded to place their money in the bank, it will soon become apparent that day-after-day new deposits will just about equal withdrawals from these accounts. Some customers will be writing checks to others who are also customers of the bank. No change in net deposits will occur. Checks written to outsiders will approximately match checks from outsiders. Suppose that over a long period of time, the difference between withdrawals and new deposits fluctuates within a range of, say, 5 percent of the average amount on deposit. With this knowledge, the banker recognizes that 95 percent of the deposited money (or perhaps only 90 percent, to leave a margin for safety) could be loaned out at interest. The interest earned from the loans enables the banker to pay interest to the depositors, and the spread between the interest charged to borrowers and the interest paid to depositors leaves money for the expenses of operating the bank and for profits to the owners of the bank (the shareholders).

There are also advantages from the point of view of the depositors. These people have wealth and can choose among many alternative ways to hold it. To obtain quick spendability (liquidity), they might hold cash but will earn no interest. To obtain dividend or interest earnings, they might purchase stocks or bonds, but their risk will be greater, and their wealth will have less liquidity. However, the depositor today can have both liquidity and interest earnings by placing funds in a bank or similar financial institution.[1] As long as the danger of bank failure and loss of deposits is minimal, there is little reason to forgo the advantages of earning interest and/or using a bank's services. In a well-run bank, the bankers, the depositors, and also those who borrow from the bank can all find the arrangement beneficial.

The partial reserve feature of banking clearly implies that money put into a bank, either by shareholders or by depositors, can be used as a reserve for a considerably greater quantity of "bank money" circulating in the economy. In times past, this bank money took the form of bank notes. Today, it takes the form of checking account balances. We shall carefully explain this process of monetary expansion later in the chapter. But first it is important to understand how partial reserve banking can also be safe banking.

BANK SAFETY In good times, banks share in the general prosperity, and bankers are caricatured as fat and greedy, enjoying a parasitic living from the success of others. When times are bad, banks share in the general adversity, and bankers are caricatured as thin and grasping, extracting the widow's mite to the wails of emaciated children. History books are filled with accounts of financial panics and bank failures, of savings lost and businesses ruined. Again, an accusing finger points at banking and the partial reserve system. Surely, the lure of profits or the "lust" for money may cause the banker to maintain the smallest possible reserve of cash and non-interest-earning reserves. But no banker wants the bank to fail, since failure will mean the loss of his or her job. How can the risk of bank failure be minimized?

BANK EXAMINERS The most common threat to bank safety arises when businesses that have borrowed from the bank are not able to repay

their loans. Perhaps the businesses were bad risks in the first place, and the loans should not have been granted. If bank loan officers make too many bad judgments, the bank will be in trouble, and poor management will be to blame. Therefore, the first line of defense against bank failure comes with **bank examiners** from agencies of the state or the federal government, who descend unannounced on the bank and assess the soundness of its operations and of the firms to which loans have been made. Reports of bad management or poor judgment in making loans will lead shareholders to install new management.

BANK "RUNS" AND DEPOSIT INSURANCE Bank examiners alone cannot ensure the safety of a bank. Bank lending is typically concentrated in the local community. Therefore, if local business conditions turn sour, many businesses that appeared sound in better times may become unable to meet their payments to the bank. If the local situation is temporary, all the bank needs is temporary help from outside, usually in the form of a loan from some other financial institution. If the community is in a long-run decline, the bank must find a way to make an orderly cutback in its operations.

Whenever doubt arises about the soundness of a bank, rumors quickly spread that the bank may fail. Few rumors are more contagious than those about impending bank failure. Lines form at tellers' windows as depositors rush to get their money out of the threatened bank. Ironically, as long as depositors are confident that their money is "in the bank," they are content to leave it there. But "if you don't have it, I want it immediately" is the theme of a "run" on a bank. As melodramatic movies so vividly show, tellers pay out the dwindling funds as slowly as possible, while a frantic effort is made to import cash from other banks.

Deposit insurance is an excellent illustration of the adage that "an ounce of prevention is worth a pound of cure." After a disastrous episode of bank failures in 1931 and 1932, the U.S. government established the Federal Deposit Insurance Corporation (FDIC). This federal agency insures bank deposits up to the amount of $100,000 per

---

1. As we mentioned earlier, interest is not paid on demand deposit balances. But NOW accounts, ATS accounts, credit union share drafts, and the like, in effect offer both checking services and interest earnings. Before the introduction of these accounts, checking service was usually offered without charge— an arrangement that offered a valuable service in place of cash interest earnings.

TABLE 12-1 Balance Sheet Total for All Commercial Banking Institutions in the United States, January 29, 1986 (in billions of dollars)

Assets		Liabilities and Net Worth	
Reserves and cash items	173.2	Demand deposits (transaction deposits)	481.3
Loans	1,383.3	Savings deposits	450.4
Securities	417.3	Time deposits	749.5
Other assets	273.1	Borrowings	292.2
		Other liabilities	119.1
		Total liabilities	2,092.5
		Net worth	154.3
	2,246.8		2,246.8

Note: Items may not all add to total because of rounding
Source: *Federal Reserve Bulletin*, April 1986, Table 1.25.

account. To get this insurance, the bank pays a premium based on the average amount of its deposits. An attractive plaque is displayed prominently by the bank to assure depositors that their money is safe. Wide publicity is given to the statement that "not a penny has ever been lost in an account insured by the FDIC." With this insurance, there is little danger that a bank will be forced to close because of a run by depositors. Most, but not all, banks purchase this insurance. Similar insurance is available to other financial institutions. For example, the Federal Savings and Loan Insurance Corporation (FSLIC) insures deposits in savings and loan associations, and the National Credit Union Administration (NCUA) insures deposits in credit unions.

WILL LARGER RESERVES PROTECT BANKS? This is an intriguing question and one that has caused confusion and frustration over the years. "Will a larger gas tank protect your car against running out of gasoline?" Driving too far between station stops can cause even the largest gasoline tank to run dry, and even the largest bank reserve (except 100 percent) could be depleted if the economic situation were bad enough. Of course, a larger gasoline tank will reduce the likelihood of running out, but the car must be heavier to haul the added weight of extra gas. Similarly, larger bank reserves

can reduce the likelihood of bank failure, but at some cost to the bank itself, which must forgo interest on a larger portion of its funds.

Though government agencies do regulate the size of bank reserves, the main reason for doing so is to give the government a way of controlling the amount of bank money (checking accounts) that the banking system can create. This is the matter of deposit expansion by the banking system, which we shall examine shortly.

The Balance Sheet of a Bank

In order to understand the deposit expansion process, it is necessary to have some acquaintance with the balance sheet of a bank. In Table 12-1, we present a simplified balance sheet showing totals for all commercial banking institutions in the United States as of January 29, 1986. Assets are listed on the left side, and liabilities and net worth on the right.

ASSETS Let us briefly explain each entry on the left side first.

RESERVES AND CASH ITEMS Reserves consist mainly of deposits that commercial banks are required by law to maintain with Federal Reserve

Banks. In the next chapter, we shall describe the Federal Reserve Banks and how reserve requirements are set. This item on the balance sheet is very important in the deposit expansion process. Cash items consist of all cash in the bank vault and in the tellers' cages, along with other miscellaneous items.

LOANS These are the IOUs that the bank holds from individuals and businesses who have borrowed from the bank. They are the main source of interest earnings for the bank. Interest earnings from these loans and from securities provide funds to pay interest to depositors, to cover operating expenses, and to pay dividends to shareholders.

SECURITIES These are mainly government bonds that banks buy and hold in order to generate interest income while at the same time retaining fairly quick access to funds.

OTHER ASSETS These consist of buildings, furniture, and equipment needed to carry on the bank's operations. This category also consists of minor items not conveniently listed elsewhere.

LIABILITIES AND NET WORTH Now let's take a look at the entries on the right side of the balance sheet.

DEMAND DEPOSITS (TRANSACTION DEPOSITS) These are amounts owed to holders of checking accounts. When a depositor writes a check, he or she is placing a demand on the bank to transfer money to someone. These **demand deposits** (or **transaction deposits**) are payable on demand. (The official designation for these accounts is "transaction deposits." The reason for this change in designation is explained in the next chapter.)

SAVINGS DEPOSITS These are amounts owed to holders of savings accounts. Technically, they are not payable on demand. Some waiting period or advance notice may be required by the bank.

TIME DEPOSITS Time deposits are obligations to the holders of accounts that have stated dates

when they will have to be paid—that is, they have fixed maturity dates. Certificates of deposit are examples of this type of account. Banks can pay somewhat higher rates of interest on these accounts since they are committed to remain in the bank for a longer period of time. This kind of account gives the bank greater flexibility in lending out this money.

BORROWINGS These are IOUs given by banks when they borrow from other financial institutions. If a bank can borrow at a low rate of interest and lend the money out at a higher rate, there is every reason to expect that it will do so.

OTHER LIABILITIES These are obligations that a bank has, like any other business, but which do not fit into other categories.

NET WORTH Assets minus liabilities equal net worth—that is, the book value of the business to its owners. As we noted in our discussion of balance sheets in Chapter 2, the net worth of a business includes the money that was paid in by original stockholders minus losses that have been suffered plus profits that have been earned but not paid out as dividends.

DEPOSIT EXPANSION AND CONTRACTION

We mentioned earlier that fractional or partial reserve banking opens the way for banks to expand the money supply. Indeed, this expansion potential is a by-product of the fractional reserve system. There is nothing illegal or magical about banks "creating" or "destroying" money. The process is not difficult to understand.

The Reserve Ratio

The **reserve ratio** is a key term in understanding how banks expand and contract the money supply. This ratio is the total of cash and official (government-approved) reserves held by the bank divided by the amount of checkable account liabilities of that bank. Checkable accounts include regular demand deposits plus other types of accounts against which checks can, in effect, be written. For simplicity, we will use the term *demand deposits* to include all of these accounts. Suppose that a bank had $20 in cash and official reserves and $100 in demand deposit liabilities. Its reserve ratio would then be 20 percent. Official reserves must be held in the form of deposits with Federal Reserve Banks or vault cash, except that sometimes banks can arrange to hold these reserves with other financial institutions, which, in turn, maintain reserve deposits with a Federal Reserve Bank.

Another term that is important to understand is the **reserve requirement**—the amount of official reserves that banks (and other depository institutions) must maintain in order to avoid penalties. The reserve requirement is generally expressed as a minimum required reserve ratio. In our example, if the reserve requirement for the bank were 20 percent, the bank would be exactly in conformity with the law. It would not have too few reserves, and it would have no **excess reserves.** This is another key idea in the expansion process. Excess reserves are official reserves over and above the reserve requirements.

The Deposit-Expansion Process

Exactly how do banks expand the money supply by expanding demand deposits? Of course, we must state at the very beginning that the process also works in the reverse direction. That is, it can work to contract the money supply as well.

Table 12-2 shows balance sheets for Bank A, which we have simplified by showing only the entries needed to explain the expansion process and by showing zero amounts initially (top panel) for each entry. We shall assume that the reserve requirement is 20 percent.

The **deposit-expansion process** starts when a new deposit is made in this bank. This is shown in the middle panel of Table 12-2. To use the simplest example, we assume that Bill Brown deposits $100 of currency that previously had

been circulating as hand-to-hand money.[2] He deposits the $100 in his checking (demand deposit) account, which is a liability entered on the right side of the balance sheet for Bank A. On the asset side, the $100 is recorded in the "reserves and cash" category. In parentheses below this entry, you will note that these reserves consist of $20 that is required and $80 of excess reserves. No expansion of the money supply has yet taken place. Even though Bill Brown's checking account balance is counted as money, only coins and currency *outside* the bank are included in the official definition of the money supply. Therefore, Bill's checking account balance simply replaces the currency that he deposited.

The stage is set, however, for an expansion of the money supply. Bank A has excess reserves in the amount of $80, given our assumed 20 percent reserve requirement. If Ron Black wants to borrow $80 and if the bank is willing to lend it to him, an expansion of the money supply will take place. This step is shown in the bottom panel in Table 12-2. Mr. Black signs a note to the bank, which it lists as an asset in the loans category, and Mr. Black takes the proceeds of his loan in currency. The reserves and cash account for Bank A is reduced to $20, all of which is required, and both Ron Black and Bill Brown have money to spend.

Since Mr. Black did not borrow the money for the sheer pleasure of paying interest to the bank, we assume that he soon spends it to buy something, say, a record turntable from the Green Radio Company. Green Radio deposits the currency in its checking account in Bank B (top panel in Table 12-3). After Bank B places the money in its reserves and cash account, it is ready (even eager) to lend out the $64, which is in excess of the prevailing 20 percent reserve requirement. The story continues. Sue Blue, who banks with Bank B, has a good credit rating and wants to borrow $64 to pay for a repair on her car. So she signs a note to Bank B, which lists it as an asset in the loans category (bottom panel in Table 12-3).

2. You will learn in the next chapter that the central bank is the most likely originating source of new deposits into the banking system.

TABLE 12-2   Deposit-Expansion Process: Bank A (amounts in dollars)

Bank A
(start)

Assets		Liabilities	
Reserves and cash	0	Demand deposits	0
(Required: __0__)			
(Excess: __0__)			
Loans	0		
Securities	0		
	0		0

Bank A
(new deposit step)

Assets		Liabilities	
Reserves and cash	100	Demand deposits	
(Required: __20__)		Bill Brown	100
(Excess: __80__)			
Loans	0		
Securities	0		
	100		100

Bank A
(loan step)

Assets		Liabilities	
Reserves and cash	20	Demand deposits	
(Required: __20__)		Bill Brown	100
(Excess: __0__)			
Loans			
Ron Black	80		
Securities	0		
	100		100

The process begins in the "new-deposit step" when Bill Brown deposits $100 in his checking account. The bank then has excess reserves of $80, which are loaned to Ron Black in the "loan step."

For convenience, Ms. Blue takes her loan in the form of a $64 addition to the balance in her checking account and writes a check for $64 to the White Motor Company to pay for the auto repair. Since we expect borrowers (Ron Black and Sue Blue) to spend their money promptly, it does not matter whether they accept the loan in cash or as an entry in their checking accounts. The bank expects the prompt departure of the borrowed money, either in cash or as soon as the White Motor Company or its bank presents Sue's check for payment.

As you probably expect, the deposit-expansion process is far from over. As soon as White Motor

TABLE 12-3 **Deposit-Expansion Process: Bank B (amounts in dollars)**

Bank B
(new deposit step)

Assets		Liabilities	
Reserves and cash	80	Demand deposits	
(Required: 16)		Green Radio Co.	80
(Excess: 64)			
Loans	0		
Securities	0		
	80		80

Bank B
(loan step)

Assets		Liabilities	
Reserves and cash	16	Demand deposits	
(Required: 16)		Green Radio Co.	80
(Excess: 0)			
Loans			
Sue Blue	64		
Securities	0		
	80		80

When cash loaned by a bank returns to the banking system as a new deposit, the stage is set for a second round of deposit expansion. In this stage, Green Radio Company deposits the $80 spent by Ron Black. Bank B now has excess reserves of $64, which it loans to Sue Blue.

deposits the $64 in Bank C (see top panel in Table 12-4), that bank finds that it has excess reserves in the amount of $51.20—the $64 deposit minus the $12.80 of required reserves. Bank C decides to put these excess reserves to work by purchasing bonds in the bond market. Bonds of the Yellow Cab Company appear to be a good buy, and on that day Grace Gray happens to be selling her holdings of these bonds. The bank buys the bonds, which it lists as an asset in the securities category on its balance sheet (see the bottom panel of Table 12-4), and, through the system of markets and brokers, Grace Gray receives a check for $51.20. She deposits the check in her checking account in Bank D, and the expansion process continues.

The deposit-expansion process is summarized in Table 12-5. It started in our example when Bill Brown put $100 of currency into a checking account. Once this money was in the banking system, the expansion process went into operation as new checking account balances were created for the Green Radio Company, the White Motor Company, Grace Gray, and others. The cumulative-totals column in Table 12-5 emphasizes that all of these balances exist at the same time and that all of them are money according to the prevailing definition. Our example assumed that money loaned out was then deposited in a different bank. However, the process would work in the same way if the money came back to the same bank that made the loan.

A **deposit-contraction process** would follow the same sequence, except that it would start with a withdrawal instead of a deposit. If the banks were in exact conformity with the reserve requirement

TABLE 12-4   Deposit-Expansion Process: Bank C (amounts in dollars)

Bank C
(new deposit step)

Assets		Liabilities	
Reserves and cash	64	Demand deposits	
(Required: 12.80)		White Motor Co.	64
(Excess: 51.20)			
Loans	0		
Securities	0		
	64		64

Bank C
(loan step)

Assets		Liabilities	
Reserves and cash	12.80	Demand deposits	
(Required: 12.80)		White Motor Co.	64
(Excess: 0)			
Loans	0		
Securities			
Yellow Cab Co.	51.20		
	64.00		64

In the third round of the deposit-expansion process, White Motor Company deposits the check written by Sue Blue, and Bank C has excess reserves of $51.20. The bank purchases $51.20 of Yellow Cab Company securities from Grace Gray.

when the withdrawal occurred, securities would be sold, and loans would be called in or not renewed. As a result, demand deposits would shrink.

The Deposit-Expansion Factor

You undoubtedly recognize that the arithmetic in Table 12-5 is like that used in Chapter 10 to explain the multiplier effect of changes in total planned expenditure on national income and product. In other words, we have a geometric progression, in which each successive round generates new deposits equal to a fixed percentage of those created in the preceding round. The reserve ratio operates in the same way that $(1 - MPC)$ did in the formula for the multiplier.

In terms of the reserve ratio actually operating in the banks, the **deposit-expansion factor** is

$$\frac{1}{\text{reserve ratio}}$$

In our example, we assumed that the banks were always in exact conformity with the legal reserve requirement, so that the reserve ratio was 20 percent at all times. In this case, the deposit-expansion factor was $1/0.2$, which works out to a value of 5.[3] The first deposit of $100 was expanded

3. We arrive at the answer in the following way:

$$1 + (0.8) + (0.8)^2 + (0.8)^3 + \cdots$$
$$+ (0.8)^n = \frac{1}{1 - 0.8} = \frac{1}{0.2} = 5$$

TABLE 12-5 Summary of Deposit-Expansion Process

	Demand Deposit Balances	
	Individual Accounts	Cumulative Totals
Bill Brown (Bank A)	$100.00	$100.00
Green Radio (Bank B)	80.00	180.00
White Motor (Bank C)	64.00	244.00
Grace Gray (Bank D)	51.20	295.20
etc. (Bank E)	40.96	336.16
etc. (Bank F)	32.76	368.92
etc. (Bank G)	26.21	395.13
. . .		
. . .		
. . .		
(nth Bank) .		$500.00
	$500.00	

Bill Brown's initial deposit is expanded by deposits for Green Radio, White Motor, Grace Gray, and others. All of these demand deposits exist at the same time, and all count as money. With a 20 percent reserve ratio, total deposits may be five times the initial deposit.

to support an added $400 in demand deposits, so that the total of demand deposits was $500. If the reserve ratio had been kept at 25 percent, the expansion factor would have been 4. If the reserve ratio had been kept at 10 percent, the expansion factor would have been 10, and so on.

Controlling the Expansion Factor

The reserve ratio, and therefore the expansion factor, is controlled through the Federal Reserve System's authority to set the official minimum reserve requirement. This is stated as a percentage of the amount on deposit in accounts that offer check-writing services. As of April 1986, the required reserve was 12 percent of such balances. We shall explain in the next chapter just how this official minimum ratio is set. For the moment, it is enough to know that the profit motive will

encourage banks to keep the actual reserve ratio fairly close to the official ratio, since excess reserves earn no interest and a deficiency in reserves will force the bank to borrow and pay interest. So the Federal Reserve System can control the deposit-expansion factor by setting the official reserve ratio.

Of course, banks may not always remain in exact conformity with the official reserve requirement, and therefore the Federal Reserve System's control of the expansion factor is less than perfect. Banks may keep some excess reserve on hand to avoid penalties from unexpected withdrawals or so that they will be ready to accommodate especially good customers when they ask for loans. These are called **desired excess reserves.** There also is a second reason why the control of the expansion factor is not exact. Our expansion process assumed that borrowers (Ron Black and Sue Blue) quickly spent every cent that they borrowed. However, if some of the funds borrowed are kept as pocket money or simply allowed to circulate from hand to hand in the economy so that the money is not returned to the banking system, the deposit expansion will stop short of its full potential. The actual expansion, therefore, is not as exact as the deposit-expansion factor and our example imply.

Controlling the Money Supply

In the United States, the money supply is regulated by (a) controlling the deposit-expansion factor and (b) by controlling the actual amount of reserves in the banking system, as will be described in the next chapter. You will learn about the Federal Reserve System, which is the "central bank" in the United States and is responsible, under legislation from Congress, for administering both of these steps in controlling the money supply.

SUMMARY

1. Most economists believe that changes in the amount of money in the economy and in the speed of its circulation can cause changes in the general price level and can also cause changes in real levels of production and employment.

2. Economists define money as anything that is generally accepted as a medium of exchange, a unit of account, a store of purchasing power, and a standard for deferred payment. At various times and places, many different things have served as money.

3. According to the definitions most widely used in the United States, the money supply consists of coins, currency, and checkable account balances. Checkable account balances are the largest component. The currency is "fiat money"; that is, the government specifies it to be legal tender.

4. Broader definitions of the money supply include forms of wealth that are somewhat less liquid than coins, currency, and checkable account balances. The forms of wealth that are almost money are called "near monies."

5. Banks are profit-seeking businesses that earn their incomes by obtaining money from investors and depositors and by buying securities and lending money to individuals and businesses. The difference between interest charged by the bank and interest paid by the bank provides money to cover expenses and to pay dividends to the bank's shareholders.

6. Banks operate with partial or fractional reserves, which means that money deposited in a bank can be used to support new checkable account balances that are created when banks make loans to customers.

7. Partial reserve banking involves some risks of bank failure. These risks are reduced by officially designated bank examiners and by deposit insurance.

8. A bank's reserve ratio is its total of official reserves divided by its total checkable account liabilities. The reserve requirement is the official reserve ratio that must be kept in order to avoid penalties. Excess reserves are those over and above the official reserve requirement.

9. Because banking is carried on with partial or fractional reserves, a new deposit gives rise to excess reserves. There is a deposit expansion when these excess reserves are loaned out or used to buy stocks and bonds. When the new

loan or the payment for the securities is itself deposited in a bank, the expansion can be repeated. The deposit-expansion factor is 1 divided by the reserve ratio actually in use in the banks.

10. The Federal Reserve System's authority to set minimum reserve requirements allows it to regulate the size of the deposit-expansion factor. This regulation is not precise, however, because some banks may not be in exact conformity with the official reserve requirement and because some of the money brought about through new loans may not be returned to the banking system.

11. The deposit-contraction factor operates to reduce the money supply. Deposit contraction is begun when deposits are withdrawn from the banking system and not deposited again. In this case, banks must sell some of their securities, call in loans, or refuse to renew loans when they fall due.

12. The Federal Reserve System's control of the money supply is carried out in two ways: it can control both the deposit-expansion factor and the amount of reserves in the banking system.

DISCUSSION QUESTIONS

1. Why is it not possible to define money in terms of its composition? Identify the four functions of money that are specified in economics. Which of them is the most basic? Why? Which is (are) most affected by inflation?

2. Write down the definition of money given in this chapter. Then explain why the words "generally accepted" are basic to this definition. What is Gresham's Law? Explain why it still works.

3. Explain how a bank note is an ancestor of modern paper currency. Does today's U.S. currency have more or less backing than did the early bank notes? Explain your answer. What does *legal tender* mean?

4. Describe two different ways in which you can add to the balance in your checkable account. Why is much of our money actually "monetized debt"? Explain.

5. Explain the term *liquidity*. Why do slight differences among assets in their liquidity create problems in measuring the money supply? Briefly summarize the types of assets included in the M1 category of the U.S. money supply.

6. What is a "run" on a bank? Since runs are always possible under partial reserve banking, why are depositors willing to expose their money to this risk? Explain how the partial reserve system operates to the advantage of all people involved.

7. Discuss the roles of bank examiners and deposit insurance in improving the safety of bank deposits. Why does a reserve requirement not guarantee safety? What is the reason for the legal reserve requirement in the U.S. banking system?

8. Without looking at Table 12-1, prepare a commercial bank balance sheet and record its major entries. Then check to make sure you have it right. Explain how electronic technology has blurred the distinction between demand deposits and savings deposits.

9. Carefully distinguish between the actual reserve ratio and the official required reserve ratio. What happens if the actual ratio is less than the requirement? What happens if the actual ratio is more than the requirement? Explain what is meant by "excess" reserves and why they are important in the economy.

10. Trace the process by which the banking system expands the amount of money when excess reserves appear. How does the official reserve requirement control the amount of this expansion? Write the formula for the deposit-expansion factor. Describe two situations that may cause the actual expansion not to follow exactly the formula for money expansion.

13 *The Federal Reserve System and Monetary Instruments*

PREVIEW As you have learned, banks operate on partial reserves, so that they are able to expand and contract the money supply. This chapter will explain how the Federal Reserve System, the central bank of the United States, regulates the money supply by controlling the operations of banks. Regulating the money supply is a key ingredient in the *monetarist* approach to macroeconomic policy, just as regulating taxes and government purchases are key ingredients in the *fiscalist* approach, which we studied in Chapter 11. Debates between fiscalists and monetarists dominated macroeconomic policy discussions in the 1960s and 1970s. In this chapter, we examine monetary instruments for macroeconomic policy.

We start by describing the beginnings of the Federal Reserve System—how it was set up after many years of dissatisfaction with an earlier system. Then we explain how the Federal Reserve System is organized through twelve district banks and describe the services that it offers. The Board of Governors of the system meets in Washington, D.C., to set policy. Many people believe these seven governors to be the most powerful non-elected officials in the country. The Federal Open Market Committee, which includes the seven members of the Board of Governors, buys and sells government securities to affect the money supply.

The second part of this chapter describes **monetary instruments,** or the tools used to regulate the money supply. In carrying out macroeconomic policy, monetary instruments are used along with the fiscal instruments. Among the monetary tools are the setting of reserve requirements for banks, the buying and selling of government securities (open market operations), the setting of interest rates on loans to banks (called discount rates), and attempts to persuade banks to cooperate with central bank policy. We explain the money multiplier concept to show how difficult it is to maintain exact control of the money supply.

Finally, we review the record of actions taken by the Federal Reserve in its job of controlling the money supply. Why did it not bail out the banks when failure threatened in 1932? Why did it raise the reserve requirements for banks in 1936? Why did it keep on buying government bonds and expanding the money supply even after World War II ended? Should the Federal Reserve Board be blamed for high interest rates and credit shortages in 1968 and later years? These questions set the stage for the following chapter, which will explain the relation of the money supply to inflation and to the level of equilibrium real national income and product.

THE FEDERAL RESERVE SYSTEM

Most industrial countries have a centralized monetary authority, generally called a central bank, which is an arm of the Treasury or the finance ministry. The central bank of the United States, called the **Federal Reserve System,** is different from most central banks because of its relative independence from the Treasury and the other offices of the administration.

The Federal Reserve System, often called the "Fed," was begun by an Act of Congress in 1913 because Americans had come to dislike the earlier system. The National Banking System, which dated from the Civil War, operated without a central bank. It had developed two major problems. These were the seasonal "money shortages" in farming areas when crops had to be financed and a susceptibility to nationwide panics because of the "pyramiding" of reserves. The seasonal money shortages arose because the amount of currency that could be issued did not respond to seasonal changes in the demand for cash.

The system's susceptibility to nationwide panics was a more serious problem. This happened because a large part of the reserves of small banks could be held as deposits in banks in larger cities and because these banks, in turn, could hold a large part of their reserves as deposits in banks in a few major cities. So, as small banks called for funds from the larger city banks and as these larger banks called for funds from the major city banks, cash demands and reserve problems arising in isolated areas would build up and create a panic. This **pyramiding of reserves** set the stage for repeated nationwide bank panics. One such panic in 1907 led to the passage of the Federal Reserve Act in 1913.

Many Americans favored a strong European type of central bank, but those in the agricultural parts of the country were suspicious of the East and "Wall Street" and wanted as much control as possible over regional monetary conditions. Because they did not really trust bankers, they wanted farmers and business people to share control of the system. Under the Federal Reserve Act, the country was divided into twelve districts, a Federal Reserve Bank was set up in each district, and a Board of Governors was charged with supervising the operation of the whole system. The new system was designed to control the money supply, to provide a more flexible currency (the Federal Reserve Note), and to be a lender of last resort that could prevent bank failures by making loans to banks when trouble arose, thus forestalling panics. Though modified by experience and additional legislation, the structure set up in 1913 is much the same today.

The Board of Governors

On the **Board of Governors** of the Federal Reserve System are seven people appointed by the president of the United States and confirmed by the Senate. Their terms are for fourteen years, with one member's term expiring every second year. Part of the reason for this long term of office is to protect the Board from short-run political pressures and so to give the Federal Reserve a degree of independence from the executive and legislative branches of the government.

The Board is responsible for directing the nation's monetary policy, which can be used either to counteract or to reinforce the fiscal policy undertaken by the president and Congress. Thus, the independence of the Board is one of the checks and balances that have been built into the U.S. system of government.

As a practical matter, however, we should not overstate the independence of the Board of Governors. Members sometimes resign before the end of their fourteen-year term, so that appointments must usually be made oftener than every two years. Also, every four years the president can choose a member of the Board to serve as chairperson.

Over the years, the monetary policy followed by the Board has generally been consistent with the fiscal policy of the president and the Congress, but on important occasions conflict has arisen. We shall examine these conflicts later in this chapter.

The Federal Open Market Committee

The **Federal Open Market Committee (FOMC)** has twelve members, seven of whom are the members of the Board of Governors. The other five members come, one each, from five of the Federal Reserve District Banks. The Federal Reserve Bank of New York always provides one of these five committee members, and the other four positions are filled, on a rotating basis, from the other Federal Reserve Banks.

The Federal Open Market Committee was not a part of the original (1913) structure of the Federal

Reserve System, but experience during the 1920s showed that the purchase and sale of securities by the Federal Reserve could have important effects on the economy. When the FOMC became an official agency of the Federal Reserve in the 1930s, informal cooperation among the banks was replaced by direct control by the Board of Governors. FOMC buying and selling of government securities in the open market is one of the most powerful tools of monetary policy.

Federal Reserve District Banks

The map in Figure 13-1 shows the locations of the twelve **Federal Reserve Banks** and the boundaries of their districts. This geographic distribution recognized the diverse interests of the various parts of the country and countered the fears of centralized banking and eastern domination that had plagued the earlier attempts to set up a central bank. Each district bank is expected to serve the particular banking and commercial interests of its district with appropriate expertise, such as ranching in Kansas City, oil and gas in Dallas, agriculture in Chicago, or trade and finance in New York. Each Federal Reserve Bank is owned by the banks in its district, which become members of the system by purchasing stock in their district bank. All **national banks** (those chartered by the federal government) must be members of the system. If state banks choose to join, they may do so. The Federal Reserve Banks generate profits from interest on the securities they own and pay dividends to their shareholding member banks. However, federal law limits the amount of dividends that can be paid. Any "excess" profits must be turned over to the U.S. Treasury.

Each Federal Reserve Bank receives deposits and handles checks for the federal government and provides many services to local banks. Among their main services to these banks are bank examinations, check clearing, and making loans. A detailed description of most of these services is best left to specialized courses in money and banking. However, their service of making loans to commercial banks is directly related to the

Federal Reserve's regulation of the money supply, which is our focus in this chapter.

Making loans to member banks is a way to meet one of the major goals in setting up the Federal Reserve System in 1913—assuring the soundness of the banking system and preventing panics and, if possible, bank failures. To achieve this goal, each Federal Reserve Bank is expected to understand the economic needs of its district and to oversee the soundness of its member banks. If a member bank has temporary difficulty, a loan from the Federal Reserve Bank can be arranged. This **lender of last resort** service ranked high among the objectives in setting up the system. Loans to member banks are carried out through a process called **discounting,** in which securities or promises from a borrower are purchased by a Federal Reserve Bank from a member bank at less than their value at maturity. The **discount rate** is the rate of interest charged on these loans. Discounting not only can help member banks but also can be an instrument for controlling the money supply.

Federal Reserve Bank Balance Sheet

A simplified balance sheet for the twelve district banks of the Federal Reserve System is presented in Table 13-1. On the asset side, the most important item is U.S. government securities. These are debt instruments that have been issued by the U.S. Treasury. They make up part of the national debt. Even though most of the national debt is held by private citizens and firms (including commercial banks), the part held by the Federal Reserve Banks is very important. Most of this part consists of short-term securities (90-day Treasury bills) that have been acquired by the Federal Reserve Banks in carrying out open market operations, which are described later in this chapter.

On the liability side of the balance sheet, the major item is the Federal Reserve Notes circulating in the economy. These notes are the legal tender currency of the United States. Two other entries on the liabilities side also are important. One of these is the reserve deposits account. In

FIGURE 13-1 The Federal Reserve System

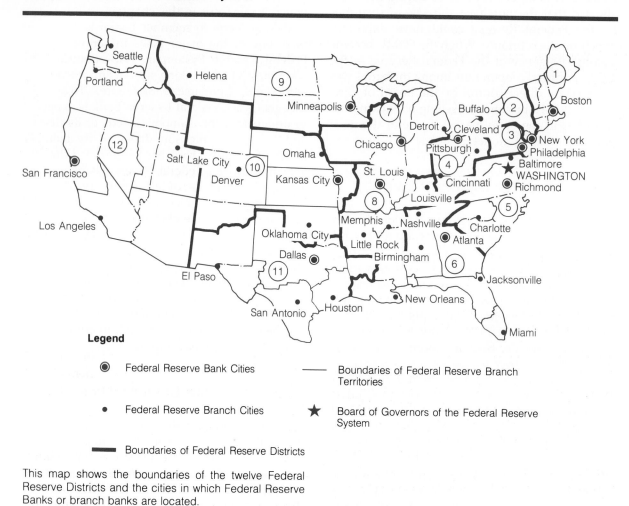

Legend

◉ Federal Reserve Bank Cities

● Federal Reserve Branch Cities

—— Boundaries of Federal Reserve Districts

—— Boundaries of Federal Reserve Branch Territories

★ Board of Governors of the Federal Reserve System

This map shows the boundaries of the twelve Federal Reserve Districts and the cities in which Federal Reserve Banks or branch banks are located.

Note: Alaska is in the Seattle Branch Territory and Hawaii in that served by the Head Office of the Federal Reserve Bank of San Francisco. Both are in the Twelfth District.

Source: Federal Reserve Bulletin, April 1986.

TABLE 13-1 Balance Sheet for Federal Reserve Banks, January 31, 1986 (in billions of dollars)

Assets		Liabilities	
U.S. Government securities	179.0	Federal Reserve Notes	174.5
Other securities	9.7	Deposits	
Other assets	38.7	Reserve accounts[a]	23.5
		U.S. Treasury	16.2
		Other	0.7
		Other liabilities	8.2
			223.1
		Capital Account	
		Paid in	1.8
		Other	2.5
Total	227.4	Total	227.4

This is a simplified balance sheet for all twelve Federal Reserve Banks.

a. Technically, these are simply deposits from depository institutions.
Source: Federal Reserve Bulletin, April 1986, Table 1.18.

describing reserve requirements in Chapter 12, we noted that official reserves must be held as vault cash or as deposits in the Federal Reserve Banks. This is the balance sheet entry that records these reserve deposits. The other important entry on the liability side of the balance sheet is the deposit of the U.S. Treasury. One of the tasks of the Federal Reserve System is to handle the checking account of the federal government.

INSTRUMENTS OF MONETARY POLICY

Now that you know the structure of the Federal Reserve System and the services it provides, we can examine how it seeks to control the U.S. money supply. As you learned in the last chapter, checking account balances are the major component of the money supply. You also know that the ability of banks to create checking account balances depends on the amount of reserves in these banks and on their reserve ratios. Federal Reserve influences on the reserve ratio and the amount of reserves are the main elements of monetary policy in the United States.

Reserve Requirements

Because cash and reserve accounts earn no interest, banks will try to keep the lowest possible reserve ratio that is safe and in keeping with the laws governing bank operations. By setting minimum required reserve ratios, the government can strongly influence actual reserve ratios. Let us see how this control operates.

CHANGING RESERVE REQUIREMENTS If you think back to the deposit-expansion process described in Chapter 12, you can easily see how important the Board's power to raise or lower official reserve requirements is. Raising the official reserve requirement will most likely raise the actual reserve ratio maintained by banks and so will lower the deposit-expansion factor. Let's suppose that the actual reserve ratio was 12 percent. In this case, the banking system could support $833.33 of checking deposits when the amount of reserves in the system was $100 ($100/0.12 = $833.33). But if the Board raised the reserve requirement so that the actual reserve ratio became 14 percent, this same $100 of reserves would support only $714.29 in checking deposits ($100/0.14 = $714.29). The Board's action could force a great reduction in the money supply. On the other hand, lowering the reserve requirement so that the actual reserve ratio became 10 percent would allow these reserves to support $1,000 of checking deposits ($100/0.10 = $1,000). The Board would have invited a large expansion in the money supply.

Raising or lowering the official reserve requirement is a powerful instrument, but it is quite sparingly used. The main problem with the reserve-requirement instrument is that changes in reserve requirements can cause embarrassing problems for ordinary commercial banks as they try to serve their customers. Increases can cause the most trouble. If a bank is operating close to the official ratio in order to serve its stockholders, it may find that an increase in this ratio forces it to deny loans to customers who depend on the bank or to borrow funds from a Federal Reserve Bank. For this reason, changing the reserve requirement is a heavy-handed and somewhat crude tool for adjusting the money supply. As you will see, there is another instrument that can perform more smoothly. Before discussing other instruments, however, we shall see how the power of the Board of Governors to influence reserves was greatly strengthened by the Monetary Control Act of 1980.

THE MONETARY CONTROL ACT OF 1980[1] The **Monetary Control Act of 1980** was landmark legislation, which broadened the Board of Governors' powers to regulate the money supply in two directions. First, the law broadened the Board's regulatory power to cover all **depository institutions.** In other words, the Board's authority is no longer limited to banks that are members of the Federal Reserve System. Under the law, the Board's reserve requirements cover all transactions accounts in member banks, nonmember banks, savings and loan associations, mutual savings banks, credit unions, and any other institution that offers depository services.

Second, the Act used the term **transactions accounts** so that the Board's authority was broadened to include "all deposits on which the account holder is permitted to make withdrawals by negotiable or transferable instruments, payment orders of withdrawal, and telephone and pre-authorized transfers (in excess of three per month) for the purpose of making payments to third persons or others."[2]

This means that any checkable account is covered, whether it is a conventional demand deposit account, an **automatic transfer service account (ATS),** a **negotiable order of withdrawal account (NOW),** a **share draft account,** or a checking account with some other name. With ATS, money deposited in a savings account is automatically transferred to a demand deposit in the exact amount needed to honor each check written by the depositor. When the check is paid, the demand deposit balance returns to zero. Interest is paid on the balance kept in the savings account.

The law set the required reserve at 3 percent on the first $25 million of net transactions accounts (accounts on which checks can be written) in each institution. It provided a formula for changing this figure—in 1986 the 3 percent is applied to the first $31.7 million. The Act also gave the Board the power to set the required reserve ratio for amounts above that figure in a range between 8 and 14 percent. As of this writing, the Board has set this rate at 12 percent.

For a long time before the 1980 law, the Board had had difficulty in regulating the money supply. There were different reserve requirements for different kinds of deposits and for different kinds of financial institutions. For this reason, the amount of required reserves would change when money was moved from one kind of account to another or from one institution to another. These problems caused the greatest trouble during the 1970s

---

1. The full name of the 1980 legislation is *The Depository Institutions Deregulation and Monetary Control Act.*

2. *Federal Reserve Bulletin,* April 1986, footnote to Table 1.15, p. A7.

with the combination of very high interest rates and the vast changes taking place in the banking industry as computers and electronic bookkeeping systems were introduced. The new equipment allowed depositors to move money from one account to another instantaneously. Also, with the high interest rates, customers were eager to take advantage of the rates being paid on savings accounts. Operational distinctions between demand deposit accounts and other kinds of accounts soon faded, as did the difference between banks and other kinds of financial institutions. In this atmosphere, the Monetary Control Act of 1980 was seen as a necessary step to help the Federal Reserve Board keep up with changing times.

Open Market Operations

Open market operations consist of the buying and selling of government securities by the Federal Reserve. As you will see, these operations allow the Board of Governors to control the *quantity* of reserves in the banking system, just as control of the reserve ratio makes it possible for the Board to control the deposit-expansion factor. Together, these two tools give the Board great power over the money supply in the United States.

Open market operations are directed by the Federal Open Market Committee (FOMC), which was described earlier. These operations are called "open market" because they are carried out in the same securities markets as those open to ordinary citizens and businesses. When the FOMC decides to buy securities, it pays the existing market price, and when it sells, it accepts the existing market price. The securities bought by the FOMC come from the holdings of private persons, banks, or business firms, and those that are sold move into these private holdings. Even though the FOMC deals only in short-term government securities, the effects of its buying and selling are quickly felt in the prices of other securities in the open market.

OPEN MARKET PURCHASES A good way of illustrating open market operations is to describe

TABLE 13-2   Open Market Purchase (amounts in dollars)

Federal Reserve Banks

Securities	+100	Reserve deposits	+100

The Banking System

Reserves	+100	Demand deposits Seller of security	+100
Loans	+400	New loans	+400
	+500		+500

When the Federal Reserve System purchases $100 of securities, its securities assets account expands by $100. When the check in payment for these securities is cleared, reserve deposits of banks increase by $100. These accounts are liabilities to the Federal Reserve System and assets to individual banks. If the reserve ratio is 20 percent, new loans can be made, so that the money supply may increase by as much as $500.

the effects of a $100 purchase of government securities by the Federal Reserve System. The person, business, or bank that sells the securities will receive a check from a Federal Reserve Bank in payment for the securities. When this check is deposited in a bank and cleared through the check-clearing system, the reserve account of the bank will be larger by $100. If the reserve ratio in the banking system is 20 percent, only $20 of these new reserves will be required for the new demand deposit. The remaining $80 is excess reserve, which the bank can use for lending. Because of the deposit-expansion process, which you studied earlier, the $100 open market purchase can expand the money supply by as much as $500.

Our hypothetical open market transaction is summarized in Table 13-2. On the balance sheet of the Federal Reserve Banks, the $100 expansion of the securities assets account is balanced by the $100 expansion of the liabilities account for bank reserve deposits. On the balance sheet for the banks in the commercial banking system, the $100 of new reserves supports $500 of new demand deposits, $100 of which came from the initial deposit and $400 from new loans made by the banks in the system. The effect on the money supply would have been the same if the security had been sold by a bank itself. New reserves would at first have come from a reduction in securities holdings, and all of these new reserves would have been "excess." The banking system could then generate up to $500 of new loans and demand deposits from these new reserves.

OPEN MARKET SALES Open market sales by the Federal Reserve System have the opposite effects from open market purchases; that is, sales contract the money supply. When the Federal Reserve sells a security, its asset account for securities shrinks. Then, when the purchaser sends his or her check to pay for it, clearing the check reduces the balance in the reserve accounts of the commercial banking system. If a 20 percent reserve ratio is being maintained by the banking system, a $100 sale of securities by the Federal Reserve will bring as much as a $500 reduction in checking account balances.

THE IMPORTANCE OF OPEN MARKET OPERATIONS The great advantage of the open market instrument is its flexibility. Since the Federal Reserve Banks are trading most of the time in the open market, they can carry out policy in a subtle and gradual way. The net purchases or net sales position of the Federal Reserve can be adjusted day by day to meet seasonal or short-run needs for money and, at the same time, can lean in either an expansionary or a contractionary direction as long-term policy may require. Changes in policy need not subject individual banks to untimely pressures, as is the case with changing reserve requirements. Through open market operations, changes in the money supply can be brought about without upsetting ordinary banking activities.

The important part that could be played by open market operations was not recognized when the Federal Reserve System was set up in 1913. However, coordination of securities buying and selling among the Federal Reserve Banks began during the financially active 1920s. Then, in the

1930s, the FOMC was established, and open market operations came under the direct control of the Board of Governors. Since that time, open market operations have become the most important instrument of monetary policy.

The Discount Rate

The third basic instrument of monetary policy is the **discount rate,** which is the rate of interest that Federal Reserve Banks charge on loans to member banks. Loans to member banks and the discount rate were expected to be major monetary control tools when the Federal Reserve was set up in 1913. The loans would supplement bank reserves and allow the needed expansion of the money supply during prosperous times. Then, during recessions, the Federal Reserve Banks would be lenders of last resort to prevent bank failures and forestall bank panics. History was unkind to both of these expectations. As a money-supply regulator, the discount rate was largely displaced by open market operations. As a lender of last resort, the Federal Reserve System failed miserably to prevent bank failures in 1932 and 1933. Today, discount rate changes serve mainly as signals of coming Federal Reserve policy, and loans to banks are used to help individual banks adjust to unexpected problems.

DISCOUNT RATE "SIGNALS" Changes in the discount rate have little *direct* impact on banks unless they need to borrow from the Federal Reserve System. If a bank has excess reserves, it will not need to borrow, nor will borrowing be necessary if the bank holds government securities that can be sold on the open market to obtain reserves. For these reasons, most banks are not directly affected by changes in the discount rate. However, these changes can have important *indirect* effects on bank lending and the money supply. A decision by the Board of Governors to raise the discount rate, for example, may be a signal that the Board plans to restrict the money supply, perhaps through future open market sales. Such action most likely will raise interest rates. In this case, the discount rate signal may suggest to bankers that they can get a higher rate of interest by putting off lending until the higher rates really appear in the money market. This can be a self-fulfilling prophecy, since lending restraint by the banks may, in fact, bring the higher interest rates that were expected. Of course, the signal can also operate in the other direction. Lowering the discount rate may lead bankers to more aggressive lending operations in anticipation of expansionary open market policies from the Federal Reserve.

DISCOUNTING AND THE FEDERAL FUNDS RATE
Borrowing by member banks through the discounting procedure is, according to Federal Reserve policy, a privilege rather than a right. Federal Reserve policy is that these loans should be made only when the bank's shortage of reserves is temporary and due to circumstances that could not reasonably have been anticipated by the borrowing bank. Thus, banks are encouraged to look elsewhere for money before asking for a loan from the Federal Reserve. The logical place to look, of course, is to banks that have excess reserves in their accounts in the Federal Reserve Bank. Balances in these accounts are called **federal funds.**

In the United States, there is a well-developed federal funds market. In this market, funds that are excess reserves for some banks are loaned to other banks that need more reserves. The rate of interest charged on these loans is called the **federal funds rate.** This rate will generally rise when economic activity and bank lending are expanding more rapidly than the money supply. The higher federal funds rate is a sign of a "tightening" money market. On the other hand, a falling federal funds rate points to an "easing" of the money market.

If the federal funds rate is lower than the discount rate set by the Federal Reserve Board, banks will clearly prefer to borrow in the federal funds market and will not come to their district Federal Reserve Bank for money. But when the money markets are tightening, the federal funds rate may rise above the discount rate, and loans from the Federal Reserve Bank can ease the problems of individual banks in adjusting to the tighter money situation. Thus, the discounting system is a safety valve for individual banks

during a time when the Board's open market operations are restrictive. In these times, of course, the Federal Reserve Banks must carefully examine requests for loans and must ration this bank credit to prevent discounting operations from canceling the effects of restrictive open market operations.

Other Instruments

Several other instruments are available to the Board of Governors besides the three that we have already mentioned. Even though reserve requirements, open market operations, and discounting are by far the most important, the other instruments do have their special uses.

MARGIN REQUIREMENTS The Board may set **margin requirements** for stock market trading. In the language of the stock market, trading "on margin" means that money from the purchaser of a stock covers only a fraction of the price of the stock being bought, while the rest of the cost is borrowed from the stockbroker. The money put in by the purchaser is called the *margin.* The broker collects interest on the money loaned to the purchaser and is also protected by receiving the power to sell the stock to recover the amount loaned if the price of the stock falls far enough to wipe out the buyer's margin. The experience in 1929 showed that this arrangement could turn a stock market decline into a stock market disaster, since sales by brokers would force stock prices still farther down. Since the 1930s, the Board has had the power to set margin requirements in a range between 25 and 100 percent of the value of the stock. At the time of this writing, the margin requirement is 50 percent.

INTEREST RATE LIMITATIONS During the 1930s, the Federal Reserve Board was given the power to set upper limits on the interest rates that could be paid on savings accounts and time deposits in banks and other financial institutions. During those troubled times, bankers were afraid that competition to win depositors could push interest rates upward and bring bank failures, which, as experience had shown, could spread widely. For this reason, legal interest rate limits were placed on savings accounts, and no interest payments at all were allowed on checking accounts. These restrictions hurt the small saver when the market interest rates rose above these legal limits, as they did during the 1970s. But, as we have noted, electronics, computer technology, and banking ingenuity offered more and more ways to escape from these limitations. These facts of life were recognized in the **Depository Institutions Deregulation and Monetary Control Act of 1980,** which began a slow phase-out, over a period of six years, of all interest rate limitations.

The phase-out of interest-rate limitations came at an especially difficult time for thrift institutions such as savings and loan associations. Many of these had made long-term mortgage loans in past years at the relatively low interest rates that then prevailed. Some of these loans were still outstanding in the early 1980s when interest rates were unusually high. Consequently, these institutions feared a profit squeeze or even bankruptcy if removal of interest-rate ceilings forced them to pay higher interest rates to their depositors. To provide relief, the **Garn–St. Germaine Depository Institutions Act of 1982** provided aid for institutions in distress and expanded the lending authority of thrift institutions so that they might earn higher rates on their lending. Nevertheless, a number of thrift institutions did not survive these difficult times.

MORAL SUASION The Board of Governors can put pressure on member banks simply by publicizing the actions that it wants them to take. Using what is often called **moral suasion,** the Board urges "cooperation" in promoting certain policy goals. Sometimes this approach is called jaw-boning. When there is danger of inflation, for example, the Board may urge "restraint" in granting new loans. Since member banks are subject to regulation by the Federal Reserve, they may find that it is wise to cooperate. Moral suasion, like the other minor instruments of monetary control, may have some limited effect on the money supply and the behavior of the banking system. However, the most important of the monetary instruments are the reserve requirements, open market buying and selling, and the discount rate for loans to member banks.

THE MONETARY BASE AND ITS MULTIPLIER

How well do all these instruments really work; that is, how precise is the control? To answer this question, we must first describe the monetary base and then the money multiplier, which ties the monetary base to the money supply itself.

The Monetary Base

The **monetary base** is made up of bank reserves along with the coins and currency circulating in the economy. The Board of Governors can influence the size of the monetary base through open market operations and lending to banks. But there are forces outside the Federal Reserve System that can also change the monetary base. For example, many U.S. dollars are held in foreign countries and are used in overseas operations. Changes in interest rates or in investment opportunities can bring money into the U.S. economy or drain it out and so affect the U.S. monetary base. Similarly, U.S. Treasury operations influence the monetary base when there are changes in the flows of tax collections and transfer payments and when national debt securities are issued or retired. Therefore, when the Board of Governors uses its open market and bank lending instruments to regulate bank reserves, it must anticipate changes that may come from these outside influences.

The Money Multiplier

The **money multiplier** is the ratio between the amount of money (such as M1) in the economy and the size of the monetary base. In November 1985, for example, this money multiplier averaged 2.861, meaning that a $1 million change in the monetary base was associated with a $2.861 million change in the M1 money supply. For the money managers of the Federal Reserve System, the money multiplier is another variable that must be taken into account in doing their job of controlling the money supply. If the money multiplier is stable, their job is easier. If it is unstable, their job is more difficult.

At least two forces can cause the money multiplier ratio to move up or down. One is that the reserve ratio actually maintained by banks can fluctuate somewhat above the legal minimum reserve ratio set by the Board if banks maintain "desired" excess reserves. Therefore, the deposit-expansion factor may fluctuate. A second reason is that there is an ebb and flow of currency and coin between bank reserves and hand-to-hand circulation in the economy. When currency and coin are in hand-to-hand circulation, they count as money, but they are not official reserves. When they are deposited in banks, they are not counted as money under the conventional M1 definition, but they become official reserves that can support several times their own worth in checking account money. In other words, bank reserves themselves move up and down as currency and coin flow into and out of the banks.

In spite of some uncertainty about how precisely monetary instruments work, there is no doubt that important changes in the money supply have resulted from actions taken by the Board of Governors. It is interesting and instructive to review briefly some of the highlights in the record of the Federal Reserve Board's use of the instruments of monetary policy.

THE HISTORICAL RECORD

Over the years that the Federal Reserve System has operated, there have been quiet intervals of "normalcy," but there also have been times when conditions changed quickly and the Board faced choices that were controversial, important, and shrouded in uncertainty. We shall begin by describing the first real test of the Board's ability to stabilize the economy.

The Recession of 1921

The Federal Reserve System was launched, in 1913, onto financial waters that soon would be stirred to great turbulence by World War I. As people tried to find a safe haven for their wealth, gold, which then was part of the money supply and could be used as reserves for loans, flowed into the United States and added to bank reserves. Businesses borrowed large sums to build factories for war production, and the government sold Liberty Bonds to finance the war effort. When the war ended, some gold flowed back to Europe, foreign demand for U.S. products slackened, and the U.S. economy slipped into a severe, though short, recession in 1921. Somewhat belatedly, the Board lowered the discount rate, which of course was an expansionary move, but otherwise the Board did very little to stop the economic decline. Supporters of the Board contend that its members were worried that expansionary policies might speed the outflow of gold. In any case, the Board did not lower reserve requirements and did not use open market operations. Critics say that the Federal Reserve Board had been too timid and had failed to ease the shock of the postwar recession.

The Stock Market Crash: 1929

Rapid expansion in the automobile and other markets made the decade of the 1920s a period of prosperity for the United States, except for farmers, who had not recovered from the loss of wartime markets. In Europe, the aftermath of the war and the Versailles peace treaty were causing problems.[3] As people again began to seek safety and profitable investment, gold flowed back into the United States, bolstering the money supply. At the same time, the national debt, which had grown during the war, provided bonds and other securities that were well suited to bank holdings and open market dealings. The Federal Reserve Banks learned that open market operations could affect the economy. Even though the economy appeared to be running smoothly, the Board did worry about increased speculation in the stock

---

3. In one of the more remarkable exhibitions of economic forecasting, the British economist John Maynard Keynes in 1919 predicted that the Versailles peace treaty would mean economic misfortune for Europe. See Keynes, *The Economic Consequences of the Peace* (1920).

market. Since it did not yet have the authority to regulate margin requirements, the Board tried in early 1929 to reduce stock market speculation by putting modest restraints on the growth of the money supply. Economists do not agree about the causes of the crash. However, when the stock market crashed later that year, the Board quickly reversed itself, lowering discount rates and buying government securities in the open market. But the blow from the stock market crash in the United States was soon followed by further problems, as conditions kept growing worse in world financial markets.

In Europe, declining economic conditions led, in 1931, to the failure of the leading banking house in Austria, the Credit Anstalt. Runs on European banks began as people withdrew gold and currencies in fear of further bank failures. First Austria, then Germany, and then Great Britain had to go back on their promises to exchange a fixed amount of gold for their paper currencies (in other words, they went off the **gold standard**). Fear spread that the United States might soon follow suit. As gold and currency started flowing out of U.S. banks, the stage was set for one of the most controversial and critical decisions yet faced by the Federal Reserve Board.

At this time (1931), the quantity of Federal Reserve Notes that could be issued was limited by the amount of gold and commercial paper (business IOUs obtained by the Federal Reserve Banks when loans were made to commercial banks) held by the Federal Reserve. The Federal Reserve Banks' holdings of both gold and commercial paper (the IOUs) were declining in 1931, and this decline threatened to force a drop in the Federal Reserve Note money supply. The Board decided not to use open market purchases to expand the money supply because that would reduce the need for local banks to borrow from the Federal Reserve, thus further reducing the central bank's holding of business IOU backing for Federal Reserve Notes. Instead, the Federal Reserve Banks *raised* discount rates and allowed further tightening of the money supply, an act that would be unthinkable to today's understanding of appropriate monetary policy. When a major bank in Detroit failed in early 1933, the governor

of Michigan closed all the banks in the state to prevent runs on other banks. Soon all the other states followed with bank closings. One of the first acts of incoming President Franklin D. Roosevelt was to declare a nationwide "bank holiday." The money supply had fallen drastically, and the Federal Reserve System had again failed to stabilize the economy.

Repairing the Monetary System

Repair of the monetary system started even before the collapse in 1933, though too late to prevent it. In 1932, new legislation (the Glass–Steagall Act) allowed the Federal Reserve System to use government bonds for backing Federal Reserve Notes, thus clearing away the obstacle that had kept the Board from using open market operations vigorously. Also under this Act, the Federal Open Market Committee was formed, further improving the ability to use open market operations. In 1933, as panic spread and gold was withdrawn from the banks, the United States went off the gold standard, as Great Britain and others had done earlier. Thus, the government was not obligated to give up its gold holdings in exchange for currency. The United States remained off the gold standard for almost two years. In 1934, when conditions were more stable, a modified gold standard was established and a higher price for gold was offered. Gold flowed back into the U.S. banking system, strengthening the reserve position of the Federal Reserve System. Excess reserves in commercial banks climbed to high levels. Strangely enough, the stage was now set for another Federal Reserve Board act that history has called a mistake.

In 1936, the large and growing excess reserves in the banking system led the Board to fear the coming of inflation, which might get out of control. For this reason, the Board doubled reserve requirements over a short period of time and used open market sales to counteract the effect of gold imports. Within a year, the economy plunged into even deeper recession. Criticism was heaped on the Board of Governors for once again having made the wrong move.

In fairness, however, it must be added that certain fiscal events were taking place at about the same time. As noted earlier, the Social Security system had started collecting taxes but few could yet collect benefits. Also, through a legislative mistake, taxes on corporations were increased significantly.[4]

Money Goes to War: 1941–1945

After the disastrous experience of the 1937–1938 recession, the chastened Board of Governors reversed itself and began to follow an expansionary or easy-money policy. In 1939, World War II started in Europe, and the U.S. economy expanded to produce war goods. After the attack on Pearl Harbor in December 1941, the U.S. economy went all out for war production. The Board of Governors promised that open market operations would support the bond market to make sure that the massive sales of war bonds would not force interest rates upward. This meant huge and continuing open market purchases and a great expansion of the money supply. The money supply grew and grew during the war, while civilian production was cut back. To hold down inflation, the government used price and wage controls as well as rationing. Congress authorized and the Board of Governors applied controls over lending and borrowing. Banks were permitted to play favorites among customers to favor war production and essential civilian needs. Money and prices had gone to war.

When the war ended, price controls were removed. Even though inflation was beginning in earnest, fear was widespread that the economy soon would fall back into recession, since this had happened in the past when wartime pressures subsided. At this time, the Board of Governors again faced important and controversial questions. If open market purchases stopped supporting bond prices, would the bond market collapse and trigger financial chaos and bank failures? The Board had been criticized for its restrictive policies in 1931 and in 1936. Should it

4. See page 194.

risk another recession? The Treasury, wanting interest costs to stay low on the greatly expanded national debt, put strong pressure on the Board to follow an easy-money policy. Under all this pressure, the Board decided to continue open market purchasing to support the bond market and to limit its inflation fight to maintaining higher discount rates and reserve requirements. Inflation spread, reaching a peak in 1948.

The "Accord" of 1951

War-related problems and inflationary conditions arose again in 1950 as the United States became involved in the Korean War. Again the Treasury wanted more open market purchases to support the bond market, but this time the Board of Governors chose to fight for its independence. After a great political struggle, open market operations were freed from the commitment to support the bond market. The "accord" was announced on March 4, 1951. The Board was again independent of the Treasury.

In the period after the accord of 1951, the Board generally followed a policy of "leaning against the wind." This meant using open market purchases and sales, as well as small adjustments in reserve requirements and discount rates, to moderate expansions and contractions of the economy. The Board was neither swept along by the winds of war nor overcome by forces it wished to oppose.

Disintermediation

The economy's performance was sluggish in the last half of the 1950s, but picked up speed in the early 1960s. Taxes were reduced in 1964 in a clear application of fiscal instruments and Keynesian economic theory. By 1966, the Federal Reserve Board of Governors detected inflationary dangers. As the "war on poverty" was waged and as hostilities increased in Vietnam, the federal budget moved deeper and deeper into deficit. Restrictive open market operations were applied, and almost no increase in the money supply was permitted.

But because the demand for loans kept on growing while the money supply was stabilized, interest rates climbed. When market interest rates rose above the legal ceiling rates that banks and other regulated financial institutions were allowed to pay, many people took their money out of these institutions in order to get higher interest on their savings elsewhere. This process is called **disintermediation.** Savings and loan companies and the home-building industry, which depends heavily on loans from them, suffered greatly from a shortage of available funds in 1967. Unfortunately, the inflationary danger that the Fed was trying to combat was only partly defused.

In 1968, the Board started using monetary tools in an expansionary direction. The reason was that the economy was beginning to contract. Gold and financial capital were flowing out of the country as the United States' competitive position in world trade grew weaker. Also, Congress raised taxes by 10 percent. To counter the economic overkill that it thought would come from the combined effect of these events, the Board expanded open market buying. By this time, the U.S. economy was starting to show signs that were contradictory according to the prevailing economic theories. Growth was lagging, unemployment was increasing, and inflation continued. In other words, the economy was beginning to suffer from *stagflation*. At the end of the 1960s, the Board tightened the money supply in an effort to slow the inflation. Interest rates rose, and disintermediation took place once again.

The Great Stagflation

The combination of inflation, rising unemployment, and sluggish economic growth is called **stagflation.** As the stagflation problem grew in the early 1970s, the Nixon administration decided to use both fiscal and monetary tools to aid production and reduce unemployment. Taxes were cut, government spending was increased, the FOMC bought securities and discount rates were lowered. To hold down inflation, President Nixon announced a freeze on prices and wage rates and a suspension of U.S. gold payments in

international transactions. However, during the control period, the money supply was expanded. When the controls were lifted, inflation burst forth with new vigor. President Ford, who replaced President Nixon after the Watergate scandal, undertook a program called "Whip Inflation Now" (abbreviated "WIN"). Money supply growth was restricted and unemployment increased.

The election victory of President Carter in 1976 brought confrontation between the Federal Reserve Board on the one hand and the president and the Congress on the other. Armed with the election mandate to expand the economy, President Carter refused to name Board member Arthur Burns (who was associated with a "tight" money policy) to another term as chairman. Burns retired, and the Board, under new leadership, expanded the money supply. Over the four years of the Carter administration, the M1 money supply grew at a yearly rate of 7.7 percent, and the inflation rate rose to around 9 percent a year, sometimes reaching a double-digit figure. Alarmed by these high inflation rates, President Carter installed a new Federal Reserve Board Chairman, Paul Volcker, and backed a tighter monetary policy.

The election of President Reagan in 1980 gave a further mandate for a strong anti-inflation policy. Restrictive monetary measures continued throughout 1981 and into 1982. Interest rates and unemployment remained high, but the inflation rate came down dramatically.

Monetary instruments can claim some, but not all, of the credit for the very significant slackening of the inflation rate in the first half of the 1980s. The sluggish economy weakened the demand for funds. In addition, restrictive monetary policy was powerfully assisted by decreases in petroleum prices, as the Organization of Petroleum Exporting Countries (OPEC) encountered increased difficulty in limiting petroleum output. Chairman Volcker continued to guide Federal Reserve policy. Although money supply increases were allowed, real interest rates—interest rates adjusted for the now much lower inflation rate[5]—

5. See Chapter 6 for an explanation of how nominal interest rates are adjusted to determine real interest rates.

were very high by historical standards. Some argued that expectations about future inflation prevented a sufficient downward movement of real interest rates.[6] Whatever the cause, high interest rates caused great trouble for some financial institutions, as mentioned earlier, and for farmers, who faced the problem of lower prices for their crops along with extremely high interest costs on their indebtedness. There is no doubt that monetary policy can be a powerful force in the macroeconomy. At the same time, the hardships resulting from high real interest rates make the restrictive application of monetary instruments a politically sensitive and controversial matter.

An Overview

As our brief history has suggested, the monetary policies of the Federal Reserve Board have often been controversial. With 20–20 hindsight, it is clear that mistakes were made in 1921, 1931, and 1936, though it would be unfair to place all the blame for these hard times on monetary policy. The Board's support for the war effort during World War II can hardly be faulted, and its fight for independence from the Treasury and its non-inflationary financing of the Korean War merit praise. During the 1950s and the early 1960s, monetary policies operated smoothly most of the time.

Monetary policies, like most other demand-side approaches, were not able to solve the complicated riddle of stagflation in the 1970s, and, as in the Great Depression of the 1930s, the Board was often blamed for unemployment. However, in 1980 and 1981, monetary instruments proved their power to bring down the inflation rate.

The relative independence of the Federal Reserve Board from control by the elected officials of the government continues to be a focus of debate. When monetary policies are unpopular, calls are heard to place monetary policy under the control of the Treasury or, by some other means, to give the president or Congress greater power over the Federal Reserve. So far, independent monetary policy has survived these attempts, providing another aspect of the checks-and-balances system in the U.S. government.

SUMMARY

1. The Federal Reserve System was established by an act of Congress in 1913 to provide a means for controlling the money supply, to assure a flexible national currency, and to be a lender of last resort to forestall bank panics.

2. The Board of Governors of the Federal Reserve System is made up of seven persons appointed by the president and confirmed by the Senate. The Board sets policy for the Federal Reserve System. The independence of the Board from the elected officials of the government is an important issue, since the Board wields great power in the economy.

3. The Federal Open Market Committee consists of the seven members of the Board of Governors plus five members from the Federal Reserve Banks. This committee directs and coordinates the purchase and sale of securities by the Federal Reserve System in the open market.

4. There are twelve Federal Reserve Districts, and a Federal Reserve Bank is located in each district. These banks, which are owned by member banks in the district, provide services to the banking and commercial interests of the district. Federal Reserve Banks provide bank examiners, make loans to member banks, operate a check-clearing system, and serve as fiscal agent for the federal government.

5. From the beginnings of the Federal Reserve System, the Board had the power to set minimum required reserve ratios for banks that were members of the system. The Monetary Control Act of 1980 broadened this power by giving the Board authority to set minimum reserve requirements for all "transactions accounts" in all depository institutions. By setting minimum required reserve ratios, the Board can strongly influence the deposit-expansion factor that relates bank reserves to the money supply.

---

6. The economic theory of inflationary expectations will be explained in Chapter 17.

6. Open market operations consist of the buying and selling of government securities by the Federal Reserve Banks in the general or open market. When securities are purchased by the system, reserves in the banking system are increased, inviting an expansion of the money supply. When securities are sold by the system, reserves in the banking system are reduced, and the money supply is restricted. Open market operations are the most actively used of all the monetary instruments of the Federal Reserve System.

7. The discount rate is the rate of interest charged by a Federal Reserve Bank on a loan to a member bank. Since these loans are intended only as temporary aid to banks that face unexpected reserve problems, the discount rate does not directly affect most banks. However, the discount rate may be read as a signal of upcoming Board of Governors' policy. A higher discount rate may suggest a tightening of the money supply, and a lower discount rate may suggest an easing of the money supply.

8. Federal funds are reserve deposits in Federal Reserve Banks. Banks may borrow federal funds from other banks as an alternative to borrowing through the discounting procedure with the Federal Reserve System. The federal funds rate is the rate of interest charged on these loans. A rising federal funds rate indicates a tightening of the money markets, and a falling federal funds rate indicates an easing of the money markets.

9. The Board of Governors has the authority to set margin requirements for stock market trading. These requirements specify the minimum percentage of the purchase price of stock that must be paid in by the purchaser himself or herself— the remainder of the purchase price being borrowed from the broker. Experience in 1929 showed that stocks owned on small margins could be "dumped" on the market, turning a modest decline into a stock market disaster.

10. During the 1930s, the Board of Governors was authorized to set upper limits on interest rates that could be paid on deposits in banks and other financial institutions. When market interest rates rose above these ceiling rates, small savers suffered and disintermediation occurred in financial markets. The Depository Institutions Dereg-

ulation and Monetary Control Act of 1980 launched a phase-out, over a period of six years, of all interest rate limitations.

11. The monetary base consists of bank reserves plus coins and currency circulating from hand to hand in the economy. The Board of Governors can influence this base by open market operations and by loans to banks. The money multiplier is the ratio between a money supply measure, such as M1, and this monetary base. If this ratio is stable, the Board of Governors can have some influence on the money supply. If the ratio or multiplier is unstable and unpredictable, Federal Reserve influence is less reliable.

12. The Board of Governors has made many controversial and important decisions over the years since the founding of the Federal Reserve System. It was severely criticized as contributing to recessions in 1933 and 1936 and to inflation after World War II and during the 1970s. Most notably, the Board has been blamed for high interest rates and the hardships that follow.

DISCUSSION QUESTIONS

1. How are Federal Reserve Board members selected? What systems have been set up to insulate, to some degree, the Board of Governors of the Federal Reserve System from control by the president or the Congress? Do you believe that the Federal Reserve Board should be more closely or less closely tied to the president and the Congress? Explain your position.

2. How are members of the Federal Open Market Committee selected? Describe the operations that are carried out by this committee. Explain how these operations affect the money supply.

3. Explain how, under the pyramiding of reserves system, a relatively minor problem of a few banks not having enough reserves to cover withdrawal requests might build up to a nationwide bank crisis. How does the system today provide help for a member bank that is short on reserves? How can an individual bank obtain help if it is not a member of the Federal Reserve System?

4. How is the help that a Federal Reserve Bank gives to member banks in its district related to the discount rate? Explain the conflict that sometimes arises between contracting the money supply in the economy and helping out troubled member banks.

5. Construct a balance sheet for the Federal Reserve Banks, showing the main entries on both the assets and the liabilities sides. Then compare your work with Table 13-1. Explain how the U.S. Government securities entry is related to the national debt. Explain how the reserve accounts entry is related to the laws that control individual commercial banks.

6. Explain how the profit motivation of commercial banks helps to assure that actual reserve ratios will stay close to legal reserve ratio requirements. If the Federal Reserve lowers the legal reserve requirement, how is the amount of checking account money likely to be affected? Explain the process that leads to this result.

7. The Monetary Control Act of 1980 broadened the Federal Reserve's authority over checking accounts in two ways. What were they? How did technological changes in the way banking was conducted create the need for these broader Federal Reserve powers?

8. By drawing a pair of balance sheets, one for the Federal Reserve Banks and the other for the banking system, show how a Federal Open Market Committee purchase of securities can expand the money supply. Compare your balance sheets with Table 13-2. Select a different legal reserve requirement and rework your balance sheets to show a different change in the money supply.

9. What are "federal funds"? If an individual bank needs to borrow money, why might it wish to borrow federal funds rather than to borrow from its Federal Reserve Bank? In terms of the money supply and the demand for loans, what

is usually happening in the economy when the federal funds rate is rising?

10. Three minor powers of the Federal Reserve are margin requirements, moral suasion, and interest rate limitations. Briefly describe how margin requirements and moral suasion may have some influence on economic activity. What did the Depository Institutions Deregulation and Monetary Control Act of 1980 do with respect to interest rate limits? Do you believe that deregulation will increase or decrease competition in financial markets? Explain.

11. What happens to the U.S. monetary base when dollars move to other countries to take advantage of investment opportunities? How does the money multiplier show the effect of a change such as this on the money supply in the United States? If you were trying to manage the U.S. money supply, would you want the money multiplier to be high, or low, or just stable? Explain.

12. The Glass–Steagall Act of 1932 allowed the Federal Reserve System to use government bonds for backing the Federal Reserve Notes. What had the system been required to use before this law was passed? How could higher discount rates bring in more of the pre-1932 legal backing to the Federal Reserve?

13. Federal Reserve policy during and after World War II was to support the price of government bonds and to keep interest rates low. Explain how the Federal Open Market Committee was involved in these operations. How did these operations affect the money supply? What was the "accord" reached in 1951?

14. What is "disintermediation"? Why did disintermediation happen in 1967 when the Federal Reserve engaged in restrictive monetary policy? Would disintermediation have happened then if the Depository Institutions Deregulation and Monetary Control Act had been in effect? Explain.

14 *Monetary Economics and Monetarism*

PREVIEW In the last chapter you learned how the Federal Reserve System (the central bank) and the banking system can use various monetary instruments to influence the supply of money in the economy. Now it is time to see how these changes in the money supply affect the equilibrium level of national income and product. The connection between changes in the money supply and changes in equilibrium national income and product is the focus of the *monetarist* approach in macroeconomic theory.

We will start our study by examining an early and simplistic monetarist model based on what is called the quantity theory of money. We will find that this simple theory leaves unanswered many questions about how the money supply may influence the output of real goods and services in the economy. To answer these questions, we go on to explain more modern monetarist theories about how the demand for money and the supply of money interact to determine interest rates and equilibrium national income and product.

Since interest rates play a key role in many monetarist theories, our next step will be to explain the difference between *nominal* interest rates, which are those advertised by banks and quoted in the press, and *real* interest rates, which are adjusted for price-level changes.[1] To illustrate the importance of this distinction between nominal and real interest rates, we will present two "scenarios" about the determination of real interest rates in the short run. The first assumes that no change in the price level (no inflation or deflation) is expected, so

that monetary instruments are able to change the real rate of interest and the equilibrium level of real national income and product. The second scenario assumes that an expansionary use of monetary instruments causes people to expect price-level increases—that is, inflation. In this case, monetary tools may have only temporary effects on real interest rates and on the equilibrium level of real national income and product. This scenario also raises questions about how inflation expectations may affect the economy.

We close the chapter with an explanation of what is known as **modern monetarism,** which contends that, in the long run, only the price level is affected by changes in the money supply. At this point, we explain how the market for loanable funds determines real interest rates and the volume of investment in the long run.

Because we believe that most human behavior is based on real values (or on what people believe are real values), most of our analysis of the relation between money and equilibrium national income and product is carried on in terms of real values. However, when we consider possible inflationary effects of changes in the money supply, nominal values may be important, especially for interest rates.

THE QUANTITY THEORY OF MONEY

The quantity theory of money has been famous in economics for a long time. It is based on a simple relationship called the **equation of ex-**

---

1. Before starting this chapter, you may wish to review the explanation of nominal and real values in Chapter 6.

change. The equation is $MV = PQ$, where M stands for the quantity of money in the economy, V stands for its **velocity of circulation** (the average number of times each dollar is used per year to buy newly produced goods and services), P stands for the price level, and Q stands for the quantity of real output for the year.

The equation of exchange is the statement that the quantity of money in the economy multiplied by the number of times the average dollar is used each year to purchase newly produced final products must be equal to the quantity of these final products multiplied by their average price.

It is easy to see why this is called the equation of exchange. The left side, MV, represents total money spent by purchasers, and the right side, PQ, represents total money received by sellers. Because the two sides of the equation must be equal by definition, the equation is more properly called an *identity*.

Since a relationship that is true by definition cannot be used to prove a cause-and-effect relation, the equation of exchange does not establish any necessary connection between the quantity of money, as a cause, and the equilibrium level of national income and product, as an effect. But it does provide a framework for a great deal of debate about the importance of money in the economy.

The equation of exchange is used in the **quantity theory of money,** which asserts that the velocity of money circulation is constant in the long run, so that changes in the quantity of money provide a good way to predict changes in gross national product (GNP), since the PQ part of the equation corresponds with the definition of GNP. In other words, if the V in the equation of exchange is constant, a 10 percent increase in the quantity of money (M) would mean a 10 percent increase in gross national product (PQ).

Much discussion has focused on the question of whether the velocity of money circulation actually is constant. Also, since neither P nor Q is necessarily constant there is the question of whether the change on the PQ side of the equation will be in the price level (P) or in the volume of real output (Q). We must, therefore, proceed to examine these questions.

Is Money Velocity Constant?

Supporters of the quantity theory contend that the velocity of circulation of money is reasonably stable and predictable in the long run, so that changes in the money supply can be used to predict long-run changes in nominal national income and product. They recognize that velocity increases when people are optimistic and spend money freely, and they recognize that velocity falls when people are pessimistic and fearful about the future. But quantity theorists reason that waves of optimism and pessimism average out in the long run. Then they point out that basic factors that influence the speed of money circulation, such as how the banking system operates and how frequently people are paid, do not change very rapidly. Thus, they conclude that, unless these basic factors change, an assumption of constant velocity of money circulation is not unreasonable for long-run forecasts.

Figure 14-1 shows the velocity of money in the United States from 1960 through 1985 as measured by dividing GNP by the M1 and the M2 quantity of money for each year. M1 velocity increased substantially over this period, and M2 velocity, although reasonably stable in the long-run trend, showed important fluctuations from year to year. Many factors probably were at work. For one thing, great technological changes were taking place in the banking industry. Computers and automatic teller machines speeded up transactions and probably helped to increase velocity as measured by M1 money. Credit cards were more widely used. Nominal interest rates were high, especially toward the end of this period, so people probably wanted to make their money work harder. Also, inflation was a problem, and people may have kept less money in accounts earning negative or low real interest to try to reduce the loss of purchasing power that they would suffer. Thus, over this twenty-six-year period, the simple quantity theory using the M1 definition of money did not do a very good job of predicting nominal national income and product.

The M2 measure of the money supply makes a better case for supporters of the quantity theory. Although velocity fluctuated widely from year to

FIGURE 14-1   **Velocity of Money in the United States, 1960–1985**

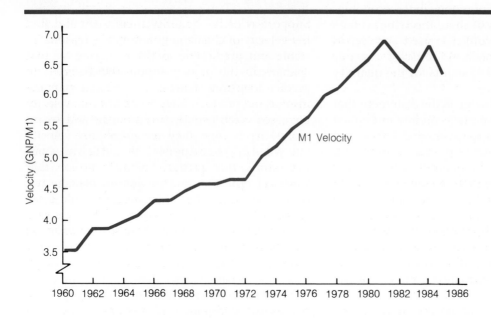

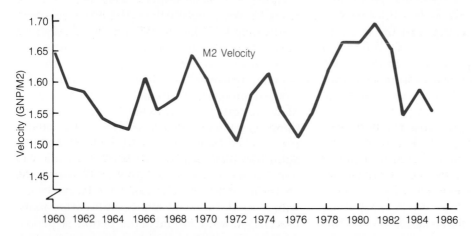

The velocity of money circulation is measured by dividing GNP by the quantity of money for each year. MI velocity increased greatly over this period. M2 velocity fluctuated from year to year but showed no long-term upward or downward trend.

Source: Economic Report of the President, 1986, Tables B-1 and B-64.

year according to this measure, the long-run M2 velocity showed little change. If long-run effects are what matter most in economic policy, the equation of exchange can be useful in guiding policy makers.

Will Money Affect *Real* Production?

Even if we accept the proposition that the velocity of money circulation (V) is reasonably constant in the long run, the equation of exchange does not tell us whether the consequences of changes in the quantity of money (M) will fall on the quantity of goods and services produced (Q) or on the price level (P). Let us suppose, for example, that the quantity of money increases by 7 percent per year and, as assumed in the simple quantity theory, that the velocity of circulation is constant. The theory predicts a 7 percent per year increase in nominal national income and product. If the volume of production (Q) also increases by 7 percent per year, the theory predicts that the price level (P) will be stable. But if the volume of production increases by less than 7 percent per year, the theory predicts some increase in the price level. If production does not increase at all, the theory predicts a 7 percent per year increase in the price level. It is clear that the simple quantity theory cannot tell us all we want to know about the relation of money to equilibrium national income and product. To gain a better understanding of this relation, modern economic theory directs our attention to how money may affect interest rates, how interest rates may affect investment, and how investment may affect production in the economy.

THE ROLE OF INTEREST RATES

You have already learned how interest rates can be important in the operation of the economy. In Chapter 9, you studied the demand curve for planned investment expenditure.[2] In Figure 9-3,

the rate of interest is the independent variable that can cause a movement along the demand curve and change the quantity of planned investment expenditure per year in the economy. The negative slope of the demand curve for planned investment means that reductions in the interest rate cause increases in the quantity of planned investment expenditure, and vice versa. Therefore, changing the money supply (M) can cause a change in planned investment expenditure and the volume of production in the economy (Q) *if* the money-supply change can alter the rate of interest. Conversely, if changing M does *not* change the rate of interest, it will not cause a change in planned investment and production (Q). In this case, changing M will change only the price level (P) in the equation of exchange, $MV = PQ$.

Before we go any further, it is essential to review the difference between real values and nominal values. This is essential because the decisions of investors and others in the economy are based on real (or on what they believe to be real) values.

Real and Nominal Values

When you studied index numbers in Chapter 6, you were introduced to the concepts of real and nominal values.[3] In the theories that you will learn in this and in the following chapters, the distinction between real and nominal values is very important. We must define these terms clearly.

Nominal values are values that are stated or measured in terms of some monetary unit. In the United States, the monetary unit is the dollar. Thus, the nominal value of an item is the number of dollars that would be exchanged for it. Nominal values have *not* been adjusted for price-level changes by dividing them by an index number or deflator.

Real values are values that are stated or measured in terms of goods and services. The real value of an item is the quantity of goods and

---

2. See pages 164–165.

3. See pages 104–108.

services that would be exchanged for it. A real value *has* been adjusted for price-level changes by applying an index number or deflator.

Two illustrations will help you understand the importance of the difference between nominal and real values. Suppose that when you were seven years old, your parents purchased a $1,000 bond, which at that time would have paid for a year's tuition at college. They hold the bond while you are growing up, and during that time the price level rises. When you go to college, they sell the bond, but the proceeds are not enough to pay a year's tuition. What has happened? The nominal value of the bond stayed unchanged at $1,000, but the real value fell to less than $1,000 in terms of the old price level. If the price level had doubled, the real value of the bond would have fallen to $500 in terms of the old price level. Your parents suffered a *real* loss of $500, though they did not suffer a *nominal* loss.

As another illustration, suppose you borrow $1,000 and promise to pay it back on some future date. The nominal value of the promise is clearly stated in terms of money. But the real (goods and services) value of the promise depends on the price level that will exist when you must pay the money. Since that time has not come yet, neither you nor the person to whom you make the promise can be entirely sure about its real value. If the price level rises, the real value will fall, and vice versa.

Behavior Based on Real Values

In the macroeconomic theories that you have studied up to now in this book, changes in measured magnitudes, or amounts, were assumed to show changes in real magnitudes.[4] In other words, decision makers responded to changes in real production, real living standards, real wealth, and real relative prices. When we reasoned that the consumption function would shift owing to changes in wealth, it was because people believed that their real wealth had changed. In the same way, when we reasoned that planned

4. See page 158.

investment would change because of a change in the rate of interest, it was the real rate of interest that was involved.

The discussion stayed with real values on the assumption that rational people respond to the facts or what they believe to be the facts. The units of measurement themselves are not crucial. For example, the weight of a bucket of water, or how hard it is to carry this load, does not depend on whether the quantity of water is measured in gallons or liters or pounds or kilograms. In other words, it depends on the real value, not on the nominal value.

Real and Nominal Interest Rates

Now that we are studying the relation of money and national income and product, the distinction between real and nominal value is especially important, because an interest rate is a price in a transaction that has a time dimension. The time lapse between borrowing money and repaying the loan provides an opportunity for price-level changes to occur. If the price level increases during this time, the loan will be paid back in dollars that have less real purchasing power than those originally borrowed. The nominal rate of interest will not correctly measure the real cost of borrowing.

There is a simple rule about the relation between real and nominal interest rates. This rule states that the difference is equal to the rate of change in the price level.[5] Here is an illustration. If the price level is *rising* by 5 percent annually, a nominal 12 percent interest rate is a real 7 percent interest rate and a nominal 9 percent interest rate is a real 4 percent interest rate. We simply subtract the inflation rate from the nominal interest rate to determine the real interest rate. Conversely, if the price level is *falling*, the real interest rate will be above the nominal interest rate. If the price level is falling by 2 percent a

5. Changes in the general price level are discussed in Chapter 6 (see pages 111–112). When both inflation rates and interest rates are extremely high, some modification of this simple rule is needed. This refinement will be left for more advanced courses.

year, a nominal interest rate of 5 percent is a real interest rate of 7 percent. The logic behind these adjustments is that the dollars used to pay back a loan will have a different purchasing power from the dollars that were borrowed. If the price level is rising, the loan will be paid back in dollars that are worth less than those initially borrowed, thus reducing the real cost of borrowing and the real return to the lender. The real interest rate is below the nominal interest rate. If the price level is falling, the loan will be paid back in dollars that are worth more than those that were borrowed, thus increasing the real cost of borrowing and the real return to the lender. Here, the real interest rate is higher than the nominal interest rate.

When the lender-borrower agreement is negotiated, neither side can be certain about the price-level change that may actually take place during the term of the loan. Each must make a best guess. In other words, it is the *expected* rate of price-level change (inflation) that each party uses to determine the difference between the nominal and the real interest rate. Of course, the two parties may not, in their own minds, be using the same expected rate of price-level change. One or the other, or both, may prove to have been mistaken, with consequent unexpected gains or losses.

As we proceed now to examine how interest rates are determined, we will use the *real rate of interest* in explaining the demand and the supply of money. It is important to remember that this is not necessarily the same as the *nominal* rate of interest that would get written into contracts and reported in the press. Nominal and real interest rates would be equal only when neither borrowers nor lenders expect any change in the price level.

THE SUPPLY OF AND DEMAND FOR MONEY

Our next job is to understand the **money market.** The money market is the economic conception of how the demand for and the supply of money interact to determine the rate of interest for an

FIGURE 14-2   The Money Market

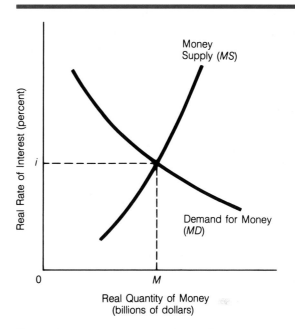

The vertical axis shows the real rate of interest—the rate *after* adjustment for changes in the price level. The horizontal axis shows the *real* quantity of money—the nominal quantity of money divided by a price-index number such as the GNP deflator. This axis shows quantities of money demanded and supplied as an asset or form of wealth. The money-supply curve (*MS*) has a positive slope and its location may be influenced by monetary policy. The demand-for-money curve (*MD*) has a negative slope and its location may be shifted by changes in the level of income and wealth in the economy.

economy. Once we understand this market, we can go on to see how the Federal Reserve System (or central bank) may be able to change the supply of money and thereby change the real rate of interest in the economy.

The economic concept of the money market is illustrated in Figure 14-2. The vertical axis shows the *real* rate of interest—the rate *after* adjustments have been made for expected changes in the price level. In our illustration of the money market, we use a single interest rate to represent the whole pattern or "family" of rates that actually exist in the economy, where there are many different interest rates reflecting differing amounts of risks. We can think of our interest rate as a "pure" rate applicable to a risk-free loan.

The horizontal axis shows some measure of the *real* quantity of money according to some accepted measure such as M1—the quantity of M1 dollars divided by a price-level index number, such as the GNP deflator.[6] Amounts on this axis show real quantities of money that are supplied and demanded as an *asset* to be held as an item of wealth in preference to other assets, such as securities, jewelry, real estate, and so on. The notion of money as an asset is important in understanding the money market.

The Demand-for-Money Curve

In explaining the demand-for-money curve, economists consider the speculative demand, the transactions demand, and the precautionary demand for holding money. We shall describe each of these and explain how they help in understanding the slope and the location of the demand-for-money curve.

SPECULATIVE DEMAND Speculative demand is mainly responsible for the slope of the demand-for-money curve. To understand this point, you must understand what speculation is and how money can be used for this purpose.

Most people think of speculation as the holding of risky assets like oil wells or uranium mines. Actually, **speculation** means taking actions based on expectations of *future changes* in the market values of assets. Imagine that you are wealthy (not an unpleasant thought) and that you want to manage your wealth to make it grow as much as you can. Managing your wealth means that you are placing it in money, stocks, bonds, real estate, and so on, depending on which forms promise you the best return.

For speculative purposes, the most important type of return on your wealth is not the rate of interest you can obtain but the gain that you can make from changes in the market value of what-

6. See page 106 for an explanation of the GNP deflator.

ever types of assets you have chosen as wealth forms. For example, if you expect the market value of bonds, stocks, or real estate to rise in the future, you will place your wealth in these promising forms and demand very little, if any, money for speculative purposes. On the other hand, if you expect the market value of bonds, stocks, or real estate to fall in the future, you will sell these assets and hold cash. In this case, you have a **speculative demand for money.**

The next step in understanding the demand-for-money curve in Figure 14-2 is to see how anticipated gains or losses on nonmoney assets are related to the real rate of interest, which is the variable on the vertical axis of the money-market graph. The fact is that there is a clear connection between the rate of interest prevailing at a given time and the likelihood that the values of stocks, bonds, and other nonmoney assets will rise or fall in the future. This connection is easily derived from the formula that converts a stream of expected future income into a present value. The **present value formula** is as follows:

$$present\ value = \frac{expected\ annual\ income\ flow}{rate\ of\ interest}$$

Consider, for example, a nonmoney asset that will pay net income of $100 a year indefinitely. If the rate of interest that can be earned on similar wealth forms is 10 percent a year, the present value of this nonmoney asset will be $1,000—that is, $100/0.10. A person would not pay more than this amount because he or she would then earn a rate of return of less than the going rate of 10 percent. Some other form of wealth would be more attractive. Similarly, the seller would not accept less than $1,000.

Let us apply this idea to our demand-for-money curve. The quantity of money demanded for speculation will be great when the real interest rates are considered "low." According to the present value formula, when interest rates are low, the present value of any given expected annual income flow is high, other things being equal. For example, if the interest rate were 3 percent, our hypothetical nonmoney asset would have a present value of $3,333, that is $100/0.03.

A speculator will sell the nonmoney asset because he or she expects that its price (present value) will fall as interest rates return to higher levels. In other words, he or she will hold money, speculating on the coming price decrease of nonmoney assets. On the other hand, the quantity of money demanded as a speculative asset will be low when interest rates are considered high because the present value of nonmoney assets then will be considered low. At an interest rate of 15 percent, for example, the asset bringing a net $100 a year will have a present value of only $667, that is $100/0.15. Speculators will hold nonmoney assets, expecting to profit when interest rates fall and the present value of these assets rises. In this way, the speculative demand for money assets provides a strong reason for the demand-for-money curve having a negative slope.

The speculative demand for money is sometimes called the *liquidity* demand for money. **Liquidity** is the "spendability" of an asset—that is, the ease with which it can be used in exchange or converted into a form that can be used in exchange. Cash and checkable accounts are fully liquid. They can be used directly in exchange for anything a person wants to buy. The liquidity demand for money simply means that people want to hold it so that they will be in a position to take advantage of opportunities to purchase other assets when favorable terms arise. When people hold money because they expect the prices of nonmoney assets to be lower in the future, their demand for liquidity is speculative.

TRANSACTIONS AND PRECAUTIONARY DEMANDS
The **transactions demand for money** arises because people want to hold some of their wealth in a form that is convenient for day-to-day buying and selling of goods and services. The **precautionary demand for money** arises because people want to be prepared for unexpected changes in the pattern of their receipts and expenditures. The role of the interest rate in determining the quantity of money demanded for these purposes can be easily understood by using the concept of *opportunity cost*. The basic point is that people who hold money receive very little interest return on this portion of their wealth. Cash earns no

interest at all and checkable accounts earn relatively low rates of interest. The amount of interest earning that is given up is the opportunity cost of holding money instead of nonmoney assets. It follows from this that the opportunity cost of holding money is greater when the rate of interest is high than when the rate of interest is low. Thus, economists expect that less money will be demanded for transactions and precautionary purposes when interest rates are high and that more money will be demanded when interest rates are low, other things being equal. In other words, the transactions and the precautionary demands for money impart a negative slope to the demand-for-money curve, just as the speculative motive did. In fact, opportunity cost reasoning also applies to the speculative demand for money, giving further support for the negative slope of the demand-for-money curve.

SHIFTING THE DEMAND-FOR-MONEY CURVE The demand-for-money curve may shift when there is a change in some variable other than the rate of interest. There are many variables that might do this. Changes in the amount of wealth, for example, are expected to affect all three of the demands for money assets. When wealth increases, these demands for money are expected to increase, and when wealth decreases, these demands are expected to decrease. However, in macroeconomic analysis, the most important shift variable for the demand-for-money curve is the level of national income and product itself. When national income and product increases, the curve is expected to shift to the right and when it decreases, the curve is expected to shift to the left.

Changes in national income and product affect all of the demands for money, but their effects on the transactions demand is especially apparent. For most people, the transactions demand for money arises because receipts and expenditures are not perfectly timed with each other. For example, suppose that you receive $700 every two weeks and that you spend $50 every day. When you receive your pay, you have $700 in money. At the end of the first day you have $650, at the end of the next day you have $600, and at the end of the fourteenth day you have no money. On the average, your money holding is equal to half of your pay, that is, $350. Now suppose that you get a 10 percent raise to $770 every two weeks and that you increase your spending also by 10 percent to $55 per day. At the end of the first day after you receive your pay, you have $715 ($770 − $55 = $715) and at the end of the fourteenth day you again have no money. In this case, your average money holding is $385 (half of $770), which is 10 percent greater than in the previous case. The 10 percent change in income has led to a 10 percent change in the transactions demand for money. In Figure 14-2, this change would appear as a shift (change in the location) of the demand-for-money curve because it was not the result of a change in the real rate of interest but was due to a change in some other variable—in this case, income. We conclude that income changes will shift the demand-for-money curve in the same direction as the change in income—that is, to the right when income increases and to the left when income decreases.

This example of the transactions demand shows no precautionary demand for money because we assume that you allow your money holding to fall all the way to nothing just before the next payday. It is more reasonable to expect that you would keep some "back-up" money on hand just in case the paycheck was late or some unusual expense, such as an illness, or buying opportunity, such as a sale, should come along. In our illustration, if you keep a $100 backup, your average money holding would have been $450 when your income was $700, and $485 when your income was $770. In each case, you would have had a $100 cash balance on hand just before you received your next pay. It seems reasonable that an increase in your income and in the volume of your routine transactions would also lead you to keep a larger backup of money. In this way, changing the level of income is a shift variable for the precautionary demand for money as well.

The Money-Supply Curve

The money-supply curve (MS) in Figure 14-2 shows the relationship between the real rate of interest and the real quantity of M1 money in the economy. The curve is drawn with a positive slope because, in the deposit-expansion process described in Chapter 12, banks will work more eagerly to expand the money supply when real interest rates are high than when they are low. This is because the profitability of loaning money will be greater when real interest rates are high, other things being equal, and banks will hold smaller amounts of "desired" excess reserves. Therefore, with a given monetary base and reserve requirement, the amount of money that is supplied will be greater when real interest rates are high.

The location of the money-supply curve is very important to the theory of interest-rate determination. The monetary instruments of the Federal Reserve (open market buying and selling, reserve requirements, and discount rates) may be able to shift this curve either to the left by restrictive policies or to the right by expansionary policies. Whether or not they can in fact shift the *real* money-supply curve is the key question in short-run real-interest-rate determination. We shall take up this question shortly.

Equilibrium in the Money Market

In Figure 14-2, the point where the MD curve crosses the MS curve identifies the equilibrium condition. At the equilibrium interest rate, i, the amount of money actually supplied is equal to the amount demanded. Given the location of these curves, no other interest rate could bring about that balance.

The equilibrating action of the interest rate becomes clear when we examine what would happen at interest rates above or below the equilibrium rate. Let us assume that i in Figure 14-2 represents a real interest rate of 5 percent. Consider a nonmoney asset that pays $100 a year to its owner. At the 5 percent rate of interest, the present value of this asset is $2,000 (that is, $100/0.05). Now think about what would happen at a real interest rate of 7 percent. At this higher interest rate, the supply of money would be greater (as shown by a movement along the money-supply curve in Figure 14-2), but the present value of the nonmoney asset would be only $1428.57 (that is, $100/0.07). At this lower price, it becomes a more attractive buy for speculators who believe that its price will go up. Now the equilibrating mechanism starts to work. Speculators use the extra money to bid for the nonmoney asset and its price is bid upward. But when the price rises above $1428.57, the yield or rate of return on the asset falls to less than 7 percent, since the asset still promises to pay only $100 per year to its owner. What this means is that no real interest rate other than i (5 percent in our numerical illustration) can be sustained, given the locations of the MS and MD curves in the money market. In order for equilibrium to exist, the real rate of interest in this market must correspond with the yield or rate of return of the nonmoney assets that are alternative assets for holding wealth.

Now that you understand the equilibrating mechanism of the money market, we can turn our attention to the important policy question of shifting the money-supply curve. The monetarist approach to macroeconomic equilibrium directs our attention to how (and whether) the central bank (Federal Reserve System) can shift the MS curve in the money market. We will present two views or scenarios about this question. The first assumes that no inflationary expectations are set in motion by an expansionary central bank action. The second scenario assumes that inflationary expectations *do* arise from such central bank actions.

MONETARY INSTRUMENTS IN ACTION: THE NO-INFLATION SCENARIO

Figure 14-3 illustrates an expansionary central bank action. We begin with equilibrium at the intersection of the MD curve with the MS_1 curve, with real interest rate i_1 and the real quantity of money M_1. Next, we assume that the central bank takes some expansionary action, such as might be carried out through open market purchases, lower reserve requirements and/or lower discount

FIGURE 14-3 Expansionary Monetary Policy (the No-Inflation Scenario)

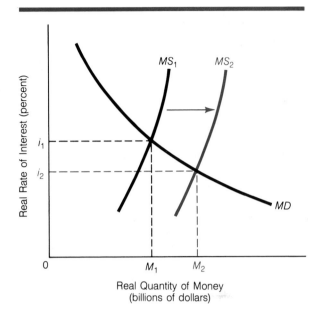

If people do not expect any change in the price level, expansionary Federal Reserve action can shift the MS curve to the right from MS_1 to MS_2. This will cause real interest rates to fall from i_1 to i_2. Contractionary action would shift the MS curve to the left and raise real interest rates.

rates. If this leads to no expectation of any change in the price level, the money-supply curve will shift to the right (from MS_1 to MS_2). *The assumption that no price-level change is expected is critical in shifting this curve.* If no price-level rise is expected, each dollar of the M1 money recorded on the horizontal axis keeps its original purchasing power. So an increase in the number of these dollars is an increase in the real money supply. As a result, the real interest rate falls from i_1 to i_2. If, instead, the Federal Reserve Board wanted to raise real interest rates, the money supply would be reduced, shifting the MS curve to the left.

The process of moving to the new equilibrium follows the steps explained earlier. When the money supply is increased, people find that they have more money (and less of other assets) than they want at the i_1 rate of interest. To gain more wealth, people will bid on such nonmoney assets as stocks, bonds, or real estate. Their bids push up the market prices of these assets, and, as you can see from the present value formula, the rise in their prices leads to a drop in the rate of interest. On the other hand, if the money supply is reduced, shifting the MS curve to the left, wealth holders will find themselves with less money than they desire at the initial interest rate. In order to hold more wealth in the form of money, they will offer to sell stocks, bonds, real estate, and so forth. These sale offers will lower market prices for these assets and cause interest rates to rise.

Transmission to Real National Income and Product

If monetary instruments are able to shift the real money-supply curve and lower the real interest rate, as shown in Figure 14-3, how will the effects be transmitted to the equilibrium level of real national income and product?

KEYNESIAN TRANSMISSION MECHANISM The **Keynesian transmission mechanism** uses the Keynesian model and stresses the importance of planned investment. It is illustrated in Figure 14-4, which combines the interest-rate-determination model (which you have just studied) with the planned-investment and the Keynesian-cross models from Chapters 9 and 10. Here is how the connections work. The Federal Reserve undertakes expansionary action by buying bonds in the open market, by reducing reserve requirements, or by reducing discount rates. This, according to the "no-inflation scenario," shifts the real money-supply curve in panel (a) from MS_1 to MS_2 (step 1). The real rate of interest falls from i_1 to i_2 (step 2). These lower real interest rates affect the volume of planned investment, as shown in panel (b). The original volume of planned investment was I_1, corresponding to the original rate of interest of i_1. When interest rates fall to i_2, the volume of planned investment rises to I_2 (step 3). Planned investment is part of total planned expenditure ($C + I + G + X - Im$). Panel (c) shows the effect of the change in planned investment

on the equilibrium level of real national income and product. When the volume of planned investment rises, other things being equal, the total planned-expenditure curve shifts from $C + I_1 + G + X - Im$ to $C + I_2 + G + X - Im$ (step 4), and the equilibrium level of real national income and product rises from Y_1 to Y_2 through the operation of the multiplier process (step 5).

When you examine the graphs in Figure 14-4 carefully, you may discover that the strength of the monetary action depends on the slopes of the curves in panels (a) and (b). At this point, we will not interrupt the explanation of monetary instruments to examine this matter further. However, it is an issue in the Keynesian–monetarist debate, which we will discuss in Chapter 16.

DIRECT TRANSMISSION   Many economists say that monetary instruments do not have to work through the complicated process of interest-rate changes, followed by planned-investment changes, and finally by changes in national income and product. They contend that changes in the money supply work directly through household budgets and consumption expenditure. For example, if Federal Reserve Banks purchase securities in the open market, the households that sell the securities receive money, which they can spend directly for consumption goods and services. The economy can expand without going through the initial step of an interest-rate change. This is called the **direct transmission mechanism.**

Feedback to the Demand-for-Money Curve

The transmission mechanism shown in Figure 14-4 does not tell the complete story of the effects of monetary actions. When the level of real national income and product changes, as it did in step 5, there will be a feedback effect in the money market. This feedback will counteract some of the initial effects of the monetary action. It operates through *shifts* in the demand-for-money curve.

When you studied the speculative, transactions, and precautionary demands for money,

FIGURE 14-4 Transmission from Change in Real Interest Rate to Change in Equilibrium Real National Income and Product

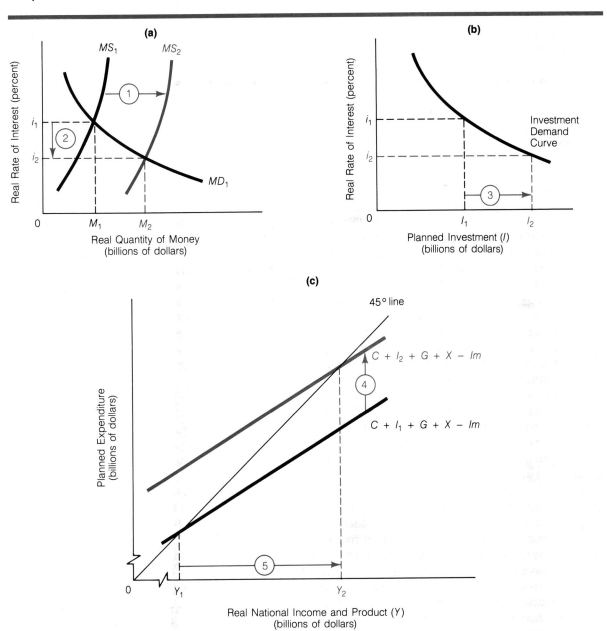

Panel (a) shows how an increase in the real money supply shifts the *MS* curve to the right (step 1) and causes a reduction in the real rate of interest (step 2). Panel (b) shows how this decrease in the real interest rate causes an increase in the volume of planned investment (step 3). Panel (c) shows how an increase in planned investment, other things being equal, causes an upward shift in the $C + I + G + X - Im$ curve (step 4). This shift in planned expenditure brings an increase in equilibrium real national income and product from Y_1 to Y_2 (step 5). The three panels together illustrate a transmission mechanism linking monetary changes to changes in equilibrium real national income and product.

you learned that changes in income and wealth could shift the demand-for-money curve. The rise in real national income and product from Y_1 to Y_2 (step 5 in Figure 14-4) could then lead to a shift in the demand-for-money curve. With higher incomes, people want more money because they are engaging in more transactions. This feedback effect is shown in Figure 14-5, which repeats Figure 14-4 and adds the feedback effects in half-tone color. The shift of MD_1 to MD_2 to the right (step 6), which is caused by the rise in equilibrium real national income and product from Y_1 to Y_2, brings an increase in real interest rates from i_2 to i_3 (step 7). This rise partly offsets the drop in interest rates from the original policy action of the Federal Reserve. The rise in the interest rate carries over to panel (b) and brings a drop in the volume of planned investment from I_2 to I_3 (step 8), which partly offsets the rise in planned investment from the first round of the process. Finally, in panel (c), we see that the partial reduction in the volume of planned investment brings a downward shift in the total-planned-expenditure curve, from $C + I_2 + G + X - Im$ to $C + I_3 + G + X - Im$ (step 9), and a drop in the equilibrium level of real national income and product from Y_2 to Y_3 (step 10). What has happened is that some of the new money that pushed interest rates down initially is now being used in hand-to-hand circulation and is no longer being used in bidding for securities and other assets.

The feedback process will repeat itself, in ever-weakening rounds, until the real national income and product reaches a new equilibrium, which will lie somewhere between Y_2 and Y_3. You must remember, however, that this whole procedure depends on whether monetary tools can in fact shift the real money-supply curve.

MONETARY INSTRUMENTS IN ACTION: THE INFLATION SCENARIO

The interest-rate-determination model that we have just examined used the assumption that the Federal Reserve System could shift the *real* money-

supply curve by using expansionary open market, reserve requirements, and discount rate instruments. However, many economists believe that expansionary monetary actions lead to price-level increases (inflation), especially when the economy is already operating at high levels of employment. They say that the inflationary effects of expansionary monetary action will cancel much of the intended increase in real output and jobs in the economy.

Figure 14-6 illustrates how this can happen. This figure reproduces Figure 14-3, but adds arrows to illustrate the effect of changes in the price level. A higher price level means a decrease in the *real* value of each dollar of the money supply because each dollar will now buy a smaller quantity of goods and services. In real terms, the units of measurement on the horizontal axis shrink, and the falling real value of the monetary unit (the dollar) moves the *real* money-supply curve to the left, back toward its original location. If we assume that there is no change in the volume of real output in the economy or in any other variable that affects prices, the rising price level will eventually cancel out the initial expansion in the money supply and the real rate of interest will return to its original level, at i_1.

Will the demand-for-money curve shift as a result of the change in the price level? This is another question for debate among economists. Transactions and precautionary demands for money probably increase along with the rising price level. People demand more money to keep up with the higher prices. But higher price levels could lower real income or wealth and cause a reduced demand for money. The strength of these effects is very uncertain. In our simple model, we assume that no shift takes place in the real demand-for-money curve, but we recognize that research must continue on this question.

Inflationary Expectations

Figure 14-6 illustrated the effect of actual inflation on the real supply of money. A similar, and perhaps more useful, application of this model arises when the expansionary use of monetary instruments leads people to anticipate rising price

FIGURE 14-5 **Feedback Effect from Real National Income and Product to the Demand
for Money in the Transmission Mechanism**

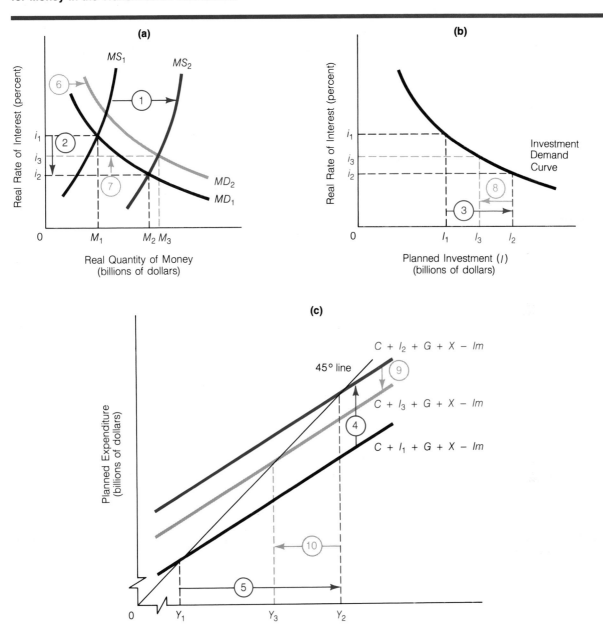

A rise in real national income and product from Y_1 to Y_2 will cause a rightward shift in the MD curve in panel (a) (step 6). The increase in real interest rates that comes from this demand shift (step 7) will bring a decrease in planned investment from I_2 to I_3 in panel (b) (step 8). This decline in planned investment will bring a downward shift in the $C + I + G + X - Im$ curve in panel (c) (step 9), and this reduction in planned expenditure will lower the equilibrium level of real national income and product from Y_2 to Y_3 (step 10). This feedback process will repeat itself in weakening rounds of interaction, approaching a new equilibrium somewhere between Y_2 and Y_3.

FIGURE 14-6 **Monetary Policy and Real Interest Rates (the Inflation Scenario)**

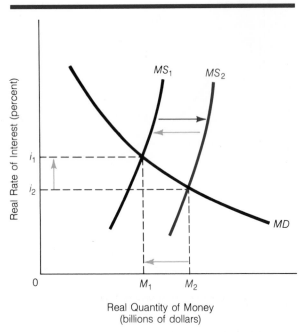

Real Rate of Interest (percent)

Real Quantity of Money
(billions of dollars)

As the price level rises, the real purchasing power of the monetary unit (recorded on the horizontal axis) decreases, causing a leftward shift in the real money-supply curve from MS_2 to MS_1. As the real money-supply curve shifts to the left, the real rate of interest rises from i_2 to i_1. This analysis suggests that an initial increase in the money supply will result in only a temporary lowering of the real rate of interest.

levels, that is, when it gives rise to **inflationary expectations.**

To illustrate the inflationary expectations model, let us assume that the initial interest rate (i_1) in Figure 14-6 represents a real interest rate of 5 percent. Now, let us assume that an expansionary use of monetary instruments leads both demanders and suppliers of money assets to anticipate a 4 percent increase per year in the price level, that is, a 4 percent inflation rate. As both demanders and suppliers build these inflationary expectations into their calculations, *nominal* interest rates will rise to 9 percent while *real* interest rates will remain at the original 5 percent level. Neither the money-supply curve (MS) nor

the demand-for-money curve (MD) will have shifted in real terms. The monetary action would be completely ineffective in changing the real rate of interest.

Inflationary expectations may, however, cause shifts in real demand and supply curves for money. For example, speculative demand for money may decrease when inflationary expectations make money assets less attractive than nonmoney wealth forms. In cases of extreme inflation, as in Argentina in 1985, virtually no one wanted to hold money balances. We must, however, leave these matters to more advanced economics courses. Our purpose here is to point out that inflationary expectations can severely limit the ability of monetary instruments to lower real interest rates in the economy. Such expectations may have played a role in keeping real interest rates high in the United States in 1983 and 1984.[7]

Temporary Changes in Real Interest Rates

Expansionary monetary actions are more likely to trigger inflationary expectations when there has been a recent experience with inflation. For example, the likelihood that expansionary monetary action would trigger inflationary expectations was much greater in 1980, when the United States had recently experienced double-digit inflation, than it was in 1986, after the inflation rate had been falling for several years. It is reasonable to suppose, therefore, that in most situations monetary expansion will bring a combination of results. Expectations of inflation might not fully cancel the effects of an increase in the money supply. There could be some lowering of real interest rates, some rise in real national income and product, some expectations of higher price levels, and some rise in nominal interest rates. As you can see, predicting the relation of money to equilibrium real national income and product is a very risky activity in these situations.

7. Further aspects of inflationary expectations theory will be examined in Chapter 17.

REAL INTEREST RATES IN THE LONG RUN

As we have just seen, there is much uncertainty about interest-rate determination through the demand and supply of money as an asset. Whether monetary instruments can influence real interest rates in the money market depends importantly on whether or not these actions create inflation or inflationary expectations. There is less uncertainty about the determination of real interest rates in the **loanable funds market,** that is, in the market that brings together those who wish to lend and those who wish to borrow funds. According to modern monetarist thinking, this is the market that determines real interest rates in the long run.

Figure 14-7 illustrates the loanable funds market. The horizontal axis shows the real (adjusted for price-level change) quantities of money demanded and supplied for loans. The vertical axis shows the real rate of interest. The supply curve represents the behavior of people who are willing to let others use part of their wealth in exchange for the payment of interest. It reflects the time preferences of these people between using their wealth for current consumption or saving it for future uses. The supply curve has a positive slope because, other things being equal, wealth holders will be willing to loan more money when real interest rates are high than when they are low. Modern monetarist economists say that central bank policy has little influence over the location of this curve.

The demand curve in the loanable funds market illustrates the behavior of borrowers. It shows the amounts that they are willing to borrow at various possible interest rates. In the loanable funds model, one of the main reasons for borrowing is to finance capital, such as plant and equipment to be used in production. The quantity that firms are willing to borrow, at any given interest rate, depends on the expected profitability of using capital in production. Modern monetarist economists contend that central bank policies have little to do with the forces that determine the location of this curve also. Instead,

FIGURE 14-7 Real Interest Rates in the Long Run

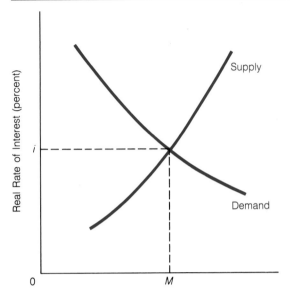

In the long run, the real rate of interest balances the amount of money that lenders are willing to lend with the amount that borrowers are willing to borrow. The willingness to borrow is related to the productivity of machines. The willingness to lend requires wealth holders to give up the use of their wealth temporarily.

its location is determined by forces that influence the expected profitability of capital itself. Inventions, favorable government policies, and promising economic conditions shift this curve to the right. Conversely, forces that reduce expected profitability shift the curve to the left. The demand curve also reflects borrowing by consumers and governments that wish to purchase goods and services today but want to postpone payment until some future time. Again, central bank actions have little effect.

Modern monetarist economists conclude that central bank policies about the money supply cannot significantly influence real interest rates in the long run. Although monetary policies may have temporary effects on real interest rates, output, and employment, their effect in the long run is mainly on the price level in the economy. Other things being equal, if the money supply rises faster than production, the price level will rise, and if the money supply rises more slowly than production, the price level will fall. But, in the long run, the volume of production itself is not determined by changes in the money supply.[8]

SUMMARY

1. The quantity theory of money holds that in the long run changes in the quantity of money bring changes in the price level and/or in the quantity of goods and services produced in the economy. This theory is based on the equation of exchange, $MV = PQ$, which actually is an identity. It fails to answer many questions about the stability of velocity and about the determination of real output.

2. Nominal values are measured in terms of some monetary unit (such as the dollar) and are not adjusted for price-level changes. Real values, on the other hand, are measured in terms of goods and services. A real value has been adjusted for price-level changes by applying an index number or deflator. Actual human behavior is believed to be based on real values or what are believed to be real values.

3. Since borrowing and lending transactions cover a period from the time when money is borrowed until it is repaid, expected price-level changes introduce a difference between real and nominal interest rates. This difference is equal to the expected rate of change in the price level.

4. A money market relates the supply and the demand for money as an asset. The supply curve reflects the quantity of money in the economy, and the demand curve reflects the transactions, precautionary, and speculative motives for holding money. The slope of the demand-for-money curve is related to the speculative demand for money. The demand-for-money curve may shift because of changes in income or wealth.

5. If no inflation occurs, an expansionary exercise of monetary instruments will shift the real

money-supply curve to the right and lower the real rate of interest, assuming that the demand-for-money curve does not shift.

6. The effects of the use of monetary instruments may be transmitted to the equilibrium level of real national income and product through a transmission mechanism involving changes in the real rate of interest, changes in the volume of planned investment, and changes in the $C + I + G + X - Im$ curve in the Keynesian-cross diagram. The strength of these effects is moderated by feedback from income changes, which further shifts the demand-for-money curve. Monetary effects also may be transmitted directly through changes in household consumption expenditure.

7. If price-level increases occur, the real money-supply curve will shift to the left, other things being equal. This shift can moderate or cancel the effects of expansionary monetary instruments and raise the real rate of interest. Economists who believe that the use of expansionary monetary instruments brings increases in the price level claim that monetary instruments can have only temporary effects on the real rate of interest.

8. If the use of expansionary monetary instruments triggers expectations of price-level increases, nominal interest rates will rise above real interest rates. Therefore, it is possible that expansionary monetary instruments could raise nominal interest rates without having any effect on real interest rates or real national income and product.

9. In the long run, real interest rates are determined by the productivity of machines (that is, capital) and the willingness of lenders to forgo the use of their wealth temporarily. Short-run real interest rates may be influenced by forces other than the productivity of capital.

10. Modern monetarist economists say that, in the long run, monetary instruments mainly affect the price level in the economy rather than the volume of real national income and product.

DISCUSSION QUESTIONS

1. Write down the equation of exchange and define each of its terms. Which side of the

---

8. A more complete explanation of the loanable funds market is presented in microeconomics.

equation is actually GNP as usually measured in the national accounting system? Explain the reasoning contained in the equation, noting why this is properly an identity rather than an equation that can be used for predictions.

2. If the nominal GNP is $1,200 billion and the quantity of M1 money averaged $300 billion during the year, what is the implicit velocity of money circulation? In Germany during the inflation after World War I, people wanted to be paid every day instead of only once each week. What would a change like that do to the velocity of circulation of money? Discuss the effect of electronic banking machines on the velocity of circulation of money in the United States since they were introduced in the 1970s.

3. In your own words, explain the definitions of nominal value and real value. Suppose that the consumer price index was 200 (1972 = 100) a year ago and is 220 today, and that a phonograph record sold for $8.00 a year ago and for $8.80 today. Has the nominal value of the phonograph record changed? Has its real value changed? Explain your reasoning.

4. Suppose you sign an agreement to borrow money and to pay a nominal interest rate of 10 percent. If you expect the price level to rise by 6 percent a year, what real interest rate do you expect to pay? If the lender expects the price level to rise by 5 percent a year, what real interest rate does he or she expect to receive? If the price level actually rises by only 4 percent a year, is the lender pleased with the outcome of the transaction? Are you pleased with the outcome? Explain.

5. Write down, from memory, the definition of speculation, and then check in the chapter (or the Glossary) to be sure it is correct. Under what expectations about future asset prices would a speculator decide to hold cash? When would this speculator decide to hold nonmoney assets instead of cash? Carefully explain how this reasoning suggests that a demand-for-money curve, drawn with the real interest rate on the vertical axis, would have a negative slope.

6. Explain the transactions demand for money. Suppose that there is an economic boom in your home town, perhaps because the price of its main product has risen on the national market. The incomes of many local people have gone up.

Since your home town is a small part of the total economy, its prosperity has not influenced the real interest rate. What will happen to the quantity of money demanded for transactions in the town? Explain why this is a shift and not a movement along the demand-for-money curve.

7. Assume that the monetary authorities increase the amount of M1 money in the economy and that no one expects this to cause any increase in the price level. What will happen to the demand for stocks and bonds and other nonmoney assets? How will this affect the prices of these assets? How will this, in turn, affect the equilibrium real rate of interest as determined in the market for money? Trace this same sequence for a reduction in the amount of money in the economy.

8. Without looking at Figure 14-4, construct the set of three graphs that illustrate the transmission of a change in the real money supply to a change in equilibrium real national income and product. Trace through the transmission system, starting with an increase in the real money supply. Check to be sure you have it right, and then write a brief description of the system. Include a discussion of the feedback effect.

9. If the money-supply curve is drawn on a graph with real values on its axes, a change in the price level could cause a shift in this curve. Which way will the money-supply curve shift if the price level increases? Why? Which way will it shift if the price level decreases? Why?

10. Suppose that a machine costs $1,000 and, for simplicity, that it never wears out or requires any operating cost. Suppose also that using this machine will increase returns to the firm that owns it by $60 a year. Would it be profitable to purchase and use this machine if the interest rate were 5 percent? If the interest rate were 10 percent? Discuss how the real rate of interest influences the amount of planned investment. Explain how a change in the productivity of machines would affect the real rate of interest if lenders kept their preferences unchanged between present and future consumption.

11. In some circumstances, an increase in the money supply may bring a rise in nominal interest rates but no change in real interest rates. Describe the circumstances and the viewpoints of lenders and borrowers that can bring about this situation.

Friedman and Monetarism: Do Not Confuse Them!

Many people have come to identify certain economic policies called monetarism with Milton Friedman (1912–   ), much as they identify certain other policies called Soviet communism with Marx and Lenin. Such identifications are seldom accurate; "Friedman and monetarism" is a case in point. Friedman's Nobel Prize in 1976 was based on much more than his monetarism.

Friedman and the Free Market

Before discussing monetarism, let us turn to Friedman himself. We shall then be able to relate Friedman's form of monetarism to his broader vision of the economy.

Friedman was a poor boy from Brooklyn, New York, who graduated from Rutgers University in both mathematics and economics during the middle of the Great Depression. Starting his career as an economic statistician, he eventually rose to the leadership of the so-called "Chicago School" of strongly free-market economists centered at the University of Chicago, where he taught for thirty years. His advice is sought by leaders all over the world, but is not always followed.

Friedman has always been a strong supporter of the free market, as indicated by the titles of two of his best-known books, *Capitalism and Freedom* and *Free to Choose.* Observing the stream of history, he believes that the market economy is a *necessary* condition—though not a sufficient condition—for the continuation of civil liberties in the long run. His view is reinforced by his own experience with what a poor boy and a member of a minority can achieve in a market economy.

The Influence of Positivism

Besides civil liberties and the free market, a philosophical doctrine called positivism has been a strong influence on Friedman, and Friedman has in turn been a leader in applying positivist ideas in economics.

Milton Friedman

Positivists believe that it is important to make it clear when one is making *positive* statements about what *is,* and when one is making *normative* statements about what *ought* to be. Only the first sort of statements are scientific, and only in the positive aspects of his subject is the specialist also an expert.

In the positivist view, the truth or falsity of a positive proposition can generally be determined only by comparing it with rival theories or explanations. To confirm or disconfirm a theory in a single case is not to prove or disprove it. The intuitive plausibility or "realism" of any assumptions on which a theory may have been based has nothing to do with whether it is true or false. Its truth or falsehood can be judged only by testing predictions based on its conclusions, as compared with other predictions based on rival theories. Such comparisons are preferably quantitative or statistical.

In the case of economics, Friedman has hoped that many controversial points traditionally presented in literary form might be settled once and for all by using statistical methods. Then, with agreement on the facts of positive economics, economists would have little difficulty in reaching agreement on the normative question of what, if anything, should be done about them. This hope does not yet appear to be borne out.

Friedman and the Negative Income Tax

Friedman is never happier than at the center of a controversy, usually in the interests of the free market. One example of so-called "Friedmanship" that has attracted much attention is Friedman's advocacy of a negative income tax as a replacement for welfare state and agricultural price support systems. He believes that the direct approach of giving money to poor people so that they will no longer be poor makes the most sense. The negative income tax would compensate only the poor, whether or not they belonged to some generally disadvantaged group. The taxpayer would save large amounts of money by dismantling the welfare bureaucracy, but many social workers and other professionals would lose their jobs. Friedman's plan is generous enough to allow many poor people to survive on negative income tax payments alone. And while his plan includes monetary incentives for people to work, it does not force them to work if they do not desire to do so.

Friedman's Monetarism

From Friedman's positivist philosophy and his "classical liberalism," the road to his form of monetarism is shorter and less winding than it may appear. Friedman observed that Keynesian policies, as carried out during the ten to fifteen years after World War II, were producing inflation,

contrary to the hopes and forecasts of their well-intentioned advocates. He also observed that what he believed to be dangerous restrictions on the market economy (wage and price controls) and on civil rights (harsh enforcement policies) were being developed as a next step. These restrictions were later known as "incomes policies," when wage and price controls as such became unpopular.

Moreover, Friedman pointed out that the difficulties with governmental management of the economy were nothing new. In a series of studies beginning with *A Monetary History of the United States,* Friedman (with Anna Jacobson Schwartz) traced a century of monetary mismanagement and its effects. He claimed that the Federal Reserve System, which was supposed to smooth out the economic fluctuations accentuated by monetary uncertainty, had actually made matters worse. It had done so especially by reducing the money supply sharply over the three years following the stock market crash of October 1929. Friedman and Schwartz believe that the crash would not have developed into the Great Depression if the American money supply had been allowed to increase at a normal rate. Friedman maintains that because of the long and variable lag between monetary growth rate changes and their price-level effects, monetary authorities have a tendency to "overshoot" the mark—to continue an easy money policy during high monetary growth long after acceleration of inflation has become unavoidable, and to continue monetary tightness and low growth long after the stage is set for recession.

Friedman has therefore proposed a monetary rule under which monetary authorities would lose their discretion. Instead, a particular monetary entity—currency plus demand and time deposits in commercial banks—should be allowed to grow at a steady rate regardless of short-term business conditions. This steady rate should be at, or slightly above, the long-term growth rate of the country's real output. Certainly such a rule is far from perfect, but it may do much better than the historical record of "fine tuning" and concentration on the short-run "feel of the market"—whatever that is.

There is some danger of such a rule creating monetary tightness and high interest rates when governments finance deficits by selling abnormally large amounts of public securities. To reduce this danger, Friedman would like domestic budgets to be balanced or in surplus at high levels of employment.

Non-Friedman Monetarism

What of the non-Friedman monetarists such as those who support a "Shadow Open Market Committee," which meets to "second-guess" the monetary policy decisions of the Federal Reserve Board? Such monetarists differ from Friedman by proposing that a different monetary target be chosen, that a different rule or set of rules be followed, or even that some monetary discretion be continued under a new generation of monetary authorities who have learned enough to avoid their predecessors' mistakes.

V *Aggregate Demand, Aggregate Supply, and Macroeconomic Policy*

- Aggregate Demand and Aggregate Supply
- Macroeconomic Policy: Demand Side
- Macroeconomic Policy: Supply Side

15 *Aggregate Demand and Aggregate Supply*

PREVIEW The chapter that you are about to study brings together almost everything that you have learned so far about macroeconomics and focuses this knowledge on two of the most important problems of our times: unemployment and inflation. It does so by carefully developing the concepts of *aggregate demand* and *aggregate supply*, which were first presented in Chapter 5.

We start by carefully explaining how aggregate-demand and aggregate-supply curves are constructed. The aggregate-demand curve makes use of both the Keynesian and the monetarist models that you have already studied. The aggregate-supply curve, on the other hand, is determined by the production capabilities of the economy and by the behavior of business firms. Supply-side economics focuses on this curve.

To help you understand the effects of shifts of aggregate-demand and aggregate-supply curves, we use them first to describe a recession–deflation chain of events that parallels what happened during the Great Depression of the 1930s. Then we present an expansion–inflation pattern that is much like the experiences of the late 1960s and early 1970s in the United States.

Throughout these exercises, we shall pay very close attention to events or policies that can start the whole process by shifting one of the curves. Then we shall explain why the aggregate-supply curve shifts as a delayed reaction to changes in the price level. This will help you understand the difference between the short-run and the long-run aggregate-supply curve and what economists mean by the natural rate of unemployment and effective full employment.

When you finish this chapter, you will be prepared for the study of macroeconomic policy, which is the subject of the next two chapters. Since macroeconomic policy operates by shifting aggregate-demand and aggregate-supply curves, a sound understanding of these ideas is needed in order to evaluate different policies.

AGGREGATE DEMAND

Figure 15-1 presents an **aggregate-demand curve**—that is, a demand curve for the whole national income and product, viewed as if it were a single good or service. The vertical axis shows various possible price levels. As you learned in Chapter 6, the price level is an average of the prices of all goods and services produced in the economy. If actual figures for different price levels were shown on the vertical axis of this graph, they would be index numbers, such as GNP deflator values, giving different price levels in terms of the price level in some selected base year. In reading this graph, movements upward show increases in the price level (inflation) and movements downward show decreases in the price level (deflation).

The horizontal axis of the graph in Figure 15-1 records real national income and product. In other words, it shows total output of goods and services in the economy, valued in dollars with a fixed or constant purchasing power. Movements to the left show decreases in real national income and product and usually go along with increases in unemployment. Movements to the right on the graph show increases in real national income and

FIGURE 15-1   The Aggregate-Demand Curve

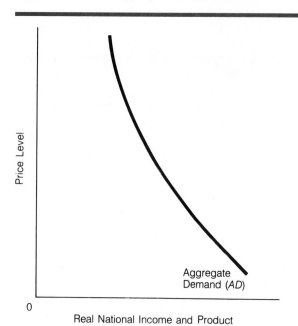

The aggregate-demand curve shows a relationship between the price level and real national income and product. It has a negative slope, suggesting that increases in the price level will cause decreases in real national income and product demanded. Price-level decreases cause increases in real national income and product demanded.

product, which usually mean decreases in unemployment. As you can see, this graph brings together inflation and unemployment, the major concerns of macroeconomic policy.

Before we go on to explain the slope and location of the aggregate-demand curve, it is important to distinguish this curve clearly from the total-planned-expenditure curve that you studied in the Keynesian model in Chapter 9. Sometimes that curve is referred to as "aggregate demand," but it is definitely not the same aggregate-demand concept that we are dealing with here. To understand the difference, remember that the aggregate-demand curve, as explained in Chapter 5, shows that quantity demanded depends on the price level. When aggregate demand is illustrated on a graph, the price level

is on one axis and the quantity demanded is on the other, so that changes in the price level cause *movements along* the aggregate-demand curve. But the price level does not appear on either axis of the Keynesian-cross graph. This means that the price level is held constant by the *ceteris paribus* assumption when the total-planned-expenditure curve is drawn. Therefore, changes in the price level do not cause movements along the total-planned-expenditure curve. Instead, they cause *shifts* of that curve. We will illustrate this in our explanation of the slope of the aggregate-demand curve, which comes next.

Slope of the Aggregate-Demand Curve

The aggregate-demand curve slopes downward to the right. This negative slope means that there is an inverse relationship between the variables shown on the axes. In other words, increases in the price level (the independent variable) bring reductions in real national income and product demanded (the dependent variable), and price-level decreases bring increases in real national income and product demanded, other things being equal.

As in explaining the slope of any curve in economics, the only variables that are allowed to change are the ones shown on the axes of the graph. In this case, these are the price level (on the vertical axis) and the quantity of real national income and product demanded (on the horizontal axis). Our reasoning is that the quantity of real national income and product demanded depends on the price level, other things being equal. Thus, the price level is our independent variable, and the real national income and product demanded is our dependent variable. We do not reason in the opposite direction, that the price level depends on the quantity of income and product demanded, because our theory is that the price level depends on the combination of both aggregate demand and aggregate supply, and not on either one individually. This is the same type of reasoning that is used in demand-and-supply models for particular products.[1] Two theories will help to explain the slope of this curve. One is the interest rate theory and the other is the real cash balances theory.

THE INTEREST RATE THEORY The interest rate theory is based on the fact that a rise in the price level shrinks the *real* quantity of money in the economy, if other things remain unchanged. This was explained in the previous chapter. In real terms, each dollar has less purchasing power than before the rise in prices. The way this theory explains the slope of the aggregate-demand curve is shown in Figure 15-2, which repeats the transmission mechanism illustrated in Figure 14-4 in Chapter 14. Panel (a) shows what happens to the real money supply when the price level increases. The money-supply curve shifts to the left, from MS_1 to MS_2. This leads to a rise in the real interest rate from i_1 to i_2. Panel (b) shows how this rise in the real interest rate reduces the volume of planned investment expenditure from I_1 to I_2. This reduction in planned investment expenditure lowers the total-planned-expenditure curve in panel (c) from $C + I_1 + G + X - Im$ to $C + I_2 + G + X - Im$. According to this demand-side reasoning, the equilibrium level of real national income and product falls from Y_1 to Y_2, as indicated by the movement of the 45-degree line intersection from E_1 to E_2. Panel (d) shows how all these responses are summarized in the slope of the aggregate-demand curve. At the initial price level of P_1, the real national income and product demanded was Y_1, as shown by point A on the aggregate-demand curve. At the new price level of P_2, the real national income and product demanded is Y_2, as shown by point B on the aggregate-demand curve. Therefore, working through the demand side of the economy, the rise in the price level has brought a reduction in national income and product. Our aggregate-demand curve therefore has a negative slope. Because this theory uses the basic Keynesian technique of linking interest rates to planned investment and national income and product, it sometimes is called the **Keynes effect.**

There are some qualifications to this model. A lot may depend on how steep or how flat the demand-for-money curve and the planned-investment-demand curve are. There also is debate about whether the demand-for-money curve would shift as a result of a change in the price level. Even in view of these qualifications, however, it still seems reasonable to draw the aggregate-demand curve with a negative slope.

THE REAL BALANCES THEORY The **real balances theory**[2] reasons that a rise in the price level will mean reductions in real wealth for the people who hold money or certain assets whose value is given in monetary terms, such as government bonds. The real goods and services equivalent of these assets is reduced by the increase in prices. This is a familiar result of inflation. As you learned in Chapters 9 and 10, reductions in wealth can cause a downward shift in the consumption function, which is part of the $C + I + G + X - Im$ curve in the Keynesian-cross diagram, just as investment shifted the curve in panel (c) of Figure 15-2. This shift will lower the equilibrium level of national income and product. In this way, the real balances theory also concludes that a rise in the price level will bring a drop in real national income and product and that the aggregate-demand curve has a negative slope.

The net strength of the real balances effect may be quite small. Often one person's loss from inflation is another person's gain. Only a small part of the total wealth in the economy, such as cash itself, is free of this counterbalancing effect.

Location of the Aggregate-Demand Curve

As with other demand curves, the relationship between the price level and the quantity of real

---

1. See Chapter 5.

2. This theory is sometimes called the **Pigou effect,** after the British economist A. C. Pigou, who analyzed how changes in wealth influence spending and saving.

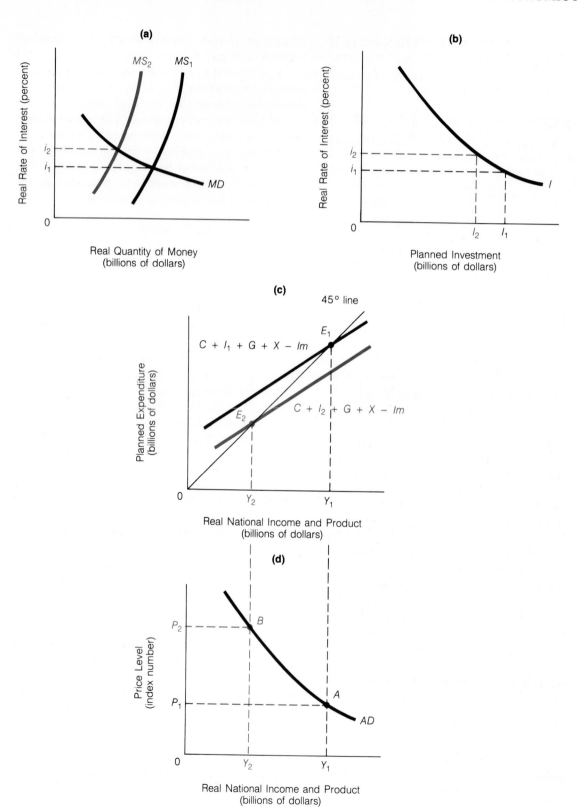

◀ FIGURE 15-2   How Changes in the Price Level Can Change Real National Income and Product Demanded

Panel (a) shows how an increase in the price level, other things being equal, will shift the money-supply curve to the left from MS_1 to MS_2, causing the real rate of interest to rise from i_1 to i_2. Panel (b) shows how this rise in the real rate of interest reduces the amount of planned investment expenditure from I_1 to I_2. Panel (c) shows how this reduction of planned investment expenditure causes a downward shift of the total-planned-expenditure curve from $C + I_1 + G + X - Im$ to $C + I_2 + G + X - Im$, lowering the equilibrium level of real national income and product from Y_1 to Y_2, as the equilibrium intersection moves from E_1 to E_2. Panel (d) shows how the end result of these responses is illustrated by the aggregate-demand curve. The quantity demanded was Y_1 when the price level was P_1, as shown by point A, and becomes Y_2 when the price level rises to P_2, as shown by point B.

goods and services demanded is based on the assumption that all other variables remain unchanged. The curve may shift if any of these other variables changes. Of course, there are many variables that may shift the aggregate-demand curve, and the fiscal and monetary policies of government affect many of them. If these policies move in an expansionary direction, the aggregate-demand curve will shift to the right, meaning that, at any given price level, a greater amount of real goods and services will be demanded. If fiscal and monetary policies move in a contractionary direction, the aggregate-demand curve will shift to the left, and a smaller amount of real goods and services will be demanded at any given price level. This explains why both fiscal and monetary policies are said to be demand-side instruments of macroeconomic policy.

SHORT-RUN AGGREGATE SUPPLY (SRAS)

An **aggregate-supply curve** shows how changes in the price level operate through the supply or production side of economic activity to change

the level of real national income and product supplied. The slope and location of this curve are very important in economics today. Supply-side economics deals with actions and events that have their impact through this curve.

Modern macroeconomics makes a very important distinction between the short-run aggregate-supply curve and the long-run aggregate-supply curve. We shall first examine short-run aggregate supply. Later in the chapter, we shall consider long-run aggregate supply.

Slope of the SRAS Curve

The short-run aggregate-supply curve (SRAS) is illustrated in Figure 15-3. We shall offer two explanations for the slope of this curve: the wage–cost lag theory and the money illusion theory.

THE WAGE–COST LAG THEORY   The **wage–cost lag theory** is the proposition that changes in costs of production lag behind or follow changes in the general price level, which is based on the prices of final goods and services produced. Consider labor costs, for example. Many workers in the economy are employed under contracts that run for one or more years into the future. When the prices of finished goods change, it may be some time before the wages of these workers catch up with the new cost of living. Even for workers not under contract, wage-rate adjustments usually are not made as frequently as are adjustments in the prices of final goods and services. Therefore, if a stable condition in the economy is upset by a change in the price level, it is likely that the prices of products sold by firms will change more than wage rates and labor costs of production. When the price level increases, the lag of labor costs increases profit margins and encourages firms to expand output, in order to get as much profit as possible while the favorable conditions last. When the price level falls, the lag will squeeze profit margins and firms will cut back on production so as not to suffer too much. Applying these ideas to the SRAS curve in Figure 15-3 suggests that a rise in the price level will lead to an increase in the quantity of real national income

FIGURE 15-3   **Short-Run Aggregate-Supply Curve**

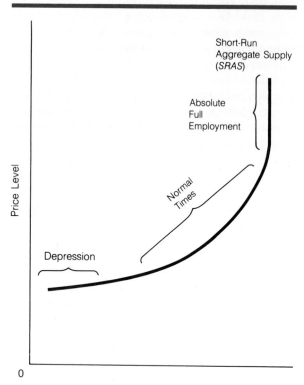

The short-run aggregate-supply curve illustrates how changes in the price level operate through the supply or production side of economic activity to affect real national income and product while behavior is influenced by wage-cost lags and by money illusion. In the depression segment, a change in the price level would change output a great deal. In the absolute full-employment segment, changes in the price level bring no change in output. In normal times, changes in the price level lead to some change in output.

labor costs, there may be some time lag after a change in the price level before these costs of production are fully adjusted. When the price level rises, the lag will cause profit margins to increase and encourage greater output, and when the price level falls, the lag will shrink profit margins and encourage firms to reduce output. Thus, these cost lags also suggest a positive slope for the short-run aggregate-supply curve.

The wage–cost lag theory is not difficult to understand, but a cautionary note is necessary at this point. There are circumstances when changes in wages and other costs of production can be the *cause* rather than the *effect* of changes in the general price level. We will have more to say later (in Chapter 17) about wage-push and cost-push theories of inflation. As you will see, those theories involve *shifts* of the *SRAS* curve rather than *movements along* this curve. Those theories do not concern us now because we are limiting our explanation to the slope as distinguished from the location of the *SRAS* curve.

THE MONEY ILLUSION THEORY   **Money illusion** is the belief that changes in nominal values are the same as changes in real values.[3] This belief can have an important influence on the economy when the price level is changing. For example, if all prices were to increase by 10 percent, there would be no change in relative prices among different goods and services and their real values would not have changed from what they were before the price-level increase. Of course, the real value (purchasing power) of money would have changed. A person under money illusion would believe, however, that the purchasing power of money had stayed the same and that the real value of goods and services had changed.

Here is how the money-illusion theory explains the slope of the short-run aggregate-supply curve. Suppose that there is an increase in the price level and that everyone in the economy operates under complete money illusion. Since wages, interest, rent, and profit are rewards for production-related (supply-side) activities, everyone

and product supplied and that a fall in the price level will lead to a reduction in real national income and product supplied. Thus, the short-run aggregate-supply curve will have a positive slope.

It is not only labor costs that may lag behind product prices when the price level changes. It is often true that firms have contracts that govern the prices they pay for raw materials and intermediate products used in production. Just as for

3. See Chapters 6 and 14 for earlier discussions of nominal and real values.

believes that the real tradeoff between work and leisure has changed in favor of more work. So everyone works harder, and real national income and product increases. In this way, behavior based on money illusion suggests a positive slope for the short-run aggregate-supply curve.

HOW STEEP IS THE *SRAS* CURVE? The steepness or flatness of the short-run aggregate-supply curve (the amount of supply response to a change in the price level) is related to other conditions in the economy. For the most part, the amount of the supply response depends on the extent to which idle resources exist in the economy.

Figure 15-3 shows a short-run aggregate-supply (*SRAS*) curve divided into three parts—an almost horizontal "depression" segment, a positively sloped "normal times" segment, and a vertical "absolute-full-employment" segment.

THE DEPRESSION SEGMENT The nearly horizontal depression segment of the short-run aggregate-supply curve describes conditions when there is a great amount of macroeconomic or cyclical unemployment. Excess capacity (unemployment and idle machines or factories) will be found in nearly all industries. In this segment wage–cost lags may be great, and a small rise in the price level can add greatly to output.

During the Great Depression of the 1930s, many economies were in the depression segment of their short-run aggregate-supply curves.

THE NORMAL-TIMES SEGMENT The positively sloping middle segment of the short-run aggregate-supply curve represents "normal times" in an economy. Increases in the price level bring a smaller increase in production than they would if unemployment were widespread. The reason this happens is that, at any particular time in an economy, some industries are enjoying good times and are running at full capacity while others are at a low point and have excess capacity. Industries operating at or near capacity will not be able to expand output as easily as would be possible in the depression segment of the curve. Their wage and cost lag may not be very large, since bidding labor and materials away from other

firms can increase the prices of these inputs and shrink profit margins. Overtime operation also would lower profit margins. Bottlenecks may occur. All of these problems reduce the output response to a rise in the price level and make the *SRAS* curve steeper.

THE ABSOLUTE-FULL-EMPLOYMENT SEGMENT The vertical segment of the short-run aggregate-supply curve illustrates **absolute full employment,** a situation in which all industries in the economy are operating at full capacity and where all workers are fully employed, except for a few caught up in frictional or structural unemployment. Since all resources are fully employed, no increase in output can be achieved through a higher price level.

Of the three segments of the short-run aggregate-supply curve, this vertical segment is the hardest to imagine as a realistic state of affairs. In a dynamic and changing society, it is hard to believe that all industries could ever be at full capacity at the same time. Perhaps all-out wartime emergencies come closest to being instances of absolute full employment. In a macroeconomic sense, the vertical segment simply illustrates the special case in which a change in the price level brings no change in real national income and product.

Location of the *SRAS* Curve

Any particular short-run aggregate-supply curve is drawn on the assumption that all variables other than the price level and the real national income and product are held constant. When there is a change in any other variable, a shift (change in location) of the short-run aggregate-supply curve may occur.

In examining shifts of the short-run aggregate-supply curve, we are interested in the two phenomena that we have already discussed in connection with the slope of this curve, that is, the wage–cost lag and the money illusion. According to our theory, with the passage of time, changes can take place in each of these variables. Specifically, both wage–cost lag and money illusion are expected to melt away with the passage of time.

Such time-related changes in these variables will shift (relocate) the *SRAS* curve.

CHANGES IN WAGE–COST LAG The lag in wages and other costs of production after a price-level change will not continue indefinitely. As time passes, the gap caused by the lag will disappear. For example, after a price-level increase, labor will demand extra wage increases as soon as possible. As these adjustments are made, the wage gap will evaporate, reducing the quantity of output that will be supplied at any given price level and shifting the *SRAS* curve to the left.

If the price level has recently fallen, the initiative to eliminate the wage–cost gap will come from firms, which then will want to lower wages and other costs. As their efforts bear fruit, the quantity of output that will be supplied at any given price level is increased and the *SRAS* curve shifts to the right.

It is worth noting, in addition, that after the shift the *SRAS* curve may have a steeper slope than it had before the shift. The reason for this is that the strength of the wage–cost lag depends not only on the level of economic activity in the economy but also on the laws and customary patterns of behavior in relations between firms and workers and between firms and their suppliers. Consider, for example, the average length or time period of a labor–management contract governing wage rates and working conditions. If price levels have been stable for some time, it may have been convenient for both labor and management to have relatively long-term contracts. But changing price levels will prompt one side or the other to want to shorten contracts in order to reduce the wage lag from future price-level changes. For example, after an experience with inflation, labor will want shorter contracts and "reopener" provisions to shorten future wage lags. Automatic cost-of-living adjustment (COLA) provisions may be added to contracts. On the other hand, if the recent experience has been with price-level declines, it is likely that firms, rather than their workers or their suppliers, will want to shorten contracts and to include reopener provisions. This also will make the new *SRAS*

curve steeper than the old one. We will return to this matter when we consider theories of inflationary expectations in Chapter 17.

CHANGES IN MONEY ILLUSION The passage of time after a price-level change will also cause money illusion to melt away. Consider what happens when people realize that *all* prices, including the prices of consumption goods that they buy, have gone up? Now they begin to realize that the changes in nominal values, which had led them to work harder, were not actually changes in real values. Their real wage, interest, rent, or profit had not gone up. When this realization dawns on them, money illusion starts to evaporate, and the tradeoff between work and leisure is re-examined. In the light of their now clearer understanding of real wages, interest, rent, and profit, people move back toward their old work habits. As this happens, the short-run aggregate-supply curve shifts to the left at all output levels less than absolute full employment. This shift occurs as the money illusion evaporates.

How long does it take for people to recognize that changes in nominal values are not also changes in real values? The answer depends on many things. How long was the price level stable before the inflation or deflation occurred? How large is the change in the price level? How rapidly is the price level changing? In actual policy making, these questions are very important, and economists spend much time discussing and researching them. For our purposes, however, it is the concept of money illusion and the concept of shifting the short-run aggregate-supply curve that are important.

Now that we have examined the forces that determine the slope and the location of the short-run aggregate-supply curve, we can offer the following definition: *the short-run aggregate-supply curve represents the relationship between changes in the price level and changes in real national income and product supplied while wage and cost changes are lagging behind a change in the price level and while money illusion due to that price-level change is altering choices between work and leisure.*

FIGURE 15-4 **Short-Run Macroeconomic Equilibrium**

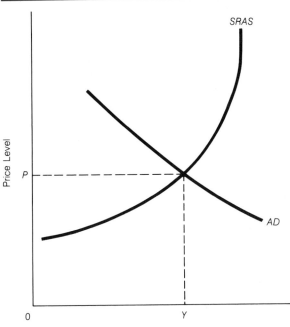

Real National Income and Product

Short-run macroeconomic equilibrium is at the intersection of the aggregate-demand (*AD*) curve and the short-run aggregate-supply (*SRAS*) curve. At the price level indicated by that intersection, the quantity of goods and services supplied is equal to the quantity demanded.

Short-Run Macroeconomic Equilibrium

Figure 15-4 illustrates the aggregate-supply and aggregate-demand concept of **macroeconomic equilibrium.** The equilibrium condition occurs at the intersection of the aggregate-demand curve, *AD*, and the short-run aggregate-supply curve, *SRAS*, with the price level, *P*, and real national income and product, *Y*. If all other variables related to the locations of these curves remain unchanged, a balance of forces will bring about this equilibrium. At any price level below *P*, the demand for real goods and services will exceed their supply, and the price level will be bid

upward. At any price level above *P*, more will be offered for sale than can be sold at that price level, and prices will be cut to lower unwanted inventories.

It is important to remember that this is only a short-run equilibrium. As we have noted, the passage of time may bring shifts in the short-run aggregate-supply curve. The importance of these shifts in aggregate supply will become clearer in the illustrations that follow. One of these shows a recession–deflation process, somewhat like that which took place in the Great Depression. The second shows an expansion–inflation process much like what took place in the United States in the late 1960s and the early 1970s. These illustrations will help you understand how the aggregate demand–aggregate supply model works and will introduce the concept of the long-run aggregate-supply curve.

RECESSION AND DEFLATION

Our first illustration of aggregate-demand and aggregate-supply analysis is a model of recession and deflation. In Figure 15-5, we start at point *A*—a short-run equilibrium condition at the intersection of aggregate-demand curve AD_1 and some point in the normal times segment of the short-run aggregate-supply curve $SRAS_1$. We assume that this equilibrium has lasted for a long enough time that people have become well adjusted to it. This assumption is important because it means that wages and costs are in step with product prices and that people have adjusted their economic behavior to the price level, P_1.

Recession

Our demonstration begins with a shift of the aggregate-demand curve to the left from AD_1 to AD_2. Such a shift may have brought about the Great Depression of the 1930s. Keynesians find that it was caused by falling planned investment due to poor business prospects after the stock

FIGURE 15-5   Recession and Deflation

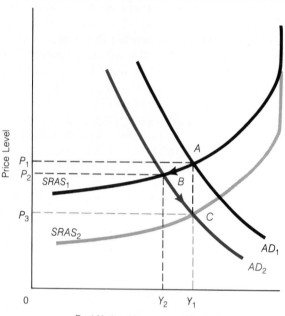

Real National Income and Product

The recession–deflation model starts with a leftward shift of the aggregate-demand curve, from AD_1 to AD_2. A new short-run equilibrium exists at B, with price level P_2 and real national income and product level Y_2. Later, $SRAS_1$ shifts to $SRAS_2$ as wage–cost lags disappear and as money illusion wears off. After this long-run adjustment has taken place, equilibrium is at C. Our illustration shows this new equilibrium at the same real national income and product (Y_1) as at the start of the process. Some economists doubt that the economy will necessarily return to the same real income and product level.

market crash. Monetarists believe that the cause was a reduced money stock due to widespread bank failures. In each view, however, there was a demand-side shock to the economy, which tended to reduce the short-run equilibrium level of real national income and product.

Figure 15-5 illustrates the consequences of such a contractionary demand shock. Unplanned inventories accumulate because of the fall in aggregate demand and, in order to rid themselves of this unwanted inventory, firms lay off workers and cut production and prices. As the aggregate-

demand curve shifts to the left, the equilibrium point moves down and to the left along the $SRAS_1$ curve from point A to point B. Unemployment rises and both output and prices decline.

The move from A to B is the first phase of the recession. Its seriousness depends on the slope of the short-run aggregate-supply curve and on how far the aggregate-demand curve shifts to the left. If the short-run aggregate-supply curve is steep, few people will lose their jobs. If it is flat, many jobs will be lost. If the initial shift in aggregate demand is severe enough, the pessimism caused by rising unemployment and falling prices may bring further leftward shifts in the aggregate-demand curve. In other words, the recession may feed on itself in a pattern called **hyperdeflation.** Probably this really did happen in the Great Depression of the 1930s. For simplicity, we do not illustrate this extra shift of the aggregate-demand curve in Figure 15-5.

Recovery by Deflation

Point B in Figure 15-5 is not a stable or long-run equilibrium position because the changes in economic conditions have set in motion forces that will shift the short-run aggregate-supply curve. The second phase of the recession–deflation process takes place with a shift in the short-run aggregate-supply curve from $SRAS_1$ to $SRAS_2$. The shift comes as the wage–cost gap disappears and as the money illusion breaks down. Moreover, the hard facts of unemployment have sapped the financial reserves of many workers. Therefore, people decide not to hold out any longer for higher wages for labor, higher interest on bonds, higher rent on natural resources, or higher prices and profits on products.

The rightward shift of the short-run aggregate-supply curve illustrates a "deflationist" solution for the problem of economic recession. The squeeze on profits, which motivated firms to reduce output and employment in the recession, is to be relieved by lowering wage rates and the prices of other inputs. According to the deflationist prescription, the fading money illusion will make these reductions acceptable to workers and other resource owners. As the *SRAS* curve shifts to the right, the equilibrium condition slides down the *AD₂* curve, bringing lower prices and greater output. Our model shows real national income and product at the new equilibrium (point *C*) to be exactly the same as they were at *A* before the initial shift in aggregate demand. However, some economists doubt that the *SRAS* curve will shift far enough to bring the economy all the way back to its original level of real national income and product.

Recovery by Reflation

In the situation that existed in the Great Depression, many people felt that solving the problem with the "deflation" solution would take too long, cause too much suffering, and endanger the political stability of the country. Over the early years of the 1930s, prices had fallen by almost 25 percent and about 25 percent of the labor force was unemployed.

Shifting the aggregate-demand curve back to its original position offers an alternative way out of a recession caused by a demand-side shock. This is recovery by **reflation**, that is, by causing the price level to return upward to a level that prevailed earlier. The "reflationist" prescription can be illustrated with the same graph that showed the "deflationist" approach. Starting from point *B* in Figure 15-5, expansionary fiscal and monetary actions can be undertaken in order to shift the aggregate-demand curve to the right, from *AD₂* back to *AD₁*. This was the route that Keynes's model indicated as a way out of the depression of the 1930s. By using expansionary fiscal and monetary policies (see Chapters 11 and 14), aggregate demand can be increased, reversing the decline that had caused the recession. Both employment and prices will return to their earlier levels as the equilibrium condition moves upward and to the right along the original short-run aggregate-supply curve, *SRAS₁*.

In retrospect, the reflationist prescription for the problems of the Great Depression appears clear and promising. At the time, however, the prospect of large and intentional government

deficits was upsetting to many people and especially to business and financial leaders. They feared unrestrained government spending and the taxes that they believed would eventually be required. The expansionary moves undertaken by the New Deal administration were timid by later standards and produced disappointing results.[4]

EXPANSION AND INFLATION

Our second illustration of aggregate demand–aggregate supply analysis is something like the one just studied, except that it pictures an expansionary process. Historically, this model parallels the expansion and inflation experience of the 1960s and early 1970s. As in the recession model, the initiating event comes from the demand side. However, this time the aggregate-demand curve shifts to the right rather than to the left. In the 1960s, fiscal and monetary instruments of government generally worked in an expansionary direction to stimulate the economy and to carry on a "War on Poverty" at home and a war in Vietnam without large rises in taxes. These expansionary policies shifted aggregate demand to the right.

Expansion

We begin at point *A* in Figure 15-6, the intersection of the initial aggregate-demand curve, *AD₁*, and the initial short-run aggregate-supply curve, *SRAS₁*. Again we assume that this situation has lasted long enough for people to have adjusted their behavior to this price level and to this level of real national income and product.

After the shift to the right of the aggregate-demand curve, the new short-run equilibrium is at *B*, where the new aggregate-demand curve, *AD₂*, intersects the old short-run aggregate-supply curve, *SRAS₁*. The rise in demand causes

4. See "The Great Depression and the Hungry Thirties," pp. 191–194.

FIGURE 15-6   Expansion and Inflation

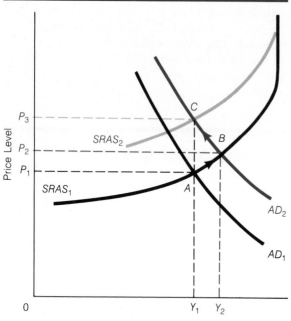

Real National Income and Product

The expansion–inflation model starts with a rightward shift in aggregate demand, from AD_1 to AD_2. A new short-run equilibrium exists at B. $SRAS_1$ shifts to $SRAS_2$ as wage and cost gaps are closed and as people get over the money illusion caused by the price-level change from P_1 to P_2. After this adjustment, equilibrium is reached at C. Our illustration shows this new equilibrium at the same real national income and product as at the start of the process.

inventories to fall below planned levels, and companies respond with higher prices (to keep inventory from being used up too quickly and to make higher profits) and with increased production to restore inventories to desired levels. In the "normal times" segment of the $SRAS_1$ curve, some industries are already operating at near or full capacity so that the demand increase pulls up the price level.

Along the path from A to B, the economy is experiencing good times. Wages and other costs of production are lagging behind increases in prices of finished goods so profit margins are attractive. Employment is increasing. Even though

wage rates are lagging behind increases in the general price level, workers are working longer hours and taking home larger paychecks. Because of the money illusion, they overestimate their increase in real income and the attractiveness of work compared with leisure.

The mixture between price increases and output increases depends on the slope of the $SRAS$ curve. If the $SRAS$ curve is quite flat, prices will rise little and output will expand significantly. But if the $SRAS$ curve is steep, as may be the case if there has been recent experience with inflation, prices may rise rapidly with only modest increases in output. In extreme situations, called **hyperinflation,** the rising prices induce further shifts of the aggregate-demand curve as people hurry to spend their income before it loses its buying power. Prices rise faster until money becomes virtually worthless and economic collapse is threatened.[5]

Stagflation

Point B does not represent a stable or long-run equilibrium for reasons that are parallel to those in the recession case. In the movement from A to B along the $SRAS_1$ curve in Figure 15-6, some people mistakenly believe that the increases in nominal wage (and profit, interest, and rent) rates represent equivalent increases in real rates. They believe that these increases in nominal wage (and profit, interest, and rent) rates have changed the real tradeoff between work and leisure in favor of working more. Because of the supposedly higher rewards, more jobs and overtime are accepted and more business ventures undertaken. However, as time passes, these people realize that some of the increases in nominal wage (and profit, interest, and rent) rates have been lost to increases in the general price level and the rising cost of living. Real wages have not increased as much as they thought they had.

As people gain a more accurate understanding of the relative prices of work and leisure, the money illusion evaporates. Workers start to play

5. See the discussion of inflation in Germany, p. 114.

"catch-up" in wage negotiations, asking for wage-rate increases in excess of productivity increases so that they can make up for the purchasing power losses they have suffered from inflation. Strikes are more frequent as wages and other costs catch up from the wage–cost lag and close the gap that had existed during the expansion. Profit margins become smaller. Through these actions, reflecting the closing of wage and cost gaps and the fading of money illusion, the $SRAS$ curve in Figure 15-6 shifts to the left, from $SRAS_1$ to $SRAS_2$ and the equilibrium condition moves along the AD_2 curve from point B to point C.

The move from B to C involves falling output, rising unemployment, and continuing increases in the price level—a combination that economists have labeled **stagflation.** Stagflation offers the "worst of both worlds" in macroeconomics. The U.S. economy and many others in the world suffered from stagflation during the 1970s, partly as a result of earlier shifts in aggregate demand and partly from supply-side shocks, which we will discuss shortly. Our illustration in Figure 15-6 suggests that equilibrium will be established at point C, when profit margins have returned to normal and people have adapted to the new price level of P_2, so that money illusion and "catching up" no longer influence behavior.

Demand-side policy alternatives for dealing with stagflation are unattractive. Shifting the aggregate-demand curve to the right promises still more inflation, whereas shifting it to the left threatens still greater unemployment. The stagflation experience of the 1970s and the unattractiveness of demand-side remedies invited economists to look more closely at the supply side of the economy, that is, to shifts of the aggregate-supply curve. We will introduce the subject of supply shocks later in this chapter and offer a full explanation of supply-side economics and stagflation in Chapter 17.

LONG-RUN AGGREGATE SUPPLY

In each of the exercises just completed, the consequences of a shift of the aggregate-demand curve were, first, a movement along the short-run aggregate-supply curve, while money illusion and wage–cost lags operated, and then a shift of the $SRAS$ curve as money illusion faded and as wages and costs caught up with other prices. Now we must ask about the relation between the price level and real national income and product supplied in the long run, after the shifts of the $SRAS$ curve have been completed.

To keep our discussion conceptually clear, suppose that no change takes place in physical production capabilities (level of technology, size and skill of the labor force, size and quantity of the stock of capital, and so on) during the time it takes for wage and cost gaps and money illusion effects to disappear. Then we can define the **long-run aggregate-supply curve** as follows: *the relationship between changes in the price level and changes in real national income and product supplied that arises as long as there is no change in physical production capability but when enough time has passed for people to adapt completely to the existing price level.* We know that the conditions set up by this definition most likely will never in fact be observed because changes in production capability are always taking place. But this definition will help us come to grips with important issues in modern macroeconomics.

Does the Price Level Affect Long-Run Aggregate Supply?

Figure 15-7 shows the long-run aggregate-supply curve that was suggested in the recession–deflation and expansion–inflation models studied earlier. We shall let the intersection of AD_1 and $SRAS_1$ (point A) show the beginning equilibrium point for both of these models. The recession–deflation process is shown by the shift of aggregate demand from AD_1 to AD_2, followed by the shift of short-run aggregate supply from $SRAS_1$ to $SRAS_2$ as wage–cost lags and the money illusion wear off. Equilibrium is finally restored at the intersection of AD_2 and $SRAS_2$ (point B). The expansion–inflation process is shown by the shift of aggregate demand from AD_1 to AD_3, followed by the shift of short-run aggregate supply from

FIGURE 15-7   **The Long-Run Aggregate-Supply Curve**

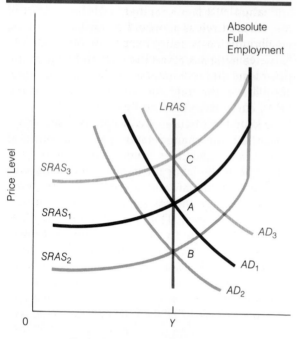

The vertical *LRAS* curve represents the long-run aggregate-supply curve that is suggested by our illustrations of the recession–deflation and the expansion–inflation processes in the economy. The recession process is illustrated by the AD_2 and $SRAS_2$ curves, and the expansion process by the AD_3 and $SRAS_3$ curves. Our models suggest that when behavior is adjusted to correct for money illusion and wage–cost lags, the *SRAS* curves shift far enough to restore real national income and product to its original level. Thus, the long-run aggregate-supply curve (*LRAS*) is a vertical line.

store completely the original level of real national income and product.

Some economists believe that the vertical long-run aggregate-supply curve is a special case and that more often the curve has a positive slope—that in the long-run, real national income and product supplied is greater at high price levels than at low price levels, other things being equal. These economists say that, even without wage–cost lags and money illusion, the price level can influence production behavior. It is the choice between work and leisure that is involved. Their argument parallels the real balances effect, which we explained earlier in connection with the aggregate-demand curve. It goes like this. At high price levels, assets whose values are given in fixed nominal amounts (such as money and government bonds) have low real purchasing power value. The low real wealth of people holding these assets persuades them to work harder and longer than they would at a lower price level. At low price levels, however, these assets have high real purchasing power, and their holders have greater real wealth, so they consume more leisure and do less work than at high price levels. These economists conclude, therefore, that the long-run aggregate-supply curve is not a vertical line but has some positive slope.

Shifts in the Long-Run Aggregate-Supply Curve

In our definition of long-run aggregate supply, we assume that there is no change in physical production capabilities, such as might come from changes in the level of technology, the size and skill of the labor force, and the size and quality of the stock of capital equipment. Now we ask what will happen if a change in physical production capability does take place. The answer is that the long-run aggregate-supply curve itself will shift. Figure 15-8 shows that when the long-run aggregate supply curve shifts to the right (from $LRAS_1$ to $LRAS_2$) and aggregate demand does not change, the price level will fall. If, instead, production capacity is destroyed because of war

$SRAS_1$ to $SRAS_3$, again as wage–cost lags and the money illusion wear off. Here, equilibrium is finally restored at the intersection of AD_3 and $SRAS_3$ (point C). In each case, we have assumed that the final equilibrium is at exactly the same real national income and product as the starting equilibrium, so that the long-run aggregate-supply curve (*LRAS*) is a vertical line. In other words, we suppose that, in each case, the short-run aggregate-supply curve shifts far enough to re-

FIGURE 15-8   Shifts in Long-Run Aggregate Supply

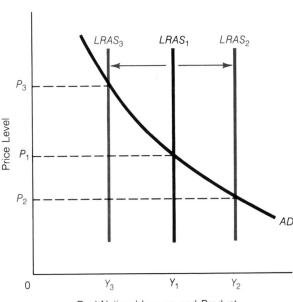

The long-run aggregate-supply curve will shift if changes take place in production capability. A shift to the right, as from $LRAS_1$ to $LRAS_2$, illustrates growth in production capability. The price level will fall if there is no change in aggregate demand. A shift to the left, as from $LRAS_1$ to $LRAS_3$, illustrates a reduction in production capability. If there is no change in aggregate demand, the price level will rise.

or some other disaster, the *LRAS* curve would shift to the left (such as from $LRAS_1$ to $LRAS_3$), so that if aggregate demand does not change, the price level will rise.

Cultural and institutional facts of life in a society are important in determining the location of the long-run aggregate-supply curve. Cultural factors may influence the way in which people divide their time between work and leisure, say, between enjoying a new car and watching the sunset. Institutional factors, such as whether the economy is organized through free markets or through central planning, may also be important. These subjects are the focus of supply-side economics, to be discussed in Chapter 17.

The Natural Rate of Unemployment

The **natural rate of unemployment** is the statistical or measured rate that would prevail in long-run equilibrium, that is, when people had fully adapted to the existing price level so that there were no distortions due to wage–cost lags or money illusion. If the *microeconomy* were functioning perfectly, each person would be on his or her own labor-supply curve. As explained in Chapter 6, this means that each person would be working exactly the number of hours per week or per month or per year that he or she wished to work at the prevailing wage rate. The balance between work and leisure would exactly match his or her preferences at this wage rate. Even though it is recognized that the microeconomy does not work perfectly, macroeconomists think of the natural rate of unemployment as being **effective full employment.**

In both the recession–deflation and the expansion–inflation exercises in this chapter, we assumed that the initial price level had existed long enough so that everyone had fully adjusted to it. Thus, there were no distortions due to wage–cost lags or money illusion. In other words, the natural rate of unemployment existed at the start of each exercise (at points *A* in Figures 15-5 and 15-6). Similarly, the natural rate of unemployment existed at the close of each of these exercises (at points *C* in these figures), since wage–cost gaps and money illusion faded out as the *SRAS* curve shifted. What happened during these exercises was that *actual* unemployment rose above the natural rate during the recession exercise and fell below the natural rate during the expansion exercise.

What will the official or "measured" rate of unemployment be when the economy is at effective full employment? At effective full employment there will be some structural, some frictional, and some seasonal unemployment. The structural unemployment exists because some industries are growing and others are contracting, so that workers must retrain and move around to qualify for different job openings. Frictional unemployment exists as people seek jobs that pay better or are more satisfying. In addition, measurement problems arise because people falsely claim to be unemployed in order to collect unemployment compensation payments. There is no macroeconomic or cyclical unemployment when the economy is at long-run equilibrium.

The natural rate of unemployment itself may change from time to time because of changes in the labor force, in the rate of change of technology and consumer tastes, in barriers to moving from one job to another, and in the content and enforcement of unemployment compensation laws. For example, it is likely that the natural rate of unemployment rose during the 1970s because of the great changes in relative prices caused by oil-price increases and because many women who had recently entered the labor force had trouble finding a job or went through several moves before finding the right job.

Just because some rate of unemployment is "natural" in the sense that macroeconomic forces tend to move the economy toward that rate, it does not follow, of course, that this rate is desirable or that nothing can be done to lower it. *Micro*economic tools may be able to lower the natural rate of unemployment and so raise the real living standard of the society in long-run equilibrium. Among these microeconomic tools are measures to improve mobility and reduce discrimination in the job market, ways to make more information available to workers, and so on.

SUPPLY SHOCKS

The recession and the expansion models in this chapter both began with a shift in the aggregate-demand curve. That is, they originated in demand-side events or shocks. Disequilibrium conditions can also be caused by shifts in the aggregate-supply curve, that is, by **supply shocks.** These can be either expansionary or contractionary. An expansionary shock might be an important technological breakthrough, the discovery of a great new natural resource, or a rise in labor force participation. Such shocks would shift the short-run aggregate-supply curve to the right.

Contractionary supply shocks can result from the destruction of productive capacity through wars or other disasters. They can also be artificially created, as when the Organization of Petroleum Exporting Countries (OPEC) cut the output of oil in the 1970s. These shocks can shift the short-run aggregate-supply curve to the left.

Figure 15-9 shows the two forms of supply shocks. In the contractionary supply-shock case in panel (a), the initial equilibrium is at A. A shift to the left in short-run aggregate supply leads to a new short-run equilibrium at B, a higher price level, P_2, and a lower level of output, Y_2. These changes follow as long as the aggregate-demand curve does not shift, because a given money supply (implied in the aggregate-demand curve) is being used to purchase a smaller amount of output.

In the expansionary supply-shock case in panel (b), the initial equilibrium is at A, and the short-run aggregate-supply curve shifts to the right. If the aggregate-demand curve does not shift, the new short-run equilibrium will be at B, with a lower price level, P_2, and greater output, Y_2. The given money supply (implied in the aggregate-demand curve) is being used to buy more goods and services.

An important assumption in each of these cases is that there is no shift in the aggregate-demand curve. But you know that the aggregate-demand curve can be shifted by means of the monetary and fiscal instruments of government policy. So it is quite possible that the government will decide that shifts in the short-run aggregate-supply curve should be met with shifts in the aggregate-demand curve. Public policy questions about shifting the aggregate-demand curve and the aggregate-supply curve will be studied in the next two chapters.

SUMMARY

1. Aggregate-demand curves and aggregate-supply curves show relationships between changes in the price level, as measured by some index number, and changes in real national income and product. These concepts are helpful in

FIGURE 15-9 **Supply Shocks**

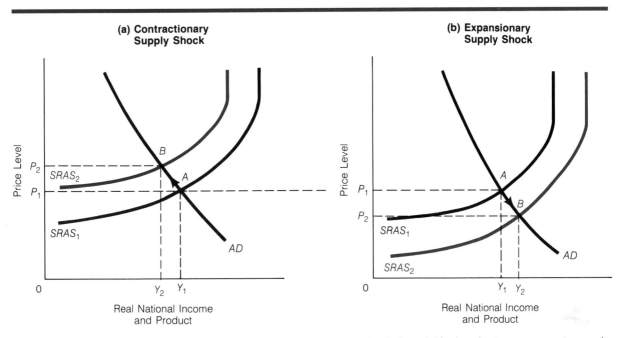

Panel (a) shows a contractionary supply shock. The short-run aggregate-supply curve, $SRAS_1$, shifts to the left because of a reduction in production capability. If the aggregate-demand curve does not shift, the new short-run equilibrium will be at B, with a higher price level and lower real national income and product. In the expansionary supply shock (panel b), the short-run aggregate-supply curve shifts to the right because of some increase in production capability. If the aggregate-demand curve does not shift, the new equilibrium will be at B, with a lower price level and larger real national income and product.

understanding the economics of inflation and unemployment.

2. Two theories help to explain the negative slope of the aggregate-demand curve. The interest rate theory is that higher price levels, if other things are equal, reduce the *real* money supply and cause higher real rates of interest, which reduce planned investment spending and thereby lower equilibrium national income and product. The real balances theory is that higher price levels lower the real value of wealth held as money or assets denominated in terms of money. These wealth reductions may reduce planned consumption spending, thus lowering the equilibrium level of real national income and product.

3. A shift in aggregate demand means a change in the quantity of real goods and services de- manded at any given price level. Many variables may shift this curve. Monetary and fiscal policies are important because they permit governments to influence many variables that change the location of this curve.

4. The short-run aggregate-supply curve shows how changes in the price level affect the quantity of real national income and product supplied in the economy. It has a positive slope because wages and other costs of production tend to lag behind changes in the price level and because, when the price level changes, the behavior of many people in the economy is affected by money illusion—the belief that changes in nominal values are the same as changes in real values. The short-run aggregate-supply curve is nearly horizontal when there is a great deal of unemployment in the economy and vertical when there is absolute full employment.

5. Money illusion and lags of wages and costs do not continue indefinitely after a change in the price level. As wages and costs catch up to the change in the prices of final goods, and as money illusion fades away, the short-run aggregate-supply curve shifts in such a way as to move the quantity supplied in the direction of the initial volume of real national income and product.

6. In macroeconomic equilibrium, the price level exactly balances the demand for real goods and services with the willingness to supply these products. This condition exists at the intersection of the aggregate-demand curve and the short-run aggregate-supply curve.

7. The recession–deflation model describes how an economy may experience a period of high unemployment and declining price levels due to a leftward shift in aggregate demand. But as the *SRAS* curve shifts to the right, the economy expands toward its original level of real national income and product.

8. The expansion–inflation model describes how an economy may experience a period of low unemployment and rising price levels due to a rightward shift in aggregate demand. But as the *SRAS* curve shifts to the left, the economy contracts toward its original level of real national income and product.

9. A situation with sluggish growth, inflation, and increasing unemployment is called stagflation. This combination of problems arises as a result of a leftward shift of the short-run aggregate-supply curve. Demand-side remedies are unattractive in this situation. The stagflation that took place during the 1970s focused attention on the supply side of economic activity.

10. Long-run macroeconomic equilibrium exists when a given price level has existed long enough so that neither wage–cost lag nor money illusion is distorting decisions in the economy. The long-run relationship between the price level and the quantity of real national product supplied (the *LRAS* curve) may appear as a vertical line on an aggregate-demand and aggregate-supply graph, although some economists believe that it has a positive slope.

11. The long-run aggregate-supply curve can be shifted by changes in production capabilities. Expansions in production capability shift the long-run aggregate-supply curve to the right. Reductions in production capability shift the curve to the left. Cultural and institutional variables may influence the location of the long-run aggregate-supply curve.

12. The natural rate of unemployment is the rate that prevails in long-run macroeconomic equilibrium. It includes frictional and structural unemployment, but not macroeconomic (or cyclical) unemployment. This natural rate may change over time if changes take place in the labor force or in the pace of other changes in the economy. In macroeconomic analysis, the natural rate of unemployment is the same as effective full employment.

13. Economic disturbances can arise from supply-side shocks, which shift the short-run aggregate-supply curve. Shocks that reduce production shift the curve to the left, and shocks that increase production shift the curve to the right.

DISCUSSION QUESTIONS

1. Draw an aggregate-demand curve, being careful to label correctly each axis on the graph. Then compare your curve with Figure 15-1. Why is it *not* correct to refer to the $C + I + G + X - Im$ curve as a demand curve?

2. The interest rate theory (or Keynes effect) about the slope of the aggregate-demand curve uses the transmission system that you learned in Chapter 14. Without looking at Figure 15-2, draw the four graphs in this transmission system and then check to be sure you are right. If the investment-demand curve is steep, will the aggregate-demand curve be steep or flat? Explain.

3. What will happen to the real value of your life insurance policies when the price level rises? Will this change cause you to divide your current disposable income between consumption and saving in a different way? Explain how your answers to these questions can lead to an understanding of the real balances theory about the slope of the aggregate-demand curve.

4. In terms of the consequences of shifts in aggregate demand, why is the short-run aggregate-supply curve rather flat when there is much unemployment and idle capacity in the economy? Contrast this situation in the economy with that which is implied by the vertical segment of the short-run aggregate-supply curve.

5. Average gross hourly earnings in private nonagricultural employment were $4.53 in 1975, and $8.58 in 1985. Assuming a complete money illusion, explain how this change would affect worker behavior according to a short-run aggregate-supply curve. After adjustment for price-level change, real wages in 1985 were almost the same as in 1970. Explain how elimination of money illusion places the economy on its long-run aggregate-supply curve.

6. Without looking at Figure 15-5, construct the graph illustrating a recession–deflation process. Then check to be sure you have it right. Using the concepts of wage–cost lag and money illusion, explain why the first phase of the process involves rising unemployment while the second phase involves falling unemployment.

7. Hyperdeflation involves a leftward shift of the aggregate-demand curve, which is induced by the hard times resulting from some ongoing contraction of the economy. Explain hyperdeflation in terms of the graph that you drew for Question 6.

8. Thinking now about the expansion–inflation process, illustrate on a graph how a rightward shift of the aggregate-demand curve brings a higher price level and a temporary increase in real national income and product. Check with Figure 15-6 to be sure you are correct. Explain the process in words, again stressing the role of wage–cost lag and money illusion.

9. Construct a pair of aggregate demand–aggregate supply graphs, one to illustrate a contractionary supply shock and the other to illustrate an expansionary supply shock. Compare your graphs with Figure 15-9. How did the drought and "dust bowl" in the 1930s in U.S. agricultural areas affect the short-run aggregate-supply curve? Discuss whether this effect slowed or speeded the movement to a new equilibrium.

10. Write down from memory our definition of the long-run aggregate-supply curve. Check to be sure you have it right. Explain how the wage–cost lag and money-illusion concepts relate to this curve. Discuss two forces (one of them social and the other environmental) that could shift the long-run aggregate-supply curve. Explain the direction of each shift.

11. Explain the reasoning that concludes that long-run macroeconomic equilibrium establishes the natural rate of unemployment. Why can this rate also be called effective full employment? How does racial discrimination or sex discrimination in labor markets affect the natural rate of unemployment? How would elimination of such discrimination change the real level of national income and product at effective full employment? Explain.

16 *Macroeconomic Policy: Demand Side*

PREVIEW Theory "informs" policy in the sense that it provides the logical connection between the outcomes that people desire to achieve and the actions that are taken to achieve them. In other words, theory is like a road map providing a guide about how to move from where you are to where you want to be. A good map does not guarantee that you will be able to complete the journey or that unexpected things may not happen along the way, but it does influence how you plan your trip. A faulty map adds great difficulty and frustration.

In this chapter, we shall explore demand-side theories that have influenced macroeconomic policy makers in the United States. These demand-side theories flow from the thinking and writing of the British economist John Maynard Keynes. We explain how several important economic policy actions of the 1930s were related to Keynes's theory.

World War II brought the U.S. economy out of the Great Depression and set the stage for prosperity and inflation in the period after the war. We continue by explaining the issues that were discussed by economists during these decades. We shall describe the debate between Keynesian and monetarist economists about the importance of interest rates in influencing the economy and about how policy makers ought to approach their job of deciding what macroeconomic actions should be taken—whether they should be guided by certain rules or whether they should be free to exercise judgment as particular situations arise.

The last part of the chapter deals with the Phillips curve, a theory that greatly influenced economic policy during the 1960s and into the 1970s. You will see that during the 1960s the Phillips curve performed in a way that led economists to be optimistic about the ability of fiscal and monetary instruments to guide the operation of the economy. Then you will see how the Phillips curve performed poorly in the 1970s, leading economists to take a second look at the theories that guided their policy making.

In studying how theory influences policy making, you may be interested in what Keynes had to say about the power of ideas:

> The ideas of economists and political philosophers, both when they are right and when they are wrong, are more powerful than is commonly understood. Indeed the world is ruled by little else. Practical men, who believe themselves to be quite exempt from any intellectual influences, are usually the slaves of some defunct economist. Madmen in authority, who hear voices in the air, are distilling their frenzy from some academic scribbler of a few years back. I am sure that the power of vested interests is vastly exaggerated compared with the gradual encroachment of ideas. Not, indeed, immediately, but after a certain interval; for in the field of economic and political philosophy there are not many who are influenced by new theories after they are twenty-five or thirty years of age, so that the ideas which civil servants and politicians and even agitators apply to current events are not likely to be the newest. But, soon or late, it is ideas, not vested interests, which are dangerous for good or evil.[1]

---

1. John M. Keynes, *The General Theory of Employment, Interest and Money* (New York: Harcourt, Brace, 1936), pp. 383–384.

KEYNES AND DEMAND-SIDE ECONOMICS

The economic theory of John Maynard Keynes is a leading illustration of the idea that theory informs policy. After it appeared in 1936 in Keynes's book *The General Theory of Employment, Interest, and Money*, his theory dominated economic policy making in nearly all market economies. Like the theories of Adam Smith during most of the nineteenth century, the influence of Keynes was both deep and widespread.[2]

As you learned in the historical discussion in Chapter 9, macroeconomic policy before Keynes was guided by Say's Identity and neoclassical economic theories. These theories suggested that the macroeconomy could manage itself quite well if wage rates and prices were flexible. Prices of some goods or services would rise if demand for them rose or if their cost of production went up. At the same time, prices of other goods or services would fall as demand for them decreased or if their cost of production fell. These individual price changes would clear markets in a fairly quick time, and there could be no "general glut" of unsold goods for very long. Cyclical or general unemployment could exist only if wage rates were too high and inflexible. For this reason, the macroeconomic theories of the time did not accept the idea that too little aggregate demand could be the cause of extended general unemployment. Therefore, no action need be taken to regulate aggregate demand. In fact, it was argued that government involvement would do more harm than good if it delayed the necessary changes in prices.

Keynes's theory showed that planned expenditure is very important in an economy. As you learned in Part III, he pointed out the main components of total planned expenditure (C, I,

G, X, and Im) and explained how they play a part in the macroeconomic performance of the economy. Consumption, the major component, gives the economy a solid base. However, its response to changes in income (the marginal propensity to consume) contributes to the multiplier effect, which brings about large changes in the level of economic activity whenever any force upsets an existing equilibrium. The planned-investment component, depending very much on the mood and expectations of business, is just such an upsetting force. Changes in planned investment can start the multiplier process and move the economy into contractions or expansions. In the theory of Keynes, government purchases (along with government tax collections) became very important because they can be controlled by policy actions. It is likely that the most powerful policy message in Keynes's theory is its justification of government budgetary (fiscal) actions to manage the aggregate performance of the economy.[3]

Coming when it did in the course of history, the effect of Keynes's theory was striking. It showed policy makers that changes in total planned expenditure could cause macroeconomic unemployment. It also showed that government action was justified in order to boost aggregate demand. No wonder Keynes stands as the most influential economist of the twentieth century!

Antidepression Economic Policies

The antidepression implications of Keynes's ideas in terms of policy can be seen in Figure 16-1, which is much like Figure 15-5. In the United States in the 1930s, depression conditions came about because of a leftward shift of aggregate demand in relation to aggregate supply. In the figure, this is pictured by the shift from AD_1 to AD_2. Short-run equilibrium is at point B, on the

---

2. The theories of Karl Marx also have been profound and pervasive. However, Marx offered little specific guidance about economic policies after a socialist government has attained power. His influence has been mainly in bringing about revolutions.

3. The foreign trade component of total spending was only a small portion of aggregate expenditure in the U.S. economy. However, Keynes noted that the application of his theory could lead countries to restrict international trade.

FIGURE 16-1   Antidepression Implications of
Keynes's Theory

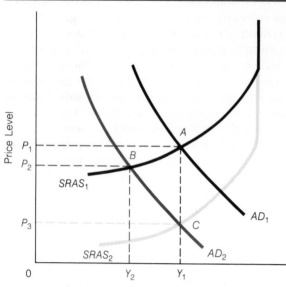

The depression conditions of the 1930s came about because of a leftward shift of aggregate demand from AD_1
to AD_2, bringing a short-run equilibrium at B and severe
unemployment. The policy implication of Keynes's theory
was to shift aggregate demand back to the right and so
restore the initial equilibrium at A. This process would be
much faster and less painful than waiting for the short-run
aggregate-supply curve to shift from $SRAS_1$ to $SRAS_2$,
which would lower the price level from P_2 to P_3 while
returning the economy to effective full employment at Y_1
(point C).

short-run aggregate-supply curve, $SRAS_1$. Keynes's
theory shows policy makers that, in cases such
as this one, shifting the aggregate-demand curve
back to the right can attack the source of the
problem and return the economy to its original
price and output level at A. In this way, unemployment can be reduced without the painful and
long-drawn-out process of shifting the short-run
aggregate-supply curve from $SRAS_1$ to $SRAS_2$ to
bring back effective full employment (at C).

In the case of the Great Depression, the social
and political structure might not have stood the

stresses that such a shift in the short-run aggregate-supply curve would have caused. The fall in
the price level (from P_2 to P_3) that would have
gone along with the shift in the short-run aggregate-supply curve would have meant that people
holding assets whose value was shown in fixed
nominal amounts would have received a rise in
real wealth while workers accepted lower nominal
wages. The possible social and political results of
such a long-drawn-out adjustment can easily be
imagined. Keynes's theory offered a way to avoid
these hardships and problems.

Although Keynes's influence on economic
thinking in the United States in the 1930s was
important, many of the actions taken were experimental and were not a full application of his
theories. As we noted in describing "The Hungry
Thirties" in Chapter 10, the earliest New Deal
efforts to fight the Great Depression took the
form of **pump-priming,** which used temporary
injections of government money in an effort to
build up business confidence and to raise planned
investment. However, this was *not* a full-fledged
application of the Keynesian theory, which requires a sustained increase in the flow of planned
expenditure.

Another ill-fated effort to raise profits and
business investment was launched through the
National Industrial Recovery Act (NIRA), passed
in 1933. Here the target was the falling price
level. As you learned in Chapter 15, a falling
price level along with a wage–cost lag and money
illusion can be partly responsible for unemployment and slack business investment. Under the
NIRA, the government encouraged industries to
set up "codes of fair competition," which generally meant cutting output and raising prices.
Again, this was not an application of Keynes's
theory. Within two years, important parts of the
NIRA were found to be unconstitutional, ending
this experiment in macroeconomic policy.[4]

In 1937 the economy relapsed into a severe
secondary depression, and the impression was

4. Although the NIRA had little immediate effect on the
economy, it contained farm price support and labor legislation
arrangements that were re-enacted and are still in effect.

that the experimental policies of the New Deal had failed to solve the problems facing the economy. Perhaps a more comprehensive and coordinated program was needed.

World War II and Inflation

Huge government purchases of war goods and large budget deficits occurred during World War II. These shifted the aggregate-demand curve to the right, into the vertical (absolute-full-employment) segment of the short-run aggregate-supply curve. Price controls held down (or postponed) much of the price-level increase that ordinarily would have come from this increase in aggregate demand. Also, households accumulated large amounts of near money (such as war bonds) because of patriotic appeals and shortages of goods and services.

When the war ended, price controls were removed promptly. In the change from the hardships of war to the comforts of peace, consumption and investment spending flooded the economy. With the benefit of hindsight, economists today can readily explain the inflation that followed the war. The removal of price controls released pressures pent up during the war. The drop in military spending was more than offset by the private sector catching up after five years of shortages, and aggregate demand remained high. People cashed in war bonds, and the Federal Reserve obediently bought securities in the open market, thus expanding the money supply.

The Employment Act of 1946

The influence of Keynes's theory is clearly evident in **The Employment Act of 1946,** which was passed soon after the war ended and before the postwar economic boom had gathered much force. Many remembered the Great Depression and knew that wars in the past had always been followed by severe recessions. The Employment Act was landmark legislation because through it the federal government clearly stated that it intended to "promote maximum employment, production, and purchasing power."

The Employment Act of 1946 established two official agencies to help carry out government responsibilities under the Act. Both are still influential. The **Council of Economic Advisers** is made up of three persons, named by the president. Along with their staff, they analyze the state of the economy and advise the president about economic actions to be taken. The Council and its staff do research and make forecasts on many parts of the economy, such as the location of aggregate-demand and aggregate-supply curves and the amount of planned spending. The Act also set up the **Joint Economic Committee** to do for the Congress much of the same kind of work that the Council does for the president. The staff of this Committee also does research and makes economic forecasts.

A law that came much later was the **Full Employment and Balanced Growth Act of 1978 (Humphrey-Hawkins).** This Act extended the government's macroeconomic responsibilities to cover price stability, reasonable economic growth, and a satisfactory position for the United States in world trade. The Humphrey-Hawkins Act set certain goals for inflation and unemployment rates. Clearly, government policy about intervention in the functioning of the macroeconomy had gone through a complete change since the pre-Keynesian period.

THE KEYNESIAN–MONETARIST DEBATE

As you remember from the discussion of central bank policies in Chapter 13, the Federal Reserve System followed a policy of purchasing securities in the open market and supporting the government bond market during and after World War II. However, in 1951, an "accord" was reached that gave the central bank greater freedom in the conduct of monetary policy. This opened an extended and still continuing discussion among macroeconomists about the best demand-side instruments to use in carrying out macroeconomic policies, which has become known as the **Keynesian–monetarist debate.**

In this debate, the *Keynesian* position includes the view that fiscal instruments (Chapter 11) are more effective than monetary instruments (Chapter 13) for carrying out macroeconomic policy. This position is sometimes called "fiscalist." The Keynesian position also includes the view that macroeconomic unemployment can last for a long time if no countermeasures are taken. For this reason, Keynesian economists feel that it is both politically necessary and socially desirable that the government step in to restore effective full employment.[5]

The *monetarist* point of view finds its roots in neoclassical economics and especially in the work of Irving Fisher (1867–1947). Fisher devised the equation of exchange (see Chapter 14) and believed that, in normal times, changes in the level of economic activity arise mainly from changes in the growth rate of the money supply. The best-known contributor to modern monetarist theory is Milton Friedman. Modern monetarist economists distinguish sharply between nominal and real values and generally see macroeconomic unemployment as temporary. In their view, if the right monetary rules are followed, there is no need to use fiscal policy to keep the economy close to effective full employment.

Concerning the question of whether fiscal or monetary instruments are more effective in carrying out macroeconomic policies, most Keynesians grant some effectiveness to monetary tools. However, they believe that money-supply actions are weak when economic expansion is needed. They also feel that the delays and uncertainty of monetary tools are great. Keynesians prefer to use changes in taxes and government purchases

to regulate the economy. They believe that these tools are faster and surer. Monetarists answer them by pointing to the historical record that shows patterns of relationships between money-supply changes and changes in nominal national income and product and by noting the cases in which monetary changes were able either to cancel or to dominate fiscal changes when the two aimed in opposite directions. We shall now look more closely at some of their points of disagreement.

Are Monetary Instruments Weak or Strong?

In the Keynesian–monetarist debate, Keynesians grant that tightening the money supply can eventually pinch off investment and slow the rate of expansion of the economy, but they say that monetary instruments are weak when used in the other direction—to increase investment, employment, and production. The issue involves the transmission mechanisms that you studied in Chapter 14 (see especially Figure 14-4).

To carry out an expansionary monetary policy, central bank instruments would attempt to shift the money-supply curve to the right so as to lower the real rate of interest. The lower real interest rate would then increase the volume of planned investment expenditure and the equilibrium level of national income and product. In suggesting that expansionary monetary policy is weak, Keynesians raise two questions, one about the demand-for-money curve and the other about the planned-investment-demand curve.

THE SLOPE OF THE DEMAND-FOR-MONEY CURVE Figure 16-2 illustrates the difference between Keynesian and monetarist views about the slope of the demand-for-money curve. This figure contains two demand-for-money curves, one labeled *MD* (Keynesian) and the other labeled *MD* (monetarist). To understand this issue in the Keynesian–monetarist debate, start at point *A*, where equilibrium would exist between money-supply curve MS_1 and either of the two demand-for-money curves. Next, shift the money-supply

---

5. The Keynesian point of view is sometimes subdivided to distinguish among **Keynesians,** who follow the work of Keynes himself, **neo-Keynesians,** who add refinements and extensions to the work of Keynes, and **post-Keynesians,** who use Keynesian and neo-Keynesian models but go beyond these to emphasize institutional features of the economy, such as monopoly power, price rigidity, and labor union influences. Our discussion most closely follows the neo-Keynesian views.

FIGURE 16-2   Keynesian and Monetarist Positions About the Slope of the Demand-for-Money Curve

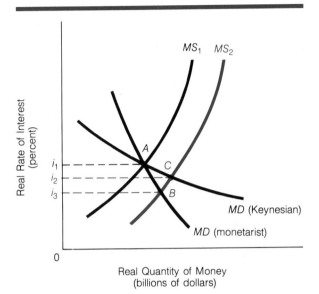

The Keynesian position is that the demand-for-money curve tends to be flat when expansionary policies are needed for the economy. This view is represented by the curve labeled MD (Keynesian). The monetarist position is that the curve has some significant negative slope, as illustrated by the curve labeled MD (monetarist). Starting from equilibrium at point A, an expansionary shift of the money-supply curve from MS_1 to MS_2 will cause interest rates to fall to i_3 at point B in the monetarist view, but only to i_2 at point C in the Keynesian view.

curve to the right, from MS_1 to MS_2, to represent an expansionary application of monetary instruments. How great a change will take place in the real rate of interest? The monetarist demand-for-money curve suggests a substantial drop in the real interest rate, from i_1 to i_3, as shown at point B. But the Keynesian demand-for-money curve suggests a smaller interest-rate decrease, from i_1 to only i_2, as shown at point C.

The issue is whether the demand-for-money curve is steep or flat. The steeper the demand-for-money curve, the more effective monetary instruments will be, other things being equal. If the demand-for-money curve is steep, shifts in the money-supply curve will bring great changes

in real interest rates, and monetary instruments can be powerful. But if the demand-for-money curve is flat, shifts in the money-supply curve will have little influence on real interest rates. Increases in the quantity of money would simply be absorbed into greater money holdings. A flat demand-for-money curve illustrates what is called a **liquidity trap.** This is a problem mainly at very low interest rates (and very high asset prices) when people hold large amounts of money waiting for these asset prices to fall (and for interest rates to rise). Economists disagree about how important it has been in the past or may be in the future.

THE SLOPE OF THE PLANNED-INVESTMENT-DEMAND CURVE   The second part of the Keynesian argument about the weakness of monetary instruments to expand the economy relates to the slope of the planned-investment-demand curve. To understand the difference between the Keynesian and the monetarist views on this question, look at Figure 16-3. This figure shows two planned-investment-demand curves, one labeled I (Keynesian), representing the Keynesian position, and the other labeled I (monetarist), representing the monetarist position. Now consider what will happen as a result of a fall in the real rate of interest from i_1 to i_2. According to the monetarist demand curve, many potential investments become profitable at this lower interest rate and the quantity of planned investment will increase from I_1 to I_3, as indicated by point C. But the Keynesian demand curve shows a smaller increase in planned investment, from I_1 only to I_2, as indicated by point B.

The actual slope of the planned-investment-demand curve depends on what really happens in the economy. If interest costs are only a small part of the total costs of investment projects or if only a small backlog of such projects exists, the curve will be steep. This view is associated with Keynesian models, which deal with recession situations and rather short-term time frames. On the other hand, a longer-term point of view usually sees a larger backlog of investment projects and finds interest costs to be a significant part of their costs. This view, often associated

FIGURE 16-3 Keynesian and Monetarist Positions About the Slope of the Planned-Investment-Demand Curve

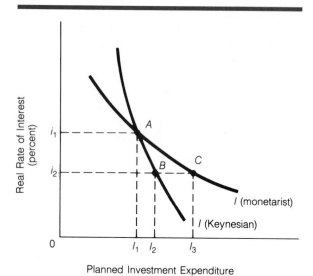

The Keynesian position is that the planned-investment-demand curve is rather steep so that a fall in the real rate of interest from i_1 to i_2 will increase the quantity of planned investment expenditure only from I_1 to I_2, as shown by the move from A to B along curve I (Keynesian). The monetarist position is that the planned-investment-demand curve is flatter, so that the indicated fall in the real rate of interest would increase planned investment expenditure all the way to I_3, as shown by the move from A to C along curve I (monetarist).

with the monetarist point of view, expects a flatter planned-investment-demand curve.

Keynesians say that expected consumer demand for final products is the major influence on investment decisions, so that *shifts* in the planned-investment-demand curve are much more important than its slope. This leads the Keynesians to call for direct government investment, for tax changes that raise the profitability of investments, and for measures aimed at increasing other components of planned spending.

The monetarists' answer comes on two levels. First, they argue that real interest rates are very important in planned-investment decisions, especially when longer-term investment plans are

considered. They state that the Keynesian stand on the interest insensitivity of planned investment simply reflects the difference between short-run and long-run thinking in economics. Long-run decisions are much more sensitive to time-related factors (such as interest rates) than are short-run decisions. On the second level, the monetarist answer is that changes in the money supply can influence the economy in ways that are entirely separate from the real rate of interest.[6] As explained in Chapter 14, this argument sets aside the whole interest rate transmission mechanism. Instead, it states that money-supply changes affect consumer spending directly without any necessary interest rate linkage. When money is expanded, consumption spending will rise. When it is reduced, consumers will spend less.

SHIFTS OF THE DEMAND-FOR-MONEY CURVE A related issue in the Keynesian–monetarist debate deals with the feedbacks on the demand for money that arise from changes in the level of real national income and product. The feedback mechanism was explained in Chapter 14.[7] There you learned how a rise in real national income and product will increase the demand for money and push real interest rates upward. These higher interest rates will lower the amount of planned investment expenditure and dampen the expansion of real national income and product. Therefore, monetarists argue that expansions started through fiscal instruments may be less effective than Keynesians believe them to be.

This debate about feedback on the demand for money again highlights differences between Keynesians and monetarists about the slope of the demand-for-money curve. Since changes in equilibrium real national income and product are expected to shift this curve to the left or to the right, its slope is important in determining the size of any resulting change in the rate of interest. This is shown in Figure 16-4. The money-supply

6. In fact, many monetarist economists contend that, in the long run, real interest rates are not affected at all by changes in the money supply. They reason that real interest rates are determined by the productivity of capital equipment and the time preferences of lenders. (See Chapter 14.)

7. See pages 262–265.

FIGURE 16-4   Interest-Rate Changes from Shifts of the Demand-for-Money Curve

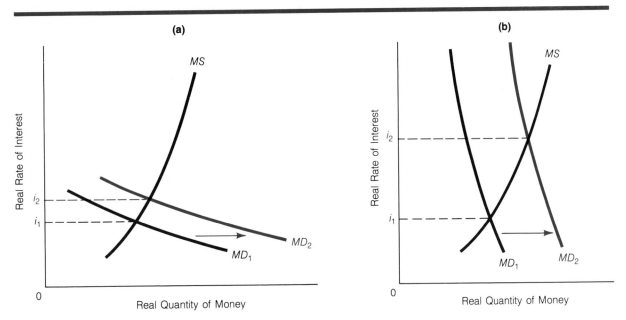

The money-supply (*MS*) curves are the same in each graph. In panel (a), the demand-for-money (*MD*) curve is quite flat, and a shift in that curve results in a small change in the real rate of interest. In panel (b), the demand-for-money curve is shifted to the right by the same distance as the demand-for-money curve in panel (a), but the change in the real rate of interest is much greater because the demand-for-money curve is steeper. Keynesians tend toward the view in the left-hand graph, whereas monetarists tend toward the view in the right-hand graph.

curve is the same in each panel of the figure. Also, the demand-for-money curve is shifted to the right by the same horizontal distance. When the demand-for-money curve is relatively flat, as shown in panel (a), this shift causes only a small rise in the real interest rate and suggests a small feedback effect. Keynesians generally accept this view of the demand-for-money curve. On the other hand, when the demand-for-money curve is steep, as in panel (b) of the figure, the same horizontal shift causes a large rise in the real interest rate and suggests a large feedback effect. Monetarists lean toward this view of the demand-for-money curve.

Should the Federal Reserve Be Independent?

As you might expect, the proper role of the Federal Reserve System is an important issue in

the Keynesian–monetarist debate. This is because an independent Board of Governors of the Federal Reserve System can use monetary instruments either to accommodate (support) or to counteract fiscal policy actions taken by the president and the Congress. At the heart of the issue is a monetary policy called **accommodation**—the use of monetary instruments to support fiscal policy initiatives and to assist government borrowing to finance budget deficits. The policy of accommodation is also known as a policy of **validation**, meaning that it provides monetary actions that reinforce fiscal actions.

One aspect of accommodation is illustrated in Figure 16-5. Suppose that government purchases have increased or that taxes have been reduced, tending to produce a deficit in the government budget and a rise in the equilibrium level of real national income and product. Because of the transactions and precautionary motives for demanding money, the demand-for-money curve

FIGURE 16-5   **Accommodation**

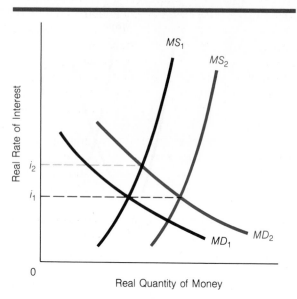

Accommodation means shifting the money-supply curve so that shifts in the demand-for-money curve do not cause changes in the real rate of interest. In this diagram, we assume that the demand-for-money curve has shifted to the right, from MD_1 to MD_2, perhaps because of an increase in national income and product. Without accommodation, the rate of interest would rise from i_1 to i_2. However, accommodation accomplished by shifting the money-supply curve to the right, from MS_1 to MS_2, can prevent this rise in the real rate of interest.

shifts to the right, from MD_1 to MD_2. Accommodation takes place if the Federal Reserve uses monetary instruments to shift the money-supply curve to the right, from MS_1 to MS_2, to prevent the rise in the real interest rate that would otherwise take place. If the real interest rate can thus be prevented from rising, no decline in planned investment expenditure need occur, and the fiscal initiative will have been accommodated or validated by monetary action. There is danger, however, that these actions may generate inflation or inflationary expectations, which, as explained in Chapter 14, could shift the MS_2 curve back to the left.

A second aspect of accommodation involves the government's sales of securities to finance its budget deficit. These sales could drive up interest rates in the market for loanable funds and crowd out private investments.[8] By purchasing government securities in the open market, the Federal Reserve System can remove the interest-rate pressure from this market while, at the same time, providing the bank reserves to expand the money supply. In this way, a monetary policy of accommodation can moderate both the crowding out and the feedback effects of an expansionary fiscal policy.

Accommodation is not always related to the government's fiscal policy actions. As you learned in our short monetary history in Chapter 13, the Federal Reserve accommodated a great rise in consumption as well as in investment spending in the years just after World War II, even though this allowed inflation to arise. In the 1970s, when OPEC raised the price of crude oil and caused a supply-side shock to the economy, the Federal Reserve again followed the route of "accommodation" by increasing the money supply and letting the price level go up.

The policy of accommodation brings together several different questions in our debate. If monetarists are correct about the (rather flat) planned-investment-demand curve and the (rather steep) demand-for-money curve, the question of whether or not to "accommodate" can lead to a conflict between the monetary authorities in the Federal Reserve and the fiscal authorities in the White House and Congress. An expansionary fiscal policy launched from the White House or the Congress could be defeated or at least greatly weakened if the monetary authorities refused to "accommodate" by increasing the money supply. In the same way, restrictive fiscal policies can be defeated or very much weakened if the monetary authorities refuse to "accommodate" by reducing the monetary growth rate. Heated discussions can arise about whether the Federal Reserve Board, whose members are appointed rather than elected and who are or have been closely connected with banking, should be trusted to use such great powers. On the other hand, the tension

8. See page 267 for an explanation of the loanable funds market.

between the fiscal and the monetary authorities can be viewed as another of the checks and balances that are part of the U.S. government system. Each side holds something of a "veto power" over the other.

Rules or Discretion?

Another question plays an important part in the debate between the Keynesians and the monetarists. Should government policy makers set certain monetary and/or fiscal policy rules and stick to them, or should they use discretion and make day-to-day judgments in deciding how to use these tools?

Keynesians usually seem to favor having the officials responsible for fiscal and monetary policy use day-by-day judgment. Sometimes this approach is called **fine tuning.** It calls for rather continuous but small adjustments in government spending, taxing, open market operations, and so forth, aimed at holding the economy near some target level of real national income and product.

The use of discretion fits well with many principles of Keynesian economics that you already have studied. Three typical Keynesian ideas are involved in the discretion, or fine-tuning, point of view. The first is that the economy, if left to itself, is unstable and can operate for long periods at less than effective full employment. The second is that the fiscal tools of government policy are reliable and effective. The third idea is that the officials who make policy judgments are able to do the right things at the right times. So the preference for using discretion follows in the tradition of Keynes, which favors active government involvement in the economy.

Monetarists usually reject each of the three points of view involved in the use of discretion in policy making. On the first point, they believe that if prices and wage rates are flexible in both directions, the economy will be fairly stable and close to effective full employment in normal times. Second, they do not believe that the standard tools of fiscal and monetary policy are effective in the long run in changing real levels of income

and production in the economy. They believe that, in the long run, both monetary and fiscal tools affect mainly the price level and have little impact on the level of real national income and product. On the third point, monetarists say that constructive use of fiscal and monetary tools is nearly impossible in practice because of the long delays and lags that are involved in using these tools.

Several types of lags are likely to arise in using discretionary instruments. First, some time is needed for economists to recognize that there is trouble in the economy, to diagnose the trouble, and to prescribe remedies. We can call this a **recognition lag.** Next, there are time lags while the government debates these remedies and goes through the legislative procedures needed to put them into effect. This we can call a **decision-making lag.** Finally, still more time passes before new programs are administered and the remedies actually take effect in the economy. This is an **implementation lag.** Taken together, these lags suggest that neither fiscal nor monetary measures can be handled quickly enough to stabilize the economy effectively. In fact, the discretionary approach could even make fluctuations worse, if, for example, measures taken to counter a contraction did not take effect until the economy had already turned the corner and started to expand.

As an additional argument against discretion and fine tuning, monetarists sometimes argue that competition between political parties and candidates biases discretionary policies in an expansionary and inflationary direction because the party in office is tempted to apply a "quick fix" to bring prosperity to the economy before the next election.

As an alternative to discretion and fine tuning, monetarists say that policy makers should adopt and stick with a few basic rules for monetary and fiscal policy. We next describe two rules illustrating this approach.

THE FULL-EMPLOYMENT BALANCED-BUDGET RULE According to the **full-employment balanced-budget rule,** Congress should decide on the amount of government purchases that the voters would desire and be willing to pay for when the economy is operating at effective full employment. Next, tax rates and transfer payment programs should be set so that net taxes would bring in enough government revenue to balance this budget when the economy reaches effective full employment. If economic growth takes place or if the desires of the citizens change, adjustments should be made in these spending and tax rates. But no changes should be made in the programs or tax rates just because the economy fluctuates around the effective-full-employment level.

If the full-employment balanced-budget rule is followed, budget deficits will arise automatically when the economy falls below effective full employment, and these deficits (accommodated by monetary adjustments) will moderate the downturn of the economy. On the other hand, budget surpluses will arise automatically when the economy operates at more than effective full employment, with strong pressures for price-level rises. The surplus would be used to pay off some of the country's debt, and monetary tools would accommodate by slowing the growth of the money supply. These actions would automatically restrain the expansion of the economy. As you can see, the rule uses the automatic stabilizers that were described in Chapter 11.

The full-employment balanced-budget rule is appealing for two reasons. First, government spending and transfer programs would be decided on their merits rather than on the basis of how well they fit the needs of the business cycle. Second, tax rates would be stable, offering a better atmosphere for business planning.

THE MONETARY GROWTH RULE   Under the **monetary growth rule,** the first step is to predict the real growth trend for the economy. This forecast takes into account the expected changes in the labor force, productivity, capital stock, technology, and so forth. Once the long-run percentage growth trend is estimated, the next step is for the Federal Reserve Board to increase the money supply by about the same percentage as the growth rate every year—year in and year out—without making any changes in the money supply

because of short-term ups and downs in the economy. In other words, if the rate of real economic growth is expected to be 3 percent a year, the money supply might be allowed to grow every year by about 3 percent. Often, the rule calls for a rate of money-supply increase a bit larger than the projected real growth trend (perhaps 3½ percent in our case) to allow a small rise in the price level or to recognize improvements in the quality of goods and services. You may notice that this rule makes use of the equation of exchange ($MV = PQ$), which was described in Chapter 14, and assumes that the velocity of circulation is constant.

THE PHILLIPS CURVE

Toward the close of the 1950s, a number of events set the stage for active demand-side macroeconomic policy in the 1960s and 1970s. In 1957, the Soviet Union beat the United States into space by launching Sputnik, an orbiting space vehicle the size of a basketball. In 1958, the U.S. economy experienced its worst recession (up to that point) since World War II. The recession and the Soviet success in space pricked the American ego and contributed to the success of John F. Kennedy's 1960 campaign slogan "Let's Get This Country Moving Again." When President Kennedy took office in 1961, Keynesian economics, which had been taught in classrooms for a generation, became the vehicle for active macroeconomic policy. Also, in 1958 an article written by A.W.H. Phillips appeared in *Economica.*[9] It described a relationship between unemployment and inflation, which became known as the Phillips curve. This theory played an important part in macroeconomic policy during the 1960s and 1970s—another example of how theory informs policy.

A **Phillips curve** is presented in Figure 16-6. The horizontal axis shows the unemployment

9. A.W.H. Phillips, "The Relationship Between Unemployment and the Rate of Change of Money Wage Rates in the United Kingdom, 1861–1957," *Economica,* November 1958.

FIGURE 16-6   A Phillips Curve

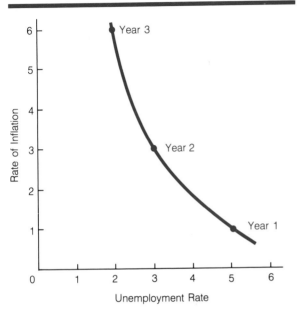

A Phillips curve is constructed by plotting the unemployment-rate and inflation-rate experience over a number of years and by constructing a line representing the pattern determined by the location of these plotted points. In the figure, year 1 had 5 percent unemployment and a 1 percent inflation rate, year 2 had 3 percent unemployment and a 3 percent inflation rate, and year 3 had 2 percent unemployment and a 6 percent inflation rate. As applied in the 1960s, the Phillips curve suggested that policy makers could choose their preferred combination of unemployment and inflation from among those located on the curve.

rate, and the vertical axis shows the inflation rate—that is, the rate of change in the price level. Suppose that the unemployment rate was 5 percent and the inflation rate was 1 percent in year 1, that the unemployment rate was 3 percent and the inflation rate was 3 percent in year 2, and that the unemployment rate was 2 percent and the inflation rate was 6 percent in year 3. Each of these years could be plotted as a point on the graph, as done in Figure 16-6. A curve fitted to these points is a Phillips curve.

In his 1958 article, Phillips used the rate of change in wage rates rather than the rate of

change in the general price level when he plotted his relationships. His curve was based on data for almost one hundred years in Great Britain. However, the Phillips curves that informed the policy of the 1960s and 1970s used the general price level, rather than wage rates, because economists were especially interested in the overall inflation rate and because they assumed that wage rates and the general price level usually would move together.

The Phillips Curve and Macroeconomic Policy

As a guide for macroeconomic policy, the Phillips curve suggests a tradeoff between inflation and unemployment. It implies that a reduction in the unemployment rate can be "bought" by accepting an increase in the rate of inflation. On the other hand, it means that a reduction in the rate of inflation can be "bought" by accepting a rise in the rate of unemployment. In the context of policy formulation in a democracy, the curve suggests that political parties and candidates can key their economic policy platforms to particular points along the Phillips curve. Parties looking for votes from workers who feel threatened by unemployment will most likely choose points toward the upper end of the curve, accepting inflation in order to save jobs. On the other hand, parties seeking votes from people who see inflation as their more serious problem will choose points toward the lower end of the curve, accepting higher unemployment (for others) in exchange for less inflation. Election results will establish the general outline for macroeconomic policy according to the Phillips-curve model.

Aside from determining its precise location, the economist's concern with the Phillips curve is to discover ways to shift the curve in order to improve the combinations available to decision makers. Clearly, a shift of the Phillips curve downward and to the left offers an improved range of choices, since the economy could then have less unemployment, or less inflation, or some combination involving less of both, com-

FIGURE 16-7   Unemployment and Inflation in the United States, 1961 through 1969

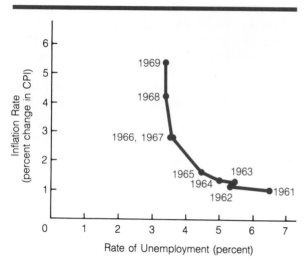

Each dot on the graph represents the combination of unemployment and inflation that existed in that year. Experience during the 1960s appeared to confirm the Phillips-curve relationship between these variables. Monetary and fiscal actions were generally expansionary and the economy appeared to move upward along the Phillips curve. In the early part of the decade, reductions in unemployment dominated the moves. In the later years, increases in the inflation rate dominated.

Source: Economic Report of the President, 1986, Tables B-35 and B-58.

pared with any point on the original curve. On the other hand, a shift of the Phillips curve upward and to the right clearly worsens the choices available, since decision makers then would have to accept either more inflation, or more unemployment, or some combination involving more of both, compared with any point on the original curve. Such movements raise the danger of stagflation for the economy.

Figure 16-7 shows the inflation–unemployment combinations that actually developed from 1961 through 1969. Most of the time during these years, fiscal and monetary actions were expansionary. The economy responded with higher and higher rates of inflation (from less than 2 percent a year in the early 1960s to almost 6 percent a year by 1969) and with reduced rates of unemployment (from almost 7 percent in 1961 to around 3½ percent in 1968). Since the Phillips curve appeared to work as a guide for economic policy, attention focused on the political aspects of choosing the appropriate point along the curve.

In the latter half of the 1960s, the United States became heavily involved in the Vietnam War. At the same time, President Lyndon Johnson pushed forward with a domestic "War on Poverty" and the building of what was called the "Great Society." These were times of great turmoil. Antiwar protests along with discontent about the rising rate of inflation helped to persuade President Johnson not to seek re-election in 1968. The election of Richard Nixon in that year showed that the American people wanted to be rid of both the war and inflation. In terms of macroeconomic policy, the election signaled a desire to lower the rate of inflation. As informed by the macroeconomic theory of the time, this meant a move downward along the Phillips curve.

Phillips-Curve Experience

Restrictive monetary and fiscal policies were followed in the early years of the Nixon administration in an attempt to slow the inflation. However, instead of moving the economy back down the Phillips curve, these efforts encountered both continued inflation and higher unemployment—the combination known as stagflation.

Figure 16-8 shows the Phillips-curve experience of the U.S. economy from 1961 through 1985. The stagflation (northeasterly) direction of the Phillips curve that the nation encountered under President Nixon was just the beginning of a generally disconcerting experience for the economy. Although the original Phillips relationship appeared from time to time, as from 1972 to 1973, from 1976 to 1979, and from 1983 to 1984, there were also periods when the economy suffered from stagflation, as from 1973 to 1974 and from 1979 to 1980, when unemployment and the price level increased at the same time.

FIGURE 16-8   **Phillips-Curve Experience in the United States, 1961 through 1985**

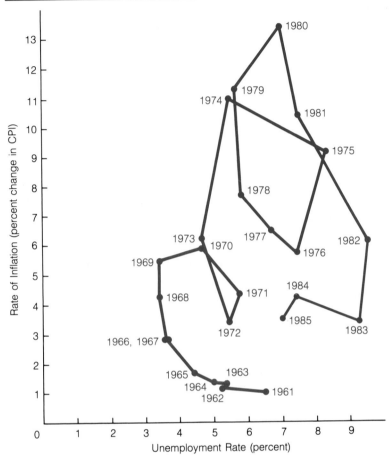

The horizontal axis shows the unemployment rate and the vertical axis shows the percentage change in the consumer price index (the inflation rate). The experience of each year from 1961 through 1985 is represented by a dot on the graph. These dots are connected in chronological order. The record since 1969 reveals that the Phillips-curve relationship is not as simple as was believed during the 1960s.

Source: Economic Report of the President, 1986, Tables B-35 and B-58.

As economists tried to understand what was happening, it became increasingly apparent that events on the supply side of the economy were causing many of the problems. Both of the stagflation periods of the 1970s (1973–1974 and 1979–1980) were associated with supply shocks brought on by great increases in petroleum prices forced by the Organization of Petroleum Exporting Countries (OPEC). Also, as you recall from Chapter 15, leftward shifts of the short-run aggregate-supply curve can come as delayed reactions to increases in the price level, as gaps caused by wage–cost lags are closed and as money illusion wears off. Both the external shocks and the reactions to inflation are aspects of supply-side economics, to be examined in the next chapter.

SUMMARY

1. The neoclassical economic theories that informed economic policy before Keynes suggested that the economy would naturally tend toward effective full employment and that government intervention not only was unnecessary but could be harmful if it delayed needed adjustments in prices and wage rates.

2. The theory of John M. Keynes, which appeared in the 1930s, explained the role of planned expenditure in the economy and showed how a depressed economy, with less than effective full employment, could continue for a long time. The theory indicated that government intervention could speed recovery.

3. U.S. macroeconomic policy in the 1930s struggled without much success to bring the economy out of the Great Depression. Pump-priming with temporary injections of government spending was attempted. It did not work. The National Industrial Recovery Act was aimed at the falling price level, but after two years it was repealed.

4. When the economy continued in a depressed condition in spite of many efforts at recovery, many people decided that the New Deal had failed and that continuous government involvement in the economy was necessary to sustain high levels of economic activity.

5. World War II brought massive increases in government purchases and huge deficits, moving the economy into the absolute full employment segment of the short-run aggregate-supply curve. Accumulated wants and reserves of spending power set the stage for postwar economic prosperity and inflation.

6. The Employment Act of 1946 announced the government's acceptance of responsibility to "promote maximum employment, production, and purchasing power" in the economy. Officials feared that, with the end of World War II, the economy would fall back into depression. This did not happen, however. The Employment Act established the Council of Economic Advisers and the Joint Economic Committee of the Congress.

7. The Keynesian–monetarist debate was the focus of economic discussion for a quarter-century after World War II. Keynesians usually argued that the economy, left to itself, was unstable and tended toward excessive unemployment. To maintain prosperity, they argued government intervention. Monetarists viewed the economy as more capable of maintaining stable conditions of reasonably full employment. They questioned the effectiveness of government intervention (both fiscal and monetary) in changing real income and production.

8. Keynesian and monetarist economists tend to disagree about the slopes of the planned-investment-demand curve and the demand-for-money curve. Because of these differences, monetarists claim that crowding out is an important economic problem and that accommodation through shifts of the money-supply curve have an important influence on the power of fiscal and monetary instruments. Keynesians tend to minimize the significance of crowding out and accommodation.

9. Keynesian and monetarist economists also tend to differ about whether macroeconomic policy decisions should be guided by "discretion" (day-by-day judgments) or by "rules" that leave less room for short-term policy adjustments.

10. The full-employment balanced-budget rule would have government purchases, transfer payments, and tax rates established in terms of what voters would be likely to prefer in times of effective full employment. This budget would balance when full employment actually prevailed. No changes in expenditure programs or in tax rates would be made because of fluctuations in aggregate economic performance. Automatic stabilizer effects would moderate economic fluctuations.

11. The monetary growth rule would direct the Federal Reserve to increase the money supply by the same percentage each year. This percentage should be about the same as the long-term real growth rate of production capacity in the economy. Money-supply changes to deal with short-term economic conditions would not be permitted.

12. U.S. macroeconomic policy became more active in the 1960s after the election of President John F. Kennedy. The Phillips-curve theory of a

predictable relation between inflation rates and unemployment rates guided economic policy during the 1960s.

13. An expansionary economic policy continued through the 1960s. Experience with the Phillips curve became increasingly unsatisfactory, with higher and higher inflation rates but smaller and smaller reductions in the unemployment rate. An attempt to move back down the Phillips curve, undertaken by President Nixon, encountered both increasing inflation and increasing rates of unemployment, which became known as stagflation.

14. Experience with the relation of inflation and unemployment throughout the decade of the 1970s turned the attention of economists to the supply side of economic activity.

DISCUSSION QUESTIONS

1. Keynes sometimes is characterized as a savior of capitalist market economic systems. Discuss the social and political stresses that go along with letting a shift of the short-run aggregate-supply curve bring an economy out of recession. Draw the recession–deflation, aggregate demand–aggregate supply graph, and illustrate a demand-side (Keynesian) solution for the depressed situation of the economy. Compare your graph with Figure 16-1.

2. The massive government spending in World War II appeared to show how Keynesian demand-side actions could bring a country out of depression. Compare this experience with your answer to Question 1. In this frame of mind, would you have voted for the Employment Act of 1946? Why or why not? Identify the two government agencies set up by this Act. What do they do?

3. Part of the debate between Keynesians and monetarists focuses on the sensitivity of planned investment spending to changes in the real rate of interest. Which group claims that planned investment is not very responsive to changes in real interest rates? Why? What is the response of the other side? Discuss how their respective time perspectives help in understanding their positions on this question.

4. Explain why the slope of the demand-for-money curve is important in the Keynesian–monetarist debate both because of movements along the curve and because of shifts of the curve. Which party in the debate contends that the curve is flat? What is a "liquidity trap" and how does it affect the power of monetary instruments?

5. If an expansionary fiscal effort is launched by the government, what action by the Federal Reserve Board would constitute "accommodation" of this move? Explain what would happen if the monetary authorities did not accommodate the expansionary fiscal policy. Discuss whether non-elected officials should have the authority to decide whether or not accommodation should take place.

6. Part of the argument for "rules" rather than "discretion" in directing macroeconomic policy is that time lags are so long that discretionary "fine tuning" doesn't work. To resolve this problem, it is sometimes proposed that the president should be given authority to change taxes or expenditure. Explain how this presidential power might make discretionary action more effective. What counterarguments can you think of to giving this authority?

7. Describe how the full-employment balanced-budget rule would operate with respect to: (a) the size of the government's purchases budget, (b) the tax rates used by the government, (c) the financing of any budget deficits that might arise, and (d) the use of any budget surplus funds. How might an elected official's desire for re-election influence the determination of the effective-full-employment level of national income and product? Explain.

8. The monetary growth rule in the Keynesian–monetarist debate provides a good opportunity to review your understanding of the mechanics of controlling the money supply. First, state what the monetary growth rule says the Federal Reserve should try to accomplish. Then explain how the monetary base and the money multiplier complicate the task assigned to the Federal Reserve. (Review the relevant section of Chapter 13 when you work out your answer to the last part of this question.)

9. Construct a graph of the Phillips curve as it appeared to exist according to U.S. data of the 1960s. Be sure to label the axes of your graph. Check with Figure 16-7 to be sure you have it right. How might political parties use this theoretical relation as a campaign platform? Discuss how the election of Richard Nixon in 1968 involved issues described by the Phillips curve.

10. Disappointment with the Phillips-curve theory led to greatly increased attention to the supply side of the economy, as you will see in Chapter 17. However, a summary of Phillips-curve problems may be helpful. To do so, describe, in turn, what happens in a "northwest" move on a Phillips-curve chart, what happens in a "northeast" move, what happens in a "southeast" move, and what happens in a "southwest" move on this chart. Which is most likely to help the re-election chances of the president in office? Which is most likely to hurt his or her re-election chances? Review U.S. political experience of the 1970s in this light.

17 *Macroeconomic Policy: Supply Side*

PREVIEW Supply-side economics focuses on shifts of the aggregate-supply curve, just as demand-side economics focuses on shifts of the aggregate-demand curve. In this chapter, you will study four kinds of aggregate-supply-curve shifts—those caused by supply shocks, by inflationary expectations, by wage and price controls, and by supply-side economic policy moves.

We begin by looking at supply shocks, which are shifts of the aggregate-supply curve that come from outside events, such as the embargo on oil and the large price rises caused by OPEC during the 1970s. Since you met these earlier in the book, only a quick review is needed here.

Next we explore the theory of inflationary expectations, which is a supply-side effect based on recent macroeconomic experience. This theory extends our earlier discussion of how the supply side of the economy can become important when wage–cost gaps close and money illusion wears off. This subject was presented in Chapter 15 in our expansion–inflation case. Here it is carried further into what is known as the theory of rational expectations.

In the third part, we describe wage and price controls. These are attempts (which generally fail in nondictatorial countries) to prevent the aggregate-supply responses that come from inflationary expectations and the fading of wage–cost lags and money illusion. Wage and price controls have often been used when it appeared that demand-side expansions might bring about too much inflation.

Fourth, we look at supply-side economics proper, where macroeconomic policy moves take the form of government attempts to bring about a shift of the aggregate-supply curve. This is the kind of supply-side economics that has become so well known in the 1980s. This strategy uses tax cuts and subsidies for business and investors to push the aggregate-supply curve to the right.

We close with a short summary of Keynesianism, monetarism, and supply-side economics—the three major guides to macroeconomic policy in market-capitalist economies. Most actual economic policies, such as those associated with particular administrations, are mixtures of these theories.

SUPPLY SHOCKS

A **supply shock** is an independent or exogenous event that shifts both the short-run and long-run aggregate-supply curves for an economy. As noted in Chapter 15, the OPEC embargo and oil price rises were supply shocks, as were the crop failures that raised food prices in the mid-1970s. Wars, floods, and other disasters are also supply shocks that lower production capacity and shift the aggregate-supply curves to the left. On the other hand, technological breakthroughs or discoveries of new natural resources are supply shocks that shift the aggregate-supply curves to the right.

Figure 17-1 pictures the sort of supply shock suffered in the 1970s because of rising oil and food prices. The initial short-run aggregate-supply curve is $SRAS_1$. The shock shifts this curve to $SRAS_2$. At any given price level, less is supplied

FIGURE 17-1   A Contractionary Supply Shock

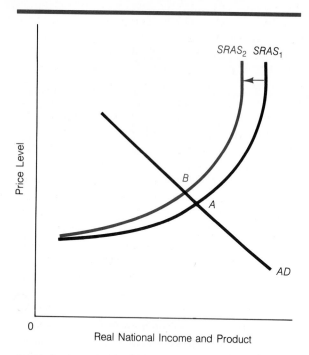

A supply shock that reduces production capability shifts the short-run aggregate-supply curve to the left, as from $SRAS_1$ to $SRAS_2$. If aggregate demand does not change, equilibrium will move from point A to point B, with a higher price level and a smaller volume of real national income and product.

after the shock than was supplied before the shock. If aggregate demand remains unchanged, the short-run equilibrium for the economy moves from point A to point B. When this happens, the price level rises, and the volume of real national income and product falls. An initial effect of a contractionary supply shock is an increase in unemployment. As you remember, the combination of rising prices, falling output, and increasing unemployment is called *stagflation*. Looking back we can see that supply shocks were important causes of the economic hard times of the 1970s.

During the early and middle 1980s, the SRAS curve for the United States (and for many other industrialized economies) shifted to the right—a move opposite from those of the 1970s. Bountiful

harvests expanded food supplies, baby-boomers increased the labor force, and world crude oil production increased due to new discoveries and the breakdown of OPEC's restrictions on production. These rightward shifts in aggregate supply contributed strongly to increases in U.S. real national income and product. At the same time, the U.S. aggregate-demand curve also shifted to the right. In terms of aggregate demand and aggregate supply analysis, the rightward shift of aggregate supply only partially offset rightward shifts in the aggregate-demand curve. The price level increased. Nevertheless, the *rate* of inflation fell from 9.7 percent for 1981 to 3.3 percent for 1985, as measured by the percentage change in the U.S. GNP implicit price deflator. Overall, expansionary supply shocks contributed greatly to the good economic times of the early and mid-1980s.

In responding to supply shocks, the first step is to develop new targets for national income and product in the economy. Estimates must be made of how far to the left or to the right the aggregate-supply curves have shifted. There must also be estimates about whether the shock has changed the growth rate of the economy, since the aggregate-supply curves normally are shifting to the right as the work force grows, technology advances, and capital accumulates. The oil shocks of the 1970s, for example, shifted the aggregate-supply curves to the left and slowed the rate of economic growth. The expansionary supply shocks of the 1980s have boosted economic growth rates, at least temporarily, but they may not have changed the long-term rate.

The second step in the policy response is to devise both demand-side and supply-side strategies in line with the new situation.

Demand-Side Responses

Demand-side responses to supply shocks use monetary and fiscal tools to shift the aggregate-demand curve. However, stagflation presents the demand-side strategies with a dilemma. Shifting the aggregate-demand curve to the left is the traditional means of fighting inflation. This may moderate the price-level effect of the shock but may mean further unemployment and still lower real national income and product. The opposite strategy of shifting the aggregate-demand curve to the right will increase the price-level effect of the shock by moving the economy upward and to the right along the new short-run aggregate-supply curve $SRAS_2$ in Figure 17-1. During the oil shocks of the 1970s, actual demand-side policy was a compromise. Monetary and fiscal instruments were used to shift the aggregate-demand curve to the right in order to moderate the unemployment caused by the shocks. But the inflationary effects of expansionary monetary and fiscal actions argued for restraint in the use of these instruments. Both inflation and unemployment rates increased.

The expansionary supply shocks of the 1980s offered much more appealing opportunities for demand-side policy. Because of these supply shifts, monetary and fiscal actions could shift the aggregate demand curve to the right with less fear of causing increased inflation rates. Thus, the impressive disinflation of the early and middle 1980s took place in spite of large government budget deficits. Although the Federal Reserve Board headed by Paul Volcker espoused restrictive monetary policy, U.S. money supply increases were substantial.

Supply-Side Responses

In the face of a contractionary supply shock, supply-side responses attempt to shift aggregate-supply curves to the right, toward their preshock locations. Often there is little that can be done to counteract the shocks themselves, since they originate outside the economy or from noneconomic events. Instead, supply-side responses must focus on the dislocations that shocks cause inside the economy.

Dislocations also occur because of expansionary supply shocks. Although the economy as a whole typically prospers from the expanded supply, specific sectors or industries can suffer hardship. For example, the domestic petroleum industry, which boomed because of the contractionary sup-

ply shocks of the 1970s, suffered severely during the expansionary supply shocks of the 1980s.

Supply shocks usually change *relative prices* in the economy as well as the general price level. In the contractionary oil shock case, for example, the prices of petroleum and petroleum-based products rose much more than other prices. Because of these changes in relative prices, jobs were lost in industries hurt by the supply shock, and the workers who held those jobs had to be retrained and perhaps relocated to qualify for jobs in industries that expanded because of the shock. While these structural changes were carried out, frictional and structural unemployment were high. Conversely, in the expansionary oil shock case, prices of petroleum and petroleum-based products fell relative to other prices. This time jobs were lost in some petroleum-related industries such as petroleum exploration and employment grew in other industries.

Worker retraining and relocation programs are among the supply-side instruments for moderating and shortening the period of economic dislocation after a supply shock. Other programs that help resources move from one industry to another include tax incentives for new investment, wage subsidies for retraining workers, and so on.

INFLATIONARY EXPECTATIONS

Inflationary expectations are anticipations that the price level will rise in the near future. These expectations can shift the short-run aggregate-supply curve in an economy. To help you understand this part of supply-side economics, we show in Figure 17-2 the main features of the expansion–inflation case from Chapter 15. As you remember, that chain of events started with an expansionary shift of the aggregate-demand curve from AD_1 to AD_2. This boosted both the price level and the volume of real national income and product as equilibrium moved upward along the $SRAS_1$ curve from A to B. The second step in the expansion–inflation process was the shift of the short-run aggregate-supply curve from $SRAS_1$ to

FIGURE 17-2   **Expansion and Inflation**

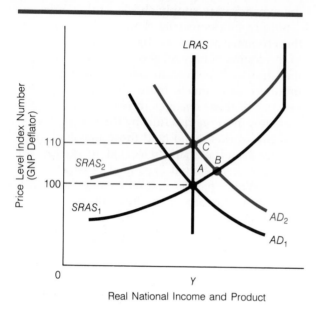

This graph illustrates the expansion–inflation process described in Chapter 15. The expansion is initiated by a shift of aggregate demand from AD_1 to AD_2, and the price level rises from 100 to 110. This rise takes place in two steps, from A to B in response to the new demand, and from B to C as money illusion and wage–cost lags wear off and the short-run aggregate-supply curve shifts from $SRAS_1$ to $SRAS_2$.

$SRAS_2$ as wage–cost lag and money illusion wore off. As this happened, the equilibrium point moved from B to C, bringing still higher prices but lowering the volume of real national income and product.

With this expansion–inflation process fresh in mind, we can now start our study of inflationary expectations. In the expansion–inflation model, the short-run aggregate-supply curve shifted to the left as the wage–cost lag and money illusion from *past* inflation wore off. In the inflationary expectations model, this curve keeps moving to the left (adding to its initial shift) because people expect more inflation is still to come. In other words, in the inflationary expectations theory, the short-run aggregate-supply curve shifts because of expectations of *future* inflation.

To show how the expectations model works, we labeled the price level in Figure 17-2 as 100 at the start of the expansion–inflation process and as 110 at the end of that process. The price level (measured in terms of the gross national product deflator) rose by 10 percent. If this happened in one year, the inflation *rate* was 10 percent a year. Even though one year is a rather short time for people to adapt their lives to this rate of inflation, we assume, for simplicity, that this is what happens. In other words, not only does $SRAS_1$ shift to $SRAS_2$ as wage–cost lag and money illusion wear off, but people come to expect that inflation will *continue* at a 10 percent rate into the future. They adjust their economic behavior to the expectation of continuing inflation.

What will happen when these inflationary expectations are fully effective? Workers and other resource owners will routinely ask for raises in their wage and other pay rates to cover the 10 percent inflation that they expect during each coming year. In a similar way, companies will routinely raise both their profit targets and their product prices by 10 percent a year. When this inflationary expectation is present, the short-run aggregate-supply curve in Figure 17-2 will keep on shifting to the left. To show you a 10 percent expected inflation rate, Figure 17-3 repeats Figure 17-2 but adds, in half-tone color, an $SRAS_3$ curve that is 10 percent higher than $SRAS_2$. This builds in our assumption that people expect inflation to continue at the same 10 percent rate that they actually experienced in the expansion–inflation process from point A to point B to point C.

Will the price level actually rise by 10 percent in the next year, as we assume people are expecting? This depends on whether monetary and fiscal policies (active shifters of the aggregate-demand curve) accommodate the expected inflation. If the aggregate-demand curve is *not* shifted, the short-run equilibrium will move from C to D. The economy will fall below effective full employment, and the price level will not rise by the full 10 percent. On the other hand, if the aggregate-demand curve is shifted to the right by exactly the correct amount to justify these inflationary expectations, as shown by AD_3 in Figure 17-3, the new equilibrium will be at E, and the inflationary expectations will be confirmed. The new price level will be 121, which is 10 percent higher than 110. If the move from C to D to E happens in one year, the actual inflation rate is 10 percent a year.

Conditions and Qualifications

The theory shows how inflationary expectations can be a supply-side force acting on the economy. We must, however, note several conditions and qualifications that apply to our simple presentation of this theory.

First, our simple model suggested that inflationary expectations arose after only a one-year experience with a given inflation rate. Probably this is too short a time period. It is more likely that several years of sustained inflation are necessary to develop really firm inflationary expectations. However, many economists believe that inflationary expectations were an important force in the economy in the 1970s, when high rates of inflation continued year after year.

Second, we should note that the inflationary expectations in our model cannot be blamed for starting the inflation, even though they may be partly responsible for continuing it. These expectations came from experience with inflation that was already going on. They are called **adaptive expectations** because people adapted their behavior to the rate of inflation that had gone on in the recent past.

Third, we must note that accommodating demand-side economic policies are needed in order for inflationary expectations to be confirmed in practice. As we said earlier, if the aggregate-demand curve is not allowed to shift from its AD_2 position (see Figure 17-3), equilibrium with the $SRAS_3$ curve (at D) will mean less than a 10 percent rise in the price level. Unemployment would have gone up, and the expected rate of inflation would not have been confirmed. In terms of the adaptive expectations theory, people would have to make yet another change in their economic behavior.

On the other hand, if demand-side actions keep on accommodating the 10 percent inflation ex-

FIGURE 17-3 Inflationary Expectations

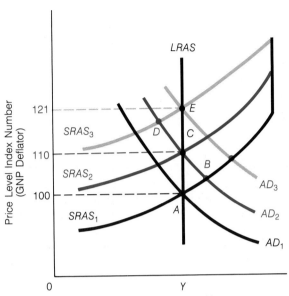

This figure reproduces the graph shown in Figure 17-2 but adds, in half-tone color, a new $SRAS_3$ curve. The initial expansion–inflation process resulted in a 10 percent increase in the price level, from 100 to 110 (point A to point B to point C). When people come to expect that this rate of inflation will continue in the future and adjust their economic behavior to this expectation, the short-run aggregate-supply curve will shift from $SRAS_2$ to $SRAS_3$. If the aggregate-demand curve remains stable at AD_2, equilibrium will be at D, and the inflationary expectations will not be confirmed. However, if aggregate demand accommodates these expectations by shifting to AD_3, the price level rises to 121 (point E), and the expectation of 10 percent inflation is confirmed.

pectation, additional pairs of $SRAS$ and AD curves will appear at ever-higher locations in Figure 17-3, with their intersections showing equilibrium conditions at higher and higher price levels. These intersections will trace the long-run aggregate-supply curve, which is either a vertical line or one with some slight positive slope. Unemployment will tend to stabilize at the natural rate.

The basic inflationary expectations theory that we have just examined has several economic policy applications. We shall now look at three of them—accelerating inflation, decelerating inflation, and the theory of rational expectations.

Accelerating Inflation

The theory of **accelerating inflation** shows what would happen if the aggregate-demand curve were shifted far enough to the right so that the price level rose even faster than people expected. In this policy, monetary and fiscal instruments would be used to shift the aggregate-demand curve even farther to the right than AD_3 in Figure 17-3. Short-run macroeconomic equilibrium would move farther up and to the right along the $SRAS_3$ curve, bringing lower unemployment and a price level above the 121 index number. In other words, unemployment would be reduced below its natural rate if the inflation rate were pushed above the expectation built into the $SRAS_3$ curve. This lower unemployment rate would be only temporary, however, because expectations soon would be adjusted upward to the higher (actual) inflation rate and the $SRAS$ curve would shift to the left again. But if aggregate demand were continually increased so that inflation expectations were never able to catch up with the actual inflation rate, unemployment might be kept below its natural rate as long as policy makers were willing to allow accelerating rates of inflation. Actual inflation rates would have to become greater and greater in order to stay ahead of expected rates so that wage–cost lags and money illusion would always remain in effect.

Decelerating Inflation

Another policy application of the basic inflationary expectations model shows how policy actions can bring down an inflation rate that has become imbedded in inflationary expectations. This is the theory of **decelerating inflation.** We shall again use Figure 17-3 to aid in our explanation.

Let us begin at point C, where the economy has just experienced a 10 percent inflation rate. With inflationary expectations for a continuing

10 percent inflation rate, the short-run aggregate-supply curve shifts to $SRAS_3$. The decelerating inflation model indicates that, at this point, policy makers may decide not to accommodate the inflationary expectations. If they refuse to accommodate and instead hold the AD_2 curve at the position indicated in Figure 17-3, short-run equilibrium will, as noted earlier, occur at point D. Unemployment will rise above its natural rate and the inflation rate will be less than 10 percent. This will force a change in expectations. As expectations adapt to the lower rate of actual inflation, the $SRAS_3$ curve will shift to the right, increasing real national income and product, lowering unemployment, and reducing the price level. Macroeconomic equilibrium will move downward and to the right along the AD_2 curve to point C. The price level will be deflated to the 110 level.

Should policy makers hold aggregate demand at the AD_2 level and force deflation on the economy? Probably not. In long-run equilibrium, the economy can operate as well at one price level as at another. Moreover, deflation can bring as much hardship as inflation. Therefore, the decelerating inflation policy favors a gradual deceleration (lowering) of the inflation rate until price stability is achieved. To do this, monetary and fiscal instruments would shift the aggregate-demand curve to the right, but not far enough to fully accommodate the prevailing inflation expectation. In this way, inflation expectations would gradually be squeezed out of the economy until price stability combined with effective full employment were realized. In Figure 17-3, this might occur at a price level of 119 or 120. When inflation expectations had been eliminated and the $SRAS$ curve stabilized, unemployment would have returned to the natural rate and real national income and product would be at Y.

The Theory of Rational Expectations

In the theories that you have just studied—accelerating inflation and decelerating inflation—inflationary expectations are assumed to arise from actual experience with inflation. They are called adaptive expectations because they arise as people adapt to the existing situation. Now we shall examine a different theory about how expectations arise. This is the theory of **rational expectations.** It assumes that expectations arise because people think about the actions taken by government policy makers and accurately predict whether or not these actions will result in inflation. In other words, these expectations arise through rational thinking processes, rather than through adaptation to existing circumstances.

The change in the assumption about how expectations arise leads to conclusions that are very different from the theories based on adaptive expectations. The main difference is that shifts of the short-run aggregate-supply curve are not delayed by waiting for workers and firms to learn from actual inflation or deflation. Instead, expectations arise almost immediately after policy decisions are made so that there is virtually no wage–cost lag or money illusion. As you remember, wage–cost lag and money illusion are the bases for the slope of the short-run aggregate-supply curve. If wage–cost lag and money illusion are weak or nonexistent, the *SRAS* curve will be very steep or, in the limiting case, vertical. Price-level changes will be so completely anticipated that they will have almost no effect on real national income and product. With no wage–cost lag, inflation will cause no temporary profits to spur firms to increase output, and with no money illusion, inflation will not lead workers to believe that the tradeoff between work and leisure has changed.

The theory of rational expectations has profound implications for macroeconomic policy. Once the economy settles into long-run equilibrium at effective full employment, efforts to expand the economy with demand-side (fiscal and monetary) instruments would be unable to change employment and real output. Workers and firms would take note of the policy decisions, anticipate the price-level effects of the proposed actions, and immediately build the new price level into their decision making. Demand-side initiatives could raise or lower the price level, but they would have no effect on employment or real national income and product.

Economists are divided on how much importance to attach to the theory of rational expectations. Most agree that expectations are important and that a distinction must be made between price-level changes that are anticipated (expected) and those that are unanticipated (unexpected). But many doubt that the public is well informed enough or sophisticated enough about macroeconomics to forecast promptly and accurately the price-level effects of government policy decisions. But there undoubtedly is some merit in the rational expectations model, especially in times when there has been recent experience with inflation. In the late 1970s and early 1980s, after a decade of serious inflation, many policy makers believed that expansionary demand-side actions would trigger widespread fears of renewed inflation and that such expectations would actually produce inflation rather than the desired real effects on output and employment. Demand-side actions clearly were less appealing.

Indexing

Indexing is a procedure that automatically adjusts wage rates, savings accounts, taxes, interest rates, bond values, and all other contracts for changes in the price level. It is designed primarily to prevent important groups (such as retirees and savings account owners) from being hurt by unanticipated inflation. But indexing also is important in inflationary expectation theories because, if compensating adjustments are made automatically, workers and firms do not have to worry about or try to anticipate price-level changes. Let us see how indexing works and how it may affect the macroeconomy. Suppose that you have an indexed savings account with a contracted interest rate of 6 percent and a $1,000 balance at the start of the year. With indexing, a 10 percent inflation during the year would automatically raise both the balance in your account and the nominal interest rate by 10 percent. Thus, your initial balance of $1,000 would be multiplied by 1.166. At the end of the year you would have $1,166 in your account, which is equivalent to the $1,060 that you would have had if there had been no inflation. Full indexing would mean similar arrangements for wage and salary agreements, government bonds, income tax rates and exemptions, and all other contract agreements in the economy. Even though the United States does not have official full-scale indexing, the federal individual income tax is indexed and many labor–management contracts have cost-of-living adjustments.

What does indexing have to do with inflationary expectation theories? Its main connection is that people would no longer need to build inflation expectations into their wage or other negotiated agreements. Ideally, negotiators could put inflation expectations out of their minds because each side could be sure that it would receive an appropriate adjustment for any inflation that might come. So *expectations* of inflation no longer would drive the economy to higher price levels by shifting the short-run aggregate-supply curve. In this sense, those who favor indexing claim that it would help fight inflation.

There is opposition to indexing as an instrument of macroeconomic policy. Many say that indexing amounts to giving up the fight to stop inflation. If all were protected from it, who would step forward to try to stop it? Also, there are doubts that indexing really could be done fairly and effectively. It is hard to imagine a truly general and complete indexing system that would not leave out some people in the society. Further arguments arise about choosing the particular price-index number to use for the system. Some indexes benefit some groups, and other indexes benefit other groups. Even if it were decided to use different indexes for different groups, the arguments in setting up the system could be endless.

WAGE AND PRICE CONTROLS

Wage and price controls are another way that economic policy works through the supply side of the economy. These controls are limits imposed by law on increases in wage rates and prices. Sometimes the controls are very precise and rigid, as when all prices and wage rates are "frozen"—

that is, when they are not allowed to change at all. At other times they are more flexible, as when an official agency is given the power to approve or disapprove proposed changes in wage rates and prices. Sometimes the controls are mandatory, meaning that persons who violate the laws may be fined or put in prison or both. When violators cannot be officially punished, the controls are said to be voluntary (sometimes called **wage and price guidelines**). When controls are used throughout the whole economy and attempts are made to coordinate wages and prices to reach a certain set of goals, the controls are part of an **incomes policy.**

Wage and price controls have been used at one time or another in most organized economies of the world. They are a standard feature of planned economies, where the major sectors of the economy normally operate under controls. In market economies, the inflationary biases of demand-side economic policies often have led to direct controls over wage rates, prices, profits, and outputs. The United States imposed a full set of controls during World War II and less-comprehensive controls during the Korean War. Wage and price guidelines were used during the 1960s and 1970s, by both Republican and Democratic administrations. In 1971, President Nixon, faced with severe inflation and serious international payments problems, placed a ninety-day freeze on all wages and prices. This was followed by a comprehensive system of controls that were applied to the economy with varying degrees of stringency until they were removed in April 1974. After these controls were removed, the price level leaped upward, leading most observers to conclude that the controls had only suppressed inflation but had not prevented it. In fact, many believed that the controls disrupted the economy so much that production was lower and the price level higher than they would have been had the controls never been used.

Changing the *SRAS* Curve

Wage and price controls are treated together with supply-side economics because their aim is to change the shape of the short-run aggregate-

FIGURE 17-4 Wage and Price Controls and the Short-Run Aggregate-Supply Curve

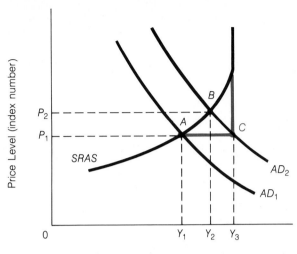

Real National Income and Product
(billions of dollars)

Wage and price controls can be used in an attempt to make the short-run aggregate-supply curve horizontal at the existing price level. Starting from equilibrium at A, a shift of aggregate demand from AD_1 to AD_2 would, in the absence of wage and price controls, produce a new short-run equilibrium at B, with price level P_2 and real national income and product Y_2. However, if wage and price controls work perfectly, the SRAS curve would become horizontal at price level P_1 and the shift in aggregate demand would produce equilibrium at C, with real national income and product of Y_3 and no change in the price level.

supply curve. This is illustrated in Figure 17-4. Suppose that equilibrium exists at point A, with price level P_1 and real national income and product Y_1. Now let the aggregate-demand curve shift to the right, from AD_1 to AD_2, perhaps from wartime spending or perhaps as a policy initiative to reduce unemployment. In this situation, the theories that you have studied lead economists to predict that short-run macroeconomic equilibrium will move to point B, with a larger real national income and product (Y_2) and a higher price level (P_2). These theories also suggest that the inflation will set the stage for a leftward shift of the SRAS curve and stagflation when wage–cost gaps and money illusion fade away. More-

over, inflationary expectations that could lead to still further leftward shifts of the short-run aggregate-supply curve may be built up.

If a national emergency is felt to exist, as is likely in these circumstances, strong sentiment may arise in favor of wage and price controls to hold prices at the original level (P_1). In terms of Figure 17-4, the aim of these controls is to make the SRAS curve horizontal at this price level. If the controls are effective and if patriotic enthusiasm encourages people to work hard, macroeconomic equilibrium might be reached at point C on the horizontal part of the SRAS curve, with price level P_1 and real national income and product at Y_3. Under these ideal assumptions about the effectiveness of wage and price controls, aggregate demand could be increased to achieve absolute full employment with no increase in the price level. Having prevented inflation, the controls might also prevent subsequent leftward shifts of the SRAS curve and the stagflation that would result.

Problems with Wage and Price Controls

Experience indicates that wage and price controls do not in practice achieve the ideal results illustrated in Figure 17-4. Part of the problem is that controls inevitably lead to rationing and other enforcement problems. In addition, the social, political, and economic compromises built into the control program sooner or later break down. Price controls and rationing were introduced in Chapter 5. Let us re-examine these problems in our present context.

Rationing of goods and services is likely to be used along with wage and price controls, especially if these controls are expected to remain in effect for very long. The reason for rationing is easily understood from the supply and demand curves shown in Figure 17-5. These curves represent seller and buyer plans and include the inflationary pressures that price and wage controls are trying to combat. For this reason, the equilibrium price P_1 shown by the intersection of these curves is above the price set by the controls, which is shown as P_2. At the controlled price,

FIGURE 17-5   Rationing and Price Controls

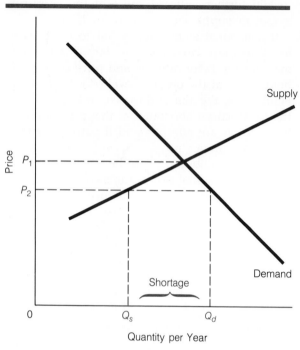

Quantity per Year

The supply curve and the demand curve include inflationary pressures that wage and price controls are designed to combat. Without controls, the equilibrium price is P_1. The controlled price for this good or service is illustrated by P_2. At this price, the quantity demanded is Q_d, where this controlled price meets the demand curve. The quantity supplied is Q_s, where the controlled price meets the supply curve. A shortage is shown by the distance between Q_d and Q_s. Rationing is used to divide up the available supply (Q_s) and to hold down pressures for prices to rise above P_2.

the quantity demanded (Q_d) is greater than the quantity supplied (Q_s), and there are shortages.

Rationing systems are intended to divide up the limited quantities of goods and services actually supplied under wage and price controls and thereby to relieve some of the upward pressure on prices. Ration coupons are issued to each individual or household for each of the various goods subject to rationing. Then, when a purchase is made, the buyer must give the merchant the required number of ration coupons along with the money price of the item bought. Aside from

the complexity of the system itself, a major problem is that illegal ("black") markets arise that do not require coupons and that sell rationed items at illegally high prices. Moreover, since rationing cannot cover all the goods and services that people want to buy, spending power not usable for rationed items may spill over and increase demand for nonrationed items, putting extra upward pressure on their prices. During wartime emergencies, patriotic appeals encourage cooperation with price controls and rationing, but problems increase the longer the system is in operation. Shortages become more severe and black markets more widespread. Only totalitarian systems can make rationing work over extended periods of time.

The second type of problem encountered by wage and price controls involves the complicated set of compromises and assurances needed to gain the political support needed to adopt and maintain controls. Besides rationing, the plan is likely to call for subsidies to industries that are asked to operate at a loss under the controlled prices and deficits for government operations that buy or import food or other goods for the public. In countries where public payrolls are a large part of total labor income, civil service wage rates are often frozen, leading to corruption, absenteeism, and poor performance on the job.

Ultimately the major problems with wage and price controls spring from hard facts of both life and arithmetic. The arithmetic fact is that it is impossible to fix the prices of two goods without automatically fixing the ratio between them. But flexibility of relative prices is essential in any economy as conditions change. The relative prices of some goods must rise, and the relative prices of other goods must fall. If these changes do not occur, shortages will appear in some markets and surpluses in others.

The facts of life are that no set of price or wage ratios can satisfy all the parties concerned even after their leaders have accepted it. For this reason, after the controls have been in place for a few months or years and the original "emergency" has somewhat subsided, they may begin to break down. Sometimes black markets expand into second economies, militants appear among the pressure groups, and there are wildcat strikes, slowdowns, and shutdowns in protest against one or another part of the system. There may be a breakdown of the controls, as in the United States after World War II and after the Nixon controls of 1971–1973 and in Britain from 1976 to 1979. At other times the country may resort to martial law or similar dictatorial methods to reinforce the system, as in Poland in 1956, 1970, and 1980–1982.

SUPPLY-SIDE ECONOMICS

So far in this chapter, we have discussed wage and price controls, inflationary expectations, and supply shocks caused by events external to the economy. All of these deal with the supply side of the economy, but they are not what is meant by supply-side economics as the term is used in the 1980s. Mainstream supply-side economists, such as those especially prominent in the first Reagan administration, are not much interested in holding the aggregate-supply curve in place in order to suppress the inflationary results of demand-side economic policies. Instead, they want to take the initiative to shift the aggregate-supply curve, both short-run and long-run, to the right. That is, they want to raise the production capability and performance of the economy.

Figure 17-6 shows how supply-side economics works. Let's say that point A stands for a recession situation or an unsatisfactorily low level of real national income and product. Assume also that policy makers have identified a real national income and product of Y_2 to be a level that could be achieved if constructive supply-side actions were taken. The main thrust of supply-side policy is to shift both short-run and long-run aggregate-supply curves to the right. In terms of Figure 17-6 (which shows short-run aggregate-supply curves only), supply-side policy makers want to shift the short-run aggregate-supply curve from $SRAS_1$ to $SRAS_2$.

Among the tools that supply-side economists want to use to shift the aggregate-supply curve are tax cuts mainly for corporations and for

FIGURE 17-6   Supply-Side Economics

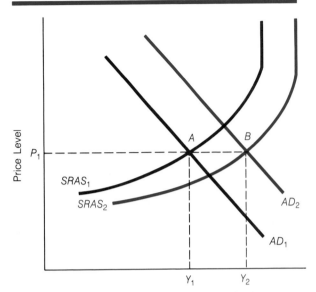

Real National Income and Product

The initial situation is real national income and product level Y_1 and price level P_1, with equilibrium at A. Supply-side action tries to shift aggregate supply from $SRAS_1$ to $SRAS_2$ through tax reductions and through deregulation. The goal is to bring the economy into equilibrium at B, with real national income and product at Y_2. Supply-side economists hope that tax cuts and expanded production will shift aggregate demand just enough to bring about this equilibrium, which maintains the original price level.

higher-income individuals, and also the freeing of private business from government regulations. These moves are intended to give a green light to investments and to innovation. Business profits, both before and after taxes, are expected to rise and to encourage more investment. The tax cuts for higher-income groups are designed to encourage saving and help provide funds for these investments. Since innovation and investment take time, these measures reveal the long-run point of view that characterizes many supply-side economists.

The tax cuts and similar measures used by the supply-siders are also expected to shift the aggregate-demand curve to the right. In Figure 17-6, we show aggregate demand shifting from

321

AD_1 to AD_2, which is just enough to hold the initial price level and to arrive at the desired equilibrium level of real national income and product at Y_2. This is a "best-case" scenario. Aggregate demand has expanded just enough to reach the target level but not far enough to set off demand-pull inflation. How likely is this to happen? In trying to answer this question, we shall describe two of the problems of supply-side economics and some responses to them as well.

Say's Identity Again?

Doubters of the supply-side approach say that by shifting aggregate demand just enough to hit their target, supply-siders come close to reasserting **Say's Identity,** that supply creates its own demand at the supply-price level. These critics say that there is no reason to expect that the expansion of production and the fiscal measures that brought it about will necessarily lead to just the right amount of aggregate demand.

The supply-siders' answer is much like that of physicians about "normal" body temperatures or the normal values of any other life sign. That is, they say that any failure of the identity is a symptom of something that is wrong with the working of the economy—such as overly high tax rates or excessive regulation. So if aggregate demand doesn't shift to the proper level, it is not the policy but "something else" in the economy that must be corrected. When that "something else" is corrected, then Say's Identity will return, just as body temperature returns to 98.6 degrees when measles or pneumonia has been cured.

The Laffer Curve

The second problem for supply-side economics has to do with the possibility that tax cuts will cause large government deficits and that financing these deficits will raise interest rates, crowding out the private investment that supply-siders hope to increase through their tax cuts.

The supply-side counterargument is based on the **Laffer curve,** pictured in Figure 17-7. The

FIGURE 17-7   The Laffer Curve

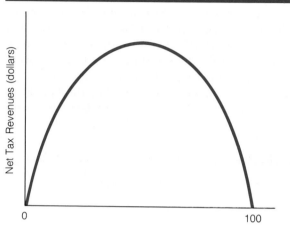

The Laffer curve illustrates the proposition that net tax revenues increase as average net tax rates increase, but only up to a point. If net tax rates go too high, net revenues actually coming into the government may fall. This is shown on the right side of the curve, where it has a negative slope. Some supply-siders suggest that the United States is on the right side of the curve so that reductions in tax rates would actually increase net tax revenues.

vertical axis shows the net tax revenues of government, and the horizontal axis shows the average net tax rate. The curve itself displays Arthur Laffer's idea of how net tax revenues respond to changes in average tax rates.[1] As you can see, no revenue would be collected if the tax rate were zero. But neither would any be collected at a tax rate of 100 percent, since no one would find it worthwhile to work if government took all the earnings. In between, the Laffer curve suggests that tax revenues will rise as average tax rates rise, but only up to a point. If tax rates rise above a certain level, the level corresponding to the peak of the curve, the work-discouraging effects of rate increases more than offset their revenue-raising effects, and total revenue falls.

1. Arthur Laffer, professor of economics at the University of Southern California and prominent advisor to President Reagan during his first administration, is at this writing an economic consultant and political candidate.

Many supply-side economists, and among them Arthur Laffer himself, claim that the United States and many other countries are on the right-hand side of the curve. If this is true, supply-side policies can avoid large deficits, and there should be no crowding out of private investment. Lower tax rates could in fact raise tax revenues. Many economists, however, are not persuaded that the United States really is on the right-hand side of the curve.

KEYNESIANS, MONETARISTS, AND SUPPLY-SIDERS

You have studied the three mainstream schools of modern macroeconomic thought—Keynesianism, monetarism, and supply-side economics. Now it is time to put them together in the context of actual policy making.

The Keynesian school of thought, which stresses the demand-side approach and was explained in detail in Chapters 9, 10, and 11, springs from the work of J. M. Keynes in the 1930s. The Keynesian approach dominated U.S. economic policy most of the time for forty years after Keynes wrote the *General Theory* but his theories could not explain or cure the stagflation that brought both inflation and unemployment to the economy in the mid-1970s.

The supply-side approach, which has been explained in this chapter and in Chapter 15, came to prominence because of the problems that arose from aggregate-supply shifts in the mid-1970s. Some of these shifts came from outside events, such as the OPEC increases in the price of crude oil, and some came as reactions to price-level increases that started in the late 1960s as results of Vietnam war spending and government Great Society programs. Supply-side economics is the youngest of today's mainstream macroeconomic doctrines, although its roots can be found in Adam Smith and classical economics. Like the Keynesians, supply-side economists are activists and believe government should take an active role in promoting the growth and vitality of the economy.

Monetarism is the third mainstream school of macroeconomic thought. In many ways, monetarism is a halfway house between demand-side and supply-side macroeconomic policy. As you learned from the historical account of the Great Depression (Chapter 10), monetarism has its doctrinal roots in neoclassical economic thought, which came after Adam Smith and the classicals but before Keynes and the Keynesians. During the past fifty years, the monetarist view has usually been expressed as a counterargument against the prevailing Keynesian positions. However, monetarist views gained prominence during the 1970s, when Keynesian solutions appeared ineffective.

Monetarism is also a halfway house in its political-economic position, favoring little or no government intervention in the economy, on either the demand side or the supply side. The standard form of the monetarism doctrine comes from Milton Friedman (1912–   ) and his followers. From his study of the historical record in the United States, Friedman concludes that government intervention or fine tuning of the economy, whether done with fiscal or with monetary tools, makes matters worse rather than better. Such action, he feels, will slow down or reverse the natural adjustments that bring about equilibrium, and will destabilize the economy. In fact, he argues that government should not try to manipulate aggregate demand in any way. For this reason, he cannot be called a demand-sider. But neither does he favor government efforts to manipulate aggregate supply. So he cannot be called a supply-sider either.

Reaganomics

Supply-side economists played a major part in the economic strategies of both Reagan administrations. However, "Reaganomics" is not supply-side alone. In fact, **Reaganomics** is less a coherent economic philosophy than a shifting balance among the positions of various groups that backed Reagan on economic grounds in the elections of 1980 and 1984. With respect to macroeconomic policy, Reagan's supporters fall into

three major groups. These are (1) the anti-inflationists, who are mostly monetarist; (2) the anti-
high-taxers, who are mostly supply-siders; and
(3) the anti-high-interest-rate group, which includes both monetarists and supply-siders. A
fourth important group, which is not primarily
economic, favors more defense spending.

Supply-side influence was apparent in major
tax reductions that were enacted early in the first
Reagan administration. The corporation income
tax was revised to offer substantial incentives for
investment. Reductions in individual income tax
rates were phased in over a three-year period
and, starting in 1985, exemptions, rates, and other
features of the tax were indexed to keep step
automatically with inflation. Meanwhile, restraints were imposed on government spending
for social programs. However, these restraints
failed to hold the line against higher budget
deficits, chiefly because of substantial increases
in defense expenditure. In both Reagan administrations, major political battles were waged on
the issues of increased defense spending, of
spending for social programs, and of tax reduction. Huge budget deficits arose. As a reaction to
these, the **Gramm-Rudman-Hollings Act,** passed
in late 1985, required a balanced budget by 1991
and established procedures for achieving this
goal.

Monetary policy made headlines, especially in
the first Reagan administration. Unemployment
rates were very high. In addition, the large budget
deficits raised fears that government borrowing
would crowd out private investments, upsetting
supply-side plans for shifting the aggregate-supply
curve. Great pressure was placed on the Board
of Governors of the Federal Reserve System to
lower interest rates and to accommodate the
government borrowing with increases in the money
supply. But the double-digit inflation experience
of the late 1970s raised fears that money-supply
increases might trigger inflationary expectations
and another bout with stagflation. Monetary policy tried, successfully in retrospect, to maintain
a knife-edge balance between too much and too
little monetary expansion.

The Reagan economic policies received considerable help from a weakening of world petroleum

prices as the Organization of Petroleum Exporting
Countries encountered both external and internal
problems. High prices reduced quantities demanded while new petroleum production from
nonmember areas (the North Sea, Mexico, and
Alaska) further reduced sales by OPEC members.
The temptation to exceed quotas set by the cartel
was irresistible to many OPEC member countries.
When they exceeded their quotas, lowered their
prices, and increased their sales, the remaining
members suffered and OPEC itself was forced, in
effect, to recognize the new lower prices for oil.

Led by declining prices for crude oil, the inflation rate in the United States declined much faster
than most economists expected in the early and
middle 1980s. Also, the pro-business policies of
the Reagan administration encouraged foreigners
to make financial investments in the United States.
The combination of relatively attractive investment opportunities, impressive reductions in the
inflation rate, and high real interest rates brought
a flood of foreign funds into U.S. financial markets
(note the connection between foreign markets
and U.S. financial markets in Figure 8-4, page
140). To a significant extent, the inflow of foreign
funds eased the pressure of government borrowing in the financial markets. By 1985 the dollar
had risen to very high levels relative to foreign
monies, encouraging imports and discouraging
exports. As of this writing, early in 1986, the
dollar had fallen back significantly from its 1985
high.

Economic Theory and Economic Policy

In the preview to Chapter 16, we observed that
"theory informs policy." We then described how
the Keynesian theory guided macroeconomic policy making in the United States in the post–World
War II period and up to the 1970s, when supply
shocks and stagflation cast a shadow over the
Keynesian approach. Monetarist and supply-side
approaches became more popular and were reflected in the policies of the latter part of the
Carter administration and in the Reagan administrations. But economic theories have great stay-

ing power. Actions taken by the Reagan administrations were at least as much Keynesian and monetarist as supply-side oriented and external events, such as the weakening of OPEC, contributed greatly to U.S. economic recovery.

As of this writing in early 1986, it is much too early to know whether the Gramm-Rudman-Hollings Act, passed in December 1985, will mark the start of a period in which less emphasis will be placed on government deficits and surpluses as instruments of macroeconomic policy. This legislation calls for a balanced federal government budget by 1991 and specifies steps that are to be taken to achieve this goal. However, it also states that the balanced budget requirement can be set aside whenever unemployment is expected to rise to unacceptable levels. In this sense, it is as much a reaffirmation as a rejection of the Keynesian theory and of the acceptability of fiscal instruments for dealing with macroeconomic unemployment.

It is not likely that Keynesian economics will be completely set aside in the years ahead any more than monetary economics could be completely set aside during the heyday of Keynesian policies in the 1950s and 1960s. Instead we are likely to see all three of the major schools of macroeconomic thought—Keynesian, monetarist, and supply-side—still playing a part in policy making. Since most nonradical economists agree with one another on at least nine-tenths of the theoretical building blocks of their discipline, modern economic policy is likely to be a mixture of demand-side and supply-side thinking. Your training in macroeconomics should help you to understand the main elements of economic policy.

SUMMARY

1. Supply shocks are events that shift the aggregate-supply curve. Shocks that reduce production shift the curve to the left, and those that increase production shift it to the right. Demand-side responses to downward supply shocks face a conflict between more inflation and more unemployment. For both contractionary and expan-

sionary supply shocks, supply-side responses try to speed adjustments to changed relative prices.

2. Inflationary expectations bring shifts to the left of the short-run aggregate-supply curve when people expect inflation and change their behavior in order to meet the coming price-level increases. If the aggregate-demand curve does not shift, inflationary expectations bring both higher prices and higher unemployment. If aggregate demand accommodates the expectations, the economy can stay at effective full employment, but the inflationary expectations will be confirmed, so that the inflation rate will continue into the future.

3. Accelerating inflation can happen if demand-side policies try to hold the economy above effective full employment. To do so, actual inflation rates must stay ahead of expected inflation rates, so that money illusion and wage–cost lags persist.

4. Decelerating inflation can be brought about if the aggregate-demand curve is shifted to the left during a time when inflation is going on or if demand-side policies refuse to accommodate inflationary expectations. Unemployment will increase and the inflation rate will decrease. When the reduced inflation rate is built into expectations, so that the short-run aggregate-supply curve shifts to the right, inflation can be brought under control and the price level stabilized.

5. Rational expectations theory suggests that people will come to recognize the inflationary consequences of demand-side policies, so that the short-run aggregate-supply curve will shift to the left almost immediately when the expansionary policies are undertaken. Thus, expansionary demand-side policies will not move the economy away from effective full employment but will only bring higher price levels.

6. Indexing is a system that automatically builds actual inflation into the terms of contracts that have a time dimension. It can be a tool to fight inflation caused by expectations, because, with indexing, people need not negotiate for higher wages or interest rates to protect themselves. However, there are difficult problems in actually setting up indexing systems.

7. Wage and price controls are attempts to change the shape of the short-run aggregate-supply curve

after expansionary demand-side actions have been taken. Price controls have often been tried, but have always failed to stop inflation when pressures for inflation persist in the economy. The main problem with controls is that usually they are not able to make needed responses to changes inside the economy.

8. Rationing is usually needed to go along with wage and price controls. This is because shortages will arise when the legal price is below the free market equilibrium price for a good or service. Rationing tries to divide up the available supply of the product and to reduce pressures for price increases.

9. Mainstream supply-side economics tries to shift the aggregate-supply curve, both short- and long-run, to the right through actions taken by economic policy. Supply-side policies usually include tax cuts for business and higher-income individuals and the freeing of private business from government regulations. The aim is to stimulate investment and innovation.

10. Problems with supply-side economic policies include the question of whether the policies that shift the aggregate-supply curve will also shift the aggregate-demand curve enough so that the added production will be demanded at the original price level. This is the question of whether Say's Identity will hold for the policies.

11. The Laffer curve illustrates another issue involving supply-side economic policies. The Laffer-curve argument suggests that reductions in tax rates may actually bring increases in government tax collections. If the Laffer argument doesn't work, supply-side economic policies might bring large government deficits that could crowd out the desired increases in private investment.

12. Modern macroeconomic policy making involves continuing interaction among the three mainstream schools of economic thought—Keynesianism, monetarism, and supply-side economics. Monetarism is a halfway house between demand-side and supply-side approaches.

13. Reaganomics is a mixture of several macroeconomic policy approaches. Most recent administrations have adopted mixtures that reflect the differing points of view that appeared to be most favored in the society at that time.

DISCUSSION QUESTIONS

1. Leftward shifts of supply curves due to external events are not very unusual in specific industries, but such shocks must be quite large and widespread to affect the aggregate-supply curve for the whole economy. Identify one or two external events (in addition to the oil embargo and food-price changes mentioned in the text) that might be large enough to be a supply shock for the entire economy and explain why their effects would be large. Consider both expansionary and contractionary shocks.

2. In the face of the stagflation effects of a leftward supply shock, many calls will be heard for demand-side action to deal with the situation. Explain the dilemma facing those favoring demand-side action in this case. If you were in a position to direct demand-side action, would you hold the aggregate-demand curve stable, shift it to the right, or compromise? Justify your choice.

3. What is the difference between a shift of the short-run aggregate-supply curve that comes from a wearing off of wage–cost lags and money illusion from past inflation and a shift of that curve that comes from inflationary expectations? Carefully explain this difference. What will happen if the shift coming from inflationary expectations is not accommodated by demand-side macroeconomic policy? What will happen if the shift is accommodated by demand-side action?

4. "You can fool some of the people all the time and all of the people some of the time, but you can't fool all of the people all of the time." How does this well-known saying relate to the proposition that unemployment can be kept below its natural rate through a policy of accelerating inflation? How does it relate to the rational expectations theory?

5. For the sake of argument, set aside the theory of rational expectations for a moment. An accelerating inflation policy justifies inflation by its effects on employment. How would you justify a policy of decelerating inflation aimed at bringing about a stable price level? Could you justify a policy of absolute deflation? Explain.

6. Check back to Chapter 6 on index numbers to find a basis for deciding whether you would

prefer to have your wage or salary indexed according to the consumer price index or the GNP deflator. What is your choice? Why? Should an indexing system use different adjustments depending on where a person lives in the country? Should farm people have a different index from city dwellers? Explain.

7. Draw an aggregate demand–aggregate supply graph, shift the aggregate-demand curve to the right, and then change the shape of the short-run aggregate-supply curve to show how wage and price controls try to prevent demand-pull inflation. Do you believe wage and price controls are justified in wartime? Are they justified in peacetime? Explain each of your answers. If you answer "yes" in one case and "no" in the other, explain the basis for the difference.

8. Suppose that prices for gasoline and for heating oil are frozen at the levels prevailing at some time during the summer, when the demand for gasoline is high and the demand for heating oil is low. What might happen when winter comes if, in a free market, the price of gasoline ordinarily would fall and the price of heating oil ordinarily would rise? Discuss your answer, considering surpluses, shortages, and pressures for easing price controls.

9. Why does supply-side economics suggest tax cuts for business and for high-income groups rather than for poor or middle-income people? Construct a graph illustrating the "best-case" scenario for supply-side expansion of the economy. Compare this graph with Figure 17-6. Why does this best case come close to asserting Say's Identity? Explain.

10. Construct a Laffer-curve diagram and compare it with Figure 17-7. Be sure the axes are labeled correctly. Why might this curve offer help to supply-side economic policies if the United States is on the right-hand part of the curve? Would the same be true if the United States were on the left-hand side of the curve? Explain. Is it necessary that the curve be drawn as smooth and symmetrical as we have shown it? Explain.

11. In what sense is monetarism a halfway house between supply-side and demand-side economics? If, after studying macroeconomic theories, you were to classify your views, would you call yourself a Keynesian, a monetarist, a supply-sider, or an "eclectic" (a mixture of all)? Explain your views. Listen to the views of others.

Macroeconomic Policy:
From the New Frontier to Supply Side

Keynesian stabilization policy reached its zenith not in Keynes's native Britain but across the Atlantic in the United States, and not during Lord Keynes's lifetime but, more than fifteen years later, in a brief five-year period under Presidents John F. Kennedy and Lyndon B. Johnson (1961 to approximately 1966).

Policies of the New Frontier

The economics of "practical Keynesianism" on the Kennedy–Johnson "New Frontier"—sometimes called "Camelot" after King Arthur's castle—may be summarized in a half-dozen propositions.

1. Like other variants of Keynesian doctrine, the economics of the New Frontier concentrated on the maintenance and increase of aggregate demand, while rather neglecting aggregate supply. Some critics have devised a short statement called "Keynes's Law," which Keynes might have rejected but which found some backing in the United States: aggregate demand creates aggregate supply until full employment is reached.[1] Also, the growth path of full-employment GNP was taken as given. It might respond to technological progress or decline, to war and epidemic, and to the discovery and exhaustion of natural resources—but not to macroeconomic policy in the ordinary monetary and fiscal senses of the term.

2. Fiscal policy (government receipts, expenditures, surpluses, and deficits) bears primary responsibility for determining the level of income and employment. Although supportive of the Employment Act of 1946, the economics of the New Frontier did not extend so far as to involve any legal obligation for the government to act as employer of last resort or otherwise provide work for everyone.[2]

To the disappointment of surviving New Dealers from the 1930s and 1940s, expansive fiscal policy to practical Keynesians meant cuts in federal tax rates rather than new programs of public expenditure. In the climate of recovery from a mild recession, these cuts raised total revenues rather than lowering them. It is questionable how long such a policy would have continued, even had President Kennedy survived and the Vietnam War not exploded. President Kennedy had read Michael Harrington's *The Other America,* the intellectual inspiration for the War on Poverty, and Walter Heller, Chairman of the Council of Economic Advisers, was preparing the groundwork for expenditure increases well before the assassination of the President.

3. Okun's Law was another basic proposition for the practical Keynesians. This law is a statistical generalization from actual U.S. experience during the 1950s and early 1960s when a real GNP growth rate of 3.75 percent a year had kept the unemployment rate approximately stable. The law stated that the measured unemployment rate would fall by one percentage point for every three percentage points by which the growth rate of real GNP exceeded 3.75 percent (and vice versa). If measured labor productivity were to rise, the 3.75 figure would rise and more rapid growth would be needed to "stay in the same place" with regard to unemployment. In addition, the 3-to-1 ratio would fall and fewer new workers would be required to accommodate any increase in the growth rate.

4. The Phillips curve was another hallmark of the economics of the New Frontier. To lower the unemployment rate, the Phillips curve maintains, one must accept some

---

1. Thus "Keynes's Law" stands Say's Law or Say's Identity (see p. 156) on its head.

2. This extension of Keynesian doctrine was proposed later, in the Humphrey-Hawkins bill of the late 1970s. It was not, however, included in the Humphrey-Hawkins Act as passed in 1978.

President John F. Kennedy

Decline of the New Frontier

The New Frontier combination of policies is credited by its supporters with keeping the American growth rates high, and the American unemployment and inflation rates both low, during the half-decade 1961 to 1965 inclusive. It also gave economics, particularly Keynesian macroeconomics, a certain scientific prestige and self-confidence, which it had seldom possessed earlier and has yet to regain. At the height of its success, such confidence led President Richard Nixon (Johnson's Republican successor) to assure the public that "we are all Keynesians now."

What closed the New Frontier was not any failure of formal economic analysis but three external shocks, to which policy was prevented from adjusting by political reasons of short-term "votefare." The first shock was the explosion of the American intervention in Vietnam to a full-scale war. The second shock was President Johnson's refusal to discontinue a second "war"—the domestic "War on Poverty"—or to raise taxes, and his determination to finance both wars at once by deficit financing and monetary expansion. (His political rationale was that raising taxes, tightening money, or postponing the War on Poverty would have increased opposition to the already unpopular Vietnam conflict.) The third shock (or after-shock) was the sudden quadrupling of the world price of oil by OPEC in 1973–1974, with a further upward jump after the Iranian revolution of 1979.

Six New Frontiersmen

Many eminent young economists assisted Lord Keynes's ghost in framing New Frontier economic ideas. From their number we have chosen a half-dozen: Walter Heller, Lawrence Klein, Arthur Okun, Paul Samuelson, Robert Solow, and James Tobin. They had many things in common. None was over forty-five years old when President Kennedy was inaugurated. All had lived as children, teenagers, or young adults through the Great Depression. All had been converted to both the New Deal and Keynesian economics. Most came from, and returned to, prestigious academic posts. Three of the six received Nobel Prizes in economics after their New Frontier days. (These prizes were awarded for the first time in 1969.)

acceleration of inflation. Price stability was estimated by Paul Samuelson and Robert Solow in 1960 to require a 6 to 7 percent unemployment rate.

5. The economics of the New Frontier admitted that money matters, but the primary role of monetary policy was to regulate the inflation rate and the (nominal) interest rate. When these could not be regulated simultaneously, it was usually considered more important to try to slow or prevent rises in interest rates than rises in the price level.

6. The practical Keynesians cared deeply about income distribution. They sought to increase the share of workers (as distinguished from property owners) in the national income and also the measured degree of equality in the personal distribution of income. Distributional considerations prompted these economists to favor low interest rates over high ones, and likewise to favor progressive direct taxes on income and estates over indirect taxes on sales in general, and on specific commodities like tobacco, liquor, and gasoline.

• **Walter Heller** (1915–   , University of Minnesota): Heller was Chairman of the Kennedy Council of Economic Advisers. Specializing in public finance and taxation, he was the principal architect of the Kennedy fiscal policy. Perhaps more important, he is a superb communicator. He retains a certain common touch that belies his expertise and eminence.

• **Lawrence Klein** (1920–   , University of Pennsylvania): Nobel laureate and author of *The Keynesian Revolution,* Klein became the macroeconomic complete-system model-builder *par excellence.* He tended to remain in the background, lest his youthful radicalism embarrass the administration, but the fundamental "numbers" of its policies were worked out and articulated by methods of his devising if not actually by his group at the Wharton School.

• **Arthur Okun** (1928–1980, Yale University and Brookings Institution): "Okun's Law" is the principal memorial of his statistical and forecasting services to the Kennedy administration, but he later served as President Johnson's last Chairman of the Council of Economic Advisers. His interest in income distribution is reflected in his best-known book, *Equality and Efficiency, the Great Trade-Off,* and his interest in labor problems in his *Prices and Quantities.* This posthumous work presented a theory of "implicit contracts" in labor relations, which keep both money and real wages rigid downward and impervious to monetary and fiscal policy, until substantial unemployment has developed.

• **Paul Samuelson** (1915–   , Massachusetts Institute of Technology): Nobel laureate and leader of his generation of American Keynesians, Samuelson has written at every level, from letters to the editor through *Newsweek* columns and twelve editions of a textbook on *Economics* to mathematical and philosophical explorations in the most learned of the scholarly journals. He has contributed to almost every branch of macroeconomics, microeconomics, international economics, mathematical economics, and economic methodology. As a student, for example, he fitted the first statistical consumption function. Rather than accepting service in Washington, Samuelson has preferred the role of power behind the intellectual throne.

• **Robert Solow** (1924–   , Massachusetts Institute of Technology): Solow's principal scholarly contributions have been in growth theory, in the study of capital and investment, and in the econometrics of production functions. He is known for his application (with Samuelson) of the Phillips curve to American data. We might mention also an essay, "The Case Against the Case Against the Guideposts," in which Solow defended "jawboning" methods of price and wage control. Like Heller, Solow is a celebrated communicator.

• **James Tobin** (1918–   , Yale University): Nobel laureate and author of a series of articles on portfolio theory, he served with Heller on Kennedy's Council of Economic Advisers. As monetary theorist, as econometrician, and on questions of income distribution, the quiet and unpretentious Tobin has retained his Keynesianism through thick and thin, including a strong and often-repeated preference for inflation (even accelerating inflation) over any tolerance of continued unemployment.

Successors to the New Frontiersmen: Monetarists and Supply-Siders

The New Frontier is by no means dead, particularly within the Democratic Party. It may well revive if the Democrats recapture control of the federal administration. For the present, however, interest has tended to focus on two rival groups of successors, almost as hostile to each other as to Keynesianism. Some of these are called monetarists and some supply-siders. Despite their mutual hostility, they are often confused in the popular press. Both have played important parts in the Reagan administrations, while struggling among themselves for the economic "soul" of the President. The supply-siders appear to have won most of the earlier battles, but the war remains undecided.

Monetarism has already been discussed in this and earlier parts of this book. Let us review its tenets briefly.

1. The money supply, however defined, is the principal determinant of aggregate demand. In particular, it is more important than autonomous expenditures. (This is a mild and general restatement of the quantity theory of money.)
2. The money supply exercises its influence not immediately but later, with a long and variable lag pattern that economists do not understand at all well. (In general, monetary influences on real income and product come before such influences on the price level, but the price-level effects often counteract the real-income ones.)
3. The historical record suggests that discretionary monetary policy, whether exercised by politicians, bankers,

businessmen, or academic experts, has not waited for the lag pattern to work itself out. The result has often been to accentuate economic fluctuations. It would therefore be better to replace such discretion by a monetary rule that would require some monetary aggregate to grow steadily at a rate approximating the long-term growth rate of real GNP, despite any resulting fluctuations in the rate of interest. But monetarists do not agree among themselves on what the monetary rule should be—whether the monetary aggregate should be the monetary base, M1, or M2, and what account (if any) should be taken of shifts in the demand for money (Keynes's "liquidity preference"), as reflected in changes in the measured velocity of monetary circulation.

4. We should also mention a subgroup, the so-called "rational expectations" school. These writers believe that the markets' responses to policy changes are rational—and in particular, that they do not include money illusion. They also believe that the economy is always in a neighborhood of equilibrium, with all Phillips curves nearly vertical and unemployment always near its natural rate. In such a world, policy exercises major influence only on the price level; it influences output or unemployment only when the markets have been deceived, or have deceived themselves, as to what the policy is. The best we can hope to do is to reduce the risk element in production costs by announcing and following policy rules—particularly rules about monetary growth.

Like the Keynesians, monetarists view macroeconomic policy largely as a matter of aggregate demand. Supply-siders, an even more variegated group than the monetarists, want to shift the emphasis back to aggregate supply, where it was in the glorious days of Say's Identity, when aggregate supply was counted on to create its own demand. Indeed, the supply-siders can be interpreted as implying, although not always as saying, that Say's Identity holds, at least in a well-run economy.

But what is a well-run economy, and how does it differ from the one we have? The supply-siders see the principal weaknesses of the present economy as the twin burdens of excessive taxation and excessive regulation. At the same time, they are not anarchists; they do not propose to dispense with either taxation or regulation altogether. They believe only that both should be cut back sharply, and that the cuts can readily be made together, since some of the costs of public regulation are borne by taxpayers. When it comes to specifics,

President Ronald W. Reagan

however, the supply-siders are disunited. They all believe that progression in the personal income tax has gone too far, and that corporate income-tax rates should be reduced sharply. When it comes to regulation, their favorite targets include antimonopoly legislation, delays in technical progress in the name of safety and health, and increases in the cost of employing labor—minimum wages, encouragement of trade unionism, and high relief standards, which reduce the labor supply.

One supply-side artifact in particular, the Laffer curve, caught the public eye in 1981–1982. The economist Arthur Laffer, then at the University of Southern California, argued that not only GNP but also the public revenue could be increased by a tax cut, and the deficit reduced. In addition to the curve itself, Laffer's evidence comes from two or three episodes in American economic history—including, interestingly enough, the New Frontier tax cuts of the early 1960s—and from the consequences of lowered top-bracket income-tax rates on the taxes received from high-income recipients, who were weaned from tax shelters to more productive activities. The "Reaganomic" record, however, has hardly borne out Laffer's rosy predictions.

The apparent failure of the Laffer curve, however, is explained away by supply-siders. Tight money and high interest rates, "imposed" by Federal Reserve "disinflation" policy—lowering the inflation rate—is their principal culprit. The high cost of credit, supply-siders believe, offset the effect of lower taxes on both economic activity and government receipts.[3]

Are the supply-siders, then, "soft on inflation"? The answer to this question appears to be both yes and no. Yes, in the sense of willingness to buy higher output with higher price levels. But no, in the sense of tolerating inflation rates approaching those of Germany in the early 1920s or China in the late 1940s, which seem to have reduced output rather than raising it.

3. Another explanation, favored by Laffer himself, is that the Reagan tax cuts, totalling 30 percent, were staggered over three years instead of being made all at once in 1981. Anticipation of lower taxes and more favorable treatment in 1983–1984 may indeed have delayed the supply-side effectiveness of the 1981–1982 reductions.

VI *International Trade, Economic Growth, and Economic Development*

- International Macroeconomics: Exchange Rates and The Balance of Payments
- Economic Growth and Development
- A New International Economic Order? North-South Confrontation

18 *International Macroeconomics: Exchange Rates and the Balance of Payments*

PREVIEW When people in one country trade with people in another country, the price levels in the two countries must somehow be related to one another. When people in one country make investments in another country, the interest rates in the two countries must somehow be related to one another. So far, in our macroeconomic analysis, we have not explored these relationships. In this chapter, we examine international macroeconomics, which does explore them.

It is quite unrealistic to presume that international economic relations do not affect economic behavior. After making this point, we start our analysis by examining how foreign exchange markets determine the value of a country's money in terms of the monies of other countries. From here, we go on to explain how governments sometimes intervene in the operation of these markets and try to control the exchange value of different monies. We discuss the question of whether foreign exchange rates should be fixed or free to find their own relationships, and we briefly review the history of exchange rate fixing schemes, from the gold standard to the present-day "dirty float" arrangement.

The second part of the chapter explains the balance of payments accounting system and what is meant by "favorable" or "unfavorable" balances of trade and payments. We trace the evolution of a country from immature debtor to mature creditor, and ask when a country has a balance of payments problem. Since many countries in the world today have balance of payments problems, we list and explain eight often-suggested solutions for these problems. A brief appendix to this chapter offers a more advanced analysis of international financial relationships.

THE WORLD IS ALWAYS WITH US

Before we plunge into the details of international trade and finance, let us note how important these topics are. In the United States, it is estimated that one out of every six workers owes his or her job to exports, two out of every five acres of farmland produce for export, and about 20 percent of industrial output is exported.

International trade and finance also play large roles in world politics. Early in the Great Depression, both the United States and the British Empire raised their **tariffs** (taxes on imported goods), trying to "export unemployment" to other countries by producing at home goods previously imported. The United States passed the high Hawley-Smoot tariff in 1930 to keep foreign goods out. At about the same time, Britain set up a system of Imperial Preference, or tariffs against non-Empire countries. Later other tariffs were added to protect the British Isles themselves. A major victim of these tariffs was Japan, a resource-poor country that depended upon its exports to pay for its imports of both food and industrial raw materials. Largely in order to avoid the serious economic effects expected from the Anglo-American blockage of their exports, the Japanese sought for themselves a "co-prosperity" sphere of influence in China and East Asia from which they could import the goods that they needed, and in which they could sell their exports, free from Anglo-American competition. In 1931 they set up a puppet government in Manchuria, as a source of iron ore, coal, soybeans, and salt for fertilizer. They also built up mines and factories in Manchuria. This aggression started Japan on the slippery slope toward Pearl Harbor.

We cannot say how the course of history would have been different if the United States or Great Britain or Japan had behaved differently in their international economic relations. Knowledge about how these international relationships operate will not guarantee the peaceful resolution of problems. But to understand them and search for solutions, we must learn the basics of international trade and finance.

FOREIGN EXCHANGE MARKETS

Let us start the study of international trade and finance with **foreign exchange markets,** which are markets in which the monies of different countries are exchanged (traded) for one another. In fact, **foreign exchange** simply means the money of other countries. The reason these markets are needed is that the people who produce and sell things want to be paid in the money of their own country. Therefore, if the buyer has only the money of another country, some exchange of monies must take place. It is a convenient simplification to suppose that a German who wishes to buy something from the United States must first buy American dollars and then buy the American good or service, or that an American who wishes to buy something from Japan must first buy Japanese yen and then buy the Japanese product.

A Two-Country Model

Figure 18-1 illustrates a foreign exchange market as it might exist between the U.S. dollar and the Japanese yen, assuming for the moment that these are the only monies in the world.[1] The quantity of dollars demanded and supplied in

FIGURE 18-1   Two-Country Foreign Exchange Market

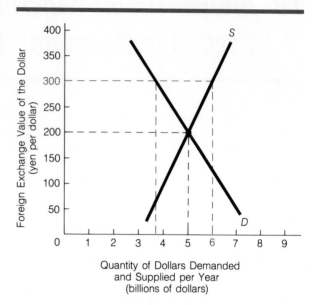

The horizontal axis shows the quantity of dollars supplied and demanded per year in international transactions. The demand comes from people and firms that wish to acquire dollars in order to complete transactions with Americans. The supply comes from those who wish to acquire foreign money (yen) in order to carry out transactions with Japan. The vertical axis shows the foreign exchange value of the dollar, that is, how many yen can be exchanged for one dollar.

international transactions is shown on the horizontal axis, and the price of these dollars is shown on the vertical axis. The price of the dollar is expressed in terms of foreign exchange, which, in this case, is Japanese yen. In this illustration, the equilibrium value of the dollar is 200 yen, balancing the quantity demanded with the quantity supplied at 5 billion dollars a year. At a higher exchange value, say, 300 yen per dollar, a greater number of dollars would be supplied, but fewer would be demanded, so that the exchange value

1. In practice, most foreign exchange transactions involve short-term government securities rather than money. But the explanation is clearer if we assume that money is exchanged.

of the dollar would tend to fall. At a lower exchange value, more dollars would be demanded but fewer supplied, pushing the exchange rate upward.

In this simple two-country illustration, part of the demand for dollars comes from Japanese who want to buy American goods and services. Some of these buyers are Japanese tourists in the United States. Others are residents of Japan who want to import American goods, such as coal or lumber, or Japanese companies that want to import American machines for their factories. Some of the demand for dollars comes from Japanese investors who want to purchase bonds or shares of stock in U.S. stock and bond markets, and some comes from Japanese who send money to relatives in the United States. A portion of the demand may also come from the Japanese government itself, if it wishes to acquire American dollars to hold as part of Japan's official reserves.[2]

The supply of dollars, on the other hand, comes from Americans who wish to buy Japanese goods or travel in Japan, who want to invest through the Japanese bond and stock markets, or who want to send money to Japanese friends or relatives. The U.S. government may even supply dollars in order to acquire yen to hold as part of its official reserves.

Multilateral Trade

Our simple model of a two-country world provides the basic idea of the demand and supply of a nation's money in international trade, but it is only of limited use in exploring international trade and finance. In practice, many countries are involved on both the demand side and the supply side of the international exchange market for dollars and other monies. In actual international finance, an American who wants to buy a Japanese product does not have to get yen directly from a Japanese who wants to buy an American product. The American may, just as well, get the

2. Official reserves will be described later in this chapter in connection with balance of payments accounting.

FIGURE 18-2   Foreign Exchange Market for the Dollar

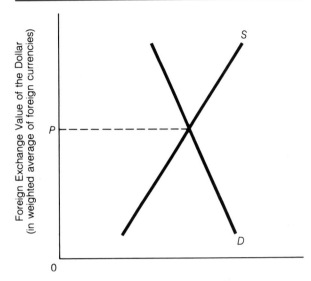

The vertical axis is measured in a weighted-average value of foreign monies. At P the quantity of dollars demanded is equal to the quantity supplied. The dollar is overvalued at exchange values above P and undervalued at exchange values below P.

yen from a German who got them by selling goods to Japan. Generally he or she buys them from banks and foreign exchange dealers who specialize in handling monies from many countries. We can still draw a graph for the U.S. dollar in the international exchange market, as in Figure 18-2, but the vertical axis now should be labeled simply as the foreign exchange value of the dollar, rather than as Japanese yen, or West German marks, or British pounds, or some other specific foreign money. For actual measurements, the units on the vertical axis are an average value of all foreign monies, "trade-weighted" by their importance in trade with the United States, without reference to capital movements involving the dollar. In practice, the units on the vertical axis are index numbers, with the exchange value of the dollar on some chosen date or base year set equal to 100. We shall simply refer to the dollar's exchange value as P so that we can say that the foreign exchange value of the dollar rises or falls, without measuring the rise or fall in any specific money. It is important to do so because the American dollar may possibly rise in its foreign exchange value even while it is falling in its exchange relation with some specific money, if that other money is rising even faster in its foreign exchange value.[3]

The Slopes of Demand and Supply Curves

In Figure 18-2, the demand and supply curves for the American dollar look much the same as demand and supply curves for actual goods and services. But there is an important difference that must be cleared up before we go on to talk about equilibrium in foreign exchange rates. Let us concentrate on the supply curve and suppose that the dollar's exchange value goes up for some reason. Does this mean that the quantity of dollars supplied to the international exchange market will increase? The answer depends on how the change in exchange value affects the behavior of the people and firms that are supplying dollars. Americans who buy foreign goods are one of these supplier groups. The increased exchange value of the dollar means that the dollar price of foreign goods has fallen. As a result, we expect that these Americans will buy more foreign goods, but we do not know how much more they will buy. Suppose that the exchange value of the dollar rises by 10 percent and that, as a result, Americans purchase 10 percent more foreign goods. Is there any change in the number of dollars supplied to the international exchange market? The answer is no, because the effective

cut in the unit price of foreign goods exactly cancels the increase in the number of these goods bought. In this situation, the supply curve of dollars in the international exchange market would be a vertical line.

This exercise tells you that when we draw a positively sloping supply curve for dollars, we are assuming that Americans (and others who supply dollars) are quite sensitive to changes in the dollar's exchange value—so sensitive in fact that their response in actual buying and investment and so on is more than proportional to the change in the dollar's exchange value. This is a reasonable assumption that is borne out by experience in normal times. It often does not hold for short time periods or in abnormal times.

The responsiveness conditions that we have just outlined for the supply curve also apply to the demand curve for the dollar. In this case, the reasoning process asks you to put yourself in the place of those who demand dollars and consider how you would respond to changes in its exchange value. More than proportionate responses to exchange value changes give this curve the negative slope shown in Figure 18-2.[4]

Equilibrium Foreign Exchange Rates

Movements toward equilibrium in foreign exchange markets operate in essentially the same way as in markets for domestic goods and services (see Chapter 5). At any exchange rate above P in Figure 18-2, the dollar is said to be "overvalued," which means that a dollar will buy more in foreign countries than it will buy at home. An overvalued dollar also means that American goods are overpriced in international trade. In this case, more dollars will be supplied than are demanded, and pressure is exerted for a decrease in the exchange value of the dollar. If the exchange value of the dollar is allowed to fall, the language of foreign

3. Of course, it is still possible and useful in many cases to express the international exchange value of the dollar in terms of some specific money. If you plan to travel to Canada, for example, you want to know the exchange rate between the American dollar and the Canadian dollar.

4. If you have already studied microeconomics, you will recognize that the slopes of foreign exchange market demand and supply curves involve the well-known concept of elasticity.

exchange says that the dollar is **depreciating.** At any exchange rate below *P,* on the other hand, the dollar is said to be "undervalued" in the sense that it will buy less in international trade than it will buy at home. An undervalued dollar also means that American goods are underpriced in international trade. Now more dollars will be demanded than supplied, and pressure will be exerted for a rise in its exchange value. If exchange rates are free to move in response to market conditions, the dollar will **appreciate** as its exchange value rises. When equilibrium exists in a free international exchange market, the dollar is neither overvalued nor undervalued.

To extend our understanding of foreign exchange rates and markets, let us think of a foreign exchange market as divided into two separate submarkets. One submarket (which will be called the "capital account" when we study the balance of payments accounting system) is limited to transactions involving stocks, bonds, bank accounts, and other financial assets. In this "capital account" submarket, equilibrium would mean that the dollar rate of return on $1,000 would be the same as the foreign-money rate of return on $1,000 worth of foreign money after conversion to U.S. dollars. This condition is called **interest rate parity.**

The other submarket (which will be called the "current account" when we study the balance of payments accounting system) is limited to transactions in goods and services. In the current account submarket, equilibrium involves a condition known as **purchasing power parity.** This means that, so far as traded goods and services are concerned, a country's money will buy as much in traded goods abroad as it will at home. (Nontraded goods and services, like homes and haircuts, are not really in the picture.)

In practice, since these two submarkets are not separated, the actual overall exchange rate lies between the purchasing power and the interest rate parity values. When the two parity values differ, neither parity condition is satisfied. A rate that over- or undervalues a currency in terms of purchasing power may nevertheless be a persistent equilibrium condition. This helps explain why

the U.S. dollar was overvalued in purchasing power terms for several years before September 1985.

FIXED VERSUS FLEXIBLE EXCHANGE RATES

Foreign exchange rates are called **free,** or **floating,** or **flexible,** when they are free to move up or down in response to shifts in demand and supply curves arising from the ordinary operations of international trade and finance. But countries have not often been willing to allow the international value of their monies to move freely. Politically persuasive arguments have generally led to **fixed exchange rates**—rates maintained through government intervention. We shall first describe how the exchange values may be fixed. Then we shall present both sides of the debate about fixed versus flexible rates.

Fixing Exchange Rates

The governments of countries that take part in international trade generally hold reserves of gold and monies (both their own and those of other countries) so as to be able to influence exchange rates if they choose to do so. During the 1960s, the United States held the foreign exchange value of the dollar above its free-market equilibrium rate as it tried to maintain a fixed rate in spite of a decline in the dollar's free-market value. The essentials of how this influence may be applied are easy to see by looking at Figure 18-3, which shows the international market for dollars. To maintain the dollar's value at, say, P_1, the United States dipped into its reserves of gold and foreign exchange and sold them for dollars. As long as the United States had enough reserves to purchase quantity *AB* of dollars per year, it could support the exchange value of the dollar at P_1. In effect, the demand curve became horizontal at the fixed rate, as shown by D_2, and the equilibrium moved to point *B.* On the other hand, if the

United States wants to push the exchange value of the dollar below the free-market equilibrium level, say, to P_2, it can take dollars from its reserves or create more dollars and sell them in the foreign exchange market. If it sells quantity EF per year, it will succeed in depreciating the exchange value of the dollar to P_2. In this case, the supply curve becomes horizontal (as shown by S_2) at the fixed exchange rate, and equilibrium moves to F. A depreciated dollar would lower the cost of U.S. goods to foreign buyers and promote U.S. exports.[5]

The Case for Flexible Rates

Those who favor flexible rates argue that they are prices like any others. They say that flexible exchange rates are better than fixed or government-controlled rates simply because free markets generally do a better job of setting prices and allocating resources than governments do. They also say that fixed rates are not really as safe and sure and stable as their advocates claim or hope. Governments, they say, often try to fix rates at levels or for time periods that are more than they can handle with the gold and foreign exchange reserves available for that purpose. When the reserves run out, drastic exchange rate changes can do more harm than the steady and moderate movements that would have come under a free-rate system. Worse yet, governments often resort to tariffs, quotas, and direct controls when their reserves start to fall too low. These direct controls reduce freedom and seriously distort world trade.[6]

---

5. Some countries, such as Nazi Germany, developed very complex multiple exchange rates. Such systems are usually combined with **exchange controls**, which require licenses to buy foreign money or forbid its use to buy luxury imports, to travel abroad, or to buy foreign securities or other assets abroad. Generally, multiple rate systems involve the central bank selling foreign exchange to importers cheaply for essential imports and selling it dearly for less important uses. An **inconvertible currency** can exist under such control systems. For example, the Soviet ruble is inconvertible because Soviet citizens must have special licenses in order to buy foreign currency legally.

6. Tariffs, quotas, and direct controls on foreign trade are discussed in the chapter on "Free Trade Versus Protection."

FIGURE 18-3   Fixing Foreign Exchange Rates

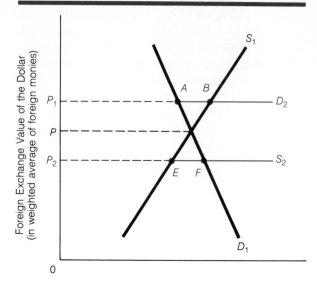

Quantity of Dollars Demanded and Supplied per Year (billions of dollars)

If the United States wants to fix the exchange value of the dollar at P_1, it can use its gold and foreign exchange reserves to demand dollars at that exchange value. The demand curve becomes horizontal at that exchange value (D_2), and equilibrium is at B, with the United States purchasing AB quantity of dollars per year. To fix the exchange value at P_2, the United States may sell dollars at that value, producing the supply curve S_2 and selling quantity EF per year.

The Case for Fixed Rates

The main argument of those who favor fixed rates is that some of the risks can be removed from international trade and especially from long-term international lending when exchange rates are fixed. Borrowers can borrow and lenders can lend with more assurance about what the exchange rates will be when the time comes to repay the loans. Also, those in favor of fixed rates say that flexible-rate systems will make exchange rates move up and down more than is really necessary or desirable for international trade. This argument comes partly from the feeling that markets, when left to themselves, may often overshoot the mark in making adjustments, and that professional speculators, who make their living by predicting exchange rate changes, may deliberately destabilize exchange markets for their own gain. However, they argue that, rightly or wrongly, governments are bound to intervene occasionally in exchange markets and that it is better for them to do so openly under a clearly defined fixed-rate system than for them to do so informally and with less clearly stated goals. They see no reason why fixed-rate systems should not work, if only countries would hold large enough reserves and if price and wage-rate levels could be made more flexible.

The Policy Autonomy Issue

Most countries and their governments believe that it is very important to protect their freedom to choose and carry out internal fiscal and monetary policies with little thought about the rest of the world. But whether this policy autonomy favors fixed or flexible exchange rates depends on whether fiscal or monetary tools are most important to the country's policy. On the one hand, freedom for expansionary fiscal policy is best protected under fixed rates. On the other hand, freedom for expansionary monetary policy is best protected under flexible rates. Let us see why this is so.

Expansionary fiscal policy generally raises government budget deficits, which must be financed. Financing a deficit means increasing the supply of government securities, which lowers their prices and raises interest rates. In the foreign exchange market these higher interest rates shift the demand curve for the nation's money to the right as foreigners seek to take advantage of these relatively higher rates of interest. Under floating exchange rates, the resulting inflow of financial capital brings about an upward valuation (appreciation) of the country's money. With this higher exchange value for its money, the country's exports may fall and imports may rise, so that the expansionary fiscal policy becomes less effective. However, under fixed exchange rates, lower financial capital outflows and higher financial cap-

TABLE 18-1 Which Exchange-Rate Regime Maximizes Internal Macroeconomic Policy Autonomy?

Primary Policy Instrument	Policy Goal	
	Expansion	Contraction
Fiscal policy	Fixed rates	Flexible rates
Monetary policy	Flexible rates	Fixed rates

ital inflows promote the expansionary policy without causing imports to increase as exports decrease.

Expansionary monetary policy, on the other hand, favors flexible exchange rates. Expanding the money supply could possibly lead to lower real interest rates in the short run (see Chapter 14). Fixed exchange rates would increase the flow of capital out of the country and would mean less investment at home. Under floating rates, however, there would be a lower exchange value for the country's money, reducing the capital outflow, encouraging exports, and discouraging imports.

For countries seeking to contract or to bring down the inflation rate, these arguments work in the other direction. As witnessed in the early 1980s in the United States, contractionary *monetary* policy raises interest rates at home and brings capital inflows. Contractionary *fiscal* policy, by lowering interest rates at home, raises capital outflows. So a country that is trying to lower its inflation rate by monetary means would favor fixed exchange rates. If such a country stresses fiscal contraction, it would favor flexible rates. Table 18-1 sums up each of these cases.

A Brief History of Exchange-Rate Systems

Historically, fixed-rate systems have been more common than floating-rate systems. Probably the best-known system for fixing exchange rates is the gold standard, which was used by most major trading countries from the 1870s to the 1930s, except for the World War I period. After World

War II, a new rate-fixing system was set up under the Bretton Woods plan and carried out through the International Monetary Fund. We shall take a look at these systems and at why the most recent system broke down in the 1970s. We shall also see how Eurocurrencies fit into this picture.

THE GOLD STANDARD   Under the **gold standard,** countries promised to back their own money with a fixed amount of gold. That is, they promised to buy their own money and pay a stated amount of gold for it. Among the countries that followed this system, exchange rates were fixed, because a money that can be exchanged for twice as much gold as another money could also be exchanged for twice as much of that other money. For this reason, the price levels in gold-standard countries were linked to one another. Except for goods and services not traded and the costs of shipping goods and gold, the price levels in the trading countries would match (inversely) the fixed exchange ratios of their monies. A country with a low-valued money would have a high price level, and a country with a high-valued money would have a low price level. The price-level difference would tend to bring purchasing power parity into international trade.

The major problems with the gold standard came in times of rapidly changing economic conditions. For example, if a recession caused prices to fall in one country, its goods would become attractive in international trade compared with the goods of countries whose prices had not fallen. In the country suffering from the recession, exports would grow, helping it to recover. Also, in order to carry out these purchases, foreigners would pay for the exporting country's goods (or its money) partially with gold or convertible monies. Under the gold standard, such "gold inflows" or increases in reserves would expand the exporting country's money supply, causing its price level to rise back toward its original level. But its trading partners would have falling exports and rising imports. They would lose international reserves, including gold, and they might suffer recession also. Of course, if price levels and wage rates could change quickly enough, the linkage would not bring much hardship and unemploy-

ment, but if wage rates and prices were slow to change, unemployment would grow. The gold-standard linkage could be uncomfortable as economies with payments deficits found themselves vulnerable to the effects of changes elsewhere in the world. A recession and unemployment afflicting one country could spread to its trading partners.

For smooth working, the gold standard requires the following three conditions:

1. At least one major trading country in the system must permit its central bank to tighten credit, raise interest rates, and contract its domestic money supply by however much might be required to maintain its gold reserves. "Eight percent," as one financial writer put it, "will bring gold from the moon." But it would also mean downward pressure on that (deficit) country's prices, wages, and employment.

2. At least one major trading country in the system, when its international accounts are in surplus, must permit its increased international reserves to exercise their (inflationary) effects on domestic costs and prices, without trying to "sterilize" these inflows by tightening credit in the interest of domestic stability.

3. At least one major trading country in the system must "make a market" for "distress goods" exported by deficit countries, despite the resulting damage to its domestic import-competing industries and work forces.

Great Britain satisfied all these conditions in the Victorian and Edwardian generations before 1914. Satisfying the last, of course, maintained world confidence in the pound sterling. Satisfying the other two conditions reduced deflationary and contractionary pressures for Britain's trading partners, at considerable sacrifice to Great Britain itself.

After World War I, the United States and (after 1925) France, both protectionist countries, took over Great Britain's leading role in the gold-standard system. Conditions 2 and 3 no longer held and the gold standard took on, for deficit countries, a pronounced deflationary bias, while concentrating the burdens of economic adjustment on these same countries. Small wonder that, in the first major test of the postwar gold standard—the Great Depression of the 1930s—it failed miserably. Country after country, including Great Britain itself in 1931 and the United States in 1933, went "off gold" in the sense that they no longer provided gold to holders of their domestic currencies, even though the price of gold remained fixed.

The mid-Depression abandonment of gold led to a six-year period (1933–1939) of **competitive depreciation** and **exporting unemployment** that lasted until the outbreak of World War II. Countries anxious to increase exports, reduce imports, and reflate their domestic price levels bid up the prices of foreign monies and thereby cheapened their own. The process was accompanied by increased protection all around and, in many countries, by exchange controls as well. The volume of world trade contracted. Resource-poor countries like Japan, and to some extent Germany and Italy, doubting their ability to prosper by trade, turned eagerly to military imperialism as a replacement, with disastrous consequences.

THE INTERNATIONAL MONETARY FUND The **International Monetary Fund (IMF)** was set up shortly before the end of World War II at a meeting of central bankers and finance ministers at Bretton Woods, New Hampshire, and is sometimes called the **Bretton Woods system.** Its major goal was to maintain stable exchange rates and to avoid competitive depreciations and devaluations. Gold and the U.S. dollar were established as joint monetary standards, tied to each other at the ratio of $35 per ounce of gold, and the exchange values of other monies were fixed ("pegged") in relation to the dollar. Thus, a new set of fixed exchange rates was set up. Next, a fund (the IMF) was established from contributions of gold and monies from the major trading countries, roughly in proportion to their trading activity. The IMF directors then could make loans from the fund to help individual countries maintain these fixed exchange rates.

To understand how the fund was expected to operate, look again at Figure 18-3. Suppose that the fixed or pegged exchange value of the country's money is P_1, where the IMF believes the

demand and supply curves will intersect in normal times. In other words, the IMF directors believe that the demand and supply curves, as shown in Figure 18-3, represent temporary circumstances and that they eventually will shift to bring equilibrium back to the P_1 exchange value. To maintain the fixed value, gold or foreign exchange in the amount of AB per time period would have to be used to support the demand for the nation's money. If the country did not have enough reserves of gold or foreign exchange to continue to pay out this quantity, an IMF loan could tide it over until demand and supply curves shifted back to "normal" positions and made the equilibrium value match the fixed value. If these shifts were not expected to take place, the IMF could deny the loan and require the country to devalue its money. Or it could set conditions for its assistance, generally in the form of lowered inflation rates and lowered budget deficits. The idea of the fund was that such devaluations would be limited and would not be permitted to lead to competitive devaluations as they had before World War II.

THE BREAKDOWN OF FIXED RATES How did the Bretton Woods system actually work out? The U.S.S.R. and the Soviet bloc never joined the IMF, and that body itself could impose its wishes mainly on the weaker developing countries, which came to resent IMF-imposed "austerity." Nevertheless, the Bretton Woods system worked reasonably well until the Vietnam War and the War on Poverty combined to put increasing downward pressure on the dollar itself, and fears arose that the United States would not have enough gold or other reserves to maintain the $35 per ounce relationship with gold. The resulting European preference for gold rather than dollars in their reserve holdings added further to this pressure. After the failure of various compromise solutions, President Nixon "pulled the plug" on the Bretton Woods system in August 1971 by refusing any longer to exchange gold for dollars even with foreign governments and central banks.

Since then, foreign exchange markets have operated under what has become known as a **dirty float.** Many developing countries have pegged their money to the dollar, in practice at least. But individual governments often try to influence the exchange value of their own money by buying or selling large amounts of foreign exchange. The result is a weak imitation of a fixed-rate system.

EUROCURRENCIES   We hear a great deal about Eurodollars today. Why are there no Eurodollar bills? Is a Eurodollar different from a U.S. dollar? Is a Euromark or Eurofranc different from an ordinary Deutschmark or Swiss franc?

To answer these questions, we turn to history. The **Eurocurrency** system began in the 1950s with the Eurodollar, which in turn seems to have begun with the Soviet Union. The Soviet authorities needed dollar reserves for purchases in the West, but they did not want to hold dollars in the United States, where the government might freeze or confiscate them if the Cold War heated up. It was tempting for them to buy pounds or francs and earn the higher interest rates that then prevailed in Western Europe, but the instability of European monies was a problem. The dollar was the world's most stable money and was widely used in contracts between and among citizens of European countries. So the Soviets devised a way to deposit their dollar funds in special dollar accounts in European banks. For the European banks, these dollar accounts could serve as reserves for dollar loans at high European interest rates—the best of both worlds, so to speak. The dollar accounts in European banks became known as Eurodollars.

The system spread. Financiers from all countries, the United States included, took advantage of it to increase their interest earnings when U.S. interest rates were low. The dollars that European banks were lending came to include not only their depositors' dollar funds in Europe but other dollar funds purchased or borrowed and then deposited in American banks. From an original base in London, the market spread all over Western Europe and beyond. When the dollar weakened in the wake of the Vietnam War, the market expanded from Eurodollars to include the other Eurocurrencies.

The Eurocurrency's main attraction is freedom. A dollar deposit in a London bank, including a London branch of a New York or San Francisco bank, is not subject to U.S. laws and regulations about reserve ratios, interest rates, and the quality of its loans, because it is located physically in Britain. But neither is it subject to British law, since the status of the British money and the ordinary British depositor are not involved. (If the British should try to regulate the Eurodollar market too much, it would soon leave London!)[7] So it has grown into a major oasis of freedom in an overregulated world (according to its friends) or a major unguided missile on the world financial scene (according to its enemies).

The Eurodollar should not be confused with the **European Currency Unit (ECU),** which is the monetary unit of the European Currency Union. There is no physical distinction between an ordinary dollar and a Eurodollar, but the ECU is a money of account, which does not exist in any physical sense. It is a weighted average of the values of a number of European Community (EC) monies. Although ECUs cannot be circulated, bank accounts may be held in them. The value of the ECU is not fixed relative to the dollar, the yen, or any other "outside" money, but it is hoped that it will fluctuate less violently than the Deutschmark, the Dutch guilder, or other member-country monies.

BALANCE OF PAYMENTS ACCOUNTS

You have just learned how demand and supply for a nation's money in foreign exchange markets determine its value in international transactions. Now we shall explain the accounting system that countries use to keep track of the international transactions that give rise to the demands for and supplies of their money. The record of transactions affecting the international demand and supply for a nation's money is that nation's **balance of payments account.** In order to introduce you

---

7. Much of the Eurodollar "market" is now international, with centers in such places as Tangier, Hong Kong, and Singapore.

to the idea of international transactions, we first present two hypothetical cases. Then we outline the U.S. balance of payments accounts.

We start by limiting our attention to a single pair of international transactions. The two are, we shall suppose, of equal size. Herr Braun, of Hamburg, Germany, has instructed his broker to buy for him $15,000 worth of International Business Machines (IBM) stock on the New York Stock Exchange on Wall Street. Payment must be made in dollars, but we suppose that Herr Braun and his broker have only German marks. At the same time, Mr. Brown, of Chicago, buys from a local dealer a $15,000 sports car made by the Toyota Company in Nagoya, Japan. Eventually Toyota wants payment in Japanese yen, but both Mr. Brown and the Toyota dealer in Chicago have only American dollars.

What do these two transactions mean in terms of U.S. international balances? Herr Braun's purchase of IBM stock is part of both the demand for American dollars and the supply of German marks in foreign exchange markets. From the American point of view, transactions such as this are usually called positive, or active, or credit, or favorable because they build up American-owned reserves of foreign currency. On the other hand, Mr. Brown's purchase of the Toyota automobile is part of both the American demand for foreign exchange (in this case the Japanese yen) and the supply of American dollars as seen by foreigners. From the American point of view, transactions such as this are usually called negative, passive, debit, or unfavorable because they draw down American reserves of foreign exchange. Later we shall see how important this distinction is and whether a positive item, leading to the accumulation of foreign exchange, is really any more favorable than a negative item, which draws down such reserves. For the moment, we shall look at the accounting system that keeps track of international transactions.

U.S. International Accounts

Actual international data cover thousands, even millions, of transactions taking place among more

than 150 countries. Few of these transactions cancel out quite as neatly as in our hypothetical cases. Also, the number of different types of transactions is much greater.

Table 18-2 presents the U.S. international accounts for 1983–1984. It summarizes the millions of transactions that took place between Americans and foreigners during those years. In reading this table, first notice the columns entitled Credit ($+$), Debit ($-$), and Balance (which may have either sign). Each transaction recorded in the international accounts system must be entered as either a credit or a debit to show its effect on the exchange value of the dollar.

What determines whether any particular transaction is recorded as a credit (positive item) or a debit (negative item) in the account? The general rule is as follows. If a certain kind of transaction normally leads to a demand for domestic (in this case, U.S.) money or a supply of foreign money, it is a positive transaction. If it generally leads to a demand for foreign money or a supply of domestic money, it is a negative transaction. This is clearly shown by the entries in the balance of trade part of the account in item 1 of Table 18-2, where exports are positive and imports are negative. Exports of U.S. goods generally mean that foreigners demand dollars and supply their own money in international exchange markets to pay for goods purchased from U.S. citizens. On the other hand, when Americans buy goods from foreigners, they must supply dollars and demand foreign money in order to pay for these imports. It is a bit harder to understand the positive and negative entries in other sections of the accounts, but the general rule holds there as well.

The next step in understanding the international accounts in Table 18-2 is to note that the different types of transactions that take place during the year are listed (and numbered) down the left side of the table. To explain how the accounting system works, we will work through the accounts from one concept of balance to the next.

BALANCE OF TRADE (MERCHANDISE) The **balance of trade** (item 1 in Table 18-2) is the easiest to understand. It is the amount by which the

TABLE 18-2   U.S. International Transactions, 1983–1984 (billions of dollars)

Account	1983			1984		
	Credit (+)	Debit (−)	Balance	Credit (+)	Debit (−)	Balance
1. Balance of trade (merchandise trade excluding military)	201.7	268.9	−67.2	219.9	334.0	−114.1
2. Invisible items						
a. Investment income	78.0	52.6	25.4	87.6	68.5	19.1
b. Military transactions (net)	—	0.2	−0.2	—	1.8	−1.8
c. Travel and transportation (net)	—	4.7	−4.7	—	9.0	−9.0
d. Other services (net)	9.6	—	9.6	9.8	—	9.8
e. Remittances, pensions, and other unilateral transfers (net)	—	8.9	−8.9	—	11.4	−11.4
3. Balance on current account [(1) + (2)]	289.3	335.3	−46.0	317.3	424.7	−107.4
4. Capital outflow (−)						
a. U.S. private assets	—	48.8	−48.8	—	11.8	−11.8
b. U.S. government assets (other than 4c)	—	5.0	−5.0	—	5.5	−5.5
c. U.S. official reserve assets	—	1.2	−1.2	—	3.1	−3.1
d. Total	—	55.0	−55.0	—	20.4	−20.4
5. Capital inflow (+)						
a. Foreign assets (other than official)	78.5	—	78.5	93.9	—	93.9
b. Foreign official assets	5.8	—	5.8	3.4	—	3.4
c. Total	84.3	—	84.3	97.3	—	97.3
6. Balance on capital account						
a. Private [(4a) + (5a)]	78.5	48.8	29.7	93.9	11.8	82.1
b. Government [(4b) + (4c) + (5b)]	5.8	6.2	−0.4	3.4	8.6	−5.2
c. Total [(4d) + (5c)]	84.3	55.0	29.3	97.3	20.4	76.9
7. Errors and omissions	16.7	—	16.7	30.5	—	30.5
8. Total [(3) + (6c) + (7)]	390.3	390.3	0.0	445.1	445.1	0.0

Source: Economic Report of the President (1986), Table B-99.

value of a country's exports of goods exceeds the value of its imports of goods. Of course, a country can have a negative or deficit balance of trade if it imports more than it exports, as the United States did in 1983 and 1984. Mr. Brown's purchase of the Toyota automobile would be recorded as an import in this part of the account.

BALANCE ON CURRENT ACCOUNT The **balance on current account** (item 3 in Table 18-2) is also

easy to follow. It simply adds the invisible items to the balance of trade. The invisible items are investment income payments, such as dividends and interest; transactions in services, as distinguished from tangible goods; and unilateral transfers, such as gifts and other transfers to or from people and governments abroad. The United States has had credit entries in invisibles due mainly to income from U.S. investments abroad. But this credit item threatens to turn into a debit item because of interest payments to foreign holders of U.S. government securities.

BALANCE ON CAPITAL ACCOUNT The U.S. figures (Table 18-2) present first capital outflows, then capital inflows, and then the balance between them. Let us go into the most detail on the first of them (row 4 of the table).

Capital exports or outflows are purchases of foreign assets and should not be confused with exports of capital goods. The foreign sellers of foreign securities, foreign real estate, or the control of a foreign firm ordinarily demand foreign money in payment; the exporters of trucks or oil-well rigs ordinarily demand domestic money. So a capital export is a debit item, whereas a capital-goods export is a credit item.

Capital outflows are subdivided into private purchases of foreign assets (row 4a), similar purchases by the government (row 4b), and changes in government's official reserves of gold, convertible foreign monies, and credits with the International Monetary Fund (row 4c).

Capital imports or inflows (purchases of American assets by foreigners, largely by Japanese in 1983 and 1984) are presented in the same way, but with no distinction as to the source of funds used for buying American assets. Thus, row (5b) corresponds to the sum of rows (4b) and (4c). The totals on row (5c) are positive credit items almost by definition, like the negative balance on row (4d).

The results of rows (4) and (5) are combined on row (6) to give balances on capital account for the private and public sectors, both singly and in combination.[8] The overall balances (row 6c) were unprecedentedly positive in 1983 and 1984, when

American inflation was low, political conditions were stable, and high rates of return could be earned on American assets.

ERRORS AND OMISSIONS When we add a country's balances on current account and capital account in Table 18-2, the theoretical result is zero by the ordinary principles of double-entry bookkeeping. In fact, the sum is never zero, and a special account called "errors and omissions" (row 7) is added to force a balance on row (8). (Specialists think their estimates of credit items are somewhat more accurate than their estimates of debit ones.) In addition to problems of sampling and adjusting for seasonal movements, the published data are marred by smuggling and fictitious valuations of goods, along with securities and money evading tariffs, taxation, exchange controls, and regulation generally. (When the American parents of a junior-year-abroad student in Paris send their offspring a $10 bill unrecorded through the mails, both French and American "errors and omissions" increase.) For some reason, the "errors and omissions" entry for the United States was unusually large in 1984.

BALANCES OF PAYMENTS After the artificial "errors and omissions" account is inserted—not an approved accounting practice—each country's international accounts are apparently in balance, as in row (8) of Figure 18-2 for the United States. So what is this thing or these things called *the* balance or balances of payments? Do not the payments always balance?

A country's balance of payments is defined as the sum of its balance of current account and its balance on whatever capital-account transactions may have been undertaken for their own sakes, rather than merely in settlement for other transactions. Economists, however, are not mind readers, so how can they know the motivations of each and every capital movement? They do not know, but use various rules of thumb to divide the capital accounts into autonomous items and settlement items.

Returning to Table 18-2, look at row (4c), indicating small drawdowns of the U.S. government's holdings of "official reserve assets" in

8. Most countries use a very different system of classifying capital movements in capital-account balances. They try to divide such movements into long- and short-term ones, and further to subdivide short-term capital movements into movements of nonliquid capital (ordinary commercial paper) and liquid capital (chiefly bank deposits). This system permits economists and statisticians to estimate a "basic" balance of payments (balance on current account plus balance on long-term capital movements) and also a "liquidity" balance of payments (basic balance plus balance on nonliquid short-term capital account).

TABLE 18-3   Balance of Payments Stages

Stage No.	Stage Description	Trade in Goods and Services	Capital-related Transactions		
			New Investments	Interest, Dividends, and Loan Repayments	Net Flow
1	Immature debtor	−	+ +	−	+
2	Mature debtor	+	+	− −	−
3	Intermediate	+	−	?	−
4	Immature creditor	+	− −	+	−
5	Mature creditor	−	−	+ +	+

This table lists five international payments stages through which a country may pass in the course of its economic development. Plus signs (+) indicate net credit balances, and minus signs (−) indicate net debit balances.

both 1983 and 1984. In balance of payments terms, this means that the American "official settlements" balance of payments—the balance on which most countries concentrate their attention—was slightly in deficit. But the American government does not itself attach any such precise meaning to that figure and does not take sides as between and among the several varieties of balance of payments concepts. What is *the* balance of payments? This remains a mystery, like "what is *the* quantity of money," "*the* rate of interest," "*the* deficit," or "*the* national debt."

Balance of Payments Stages

A country's balances of trade and capital movements generally go through several stages of balance and imbalance in the course of economic growth and development. Table 18-3 illustrates one theory about how this happens. Plus signs (+) indicate credit balances, and minus signs (−) indicate debit balances. According to this view, a country such as the United States moves from the stage of an "immature debtor" to that of a "mature creditor" in the following way.

1. An **immature debtor,** such as the North American colonies in the seventeenth century, imports

goods and especially real capital goods. The result is a deficit in the goods and services entries of the balance of payments accounts. Payment is through capital inflow from abroad, which is a positive item in the capital account. There is some return flow as loans are repaid, but the net flow still is positive.

2. A **mature debtor,** such as the American colonies in the eighteenth century and the United States through much of the nineteenth century, has developed agricultural exports (wheat, cotton, and tobacco), which turn its trade balance positive. It continues to import capital, but its return flow of dividends, interest, and loan repayments has become much larger over the years and the net flow is now negative.

3. There is often an intermediate stage, which was cut short in the United States by World War I. The trade balance remains normally positive, but the country begins a net export of capital, mainly to less developed countries like Canada and Mexico. The return flow of dividends, interest and loan repayments due to previous European loans and investments in America continues so that the combined return-flow account may go either way. The net flow is generally negative.

4. An **immature creditor,** like the United States from the end of World War I through World War II and until about 1960, exports enough capital to balance both return flows and continuing trade surpluses.

5. From the point of view of the payments balance, a **mature creditor,** like the United States today, tends to live off its income from investments abroad. Repayments from past capital exports exceed its present capital exports. The country's trade balance also turns negative, because some of its natural resources have been depleted and it has become a high-living, high-cost country. It is not unusual for a rich mature creditor country's receipts from repayment of past loans from any particular poor country to exceed its new exports of capital to that country, so that money appears to be flowing from the poor country to the rich one. The flow between many Latin American countries and the United States as they repay loans seems to be following this pattern and causing great resentment.

Favorable or Unfavorable Balance?

An active, positive, or surplus balance of trade or payments is often called a **favorable balance.** It is thought to be a good thing. On the other hand, a passive or negative balance is often called a deficit or **unfavorable balance**—a bad thing. These terms were developed by the mercantilist school of political economy, which dominated Western economic thought for 250 years ending in about 1750 and which is now being revived under the banner of protectionism. According to mercantile theory, which has never died, gaining and keeping positive international balances and accumulating treasure should be among the major goals of a country's trade policy.

The mercantilist policy makes a good deal of sense when the macroeconomy's main problem is achieving or maintaining high employment, since exports add to aggregate demand and imports often have a negative effect. But when the main problem is inflation, or too little domestic aggregate supply, the reverse of the mercantilist policy makes sense. In order to control inflation, a negative balance is a good thing and a positive balance is a bad thing. Countries may restrict exports to hold down prices at home. For exam-

ple, in the 1970s the United States put restrictions on the export of Alaskan oil, building materials such as lumber, and animal feed such as soybeans. When a country is experiencing stagflation, with *both* unemployment and inflation, there is no general answer to the question of whether a positive or a negative balance is better.

BALANCE OF PAYMENTS PROBLEMS

Every country has a balance of payments that is generally either in surplus or in deficit according to some balance concept. Only rarely will a country have an actual balance. It does not follow, however, that every country has a payments *problem*. A country has a payments problem only when the international situation puts it under great pressure to change its economic policies.

No country with a reasonably steady balance of payments surplus has a payments problem. True, its portfolio of international assets may accumulate too much foreign exchange and gold and too few earning assets like securities and real estate. Also, its surplus may be contributing to a depression in some other countries that are not exporting as much as they would like. For example, the U.S. policy of accumulating gold after World War I was criticized as contributing to depression in Europe. But a surplus country is under no immediate pressure from abroad to change its ways. It is free to wait to make up its mind about what to do. The situation may change, or other countries may do the reacting. Such freedom from pressure is the meaning of freedom from payments problems.

Nor does a country have payments problems immediately when its balance of payments becomes negative. It has no payments problems if it has accumulated enough reserves in the past or if it produces large amounts of a payment item such as gold, or if its deficits are guaranteed by some internationally acceptable agency. In 1951, during the Korean War, the United States began a long series of deficits. For the rest of the decade, the series was broken only once, at the time of the 1956 Arab-Israeli War. But the United States remained unaware of any payments problems because of large American gold reserves and the willingness of most European creditor nations to hold U.S. dollars.

A country has a payments problem only when its negative balance is so large, compared with its reserves, that it cannot simply continue to settle its deficits by paying out (exporting) its reserves of gold or money that surplus countries will accept. It also has a problem when other countries doubt its political willingness to take steps to lower its deficit and will not themselves help it to do so.

A country may have *trade* problems without balance of payments problems, and vice versa. An example was the United States in the mid-1980s. Strongly negative balances of trade and on current account were offset by strongly positive balances on capital account—foreign purchases of American securities, real estate, and other dollar assets. The offset precluded balance of payments problems but it did not solve the low-profit and unemployment problems of American export- or import-competing industries—the Kansas wheat farmer or the Ohio Valley steel worker.

Solutions for Payments Problems

We will discuss eight groups of remedies for payments problems. They may be applied singly or more often in combinations.

THE CLASSICAL MEDICINE The classical medicine, often called the **price-specie flow,** is expected to solve payments problems automatically by the operation of the gold standard. A negative official settlements balance leads to the loss of gold reserves to the country's trading partners. The loss of these reserves means a decline in the country's monetary base (see Chapter 13). Reduction in the monetary base leads to a falling domestic money supply, then to a falling domestic price level, and finally to more positive trade and current account balances. At the same time, the countries receiving the additional gold reserves will have higher money supplies and higher

prices, leading to lower balance of payments surpluses. These flows of reserves are expected to continue until the deficit country achieves a balance of its international payments.

The classical medicine is bitter. The bitterness is due to unemployment and loss of output when wage–cost lags and money illusion delay adjustments to the falling money supply and price level (see Chapter 15).

DEPRECIATION AND DEVALUATION If a country's money is guaranteed to be exchangeable for a given amount of reserves, such as gold or acceptable foreign monies, the amount of gold or foreign money in the guarantee can be reduced. This is called **devaluation,** and it lowers the international exchange value of the money. If the money is not tied to gold or some other base, the country may have been supporting its international exchange value through operations in the official reserve section of the balance of payments accounts. In this case, by lowering the level of support given to it, the money can be **depreciated.** Here again, the international exchange value of the money will fall.

The effects of depreciation or devaluation are seen as lower prices for the depreciating country's money abroad and higher prices of foreign money at home. Because the depreciating country's exports have become cheaper abroad and its imports are now more costly at home, the country's payments balance is expected to become more positive. Devaluation often causes the country to export more goods and to find substitutes for imported goods, thus raising the level of income and employment at home. These changes may give rise to greater demand for credit and higher interest rates. Capital outflow may become smaller if devaluation seems to be working and confidence rises. This scenario supposes the demands and supplies of the country's exports and imports to be fairly responsive to exchange value changes.

Though devaluation and depreciation are not the same thing as inflation, they have inflationary effects that seem to spread through the depreciating country's whole economy. Increasing demand for exported goods as well as for import-competing goods raises their domestic prices.

Higher prices for imported raw materials (like oil in industrial countries) lead to cost and price rises in goods of all kinds. Higher prices of imported food and other important items that increase the cost of living lead to demands for raising wages to pay for them. If these raises take place, there are further pressures on monetary authorities to accommodate with expansionary policies, which raise price levels.

Domestic inflation, if it takes place, often undoes any good that the original devaluation had done to the balance of trade because it makes export goods more costly abroad and imported goods cheaper at home. Also, the prospect of inflation or accelerating inflation encourages capital outflow. Just as reduced capital outflow makes matters easier (as we said above), greater capital outflow makes them more difficult. For these reasons, devaluation and depreciation seemed to be less appealing in the 1970s and mid-1980s than they were in the 1960s, except in countries like the United States, where the dollar appreciated from 1982 to 1985.

ABSORPTION   The absorption approach asks domestic consumers and producers to bear the burdens of solving the balance of payments problem. During and right after World War II, some of the European countries, including Britain, were living beyond their means. They were demanding output beyond their productive capacity, mainly because they had to repair war damage. For this reason, they had a large payments deficit. The United States, Britain's main creditor, urged the British to devalue their currency, as indeed they finally did in the fall of 1949 and several times afterward. However, a number of British and European economists worked out another strategy, which came to be called the absorption approach.

As you know, in an open economy, the equilibrium real national income and product (Y^*) is equal to domestic consumption, investment, and government purchases ($C + I + G$) plus net exports ($X - Im$). Here we define domestic consumption as $C + I + G$ and the foreign balance as $X - Im$. To improve the balance of payments, net exports should be raised (to a smaller negative value). This would be done by reducing domestic absorption of both imports and domestic output through an austerity program enforced by high taxes and strict rationing. This would lessen the inflationary pressure and the need for devaluation.

The costs of the absorption approach are mainly two. The obvious one is the burden on consumers and investors who must live under the austerity program. More important perhaps in the long run may be the threats to the citizens' freedoms and civil rights involved in enforcing high taxes and strict rationing over long periods.

The absorption approach has been used in some countries even when there was no inflationary problem, and when unemployment was present. If the goal is to raise real national income and product without causing deficits in the balance of payments that are too high, there may be a combination of controls on imports and government-directed investment in export industries. This direction takes the form of special favors (subsidies) for present and potential export industries. Such treatment causes complaints of unfair competition from the country's competitors on the world market. In the United States, the steel and automobile industries have complained about such competition from both Europe and Japan.

MONETARY APPROACH   So far, all of the approaches have centered on raising a country's trade balance. The monetary approach, however, focuses on lowering the capital outflow and encouraging capital inflow. Fighting inflation is an important part of this approach. If one's own money is inflating more rapidly than foreign monies are, foreign assets, including foreign durable consumption goods, become more desirable. Holding foreign money, securities, and durable goods is seen as a hedge or protection against inflation at home. The payments problems that result from these actions are attacked through an anti-inflationary monetary policy—that is, by limiting the growth of the money supply through open market operations, reserve requirements, and discount rates. Exchange rates should *not* be devalued because, as we have seen, devaluation generally sets the stage for more inflation.

It has been easy for economic statesmen to advise their neighbors and trading partners to solve their payments problems by anti-inflationary measures. But it has proved much harder for democratic countries to put these measures into practice long enough and consistently enough to show the international financial community that they mean business. Switzerland, West Germany, and later Japan have had more luck with it than most other countries. The United States may be said to have attempted it after 1981.

PROTECTIONISM Perhaps the most popular answer to payments problems has been **protectionism**—protecting export industries by direct or hidden subsidies and protecting import-competing industries by tariffs (taxes on imports) and other restrictions on imports such as quotas and time-consuming customs procedures. These devices are most attractive when a negative trade balance is combined with a rise in unemployment in key political areas at home. These conditions were met in the United States in the 1970s and early 1980s with the hardest-hit states of Pennsylvania, Ohio, and Michigan being centers of the steel and auto industries and very important politically. Protection is also favored when it can be used to attract foreign capital. Canada has been very successful in using protection to attract **tariff factories.** These are factories built by foreign companies and protected by Canada's tariffs. Protectionist measures force a reduction in the supply of imports, which is followed by a rise in their prices. The costs are borne largely by the consumers of the protected goods.[9] In the 1980s, the United States attracted foreign (especially Japanese) investment capital by threats of increasing protection, especially import quotas and "domestic content" legislation.

Generalized (macroeconomic) protection tries to deal with overall payments problems rather than with those connected with specific industries. It calls for a flat overall tax on *all* imports, even on necessary raw materials and other goods that ordinarily would be admitted free. This plan

9. These matters are examined further in the chapter on "Free Trade versus Protection."

has the same macroeconomic effects as any other form of protection. However, its benefits are centered less on particular industries and its burdens are centered less on particular consumer groups.

Capital-export restrictions are another kind of macroeconomic protection. The American form of capital-export restriction (under President Johnson) was an interest-equalization tax on purchases of foreign securities earning higher rates of interest than those in the United States. Other countries directly and openly use foreign exchange taxes, exchange controls, and exchange rationing. An often-used device in debtor countries is to require domestic reinvestment of interest, dividends, or repayments of foreign debt. These payments can be received but cannot be sent back home. All of these measures are intended to hold down interest rates and to create jobs in the country's economy at home.

PASSIVITY AND RENEGOTIATION   A country may react passively to its payments problems. It may choose to do nothing about them except to wait for other countries or international organizations to help them out for reasons of political alliance, sympathy, or fear of debt repudiation. Cases of such aid are the American Marshall Plan for Western Europe after World War II, the Soviet aid to Cuba, and North Korea's strategy of continual postponement of debt interest and repayment to its many creditors. The World Bank, formerly called the International Bank for Reconstruction and Development, is the best known of a number of international bodies whose long-term loans can help to solve or postpone a country's payments problems.

The International Monetary Fund, which was described earlier in this chapter, is another international agency that may provide help to a nation suffering a balance of payments problem. Originally, the fund came from gold and foreign exchange paid in by member nations. Later, however, the IMF was permitted to issue **special drawing rights** (also called **SDRs** or **paper gold**) that countries could use to meet international payment obligations, much as they might use gold or foreign exchange if they had any. A grant of special drawing rights from the IMF is another way that a country may solve or postpone its payments problems.

During the 1980s, deficit countries have often demanded renegotiation of the interest and principal payments on loans from governments, banks, and international organizations. Renegotiation is a code word for postponing or stretching out the payment of interest or repayment of principal on a country's foreign debt. In many less developed countries, the debts were contracted to pay for OPEC oil. In other cases, debts were contracted to help oil-exporting countries industrialize quickly on the assumption that oil prices would keep on rising. The resulting increase in Latin American debt in particular (to nearly $1 trillion) is the major debt problem of the mid-1980s.

LOCOMOTIVE THEORY The **locomotive theory** is also passive as far as the deficit countries are concerned. It has been offered by large countries with payments problems, like the United States in the late 1970s. The United States claimed that the American deficit was a contribution to a free-world cause and called on America's creditors to return the favor by helping the United States.

The Carter administration explained a large and rising American balance of payments deficit as aid to the free world's and the developing world's recovery from the OPEC oil shock of 1973–1974. According to this theory, the United States, by expanding its economy and letting its inflation rate rise, was acting as a locomotive to the European Community and Japan. President Carter called on the two largest and strongest creditor countries, West Germany and Japan, to adopt expansionary policies and in this way to increase their capital exports to and their imports of goods from the United States. The creditor countries refused to do so except in a token way, largely because of fears that expansion would mean mainly increased inflation. The locomotive theory, however, is not dead but merely resting in the roundhouse.

COUNTERTRADE **Countertrade** is a fancy name for barter. Just as barter is the normal form of trade among people short of money, countertrade

is important in the trade relations of, and especially between, countries with payment deficits. It has been estimated that as much as 20 percent of international trade is countertrade.

One great advantage of countertrade is ideological; if the Party or the Maximum Leader or the Great Helmsman thinks money an invention of the Devil or the capitalist class, it is important to show that, after the revolution, it can be dispensed with. Another great advantage is psychological; neither trading partner need recognize or acknowledge the international distrust of its money. Also, if the exchange ratio between the countertrade goods differs markedly from their relative world-money prices, countertrade is a cover for the country whose goods are overpriced to exploit the other. The USSR is said to exploit Cuba by overpricing Soviet oil and armaments relative to Cuban sugar.

When countertrade requires bilateral balancing between each pair of partners, with only minimal "swing credit," the system loses the advantage of multilateralism. When a country accepts, in disposing of an export surplus, goods it does not want except to re-export for whatever it does want, countertrade involves unnecessary transaction costs. When Country A imports oil from Country C by countertrade, having previously purchased it from Country B, the saving of its exchange reserves may be more than cancelled by the added cost of adjusting its refineries to handle C's oil instead of B's oil. (Petroleum is by no means a standard commodity.) When not inspired by ideological considerations, countertrade is often a desperate measure by a country that cannot dispose of its exports at world prices and wishes to hold on to its limited international reserves for other uses.

U.S. Payments Solutions

Countries use a changing combination of possible methods of meeting or dodging balance of payments problems. The United States has combined and alternated between devaluation, protection, and locomotive remedies since it realized in the late 1950s that its balance of payments problem was becoming serious. The many domestic and foreign critics of the U.S. record have called for heavier use of both classical and monetary approaches. The absorption approach has not been important in the United States because it depends on controls, which American business people fear would be administered much of the time by antibusiness bureaucrats.

The U.S. trade difficulties of the 1980s have been problems with the trade and current accounts, not with the balance of payments as a whole. The problems arose as tax cuts and enlarged defense expenditures produced record peacetime deficits in the federal budget. To finance these deficits, government securities were issued in a volume that could be sold only at low prices and high interest rates. These high interest rates attracted foreign financial capital—a positive capital account entry that raised the value of the dollar well above purchasing power parity. The high interest rates discouraged domestic private investment and the high-valued dollar made American exports expensive abroad and foreign imports relatively cheap in the United States. The result was a strong negative tilt in the balance of trade. The payment of debt interest to foreigners added a negative element to the current account balance.

With wage rates that adjusted only slowly, the increase in unemployment that came with the negative trade balance was not offset by stimulative effects from the positive capital account balance. The unemployment problems were serious, but the United States did not have a balance of payments problem.

SUMMARY

1. Open economies cannot conduct macroeconomic policies as though they were closed to international trade and capital movements. What the rest of the world does affects the economy of a country.

2. The money of one country is exchanged for the money of another country in foreign exchange markets. These markets are needed in interna-

tional trade because people wish to be paid in the money of their own country.

3. The intersection of the demand curve and the supply curve in the foreign exchange market indicates the equilibrium foreign exchange value of a nation's money. Purchasing power parity exists when the buying power of a country's money is the same at home as abroad. If its exchange value is above purchasing power parity, a nation's money is overvalued in international trade. If its exchange value is below purchasing power parity, it is undervalued in international trade. Because interest-rate differences also affect exchange values, purchasing power parity is rarely realized in practice.

4. Countries may try to fix the exchange value of their money above its purchasing power parity by using their gold and foreign exchange reserves to supplement the demand for their money. They may fix its exchange value below purchasing power parity by selling their own money in the foreign exchange market.

5. The argument for flexible exchange rates is that they do a more efficient job of pricing goods and allocating resources than do government-controlled rates. Moreover, government attempts to control rates often break down and cause serious problems.

6. The argument for fixed exchange rates is that they reduce uncertainty and thus help international trade and investment. Moreover, since governments usually influence exchange rates anyway, it is better that it be done openly.

7. Many countries wish to maintain their freedom to carry out domestic macroeconomic policy without adverse effects from international trade and capital flows. Whether this suggests flexible exchange rates or fixed exchange rates depends on whether the policies are expansionary or contractionary and on whether they are carried out with fiscal or monetary instruments.

8. Under the gold standard, monies are linked to each other because each is guaranteed to be exchangeable for a stated amount of gold. Under this system, gold and trade flows tend to force the price levels in gold-standard countries into fixed relationships, corresponding inversely to the gold backing of their monies. A gold-standard system collapsed in the unstable economic conditions following World War I.

9. The International Monetary Fund was set up after World War II to make loans to countries to help them hold the exchange value of their monies in line with fixed exchange rates approved by the IMF directors. This fixed-exchange-rate system broke down in 1971 when the United States refused to continue to exchange gold for dollars, thus letting the reserve money itself float in foreign exchange value.

10. Eurocurrencies are deposits of foreign monies in European banks. These deposits are free from their issuing government's controls over reserve ratios, interest rates, and the quality of loans. The advantages of this freedom from control have led to a great expansion of Eurocurrency accounts.

11. Balance of payments accounts record transactions that involve demands (credit entries) and supplies (debit entries) for a nation's money in international payments. Four widely recognized concepts of balance are (a) the balance of trade, (b) the balance on current account, (c) the balance on capital account, and (d) the official settlements balance of payments.

12. It is sometimes suggested that countries move through several balance of payments stages in the course of economic development. They start as immature debtors and end as mature creditors, living off dividends and interest from previous investments abroad.

13. Following mercantilist views, a positive payments balance usually is considered favorable and a negative balance is unfavorable. However, in terms of macroeconomic policy, these judgments depend on whether the goal is to expand the economy or to fight inflation.

14. Countries have balance of payments problems when persistent deficits threaten to make them change their economic policies.

15. Of eight potential solutions for payments problems, six involve action initiated by the country facing the problem. These are (a) the "classical medicine" of price-specie flow and contraction of the monetary base, (b) currency depreciation and devaluation to expand exports and reduce imports, (c) the absorption approach of reducing domestic expenditures, (d) the monetary approach of reducing domestic inflation, (e) protectionism to exclude foreign goods and discourage investment abroad, and (f) barter transactions called "countertrade."

16. The other two solutions to payments problems are passive in that the country with the problem does little or nothing and waits for its trading partners or others to act to resolve the problem. Renegotiation asks creditors to postpone repayment dates on obligations of the debtor country. The locomotive theory asks a country's trading partners to inflate their price levels and thereby relieve the deficit in the country with the payments problem.

17. The U.S. trade difficulty of the mid-1980s has been not its balance of payments but strongly negative balances of trade and current account. These were balanced by positive figures on capital account, representing capital inflows.

DISCUSSION QUESTIONS

1. Construct a graph showing the demand and supply for U.S. dollars in the foreign exchange market. Describe an action that the U.S. government might take or a development in the U.S. economy that would cause the dollar to depreciate in exchange value. Use your graph to illustrate why this would happen.

2. What interests in the American economy benefit when the dollar rises on the international exchange markets? What interests benefit when the dollar falls?

3. What is the difference between fixed and flexible exchange rates? What are the advantages and disadvantages of each for the United States?

4. It is often proposed in conservative circles that the United States return to the gold standard, but not to the pre-1971 gold price of $35 an ounce. How do you think an appropriate gold price might be estimated? What would happen if the estimate were seriously wrong in either direction?

5. What are Eurodollars? Why are they important to an entrepreneur?

6. Explain how it can happen that a country can have a positive balance of trade at the same time that it has a negative balance of payments, or vice versa.

7. Explain why an export of a country's capital and an export of capital goods (such as machinery) have opposite effects on a country's international balances.

8. In what circumstances would the price-specie flow (or classical medicine) for solving payments problems result in the loss of output and unemployment?

9. The text describes the locomotive theory as "waiting in the roundhouse" for another trial run. Do you expect this to happen soon? Why or why not?

Appendix: Payments Equilibrium

Our discussions of foreign exchange markets and the balance of payments accounts have shown that when a country engages in international trading and investing, its economy is linked with the outside world. Therefore, achieving and maintaining a balance with the outside world is part of the macroeconomic problem for a trading country. In this appendix, we outline the concept of payments equilibrium and show how the outside world is an important force in shaping a country's aggregate economic situation.

Payments equilibrium is any situation in which a country's balance on current account is matched by an equal but opposite balance on its capital account. A graphic illustration of payments equilibrium is presented on this page in Figure 18-4. On this graph, the horizontal axis measures a country's real national income and product, and the vertical axis shows the real rate of interest. As you will see, for a trading nation, the real rate of interest is a link to the outside world. At point E, which is called a **macro-dot,** the economy is at internal macroeconomic equilibrium (see Chapter 15). The real interest rate at point E satisfies two conditions at the same time. First, this rate is such that the flow of total planned expenditure $(C + I + G + X - Im)$ exactly matches real production on a Keynesian-cross diagram, such as the one you studied in Chapter 9. Second, at this real interest rate, the demand for the country's stock of money is equal to its supply, counting quantities demanded and supplied by both domestic and foreign operations.

Let us now examine the balance of payments line (BP) in Figure 18-4. This line shows the different combinations of real interest rates and real national income and product that would produce equilibrium in the international accounts. To understand why BP curves generally slope upward, start at point E and suppose an increase in real national income and product. Some part

of this increase will normally be spent on imports, with no balancing increase in exports. In itself, this change turns the country's payments balance negative. To maintain payments balance (that is, to keep the country on the BP curve), there must be an offsetting increase in the interest rate, to attract capital imports, which are a positive entry in the balance of payments. Therefore, we have

FIGURE 18-4 Payments Balance, Surplus, and Deficit

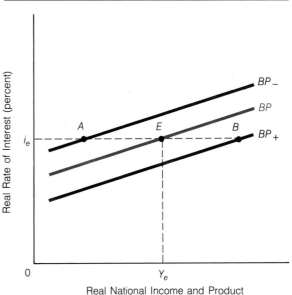

Point E is a macro-dot indicating a position of internal macroeconomic equilibrium, with real national income and product at Y_e and the real interest rate at i_e. The balance of payments line BP identifies income and interest rate combinations that provide payments equilibrium in the international accounts. A BP line passing through point E satisfies the conditions for both payments equilibrium and internal macroeconomic equilibrium. If the BP line passes above E, as does BP_-, a payments deficit is incurred at E. Solving this problem calls for either higher domestic interest rates or a lower national income and product, which is shown by a move from E to A. A BP line below E, as shown by BP_+, involves a payments surplus at E. Solving this problem requires either lower interest rates or expanding real income and product, a move from E to B.

real national income and product and real interest rates both moving in the same direction, which means an upward-sloping *BP* line.

If domestic equilibrium (the macro-dot *E*) lies on the payments equilibrium line (*BP*), a country's internal and external equilibria are consistent with each other. But this is a special case. What will happen if its internal equilibrium involves a different real interest rate from the one needed to provide a balance in its international payments? If the *BP* line lies above or below point *E*, the country has a payments surplus or deficit when operating at internal macroeconomic equilibrium.

Note the line that we have labeled BP_- in Figure 18-4 and interpret it as follows. At domestic equilibrium income and product level Y_e, the country's macro-dot is at *E*, with the real interest rate of i_e, but the balance of payments line BP_- shows that its payments balance is negative. The country's real interest rate is too low to attract enough capital inflow to offset its negative balance on current account. To balance its payments at income and product level Y_e, this country should allow its interest rate to rise. By similar reasoning, the line BP_+ in Figure 18-4 shows cases where the interest rate for internal equilibrium is so high that it generates enough capital inflow to put the country's payments balance in surplus. Lower domestic interest rates would be needed to bring about payments balance.

Rather than trying to adjust its domestic interest rates, a country might change its domestic real national income and product instead, though this is politically harder to do. In this case, if a country had internal equilibrium at *E* but kept on running a balance of payments deficit, it might lower real national income and product until it reached a payments balance at *A*. The falling income and product will lower imports and perhaps raise exports, bringing about the payments balance. This move, however, would most likely mean a severe depression. If the country were running a payments surplus at *E*, one remedy might be to expand real national income and product so as to reach equilibrium at *B*. Unfortunately, this move might be impossible because of limits to a country's aggregate-supply capability.

This exercise shows that, in an open economy, macroeconomic policy cannot ignore the international sector.

DISCUSSION QUESTIONS: APPENDIX

1. Briefly explain the meaning of payments equilibrium. What is a macro-dot?

2. Suppose that a country is in domestic equilibrium, with a particular combination of real national income and product and interest rate, but is running a balance of payments deficit. What interest rate policy might correct this problem? Explain why. What real income and product policies would help? Explain.

19 *Economic Growth and Development*

PREVIEW We begin with two propositions. First, the Third World of less developed countries is much more than a group of homogeneous, overpopulated rural slums or backwaters that look pretty much alike and that are scattered here and there in isolated pockets all over the world. A great majority of the world's population lives in the underdeveloped, undeveloped, or less developed countries, often called LDCs. These countries vary widely among themselves in many ways. Like the more developed countries (MDCs), they are becoming more and more urbanized.

Our second proposition is that economic growth is not economic development. Economic growth is basically an objective idea. It is measured in terms of GNP, either in total or (more often) per capita. Its definition remains somewhat arbitrary, and it is a poor measure of economic welfare (see Chapter 1). Economic development, on the other hand, is more subjective and purposeful. The end point of economic development is supposedly welfare or modernization in some sense of these vague terms. A country may grow without development, or it may develop without growth. We believe that both of these propositions are more widely understood than they were a generation ago, but neither is understood as widely as we think it should be.

After distinguishing between growth and development, our next subject is development theory. Why have some countries developed more rapidly than others? How do we explain differences in development? What hope is there for development of the present-day LDCs? There is as yet no agreed-upon answer. We look at a number of rival views.

Next we outline two economic growth theories and ask whether growth is a "good thing." What are its costs? Can it be expected to continue much longer? We shall examine both optimistic and pessimistic views on this unsettled question.

Finally, we discuss income distribution. We contrast the "growth first distribution later" views implied in the work of Simon Kuznets with the "redistribution with growth" stand of the World Bank and the so-called basic human needs approach, which sacrifices growth to development. We also explain the distributional meaning of the "economic dualism," which often goes along with growth.

GROWTH IS NOT DEVELOPMENT: DEVELOPMENT IS NOT GROWTH

Economic growth means higher total or (usually) per capita GNP. What is the difference, in economic terms, between growth and development? In speaking of his own country, Premier George Papandreou of Greece said, "The figures prosper but the people suffer." What he meant was that measured GNP in Greece, or anywhere else, can rise while the person in the street or behind the plow is worse off than before, either absolutely, or as compared to the rich, or both. (Suppose that income distribution became more uneven while growth was taking place.) Also, measured GNP may increase primarily from goods and services that critics call "decadent" rather than "civilized."

Economic development means that progress is taking place in some sense that brings gains in welfare and makes life better for the people. For example, we may look at development through the eyes of those who favor the **basic human needs (BHN)** approach. In this view, a country is developing only when a steadily falling percentage of its people lacks good food, clean water, decent shelter, basic health care, elementary education, and a means of presenting their views to their governments through petitions or demonstrations. It makes no difference whether growth as measured by GNP slows down or even turns negative. There can be development even if there is no growth. "To Hell with GNP!" is the way Japanese environmentalists put the point. In many industrializing LDCs, such as India, "development" has meant more heavy industry, so that any rise in GNP due to traditional farming and handicrafts is not taken seriously. The British Overseas Development Ministry (which backs the basic human needs approach), the Japanese environmentalists, and the Indian planner are all in favor of development but are less interested in measured growth.

Economic development means different things to different groups. To many Americans, it means progress toward a goal not too different from an idealized version of today's American economy. To many Russians, the development goal is an idealized form of the present-day Soviet economy. To members of certain countercultures, the development goal is a world of idealized *Kibbutzim,* communes, labor-managed companies, or encounter groups, sharing, perhaps, the ideal of "plain living and high thinking" or "appropriate" technology, "equitable" distribution of income and wealth, or "respect for the environment."

THE VAST AND VARIEGATED MAJORITY

Statistics cannot bleed. Nevertheless, we offer some facts in Table 19-1. It includes only 126

countries out of about 160 in the world, and it is really far from accurate or complete. However, it does show how countries and "worlds" differ. In this table, the so-called **First World** comprises the non-Communist more developed countries (MDCs) of Western Europe and North America, plus Australia, Japan, and New Zealand. The **Second World** comprises the European Communist countries regardless of their economic levels. The **Third World** includes all other countries. However, the poorest of the poor are sometimes separated out as a **Fourth World.** The status of particular countries is often dubious; China, Cuba, Ethiopia, and Yugoslavia are examples. In addition, Table 19-1 follows the World Bank practice of separating out five high-income oil exporters (Kuwait, Libya, Oman, Saudi Arabia, and the United Arab Emirates) into a special category all their own.[1]

Per Capita Income

The GNP references are to GNP per capita. This is because the individual welfare of each person or family is connected more closely with per capita GNP than with total GNP. But if one of the social goals of a nation, race, or religious group is to achieve a large population, for reasons such as "cannon fodder," insurance against some enemy's intentions, or "propagation of the true faith," then total GNP becomes more important than per capita GNP. Per capita income is much larger in the First World than in the Third World (see column 2 of Table 19-1). With less than one-sixth of the 126-country population in 1983, the First World received over three-quarters of the estimated total income. Of course, these statistics do not give the whole picture about population

1. Although the Soviet Union and the other Second World countries publish usable population figures, the World Bank, from whose publications Table 19-1 is derived, now believes that usable GNP figures can be compiled only from data for Hungary, so that the table's income figures are computed from a reduced sample (119 countries instead of 126). The last two columns of the table therefore are biased upward by the exclusion of Second World income estimates.

TABLE 19-1 Four Worlds and Five Oil Countries: Population, Income, and Growth, 1983

| | Population (millions) (1) | GNP ($ per capita) (2) | GNP (billions of dollars) (3) | Percent of Total | | (5) as percent of (4) (6) |
				Pop. (4)	GNP (5)	
First World						
Industrial market economies						
(19 countries)	728.9	11,060	8,061.6	15.7	77.4	493.0
United States	234.5	14,110	3,308.7	5.1	31.8	623.5
US and Canada	259.4	n.a.	3,615.2	5.6	34.7	619.6
Second World						
European nonmarket economies						
(8 countries)	386.0	n.a.	n.a.	8.3	n.a.	n.a.
High-income oil exporters						
(5 countries)	17.9	2,370	221.4	0.4	2.1	525.0
Third World						
Middle-income economies						
(59 countries)	1,165.2	1,310	1,526.4	25.1	14.7	58.6
Sub-Saharan Africa (9)	148.2	n.a.	n.a.	3.2	n.a.	n.a.
Lower-middle income (37)	665.1	750	498.8	14.4	4.8	33.3
Upper-middle income (22)	500.1	2,050	1,025.2	10.8	9.8	90.7
Fourth World						
Low-income countries						
(35 countries)	2,335.4	260	607.2	50.4	5.8	11.5
China and India	1,752.3	280	490.6	37.8	4.7	12.4
Sub-Saharan Africa (21)	245.2	220	53.9	5.3	0.05	9.4
Totals:						
126 countries	4,633.5	—	—	99.9	—	—
119 countries	—	—	10,416.8	—	100.0	—

Notes: Low-income, under $400; lower-middle, $400–1,500; upper-middle, $1,500–7,000; high-income oil exporters, over $6,000; industrial countries, over $4,500. (There is some overlapping.)

Figures are as of 1983. Monetary unit, U.S. dollar of 1983 purchasing power.

Of the middle-income sub-Saharan African countries, all but one (South Africa) are lower-middle.

Of the 8 OPEC members not classified as high-income, 4 are lower-income and 4 are upper-middle.

The terminology "First" through "Fourth World" are our own and not used by the World Bank or in the *World Development Report 1985.*

Source: World Bank, *World Development Report 1985,* Annex Table 1, pp. 174f. Used with permission.

and income. Just as there are poor people in the richest of countries, so there are rich people in the poorest countries. There are poor people in New York or Los Angeles, and rich people in Dacca (Bangladesh) or Nairobi (Kenya). Moreover, a country's economic situation can change rapidly. In the mid-1950s, Libya was considered a "hopeless case"—but then oil was discovered there! Finally, the Third World differs from, say, the Appalachia region of the United States because of the large and growing number of world-class cities with populations in the millions. Mexico City, for example, may soon pass New York City in population, if it has not already done so. Bangkok in Thailand, Bombay and Calcutta in India, Cairo in Egypt, Caracas in Venezuela, Ibadan and Lagos in Nigeria, Jakarta in Indonesia, São Paulo in Brazil are all in this class, and there are many more.

Differences in Living Standards

Per capita income differences between MDCs and LDCs probably exaggerate differences in living standards. This is because activities like baking bread, making clothes, and building homes involve the market in the First World (and so are included in GNP and national income estimates) but involve only households in the Fourth World (and so are excluded from the statistics). Nevertheless, the difference is huge. Here is a picture of the difference between life in the United States and in an urban area of some Fourth World country, taken from Robert Heilbroner's *The Great Ascent*.[2] We have adjusted some numbers for the inflation that has occurred since that book's publication (1963). Unfortunately, the facts need no adjustment:

2. Robert L. Heilbroner, *The Great Ascent* (New York: Harper, 1963), pp. 23–27. Abridged and adapted from "The Tableau of Under-Development" in *The Great Ascent* by Robert L. Heilbroner. Copyright © 1963 by Robert L. Heilbroner. Reprinted by permission of Harper & Row, Publishers, Inc.; and by permission of William Morris Agency on behalf of the author.

[Let us imagine] how a typical American family could be transformed into an equally typical family of the under-developed world.

We begin by invading the house of our American family to strip it of its furniture. Everything goes: beds, chairs, tables, TV set. . . . Each member of the family may keep his oldest suit or dress, a shirt or blouse. We permit a pair of shoes to the head of the family, but none for the wife or children.

We move into the kitchen. . . . The box of matches may stay, a small bag of flour, some sugar and salt. A few moldy potatoes, already in the garbage can, must be rescued, for they will provide much of tonight's meal. We leave a handful of onions and a dish of dried beans. We take away: the meat, the fresh vegetables, the canned goods. . . .

. . . Next we take away the house. The family can move to the toolshed. It is crowded, but "it is not uncommon for a family of four or more to live in a bedspace, that is, on a bunk bed and the space it occupies—sometimes in two or three tiers—their only privacy provided by curtains."

All the other houses in the neighborhood have also been removed; our suburb has become a shantytown. Our family is fortunate to have a shelter. . . . [In] Cali, Colombia, "on one hillside alone, the slum population is estimated at 40,000—without water, sanitation, or electric light. And not all the poor of Cali are [so] fortunate. Others have built their shacks on land which lies beneath the flood mark. To these people the immediate environment is the open sewer of the city, which flows through their huts when the river rises."

Communication must go next. No more newspapers, magazines, books—not that they are missed, since we take away our family's literacy as well. Instead, in our shantytown we will allow one radio.

Now government services must go. No more postman, no more fireman. There is a school, but it is three miles away. . . . There are no hospitals or doctors nearby. The nearest clinic is 10 miles away and tended by a midwife. It can be reached by bicycle, provided the family has a bicycle, which is unlikely. Or one can go by bus—not always inside. . . .

. . . We will allow our family a cash hoard of $20. Meanwhile the head of the family must earn his keep. As a peasant cultivator with three acres, he may raise the equivalent of $500 to $1,500 worth of crops a year. If he is a tenant farmer, a third or so will go to his landlord, and probably another 10% to the local moneylender. But there will be enough to eat. Or almost enough. The human body requires an input of 2,000 calories [a day] to replenish the energy consumed by its cells. If our displaced American fares no better than an Indian peasant, he will average no more than 1,700–1,900. His body, like any insufficiently fueled machine, will run down. . . .

This is only an impression of life in the underdeveloped lands. It is not life itself. There are lacking the things that underdevelopment gives as well as those it takes away: the urinals smell of poverty, the disease, the flies, the open sewers. And there is lacking a softening sense of familiarity. A [scene], shocking to American eyes, is less shocking to eyes that have never known any other. . . . When we are told that half the world's population enjoys a standard of living "less than $300 a year," this is what the figures mean.

The Widening Gap

As shown in column 4 of Table 19-1, approximately three-quarters of the world's people live in Third World countries, half of them in the Fourth World. But even these percentages are probably biased, since most of the omitted countries are small, poor LDCs. In addition, the Third World's income is growing more slowly than that of either the First or the Second. This is the "widening gap" of which the Third World countries complain.

THEORIES OF DEVELOPMENT AND UNDERDEVELOPMENT

As yet there is no generally accepted theory that explains why some countries have developed and why others have not. Historically, however, there have been a number of different development and underdevelopment theories.

Adam Smith's Development Theory

Oldest in time is the sunny optimism of Adam Smith (1723–1790), as seen in the following words quoted from an essay on development, written in 1755, twenty-one years before his *Wealth of Nations*:

> Little else is requisite to carry a state to the highest degree of opulence, from the lowest barbarism, but peace, easy taxes, and a tolerable administration of justice; all the rest being brought about by the natural course of things.

This is less simple-minded than it sounds, for Smith goes on:

> All governments which thwart this natural course, which force things into another channel or which endeavor to arrest the progress of society at a particular point, are unnatural, and to support themselves are obliged to be oppressive and tyrannical.

How many of today's LDCs, either as colonies or as independent countries, have enjoyed "peace, easy taxes, and a tolerable administration of justice" under governments not "oppressive and tyrannical"? The Chinese case is instructive. For 109 years (1840–1949), the country had one civil or international war after another, from the Opium War to the conquest of power by Mao Zedong's Communists. With peace came development, for which communism claims the credit.

In Book III of *The Wealth of Nations*, Adam Smith spelled out "the natural course of things," mentioned in the quotation. It leads from agriculture to manufacturing, and finally to (foreign) trade. But even so, "Smith on Development" seems to a present-day reader to underestimate the problems and the roadblocks. At the very least, he might have noted the danger of population explosion, and the need to obtain natural resources that the developing country may not have within its own borders.

Marxian Theories

It is no surprise to find Karl Marx (1818–1883) and his followers less cheerful than Adam Smith about development under capitalism. Their conclusions, however, are based on more than the intuitive emotionalism of much Marxist political activism. Let us see how the Marxist answer is derived.

EXPLOITATION AND THE FALLING RATE OF PROFIT The key proposition in Marxian economics is that all value comes from labor and, for that reason, the profits of capitalists arise from the exploitation of labor—that is, by taking from workers some of the fruits of their labor. In Marxian reasoning, capitalist profits are plowed back into production through ever-rising investments in machines. But this increasingly capital-intensive method of production lowers the proportion of new labor input, in this way allowing the capitalist fewer chances for further exploitation. The result is a falling rate of profit, for each dollar invested. The capitalist's responses to this falling rate of profit are the keys to Marxist forecasts of economic suffering, the collapse of capitalism, the rise and fall of imperialism, and the problems of the Third World. Rather than raising their consumption as the classical economists expected, Marxists contend that capitalists will keep on accumulating and simply hoard money or cash balances. The results of this hoarding, as Keynes would agree, are stagnation, unemployment, and misery, ending, Marxists say, in revolution and capitalist downfall.

IMPACT ON THE THIRD WORLD After Marx's death, the writings of his followers spelled out what the falling rate of profit would mean for imperialism and the Third World. In the view of Lenin (1870–1924), the great theorist of imperialism, Third World countries will be brought into the capitalist system. As capital accumulates, it will be exported there, and native people will be put to work at lower (more exploitative) wages than are paid in the more developed countries. In this way, stagnation in the MDCs can be slowed down or even reversed, and the capitalist system can continue onward and upward for a while. But the LDCs themselves will neither grow nor develop. The profits from their businesses go mainly to MDC residents.

Other Marxists, especially Rosa Luxemburg (1871–1919), saw imperialism somewhat differently. In "Red Rosa's" view, to keep up employment and get rid of goods that its own consumers could not buy at profitable prices, each capitalist country would take over LDC areas as happy dumping grounds. The poor LDCs would pay for these goods mainly by selling their assets, meaning the control of their land and mineral resources. The final results of "Luxemburg" imperialism were to be no different from those of "Lenin" imperialism.

Both Lenin and Luxemburg predicted that the end will come because the Third World too is limited in size. The rival imperialist powers will clash over colonization or control of the most promising LDCs. Within its LDCs, each imperialist power will face "liberation movements" that are pitted against the mother country and against its allies in the native capitalist class. The United States fought Spain over Cuba, the Philippines, and Puerto Rico. Later the U.S. fighting in Vietnam gave rise to civil disobedience and rioting in the United States itself. The end result of all this warfare and revolution, the Marxists say, will be the downfall of capitalism, for the wars will spread beyond the Third World. As Lenin put it during World War I, "The road to London and Paris leads through Peking and Calcutta."

Marxist views have been strong in Third World countries. Much of the demand for a New International Economic Order (the subject of the next chapter) is based on Marxian analysis, even though many Third World Marxists wish to remain outside the Soviet or Chinese sphere of influence.

Dependencia Theories of Underdevelopment

Dependencia (dependency) theories of LDC underdevelopment spring from the Third World, particularly from Latin America. This is why they are known by their Spanish name. They are forms of neo-Marxism, in which MDC protectionists and labor unions play "bad guy" roles alongside MDC capitalists. They go beyond standard Marxism to argue that the prosperity of the First World is *dependent upon* the poverty of the Third—"They are rich because we are poor." And similarly, the poverty of the Third World is *dependent upon* the prosperity of the First.

To understand *dependencia* theory, let us go back in time to Europe of the sixteenth, seventeenth, and eighteenth centuries. The dominant economic thinking of the time was *mercantilism.* In England, France, the Netherlands, Spain, and elsewhere, "the mercantile system" took different forms, but all agreed that the goal of a state's economic activity was to strengthen its political (military) power in Europe. This is the key to mercantilist doctrine. The aim was to win colonies in faraway lands, first as sources of precious metals and industrial raw materials for the mother country, and second to keep such riches away from that country's rivals. It was believed to be dangerous for colonies, especially for their non-European natives, to develop any kinds of modern industry that would compete with mother-country producers or provide economic bases for revolt and independent political existence.

According to a number of writers, both the present MDCs and the present LDCs were undeveloped at the start of the mercantilist age, but the MDCs had the edge in military technology. This they used to gain control over the rest of the world, profiting from the world's resources and confining "the natives" to low-paid unskilled work. And the gains that resulted from such exploitation financed the subsequent Industrial Revolution and prosperity. To quote Premier Jawaharal Nehru of India, Britain's Industrial Revolution was "financed by the loot of Bengal."

Mercantilism never died. After their American colonies won their freedom, the mother countries and other powers kept on using colonies as raw material sources by putting high tariffs (import taxes) on their manufactures and other finished goods while admitting their food and raw materials tax-free, even though they competed with the mother country's own farmers and landlords. Still mainly for military reasons, MDCs tried for some time to control the "trade secrets" of the Industrial Revolution against all others, even their old colonies. Students of U.S. economic history may remember Samuel Slater, who memorized the blueprints of advanced British textile machinery whose export was against the law, brought his secret to Rhode Island, and started the New England textile-manufacturing business.

Later in the nineteenth century, as labor movements developed in Western Europe and the United States, skilled workers came more and more to support what is called neomercantilism. Modern industry offered more skilled jobs than farming had, and these jobs were more highly paid than unskilled ones. Workers and their unions demanded protection against low-wage LDC competition, with the same results for the LDCs as they had known under the older military mercantilism.

Dependency is more than a political or economic matter. It has its psychological aspects too. Europeans and their descendants took over most managerial jobs in the modern sectors of LDC economies, both colonial and ex-colonial. The natives' feelings toward them were mixed. Of course, there was resentment against them as well as against other foreigners, such as Chinese and Indians, who held jobs that the natives could not or would not take. But at the same time, natives looked at people from Europe, the United States, or Japan as having superior knowledge and skills, and even doubted their own abilities to run their own affairs. For these reasons, many LDCs remain psychologically dependent on foreign advisers and hesitate to compete with MDC goods on world markets.

Also, technical progress has had different effects on manufacturers in MDCs and on farm products and raw materials in LDCs. In the LDCs, progress led to higher outputs and lower prices on competitive export markets. But in the MDCs, progress appeared to be used mainly to raise profits and wages while holding prices steady or raising them. In the LDCs, the prices of exports generally seemed to fall as compared to the prices of imports. The opposite seemed to be true for the MDCs. These tendencies have been stressed by *dependencia* writers.

Dependencia thinking is an important basis for LDC pressure for bigger and better OPECs, price supports for their countries' exports of goods, and for what is called "redeployment," or transfer, of a higher percentage of world manufacturing capacity into LDC countries from the MDCs. (Because of the lower wage scales in the LDCs, some redeployment is occurring in textiles, clothing, and shoes, to the great concern and dismay of the U.S. labor movement.)

Rostow's Institutional Stage Theory

W. W. Rostow's influential *Stages of Economic Growth* is subtitled "A Non-Communist Manifesto." It may be regarded as an argument not only against Marxism but also against *dependencia* theory, which was not well known when Rostow was writing (1960). Rostow's work is an example of an institutional stage theory.

The Rostow stages of growth are five in number: (1) traditional society, (2) preconditions for take-off, (3) take-off itself (the kernel of the theory), (4) drive to maturity, and (5) high mass consumption.

We need say little about stage 1. Even though economic activity is limited largely to farming and handicrafts and per capita income is low and stationary, life is not always as miserable as that portrayed by Heilbroner earlier in this chapter.

In stage 2, which may last a long time and in which many LDCs now find themselves, there may develop Adam Smith's combination of "peace, easy taxes, and a tolerable administration of justice." In this stage countries often have some accumulation of **social overhead capital** (roads and harbors, schools and public health facilities), and also one or more leading industries (textiles and transportation in Britain and the United States, oil extraction and refining in the OPEC countries).

The take-off (stage 3) is quite sudden when it comes. It covers just about one generation. Rostow's estimates are 1783–1802 for Britain, 1843–1860 for the United States, 1850–1873 for Germany, 1878–1900 for Japan, 1890–1914 for (Czarist) Russia. It is marked by two features. One is the spread of modern methods from the leading sectors to the rest of the economy, which supplies their raw materials and purchases most of their products. The second feature is a sudden sharp rise in saving and investment, often aided by an influx of foreign capital.

After the take-off, Rostow believes the drive to maturity (stage 4) is a much easier matter because it is aided by reinvestment of the gains from take-off—or the force of compound interest. However, take-offs may be followed by crashes, as in Mexico

under Porfirio Díaz (due to revolution) and Russia under Nicholas II (due to World War I). Maturity itself is described by Rostow in terms of higher average labor skills, a shift in economic leadership from self-made "robber barons" to professionally trained managers, and a certain "boredom with the miracle of industrialization," leading to moves in other directions. It was supposedly reached in Britain about 1850, in the United States about 1910, in Japan about 1940, and in (Soviet) Russia in about 1950.

Once maturity (stage 5) is achieved, Rostow says, it can be used in some combination of three ways: militarism and imperialism, the welfare state, and high mass consumption. Rostow favors some judicious combination of the last two. He criticizes Germany and Japan for concentrating on the first for as long as they did, and believes that the Soviet Union still has its choice to make. He believes that the United States used too much of the gains from growth to pay for a postwar "baby boom." His advise to the LDCs is to speed up their take-offs, and he pays little attention to whether MDC policy speeds up or slows down LDC growth. You should also remember that Rostow sees nothing inevitable in this whole evolution.

THEORIES OF ECONOMIC GROWTH

As we have said, economic growth is different from economic development. Economic growth means higher per capita personal income and higher standards of living, but does not involve the cultural and qualitative changes that are important in development. We shall outline two theories of economic growth and then consider whether growth is a "good thing."

The Neoclassical Theory

The neoclassical theory is a supply-side explanation of growth. The main idea can be summed

TABLE 19-2   Levels and Rates of Change of U.S. Productivity in Selected Years, 1950–1984

A. Levels (index numbers, 1977 = 100)					
	1950	**1960**	**1970**	**1980**	**1984**
All private business					
Output per hour of labor	49.7	64.8	86.1	98.7	107.1
Output per unit of capital services	98.6	98.5	98.5	95.6	97.4
Multi-factor productivity	63.6	75.4	90.2	97.6	103.7
Manufacturing only					
Output per hour of labor	49.4	60.0	79.2	101.7	115.6
Output per unit of capital services	94.5	88.0	91.8	90.7	96.0
Multi-factor productivity	59.9	67.0	82.3	98.8	110.4

B. Annual Rates of Growth, 1977–1984							
	1977–78	**1978–79**	**1979–80**	**1980–81**	**1981–82**	**1982–83**	**1983–84**
All private business							
Output per hour of labor	0.5	−1.2	−0.6	1.9	0.2	2.9	3.2
Output per unit of capital services	1.8	−1.5	−4.9	−1.6	0.8	3.0	5.5
Multi-factor productivity	1.0	−1.3	−2.2	0.7	0.5	2.9	4.1
Manufacturing only							
Output per hour of labor	0.9	0.7	0.1	3.1	2.1	4.2	3.6
Output per unit of capital services	1.5	−2.0	−9.7	−0.9	−8.4	5.7	9.6
Multi-factor productivity	1.1	−0.1	−2.2	1.8	−0.5	4.6	5.2

Source: *Monthly Labor Review* (December 1985), Table 28, p. 86.

up in a simple way: a country's growth rate is the weighted sum of the growth rates of the quantity and the quality of each of its productive inputs plus a factor reflecting technical progress. Each input is weighted by its share in the national income and product.

The detailed accounting and statistical techniques used to support this theory are difficult and often controversial. A sample of such computations, made for the United States by the Bureau of Labor Statistics, is presented in Table 19-2. Note the important distinction between the *levels* of productivity in part A of this table and the *rates* of productivity growth in part B. It was the second of these that aroused most interest

when many of them not only turned down but turned negative in the late 1970s and early 1980s. In making sense of the figures, we should recall that "units of capital services" are overestimated in recession periods by the inclusion of machinery and equipment that is available but not actually in use. Also, automation and robotization in the mid-1980s raised "labor" rather than "capital" productivity because the equipment itself is expensive and because it makes possible increases in output with minimal increases in employment.

Table 19-3, estimated by John W. Kendrick of George Washington University, deals with the slowing of U.S. private sector growth that followed the oil shock of 1973 and was perhaps also

TABLE 19-3   Sources of Growth in Real Gross Product for the U.S. Domestic Economy, 1948–1981, with Projections to 2000

Source of Changes in Real Gross Product	1948–73	1973–81	1981–90	1991–2000
Changes in variables influencing productivity				
1. Advances in knowledge	1.4	0.7	1.2	1.0
2. Changes in labor quality[a]	0.5	0.6	0.9	0.9
3. Changes in quality of land	—	−0.2	−0.3	−0.3
4. Resource reallocations	0.4	0.1	—	—
5. Volume changes[b]	0.3	−0.3	0.6	0.4
6. Net government impact[c]	—	−0.2	−0.1	−0.1
7. Other productivity variables[d]	−0.6	−0.6	−0.5	−0.5
Subtotal (total factor productivity)	2.0	0.1	1.8	1.4
Changes in quantity of productive resources	1.7	2.0	2.2	1.8
Total change in real gross product	3.7	2.1	4.0	3.2

Note: Figures are averages of annual percentage rates of change.
a. Includes changes arising from education and training, health, and age-sex composition of labor force.
b. Includes effects of economies of scale and intensity of demand.
c. Includes services to business and the effects of government regulations.

d. Includes the ratio of actual efficiency to potential efficiency and items not elsewhere classified.
Source: John W. Kendrick, "Long-term Economic Projections: Stronger U.S. Growth Ahead," *Southern Economic Journal* (April 1984), Table 1, p. 953.

influenced by the environmentalist movement within the United States itself. Kendrick makes optimistic projections for the last nineteen years of the present century. He estimates that the growth rate of real gross product in the United States was 3.7 percent a year over the quarter century from 1948 to 1973, then fell to 2.1 percent a year from 1973 to 1981, but is expected to recover to 4.0 percent in the decade from 1981 to 1990 and to 3.2 percent in the last decade of the century. Productivity gain follows a similar pattern, falling almost to zero in the oil-shock period. Advances in knowledge and changes in labor quality made important contributions to productivity and growth in all periods studied. Other forces estimated by Kendrick seem to be neutral or negative.

Neoclassical growth theory says nothing about the level of employment of labor and capital, and it is often accused of assuming full employment. This is not quite true, however. What is assumed rather is that the microeconomic market and macroeconomic policy will work together to keep employment rates fairly steady over time. When, in fact, employment rates are falling—the so-called "stagnation" or "mature economy" thesis—neoclassical growth forecasts tend to be too optimistic. When these rates are rising, the error is one of too much pessimism.

Keynesian Theories

The Keynesian growth models and the theories of Sir Roy Harrod in Britain and Evsey Domar in the United States dominated economic literature for a generation after World War II. We limit ourselves to a simpler early model by Harrod. It involves only three quantities: the economy's saving rate (percent of national income devoted to saving), the **capital/output ratio** (the amount of additional capital needed for a one-unit output increase), and the growth rate itself. Harrod's result is very straightforward. The rate of growth is the economy's saving rate divided by its capital/output ratio:

$$\text{economic growth rate} = \frac{\text{saving rate}}{\text{capital/output ratio}}$$

Harrod's system is very convenient in comparing two or more cases over time or space. For example, Table 19-4 compares growth in the United States and Japan over the period of "miracle" Japanese growth from the late 1950s to the oil shock of 1973. During this period the Japanese not only saved (and invested) a higher proportion of their income than did the Americans but also needed less capital per unit of expansion. (Japan was apparently using capital more effectively than the United States, or the productivity of capital was higher there—perhaps because the capital stock was newer.)[3]

IS GROWTH A GOOD THING?

Most of us would rather be rich than poor, or at least we would like to have some of the comforts of life. Only a few of us really seek plain living, with or without high thinking. Those few become hermits, join communes, vow allegiance to Lady Poverty, and remember the sad Emperor of China. (His psychiatrist proposed to cure his depression by having him sleep in the shirt of a happy man. When the happy man was found, he had no shirt!)

Advantages of Growth

The consumption advantages of higher income, and thus of growth, are clear despite the tendencies of MDC people to "dig their graves with

3. More advanced versions of the model, using higher mathematics, lead to unstable or "knife-edge" equilibrium growth paths. This means that constant intervention, presumably by government bodies, is needed to prevent the national income from rising without bound whenever it goes above the growth path or falling at least to zero whenever it drops below this path.

TABLE 19-4   Harrod Model: U.S. and Japanese Growth (1958–1973, approximately)

	U.S.	Japan
1. Saving rate (percent)	16	30
2. Capital/output ratio	4	3
3. Growth rate (1 ÷ 2)	4	10

Note: This table does not involve the "knife-edge equilibrium" instability of more advanced Harrod-Domar models.

their teeth" and bang each other with automobiles. There are also security advantages if crime and environmental pollution can be controlled and if basic welfare can be assured without too great a cost in individual freedom or the right to privacy. There seems no doubt that the average MDC worker lives better than the medieval lord and lady did in their unheated castle, covered with "ermine and vermin," and expecting death or major illness before the age of fifty.

For society, growth yields a dividend, which can be used to raise the standard of living for those at the lowest levels and even redistribute income and wealth above these lowest levels without absolute loss to the "haves" or the community. The moral of Lester Thurow's *Zero-Sum Society* is that "doing something about poverty" is more costly to the rich and the middle class when the country's per capita income is stagnant than when it is growing.

The same principles hold between countries. MDCs can be expected to offer more aid to LDCs when MDC income per capita is growing than when it is not. And the more that world income growth slows down, the greater the likelihood that the LDCs must give up all ambition for catching up with today's MDCs.

Antigrowth Arguments

Antigrowth literature is not quite so old (among economists) as progrowth literature, but it too dates back at least to the English classical school.

David Ricardo (1772–1823), the greatest economist of his time, feared that growth would end in a "stationary state" as capital accumulated. Since capital was subject to diminishing returns, profits would fall to a low point, and net saving and investment would then fall to zero. This prediction, though less extreme than Marx's, helped to give economics the name of "dismal science."

JOHN STUART MILL   John Stuart Mill (1806–1873) did not agree. His *Principles of Political Economy* (1848) included a *defense* of the stationary state and an attack on what we now call **growthmanship** (an overemphasis on measured economic growth). Here is a quotation:

I cannot regard the stationary state with . . . unaffected aversion. . . . [It] would be a very considerable improvement on our present condition. I am not charmed with the ideal of life held out by those who think that the normal state of human beings is that of struggling to get on: that the trampling, crushing, elbowing, and treading on each other's heels, which form the existing type of social life, are the most desirable lot of human kind, or anything but the disagreeable symptoms of one of the phases of industrial progress.[4] . . . [The] best state of human nature is that in which, while no one is poor, no one desires to be richer, or has any reason to fear being thrust back by the efforts of others to push themselves forward. It is only in the backward countries of the world that increased production is still an important object; in those most advanced, what is economically needed is a better distribution. . . .

. . . Nor is there much satisfaction in contemplating the world with nothing left to the spontaneous activity of nature; with every rood [unit of measure] of land brought into cultivation, which is capable of growing food; every flowery waste ploughed up, all quadrupeds

4. At this point Mill's first edition paid its respects to the United States. "The northern and middle states of America are a specimen of this stage of civilization in very favourable circumstances; the proportion of capital to land is such as to ensure abundance to every able-bodied member of the community who does not forfeit it by misconduct. All that these advantages seem to have done for them is that the life of the whole of one sex is devoted to dollar-hunting, and of the other to breeding dollar-hunters." This passage was later dropped.

or birds which are not domesticated for man's use exterminated as his rivals for food, and scarcely a place left where a wild shrub or flower could grow without being eradicated as a weed. If the earth must lose that great portion of its pleasantness which it owes to things that the unlimited increase of wealth and population would extirpate from it, I sincerely hope, for the sake of posterity, that they will be content to be stationary, long before necessity compels them to it.

A stationary condition of capital and population implies no stationary state of human improvement. There would be as much scope as ever for mental culture, and moral and social progress; as much room for improving the Art of Living, and much more likelihood of its being improved, when minds cease to be engrossed by the art of getting on.

EZRA MISHAN   The twentieth-century equivalent of Mill (in his antigrowth opinions) has been Ezra Mishan, author of *The Costs of Economic Growth* and *The Economic Growth Debate.* Mishan puts Mill's points in today's context. He sees industry, urban sprawl, the automobile, and tourism as great dangers to the environment. And he fears the effects on human life of radio, television, air travel, the computer, herbicides, pesticides, the civilian and military applications of nuclear technology, and other recent inventions.

ERICH SCHUMACHER   From Mill and Mishan we pass to Erich Schumacher, who wrote *Small is Beautiful,* subtitled "Economics as if People Mattered." Most economists, incidentally, will agree that they do! Schumacher is not against growth but against *growthmanship.* He wants a world in which people live in greater harmony with their natural environment than they do in large cities. In such a world, people will have interesting jobs, which they need not fear losing to machines or to robots. He wants people to know where their work fits into some useful finished product, and to be regarded as something more than faceless numbers on time cards or stations on assembly lines. He believes that excessive concern for higher measured growth has pushed the division of labor, the substitution of machinery for human skills, the alienation of the worker, and the pollution of the environment too far. These trends not only should be prevented from spreading to the LDCs but should be reversed in the MDCs. The key to this better world is "appropriate technology," an undefined term in Schumacher's book. It may not always exist. A major task is to develop it when it does not, as well as to apply it when it does exist despite any sacrifice in growth.

LIMITS TO GROWTH Another strain of anti-growth literature tells us that growth will end in catastrophe. "Technical fixes" for one problem will give rise to other problems—or make other problems worse. The best-known "model of doom" is *Limits to Growth,* published by an international group of engineers, natural scientists, and social scientists headquartered in Rome and calling themselves the Club of Rome.

The Club-of-Rome analysis of growth begins with an undeniable mathematical fact. Growth of any quantity at any constant rate "explodes," going beyond any finite upper limit. For this reason, it is impossible, in the long run, unless the upper limit is itself growing at the same rate (or at a higher one). But given a finite limit set by the earth's resources growing only slowly or not at all (and they may be falling!), the growth rate must eventually fall toward zero.

The Club-of-Rome pessimism, however, is more immediate than we have suggested so far. If population, especially in the LDCs, continues to explode, and if per capita real income and product levels as a consequence decline, some terrible combination of fatal maladies lies ahead in the short-term future (twenty-first century). There will be starvation, war, and disease if the food supply runs out. If countries return to agricultural production, living standards will fall sharply. There will be a sharp rise in environmental pollution if "technical fixes" are used to keep total output rising on a limited resource base. *Limits to Growth* spells out these alternatives in the language of computer simulation. However, the underlying statistical proofs for the equations fed into the computers are not always made clear. The Club of Rome sees "hope" only in drastically limiting population in the short-term future.

GROWTH AND INCOME DISTRIBUTION

How is economic growth related to equality and inequality in income distribution? We shall give three different views on this question.

The Kuznets Hypothesis

Analyzing historical growth and income distribution statistics for the present MDCs, the Nobel Prize economist Simon Kuznets has noted a pattern of inequality over time. As development progresses, measured inequality has first risen and then fallen in most countries. At the same time, labor's share of income first fell and then rose.[5]

In the Kuznets model, three factors are interwoven to explain the pattern of rising and falling inequality. Part of the explanation is that capital accumulation first feeds on profits and inequality, but later declines as diminishing returns set in for capital. Population and labor force growth also play a role. Population growth rates go up at first, increasing inequality, but go down later, raising wages and reducing inequality. Third, as time passes, highly paid skills are learned by a larger part of the work force, reducing the proportion of low-paying jobs.

What this theory means for the LDCs is presented in the following quote from the Canadian economist Harry G. Johnson:

> There is a conflict between economic efficiency and social justice. The importance of this conflict is likely to vary according to the state of economic development.

5. The "macroeconomic history" of *American Inequality,* by Jeffrey Williamson and Peter Lindert (1981), uses more data than was available to Kuznets himself.

Kuznets notes incidentally that the mid-nineteenth century, when Karl Marx was writing, marks the period of the greatest inequality in Great Britain, where Marx was living in exile. Could Marx have assumed, from what was happening in his lifetime, that the trend toward inequality would continue unchanged?

The more advanced a country is, the more likely are its citizens to have consciences about the distribution of income, and the higher the level of income reached, the less serious will be any slowing down of the rate of growth brought about by redistribution policies. An advanced country can afford to sacrifice some growth for the sake of social justice. But the cost of greater equality may be great to any economy at a low level of economic development. It would therefore seem unwise for a country anxious to enjoy rapid growth to insist too strongly on policies aimed at ensuring economic equality.[6]

Redistribution with Growth

Johnson's advice has not sat well with LDC political leaders, who either represent the political Left in their countries or fear leftist revolution in the short run if they wait for the Kuznets turning point. They want *Redistribution with Growth*, which is the title of a joint study by economists at the World Bank and at the Institute of Development Studies in England. According to this study, redistribution with growth can come about by "appropriate technology" and an "appropriate product mix," which substitutes labor, especially semi-skilled labor, for capital goods and the more highly skilled specialties of the labor aristocracy. It can also come about by pouring capital into the LDCs either free of interest charges or on special terms from MDC governments or from international bodies. In either case, MDC taxpayers would eventually foot the bill.

Basic Human Needs

More extreme than redistribution with growth is the basic human needs strategy, already described. It aims directly at economic development, meaning by "development" first the reduction and finally the end of poverty and alienation. It is not concerned with the measured rate of eco-

nomic growth. It is less popular in most LDC government circles than in MDC universities and in international organizations. (The LDC civil service is an important part of the country's urban labor aristocracy.)

DUALISM AND ENCLAVES

Imagine an MDC visitor returning to a Third World country after a lapse of five or ten years. The visitor will generally land at a major city airport, and spend the first few days in and around that city. Before leaving, the visitor will usually travel for some distance into the surrounding countryside.

What differences is he or she likely to find? Probably much of the capital or any other major city (aside from the slums) will seem more "modern" than it was during the earlier visit. There will be more pavement, more automobiles, more Western-style buildings, more neon signs, more billboards, and so on. But on a trip fifteen to twenty miles out into the farming areas, the banana trees or rice paddies will seem largely unchanged unless the traveler visits a model farm or commune.

This is the visual aspect of **economic dualism.** Dualism may be looked on as another distribution problem, a regional one, between the large cities and the rural areas. The cities, and particularly the areas where foreigners live and work, can easily become islands, or enclaves, of modernization and prosperity in otherwise stagnant and miserable LDCs.

SUMMARY

1. Economic growth and economic development are not the same thing, though the two often go together. Growth is a basically quantitative matter of rising GNP, in total or (usually) per capita terms. Development is progress toward some specific goal or set of goals. These goals differ

6. Harry G. Johnson, *Money, Trade, and Economic Growth,* 2nd ed. (London: Unwin, 1964), p. 159.

from person to person, and may be quite unrelated to measured growth.

2. Of 126 countries reporting to the World Bank, nearly 100 are regarded as LDCs belonging to the Third World and with average per capita income of about $600 a year. The First World comprises the essentially capitalist industrialized MDCs. The Second World includes centrally planned (socialist) countries with widely different degrees of development.

3. Within the Third World is a group of so-called Fourth World countries, 35 or more in number and with per capita income of about $260. These are the poorest of the poor. Sometimes included in the Third World are a few relatively rich oil-exporting countries and a larger number of newly industrializing countries.

4. The Third World (including the Fourth) has three-quarters of the world's population but receives only about one-fifth of world income. There are, however, some wealthy people even in Fourth World countries, just as there are people below the poverty line in rich countries.

5. The Third World is not merely a set of rural backwaters. It includes many large and growing cities of over a million inhabitants, and the number of such cities is increasing.

6. There is no generally accepted theory of economic development. We present instead a sample of four theories.

7. Adam Smith was a development optimist. He believed that growth required little beyond "peace, easy taxes, and a tolerable administration of justice."

8. Karl Marx and his followers—among them Lenin and Rosa Luxemburg—were pessimists about capitalist development. They saw development as leading to stagnation, imperialism, and war by a number of alternative routes.

9. *Dependencia* theory, pessimistic and influenced by Marxism, bases much of its argument on neomercantilism as well as capitalism generally. The division of labor between LDCs and MDCs, or between the mother country and her colonies, plays an important part in this theory.

10. The most striking feature of W. W. Rostow's stage theory of economic growth is its stress on a single-generation "take-off" in which saving rates rise and "leading industries" increase sharply in both number and importance.

11. Neoclassical (supply-side) growth theory focuses on the separate growth rates of technology and of the quantities and qualities of the major inputs to production.

12. Keynesian (demand-side) growth theory is represented here by the simplest Harrod model. It shows the growth rate to be the quotient of two ratios: the saving rate (percentage of income saved) is the numerator, and the capital/output ratio (the net amount of additional capital demanded to increase output by one unit) is the denominator.

13. Growth and development are generally accepted as desirable. One especially important advantage of growth is that it opens up the possibility of aiding the poor and redistributing income without causing absolute injury to the rich and the middle classes.

14. Objections to growth, especially uncontrolled growth, have been raised by a number of writers. Their grounds relate mainly to the environment, the population explosion, the neglect of the poor, the alienation of workers, and the decline of the arts. Writers cited are John Stuart Mill, Ezra Mishan, and Erich Schumacher.

15. The Club of Rome's *Limits to Growth* goes further. These writers see disaster (starvation, resource exhaustion, or pollution) as resulting from economic growth unless population is stabilized quickly.

16. The growth process in the present MDCs has been marked, according to the Kuznets hypothesis, by rising income inequality in its early stages—a trend that is later reversed.

17. The World Bank seeks to correct the pattern of inequality in the present LDCs. The Bank's efforts have stressed the basic human needs strategy and "appropriate technology" that keeps up the demand for semi-skilled labor in meaningful jobs.

18. Another distributive problem is the dualism between urban (industrial) and rural (agricultural) areas, as well as between modern and traditional industries, which usually accompanies growth.

DISCUSSION QUESTIONS

1. Describe a pattern of economic change in "Faroffistan" that you would consider economic growth but not economic development.

2. Similarly, describe a pattern that you would consider economic development but not economic growth.

3. Differentiate among First, Second, Third, and Fourth World countries.

4. If you were expanding Adam Smith's prescription for growth, what factors would you propose to add to his "peace, easy taxes, and a tolerable administration of justice"?

5. Compare Marxist-Leninist growth theory with the neo-Marxian or *dependencia* point of view.

6. Summarize the neoclassical theory of economic growth.

7. Briefly explain the Harrod formula stated in the text and used as the basis for Table 19-4.

8. Which side do you think has the better of the debate as to the desirability of economic growth? Explain your answer.

9. How does the Kuznets hypothesis explain the pattern of growth and income distribution in the MDCs?

10. What is the basic human needs approach to growth and income distribution?

20 *A New International Economic Order?*
North-South Confrontation

PREVIEW Since about 1960, economic relations between the First World (the "North") and the Third World (the "South") have deteriorated. Many of the Southern countries feel that the Northern countries have been able to develop their industrial base and to prosper because of cheap raw materials and labor from the Southern countries. For this reason, the South has voiced a set of demands through several United Nations agencies that are aimed at improving economic conditions in the Third World.

After briefly describing the nature of this North-South conflict, we outline the South's proposals for a new international economic order (NIEO) and the responses by countries of the North to the South's demands. Then we consider fourteen of the major demands in some detail. These demands range from those dealing mainly with economic matters such as trade balances to those that are mostly political, such as the law of the sea. Finally, we describe the weapons that some of the countries and leaders of the South seem ready to use against the North.

THE NATURE OF THE CONFLICT

During the three or four generations before World War I, a key policy question in economics was an international one: free trade or protection? Most conventional economists were on the side of free trade, whereas others favored some form of protection.

Now, at the end of the twentieth century, a different split threatens. The issue is the desir-

ability of a **New International Economic Order (NIEO),** which would possibly give the poorer countries a better chance to grow and develop. Conventional economists believe that the existing international economic order works quite well, though it could be improved by getting rid of protectionist abuses. With all its faults, they say, the existing order works better than the NIEO proposals are likely to work in practice. Others, however, see no hope in the existing system. They see the present order as doomed and propose to move ahead with the new order.

To some extent the conflict is geographic. Although differing among themselves (and also internally) about the desirability of freer trade, the more developed countries (MDCs) of the temperate zone ("the North") are more or less satisfied with the existing order, in which they have prospered. On the other hand, the less developed countries (LDCs, or "the South") tend to blame the present international order for their inability to grow and develop. They generally support some form of NIEO, though with only a shaky and ever-changing agreement as to its nature and meaning.[1]

---

1. The North-South geographic split should not be taken literally. The "North" includes several MDCs from the temperate zone of the Southern Hemisphere. Australia, New Zealand, and South Africa are examples. The "South" includes most of the tropical countries of the Northern Hemisphere, lying between the Equator and the Tropic of Cancer in Latin America, Africa, and Asia. If there is a geographic North-South split, the dividing line is not the Equator but the Tropic of Cancer.

TABLE 20-1   The Major New International Economic Order (NIEO) Proposals

LDC Trade	LDC Receipts of Capital and Transfer Payments	LDC Internal Economies	Essentially Political Issues
1. Preferential access of LDC exports to MDC markets 2. Higher and more stable world prices of LDC export goods (stockpiling of goods) 3. LDC cartels to raise world prices of LDC export goods 4. Redeployment of world industrial capacity to LDCs	5. Increased MDC aid (reparations) to LDCs 6. LDC access to international lending on concessional (preferential) terms 7. Rescheduling of existing LDC debts to MDC institutions and to international organizations 8. Linkage of special drawing rights (or "paper gold") to LDC aid receipts	9. Transfer of technology to LDCs; development of "appropriate technology" for LDCs 10. LDC control of multinational corporations within their borders	11. International control of the open sea— "law of the sea" 12. Division of control of international financial organizations between MDCs and LDCs 13. Respect for LDC sovereignty; unconditionality of financial aid; limitations on appeal to international tribunals 14. MDC disarmament, which would free resources for purchases of LDC goods, and for sale or transfer to LDCs

The South's (the LDCs') demands are voiced mostly at and through a number of United Nations (U.N.) bodies.[2] However, North-South issues have also been on the agenda of the World Bank (which makes international long-term loans), the International Monetary Fund (which regulates exchange rates and gives short-term balance of payments support to deficit countries), and a wide variety of other world organizations. These demands have increased over the years in both number and variety. Economic and political issues are intertwined. No single LDC feels very strongly about every one of them, but a number of LDCs have been able to present a united front in supporting them both separately and as a group.

We shall offer a brief overview of the NIEO demands and the responses from MDCs. Then we shall examine specific demands in more detail.

The NIEO Demands: Fourteen Major Proposals

Table 20-1 lists fourteen of the most important NIEO proposals. The list begins with demands that are mainly international and economic (trade issues and demands about capital movements), goes on to those that are domestic and economic, and finally to primarily political demands.

2. Among these U.N. bodies are the General Assembly, the Economic and Social Council (ECOSOC), the U.N. Conference on Trade and Development (UNCTAD), the U.N. Industrial Development Organization (UNIDO), the U.N. Economic Councils for individual regions (Latin America, Africa, Asia and the Pacific), and many more.

The list of demands has been growing longer over the years, as LDCs have failed, as a group, to catch up with the MDCs. A possible near-future addition to the list may be some form of international taxation by a U.N. agency to aid Third World countries. Another proposal would single out for taxation the countries that benefit from the "brain drain," which occurs when people educated in Third World countries live and work in the First World, taking away from their homelands their skills or "human capital."

MDC Replies and Strategies

The replies of MDCs have ranged from acceptance to outright rejection. At one extreme are the countries that are so receptive to LDC demands that they are looked upon as being MDC branches of the LDC. Sweden has come the closest to this position. At the other extreme are those countries that "stonewall," or simply refuse to discuss the issues, to offer compromises, to bargain, or to reach any agreement at all. (The United States has been accused of such attitudes.)

The MDC replies have also varied from time to time, from country to country, from proposal to proposal, and from political party to political party, within each of these countries. Socialist parties and neutral countries have generally been more sympathetic to LDC arguments than have capitalist countries with large defense budgets. The reaction has also depended on the state of East-West (First World–Second World) relations. When relations between the United States and the Soviet Union have improved, each side has become less interested in LDC problems. In contrast, the Cold War has meant competition to win over the LDCs.

Many strategies have been used by the MDCs in responding to the LDC demands. One is "tokenism," which means granting limited and conditional concessions. For example, a country may allow access to its markets only for a small group of LDC-manufactured exports, or only for a short time, or only for small quantities (quotas), or only for a certain group among the LDCs. In one such case, France allowed access to its markets only for French-speaking former colonies in Africa. These concessions may also be subject to withdrawal if MDC business or labor claims to be injured by them. Still another strategy is "buck-passing," or the granting of concessions subject to legislative approval, which is not expected to be gained. It is easy for American diplomats at world conferences to promise more foreign aid, when they know that Congress will not appropriate the funds! Finally, there is the strategy of "splitting" the LDC bloc in different ways, as by separating the exporters and importers of oil, or separating the low-income from the middle-income LDCs. This tactic has not been generally successful.

TRADE ISSUES

What are the economic merits of the individual LDC proposals that together form the NIEO? We shall try to be objective and unemotional in our answer. Of course, the search for objectivity often leads to uncertainty when technical questions come up. However, the alternative would be simply to place our trust in intuition and emotion, or in the inspiring words of particular leaders living or dead. Picking and following a popular leader does give certainty and easy answers like a slogan or shouting "Right on!" But all too often there are regrets the next day, the next year, or the next decade.

For the economist, the most important of the NIEO issues are concerned with LDC trade. If the new order could provide the LDCs not only access to MDC markets for their potential manufactured exports but also higher prices for their present agricultural and raw material exports, the worst of their troubles might well be over. The gap between LDC and MDC incomes might close rapidly, and the demand for a new order might disappear.

Preferential Access to MDC Markets

Most who represent or speak for the LDCs are anything but free traders. They do not care

FIGURE 20-1   Wage-Rate Equalization by LDC Access to MDC Markets

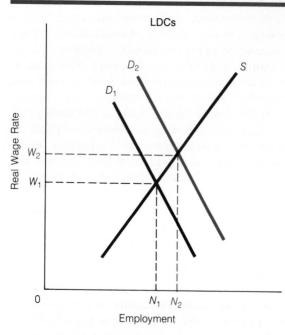

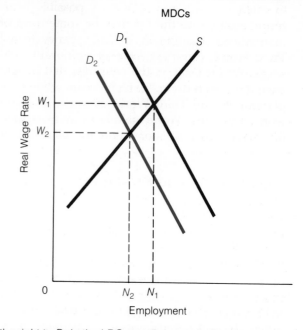

In these graphs, W_1 is the real wage rate and N_1 is the number employed when LDC products are effectively excluded from MDC markets. The real wage rate W_1 is much higher in the MDCs than in the LDCs.

With freer trade, world demand shifts from MDC to LDC products, increasing demand for LDC labor (D_1 shifts to the right to D_2 in the LDC panel), but reducing demand for MDC labor (D_1 shifts to the left to D_2 in the MDC panel). Employment and wage rates both rise in the LDCs, but both fall in the MDCs. As a result, the two wage rates W_2 are closer together than the original wage rates W_1.

whether or not the MDCs open their home markets to each other's manufactures. They want preferential access for LDCs alone. Nor do LDCs propose to offer MDCs access to their own markets in return for access to MDC markets. Nevertheless, we shall limit our discussion to what would most likely happen if LDCs had access to MDC markets in a freer-trade situation, with fewer protective tariffs, quotas, or export restrictions.

The LDCs are low-wage countries with low-skilled workers. At first, their manufactured exports would be light manufactures, such as textiles, clothing, shoes, parts and components, and assembly services. These industries are labor-intensive and use unskilled and semi-skilled labor. (A labor-intensive industry is one calling for

much labor for each unit of product.) The LDC advantage in world markets is the cheapness of their low-skilled labor.

If the LDCs could more freely export the products of their cheap low-skilled workers, the demand for these workers would rise, and with it the wages of the workers in LDC cities. But the low-wage goods from LDCs would surely lower the demand for the low-skilled MDC workers who compete with them. For this reason, the real wages and/or employment of such MDC workers would fall. In other words, trade would make real wage rates and real incomes to the factors of production more nearly equal across countries.

Figure 20-1 illustrates how this would happen. The left-hand panel shows the situation in the LDCs. The initial wage rate is W_1, and the initial employment level is N_1. Increased exports cause the demand curve for workers to shift to the right from D_1 to D_2. The wage rate rises to W_2, and employment rises to N_2. The right-hand panel shows the situation in MDCs, where wage rates are at first much higher than in the LDCs. The competition from imports from the LDCs shifts the demand curve to the left, from D_1 to D_2, which lowers the real wage rate from W_1 to W_2 and, at the same time, lowers employment from N_1 to N_2.

This point, however, leads us to a problem of income distribution. Viewing the world as a whole, we can see that freer access of LDC exports to MDC markets would make the income distribution more nearly equal by raising LDC wages and employment in cities. But within any one MDC, the result would be just the opposite. The MDC workers in labor-intensive industries who would lose their jobs or be downgraded would be, as we said, mainly the low-skilled or semi-skilled people. These are the people already disadvantaged by age, race, or sex; by poor schooling or ignorance of the MDC language; and by every kind of handicap. They would not be the MDC "labor aristocracy" but would be those at the bottom of the MDC total-income and wage-income ladders.

At the same time that real wage rates would be partly or completely equalized between MDCs and LDCs, interest and profit rates would tend to be equalized as well. In the new LDC manufacturing export industries, profits would rise, and in the MDC import-competing industries, they would fall. Capital would move away from the relatively low-interest, low-profit MDCs to the high-interest, high-profit LDCs. Within the MDCs, gains that would result from this capital movement would go to the (generally wealthy) recipients of interest and profit. Capital export might cause further losses to MDC workers through less backing from capital and capital goods, lower productivity, and lower demand for labor across the board.

Those who favor "more equality" often do not face up to this distributional problem. If the desire is for equality of *world* income, access to MDC markets for the products of LDC labor is one way

to go. A quicker way would be the immigration of LDC working people into MDC labor markets. But if we mean only, or mainly, equality of *domestic* income, MDC citizens should oppose LDC demands for access to their markets. Most likely this dilemma will play a larger and larger part over time in discussions of world economic problems.

Although labor and wages are important, we should not forget consumers and the prices of goods. Trade equalizes prices of goods across countries, and also the real wage rates and real prices of nonlabor productive inputs, such as machinery. In the present case, this means that MDC consumers of light manufactured goods gain by freer LDC access to MDC markets. It also means, however, that LDC consumers of these goods—and of the other goods from which labor might shift in order to enter export industries—would lose. When freer trade causes LDC farm land and workers to shift from subsistence agriculture (food consumed on the farm by the farmers themselves) to cash crops for export (sugar, coffee, bananas, and flowers), the suffering consumers may include most of the LDC people.

Stockpiling of Goods

The South's position on storable goods, such as grain, and industrial raw materials is that international stockpiles or "buffer stocks" should be set up to make sure that the producers will have stable and profitable prices at all times, and to protect them from changes in demand that are caused by MDC business cycles. An internationally financed organization would buy and store surplus goods in MDC recession years and then sell them in MDC boom years. At the same time, it would iron out the price effects of weather and similar supply-side disturbances.

To understand the South's position, one must realize that many LDCs are *monocultural*. That is to say, their source of foreign exchange is the export of a single or a very few goods whose world markets are sensitive to cyclical problems in the buying countries (MDCs). The United

States, particularly the South and West, was in such a position before the Civil War, when the major U.S. exports were cotton, tobacco, and wheat. Today many Latin American countries depend for their prosperity on the markets for coffee, sugar, and/or bananas. A few other examples from the LDCs are Sri Lanka's tea, Malaysia's tin and rubber, Ghana's cocoa, and Zambia's copper.

The South's position is supported by the **Prebisch thesis**—that the market system has developed in a way that is unfair to agricultural and raw material producers.[3] Just why did the market develop in this way? To begin with, because there are usually many small firms in this market, the producers of agricultural products and raw materials are not able to restrict output to raise prices. Their answer to technical progress has been simply to raise their output (supply). On the other hand, both employers and workers who produce manufactured goods often are organized. Their reaction to progress has been to raise wage rates and profit margins through collective (and collusive) bargaining. For this reason it is said that the terms of trade, both between raw materials and manufactured goods and between LDCs and MDCs, have been twisted in favor of the manufactured goods and the MDCs. Whether or not the Prebisch thesis is valid, it has become an article of faith among many Third World intellectuals and partisans.

The several stockpiling plans that the countries of the South seek for individual goods do not call for separate enterprises. They are to be brought together in a Common Fund, so that net losses on one good can be paid from net profits on another. The Common Fund itself is to be financed by the United Nations. This means that the MDC taxpayers would provide most of the money. If the Common Fund has enough resources, it is also to offer low-interest loans to LDC development plans of all sorts.

Cartels

Inspired by the success of OPEC (Organization of Petroleum Exporting Countries) in the 1970s, the South has favored similar producer-ruled combinations, called **cartels**. By cutting back production, a cartel attempts to raise the price of the controlled commodity and the income of the cartel members. As a matter of theory, it is clear that world real income is decreased when production is cut back and prices are raised.[4] But OPEC proved that cutting production and raising prices can help certain countries in certain cases for a certain length of time. It can also hurt the MDCs. For many resentful LDCs, "The enemy of my enemy is my friend," even when they are themselves hurt.

The South regrets and the North rejoices that government cartels for copper, tin, or rubber have not duplicated even the temporary success of OPEC. There are four main reasons why they have failed. (1) In most cases, natural substitutes are available. (2) As a result of technical progress, there are *manufactured* substitutes for the good. (3) The geographical spread of production is often so wide that the cartel cannot really control it. (4) Consumers find that they are able to get along with less of the good even when there are no close substitutes, as in the case of gasoline in the United States.

Redeployment of Industries

The term *redeployment* may inspire visions of Soviet troops taking apart factories in Germany or Manchuria and setting them up again in the Soviet Union. Nothing quite so drastic has been proposed. However, one of the South's major goals is to increase the LDC share of world manufacturing capacity and output to 25 percent by the year 2000.

---

3. The *Prebisch thesis* is named for Raul Prebisch, a noted Argentine development economist. A similar argument has been used within the United States in support of price "parity" for agricultural goods.

4. World *wealth*, however, is another matter in the case of exhaustible resources. Oil or coal in the ground may turn out to be a more desirable asset than the immediate income or MDC assets for which they can be exchanged.

How can this be done? The plan is for *new* capacity to be concentrated mainly in the LDCs. However, even though the plan does not call for any physical movement of existing plant and equipment, the costs to the MDCs would be very real. As we have said, the industries to be redeployed are mainly[5] unskilled-labor-intensive ones suited for workers with little formal education and few industrial skills. If these industries—such as textiles and clothing—decline in the MDCs, the workers who lose their jobs will be mostly from the bottom of the income distribution. What is to become of them? Who else will hire them? Are they to live for the rest of their lives on nothing but "make-work" or transfer payments?

CAPITAL MOVEMENTS AND TRANSFER PAYMENTS

Another group of proposals is concerned mainly with the transfer of capital to LDCs in the form of direct aid from the MDCs or special lending arrangements.

Aid—Charity or Reparations?

The most important proposal on foreign aid appeared in 1980 in the so-called Brandt Report, entitled *North-South: A Program for Survival*, prepared with U.N. support. It proposed that foreign aid from each MDC should rise to 0.7 percent of GNP a year by 1985 and to 1.0 percent by the year 2000. The U.S. GNP was approximately $4 trillion in 1985, so that the Report would have called for a U.S. contribution of about $28 billion. If we conservatively estimate U.S. GNP at a $6.5 trillion level for the year 2000 (in 1985 dollars),

the U.S. contribution would have to be $65 billion (in 1985 dollars).

These transfers are proposed both as charity and as reparations. We shall not dwell on the charitable aspect here, but recall the miserable conditions of LDC life, particularly Fourth World life, described in the previous chapter. The more controversial reparations aspect is founded on the *dependencia* theory, which was also presented in that chapter. We need not prepare a detailed "balance sheet of imperialism" as a whole, or decide whether imperialism was either better or worse than its possible alternatives. The LDC argument is simply that the major *gains* from colonial and imperialist adventures went to certain persons and classes in the MDCs and helped to start some of these countries on the road to development. According to the *dependencia* theory, the major *losses* went to certain persons and classes in the LDCs, setting most of these countries on the road to underdevelopment. It is worth noting that the biggest developmental success stories outside Europe were countries that escaped European imperialism altogether (like Japan) and countries settled by Europeans who won their freedom fairly early in their history (as did the United States, Canada, and Australia).[6] Aid is thought of as reparation or payment to restore the balance, even though the present generation of Americans had nothing to do with the Mexican War, and the present generation of English people had nothing to do with the conquest of India.

In the North, aid is thought of as a free gift, but this is not always the view in the South. It has in fact been common for aid funds to be "tied" to the purchase of equipment from the granting country, to projects approved by the granting country, and to support of the granting country's nationals stationed in the receiving country to give technical assistance or to supervise the uses to which aid money is put. Some have been tied to military aid. Much aid money is "wasted" on "overpriced" equipment and/or

---

5. But not exclusively, as witness the meteoric rises of the Korean auto, steel, and shipbuilding industries! The "four modernizations" of Deng Hsiao-ping in China include "economic modernization," which implies Korea on an enormously larger scale.

6. Hong Kong (since 1950) is an exception to this generalization. So are Korea and Singapore.

personnel from the granting country. Also, there are often restrictions on the receiving country's production of goods that might compete with the granting country's industries and labor. Sometimes it is claimed that the aid bureaucracy is a "cover" for the granting country's secret agents who might otherwise not be admitted into the receiving country. Aid may also be subject to cutoffs if the receiving country makes political decisions or installs a government that the granting country considers unfriendly. Thus some U.S. laws call for ending economic aid to countries that nationalize U.S. company assets without payment of adequate compensation. It surprises nobody that the South opposes all forms of "tying" aid or having "strings attached" to it.

The five main Northern, or MDC, objections to foreign aid are easily stated:

1. Both public and private sectors have attractive uses at home for the funds and resources involved. Both individual cases of poverty and pockets of poverty remain within their own boundaries.
2. Often there is LDC "ingratitude" for aid received in the past. This is especially likely when those presently in the LDC government are political opponents of the regime that had received the aid.
3. LDC products helped by the aid often compete with the exports and with the domestic production of the granting country. The United States gave textile mills to the Republic of Korea after the Korean War (1950–1953). Products of these mills were being imported into the United States as early as 1965.
4. Often the aid fails to reach the targets expected by the MDC taxpayers if not the MDC government. Whether by reason of corruption or the traditional working of the receiving country's government, much aid seems to be a transfer "from poor people in rich countries to rich people in poor countries."
5. Often, there is a concentration of official aid in the LDC public sector, when, according to MDC opinion, the LDC private sector is more productive, more efficient, and unduly neglected.

Concessional Lending

The second-best source of LDC development aid is the **concessional loan.** Unlike grant aid, concessional loans must be repaid. But generally they are long-term loans at rates of interest well below the international market rates on such loans. After allowing for inflation, one finds that concessional rates of interest are usually negative so that real loan repayment is only partial.

Private sector banks and other financial institutions seldom make concessional loans deliberately, though they may do so by mistake or under government pressure. To whom, then, can the LDCs turn for these loans? Governments—mainly but not only MDC governments—sometimes make concessional loans, most often to present or potential political allies. The more frequent source of such loans, however, is an international agency. The most important single source of loans has been the World Bank, originally called the International Bank for Reconstruction and Development (IBRD) in Washington, D.C. There are many regional institutions as well. The Asian Development Bank in Manila is one, and the Arab Monetary Fund in Abu Dhabi is another. The South would like to see the capital of these lending institutions increased so that they can make more loans. The South would also like these loans to be freer from any requirements that receivers make profits or avoid losses, or practice any form of austerity.

Debt Renegotiation

Loans, either public or private, solve or postpone LDC payments problems as well as grants do, but their "service" (interest charges and principal repayments) makes these payments problems worse. As noted in Chapter 18, it is by no means unusual to find capital flowing from poor to rich countries when past years' loans are falling due, and when new loans are not forthcoming.

Most LDC loans contracted before 1973 were expected to be repayable, at existing tax rates, out of the proceeds of the growth that they assisted. Some of them, especially the private ones, were expected to be **self-liquidating loans.**[7] Following the rise of OPEC, however, new problems arose. Some loans were diverted from growth to paying for oil imports at high OPEC prices—that is, from positive economic growth to avoiding economic decline due to shortage of fuel, or from moving ahead to "running in place." Too little attention was paid to the servicing of the loans. Another set of loan problems arose in 1983 as world oil prices fell. Some oil-producing LDCs had undertaken large debts, expecting to make repayment from sales of oil at high prices. As prices fell, several of these countries defaulted or threatened to default. For the United States, the most important of these cases was Mexico, which had borrowed particularly heavily in anticipation of *rising* oil prices. The total of all LDC debts, new and old, was estimated at nearly $1 trillion in 1985, of which $360 billion were owed by Latin American countries. Fidel Castro has repeatedly asserted that these sums can never be repaid and should be cancelled outright. Among the creditors have been the principal banks of New York City and other world financial centers, which "recycled" deposits from OPEC countries into loans to LDCs. Wholesale LDC defaults on loans would endanger not only the profits of many of the world's largest banks but also the liquidity and the safety of their depositors, not to mention the future of the "recycling" mechanism itself.

When oil prices were high, the North may have expected the countries of the South that do not produce oil to join in some form of action by oil importers against OPEC. This did not happen. Indeed, the MDC countries themselves did not present a common front against OPEC. Instead, the non-oil South demanded **debt renegotiation**—

7. When a public or a private corporation borrows money to build a railroad or an electricity-generating facility, and the loan is to be repaid from freight charges by the railroad or the sale of electric power, the railroad or electric plant is said to be self-liquidating. Loans to build public highways, hospitals, or schools are seldom technically self-liquidating, but they may still be paid without strain from the higher incomes resulting from the added facilities.

changing the terms of the loans. Specifically, the South proposes the "stretching out" of LDC debts without increases in nominal interest rates and without prejudice against new loans. These new loans would allow them to continue to buy oil and might allow a number of the drought countries of sub-Saharan Africa to buy food as well.

Even though renegotiation of the stretch-out kind may avoid formal repudiation or default, during inflationary times it is a partial repudiation when measured in real terms. On the other hand, it is no more "unreasonable" than the renegotiation requests of many governments in financial trouble. New York City has been the best-known American example.

Paper Gold

Gold coin and bullion (the metal itself) are accepted and held as international reserve assets (see Chapter 18). For this reason, gold production automatically improves the payments position of South Africa, the Soviet Union, and other countries where mines are located. That is to say, it reduces their balance of payments deficits or increases their surpluses.

It is natural for non-gold-producing LDCs with international payments problems to envy the gold producers and seek equal status with them. They have tried to use the international agencies for this purpose, particularly the special-drawing-rights (SDRs) system of the International Monetary Fund (IMF). As explained in Chapter 18, special drawing rights are entries on the IMF's books—assets of countries holding them and liabilities of the IMF itself. They are issued by the IMF to help countries deal with balance of payments problems. Like gold, they can be used by deficit countries to settle international balances. For this reason, they are called "paper gold."

The LDCs want the issuance of SDRs to be tied to development financing. The NIEO proposal is to give the South the lion's share of each new SDR issue, and to have many such issues. The share of each country in each new issue would be determined by some combination of formula and bargaining.

LDC INTERNAL ECONOMIES

The next set of proposals deals with ways in which the internal economies of the LDCs might be improved through the transfer of MDC technology to LDCs and through LDC control of multinational corporations within their borders.

Technology Transfer

Companies that hold patents and know how to use them efficiently often refuse to license the use of these patents in LDCs, particularly by LDC public agencies. Or they may exact conditions that the LDCs feel are unfair, such as high royalty payments, prohibitions on exports that compete with the patent owner's own goods, and control by the patent owner over the patent's use in the LDC.

One part of the South's NIEO proposal on technology is the compulsory licensing of MDC patents to an international agency. This agency would be supported by MDC taxpayers but would act on behalf of the LDCs. The LDCs could then get MDC patents free of charge or at a low cost. If MDC patent owners set unacceptable conditions on licenses to the international agency, the world rights to their patents might be limited or taken away, or the differences might be made subject to binding international arbitration.

A second part of the South's NIEO proposal on technology relates not to current but to what is called "appropriate" technology for the LDCs. Most Northern technology now in use has been designed in and for countries with fairly cheap capital and with costly but skilled labor. It is poorly suited to LDCs, which generally have scarce capital and unskilled, though cheap, labor. For this reason, the use of Northern technology in the South may not be economical. Or, even when it is, it may add to the using country's unemployment by putting native labor-intensive producers out of business. What the South feels is appropriate technology is more unskilled-labor-intensive than Northern technology. It is also less polluting for the environment, and sometimes smaller-scaled. However, the South wants it to be equal in economic efficiency to MDC technology under LDC conditions.

Such appropriate technology is not often found outside the laboratory. The NIEO proposal is for LDC-ruled international agencies to be given control over enough money and investment processes to allow the appropriate technologies to develop rapidly in many fields at the same time. It calls for this development to take place on the shop floor or at least in the pilot plant, and not just in the laboratory. The South is sure that with enough investment it can develop a good deal of appropriate technology in fairly short order—as the North developed nuclear power and space exploration. The North is not so sure, and it worries about "throwing money at problems."

Control of Multinationals

Multinational or transnational corporations have become the "big bad wolves" of international development. Let us try to examine them and their activities as objectively as we can.

The typical multinational corporation (MNC) is no corner grocery. By the standards of most LDCs, it is *big*—sometimes larger than the LDC's own "host" government—even when unnoticed by such directories as the *Fortune 500*. Its power center is in an MDC, even when its official home office is far away in some place safe from taxation and publicity. For many reasons—such as savings on tariffs, taxes, regulations, wages, raw materials, and transportation—it has chosen to diversify its activities internationally. Because it is profitable to do business in LDCs, the MNC generally gives (and boasts of giving) development aid to its LDC host countries. This aid may include capital, technology, entrepreneurship, and urban development. It may have come into its host country only by invitation, possibly reinforced by special concessions. It remains there only by permission of the host government—

modified sometimes by a long-term contract that is intended to guarantee certain rights for a term of years. So what is all the fuss about? And how is the North involved?

Here are three types of cases illustrating what the fuss may be about:

1. The regime that invited the MNC to operate in its country has been replaced by another regime, which claims the invitation was a corrupt mistake. The new regime proposes unilaterally to change the terms under which the MNC is operating in the country, or to expel the MNC altogether. The South wants such unilateral actions legitimized under international law.

2. The LDC proposes to tax the MNC on that part of its net income that was earned there. How can the LDC Finance Ministry find out what total MNC profits were and then estimate the proportion attributable to its LDC operations? Clearly, access to MNC books and records is required. But these records are located in the MNC's home office in its home country, where it is difficult for LDC investigators to get at them. The South would like MNC home governments forced to make MNC books and records available to governments in all the host countries in which the MNC does business, not only for tax purposes but to help with quality controls, tariff duties, and other host-country laws and regulations.

3. Like other companies, MNCs often involve themselves in host-country politics to secure favorable regimes and favorable treatment. Sometimes the MNC may also seek the help of its home country's embassy in the LDC, or even of its government back home. When such help is given, and when it is decisive, the situation is called **neocolonialism.** Or when the MNC feels it has suffered too much from some action against it—as when its property is confiscated without what it considers adequate compensation—it may try to persuade its home government to take action against the host-country LDC. "Action" may mean reduction of aid, reduced purchases of host-country exports, or even collaboration with rebels against the defending regime. Such policies are called *destabilization*, and the South wants them outlawed.

Much of "the fuss" does not raise the question of alternative sources of what the MNCs have to offer. There simply are complaints that the companies are neither generous nor idealistic and that they are foreigners as well. In addition, there is regret that because the host country was so poor or its leaders were so corrupt, it did not make a better deal with the MNCs in the first place. But the major problem generally is that one or a few of these huge companies have become almost a second government in the host country, rivaling the country's real government in political and economic power. The MNCs and also their home countries see conflict, when it arises, as a blow to liberty caused by the government in the LDC. But to the host country and particularly its left wing, the same conflict appears as an imperialistic, racist, or exploitative attack.

ESSENTIALLY POLITICAL ISSUES

The last group of NIEO demands are mainly political issues. However, each proposal has important worldwide economic effects.

Law of the Sea Proposals

The open seabed, outside any country's territorial waters, contains surface deposits of rare metals, particularly manganese, in what engineers believe are large enough amounts to make them worth mining. But when a company incorporated in Country A and another company incorporated in Country B wish to explore overlapping seabed areas, who is to decide between them?[8]

As part of the new order, the South demands that a United Nations agency—with each country having one vote, but no veto power—be set up with exclusive rights to license and/or carry on seabed exploration. It is hoped that this agency

8. When English, French, and Spanish land grants in the wilds of North America overlapped with each other—ignoring Indian rights—the result was warfare. Nobody wants to repeat that experience.

will earn large revenues, which are to be distributed as development aid to LDCs, even to the landlocked countries.

World Bank and IMF Voting Rights

Voting rights in the World Bank and the International Monetary Fund (IMF) are presently related to financial contributions in such a way that single directors represent whole blocks of LDC members, while the United States and the European Community (EC) have veto powers over the agency's policies. Each LDC may increase its power within the World Bank and IMF by raising its contribution, as Saudi Arabia has done, but this choice is not open to any of the poorer countries of the South.

The South demands changes in the World Bank and the IMF to increase the voting strength of present and potential debtor countries. Such a move means a reduction in the voting strength of the presently dominant creditor countries of the North. At first glance, it seems more natural for a bank, whose revenue comes mainly from loans, to be controlled by the lending (creditor) interests that have organized it. But the checkered histories of many commercial banks in many countries, including both public and private institutions in the United States, offer many cases where directors chosen from among major "customers" (borrowers) actually control bank policy in the interest of debtors.[9] However, the results of such experience are not usually the best, either for the banks themselves or for their depositors.

Sovereignty

Suppose that a major power, or a known friend of a major power, takes over foreign-owned natural resources or other property within its borders. Suppose that it tolerates or even inspires antiforeign mob violence, refuses to protect foreigners' civil rights, or otherwise violates peacetime international law. In most cases, very little is done about it. "Gunboat diplomacy" is not often used against the offending country, nor can the offender be brought before international courts of law or sued unless it agrees. Immunity from lawsuits is a part of political sovereignty. In other words, the large countries' sovereignty is respected "short of war," despite their violations of international law.

The South, especially the self-styled nonaligned countries among the LDCs, seeks the same respect. The main targets of their opposition are MDC export boycotts of "sensitive" materials and technology, boycotts on imports from LDCs, punitive cutoffs of aid, or condemnations by the United Nations or other world bodies. (The term **boycott** means to refuse to engage in trade with another country or firm in specific goods of that country or firm.) Examples are the U.S. boycott of Castro's Cuba, the law barring economic aid to countries that take over American-owned property, and the U.S. appeal to international bodies when it tried to get the release of hostages from Khomeini's Iran.

Disarmament

Most of the NIEO proposals would put a burden on the North for the benefit of the South. Citizens of the North would have to pay for many of the proposed programs, either as taxpayers or through higher prices for goods bought from LDCs. The 1980 Brandt Report recognized this burden sympathetically and suggested that greater aid for LDCs be paid for by cutting military spending throughout the world. We give a few interesting statistics from the report:

> The annual military bill is approaching $450 billion, while official development aid accounts for less than 5 percent of this figure. . . . The military expenditure of only half a day would finance the whole malaria eradication programme of the World Health Organization. . . . A modern tank costs about $1 million; that amount could improve storage facilities for 100,000 tons of rice and save 4,000 tons or more annually; one

9. Here are two examples. In the private sector, the Penn Square Bank in Oklahoma City became a "cash cow" for speculative oil and gas ventures. In the public sector, the Export-Import Bank lends at concessionary rates to American exporters and also to importers of raw materials and other goods not competitive with domestic industry.

person can live on just over a pound of rice a day. . . . For the price of one jet fighter ($20 million) one could set up about 40,000 village pharmacies. . . . One-half of one percent of one year's world military expenditure would pay for all the farm equipment needed to increase food production and approach self-sufficiency in food-deficit low-income countries by 1990.[10]

A BOYCOTT WEAPON?

We have pointed out the refusal of most Northern countries to make more than token concessions to the South's one-sided NIEO proposals. Now that we have outlined the details, we may ask, "Why should the North pay any attention to them at all?" And why, for that matter, should a general book like this one devote space to such one-sided demands?

The South's great economic weapon, which some countries and leaders—possibly an increasing number—seem ready and willing to use, is "self-reliance." What is meant by "self-reliance" is an economic boycott of most of the First World by most of the Third World. Exports, imports, aid, capital movements, and debt repayments would all be reduced to a trickle. A parallel in history is the "one ship a year" that Tokugawa Japan allowed the Dutch (representing the whole Western world) to bring to Nagasaki (Japan's only open port) over a period of about 225 years ending in the mid-nineteenth century.

In the short run, self-reliance would hurt both North and South economically. Who would suffer most? Some who speak for the South hope and believe that the North could not stand the strain because its "post-industrial" development has gone beyond agriculture and manufacturing and because its people are used to affluent lifestyles. The South, at worst, could simply continue enduring poverty as it has been doing in the past. At best, it could "learn by doing" and speed up its own growth by developing new technologies and substitutes for its imports and by freedom from the burden of debts and service charges.

10. Willy Brandt et al., *North-South: A Program for Survival* (Cambridge, Mass.: MIT Press, 1980), p. 14.

The various LDCs could help one another, and the "self-reliance" movement might gain the support and aid of the Second World, as Cuba has been supported by the Soviet Union.

The 1973–1974 crude oil boycott of the United States and the Netherlands by the Arab members of OPEC is proof of the North's vulnerability, according to advocates of Third World self-reliance. Generalizing this experience to more countries and to total trade and payments, the South's Marxist and semi-Marxist spokespersons expect that a boycott would force the North to give in on most or all the NIEO issues that we have described. The socialists among them also feel that neither capitalism nor the market economy could survive, as both are somehow dependent on continued prosperity based on the present international order.

SUMMARY

1. Economic relations between the industrialized MDCs of the First World (the North) and the LDCs of the Third World (the South) have deteriorated since about 1960. Evidence of this deterioration is the South's demand for a New International Economic Order (NIEO) to replace the present system. Many LDCs consider the present system exploitative and blame it for their underdevelopment.

2. While there is no complete agreement as to what NIEO might look like, we have listed some fourteen points, grouped as follows:

   a. *Problems of trade:* Access of LDC-manufactured exports to MDC markets; international financing of raw-material, price-stabilization, and price-support schemes; legitimation of OPEC-like cartels among LDCs; redeployment of world industrial capacity to LDCs.

   b. *Problems of capital movements:* Increased unconditional foreign aid (official development assistance); increased unconditional lending on concessionary terms; rescheduling (postponement) of LDC international debts; linkage of special drawing rights (SDRs) to LDC development.

   c. *Problems of LDC internal economic policies:* International provision and development of appropriate technology for LDCs; international cooperation in regulating multinational corporations and their activities in LDCs.

d. *Essentially political issues:* Use of seabed resources for LDC development; LDC control of the World Bank and International Monetary Fund (IMF); unconditional recognition of LDC sovereignty over natural resources and capital located within their borders; MDC disarmament as an aid to development.

3. The one-sidedness of many of these demands reflects the South's feeling that the existing international economic order has allowed, if not supported, the exploitation of the South's labor and resources for the sake of the earlier development of the North. Their demands, therefore, embody a general feeling that payment and reparations are justified.

4. The North has not responded significantly to the South's demands. The confrontation may lead to an economic boycott or "self-reliance" on the part of the South or an alliance of LDCs. This would mean a drastic reduction in North-South economic relations, from which both parties would lose. Those who speak for the South believe that the loss to the North would be greater than to the South and that a boycott policy could lead to the establishment of a new order, and perhaps to the downfall of the capitalistic and market economies of the North.

DISCUSSION QUESTIONS

1. Who are the principal participants in the North-South controversy? What are the principal political and economic issues in this controversy?

2. Summarize the existing international economic order that the South is attacking. Are its free-trade or its protectionist features most under attack?

3. Discuss the positions of organized labor and organized agriculture in the United States and other industrial countries in the North-South controversy.

4. Why have the U.N. agencies sided generally against the North in the North-South controversy? What significance should be attached to this fact?

5. What is the Prebisch thesis, and how does it support the South's position on the stockpiling of goods?

6. Do you agree that direct aid and concessional loans are owed by the industrial countries to LDCs as reparations? Why or why not?

7. What is meant by neocolonialism? Can it be justified in the cases of any LDCs? Why or why not?

8. What are some of the charges that the LDCs make against multinational corporations operating within their borders? Are they valid? Explain.

9. Do you think the U.S. government should revise its attitudes in the North-South controversy? Why or why not?

10. Some LDCs are oil exporters, but most of them are oil importers. Nevertheless, the solidarity of the South in the North-South controversy was not broken by the rise of OPEC. How do you explain this?

11. Would an economic boycott of industrial countries like the United States by the LDCs, aided by the socialist countries, destabilize the economies of the North more seriously than it would injure the South? Explain.

Japan's Economic Miracles and the International Economy

The existing system of international economic relations—"the old international economic order"—has come under economic attack as an exclusive club run by the industrial countries of North America, Western Europe, and now Japan for their own advantage, with its rules rigged to make it almost impossible for outsiders to share its benefits. For example, workers from poor countries cannot immigrate freely into rich countries, and the products of their cheap labor are imported freely into rich countries only if they do not compete with these countries' products.

If we examine the historical record, however, there is one country that has risen from the ranks of the underdeveloped to the ranks of the industrial countries without being heavily populated by people of European origin. That country is Japan.

Japan has experienced not one but two "economic miracles" during the period since 1853, when Commodore Matthew C. Perry and his American naval squadron forced Japan to open itself to the West against its own will. The first was a miracle of *development* during the Meiji Era (1868–1912, between the end of the American Civil War and the beginning of World War I). The second economic miracle has been a miracle of *reconstruction* following Japan's defeat in World War II and the destruction of some 25 percent of the country's total stock of physical capital, and seven years of American occupation (1945–1952). We shall examine each period in turn, with special attention to the *international economics* of each miracle.

These miracles occurred despite the lack of certain aids to growth. Japan had few natural resources in 1853, and many of those that Japan had then are depleted or inadequate today. Nor was the population sparse in relation to the available resources. Japan's population in 1853 was 30 million (in an area slightly smaller than the state of California). Its 1981 population was estimated at 118.5 million, or 52 percent of the U.S. population (including Alaska and Hawaii). In Japan during the Meiji Era, there was no foreign aid at all, and its few loans from abroad were all on a strictly commercial basis.[1] Japan was never a colony, but "unequal treaties" with the Western powers established foreign concessions in various "treaty ports" until 1899, and limited Japan's import tariffs to the 5 percent level.

The First Miracle

How could Japan rise over the forty-five-year Meiji Era to become an important world economic power? We shall explain Japan's success in terms of the availability of human capital, the opportunity to develop it further, access to world markets to import the materials Japan lacked, a government that desired economic growth and was proud of it for both civilian and military reasons, and a population more willing (or more compelled) than others to sacrifice consumption and to work hard.

THE PRE-MEIJI ERA   In the words of Adam Smith that we have quoted already, the three requisites of economic growth are "peace, easy taxes, and a tolerable administration of justice." Japan under the Tokugawa family of Grand Marshals (Shoguns) had the great advantage of 250 years of peace before Commodore Perry's arrival. To ensure and preserve this peace, Japan had isolated itself for 200 years of that period,[2] except for Nagasaki Harbor, where a little trade was carried on with the Dutch and Chinese. Of course, any major European power might have forced its way in, but Japan was at "the end of the line" from Europe, much farther than India or China. Also, there was little to attract Europeans there

1. One of these financed Japan's first railway, which covered the 25 miles between Tokyo and Yokohama.

2. This isolation policy followed a "Christian Century" (1540–1640 approximately) of contact with Europeans, especially Spaniards and Portuguese, whom the Tokugawa Shoguns came to suspect of the desire to take over the country.

Japanese silk factory, Meiji Era

when they were busy fighting each other and colonizing the Americas, the Indies, Siberia, and so on.[3]

Japan's cultural tradition was another point in its favor. While preserving a fierce national pride in "things Japanese," the Japanese had shown themselves unusually willing and able to learn from foreigners—from the Chinese in earlier times and more recently from the Europeans during the "Christian Century" and from the Dutch in Nagasaki. The assimilation of Western products and processes was therefore easier for the Japanese than for any other Asian country. The Japanese were relatively literate and, during the period of Tokugawa peace, they had developed a wide range of both fine arts and everyday handicrafts, as well as harbors, schools, and even roads.

3. In the twenty years after Perry's visit, Japan was still weak, but the Westerners were busy elsewhere. For example, the Crimean War, the unifications of Germany and Italy, the Indian Mutiny, the American Civil War, and the French effort to set up a Mexican Empire occupied the attention of the Western powers. It was thus relatively easy for Japan to avoid becoming a colony or being divided into spheres of foreign influence.

Japan was also fortunate in the early rise of its silk industry, since exports of silk and silk fabrics financed nearly 40 percent of Japan's imports in the Meiji Era. Had rayon and nylon existed in the late nineteenth century, Japanese economic history would have been decidedly different. The rise of silk as Japan's staple export industry was aided by the misfortunes of rival silk producers—silkworm disease in France and Italy, and a great civil war, the so-called Taiping Rebellion, in central China.

ECONOMIC POLICIES IN THE MEIJI ERA We date the Meiji Era from 1868, when Tokugawa rule was overthrown in a near-bloodless revolution, giving the fifteen-year-old Meiji Emperor a new set of advisers. They were the "Meiji statesmen," revered in Japan like the "founding fathers" in the United States. Because these men all feared the fate of India, which became a British dependency, or of China, which had been divided into areas of foreign dominance, they made a number of wise economic decisions.

For example, they not only displaced a dominant military caste (the *samurai*) but successfully transformed the members of this class into policemen, teachers, bureaucrats, and business people while opening the higher ranks of the armed services to people of other classes. This move is important because, in many LDCs, the business class is composed largely of lower-class people and of racial or religious minorities not respected by the citizens generally, while the higher military and administrative ranks are reserved for middle- and upper-class people. The result is a sort of group or class conflict, which Japan has been spared.

The Meiji statesmen also devised a system of pilot plants, especially in textiles and shipbuilding. The government established such plants and bore the losses involved in adapting them to Japanese conditions. Then after the "teething troubles" had been overcome, and after skilled Japanese workers had been trained, these plants not only became models for private industry in general but were themselves sold (usually at substantial losses) to favored private companies.

These leaders provided Japan with a financial system that kept inflation under reasonable control. During the Meiji Era, the price level approximately doubled, a mild inflation rate by later standards, and the inflation process was itself interrupted by periods of deflation, particularly in the late 1880s.

Another of the Meiji policies was a regressive fiscal system, based mainly on taxes levied on agricultural land and improvements. This system has been faulted for falling most heavily on the poor peasants in the countryside. At the same time, however, it provided for public capital formation, estimated at over 40 percent of the total investment of the Meiji Era—or more than half if military capital in the form of arsenals, navy yards, warships, and the like, is included. This capital went largely into the social and military underpinnings of development. Higher education and technical training played especially important parts as well.

While building up more military and naval strength than proved really necessary to repel foreign aggression, the Meiji statesmen resisted for over twenty-five years all temptations to engage in costly military adventures overseas. When they did expand to the Asian continent, the expansion was primarily into the Korean peninsula, which the Japanese saw as a possible springboard for invasion of Japan by some Russo-Chinese alliance. (Japanese expansion into China proper came only later.)

THE OPEN WORLD ECONOMY We have left to the last a neglected aspect of Japanese growth, namely, the openness of the world economy. By building up export industries on a cheap-labor basis, Japan was able to increase exports enough to purchase from abroad the essential food[4] and raw materials needed for the people and the economy. Free trade was not the rule, except in Great Britain, but tariffs were low. Also, "cheap coolie labor" and "unfair competition" arguments against Japanese exports were ineffective. The old international economic order, then, helped Japanese growth rather than slowing it down. But this was the pre-1914 economic order. Had Meiji Japan been faced with our present structure of tariffs, quotas, and administrative protection, it is very doubtful whether its history would have been a success story, let alone an economic miracle.

The Second Miracle

Only a generation elapsed between the end of the first miracle of development and the beginning of the second miracle of reconstruction—which eventually went far beyond mere reconstruction!

4. Japan was self-supporting in rice until about 1890.

The main source of the second miracle seems also to have been human capital—the volume of inexpensive labor, much of it now highly educated, trained, and skilled, released into the civilian economy from the armed forces, the war industries, and the short-lived Japanese Empire overseas, mainly in Korea and North China. This was Japan's major gain from the restoration of peace— if we again look back to Adam Smith.[5]

THE AMERICAN CONTRIBUTION Another gain from the restoration of peace was the availability of foreign, particularly American, civilian technology. Japan had fallen far behind during its concentration on military expansion. With human capital available, the catching-up process was much faster than most observers had expected it to be.

The Japanese postwar inflation, which raised prices in 1948 to 300 times their levels of 1936, of course had a disruptive effect. But it had one important benefit as well. It permitted Japanese firms in war industries to pay off their debts in inflated yen. Without the inflation, these firms would have been bankrupted when the American occupation forces forbade the Japanese government to pay for materials supplied during the last months of the war.

Nor should we forget the role of American aid, partly in outright gifts and partly in low-interest loans. The total amount was $2 billion. This aid warded off large-scale famine during 1945–1947. Later on, it included machinery, which restored Japanese productive capacity in a number of industries, especially textiles.[6]

5. Why did not these people simply become unemployed, as similar people might in the United States following a sudden disarmament? Because, in the inflationary disruption of 1945, there were literally no facilities for unemployment insurance or relief in Japan. "We could not afford to be unemployed," as one of them put it. Some people probably worked for starvation wages, and others were reduced to beggary and crime. Some people undoubtedly starved or froze to death, and others were scarred as long as they lived by the horrible winter of 1945–1946. But large-scale unemployment never developed.

6. The wartime Allied plan had been to build up China as a replacement for the Japanese "workshop of Asia," and also as a showpiece of capitalism. Much Japanese equipment was to be transferred, primarily to China but also to the Philippines and other Southeast Asian nations that Japan had occupied. These plans were reversed when it became obvious that General Chiang Kai-shek would not win the Chinese Civil War with Mao Zedong's Communists, or restore peace to the Chinese mainland.

AFTER INDEPENDENCE After the end of the American occupation in 1952, and the accompanying end of American aid, there remained some doubt that Japan could balance its international payments without some slowdown in the improvement of its living standard. However, "special procurement" of both civilian and military supplies for United Nations forces in Korea, and later for American efforts in Indochina, helped to ease the transition to complete independence for the Japanese. By the late 1950s, Japan no longer needed such support and took off on Premier Hayato Ikeda's program for doubling the national income in the decade of the 1960s. In fact, the doubling took only seven years. The planning had been too modest!

WORLD TRADE EFFECTS On the international economic front, postwar Japan faced quite different market situations in North America, in Western Europe, and in the Third World. The North American markets were relatively open for a long time. However, North America, including both Canada and the United States, has tended to restrict Japanese exports as Japanese competition has become stronger, especially in periods of recession, despite the increasing volume of Japan's raw material and agricultural imports. The restrictions have taken the form primarily of "voluntary" agreements by the Japanese to restrict their exports of an increasing range of products. Western Europe, which was racing with Japan to recover from the damage of World War II, has tended toward extreme and discriminatory hostility toward Japanese exports. The Third World countries have taken positions somewhere in between. Those with positive trade balances with Japan, due to raw material exports, tend to cooperate with Japanese efforts. So do those desirous of attracting Japanese capital. On the other hand, many LDCs would prefer to build up finished and skilled-labor-intensive products like steel rather than raw materials like iron ore or coal. Also, Japanese investors, especially the large multinational companies, have not been much more popular in their host countries than have American or European ones.

It would again appear that the existing international economic order, especially its open-economy aspects, has helped rather than hindered Japanese recovery and growth. If the whole world had adopted the anti-Japanese policies of the European Community, it is doubtful that the recovery could have succeeded at all. After the oil and other shocks of the early 1970s, the failure of Japanese economic growth to resume its "miraculous" pace of the 1960s can be blamed in large part on the increasing protectionism of Japan's other trading partners, including the United States.[7]

Japanese Protectionism

Considering the debt of Japan's "miracles" of export-led growth[8] to the relatively open international markets for Japanese exports, one might expect public opinion in Japan itself to be strongly internationalist and free-trade-oriented. But such has never been the case, even when the "unequal treaties" of the Meiji Era were forcing Japan into the near-free-trade position we have outlined.

Historical reasons for Japanese protectionism and mercantilism are actually not difficult to find.[9] The country has been dependent on the rest of the world for nearly all of its principal raw materials and (since 1890) for an important percentage of its basic foodstuffs as well. The problem of paying for these imports has been ever present. Trade deficits and current-account deficits have led to import squeezes, and import squeezes have ended promising economic expansions. Fears of being cut off from world markets by boycotts, or of being outbid by the West in the competition for raw materials, prompted Japanese expansion into markets she expected to dominate as both exporter and importer, first Manchuria and then China proper, in the 1930s. They also prompted

Japan's "co-prosperity" move into the rice-, oil-, and rubber-producing lands of Southeast Asia in 1940–1941. This move required, so the military believed, the accompaniment of the simultaneous attacks on Pearl Harbor, Hong Kong, the Philippines, and Singapore that spread World War II to the Pacific. For twenty years after Japan lost that war, the import squeeze was still on. Japan has had less than a generation to realize that its trade problem has shifted from trade deficits to trade surpluses, both with the world as a whole and with its principal single trading partner, the United States.

Japanese protectionism has taken various forms. In view of the need to husband resources to pay for essential imports, it was long considered unpatriotic to complicate the country's problems by importing nonessentials when domestic substitutes were available. The current argument is rather that imports are overpriced. And if not unduly expensive, they are poorly made, with a dangerously high proportion of "lemons."[10] Or they are inadequately serviced, or important instructions are not written in good Japanese, or they are poorly adapted to Japan's damp climate, or they are too big and clumsy for the small size of the Japanese family and its typical housing unit, and so on.

Since the recovery of full independence in 1952,[11] Japan has translated these attitudes into trade policy, primarily into administrative protection. Except on agricultural products, Japanese tariffs have been both low and unimportant. Quotas, initially fairly numerous and stringent, are now largely confined to agricultural products and high-technology goods in which Japan anticipates becoming competitive in the near future. (Automobiles were a prime example in the 1950s, calculators and computers in the 1970s.) But the Japanese pattern of administrative protection—slow, detailed, meticulous certification, inspection, and testing, combined with refusal to accept foreign test data—is another matter. These tests, certifications, and inspections, moreover, are sometimes applied to every item and not merely to

7. There are other reasons as well: Japan had at least caught up with Western technology; shortages of labor were developing; the high cost of energy affected Japan as much as, or more than, any other country; investment was being shifted to environmental protection, to residential housing, and to "welfare state" institutions rather than being concentrated, as previously, in the construction of "factories, factories, and factories."

8. We speak of growth as "export-led" when the real growth rate of a country's exports systematically exceeds the growth rate of its GNP as a whole.

9. Mercantilism is an elaborate system aiming at growth in both economic and military power. It features the accumulation of international reserves (primarily precious metals) by encouraging exports and discouraging imports, expanding the working population, keeping both wage and interest rates low, and planting colonies to supplement the country's resources. Mercantilism reached its zenith in eighteenth-century Europe, but has never died out, and achieves frequent revivals in various countries.

10. This is the key Japanese objection to buying American "high-tech" products even before Japan has developed anything equally up-to-date. It reflects a general Japanese prejudice against foreign workers as lazy, careless, and overpaid.

11. In the initial years of the American Occupation (1945–1949) a special license was required for *any* private Japanese individual or company to import *anything* from *anywhere*. Japanese protectionism has never approached this degree of severity.

Japanese electronics, the postwar miracle

a small sample from each lot of imports. They are the basic "headache" of the foreign exporter. They are carried on by civil servants who cannot be removed except for cause, who see their role as an activist one—to protect Japanese buyers from the inferior products of dishonest foreigners and their sloppy work force. (In addition, some of these civil servants take post-retirement jobs with the Japanese competitors of the disadvantaged foreigners.)

Japan is also a land of the established business network, supported by public opinion against the interloper, particularly the foreign interloper. To understand this system in its simplest form, suppose a set of four firms (A, B, C, D) and a bank or other financial institution E. Firm A sells to Firm B, which sells to Firm C, which sells to Firm D, with some value added at each stage. This group has existed for generations in close to its present form; "everybody" knows "everybody else." Enter now an interloper, a foreign firm or its Japanese representative, whom we shall call B′. B′ proposes substantially to displace B as a supplier to C, thereby injuring not only B but also B's supplier A. The expected (and usually approved) responses to the threat from B′ include pressure by A and B not only on C (not to buy from B′) but on D (to boycott C if C does buy from B′). This pressure on C and D may be joined by the bank E, if the A or B account is of sufficient importance to E. . . . Such networks are not, of course, unique to Japan. They may be found in small towns and in neighborhood luncheon and "service" clubs in the United States, for example. But the networking process seems significantly better established and more widely accepted in Japan than in America or Europe, especially when it is directed against the dreaded or despised imports.

Conclusions

Do these practices, taken together and in conjunction with others omitted in this essay,[12] add up to a degree of "market closure" significantly greater than that encountered in other imperfect foreign markets in this imperfect world? Surely the answer depends upon the particular market one is discussing and the particular international comparisons one is in a position to make. Clearly many potential exporters to Japan think that they do, but their complaints may reflect little more than the greater strength and resourcefulness of Japanese competitors as compared with competitors elsewhere.

When the anger of these potential exporters is added to the unavoidable resentment of the industries competing with Japanese exports, the Japanese-American trade conflict becomes more serious and more acute politically than such conflicts normally are. (In the normal cases, the export- and the import-competing interests line up on opposite sides of the political-economic fence.)

Furthermore, such market closure as exists can hardly be blamed upon or remedied by the present Japanese government. In 1965, the bilateral trade balance shifted from the traditional American surplus to a growing and now gigantic Japanese one. Since that date, successive Japanese governments have striven for market opening. Yasuhiro Nakasone, premier as these lines are written, has been a leader in this respect. The Ministry of International Trade and Industry—the "notorious MITI" of the Japan-bashers—has followed the official line. But Japan is not a dictatorship, and many Japanese, within the ruling Liberal Democratic Party as well as the opposition parties, resent any further governmental "yielding to foreign pressures." Opposition, foot-dragging, and compromise have all been strong, and the effects of Japanese market-opening measures are as yet only barely visible above the famous "bottom line" as far as a number of American export industries are concerned, from beef and citrus and wood products to drugs and communications equipment and electronics.

12. For example, favoritism to domestic suppliers in purchases by the Japanese government, by government industries, and by beneficiaries of government subsidy (such as the private universities).

VII *The Behavior of Consumers and Firms*

- Consumer Choice
- Market Demand and Elasticity
- Business Firm Choice
- Market Supply and Elasticity

21 *Consumer Choice*

PREVIEW In this chapter we begin the study of microeconomics, the part of economics that focuses on the behavior of particular decision makers within the economy. We start with the concept of the individual demander, which we introduced in Chapter 5.

Opening with a brief review of the demand curve, we then go on to present a more detailed explanation of why individual consumers spend their incomes the way they do. We look behind that curve at the underlying forces at work and show how the demand curve is derived. Economists have offered a number of theories of consumer behavior. Here we discuss the best-known one, which is called *utility analysis*. (The appendix to this chapter offers a second, widely held approach, called *indifference curve analysis*.)

The explanation of utility analysis is followed by two extensions of this theory: *consumers' surplus* and the *paradox of value*. The first one explains why it is that consumers generally gain satisfaction from their market transactions. The second allows us to explain the apparent paradox, or contradiction, that consumers often pay higher prices for less useful goods than they do for more important ones.

people demand greater quantities of goods and services at low prices and fewer at high prices. However, not wishing to rely on intuition alone, we offered in Chapter 5 an explanation consisting of two parts—the income effect and the substitution effect. The income effect is the effect that a price change has on a person's real income or purchasing power. The substitution effect is the effect that a change in price has on relative prices of substitutable goods. Together, the two effects suggest that people buy more of a good when its price is lower because they have now become "richer" and because they now find that substitute goods have become relatively more expensive. On the other hand, they suggest that people will buy less of a good when its price is higher because the higher price causes them to be "poorer" and substitute goods to be relatively cheaper. Though this explanation may be adequate, further insight into the reasons behind consumer behavior will be helpful.

REVIEW OF THE DEMAND CURVE

In Chapter 5 we suggested that it was reasonable to expect an inverse relationship between the quantity demanded and the price of a good or a service. Most students find it quite obvious, and also consistent with their own experience, that

UTILITY ANALYSIS

Utility analysis attempts to explain the underlying forces of consumer behavior. It dates back to the 1870s, when the British economist William Stanley Jevons, the Austrian economist Karl Menger, and the French economist Leon Walras introduced the theory to analyze why consumers buy what they do.

Assumptions of Utility Analysis

Utility analysis relies on the following key assumptions:

1. Consumers are rational.
2. Utility, meaning expected satisfaction, is for each consumer a measurable quantity.
3. Marginal utility (the additional utility gained from consuming one more unit of a product) decreases as the consumption rate of a particular product increases.
4. Total utility increases as the consumption rate of a particular product increases.
5. Consumers have limited income with which to buy all the goods and services they want.
6. Consumers know the prices of all goods and services that they might buy.

These are the six main assumptions of utility analysis. You may remember from Chapter 3 that simplification and isolation are necessary in order to see and understand relationships between particular variables. Some of these assumptions may not fully describe reality, and some may not apply in all cases. But they are helpful in understanding the important relationships that are revealed in utility analysis theory. We shall take a closer look at each of these assumptions in the following paragraphs.

CONSUMER RATIONALITY   What economists mean by a **rational consumer** was briefly described in our discussion of rationality in Chapter 3. A consumer is assumed to be rational, meaning that he or she seeks to maximize his or her satisfaction. It is therefore rational to try to get the most out of one's income by selecting the mix of goods and services that promises to offer the greatest amount of personal satisfaction. For example, if a person is faced with the choice of buying a dollar's worth of bananas or a dollar's worth of ice cream, and if the person prefers the ice cream to the bananas, it would not be rational for him or her to purchase the bananas.

MEASURABLE UTILITY   **Utility** is a measure or expression of an individual consumer's expected,

or anticipated, satisfaction. As we have said, this may be either more or less than this person's actual satisfaction. Utility theory assumes that total and marginal utility are measurable. The measure of utility (unit of anticipated satisfaction) is often called a **util.** Try to imagine assigning a util value to things you are planning to consume. Of course, people do not assign these util values to goods and services in real life. However, the theory predicts that people act as if they do—as if they have roughly calculated utility schedules in their minds as they do their shopping. The theory also predicts that, at least in the long run, utility, measured in utils, has more power in determining consumption patterns than, say, the facts about a person's routine behavior.

Utility is subjective, or personal, in its meaning. The absolute number of utils assigned to a unit of a good or service by a person means nothing in itself. What is important is how that absolute number relates to the number that the person assigns to other units of the same good or service and to other available goods and services. For example, if an individual assigns 100 utils to the first potato at a meal, 50 utils to the second potato at this meal, and 1,000 utils to a steak at this same meal, it can be determined that this person likes the first potato twice as much as the second potato and the steak ten times as much as the first potato and twenty times as much as the second potato. The individual could have expressed exactly the same tastes by assigning 2 utils to the first potato, 1 util to the second potato, and 20 utils to the steak. The second example simply uses a different scale, with the utility ratios left unchanged.

Modern economists who concern themselves with consumer welfare limit or qualify the measurability of utility in a very important way. They hold that utility comparisons can be legitimately made by a single individual, but that it is *not* valid to compare the satisfaction or utility that two different individuals receive from the same good or service. There is no comparable scale. Both an ascetic monk and a high-living playboy may assign 1,000 utils to a steak and 100 utils to a potato, so that they would both be expressing a 10 to 1 ratio. However, no one can be sure from this fact that the two receive the same satisfaction from the steak or the potato.

Economists realize that a person's expression of utility is not formed in a vacuum, but that it reflects one's social environment. Most of us have taboos against eating human flesh or buying slaves, but in other times or other societies we might feel differently. Orthodox Jews and Moslems will not eat pork, orthodox Hindus will not eat beef, and orthodox vegetarians will not eat meat of any kind or fish or sometimes eggs. People brought up in Italian households will seek carbohydrates largely from pasta in the form of spaghetti, ravioli, lasagna, and so on. People brought up in Oriental households will seek them largely from plain boiled rice. In the same way, people may value particular consumption patterns mainly to show how rich (or poor), how modern (or traditional), or how intellectual (or anti-intellectual) they are (or wish they were). The American economist Thorstein Veblen spoke of "conspicuous consumption" both of the rich showing off their wealth and of the poor pretending to be richer than they were. All such behavior may be entirely rational to the consumer who engages in it, whatever you, or we, or the rest of the world may think about it.

DIMINISHING MARGINAL UTILITY   Another essential ingredient in the theory of utility analysis is the assumption of **diminishing marginal utility.** This assumption is that over a certain time period a person's added satisfaction grows less as he or she consumes more and more units of the same good or service. It is another way of saying that additional units of the same good or service in a specified period of time satisfy less and less pressing wants. For example, diminishing marginal utility suggests that a person will gain more satisfaction from eating the first apple than the second apple, which in turn provides more satisfaction than the third apple, and so on—when all the apples are eaten at one sitting. Note that the consumption activity is defined over a certain period of time. It is *not* assumed that an apple eaten next week will not provide just as much satisfaction as one eaten today. Similarly, it suggests that a first lamp in a room will provide

more satisfaction than the second lamp in that room and that under usual circumstances a second car wash during the period of a week provides less utility than does a first car wash.

In a world where individuals can choose among many different goods and services, diminishing marginal utility also expresses a philosophy of "variety as the spice of life." Most people prefer to have one or a few of a lot of different goods and services rather than a great many of only a few goods and services. For example, you may buy only two pounds of apples because you prefer also to buy some oranges, pears, and bananas, rather than more apples.

Exceptions to diminishing marginal utility are rarely observed. They can usually be classed as cases of addiction, compulsive buying, conspicuous consumption, or set completion. An example of addiction is an alcoholic, who, at one sitting, derives more satisfaction from a third drink than from a second drink and even more from a fourth drink than from a third, and so on—for a while. Compulsive buying may be a form of addiction, where the individual gets "turned on" by the act of buying. Conspicuous consumption—consuming in order to impress others—may take the form of owning an unusually large quantity of some good: many rings on one's fingers or several poodles to strut around with. An illustration of set completion would be a stamp collector, whose satisfaction from additional stamps to complete a set (such as stamps portraying U.S. presidents) increases as he or she gets closer to completing the set. The theory of utility analysis recognizes these as exceptions. They are rare enough so that they may be neglected.

Let us illustrate diminishing marginal utility with a numerical example. Consider the case of Terry Smith, a college student, whose marginal-utility schedule for sweaters is presented in Table 21-1. The first sweater that she might consume during the year would give her 1,500 utils, but the second one gives only 1,200 utils, and the seventh sweater just 500 utils. Terry's marginal-utility curve is shown in Figure 21-1. The negative slope of the whole curve reflects diminishing marginal utility.

INCREASING TOTAL UTILITY The **total utility** that a person gains from any good or service is the sum of all the marginal utilities that he or she gains from successive units consumed. For example, Terry Smith's total-utility schedule for sweaters in Table 21-2 is derived from the marginal-utility schedule in Table 21-1. As she consumes more and more sweaters, the total utility increases by the amount of the marginal utility that she gains from each additional one. The assumption of **increasing total utility** is expressed in the fact that each additional sweater provides her with additional utility—her marginal utility continues to be positive. Terry's total-utility curve is shown in Figure 21-2. It is positively sloped throughout its length (total utility increases with more sweaters). However, it rises at a decreasing rate, reflecting Terry's diminishing marginal utility (total utility increases by less and less for each additional sweater).

The possibility of a negatively sloped segment of a total-utility curve does exist. The assumption of diminishing marginal utility does not rule out the possibility that marginal utility could become negative. You can certainly come to have a real dislike for additional units of something after a point. You can get quite "sick" of it. Taken to the extreme, diminishing marginal utility will likely become negative marginal utility sooner or

FIGURE 21-1 Terry Smith's Marginal-Utility Curve for Consumption of Sweaters During the Next Year

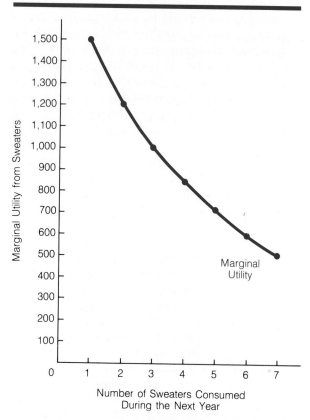

The numbers from Table 21-1 are plotted on the graph to establish the points along Terry Smith's marginal-utility curve. The curve conforms to the assumption of diminishing marginal utility—that during some specified time period an individual's added satisfaction diminishes as he or she consumes additional units of the same good.

TABLE 21-1 Terry Smith's Marginal-Utility Schedule for Consumption of Sweaters During the Next Year

Unit of Sweater	Marginal Utility
First	1,500
Second	1,200
Third	1,000
Fourth	840
Fifth	720
Sixth	600
Seventh	500

The numbers are the arbitrary absolute values that a particular hypothetical person, Terry Smith, assigns to the extra satisfaction that she would receive from each additional sweater that she might consume during the year.

later. A Swedish economist, Staffan Burenstam Linder, wrote *The Harried Leisure Class*, about the plight of people without time to enjoy all the goods they had accumulated. He suggested that their marginal utility not only was diminishing but also was negative, and thus that their total utility might be greater if they had fewer goods. As the Scottish historian and philosopher Thomas Carlyle put it, "Things are in the saddle and ride mankind." But since consumers generally have a very large number of goods and services from which to select their purchases, since these goods and services are not free, and since consumers have limited incomes, it is not likely that they will consume so much of any one good or service that negative marginal utility is actually reached. Moreover, extending consumption when marginal utility is negative violates our first assumption that the consumer is rationally seeking to maximize satisfaction. The theory of utility analysis recognizes decreasing total utility as an exception, rare enough that it may be neglected.

INCOME So far our discussion has covered only consumer preferences. Two other important variables involved in utility analysis theory are income and the prices of goods and services.

Utility analysis assumes the income (here defined as the broader concept of buying power) of an individual to be limited. It may be $10 a week or $1 million a week, but some income limit is assumed to exist. Individuals cannot buy unlimited amounts of goods and services; they must choose among goods and services. They must "live within their income," if we include in *income* the proceeds of selling or mortgaging their accumulated wealth and the limits on their lines of credit. (Economists know that people—even

TABLE 21-2   Terry Smith's Total-Utility Schedule for Consumption of Sweaters During the Next Year

Number of Sweaters	Total Utility
1	1,500
2	2,700
3	3,700
4	4,540
5	5,260
6	5,860
7	6,360

The total-utility numbers are the arbitrary absolute values that a particular hypothetical person, Terry Smith, assigns to the total satisfaction that she receives from alternative quantities of sweaters that she might consume during the year. As she consumes successively more sweaters, her total utility increases by the amount of the marginal utility that she gains from each additional one.

FIGURE 21-2   Terry Smith's Total-Utility Curve for Consumption of Sweaters During the Next Year

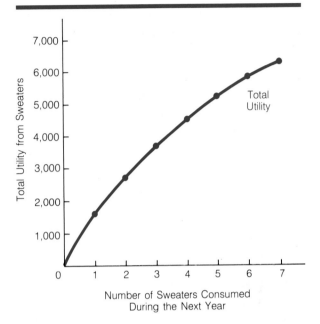

The numbers plotted from Table 21-2 establish the points along Terry Smith's total-utility curve. The curve conforms to the assumption of increasing total utility—that during some specified time period an individual's total satisfaction increases by diminishing amounts as he or she consumes greater total amounts of the same good.

economists!—can go bankrupt through overconsumption.) We may look upon saving as the purchase of future buying power. Although future buying power is hardly a consumption good like food or clothing, it obviously yields utility.

PRICE The last assumption made in utility analysis theory involves price. In order to make rational choices among products, individuals are assumed to know and to take account of the prices of all goods and services that they might buy. Frequently it is very easy to discover the price. Many goods are tagged. The price is stamped right on a container of milk or the price tag attached to a shirt or a belt. For many services the price is announced "up front." The price of admission to a movie house is clearly displayed at the box office, and the price of a haircut can usually be found on a price board. Occasionally, however, prices may be more difficult to determine. What is the price of a rare stamp that was last sold at an auction in 1962? What is the price of the "price negotiable" skis advertised in the classified section of a local newspaper? Indeed, what is the price of a new car in the dealer's showroom which flaunts a *list price* of $16,807, but which you know you can buy for considerably less? The rare stamp, the skis, and the new car all have prices. The price of each will be determined jointly by the seller and buyer at the time of the actual transaction. The theory of utility analysis assumes that the individual either knows *transaction prices* or can estimate them closely.

Again we realize that this assumption is less than realistic. Many people actually are ignorant of many prices. But the theory of utility analysis sets this problem aside in order to penetrate as deeply as possible into the pure logic of choice.

Utility and Demand

Having examined the six main assumptions of utility analysis, we are now ready to show how it can predict consumer demand. We bring together the variables of satisfaction (expressed in utils), income, and prices. In order to make rational choices among different mixes of goods and services, we must weigh prices against our expected utility. For example, Terry Smith, whose marginal-utility and total-utility schedules and curves appeared earlier, may be choosing among sweaters and shirts to replace her clothing destroyed in a fire. She may like a sweater (she assigns 600 utils to that unit) twice as much as a shirt (she assigns 300 utils to that unit). However, the sweater may be priced three times as high as the shirt ($24 compared to $8). In this case, Terry would buy the shirt because she can gain 300 utils by spending $8 as opposed to 600 utils by spending $24. She obtains 37.5 utils per dollar (300/$8) spent on the shirt compared to only 25 utils (600/$24) from each dollar spent on the sweater. In other words, in making this choice,

she will decide in favor of the alternative that offers the greater amount of marginal utility per dollar of expenditure. Only when she maximizes the marginal utility that she gains from each dollar that she spends will she be able to maximize her total utility from her total expenditures.

CONSUMER EQUILIBRIUM At this point we can combine the assumptions of utility analysis into a method of explaining consumer choice. The theory predicts that, in making each choice, the consumer will decide in favor of the alternative with the greatest marginal utility per dollar. When this is done, the assumption of diminishing marginal utility holds that the next unit of this good will offer less marginal utility per dollar than the one just purchased. Following this reasoning to its logical conclusion, we find that, in maximizing satisfaction, the consumer will purchase a mixture of goods and services such that their marginal utilities per dollar will be equal to one another.

If an individual at first fails to equate the marginal utility per dollar spent on one good or service with that of another, that person will later have the chance to increase his or her total utility by buying a little less of the good that is lower in marginal utility per dollar and a little more of the one that is higher. Only after a person has made all of his or her purchases and finds that the marginal utility per dollar received from each good or service is the same, has that person achieved **consumer equilibrium**—the maximum possible utility or satisfaction.

To state the consumer equilibrium rule more generally, where an individual buys goods and services A through N, thereby exhausting his or her income, the person will maximize his or her satisfaction if

$$\frac{\text{marginal utility of good } A}{\text{price of good } A} =$$

$$\frac{\text{marginal utility of service } B}{\text{price of service } B} =$$

$$\cdots = \frac{\text{marginal utility of good } N}{\text{price of good } N}$$

TABLE 21-3 Terry Smith's Utility Schedules for Consumption of Sweaters and Shirts During the Next Year

Utility for Sweaters			Utility for Shirts		
Unit	Marginal Utility	Total Utility	Unit	Marginal Utility	Total Utility
1	1,500	1,500	1	325	325
2	1,200	2,700	2	300	625
3	1,000	3,700	3	281	906
4	840	4,540	4	264	1,170
5	720	5,260	5	250	1,420
6	600	5,860	6	240	1,660
7	500	6,360	7	234	1,894
			8	228	2,122
			9	223	2,345
			10	218	2,563
			11	214	2,777
			12	210	2,987
			13	206	3,193
			14	203	3,396
			15	200	3,596

The marginal utilities and total utilities assigned by Terry Smith for sweaters are repeated from Tables 21-1 and 21-2. Similar information is provided for her with regard to shirts. Sweaters are priced at $24 each and shirts at $8 each.

or, simplified, if

$$\frac{MU_A}{P_A} = \frac{MU_B}{P_B} = \cdots = \frac{MU_N}{P_N}$$

Let us return to Terry Smith and her depleted wardrobe. Table 21-3 presents her marginal-utility and total-utility schedules for sweaters from Tables 21-1 and 21-2 and adds similar information about her utility schedules for shirts. We know that sweaters are priced at $24 each and shirts at $8. With the added information that Terry can spend only $168 of her income for the year on these items, we can calculate her consumer equilibrium allocation between sweaters and shirts and be well on our way to predicting her actual buying behavior.

Suppose that she spent all of her $168 on 2 sweaters (2 × $24 = $48) and 15 shirts (15 × $8 = $120). Her marginal utility per dollar from sweaters (1,200/$24 = 50) would then exceed her marginal utility per dollar from shirts (200/$8 = 25). Her total utility would be 6,296 (2 units of sweaters yield 2,700 utils and 15 units of shirts yield 3,596 utils; 2,700 + 3,596 = 6,296). If, instead, Terry had bought 6 shirts (9 fewer) and 5 sweaters (3 more), her marginal utility per dollar from the two goods would have been equal (240/$8 = 720/$24). She would have lost 1,936 utils by buying 9 fewer shirts (3,596 − 1,660 = 1,936), but she would have gained 2,560 utils by buying 3 more sweaters (5,260 − 2,700 = 2,560). Since she was able to buy the 3 additional sweaters with the $72 that she gained from not buying the seventh through fifteenth shirts, she experiences a net gain of 624 utils (2,560 − 1,936). Thus, when Terry buys 5 sweaters and 6 shirts, equating her marginal utility per dollar between sweaters

FIGURE 21-3 Terry Smith's Demand Curve for Shirts

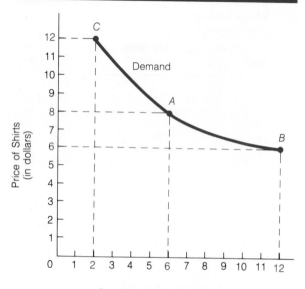

Quantity of Shirts Demanded
During the Next Year

With her income and the prices of other products held constant, Terry's consumer equilibrium solutions occur where her marginal utility per dollar spent on shirts is equal to her marginal utility per dollar spent on every other product that she buys. These solutions establish the points along her demand curve. The resulting demand curve conforms to the normal negative relationship between price and quantity demanded.

and shirts, her total utility will be 6,920. This is the greatest total utility that she can attain, given her utility schedules, the amount of money that she can spend on sweaters and shirts ($168), and the prices that she must pay ($8 per shirt and $24 per sweater).

DERIVATION OF THE DEMAND CURVE Since utility analysis enables us to predict that Terry Smith will demand 6 shirts at a price of $8 per shirt, it provides us with a point on her demand curve for shirts. This is illustrated as point A in Figure 21-3. It follows that additional points on Terry's demand curve for shirts—at different prices of shirts—can be derived in the same manner. At a

lower price for shirts (and the same price for sweaters), Terry's marginal utility per dollar spent on shirts will increase while her marginal utility per dollar spent on sweaters will remain the same.

For example, if shirts went down in price to $6 per unit, her marginal utility per dollar spent on the sixth shirt would rise to 40 (240/$6 = 40), which would then be higher than her marginal utility per dollar spent on the fifth sweater (which remains at 30). Terry will therefore want to buy more shirts and fewer sweaters in order once again to equate her marginal utility per dollar spent on the two items. Specifically, she will want to buy 12 shirts (6 more than before the price decrease) and 4 sweaters (1 less than before). Her marginal utility per dollar spent on shirts will then be 35 (210/$6 = 35), which is equal to her marginal utility per dollar spent on sweaters (840/$24 = 35), and her $168 will again be entirely spent. This provides us with a second point on Terry's demand curve—at a price of $6 per shirt, she will demand 12 shirts (this is point B in Figure 21-3).

At prices higher than the original $8 per shirt, Terry's marginal utility per dollar spent on shirts will decrease, while her marginal utility per dollar spent on sweaters will remain the same. For example, if shirts went up in price to $12 per unit, her marginal utility per dollar spent on the sixth shirt would fall to 20 (240/$12 = 20). Terry will therefore want to buy fewer shirts and more sweaters in order once again to equate her marginal utility per dollar spent on the two items. Specifically, she will want to buy 2 shirts (4 fewer than she bought at the original $8 price) and 6 sweaters (1 more than originally). Her marginal utility per dollar spent on the second shirt will then be 25 (300/$12 = 25), which is equal to her marginal utility per dollar spent on the sixth sweater (600/$24 = 25), and her $168 will again be entirely spent. This example provides us with a third point on Terry's demand curve—at a price of $12 per shirt, she will demand 2 shirts (point C in Figure 21-3).

In Figure 21-3 we have joined the three points that we derived in order to illustrate Terry's demand curve for shirts. The curve reflects the normal negative relationship between price and quantity demanded that was introduced in Chapter 5.

Is the Consumer Sovereign?

Consumer sovereignty means that the consumer is "king" or "queen" and so does as he or she pleases. Subject only to income limitations and the prices that must be paid, the consumer determines the mix of goods and services to purchase. Some economists, such as John Kenneth Galbraith in *The New Industrial State,* point out that consumers are uninformed or misinformed about the thousands of goods and services among which they choose, and can be easily pressured by salesmanship and advertising. You may have heard the definition of the American consumer as a person who "buys goods he does not really want for prices he cannot really afford, because of advertising he does not really believe, to impress other people he does not really care about."

The view that consumers are frequently manipulated by sellers probably arises because of the massive amount of advertising and promotion to which consumers are subjected in a market-capitalist system. Are consumers told what satisfies them most? Do they believe what they are told? If the answer is "yes," isn't the producer sovereign rather than the consumer? These are questions of fact (positive economics), and the evidence is mixed. Certainly some advertising campaigns are successful. We see them over and over in newspapers, magazines, and television. But many advertising campaigns fail. They soon disappear from the media. Do more campaigns succeed than fail? Would the answer to this question be decisive with respect to the "validity" of utility theory? Is the question whether utility analysis is "true or false," or are there degrees of acceptance for the theory? How much faith do you choose to place in utility analysis? So far as the theory itself is concerned, utility analysis merely accepts consumers' preferences, no matter how they are formed. How they are formed is a separate question.

Those who question the validity of utility analysis raise a very important set of questions. No doubt, there is much consumer ignorance. Consumers can only guess at the amount of satisfaction that they will derive from goods and services with which they have had little or no experience. However, utility analysis does not assert that consumers maximize their satisfaction under perfect conditions, but only that they act as though they are doing the best they can with the limited and biased information they possess. If they are disappointed after making one purchase, the theory predicts that they will alter their purchases the next time they shop.

The root of the issue is whether consumer choice should be in the driver's seat in determining what to produce with an economy's resources. The word "should" tells you that this involves a value judgment. It is in the realm of normative rather than positive economics. If consumers should not be given this power, to whom should it be given?

EXTENSIONS OF UTILITY ANALYSIS

Utility analysis provides a method for exploring some interesting and frequently puzzling observations about consumer behavior. At this point, we shall limit ourselves to only two. The first, called **consumers' surplus,** suggests that consumers are really very lucky because in most cases they gain in utility to the extent of receiving "more than they pay for," or even "something for nothing." The second and related observation is the so-called **paradox of value,** or the fact that consumers sometimes pay lower prices for goods and services that they consider to be essential than for goods and services that they consider luxuries and use in a frivolous manner.

Consumers' Surplus

Alfred Marshall (1842–1924), the British economist, described consumers' surplus as follows:

... the price which a person pays for a thing can never exceed, and seldom comes up to that which he would be willing to pay rather than go without it: so that the satisfaction which he gets from its purchase generally exceeds that which he gives up ... and he thus derives from the purchase a surplus of satisfaction. The excess of the price which he would be willing to pay rather than go without the thing, over that which he actually does pay, is the economic measure of this surplus satisfaction.[1]

Let us illustrate consumers' surplus by returning to Terry Smith and her shirt purchases. Figure 21-4 reproduces (from Figure 21-3) Terry Smith's demand curve for shirts that we derived by using utility analysis. Recall that at a price of $12 per shirt she was willing to buy 2 shirts. However, she would buy more than 2 if the price were lower—we found that at $8 she would buy 6 shirts. The extra satisfaction (marginal utility) that she gained from each of the 4 additional shirts was successively lower, but the price reduction made them worth the money. Terry's total satisfaction from the 4 additional shirts is the sum total of the marginal satisfaction that she receives from each of the third through sixth shirts. Her satisfaction from the 4 additional shirts is therefore pictured as the shaded area under her demand curve between the second and sixth shirts. But she pays only $8 per shirt, so that her expenditure for these 4 additional shirts is $32. This is the shaded and striped rectangular area between the second and sixth shirts and below the horizontal line drawn at the $8 market price. The shading indicates that satisfaction is being realized, and the stripes indicate that payment in full is being made for this portion of the marginal utility. From the additional shirts, she is gaining consumers' surplus represented by the shaded area that is left unstriped. This is the satisfaction that Terry receives from shirts 3 through 6, over and above the amount that she paid to obtain these additional shirts. Although it is not shaded in Figure 21-4, she received some consumers' surplus from shirts 1 and 2 before the price decrease and even more from them after the price decrease.

1. Alfred Marshall, *Principles of Economics,* 8th ed. (New York: Macmillan, 1948), p. 124.

FIGURE 21-4 Terry Smith's Consumers' Surplus from Shirts 3 through 6

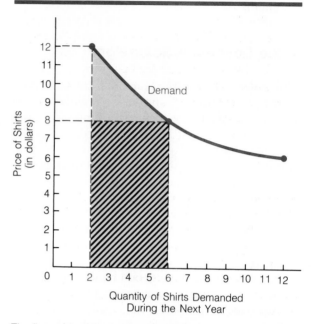

The figure reproduces Terry's demand curve for shirts from Figure 21-3. At a price of $12 she demands 2 shirts and at a price of $8 she demands 6 shirts. Her total satisfaction from the third, fourth, fifth, and sixth shirts is shown as the shaded area under her demand curve. She pays the market price of $8 for each of these shirts (the shaded and striped area). The difference between these two areas—the satisfaction that she receives minus the amount that she paid for them—is her consumers' surplus from these 4 shirts, and is shown as the shaded area that is left unstriped.

Consumers' surplus is the result of two important facts of economics—one related to consumer behavior and the other related to markets. The first is that people are normally willing to buy more and more of a particular good or service only at lower and lower prices because additional units of the same good or service satisfy less and less pressing wants. This fact is expressed in the concept of diminishing marginal utility. The second fact of economics is that if a uniform price prevails in a market, the price consumers pay for each unit of a good or service represents the value they place on the last unit (the marginal unit) bought. Taking these two facts together, we see that, except for the last unit purchased, consumers receive satisfaction or utility from each unit bought that is greater than what they actually pay for it. Expressed in terms of utility analysis, consumers' utility per unit consumed decreases as they consume more units over some time period. But consumers pay only according to the utility they receive from the last unit bought. Therefore, they get an increase in utility that they need not pay for.

Paradox of Value

The other puzzling observation that utility analysis helps to explain is the *paradox of value*. Adam Smith expressed the paradox as follows:

> The things which have the greatest value in use have frequently little or no value in exchange; and on the contrary, those which have the greatest value in exchange have frequently little or no value in use. Nothing is more useful than water: but it will purchase scarce anything; scarce anything can be had in exchange for it. A diamond, on the contrary, has scarce any value in use; but a great quantity of other goods may frequently be had in exchange for it.[2]

What Adam Smith observed in the eighteenth century is just as readily seen today. Now, however, we have some economic concepts (including consumers' surplus) that allow us to explain this apparent paradox. **Value in use** is total satisfaction, while **value in exchange** is determined not by total satisfaction but rather by what people are willing to pay for the last unit they buy. Although we expect the total satisfaction from water to be much higher than that from diamonds, the additional satisfaction gained from the last unit of water is expected to be very low compared with diamonds, since water is plentiful in most areas and the typical consumer buys so many more units of water than of diamonds. This fact may be observed in Figure 21-5, where two marginal-utility (satisfaction) curves are pictured for a typical consumer of both water and diamonds. For early units of water, which most

2. Adam Smith, *The Wealth of Nations* (New York: The Modern Library, 1937), p. 28.

FIGURE 21-5 Paradox of Value

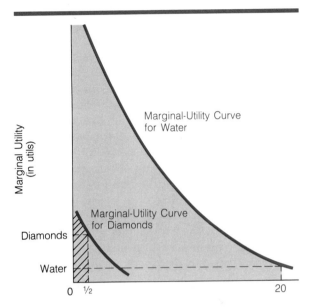

Quantity of Water (in thousands of gallons)
and Diamonds (in carats)
Demanded per Time Period

Pictured here is a person's marginal-utility curve for water and, superimposed on it, the same person's marginal-utility curve for diamonds. The shaded area under the marginal-utility curve for water represents the total utility the person gains from the 20,000 gallons of water consumed. The shaded and striped area under the marginal-utility curve for diamonds represents the total utility the person gains from the ½ carat of diamonds consumed. Marginal utility is merely read off each curve at the point of quantity actually purchased. "Value in use" is shown by the total utility, and "value in exchange" by the marginal utility of the last unit purchased. Since the total utility for water is seen to be much greater than the total utility for diamonds, whereas the marginal utility of diamonds is seen to be greater than the marginal utility of water, the "paradox of value" is resolved.

consumers consider to be essential for their survival, marginal utility is very much higher than it is for diamonds. But the marginal utility for water declines as a large number of units are consumed, so that for most consumers at equilibrium the marginal utility for diamonds is actually much higher than the marginal utility for water. For example, note that the consumer pictured in

Figure 21-5 may be reaching consumer equilibrium (equating marginal utility per dollar spent on diamonds and on water) when he or she is consuming ½ carat of diamonds and 20,000 gallons of water. Since total utility (satisfaction) is the sum of the marginal utilities received from each unit bought, it can be read as the area under each marginal-utility curve up to the last unit bought. The very much larger area under the marginal-utility curve for water (shaded) than under the marginal-utility curve for diamonds (shaded and striped) shows the difference in "value in use" between the two products. However, the marginal utility for the last unit of water is shown to be below that for the last unit of diamonds, explaining the higher "value in exchange" of diamonds. The relative abundance of water compared to diamonds explains why the price of the marginal unit of water is much less than the price of the marginal unit of diamonds. For each of these products, the difference between the "value in use" (total utility) and the "value in exchange" (marginal utility) times the number of units consumed is consumers' surplus. It is very large for water, much smaller for diamonds.

SUMMARY

1. Utility analysis is a theory used to explain why consumers choose as they do. It examines the forces behind the demand curve and how the demand curve is derived.

2. Utility analysis relies on six key assumptions. These are that (a) consumers are rational, (b) utility can be measured, (c) marginal utility diminishes as consumption goes up, (d) total utility increases as consumption rises, (e) incomes are limited, and (f) prices are known.

3. Consumer rationality means that consumers seek to maximize their satisfaction.

4. Utility is defined to mean satisfaction, which is measured in terms of utils. Utility is subjective in nature so that when a person assigns a certain amount of utility to a unit of a product it is meaningful only in terms of its relationship to that same person's assignments of utility to other units of that product or to other goods and services.

5. Diminishing marginal utility means that during some specified time period an individual's added satisfaction diminishes as he or she consumes additional units of the same product.

6. The meaning of increasing total utility is that a person will continue to attain positive satisfaction from consuming additional units of the same product—at least over the range of consumption that is consistent with the assumption of rationality. Because of the assumption of diminishing marginal utility, as the person consumes additional units of the same product over a specified period of time, he or she will find that utility will increase at a decreasing rate.

7. A consumer will maximize total utility or satisfaction (reach "consumer equilibrium") when his or her total purchasing power is spent so that marginal utility per dollar for each product is the same as for every other product purchased.

8. An individual's consumer equilibrium position at any particular price for a product establishes a point on that individual's demand curve for that product. By joining a number of such points, an individual's demand curve for a product can be drawn.

9. Utility analysis explains that the consumer buys what he or she pleases. Some economists believe that consumer ignorance and consumer manipulation by sellers (through advertising) is so widespread that marginal-utility theory is largely irrelevant and useless in explaining consumer behavior. They reject the view that the consumer is truly "sovereign" in deciding what to buy.

10. Consumers in competitive markets receive consumers' surplus—value received for which they do not have to pay. This happens because of diminishing marginal utility and because consumers usually pay a uniform price for all units of the same good or service—a price representing the value that they place on the last unit bought.

11. Consumers often pay far lower prices for goods and services that are called essential than they pay for goods and services considered unimportant. This phenomenon is referred to as the "paradox of value." The paradox is resolved when one understands that price or "value in exchange" is based on marginal utility whereas the importance of a product or its "value in use" is based on total utility.

DISCUSSION QUESTIONS

1. "Diminishing marginal utility is sufficient reason for a government program that takes from the rich and gives to the poor." Do you agree? Explain.

2. Discuss three instances in which you did not experience diminishing marginal utility. How important are such instances in your overall buying pattern? Do they involve a significant proportion of your total expenditures?

3. Bonnie spends her income according to the assumptions of the theory of utility analysis. How would her pattern of purchases be different if she did not experience diminishing marginal utility?

4. The utility analysis theory of consumer choice assumes that a person's total utility derived from a good or a service always increases with additional units of that good or service within a specified period of time. However, you can probably think of dozens of hypothetical examples that do not comply with this assumption. Give at least three. Why, then, does this assumption still allow us to make reasonably good predictions about consumer choice? Why is this not a particularly heroic assumption to make?

5. Carefully explain why Martin maximizes his satisfaction when, after he has made all of his purchases, the marginal utility per dollar spent is the same for all the goods and services he bought.

6. Assume that the following tables are Ms. Rational's utility schedules.

Clothing ($10 per Unit)

Units	Marginal Utility	Total Utility	Total Expenditure ($)
1	10,000	10,000	10
2	5,000	15,000	20
3	3,500	18,500	30
4	2,000	20,500	40
5	1,000	21,500	50
6	500	22,000	60
7	300	22,300	70

Food ($1 per Unit)

Units	Marginal Utility	Total Utility	Total Expenditure ($)
1	10,000	10,000	1
2	8,000	18,000	2
3	5,000	23,000	3
4	2,000	25,000	4
5	800	25,800	5
6	400	26,200	6
7	250	26,450	7
8	200	26,650	8
9	150	26,800	9
10	100	26,900	10
11	75	26,975	11
12	50	27,025	12

Concerts ($5 per Unit)

Units	Marginal Utility	Total Utility	Total Expenditure ($)
1	1,200	1,200	5
2	1,000	2,200	10
3	500	2,700	15
4	400	3,100	20
5	200	3,300	25

Assume also that Ms. Rational has a disposable income of $75 per week, and that she cannot buy partial units. How many units of clothing, food, and concerts will she buy in this world of just three goods and services?

7. How does the issue of consumer sovereignty affect the validity of the utility analysis theory of consumer choice?

8. Why are sellers so "kind" as to offer buyers the benefit of consumers' surplus?

9. Distinguish between "value in use" and "value in exchange." How are these two concepts related to total utility and marginal utility?

10. Devise a pricing scheme for selling shoes that does not permit the consumer to gain any consumers' surplus.

Appendix:
Indifference Curve Analysis

Indifference curve analysis is a theory of consumer behavior that expresses the consumer's tastes in the form of curves (indifference curves). Since it dates back to the 1930s, it is a newer approach to consumer behavior than utility analysis. It is based on less restrictive assumptions, but many students consider it more complex. Whereas utility analysis assumes that satisfaction can be measured, indifference analysis assumes only that it is possible to rank different combinations of goods in order of preference. For example, utility analysis assumes that each of us is able to measure our taste for goods X and Z by assigning a certain number of utils to each. Thus we may indicate that we derive 3.5 times as much satisfaction from X as from Z or that we like Z twice as much as X. In contrast, the indifference approach assumes only that we like one combination of X and Z more than we like another combination of them, or that we just don't care which of these two combinations we consume (are indifferent between them).

THE INDIFFERENCE CURVE AND MAP

An indifference curve is made up of a very large number of points—an infinite number, since we draw it as a smooth line. Each point represents a different combination of goods and/or services that a particular individual might consume. A single **indifference curve** includes all the combinations that will satisfy the individual equally well. That is to say, the individual is indifferent as to whether he or she consumes one or another combination of goods and/or services on the same indifference curve. Figure 21-6 pictures an indifference curve for Jim Gallo, who lives in the limited world of food and clothing. Looking at only three points on Jim's indifference curve

(1, 2, and 3), we see that they all represent different combinations of the two goods. (Point 1 is 110 units of food plus 40 units of clothing, point 2 is 50 units of food plus 80 units of clothing, and point 3 is the combination of 27 units of food and 120 units of clothing.) Jim does not care which of these combinations he consumes or whether he consumes some other combination of food and clothing that can be read off the same indifference curve.

Indifference analysis assumes that many such indifference curves may be derived for an individual. An infinite number of indifference curves representing an individual's preferences is called an **indifference map.** Five indifference curves from Jim Gallo's indifference map appear in Figure 21-7. We can use this diagram to show that Jim would like to be on as high an indifference curve (farthest to the northeast) as he possibly can. That is, indifference analysis suggests that he prefers any combination on curve B to any combination on curve A, any combination on curve C to any on curves A or B, any on curve D to any on curves A, B, or C, and, finally, any combination on curve E to all the others. This follows if we assume that he prefers more of both goods to less of both goods. For example, it is easy to see that Jim prefers combination 4 on indifference curve D to combination 2 on indifference curve C because it entails more of both food and clothing. However, we can go further and conclude that Jim also prefers combination 4 to combination 3, even though combination 4 provides less clothing than does combination 3. Since Jim is indifferent between combination 2 and combination 3 (they are both on the same indifference curve C) and since he prefers combination 4 to combination 2, indifference-curve logic concludes that he also prefers combination 4 to combination 3.

Relationships Among Indifference Curves

Does indifference-curve logic allow for the possibility of indifference curves to cross? In other words, is it possible for two different indifference curves on a single indifference map to have a common point? The answer is "no." Imagine that indifference curves *C* and *D* from Figure 21-7 intersect so as to make points 2 and 4 a single common point. (You may wish to draw them on a piece of paper.) In one direction from the intersection, curve *D* then lies above (to the northeast of) curve *C*, while curve *C* lies above curve *D* in the other direction. This situation denies indifference-curve logic. At the point of intersection in such a construct, Jim Gallo is indifferent between being on indifference curve *C* or *D*, since that point represents the same combination of food and clothing. Yet at all other points, he prefers being either on indifference curve *D* because it lies above indifference curve *C* or on indifference curve *C* because it lies above indifference curve *D*. Thus he would no longer

FIGURE 21-7   Five Indifference Curves on Jim Gallo's Indifference Map

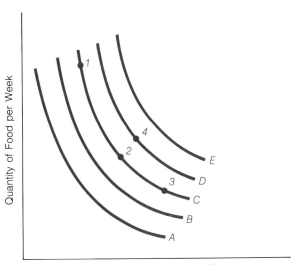

Quantity of Food per Week

Quantity of Clothing per Week

Shown here are five indifference curves from Jim Gallo's indifference map. The higher the curve he can reach (the farthest to the northeast), the better off he will be. Jim prefers any combination of food and clothing represented on curve *E* to any on curves *A*, *B*, *C*, or *D*. Similarly, he prefers a combination of food and clothing represented on curve *D* (such as the one marked 4) to any on curves *A*, *B*, or *C* (including such combinations as 1, 2, and 3 on curve *C*), and so on.

FIGURE 21-6   Jim Gallo's Indifference Curve

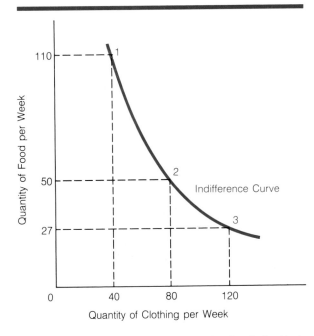

Quantity of Food per Week

Quantity of Clothing per Week

Pictured here is an indifference curve for Jim Gallo. He is equally well satisfied by each combination of food and clothing that is represented along this curve. He is indifferent among the three combinations that are marked and specified on this curve, as he is among all other combinations of food and clothing that can be read off this same indifference curve.

be indifferent among all points along the same indifference curve.

The Shape of Indifference Curves

Jim Gallo's indifference curves were drawn on the basis of two assumptions that are characteristic of indifference analysis. First, his indifference curves are negatively sloped, and, second, they are bowed inward toward (are *convex* to) the origin.

A negatively sloped or downward-sloping indifference curve indicates that the individual considers the goods measured on the axes to indeed be desirable—more is always preferred to less. Some quantity of one good must be given up when some of the other good is added in order for the individual to remain equally well off. By contrast, let us briefly examine the meaning of positively sloped indifference curves, as it sometimes helps to see the results of other assumptions. A positively sloped or upward-sloping indifference curve would mean that the person was indifferent among combinations that included more of both things and less of both things. This sort of curve would make sense only if one of the things was a "bad" (something the individual wanted less of, such as garbage), and the other was a good. Each point on such an indifference curve would represent a particular combination of the "good" and the "bad," and the individual would be indifferent among all of these combinations.

An indifference curve that is a horizontal or a vertical straight line tells us that one axis measures a good and the other an "I don't care"—a product that neither adds to nor subtracts from the individual's well-being. A horizontal straight-line indifference curve indicates that the horizontal axis measures the "I don't care." The person cares only about how much he or she gets of the good on the vertical axis and is indifferent among the various amounts of the "I don't care" with which it is combined. Similarly, a vertical straight-line indifference curve shows that the "I don't care" is measured on the vertical axis. This time the person cares only about how much he or she gets of the good on the horizontal axis and is indifferent among the various amounts of the "I don't care" with which it is combined.

The second assumption of the theory is that indifference curves have the sort of curve pictured in Figures 21-6 and 21-7—convex to the origin. This convexity indicates that individuals desire variety. The theory predicts that if a consumer has, for example, a large quantity of food and a relatively small quantity of clothing, a large additional amount of food must be added if another unit of clothing is eliminated in order to allow him or her to maintain the same level of satisfaction. The same principle works if he or she has a lot of clothing in comparison to food.

Perhaps this convex-curve assumption reminds you of the diminishing-marginal-utility assumption used in utility analysis. There, utility diminished in terms of utils. Here, it appears as a changing "tradeoff" rate between goods. If an individual's indifference curves were bowed out instead of bowed inward to the origin, they would indicate the opposite. Such curves would show that added units of the good of which the person had a relatively large amount were valued more highly than added units of the good of which he or she has relatively little.

Finally, if the indifference curves had no curvature at all but were instead straight lines (but not vertical or horizontal ones), they would indicate that the goods measured on the axes were perfect substitutes for each other. The tradeoff rate between the goods would be the same no matter in what proportion the goods were held. Only the same good appearing on both axes would be a case of perfect substitutes, but near-perfect substitutes such as $5 bills and $10 bills exchanged on a two-for-one basis would come close.

THE BUDGET LINE

Indifference analysis involves consumer preferences, consumer income, and the prices of goods and services. So far, our discussion of the indifference approach to consumer behavior has dealt only with preferences (the indifference map). The income and price variables that act as constraints, or limits, on what the individual is able to buy can be expressed in the form of a budget line. The **budget line** shows the combinations of the goods and/or services measured on the axes that can be purchased by an individual who has a particular income and who faces particular prices for those goods and/or services.

We can construct a budget line for Jim Gallo, whose preferences we have previously mapped. Suppose that his income is $100 per week, that food sells for $5 per unit, and that the price of clothing is $10 per unit. The line in Figure 21-8 extends down from 20 units of food to 10 units of clothing. If Jim were to spend his entire $100 income on food, he could buy 20 units of food ($100/$5 = 20); on the other hand, if he were to spend his entire income on clothing, he could buy 10 units of clothing ($100/$10 = 10). In

FIGURE 21-8   **Jim Gallo's Budget Line**

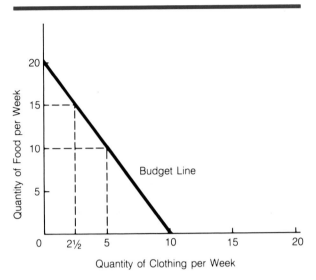

Jim Gallo's budget line pictures the constraints that are placed on his ability to purchase food and clothing by his income and the prices of food and clothing. His income is $100 and food sells for $5 per unit and clothing for $10 per unit. If he buys none of the other, he can buy 20 units of food or 10 units of clothing. Between these two extremes lie many alternative combinations that offer him positive amounts of both food and clothing. Two such alternative combinations are marked—15 units of food plus 2½ units of clothing and 10 units of food plus 5 units of clothing.

between these two extremes are many other combinations. Two such combinations, shown in Figure 21-8, are 15 units of food plus 2½ units of clothing and 10 units of food plus 5 units of clothing. Given his income and the prices of food and clothing, Jim can afford to buy any combination on his budget line or beneath it, but he cannot afford any combination outside his budget line.

The budget line will shift if either price or income changes. Panel (a) in Figure 21-9 illustrates budget-line shifts that occur if income changes while prices remain the same. If Jim's income decreases to $80 per week, the budget line will shift to the left, so that it will extend from 16 units of food to 8 units of clothing. The new budget line is derived in the same way as the original one. If Jim spent his entire $80 of income

on food, he could buy 16 units of food ($80/$5 = 16). On the other hand, if he spent all of his $80 income on clothing, he could buy 8 units of clothing ($80/$10 = 8).

Similarly, an increase in Jim's income to, say, $120 a week will shift his budget line to the right, so that it extends from 24 units of food to 12 units of clothing. If Jim spent all of his $120 of income on food, he could buy 24 units of food ($120/$5 = 24). On the other hand, if he spent his entire $120 of income on clothing, he could buy 12 units of clothing ($120/$10 = 12).

Panel (b) in Figure 21-9 shows budget lines at several different prices of clothing, assuming that the price of food and Jim's income both remain the same. If the price of clothing increases to $20 per unit, the budget line intersects the horizontal axis at 5 units. The most clothing that Jim's $100 income can now buy is 5 units ($100/$20 = 5). If, instead, the price decreases to $5, the budget line intersects the horizontal axis at 20 units. Jim's $100 income can now buy 20 units of clothing ($100/$5 = 20). Panel (c) in Figure 21-9 shows similar shifts of budget lines when the price of food changes while the price of clothing and Jim's income remain the same. The shift to the left reflects an increase in the unit price of food, and the shift to the right reflects a decrease in the unit price of food.

CONSUMER EQUILIBRIUM

An individual's indifference map expresses what that person would *like* to consume, and an individual's budget line tells what that person is *able* to consume. When the two are put together, the consumption pattern that maximizes that individual's satisfaction can readily be determined. Superimpose the individual's budget line on his or her indifference map and seek the point where it is *tangent* to (where it just touches) an indifference curve. This point identifies the combination of goods and/or services that will maximize that person's satisfaction under the given income and price constraints.

Figure 21-10 shows the case of Jim Gallo. Recall that Jim's income is $100 per week and that food

FIGURE 21-9   Budget-Line Shifts

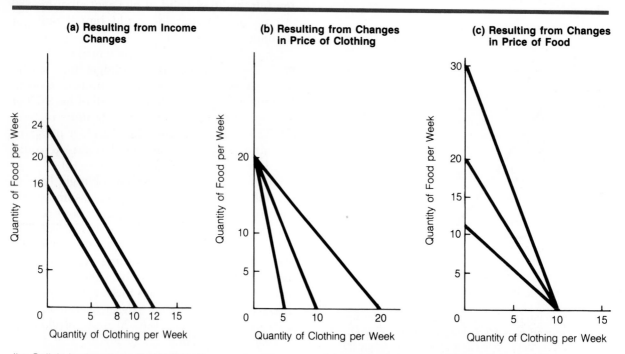

Jim Gallo's budget line will shift if his income changes or if the price of clothing and/or food changes. Panel (a) reproduces Jim's budget line from Figure 21-8 and then shows the parallel inward shift that occurs as a result of his income dropping to $80 and the alternative parallel outward shift resulting from his income increasing to $120. Panel (b) again reproduces Jim's budget line from Figure 21-8 and then shows the inward shift that occurs as a result of the price of clothing increasing to $20 and alternatively the outward shift resulting from the price of clothing decreasing to $5. Panel (c) also reproduces Jim's budget line from Figure 21-8, but this time shows the inward shift of the budget line that results from an increase in the price of food and the outward shift resulting from a decrease in the price of food.

sells for $5 per unit and clothing for $10 per unit. If we superimpose his budget line (Figure 21-8) on his indifference map (Figure 21-7), we can find the point where it is tangent to an indifference curve. He would like to reach indifference curve E, but since it lies completely outside of his budget line (as do indifference curves D and C), he cannot. On the other hand, he can reach a number of points on indifference curve A, two of which will exhaust his income. (These combinations are 15 units of food plus 2½ units of clothing and 4 units of food plus 8 units of clothing.) But by choosing a different combination, Jim is able to reach the higher indifference curve B. Indifference curve B is just tangent to his budget line, which

means that he can reach no higher indifference curve. The combination of 8 units of food plus 6 units of clothing is a solution that uniquely maximizes satisfaction for Jim. He could have spent his $100 per week in any number of different combinations along his budget line, but his satisfaction is maximized *only* when he buys 8 units of food plus 6 units of clothing.

In summary, the indifference curve analysis approach to consumer behavior relies on three pieces of information to predict what an individual will consume: (1) the person's preferences, (2) the person's income, and (3) the prices of the goods and services that the person has to choose from. It makes the same assumptions as does

FIGURE 21-10 Jim Gallo's Consumer Equilibrium Solution

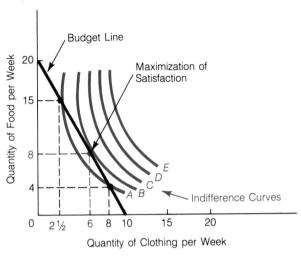

Jim Gallo's budget line (from Figure 21-8) is superimposed on his indifference map (from Figure 21-7) to show his "consumer equilibrium"—the combination of food and clothing that, given his income and the prices of food and clothing, maximizes his satisfaction. Indifference curve *B* is the highest one that Jim can reach, since his budget line is just tangent to it. The combination of 8 units of food plus 6 units of clothing is the solution that uniquely maximizes satisfaction for Jim.

utility analysis except that it does not assume that utility can be measured. Instead, it assumes that consumers can rank-order the desirability of different combinations of goods and/or services. Preferences are expressed by the indifference map; income and prices determine the budget line. The point where the budget line is tangent to one of the indifference curves represents the consumption pattern that maximizes satisfaction. In other words, it represents "consumer equilibrium."

DERIVING A DEMAND CURVE

What you have learned about indifference curves and budget lines allows you to see that this theory of consumer behavior contains all the ingredients

FIGURE 21-11 Derivation of Jim Gallo's Demand Curve for Clothing

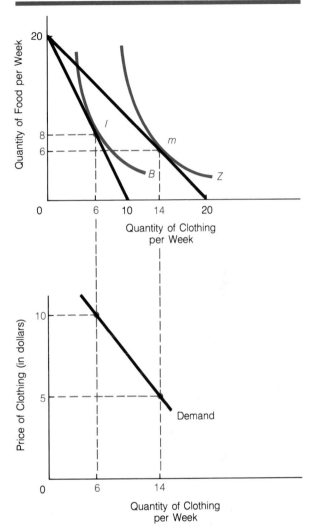

The top panel shows a shift to the right of Jim Gallo's budget line in response to a decrease in the price of clothing. The original equilibrium point of *l* was maintained when the price of clothing was $10 per unit, given food at $5 per unit and Jim's income of $100 per week. The new equilibrium *m* is attained as a result of a decrease in the price of clothing to $5, the price of food and Jim's income remaining the same.

The lower panel shows the two points on Jim's demand curve for clothing that were derived in the upper panel. With no change in the price of food and no change in Jim's income, Jim demands 6 units of clothing when clothing sells for $10 per unit and 14 units of clothing when clothing sells for $5 per unit.

required to derive a demand curve. In fact, we have already determined one point on Jim Gallo's demand curve for food and one point on his demand curve for clothing. Let us concentrate on his demand for clothing.

Figure 21-10 shows that Jim demands 6 units of clothing when clothing is priced at $10 per unit, given that the only other product in the world, food, is priced at $5 per unit and that his income is $100 a week. The top panel of Figure 21-11 reproduces that equilibrium situation at point *l*. Jim's indifference curve *B* is tangent to his budget line, which reflects the $10 price of clothing, the $5 price of food, and Jim's $100 income. In the lower panel of Figure 21-11 we have plotted the point showing that Jim demands 6 units of clothing when clothing sells for $10 per unit.

Suppose now that the price of clothing falls to $5 per unit while the price of food and Jim's income remain the same. Jim's budget line, shown in the top panel of Figure 21-11, shifts to the right. (See the same case in Figure 21-9b.) A new consumer equilibrium is reached at *m*, where Jim's indifference curve *Z* is tangent to his new budget line. At $5 per unit of clothing, $5 per unit of food, and $100 per week income, Jim wants to buy 14 units of clothing. This case is reflected as a second point on Jim's demand curve in the lower panel of Figure 21-11. Other points on Jim's demand curve can be derived in a similar way for other prices of clothing.

BEHAVIORAL PREDICTIONS

Not all economists accept the "rationality" assumptions that we have described. Among the "behavioral" opposition is the Nobel laureate economist Herbert Simon. This opposition claims that a different explanation of consumer behavior fits the facts better, and that it too can be shown on an indifference map. Suppose that some indifference curve (crossed by the budget line) represents the consumer's "aspiration level." Once the consumer reaches that level, he or she is satisfied and does not care for anything more. Such a satisfied consumer, given his or her budget

line, may choose *any* consumption pattern on this budget line that is not below his or her aspiration level. Most likely he or she will choose the point on the budget line that follows the pattern of the consumer's established routine—where he or she consumes the same proportions of the goods or services as in the past. The point of tangency has little or nothing to do with this choice, but rather it is the pre-established routine that influences consumer behavior.

DISCUSSION QUESTIONS: APPENDIX

1. Using your knowledge of indifference curves, logically explain why Mary will probably be eager to reach a higher indifference curve than the one that she is currently on.
2. Draw each of the following indifference curves as described *and* tell what the indifference curve indicates about how the person views the products on the axes:
   a. a positively sloped indifference curve
   b. a vertical straight-line indifference curve
   c. a horizontal straight-line indifference curve
   d. a negatively sloped, straight-line indifference curve
   e. a negatively sloped, bowed-out (concave to the origin) indifference curve
3. Explain why Beatrice maximizes her satisfaction when she consumes that combination of goods represented at the point where her budget line is tangent to her indifference curve.
4. What may account for each of the following?
   a. a change in the shape of a person's indifference curves
   b. a parallel shift to the right of a person's budget line
   c. a parallel shift to the left of a person's budget line
   d. a person's tangency solution above and to the right of his or her previous tangency solution
   e. a shift to the right of all points on a person's budget line except for the point where he or she selects none of the good labeled on the horizontal axis

22 *Market Demand and Elasticity*

PREVIEW Chapter 5 introduced the concept of consumer demand. Consumers were seen to demand larger quantities of goods and services at lower prices and smaller quantities at higher prices. Both an individual consumer-demand curve and a market-demand curve were explained. Further insight into this negative relationship between quantity demanded and price was given in Chapter 21. There utility analysis was used to trace an individual consumer's demand schedule and curve for a good or a service.

In this chapter, we expand on the subject of market demand. We begin by explaining how the demands of individual consumers are added together to form a market-demand curve. Then we look at one important characteristic of market demand—elasticity, or the degree of responsiveness to changes in price or income. In studying the *price elasticity of demand*, you will discover why quantity demanded is much more responsive to price changes for some products (goods and services) than for others and what difference that fact makes to business decision makers. We also apply elasticity to changes in demand for one product caused by a change in price of a related product (called *cross elasticity of demand*). Finally, we apply elasticity to changes in the demand for a product caused by a change in income (called *income elasticity of demand*).

THE MARKET-DEMAND CURVE

Chapter 21 showed how economists explain the source of an individual consumer's demand schedule and curve. We move on now to show how these may be added together to form a **market-demand** schedule and curve. The market-demand schedule and curve sum up or combine all the individual consumers' demands for a particular product in a particular geographic area. This is what concerns sellers. Business firms want to know how much they can sell at alternative prices in various markets. Which consumer happens to buy their product doesn't really interest them very much except insofar as that knowledge might enable them to raise the total demand. Normally a business firm doesn't care whether more demand stems from John and Alice than from Mary and Jim or whether the reverse is true.

Suppose that these four consumers—John, Alice, Mary, and Jim—constitute the entire market for fruit in a very small village. Their individual consumer-demand schedules are shown in Table 22-1 and then plotted and drawn as demand curves in Figure 22-1. The market-demand schedule and market-demand curve are then derived by horizontally adding them together. When fruit is offered at $0.25 per pound, for example, the quantity demanded by the four consumers adds up to 370 pounds per year (100 + 50 + 140 + 80 = 370), but when the price is $1.00 per pound, the market demand drops off to 140 pounds per year (40 + 10 + 60 + 30 = 140). The market demand at the four different prices is shown in the far right column of the demand schedules in Table 22-1 and plotted as the market-demand curve in Figure 22-1.

TABLE 22-1 Four Individual-Demand Schedules and the Market-Demand Schedule for Fruit

Price of Fruit (dollars per pound)	Individual Quantity Demanded (pounds of fruit per year)				Market Demand (pounds of fruit per year)
	John	Alice	Mary	Jim	
0.25	100	50	140	80	370
0.50	70	30	100	50	250
0.75	50	20	80	40	190
1.00	40	10	60	30	140

Shown here are four individual-demand schedules for fruit. Since these four people constitute the entire market, the horizontal sum of their demands is the market-demand schedule.

Market-Demand Shifts

It is not surprising that the market-demand curve shows the same negative relationship between price and quantity demanded as do individual-demand curves. As we explained in Chapter 5, individual demand in the schedule sense relates the quantity demanded for a product to the price of that product, while keeping constant other influencing variables—in particular, preferences, income, and the prices of related goods and services. When variables other than the price of this product are allowed to change, shifts in individual-demand curves may occur. The same must, of course, hold for market demand since it is merely the sum of individual demands. If, as a total for all these consumers, preferences for the product increase, or if income goes up, or if the price of a good substitute product increases, or if the price of a complement decreases, the market-demand curve will shift to the right (*ceteris paribus*). On the other hand, if preferences decrease or income goes down for the total of these consumers, or if the price of a good substitute product decreases, or a complement's price increases, the market demand will shift to the left (*ceteris paribus*).

In dealing with market-demand curves, two more influencing variables must be considered. The first is that market demand may grow or decline with the numbers of consumers that it includes. Extending our example, Linda and Larry may move into the village where only John, Alice, Mary, and Jim lived before. Linda's and Larry's individual-demand schedules for fruit must then be added to the others, thus shifting the market-demand curve to the right. However, the market-demand curve would shift to the left if one of the inhabitants of the village died or moved away.

In considering market demand, the second variable to be added is the distribution of income among consumers. The combined income of the four inhabitants of our village may remain the same, but the *distribution* of income among them may change. Suppose that John, Alice, Mary, and Jim all earned incomes of $25,000 per year. Then suppose that Alice receives a big promotion, raising her income to $85,000 and John, Mary, and Jim lose their jobs, so that each of their incomes falls to only $5,000 (unemployment compensation). Even though their combined income is still $100,000, we can well imagine that the additional fruit demanded by Alice, who is now much richer, may be more than offset by the much lower amount demanded by the three other people, whose incomes were so severely reduced.

PRICE ELASTICITY OF DEMAND

By now, you should feel comfortable with the idea that market-demand curves are negatively sloped—at lower prices consumers demand more,

FIGURE 22-1 **Four Individual-Demand Curves and the Market-Demand Curve for Fruit**

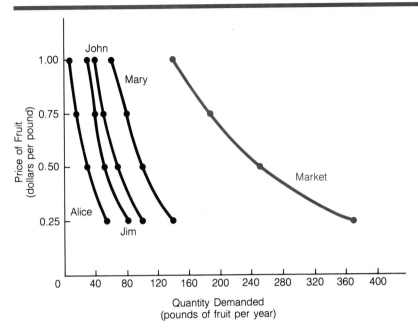

The graph shows four individual-demand curves for fruit, which have been plotted from the demand schedules given in Table 22-1. Since these four people constitute the entire market, the horizontal sum of the curves is the market-demand curve.

and at higher prices they demand less. Thus we can turn our attention to the *sensitivity* of that relationship. Just how sensitive or responsive is the quantity demanded to a change in price? We recognize that price sensitivity of demand may be greater for some goods or services than for others and that, even for the same product, this sensitivity may be greater at some price levels than at others. For example, the demand for cars may be more responsive to price than is the demand for table salt. In the case of gasoline, the quantity demanded has been found to be much more sensitive to price change in the vicinity of $1 a gallon than in the vicinity of 50 cents a gallon. The concept that economists use to measure this degree of responsiveness is called the **price elasticity of demand.** It is one of the several elasticity concepts that will be used in this book. All elasticity concepts describe the responsiveness of one variable to a change in another variable. The price elasticity of demand describes how

great a change in quantity demanded results from a change in the price. The response may range from none at all to a very large one. Elasticity of demand is defined so that it can be measured and expressed numerically.

The Relationship Between Relatives

The price elasticity of demand (E_D) may be expressed in the following form:

$$E_D = \frac{\text{the percentage change in the quantity demanded}}{\text{the percentage change in the price that caused it}}$$

Notice that the concept shows a relationship between relative amounts—a ratio between percentage changes—and *not* between absolute numbers. Recall from Chapter 3 the discussion of

TABLE 22-2 Elasticity Coefficients Calculated from a Market-Demand Schedule for Sweaters

Price (dollars per sweater)	Market Demand (millions of sweaters per year)	Price Elasticity of Demand Calculation	Elasticity Coefficient
$20	150		
		$\dfrac{\dfrac{125-150}{150+125}}{\dfrac{30-20}{20+30}} = \dfrac{\dfrac{+25}{275}}{\dfrac{10}{50}} = \dfrac{\dfrac{+1}{11}}{\dfrac{1}{5}} = \dfrac{1}{11} \times \dfrac{5}{1} = \dfrac{5}{11}$ or −0.45	or the absolute value of −0.45, which is 0.45
$30	125		
		$\dfrac{\dfrac{75-125}{125+75}}{\dfrac{40-30}{30+40}} = \dfrac{\dfrac{-50}{200}}{\dfrac{10}{70}} = \dfrac{\dfrac{-1}{4}}{\dfrac{1}{7}} = \dfrac{-1}{4} \times \dfrac{7}{1} = -\dfrac{7}{4}$ or −1.75	or the absolute value of −1.75, which is 1.75
$40	75		
		$\dfrac{\dfrac{20-75}{75+20}}{\dfrac{60-40}{40+60}} = \dfrac{\dfrac{-55}{95}}{\dfrac{20}{100}} = \dfrac{\dfrac{-11}{19}}{\dfrac{1}{5}} = \dfrac{-11}{19} \times \dfrac{5}{1} = -\dfrac{55}{19}$ or −2.89	or the absolute value of −2.89, which is 2.89
$60	20		

"slope"—the concept that related the *absolute* change in one variable to an associated *absolute* change in another variable. Slope is not the same thing as elasticity. In trying to establish the price elasticity of demand, we are *not* asking how the absolute quantity demanded responds to the absolute change in price or, for example, how many fewer pairs of shoes consumers will demand when the price is $2 higher. Instead, the price elasticity of demand relates the *percentage* changes. It answers the question, "By what percentage will the quantity of shoes demanded change in response to a certain percentage change in price?" Knowing that the price of shoes went up by $2 and that consumers responded by demanding 100,000 fewer pairs tells us very little about elasticity—only that there was a negative response. Was the $2 a big price change or not? Was the 100,000-pair response a substantial de-

crease or a minor one? If the shoes had been of an inexpensive variety that had previously sold for $20, the price increase would have been 10 percent. If, instead, they were made of fine leather and had earlier sold for $100, the $2 increase would have amounted to only 2 percent. Likewise, for the quantity demanded, the 100,000 decrease would have been only 5 percent if 2,000,000 pairs of shoes had been demanded before, but would have been 50 percent if only 200,000 had been previously demanded.

Putting these facts together, we see that our initial information, which told us only of the $2 increase in price and the resulting 100,000 decrease in the quantity demanded, did not reveal much about the demand response. However, as we learn about percentage changes, the picture becomes clearer. A 5 percent decrease in the quantity demanded (from 2,000,000 to 1,900,000) in response to a 10 percent price increase (from $20 to $22) would have been a meager response compared with a 50 percent decrease in the quantity demanded (from 200,000 to 100,000) in response to a 2 percent price increase (from $100 to $102).

The fact that elasticity relates percentage changes means that it is independent of the unit of measurement used. The elasticity of a product measured in tons can be compared with one measured in ounces, as can goods priced in dollars be compared with others that are priced in pennies or for that matter in German marks or Japanese yen. If, in our previous example, we had chosen to price shoes in pennies instead of dollars or if the quantities demanded had been measured in dozens of pairs of shoes instead of single pairs, we would still have gotten the same answer using elasticity. However, if we had compared absolute changes—if we had used slope instead of elasticity—and had changed the price unit from dollars to pennies, the ratio of the absolute change in quantity demanded to the absolute price change would have become 100 times smaller.

The Numerical Value of Elasticity

We have defined price elasticity of demand as the percentage change in quantity demanded divided by the percentage change in the price that caused it. This relationship can be shown in formula form as follows:

$$E_D = \frac{\Delta Q_D / \overline{Q}_D}{\Delta P / \overline{P}}$$

Here ΔQ_D is the change in quantity demanded, $\overline{Q}_D$ is the average quantity demanded, ΔP is the change in price, and $\overline{P}$ is the average price. The numerators of the two fractions, ΔQ_D and ΔP, are quite easy to understand, since they are figured simply by subtracting the original quantity demanded from the new quantity demanded and the original price from the new price. The denominators of the two fractions, $\overline{Q}_D$ and $\overline{P}$, need to be explained further. We choose to use average

price and average quantity (the sum of the original price and the new price divided by 2, and the sum of the original quantity and the new quantity divided by 2). This method is much better than using either the original price and quantity or the new price and quantity in the denominators because the use of original or new prices and quantities will make the whole expression confusing. In other words, we would get one percentage change using the original price (or quantity) and a different percentage change using the new price (or quantity). If we stick to averages in the denominators, our elasticity measure will be the same for rising prices (and resulting quantity decreases) as for falling prices (and resulting quantity increases). So let's say that Q_{D_1} is the original quantity demanded and Q_{D_2} is the new quantity demanded and that P_1 is the original price and P_2 is the new price. The formula for computing elasticity would then appear as follows:

$$E_D = \frac{\dfrac{Q_{D_2} - Q_{D_1}}{(Q_{D_1} + Q_{D_2})/2}}{\dfrac{P_2 - P_1}{(P_1 + P_2)/2}}$$

When the twos cancel out, it would be:

$$E_D = \frac{\dfrac{Q_{D_2} - Q_{D_1}}{Q_{D_1} + Q_{D_2}}}{\dfrac{P_2 - P_1}{P_1 + P_2}}$$

Table 22-2 gives three examples of how the numerical value of elasticity is calculated. Four prices, with the corresponding quantity demanded at each, are shown on a market-demand schedule for sweaters. Calculated is the elasticity between $20 and $30, between $30 and $40, and between $40 and $60. The numerical value, or the *elasticity coefficient*, may be expressed in fraction or decimal form. Since the relationship between price and quantity demanded is negative, the price elasticity of demand coefficients will be negative. However, by convention, economists usually use the absolute values of the coefficients, which means that the signs are ignored.

Let us work through the first of the three examples in Table 22-2. At the original price of $20, 150 million sweaters are demanded. At the higher price of $30, only 125 million sweaters are demanded. Plugging the quantities into the top half of the elasticity formula, as shown in the table, we subtract 150 million (Q_{D_1}) from 125 million (Q_{D_2}) and divide by the sum of these quantities (275 million, which is $Q_{D_1} + Q_{D_2}$). In the lower half of the elasticity formula we subtract $20 ($P_1$) from $30 ($P_2$) and divide by the sum of the prices ($50, which is $P_1 + P_2$). Dividing through by the least common denominator, we get $\frac{-1}{11}/\frac{1}{5}$. By inverting the denominator fraction and then multiplying, we get an elasticity coefficient of $-\frac{5}{11}$ or -0.45, or the absolute value of -0.45, which is 0.45.

Elasticity Categories

How should we interpret price elasticities of demand such as those shown in Table 22-2? An elasticity coefficient of 0.45 means that for every 1 percent increase in price, the quantity demanded decreases by somewhat less than one-half percent (0.45 of 1 percent). Similarly, the elasticity coefficient of 1.75 means that for every 1 percent increase in price, the quantity demanded falls by 1¾ percent. You can immediately see a major difference between these two cases. In the first case the percentage response in the quantity demanded was less than the percentage change in the price that caused it. In the second case (and also in the third case) in the table the percentage response in quantity demanded was greater than the percentage change in price.

To describe such different degrees of elasticity, economists have grouped all possible cases into five categories. We have already taken note of the two most important ones. Whenever the percentage response in the quantity demanded is less than the percentage change in the price that caused it, with both expressed in absolute values, demand is said to be **inelastic.** That is, the elasticity coefficient is less than 1 in absolute value. And whenever the percentage response in the quantity demanded is greater than the percentage change in the price that caused it, in

absolute values, demand is said to be **elastic.** Here the elasticity coefficient is greater than 1 in absolute value. The third category is the case that is just on the borderline between inelastic and elastic. Called **unitary elasticity,** it is where, in absolute value, the percentage response in the quantity demanded is exactly equal to the percentage change in price that caused it. Here the elasticity coefficient is 1 in absolute value. Such a case would be a 10 percent decrease in price leading to a 10 percent rise in the quantity demanded. The last two categories are the extreme cases of inelastic and of elastic demand. The extreme case of inelasticity, called **perfectly inelastic,** is when a price change causes no quantity response at all. The elasticity coefficient is zero. Finally, the extreme case of elasticity, called **infinitely elastic** (or **perfectly elastic**), is when a price change causes an infinite—greater than we can ever count—response in the quantity demanded.

Table 22-3 sums up the five elasticity categories and gives an example showing what the demand curve might look like for each. The inelastic demand curve is shown to be much steeper than the elastic demand curve. Over the same price range, this relationship will always hold as long as the axes are scaled in the same way. The unitary elastic demand curve is drawn so that the price times the quantity demanded is equal for all points on the curve. (Mathematicians call the shape a "rectangular hyperbola.") The perfectly inelastic demand curve is always parallel to the vertical axis, since the same quantity (80 in our case) will be demanded regardless of the price. The infinitely elastic demand curve is always parallel to the horizontal axis, since at any price above the current price ($10 in our case) the quantity demanded will be zero and at the current price the maximum quantity demanded will be infinite.

Determinants of Price Elasticity of Demand

Price elasticity of demand varies greatly among different products and also for the same product at different prices and for different periods of

TABLE 22-3   Price Elasticity of Demand Categories

Elasticity Category	Relationship Between Price and Quantity Demanded	Elasticity Coefficient	Numerical Example	Diagram of Demand Curve for This Example
Inelastic	In absolute values the percentage change in the quantity demanded is smaller than the percentage change in the price that caused it.	less than one (in absolute value)	A price increase from $10 to $20 causes quantity demanded to decrease from 60 to 40.	
Elastic	In absolute values the percentage change in the quantity demanded is greater than the percentage change in the price that caused it.	greater than one (in absolute value)	A price increase from $10 to $20 causes quantity demanded to decrease from 120 to 20.	
Unitary elastic	In absolute values the percentage change in the quantity demanded is exactly equal to the percentage change in the price that caused it.	one (in absolute value)	A price increase from $10 to $20 causes quantity demanded to decrease from 80 to 40.	
Perfectly inelastic	Any change in the price causes no response at all in the quantity demanded.	zero	A price increase from $10 to $20 causes no change in the quantity demanded.	
Infinitely elastic	Any change in the price causes a limitless (infinite) response in the quantity demanded.	∞ (infinity)	At any price above $10, the quantity demanded will be zero, and at the $10 price, quantity demanded is indefinitely small or large.	

TABLE 22-4 Selected Short-Term Price Elasticities of Demand

Product	Elasticity
China, glassware, tableware	1.54
Electricity (household)	0.13
Furniture	1.01
Legal services	0.37
Medical care	0.31
Natural gas (household)	0.15
Restaurant meals	2.27
Shoe cleaning and repairing	1.31
Stationery	0.47
Telephone	0.30
Tobacco products	0.46
TV repair	0.47

Source: H. S. Houthakker and Lester D. Taylor, *Consumer Demand in the United States: Analysis and Projections,* 2nd ed. (Cambridge, Mass.: Harvard University Press, 1970), pp. 66–128.

time. What do you think will be important in determining a product's price elasticity of demand? If you were asked to decide whether the demand for a good wrapped in a large black box—you have no idea what is inside—is relatively elastic or relatively inelastic, what sort of information would you look for? Of course, data on both price and quantity demanded would be best, but if that were not available, you might seek answers to the following questions:

1. Are consumers generally able to find close substitutes for this good?
2. What proportion of consumers' incomes is normally spent on this good?
3. Is this good generally considered a necessity or a luxury?
4. How much time are consumers generally given to adjust to a new price for this good?

The closer the substitutes available to consumers, the more elastic will be the demand for a product. If a good increases in price, the availability of close substitutes enables a consumer to switch to another good that is now relatively cheaper. Similarly, when a person uses a variety of products that are good substitutes for each other and one of them decreases in price, he or she will have a tendency to demand proportionately more of that good because it is now relatively cheaper. Table 22-4 lists a number of products along with estimates of their price elasticities of demand. The demand for restaurant meals is probably the most elastic short-term price elasticity of demand among those shown in Table 22-4, because most consumers believe that home meals are close substitutes for restaurant meals. By contrast, most people find only few and poor substitutes for household consumption of electricity and gas. The same appears to be true for legal services, medical care, and telephone service. Notice the rather inelastic coefficients for these products in Table 22-4.

A second determinant of price elasticity of demand appears to be the percentage of household income spent for the product. Price elasticity appears to be low when the portion of income spent for it is low, and high when the portion of income is high. The slightly elastic short-term demand elasticity of 1.01 for furniture (see Table 22-4) would probably be much more inelastic if the average piece of furniture were not priced so high, making it a large proportion of most households' incomes. By contrast, take the classic example of table salt. Even if the price of table salt rose by 50 percent, the increase might amount to only as little as 10¢ a month for the average household. Ten cents is surely a small portion of the income of most households. Because they would not be forced to cut back their purchases of salt very much, we would expect the price elasticity of demand to be very low (very inelastic).

The third determinant of demand elasticity is whether people consider the product to be a necessity or a luxury. A product that is felt to be a "necessity" tends to be more inelastic, whereas a product considered to be a "luxury" tends to be more elastic. Household consumption of electricity and natural gas, legal services, medical care, and telephone serve as good examples of necessities. Table 22-4 shows their elasticity coefficients to be very low. Restaurant meals and china, glassware, and tableware, though not the best examples of luxuries, fit that description better than the other products in Table 22-4. Note that their elasticity coefficients are the highest among the twelve selected products.

Finally, the time allowed for consumers to adjust to a new price is an important determinant of the price elasticity of demand. The longer the time interval, the more elastic will be the demand. If there is very little time for adjustment—not enough time to break the habit or to use up enough of a complementary durable good—demand is likely to be relatively inelastic. Although we saw in Table 22-4 that the short-term elasticity coefficient for tobacco products is 0.46, the same study estimates it at 1.9 in the "long run." The habit of smoking is usually not broken overnight. In fact, it takes some time for most people to cut down. The elasticity coefficient for gasoline has been estimated to be about three to four times higher in the "long run" than in the short term. This difference is explained by the fact that people who own "drivable" gas-guzzlers find that it pays to hold on to those cars, even in the face of sharply increasing gasoline prices. Once the gas-guzzlers break down, people will generally buy smaller cars to replace them.

We have explained four determinants of the price elasticity of demand. Actual products may have several of these characteristics, and they may be either contradictory or reinforcing. It is much harder to predict the elasticity for, say, vacation trips than for table salt. There are few close substitutes for a vacation trip, but it usually takes a large proportion of a person's income and it is generally not considered a necessity. On the other hand, table salt has no good substitutes, it is a small proportion of most people's incomes, and it is considered a necessity by most people.

Price Elasticity of Demand and Total Revenue

Business firms are keenly aware of elasticity. Why shouldn't they be? The price elasticity of demand will determine whether a price change will lead to an increase or a decrease in their total revenue. **Total revenue**—or the total receipts that a company receives from selling its products—is figured by multiplying the quantity demanded of the product by the price per unit.

$$TR = P \times Q_D$$

where TR is total revenue, P is the unit price of the product, and Q_D is the quantity demanded of the product.

From your earlier study of demand, you know that when a company changes the price of a product that it sells, it can be pretty sure that the quantity demanded will move in the opposite direction. But will the price change increase or decrease total revenue? A price rise does not necessarily mean a higher total revenue. Neither does a price cut necessarily mean that total revenue will go down. The impact on total revenue depends upon the degree to which the quantity demanded responds to the price change that caused it—in other words, to the price elasticity of demand. For this reason, the following relationships will hold:

Price Elasticity of Demand	Direction of Change in Total Revenue When Price Falls	Direction of Change in Total Revenue When Price Rises
elastic	increase	decrease
inelastic	decrease	increase
unitary elastic	constant	constant

When demand is elastic, the percentage change in quantity demanded is greater in absolute value than the percentage change in price. So if price falls, the increase in quantity demanded will more than offset the decrease in price, and total revenue will go up. When price rises, total revenue will go down because the decrease in quantity demanded will more than offset the rise in price. In the case of inelastic demand, in absolute values the percentage change in quantity demanded is less than the percentage change in price. A decrease in price will more than offset the increase in quantity demanded, and total revenue will drop. When price rises, total revenue will rise because the increase in price more than offsets the decrease in quantity demanded.

Finally, when demand is unitary elastic, the percentage changes in price and quantity demanded are exactly equal in absolute values. For this reason the two forces will cancel each other out, and total revenue will not change. Sometimes it is easier to see the relationships that we have been describing by looking at numerical

TABLE 22-5 Relationship Between Price Elasticity of Demand and Total Revenue

Price Elasticity of Demand	Price (dollars per unit)	Quantity Demanded (units per time period)	Total Revenue (in dollars)
Elastic (1.5)	5	300	1,500
	10	100	1,000
Inelastic (0.6)	5	300	1,500
	10	200	2,000
Unitary elastic (1.0)	5	400	2,000
	10	200	2,000

examples. In Table 22-5 you can see what happens to total revenue when the price rises (read down) or the price falls (read up) under elastic, inelastic, and unitary elastic conditions.

When demand is elastic (coefficient of 1.5 in our case) and price rises from $5 to $10, the quantity demanded falls from 300 to 100, so that total revenue (price times quantity demanded) drops from $1,500 to $1,000. Under the same conditions, a drop in price from $10 to $5 will cause total revenue to rise from $1,000 to $1,500.

When demand is inelastic (coefficient of 0.6 in our case) and price rises from $5 to $10, the quantity demanded falls from 300 to 200, so that total revenue rises from $1,500 to $2,000. Under the same conditions a drop in price from $10 to $5 will cause total revenue to fall from $2,000 to $1,500.

When demand is unitary elastic (coefficient of 1.0), a price change in either direction will cause an equal percentage response in quantity demanded in the opposite direction, so that total revenue will remain at $2,000.

CROSS ELASTICITY OF DEMAND

So far, we have been dealing only with the relationship between the quantity demanded for a product and the price of the *same* product. **Cross demand** relates the quantity demanded for a product to the price of a *different* product. This functional relationship may be expressed as

$$Q_{DA} = f(P_B), \text{ ceteris paribus}$$

where Q_{DA} is the quantity demanded of good A, f is the symbol for function (which may be read "depends on"), P_B is the price of good B, and *ceteris paribus* means that all other variables are held constant.

It follows that the **cross elasticity of demand** relates the percentage change in the quantity demanded for *one* product to the percentage change in the price of a *different* product, with other variables held constant. The cross elasticity of demand (E_C) may therefore be expressed as follows:

$$E_C = \frac{\text{the percentage change in the quantity demanded for one product}}{\text{the percentage change in the price of a different product that caused it}}$$

For goods A and B the formula for figuring cross elasticity is

$$E_C = \frac{\dfrac{Q_{DA2} - Q_{DA1}}{(Q_{DA1} + Q_{DA2})/2}}{\dfrac{P_{B2} - P_{B1}}{(P_{B1} + P_{B2})/2}}$$

After the twos cancel out, it is

$$E_C = \frac{\dfrac{Q_{DA2} - Q_{DA1}}{Q_{DA1} + Q_{DA2}}}{\dfrac{P_{B2} - P_{B1}}{P_{B1} + P_{B2}}}$$

Here Q_{DA1} is the original quantity demanded for good A, Q_{DA2} is the new quantity demanded for good A, P_{B1} is the original price of good B, and P_{B2} is the new price of good B.

Recall from Chapter 5 that the demand curve of a product shifts as the result of a change in the price of a related product and that economists have described two kinds of relationships—substitutes and complements. When two products are **substitutes**—readily interchangeable—the cross elasticity of demand will be positive.[1] A rise in the price of one will increase the demand for the other, and a drop in the price of one will lead to less demand for the other. For example, when the price of beer goes up, the demand for ale will go up. In other words, at higher prices of beer many people will switch over to buying ale. Likewise, when the price of beer goes down, the demand for ale goes down as people switch from ale to beer. A high positive cross elasticity between two products means that they are close substitutes, whereas a low one means that not much substitution takes place when one product changes in price. A 10 percent rise in the price of beer may bring about a 30 percent increase in the demand for ale (cross elasticity coefficient of 3.0). Yet a 10 percent rise in the price of beer may cause only a 1 percent increase in the demand for brandy (cross elasticity coefficient of 0.1).

When two products are **complements**—used along with each other—the cross elasticity will be negative. A rise in the price of one will decrease the demand for the other, and a drop in the price of one will increase the demand for the other. When the price of typewriters goes up, the demand for typewriter ribbons will go down. This happens because at higher prices of typewriters, the price of the combination made up of typewriter and ribbon rises, so that the quantity demanded for typewriters goes down and the demand for ribbons goes down. When the price of typewriters *decreases*, the demand for typewriter ribbons will go up, since the combination of the two complementary goods goes down in price. A large negative cross elasticity between two products means that they are close complements, whereas a small one means that the complementary relationship is weak. A 10 percent decrease in the price of typewriters may lead to a 20 percent rise in the demand for typewriter ribbons (cross elasticity coefficient of −2.0). Yet a 10 percent drop in the price of writing paper may cause

TABLE 22-6 Cross Elasticities of Demand for Three Pairs of Products

Product Pairs	Cross Elasticity Coefficient
The price of butter and the demand for margarine	0.81
The price of pork and the demand for beef	0.28
The price of animal foods and the demand for flour	0.56

Source: Herman Wold and Lars Jureen, *Demand Analysis: A Study in Econometrics* (New York: John Wiley & Sons, Inc., 1953). Copyright © 1953 by John Wiley and Sons, Inc. Reprinted by Greenwood Press, Westport, Connecticut, 1982. Used with permission.

only a one-half percent increase in the demand for pens (cross elasticity coefficient of −0.05).

Some actual estimates of cross elasticities of demand have been made by Herman Wold and Lars Jureen. They appear in Table 22-6. Note that, while all three pairs of products were found to be substitutes, margarine for butter was found to be a much better substitute than beef for pork.

Cross elasticity of demand was used in a very important antitrust case, to which we shall refer again in a later chapter. In 1956 the Supreme Court of the United States found the Du Pont Company innocent of monopolizing cellophane production on the grounds that the cross elasticity of demand between cellophane and other flexible packaging materials such as polyethylene, aluminum foil, and waxed paper was positive and very high.[2] The Du Pont Company had been accused of illegally monopolizing the production of cellophane because it produced about 75 percent of the cellophane sold in the United States. The Du Pont Company's defense was that the cross elasticity of demand between cellophane and the other flexible packaging materials was so high (they were such good substitutes) that the

1. Be sure to recognize that the convention of ignoring the sign for price elasticity of demand coefficients *cannot* be carried over to cross elasticity of demand coefficients.

2. U.S. v. E.I. Du Pont de Nemours and Co., 351 U.S. 377 (1956).

relevant industry was not cellophane, but rather flexible packaging materials, of which Du Pont held less than 20 percent of the market.

INCOME ELASTICITY OF DEMAND

So far, we have been dealing with the relationship between the quantity demanded for a product and the price of either the same product or a different product. **Income demand** relates the quantity demanded for a product to the income level of the consumers or potential consumers of that product. This functional relationship may be expressed as

$$Q_{Dx} = f(Y), \text{ ceteris paribus}$$

where Q_{Dx} is the quantity demanded of good X, f is the symbol for function, Y is the symbol for the income level of consumers and potential consumers of X, and *ceteris paribus* means that all other variables are held constant.

It follows that the **income elasticity of demand** relates the percentage change in the quantity demanded for a product to the percentage change in the income level of the consumers or potential consumers of the good or service, with all other variables unchanged. Therefore, the income elasticity of demand (E_Y) may be expressed as follows:

$$E_Y = \frac{\text{the percentage change in the quantity demanded for a product}}{\text{the percentage change in the level of income}}$$

The formula for figuring income elasticity of demand is

$$E_Y = \frac{\dfrac{Q_{D_2} - Q_{D_1}}{(Q_{D_1} + Q_{D_2})/2}}{\dfrac{Y_2 - Y_1}{(Y_1 + Y_2)/2}}$$

After the twos cancel out, we have

$$E_Y = \frac{\dfrac{Q_{D_2} - Q_{D_1}}{Q_{D_1} + Q_{D_2}}}{\dfrac{Y_2 - Y_1}{Y_1 + Y_2}}$$

Here Q_{D_1} is the original quantity demanded for the product, Q_{D_2} is the new quantity demanded, Y_1 is the original income level, and Y_2 is the new income level.

Again recall from Chapter 5 that the demand curve of a product shifts as a result of a change in the level of income. For most products we expect this relationship to be positive, because people demand more of a product when they can afford more. Where there is a positive relationship between the demand for a product and income, economists call that product **normal**.[3] As you know, students are likely to buy more automobiles, more dinners at a restaurant, and more stereo records when their income is higher. A high positive income elasticity of demand for a product means that a change in the level of income will bring about a strong demand response in the same direction. A 10 percent increase in a college student's income may cause him or her to buy 50 percent more restaurant dinners (income elasticity coefficient of 5.0).

Goods and services differ widely in their income elasticities of demand. In general, goods and services considered to be luxuries, such as jewelry and furs, tend to have high income elasticities, and those considered to be necessities, such as salt and detergent, tend to have low income elasticities. The proportion of income spent on a good or service is an important determinant of how income elastic it is. Table 22-7 lists several products, along with estimates of their income elasticities of demand. The first five products are found to be normal. Automobiles, a fairly high-priced item, were found to be quite income elastic (a 1 percent increase in income causes a 3 percent increase in the demand for automobiles). On the other hand, coffee was found not to be very income elastic.

3. The income elasticity of demand coefficient is positive for normal goods and services. Even though most goods and services are normal, the sign may not be ignored.

TABLE 22-7 Income Elasticities of Demand for Selected Products

Product	Income Elasticity Coefficient
Automobiles	3.00
Beer	0.93
Fruits and berries	0.70
Cigarettes	0.50
Coffee	0.29
Margarine	−0.20
Flour	−0.36

Sources: Gregory C. Chow, Demand for Automobiles in the United States (Amsterdam: North Holland Publishing Company, 1957); T. F. Hogarty and K. G. Elzinga, "The Demand for Beer," Review of Economics and Statistics, May 1972; Herman Wold and C. E. V. Leser, "Commodity Group Expenditures Functions for the United Kingdom, 1948–1957," Econometrica, January 1961; S. M. Sackrin, "Factors Affecting the Demand for Cigarettes," Agricultural Economics Research, July 1962; John J. Hughes, "Note on the U.S. Demand for Coffee," American Journal of Agricultural Economics, November 1969.

In some rare cases people demand more of a product when their income is low and less of the product when they have a higher income. Where such a negative relationship between demand and income exists, economists call the product **inferior.** For example, people may buy fewer potatoes and fewer bus tickets when their income is higher, since at higher income levels they may substitute some meat for some potatoes and an automobile for the bus. A 25 percent increase in a person's income may cause him or her to buy an automobile and thus buy 95 percent fewer bus tickets (income elasticity coefficient of −3.8).

Looking back at Table 22-7 once more, we see that Wold and Leser estimated negative income elasticities for both margarine and flour in mid-twentieth-century Britain.

SUMMARY

1. A market-demand schedule and curve are derived by horizontally adding together all of the individual consumer-demand schedules and curves

in a market that is clearly defined on the basis of both product and geography.

2. Shifts in market-demand curves occur for the same reasons that cause individual consumer-demand curves to shift. (These reasons are changes in preferences, changes in income, and changes in prices of related goods and services.) In addition, market-demand curves may shift because of changes in the number of consumers that are included in the market and the distribution of income among the consumers.

3. Elasticity is a concept used to describe the responsiveness of one variable to a change in another variable. The changes are measured in percentages, and not in absolute numbers. This means that elasticity is independent of the unit of measure that is used.

4. Price elasticity of demand measures the percentage change in the quantity demanded of a product in response to a percentage change in the price of that product.

5. There are five categories of elasticity. Demand is *elastic* when in absolute values the percentage change in the quantity demanded is greater than the percentage change in the price that led to it. Demand is *inelastic* when in absolute values the percentage change in the quantity demanded is less than the percentage change in the price that caused it. Demand is *unitary elastic* when in absolute values the percentage response in the quantity demanded is exactly equal to the percentage change in price that generated it. Demand is *perfectly inelastic* when a price change causes no quantity response at all. Demand is *infinitely elastic* when a price change causes an infinite response in the quantity demanded.

6. The price elasticity of demand of a product depends upon: (a) whether there are good substitutes available for it, (b) the proportion of consumer incomes spent on it, (c) whether the product is a luxury or a necessity, and (d) the amount of time that consumers have to adjust to the price change.

7. Whether a firm's total revenue from sales of a product will increase, decrease, or remain the same when it changes the price of the product will depend upon the price elasticity of demand for that product.

8. Cross elasticity of demand relates the percentage change in the quantity demanded for a product to the percentage change in the price of another product. It is positive for substitute products and negative for complements.

9. Income elasticity of demand relates the percentage change in the quantity demanded for a product to the percentage change in consumer income. It is positive for normal products and negative for inferior products.

DISCUSSION QUESTIONS

1. A market-demand curve may shift to the left or to the right for a number of different reasons. List and briefly explain the five reasons that were discussed in the chapter. Which of these reasons also apply to individual-demand curves, and which are unique to market-demand curves?

2. Using the formula provided in the chapter, calculate the price elasticity of demand for each of the following cases:

a. The price of a certain cough syrup increases from $5 to $10 a bottle, which causes the quantity demanded for this cough syrup to decrease from 1,000 bottles per day to 700 bottles per day.

b. The price of a certain type of shirt increases from $18 to $19, which causes the quantity demanded for these shirts to decrease from 100,000 units per month to 75,000 units per month.

c. The price of a certain computer game decreases from $40 to $32, which causes the quantity demanded for this game to increase from 3,000 units per year to 5,000 per year.

3. Referring to the three cases given in the previous question, determine whether the demand for each product is elastic, inelastic, or unitary elastic.

4. Provide a numerical illustration of a case in which demand is unitary elastic. What is the elasticity coefficient?

5. Provide a numerical illustration of a case in which demand is perfectly inelastic. What is the elasticity coefficient?

6. Explain how each of the following characteristics or circumstances relating to a particular good or service is expected to affect its price elasticity of demand:

a. A small portion of most consumers' incomes is spent on it.

b. Most consumers consider it a necessity.

c. Most consumers find that rather close substitutes are available for it.

d. The change in the quantity demanded is measured only a few hours after its price changed.

e. Most consumers consider it a luxury.

f. It is a big-ticket product, so that most consumers find that a large part of their income is spent on it.

g. The change in the quantity demanded is measured five years after its price changed.

7. If you know whether the price of a good has gone up or down and if you know whether its price elasticity of demand is elastic, inelastic, or unitary elastic, you can determine whether the seller's total revenue has gone up, down, or remained the same. Provide numerical illustrations to show this statement to be accurate.

8. Discuss the difference between the price elasticity of demand concept and the cross elasticity of demand concept.

9. From your own experience, give five examples of pairs of products that you consider to be good substitutes. Provide five more examples of pairs of products that you consider to be complements. Of these ten examples, which do you suppose would have the highest positive cross elasticity of demand coefficient? Which do you suppose would have the highest negative cross elasticity of demand coefficient?

10. If you know that Linda's consumption of potatoes fell from 200 pounds a year to 150 pounds a year when her income went up from $15,000 a year to $24,000 a year, you are able to calculate Linda's income elasticity of demand for potatoes. What is it? What do economists call this kind of a good?

23 *Business Firm Choice*

PREVIEW In the last two chapters we examined the demand side of product markets—the principles of consumer choice that economists use to predict what products will be demanded and in what quantities. In this and the next chapter we look at the supply side of product markets. This means that our interest turns to business firms, which concern themselves with production decisions. We shall therefore focus on the principles of business firm choice that economists use to predict what products will be supplied and in what quantities.

You may not be able to "wear the shoes" of the businessman or businesswoman quite as comfortably as those of the consumer. After all, each of us is a consumer, but only a small fraction of the population is likely to be engaged in making business decisions. However, it will be helpful for you to keep in mind the rationality assumption that economists make about business firms—namely, that they seek to maximize profits.

In this chapter you will study the fundamentals of production. Business firms seek an efficient way of combining inputs to produce certain outputs. The production function describes that relationship in terms of actual inputs and outputs. It cannot change during what economists call the short-run and long-run time periods. It is, however, subject to change in the very long run. You will see that business firm decision makers must be concerned with all three of these time periods at once.

Next you will learn a general theory of production in the short run. You will see what happens to output (goods or services produced) as a business firm adds more and more units of a variable input (such as the number of workers) to some other inputs that the firm cannot change (such as the size of a factory building). Then you will study the same case from the cost side. A whole family of business-cost concepts—seven in all—are defined, and the relationships between them are explained.

We then go on to discuss production in the long run. Economies and diseconomies of scale, as well as the important relationship between short-run and long-run average total cost, are explained.

Finally, we discuss production in the very long run, where inventions and innovations give rise to technological changes. Here we introduce the concept of *productivity* and explain the major determinants of productivity changes.

An appendix to the chapter, using a tool much like that used in the appendix to Chapter 21, shows one way of finding a firm's best input combination in the long run.

PRODUCTION

Production is the transformation of inputs into outputs. The **inputs** are the resources that we described in Chapter 4: labor, natural resources, and capital. These factors of production may appear in their original state, such as unskilled human labor or raw materials, or they may be the result of an earlier production process, as is the case with machines or semifinished goods. The **outputs** are the economic goods and services that business firms produce for sale to consumers,

TABLE 23-1   Input Combinations Resulting from Different Methods of Production for Producing Ten Dozen Pairs of Shoes per Day

Production Method	Quantity of Shoes Produced per Day (in dozens)	Number of Shoe Workers (in 8-hour days)	Number of Shoemaking Machines (in 8-hour days)
A	10	30	10
B	10	25	7
C	10	22	5
D	10	20	6
E	10	20	5

other business firms, and governments. For example, a company that manufactures shoes may transform such inputs as labor, shoemaking machinery, leather, nails, and laces into a variety of shoe outputs that are sold to individuals, to shoe stores, or to the U.S. Navy.

Technical Efficiency

Since economically rational business firms engage in production in order to obtain profits, they do not wish to use production methods that waste resources. Therefore, the first step in analyzing the behavior of firms in production is to understand what is meant by **technically efficient** methods of production. No waste of resources occurs when a technically efficient method of production is used. This means that no other method of production will yield the same output by using a lower quantity of any input without using a higher quantity of some other input. Combinations that are not technically efficient use more of at least one input and the same amounts of other inputs to yield the same output as another method of production. Table 23-1 illustrates this point. Five different production methods are shown (A through E), all of which yield 10 dozen pairs of shoes per day. Only production method E is technically efficient. Production methods A and B use more workers and more machines than does E, and so are technically inefficient. Production method C uses the same number of

machines as E but requires two more workers. Production method D uses the same number of workers, but one more machine. Hence, both C and D are also technically inefficient.

Once the technically inefficient production methods have been weeded out, the way is clear to understand a basic economic concept about the behavior of firms—the production function.

THE PRODUCTION FUNCTION   The relationship between the physical units of inputs and outputs in the production process is expressed in a firm's production function. A **production function** shows the maximum output that can be obtained from given amounts of inputs as of a specified point in time. The word "maximum" shows that it includes only technically efficient input combinations. The production function can also describe the minimum amount of inputs needed to support a certain level of output. It tells us what is possible at the present level of technological development. For example, the production function may show that a certain quantity of shoes can be produced each day, given any one of a number of combinations of shoe workers and shoemaking machinery.

A general statement of a production function for a good or service is as follows:

$$X = f(A, B, C, \ldots N)$$

Here X is the quantity of output per unit of time, and A, B, C, all the way to N, are the quantities

TABLE 23-2 Minimum Input Combinations for Producing Ten Dozen Pairs of Shoes per Day

Quantity of Shoes Produced per Day (in dozens)	Number of Shoe Workers (in 8-hour days)	Number of Shoemaking Machines (in 8-hour days)
10	100	1
10	50	2
10	25	4
10	20	5
10	10	10
10	5	20
10	4	25
10	2	50
10	1	100

of different inputs used to produce the output. It is convenient to simplify the general statement of the production function by grouping all of the different inputs that are actually used under just two headings: labor and capital. (Natural resources are here assumed to be part of capital.) We can then write the following:

$$X = f(L, K)$$

Here again X is the quantity of output per unit of time, L is the quantity of labor used to produce X, and K is the quantity of capital used to produce X.

To illustrate this concept, we return to the case of shoe manufacturing. Suppose that shoes can be produced by using only combinations of shoe workers (L_s) and shoemaking machinery (K_s) as inputs and that, using only technically efficient combinations, the exact relationship between them and the quantity of shoes produced (S) is as follows:

$$S = \sqrt{L_s \cdot K_s}$$

Shoe output will be measured in dozens of pairs of shoes per day and the inputs on the basis of a standard eight-hour day. This production function may then be read as follows: The maximum

quantity of shoes produced per day is equal to the square root of the number of shoe workers working an eight-hour day multiplied by the number of shoemaking machines operating for eight hours.[1]

If a certain shoe manufacturer wishes to produce 10 dozen pairs of shoes per day, the production function would indicate the following relationship:

$$10 = \sqrt{L_s \cdot K_s}$$

It shows the way in which a firm can substitute one input for another without changing its total output. Note that $L_s \cdot K_s$ must always be equal to 100, so that the square root is always equal to 10. Alternative labor–capital combinations for our hypothetical shoe manufacturer are presented in Table 23-2. Given its production function, the firm cannot produce 10 dozen pairs of shoes per day with fewer inputs than those shown in Table 23-2. We are assuming that no fractional units of either workers or machines can be employed. (In other words, we assume that the firm cannot hire

1. Recall that the square of a number is that number multiplied by itself. The square root of a number is merely the reverse of that calculation. As in the example we shall use here, the square of 10 is 100 and the square root of 100 is 10.

TABLE 23-3   Minimum Input (Technically Efficient) Combinations and Total Cost for Producing Ten Dozen Pairs of Shoes per Day

Quantity of Shoes Produced per Day (in dozens)	Number of Shoe Workers (in 8-hour days at $60 a day)	Number of Shoemaking Machines (in 8-hour days at $50 a day)	Total Cost per day (in dollars)
10	100	1	6,050
10	50	2	3,100
10	25	4	1,700
10	20	5	1,450
10	10	10	1,100
10	5	20	1,300
10	4	25	1,490
10	2	50	2,620
10	1	100	5,060

part-time workers or rent machines for part of a day.) The table shows nine different technically efficient ways of producing 10 dozen pairs of shoes per day. Comparing two of the alternatives from Table 23-2, we see that this firm can use a fairly high ratio of shoe workers to shoemaking machinery such as 25 workers and 4 machines ($10 = \sqrt{25 \times 4}$) or a low ratio of shoe workers to shoemaking machinery such as 2 workers and 50 machines ($10 = \sqrt{2 \times 50}$).

The preceding discussion makes the implicit assumption that business firms "know" their production functions. In reality, they often do not. Not enough information may be available, and business firms may not be willing to spend what it costs to find out about all of the possible input–output relationships. Just the same, we shall continue to make this simplifying assumption on the grounds that firms do have a pretty good idea about many of their most immediate tradeoffs.

Economic Efficiency

The production function shows the various technically efficient input combinations that can be used to produce a given quantity of output. But which of these technically efficient alternatives should a firm adopt? The production function cannot answer this question. Rather, the answer is based on **economic efficiency**—the technically efficient method with the lowest cost to the firm. We continue our shoe example to make this point clear. Table 23-3, besides repeating the nine technically efficient combinations shown in Table 23-2, gives a cost figure for each of them. We arrive at these cost figures simply by adding together the cost of workers and the cost of machines for each combination. For example, the firm can employ 5 workers at a rate of $60 per worker per day, or $300, and use 20 machines at a cost of $50 each per day, or $1,000, so that the combination of 5 workers and 20 machines costs the firm $1,300. We assume that the small firm in our example does not influence input prices, so that the cost of shoe workers is $60 per day and the cost of shoemaking machines is $50 per day for all quantities shown in Table 23-3. The total-cost figures allow us to determine which combination is economically efficient. The answer is, of course, 10 workers and 10 machines, since the total cost of $1,100 for that combination is less than for any other.

THREE TIME SPANS FOR DECISION MAKING

When a business firm enters an industry, it comes in at a certain size or capacity to produce. It has already made a number of commitments that reduce its immediate flexibility. Besides having built a certain size plant, it may have contracted to buy a minimum amount of some material inputs for a certain length of time or hired some workers or leased some land for a number of years. For example, automobile firms commonly enter into long-term agreements to purchase steel and tires from suppliers, and professional ball clubs enter into employment contracts with some of their players covering several years.

At any given time, a firm is expected to be less than perfectly flexible, since it faces some fixed obligations. The **short run** is defined as the period of time during which at least one of the firm's inputs cannot be varied.[2] It would be ideal if we could say exactly how long the short run generally lasts. But we cannot. For a small housepainting firm that wishes to expand, the short run may be only the two days that it takes to hire one more painter and buy the equipment that he or she needs. By contrast, a steelmaking firm may find that the short run lasts four years, since that is how long it takes to get delivery on a new basic oxygen furnace and to put up a building around it. In other words, the steel firm has a commitment to its present plant for four more years.

The second time span in which business decisions are made is called the **long run.** It is a period of time long enough to make all the changes that a firm wants to make within the limits of its existing production function. That is, the level of technological development does not change, even though all of the inputs that are recognized in the firm's production function are variable. In the long run, for example, a firm would be able either to double its capacity by building another plant and training additional workers or to produce only a third as much as it could before by selling off enough of its machines and letting go enough of its workers.

Business decisions also involve what economists refer to as the **very long run.** This is a period of time long enough so that a whole new technology can be introduced and the production function itself can be changed. The shoe manufacturer in our earlier example would no longer be bound by the alternatives offered in Table 23-2, since a new shoemaking machine or a new organizational system may now enable only 15 shoe workers and 4 shoemaking machines to produce 10 dozen pairs of shoes per day.

Business firms do *not* make short-run decisions in the short run, long-run decisions in the long run, and very-long-run decisions in the very long run. Instead, they make decisions in all three at the same time. A business decision maker decides the quantity and mix of products to produce and the prices to charge for them in the relatively inflexible environment of the short run. But at the same time the businessperson must also plan for the long run. If more steelmaking capacity is wanted in four years, the order for the furnace must be placed right now. Furthermore, firms must coordinate their short-run and long-run decisions with their very-long-run decisions. A firm must determine how much of its resources will be devoted to research, development, and adaptation.

PRODUCTION IN THE SHORT RUN

The short run is a time period during which a business firm is not perfectly flexible because at least one of its inputs cannot be varied. Important production decisions must be made in the short run. Economists have formulated some useful theories that allow us to make some generalizations about short-run production.

---

2. Some economists also like to recognize the *very short run,* a time period so short that the firm is unable to vary any of its inputs. We choose not to include the very short run in our discussion since it adds little to the analysis of business firm choice.

TABLE 23-4   Short-Run Production in Hypothetical Shoe Firm

(1) Quantity of Fixed Input (machines used for 8 hours per day)	(2) Quantity of Variable Input (workers working 8-hour days)	(3) Total Product (pairs of shoes per day)	(4) Marginal Product (pairs of shoes per day)	(5) Average Product (pairs of shoes per day) (3) ÷ (2)
3	0	0		0
3	1	3	3	3
3	2	7	4	3½
3	3	10	3	3⅓
3	4	12	2	3
3	5	13	1	2⅗
3	6	12	−1	2

Suppose that a shoe manufacturing firm can vary the number of shoe workers that it employs, but that it cannot change the number of its shoemaking machines. (Even though we are again using an example in which shoe workers and shoe machines are the only inputs necessary to produce shoes, it is not the same example that we used earlier in the chapter in our discussion of technical efficiency. For the sake of simplicity, we have switched to fewer workers and machines producing single pairs instead of dozens of pairs of shoes.) The numbers in Table 23-4 are strictly hypothetical, but the relationships are what economists predict about short-run production. Column 1 shows that the firm has fixed inputs (those it cannot change) of 3 units. It cannot in the short run increase or decrease the number of shoemaking machines. Column 2 gives the number of workers hired to produce shoes. This is a variable input—that is, this number can be changed in the short run. Column 3 shows the **total product**—the number of pairs of shoes per day that are produced when a certain number of shoe workers is employed to work with the 3 shoemaking machines. No shoes are produced when no workers are hired. The firm produces 3 pairs per day when 1 worker is employed, 7 pairs per day with

2 workers, and so on. Column 4 shows the **marginal product**—that is, the number of additional pairs of shoes per day that are produced as a result of employing one more worker. The first worker adds 3 pairs of shoes per day to the firm's output (3 − 0). The second worker adds 4 pairs per day (7 − 3), the third worker adds 3 pairs per day (10 − 7), and so on. Be sure to recognize the fact that the marginal product of a worker—say, the third worker—is not the output produced by the third worker but rather the addition to the total output as a result of employing the third worker. The last column shows **average product**—the total number of pairs of shoes produced per day divided by the number of workers employed (column 3 divided by column 2). Average product is 3 when 1 worker is employed (3 ÷ 1), it is 3½ when 2 workers are employed (7 ÷ 2), and so on.

All of these measures—total product, marginal product, and average product—are related to one another in simple mathematical ways. They are alternative ways of describing relationships between inputs and outputs. The patterns shown in the table represent those that economists predict will exist in the short-run time period. Let us describe these patterns further.

Increasing, Diminishing, and Negative Returns

Short-run production theory predicts that when a firm adds successive units of a variable input to certain fixed inputs, it may first result in increasing marginal product, then will result in diminishing marginal product, and eventually in negative marginal product. There are sound, logical reasons for these expectations.

The best illustration of **increasing returns** is our example of the second worker adding more product (4 pairs of shoes per day) than was added by the first worker, who added only 3 pairs of shoes per day to the firm's output. There are several ways to explain why increasing returns occur. The higher marginal product may be gained by specialization. One worker operating a number of different machines may be a "jack of all trades, but a master of none," whereas performing fewer different tasks may cause a worker to become expert and thereby to increase the rate of output. Also, one worker handling three machines may spend a great deal of time moving from machine to machine, whereas two workers may greatly reduce this time loss. A third way to explain this pattern is to imagine that one worker alone is not able to take full advantage of the capabilities of three machines. Some machines may have "down time" while the worker is busy with another machine. Adding the second worker allows more effective use of the machines' potential. Even though it may seem a bit unfair to the machines, we attribute the production increase to the additional worker. This explanation makes sense in the short run. Since the firm cannot change the number of machines, its decisions are made in terms of the variable input.

Diminishing returns occur when the marginal product is falling—that is, when the marginal product of each additional worker is smaller than the marginal product of the worker hired just before. It is an essential feature of short-run production that, after some point, each successive addition to a firm's variable input will result in a smaller addition to the firm's output. As shown in Table 23-4, diminishing returns set in with the hiring of the third worker, who adds only 3 pairs of shoes per day to the total product, as compared with 4 pairs per day added by the second worker. The total product increases. But in our example the gain (marginal product) from the third worker is not as great as the gain from the second worker. Diminishing returns have set in.

In these examples, we are assuming that there is no difference in the quality, diligence, or skill of these workers. The third worker is just as "good" as the second worker. The only thing that is changing is the ratio or mixture between workers and machines. As we add successive units of the variable input to the fixed amount of some other input, the mixture changes. It is the changing mixture that is responsible for the changing levels of the marginal product.

There are **negative returns** when the marginal product of a unit of variable input is negative—that is, when the total product is less when using this additional unit of input than it was before it was used. In our example, negative returns set in with the hiring of the sixth worker. The total product falls from 13 pairs of shoes per week to 12 pairs. The sixth worker is "excess baggage" and gets in the way of the others when there are only three machines available. We doubt that a profit-seeking firm would ever intentionally expand its operations to hire this worker, but mistakes do happen.

The Stages of Production

In Figure 23-1 we have plotted the data from Table 23-4. The horizontal axis of each graph in this figure shows quantities of the variable input—shoe workers in our shoemaking example. The vertical axes represent different measures of production. The total product is shown on the vertical axis of the upper graph. The average product and marginal product are shown on the vertical axis of the lower graph.

The horizontal axes in these graphs are divided to show three stages of production. In stage I the average product is increasing, and the marginal product is above it. In Stage II the average product

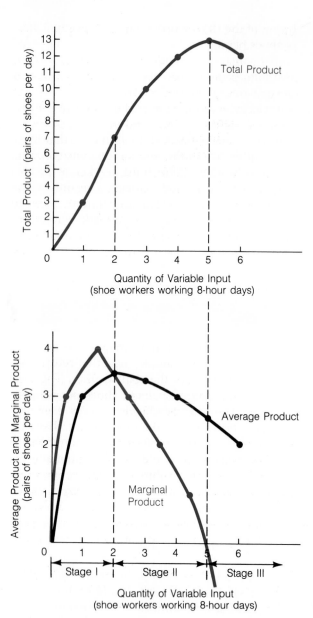

The numbers plotted from Table 23-4 establish the points along the three curves. The total-product and average-product points are plotted at the end points of the units of the variable input, while the marginal-product points are plotted as midpoints. The upper graph shows the total-product curve, first increasing at an increasing rate (where marginal product is increasing), then increasing at a decreasing rate (where marginal product is decreasing yet remains positive), and then decreasing (where marginal product is negative). The lower graph shows average product rising where marginal product is above it and average product falling where marginal product is below it.

Stage I is shown to be the range in which average product is increasing. Average product is at its peak (after 2 workers are employed) at the borderline between Stages I and II. In Stage II average product is falling, but marginal product remains positive. Total product is at its peak (after 5 workers are employed) at the borderline between Stages II and III. Stage III is shown to be the range in which total product decreases and marginal product is negative.

is decreasing, but the marginal product is still positive. In Stage III the marginal product is negative. Another way to see these stages is to note that the peak or the highest average product separates Stage I from Stage II and that the peak or the highest total product separates Stage II from Stage III. A third approach notes that average and marginal product are equal at the separation between Stage I and Stage II and that marginal

product becomes negative at the separation between Stage II and Stage III. Finally, note that these relationships all arise because total product is rising at an increasing rate in much of Stage I, rising at a decreasing rate in Stage II, and falling in Stage III. Division of the production function into three stages will help you to understand the behavior of the firm in the short run.

These different relationships should not be surprising once you know that all these curves (total, average, and marginal) are mathematically derived from the same set of data—the production function as applied in short-run production theory. Once you understand the mathematical relationships, it is not hard to recognize the characteristics of each stage. However, the relationship between the marginal product and the average product deserves a closer look.

Whenever marginal product is *higher* than average product—whether marginal product is rising or falling—average product must be rising. Likewise, whenever marginal product is *below* average product—whether marginal product is rising or falling—average product must be falling.

Therefore, when marginal product is neither higher than nor lower than average product—that is, when they are equal to each other—average product is no longer rising, nor has it yet begun to fall, so it is at its peak. This relationship always holds. It is a mathematical relation. In a sense, the marginal product "causes" the average product to rise or fall, or remain the same. The relationship is easily understood if we think in terms of sports averages such as in bowling or baseball. Suppose that a baseball player is carrying a .250 batting average in 45 games as a result of 50 hits in 200 times at bat. The player's average will increase or decrease or remain the same depending on his or her success in getting hits in the forty-sixth (the marginal) game. If the player's marginal performance is above .250, his or her average will increase. For example, 2 hits in 4 times at bat—a marginal performance of .500—will cause the player's average to climb to .255 ($52 \div 204$). On the other hand, a marginal performance below .250 will decrease the player's average. No hits in 4 times at bat during the forty-sixth game—a marginal performance of zero—will cause the player's average to decline to .245 ($50 \div 204$). Of course, his or her marginal performance could exactly equal .250—1 hit in 4 times at bat—so that the player's average would remain unchanged at .250 ($51 \div 204$).[3]

COSTS IN THE SHORT RUN

So far we have presented a general theory about the relationships between a business firm's physical inputs and outputs in the short run. Of course, a firm's inputs cost the firm something. Since we assume that business firms want to make the highest possible profit, it follows that they want to produce the output of their choice at the lowest

possible cost. Therefore we must bring cost into our discussion.

Economists view cost in terms of what is given up to attain something else. (See the discussion of opportunity cost in Chapter 4.) From the point of view of society, cost is the value of all the resources (labor, capital, and natural resources) that are used in production. From the point of view of a business firm, cost is a narrower concept. It is merely what the firm itself gives up to hire inputs that it uses in producing outputs. When a firm uses resources but does not itself incur that cost (as when a firm pollutes a river by dumping waste products into it), it is considered a cost to society but *not* to the firm.[4] Since this chapter deals with business firm choice, the costs to society that are not costs to business firms will not be considered.

Explicit and Implicit Costs

Some costs incurred by business firms are more easily identified than others. It is important, however, that all costs to firms be recognized and included in their decision-making calculations. For example, a couple who own a small independent grocery store incur many different costs. Among these costs are payments for the groceries they buy as stock, the salary they pay a clerk, the gas and electric bill, and the rent for the shop. Economists call these **explicit costs**—money payments for the use of inputs. Other costs are incurred for inputs for which no such obvious payment is made. These **implicit costs** also divert resources from other uses, but money payment is not actually made. The husband (Papa) works, let us say, seventy hours a week but never collects a salary check. His wife (Mama) works only "part-time"—forty hours a week—but she doesn't receive a salary check either. Also, the couple may have $50,000 tied up in store capital (shelving, refrigerator and freezer cases, and a stock of groceries), for which they receive no obvious return. At the end of each week the owners take

---

3. For those of you who are not sports enthusiasts and are therefore unfamiliar with the intricacies of baseball batting averages, try examining the relationship between your overall grade point average (GPA) and your grade in a marginal course. For example, if you receive an "A" (4 point) in this class, as you will no doubt do, it will raise your GPA, which, let us say, was somewhat below a 4 point.

4. This point will be more fully explained in our discussion of externalities in a later chapter.

TABLE 23-5   Costs for Hypothetical Shoe Firm

(1) Variable Input (number of shoe workers)	(2) Total Output (pairs of shoes produced per day)	(3) Total Fixed Cost (TFC) per day	(4) Total Variable Cost (TVC) per day	(5) Total Cost (TC) per day	(6) Marginal Cost (MC) per day	(7) Average Fixed Cost (AFC) per day	(8) Average Variable Cost (AVC) per day	(9) Average Total Cost (ATC) per day
0	0	$150.00	$ 0	$150.00		—	—	—
					$20.00			
1	3	150.00	60.00	210.00		$50.00	$20.00	$70.00
					15.00			
2	7	150.00	120.00	270.00		21.43	17.14	38.57
					20.00			
3	10	150.00	180.00	330.00		15.00	18.00	33.00
					30.00			
4	12	150.00	240.00	390.00		12.50	20.00	32.50
					60.00			
5	13	150.00	300.00	450.00		11.54	23.08	34.62

out of the cash register the amount of money not needed to pay their current bills (explicit costs). They probably call it "profit." Actually, it goes largely to help cover implicit costs. The grocery store owners could probably be employed in a nearby supermarket for $6.50 per hour, and the $50,000 investment in the store could be deposited in a bank where it would earn 10 percent interest. Therefore, the implicit cost of their labor is $37,180 per year (5,720 hours × $6.50 per hour) and the implicit cost of the store capital is $5,000 per year (0.10 × $50,000). Papa and Mama may be under the impression that they are making $50,000 profit this year. An economist might be ornery enough to point out that their implicit cost, which they disregarded, is $42,180 ($37,180 + $5,000 = $42,180), so that their profit is only $7,820 ($50,000 − $42,180 = $7,820).

Total Costs of Production

In the short run, a firm's total cost may be broken down into total fixed cost and total variable cost.

TOTAL FIXED COST (TFC)   The **total fixed cost (TFC)** is the cost that does not vary with the quantity of output that a firm produces. It will be the same whether a firm produces 5 units per day or 5,000 units per day or even zero units per day. For the hypothetical shoe manufacturer in our previous example, fixed input consisted of three shoemaking machines (see Table 23-4). Each machine costs $50 per eight-hour day, so that TFC is $150 per day. Table 23-5 gives the cost figures for this firm. Column 3 shows TFC to be $150 for the whole range of output from zero production to an output of 13 pairs of shoes per day. Figure 23-2 shows a total-fixed-cost curve for this example. Note that it is a horizontal straight line at $150.

TOTAL VARIABLE COST (TVC)   Those costs that are not fixed are called variable costs. The **total variable cost (TVC)** is the cost that varies with the quantity of output that a firm produces—the higher the output, the higher the total variable cost, and vice versa. (Most labor and material input costs are in this category.) But while the

FIGURE 23-2 Total-Cost Curves for Hypothetical Shoe Firm

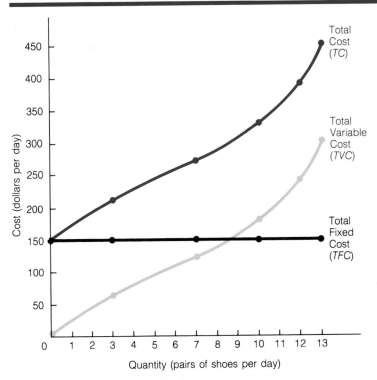

The numbers plotted from Table 23-5 establish the points along the three total-cost curves that are drawn for our hypothetical shoe firm. *TFC* is shown as a horizontal straight line, since *TFC* does not vary with output. The curve *TVC* is positively related to output and increases at a decreasing rate over the range of output (0–7 pairs) where the firm's marginal product increases and after that (7–13 pairs) increases at an increasing rate, since diminishing returns have set in. The curve *TC* is the vertical sum of the *TFC* and *TVC* curves. It has the same shape as the *TVC* curve because a constant ($150) is added to *TVC* at every level of output.

relationship between a firm's output and its *TVC* is positive, it is not expected to be proportional. In fact, it would be inconsistent with short-run production theory if we now found that, say, each time a firm doubled its output it would also double its *TVC*. What did we learn in our discussion of production in the short run? At very low levels of output, a firm is expected to experience increasing returns, so that its marginal product rises. At a somewhat higher level of output (but still in Stage I), diminishing returns set in, so that the firm's marginal product falls. Therefore *TVC*—the cost of the inputs needed to

produce the additional output—will rise with output at a *decreasing rate* until diminishing returns set in. We can illustrate this point by looking at the second and fourth columns in Table 23-5. The *TVC* for producing 3 pairs of shoes is $60, but a doubling of *TVC* to $120 will more than double the number of shoes—from 3 pairs to 7 pairs—that can be produced. For this range of output, *TVC* related to the output of shoes has increased at a decreasing rate, since the firm is experiencing increasing returns. The *TVC* for producing 7 pairs of shoes is $120, but a doubling of *TVC* to $240 will less than double the number of shoes—from

7 pairs to 12 pairs—that can be produced. For this range of output (and beyond) *TVC* related to the output of shoes has increased at an *increasing rate*, since the firm is experiencing diminishing returns. Figure 23-2 shows a *TVC* curve for this example. Note that it is not a straight line, but rather that it is bowed up (increasing at a decreasing rate) in the range of increasing returns and bowed down (increasing at an increasing rate) afterward, when diminishing returns prevail.

TOTAL COST (*TC*)   The last of the family of total-cost curves is the total cost itself. **Total cost (*TC*)** is the sum of *TFC* and *TVC*. For our shoe firm, *TC* is presented in column 5 of Table 23-5. Each cost figure in that column is derived by adding together the costs in columns 3 and 4. Figure 23-2 pictures the total-cost curve for our example. Note that it has exactly the same shape as the variable-cost curve, except that it is higher by the amount of *TFC*. At every level of output (including zero) the vertical distance between the total-variable-cost curve and the total-cost curve is $150.

Average Costs of Production

Besides the total-cost concepts, economists are often interested in costs per unit. The unit cost is found by dividing the same three cost concepts just discussed by the output level.

AVERAGE FIXED COST (*AFC*)   **Average fixed cost (*AFC*)** is the total fixed cost divided by the quantity of output. For our shoe firm, *AFC* is given in column 7 of Table 23-5. The figures are derived by dividing column 3 by column 2. For zero output, *AFC* is not defined, since we cannot divide a number by zero. For an output of 3 pairs of shoes, *AFC* is $150 divided by 3, or $50. As output increases, *TFC* ($150) is spread over larger and larger levels of output, so that *AFC* continuously declines. Yet, as long as there is still some *TFC*, *AFC* cannot be zero. An average-fixed-cost curve conforming to our example is shown in

Figure 23-3. Note that it continuously slopes downward but will never reach the horizontal axis because it will always be positive.

AVERAGE VARIABLE COST (*AVC*)   **Average variable cost (*AVC*)** is the total variable cost divided by the quantity of output. For our shoe firm, *AVC* is shown in column 8 of Table 23-5 and is the result of dividing column 4 by column 2. Average variable cost falls during early levels of production and increases after that. Just as we explained *TVC* by recalling our discussion of *marginal* product, we can explain *AVC* by remembering what we learned about *average* product. In Stage I, where the hiring of successive units of a variable input (at a fixed price of, say, $60 per day as in our example) results in an increase in average product, *AVC*—the variable cost per unit of output—must be falling. In Stage II the opposite happens. The hiring of successive units of the variable input (assuming its price does not change) results in a decline in average product and therefore a rise in *AVC*. An average-variable-cost curve for our example is pictured in Figure 23-3. Note that it is U-shaped.

AVERAGE TOTAL COST (*ATC*)   **Average total cost (*ATC*)** is the total cost divided by the quantity of output. It is the sum of *AFC* and *AVC*. For our shoe firm, *ATC* may be found in column 9 of Table 23-5 and can be figured either by dividing each figure in column 5 (*TC*) by the corresponding quantity in column 2 (Total Output) or by adding together columns 7 (*AFC*) and 8 (*AVC*). Average total cost decreases over a greater range of output than *AVC*, but eventually when the rise in *AVC* is greater than the fall in *AFC*, *ATC* will rise. Figure 23-3 shows the average-total-cost curve for our example, which is U-shaped. Note that the average-total-cost curve is far above the average-variable-cost curve at early levels of output—where *AFC* is high. Also note that the average-total-cost curve and the average-variable-cost curve are relatively close together at higher output levels, where *AFC* is low. Of course, they will never actually meet, since *AFC*, which is the difference between *AVC* and *ATC*, will always be positive in the short run.

FIGURE 23-3 Average-Cost Curves for Hypothetical Shoe Firm

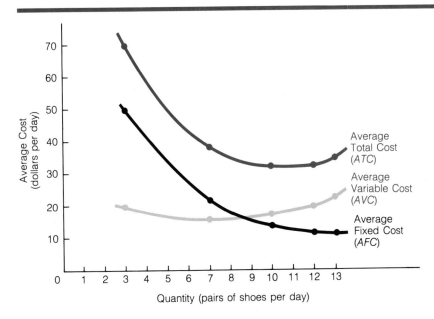

The numbers plotted from Table 23-5 establish the points along the three average-cost curves that are drawn for our hypothetical shoe firm. The curve AFC continuously declines since, as output increases, TFC must be divided by larger and larger quantities. The curve AFC remains positive—does not touch the horizontal axis—because TFC is positive. The curve AVC is U-shaped, since it decreases when the firm's average product increases and increases when its average product decreases. The curve ATC is the sum of the AFC and AVC curves. It is also U-shaped. At early levels of output, it is far above AVC because AFC is high. At high levels of output, ATC is much closer to AVC since AFC is low.

Marginal Cost of Production

The last short-run cost concept to be explained is marginal cost. **Marginal cost (MC)** is the addition to total cost when one more unit of output is produced. Column 6 of Table 23-5 presents MC for our hypothetical shoe firm. Notice that the figures in column 6 are not placed on the same horizontal lines as all the other numbers in the table, but are read between those lines. Also, since successively adding variable inputs (in column 1) does not increase output (in column 2) by single units, we *cannot* find MC merely by subtracting (in column 5) one total-cost figure from the next. Instead, MC is found by dividing the additional cost of hiring another unit of the variable input by the additional output that it helps to produce. For example, in Table 23-5, the MC of $15 connected with hiring the second shoe worker is found by dividing the additional cost of hiring the second worker ($60) by the increase in output (4 pairs of shoes) gained by hiring that worker. Another way to calculate marginal cost in Table 23-5 is to divide the increase in total cost (column 5) by the associated increase in output (column 2).

Marginal cost decreases over early production levels and rises afterward. Earlier in this chapter, when we discussed the shape of the total-cost curve, we explained that when marginal *product* is rising, total *cost* must be increasing at a decreasing rate and when marginal *product* is falling, total *cost* must be increasing at an increasing rate. Since MC is the rise in total cost when output

FIGURE 23-4   Marginal-, Average-Variable-, and Average-Total-Cost Curves for Hypothetical Shoe Firm

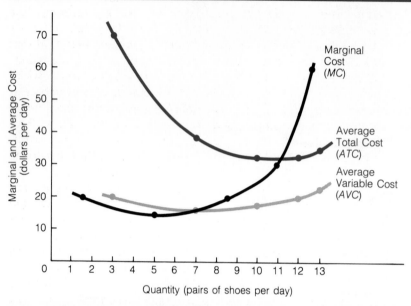

The numbers plotted from Table 23-5 establish the points along the three curves that are drawn for our hypothetical shoe firm. The curves *ATC* and *AVC* are the same as drawn in Figure 23-3. The curve *MC* is U-shaped. It decreases when the firm's marginal product is increasing and then increases when its marginal product declines. The curve *MC* intersects the minimum points of the *ATC* and *AVC* curves, since it must be below them when they are falling and above them when they are rising.

increases by an additional unit, *MC* is the rate of change or the *slope* of the total-cost curve. Therefore, when marginal product is rising so that total cost is increasing at a decreasing rate, *MC* falls. When marginal product is falling so that total cost increases at an increasing rate, *MC* rises.

Figure 23-4 pictures the marginal-cost curve of our hypothetical shoe firm. Note that it is U-shaped. In the same figure we have drawn the firm's average-variable-cost and average-total-cost curves so that you may see their relationship to the marginal-cost curve. Notice that the marginal-cost curve intersects both the average-variable-cost curve and the average-total-cost curve at their lowest points. When *MC* is below *AVC* and *ATC*, it causes them to fall. When *MC* is above *AVC* and *ATC*, it causes them to rise. Only when *MC* is equal to *AVC* is *AVC* neither falling nor

rising (and at its lowest point), and only when *MC* is equal to *ATC* is *ATC* neither falling nor rising (and at its lowest point). Recall the comparison to baseball batting averages that we used earlier in this chapter in explaining a similar relationship between the marginal-product and average-product curves. Those were, inverted U-shaped curves, whereas here we have U-shaped curves, but the relationship holds just as well.

PRODUCTION IN THE LONG RUN

In the long run, business firms can vary any and all of their inputs. For this reason, even though they are still subject to the same production function, they face no fixed costs. There is no longer—as there was in the short run—a need to be concerned about adjusting variable inputs to fixed inputs. Firms simply seek out their lowest-cost methods of producing their desired levels of outputs. Our shoe firm, for example, was able to raise its output in the short run only by adding workers, since the number of shoemaking machines was fixed. But in the long run, it can add (or eliminate) as many shoemaking machines as it wants. It can also build a new factory building that uses a method of production better suited to its planned output level. Or it can sell off some of its production facilities and change its method of production to suit its smaller operation.

Total costs in the long run are made up entirely of variable costs. Therefore, of the seven cost concepts that we explained in our discussion of the short run (*TFC, TVC, TC, AFC, AVC, ATC, MC*), only three remain in the long run. These are long-run total cost, long-run average cost, and long-run marginal cost.

Long-run total cost (*LRTC*) is the total cost of producing a certain level of output when a firm is able to vary all of its inputs. For example, when the Boeing Company plans for the production of a new-generation aircraft, it does not allow itself to be restricted by its present resources. Long-run planning may be for the beginning of production ten years from now, which gives Boeing the opportunity to make all of the facility and work force changes that it wishes.

Long-run average cost (*LRAC*) is the long-run total cost divided by the quantity of output. **Long-run marginal cost (*LRMC*)** is the addition to *LRTC* when one more unit of output is produced. The mathematical relationships among total, average, and marginal values are the same for long-run costs as for short-run costs. However, we must explore long-run cost and production theory in order to understand how these costs vary with output.

Effects of Plant Size on Long-Run Average Cost

Economic theory suggests that there are predictable results from changing the size of a firm's

plant. According to the theory, plants that are set up to produce a low volume of output are not able to use certain known methods of production. They cannot effectively use an assembly-line method, for example. But a firm that sets up a plant to produce a greater volume may find that it does pay to use an assembly line in production. In fact, the larger-volume plant offers a wider range of choice about methods of production. If some of these added choices allow the firm to produce goods at a lower average total cost than would be possible in the small-volume plant, economies of scale exist. Economic theory predicts that this advantage will not last forever. At some point, constant returns set in, and larger plant size will no longer bring about lower average total cost. Economic theory even predicts that plants can be too large. Muscle-bound giants could experience higher average total cost than smaller plants. Thus, even diseconomies of scale are possible. Let us carefully define and illustrate the economists' concepts of economies, constant returns, and diseconomies of scale.

ECONOMIES OF SCALE **Economies of scale** are long-run increasing returns. They occur when a firm has a more-than-proportionate rise in its output because of increasing its inputs. For example, if a firm were to double total inputs, and if its output more than doubled as a result, economies of scale would exist. The importance of economies of scale over a fairly extensive range of output may be seen in the example of General Motors' stamping operations. A few years ago General Motors used a single die set, valued at about $500 million, in the manufacture of car bodies for many different car lines both within the same division, such as Chevrolet or Buick, and across divisional lines. The company maintained that if it had used specialized dies to stamp out panels such as hoods, doors, fenders, deck lids, underbodies, and roofs for each individual car model, its average total cost would have been substantially higher.[5]

5. General Motors Corporation, *Competition and the Motor Vehicle Industry*, April 1974.

FIGURE 23-5   Cost Curves with Economies of Scale

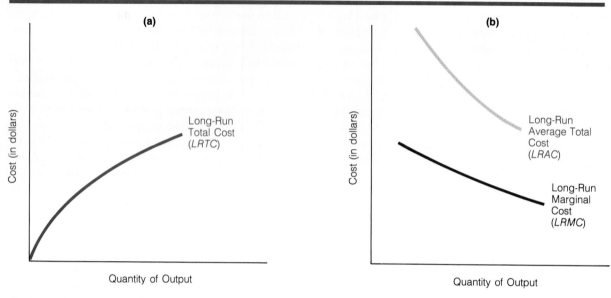

A firm's three long-run cost curves under conditions of economies of scale are shown here. Panel (a) pictures the *LRTC* curve increasing at a decreasing rate. Therefore,

panel (b) shows the *LRAC* and the *LRMC* curves sloping downward to the right. Since *LRAC* is falling, *LRMC* must be below it.

Figure 23-5 pictures a firm's three long-run cost curves under conditions of economies of scale. Panel (a) shows its *LRTC* curve. It increases at a decreasing rate, showing that when input prices remain constant and output doubles, total cost will less than double. Panel (b) shows the *LRAC* curve and the *LRMC* curve for the same firm. These curves slope downward to the right because *LRTC* rises at a slower rate than output. The *LRMC* curve lies below the *LRAC* curve for the usual reason. When marginal cost is below average cost, average cost must be falling.

CONSTANT RETURNS TO SCALE   Constant returns to scale are long-run returns when an increase in output is exactly proportionate to the increase in inputs. For example, a firm finds that doubling total inputs causes its output also to double. Figure 23-6 pictures a firm's three long-run cost curves under conditions of constant

returns to scale. Panel (a) shows its *LRTC* curve as a straight line coming out of the origin. When input prices remain constant and output doubles, total cost will also double. Panel (b) shows that the *LRAC* curve and the *LRMC* are both constant (the same at each level of output) and are equal to each other. (Recall that when average total cost is neither rising nor falling, marginal cost must be equal to it.)

DISECONOMIES OF SCALE   Diseconomies of scale—the opposite of economies of scale—are long-run decreasing returns. They occur when a firm has a less-than-proportionate increase in its output as a result of increasing its inputs. For example, a firm finds that doubling its inputs causes its output to less than double. Scaled-up process vessels and machines may become difficult for workers to handle or require special facilities to house them. As an instance, cement

FIGURE 23-6   Cost Curves with Constant Returns to Scale

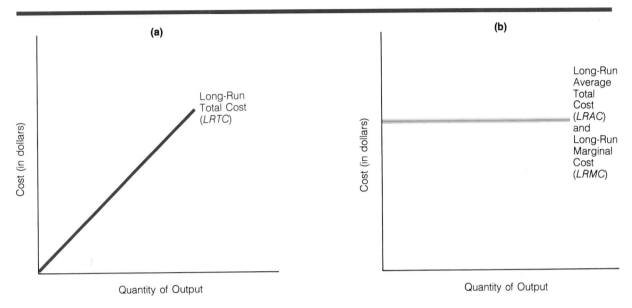

A firm's three long-run cost curves under conditions of constant returns to scale are shown here. Panel (a) pictures the *LRTC* curve increasing at a constant rate. Therefore, panel (b) shows the *LRAC* and the *LRMC* curves as the same horizontal straight line. The curves *LRAC* and *LRMC* are the same at each level of output and are equal to each other.

---

kilns experience unstable internal aerodynamics above a capacity of 7 million barrels a year.[6] Figure 23-7 shows a firm's three long-run cost curves under diseconomies of scale. Again, panel (a) pictures its *LRTC* curve. It is rising at an increasing rate, showing that at constant input prices when output doubles, total cost will more than double. The companion graph, in panel (b), again shows the same firm's *LRAC* and *LRMC* curves. This time they are increasing, since *LRTC* rises at a faster rate than does output. The *LRMC* curve lies above the *LRAC* curve. When *ATC* is rising, *MC* must be above it, or when *MC* is above *ATC*, *ATC* must be rising. Now look back at Figures 23-5, 23-6, and 23-7 and compare the *LRTC*, *LRAC*, and *LRMC* curves in each figure.

6. F. M. Scherer, *Industrial Market Structure and Economic Performance*, 2nd ed. (Chicago: Rand McNally, 1980), p. 84.

THE CAUSES OF ECONOMIES AND DISECONOMIES OF SCALE   Economies and diseconomies of scale stem from a change in the relationship among a firm's inputs within a plant. (A *plant* is a factory or other production facility in a particular geographic location. A firm may operate only one plant or a number of plants.) As a firm changes the level of output of a plant, it often adopts a different method of production or technology—the one that is expected to offer a lower average total cost. Large plants typically use a significantly different mode of production than do small plants in the same industry. Though it pays to use very specialized machines and workers in a very large operation, it does not pay in a relatively small one. The cost advantages gained through such specialization largely explain economies of scale. For example, a firm producing cars at a rate of 100 per year would want to use a very simple technology—a few highly versatile workers and

FIGURE 23-7   Cost Curves with Diseconomies of Scale

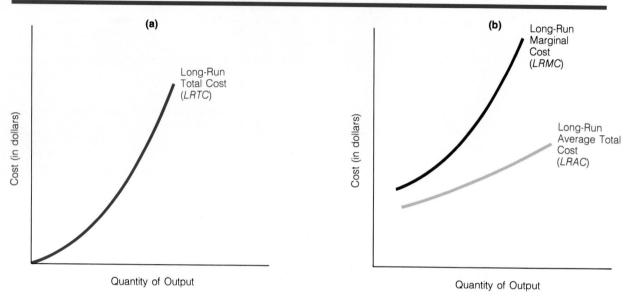

A firm's three long-run cost curves under conditions of diseconomies of scale are shown here. Panel (a) pictures the *LRTC* curve increasing at an increasing rate. Therefore, panel (b) shows the *LRAC* and the *LRMC* curves sloping upward from left to right. Since *LRAC* is rising, *LRMC* must be above it.

a few fairly simple machines. By contrast, a firm producing 400,000 cars per year in a plant would use an assembly-line method, which calls for very specialized workers, sophisticated machines, and an elaborate organization. In between the 100-per-year and the 400,000-per-year plants are many plants of different sizes in which a firm might wish to produce in the long run. As the output level becomes larger, it calls for a somewhat different technology and, presumably, a lower cost in terms of inputs per unit of output. It is reasonable to expect that such gains from specialization will come to an end at some level of output. After that point, there might be a range of output over which the firm can realize only constant returns to scale. Finally, at a very large plant size, diseconomies of scale will set in. As in the case of economies of scale, these are caused by a change in input relationships. For example, when an automobile plant gets so large, say, above the 800,000-cars-per-year level, that it re-

quires several layers of management—managers of managers who manage other managers—the increased ratio of managers to production workers may bring about diseconomies of scale.

Figure 23-8 illustrates the *LRAC* curve for the hypothetical car firm example. For the output range up to 400,000 cars, the firm experiences economies of scale, so that the *LRAC* curve is like the one drawn in Figure 23-5. Plant sizes between 400,000 and 800,000 cars per year offer constant returns to scale; this range of the *LRAC* curve resembles the one drawn in Figure 23-6. Finally, plants that produce more than 800,000 cars per year experience diseconomies of scale, so that portion of the *LRAC* curve resembles the one we drew in Figure 23-7.[7]

7. All along we have been assuming a single underlying production function. However, no single mathematical production function will give rise to the three distinct portions of the long-run average-cost curve shown in Figure 23-8.

FIGURE 23-8   Economies, Constant Returns, and Diseconomies of Scale for a Hypothetical Automobile Firm

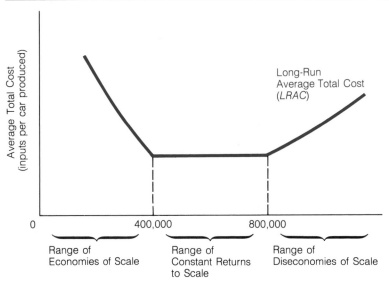

Quantity of Output (cars produced per year)

The *LRAC* curve shown here is that of a hypothetical automobile firm. Larger and larger plants up to the one used to produce 400,000 cars per year bring lower *LRAC*.

Plants that produce between 400,000 and 800,000 cars per year experience the same *LRAC*. Even larger plants bring higher and higher *LRAC*.

The Relationship Between Long-Run and Short-Run Average Total Costs

The long-run nature of economies, constant returns, and diseconomies of scale is clearly illustrated by the relationship to short-run cost curves. The long-run average-cost curve is made up of points from all the short-run average-total-cost curves. At every possible output level, there is a point on some short-run average-total-cost curve that indicates the lowest average cost at which that quantity of output can be produced. All such points taken together over the whole range of possible outputs define the long-run average-cost curve. Figure 23-9 shows the same *LRAC* curve that we drew for our hypothetical automobile firm in Figure 23-8. It also shows six short-run *ATC* curves. These short-run *ATC* curves indicate the presence of some fixed inputs—a certain plant

size—so that each describes operations within a plant of a particular size. Every point on the *LRAC* curve shows the lowest cost per unit of output at which a certain quantity level of output may be produced.

For example, ATC_1 represents a plant that can produce 150,000 cars per year at the lowest possible average total cost in the long run. This is the output level at which ATC_1 is tangent to (touches) the *LRAC* curve. Likewise, ATC_6 represents a plant that can produce 1,150,000 cars per year at the lowest possible average total cost in the long run. In between we show four more short-run average-total-cost curves (ATC_2, ATC_3, ATC_4, and ATC_5) representing plants of four other sizes out of the huge number that could be drawn.

Figure 23-9 reveals that the U-shaped, short-run average-total-cost curves that are tangent to the constant-returns-to-scale part of the *LRAC*

FIGURE 23-9   Relationship Between Long-Run and Short-Run Average-Total-Cost Curves for a Hypothetical Automobile Firm

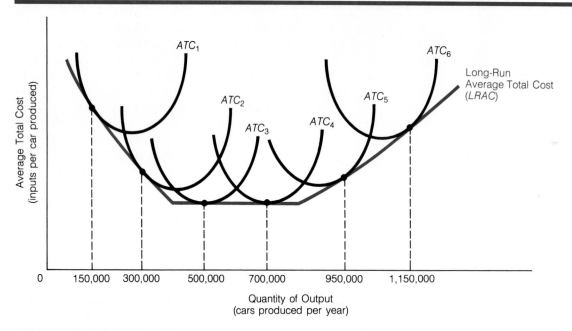

The $LRAC$ curve and the six short-run ATC curves belong to the same hypothetical automobile firm shown in Figure 23-8. Each of the six short-run ATC curves describes operations within a certain-sized plant, and the $LRAC$ curve shows the lowest cost per unit at which any level of output may be produced. Along the economies-of-scale portion of the $LRAC$ curve, short-run ATC curves such as ATC_1 and ATC_2 are tangent at a level of output that is less than the one associated with minimum average total cost of production in that plant. Along the diseconomies-of-scale portion of the $LRAC$ curve, short-run ATC curves such as ATC_5 and ATC_6 are tangent at a level of output that is greater than the one associated with minimum average total cost of production in that plant. Only along the constant-returns-to-scale portion does minimum short-run ATC coincide with minimum $LRAC$.

curve, such as ATC_3 and ATC_4, are tangent at their lowest points. (That is, no other level of production in those plants would yield lower cost per unit.) By contrast, ATC_1 and ATC_2, which are tangent along the economies-of-scale part of the $LRAC$ curve, are tangent at a level of output that is less than the one associated with lowest average total cost of production in that plant. Likewise, ATC_5 and ATC_6, which are tangent along the diseconomies-of-scale part of the $LRAC$ curve, are tangent at a level of output that is greater than the one associated with lowest-average-total-cost production in that plant.

These facts may suggest that in the short run a firm will wish to expand output in plants with curves such as ATC_1 and ATC_2 and to contract output in plants with curves such as ATC_5 and ATC_6 in order to produce at the lowest point of its short-run ATC curve. However, in the long run—when a firm is able to change the size of its plant—it hopes to produce along the constant-returns-to-scale part of its $LRAC$ curve in a plant with a curve like ATC_3 or ATC_4.

The relationships in Figure 23-9 provide interesting food for thought. In the economies-of-scale part of the $LRAC$ curve, short-run efficiency implies that the plant is a bit too large. That is, the lowest-cost way to produce a given output in the long run is to have a plant that is a little too large and to leave some of this capacity unused (wasted). This situation implies that the economies of scale made possible by the extra plant size more than make up for the "waste" of operating at less than capacity. An opposite set of possibilities can be seen in the diseconomies part of the *LRAC* curve.

PRODUCTION IN THE VERY LONG RUN

Besides the short-run and long-run decisions that are subject to its production function, a business firm also makes decisions that have the potential of changing its production function. These decisions are classified as being very long run in nature. They deal with such activities as research, development, invention, and innovation. The firm's purpose is to increase its profits through the discovery of new and better products for consumers and new, lower-cost production methods that raise its productivity.

Invention and Innovation

Invention is the discovery of a new product or a new technical tool or process. A large percentage of the products and processes that we use and take for granted in the United States today were not even imagined, say, one hundred years ago. Among these are television sets, computers, penicillin, and synthetic materials. Some inventions are the work of private persons, but more and more often they are the product of company or university research.

Innovation is the development of an invention from the original idea to a practical use. Innovation, even more than invention, stems from a firm's decision to use its resources for research and development (R&D). For example, Chester Carlson invented xerography in 1938. However, the first Xerox photocopying machine was not introduced to the market until 1959. During those twenty-one years, the Battelle Development Company and then the Haloid Corporation (later called the Xerox Corporation) worked to make a useful machine from Carlson's invention. They took the basic idea of xerography and overcame some important physics and engineering problems to develop a single-unit copier that outperformed all other copying machines available at the time.

Productivity and Business Decisions

Very-long-run business decisions will have an effect on productivity. **Productivity** is the amount of output produced by a unit of resource input during a given span of time. Generally, productivity is expressed in terms of product output per hour of labor input. Of course, labor uses capital and natural resources to produce output, so that this measure also captures changes in how these other inputs are used and combined.

Over the past two to three hundred years, impressive productivity gains have been made in most of the industrialized countries of the world. Their standards of living—measured by the amount of goods and services consumed by the average citizen—have dramatically increased. How can we explain these changes? The most important reasons for these productivity increases come under two fairly broad headings: (1) input substitution and (2) increasing quality of inputs.

INPUT SUBSTITUTION Input substitution means using a more productive input in place of one that is less productive. Recall from our earlier discussion that some such substitution takes place in the long run when one known technology replaces another as the scale of operation is changed. Input substitution becomes very long run when the change is brought on by **technological progress**—an advance in knowledge of the industrial arts and/or improved techniques of organizing production. In the very long run, input substitution may be limited to a single resource class (one machine for another, or one kind of skilled worker for another) or may be between different resource classes such as capital for labor. In fact, important productivity gains have been made by substituting capital for labor. One construction worker running a power shovel may be more productive than ten workers using hand shovels. One farmer with a combine may outproduce fifty farmers using only hand tools. One manager using a computer may be able to coordinate a firm's productive activity with greater precision than could an army of managers without that tool.

QUALITY OF INPUTS The second reason why productivity may increase is that the quality of many of the inputs improves. As you have already seen, technological progress may improve the quality of capital. Education and training enhance the quality of labor. Firms may also discover higher grades of raw materials or be able to purchase better-quality semifinished inputs. The upgrading of some inputs without others may, however, do little to raise productivity. Higher productivity often calls for a balanced improvement in the quality of inputs. For example, a modern plant with the latest capital equipment will likely yield a low quantity and quality of output if it is operated by poorly trained and undereducated workers. Can the quality of inputs decrease? If high-quality mineral resources are used up, so that lower-quality ones must be used, productivity may go down.

Productivity in the United States

Throughout most of its history the record of productivity growth in the United States has been impressive. U.S. productivity today is the highest in the world, but over the period of the last two decades its growth has trailed such countries as Japan and Germany. From 1948 to 1968 U.S. productivity rose at an average annual rate of 3.2 percent. From 1968 to 1973 the annual increase was just under 2 percent and the remainder of the 1970s saw an average annual increase between 0.5 and 1 percent. Since then the rate has increased, but it is too soon to tell whether this

means that there has been a reversal of the declining trend. Why did the decline in the U.S. productivity increases take place? Some blame government, arguing that government regulations hinder productivity growth, that tax policies do not offer enough incentives for firms to spend large amounts on R&D, and that there is not enough direct government R&D support. Some blame labor unions, claiming that they prevent firms from making changes that may lead to greater efficiency. During the 1970s many blamed soaring energy prices fueled by the OPEC cartel. Others argue that faltering productivity growth has been due largely to the huge rise in employment in the service industries, where productivity is more difficult to increase. Finally, there are those who contend that U.S. business managers have lost their entrepreneurial spirit and are simply no longer willing to make risky very-long-run commitments. Probably, the answer is some combination of these reasons. Our theory suggests that very-long-run decisions are based on expectations of payoffs. If firms see a likelihood that R&D spending will lead to profitable new products and/or processes, there will be a tendency for productivity to increase.

SUMMARY

1. Business firms engage in production, which is the transformation of inputs into outputs.

2. Technically efficient input combinations are those that cannot be improved upon. That is, the equivalent output cannot be obtained by using less of some input without using more of some other input.

3. Technically efficient relationships between a firm's physical units of inputs and outputs are expressed in its production function. It presents the maximum output that can be obtained from given amounts of inputs at a given level of technological development or the different technically efficient combinations of inputs that can produce a given output.

4. An input combination is economically efficient if it produces a given output at the lowest possible cost.

5. Firms make decisions for three different time spans: the short run, the long run, and the very long run. The short run allows a firm the least amount of flexibility because at least one of its inputs cannot be varied. The long run allows complete flexibility within the firm's production function. In the very long run, a firm's production function can be altered through technological change.

6. The theory of production in the short run predicts that when a firm adds successive units of a variable input to some fixed inputs, it will first result in increasing returns (rising marginal product), then diminishing returns (falling marginal product), and eventually in negative returns (falling total product and negative marginal product).

7. The theory of production in the short run separates production into three stages. In stage I total product rises, average product rises, and marginal product first rises and then falls. In stage II total product rises at a decreasing rate, marginal product falls, and average product falls. In stage III total product falls, marginal product is negative, and average product continues to fall.

8. Business firms are assumed to want to maximize their profits and therefore to want to minimize the costs of what they choose to produce. Economists separate a firm's costs into seven short-run cost concepts. These are: *TC, TFC, TVC, ATC, AFC, AVC,* and *MC.* They are related in the following ways:

$TC = TFC + TVC$
$ATC = TC \div$ quantity of output
$ATC = AFC + AVC$
$AFC = TFC \div$ quantity of output
$AVC = TVC \div$ quantity of output
$MC =$ the change in *TC* when output changes by one unit

9. The economic theories of increasing and diminishing returns determine the shape of a firm's short-run cost curves.

10. In the long run, there are three cost concepts: *LRTC, LRAC,* and *LRMC.* When *LRTC* increases at a decreasing rate, *LRMC* will be below *LRAC,* which is falling. Such long-run increasing returns are called economies of scale. When *LRTC* in-

creases at a constant rate, *LRMC* and *LRAC* will be constant and equal. This condition is called constant returns to scale. When *LRTC* rises at an increasing rate, *LRMC* will be above *LRAC,* which is rising. Such long-run decreasing returns are called diseconomies of scale.

11. At increasingly higher levels of output, *LRAC* is expected first to decrease, then to level off, and finally to increase. Each larger and larger output level calls for the adoption of a somewhat different method of production. At first there are gains from specialization, but eventually these fade out, and finally wasteful bureaucracy is expected to set in.

12. The *LRAC* curve is made up of points from all the short-run *ATC* curves. Each short-run *ATC* curve represents a certain-sized plant. In the long run, economists predict that a firm will choose a plant that offers minimum *ATC* at the level of output it wishes to produce. Only in the constant-returns-to-scale range of output will a firm achieve both minimum short-run and minimum long-run *ATC.* In the output ranges of economies and diseconomies of scale, short-run minimum *ATC* will not coincide with long-run minimum *ATC.*

13. Very-long-run business decisions involve invention and innovation. Invention is the discovery of a new product or process, and innovation brings it to practical use.

14. Very-long-run business decisions affect productivity. Productivity—usually measured in terms of product output per hour of labor input—can be changed by input substitution and by changing the quality of inputs. Productivity increases have slowed significantly in the United States over recent decades.

DISCUSSION QUESTIONS

1. The production function describes a set of alternative input combinations that are all technically efficient. What is meant by technical efficiency? Distinguish between technical efficiency and economic efficiency. Are all economically efficient methods of production technically efficient as well?

2. Distinguish among the three time perspectives for decision making—short run, long run, and very long run. Suppose that you are a high-level decision maker for a firm that manufactures and sells tires. Give two examples of short-run decisions you might have to make, two examples of long-run decisions, and two examples of very-long-run decisions.

3. Distinguish between diminishing returns and negative returns. Which do you expect firms to experience more frequently? Why?

4. "The theory of diminishing returns has a rather bleak prediction to offer. As time goes on, we shall get lower and lower returns." Do you agree? Why or why not?

5. Without looking at Figure 23-1, draw a total-product curve on a set of axes that measures total product along the vertical axis and the quantity of a variable input along the horizontal axis. Compare your diagram with Figure 23-1 to be sure you have it right. Using the concept of *marginal product*, explain why the theory of production suggests that the total-product curve looks this way in the short run.

6. Discuss the relationship between the marginal-product and the average-product curves in the short run. Specifically, explain their relationship:

    a. in Stage I
    b. in Stage II
    c. at the borderline between Stage I and Stage II

7. Without looking at Figures 23-2 and 23-3, on a single set of axes draw a total-cost curve, a total-fixed-cost curve, and an average-fixed-cost curve as you would expect them to look for a particular firm in the short run. Compare your diagram with Figures 23-2 and 23-3 to be sure you drew the curves correctly. Using what you learned about increasing and diminishing returns, carefully explain why the total-cost curve is shaped as it is. Then explain the relationship between the total-fixed-cost curve and the average-fixed-cost curve. When will the average-fixed-cost curve reach the horizontal axis?

8. Without looking at Figure 23-4, draw an average-variable-cost curve, an average-total-cost curve, and a marginal-cost curve on a single set of axes, as you would expect them to look for a particular firm in the short run. Compare your diagram with Figure 23-4 to be sure you have it right. Explain why the marginal-cost curve intersects the average-variable-cost curve and the average-total-cost curve at their minimum points. Why is average total cost far more in excess of average variable cost at low quantities of output than at high quantities of output?

9. Economists use seven different cost concepts to analyze a firm's production decisions in the short run, but only three in the long run. True or false? Explain.

10. Why is a firm's long-run average-cost curve expected to be U-shaped? (What accounts for the negatively sloped and then the positively sloped segments?)

11. "A firm would be foolish not to increase its level of output as long as it is operating on the negatively sloping portion of its long-run average-cost curve." True or false? Explain.

12. Distinguish between invention and innovation. Explain how either may affect productivity through input substitution and through increasing the quality of inputs.

Appendix:
A Firm's Best Input
Combination

How can a firm find the combination of inputs that allows it in the long run to produce the output that it wants at the lowest possible cost? To answer this question, we use a tool not very different from the one we used in the appendix to Chapter 21. If you understand the indifference-analysis approach to the theory of consumer behavior, you will probably find the material in this appendix quite easy to follow. In order to find the right combination, a company must know both the technically efficient combinations of inputs that can be used to produce different levels of output and the prices of these inputs. Remember that the technically efficient combinations are shown by a firm's production function. By using input prices, it is possible to discover the com-

bination that is economically efficient—the least-cost input combination.

To show how the best input combination may be found, we shall first present graphically the combinations of inputs offered by a company's production function and then picture their input prices. Finally, we shall combine the two.

ISOQUANTS

The word **isoquant** means "same quantity." Economists use this term to describe a curve (based on a firm's production function) that shows all of the technically efficient input combinations for producing a certain quantity of output. Each point on an isoquant shows a different combination of inputs that can be used to produce a specified quantity of output. Table 23-6 presents a number of labor–capital combinations for three different quantities of output that a shoe company might produce. We have used the same two-input (shoe

TABLE 23-6 Technically Efficient Combinations for Producing Ten Dozen, Eight Dozen, and Six Dozen Pairs of Shoes per Day

10 Dozen Pairs of Shoes per Day		8 Dozen Pairs of Shoes per Day		6 Dozen Pairs of Shoes per Day	
Number of Shoe Workers (in 8-hour days)	Number of Shoemaking Machines (in 8-hour days)	Number of Shoe Workers (in 8-hour days)	Number of Shoemaking Machines (in 8-hour days)	Number of Shoe Workers (in 8-hour days)	Number of Shoemaking Machines (in 8-hour days)
100	1	64	1	36	1
50	2	32	2	18	2
25	4	16	4	12	3
20	5	8	8	9	4
10	10	4	16	6	6
5	20	2	32	4	9
4	25	1	64	3	12
2	50			2	18
1	100			1	36

FIGURE 23-10   **Three Alternative Isoquants**

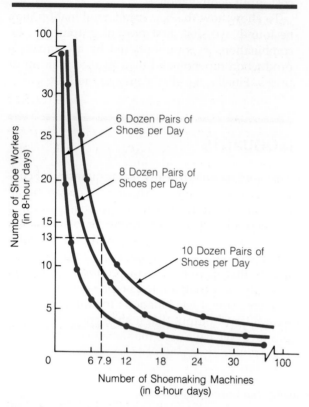

The numbers plotted from Table 23-6 establish the points along the three isoquants for a hypothetical shoe firm. Each isoquant shows all of the technically efficient combinations of workers and machines that will enable this firm to produce the quantity of shoes specified for that isoquant. For example, 10 dozen pairs of shoes per day can be produced by employing 20 shoe workers and 5 shoemaking machines or by employing only 13 workers but using 7.9 of the machines (7 for the full 8-hour day and an eighth machine for nine-tenths of the day).

workers and shoemaking machines) production function that we used earlier in this chapter. Table 23-6 shows nine different combinations for producing 10 dozen pairs of shoes per day, ranging from using 100 workers plus 1 machine to using 1 worker plus 100 machines. Also shown are several different combinations for producing 8 dozen and 6 dozen pairs of shoes per day.

The alternative combinations for each of the three quantities of output shown in Table 23-6 have been plotted in Figure 23-10. A smooth line drawn through the alternative combinations for each of the output levels enables us to read off a large number of additional combinations of the two input levels for each of the three quantities of output. For example, besides the points plotted from the two left-hand columns of Table 23-6, we can see that 13 workers and 7.9 machines will also produce 10 dozen pairs of shoes per day (assuming that machines can be rented on a part-time basis).

Isoquants have been drawn for 10 dozen, 8 dozen, and 6 dozen pairs of shoes per day. The figure does not show the isoquant for 2 dozen, for 76 dozen, or for 300 dozen. But there is an isoquant for every quantity of output that a firm could possibly produce. All of these isoquants—an infinite number—on a single graph are called an **isoquant map.** Since each one refers to a different output, no two isoquants on an isoquant map can ever touch each other. After all, each one is made up of all of the technically efficient possibilities for producing a particular quantity. If two touched, the common point would represent the minimum quantities of all inputs for two different quantities of output. For example, if the isoquant for 6 dozen pairs of shoes touched the isoquant for 8 dozen pairs of shoes, it would indicate that both quantities could be produced with the same combination of the inputs. That is to say, it would take no more inputs to produce 8 dozen than to produce 6 dozen. But since it is clear that 6 dozen can be produced with fewer inputs than 8 dozen, the input combination at the common point cannot be on the isoquant for both 6 dozen and 8 dozen pairs of shoes.

ISOCOST LINES

The isoquant map graphically illustrates a firm's production function for all possible quantities of output it may wish to produce. But in order to be able to decide on the best input combination

FIGURE 23-11   Three Alternative Isocost Lines

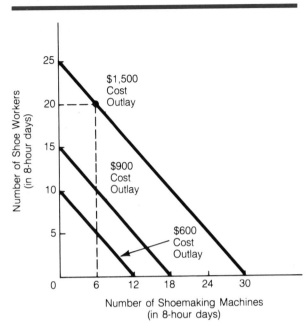

Three isocost lines for our hypothetical shoe firm are drawn. Each isocost line shows all of the different combinations of shoe workers and shoemaking machines that the firm can buy for a specified cost outlay. For example, the firm can spend $1,500 on 25 shoe workers or on 30 shoemaking machines, or on 20 workers plus 6 machines. The slope of the isocost line is the ratio of the price of shoemaking machines to the wage rate of shoe workers—$50 to $60.

for a firm, input costs must also be brought into the picture. Shoe workers receive a wage, and shoemaking machinery must be bought or rented. These costs are expressed in the form of isocost lines. An **isocost line** (meaning "same cost") shows the combinations of inputs a firm can buy for a given cost outlay. For every possible cost outlay there is an isocost line. The slope of the isocost line is the ratio of the per unit costs—the prices—of the inputs. The line becomes steeper or flatter as the cost of one of the inputs increases in relation to the cost of the other.

Our example of the shoe manufacturer can also be used to illustrate isocost lines. If we know that a shoe worker receives a wage of $60 per day

and that a shoemaking machine costs $50 per day (based on purchase price or rental fees, maintenance, and the fuel required to run it), we can draw some isocost lines for several different cost outlays (see Figure 23-11). In the case of the $1,500 cost outlay, if the firm were to spend it all on workers, 25 workers could be hired ($1,500/$60 = 25). Or the firm could have 30 machines ($1,500/$50 = 30) if it were to spend all $1,500 on machines. In between these two extremes there are many other combinations. One such combination, as shown in Figure 23-11, is 20 shoe workers and 6 shoemaking machines. The other two isocost lines are constructed in the same way. With a cost outlay of $900, the most workers that the firm could hire is 15 ($900/$60 = 15), or the most machines it could have is 18 ($900/$50 = 18). The two extreme alternatives when the cost outlay is $600 are 10 workers ($600/$60 = 10) and 12 machines ($600/$50 = 12).

FINDING THE BEST INPUT COMBINATION

A firm's isoquant map expresses its production function at different levels of output. Its isocost lines show input combinations possible at different total-cost outlays. When the two are put together, the best input combination for any given level of output for the firm can be readily determined. It is the one that will allow the firm to produce the desired quantity at the lowest possible cost. In the case of our shoe firm, we begin in Figure 23-12 by drawing the isoquant that corresponds to the quantity the firm wishes to produce. Suppose that, on the basis of its expected sales, the firm decides to produce 10 dozen pairs of shoes per day. Thus, in Figure 23-12, we have added the firm's isocost lines developed in Figure 23-11 to the 10-dozen isoquant from Figure 23-10. Figure 23-12 shows that both the $600 and the $900 isocost lines do not represent enough cost outlay to produce 10 dozen pairs of shoes. Both are shown to be below the 10-dozen isoquant and are only enough for a lower level of output. The

FIGURE 23-12   Looking for the Best Input Combination to Produce Ten Dozen Pairs of Shoes per Day

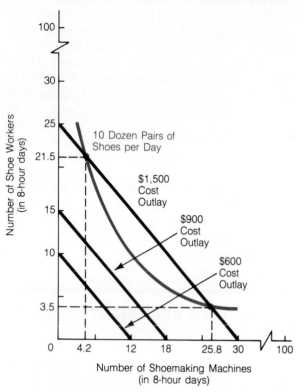

FIGURE 23-13   Best Input Combination to Produce Ten Dozen Pairs of Shoes per Day

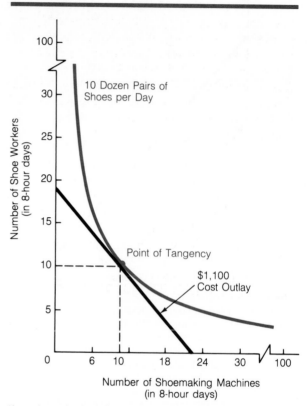

The isoquant for 10 dozen pairs of shoes per day has been added from Figure 23-10 to the set of isocost lines that were shown in Figure 23-11. If this shoe firm wishes to produce 10 dozen pairs of shoes per day, it is evident that neither the $600 nor the $900 cost outlay is enough. (At every point, the 10-dozen isoquant lies above the $600 and the $900 isocost lines.) We see that $1,500 is enough. The $1,500 isocost line is twice intersected by the 10-dozen isoquant. Ten dozen pairs of shoes per day can be produced with 21.5 workers plus 4.2 machines or with 3.5 workers plus 25.8 machines. However, neither of these combinations represents the lowest-cost method of producing 10 dozen pairs of shoes. There are surely isocost lines (not drawn here) between the $900 one and the $1,500 one that will allow the firm to produce 10 dozen pairs of shoes per day. The isocost line that represents the lowest cost outlay that will enable the firm to produce 10 dozen pairs of shoes per day will be shown in Figure 23-13.

If our hypothetical shoe firm wishes to produce 10 dozen pairs of shoes per day, its best input combination will be 10 shoe workers plus 10 shoemaking machines. Given the assumed wage rate for shoe workers and price for shoemaking machines, the $1,100 isocost line represents the lowest possible cost of producing 10 dozen pairs of shoes per day since it is just tangent to the 10-dozen isoquant.

remaining isocost line ($1,500 cost) is enough. It intersects the isoquant at two places. Ten dozen pairs of shoes per day can be produced with 21.5 workers plus 4.2 machines or with 3.5 workers plus 25.8 machines, at a cost of $1,500 per day in each case. Could the firm do better? Could it produce the 10 dozen pairs of shoes per day at a lower cost? The answer is "yes." Any isocost line that lies below the $1,500 line but is high enough to reach the 10-dozen isoquant will enable the firm to produce 10 dozen pairs of shoes per day at a lower cost than $1,500 per day. The isocost line that corresponds to the lowest possible cost is the one just tangent to the isoquant. This isocost line is illustrated in Figure 23-13, and it turns out to be the one at $1,100. This isocost line is drawn parallel to the others (has the same steepness) and thus shows that the ratio of $60 to $50 between the input prices has been maintained. The point of tangency—the only point at which 10 dozen pairs of shoes per day can be produced for $1,100 per day—shows that the firm will use the input combination of 10 shoe workers and 10 shoemaking machines. This combination is the only solution that minimizes the cost of producing 10 dozen pairs of shoes per day.

In summary, given the facts that the firm wishes to produce 10 dozen pairs of shoes per day, that shoe workers cost $60 per day, and that shoemaking machines cost $50 per day, employing 10 shoe workers and operating 10 shoemaking machines is the best input combination for the firm.

DISCUSSION QUESTIONS: APPENDIX

1. Carefully define an isoquant. Why is it that no two isoquants on the same firm's isoquant map can touch each other? You probably studied indifference curves in the appendix to Chapter 21. If you did, discuss some similarities and some differences between isoquants and indifference curves.

2. Explain why a firm produces any given level of output with the best combination of inputs where one of its isoquants is tangent to its isocost line.

3. A profit-maximizing firm will always try to reach the highest isoquant that it can on its isoquant map. True or false? Explain.

24 *Market Supply and Elasticity*

PREVIEW In this chapter we continue our discussion of the supply side of product markets. The last chapter presented the fundamentals of production theory. With this background, you are ready to learn how business firms determine the supply of products that they will offer. We assume that firms act in a rational way, which means that they will supply products according to the principles of profit maximization and loss minimization. In other words, they want to make as high a profit or as low a loss as possible. But the term *profit* and the term *loss* are used differently in different fields. You will see that the economist's definition is not the same as the one used by the accountant.

In this chapter you also will study the logic that is used by economists to arrive at predictions about the quantity of output that firms will actually supply. This reasoning involves both the revenue side and the cost side of firms' operations. We use the concepts of total revenue and total cost as well as marginal revenue and marginal cost to explain equilibrium-supply solutions.

We shall also ask the age-old question, "To supply or not to supply?" You will see that the answer may be different in the short run than in the long run. The short run question is: When will a rational business firm decide to shut down? The long run question is: When will a rational business firm decide to exit from an industry?

Finally, we describe the price elasticity of supply. It is the same elasticity concept that we applied earlier to demand. Here you will learn why the quantity supplied is much more responsive to price changes for some products than it is for others.

RATIONAL BUSINESS FIRMS

Recall from Chapter 3 that economists often assume that business firms act rationally—that they try to maximize their profit and minimize their loss. Important theories of the firm make this assumption in order to simplify what is really a very complex set of motives that influence business firm decision makers.

How realistic an assumption is profit maximization? Does it allow economists to make fairly reliable predictions? It is hard for us to give a simple answer. We realize that firms have goals other than making the maximum profit and that even when firms aim for maximum profit, they may be frustrated and fail to achieve it. But probably there is no other simple assumption, at least for the long run, that allows economists to make better predictions.

We know that firms must make their decisions in a world of uncertainty. They do not know what will happen tomorrow. The best they can do is to assign probabilities to particular outcomes. Suppose that a builder who is trying to decide whether or not to build another house this month assigns probabilities to two different selling prices. If the builder assigns a probability of .8 to successfully selling the house at a profitable price and .2 to having to sell it at a loss, the builder may decide to go ahead and build the house. If, instead, the probabilities were reversed (.8 that the house would be sold at a loss), the builder would probably not build the house. But how reliable are a builder's predictions? Can we expect the builder to assign the correct probabilities? It is hard to say. Some business people are very well informed about business conditions, and others are not. Also, it is important to recognize that predictions depend on the time period over which business people attempt to maximize profits. How many years into the future are being considered?

Another problem with the profit maximization assumption is that large and complex companies have so many layers of decision making that even if the top management wants to maximize profits, it may not be able to do so. The sales department is often more interested in maximizing sales than profit. The marketing department usually wants to maximize sales per dollar spent on advertising. In the accounting department the aim may be to maximize cash flow. And the research and development department may be more interested in making an exciting new discovery than in just how much this discovery will contribute to company profits. Therefore, directives from top management may be compromised, so that profit is lower than it would be if a strict profit maximization policy were followed.

A final reason why the profit maximization assumption may not lead to entirely reliable predictions is that top management itself has goals that are not always consistent with profit maximization. Herbert Simon, a Nobel Prize–winning economist, suggests that many managers **satisfice**—that is, seek satisfactory profit instead of maximum profit. Satisfactory profit for a firm may be an amount of profit that leaves the firm's stockholders and members of the board of directors satisfied with the firm's performance. Besides satisficing, top managers are concerned with the security of the firm. They want to make sure that it will still be around in twenty-five years, fifty years, or more. For this reason they are often willing to trade off some profit for greater diversification or a better public image, both of which may add to the security of the firm. Top

managers may have personal goals that are not entirely consistent with maximum profit for the firm. Since the money they earn is at least as closely related to the size of the firm (measured in sales or assets) as to its profitability, managers may lean toward maximizing growth rather than profit. They are also concerned with the security of their positions. Profit improvement and steady year-after-year profit may make their jobs safer than a very high profit in one year but a much lower one in another year. Of course, managers are motivated by more than money and security. They seek prestige, power, and glory, too. Being written up in *Fortune* magazine or in *Business Week* and being recognized when approaching the first hole at the country club may be more readily achieved through the firm's growth than through the firm's profitability.

Where does our discussion of business goals leave us? We hope a bit wiser and more tolerant of how hard it is to predict in a world of uncertainty and multiple goals. We find that we do not make better predictions when we redefine a rational business decision maker as one who tries to maximize sales or security or any of the just-mentioned personal goals of managers. Therefore, even though we know it does not capture all of a firm's goals, profit maximization remains as the best single simple assumption about how business firms behave.

THE MEANINGS OF PROFIT

A wise old trader (who never had a course in principles of economics) once advised, "Buy sheep and sell deer." The play on words, of course, refers to making a profit when one can buy "cheap" and sell "dear." This advice recognizes that **profit** is the difference between cost and revenue or the difference between what a firm gives up to produce a product and what the firm takes in from the sale of that product. When revenue is greater than cost, the firm is said to have made profit. When cost is greater than revenue, it has experienced negative profit, or loss.

Unfortunately, these commonly understood definitions are complicated by accountants and economists not always defining cost in the same way. Remember from Chapter 23 (see pp. 441–442) Mama and Papa, who own a grocery store and who "forget" to pay themselves wages for the hours that they work and interest for the money that they have tied up in store capital. We called such items "implicit costs" and argued that they are just as much a part of a firm's costs as are those that are transacted ("explicit costs") such as a clerk's wages and the utility bill.

Accountants, who are most interested in the funds that flow to and from a business firm, often neglect to include some of the implicit costs. It is customary for accountants to include depreciation of plant and equipment and the rental value of property. But wages not paid to owners and the return on money that owners have in their businesses are usually omitted. Thus accountants may overstate the amount of profit that is earned by a firm. Economists, who use the concept of opportunity cost, include implicit costs and so give a more realistic picture of a firm's profit.

It follows that an amount of profit that accountants consider to be "normal" for a firm to earn is recognized by economists as a cost of doing business. Therefore, if it takes $42,180 a year of "accounting profit" to keep Mama and Papa operating their grocery business, that is the amount of *normal profit* in this example. Accounting profit greater than $42,180 in this example is called *greater-than-normal profit* or **economic profit.** Accounting profit of less than $42,180 in this example is called *less-than-normal profit* or **economic loss.** If economic loss persists, the firm will likely go out of business.[1]

In summary, profit is simply the difference between total revenue and total cost. But we must

---

1. In the short run, a firm earning less-than-normal profit or economic loss may remain in business since its revenue may exceed its variable cost and thus reimburse the firm for part of its fixed cost. If the firm shut down its operation, it would lose all of its fixed cost. We shall elaborate on this point later in this chapter.

be sure that just as all of a firm's receipts are included in its total revenue, all of its costs, explicit and implicit, are included in its total cost. **Normal profit**—the return to enterprise that the firm must receive in order for it to be willing to continue its operation—is treated as a cost by economists. It is a dollar amount that is not high enough to be economic profit, yet not low enough to be economic loss. Firms try to earn an economic profit in the long run and will go out of business if they earn an economic loss. Just how to determine the amount of profit a firm is able to earn is discussed in the next section.

IDENTIFYING THE PROFIT-MAXIMIZING LEVEL OF OUTPUT

An economist who wishes to predict the quantity of output that a firm will supply must examine the costs and the revenues that are associated with alternative output levels of that firm. Only then can the amount of profit or loss be determined. The logic of the profit-maximizing solution may be seen in two different ways: one using total cost and total revenue and another using marginal cost and marginal revenue.

Total Cost and Total Revenue

Total cost, as you have seen, includes all the costs—explicit and implicit—that a firm incurs in production. **Total revenue** is the total amount of receipts or income that a firm obtains from selling what it produces. Over any period of time, the difference between a firm's total revenue and its total cost is its profit or loss. Suppose that we have reliable total-cost and total-revenue data for a firm that produces yachts. Table 24-1 shows this information along with the profit or loss that would be realized for different numbers of yachts that this firm could produce. Total revenue is seen to increase with increases in the number of yachts sold each year. However, the amount of the increase goes down as more units are sold. This happens because we assume a normal down-

TABLE 24-1 Total Revenue, Total Cost, and Profit Data for a Hypothetical Yacht Firm

Output of Yachts (per year)	Total Revenue (in thousands of dollars)	Total Cost (in thousands of dollars)	Profit or Loss (in thousands of dollars)
0	0	50	−50
1	300	400	−100
2	575	575	0
3	825	700	125
4	1,050	835	215
5	1,250	985	265
6	1,425	1,160	265
7	1,575	1,370	205
8	1,700	1,700	0
9	1,800	2,180	−380
10	1,875	2,860	−985

ward-sloping demand curve, which means that in order to sell more units, the firm has to lower its price. Thus, total revenue is $300,000 when the firm sells 1 yacht, but $575,000 when it sells 2 at a price of $287,500 each, $825,000 when it sells 3 at a price of $275,000 each, and so on. Ten yachts a year cannot be sold for more than $187,500 each.

Total cost also goes up with increases in sales. You learned in the previous chapter that cost and output are positively related, but that during early levels of output we may expect increasing returns (total cost rising at a decreasing rate) and that at higher output levels diminishing returns will set in (total cost rising at an increasing rate). Increasing returns occur over the output range of zero to 3 yachts. After that, diminishing returns set in.

When the firm sells no yachts, it loses $50,000, the amount of fixed costs that it incurs. When the company sells 1 yacht, it loses $100,000, since the total cost of producing that unit is $400,000, though it can sell the yacht for only $300,000. At 2 units of output the firm breaks even, since the total cost is equal to the total revenue. (Remember that "breaking even" means that the firm does earn "normal profit" but that "economic profit" is zero.) Producing 3 yachts is profitable ($125,000),

4-unit production brings a higher profit ($215,000), and producing 5 or 6 yachts a year is even more profitable ($265,000). Over the range from zero to 5 units, the total revenue rises faster than the total cost, so that loss falls or profit rises. At output levels higher than 6, profit drops because the total cost rises faster than the total revenue. At 8 units the firm again breaks even, and above that amount, it has a loss.

It is clear from the data in Table 24-1 that the company—which is assumed to be a profit-maximizing firm—will not produce less than 5 yachts or more than 6 yachts a year. However, we cannot predict whether the firm will produce 5 units or 6 units. Because the company produces and sells very few yachts, the data are quite "lumpy." Somewhere between producing 5 and 6 yachts there may be a unique point where profit would theoretically be at a maximum. But that point may be at 5½ units, and we all know that half a yacht would sink. When the good can be more easily divided, or when we allow the firm to have inventory to carry over to the next year, we approach a single profit-maximizing level of output.

Of course, we could predict whether our firm will produce 5 or 6 yachts by bringing more variables into our theory. For example, we may reason that the firm's size is positively related to its security and to the individual managers' goals such as compensation, job security, and prestige. On that basis we might predict that this company will produce 6 yachts a year, and not 5. However, we might also reason that the firm's size is positively related to more work, responsibility, and hassles for managers. On that basis we might predict that the company will produce 5 yachts a year, and not 6. We see, then, that additional variables may be relevant but do not give economists the simple generalization that is offered by the profit-maximization assumption. Also, there is generally no need for predictions to be narrowed down to a single level of output. The cost and revenue data are usually not so reliable that one can reasonably expect to gain very much greater precision from doing so. Based on the assumption of profit maximization alone, we are left with our prediction that this firm will produce 5 or 6 yachts a year.

Marginal Cost and Marginal Revenue

A second way to see the logic that leads us to the profit-maximizing level of output is to use the concepts of marginal cost and marginal revenue. We have seen that marginal cost is the addition to a firm's total cost that comes from producing one more unit of output. Likewise, marginal revenue is the addition to a firm's total revenue that comes from selling one more unit of output.

Let us return to our example of the yacht firm. Table 24-2 repeats the data in Table 24-1 but adds columns for marginal revenue and marginal cost. (The amounts in these two new columns are printed on lines lying between units to show that they refer to the *changes* that take place in total revenue and in total cost each time one more yacht is added to the firm's level of total output.) Notice that since the company must lower its price in order to sell more, marginal revenue falls as more yachts are produced and sold. Marginal cost goes down as increasing returns are experienced for up to 3 yachts. But after that point marginal cost goes up as diminishing returns set

in. Under these conditions, marginal-cost and marginal-revenue data allow us to find the level of output that will maximize a company's profit. The rule is as follows: A firm will maximize its profit when it produces that level of output at which marginal revenue equals marginal cost, as long as marginal revenue is greater than marginal cost at somewhat lower levels of output and marginal cost is greater than marginal revenue at somewhat higher levels of output.

Why this rule will always hold can be seen by studying the data in Table 24-2. We shall not concern ourselves with the zero-to-1 range of output, since it is excluded by the profit-maximization rule. (Marginal cost is higher than marginal revenue for the first unit of output.) Marginal revenue is equal to marginal cost between 5 and 6 units of output. To see that this must be the profit-maximizing level of output, we shall look at the alternatives of producing less than 5 units and producing more than 6 units. At a production level of 3 yachts, the firm is encouraged to raise output, since producing the fourth yacht adds more to revenue than it does to cost. Because the marginal revenue is $225,000 and the marginal cost is $135,000, producing 4 yachts a year instead of 3 raises the firm's profit by $90,000. The same reasoning explains why the firm would rather produce 5 yachts than 4. Because the marginal revenue of $200,000 is greater than the marginal cost of $150,000, the company would give up $50,000 of profit if it did not produce the fifth yacht. When the firm considers whether or not to produce 6 yachts, it finds that marginal cost is equal to marginal revenue (both $175,000). Revenue rises just as much as cost does, so that profit is not changed. As we found in our earlier discussion about total revenue and total cost, if we wish to predict on the basis of profit maximization alone, we are not able to say whether the firm will produce the sixth yacht or not, since there is neither a profit incentive nor a profit penalty for doing so.

In raising production from 6 to 7 units, the firm's marginal cost of $210,000 is greater than its marginal revenue of $150,000. This means that the company adds more to total cost than to total revenue when it produces the seventh unit. Profit

TABLE 24-2 Revenue, Cost, and Profit Data for a Hypothetical Yacht Firm

Output of Yachts (per year)	Total Revenue (in thousands of dollars)	Marginal Revenue (in thousands of dollars)	Total Cost (in thousands of dollars)	Marginal Cost (in thousands of dollars)	Profit or Loss (in thousands of dollars)
0	0		50		−50
		300		350	
1	300		400		−100
		275		175	
2	575		575		0
		250		125	
3	825		700		125
		225		135	
4	1,050		835		215
		200		150	
5	1,250		985		265
		175		175	
6	1,425		1,160		265
		150		210	
7	1,575		1,370		205
		125		330	
8	1,700		1,700		0
		100		480	
9	1,800		2,180		−380
		75		680	
10	1,875		2,860		−985

will be $60,000 less than it would have been if the company had produced only 6 yachts. Producing more than 7 yachts a year lowers profit even more. An output level of 8 yachts a year lowers profit to the breakeven point. (Remember that "breaking even" means that the company does earn "normal profit" but that "economic profit" is zero.) The eighth yacht adds $125,000 of revenue for the firm, but it also means that it has added costs of $330,000. The difference between the marginal revenue and the marginal cost ($205,000) is a drop in profit that the company can avoid by not producing the eighth yacht.

In summary, a profit-maximizing firm will not produce less output than the amount at which a rising marginal cost is equal to marginal revenue. As long as marginal revenue is greater than marginal cost, more output will add more to revenue than to cost, and a company would be giving up profit by not producing more. Likewise, a profit-maximizing firm will not produce more output than the amount at which a rising marginal cost is equal to marginal revenue. If marginal cost is greater than marginal revenue, more output will add more to cost than to revenue, and each added unit of output will lower profits.

Graphic Presentation of Profit Maximization

To show the profit-maximizing solution as a diagram, we have plotted the data from Table 24-2 on two sets of axes on Figure 24-1. Total revenue and cost are shown in the top part and marginal revenue and cost in the lower part.

As shown in the top panel, total revenue rises by decreasing amounts over the whole range of

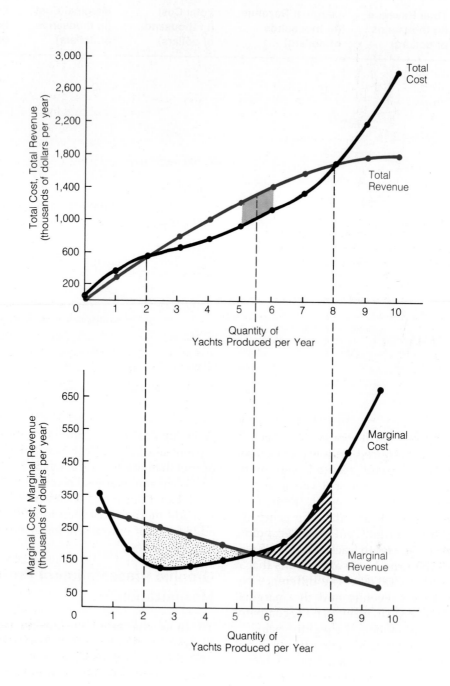

◀ **FIGURE 24-1   Profit Maximization for a Hypothetical Yacht Firm**

The top panel shows the yacht firm's total-cost and total-revenue curves. At production levels of less than 2 yachts a year or more than 8 yachts a year, total cost exceeds total revenue and thus a loss is incurred. The firm just breaks even if it produces either 2 or 8 yachts a year. The firm realizes a profit if it produces more than 2 but less than 8 yachts per year. Within this profit range, total revenue lies above total cost by the greatest amount when the firm produces 5 or 6 yachts a year. This dual profit-maximization solution is shown as the shaded area between the curves.

The lower panel shows the same firm's marginal-cost and marginal-revenue curves. We analyze only the range from one breakeven point to the other. Between the output levels of 2 and 5½ yachts a year, marginal revenue exceeds marginal cost. This is shown as the dotted area. Between the output levels of 5½ and 8 yachts a year, marginal cost exceeds marginal revenue. This is shown as the striped area. Profit maximization takes place at the level of output where the firm's marginal-cost curve intersects its marginal-revenue curve from below. This is at 5½ yachts a year. Since half of a yacht cannot be sold, the firm maximizes its profit when it produces either 5 or 6 yachts a year. The shaded areas to the right and to the left of the intersection represent equal amounts of marginal profit that is sacrificed to the need to produce whole units.

output. Total cost rises by decreasing amounts up to 3 yachts and then by increasing amounts over the remaining range. Total cost is higher than total revenue for fewer than 2 yachts, and so the company has a loss (less-than-normal profit, or economic loss) over that very low range of output. At a production level of 2 yachts a year, total cost is equal to total revenue (the curves intersect). In this case the company is just breaking even (only normal profit is earned). The firm makes a profit (greater-than-normal profit, or economic profit) over the range of output between 2 and 8 yachts. Total revenue is above total cost over that range. Producing 8 yachts a year again finds the company just breaking even (the curves intersect). At levels above 8 yachts a year, the total-cost curve is above the total-revenue curve, so that the firm shows a loss (less-than-normal profit or economic loss). Within the profit range, where total revenue is above total

cost, the greatest vertical distance between total revenue and total cost appears at the level of output between 5 and 6 yachts. This is, of course, the same solution that we described earlier. Since the data are lumpy, rather than continuous, the solution appears as a range on the figure (the shaded part between the total-revenue and total-cost curves) rather than as a single point.

The lower panel of Figure 24-1 pictures the marginal-revenue and marginal-cost curves of our yacht-producing firm. Each level of output along the horizontal scale corresponds to the level in the upper panel, though the vertical scale is stretched out so that you can see the details more clearly. Note that the marginal-revenue curve slopes downward over the whole output range. This corresponds to the total-revenue curve, which increases by decreasing amounts (upper panel), from which it is derived. The marginal-cost curve falls at early levels of output and rises afterward. It decreases over the output range where total cost rises by decreasing amounts and then increases when total cost rises by increasing amounts.

Because of our lumpy data, we shall begin our analysis in the lower panel of the figure at the breakeven output of 2 yachts a year. At that point we see that marginal revenue is higher than marginal cost. It remains higher up to the production level of 5½ yachts. This means that, within that output range, the production of every additional yacht causes revenue to rise more than cost, so profit goes up. At output levels beyond 5½ yachts, marginal cost lies above marginal revenue, so that the firm adds more to cost than to revenue and profit goes down. Producing 8 yachts a year will again allow the company only to break even. We see then that the dotted area to the left of the intersection at 5½ yachts (the excess of marginal revenue over marginal cost between the output levels of 2 and 5½) is exactly equal to the striped area to the right of the intersection (the amount of marginal cost in excess of marginal revenue between the output levels of 5½ and 8). At production levels greater than 8 yachts a year, the company suffers a loss (earns less-than-normal profit or economic loss).

Where marginal cost intersects marginal revenue from below is the profit-maximizing level of

TABLE 24-3 Four Alternative Short-Run Cases for the Verbo Company

	Case 1	Case 2	Case 3	Case 4
Variable cost	$ 5,000	$ 5,000	$ 5,000	$ 5,000
Fixed cost	10,000	10,000	10,000	10,000
Total cost	15,000	15,000	15,000	15,000
Total revenue	16,000	11,000	9,000	4,000
Profit (+) or loss (−) if Verbo operates	+1,000	−4,000	−6,000	−11,000
Profit (+) or loss (−) if Verbo shuts down	−10,000	−10,000	−10,000	−10,000
Expected decision by Verbo	Operate	Operate	Operate	Shut down

output. At that volume of production, the company takes advantage of all units of output at which marginal revenue is greater than marginal cost, yet does not produce so much that marginal cost is higher than marginal revenue. Of course, we still have the problem caused by the lumpy data. We cannot predict that the company will produce 5½ yachts (remember that half a yacht will not float). For this reason, the company is said to maximize its profit when it produces either 5 or 6 yachts a year. In the lower panel of Figure 24-1 the small shaded area to the left of the intersection of marginal cost and revenue is equal to the shaded area to the right of that intersection. Each of these shaded areas shows the amount of marginal profit that is lost because of the need to produce whole units.

To Supply or Not to Supply?

So far we have taken it for granted that all firms will supply a product. The question was only how much. In fact, a firm may choose not to supply anything at all. The decision to produce nothing at all may come in two different ways. One involves a long-run decision and the other involves a short-run decision.

LONG RUN: EXIT Recall that the long run is a period of time long enough for a firm to make all the adjustments in production that it wishes.

There is no fixed cost in the long run. If, in this case, a firm supplying its profit-maximizing quantity cannot earn at least a normal profit, economists predict that it will leave the industry. Since economists consider normal profit to be a cost of doing business, the company would find that its opportunity cost of staying in this business is simply too great. Total revenue would not cover total cost. The rational business firm—one that will minimize its losses—will exit. No loss at all is better than even a small loss.

SHORT RUN: SHUT DOWN In the short run, however, there is a good reason why a rational firm may continue to operate even though it does have a loss. That reason is the presence of fixed cost. In the short run, a firm's total cost is made up of both fixed cost and variable cost. Fixed cost cannot be shed, even by shutting down. For this reason, if a firm supplying its profit-maximizing quantity of output can earn enough to recover all of its variable cost and at least some of its fixed cost, it will pay for it to operate. In other words, according to the principle of loss minimization, it is better for a firm to lose only some of its fixed cost rather than to lose all of it. On the other hand, economists predict that if a company producing its profit-maximizing quantity of output in the short run is not even able to recover its variable cost, then it will shut down.

Let us predict the short-run decision that a rational business firm, the Verbo Company, would be expected to make under each of four alternative sets of conditions. Table 24-3 shows these four cases. We assume that the cost conditions—$5,000 of variable cost, $10,000 of fixed cost, and therefore $15,000 of total cost—are the same in all four cases. However, total revenue is different in each of the cases: $16,000 in case 1, $11,000 in case 2, $9,000 in case 3, and only $4,000 in case 4.

In case 1, Verbo earns $1,000 of profit by operating the business. Shutting down would cause it to have a loss of $10,000, the amount of the fixed cost, since variable cost and total revenue would become zero. This would make Verbo $11,000 worse off. We would therefore expect Verbo to operate.

In case 2, Verbo suffers a loss of $4,000 by operating the business. Our first inclination might be to think that it would want to shut down. But would it be better off by shutting down in the short run? The answer is "no," because Verbo's total revenue exceeds its variable cost by $6,000, so that by operating it will lose $6,000 less than if it shut down. If it were to shut down, it would lose its entire fixed cost of $10,000, whereas by operating it can cut its losses to $4,000.

In case 3, Verbo suffers a loss of $6,000 by operating the business. In this case, it still pays for Verbo to produce. Its total revenue of $9,000 is enough to offset its variable cost of $5,000. Notice that production at a loss does not require revenue sufficient to cover fixed cost. The shutdown decision is made on the basis of the relationship between revenue and variable cost.

In case 4, Verbo suffers a loss of $11,000 by operating the business. In this case, it will want to shut down because that will enable it to cut its losses to $10,000. Its total revenue of $4,000 is not enough to offset its variable cost of $5,000. By shutting down, it can bring both total revenue and variable cost to zero and thus suffer only the loss of the $10,000 of fixed cost.

ELASTICITY OF SUPPLY

The concept of elasticity was presented earlier in the book and in Chapter 22 we applied it to demand. Here you will learn about the elasticity of supply. The basic idea is the same—the degree of responsiveness—but of course it takes on a different meaning when applied to supply.

The supply curve that we constructed in Chapter 5 was defined in the schedule sense. It related certain quantities of supply to a number of different prices. We saw that it was positively sloped, since sellers, whose costs were held constant, found it profitable to supply more at higher prices and less at lower prices. The degree of that response, or the sensitivity of that quantity–price relationship, is numerically measured by the elasticity concept.

The **price elasticity of supply (E_S)** may be stated in the following form:

$$E_S = \frac{\text{the percentage change in the quantity supplied}}{\text{the percentage change in the price that caused it}}$$

This is a ratio of percentage changes and so is independent of the units of measure (pounds, pairs, inches, dollars, and so forth) that may be used. In formula form it may be expressed as follows:

$$E_S = \frac{\Delta Q_S / \overline{Q}_S}{\Delta P / \overline{P}}$$

Here ΔQ_S is the change in quantity supplied, $\overline{Q}_S$ is the average quantity supplied, ΔP is the change in price, and $\overline{P}$ is the average price. The formula used in the computation can also be stated as follows:

$$E_S = \frac{\dfrac{Q_{S_2} - Q_{S_1}}{(Q_{S_1} + Q_{S_2})/2}}{\dfrac{P_2 - P_1}{(P_1 + P_2)/2}}$$

or since the twos cancel out, as

$$E_S = \frac{\dfrac{Q_{S_2} - Q_{S_1}}{Q_{S_1} + Q_{S_2}}}{\dfrac{P_2 - P_1}{P_1 + P_2}}$$

TABLE 24-4 Elasticity Coefficients Calculated from a Market-Supply Schedule for Sweaters

Price (dollars per sweater)	Market Supply (millions of sweaters per year)	Price Elasticity of Supply Calculation	Elasticity Coefficient
$20	100		
		$\dfrac{\dfrac{125-100}{100+125}}{\dfrac{30-20}{20+30}} = \dfrac{\dfrac{25}{225}}{\dfrac{10}{50}} = \dfrac{\dfrac{1}{9}}{\dfrac{1}{5}} = \dfrac{1}{9}\cdot\dfrac{5}{1} = \dfrac{5}{9}$ or 0.56	
$30	125		
		$\dfrac{\dfrac{175-125}{125+175}}{\dfrac{40-30}{30+40}} = \dfrac{\dfrac{50}{300}}{\dfrac{10}{70}} = \dfrac{\dfrac{1}{6}}{\dfrac{1}{7}} = \dfrac{1}{6}\cdot\dfrac{7}{1} = \dfrac{7}{6}$ or 1.17	
$40	175		
		$\dfrac{\dfrac{400-175}{175+400}}{\dfrac{60-40}{40+60}} = \dfrac{\dfrac{225}{575}}{\dfrac{20}{100}} = \dfrac{\dfrac{9}{23}}{\dfrac{1}{5}} = \dfrac{9}{23}\cdot\dfrac{5}{1} = \dfrac{45}{23}$ or 1.96	
$60	400		

Here Q_{S_1} is the original quantity supplied, Q_{S_2} is the new quantity supplied, P_1 is the original price, and P_2 is the new price.

Table 24-4 gives three examples of how the numerical value of elasticity, or the elasticity coefficient, is figured. We have used the same good (sweaters) and the same four prices as we did for demand in Table 22-2. Of course, the supply responses are positive, whereas the demand responses in Table 22-2 were negative. Again, by convention, we do not use the sign.

Elasticity Categories

Price elasticity of supply categories are the same as those used for demand (see Chapter 22, pp. 424–425). In Table 24-4, the elasticity coefficient of 0.56 is inelastic (smaller than 1.0) and means that for every 1 percent rise in price, the quantity supplied increased by a bit more than ½ percent (0.56 of 1 percent). The other two examples in

Table 24-4 show elastic (larger than 1.0) supply, since for every 1 percent rise in price, the quantity supplied increases by more than 1 percent (1.17 percent and 1.96 percent).

Table 24-5 presents all five categories for supply elasticity, as did Table 22-3 for demand elasticity. Notice that the definitions and examples are alike. The inelastic supply curve is steeper than the elastic one, and the perfectly inelastic supply curve is a vertical straight line, whereas the infinitely or perfectly elastic supply curve is a horizontal straight line. The only elasticity category in which the supply curve is not similar (although sloping in the opposite direction) to the demand curve in the same category is unitary elasticity. The demand curve of unitary elasticity is a rectangular hyperbola, but the supply curve of unitary elasticity is a straight line drawn through the origin. The amount supplied changes in fixed proportion with the price. A 12 percent rise in the price of basketballs causes sellers to increase the supply of basketballs by 12 percent.

TABLE 24-5   Price Elasticity of Supply Categories

Elasticity Category	Relationship Between Price and Quantity Supplied	Elasticity Coefficient	Numerical Example	Diagram of Supply Curve for This Example
Inelastic	The percentage change in the quantity supplied is smaller than the percentage change in the price that caused it.	less than one	A price increase from $10 to $20 causes quantity supplied to increase from 40 to 60.	
Elastic	The percentage change in the quantity supplied is greater than the percentage change in the price that caused it.	greater than one	A price increase from $10 to $20 causes quantity supplied to increase from 20 to 120.	
Unitary elastic	The percentage change in the quantity supplied is exactly equal to the percentage change in the price that caused it.	one	A price increase from $10 to $20 causes quantity supplied to increase from 40 to 80.	
Perfectly inelastic	Any change in the price causes no response at all in the quantity supplied.	zero	A price increase from $10 to $20 causes no change in the quantity supplied.	
Infinitely elastic	Any change in the price causes a limitless (infinite) response in the quantity supplied.	∞ (infinity)	At any price below $10 the quantity supplied will be zero, and at the $10 price, quantity supplied is indefinitely small or large.	

Determinants of Price Elasticity of Supply

Actual elasticities of supply vary greatly among goods and services. Elasticity of supply is determined largely by two factors: (1) the change in average total cost that is incurred by a firm when it changes the quantity of its output, and (2) the time that it takes a company to raise or to lower its output. These two factors are like those for the elasticity of demand, which we described earlier.

CHANGES IN AVERAGE TOTAL COST Remember that the availability of good substitutes was one of the factors influencing demand elasticity. For supply elasticity the corresponding influences come from the changes in average total cost to a company when it raises or lowers output in response to price changes.

When labor, capital, and natural resources flow easily into and out of production, we say that they are readily substitutable. This means that resources can easily be switched from producing one product to producing another. In this situation, we expect the supply of such goods and services to be relatively elastic. This may be illustrated by what happens to a firm's average total cost when the level of output is changed. Let us suppose that the price of women's evening gowns goes up 10 percent. The garment workers who make dresses, blouses, robes, and other clothing, as well as the cutting and sewing machines that they use, can easily be switched to evening gowns without paying the higher wages that might be needed to train new people or the extra money needed to buy new machines. It follows, then, that average total cost will be bid up only slightly, if at all, as the level of output increases, and that evening gown production will become more profitable. We would expect that the 10 percent price rise together with no important rise in average total cost would cause companies to respond with an output increase of greater than 10 percent. If, on the other hand, increases in output could be managed only by bidding up the prices of inputs or by using only relatively poor (high-cost) substitute inputs, we would expect relatively inelastic supply. This

would happen if key resources are very specialized and thus are very hard or even impossible to switch to another use. For example, the supply of works of art by a well-known contemporary painter would be very inelastic since no one else is able to produce that artist's paintings. If the price of such works doubled, he or she might produce only 5 or 10 percent more paintings, so that supply elasticity would be very low. The limit case is that of a dead artist, where supply elasticity would be zero (perfectly inelastic), since no matter how much the price goes up, no more of this artist's paintings can be produced.

ADJUSTMENT TIME The second determinant of the price elasticity of supply of a product is the length of time needed for adjustment. This same time variable was explained in the demand elasticity discussion. A price change may cause only a very small response in the quantity supplied after a short time, but, as time passes, that response may increase. For example, suppose that the price of steel increases by 20 percent. Steel firms might quickly respond by hiring more labor and buying more iron ore and other material inputs. Still, they might find that they can raise output by only 10 percent, representing a supply elasticity of 0.5. Production increases are limited by the number of furnaces that they have. Of course, furnaces are major pieces of capital equipment for steel companies. They must be ordered in advance, factories must be built to house them, and their operation must be well timed with the operations of the existing furnaces. This process may take several years to complete. If the steel companies decide that the 20 percent price rise will be permanent, they will probably increase their productive capacity. Then, over the next five years, production may, for example, rise by 40 percent, representing a supply elasticity of 2.0. Instead of the supply being inelastic (0.5) as it was for the short time after the price rise, it would be quite elastic (2.0) for the five-year period. In general, then, price elasticity of supply is likely to be higher for long time periods than for short time periods.

Adjustment time is more important in determining elasticity of supply in some industries than it is in others. Some industries, including

TABLE 24-6 Estimated Short-Run and Long-Run Price Elasticities of Supply
for Selected U.S. Fresh Vegetable Markets, 1919–1955

Fresh Vegetable Market	Short-Run Price Elasticity of Supply	Long-Run Price Elasticity of Supply	Ratio of Long-Run to Short-Run
Beets	0.13	1.0	7.7
Cabbage	0.36	1.2	3.3
Carrots	0.14	0.9	6.4
Celery	0.14	1.0	7.1
Cucumbers	0.29	2.2	7.6
Cauliflower	0.14	1.1	7.9
Eggplant	0.16	0.3	1.9
Green lima beans	0.10	1.7	17.0
Green peas	0.31	4.4	14.2
Green peppers	0.07	0.3	4.3
Lettuce	0.03	0.2	6.7
Onions	0.34	1.0	2.9
Spinach	0.20	4.7	23.5
Tomatoes	0.16	0.9	5.6
Watermelons	0.23	0.5	2.2

Source: Marc Nerlove and William Addison, "Statistical Estimation of Long-Run Elasticities of Supply and Demand," *The Journal of Farm Economics,* November 1958, pp. 861–880. Used by permission of the American Agricultural Association.

steel, call for large capital inputs. Other industries, like airlines, employ highly skilled workers—pilots—who require long training periods. Both of these industries are most likely to have larger supply elasticities for long periods than for short periods. By contrast, an industry like window cleaning uses only minor capital goods—a pail, a squeegee, and a strong belt—and it employs low-skilled workers. It should have only a slightly larger elasticity of supply for long time periods than for short time periods.

Unfortunately, there are not many studies available that compare carefully measured short-run versus long-run supply elasticities. However, one such study by Nerlove and Addison provides some interesting results for a number of U.S. fresh vegetable markets. Table 24-6 lists estimates of short-run and long-run price elasticities of supply. Notice that the short-run elasticities are significantly lower than the long-run equivalents. Prices and supplies were studied over a thirty-five-year period, and the short run was taken as

one production period. The column farthest to the right shows the ratios between the long-run and short-run elasticities. They range from a close to doubling for eggplant to a multiple of over 23 for spinach.

SUMMARY

1. For many important theories of the firm, economists assume that business firms are rational. Rational business firm behavior is defined as attempting to maximize profits and minimize losses.

2. Economists recognize that firms will not strictly maximize profits. They must make their decisions in the face of uncertainty. Also, firms are often so complex that top management directives aimed at maximizing profits may be compromised. Moreover, firms' top management often pursues goals that are not completely consistent with profit maximization.

3. Economists and accountants do not define profit in the same way. Accountants concentrate on the funds that flow to and from a firm and tend to ignore implicit costs. What is considered "normal" for a firm to earn or the minimum that a firm has to earn in order for it to be willing to continue in its present business activity is considered part of "profit" by accountants, but recognized as "cost" by economists. Such cost is called "normal profit." Profit in excess of this amount is called "greater-than-normal profit" or "economic profit." "Less-than-normal profit" or "economic loss" will cause a firm to go out of business in the long run.

4. The level of output at which a firm will maximize its profit or minimize its loss may be identified by examining its total cost and total revenue or its marginal cost and marginal revenue. A firm will maximize its profit at the level of output at which its total revenue exceeds its total cost by the greatest amount. Similarly, a firm will maximize its profit at the level of output at which its marginal cost is equal to its marginal revenue, so long as marginal revenue is greater than marginal cost at somewhat lower levels of output and marginal cost is greater than marginal revenue at somewhat higher levels of output.

5. In the long run, a firm will go out of business (exit from its industry) if it cannot earn at least normal profit. In the short run, when some of a firm's cost is fixed, it will operate if it can earn enough to recover all of its variable cost and at least some of its fixed cost. If, however, it cannot recover all of its variable cost, the firm will shut down.

6. Price elasticity of supply measures the percentage change in the quantity of a product supplied in response to a percentage change in the price of that product. (This is analogous to the price elasticity of demand concept discussed in Chapter 22.)

7. There are five categories of elasticity. Supply is elastic when the percentage change in the quantity supplied is greater than the percentage change in the price that generated it. Supply is inelastic when the percentage change in the quantity supplied is less than the percentage change in the price that generated it. Supply is unitary elastic when the percentage change in the quantity supplied is exactly equal to the percentage change in price that generated it. Supply is perfectly inelastic when a change in price causes no response at all in the quantity supplied. Supply is infinitely elastic when a change in price causes an infinite response in the quantity supplied.

8. The price elasticity of supply of a product depends on (a) the change in average total cost that is incurred by a firm when it alters the quantity of its output and (b) the time that it takes a firm to expand or to contract its output in response to a change in the price of the product.

DISCUSSION QUESTIONS

1. The theory of the firm relies heavily on the assumption that business firms act in a rational manner. Economists define a rational firm as one that tries to maximize its profit. Discuss three reasons why this rationality assumption may not lead to entirely reliable predictions concerning what firms will and will not do.

2. Carefully distinguish between the accountant's concept of profit and the economist's concept of profit. In your answer be sure to show how the economist's terms of normal profit, economic profit, and economic loss fit in. Does zero economic profit mean that the firm earns no accounting profit? Under what conditions might a firm's economic loss be an accounting profit?

3. You learned that a firm will maximize its profit when it produces the level of output at which its total revenue exceeds its total cost by the greatest amount and that this is also where its marginal revenue is equal to its marginal cost. Explain why this is so.

4. Without looking at Figure 24-1, draw a firm's negatively sloped marginal-revenue curve and its U-shaped marginal-cost curve so that the latter intersects the former at two different levels of output. Compare your diagram with Figure 24-1 to be sure you have it right. Which output level is the one at which this firm maximizes its profit? Why? Why is the other not a profit-maximizing output?

5. "Economics makes a big deal out of a very simple point. Everyone knows that a firm wants to have its marginal revenue exceed its marginal cost by the greatest possible amount." Do you agree? Explain.

6. "A company makes a long-run decision to go out of business. It necessarily follows that this firm is unable to earn either economic profit or normal profit." True or false? Explain.

7. "A company makes a short-run decision to operate instead of shutting down. It necessarily follows that this firm is able to earn either economic profit or normal profit." True or false? Explain.

8. Would you expect a firm that has fixed cost of $100,000 a day, variable cost of $300,000 a day, and total revenue of $360,000 a day to operate in the short run? Why or why not? Under the same total cost and revenue conditions, do you expect it to stay in business in the long run? Why or why not?

9. Using the formula provided in the chapter, calculate the price elasticity of supply for each of the following cases:

   a. The price of certain shoes decreases from $50 to $42 a pair, which causes the quantity supplied of these shoes to decrease from 500,000 pairs a month to 450,000 pairs a month.

   b. The price of a certain kind of calculator increases from $8 to $12, which causes the quantity supplied of these calculators to increase from 20,000 a week to 40,000 a week.

   c. The price of a certain kind of vacuum cleaner increases from $95 to $100, which causes the quantity supplied of these vacuum cleaners to increase from 900,000 a year to 920,000 a year.

In each of these three cases, determine whether the supply is elastic or inelastic.

10. Why is it that elasticity of supply measurements are independent of the unit of measurement? Does that increase or decrease the usefulness of this concept?

11. Without looking at the diagrams in Table 24-5, draw a perfectly inelastic supply curve for a product. Compare your diagram with the perfectly inelastic supply-curve diagram in Table 24-5 to be sure you have it right. Give two examples of products that might logically have perfectly inelastic supply curves.

12. Actual elasticities of supply vary greatly among goods and services. Discuss two important determinants of the price elasticity of supply.

Neoclassical Economics:
The Complacent Science

We have spoken of classical economics as the dismal science, a nickname that best described certain theories of Malthus and Ricardo.[1] Malthus, as you will recall, saw population pressure holding wages at or near a bare subsistence level as the economy grew. Ricardo believed that the gains of progress would go mainly to the idle landowning classes, as land rent rose steadily under the pressure of population. At the same time, profits would decline because the accumulation of capital was subject to diminishing returns. Ricardo also saw growth ending in a stagnant state after profits had fallen to the point where capitalists would save no more than would make up for the consumption of raw materials and the depreciation of capital.

These dire predictions did not all come true. In fact, real wages began to rise sometime during the middle of the nineteenth century, and the stationary state seemed to have been pushed ever further into the future.

Dissent from the Classical Theory

Dissent from the classical views took many forms. The greatest of the dissenters was Karl Marx (1818–1883), whose theories we discuss in Chapter 39. However, many early opponents of classical economics wanted to get away from all abstract or deductive theory. These people wanted to substitute what we would now call economic history, economic sociology, or "institutional economics." But beginning in the 1870s,[2] a new kind of economic theory took over, which was later called "neoclassical economics." Outside the English-speaking world, its main center was in Austria. In fact, today's "Austrian school" is purely neoclassical. This new theory was based on demand rather than supply, on utility rather than cost, and on marginal quantities rather than average ones. Its rapid rise to prominence has been called the "utility revolution" or the "marginalist revolution" in economic thought.

Why did the neoclassical ideas win out when they did? Because the first volume of Karl Marx's *Capital* appeared in 1867, some saw the popularity of neoclassical economics as an evasion of the conclusions that Marx had drawn from the labor theory of value.[3] Another explanation was the use by some neoclassical writers of mathematical methods and physical analogies at a time when the natural sciences and mathematics were riding high.

The Complacent Revolutionaries

In calling the neoclassical economists and their followers "complacent," what do we mean? For one thing, we mean that they were not dismal. Like many Western Europeans and North Americans of the generation that ended in 1914, they looked back on a century of progress and expected another prosperous century to follow. (Alas, posterity was to disappoint them!) They were not utopians, but some may have been optimistic enough to hope that a better world might be only a century or so away "in the natural course of things."

Few were rigid in their beliefs. Most would be considered today people of good will and liberal reformers— some very stuffy, others quite erratic. However, most were not very active politically, and none shed blood at any barricade. In fact, most of them were professional economists, who taught at well-known universities for much of their later lives. Coming mainly from the middle classes, they passed most of their time surrounded by cultured upper-middle-class people. Many devoted

---

1. Even though other important classical economists like Adam Smith and John Stuart Mill were much less dismal than Malthus and Ricardo, one good epithet is often worth a hundred facts.

2. However, these ideas were really much older. For example, J. B. Say, of "Say's Identity" fame, had proposed a utility theory of value and price early in the century.

3. The labor theory of value is explained in Chapter 39.

themselves to the interests of the poor, as seen from "the other side of the tracks." However, as Robert Heilbroner put it in his *Worldly Philosophers,* they saw the world as composed of sheep without wolves. Reasonable optimism plus their reasonably comfortable and quiet lives made them complacent.

Who were the most important of these "revolutionists"? In the first generation of the 1870s, they were William Stanley Jevons of England, Carl Menger of Austria, and Léon Walras of France. These men were all professional economists, who wrote independently of each other. But all concentrated on the problems of microeconomics—the allocation of scarce resources among alternative uses—rather than on growth and development. In the next generation, the English leaders were Alfred Marshall, F. Y. Edgeworth, and A. C. Pigou. In America, they were J. B. Clark, Irving Fisher, and F. W. Taussig. The European leaders were Eugen von Böhm-Bawerk of Austria, Vilfredo Pareto of Italy, and Knut Wicksell of Sweden. Of this whole group, the most influential in English-speaking countries, and by a wide margin, has been Alfred Marshall. Marshall's *Principles of Economics*, first published in 1890, went through eight editions during its author's life. It replaced Mill's *Principles of Political Economy* as the standard advanced text for its subject in its generation.

Alfred Marshall (1842–1924)

Contributions of the Neoclassical Economists

Neoclassical economics became less popular after 1914 because it failed to speak "with one voice" on the great problems of the day: the war economy of World War I, the postwar adjustment in the early 1920s, and finally the Great Depression. Individuals, of course, talked very good sense on particular aspects of all these problems. In the case of the depression, it has been argued that the strongly neoclassical University of Chicago economics faculty as a group had an excellent record throughout the crisis. But one swallow does not make a summer, and Chicago was only one campus among many.

If they couldn't handle the postwar readjustment, the Great Depression, or other major problems of their day, why bother with these economists' ideas at all? We are interested in them mainly because so many of our contemporary ideas, especially our microeconomic ideas, spring from these writers' works. Let us note them briefly.

One of their ideas was that economics could and should aspire to the status of a pure science. These economists felt that the subject should rise above the debating-tool status that was implied by its older name, political economy.

Another of the neoclassical ideas, as mentioned earlier, was that economics should concentrate on problems of the allocation of resources under given conditions. That is, it can best proceed by examining conditions as though they changed only by small marginal increments and only one at a time, other things being equal. Their principles were most concerned with the "special case" of the more developed countries that had market systems.

In the neoclassical view, demand is determined by the marginal utilities of various goods to individual people. It is at least as important a determinant of value and price as are cost and supply. Marshall speaks of demand and supply as the two blades of a pair of scissors, neither one capable of cutting by itself. More extreme writers try to reduce "cost" further to the utility of alternative products, and to the utility of leisure as opposed to work.

Marginal productivity analysis, often with ethical implications, was worked out mainly by J. B. Clark. The first welfare economists were Edgeworth, Pareto, and Pigou. They derived conditions under which a policy change could be objectively called socially superior or inferior.

Most of the "apparatus" of microeconomics today comes from Marshall's work. The standard diagrams showing supply and demand, elasticity, and the distinction between the short-run and long-run periods were all developed, though not necessarily originated, by Marshall. The use of economic models to determine unknowns in a general equilibrium system comes from Walras. Among those who developed real (nonmonetary) interest theory were Böhm-Bawerk, Fisher, Clark, and their followers.

The term "macroeconomics" was unknown in the heyday of neoclassical economics. To some macroeconomic concepts, however, the neoclassical writers also made important contributions. On the monetary side, equations of exchange relating to money, incomes, and prices were developed by Fisher in the United States and by Pigou in Britain. Fisher went on to develop the quantity theory of money—really a quantity-of-money theory of the price level—more fully than had ever been done before. He also worked on schemes of price-level stabilization. In monetary interest theory, too, Fisher's name is important, though it was Wicksell who provided the most useful stepping stone to contemporary thinking.

In his *Structure of Scientific Revolutions*, the philosopher and historian of science Thomas Kuhn distinguishes normal from revolutionary science. Normal science solves more or less routine problems. Revolutionary science concentrates on discovering anomalies in the earlier theory and on developing new or modified theories for the normal science of the next era.

When we apply these ideas to economics, neoclassical economics, like many other kinds, is mainly normal science or "puzzle-solving." Its problem may be that, since about 1914, it has come to contain so little beyond this level, and to pay so little attention to the real-world anomalies that have developed.

VIII Market Structures and Economic Performance

- Pure Competition
- Monopoly
- Monopolistic Competition and Oligopoly
- Oligopoly: The Real World

VII Market Structures and Economic
Performance

- Pure Competition
- Monopoly
- Monopolistic Competition and Oligopoly
- Oligopoly: The Real World

25 *Pure Competition*

PREVIEW The last two chapters have helped you to understand some of the most important concepts that economists use to predict the actions of business firms. Because all firms are assumed to be rational, what each will supply depends upon its costs and revenues.

In this and the next several chapters, we view firms in the context of their markets. Every business firm operates in one or more markets, and not always on the same side of the market. For example, General Motors Corporation is a buyer in the steel market and a seller in the automobile market. You will learn that the way in which markets are organized has an important effect on consumer welfare. A large number of buyers may be exploited by a single seller, whereas those buyers might get a much better deal if the market were composed of several or a great many sellers.

In this chapter we shall briefly introduce four sellers' market structures—pure competition, pure monopoly, monopolistic competition, and oligopoly—and then focus on the first of these. Monopoly will be presented in Chapter 26, monopolistic competition in Chapter 27, and oligopoly in both Chapters 27 and 28.

In this chapter, after carefully defining pure competition, we explain the model. Alternative short-run equilibria, as well as long-run equilibrium, are described. You will see that, although some industries come quite close to it, the pure competition model is an abstract idea and not exactly representative of any real-world industry.

Pure competition is sometimes held out to be the "best of all possible worlds"—the ideal market structure—if only it could be attained. We shall examine the basis of such arguments and end by presenting some arguments in opposition to this point of view.

FOUR SELLERS' MARKET STRUCTURES

Classification is a tricky business and often involves a number of arbitrary distinctions. However, most economists feel comfortable with the idea of four different sellers' market structures: (1) pure competition, (2) pure monopoly, (3) monopolistic competition, and (4) oligopoly. There are three important bases for distinguishing among these types. The first is the number of firms that sell in the market. The second is whether or not the product is differentiated. That is, do all firms in the market sell the same standardized product, or do buyers believe there are differences among the products sold by the different firms? The third is how easy it is for new firms to enter the market.

In **pure competition** there are a large number of firms in the market. Each firm sells a standardized product. Entry to the market is perfectly easy. At the opposite pole is a **pure monopoly** market, with only a single seller. No product differentiation or entry into the market is possible. In fact, there is no other product offered in the market, and entry is completely blocked. **Monopolistic competition,** like pure competition, is a market type in which there are many sellers and entry into the market is easy. Unlike pure competition, however, each firm sells a somewhat different product. Buyers are not indifferent between the product sold by one firm and that sold

TABLE 25-1   Structural Characteristics of Four Different Seller Market Types

Market Type	Distinguishing Structural Criteria		
	Number of Firms	Product Differentiation	Ease of Entry
Pure competition	many	none	easy
Pure monopoly	one	none	impossible
Monopolistic competition	many	some	easy
Oligopoly	few	varying amounts	varying degrees of difficulty

by another in a monopolistically competitive market. Finally, **oligopoly** is a market type in which there are few sellers. The degree of product differentiation among the firms ranges from very little in some markets to a great deal in others. The ease of entry also differs from market to market, but generally it is not very easy to enter an oligopoly market.

Table 25-1 summarizes the relationships among the four sellers' market structures based on the three distinguishing features of markets.

These different market structures, which will be much more fully explained in this chapter and the next three, give rise to different patterns of behavior by firms. For example, firms in pure competition can readily ignore their rivals in the market, but those in an oligopoly market must pay a great deal of attention to what their rivals do and might do. In turn, how firms conduct their rivalry in a market strongly affects the economic performance of that market. Consumers may pay lower prices for better products when buying from a monopolistically competitive firm than when buying from a pure monopolist.

PURE COMPETITION

The term **competition** is used in two different senses in economics. First, it may be used to describe *rivalry* among sellers or buyers. One firm may be said to "compete" with another for a certain buyer's business, or one buyer may "compete" with another to obtain certain products from a seller. Adam Smith recognized competition in this "rivalry" sense more than two hundred years ago in his *Wealth of Nations*. That is still a common way to use the term. Most business people today think of competition as meaning the striving among a number of rivals in a contest aimed at obtaining the purchase or the sale of a particular product. The second sense in which competition is used in economics is as a label for the specific market type that we are about to discuss: the market structure called *pure competition*. It is important not to confuse the two meanings. Competition in the rivalry sense may be used in referring to *any* market in which there are rivals. However, pure competition refers *only* to the specific market structure that bears this name.

Pure competition describes a market in which there are so many firms that each acts as though it can exert no control over price. In pure competition, each individual firm sells such a tiny part of the total market supply that it assumes its actions have no effect on the market price. Because a small wheat farm is just one of over a million farms in the same market, it is very unlikely to produce less wheat this year in an attempt to raise the price of wheat. Likewise, an owner of 100 shares of General Motors stock is not likely to hold off selling 50 of them on the ground that this would depress the price of his or her remaining 50 shares. Over 296 million shares of General Motors stock are outstanding, and tens of thousands are generally traded every day. Thus, the owner feels that the additional supply of 50 shares is quite insignificant.

Of course, the equilibrium price really *is* affected by a change in a seller's supply. However, the price change may be so small (for example, one ten-thousandth of a cent) that it is not even noticed. The important characteristic of pure competition is that each firm *believes* that it cannot change the price. For this reason, it assumes the role of a **price taker,** one that accepts the price as given and therefore does not adjust its own sales so as to try to influence that price.

Conditions for Pure Competition

A purely competitive market requires: (1) many sellers, (2) standardized product, (3) no artificial restrictions placed upon price or quantity, and (4) easy entry and exit to and from the market. Each of these conditions bears a relationship to our definition of pure competition.

MANY SELLERS We are not able to say whether the minimum requirement of "many firms" means 1,000 or 50,000 firms. We can only say that the number of firms must be large enough so that each firm (because it is such a small part of the market) believes that it cannot affect the market price by selling more or less.

STANDARDIZED PRODUCT The product of the various firms in the market must be so standardized (so much like one another) that customers do not prefer one seller's product over another's. Since buyers do not care which seller's product they purchase, any firm that raised its price above the price charged by its competitors ("rivals") would lose all of its sales. If the products of the various firms were differentiated, then a company could affect the price by changing the quantity

that it offers for sale. In such a case, we would *not* have pure competition.

NO ARTIFICIAL RESTRICTIONS Any artificial restriction on the free movement of prices or on the quantity of output keeps a market from being purely competitive. Pure competition cannot exist under government price setting (such as price freezes) or agreements among competitors as to prices or the quantities to be sold (such as a collusive deal that involves price fixing). Any action of this sort prevents the free market forces from determining the market price. The firms would no longer be price takers since either through effective lobbying they persuade the government to set the price or through effective collusion the price is set by the sellers themselves.

EASY ENTRY AND EXIT Sellers must be free to enter and to leave a purely competitive market, and a newly entered firm must be able to sell its product as easily as a long-established firm. Any barriers to entry into a market would be inconsistent with the pure competition model.

Perfect Competition

Pure competition may be taken one step further to what economists call **perfect competition.** Besides the pure competition conditions that we just described, buyers and sellers in a perfectly competitive market also have complete and continuous knowledge of all bids and offers made in the market and the full mobility to take immediate action. In a strongly competitive setting, this perfect knowledge, combined with the full mobility to take advantage of it, results in a market in which there is only one price prevailing at any given time. To explain this condition, we shall use the case of a large trading village where farmers and merchants meet once a week in the village square to sell and buy corn. Suppose that in one part of the square farmers were selling— and merchants were buying—large amounts of corn for $3 a bushel. If a farmer knew about those transactions and was able to get over to that part

FIGURE 25-1   **Market and Firm in Pure Competition**

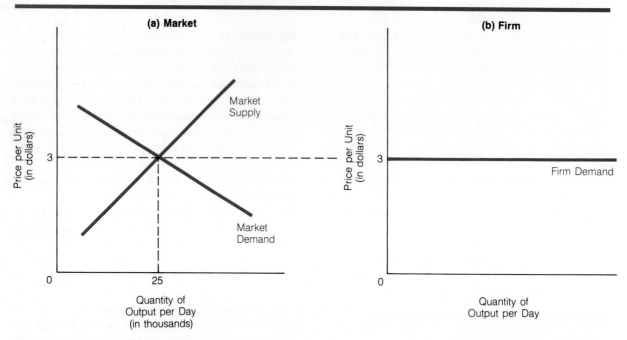

Panel (a) shows a market-demand curve and a market-supply curve for a purely competitive industry. Their intersection marks the equilibrium level of daily output of 25,000 and the equilibrium price of $3 per unit for this market. Panel (b) shows the demand curve of a typical firm in this market. The demand curve is drawn as infinitely elastic at $3 because the firm considers itself to be powerless to change this price and believes that it can sell all it wants at this market price.

of the square, he or she would not be willing to sell corn anywhere else in the square for less than $3 a bushel. Likewise, a knowledgeable, mobile, and competitive merchant would not be willing to buy corn anywhere else in the square for more than $3 a bushel. That single price of $3 would be the only one that could prevail at that particular time and place.

THE PURE COMPETITION MODEL

So far you have learned that individual firms in a purely competitive market are powerless price takers. The only decision that each needs to make is whether to produce and, if so, how much. The pure competition model that you will learn next clearly shows the outcome of this decision, for both the short run and the long run.

The Firm Versus the Market

In dealing with the pure competition model, it is essential to keep separate the concept of the individual economic enterprise, which we call the *firm,* and the group of competing firms or the industry, which constitutes the *market.*

The market-demand curve (the demand that faces the whole industry) is expected to be a normal downward-sloping curve. The product of this industry competes with the products of other industries. Because of the substitution effect, a larger quantity is demanded at lower prices and a smaller quantity is demanded at higher prices.

TABLE 25-2 Revenue for a Purely Competitive Firm

(1) Market Price	(2) Quantity Sold	(3) Total Revenue	(4) Average Revenue	(5) Marginal Revenue
$3	5	$15	$3	
				$3
3	6	18	3	
				3
3	7	21	3	
				3
3	8	24	3	
				3
3	9	27	3	

When this is combined with the income effect, which explains that buyers can afford more at lower prices and less at higher prices, the result is a normal, negatively sloped demand curve. Such a market-demand curve is pictured in panel (a) of Figure 25-1.

The market-supply curve (the total supply that is offered by all the firms in the industry) is expected to be a normal upward-sloping curve. As explained in Chapter 5, profit-minded companies are willing to supply more at higher prices and less at lower prices, other things being equal. Such a market-supply curve is also pictured in Figure 25-1a.

At the intersection of the market-demand and market-supply curves is the equilibrium market output and price. Panel (a) of Figure 25-1 shows that 25,000 units are bought and sold each day at a price of $3 per unit.

As explained earlier, each pure competitor firm takes this price ($3) as a set fact. So from the firm's viewpoint, it faces a perfectly flat or infinitely elastic demand curve, as shown in panel (b) of Figure 25-1. The firm believes that it can sell all it wants to at the market price of $3. It also is aware that it can sell none of its standardized product at a higher-than-market price, say $3.01, and that it would be foolish to offer any at a lower-than-market price, say $2.99, since it can sell all it wants to at the $3.00 market price.

Demand and Revenue for the Firm in Pure Competition

A firm's demand schedule and curve allow us to find its various revenue schedules and curves. The price that a firm charges multiplied by the quantity of output that it sells is the **total revenue** that the firm receives. Table 25-2 shows five different quantities of output that a pure competitor firm might sell. Suppose that market price is $3 per unit. If it decides to sell 5 units a day, it receives total revenue of $15. Total revenue is $18 for 6 units, $21 for 7 units, and so on. Each time the firm raises its output by one unit, total revenue increases by a constant amount equal to the market price. Figure 25-2 shows the total-revenue curve for the company whose data appear in Table 25-2. For a pure competitor, this curve is always a straight line drawn with a positive slope out of the origin.

Average revenue is total revenue divided by the quantity of goods sold. In Table 25-2, column 3 divided by column 2 equals column 4. Average revenue is the price per unit as a buyer looks at it and the revenue per unit from the firm's point of view. Therefore, an average-revenue curve is just another name for a demand curve. Figure 25-2 shows that they are one and the same.

We demonstrate the relationships as follows:

$$TR = P \cdot Q$$

$$AR = \frac{TR}{Q}$$

$$AR = \frac{P \cdot Q}{Q}$$

$$AR = P$$

where TR is total revenue, AR is average revenue, P is the price per unit of the product, and Q is the quantity of units of the product sold.

Marginal revenue, as you will remember from the last chapter, is the extra total revenue that a firm receives when it sells another unit of output. Since a pure competitor firm can sell all it wants to at the market price, it is the market price that the firm receives when it sells an additional unit.

FIGURE 25-2   Revenue for a Firm in Pure Competition

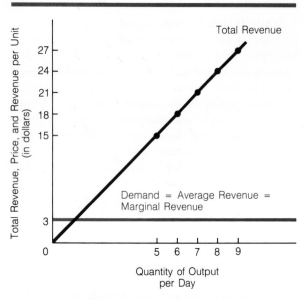

The linear curve drawn out of the origin is a purely competitive firm's total-revenue curve. It takes this shape because total revenue is price times quantity, and in pure competition, price remains the same as quantity is varied. In this example, the market price is $3, so that as the firm increases its level of output by one, total revenue increases by $3.

The horizontal curve drawn at $3 is this firm's demand curve (as in Figure 25-1, but graphically lower down because the scaling is less stretched out here) and is also its average-revenue curve and its marginal-revenue curve. Average revenue is the price per unit or the revenue per unit and is therefore just another name for a demand curve. Marginal revenue—the extra revenue that a firm receives when it sells an additional unit of output—is equal to the market price in pure competition.

In pure competition, marginal revenue will always be equal to price. Table 25-2 shows that whenever the firm decides to sell one more unit of output, its marginal revenue—its addition to total revenue—will be the market price of $3. Figure 25-2 shows that the pure competitor firm's demand (average-revenue) curve is also its marginal-revenue curve.

To summarize, in the case of pure competition, a firm's infinitely elastic demand curve, which is

drawn at the market price, is not only its average-revenue curve but also its marginal-revenue curve.

Supply and Cost for the Firm in Pure Competition

We have described a purely competitive market as one in which firms believe that they can sell all they want to at the market price. In order to determine just how much each firm wants to sell—how much supply each firm will offer—we will use the concepts that you learned in Chapter 24. There you learned that rational firms—those that maximize profit or minimize loss—will seek to supply the level of output at which their total revenue exceeds their total cost by the maximum amount and so where their marginal revenue is equal to their marginal cost.

To illustrate this point, in Figure 25-3 we have redrawn the pure competitor's total-revenue curve from Figure 25-2 and, beneath it, its marginal-revenue curve, also from Figure 25-2. In the lower graph, the vertical scaling has been stretched out (as in Figure 25-1) so that you can see it better. We have added the firm's short-run total-cost curve in the upper diagram and its short-run marginal-cost curve in the lower one. These data are taken from Table 25-3, which also repeats the total-revenue and marginal-revenue data from Table 25-2. Profit maximization takes place at between 7 and 8 units. At this level of output, the pure competitor's marginal cost of $3 is equal to its marginal revenue of $3, which is the prevailing market price. Given the requirement of having to produce whole units, producing either 7 or 8 units is an equilibrium situation because the firm is obtaining maximum profit.

With this reasoning—and with what you learned in the previous chapter about when a firm will shut down rather than produce in the short run—we are able to show that a pure competitor's marginal-cost curve (above its average variable cost) is also its short-run supply curve. You can see this by examining the three diagrams in Figure 25-4. Panel (a) pictures five alternative market equilibria. Each change in market price and output (such as from $3 and 25,000 units to $4 and 35,000 units) is brought about by a shift in market demand. Panel (b) pictures the effect on a typical firm—the firm that we studied earlier in this chapter—in this purely competitive market. The firm's five alternative horizontal demand curves correspond to five different market equilibria. Each is labeled to show that it is also the firm's average-revenue and marginal-revenue curve. In order to determine how much this firm will supply at each price, we examine its marginal-cost and average-variable-cost curves. Supply takes place where the firm's marginal cost is equal to its marginal revenue (the price). For example, at a price of $3, the firm will supply between 7 and 8 units per day, and at $5 it will supply between 9 and 10 units per day. Recall from the last chapter that the only exception to this rule is when, in the short run, a firm's revenue is not enough to cover its variable cost. In that case—when it stands to lose more than its fixed cost—the firm will minimize its loss by shutting down. In the short run, the firm will produce no output as long as its average revenue cannot at least cover its average variable cost. Therefore, that part of a pure competitor firm's marginal-cost curve that lies below its average-variable-cost curve is not part of its supply curve. In our example, the part of the marginal-cost curve that lies below $1 is not part of the firm's supply curve since the firm would not supply any output at prices under $1. Finally, panel (c) shows what we have now demonstrated—that the pure competitor's short-run supply curve is the part of its marginal-cost curve that lies above its average variable cost.

Once we have found a typical firm's short-run supply curve, it takes only simple summation to derive the short-run market-supply curve. A market-supply curve is the sum of the supply curves of all the individual firms in that market.[1] If marginal cost for firms changes, market supply will change. Of course, since in pure competition each individual firm's supply represents only a very small part of market supply, any change in marginal cost for only one or a few companies will not affect market supply very much.

1. We assume that the market is not so significant as to have supply changes affect resource prices.

FIGURE 25-3 Equilibrium Output of a Purely Competitive Firm

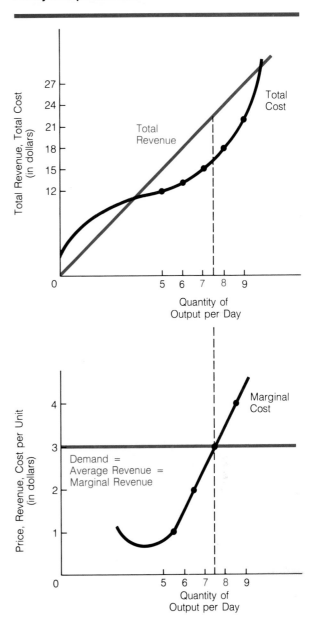

The level of output at which this purely competitive firm maximizes its profit is 7 or 8 units. This is shown in the upper diagram by where the firm's total-revenue curve exceeds its short-run total-cost curve by the greatest amount and in the lower diagram by where its short-run marginal-cost curve intersects its marginal-revenue curve from below.

TABLE 25-3   Revenue and Cost for a Purely Competitive Firm

(1) Market Price	(2) Quantity Sold	(3) Total Revenue	(4) Marginal Revenue	(5) Total Cost	(6) Marginal Cost
$3	5	$15		$12	
			$3		$1
3	6	18		13	
			3		2
3	7	21		15	
			3		3
3	8	24		18	
			3		4
3	9	27		22	

Profitability of Firms In Pure Competition

How profitable are purely competitive firms? The answer depends upon whether we are dealing with the short run or the long run. Before presenting these cases, let us quickly review what you learned in Chapter 24 about how economists define profit. Normal profit (an amount of profit that is equal to a firm's opportunity cost of remaining in its market) is considered a cost. Economic profit, then, is a return that is greater than opportunity cost. A return less than opportunity cost is an economic loss. With these definitions in mind, we shall look at short-run and long-run equilibrium in pure competition.

SHORT-RUN EQUILIBRIUM   In the short run, firms in pure competition may have an economic profit, an economic loss, or just a normal profit. Figure 25-5 pictures the three possible short-run equilibrium positions. (These are not a continuation of our previous example. We have chosen to use a less lumpy example for the remainder of this chapter so that we shall no longer be bothered with dual solutions.) Each of the three diagrams shows a company's profit-maximization position when it faces a market price of $10. Its marginal-cost curve (MC) intersects its marginal-revenue

curve (D = AR = MR) from below at an output level of 20,000 units a day. To enable us to see whether the firm is earning economic profit, normal profit, or suffering economic loss, we show an average-total-cost curve (ATC) in each of the three diagrams. Note that average total cost (cost per unit of output) at the equilibrium output is different in each of the three cases shown. At the equilibrium point in each panel, the vertical distance (if any) between average total cost and average revenue (price) shows the deviation from normal profit per unit of output. In panel (a), the company is earning an economic profit. At equilibrium, average revenue is $3 higher than average total cost ($10 − $7 = $3). The firm in panel (b) is experiencing an economic loss. At equilibrium, average total cost is $2 higher than average revenue ($12 − $10 = $2). Since it sells 20,000 units per day, the firm suffers a total economic loss of $40,000 a day ($2 × 20,000 = $40,000). In this diagram we have included the firm's average-variable-cost curve (AVC) to show that it will indeed supply the 20,000 units, since at that level of output its average revenue is greater than its average variable cost. If average variable cost had been greater than average revenue at equilibrium, the firm would of course have shut down. In panel (c), the firm has neither an economic profit nor an economic loss, as it is earning just a normal profit. At equilibrium, its

FIGURE 25-4 Derivation of a Purely Competitive Firm's Short-Run Supply Curve

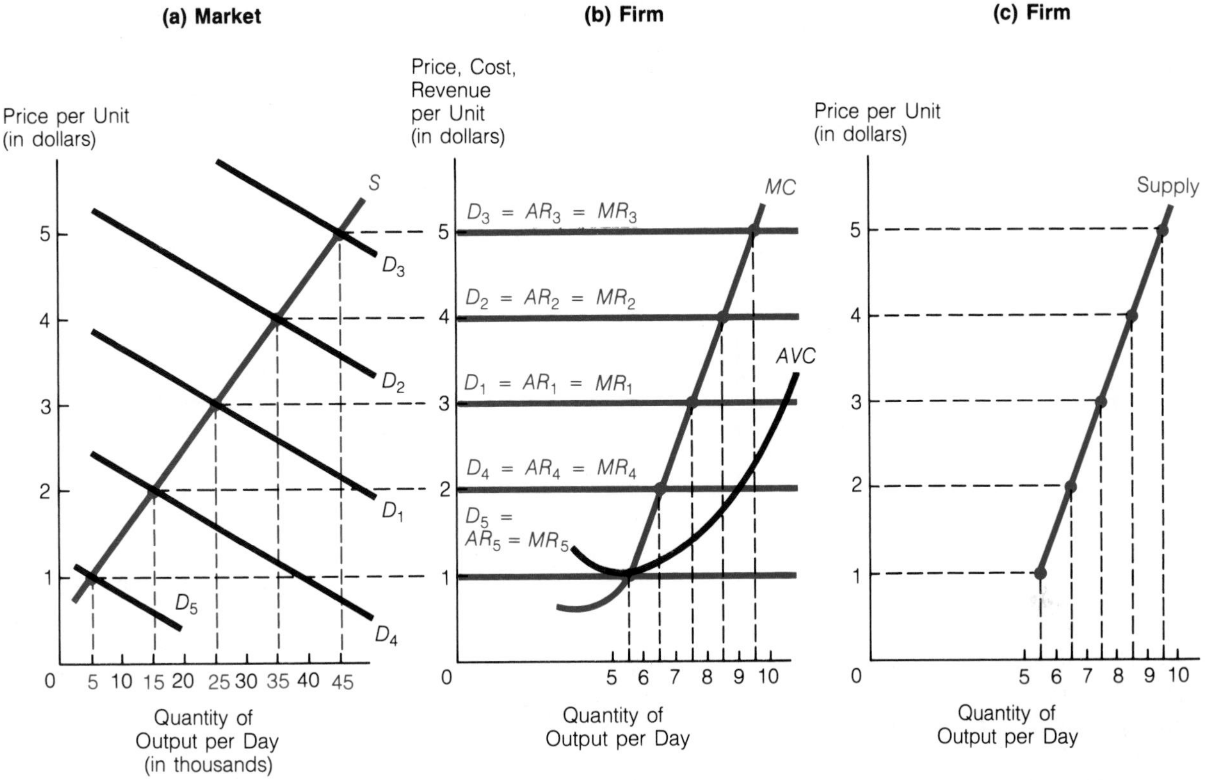

(a) Market **(b) Firm** **(c) Firm**

Panel (a) shows five different market equilibria. Here S is the market-supply curve, D_1 is the original market-demand curve, D_2 and D_3 are higher market-demand curves, and D_4 and D_5 are lower market-demand curves. Panel (b) shows five horizontal demand curves that face a typical firm in this purely competitive industry. Each corresponds to one of the market equilibria, and the subscripts specify to which one. Each demand curve ($D_1 = AR_1 = MR_1$ to $D_5 = AR_5 = MR_5$) is also the firm's average-revenue and marginal-revenue curve. The firm's marginal-cost curve is MC. Where MC intersects marginal revenue from below

is the level of output which maximizes the firm's profit: at between 5 and 6 units when the market price is $1, at between 6 and 7 units when the market price is $2, and so on. The firm's average-variable-cost curve (AVC) is included to show when the firm will shut down. In the short run, a firm will offer output only if its revenue can at least cover its variable cost. That portion of the marginal-cost curve that lies above $1 is the firm's supply curve and is reproduced in panel (c). The portion of the firm's marginal-cost curve that lies below average variable cost is not part of the firm's supply curve.

average revenue ($10) is equal to its average total cost ($10).

Will the three alternative equilibrium positions pictured in Figure 25-5 persist? Yes, they will, in the short run. Remember that the short run is defined as a period of time that is not long enough for firms to make all the adjustments that they would like to make. There is always some fixed

cost in the short run. When the companies in the market suffer an economic loss, they would like to exit from the market, but the short run does not allow enough time for them to liquidate their assets and leave. By contrast, when the companies in the market earn an economic profit, it is likely that firms in other markets or entirely new firms would like to enter this market. Again, the short

FIGURE 25-5   Three Alternative Short-Run Equilibrium Profit Positions for Firms in Pure Competition

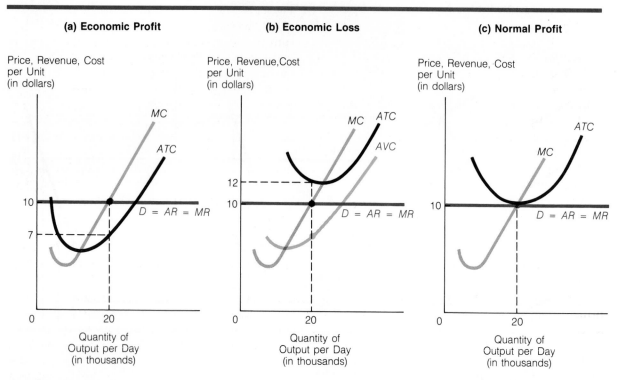

From left to right, the three diagrams show purely competitive firms that are experiencing an economic profit, an economic loss, and just a normal profit. Each of the three possible short-run equilibrium positions shows a firm's profit-maximization position when it faces a market price of $10. Each has the marginal-cost curve (MC) intersecting the marginal-revenue curve (D = AR = MR) from below at an output level of 20,000 units per day. At that equilibrium level of output, average total cost (ATC) is $7 in panel (a),

$12 in panel (b), and $10 in panel (c). Since average revenue (D = AR = MR) is $10 in all three cases, panel (a) has average revenue exceeding average total cost by $3, panel (b) has average total cost exceeding average revenue by $2, and panel (c) has them equal. In panel (b), where economic loss occurs, the firm's average-variable-cost curve (AVC) is below average revenue at equilibrium, so that the firm will not choose to shut down.

run does not allow enough time for these changes to take place.

LONG-RUN EQUILIBRIUM   In the long run, there is enough time for firms to adjust their previously fixed inputs so that they can leave or enter a market. In fact, "easy" exit and entry is a condition of the pure competition model. Whenever firms suffer an economic loss, the model dictates that in the long run they will exit from the market,

and whenever firms earn economic profit, the model dictates that in the long run new firms will enter the market. As you will see, under conditions of economic loss, the exit of some firms allows the remaining companies to earn normal profit. Similarly, under conditions of economic profit, the entry of new firms eats away the economic profit and leaves all the companies with normal profit. Thus, no matter whether firms had an economic loss, an economic profit, or just a normal profit in the short run, all will earn just normal profit in long-run equilibrium. These facts are illustrated in Figure 25-6. The top half shows the effect that exit has on market supply and so also on the equilibrium market price upon which firms act. The bottom half shows the effect that entry has on market supply and on the equilibrium price.

In the top half of Figure 25-6 (panels a and b) we begin by showing a firm with an economic loss in the short run (as in Figure 25-5b) and the market that it is in. The market is in short-run equilibrium when it supplies 200 million units of output per day at a price of $10 per unit. The firm is suffering an economic loss of $4 per unit (at equilibrium output of 20,000 units per day its average total cost is $14 while its average revenue is $10). In the long run, firms will begin to exit. As firms leave the market, the short-run market-supply curve shifts to the left because it is now composed of the marginal-cost curves of fewer firms. Long-run equilibrium occurs at the lower level of market output of 150 million units and at the higher price of $12 per unit. The companies that remain in the market earn just a normal profit. The typical surviving firm pictured in our example is in long-run equilibrium when it now produces 25,000 units per day at a price of $12 per unit.

In the bottom half of Figure 25-6 (panels c and d) we begin by showing a firm with an economic profit in the short run (as in Figure 25-5a) and the market that it is in. The market is in short-run equilibrium when it supplies 200 million units of output a day at a price of $10 a unit. The firm is earning an economic profit of $1 a unit (at equilibrium output of 20,000 units a day its average revenue is $10 and its average total cost is $9). In the long run, firms will enter this market. As firms enter, the short-run market-supply curve shifts to the right (panel d) because it is now composed of the marginal-cost curves of more firms. Long-run equilibrium occurs at the higher market output of 250 million units and at the lower price of $8 per unit. The firms in the market earn normal profit. The typical firm pictured in our example is in long-run equilibrium when it produces 15,000 units a day at $8 a unit.

Long-Run Market Supply

You have learned that the short-run market supply curve in a purely competitive market is the sum of the marginal-cost curves of the firms in that market. As firms leave or enter the market, the supply curve shifts to the left or right. Now we must examine the long-run supply curve—that is, the curve that shows the effects of entry and exit in response to changes in market demand. The shape of the long-run market-supply curve is caused by *shifts* in the cost curves of the individual firms that come with expansion and contraction of total output in the market. This adds a new aspect to the explanation of cost and price in the long run.

We shall discuss three possible cases: (1) long-run supply in a constant-cost market, (2) long-run supply in an increasing-cost market, and (3) long-run supply in a decreasing-cost market. In each case we shall begin with the market in long-run equilibrium so that each firm earns just a normal profit. Then we shall assume a rise in market demand that will allow firms to earn an economic profit in the short run.[2] Then in the long run, when other firms enter the market, you will learn how the new market equilibrium is formed: at the same price in the constant-cost case, at a higher price in the increasing-cost case, and at a lower price in the decreasing-cost case.

THE CONSTANT-COST CASE   In the constant-cost case, long-run changes in the level of market output do not affect the average total cost of producing the output, so that long-run prices remain the same. The presence of more or fewer firms in the market does not affect the cost to individual firms. Each firm's average total cost curve remains the same from one long-run equilibrium to the next.

As the market expands, there is greater demand for the types of labor, capital, and natural

---

2. We could, of course, alternatively assume a decrease in market demand, which would cause firms to earn an economic loss or even shut down in the short run. But since it turns out to be nothing more than the same cases backward, we have decided to economize on space and ask you to work out those cases on your own.

The Case of Exit

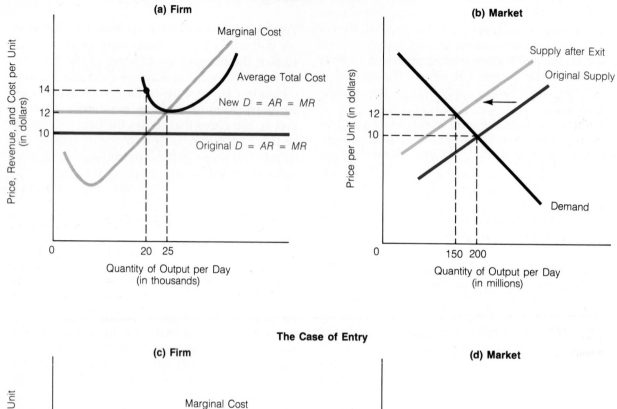

(a) Firm

Marginal Cost

Average Total Cost

New $D = AR = MR$

Original $D = AR = MR$

Price, Revenue, and Cost per Unit (in dollars)

14
12
10

0   20 25

Quantity of Output per Day
(in thousands)

(b) Market

Supply after Exit

Original Supply

Demand

Price per Unit (in dollars)

12
10

0   150 200

Quantity of Output per Day
(in millions)

The Case of Entry

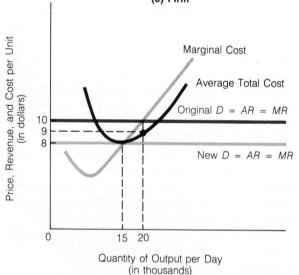

(c) Firm

Marginal Cost

Average Total Cost

Original $D = AR = MR$

New $D = AR = MR$

Price, Revenue, and Cost per Unit (in dollars)

10
9
8

0   15 20

Quantity of Output per Day
(in thousands)

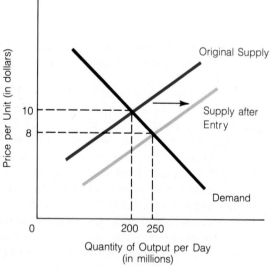

(d) Market

Original Supply

Supply after Entry

Demand

Price per Unit (in dollars)

10
8

0   200 250

Quantity of Output per Day
(in millions)

resources that are used by the firms producing the product exchanged in this market. If these inputs are in abundant supply, if they are unspecialized, or if the market uses only a very small part of their available supply, the increased demand will bring no significant change in the prices of these inputs. Therefore, the average- and marginal-cost curves of the firms in the market will not shift because of the market's expansion. After new firms enter, the average total costs of the companies in the market will be the same as they were before the expansion of the market. In

◄ **FIGURE 25-6 Achieving Long-Run Equilibrium Through Exit or Entry in Pure Competition**

The top two diagrams (panels a and b) show a market in which an economic loss is suffered in the short run and how exit eliminates such loss in the long run. Short-run equilibrium in the market occurs where the market-demand curve intersects the original market-supply curve at an output of 200 million units and a price of $10. For the firm, short-run equilibrium is where its marginal-cost curve intersects its original marginal-revenue curve (original $D = AR = MR$) at an output of 20,000 units. The firm's average total cost is $14 at equilibrium, so that the firm suffers an economic loss of $4 per unit ($14 − $10 = $4). In the long run, firms will exit, so that the market-supply curve will shift to the left, as shown in panel (b). A new market equilibrium (long-run) is established where the market-supply-after-exit curve intersects the market-demand curve at an output level of 150 million and a price of $12. The typical firm that remains in the market now faces a new demand curve at $12 (new $D = AR = MR$). It adjusts its daily level of output to 25,000 units (where its marginal-cost curve intersects its new marginal-revenue curve). At this long-run equilibrium point, the firm's average-total-cost curve is tangent to its average-revenue curve, showing that it earns just a normal profit.

The bottom two diagrams (panels c and d) show a market in which economic profit is earned in the short run and how entry eliminates such profit in the long run. Short-run equilibrium in the market occurs where the market-demand curve intersects the original market-supply curve at an output of 200 million units and a price of $10. For the firm, short-run equilibrium is where its marginal-cost curve intersects its original marginal-revenue curve (original $D = AR = MR$) at an output of 20,000 units. The firm's average total cost is $9 at equilibrium, so that the firm enjoys an economic profit of $1 per unit ($10 − $9 = $1). In the long run, firms will enter, so that the market-supply curve will shift to the right, as shown in panel (d). A new market equilibrium (long-run) is established where the market-supply-after-entry curve intersects the market-demand curve at an output level of 250 million and a price of $8. The typical firm now faces a new demand curve at $8 (new $D = AR = MR$). It adjusts its daily level of output to 15,000 units (where its marginal-cost curve intersects its new marginal-revenue curve). At this long-run equilibrium point, the firm's average-total-cost curve is tangent to its average-revenue curve, showing that it earns just a normal profit.

the long run, costs are constant. Let us examine the case of constant cost in graphic form.

We begin in Figure 25-7b with a purely competitive market in long-run equilibrium. The market short-run supply curve (S_1) intersects the market-demand curve (D_1) at a level of output of 200 million units a day and at a price of $10 a unit. The firm diagram in Figure 25-7a pictures a typical firm in that market. It accepts the market price of $10 and maximizes its profit by producing 20,000 units per day. At this level of output the firm's marginal-cost curve (MC) intersects its marginal-revenue curve ($D_1 = AR_1 = MR_1$) from below. We know that it is in long-run equilibrium since its average-total-cost curve (ATC) is tangent to its average-revenue curve ($D_1 = AR_1 = MR_1$), showing that it is earning just normal profit.

Now suppose that this long-run equilibrium is upset by a rise in the demand for the output produced by the firms in this market. This change is shown in panel (b) as a shift to the right of the market-demand curve from D_1 to D_2. The market

price rises to $16 and daily market output to 280 million units. The typical firm reacts to the higher market price by supplying 28,000 units a day, as shown where its marginal cost (MC) intersects its new marginal-revenue curve ($D_2 = AR_2 = MR_2$). This short-run equilibrium allows the firm to earn economic profit of $4 a unit (average revenue is $16 and average total cost is $12). We know that, in the long run, economic profit will draw more firms into the market. Their entry is shown in panel (b) as a shift to the right of the market short-run supply curve, from S_1 to S_2. A new long-run market equilibrium is reached at an output level of 360 million units and, once again, at a price of $10. The typical firm again sells at $10 a unit, so that its previous long-run equilibrium is restored. It once again produces 20,000 units a day. This is true because there has been no shift of its cost curves.

This example helps us to identify two points on this market's long-run supply curve: the original point at 200 million units and the new one

FIGURE 25-7   Long-Run Market Supply in Pure Competition—The Case of Constant Cost

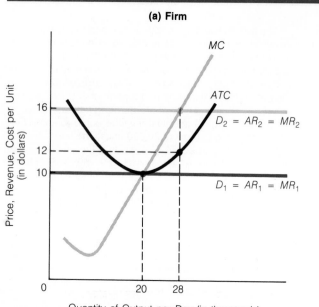

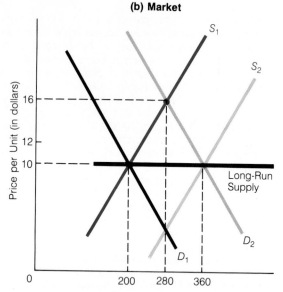

This purely competitive market is in long-run equilibrium where the short-run market-supply curve (S_1) intersects the market-demand curve (D_1) so that the daily output is 200 million units, which sell at $10 each. The typical firm shown produces 20,000 units per day.

This long-run equilibrium is disrupted by a shift to the right of the market-demand curve (D_1 to D_2). A short-run equilibrium is reached where the new demand curve (D_2) intersects the supply curve (S_1) at an output of 280 million units per day, sold at $16 per unit. The firm's new demand curve is $D_2 = AR_2 = MR_2$. The firm is in short-run equilibrium when it adjusts its output to 28,000 units per day so as to

earn $4 a unit economic profit. In the long run, firms will enter this market. This entry is reflected in the market diagram as a shift to the right of the short-run market-supply curve (S_1 to S_2). A new long-run market equilibrium is attained where S_2 intersects D_2 so that the market now sells 360 million units at the original price of $10 each. The firm reverts to its original long-run equilibrium position. It again produces 20,000 units per day. The increase in market production from 200 million to 360 million per day did not affect average total cost. The long-run supply curve is perfectly elastic.

at 360 million units. Notice that both appear on the same horizontal straight line. Because the rise in market production from 200 million to 360 million did not affect firms' costs, the long-run equilibrium remained at $10. Whenever average total cost does not change with a change in the level of output produced in a market, the market's long-run supply curve will be infinitely elastic.

THE INCREASING-COST CASE   In the increasing-cost case, long-run increases in the level of market

output raise the average total cost of producing the output, so that the price rises in the long-run adjustment to the larger volume. Each firm's average total cost increases as the market reaches higher and higher long-run equilibrium levels of output. The rising output occurs in markets that are large enough so the resources they use represent a significant part of the total demand for those resources. For example, when output is increased in an industry (market) that accounts for as much as, say, 25 percent of the demand

FIGURE 25-8   Long-Run Market Supply in Pure Competition—The Case of Increasing Cost

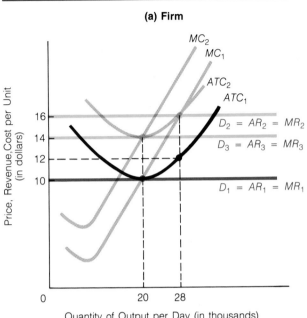

(a) Firm

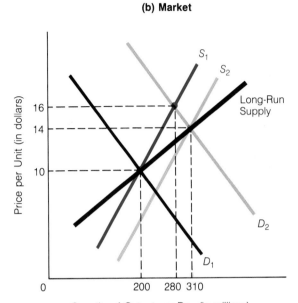

(b) Market

This purely competitive market is in long-run equilibrium where the short-run market-supply curve (S_1) intersects the market-demand curve (D_1), so that the daily output is 200 million units, which sell at \$10 each. The typical firm shown produces 20,000 units per day.

This long-run equilibrium is disrupted by a shift to the right of the market-demand curve (D_1 to D_2). A short-run equilibrium is reached where the new demand curve (D_2) intersects the supply curve (S_1) at an output of 280 million units per day, sold at \$16 per unit. The firm's new demand curve is $D_2 = AR_2 = MR_2$. The firm is in short-run equilibrium when it adjusts its output to 28,000 units per day. The firm earns an economic profit of \$4 per unit. In the long run, firms will enter this market. This fact is reflected in panel (b) as a shift to the right of the short-run market-supply curve (S_1 to S_2). The new firms bid up resource prices so

that the new long-run market equilibrium—where S_2 intersects D_2—takes place at a higher price (\$14) than the previous long-run equilibrium price. The new long-run equilibrium market level of output is 310 million. The higher resource prices are reflected in the upward shifts of the typical firm's average-total-cost curve (from ATC_1 to ATC_2) and marginal-cost curve (MC_1 to MC_2). The new long-run equilibrium for the firm is where its new marginal-cost curve (MC_2) intersects its new marginal-revenue curve ($D_3 = AR_3 = MR_3$). The firm again produces a daily level of output of 20,000 units at the new market price of \$14.

The market diagram (panel b) shows the long-run market-supply curve as a positively sloped curve. The increase in market output (from 200 million to 310 million) raises firms' average total cost by \$4 and thus the market price by the same amount (from \$10 to \$14).

for polymer chemicals, or for platinum, or for basic oxygen furnaces, we would expect the prices of these fairly specialized inputs to be bid up quite a bit. Let us examine the case of increasing cost in graphic form.

As in the constant-cost case, we begin with a purely competitive market in long-run equilib-

rium. The market diagram in Figure 25-8b shows the market short-run supply curve (S_1) intersecting the market-demand curve (D_1) at a level of output of 200 million units a day and at a price of \$10 a unit. And the firm diagram in Figure 25-8a shows a typical company in that market maximizing its profit by producing 20,000 units a day at the $10 price. Since it is in long-run equilibrium, it is earning just a normal profit.

Now suppose, as we did in the constant-cost case, that this long-run equilibrium is upset by a rise in the demand for the goods or services produced by the firms in this market. This is shown in panel (b) as a shift to the right of the market-demand curve, from D_1 to D_2. The market price rises to $16 and daily market output to 280 million units. As in the constant-cost case, the typical firm reacts to the higher market price by increasing its level of output to 28,000 units a day. It earns an economic profit of $4 a unit in this short-run equilibrium position. In the long run, new firms are attracted into the market. Their entry is shown in panel (b) by a shift to the right of the market short-run supply curve, from S_1 to S_2. A new long-run market equilibrium is reached but, unlike the constant-cost case, at a price above the earlier long-run equilibrium price (at $14 a unit instead of $10 a unit). Why? Because the firms that entered the market bid up resource prices so that average total cost increased for all the firms in the market. This can be seen in Figure 25-8a. The typical firm's average-total-cost curve shifted up from ATC_1 to ATC_2 and its marginal-cost curve shifted up from MC_1 to MC_2. The firm, now facing a $14 market price, is once again in long-run equilibrium—this time, at the point where its new marginal-cost curve (MC_2) intersects its new marginal-revenue curve ($D_3 = AR_3 = MR_3$) from below. Its new average-total-cost curve (ATC_2) is tangent to its new average-revenue curve ($D_3 = AR_3 = MR_3$), so that it is earning just a normal profit.

This example allows us again to identify two points on this market's long-run supply curve: the original point at 200 million units and the new one at 310 million units. Notice that the curve drawn through these two points—the long-run market-supply curve—is positively sloped. Along with the rise in market production from 200 million to 310 million, there was a $4 increase in average total cost and thus a $4 increase in price. Whenever average total cost rises with the level of output produced in a market, that market's long-run supply curve will be positively sloped.

THE DECREASING-COST CASE In the decreasing-cost case, long-run increases in the level of market output lower the average total cost of producing the output, so that prices decrease in the long-run adjustment to greater demand. Because more firms are present in the market, the cost to individual firms goes down. Each firm's average total cost decreases as the market reaches higher and higher long-run equilibrium levels of output. Cases of decreasing cost are expected to be found far less often than either increasing- or constant-cost cases. In order to have a case of decreasing cost, the presence of new firms in a market must bring about lower average total cost for all the firms in that market. For example, let us assume that the coal-mining firms supplying a certain market are located in a single huge coal-mining area. A major problem facing them is the water that builds up in their mine shafts and that has to be pumped out. Suppose now that there is a sharp rise in the demand for coal from this area. In the short run, the firms earn an economic profit, but in the long run, this profit slowly falls as new firms enter the market. But the additional pumping by the new firms means that there is less water to be pumped out by the original firms. As a result, all firms have lower average total cost since each is required to pump out less water. Let us examine the case of decreasing cost in graphic form.

As in the two earlier cases, we begin with a purely competitive market in long-run equilibrium. The market diagram in Figure 25-9b shows the market short-run supply curve (S_1) intersecting the market-demand curve (D_1) at a level of output of 200 million units a day and at a price of $10 a unit. The firm diagram in Figure 25-9a shows a typical company in that market maximizing its profit by producing 20,000 units a day at the $10 price. Its average-total-cost curve (ATC_1) is tangent to its average-revenue curve ($D_1 = AR_1 = MR_1$), so that it earns just a normal profit.

Now suppose, as we did in the previous two cases, that this long-run equilibrium is upset by a rise in the demand for the output produced by the firms in this market. This is shown in Figure 25-9b as a shift to the right of the market-demand curve, from D_1 to D_2. The market price rises to

FIGURE 25-9 Long-Run Market Supply in Pure Competition—The Case of Decreasing Cost

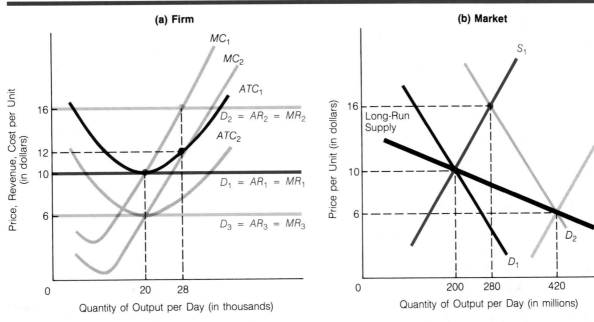

(a) Firm
(b) Market

This purely competitive market is in long-run equilibrium where the short-run market-supply curve (S_1) intersects the market-demand curve (D_1) so that the daily output is 200 million units, which sell at $10 each. The typical firm shown produces 20,000 units per day.

This long-run equilibrium is disrupted by a shift to the right of the market-demand curve $(D_1$ to $D_2)$. A short-run equilibrium is reached where the new demand curve (D_2) intersects the supply curve (S_1) at an output level of 280 million units per day, sold at $16 per unit. The firm's new demand curve is $D_2 = AR_2 = MR_2$. The firm is in short-run equilibrium when it adjusts its output to 28,000 units per day. The firm earns an economic profit of $4 per unit. In the long run, firms will enter this market. Their entry is reflected in panel (b) as a shift to the right of the short-run market-supply curve $(S_1$ to $S_2)$. The additional firms cause average total cost to decrease so that the new long-run

market equilibrium—where S_2 intersects D_2—takes place at a lower price ($6) than the previous long-run equilibrium price. The new long-run equilibrium market level of output is 420 million. The lower cost is reflected in the downward shifts of the typical firm's average-total-cost curve (from ATC_1 to ATC_2) and marginal-cost curve (MC_1 to MC_2). The new long-run equilibrium for the firm is where its new marginal-cost curve (MC_2) intersects its new marginal-revenue curve ($D_3 = AR_3 = MR_3$). The firm again produces a daily level of output of 20,000 units at the new market price of $6 (panel a).

Panel (b) shows the long-run market-supply curve as a negatively sloped curve. The rise in market output (from 200 million to 420 million) decreased firms' average total cost by $4 and thus the market price by the same amount (from $10 to $6).

$16 and daily market output to 280 million units. As in the other cases, the typical firm reacts to the higher market price by increasing its level of output to 28,000 units a day. It earns an economic profit of $4 per unit in this short-run equilibrium position. In the long run, new firms are attracted into the market. This is shown in panel (b) by a shift to the right of the market short-run supply

curve, from S_1 to S_2. A new long-run market equilibrium is reached, but unlike the other two cases, at a price below the original long-run equilibrium price (at $6 a unit instead of at $10 a unit). Why? Because the firms that entered the market caused a reduction in average total cost for all the firms in the market. This effect can be seen in panel (a) of Figure 25-9. Our typical firm's average-total-cost curve shifted down from ATC_1 to ATC_2, and its marginal-cost curve shifted down from MC_1 to MC_2. The firm, now facing a $6 market price, is once again in long-run equilibrium—this time, at the point where its new marginal-cost curve (MC_2) intersects its new marginal-revenue curve ($D_3 = AR_3 = MR_3$) from below. Its new average-total-cost curve (ATC_2) is tangent to its new average-revenue curve ($D_3 = AR_3 = MR_3$), so that it is earning just a normal profit.

Again we have identified two points on a long-run market-supply curve: the original point at 200 million units and the new one at 420 million units. In this case, the curve drawn through these two points—the long-run market-supply curve— is negatively sloped. Along with the rise in market production from 200 million to 420 million was a $4 decrease in average total cost and thus a $4 decrease in price. Whenever average total cost decreases with an increase in the level of output produced in a market, that market's long-run supply curve will be negatively sloped.

EVALUATION OF PURE COMPETITION

Though some actual industries approach the pure competition situation, the model is an abstract idea, not exactly representative of any real-world industry. Why in the world, then, have we used so much of our scarce space in this book to explain this model and asked you to spend your scarce time to read and study it? Did we practice good economics? We believe that the answer is "yes." First, the pure competition model gives us a yardstick for comparing actual characteristics of industries. Discovering how close a firm or industry comes to meeting the conditions of pure competition may help in predicting the actions of firms and the market equilibrium that will result.

Second, even though the pure competition model is an extreme case, some real-world industries do in fact come quite close to it. Therefore the model allows us to do a better job in analyzing these industries. Many small wheat farms, corn farms, and poultry farms in the United States are price takers. So are most sellers of shares of stock in the New York Stock Exchange. And relatively small coal-mining, silver-mining, and gold-mining firms are price takers as well. All of these and many others operate in markets with many sellers, and what they sell is quite standardized. However, they are not perfect examples of pure competition. To the extent that there is cooperative organization, such as a regional wheat sellers' cooperative, or government intervention, such as the U.S. government deciding to sell a large amount of silver out of a stockpile, the examples do not conform to the model. Also, these examples suffer from the fact that there are generally some exit and entry barriers that prevent free movement of resources out of and into these markets. For example, some farmers have decided to stay on their farms in the face of economic loss because they prefer to live there. They have decided to support their farming business with earnings from extra jobs.

Finally, the pure competition model involves relationships among variables that are also relevant in markets other than pure competition. Therefore, understanding this model helps in learning other models. Its usefulness will become clear in the next two chapters, where we explain the other market types.

The Virtues of Pure Competition

Would pure competition be desirable for our society, or would we be better off with markets containing at least some elements of monopoly? The answer must involve a value judgment. Those who favor pure competition argue that it would result in the "best of all possible worlds." Such arguments may be separated into political and economic ones.

POLITICAL ARGUMENTS A purely competitive society will have no big business, no big labor, and no big government. All the actors on the economic scene are powerless, one against the other. There is no centralized power that can dictate behavior. All power rests in the hands of the impersonal market forces of supply and demand, and, as Adam Smith explained in his *Wealth of Nations,* those hands are invisible.

Each of the many firms that make up a market simply adjusts its level of output according to market conditions. Labor has no reason to bargain for wage increases because gaining higher wages from companies that earn just a normal profit can result only in the loss of jobs. Likewise, there is no reason for government to intervene in the market process.[3] Any temporary excess demand or excess supply will be quickly eliminated by the market.

Furthermore, pure competition offers freedom of opportunity or "free enterprise." Anyone desiring to enter a business is free to do so. There are no barriers placed in the way. If you want to establish a new pizzeria in your town, you need no Department of Health certificate. If you want to open a bar, you need no liquor license. And if you want to own and drive a taxicab in New York City, you need no medallion.

ECONOMIC ARGUMENTS   There are a number of persuasive economic arguments in favor of pure competition. Three of them become clear when you look at the pure competition long-run equilibrium firm diagram (Figure 25-10). You can see that at equilibrium (1) the price charged is equal to the firm's marginal cost, (2) the firm earns just a normal profit, and (3) the firm produces at the minimum point of its average-total-cost curve. Let us see how each of these results benefits society.

When a firm charges a price that is equal to marginal cost, that is, when $P = MC$, any consumer who is willing and able to pay what it costs the firm to produce one more unit will be able to buy and consume it. This happens only in the case of pure competition. In the next two chapters, you will see that firms in all other market types charge a price that is higher than their marginal cost.

3. Of course, government may do things that affect the demands or costs with which the markets operate. Government may force firms to pay the pollution costs that they impose on the rest of society. Also, it may force a redistribution of income and wealth.

When a firm earns just a normal profit, its earnings are exactly equal to its opportunity cost. If it earned any less, it would leave the industry, but it takes no more than what it is earning to keep it in this business. In the next two chapters, you will see that the reason why firms are able to earn an economic profit in the long run is that resources are somehow prevented from flowing in. Those outside the industry who would like to share in the economic profit and whose resources would be more productive here than where they are currently used are not able to enter. Too many resources are then devoted to other markets and not enough to this one, which is poor resource allocation.

Finally, when a firm produces at the minimum point of its average-total-cost curve, the least amount of resources are being used to produce that level of output. Firms that produce at any higher average total cost suffer an economic loss and are forced out of the industry. Only those that waste no resources remain.

These three favorable aspects of pure competition can be seen on a diagram such as our Figure 25-10, but there are two others that are not readily visible on a diagram. The first is that none of the economy's scarce resources are devoted to advertising or promotion. Although a great deal of advertising is useful insofar as it provides important information to consumers, economists generally agree that much advertising is wasteful. Ads that say, "My product is better—buy it" are simply canceled out by rival ads that offer a similar message. Advertising is inconsistent with the pure competition model. Why should a firm add to its cost when the product that it sells is so standardized that it cannot be distinguished from the output of other firms? Furthermore, why should a firm advertise when it can already sell all that it wants to at the going market price? Advertising just doesn't make any sense in a pure competition context.

Another way in which pure competition might benefit society is that purely competitive firms are pushed to adopt quickly any new and better product or new and cost-saving technological process. Any pure competitor who lags behind its rivals will have an economic loss and be forced

FIGURE 25-10   A Purely Competitive Firm in Long-Run Equilibrium

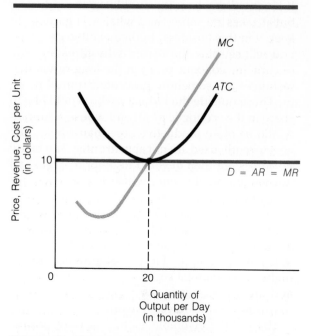

This purely competitive firm is in long-run equilibrium. It faces an infinitely elastic demand curve at a price of $10. Its marginal-cost curve (*MC*) intersects its marginal-revenue curve (*D = AR = MR*) from below at a daily level of output of 20,000 units. This profit-maximizing position earns normal profit for this firm since its average-total-cost curve (*ATC*) is tangent to its average-revenue curve (*D = AR = MR*).

to leave the industry. In other market types, firms that believe it doesn't pay for them to introduce a new product or process right away may be able to sit on it for a while, so that it is the consumer who loses in this case.

The Failings of Pure Competition

By now you are likely to be in favor of pure competition. But before you join the "Pure Competition Movement," it is only fair to point out some failings of this "ideal" market. There are at least three reasons why we might not want all industries to be purely competitive.

First, standardized products may not be what consumers want, and variety may well be worth a somewhat higher price. Imagine that the sweater industry were purely competitive. This would mean that wherever you shopped, you would be offered only a few standardized varieties of sweaters—perhaps only one. You could not choose among different colors, stitches, designs, fiber content, and brand. Would you miss that? Most people would. A much lower price may be enough to make up for a lack of variety, but that requires a value judgment that we can only make for ourselves.

Second, the incentive of economic profit may be necessary to persuade companies to carry on progressive research and development programs. If a purely competitive firm makes an important product discovery, it will not be able to take advantage of it alone very long. Since products are standardized, all the firms in the industry will be able to take advantage of the discovery as soon as it is made. Similarly, if a purely competitive firm makes an important cost-saving process discovery, it will not be able to exploit it for very long. After all, in the long run, only normal profit can be earned. Firms that are aware of these facts will not be willing to risk their money in research and development. Coupled with this lack of incentive is a possible lack of money available for this purpose. Because pure competitors earn only a normal profit, they do not have opportunities to finance research and development from long-run economic profit.

Finally, in many industries a few large firms are able to produce the demanded level of output at lower average total cost (taking advantage of economies of scale) than could many small producers. In many industries there is simply not enough demand in the market to accommodate a large number of firms big enough to take advantage of all the economies of scale that exist. Even if each purely competitive firm produces at the minimum point along its average-total-cost curve, that point may not be the same as the minimum average total cost at which much larger firms are able to produce. For example, suppose that we broke up the existing auto manufacturing firms in the United States into 100,000 separate companies. Each firm becomes a price taker, so that for all practical purposes pure competition is achieved. Each of these 100,000 firms might plan to sell about 100 cars a year. Their production method would probably make use of far more labor and unsophisticated capital than big auto firms actually use. As a result, each firm's minimum average total cost might be, say, $50,000, which in pure competition is also the price that is charged. By contrast, three or four firms can use a mass-production method that captures important economies of scale and can sell cars at around $10,000.

Taken together, these three failings of pure competition help to explain why most economists would not be in favor of having all of our industries conform to the pure competition model.

SUMMARY

1. Economists classify sellers' markets into four different structures or types. These are: (a) pure competition, (b) pure monopoly, (c) monopolistic competition, and (d) oligopoly. The structural criteria used to classify them are the number of sellers, the existence of product differentiation, and the ease of entry. A market's structure affects the behavior of firms, which in turn affects the market's economic performance.

2. The term *competition* may be used in the sense of rivalry or in the sense of the pure competition market type. Pure competition describes a market in which there are so many firms selling a standardized product that each one acts as a price taker. Besides the conditions of many sellers and a standardized product, pure competition requires that no artificial restrictions be placed upon price or quantity and that easy entry and exit are available. Perfect competition requires all of the conditions of pure competition plus complete knowledge and full mobility.

3. The pure competition model describes how the market sets equilibrium price and quantity and then how each typical firm adjusts its output to that market price.

4. The market-demand curve is negatively sloped, but since each firm believes that it is powerless to affect the price, an individual firm's demand curve is infinitely elastic. A firm's total-revenue curve will therefore be a positive linear curve drawn out of the origin. Average revenue is the price per unit and so is just another name for the demand curve. Since a firm does not have to lower its price in order to sell more, its marginal-revenue curve is the same as its demand curve.

5. Since firms maximize their profit when they produce the level of output that equates their marginal cost and marginal revenue, a purely competitive firm's marginal-cost curve, above its average variable cost, is also its short-run supply curve. A short-run market-supply curve is the sum of all the individual firm-supply curves in a market.

6. In the short run, firms in pure competition may experience an economic profit, an economic loss, or a normal profit. In the long run, economic profit invites entry, and economic loss causes firms to exit, so that in the long run all purely competitive firms earn just a normal profit.

7. A purely competitive market's long-run supply curve may reflect constant cost, increasing cost, or decreasing cost. In a constant-cost industry, long-run changes in the level of market output do not affect firms' average total costs, so that long-run prices remain the same. In an increasing-cost industry, long-run increases in the level of market output increase firms' average total costs, so that long-run prices increase. In a decreasing-cost industry, long-run increases in the level of market output decrease firms' average total costs, so that long-run prices decrease.

8. The pure competition model is an abstract idea, and not exactly representative of any real-world industry. However, it provides a norm or yardstick against which actual industries can be compared. Some industries approach this norm. Also the model involves important relationships that are relevant to other market types.

9. Pure competition is often held up as an ideal market situation. Its virtues may be divided into political arguments and economic arguments. Among the political arguments are: (a) that power is decentralized, (b) that the impersonal market forces of supply and demand determine results, and (c) that it provides freedom of opportunity. Among the economic arguments are: (a) that each firm charges a price equal to its marginal cost, (b) that each firm earns normal profit, (c) that each firm produces at the minimum point of its average-total-cost curve, (d) that no resources are wasted on unproductive advertising or promotion, and (e) that firms are pushed to quickly adopt new and better products and new and cost-saving technological processes.

10. Pure competition may not be all that it is cracked up to be. The failings of pure competition are: (a) that consumers are denied variety, (b) that there is a lack of incentive for firms to carry on research and development, and (c) that average total cost may be high because of the firms' inability to take advantage of important economies of scale.

DISCUSSION QUESTIONS

1. Firm X and firm Z sell in the same market. Firm X and firm Z compete with each other for the sale of their products to buyers. From this information alone, can you determine whether or not firms X and Z are pure competitors? Explain.

2. Purely competitive firms are price takers. Carefully explain what it means for a firm to be a price taker. What conditions must be present in order for a firm to be a price taker?

3. In the market structure of pure competition, the market-demand curve is shown as a negatively sloped function. However, each individual purely competitive firm's demand curve appears as a horizontal straight line. Explain this seeming inconsistency.

4. Explain each of the following statements as it pertains to the purely competitive market model:
   a. An individual firm's demand curve is the same as its marginal-revenue curve.
   b. An individual firm's demand curve is the same as its average-revenue curve.
   c. The portion of an individual firm's marginal-cost curve that lies above its average variable cost is the same as its supply curve.

5. In the short run, a purely competitive firm may earn an economic profit, a normal profit, or an economic loss. Without looking back at Figure 25-5, draw a diagram showing each of the three situations below:
   a. a short-run equilibrium for a purely competitive firm that is earning economic profit
   b. a short-run equilibrium for a purely competitive firm that is earning normal profit
   c. a short-run equilibrium for a purely competitive firm that is earning economic loss.
Compare your diagrams with the ones in Figure 25-5 to be sure you have them right. In each of these three cases, what will happen in the long run? (Discuss the process through which the change, if any, will take place.)

6. Why is it that an increase in the market demand for a product produced in a purely competitive industry will sometimes cause the long-run equilibrium price for that product to increase? You may wish to explain this both verbally and by using a diagram.

7. "It is really a waste of time studying pure competition since economists are very hard pressed to find actual industries that conform to all the conditions of the pure competition model." Do you agree? Why or why not?

8. Discuss the arguments for and against using the long-run pure competition equilibrium solution as an ideal to which all of our actual industries should conform.

26 *Monopoly*

PREVIEW One down, three to go. In the last chapter we took a close look at pure competition, the first of the economist's four market structures or types. In this chapter we examine the second one, pure monopoly. Then in the next two chapters we cover the remaining two, monopolistic competition and oligopoly.

As with the term *competition,* economists use the term *monopoly* in various ways. In order to avoid confusion, we begin the chapter by discussing the differences between pure monopoly, actual monopoly, and monopoly control. You will learn why many actual monopolies exist and how they are able to keep their monopoly positions. Some will be described as "natural" monopolies and these may or may not be "government-enforced." Other actual monopolies may be created by government even though they are not natural monopolies. We shall introduce government regulation of monopolies here, but wait until Chapter 34 to explain the reasons behind such regulation and the degree and variety of government regulations.

Pure monopoly, like pure competition, is a useful, yet unrealistic, model. In some important ways, it can be seen as an extreme opposite of pure competition. A pure competition market is made up of a large number of firms, and a pure monopoly market is composed of a single firm. And whereas purely competitive firms are price takers, the pure monopolist is a price maker.

After presenting both short-run and long-run equilibrium positions for a pure monopolist, we evaluate them in light of what we know about pure competition. We then point out the inefficient nature of pure monopoly as compared to pure competition, but add words of caution about the meaning of such conclusions.

Finally, we explain how monopolists may increase their profits by engaging in price discrimination. We look at the requirements for successful price discrimination and evaluate its effects.

PURE MONOPOLY, ACTUAL MONOPOLY, AND MONOPOLY CONTROL

In the last chapter you studied a pure form of competition. Here we begin with a pure type of monopoly and then consider several more realistic forms.

Pure Monopoly

Pure monopoly, like pure competition, is an extreme market type and does not exist in the real world. Pure monopoly describes a market in which there is only a single seller. No acceptable substitutes are available for the product that the pure monopolist offers for sale. It is a market in which there is no competition—now or in the future—because entry into the industry is effectively barred. For this reason, the pure monopolist does not significantly affect other firms by such actions as price changes or advertising campaigns. Similarly, the actions of other firms do not significantly affect the pure monopolist. This substantial amount of isolation and lack of concern about rivals or would-be rivals is what puts the "pure" in pure monopoly.

Actual Monopoly

No firm that we can actually identify—be it the only seller of natural gas in a region, the only seller of bus service in a city, or the only seller of a certain drug in the whole country—is an "island unto itself." Although in all three of these examples we are correct in applying the "monopoly" label, none is an example of a pure monopolist. We choose to call them **actual monopolies.** Each is the only seller in its market. However, sellers in other markets offer more-or-less good substitutes, potential competition cannot be ruled out, and the government protection that some of them enjoy may be taken away or altered.

GOVERNMENT-ENFORCED MONOPOLY   Actual monopolies are often "government-enforced" monopolies. They are common in public utility industries such as natural gas, electric power, telecommunication, and local public transportation. Generally, they are confined to a particular geographic area and regulated by one or more government agencies. Let's return to our example of the only seller of bus service in a certain city. Such a firm most likely has an exclusive franchise to offer bus service in that city, so that it does not face competing bus lines. However, it does face other kinds of competition. There are private cars, bicycles, taxis, and possibly a subway available as substitute transportation. Even walking may offer a practical alternative for covering a short distance. The bus monopolist affects other firms by its actions—for example, a large fare decrease may hurt the taxicab companies. Similarly, actions of other firms affect the seller of bus service. For example, the introduction of beautiful new subway trains may cause people to switch from bus travel to subway travel.

Our example of the natural gas firm that has a monopoly in a certain region may be a somewhat stronger (closer to pure monopoly) case of actual monopoly. Of course, consumers of gas are able to substitute oil, electricity, or even coal, wood,

or solar energy to heat their homes. But if they already own gas furnaces, they might feel compelled to buy gas from the monopolist, at least for a while, even after the price goes up much higher.

In both the bus and natural gas cases, the future position of the firm as a monopoly is not safe. Besides the prospects of lower prices and better service by competing and potentially competing firms in similar markets, the government that granted the exclusive franchise might decide to make it less exclusive or simply take it away. Government-enforced monopolies of this sort are discussed further in Chapter 34.

Another kind of government-enforced actual monopoly arises from the government granting a patent to a firm. A **patent** is a right of temporary limited monopoly over a new product or process granted to its inventor or to a company that purchases the right from the inventor. In the United States a patent is valid for seventeen years. The reason most often put forward for granting them to companies is that it is fair to compensate a firm for the time, effort, and money usually spent in the invention (research and development) process. However, the main reason why most countries have a patent system is to stimulate invention. It is believed to be a strong incentive that encourages firms to risk large sums of money in research.

Earlier we used an example of the only seller of a certain drug in the whole country. Such a monopoly most likely depends on a patent. No other firm may sell that drug until the patent expires. Even during this seventeen-year period, however, the firm is not a pure monopolist. In most such cases, rival companies sell other drugs that have slightly different chemical structures but still offer about the same medicinal value for the illness to be treated. Most likely these rivals also have patents on their drugs, so that competition takes place among several actual monopolists. If, indeed, a drug firm were the only one to hold a patent on a certain kind of drug and if the volume of expected sales and profit were high enough, other companies would try to develop and obtain a patent on an acceptable substitute as quickly as possible. Even if they failed, the actual monopolist's patent, which was probably obtained years before the drug was first offered for sale, would run out before very long.

MONOPOLY WITHOUT GOVERNMENT ENFORCE-MENT Some actual monopolies do not rely on government at all. They may exist simply because it doesn't pay for more than one firm to operate in a certain market or industry. Examples of actual monopolies that exist without government enforcement are found in many small-town service industries. The only obstetrician in a small town is an actual monopolist, as he or she doesn't compete very much with the local general practitioners or with other obstetricians who are some distance away. The same may be said for the only divorce lawyer, the only funeral director, the only commercial real estate broker, and the only fancy restaurant in town. Other firms offering such services are not prevented from entering the market. The license that they might need is not a big problem. The reason why firms do not enter this market is that they believe that it would not pay for them to do so. The small amount of business in the market does not justify starting a second firm. The actual monopoly's fixed cost is in place, and demand is not great enough for it to operate at or near full capacity. Therefore, the marginal cost of providing the service is less than the average total cost. If, instead of one firm, two firms were to compete in such a market, each would find that its marginal cost would be below its average total cost so that it would charge a price below its average total cost. In the long run, after some period of fierce competition resulting in an economic loss, the weaker of the two firms would go out of business. Suppose, for example, that there are two dentists in a small town that offered only enough patients to keep one dentist busy. If each had total cost of $3,000 a week (for an office, equipment, personnel, and the like), each had ten patients a week (average total cost of $300), and each found marginal cost to be $25, the competition for patients might very well drive the price down to just over $25. Even at $30 per patient, each of these dentists suffers an economic loss of $2,700 a week ($30 × 10 = $300, $3,000 − $300 = $2,700). After a while, one of

them will head for greener pastures. The remaining one becomes an actual monopolist.

NATURAL MONOPOLY Some actual monopolies are natural monopolies. These may be government enforced, such as our example of the natural gas firm, or exist without government enforcement, such as our example of the dental monopoly in a small town.

A **natural monopoly** refers to a market in which a single seller is required for efficient production. More than one firm producing in this market would greatly increase average total cost. In such a market, economies of scale—the decrease in long-run average total cost as the level of output is expanded—are so important in relation to demand that only a single firm can take full advantage of them. Natural monopolies usually involve services that are provided to specific geographical markets. Later, in Chapter 34, we shall discuss government regulation of natural monopolies.

Monopoly Control

Monopoly control (or monopoly power) refers to the degree of control or power that a firm has over the price of the product that it sells. Monopoly control does not, as the words unfortunately seem to imply, refer only to monopolists. In fact, all firms, except those in purely competitive industries, have some degree of monopoly control. In pure competition, all firms are price takers, so that each can exert no power over price. (Remember from the last chapter that a purely competitive firm cannot sell any output at a price even slightly above the price set in the market.)

A pure monopolist has more power over price than other types of firms, but this fact does not mean that such a firm faces a perfectly inelastic demand curve. When a pure monopolist raises the price of its product, it will sell less. The higher price causes consumers' real incomes to fall (the income effect) and the quantity demanded of that product to fall. The substitution effect would be very weak since no acceptable substitutes are available for a pure monopolist's product. For example, if a pure monopolist of parachutes raised the price of all parachutes, very few people would find another product to substitute for a parachute.[1]

Actual monopolists have less monopoly control than do pure monopolists. Somewhat better substitutes are available, and there is the threat of other companies entering the market. As you will see, firms that operate in oligopolistic markets have less monopoly control than do monopolists, and those in monopolistic competition have even less. The particular degree of monopoly control varies from industry to industry and from firm to firm.

THE PURE MONOPOLY MODEL

At this point you should have a clear understanding of pure monopoly as a market structure in which a single firm sells a product for which there is no acceptable substitute. We now turn our attention to the pure monopoly model, which will allow us to predict the level of output that such a company would offer and the price that it would charge.

In the pure competition model in the last chapter, we drew separate diagrams for the market and for a typical firm in that market. In pure monopoly only one diagram needs to be drawn, since the firm and the market (industry) are one and the same.

Demand and Marginal Revenue

The pure monopolist faces the demand curve for the whole market. Its negative slope is explained by a normal income effect and a normal (but weak) substitution effect. Consumers can afford to buy more at lower prices and less at higher prices. Changes in relative prices will cause them to make some switches from or to products in

1. This example does not hold for all uses of parachutes. For example, some sports parachutists might switch to another sport. But remember, pure monopoly does not exist in the real world.

FIGURE 26-1   Demand and Revenue for a Pure Monopolist

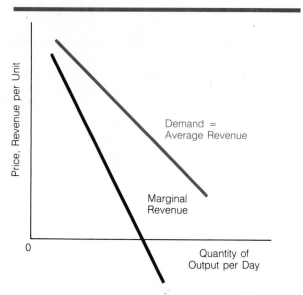

Shown here is a pure monopolist's demand (average-revenue) curve and the accompanying marginal-revenue curve. The marginal-revenue curve lies beneath the demand curve because the monopolist must lower its price in order to sell more, and in most instances, the new lower price must be charged for all units of output to all of the monopolist's customers.

other markets. Figure 26-1 illustrates a pure monopolist's demand curve. As we explained in our discussion of pure competition, the demand curve facing a firm is also its average-revenue curve (the price per unit of output that the firm receives at each different level of output). We have labeled it accordingly.

In Figure 26-1 we have also drawn this pure monopolist's marginal-revenue curve, which shows the addition to its total revenue each time it raises its level of output by one more unit. The relation between the demand (average-revenue) curve and the marginal-revenue curve that we see in Figure 26-1 is very different from the relation between these curves that we saw in the pure competition model. In pure competition a firm's marginal-revenue curve is the same as its demand curve, but in pure monopoly the firm's marginal-revenue curve lies below its demand curve. Here

TABLE 26-1 Derivation of Marginal Revenue in Pure Competition and in Pure Monopoly

(1) Quantity of Output (per day)	Pure Competition					Pure Monopoly				
	(2) Price ($)	(3) Total Revenue ($)	(4) Gain ($)	(5) Loss ($)	(6) Marginal Revenue ($)	(7) Price ($)	(8) Total Revenue ($)	(9) Gain ($)	(10) Loss ($)	(11) Marginal Revenue ($)
3	10	30				10	30			
			10	0	10			9	3	6
4	10	40				9	36			
			10	0	10			8	4	4
5	10	50				8	40			
			10	0	10			7	5	2
6	10	60				7	42			

we can recognize the basic difference between the two market types. In pure competition a firm does not have to lower its price in order to sell a larger quantity of output. But in the case of the pure monopolist—in fact, in any market where an individual firm faces a demand curve that is negatively sloped over the range of the firm's possible output—price must be lowered in order to sell more. In most cases, lowering the price does not mean that the monopolist is able to lower the price of only the last unit to be sold. Usually the firm must lower the price of all the units that it sells. Thus marginal revenue declines, not just because the monopolist must lower its price of the additional (marginal) unit in order to sell it, but also because it must then sell all of its output at this new lower price. In most cases, if the monopolist tried to lower the price of only the additional unit that it wants to sell, all of its potential buyers would be willing to buy only that lower-priced unit. Thus, in order to sell all that it wants to sell, the monopolist charges the new lower price to all of its customers.

As an illustration of this important difference between pure monopoly and pure competition, let us look at the example shown in Table 26-1. Over the range of four different levels of output (column 1), the left side of the table (columns 2–6) provides data for a purely competitive firm and the right side (columns 7–11) for a pure

monopolist. The purely competitive firm is a price taker at the market price of $10, shown in column 2. It can sell any of the levels of output at $10 a unit and does not have to lower its price in order to sell more. Its total revenue (price times quantity) is given in column 3. Column 4 shows its gain from selling an additional unit, which is the $10 price. Nothing is subtracted in column 5 (loss due to price reductions on the previous volume of sales) because the firm does not have to lower its price to make an additional sale. Finally, column 6 shows the firm's marginal revenue. As you already know, this is the change in the firm's total revenue when it sells one more unit. More important for our purpose here, however, marginal revenue is also the firm's gain (column 4) minus its loss (column 5).

Figure 26-2 shows the situation in graphic form. Panel (a) pictures the purely competitive firm's marginal revenue and is keyed to the case in which its level of output changes from 3 to 4 units per day. Its demand curve ($D = AR = MR$) is infinitely elastic at the $10 market price. Its marginal revenue between selling 3 and 4 units is shown as the shaded vertical rectangle ($1 \times \$10 = \$10$).

However, the pure monopolist firm, which faces a negatively sloped demand curve, will have decreasing marginal revenue. In our example in Table 26-1, we again begin with a price of $10, at

FIGURE 26-2   Derivation of Marginal Revenue in Pure Competition and in Pure Monopoly

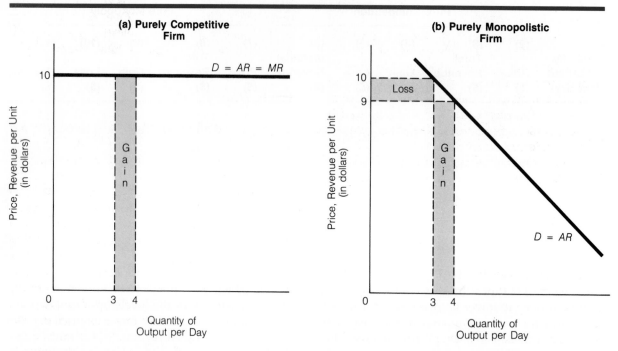

Panel (a) shows a firm in pure competition and panel (b) a firm in pure monopoly. Originally, both sell 3 units of output per day at a price of $10 per unit. Both wish to increase their level of output to 4 units per day. In (a), the firm in pure competition merely produces one more unit and sells it at the $10 market price. Its marginal revenue is the price of $10, which is represented by the shaded vertical rectangle. In (b), the pure monopolist must lower

its price to $9 in order to sell 4 units per day. That gain of $9 is shown as the shaded vertical rectangle. But the monopolist must now sell all of its output at $9 per unit (not just the fourth unit), so that it loses $3, which is shown as the shaded horizontal rectangle. The pure monopolist's marginal revenue is derived by subtracting the horizontal (loss) rectangle from the vertical (gain) rectangle—$6 ($9 − $3 = $6) in this case.

which the firm can sell 3 units. But, as shown in column 7, the monopolist can sell more only by lowering its price. It can sell 4 units at $9 per unit, 5 at $8, and 6 at $7. This causes total revenue (price times quantity, which is shown in column 8) to increase by decreasing amounts. The gain from selling another unit (column 9) is partially offset by the loss (column 10) that results from having to sell the previous quantity of output at a lower price. For example, lowering the price from $10 to $9, so that 4 units can be sold instead of only 3, offers a gain of $9, which is the price received for the fourth unit. But the price decrease also causes a loss of $3, stemming from the $1

lower price received for each of the first 3 units. Marginal revenue (column 11) can then be calculated either by subtracting the previous total revenue from the new one or by subtracting the loss (column 10) from the gain (column 9). Panel (b) of Figure 26-2 pictures the loss and the gain that this pure monopolist experiences when it decreases its price from $10 to $9 in order to increase its sales from 3 to 4 units per day. It gains $9, which is shown by the shaded vertical rectangle (1 × $9 = $9). However, as it must now sell all of its output at $9 per unit, it also loses $3, which is shown by the shaded horizontal rectangle (3 × $1 = $3). The monopolist's marginal revenue is then derived by subtracting the horizontal (loss) rectangle from the vertical (gain) rectangle. In this example, marginal revenue is $6 ($9 − $3 = $6).

Marginal revenue may be positive (as in our example), it may be negative (when the revenue loss exceeds the revenue gain), or it may be zero (when the revenue loss just equals the revenue gain). But in all three cases the marginal revenue is less than the price charged by the monopolist. For this reason, the marginal-revenue curve lies below the demand curve in Figure 26-1. At lower and lower prices, marginal revenue is less and less. Eventually it becomes zero and then negative.

Relationship to Elasticity

In Chapter 22 (see pages 427–428) you learned how the price elasticity of demand affects a company's marginal and total revenue. We showed that when the demand is price elastic, a decrease in the price causes the company's marginal revenue to be positive and its total revenue to go up. The reasoning offered was that the percentage rise in the quantity demanded more than offset the percentage decrease in the price. Also, when demand is price inelastic, a drop in price lowers the company's total revenue and causes its marginal revenue to be negative. This time the percentage rise in the quantity demanded is not enough to offset the percentage decrease in price. Finally, with unitary elastic demand, marginal revenue is zero, and total revenue does not change. The percentage changes in the quantity demanded and in the price are equal but opposite, so that they cancel each other out.

We review these relationships in Figure 26-3. The top part shows a straight-line demand and average-revenue curve and a marginal-revenue curve for a pure monopolist. The bottom part shows the same company's total-revenue curve. (At any level of output, total revenue is found either by adding together all the marginal revenue up to that output or by multiplying the price by the level of output.) Over the range of output from 0 to B, the demand is elastic, the marginal

revenue is positive, and the total revenue rises. At the output level of B, the demand is unitary elastic, the marginal revenue is zero, and the total revenue is at its maximum. Over the range from B to T, the demand is inelastic, the marginal revenue is negative, and the total revenue falls.

Equilibrium Output and Price

In pure competition, the firm is a price taker and simply adjusts its output to the level at which it maximizes its profit. By contrast, in pure monopoly, the firm is a price maker and chooses the combination of output and price that maximizes its profit. The price taker versus the price maker distinction is the key to your understanding of the essential difference between pure competition and pure monopoly. However, the term *price maker*, which implies the possession of full information and the ability to act upon it in every case, should be strictly limited to pure monopoly. Actual monopolists and firms with varying degrees of monopoly control might be better labeled *price searchers*. A **price searcher** is a firm that is able to choose the price for its product, but because it lacks perfect information, it must search for its profit-maximizing price.

In Chapter 24 (see pages 464–470) you learned the logic and techniques used to find the equilibrium output of a firm that faces a negatively sloped demand curve. We showed how a hypothetical yacht firm maximized its profit when it produced the level of output at which its total revenue exceeded its total cost by the greatest amount and at which its marginal revenue equaled its marginal cost. We use the same logic and techniques to find the equilibrium level of output for a pure monopolist. In Figure 26-4, the top part shows a pure monopolist's total-cost and total-revenue curves, and the bottom part shows the corresponding marginal cost and marginal-revenue curves. Profit is maximized when the company produces Q units a day. In this example, Q units a day is the equilibrium level of output. What is the equilibrium price? Logically, it is the highest price that the monopolist will be able to get from buyers for this level of output. How

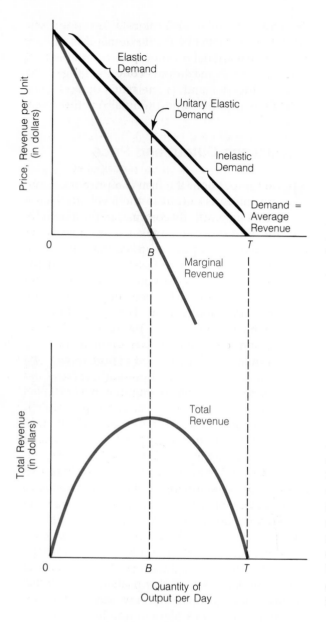

FIGURE 26-3   Elasticity of Demand and Revenue
for a Pure Monopolist

Shown here are three revenue curves for a pure monopolist—average revenue (demand) and marginal revenue in the top panel and total revenue in the bottom panel. The relationship between them and the price elasticity of demand for the product that this monopolist produces can be observed. Over the output range from 0 to B, demand is elastic, marginal revenue is positive, and total revenue increases. At the output level of B, demand is unitary elastic (since this is a straight-line demand curve, it is at the midpoint of the demand curve), marginal revenue is zero, and total revenue is at its peak. Over the output range from B to T, demand is inelastic, marginal revenue is negative, and total revenue decreases.

where the vertical perpendicular drawn from the equilibrium quantity intersects the demand curve and then drawing a horizontal perpendicular from that point of intersection to the price axis.)

Short-Run and Long-Run Profit

A pure monopolist, like any other firm, may have an economic profit, an economic loss, or just a normal profit in the short run. And like any other company, a pure monopolist will shut down if its revenue is not high enough to cover its variable cost in the short run, and it will leave the industry (causing the industry to disappear) if it cannot earn at least a normal profit in the long run. Unlike firms in pure competition, a pure monopolist may, however, earn an economic profit in the long run.

THE SHORT RUN   Figure 26-5 pictures four different short-run profit (or loss) situations for a pure monopolist. Panel (a) presents the case most often associated with pure monopoly. Here the company is earning an economic profit. The equilibrium level of output is Q, since this is where the company's marginal-cost curve (MC) crosses its marginal-revenue curve (MR) from below. The equilibrium price is P, since the vertical perpendicular drawn from Q hits the

much that is will be determined by the demand curve that the monopolist faces. In the bottom part of Figure 26-4 we show this pure monopolist's demand curve. Like any other demand curve, it indicates the maximum price that buyers are willing and able to pay for each different level of output. We see that the monopolist in our example is able to charge a price of P. (This equilibrium price is always determined by finding

FIGURE 26-4   Equilibrium Output and Price for a Pure Monopolist

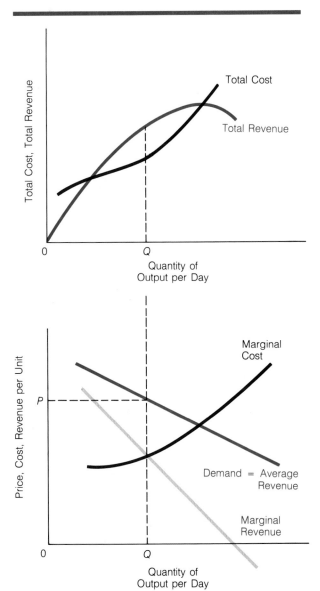

The top panel shows this pure monopolist's equilibrium output at Q. This is where its total revenue exceeds its total cost by the maximum amount. The same equilibrium is observed in the bottom panel. At output Q the monopolist's marginal-cost curve intersects its marginal-revenue curve from below. The firm will charge a price of P, since the demand curve indicates that this is the highest price that consumers are willing to pay for output Q.

demand curve ($D = AR$) at point A. If, as in this case, the price or average revenue exceeds the average total cost for some positive volume of output, the firm earns an economic profit. The amount by which average revenue (point A) exceeds average total cost (point B) is the firm's average (per unit of output) economic profit. Its total economic profit ($AB \times 0Q$) is shown as the shaded rectangle (P-AC-B-A).

Panel (b) shows a pure monopolist that is earning just a normal profit. We show its equilibrium output level of Q and price P. At equilibrium output, the company's average total cost is exactly equal to its average revenue (the average-total-cost curve is tangent to the average-revenue curve at point A), so that no economic profit is earned.

The other two panels show situations that you might not expect. However, even pure monopolists may run into trouble. They may find that they have a monopoly on a product that is quite costly to produce, and the world is not breaking down any doors to get to it. In other words, the equilibrium price for the product is below the average total cost of producing it. Panel (c) shows a monopolist suffering an average (per unit of output) economic loss, represented by the vertical distance from point A to point B and a total economic loss represented by the shaded rectangle P-AC-B-A. This is the very best that this monopolist can do in the short run. It minimizes its economic loss by producing the output level of Q and charging the price of P. Furthermore, it pays for this firm to keep operating rather than to shut down, since at equilibrium its average revenue (point A) is above its average variable cost (point C). If it shut down, its total economic loss would grow by an amount represented by the rectangle VC-P-A-C.

Finally, panel (d) shows the case of a monopolist that finds itself in a situation where it is better to shut down than to operate at all. At the level of output (Q) that equates the firm's marginal cost and marginal revenue, its average variable cost (point C) is greater than its average revenue (point A). The firm minimizes its economic loss by shutting down, so that it will lose only its fixed cost but will avoid the further loss represented by the rectangle P-VC-C-A.

(a) Economic Profit

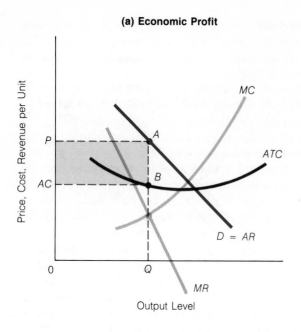

(b) Normal Profit

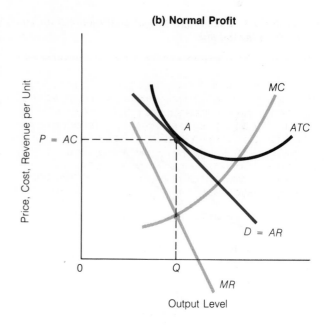

(c) Economic Loss (Operate)

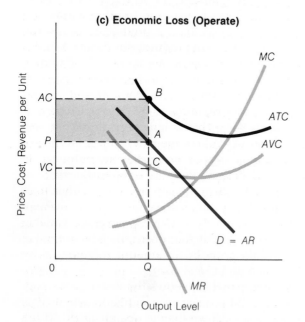

(d) Economic Loss (Shut Down)

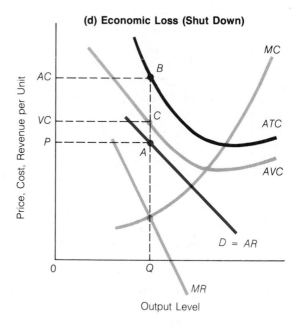

THE LONG RUN   Recall that in the long run all costs are variable. There is enough time to allow firms to make any and all adjustments that they wish to make. Such adjustments could possibly turn things around for a pure monopolist that had been suffering an economic loss in the short run. It might now be able to modernize or change the size of its plant enough to earn at least a normal profit. If that can be done, the firm will remain in the industry. On the other hand, if that cannot be done, the monopolist leaves the industry in search of more profitable ventures.

Monopolists that earned normal or economic profit in the short run may be able to do even

◄ **FIGURE 26-5 Four Alternative Short-Run Profit (or Loss) Situations for a Pure Monopolist**

Shown here are four possible short-run profit or loss situations for a pure monopolist. In each instance the firm's marginal-cost curve intersects its marginal-revenue curve at output Q, and the demand curve that it faces indicates that it should charge a price of P. Panel (a) shows the firm's average revenue above its average total cost at equilibrium, so that it is earning an economic profit, represented by the shaded area. Panel (b) shows the firm's average total cost equal to its average revenue (point A) at equilibrium, so that it is earning just a normal profit. Panel (c) shows the firm's average total cost above its average revenue at equilibrium, so that it is suffering an economic loss, represented by the shaded area. The firm will not want to shut down, because its average revenue (point A) exceeds its average variable cost (point C). Panel (d) shows that both the firm's average total cost and average variable cost exceed its average revenue at equilibrium, so that it will want to shut down and produce nothing.

better in the long run. Long-run adjustments may help a firm that was earning just normal profit in the short run to make an economic profit in the long run. And since the pure monopoly model assumes that firms would rather earn more than less economic profit, a company already earning an economic profit in the short run may improve upon it in the long run.

Notice that the effects of long-run adjustments are very different in the pure monopoly than in the pure competition model. In the pure competition model, short-run economic profit automatically brought new firms into the industry, so that all the pure competitors earned just a normal profit in the long run. In pure monopoly, no other firm can enter the market. Firms in other industries or completely new firms that would love to share in the economic profit enjoyed by the pure monopolist are denied entry. Thus a pure monopolist may earn an economic profit in the long run, now and presumably forever, safe in the knowledge that no one can break its hold on an exclusive and rewarding market.

EVALUATION OF PURE MONOPOLY

Would you like to be a pure monopolist? If you are as greedy as most of us, your honest answer is probably "yes." Would you like to live in a country in which many important markets are monopolized? The consumer in you probably says "no." From the two market-structure models that

you have studied—pure competition and pure monopoly—you have already learned enough to figure out that you would most likely pay higher prices for goods and services bought from monopolists, and so would be able to afford less of them. To help you review what you have learned, Figure 26-6 compares the two long-run equilibrium positions. Since the figure pictures one specific market, it is assumed that the market demand is the same whether the structure of this market is that of pure monopoly or pure competition. We also assume that marginal cost is the same no matter which of these market structures exists. Thus, the demand curve drawn in Figure 26-6 applies to both pure monopoly and pure competition. The positively sloped curve in the figure is both the market-supply curve in pure competition (the sum of the firms' marginal costs) and the marginal-cost curve of the pure monopolist. If the industry were purely competitive, the equilibrium price and the level of market output would be found at the intersection of the market-supply and market-demand curves: Q_{PC} level of output and P_{PC} price. If, instead, the industry were purely monopolistic, the equilibrium level of output would be limited to Q_{PM} and the equilibrium price would be the much higher P_{PM}.

Price, Marginal Cost, and Resource Allocation

It is clear from looking at Figure 26-6 that in pure competition consumers are able to buy products

FIGURE 26-6 Comparison of Long-Run Equilibrium Positions in Pure Competition and Pure Monopoly

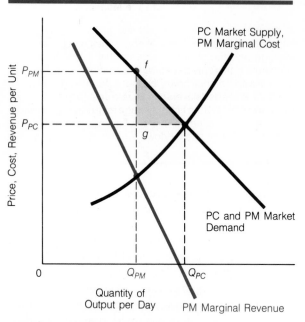

The market-demand curve is assumed to be the same for pure competition and pure monopoly (PC and PM market demand). The market-supply curve in pure competition, which is the sum of the firms' marginal-cost curves, is assumed to be the same as the pure monopolist's marginal cost (PC market supply, PM marginal cost). The equilibrium price and level of market output in pure competition are P_{PC} and Q_{PC}, respectively. The equilibrium level of output in pure monopoly is Q_{PM}, and the price is P_{PM}.

In pure monopoly, as compared with pure competition, consumers who demand the product at prices within the range from just above P_{PC} to just below P_{PM} will be denied the opportunity to buy it. So consumers not only pay a higher price, but must make do with less of the product. This additional welfare loss is shown by the shaded triangle, called the welfare-loss triangle.

---

at a price equal to the seller's marginal cost, but that in pure monopoly they must pay a price that exceeds the seller's marginal cost. This difference in price results from the fact that pure monopolists face negatively sloped demand curves instead of the horizontal ones faced by individual firms in pure competition. What an additional sale is worth to a pure monopolist (its marginal revenue) is less than what it is worth to a consumer (the price or average revenue). But what an additional sale is worth to a pure competitor (its marginal revenue) is equal to what it is worth to a consumer (the price or average revenue).

In pure monopoly, consumers are denied output equal to the difference between Q_{PM} and Q_{PC} in Figure 26-6. Consumers who demand the product at prices within the range from just above P_{PC} to just below P_{PM} will be denied the chance to buy it. So besides having to pay a higher price for the product that they buy, they must make do with less of the product. This additional welfare loss is shown by the shaded triangle in Figure 26-6. This **welfare-loss triangle** represents the amount of economic welfare that is lost to consumers of this product because it is produced and sold by a monopolist instead of by purely competitive firms.

We can restate this point about welfare in terms of resource allocation. The pure competition market structure offers greater welfare to society than does pure monopoly because it allows impersonal market forces to determine the flow of resources. In pure competition, resources are devoted to producing additional units of a product as long as the price that buyers are willing and able to pay for another unit is greater than the additional cost of producing that unit. When price equals marginal cost, the equilibrium level of output is reached. By contrast, pure monopoly limits output and blocks entry to the market, so that fewer resources are devoted to producing the product. Equilibrium takes place at a lower output level and at a price that is greater than the additional cost of producing further units of the product.

Resource Transfer

We can see how monopoly prevents socially desirable resource allocation by examining the change in the value of output that results from a transfer of resources from a purely competitive market to a monopolized one. If, indeed, monopoly keeps resources from flowing to their most desirable social use, then a government action forcing a transfer of resources from a purely competitive market to a pure monopoly market

FIGURE 26-7   Resource Transfer from Pure Competition to Pure Monopoly

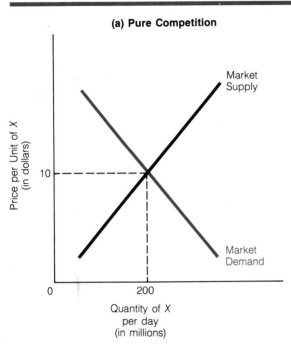

(a) Pure Competition

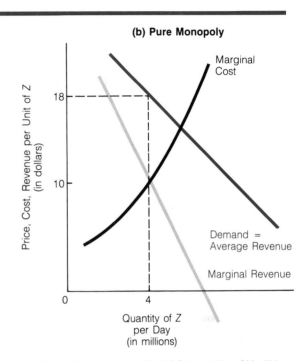

(b) Pure Monopoly

That monopoly prevents socially desirable resource allocation is shown by the results of a transfer of $100 worth of resources from a purely competitive industry (panel a) to a pure monopolist (panel b). At the time of the transfer, both the purely competitive market for X (selling 200 million units of X per day at a price of $10 per unit) and the monopoly market for Z (selling 4 million units of Z per day at a price of $18 per unit) are in long-run equilibrium. Transferring $100 worth of resources from the purely competitive industry means that 10 fewer units of X will be produced (price is equal to marginal cost), thus reducing the value of output by $100. Since the marginal cost of producing Z is also $10, the transfer of the $100 worth of resources to the pure monopolist causes it to produce 10 additional units of Z, valued at $180 (10 × $18 = $180). The forced transfer thus increased the combined value produced by these two industries by $80.

would be expected to result in a higher value of what the two markets produce. A hypothetical example is set forth in Figure 26-7. We picture a purely competitive market that sells product X and a pure monopoly market that sells product Z. They are both in long-run equilibrium. Panel (a) shows that the purely competitive firms in this market have a combined daily level of output of 200 million units of X, each selling at a price of $10. Panel (b) shows a pure monopolist selling 4 million units of Z at a price of $18 each. Now suppose that the government forces a transfer of $100 worth of resources from the industry that

produces X to the industry that produces Z. What effect will this transfer have on the value of output produced by these two industries? Since the marginal cost of producing X is $10 (marginal cost is equal to price in pure competition), 10 fewer units will be produced by the purely competitive industry. The value of output produced by that industry has been reduced by just over $100. (The market-supply curve shifts ever so slightly to the left, so that the equilibrium price rises by an insignificant amount.) The $100 worth of resources are then transferred to the pure monopoly market. The marginal cost of producing

Z is also $10, so that 10 more units of Z can be produced. Since the price of Z is $18, the value of output by this industry is increased by almost $180. (The slightly higher level of output lowers the equilibrium price by an insignificant amount.) The transfer of $100 worth of resources from a purely competitive market to a pure monopoly market caused the combined value of these industries' outputs to increase by almost $80 ($180 gain in value of Z less $100 loss in value of X). Put in national terms, the real gross national product increased by almost $80. In our example, the transfer forced a flow of resources that would not otherwise have happened. If the forcing of resources into pure monopoly markets results in a higher total value of goods and services for society, then we have illustrated our argument that the restriction of output in pure monopoly causes an undesirable allocation of society's resources.

Beyond Resource Allocation

So far our evaluation of pure monopoly has centered on comparing the long-run equilibrium of this model with that of the model for pure competition. We concluded that pure competition offers a more efficient way of allocating resources. But that is not the end of the story. Much was swept under the rug in the process of that limited analysis. Let us focus now on a few of those sweepings. First, we accepted the firms' costs as given by the existing resource prices and the state of technology. However, there is reason to expect that costs will not be alike in these two very different types of markets. Second, we did not look beyond the long run to what we called, in Chapter 23, the very long run. The prospects for progress differ greatly between these two market types. Finally, we did not address the question of equity. The most efficient allocation of resources may not be accompanied by a socially acceptable distribution of income and wealth.

COSTS OF PRODUCTION   In pure monopoly there is no competition. Thus there are no rival firms to push the monopolist to produce at the lowest

possible level of average total cost. Monopolists have been known to pay themselves (the top management) huge salaries, build themselves monuments, and hire friends and relatives for the best jobs. Paying top management more than their opportunity cost, building Taj Mahal-like executive office buildings, and hiring an incompetent son-in-law to be vice-president in charge of useless information does not add up to minimizing cost. This lack of motivational efficiency, often displayed by monopolists, is called **X-inefficiency.** So whether monopolists operate at the minimum point on their average-total-cost curves (and they probably will not) may be less important than whether they are likely to operate on the lowest average-total-cost curve available to them. To the extent that monopolists are X-inefficient— engage in high-cost internal practices—they operate on higher average-total-cost curves than do pure competitors.

An argument that leads to the opposite conclusion is that a monopolist may be more able to take advantage of economies of scale than a pure competitor. In many industries, there is not enough demand to accommodate a large number of firms, each large enough to take advantage of the most important economies of scale.

PROGRESS   Progress in industry refers to the discovery and production of new and better products as well as the discovery and putting to use of new cost-saving technology. In Chapter 23, where we introduced the economist's time-period language, we spoke of such discoveries as coming in the very long run. Should we expect a pure monopolist to be progressive? Would pure monopoly or pure competition be more likely to lower (shift down) the average-total-cost curve in the very long run? We have no clear answers.

On the one hand, as we said in the last section on cost, monopolists are not pushed by competition. Will a monopolist bother to pursue a really effective research and development program? Quite possibly not. Monopolists "have it made in the shade" and may just take a good snooze while collecting their profits. For example, U.S. Steel, which had substantial monopoly control in the American steel industry before the appearance of serious foreign competition, has been accused of such behavior. Whether it was guilty is a matter on which there is no agreement.

On the other hand, although a monopolist is not pushed by competition, it may very well be pushed by good sense and greed. Management may realize that while it has complete control over a product now, in the future some other company may discover a new product that consumers prefer. The monopolist may also realize that it can take advantage of any improvement in the product and any cost-saving gained through technological advances. Because of this incentive and the likelihood that the monopolist has earned an economic profit and so has the money to fund research and development, we have a pretty strong case for expecting substantial progress in monopoly markets. By contrast, recall from Chapter 25 the discussion of progress in pure competition industries. We suggested that because there was little incentive and money available, progressive research and development programs would probably not take place.

EQUITY FOR CONSUMERS Monopolists are not generally thought of in a very kindly way. They are believed to milk consumers for all they can get, and since they have no competitors, they are thought to get plenty. Well-known examples of monopolists are the Rockefellers, the Du Ponts, the Mellons, and other great "robber barons" during the late nineteenth and early twentieth centuries in the United States. Was it fair for them to amass great monopoly fortunes while most Americans had modest incomes? Is monopoly consistent with justice? Many people answer such questions out of both sides of their mouths. "No," they say, John D. Rockefeller's monopolization of the U.S. oil industry in the late nineteenth century was not fair. "Yes," they say, the monopolies based on patents held by Xerox and Polaroid in the 1960s and 1970s were fair since their stockholders came from all walks of life and even included widows and orphans. Immediately we see that value judgments creep in. Not wishing to impose our values on you, what can we objectively conclude about equity? The conclusions must be drawn from the pure competition

and pure monopoly models. No matter whether monopoly profits go into the pockets of robber barons or widows and orphans, sellers have the advantage over buyers. By limiting output and raising price, monopolists can become better off at the expense of consumers. Glancing back at Figure 26-6, which compares the long-run equilibrium solutions of pure competition and pure monopoly, you can see that monopoly not only decreases the welfare of consumers of their product by the shaded amount of the welfare-loss triangle but also transfers welfare from buyers to the monopolist. The concept of consumers' surplus—the amount that consumers are willing to pay for a unit of output in excess of what they have to pay to obtain it—was explained in Chapter 21 (see pages 407–409). The amount of consumers' surplus that would be received by consumers of the product in pure competition, but that is transferred to the seller in pure monopoly, is shown in Figure 26-6 by the rectangle P_{PC}-P_{PM}-f-g, which is formed by the price difference between the two market structures $(P_{PM} - P_{PC})$ multiplied by the amount that is sold by the monopolist (Q_{PM}). This consumers' surplus is denied to them in pure monopoly.

PRICE DISCRIMINATION

Earlier in this chapter we assumed that a pure monopolist will charge the same price to all of its customers. The assumption was based on the reasoning that if a monopolist tried to increase its sales by offering a lower price to some customers, its other customers would not be willing to pay any more than this new lower price. We now relax this assumption and introduce the possibility of price discrimination. When a monopolist finds it possible to practice price discrimination, it is able to improve its profit beyond the amount provided by the usual "marginal cost equals marginal revenue" profit-maximization solution. Before we show how price discrimination is practiced, let us carefully define and set out the requirements for price discrimination.

Price Differentials and Price Discrimination

How many times have you noticed different prices for what appeared to be the same good or service? Most likely your answer runs into the hundreds. One example might be the price of prescription drugs for senior citizens versus the price for the rest of the public. Others are the admission price to musical, theatrical, or sports events for students versus that for the rest of the public, and the airplane, train, or bus fares for children versus the fares for adults. You could also point out the different prices of certain automobiles sold in Detroit and those sold in San Francisco. These, and thousands more, are cases of **price differentials,** but not necessarily price discrimination. A price differential exists whenever a firm follows the practice of selling the same product at the same time to different buyers at different prices. **Price discrimination** takes place only when a price differential is not justified by a difference in cost to the seller. Our prescription drugs, admissions, and transportation fares examples are cases of price discrimination. The drug costs the same to the seller whether it is sold to a twenty-year-old person or to an eighty-year-old person. A student takes up a seat in a theater or a stadium just as a nonstudent does. And children (but not babies) take up an airplane, train, or bus seat as do older people. By contrast, the automobile example turns out to be a case of a price differential, not of price discrimination. To explain why, let us assume that the automobile in our example is produced in Detroit and, when sold to a nearby dealer, is sold for $10,000. But a San Francisco dealer must pay a delivered price of $10,800. If the $800 difference in price simply reflects the difference in transportation cost (say, the cost of shipping an auto within the Detroit area is $100, but shipment to the West Coast is $900), it is not a case of price discrimination. Logically, the definition of price discrimination may be extended to include price equality for the same product sold at the same time to different buyers despite cost differences incurred by the seller. So if the Detroit-based auto manufacturer charges both its Detroit and San Francisco dealers the same delivered price, disregarding the $800 difference in transportation cost, it would be a case of price discrimination.

Prerequisites for Price Discrimination

Price discrimination is possible only if certain conditions or prerequisites are present. These are that: (1) the seller has monopoly control, (2) the seller is able to separate buyers into different markets with different price elasticities of demand, and (3) the seller is able to prevent low-price buyers from reselling the product to high-price buyers.

MONOPOLY CONTROL   In order to practice price discrimination, the seller must either be a monopolist or at least have a substantial amount of monopoly control. In other words, the seller must be able to have some control over price. One group of buyers would be willing to pay a higher price than another group only when they had no reasonable alternative. If they were able to buy a like product at a lower price from a different seller, they would do so, and no price discrimination would take place. Adults would not be willing to pay more than children for a seat on an airplane if they could fly to the same destination on another airline that charged children's prices to people of all ages. But when only one airline flies this route or the airlines that fly this route charge the same discriminating prices, adult passengers face monopoly control and must grin and bear it.

DIFFERENT ELASTICITIES   The second prerequisite for price discrimination is the ability of the monopolist to divide buyers into two or more groups whose demand curves have different price elasticities over a given price range. Recall that the price elasticity of demand (see pages 421–428) refers to the degree of responsiveness of the quantity demanded to a change in price. Buyers who have no good alternatives may respond to a substantial price rise by buying almost as much as before. Buyers who have good substitutes available will purchase far less in reaction to a price hike. An electric power firm, for example, might separate its industrial customers from its residential customers. If the price charged by the power firm were very high, industrial users might decide to generate their own power. Households, however, with no good substitutes available, might be a little more careful about turning off the lights and lowering the thermostat at night, but otherwise they would continue to demand the service.

PREVENTION OF RESALE The final condition necessary for price discrimination is the ability to prevent arbitrage. **Arbitrage** is the purchase of a product in one market for the purpose of immediately reselling it in another market in order to take advantage of a price difference. A price-discriminating monopolist must be able to prevent the customers who buy the product at the lower price from reselling it to those customers who are faced with the higher price. For example, if a shirt manufacturer charges $12 per shirt to one group of retailers and $9 per shirt to another group of retailers, this price discrimination cannot be maintained if those retailers who buy at $9 resell shirts to the other group at less than $12. However, reselling is often prevented by a lack of communication among buyers or because of the nature of the good or service. Services, for example, are almost impossible to resell. How do you resell an appendectomy or a haircut? Also, airlines and movie theaters can quite easily enforce the rule that children are not allowed to resell their tickets to adults. Some goods such as certain fruits and vegetables or daily newspapers are difficult to resell because they are perishable or soon out of date. An extraordinary attempt at maintaining price discrimination is a case where two sellers, Rohm & Haas and Du Pont, sold a plastic molding powder to industrial users for $0.85 per pound and to denture manufacturers for $22.00 per pound. When the industrial buyers began to recognize the chance for arbitrage, Rohm & Haas, in its effort to maintain the profitable

price discrimination, allegedly planted a rumor that the powder sold to industrial users contained a bit of arsenic.[2]

Another example of price discrimination that is generally quite easy to maintain is found in international trade. Firms may sell their products at a lower price to buyers in a foreign country than to buyers in their own country. This international price discrimination is called **dumping.** Firms may choose to engage in dumping because they have excess capacity, yet don't want to lower their prices to all of their customers. Or dumping might be part of a government's trade policy, in which case the sellers would be subsidized in some way. In several cases, Japanese steel firms have been accused of dumping steel products in the U.S. market with help from their government. And it is said that the U.S. government has often dumped farm products in foreign markets.

Profit Improvement Through Price Discrimination

You have learned that a nondiscriminating monopolist will maximize its profit when it produces the level of output at which its marginal-cost curve intersects its marginal-revenue curve from below and when it charges the price indicated by its demand curve at that quantity of output. You will see how a price-discriminating monopolist can do better than that.

Price discrimination calls for a monopolist to separate customers into two or more groups with different price elasticities of demand and, of course, with no chance of reselling the product to each other. Let us imagine that a power company separates its customers into two groups—residential and industrial. Figure 26-8 pictures this case. Panel (a) shows the demand curve and the accompanying marginal-revenue curve facing the firm from its industrial customers. Panel (b) shows the same curves with regard to residential customers. Notice that the demand curve of the

2. G. W. Stocking and M. W. Watkins, *Cartels in Action* (New York: Twentieth Century Fund, 1946), pp. 402–404.

FIGURE 26-8   Price Discrimination Among Industrial and Residential Customers by a Hypothetical Power Company

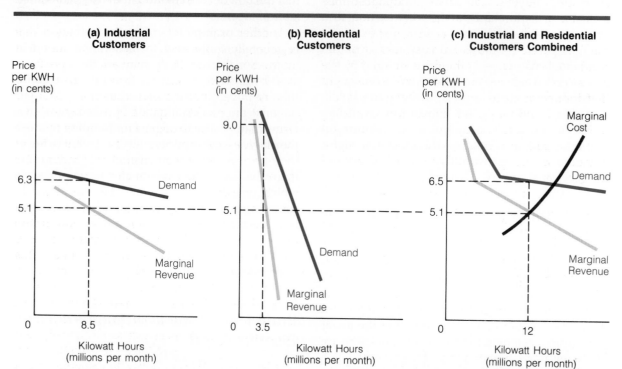

Shown here is the case of a power company that is able to separate its customers into two groups. Panel (a) shows the first group, which is made up of industrial customers, who have relatively elastic demand. Panel (b) pictures the second group, which is made up of residential customers, who have considerably less elastic demand. Panel (c) combines the demand and marginal-revenue curves of the two groups. It also includes the power firm's marginal-cost curve, so that equilibrium output may be determined at 12 million KWHs per month. Were the power firm unable to practice price discrimination, it would charge all its cus-

tomers 6.5 cents per KWH and achieve total revenue of $780,000 (12 million × 6.5 cents). If the firm is able to practice price discrimination, it will allocate its output between the two groups so as to equate their marginal revenues (8.5 million KWHs to industrial customers and 3.5 million KWHs to residential customers). Industrial customers will pay 6.3 cents per KWH, and residential customers will pay 9.0 cents per KWH. The power firm's total revenue increases to $850,500 (8.5 million × 6.3 cents + 3.5 million × 9.0 cents).

residential group is much less elastic (the quantity demanded is less responsive to price changes) than the demand curve of the industrial customers. In panel (c) we have added together the demand and marginal-revenue curves for the two groups. Assuming that the firm incurs no cost differences in serving the two groups, we have drawn a single marginal-cost curve for the combined output for industrial and residential customers. We can now predict how much output—

measured in kilowatt hours (KWHs)—the monopolist will want to produce. Its marginal cost and marginal revenue of a KWH are both 5.1 cents when it produces 12 million KWHs per month.

If the firm were a nondiscriminating monopolist, it would charge all its customers 6.5 cents per KWH and find that its marginal revenue received from industrial customers greatly exceeds its marginal revenue from residential customers.[3] By practicing price discrimination, the company can raise its profit. Output can be allocated between the two groups so that the marginal revenue from each is the same. Industrial customers will therefore be assigned 8.5 million KWHs and residential customers 3.5 million KWHs. Their respective demand curves show that industrial customers are willing to pay 6.3 cents per KWH for the 8.5 million units and that residential customers will pay 9.0 cents for each of the 3.5 million KWHs. As a nondiscriminating monopolist, the firm in this case would receive total revenue of $780,000 per month (12 million × 6.5 cents), but as a price discriminator its total revenue would be $850,500 (8.5 million × 6.3 cents + 3.5 million × 9.0 cents). Since the monopolist's cost is the same in either case, price discrimination improves its profit by $70,500 per month ($850,500 − $780,000).

Evaluation of Price Discrimination

Price discrimination is a controversial subject. It can either promote or reduce consumer welfare.

HARMFUL PRICE DISCRIMINATION The practice of price discrimination reduces consumer welfare by making it possible for monopolists to siphon off consumers' surplus. Price discrimination enables monopolists to "charge what the traffic will bear" so that each buyer or group of buyers will be forced to give up some or all of their consumers' surplus.

Price discrimination can seriously hurt competition by helping to increase the degree of monopoly control held by one or a few firms in

an industry that they already dominate. A large and powerful firm may purchase some of its inputs at prices much lower than those paid by its smaller rivals, if it is able to pressure its suppliers into practicing price discrimination in its favor.[4] The resulting competitive advantage may help such a firm to force its rivals into submission so that it emerges with a still larger share of the market. For example, suppose that in a certain city there are ten retail stores that sell garden tractors. Further, suppose that one of these retailers sells about half of the tractors, far more than any other single store in town. This retailer might try to use its relative success to gain a price advantage from each of the several manufacturing firms that sell the tractors to the retailers. Each tractor producer might agree to practice price discrimination in order to keep this large retailer's business. Such price discrimination would allow the large retailer to gain an even larger share of the market, since it could afford to undercut its competitors' prices. Of course, the benefit to consumers would be short-lived if competing retailers were forced to leave the market. Quite possibly the retailer that benefited from the tractor manufacturers' price discrimination would become a monopolist, free to raise the price substantially above competitive levels.

Price discrimination may also be harmful when it eliminates socially desirable price competition. An industry agreement calling for each firm, no matter where it is located, to charge the same price for delivered goods is a form of pricing that discriminates against buyers who receive goods from nearby suppliers. This kind of price discrimination is known as a **basing-point system.** Probably the most famous case of basing-point pricing is the "Pittsburgh Plus" system used by the American steel industry from 1900 to 1924. It ensured that the same prices would be charged for all steel mill products to all buyers. When a steel mill far away from Pittsburgh sold steel products to a buyer in its home town, it would charge a standard mill price plus the freight charges for shipping steel from the Pittsburgh

3. In order not to complicate the main points in Figure 26-8, we have not shown the marginal revenues from the industrial customers versus the residential customers that the power firm would receive if it were not practicing price discrimination. To see that marginal revenue from the industrial customers would be much higher than from the residential customers, just extend the horizontal perpendicular drawn at 6.5 cents to the left. Where it intersects each group's demand curve, draw a vertical perpendicular down to that group's marginal-revenue curve. That will enable you to read off marginal revenue of 5.6 cents for industrial customers and 0.2 cents for residential customers.

4. In Part IX of the book we shall refer to such power or control by a firm on the buying side as "monopsonistic."

area. Such a freight charge was made even though the product was not actually shipped over that distance. In the case where a steel producer based outside Pittsburgh shipped steel to a customer based in the Pittsburgh area, the seller had to absorb the freight charges. Whether a producer charged artificial freight costs or absorbed real freight costs, the result was always the same—the same delivered price in any particular area.

BENEFICIAL PRICE DISCRIMINATION Price discrimination may also offer some benefits for society. Few people are upset when doctors or lawyers charge lower fees to poor persons than to higher-income people. Prohibiting this sort of price discrimination might very possibly raise prices for the poor (often meaning that the service will not be rendered at all) without reducing prices very much for those with higher incomes.

Price discrimination may also lead to greater consumer welfare when it is practiced in an experimental and independent way. When price discrimination is used to experiment with lower prices and to compete more forcefully with rivals, the consumer may emerge as the winner. In an industry where a few firms have substantial monopoly control and charge the same price for a product, price concessions by one of these firms to a few customers may be just what is needed to stir things up. Other firms may then meet or even undercut the lower price, and before long the new competitive climate may have lowered the price to all customers.

SUMMARY

1. Pure monopoly is an extreme market type in which there is only a single seller. No acceptable substitutes are available, and entry into the market is barred. The pure monopolist and the industry are one and the same.

2. Actual monopoly is a real-world form of monopoly. An actual monopolist is the only seller in its market, yet it competes with rivals in other markets, recognizes potential competition, and may be subject to government regulation.

3. Actual monopolies may or may not be "government-enforced." Government-enforced monopolies may be firms that have received an exclusive franchise from the government or that have been granted a government patent. Actual monopolies may or may not be "natural monopolies." Natural monopolies are those that owe their monopoly status to the particular cost conditions in their industries. Economies of scale are so important in relation to demand in such markets that only a single firm can take full advantage of them.

4. Monopoly control refers to the degree of control or power that a firm possesses over the price of the product that it sells. All firms except those that are in purely competitive industries possess some degree of monopoly control.

5. A pure monopolist is expected to face a negatively sloped demand curve. Its marginal-revenue curve slopes beneath its demand curve because price must be lowered in order to sell more and because the new lower price must be charged for all units of output to all of the monopolist's customers.

6. When demand is elastic, marginal revenue is positive, and total revenue is rising. When demand is unitary elastic, marginal revenue is zero, and total revenue is at its maximum. When demand is inelastic, marginal revenue is negative, and total revenue is falling.

7. A pure monopolist will maximize its profit at the level of output at which its total revenue exceeds its total cost by the maximum amount, which is also where its marginal cost and marginal revenue are equated. The price it will charge is determined by the demand curve that it faces.

8. In the short run, a pure monopolist may experience an economic profit, just a normal profit, or an economic loss. If its revenue is not enough to cover its variable cost, it will shut down. In the long run, a pure monopolist may experience an economic profit or just a normal profit.

9. Given a certain market demand for a product and a certain cost to produce it, pure monopoly as compared with pure competition offers its consumers less output at higher prices. Purely competitive firms offer consumers greater welfare

than does pure monopoly since the purely competitive firm charges a price that is equal to marginal cost, whereas the monopolist charges a price in excess of marginal cost.

10. More efficient resource allocation is provided by purely competitive firms as compared with pure monopoly. This fact is demonstrated by forcing a transfer of resources from a purely competitive industry in long-run equilibrium to a pure monopoly market also in long-run equilibrium. Because price is equal to marginal cost in pure competition and price is higher than marginal cost in pure monopoly, a given dollar value of resource transfer will increase the combined value of output produced by the two industries.

11. Pure monopolists may operate on higher average-total-cost curves than do their counterparts in pure competition because they are not pushed by competitors to produce at the lowest cost possible. However, a monopolist may produce at lower average total cost than its counterparts in pure competition because it is large enough to capture economies of scale not available to smaller pure competitors.

12. Through effective research and development, the average-total-cost curve may be shifted downward in the very long run. There is no clear answer as to whether or not monopoly will foster such progressive actions. On the one hand, a monopolist is not pushed by competitors and may simply not bother, but on the other hand, monopolists have the incentive of long-run economic profit and probably the money to carry out research.

13. Pure monopoly may or may not be consistent with equity. Monopolies owned largely by a few individuals or families promote an unequal distribution of income and wealth. But when the stock of monopolies is widely held and includes large numbers of widows and orphans, they cannot be condemned on the basis of equity.

14. When a firm sells the same product at the same time to different customers at different prices, there is a price differential. Price discrimination takes place when a price differential is not justified by a difference in cost to the seller. In order to practice price discrimination, the seller must possess monopoly control, must be able to

separate buyers into different markets with different price elasticities of demand, and must be able to prevent low-price buyers from reselling the product to high-price buyers.

15. By practicing price discrimination, a monopolist may be able to improve its profit position. It may be able to earn more profit than it would if it were simply equating its marginal cost and marginal revenue and charging a single price determined by its demand curve.

16. The practice of price discrimination sometimes is detrimental to society's welfare and at other times is quite beneficial. Price discrimination may serve as a vehicle for an already powerful firm to gain even greater monopoly control and may also be used as a way to eliminate price competition in markets where such competition is socially desirable. On the other hand, price discrimination may be used to provide greater equity and also to lessen monopoly control.

DISCUSSION QUESTIONS

1. Carefully distinguish between pure monopoly and actual monopoly. Why is your local telephone company not a good example of a pure monopolist?

2. Actual monopolies may or may not be government enforced. Those that are government enforced may or may not be natural monopolies. Explain these two statements by carefully defining each of the four situations and providing an example for each.

3. "Only monopolists possess monopoly control." True or false? Explain.

4. A purely competitive firm's demand curve is equal to its marginal-revenue curve. Carefully explain why this is not the case for a pure monopolist's demand curve. What is the relationship between a pure monopolist's average revenue and marginal revenue?

5. Explain the relationship between the total-revenue, average-revenue, and marginal-revenue curves for a monopolist. Why is price elasticity of demand unitary when marginal revenue is zero?

6. Without looking at Figure 26-5, draw a diagram showing a pure monopolist earning an economic profit in the short run. Compare your diagram with panel (a) in Figure 26-5 to be sure you have it right. What long-run adjustments do you expect?

7. An outstanding difference between the long-run equilibrium conditions for pure competition and pure monopoly is that in pure competition price is equal to marginal cost, whereas in pure monopoly price is greater than marginal cost. What is the explanation for this difference? What important welfare implication can be drawn from this difference?

8. Make a case for each of the following:

a. X-inefficiency is more likely to occur in a monopoly structure than in other market structures.

b. The opportunity for taking advantage of existing economies of scale is more likely in monopoly than in other market structures.

c. Progress stemming from research and development is less likely to occur in a monopoly market structure than in other market structures.

d. A monopolist is likely to conduct more research and development than a pure competitor.

e. Monopolists take unfair advantage of consumers.

9. Distinguish between a price differential and price discrimination. Give an example of a price differential that is not price discrimination. In your example, what change would have to occur to make it price discrimination?

10. From the point of view of the seller, carefully explain the preconditions that are necessary in an industry before price discrimination can be successful.

11. A monopolist that sells its output to customers in different markets may find that charging the same price to all of its customers in all of the different markets results in a much higher marginal revenue from sales to some markets than to others. Given that this monopolist is able to practice price discrimination, will price discrimination enable it to increase its profit? Why or why not?

12. Price discrimination may be used to eliminate price competition among the firms in an industry. Explain how a basing-point system may accomplish this end.

27 *Monopolistic Competition and Oligopoly*

PREVIEW   In Chapter 25, when we began our study of sellers' market structures, we introduced four different types—pure competition, pure monopoly, monopolistic competition, and oligopoly. So far we have explained the first two. That leaves monopolistic competition and oligopoly yet to be covered.

The first part of this chapter deals with monopolistic competition. After defining its meaning, we discuss its origins and explain its major characteristics. Monopolistic competitors vie with one another on both price and nonprice bases. That gives us the chance to discuss the role of advertising in competition and to explain some of its advantages and disadvantages for society. We then introduce the monopolistic competition model and, as we did with pure competition and pure monopoly, we carefully examine the short-run and long-run equilibria. That leads us to an evaluation of this market structure, both on its own and as compared with pure competition and pure monopoly. Here we point out certain important similarities and differences among these market types.

The second part of this chapter deals with oligopoly. We define oligopoly and explain its most important characteristic—interdependence. You will see that, of the four market structures, oligopoly comes the closest to industries as we know them.

Of the four market models, however, oligopoly turns out to be the most complicated and hardest to understand. We shall explain why we are not able to determine short-run and long-run equilibria *in the same way* that we did for the other three market types. But we shall not leave you high and dry. You will learn about several oligopoly theories that predict certain price and level-of-output equilibria. These are based on such ideas as reaction, the kinked demand curve, game theory, collusive agreements, price leadership, and rules of thumb. Finally, we shall evaluate oligopoly and compare it with the other market types.

MONOPOLISTIC COMPETITION

The models for pure competition and pure monopoly market structures date back almost one hundred years. Alfred Marshall explained them in his *Principles of Economics,* published in 1890. For the next forty years, these were the only models that economists could use to analyze firm and industry behavior. In the early 1930s, however, two economists, Joan Robinson of Cambridge University in England and Edward Chamberlin of Harvard University in the United States, introduced a third market model. They worked independently, but published their results at about the same time. Their model of market organization is what we refer to as monopolistic competition.

Robinson and Chamberlin were disturbed about the separation of the ideas of competition and monopoly and suggested that the two be blended. They pointed out that nonidentical sellers offer nonidentical products, so that every seller is really a monopolist of its own good or service. Yet they understood that these monopolists compete against each other in certain fairly distinct markets or industries. Their logical conclusion was that most firms are really competing monopolists operating in a type of market that may be called **monopolistic competition**.[1]

Conditions for Monopolistic Competition

A monopolistically competitive market requires: (1) a large number of independent sellers, (2) product differentiation, and (3) fairly easy entry and exit. We shall take a look at each of these conditions next.

LARGE NUMBER OF SELLERS The condition of a large number of sellers may remind you of our "many sellers" condition in pure competition. However, it turns out to be not quite so extreme. You learned that pure competition required so many firms that each one believed it could not affect the price. Monopolistic competition requires only a large enough number of firms so that each one believes that the other firms in the market will ignore its actions. Each independently operated firm in the industry must have a small enough market share so that it believes its actions will bring no reactions from competitors. For example, suppose there is an industry made up of 100 firms, each selling 1,000 units of output per day. Now, if one of these firms decides to lower its price by 10 percent, so that its sales rise by, say, 20 percent (assuming price elasticity of demand of 2), this firm would take away only 200 units of sales from its 99 competitors, or about 2 from each. Since this firm believes that each of its rivals' sales will drop only from 1,000 to 998 (a rather small percentage), it will expect its rivals hardly to notice it and not to react at all.

PRODUCT DIFFERENTIATION The condition of product differentiation is the most important distinction between monopolistic competition and pure competition. **Product differentiation** means

that basically similar products are changed in some way to create some differences among them in the eyes of consumers. Recall that in pure competition there is no product differentiation. In pure competition the product is completely standardized, and consumers couldn't care less whether they buy from one firm or another in the same industry. Of course, product differentiation is also inconsistent with pure monopoly. In that market structure, consumers find no acceptable substitute for what the monopolist sells.

The term "product differentiation" covers a lot of ground. In the words of Edward Chamberlin, "it may be real or fancied." It does not matter which, as long as the difference is important to buyers and therefore influences consumer preference. For example, identical peaches that come from the same orchard and are processed in the same way are seen as different products when some are canned under the label of one firm and others carry a different firm's brand name. Some consumers are willing to pay a few cents more per can for Del Monte brand peaches, and other consumers are willing to pay more for the Libby brand.

In other cases, the product differentiation may take the form of a minor technical product difference, such as embossed versus clear plastic wrap or swivel versus stationary two-track razors. Or it may go beyond the basic character of the product and include such features as packaging, color, and size. The location of the firm may be crucial as well. The grocery store around the corner is able to sell at somewhat higher prices than the supermarket in a shopping center several miles away. Finally, certain characteristics of the seller rather than of the product itself may play a major role in product differentiation. The reputation of a certain company in terms of its outstanding efficiency, courteousness, or trustworthiness differentiate it from other companies that are not held in as high regard by consumers. Monopolistic competition recognizes that all of these characteristics are "purchased" when a customer buys the product.

FAIRLY EASY ENTRY AND EXIT The final condition required for monopolistic competition is that

---

1. Actually, the term *monopolistic competition* is Chamberlin's. His book is titled *The Theory of Monopolistic Competition,* and Robinson's book is *The Theory of Imperfect Competition.* Both were published in October 1932.

firms outside the industry find it fairly easy to enter and that firms established in the industry find it fairly easy to exit. Entry and exit are not free, as they are in pure competition. The presence of product differentiation means that new firms would not be likely to gain immediately the level of consumer acceptance attained by long-established firms. But no great barriers exist, since new firms need to add only a small percentage of the industry's level of output. Likewise, exit is somewhat more costly than in pure competition. When a monopolistically competitive firm leaves its industry, it loses the consumer acceptance that it had managed to build up.

Real-World Markets?

Some actual markets come close to being monopolistically competitive. Retail markets in fairly large cities, such as gas stations in Milwaukee, men's clothing stores in Boston, and Chinese restaurants in San Francisco, are reasonably good examples. Each of these markets is made up of a fairly large number of firms that sell products that are somewhat differentiated from each other. But while each of the many firms has a small share of the total market, they do not completely ignore each other. Generally, the owner or the manager of a gas station does keep an eye on the price charged at other gas stations in the neighborhood, the clothing store operator makes it his or her business to know other retailers' prices for certain items, and restaurant owners or managers are aware of the menus (including prices) of at least some of their major competitors. To the extent that firms do look over their shoulders to see what competitors are doing, the important characteristic of independent action is missing, and the industry only approaches the monopolistic competition market structure.

Advertising

Advertising plays a part in the product differentiation condition of monopolistic competition. However, it is a controversial area in economics.

Among the major arguments are those concerning: (1) the effect of advertising on economic freedom, (2) the effect of advertising on the efficiency of providing information to consumers, (3) the effect of advertising on competition, and (4) the effect of advertising on the cost of production.

ADVERTISING AND ECONOMIC FREEDOM   Advertising is said to be a hallmark of a free-enterprise economy. Free-enterprise capitalism depends on the ability of firms and individuals to engage in any business that they wish and to tell people that they are ready, willing, and able to provide the good or service that they seek to sell. The most common means of doing so are to use billboards and a sign above the place of business, radio and television commercials, and advertisements in newspapers and magazines. What is so controversial about doing these things? Why is there a question of economic freedom? Who would deny business people the "right" to communicate their message? A number of people would.

There are many complaints about the nuisance caused by a great deal of advertising—heavy magazines and newspapers in which there is little to read, ugly billboards along roads, and commercials interrupting one's favorite television and radio programs. There are also attacks on serious philosophical and economic grounds. It is argued that advertising threatens "consumer sovereignty"—that what consumers want should dictate what business firms produce, and not the other way around. A great deal has been written about how business firms use psychology, prey on the consumer's subconscious mind, and in other ways persuade people to buy products that they really didn't want in the first place.

Vance Packard, a popular writer in the 1950s, recognized this threat to consumer sovereignty. In *The Hidden Persuaders*, Packard writes about the motivation research that goes into preparing many advertising campaigns. He quotes the head of a major Chicago research firm, who explains that "motivation research is the type of research that seeks to learn what motivates people in making choices. It employs techniques designed to reach the unconscious or subconscious mind because preferences generally are determined by factors of which the individual is not conscious. . . . Actually in the buying situation the consumer generally acts emotionally and compulsively, unconsciously reacting to the images and designs which in the subconscious are associated with the product."[2] Packard argues that to be successful in selling a product, business firms sell "emotional security," "reassurance of worth," "ego gratification," "creative outlets," "love objects," "sense of power," "sense of roots," and "immortality."[3]

Since most advertising is done by private business firms, a companion argument is that advertising causes too large a percentage of a country's resources to be used for producing private rather than public goods and services. The hidden persuaders force an extra car into your garage rather than good streets to drive your fast car on and a nice park to drive it to.

ADVERTISING AND INFORMATION   Advertising is said to provide useful information to consumers. Consumers cannot possibly know everything there is to know about every product at every moment in time. At which grocery store can you get the best buy on frozen pizza today? Where can you get the best deal on a bicycle? And how can you best satisfy your sweet tooth today? Firms recognize that, by providing information, they can attract more sales. Telling people about the characteristics of products, their prices, and where to buy them often translates into sales. The A&P Company reasons that if consumers know that the company is offering Whamo Italian pepperoni fourteen-inch pizzas at $2.87 today, they will jam the aisles to buy them. Likewise, the Brach Candy Company believes that if consumers see a picture of their delicious-looking chocolate kisses, they will recognize their ability to satisfy the craving that they have for sweets. Their view is that advertising provides mutual benefits—consumers receive information, and business firms make sales. In fact, proponents of advertising go even one step further. They argue that advertising is

a very efficient way of providing information because once consumers "learn" that the best buys are at A&P or that Brach candies are delicious, the store or brand loyalty built up through advertising saves them the trouble of searching for better products in the future.

But to what degree is advertising actually informational? Critics of advertising see little information given in the soft drink ad that pictures a beautiful woman and a handsome man enjoying a certain brand of soft drink together at the beach, or the many cigarette, beer, and automobile ads that carry no message other than "Buy mine, it's best." Such advertisements are largely self-canceling, leaving consumers no better informed than they were in the first place.

Advertising uses scarce resources. Almost 3 percent of U.S. national income (about $90 billion) is devoted to advertising. Are consumers getting $90 billion worth of information? As we have indicated, some advertisements provide little information and are clearly wasteful. But it would be foolish to condemn advertising in general. Just leaf through a trade magazine and read the ads for industrial products. They are usually chock-full of details about the product, how it can be used, and other useful information.

ADVERTISING AND COMPETITION   Advertising is at the heart of what economists call nonprice competition. Along with price competition, it is a means by which firms compete with each other. Does it follow, then, that advertising causes an industry to be more competitive? The answer is "no." In fact, successful advertising accomplishes the opposite. Besides trying to shift customers' demand curves for their products to the right (to sell more at any particular price), firms also advertise in order to make their demand curves less elastic. Firms hope to gain greater control over price by making their competitors' products appear to be poorer substitutes. For example, suppose that a firm faced the flatter (more elastic) demand-curve segment shown in Figure 27-1 and that at equilibrium it sold 40,000 units per day at a price of $7 per unit. The firm does not advertise and has relatively little control over price. It is not a pure competitor that has no control over its price, but at somewhat higher prices it will

2. Vance Packard, *The Hidden Persuaders* (New York: Pocket Books, 1957), p. 5.

3. Ibid., pp. 61–70.

lose a lot of its sales. Its demand curve before advertising indicates that if it decided to raise its price to $9, its sales would drop by half to 20,000 units a day. Now suppose, instead, that the company did advertise so that its demand curve for prices above $7 is much steeper (less elastic). The advertising has the effect of making rivals' products appear to be poorer substitutes. Many customers are now so convinced that this product is better that they are willing to keep on buying it in spite of a somewhat higher price. If the firm is again at equilibrium when it sells 40,000 units at $7 each, the same $2 rise in price to $9 will cause its level of sales to drop by only 10,000 units to 30,000. Advertising has made poorer substitutes of its competitors' products, allowing it to gain monopoly control.

Another way in which advertising has an impact on competition in an industry is through its influence on entry by new firms. Successful advertising by established firms in an industry may create an important entry barrier. If established firms have gained great consumer acceptance through advertising—making their brand names household words—a new company with an unknown name may find it very hard to compete effectively. For example, we find few companies interested in entering the toothpaste, detergent, or beer industries, perhaps because of the large amount of consumer acceptance that firms in those industries have gained through their advertising. Some economists are so concerned about the lack of interest in entering such industries that they favor a complete ban on advertising. But would that work? Perhaps it would just solidify the monopoly control of the established firms. It would mean that no new company could enter and communicate with consumers. The few companies that successfully enter industries in which consumers are brand conscious are those that enter with a very large dose of advertising. This allows them to gain consumer acceptance and some respectable market share. If advertising were banned in such industries, almost no possibility of entering would exist, and that important aspect of competition would disappear.

ADVERTISING AND PRODUCTION COST Another controversy about advertising centers on whether

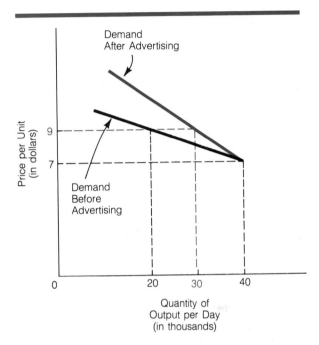

FIGURE 27-1 **The Effect of Advertising on the Elasticity of Demand**

The flatter demand-curve segment (labeled "demand before advertising") belongs to a firm that sells 40,000 units per day at $7 per unit without doing any advertising. At the higher price of $9, it would lose half of its sales. The steeper demand-curve segment (labeled "demand after advertising") belongs to the same firm after it has made its competitors' products appear to be poorer substitutes through advertising. At the higher price of $9, it would now lose only a quarter of its sales.

advertising raises or lowers the cost of producing goods and services and, in turn, the prices paid by consumers. We have already pointed out that advertising uses resources; so of course advertising costs are part of the total cost that firms spend on production. But, it is argued, advertising shifts demand curves to the right. Since many firms operate on the negatively sloping part of their long-run average-total-cost curves, economies of scale that result from advertising more than compensate for the advertising costs. It is impossible to generalize on this important point. Advertising may or may not shift a product's demand curve to the right. If it does, it may shift it a little or a great deal. In industries where advertising is

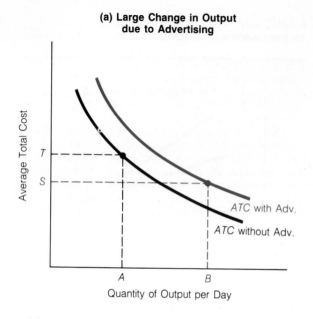

(a) Large Change in Output
due to Advertising

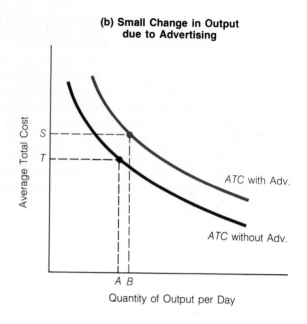

(b) Small Change in Output
due to Advertising

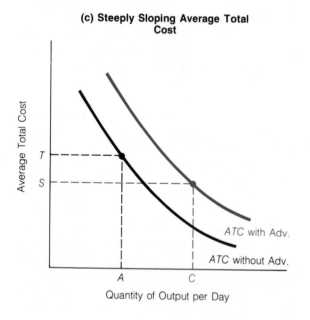

(c) Steeply Sloping Average Total
Cost

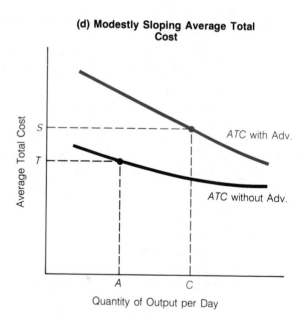

(d) Modestly Sloping Average Total
Cost

largely self-canceling, firms' demand curves may not shift at all. Companies may advertise only for defensive reasons. They recognize that if demand for one product rises, it may be at the expense of a competitor's product. Individual firms may be trying to keep their demand curves from shifting to the left. Also, firms may or may not be operating on the negatively sloping part

of their long-run average-total-cost curves. If they are on the decreasing part, the curve may be sloping either steeply or very gradually.

Figure 27-2 pictures four different cases. In panels (a) and (b), the long-run average-total-cost curves (both with and without advertising cost included) are the same. However, the change in sales (output) due to advertising (the horizontal

◄ **FIGURE 27-2**   **Four Alternative Effects of Advertising on Long-Run Average Total Cost**

Each of the four diagrams shows two long-run average-total-cost curves, one without advertising and one with advertising. Since advertising uses resources, the latter is always above the former. In all four diagrams, the horizontal distance (A to B or A to C) measures the demand response to advertising and the vertical distance (T to S) the change in average total cost that results from the combination of the demand response to advertising and the economies of scale. Economies of scale are illustrated by the slope of the average-total-cost curves.

In panels (a) and (b), the slopes of the cost curves are the same, but the demand response to advertising is much greater in panel (a). In that case, the distance between A

and B is so great that the economies of scale outweigh the advertising costs, providing the firm with lower average total cost (T to S). Panel (b) shows that the advertising cost outweighs the economies of scale, resulting in higher average total cost for the firm (T to S).

In panels (c) and (d), the demand response to advertising is the same (A to C), but the slope of the cost curves is much greater in panel (c). In that case, the economies of scale outweigh the advertising costs, providing the firm with lower average total cost (T to S). Panel (d) shows that the advertising cost outweighs the economies of scale, resulting in higher average total cost for the firm (T to S).

---

distance between quantity A and quantity B) is much greater in panel (a) than in panel (b). In panel (a), the sales (output) response is so great that average total cost with advertising is lower than average total cost without advertising (S is below T). In panel (b), the sales (output) response to advertising is so small that average total cost with advertising is higher than average total cost without advertising (S is above T).

In panels (c) and (d) of Figure 27-2, the sales (output) responses to advertising (the horizontal distance between quantity A and C) are the same. However, the slopes of the long-run average-total-cost curves (with and without advertising cost included) are much steeper in panel (c) than in panel (d). In panel (c), average total cost falls so quickly as output rises (economies of scale are great) that average total cost with advertising is lower than average total cost without advertising (S is below T). In panel (d), the decline in average total cost that goes with increases in the level of output is much less (economies of scale are relatively small). As a result, average total cost with advertising is greater than average total cost without advertising (S is above T).

The Monopolistic Competition Model

We are now ready to explain the monopolistic competition model. In some respects it is like the pure competition model. Economic profit, eco-

nomic loss, or normal profit may be earned by monopolistically competitive firms in the short run. In the long run, entry or exit plays a major role to ensure that each firm earns only normal profit. An important difference between monopolistic competition and pure competition is that monopolistically competitive firms may be making changes in their advertising expenditures, which affect their costs.

SHORT-RUN PRICING AND OUTPUT   Figure 27-3 pictures three alternative short-run equilibrium profit positions for a typical firm in monopolistic competition. Notice that the demand or average-revenue curve (D = AR) in each of the diagrams has a negative slope. This slope shows that even though the companies have many competitors that sell fairly close substitutes, each firm has some control over price—that is, some monopoly control. It means that a monopolistically competitive firm will not lose all of its customers when it raises price a bit, and that in order to sell a higher level of output, it must lower its price. Lying below each demand curve is the firm's marginal-revenue curve (MR). As we said in the discussion of pure monopoly (see pages 508–511), the marginal-revenue curve always lies below a negatively sloped demand curve. Also pictured in each of the three diagrams is this typical firm's average-total-cost curve (ATC) and marginal-cost curve (MC). These curves are drawn in the usual way, with the marginal-cost curve

FIGURE 27-3   Three Alternative Short-Run Equilibrium Profit or Loss Positions for a Typical Firm in Monopolistic Competition

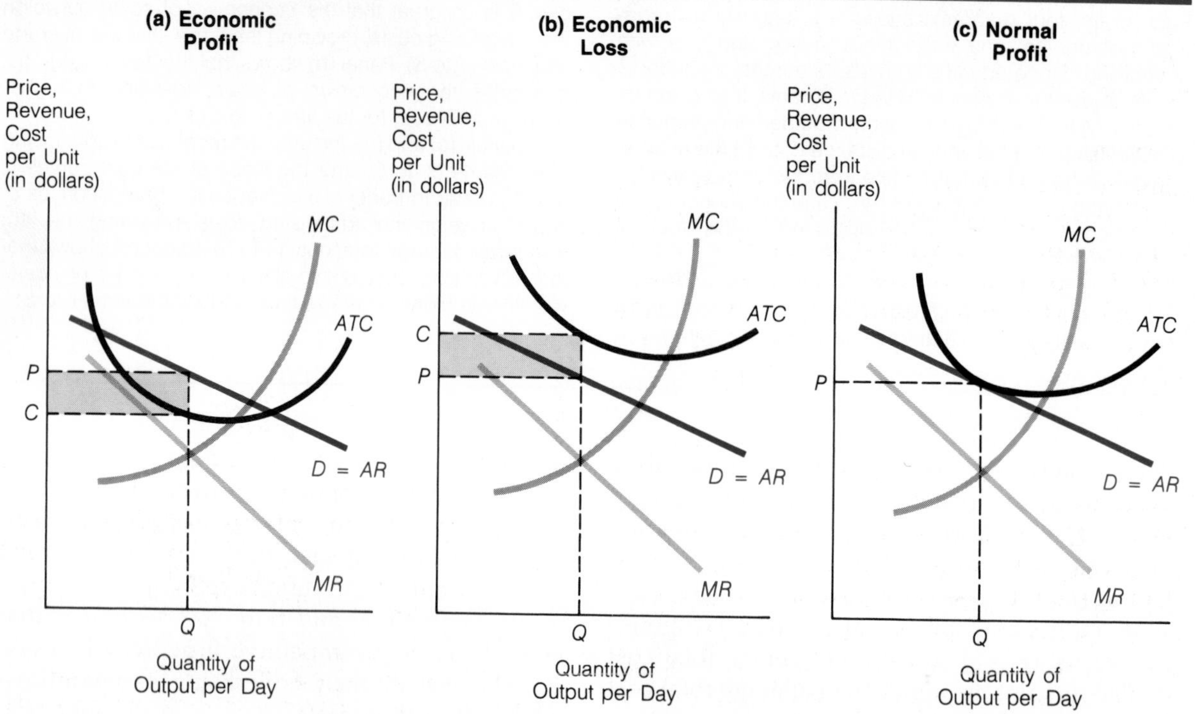

Each diagram shows a possible short-run equilibrium point for a firm in a monopolistically competitive market. Each pictures the firm's demand or average-revenue curve (*D = AR*), its marginal-revenue curve (*MR*), its marginal-cost curve (*MC*), and its average-total-cost curve (*ATC*). Profit maximization occurs where the firm's marginal-cost curve intersects its marginal-revenue curve from below. Thus in each diagram the firm wishes to produce a level of output of *Q* and charge a price of *P*.

In panel (a), at equilibrium the firm's average revenue exceeds its average total cost by the vertical distance *PC*, so that the shaded area represents its economic profit. In panel (b), at equilibrium the firm's average total cost exceeds its average revenue by the vertical distance *CP*, so that the shaded area represents its economic loss. In panel (c), at equilibrium the firm's average total cost is equal to its average revenue (the *ATC* curve is tangent to the *D = AR* curve), so that it earns a normal profit.

intersecting the minimum point of the average-total-cost curve. However, they include not only the cost incurred in making the product—as in pure competition—but also the cost incurred in trying to differentiate the company's product. Thus, advertising and promotional costs are included in the cost curves.

Profit maximization occurs where the firm's marginal-cost curve crosses its marginal-revenue curve from below, so that in each of the three diagrams the firm wishes to produce *Q* units of output a day. According to its demand curve, the

highest price at which it can sell this output is price *P*. Thus, the short-run equilibrium in each of the three diagrams is the same—an output level of *Q* and a price of *P*. However, the profit (or loss) situation is different in each of the three diagrams.

In panel (a), the firm is earning economic profit. At equilibrium output *Q*, its average revenue exceeds its average total cost by the vertical distance *PC*. The shaded area (*PC × Q*) represents its economic profit. Panel (b) shows a case of economic loss. At equilibrium output *Q*, the firm's average total cost exceeds its average revenue by the vertical distance CP.[4] The shaded area ($CP \times Q$) represents its economic loss. Finally, panel (c) shows the case of a normal profit. At equilibrium output Q, the average-total-cost curve is tangent to the average-revenue curve.

LONG-RUN PRICING AND OUTPUT What will happen in the long run? The answer is the same as for pure competition. Each firm will earn only a normal profit. Some companies will enter if there is short-run economic profit. Some will exit if there is short-run economic loss. In the case of short-run economic profit (Figure 27-3a), the entry in the long run will shift the typical firm's demand curve down and to the left because the market demand is now divided among more companies. The economic profit begins to grow smaller. Likewise, in the case of short-run economic loss (Figure 27-3b), as firms leave the industry, the remaining firms' demand curves shift up and to the right. This happens because the market demand is now divided among fewer firms. In this case, the economic loss begins to grow smaller.

Demand shifts brought on by entry or exit may not entirely explain why economic profits and losses grow smaller in the long run. Two other factors may be at work. First, as we explained in our discussion of pure competition, industries may be characterized by rising or falling cost, so that the average-total-cost and marginal-cost curves of firms in these industries may shift in the long run. Second, monopolistically competitive firms' average-total-cost and marginal-cost curves also may shift because of changes in the amounts that they spend on advertising. They may try to raise or protect their profit by spending more on advertising. If one company or only a few of them do this, we might expect that their efforts would be rewarded. However, since the "typical" firm (the one we are describing) represents the actions of the many firms in monopolistic competition, the sales gains attempted through this advertising will not be realized, as all the adver-

4. Although the average-variable-cost curve is not drawn, it is assumed that at equilibrium output Q, average revenue exceeds average variable cost, so that the firm will not shut down.

FIGURE 27-4 **Long-Run Equilibrium for a Typical Firm in Monopolistic Competition**

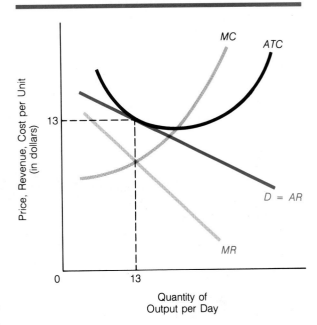

Shown here is a monopolistically competitive firm in long-run equilibrium. Its marginal-cost curve (*MC*) intersects its marginal-revenue curve (*MR*) from below at a daily level of output of 13 units, and its demand or average-revenue curve (*D = AR*) shows that it can sell this output at $13 per unit. At equilibrium its average total cost (*ATC*) equals its average revenue (the *ATC* curve is tangent to the *D = AR* curve), showing that the firm earns only a normal profit.

tising will cancel itself out. Instead of large sales increases, the typical company will have higher cost but little, if any, change in output.

Figure 27-4 shows a typical monopolistically competitive firm in long-run equilibrium. Whether that equilibrium was reached through entry or exit, through shifts of cost curves, or through some combination of the two, it offers the typical company only a normal profit.

Evaluation of Monopolistic Competition

In evaluating monopolistic competition, we first ask about the realism of the model. How well does the monopolistic competition model explain what happens between the rather unrealistic extremes of pure competition and pure monopoly? Next, we compare it with pure competition and give the arguments on both sides as to which is the more appropriate "ideal."

HOW REALISTIC IS MONOPOLISTIC COMPETITION? We first presented monopolistic competition as a market structure that is realistic and for this reason appropriate to use in analyzing many existing industries. It is a model that recognizes that firms have negatively sloping demand curves but are not pure monopolists, and that they compete with each other but are not pure competitors. The model also covers both price and nonprice competition, so that the effects of advertising can be analyzed. Just the same, after more than fifty years of familiarity with the monopolistic competition model, economists generally agree that its direct application to the real world is quite limited.

The problem is that monopolistic competition describes a market in which sellers are not interested in their rivals' responses. All actions are assumed to take place at the same time rather than in response to one another. Thus, impersonal market forces—as in the case of pure competition—determine what firms do and ensure that only a normal profit is earned in the long run. But in the real world, it is usual for companies to react to each other and to expect rival firms to act and react in certain ways. For this reason, critics say that the model does not give a "realistic" view of the world.

COMPARISON OF MONOPOLISTIC COMPETITION WITH PURE COMPETITION Even though the monopolistic competition model does not describe real-world markets very much better than the pure competition model does, the question of deciding which is the more appropriate "ideal" still remains. If it were in effect, which of these two market structures would offer greater consumer welfare?

Those who would vote for pure competition ask us to compare the long-run equilibrium po-

FIGURE 27-5   Comparison of Monopolistic Competition with Pure Competition

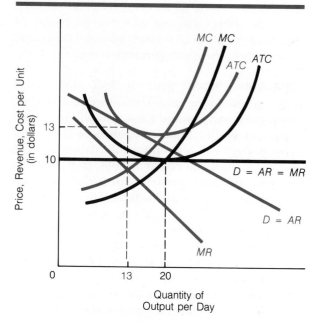

The diagram showing a monopolistically competitive firm in long-run equilibrium, which was drawn in Figure 27-4, has been printed in blue along with the diagram showing a purely competitive firm in long-run equilibrium (from Figure 25-10), which has been drawn in black. The monopolistically competitive firm has higher costs brought on by product differentiation. Output is restricted, and the price is higher than in pure competition.

sition of a typical firm in pure competition with the long-run equilibrium position of a typical firm in monopolistic competition. Figure 27-5 allows us to do so. We have combined Figure 25-10 (showing a purely competitive firm in long-run equilibrium) and Figure 27-4 (showing a monopolistically competitive firm in long-run equilibrium). To distinguish between them, the pure competitor's curves are drawn in black and the monopolistic competitor's in blue. Notice that the purely competitive firm's demand curve is infinitely elastic and the same as its marginal-revenue curve. However, as you can see, the monopolistically competitive firm faces a negatively sloped demand curve with its marginal-revenue curve lying beneath it. Also notice that the average-total-cost and marginal-cost curves are higher for the monopolistic competitor, reflecting the amounts it spends on advertising. In this case, we find that the firm in pure competition will sell 20 units a day at a price of $10 and the firm in monopolistic competition sells 13 units a day at a price of $13.

Economists who believe that pure competition is the ideal will quickly point out that purely competitive firms will sell more goods or services at a lower price. This will always happen because price is equal to marginal revenue and to marginal cost in pure competition, but price is above marginal revenue and marginal cost in monopolistic competition. Figure 27-5 also shows that monopolistic competitors produce on higher average-total-cost curves than pure competitors do and that they do not produce at the lowest point of their average-total-cost curves, as pure competitors do. The monopolistically competitive company in this figure has a price and average total cost of $13, which is $3 above the price and average total cost of the pure competitor. About $2 of that cost difference is explained by the amount spent on advertising, and about $1 by the monopolistically competitive company producing on the downward-sloping part of its average-total-cost curve rather than at the lowest point, where its marginal-cost curve crosses its average-total-cost curve.

Those who favor monopolistic competition admit to all these points. However, they still say that monopolistic competition is the more attractive ideal. They base their argument on the view that it is worth paying somewhat higher prices for a lower level of output in order to gain product differentiation. They argue that in pure competition the gains in consumer welfare stemming from greater efficiency are outweighed by the loss in consumer welfare resulting from having only standardized products available in the marketplace.

Who is right? That is difficult to say, since the answer is based on value judgments. The tradeoff between the greater efficiency offered by the pure competition model and the product differentiation offered by the monopolistic competition model cannot be measured in any objective way.

OLIGOPOLY

At the beginning of Chapter 25, we introduced **oligopoly** as a sellers' market that is made up of a few firms producing anywhere from rather standardized to quite differentiated products and that may be fairly easy or quite difficult to enter. The key to understanding this market type is to get a good grasp on what the economist means by "few firms."

Fewness

It was quite clear when we told you that a pure monopoly is made up of a single firm. It was less clear when we observed that pure competition and monopolistic competition require many firms. We had to explain what is meant by "many." In pure competition it means the presence of so large a number of firms that each one acts as a price taker. In monopolistic competition it means that there are so many firms that each one can safely ignore the others. Now we state that in oligopoly there are "few" firms. So we must explain what is meant by "few." Again the definition depends on how the firms in a market behave in relation to each other. It cannot be easily defined in numerical terms. Instead, it must be interpreted operationally. Fewness means **interdependence** among firms. It means that firms will worry about each other. They will consider their rival firms' potential reactions to any action that they are thinking of taking. For example, an oligopolist would not change the price of its product, the quality of its product, or its advertising outlay without at least taking into consideration what the response of its rivals might be. Three or four firms in an industry are surely "few firms," but thirty-five or fifty-five may or may not be. Where the line is drawn depends upon the maximum number of firms an industry can accommodate before it becomes a "many firms" monopolistically competitive industry.

Fewness means interdependence, and interdependence among oligopolists is expressed in how they make important economic decisions.

What one of these firms will do depends upon what it believes that its rivals will do in response, and each rival in the industry makes decisions in the same way.

The Real World

Real-world industries are more often characterized by oligopoly than by any of the other three market types. In other words, "fewness" or interdependence is a common industry trait. It is found over a very wide range of industries. No one is surprised to find interdependence among four or five giant firms that dominate an industry. Surely the cereal breakfast foods industry, the computer hardware industry, the passenger car industry, and the cigarette industry are examples of oligopolies. More surprisingly, interdependence is also found in many industries made up of relatively small firms. The half-dozen gas stations in your neighborhood make up an oligopoly industry. So do the "better" men's clothing stores in town, the scrap metal dealers within a twenty-mile radius, and television repair shops in a town or a neighborhood within a large city. Between the giant and the small are countless medium-sized firms grouped in oligopoly industries. Ready-mixed-concrete firms in a metropolitan area, women's and misses' dress manufacturers in various price categories, and bottlers of soft drinks in certain regions are examples. In fact, you probably realize that it is a great deal easier to think of examples of oligopoly industries than to think of examples of any of the other three market types. Interdependence among firms in an industry is the *usual* case, not the exception. Except for the monopoly (a single firm), an industry is made up of a group of competing firms, and that group usually conforms to "fewness." There are many thousands of gas stations in the United States, just as there are many thousands of "better" men's clothing stores and television repair shops, but there is no nationwide gas station, men's clothing store, or TV repair shop industry. To find appropriate industry definitions, product categories must be geographically broken down. A person living in Paw Paw, Michigan, is quite unlikely to have his or her TV set repaired in Bangor, Maine. Nor will you ordinarily gas-up at a station twenty-five miles away from your home, school, or place of work. We shall say more about industry boundaries in the next chapter. Our primary aim here is to show you how common the oligopoly structure is.

Oligopoly Models

The difference between oligopoly and the other three market structures becomes very clear when we discuss oligopoly models. Oligopolists do not determine their level of output and their prices by examining only consumer demands and production costs. In contrast to the other three market types, oligopolists also consider the effects of rivals' expected responses. This means that the demand curve faced by an oligopolist is not derived simply from consumer data but also includes what rivals are likely to do in reaction to any output level and price change. For example, an oligopolist in an industry with nine other firms may estimate that, at a price of $10, consumers will buy 1,000 units a day from the whole industry. The oligopolist may further estimate that, if all ten firms charge $10, it can sell 150 units a day. But if it lowers its price to $9 and the other firms keep their price at $10, it can sell 700 a day. However, it may reason and know from experience that the $9 price would cause its rivals to cut their prices as well. Depending upon the price elasticity of demand for the product, the oligopolist would then expect its sales to rise to, say, 160 a day. It is even quite possible that the cutthroat nature of the industry would cause rival firms not just to follow but actually to undercut the $9 price. If others charged $8, the company in our example might lose all but a few very loyal customers.

This simple example shows how much more complicated it is to determine demand curves for oligopolists than for firms in the other three market types. However, it is not impossible. It just means that in order to determine an oligopolist's demand curve, other variables beyond the usual ones must be taken into account. These are called **experience variables**—the oligopolist's knowledge of previous rival reactions to price changes in the industry, the personality traits of key managers of rival firms, and the political effects of the rivals' reactions. It is difficult but essential for the economist to evaluate this kind of material when dealing with an oligopolistic market.

A fairly large number of different oligopoly models have been offered by economists. We shall describe the most important of these: (1) early duopoly models, (2) the kinked-demand-curve model, (3) game theory, and (4) oligopoly coordination models.

EARLY DUOPOLY MODELS The first attempt at explaining oligopoly came from Augustin Cournot in 1838. Cournot's model introduced the concept of rival firms reacting to each other. His model described a **duopoly,** an industry made up of two sellers. He assumed that with a fixed price for a standardized product each firm would produce a level of output that, together with its rival's output, would bring it the maximum profit. The key assumption made by Cournot was that each company always believes that the other will keep on producing the same level of output as it presently does.

Later economists refined the Cournot model using price rather than output as the key decision variable. However, the assumption that each company expects the other to keep on doing what it is doing was retained. This unreasonable assumption, which implies that firms are not able to learn and to anticipate each other's moves, leads to less-than-very-useful predictions. Even so, the contribution made by Cournot and his followers was an important one. It introduced *reaction* into industry models.

THE KINKED DEMAND CURVE In the late 1930s several economists introduced a theory of pricing in oligopolistic industries that relies on the idea of a kinked demand curve. A **kinked demand curve** is made up of two segments of a firm's demand curve, which are divided at the industrywide price that has been established. The demand segment relating to lower prices is less elastic than the demand segment relating to higher prices. The reason is that rival firms are expected to match price reductions quickly and fully, since

FIGURE 27-6   A Kinked Demand Curve

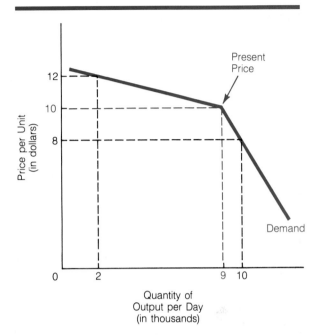

Shown here is a kinked demand curve for an oligopolistic firm that is presently producing 9,000 units of output per day and selling them at the industrywide price of $10 per unit. The demand segment for prices higher than $10 is much more elastic than the segment for prices below $10. If the firm increases its price by $2 to $12, its sales will decline by 7,000 to 2,000 units. But if it lowers its price by $2 to $8, its sales will only increase by 1,000 to 10,000 units.

they want to keep their market share. But they are expected to follow price rises only slowly and partially since they would like to increase their market share. Figure 27-6 shows a kinked demand curve as it might appear to a firm in an oligopolistic industry. The firm, which presently charges the industrywide price of $10, expects that if it raises the price to $12, it will cause a large decrease in the quantity demanded—from 9,000 down to 2,000 units—because few competitors will match the increase. By contrast, the firm expects that if it decreases the price to $8, this cut will be matched by almost all of the firm's rivals, so that it will sell only 1,000 more units. The theory states that usually oligopolists will not find either prospect very attractive and so will have a tendency not

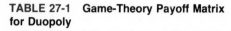

TABLE 27-1 Game-Theory Payoff Matrix for Duopoly

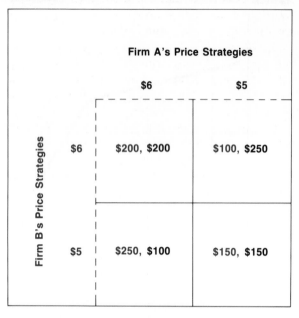

		Firm A's Price Strategies	
		$6	$5
Firm B's Price Strategies	$6	$200, $200	$100, $250
	$5	$250, $100	$150, $150

comma) is Firm B's payoff, and the second number is Firm A's payoff. Reading across the table, you can see that by charging a price of $6, Firm B can earn either $200 or $100 (depending upon what Firm A charges), or by charging $5, it can earn either $250 or $150 (depending upon what Firm A charges). Similarly, reading down the table, you can see that by charging a price of $6, Firm A can earn either $200 or $100 (depending upon what Firm B charges), or by charging $5, it can earn either $250 or $150 (depending upon what Firm B charges). Which strategy will the firms choose, and what will be the outcome? The answer depends upon what you assume. One popular game-theory assumption is that each firm will try to avoid the worst possible outcome. In our example this would mean that both firms would charge a price of $5, since this allows them to avoid the risk of earning only $100. The solution is found in the lower-right box—each firm earns $150. Each would have liked the other to charge $6, so that it could earn $250 instead of $150. That is likely to be impossible to achieve, since it would mean that the other firm would earn only $100. However, the solution of $150 profit for each is lower for both of them than it needs to be. If each charged $6, they could be in the upper-left box, where each would earn $200. But given the assumption that each will act so as to avoid the worst possible outcome, they would have to cooperate with each other to reach the more favorable solution.

The game in our example is one of many that can be used to analyze oligopoly markets. Depending upon the rules of the game, a specific solution can be found for each set of assumed behaviors.

to change the price at all. Fairly rigid prices are consistent with what is generally found in actual oligopoly industries. A fundamental objection to the kinked-demand-curve theory is that it does not explain how the industrywide price was established in the first place.

GAME THEORY A third approach that economists use to analyze oligopoly was developed by John von Neumann and Oskar Morgenstern in their classic book, *Theory of Games and Economic Behavior*, published in 1944. **Game theory** allows economists to liken the relationship between competing oligopolists to a game of cards (especially poker) or chess, and even to war. It helps to identify the conflict relationship among oligopolists and the incentive that they have for cooperation.

Table 27-1 illustrates a "payoff matrix," which shows the results of various strategies that can be adopted by rival duopolists A and B. We assume that each has only two alternative price strategies, charging $6 per unit or $5 per unit. The dollar figures in the boxes are the profit payoffs that the firms receive as a result of the combination of strategies represented by that box. The first number that appears (to the left of the

OLIGOPOLISTIC COORDINATION Under the heading of oligopolistic coordination there are three practices found in oligopolistic industries that can help us make better predictions of the equilibrium level of output produced by firms and the equilibrium price charged by firms. These are: (1) collusive agreement, (2) price leadership, and (3) rules of thumb.

COLLUSIVE AGREEMENT Collusion takes place when firms in an industry agree among themselves to take actions that will improve their mutual well-being. It is a cooperative effort to gain monopoly control in order to gain a high economic profit. The smaller the number of companies in an industry, the easier it is to collude. Of course, collusion is inconsistent with the pure competition and monopolistic competition models, but it is likely to happen in oligopoly. In oligopoly there is a tendency for the firms in an industry to maximize their joint profit and to divide that profit in some prearranged way. We shall go no further here than to point out this tendency. There are both natural and legal reasons why collusion does not usually take place. In Chapter 34 we shall deal with collusion more fully in our discussion of government antitrust policy.

PRICE LEADERSHIP In an oligopolistic industry, firms that are prevented from colluding may still find it fairly easy to coordinate their pricing behavior by means of **price leadership.** This is a practice that allows oligopolists to coordinate their price adjustments to changes in demand or cost conditions without engaging in collusion. As the term implies, price leadership means that one or more firms announce a price change, and all the other firms quickly follow the price leader's action. Price leadership can be explained best by asking and answering the question: Why do firms follow a particular firm in their industry when it raises or lowers its price? Economists give three different answers: (1) One firm in the industry (the leader) is so dominant that the others do not have much choice but to follow. (2) The price leader is seen as a barometer of market conditions, so that the other firms will want to imitate this respected firm. (3) By following the price change of any major firm, it is possible to avoid price competition. Let us look more closely at each of these answers.

Dominant-firm price leadership describes the condition of a firm so powerful compared with the other firms in the industry that the other firms accept its price as the one prevailing throughout the industry. This is something like the condition of a firm in pure competition which is convinced that it cannot affect price and so accepts the price set by the industry. In other words, dominant-firm price leadership takes place

when the small firms believe that they will not be able to sell at a higher price than that charged by the dominant firm and that they can sell all they want to at the "going" price.

Barometric-firm price leadership takes place when the firms in an industry consider one firm's price changes to be a good barometer of the market climate. The barometric price leader is usually a large and important firm in the industry. But, more important, it is a firm that historically has been proved to be "correct" in its evaluation of changing market conditions and in its price changes in reaction to them. The firms want to follow the price of the barometric price leader. They are neither forced to follow, as in the dominant-firm case, nor trying to avoid price competition, as in the case we are about to discuss.

Price leadership to avoid price competition may occur when collusion is considered undesirable or impossible. It is based on the realization by the firms in an oligopolistic industry that they will be more profitable if they charge the same price than if they engage in price competition. If one of several large and important firms in such an industry changes its price, all the other firms will follow in order to eliminate price competition.

RULES OF THUMB Another means of coordinating the firms in an oligopoly industry is for them to follow some rules of thumb or industry "conventions" that have been developed over some period of time. These rules of thumb may involve variables such as the nature of the product, advertising, research and development, and, most important, price. Interdependence among firms, the hallmark of oligopoly, causes oligopolists to keep a very close watch on each other. Companies discover from their rivals' responses just what actions are considered acceptable or unacceptable. Certain actions by firms may cause hardly any response, and certain other actions may bring strong retaliation by rivals. When these responses become known and accepted, they appear as rules of thumb.

In the important matter of pricing, the rule of thumb may be a **cost-plus price principle** such as the retailers in a certain industry adding 25 percent to the cost of the products that they purchase from the manufacturers. If all the retailers in that industry purchase from the same manufacturers, the 25 percent rule will assure all the firms that their prices will not be undercut by their competitors.

Rules of thumb may also surface in the particular dollars-and-cents price that is charged by firms. At retail, jeans are customarily sold at $19.95 or $22.95 or $29.95, but not at $19.40 or $22.31 or $29.00. Therefore, if retailers are selling certain jeans at, say, $21.95 and manufacturers raise the price to them by 40 cents, it is likely that the rule of thumb followed for pricing jeans will bring all the competing retailers' prices up to $22.95. Again, without collusion or leadership, each oligopolist will be able to predict easily what rival firms will charge.

Evaluation of Oligopoly

We are now ready to evaluate oligopoly. With certain qualifications and changes, many of the pros and cons of oligopoly are like those that we offered for pure monopoly and, to a lesser extent, for monopolistic competition.

Figure 27-7 pictures an oligopolist earning an economic profit in the long run. It sells 100 units a day at $18 a unit and earns an economic profit of $300 a day ($18 − $15 = $3; $3 × 100 = $300). The figure looks like the long-run equilibrium for a monopolist earning an economic profit. Of course, we realize that the monopolist's demand curve was based on consumer data alone, whereas the demand curve in Figure 27-7 includes, in addition, this oligopolist's expectations of what its rivals will charge at each possible price. As in pure monopoly and monopolistic competition, the oligopolist charges a price that is higher than marginal cost (Figure 27-7 shows the price to be $8 above marginal cost). The demand curve is expected to be somewhat more elastic than in pure monopoly and somewhat less elastic than in monopolistic competition. However, the particular elasticity of demand at equilibrium varies greatly from one oligopolistic industry to another.

At any given cost structure, the price that is charged in oligopoly will be much higher than pure competitors would charge and probably somewhat higher than what a typical firm in

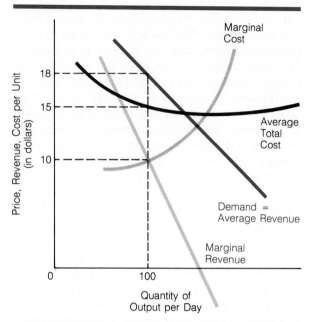

FIGURE 27-7   Oligopolist in Long-Run Equilibrium

Shown here is an oligopolist earning an economic profit in the long run. It produces 100 units per day and sells them at $18 per unit. Since its average total cost is $15, it earns an economic profit of $3 per unit or $300 per day.

monopolistic competition would charge. But an oligopolist's price is not expected to be quite as high as what a pure monopolist would charge. It follows that the level of output offered in oligopoly will be lower than in pure competition and monopolistic competition but higher than in pure monopoly. As in pure monopoly, but to a lesser extent, oligopolists restrict output. They also make it less than inviting to firms that might like to enter the industry. The results are again resource misallocation and a loss of welfare for society. Let us look a little closer at the extent to which prices, costs, and progress in oligopoly differ from those in the other three market types.

PRICE RIGIDITY IN OLIGOPOLY   One major difference between oligopolists and firms in the other three market types is that oligopolists are much slower to change their prices. In the three market structures in which firms act independently of each other, the smallest change in demand or cost will cause firms to set a new profit-maximizing price. However, in oligopoly, prices tend to be sticky or rigid because oligopolistic firms are never quite sure of the boundaries of acceptable action. They realize that the effects of being misinterpreted by rivals might be very severe—as in the initiation of a price war. For this reason, price rigidity appears as a normal oligopolistic price strategy. Firms take a "leave well enough alone" attitude and normally change the price only when it is safe to do so according to industry convention. Oligopolists commonly resort to various forms of nonprice competition, such as advertising and product changes, sometimes because these are believed to be more effective than price changes, but often as a "safer" way of achieving the same result.

COSTS IN OLIGOPOLY In our evaluation of pure monopoly in Chapter 26, we said that monopolists might not be pushed to produce on the lowest average-total-cost curve available to them. However, we also said that they might achieve quite a low average total cost since they are likely to be large enough to take advantage of economies of scale. The first point may or may not hold for oligopoly. If there is quite a bit of competition among the firms in an oligopolistic industry, each would be pushed to produce on its lowest available average-total-cost curve. But if there is effective collusion among the firms or if there are conventions that discourage active competition, the result may not be very different from that in pure monopoly.

The second point—the ability to take advantage of economies of scale—probably applies to oligopoly almost as well as to monopoly. The number of firms in an oligopolistic industry is likely to be related to the number of efficient firms that the industry is able to accommodate. There may be fewer, but seldom more. For example, given today's technology for producing automobiles, the demand for automobiles in the United States may only be great enough to accommodate five to ten efficient firms. If fifty fairly equal-sized auto firms produced for the U.S. market, they would surely incur a very high average total cost. They would not be able to take advantage of important economies of scale.

PROGRESS IN OLIGOPOLY Remember that progress occurs in the very long run and refers to the discovery and production of new and better products and the discovery and putting to use of new cost-saving technology. Would you expect oligopolists to be progressive? Again our answer is not very different from the one we gave in the last chapter regarding the progressiveness of pure monopolists. We suggested that, on the one hand, monopolists "have it made in the shade" and so might not bother to do much effective research and development. On the other hand, they probably have the incentive and the means to do a great deal of both.

The expression "having it made in the shade" is much less descriptive of oligopolists than of monopolists. With the exception of outright collusion, oligopolists cannot generally afford to be as complacent as monopolists. Generally, but not always, oligopolists face enough competition or potential competition to cause them to "bother" about carrying on research and development. In fact, most privately financed research and development is done by oligopolists. Whether more competition would raise or lower the amount spent on research and development is a matter of opinion.

The incentive to carry on research and development and the means to pay for it are on the average almost as great for oligopolists as for monopolists. Oligopolists often have a great deal of monopoly control, and many receive long-run economic profit. Joseph Schumpeter, a noted economist who taught at Harvard University during the 1930s and 1940s, argued that research and development was the backbone of competition in capitalist countries. He wrote that "the fundamental impulse that sets and keeps the capitalist engine in motion comes from the new consumers' goods, the new methods of production or transportation, the new markets, and the new forms of industrial organization the capitalist enterprise creates."[5] The capitalist businesses that Schumpeter writes about are the oligopolies that make up most of the industries in the United States as well as in the other industrial countries.

5. Joseph A. Schumpeter, *Capitalism, Socialism, and Democracy* (New York: Harper & Brothers, 1950), p. 83.

SUMMARY

1. In the early 1930s a third market structure model—monopolistic competition—was introduced. Monopolistic competition describes a market in which there are many sellers, each of which sells a somewhat differentiated product.

2. Just as in pure competition and pure monopoly, monopolistically competitive firms make all of their decisions independently of each other. Each firm believes that any action on its part will not cause a reaction on the part of its competitors.

3. Some actual industries come close to being monopolistically competitive. However, upon closer inspection, it is usually found that the firms do not completely ignore each other, and so the crucial market characteristic of independent action is not met.

4. The product differentiation characteristic of monopolistic competition is related to the controversial subject of advertising. Advertising is claimed to be, on the one hand, a pillar that supports free enterprise and, on the other, an obstacle to economic freedom since it threatens consumer sovereignty. Advertising can be valuable by providing information, but it can also be wasteful when it provides very little information. Because advertising is an important form of non-price competition, it encourages more vigorous competition among firms. Yet if successful, it can result in less competition, since it can cause the demand for a firm's product to become less elastic. Advertising uses scarce resources, and so it adds to the cost of producing products. But it may also stimulate sales so that firms are able to take advantage of economies of scale.

5. Similar to pure competition, monopolistically competitive firms may earn an economic profit, an economic loss, or a normal profit in the short run, but may earn only a normal profit in the long run. Long-run equilibrium is assured by a combination of entry and exit and changes in the amount that firms spend on advertising.

6. Though neither pure competition nor monopolistic competition characterizes most real-world industries, economists debate about which one would provide greater consumer welfare and thus about which model should be considered the more appropriate ideal. Those who favor pure competition point out that purely competitive firms produce more output and charge a lower price. Their opponents argue that some sacrifice in output and price is not too much to pay for the differentiation of products provided by monopolistically competitive firms.

7. Oligopoly describes a market in which there are few firms. "Fewness" here means interdependence. An industry is said to be oligopolistic when it is made up of few enough firms to have each one consider its rivals' reactions before taking any action itself.

8. Real-world industries are more often oligopolies than any other market type. Interdependence among firms in an industry is the usual case, not the exception. In a large country like the United States, even when thousands of different firms sell the same product, they are often broken down into hundreds of different, geographically separated, oligopolistic industries.

9. Oligopolists do not determine the amounts that they produce and the prices that they charge by examining only consumer demands and production costs. Oligopolists also consider what their rivals are likely to do in reaction to the output levels and prices that they choose. Thus, in order to determine oligopolists' demand curves, "experience variables" such as the toughness of rival managers must also be considered.

10. Early duopoly models introduced the concept of rival firms reacting to each other. The earliest was an output reaction model presented by Augustin Cournot. These models were not directly applicable to real-world oligopolies, however, since they assumed that firms were unable to learn from experience and to anticipate each other's reactions.

11. The kinked-demand-curve theory of oligopoly pricing is based on the expectation that rival firms are more likely to match price reductions than price increases. This causes the demand segment above the existing price to be more elastic than the demand segment below the existing price. Since neither prospect is attractive to oligopolists, the theory predicts fairly rigid prices.

12. Game theory helps to identify the conflict relationship among competing oligopolists and the incentive that they have to cooperate. Depending upon the rules of the game (assumptions about behavior), a specific solution can be determined.

13. Oligopolistic coordination models (including collusive agreement, price leadership, and rules of thumb) are helpful in predicting price and output equilibria in oligopolies. Collusion is a cooperative effort by competing oligopolists to gain monopoly control. Price leadership is the oligopolistic practice of having one or more firms in an industry announce a price change, and all the other firms quickly following the price leader's action. Price leadership may be of the dominant-firm, barometric-firm, or avoidance-of-price-competition variety. Rules of thumb are industry conventions such as cost-plus pricing or a certain pattern of pricing that has the effect of keeping rivals in the same mold.

14. Oligopolists may earn a normal profit or an economic profit in the long run. They will restrict output and charge a price in excess of marginal cost. Prices in oligopoly tend to be more rigid than in any other market structure. Average total cost in oligopoly may or may not be high, depending upon the amount of competition among rivals. Given the degree of competitiveness, oligopoly firms are usually large enough to take advantage of economies of scale. Oligopolies are expected to be quite progressive, since they usually face some competition or potential competition and have the means to engage actively in research and development.

DISCUSSION QUESTIONS

1. Explain the "competing monopolists" concept that characterizes the monopolistic competition market structure.

2. Actual markets only approach the monopolistic competition market structure. What important condition of the monopolistic competition model is missing in most real-world industries? Give three examples of actual industries (but not the same ones as in the chapter) that conform to all but this one condition of monopolistic competition.

3. In your opinion, does advertising infringe upon consumer sovereignty? In your own case, do you buy what you really want, or are you very much affected by advertising? Why should we be concerned about this issue?

4. Larry says to Linda, "I would like to have firms compete more vigorously than they now do. Therefore I would like to see them increase the amount of advertising that they do." Linda replies, "I am also in favor of more competition, but I favor less advertising. Advertising is used by firms in an attempt to limit or decrease competition." Who is right? Why?

5. Without looking at Figure 27-3, draw a diagram showing a monopolistically competitive firm that is earning economic profit in the short run. Compare your diagram with panel (a) in Figure 27-3 to be sure you have it right. What will happen in the long run? (In addition to the change, if any, discuss the process that will take place.)

6. Some economists argue that pure competition is the ideal market type since it offers the greatest amount of consumer welfare. Others disagree and make the case that monopolistic competition is the more appropriate ideal market structure because it actually offers greater consumer welfare than does pure competition. First taking the side that pure competition is ideal and then taking the side that monopolistic competition is the ideal, on what differences between the two market types would you base your arguments?

7. Of the four market types that economists use to analyze industries, only oligopoly is characterized by fewness. What is meant by "few firms" in a market? What difference does it make whether an industry is composed of "few" or "many" firms?

8. "Oligopoly is the market type that accurately describes most industries in the United States." Do you agree? Why or why not?

9. A theory of pricing in oligopoly markets assumes that oligopolies face kinked demand curves. What is a kinked demand curve? What causes the kink in a kinked demand curve? What explanation does this theory offer for the way that an industrywide price at the point of the kink is established in the first place?

10. Given the following payoff matrix for rival duopolists X and Z and the game-theory assumption that each of the firms will try to avoid the worst possible outcome, which strategy (prices) will the firms choose, and what will the outcome be?

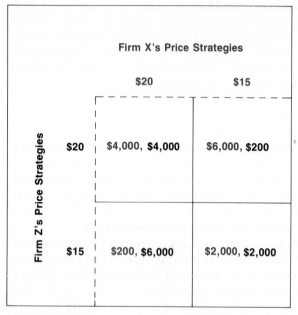

Firm X's Price Strategies

		$20	$15
Firm Z's Price Strategies	$20	$4,000, $4,000	$6,000, $200
	$15	$200, $6,000	$2,000, $2,000

Note: The dollar figures in the boxes are the payoffs that the firms receive as a result of the strategy that each chooses. The number that appears to the left of the comma is Firm X's payoff, and the number to the right of the comma is Firm Z's payoff.

11. Oligopolistic coordination may take place through price leadership. Describe what economists mean by the practice of price leadership. Distinguish among the three types of price leadership: dominant-firm price leadership, barometric-firm price leadership, and price leadership to avoid price competition.

12. In Figure 27-7 we drew a diagram of an oligopolist in long-run equilibrium. The diagram looks very much like one of the diagrams we drew for a monopolist in long-run equilibrium. Is there an important "hidden" difference? If so, what is it?

13. Applying what you have learned about the oligopoly market structure, explain each of the following statements:

a. Oligopolists are often reluctant to lower the price of a good that they sell and may be likely to resort to nonprice competition.

b. The degree of rivalry among the firms in an oligopoly industry helps to determine whether the firms in that industry produce on their lowest available average-total-cost curves.

c. Firms in oligopoly industries are expected to be quite progressive.

28 *Oligopoly: The Real World*

PREVIEW As you have learned, few industries come very close to the market structure of pure competition, pure monopoly, or monopolistic competition. In fact, most of our industries can best be described as oligopolies. An important social welfare question that must be asked, then, is whether or not an oligopolistic market is able to allocate resources well enough to meet people's wants. In other words, can a primarily capitalist economy such as the United States depend on oligopolistic companies to behave competitively enough to do what is best for society? This is a hard question to answer, partly because it is normative. Also, the answer may be very different for one industry than it is for another.

This chapter deals with how oligopolistic industries are organized and how, from the point of view of society, that kind of organization influences their economic performance. Competition among oligopolistic firms should be vigorous enough to cause them to operate efficiently, to offer a good variety of products, to invent and innovate better processes and products, and to pass productivity gains on to the consumer through lower real prices.

Here we introduce some concepts that economists use to determine the degree of competition in an economy and in specific industries. We begin with the idea of *economic concentration*, which measures the number and size distribution of firms. We show how this measure is used, the problems that surround it, its level, and its recent trends. Next we explain that firms grow either from within through building or from without through *merger*. Three kinds of mergers—horizontal, vertical, and conglomerate—are described, and their relationships to economic concentration and competition are

assessed. The "urge to merge" has been strong. So we shall offer some reasons that help to explain why.

We also present another important economic idea that affects competition in oligopolies—the *condition of entry*. Potential entry depends upon whether certain "entry barriers" are present and to what degree they work in keeping companies from entering the industry. Four barriers that we describe are capital requirements, product differentiation, absolute cost differences, and the minimum optimal scale effect.

ECONOMIC CONCENTRATION

Economic concentration measures the control of economic activity in an industry, in a major part of an economy, in a whole economy, or in a region of the world. It may be measured by a **concentration ratio,** which expresses the percentage share of some key variable such as sales or assets accounted for by the largest firms. For example, of the 139 companies in the greeting card industry in the United States, the 4 largest accounted for 84 percent of the sales and the 8 largest for 89 percent of the sales in 1982. These figures are an example of *market* concentration ratios. *Aggregate* concentration ratios, however, cover a much wider area of economic activity. Out of about 200,000 manufacturing corporations in the United States in 1984, the 200 largest held

TABLE 28-1   U.S. Aggregate Economic Concentration: A Sample of *Fortune* Magazine's Data for 1985

I. U.S. Industrial Sector

Rank (by sales)	Company	Sales (in hundreds of thousands of dollars)	Cumulative Percentage of 500 Largest
1	General Motors	96,372	5.3
2	Exxon	86,673	10.1
3	Mobil	55,960	13.2
4	Ford Motor	52,774	16.1
5	IBM	50,056	18.9
6	Texaco	46,297	21.5
7	Chevron	41,742	23.8
8	AT&T	34,910	25.7
9	E. I. Du Pont de Nemours	29,483	27.4
10	General Electric	28,285	28.9

II. U.S. Commercial Banking Sector

Rank (by assets)	Company	Assets (in hundreds of thousands of dollars)	Cumulative Percentage of 100 Largest
1	Citicorp	173,597	9.9
2	BankAmerica	118,541	16.7
3	Chase Manhattan	87,685	21.7
4	Manufacturers Hanover	76,526	26.1
5	J.P. Morgan & Co.	69,375	30.0

III. U.S. Retailing Sector

Rank (by sales)	Company	Sales (in hundreds of thousands of dollars)	Cumulative Percentage of 50 Largest
1	Sears Roebuck	40,715	12.8
2	K Mart	22,420	19.8
3	Safeway Stores	19,651	25.9
4	Kroger	17,124	31.3
5	American Stores	13,890	35.6

TABLE 28-1 **(Continued)**

IV. U.S. Transportation Sector

Rank (by sales)	Company	Sales (in hundreds of thousands of dollars)	Cumulative Percentage of 50 Largest
1	Burlington Northern	8,651	8.3
2	United Parcel Service	7,687	15.7
3	CSX Corp.	7,320	22.7
4	Santa Fe Southern Pacific	6,438	28.9
5	UAL	6,383	35.0

Source: Fortune magazine, April 28 and June 9, 1986, © 1986 Time Inc. All rights reserved. Used with permission.

about 61 percent of the country's manufacturing assets.[1]

Economic concentration ratios are gathered as a quantitative measure of potential monopoly control. The presumption is that there is a high level of monopoly control—and for this reason too little competition—in an economy where only a handful of giant companies control a very high percentage of the assets, sales, or profits in important sectors such as manufacturing, transportation, finance, or retailing. The same presumption applies in individual markets or industries. So the greeting card publishing industry just mentioned is presumed more likely to suffer from too little competition than is the women's and misses' dresses industry, where the 4 largest of the 5,489 firms operating in that industry accounted for only 6 percent of the sales in 1982.

Aggregate Economic Concentration

Aggregate economic concentration relates to the share of economic activity undertaken by the largest firms in a region of the world, in an

1. U.S. Bureau of the Census. *Statistical Abstract of the United States: 1986* (106th edition), Washington, D.C., 1985.

economy, or in some major sector beyond traditional market or industry lines. Each year *Fortune* magazine publishes data on the largest U.S. and foreign firms. The data cover the 500 largest U.S. manufacturing and mining firms (the *Fortune* 500), the 500 largest U.S. nonindustrial firms (the *Fortune* Service 500), the 500 largest foreign manufacturing and mining firms (the *Fortune* International 500), and the 100 largest foreign commercial banks.

THE LARGEST U.S. FIRMS Table 28-1 gives a sample of 1985 *Fortune* data that throws some light on U.S. aggregate economic concentration. Part I lists the sales of the 10 largest industrial firms in the United States and their cumulative percentage of the sales of the 500 largest U.S. industrial firms. Note that General Motors (one-fifth of 1 percent of the 500 largest firms) accounted for over 5 percent of their sales. One percent of these firms (the top 5) accounted for nearly 19 percent of the sales of the top 500, and 2 percent (the 10 firms listed) accounted for nearly 29 percent of their sales.

Table 28-1 also gives aggregate concentration data for three nonindustrial sectors of the U.S. economy. The commercial banking sector's aggregate concentration, as measured in assets, is quite high. The 5 firms listed (5 percent of the

TABLE 28-2 **Foreign Aggregate Concentration:** *Fortune* **Magazine's Ten Largest Industrial Firms Outside the United States, 1984**

Rank (by sales)	Company	Country	Sales (in hundreds of thousands of dollars)	Cumulative Percentage of 500 Largest Firms
1	Royal Dutch/Shell Group	Neth.-Britain	84,865	4.5
2	British Petroleum	Britain	50,662	7.2
3	ENI (Petroleum)*	Italy	25,798	8.6
4	Toyota Motor	Japan	24,111	9.9
5	IRI*	Italy	23,354	11.1
6	Unilever	Britain-Neth.	21,599	12.3
7	Elf Aquitaine (Pétroles)*	France	20,662	13.4
8	Matsushita Electric	Japan	19,993	14.4
9	Pemex (Petroleum)*	Mexico	19,405	15.5
10	Hitachi	Japan	18,486	16.4

*Government-owned.

largest 100 firms) accounted for 30 percent of their total assets. In retailing, sales of the 5 largest firms account for close to 36 percent of the largest 50 firms' sales. Finally, in the transportation sector, the largest 5 firms account for 35 percent of the sales of the 50 largest.

THE LARGEST FOREIGN FIRMS Table 28-2 provides aggregate concentration data for industrial firms outside the United States. However, it is not comparable to Table 28-1 since what it shows is not for a single country, but rather for a large number of foreign countries combined. On a country-by-country basis, aggregate concentration may be higher, lower, or about the same as in the United States. Also, the *Fortune* data do not include Soviet bloc or communist Chinese firms. Our purpose in presenting Table 28-2 is to help you recognize the names of major foreign firms and to show you that, although they are giant firms, they are on average somewhat smaller than the ten largest U.S. industrial firms.

To give you further background on non-U.S. aggregate concentration, Table 28-3 presents a breakdown by country of the largest 500 foreign industrial firms in 1984. Notice that Japan boasts by far the most large firms, with Great Britain and West Germany in second and third place, respectively. Together those three countries account for more than half of the total (280 of 500 firms). If Canada, France, and Sweden are included, over 73 percent (367 of 500 firms) are accounted for.

Aggregate concentration data focus, not on competing firms, but merely on firms in the same region of the world, or in the same economy, or in the same sector within a region or economy. Exxon, which produces petroleum, does not compete with General Motors, which is in the automobile and truck industry. Sears Roebuck, a general merchandise retailer, competes only marginally with Kroger, which sells primarily food products. To the extent that British Petroleum and Pemex serve different geographic markets, they do not compete, in spite of the fact that they deal with the same product. Toyota Motor, which produces automobiles, and Unilever, which produces food products, soaps, and cosmetics, compete hardly at all. But the power that can stem from sheer size is of great concern to some economists. They argue that the economic and political advantages gained through size alone may enable a firm to control particular markets in which it is involved.

TABLE 28-3 *Fortune* Magazine's 500 Largest Foreign Industrial Firms:
Rank Breakdown by Country, 1984

Country	Rank Breakdown 1–100	101–200	201–300	301–400	401–500	Total
Argentina	1	0	0	0	0	1
Australia	1	0	4	1	4	10
Austria	0	2	1	0	1	4
Bahamas	0	0	0	1	0	1
Belgium	1	2	1	1	0	5
Brazil	1	0	1	0	5	7
Britain	13	20	23	13	6	75
Britain/Netherlands	1	0	0	0	0	1
Canada	7	8	7	9	4	35
Chile	0	0	0	2	0	2
Colombia	0	0	1	0	0	1
Finland	1	0	0	2	4	7
France	9	7	6	10	2	34
Germany	15	13	8	4	15	55
Greece	0	0	0	0	1	1
India	1	2	0	1	0	4
Ireland	0	0	0	0	1	1
Israel	0	1	0	0	0	1
Italy	4	3	0	2	3	12
Japan	26	23	33	37	31	150
Kuwait	1	0	0	0	0	1
Luxembourg	0	0	0	0	1	1
Mexico	1	0	0	1	1	3
Netherlands Antilles	1	1	0	0	0	2
Netherlands	3	0	2	2	2	9
Netherlands/Britain	1	0	0	0	0	1
New Zealand	0	0	1	0	0	1
Norway	0	2	0	0	1	3
Pakistan	0	0	0	0	1	1
Panama	0	0	0	0	1	1
Peru	0	0	0	1	0	1
Philippines	0	0	0	1	0	1
Portugal	0	0	1	0	0	1
South Africa	1	0	3	3	2	9
South Korea	5	2	2	0	1	10
Spain	0	2	1	2	4	9
Sweden	1	4	1	6	6	18
Switzerland	3	5	3	1	0	12
Taiwan	1	0	0	0	2	3
Turkey	0	3	0	0	0	3
Venezuela	1	0	0	0	0	1
Zaire	0	0	0	0	1	1
Zambia	0	0	1	0	0	1

Source: The 500 Largest Industrial Companies Outside the U.S., *Fortune*, August 19, 1985, © 1985 Time, Inc. All rights reserved.

TABLE 28-4   Aggregate Economic Concentration in U.S. Manufacturing from 1947 to 1982, Share of Total Value Added[a] by Manufacture— Accounted for by Largest U.S. Manufacturing Companies

Company Rank Group	Percentage of Total Value Added by Manufacture							
	1947	1954	1958	1963	1967	1972	1977	1982
Largest 50 companies	17	23	23	25.0	24.6	24.5	24.4	23.9
Largest 100 companies	23	30	30	32.7	32.8	33.1	33.4	32.8
Largest 150 companies	27	34	35	37.4	37.9	38.8	39.5	38.7
Largest 200 companies	30	37	38	40.9	41.7	43.1	43.8	43.2

a. Value added is the difference between the value of materials that a firm buys and the value of what it sells.

Source: Bureau of the Census, U.S. Department of Commerce, 1982 Census of Manufacturers, Concentration Ratios in Manufacturing, Subject Series, MC 82-S-7, April 1986.

CHANGES IN THE U.S. ECONOMY SINCE THE CIVIL WAR   Great changes have taken place in the U.S. economy since the Civil War (1861–1865). At that time, the United States was accurately described as an agricultural country, because manufacturing was confined to small-scale plants, largely in the New England and Middle Atlantic states. Economic concentration was then at a very low level. Since that time, however, technological and organizational changes have completely altered the character of the economy. The large corporation has become the dominant form of business, and the level of economic concentration has increased greatly.

In 1932, economists Adolf Berle and Gardner Means called attention to this growing aggregate concentration. They reported that during the period from 1909 to 1929 the 200 largest nonfinancial corporations in the United States were growing at a much higher rate than were all other U.S. nonfinancial corporations. They projected these growth rates into the future and concluded that, if no obstacles were placed in the way, the top 200 U.S. firms would control all U.S. business by the early 1970s. Of course this has not happened. But aggregate concentration—at least in manufacturing—has continued to increase in the United States. Table 28-4 gives some indication of this fact in terms of the value added. (The **value added** is the difference between the value

of materials that a firm buys and the value of what it sells.) The table compares the largest 50, 100, 150, and 200 manufacturing corporations in the United States for selected years from 1947 to 1982. Though economic concentration was greater in 1982 than in 1947, the increase has been moderate since 1954. Most economists believe that the big jump from 1947 to 1954 should not be given great importance since it was primarily due to adjustments after World War II. For the years 1963 to 1982 we have added a decimal place to the percentages in the table, because the changes have been so slight that rounding off would distort these figures. During those years the percentage of total value added in manufacturing accounted for by the 50 largest U.S. manufacturing firms actually fell by over a percentage point. The percentage of total value added in manufacturing accounted for by the 100 largest U.S. manufacturing firms was the same in 1982 as in 1967 and the 150 and 200 largest firms decreased their shares from 1977 to 1982.

Market Concentration

We return to **market concentration**—the number and size distribution of firms in a specific industry or market. Examples of concentration ratios among groups of firms competing in particular markets,

TABLE 28-5 Standard Industrial Classification: An Example

Standard Industrial Classification Code	Designation	Name
20	Major industry group	Food and kindred products
201	Industry group	Meat products
2011	Industry	Meatpacking
20111	Product class	Fresh beef
2011112	Product	Whole-carcass beef

such as the greeting card publishing or women's and misses' dresses industry, were given earlier. But industries are not as easy to define as it may appear. If concentration ratios are to be used as indicators of competition, the definition of an industry must correctly describe a readily identifiable group of competing firms. However, most firms produce many different things and may sell them in widely separated geographic areas. For this reason, a workable classification system is required.

SIC PRODUCT CODES Industry definitions used by the U.S. Bureau of the Census in taking the Census of Manufacturers for the United States are set forth in the **Standard Industrial Classification (SIC) system.** Table 28-5 shows how this system is set up. The outputs of firms are divided into industry and product groupings, which are coded with numbers having from two to seven digits. Each time that another digit is added, the groups become narrower. Table 28-5 gives one example. The food and kindred products group shown in this table is one of 20 two-digit "major industry groups" in the manufacturing sector. Some others are textile-mill products and petroleum and coal products. These 20 major groups are further divided into 143 three-digit "industry groups," one of which (under food and kindred products) is meat products. The classification is then further narrowed to 452 four-digit "industries," such as meatpacking in our example. These in turn are separated into over 1,400 five-digit

"product classes," an example of which in this sequence is fresh beef. To leave room for possible future expansion, there is no six-digit coding. Finally, all of manufacturing is divided into about 11,000 different seven-digit "products." Whole carcass beef is one product in the sequence that we followed.

DIFFICULTY OF OVERSTATEMENT AND UNDERSTATEMENT How well does the SIC work? Can we confidently use the concentration ratios published by the Bureau of the Census in its Census of Manufacturers? Our answer is twofold: "Yes," the data taken from questionnaires filled out by firms are reliable, but "No," they do not always lend themselves to the kind of analysis of markets that economists would like to do. However, if we recognize their limitations, we can make certain adjustments. Only then can we avoid seriously overstating or understating the concentration in actual markets.

BROAD AND NARROW DEFINITIONS The most widely used SIC category is the four-digit "industry." However, it may not properly define the market—that is, the group of competing firms. If the four-digit definition is too broad, it will understate the actual concentration; if it is too narrow, it will overstate the actual concentration.

In Table 28-6 we have listed a few of the over 450 four-digit SIC "industries." The number of firms in the industry and the 4-firm and 8-firm concentration ratios based on value of shipment

TABLE 28-6 Some 4-Firm and 8-Firm Concentration Ratios Based on Value of Shipments, 1982

SIC Code	Industry	Number of Firms	4-Firm Ratio	8-Firm Ratio
2062	Cane sugar	19	65	91
2063	Beet sugar	14	67	95
2371	Fur goods	503	12	19
2521	Wood office furniture	430	22	32
2522	Metal office furniture	224	45	59
2652	Setup paperboard boxes	241	15	26
2711	Newspapers	7,520	22	34
2834	Pharmaceutical preparations	584	26	42
3221	Glass containers	41	50	73
3273	Ready-mixed concrete	4,161	6	9
3334	Primary aluminum	15	64	88
3411	Metal cans	168	50	68
3523	Farm machinery and equipment	1,787	53	62
3711	Motor vehicles and car bodies	289	92	97
3721	Aircraft	139	64	81

Source: Bureau of the Census, U.S. Department of Commerce, *1982 Census of Manufacturers*, Concentration Ratios in Manufacturing, Subject Series, MC82-S-7, April 1986.

(sales) in 1982 are given for each. The 4-firm concentration ratio presents the percentage share of that industry accounted for by the largest 4 firms in that industry, and the 8-firm concentration ratio presents the percentage share of that industry accounted for by the largest 8 firms in that industry. To make this clear, let us see what information is presented in the first line of Table 28-6. First, it tells us that in 1982 there were 19 firms producing cane sugar in the United States. Second, the 4 largest among them accounted for 65 percent of the total amount of cane sugar sold by these 19 firms. Third, the 8 largest firms accounted for 91 percent of industry sales. Thus, we can infer, that the remaining 11 firms accounted for only 9 percent of the total sales of the cane sugar industry.

Pharmaceutical preparations (2834), farm machinery and equipment (3523), and aircraft (3721) are generally regarded as too broad in their definitions and so understate economic concentration. The pharmaceutical firm that specializes in antibiotics competes very little with one that specializes in birth control pills. In that "industry," concentration ratios based on five-digit product classes or on seven-digit products may offer a better picture of the state of competition. A similar, but possibly weaker, case may be made for the farm machinery and equipment and the aircraft industries. Tractors are not good substitutes for combines, and small private planes do not compete with large commercial planes.

On the other hand, some industries are defined too narrowly in the SIC system so that concentration ratios overstate the concentration. Table 28-6 lists the cane sugar industry (2062) and the beet sugar industry (2063) as separate four-digit industries, but the difference in their products is hardly noticeable to consumers. Also, wood office furniture (2521) and metal office furniture (2522) are good substitutes in consumption, as are glass containers (3221) and metal cans (3411).

OMISSION OF FOREIGN COMPETITION The concentration data that are offered by the Bureau of the Census cover only U.S. production and omit imports from foreign countries. Omitting this foreign competition leads to significantly over-stating economic concentration in some U.S. markets. For example, Table 28-6 shows that the 4-firm concentration ratio for motor vehicles and car bodies (3711) is 92 percent. Surely this figure is misleading, since U.S. auto firms strongly compete with such firms as Toyota Motor, Nissan Motors, Volkswagenwerk, and Daimler-Benz, to name just a few.

REGIONAL MARKETS U.S. concentration ratios are calculated on a national basis, when, in fact, actual markets often cover only a region or just a small local area. This may cause a serious understatement of economic concentration. In Table 28-6 are three good examples: setup paperboard boxes (2652), newspapers (2711), and ready-mixed concrete (3273). The 4-firm concentration ratio for setup paperboard boxes is 15 percent. However, the actual markets for setup paperboard boxes are regional rather than national and are estimated to have an average 4-firm market concentration of about 75 percent.[2] Likewise, the 4-firm concentration ratio of 22 percent for newspapers tells us little about competition in that line of business. Most of the cities in the United States have only one major daily newspaper. These newspapers may compete with those of other cities (such as the *New York Times* or the *Washington Post*) to some extent, but for printed local news they are monopolists with a concentration ratio of 100 percent. Finally, 6 percent is a very misleading 4-firm concentration ratio for ready-mixed concrete. Because of the very high shipping cost, the actual markets are generally no wider than the size of a metropolitan area, and concentration ratios are quite high.

THE HERFINDAHL-HIRSHMAN INDEX An alternative measure of market concentration is the **Herfindahl-Hirshman Index (HHI).** Market concentration ratios focus on only some of the firms in a market (the 4 or 8 largest) and they do not account for the distribution of the market shares among the firms included in the ratios (a market

with a 52 percent 4-firm concentration ratio may be made up of one firm with 46 percent and each of the other firms with 2 percent or it may be made up of four equal-size firms, each with a 13 percent market share). These shortcomings are eliminated by the HHI, which includes all of the firms in a market and gives proportionately greater weight to the market shares of the larger firms in the market.

The HHI is calculated by summing the squares of the individual market shares of all the firms in the market. For example, a market consisting of six firms with market shares of 40 percent, 30 percent, 10 percent, 10 percent, 5 percent, and 5 percent has an HHI of 2,750 ($40^2 + 30^2 + 10^2 + 10^2 + 5^2 + 5^2 = 2,750$). The HHI ranges from 10,000 in the case of a monopoly to a number approaching zero in the case of an industry made up of a huge number of firms.

EVALUATION OF MARKET CONCENTRATION In spite of the difficulties that we noted, concentration can be very revealing about the power that a few firms hold in oligopoly markets. Agreement among companies to limit or eliminate competition is much more likely among a few giant firms that control a large share of a market than it is among a larger number of small firms. Pricing and product decisions made in a collusive atmosphere come close to monopoly pricing and can harm consumers in the same way.

At least, studying concentration is a good starting point for analyzing an industry. If an industry is defined correctly—not too broadly, either in terms of product or geography—it is very likely that there will be some competition among the firms when the level of concentration is fairly low. But among industries with quite high levels of concentration there are very great differences in the amount of competition that exists. To be able to judge the amounts of competition more fully in oligopolies, we must study other characteristics such as the degree of product differentiation among the firms in the industry, cost structures of the firms, and the ease of entry into the industry.

Concentration is surely not the only indicator of the competitive climate in an industry. But, concentration is one of the few quantitative

2. United States Senate, *Hearings on Economic Concentration,* Part 8, Frank J. Kottke, 1970, p. 5388.

measures in an area of economics where analysis is often based on fairly qualitative evidence. It is tempting to depend too heavily on such a measure. For this reason, we must be careful not to assume that a high degree of concentration always indicates a lack of competition.

MERGER

How did the United States and other industrial countries arrive at the high levels of aggregate and market concentration that they have today? The answer is that they reached their present levels in two ways—through internal growth and through external growth of firms. *Internal growth* is growth by building, which means adding to firms' productive capacities. *External growth* is growth by **merger,** or acquiring other companies. Both forms of growth are commonplace. Though many firms have grown mostly through internal means, others have combined internal growth with merger.

Most economists argue that internal growth is better than merger for society because firms that grow in the face of competition must meet and pass the test of the market. Growth by merger does not offer the same assurance of competitive success. Any firm that can swing a deal using cash, bonds, or stock in an amount acceptable to the owners of the company being acquired can grow by merger.

Whether internal growth leads to higher aggregate or market concentration depends upon whether it is the larger or the smaller firms that are doing most of the growing. On the other hand, merger may or may not change the market concentration, depending on the kind of merger, but it will mean fewer and larger firms in the economy and so must lead to a higher degree of aggregate concentration.

Types of Mergers

Mergers are of three kinds: horizontal, vertical, and conglomerate. In a **horizontal merger,** a firm merges with another firm in the same activity, on the same level, and serving the same geographic market. For example, the merging of two small supermarket chains that operate in Chicago, Illinois, would be a horizontal merger. They both sell groceries, so they are engaged in the same activity. Because they both sell at retail, they are on the same level. And because they both sell to the people of Chicago, they serve the same geographic market.

Vertical merger occurs between companies at different levels of a particular business activity. That is, a firm merges with another firm that has served or could have served either as its supplier or as its customer. Examples are an automobile manufacturer acquiring a company that produces spark plugs, or a shoe manufacturer taking over a chain of retail shoe stores.

Conglomerate merger takes place when a firm acquires another firm engaged in a different industry. Conglomerate mergers are further divided into product extension, geographic market extension, and relatively pure conglomeration.

A **product extension conglomerate merger** occurs when a firm acquires another firm in an allied industry—a company whose product is functionally associated with that of the acquirer. When Procter & Gamble, a major detergent and soap producer, acquired Clorox, a major liquid bleach producer, a product extension conglomerate merger took place.[3] Detergent and liquid bleach are complements. That is, consumers use them together to wash their clothes. Also, they are found close to each other on grocery store shelves and can be advertised together.

A **geographic market extension conglomerate merger** takes place when a firm acquires another firm that is in the same business activity and on the same level, but is serving a different geographic market. Suppose that the supermarket chain in Chicago, referred to earlier, acquired a chain of supermarkets located in San Diego, California. This would be a case of market extension. They are both in the same line of business,

3. This merger was later disallowed in Federal Trade Commission v. The Procter & Gamble Company, 87 S. Ct. 1224 (1967).

but they are not in the same industry or market since they serve two different populations.

Finally, interindustry mergers that are neither product extension nor market extension may be described as **relatively pure conglomerate mergers.** In an absolutely pure conglomerate merger, there would be no relationship at all between the companies' activities. Cases of this sort are almost impossible to find. "Relatively pure" is the real-world equivalent. Here the acquiring and the acquired companies are engaged in quite different lines of business, yet there may be some slight relationship between them. Textron, a company that was originally in the textile industry, made a large number of relatively pure conglomerate mergers. During a period of about ten years, Textron acquired companies producing aircraft and parts, electronic equipment, optical instruments, bathroom fixtures, broadcasting equipment, glue, paints, plywood, chain saws, underwater exploration equipment, shoes, storm doors, golf carts, watch bracelets, poultry, and tourist travel. It probably seems to you that there is absolutely no relationship among these lines of business. True, the relationships are fairly remote, but not necessarily zero. The research scientist working on a better paint may also have ideas about better glue. The accounting department, as well as the advertising department, may provide equally good service to all the divisions. In particular, top management may be expected to provide its skills across the board.

Merger Movements

There have been four fairly distinct merger movements in the United States. The first was around the turn of the century. It took place in reaction to the great technological changes in communications, manufacturing, and transportation of that period. The mergers were largely horizontal and formed dominant new companies. This was the time when Du Pont, General Electric, Eastman Kodak, International Paper, U.S. Steel (changed to USX Corporation in July 1986), American Can, Standard Oil (later to become Exxon, Mobil, and Standard Oil of California, Indiana, and Ohio),

and many others were formed through merger. Competition took a back seat to substantial monopoly control by these newly created giants. For good or for ill, the United States would never be the same again.

A second wave of mergers occurred during the decade after World War I. Most of these were horizontal, but more vertical and conglomerate mergers took place than at any time before. The horizontal mergers did not shape the giant "number one" firms as they did in the earlier merger wave. Instead, large "number two" firms were created, such as Continental Can and Bethlehem Steel. Economist Jesse W. Markham estimates that about 12,000 American firms disappeared through mergers between 1919 and 1930.[4]

The third wave of mergers took place from 1967 to 1970. What sharply distinguished this merger wave from the earlier ones was that it was made up largely of conglomerate mergers. According to the Federal Trade Commission, conglomerate mergers accounted for about 85 percent of all manufacturing mergers during those four years.

The fourth merger wave began in the mid-1970s and continues into the mid-1980s. It is composed largely of conglomerate and horizontal mergers. It is recognized as a merger wave more because of the huge size of the transactions than because of the number of mergers taking place. The annual dollar value of acquired assets increased about sixfold from 1972 to 1979, and the years 1980 to 1985 saw still more dramatic increases. In 1981 about $70 billion of assets were acquired, including acquisitions by Du Pont of Conoco Oil and by U.S. Steel of Marathon Oil, which together amounted to almost $14 billion of acquired assets. In 1984 over $122 billion of assets were acquired, close to $30 billion of which were involved in just three petroleum industry transactions—Texaco's takeover of Getty Oil ($10.2 billion), Mobil's of Superior Oil ($5.7 billion), and Chevron's of Gulf Oil ($13.3 billion). In 1985,

4. Jesse W. Markham, "Survey of the Evidence and Findings on Mergers," in National Bureau of Economic Research, *Business Concentration and Price Policy: A Conference of the Universities—National Bureau Committee for Economic Research* (Princeton, N.J.: Princeton University Press, 1955), pp. 168–169.

TABLE 28-7   Large Acquisitions[a] in Manufacturing and Mining by Type of Merger, United States, 1948–1979

Type of Merger	Number	Percent
Horizontal	331	16.4
Vertical	201	9.9
Conglomerate	1,491	73.7
Total	2,023	100.0

Type of Conglomerate Merger	Number	Percent of Conglomerate
Product Extension	870	58.4
Geographic Market Extension	78	5.2
Relatively Pure	543	36.4
Total	1,491	100.0

a. The Federal Trade Commission defines a large acquisition as one in which the acquired firm has assets of $10 million or more.

Source: Bureau of Economics, Federal Trade Commission, *July 1981 Statistical Report on Mergers and Acquisitions, 1979,* Table 19, p. 109.

acquisitions valued at close to $140 billion were completed.

Until recently, data classified by type of merger were prepared by the Federal Trade Commission (FTC), a government agency charged with the responsibility of maintaining competition in U.S. markets. The FTC has estimated that of the 2,023 large mergers in the manufacturing and mining sectors during the thirty-two-year period of 1948 to 1979, almost three-quarters of them were conglomerate. Table 28-7 presents the FTC findings for that period.

Why the Urge to Merge?

Why do firms have such a strong urge to merge? Why do they so often prefer external growth to internal growth? There are a large number of clear advantages for the management of the acquiring firm in growth through merger. We shall briefly discuss six of them.

First, if there is excess demand for a firm's products and more plant capacity is desired, the quickest way to get it may be through acquisition.

Expansion of the firm's own facilities may take so long that good will can be lost because customers become dissatisfied.

The second advantage for managers is that merger may be "cost effective" (the lowest-cost way), both in terms of the price paid for the acquired facilities and in terms of financing the expansion. The price paid for the acquired firm may be well below the "book value" (accounting value) of its assets. It is fairly common to find firms' stock prices to be severely undervalued during a poor stock market period. An offer by a would-be acquirer of a price somewhere between the current stock price and the "book value" may please the stockholders and yet be a bargain for the acquiring firm. As to financing, if the firm built its own plant, it might have some difficulty either in borrowing the required funds or in selling its not very well recognized stock to investors in a public distribution. However, in all but relatively pure conglomerate mergers, the sellers might very well know and respect the acquiring company's management and so would be more willing to accept payment in the form of the acquirer's stock.

A third reason is that a firm wishing to diversify into a new product or geographic market (conglomerate) or to use a new process in its present industry may find it advantageous to do so through merger. It would likely be easier, quicker, and less risky than starting from scratch. Merger allows the firm to gain instant experience and not make the mistakes of a newcomer.

A fourth motive for mergers—illustrated by the tremendous surge during the late 1960s—is the expectation of speculative gain. Consider the so-called "go-go" conglomerates of that period. The investing public was sold the idea that some firms had spectacular growth potential. So they merited an unusually high "price-earnings ratio" (the ratio between the price of a share of a firm's stock and the earnings per share of that firm). A growth firm might be said to "merit" a 50-to-1 price-earnings ratio. For example, if it then acquired an ordinary firm that Wall Street had given only a 10-to-1 stock price-earnings ratio, the stock price of the growth firm would increase by $50 for every $1 of earnings provided by the acquired firm. The growth firm could therefore make an offer to the owners of the ordinary firm that would allow both sets of owners to make more money. The owners of the growth firm might offer the owners of the ordinary firm $20 for each $1 of the ordinary firm's earnings (double the value as determined by the 10-to-1 stock price-earnings ratio). But when each $1 of earnings from the ordinary firm is added to the earnings of the growth firm, it adds $50 to the value of the stock of the growth firm. The magic show is complete; the stockholders of both the acquired and the acquiring firm have made large gains.

Some growth firms of the late 1960s became specialists in merger. It did not matter very much what business the acquired firm was in, as long as the stock price-earnings ratio was low. Since the growth of go-go conglomerates depended on merger, they had to make acquisitions continuously to maintain their growth status. Once the investing public reacted to nagging doubts about the go-go conglomerates, the bubble burst. The stock price-earnings ratios of the growth firms fell, making it harder for these companies to find acquisition candidates with very much lower stock price-earnings ratios. This drop in the ratio added to the investing public's doubts and had a snowballing effect. Following such a pattern, one of the "hottest" go-go conglomerates, Ling-Temco-Vought, sold for $169.50 per share of stock in 1967 and for $7.12 per share in 1970.

The 1980s have witnessed another form of speculation. Mergers are not always "friendly" or welcomed by the managements of potentially acquired firms. *Hostile takeovers*, in which acquiring firms are able to consummate mergers by virtue of buying controlling quantities of stock, constitute a threat to the managements of potentially acquired firms. *Raiders* such as T. Boone Pickens, Carl Icahn, Irwin Jacobs, and Sir James Goldsmith have made huge speculative gains. A raider may quietly buy up large blocks of stock to obtain enough to threaten a takeover of the company. The merger may actually take place or the raider may extract *greenmail*—selling the stock to the company at a premium price offered by the defending management.

A fifth reason for merger is managerial pursuit of growth. Merger is often the quickest and most likely way for top managers to boost sales and asset growth and in this way to gain personal prestige, better pay, and job security.

Many studies conducted during the past twenty years or so have shown, however, that mergers are not very profitable for the long-term owners of the acquiring firms.[5] So growth through merger is pursued by managers, rather than by owners. On the average, firms that have grown through merger have not been more profitable than comparable firms that have grown mostly from within.

Finally, a sixth motive for merger—one that directly affects the public interest—is the desire to get rid of a competitor and in this way to give the company more monopoly power. A horizontal merger will, by definition, eliminate a competitor. Often a firm finds it attractive to expand by growing in absolute size and at the same time ridding itself of a major competitor. Potential

5. For a good survey of merger studies, see Dennis C. Mueller, "The Effects of Conglomerate Mergers: A Survey of the Empirical Evidence," *Journal of Banking and Finance* (1977), pp. 315–347.

competition may be reduced through conglomerate merger when a company seeking to diversify into a new product or geographic market immediately takes over the acquired firm's market and so need not compete with it.

Merger, Concentration, and Competition

Are mergers harmful to society? Do they raise economic concentration and in turn decrease competition? The relationships between merger, economic concentration, and competition are far too complicated to permit simple "yes" or "no" answers to such questions. The answer in terms of a certain sector or market depends very much upon the kind of merger, the size and power of the acquiring and the acquired firms, and the competitiveness of the involved sector or market before the merger took place.

Horizontal mergers are the most suspect. They increase concentration by decreasing the number of competitors in an industry. It does not always follow, however, that competition in the industry will lessen. Surely, if the largest and most powerful firm in an industry takes over a rival firm, competition will suffer. But in an industry in which the two or three largest companies have a good deal of monopoly control, a merger between, say, the fifth- and seventh-largest companies in that industry may in fact lead to greater competition.

Vertical mergers generally will not affect market concentration since the acquiring and the acquired companies do not operate on the same level of business activity. A firm acquiring a supplier or customer firm will lessen competition only if that merger hurts its competitors. Sometimes a company is able to gain a sure flow of an important input by acquiring a key supplier while its rivals remain threatened with interruptions in the supply of that input. In such cases the vertical merger may mean less competition in that industry.

Conglomerate mergers are the hardest to judge. They will raise aggregate concentration in a sector or an economy but, by definition, will be neutral in terms of market concentration. U.S. Steel's

acquisition of Marathon Oil had no immediate effect on concentration in either the oil or the steel industries. The effect that conglomerate mergers have on competition (as distinct from concentration) has been hotly debated by economists for the past twenty years or so. Those who argue that conglomerate mergers do not threaten competition point out that competition takes place in markets and that these mergers do not affect a company's monopoly control in any market. Those on the other side feel strongly that such mergers do, however, affect a firm's economic control or power, which is a result of its size and its conglomeration. They say that conglomerates have "deep pockets," full of monopoly control profits gained in other markets, which can now be temporarily emptied into their newly gained subsidiaries enabling them to spend more (such as advertise more) and charge an unfairly low price. A companion attack on conglomerate mergers has to do with the chances that they offer for reciprocal selling. These "I'll buy from you and you buy from me" deals with other companies shut off sales to those who would like to compete, but are not conglomerate enough to be able to offer equal reciprocal buying opportunities. Finally, it is argued that conglomerate mergers often take the place of internal conglomerate growth. The reasoning is that if the conglomerate merger were not allowed, the would-be acquirer would enter the industry anyhow. If the industry in question is highly concentrated and not very competitive, such entry would increase competition. On the other hand, entry by conglomerate merger would fail to take advantage of the chance to increase competition.

POTENTIAL ENTRY

The performance of an oligopoly depends very much on the amount of monopoly control held by the established firms in that industry. The less monopoly control or the more competition there is among the firms in an industry, the better we expect that industry to perform for society. So far in our discussion of oligopoly we have limited our attention to the relationship among the companies that make up an oligopoly. Now we look beyond the established firms in such an industry. We know that a further important determinant of the amount of monopoly control in an industry is the likelihood of entry into that industry.

This likelihood or condition of **potential entry** will importantly affect what established firms in an industry can and will do. The established firms in an industry that is fairly easy to enter may be very slow to raise their prices for fear that such an action would invite new competitors. In contrast, the established firms in an industry that is rather hard to enter are more apt to raise their prices, since the entry of new companies is not so likely.

The Entry Concept in Economics

Entry is the act of coming into an industry by a new firm, which adds capacity to that industry. It takes place when a company that has not been producing in an industry joins that industry. The entering company may be one that did not exist before, or it may be an established firm in another industry that has decided to change industries or to expand into another industry. Economists see entry as taking place only if a new company in an industry adds to the capacity of that industry. When an established firm in one industry just acquires a firm's capacity in another industry but does not add to it, no real entry has taken place. Nor is it entry if an already established company in an industry simply increases its own capacity to produce. So entry calls for adding to an industry's capacity as well as adding a new firm to the industry.

The idea of entry has for a long time been used by economists as an important part of economic theory. In pure competition, as explained by the well-known economist Alfred Marshall (1842–1924), entry and exit bring about the long-run equilibrium of an industry (see Chapter 25). Similarly, entry is relied upon to a considerable extent to attain the long-run equilibrium state in monopolistic competition. Yet entry was for some time a rather neglected part of oligopoly theory.

When the amount of competition was studied in an industry, the emphasis was on the established competition and not on potential, or possible, competition. For example, a study seeking to discover the amount of monopoly control in the casualty insurance industry might have been limited to looking at the state of competition that already existed among established casualty firms. However, since companies in the life insurance industry were potential entrants, the chances of their entering the casualty business should also have been explored. Without these possible entrants, the casualty companies might have acted very differently. They might, we suppose, have charged higher prices and made higher profits.

A clear statement that potential competition strongly affects the actions of the established firms in an industry did not appear until Joe Bain of the University of California at Berkeley wrote *Barriers to New Competition* in 1956. Bain's work extended the theory of oligopoly beyond dealing only with the relationship among established firms to dealing with the relationship between established firms and potential entrants. Bain noted that interdependence, the main feature of oligopoly, includes the interdependence between established companies and potential entrants.

The Condition of Entry

Not all oligopolistic industries are equally easy to enter. Sometimes a potential entrant has an advantage over the established firms in an industry. A company may hold a patent on a process that, after entry, allows it to produce at lower average total cost than can the established companies. On the other hand, sometimes entry into an industry is completely blocked. This might be a case where the government gives a company an exclusive franchise such as for telephone service or natural gas service within a certain geographic area. However, most cases are somewhere in between these two. Established firms have some important advantages over possible entrants but are not able to keep them out without making some major sacrifices. A measure of the **condition of entry,** as Bain calls it, is found in the "extent to

TABLE 28-8 An Evaluation of the Condition of Entry for Eighteen U.S. Manufacturing Industries

Standard Industrial Classification (SIC)	Industry	Condition of Entry
2094	Animal and marine fats and oils	Fairly easy
3498	Fabricated pipe and fittings	Fairly easy
3111	Leather tanning and finishing	Fairly easy
2013	Meat processing	Fairly easy
2311	Men's and boys' suits and coats	Fairly easy
2328	Work clothing	Fairly easy
3351	Copper rolling and drawing	Medium
2515	Mattresses and bedsprings	Medium
3652	Phonograph records	Medium
3576	Scales and balances	Medium
3317	Steel pipe and tube	Medium
2822	Synthetic rubber	Medium
3624	Carbon and graphite products	Fairly difficult
2073	Chewing gum	Fairly difficult
2111	Cigarettes	Fairly difficult
3641	Electric lamps	Fairly difficult
3717	Motor vehicles and car bodies	Fairly difficult
3612	Transformers	Fairly difficult

Source: P. David Qualls, "Market Structure and Price Behavior in U.S. Manufacturing, 1967–1972," Federal Trade Commission Working Paper No. 6, March 1977.

which established sellers can persistently raise their prices above a competitive level without attracting new firms to enter the industry."[6] In some industries the established firms can sell their output at a price much higher than the lowest average total cost at which it can be produced and yet keep new companies from entering. In others they can bar entrants only by keeping their price within a narrow range above their lowest average total cost. A few of the American four-digit SIC manufacturing industries that are believed by authorities to be fairly easy to enter, fairly difficult to enter, and of medium difficulty to enter are listed in Table 28-8. We have chosen six in each of these categories from

6. Joe S. Bain, *Barriers to New Competition* (Cambridge, Mass.: Harvard University Press, 1956), p. 3.

a much longer list prepared by P. David Qualls, formerly with the Federal Trade Commission.

The Barriers to Entry

Why is it that the condition of entry varies so much from one industry to another? Why is it, for example, that manufacturers of fabricated pipes and fittings cannot raise their prices very much above their lowest average total cost before new companies are attracted into the industry, whereas cigarette or chewing gum manufacturers can? The answer lies in the type and height of entry barriers faced by potential entrants. We shall describe four kinds of barriers: (1) capital requirements, (2) product differentiation, (3) absolute-cost differences, and (4) minimum optimal scale effect.

CAPITAL REQUIREMENTS The **capital requirement** entry barrier refers to the amount of money needed to get the capital goods—plant and equipment—for a new firm to compete adequately with the established firms in the industry. For example, a company may need much more than a billion dollars to enter the automobile industry in such a way as to compete with the established U.S., Japanese, and European auto manufacturers. On the other hand, with a few simple tools and a pickup truck one can go into the business of building single-family homes. Given equal risk, the higher the capital requirement, the higher the entry barrier. (The amount of risk cannot be overlooked because it may be easier to raise large sums of money to enter a "sure bet" industry than smaller sums to enter an industry in which there have recently been many failures.)

PRODUCT DIFFERENTIATION A second entry barrier involves the extent to which companies differentiate their products. The greater the degree of **product differentiation** (see Chapter 27, p. 528)—and the resulting consumer acceptance of established firms' products—the higher is this barrier to entry. For example, a new firm selling a standard grade of bituminous coal might find almost no product differentiation disadvantage in relation to companies that have been in the bituminous coal business for many years. However, a new firm might find it very hard to sell its new brand of headache pills, razor blades, toothpaste, or detergent. The reason for this difficulty is that customers have generally accepted certain brands of these household products and are slow to try a new, unknown one. To overcome this high degree of consumer acceptance, new companies have sometimes had to hand out free samples or temporarily cut the price. But this approach can be very costly. Hence, product differentiation can be an important barrier to entry. In his study of twenty manufacturing industries, Bain found that product differentiation advantages of established firms "loom larger than any other source of barriers to entry."

ABSOLUTE-COST DIFFERENCES A third entry barrier is measured by the **absolute amount of**

FIGURE 28-1 Absolute-Cost Differences Between Established Firms and a Potential Entrant

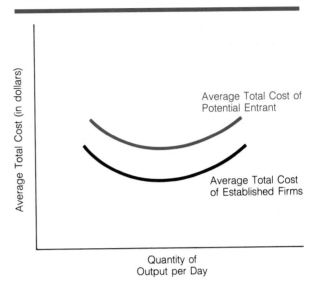

The average-total-cost curve of established firms is shown to be lower than the average-total-cost curve of a potential entrant. The vertical distance between them at the level of output at which a potential entrant plans to operate measures the absolute-cost entry barrier faced by that potential entrant.

cost difference (per unit of output) existing between established firms in an industry and potential entrants. The established companies may have lower average total costs over the whole range of output that could possibly be supplied. Figure 28-1 pictures an average-total-cost curve facing an established company and one that would be faced by a potential entrant to a certain industry. What might account for such a cost difference? For one thing, the established firms may have exclusive access to the highest-grade and most favorably located raw materials needed in production. They may own the best and closest timberland or mines or farmland. A new company may be able to overcome the established firms' control only by paying higher production and transportation costs than those of established firms. The established companies may also hold patents on the best production techniques, which are either unavailable to potential entrants or

FIGURE 28-2   Minimum Optimal Scale Effect

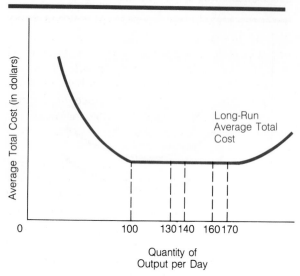

Shown is the long-run average-total-cost curve faced by the firms in a certain industry. Firms in this industry experience economies of scale up to the production level of 100 units per day, which is the minimum level of output at which a potential entrant would be able to attain low enough average total cost to be competitive. The output levels of the four established firms that now comprise the industry are marked on the horizontal axis (130, 140, 160, 170). The minimum optimal scale effect entry barrier depends upon how much an entrant adding 100 units to the industry supply of 600 units will depress the equilibrium price in this industry.

low interest rates compared with those that new companies have to pay when they enter the industry. In the 1950s, businesses were able to sell forty-year bonds that paid about 4 percent interest. However, they had to pay about four times that much in the early 1980s.

MINIMUM OPTIMAL SCALE EFFECT   The last in our list of entry barriers is the **minimum optimal scale effect** barrier. This is the effect on the price of the product that cannot be avoided when a new company successfully enters the industry. The size of the unavoidable change in price is determined by the smallest possible addition to the output of the industry that the new firm must make if it is to survive in the industry. If the entering company has to produce a very large percentage of the total industry output in order to keep its average total cost low enough to be competitive, it will add greatly to the supply of the industry. With a given demand curve, this added supply would cause the equilibrium price to fall sharply. This would amount to an important entry barrier, since the lower price after entry would be faced not only by the established companies but also by the new one. A potential entrant, which would be attracted by the price and profit in an industry before entry, would have to anticipate the degree to which price and profit would be forced down because of its own entry.

The minimum optimal scale effect is measured by the minimum optimal output of an entrant as a percentage of the existing total output of the industry. Sometimes an entering company adds only a very small percentage to industry output while reaching competitively low average-total-cost production. In such a case, the added supply might easily be absorbed in the market, so that this barrier would not be very important.

Figure 28-2 pictures a case in which the minimum optimal scale is 100 units of output a day. The industry in this case is made up of four companies that together produce 600 units a day (130, 140, 160, and 170). A potential entrant must produce at least 100 units a day to have a low enough average total cost to be competitive. The ratio of 100 to 600 (16.7 percent) expresses the

available only through the payment of royalty fees. In either case the entering company would be at a cost disadvantage—in the first case because it would have to use a higher-cost production technique and in the second case because it would have to pay a fee to one or more of the established companies.

Another source of an absolute-cost advantage for the established firms is that potential entrants may not be able to hire key inputs or to raise money on terms as favorable as those available to the established firms. A new company may have to pay much higher salaries to attract top managers and technical workers. Also, the established companies may be operating with long-term funds that were borrowed earlier at very potential for downward impact on price. This shows the minimum optimal scale effect. If the minimum optimal scale had been 50 units a day instead of 100 or if the industry daily output had been 1,200 instead of 600, the ratio would be only 1 to 12 (8.3 percent) and the entry barrier only one-half as high. Since price elasticity of demand (see Chapter 22) may be different in some industries than in others, the percentage gives only a rough idea of the real effect.

OLIGOPOLY AND SOCIAL WELFARE

In the preview to this chapter we asked whether or not oligopolistic industries can be expected to perform well enough to meet people's wants. We warned you that this is a hard question to answer because it is normative and because it is difficult to generalize for all oligopolistic industries. To help in answering this question, we developed the concepts of economic concentration, merger, and the condition of entry. It is doubtful that an economy with high aggregate concentration, high market concentration, rampant mergers, and high entry barriers would perform very well for society. We suspect that the oligopolies, unchecked by government in such an economy, would not be very efficient or very progressive. Both absolute and relative bigness of firms can be expected to inhibit competition. Individual companies would have such a large amount of monopoly control that they could restrict output and charge very high prices. Also, it is likely that they would be much larger than they need to be to achieve economies of scale and to carry on progressive research and development.

But differences of opinion are found among economists who study and interpret the sort of data that we have presented in this chapter. Some believe that aggregate concentration is too high in the United States and that many key U.S. industries are not competitive enough. They offer as evidence of this point the high market concentration often gained through mergers and the high barriers to entry. Others believe that the

power attributed to absolutely large firms is exaggerated and that the level of economic concentration of most American industries is not much higher than is needed to achieve important economies of scale. They point out that since the great majority of mergers in the United States are conglomerate, they do not have a bad effect on competition, and that the entrance of foreign companies into U.S. markets shows that the entry barriers to many U.S. industries are not very high.

Who is right? Both sides make valid points. Certain oligopolistic industries are quite competitive in the rivalry sense and perform very well for society. Yet other oligopolistic industries are not competitive enough, causing social welfare to suffer. In Chapter 34 we take a look at the U.S. record and see what role the government can play in regulating oligopolies.

SUMMARY

1. Economic concentration measures the control that the largest firms have of a particular economic activity in a region of the world, an economy, a sector of an economy, or an industry. The presumption is that competition and concentration are negatively related.

2. Aggregate economic concentration measures concentration beyond traditional industry lines. It is most often used to measure the share of economic activity undertaken by the largest firms in a major sector of an economy, but sometimes it is used in the context of a whole economy or even a region of the world.

3. Aggregate economic concentration does not focus on competing firms. The interest in aggregate concentration stems from the belief that the economic and political advantages gained through size alone may enable a firm to control particular industries in which it is involved.

4. Market concentration measures the control of the leading firms within a group of competing firms.

5. To help solve the problem of defining industries or markets (the group of competing firms), the U.S. government has designed an elaborate

classification system called the Standard Industrial Classification (SIC). This system divides the outputs of firms into groups beginning with a small number of broad, two-digit major industry groups and ending with a large number of narrow, seven-digit products.

6. Market concentration levels may be measured by traditional 4-firm and 8-firm concentration ratios or by calculating Herfindahl-Hirshman Indexes (HHIs), which take account of all the firms in a market and the distribution of their market shares.

7. The U.S. concentration ratios that are published by the Bureau of the Census may be quite revealing, but should be viewed with caution as they may contain some serious overstatements and understatements of concentration in actual industries. These may result from: (1) too broad or narrow a definition of the industry product, (2) the omission of foreign competition, and (3) the use of national rather than regional or local geographic scope.

8. High levels of economic concentration may be reached by firms growing either internally through building or externally through merger. Economists usually favor internal growth because it must be accomplished in the face of competition.

9. Mergers are of three different types: horizontal, vertical, and conglomerate. In a horizontal merger a firm acquires another firm engaged in the same activity, existing on the same level, and serving the same geographic market. In a vertical merger a firm acquires another firm that is either in a buyer or a seller relationship to it. In a conglomerate merger a firm acquires another firm engaged in a different industry. Conglomerate mergers are further broken down into product extension, geographic market extension, and relatively pure conglomeration.

10. There have been four fairly distinct merger movements in the United States. The first took place around the turn of the century and was largely horizontal. The second came just after World War I and was again primarily horizontal, though some vertical and conglomerate mergers also took place. The third merger wave came in the late 1960s and was predominantly conglomerate in nature. The latest merger movement began in the mid-1970s and reaches into the mid-1980s. It is composed primarily of conglomerate and horizontal mergers.

11. Firms often prefer merger to internal growth for the following reasons: (a) It may be the quickest way to expand plant capacity. (b) It may be the lowest-cost way to grow or the easiest to finance. (c) It may be the lowest-risk way to diversify. (d) It may be a way to capture speculative gains. (e) It may best suit the personal goals of managers as distinct from owners of the firm. (f) It may increase a firm's monopoly control by eliminating a competitor or a potential competitor.

12. An important determinant of the degree of monopoly control in an industry is the likelihood of entry into that industry. Entry, as defined in economics, requires an addition to industrial capacity plus the addition of a new firm to an industry. Just as interdependence exists between the established firms in an oligopolistic industry, interdependence also exists between those established firms and potential entrants.

13. Some industries are harder to enter than others. A measure of the "condition of entry" is the extent to which established firms are able to charge high prices and earn economic profit without attracting new firms into their industry.

14. An industry's condition of entry depends upon the type and height of the barriers to entry in that industry. There are four kinds of barriers: (a) capital requirements, (b) product differentiation (c) absolute-cost differences, and (d) minimum optimal scale effect.

15. The capital-requirement barrier is determined by the amount of money that an entrant must have in order to acquire the plant and equipment that it needs to compete with established firms. The product-differentiation barrier is caused by established firms' ability to differentiate their products and thus gain consumer acceptance, which is difficult for an entrant to overcome. The absolute-cost barrier exists when established firms in an industry experience lower average total cost than an entrant can achieve. Finally, the minimum optimal scale effect barrier relates to how much an industry's price will be depressed by the additional output supplied by an entrant operating at minimum optimal scale.

DISCUSSION QUESTIONS

1. Distinguish between aggregate economic concentration and market economic concentration. Give an example of each. Which do you think is more important to study if you wish to analyze the competitiveness of an economy?

2. "The economic concentration data that appear each year in *Fortune* magazine are aggregate concentration data." True or false? Explain.

3. Define what is meant by "value added." Using "value added" as the measuring variable, describe the change in aggregate economic concentration in the U.S. manufacturing sector from the mid-1950s to the early 1980s. (Before answering, look at Table 28-4.)

4. Explain the Standard Industrial Classification (SIC) system that is used in the United States to report market concentration data. Why might you want to use a four-digit classification to describe a certain industry and a five-digit classification to describe a different industry?

5. Joe says to Alex, "The government ought to go in there and break up some of the big corporations in the XYZ industry—after all, the four-firm concentration ratio is 73 percent." "Wait a minute," Alex replies. "There are a lot of difficulties surrounding those figures. There are certain things that I would want to find out about before I'd be ready to make such a recommendation." What might Alex have in mind?

6. Distinguish between internal and external growth of companies. Why would most economists prefer to see firms that are already large grow through internal means rather than through external means?

7. Distinguish among the three categories of mergers that economists use. Give a hypothetical example of each. How do you suppose each affects economic concentration?

8. Economists divide conglomerate mergers into three categories. Distinguish among them and provide a hypothetical example for each. What effect would each of these have on market economic concentration?

9. Growth through merger has been rather common in the United States. Discuss several reasons why firms choose to grow this way.

10. An industry's "condition of entry" depends upon the extent to which four barriers to entry exist in that industry. Briefly explain each of these barriers.

11. In addition to the amount of money necessary to enter an industry in which the minimum optimal scale is very large in relation to total output, what other conditions would keep firms from entering such an industry?

12. "Economists are of a single mind. They readily agree that oligopolistic industries are a detriment to public welfare and, whenever possible, should be done away with." Are these statements true or false? Explain.

Living with Oligopoly

Everyone knows that the "competition" he or she observes among sellers—retailers or professional people—is somehow different from the "pure" competition of economics books. (By the way, pure unregulated monopoly is at least as rare as pure competition!)

Something similar is true of the buying side of other markets, such as employers or the "middlemen" buyers of the farmer's crops or the manufacturer's output. The question is not whether the so-called imperfections of competition exist—they certainly do—but of their importance, especially their long-run importance. Two prominent subquestions under this head are:

1. What are the more obvious symptoms of the grosser departures from pure competition, which on the supply side of the market are called monopolistic competition, oligopoly, and sellers' cartels, and on the demand side are called oligopsony (buyers' oligopoly) or buyers' cartels?

2. What principal defenses does the market system itself provide for those who feel themselves victims of oligopolistic behavior? And what additional economic and political defenses are open to their victims, short of overthrowing the market system altogether?

The main body of this essay is divided into two parts, one part dealing with each of these questions.

Not Size but Price Behavior

The danger sign of oligopoly in action—the smoking gun at the murder scene or the sugar content of the diabetic's blood and urine—is *not* size but *price behavior,* which includes a wide range of specifics. For an organization, or union, or cartel of a town's or a county's "independent" grocers, or druggists, or gasoline station proprietors can and often does exercise a higher degree of monopoly-type control within its own bailiwick than do the local branches of the regional or national chains it claims to combat under the label of "antimonopoly."

Here are three specific price behaviors that should lead the watchful consumer to suspect oligopoly at work:

1. Confining competition to "quality" and "service," so that price is 95 or 98 percent excluded. Dogged refusal to cut prices *openly,* for *all* purchasers, and for *indefinite* periods. ("This week only" and "One to a customer" are the common substitutes, not to mention "Just for you, and don't tell anyone.")

2. Along with this, pressure to keep competitors from cutting *their* prices below cost plus a reasonable markup. This may be done by legislation or administrative decree on particular products; milk is a frequent example. For branded goods, the standard device is to connive with manufacturers on resale price maintenance, under the excuse of orderly marketing.

3. Advertising and slogans like "Costs more—worth it" and "New and improved," encouraging the gullible to judge quality by price. (If this year's model is "new and improved," precisely *what* is "new," *wherein* lies the "improvement," and *how large* is the price increase not mentioned in the advertising?) Occasionally this trick extends to not only concealing one's own prices (till the bill is presented) but forbidding competitors to advertise or display their (lower) ones, or indeed to mention price at all in their displays or publicity.

A second smoking gun, less smoky than the first, is *parallel action.* A worker is fired by Company A in City X. There is no job for him or her in other firms in A's industry or X's trading area. This looks like blacklisting. It can be applied as readily to the family farmer or small manufacturer who has trouble with a large corporate buyer as to the worker who has trouble with his or her bosses. Again, if you are not judged creditworthy by the Impregnable National Bank, you may somehow find that no "competing" bank in town will lend to you either. Or, after your life or health or auto insurance application with Oversize Mutual has been rated with extra premiums or exclusions, no competing insurance company will offer better terms. All such cases may of course be coincidental. Or they may be the "scientific" results of the application of "scientific" standards. But don't bet against some element of communication and collusion between ostensible competitors!

Institutional Defenses

The real-world person in the real-world street is, however, far from helpless against real-world oligopoly. Some of his or her defenses are institutional, built into the market system itself. Others require supplementing the market system by organization, legal action, or legislative lobbying. (The market, like Benjamin Franklin's God, helps those who help themselves.) More drastic action requires partial or complete replacement of the market system by regulation, socialization, or even violent revolution.

Let us concentrate first on the institutional defenses, which vary from one oligopolistic industry to the next. We divide them into seven sorts.

1. Inter-industry Competition   At the turn of the century, the Pacific Southwestern (modeled on the Southern Pacific Railroad) was "The Octopus" of Frank Norris's muckraking novels and every big city had one or more streetcar and gas-company tycoons. Three generations later, the railroads are in trouble, the streetcars are dying, and the gas companies (often regulated) are fighting for their lives against electric and fuel-oil competition. Steel competes with lighter metals like aluminum—sometimes even with plastics. Tin is (practically) gone from the old tin can, which itself competes with glass, cardboard, plastics, and with freeze-drying processes. And what would an oligopoly position in the stagecoach, buggy-whip, or livery-stable industry be worth today?

2. Consumer Mobility   At the turn of the century, every Main Street or crossroads merchant, in his bank, his general store, or his ice-coal-hay-grain-and-feed establishment, had a considerable measure of local oligopoly, which he sometimes exercised to the full. Three generations later, the potential customer has the choice of a dozen or more shopping centers within driving radius, perhaps an entire metropolitan area. Mobility extends over still longer distances by phone, by mail, or in some cases by airplane.

3. International Competition   "The tariff is the mother of the trusts," said Henry Havemeyer of the old Sugar Trust during the Taft administration just after the first decade of the twentieth century. He was right, if by "the

Imported cars, an alternative for the American consumer

tariff" he meant protection in general. And by the same token, "Free trade is the Lord High Executioner of the Trusts." Cheap foreign imports—frequently of bargain-basement quality, frequently products of cheap labor, and sometimes produced by "runaway" domestic companies—have become since World War II a major defense of American consumers against American oligopolists in both industry and the trade union movement.

4. Consumer Surrogates   A surrogate or "attorney in fact" is an official or unofficial representative of people unable or unwilling to represent themselves. For the ordinary consumer, this role is often played by a subset of firms called "price-cutters." Whereas oligopolists compete mainly on quality and service, surrogate firms compete almost entirely on price. They are often mail-order houses, discount houses, or chain stores. When the oligopolists sell nationally advertised brands, the price-cutters concentrate on "off-brands," "store-brands," or unbranded "generics." To the oligopolists' "Costs more—worth it" they reply, "Just as good—for less." Unfortunately for the consumer, successful consumer surrogates tend to change strategy and go "up-market"— with higher prices, atmosphere, ambience, and all—to join the oligopoly club. Fortunately for the consumer, other surrogates often take their place. (In the auto industry, Ford which charged $385 for a brand-new Model T "tin Lizzie," played the surrogate role in the 1920s, to be succeeded by the Volkswagen "beetle" of the next generation, and later still, by an international bevy of "econoboxes."

Discounters that have cut into the sales of major department stores such as Gimbels, above, at 33d street in Manhattan.

Source: The New York Times, June 20, 1986, p. D1

5. Contestable Markets These are also called "potential competition." The basic idea is simple; firms are in business to make money and are not bound to any particular product line. The more venturesome they are, the more willing they are to try their hands at some other field in which other firms are making excess profits. (The Duke interests shifted from tobacco to electric power and nuclear energy; the Mellons, from real estate and banking to aluminum, coke, and petroleum; railroads have branched into real estate, steel companies into petroleum refining, oil companies into department stores and entertainment.) In any oligopolistic business, a significant probability exists that exercising its powers to gouge the consumer will attract the lightning of both

small newcomers and conglomerate competitors, just as "ripe" dead animals attract the scavenging efforts of vultures, hyenas, jackals, and bacteria. It is the contention of William J. Baumol and others that real-world oligopolistic markets are in fact sufficiently contestable so that real-world oligopolists cannot, if they are to maintain their positions, act much differently from pure competitors in similar situations.

Some writers, Joseph Schumpeter most particularly, stress contestability by innovation, meaning new products or new processes. This course of action he calls "creative destruction." We have already mentioned cases of this kind under other heads—the railroads, the gas companies, and so on.

6. New-Used Competition For durable goods—autos, trucks, tractors, and farm machinery are examples—an oligopolist's principal competitors include some of its own customers of the past few years. There are more used-car lots (not to mention private small-scale suppliers) than new-car dealers and manufacturers combined. If you can't afford this year's "new and improved" price increase, or this year's "lemon" probability, why not try last year's model, with its price cut to compensate for both wear and tear and the loss of the intangible attribute called "newness." (If, that is, you can be reasonably sure of not sampling last year's bumper "lemon" crop!)

7. Do-It-Yourself This is a case of "last but not least," especially if we consider its expansion into barter arrangements and the so-called "second economy." Obvious examples of do-it-yourself include growing produce in suburban backyards, home laundering, barbering, tailoring, and medical practice. For the mechanically adept, the range is much greater; a wide range of home and vehicular maintenance and repair, furniture making (partial or complete), light trucking, and other hobbies expanded to save money. The extension to barter—"I'll fix your roof and plumbing if you care for my family's teeth"—are obvious. They can expand further to a network of avoidance and evasion, not only of oligopoly and cartel arrangements but also of taxation, licensing, trade union rules, and regulations of all kinds. Estimates of the size of the American second or underground economy run between 10 and 25 percent of the first or above-ground economy, but also cover large-scale criminal activities—drugs, prostitution, extortion, and racketeering not elsewhere classified.

Active Defenses

Active defenses against oligopoly and cartels go further and faster than the passive institutional defenses we have discussed. Some such defenses are erected against buyers' oligopoly (oligopsony). One is the trade union movement with its direct action (strikes and slowdowns). Another is the farm movement with its indirect action (legislative lobbying and political pressure). Our question here is, rather, why is the American consumer movement so weak? Why isn't it, for example, a powerful force against protectionism in international trade? (Consumer movements are much stronger in northern and western Europe.)

One reason follows from the institutional defenses themselves. The market does much of the consumers' work for them; few oligopoly or cartel abuses are big enough or permanent enough to keep the ordinary consumer angry enough to do more than complain. OPEC, perhaps because it was foreign, was an exception in the decade after 1973.

Second, if consumers literally lived by bread alone, they would surely organize against any oligopoly or cartel of bakers or flour millers, just as the machinist or the dairy farmer, whose incomes depend on the prices, respectively, of machinists' labor and dairy products, organize against oligopsonists who hold those prices down. But the vast majority of real-world consumers scatter their resentments randomly over so many people and professions ("Rich man, poor man, beggarman, thief/ Doctor, lawyer, Indian chief") with no consensus about whom to deal with first. This is not to deny that consumer guides and testing services, like the magazines *Consumer Reports* and *Consumer Digest,* survive by catering to a minority of consumers.

A third reason is political. The representative consumer activist is antibusiness, and two aspects of being antibusiness are to be prolabor and profarmer. But where high union wages and high farm prices translate into high consumer prices, what is there to do but mutter vaguely about "middlemen" and "profiteers" and "soaking the rich"? Also, many consumer activists are during working hours themselves employees of oligopolistic companies, members of oligopolistic unions, or practitioners of oligopolistically organized professions. (How is the cost of health care to be reduced, without reduction in the quality, if the services of doctors, nurses, hospital administrators, and hospital staffs are all sacrosanct?)

And so the consumer, often also a producer, goes his or her not-so-merry way, pacifying his or her conscience for oligopolistic activities on the production front by resentment, probably exaggerated, as a consumer of the ill-gotten gains of all the other oligopolies and cartel members. This is not an inspiring sight, but it may be closer to Utopia than to the Gulag Archipelago.

IX *Resource Markets*

- Resource Supply and Demand
- Labor, Wages, and Collective Bargaining
- Capital, Interest, and Investment

29 *Resource Supply and Demand*

PREVIEW In Parts VII and VIII you studied product, or output, markets. Part IX deals with resource, or input, markets. Supply and demand interact in resource or input markets in much the same way as they do in product or output markets. However, the supply of resources and the demand for them change the parts that the actors play on the economic stage. In the output markets, businesses supply and consumers demand; in the resource markets, the business firms are the demanders, while the people who own the labor, natural resources, and capital are the suppliers.

In a certain sense, this chapter offers you little that you haven't already learned. Your main challenge will be to apply some ideas that you learned earlier in a different context. You will have to keep reminding yourself that you are now studying demand from the viewpoint of a profit-maximizing firm and supply from the viewpoint of the owners of the factors of production (labor, natural resources, and capital).

We begin by reviewing the definitions of the resources. We recognize that enterprise or entrepreneurship should be separated out of the labor category. But where does labor end, and where does entrepreneurship begin? Why are certain labor skills or human capital sometimes classified as capital? And where do you draw the line between land that is a natural resource and land that should be classified as capital?

Next we discuss the supply of resources. We explain the difference between the supply of a resource for all the uses to which it can be put and the supply of a resource for a specific use. You will see that the supply curve for a resource is generally positive—as it is for products—but that it will vary in slope depending upon

the resource's opportunity cost. You will also learn about the price elasticity of resource supply and some of the more important determinants of supply elasticity.

Turning next to the demand side, we explain why the demand for resources is called a "derived demand." We also describe the price elasticity of resource demand and its main determinants. Then we present marginal productivity theory. Given certain simplifying assumptions, it explains the amounts of a specific resource that profit-maximizing companies will demand at different resource prices. Next, we combine supply and demand to discover the equilibrium level of resource quantity and price. The earnings that owners of resources receive are broken down into transfer earnings and economic earnings. Transfer earnings are the part that is equal to what a resource can earn in its next-best use, and economic earnings account for the rest. Finally, we deal with the economic and public policy implications of resource earnings made up only of transfer earnings, only of economic earnings, or of certain mixes of the two.

THE RESOURCES REVISITED

In Chapter 4 we explained that production brings together certain inputs, which we called the factors of production or resources. At that point in the book, we separated them into three broad categories: (1) labor, (2) natural resources, and (3) capital. Here we make one change. We separate enterprise or entrepreneurship out of the labor category. So here we look at four kinds of resources and the payments, or returns, that each receives:

1. Labor resources, which receive wages
2. Entrepreneurial resources, which receive profit
3. Natural resources, which receive rent
4. Capital resources, which receive interest.

Labor Resources

Labor covers most forms of human work that are or can be directed toward production. It includes the labor of the assembly-line worker and of the computer programmer. The only kind of human work that we are not classifying as labor is the entrepreneur's effort. Entrepreneurship is different from management or administration. Managerial and administrative jobs are considered to be labor, but entrepreneurship is that special kind of human effort that sets the course that a company will take. An entrepreneur makes the key decisions about the use of labor, natural resources, and capital. Labor receives wages (in some cases called salaries) in return for its productive work. An entrepreneur does not. Instead, he or she receives a residual payment called profit or incurs a loss. Whatever is left over after labor, natural resources, and capital are paid goes to the entrepreneur.

Entrepreneurial Resources

As leaders of business firms, **entrepreneurs** seek the best opportunities for production and coordinate all the other resources in order to carry them out. An entrepreneur is one who visualizes needs and takes the necessary actions to initiate the process by which they will be met. This often means taking risks and innovating. In the construction business, an entrepreneur might decide to build a new housing project. He or she decides where to build it, what kind of housing it will be, what materials to use, how much and what kind of labor and capital to employ, plus the million and one other questions that arise in leading such an enterprise. Of course, the entrepreneur can never be sure of the results of these

decisions. Perhaps a different building site would have been better. Possibly mortgage rates will rise after the project is started. The technology that was chosen may turn out to be a mistake because of some change in a labor market that greatly reduces the cost of certain workers. Just the same, the entrepreneur must make decisions about all these things, and more, before the project gets under way.

Natural Resources

Natural resources are the "gifts of nature" that can be used to produce goods. Land in its natural state is an essential input for most production. Raw materials such as crude oil, iron ore, and water are also important natural resource inputs for much that is produced. Finally, vegetation that grows without anyone planting it and animals such as fish that are generally not domesticated are also natural resources. Payment for the use of natural resources is called rent.

Capital Resources

Capital is made up of goods and skills that are used as inputs for production. Factory buildings, tools, and equipment are examples of **capital goods,** and the abilities to heal the sick, operate a lathe, and program a computer are examples of capital skills or **human capital.** Unlike the other resources, capital must first be produced itself before it is available for use in further production. Capital is produced, not for final consumer use, but rather for entrepreneurs to use, along with labor and natural resources, in producing goods and services for final consumption. Payment for the use of capital is called interest.

Resource Packages

Before we continue our discussion of the four categories of resources, you should understand that in the real world it is actually very difficult to know where one resource ends and another one begins. They are not as easy to separate as

TABLE 29-1 Functional Distribution of National Income in the United States, Selected Years, 1929–1985 (percentages)

Year	Compensation of Employees (Wages and Fringe Benefits)	Proprietors' Income	Rental Income	Corporate Profits	Interest
1929	60.5	17.1	5.8	11.4	5.6
1940	65.6	15.8	3.4	11.1	4.1
1945	67.9	17.3	2.8	10.8	1.2
1950	64.8	16.2	3.2	14.6	1.3
1955	67.2	13.5	3.6	14.0	1.7
1960	69.8	12.3	3.6	11.6	2.7
1965	68.3	11.1	3.1	13.9	3.6
1970	74.3	9.6	2.2	9.0	4.9
1975	73.6	9.7	1.0	9.1	6.5
1980	74.3	8.2	0.3	8.0	9.1
1985	73.8	7.5	0.4	9.3	8.9

Note: For some years, percentages do not add up to 100 percent because of rounding.

Source: Economic Report of the President, 1986, Table B-23.

our classification implies. Very rarely do we find a productive resource that does not include some capital. In fact, capital is a part of almost all labor, entrepreneurship, and natural resources. Labor that is totally untrained and uneducated is little more than brute force and, with no tools or machines with which to work, will probably be very unproductive. The same may be said for entrepreneurship. An untrained and uneducated entrepreneur will probably lack the vision to see business opportunities as well as the ability to combine resources effectively in a business firm. Natural resources, too, are of little use without the knowledge and skills of people who are able to use them productively. Often capital goods are needed to turn a pure natural resource into a productive input.

You can see, then, that production usually requires the use of certain combinations of resources or **resource packages** that cannot be separated except in theory. For example, a company that is building a housing project must have the land leveled, holes dug in the ground for foundations, wood put together in certain ways, bricks cemented together, and so on. The entrepreneur has many choices to make, but these are choices among different resource packages, and

not choices about whether or not to use labor or capital or natural resources. The houses must be built on land that is prepared by labor and capital. The foundations must be dug by more or less skilled labor using more or less sophisticated capital equipment. The carpentry and the brickwork also call for combinations of labor and capital. So it is clear that entrepreneurs must base their decisions on the productiveness of alternative resource packages at particular prices.

THE FUNCTIONAL DISTRIBUTION OF INCOME

Before we turn to the supply and demand for resources, let us examine their relative shares of U.S. national income. Table 29-1 shows these shares for selected years since 1929.

Several facts about the functional distribution, or relative resource shares, become clear from studying the table. Compensation of employees (labor's share) is the largest share by far and has increased over the past half-century. Proprietor's income (the net profits of unincorporated businesses) and rental income are relatively small shares of the total and have decreased. Corporate profits and interest also are relatively small shares, but have fluctuated over the years.

Certain problems arise in relating these statistics to our four-part classification of resources. Because proprietor's income is a mixture of wages, rent, interest, and profit, it combines some income from all the noncorporate categories. On the other hand, the rental income data do not include rental income received by proprietorships or corporations. Therefore, some caution should be used in interpreting changes in shares over time. To the extent that corporations have replaced large numbers of small unincorporated businesses, the share of income has shifted away from proprietor's income to all the other categories. The most important shift has been to compensation of employees. Suppose that the Ma and Pa grocery goes out of business when the new A&P grocery opens up, but that Ma and Pa are able to get jobs at the new A&P. In the statistics, compensation of employees has gone up and proprietor's income has gone down, but the actual growth in labor income is not as large as the statistics suggest. Much of the income of proprietors, like Ma and Pa, was probably labor income in the first place. Also, to the extent that title deeds to natural resources are sold by individuals to organized businesses, the rental income share will show a decrease, and corporate profits and proprietor's income will show a gain. In fact, rental income may be as great as ever.

THE SUPPLY OF RESOURCES

At any time there are certain amounts of resources in existence. There are only so many people in the world or in a country, only a certain amount of recognized natural resources, and only a certain amount of capital goods and human capital. However, it would be nonsense to dismiss the supply side of resource markets on the ground that the total quantity of each resource is fixed. Supply explores the quantities that are *offered* at various prices. Every waking hour of every "working-age" person is a potential hour of labor,

but that vast amount is only remotely related to the actual supply of labor. We expect that much more labor of any kind will be supplied at high wages than at low wages. The same positive relationship is expected for specific uses of labor, as well as for all uses of labor put together. It is also expected for the other resources. More natural resources will be offered at higher rents and less at lower rents. More capital will be produced and offered at higher interest payments and less at lower interest payments. In the same way, higher profit will attract more entrepreneurs, and economic loss may cause them to seek employment as workers.

It makes a considerable difference whether we are examining a supply response for all uses of a resource or for just one specific use of that resource. For example, we may want to know how much more labor will be offered after an across-the-board 10 percent wage increase for all workers in the United States. Or we may want to know only about the change in the quantity of hospital nursing labor that is supplied when the wages of hospital nurses are raised 10 percent, if all other wage rates remain the same. In the first case, the supply response will depend upon how many people who are already working will decide to work more hours than before the wage increase and on how many people who were not part of the labor force before will be persuaded to offer their services at the higher wage rate. In the specific-use case of hospital nursing, the supply response will not be limited to how many working hospital nurses will decide to offer more hours of work and how many trained nurses not in the labor force will decide to enter or re-enter hospital nursing. This response will also be affected by how many nonhospital nurses—such as nurses in doctors' offices, in schools, in factories, and in nursing homes—will switch over to hospital nursing.

Supply for All Uses

The preceding discussion has probably convinced you of two important facts about the supply of resources. The first is that supply responses are normally positive—more of a resource is expected to be supplied at higher prices and less at lower prices. Second, the supply for all uses of a resource is normally less responsive to a change in the price of that resource (less elastic) than is the supply for a specific use.

In this section we shall focus our attention on the supply for all uses of a resource. We expect positive supply responses to price changes, and we expect elasticity to increase with the passage of time. As with all responses, the greater the length of time between a change in price and when the quantity response is measured, the more elastic the response will be.[1] For example, after one month a 10 percent increase in the price of a natural resource such as coal or silver may bring about only a 5 percent increase in the quantity supplied of that natural resource. But after two years, when established firms in the coal- or silver-mining business have had time to make many more adjustments and new firms have had time to enter these industries, the supply response to the original 10 percent price increase may be as high as 15 or 20 percent.[2]

SUPPLY FOR ALL USES OF LABOR The supply of labor that is offered in a country depends upon many things. Some important variables include: (1) the size of the population, (2) the age distribution of the population, (3) the proportion of the population that chooses to participate in the labor force, (4) the proportion of the year, week, or day that those participating in the labor force choose to work, and (5) the age when people normally enter the labor force and the age when they normally retire. Also, the country's customs, laws, and attitudes influence who should work, for how long each year, week, or day, and over what periods of their lives. In the next few pages, we take a closer look at these five major influences on the supply of labor for all uses.

1. Recall our discussions of price elasticity of demand on the output side in Chapter 22 and price elasticity of supply on the output side in Chapter 24.
2. For the moment we ignore the possibility that speculation about future prices of coal or silver might persuade owners to leave the resource in the ground.

SIZE OF POPULATION The size of the population and its rate of growth are important determinants of the supply of labor. Population growth varies for many reasons including ignorance about birth control, religious and moral beliefs, usefulness of children as farm workers, the security of having children to take care of aged parents, life expectancy, and so on. The size of some populations is kept down by extreme poverty, and the size of others is kept down by substantial wealth.

The size of the population of a country is affected not only by birth and death rates but also by immigration. It is common for people who live in poorer countries with few opportunities for work to emigrate to wealthier ones. In the United States, the history of the labor supply is closely tied to immigration, mainly from Europe in earlier years and from Mexico and other Latin American countries in more recent years. However, the supply of labor through immigration may not be permanent. During the past two decades, countries like Germany and Italy have had a large number of temporary immigrants from countries like Yugoslavia and Turkey. Generally these people work in the host country for ten years or so and, after saving some money, return to their own country.

AGE DISTRIBUTION Two countries with populations of about equal size may not have the same labor supplies, since their age distributions may be very different. One of the countries may have a smaller labor supply because its population includes a large percentage of old people above working age. The other country may have a much greater supply of labor since its age distribution is more concentrated around the working years. Of course, a country that hosts a large number of temporary immigrants who come for the purpose of finding better jobs will have a larger proportion of working-age people than the country from which the workers emigrate.

LABOR FORCE PARTICIPATION RATE Not every working-age person is willing or able to participate in the labor force. Because some people are physically or mentally handicapped, they cannot perform most kinds of work. "Housewives" or "househusbands" choose not to supply their labor to business firms or governments so that they can take care of their young children and their homes. Many people will decide to spend extra years in school or to retire earlier than is usual. Others who have inherited wealth or have income from property may simply decide to spend their time in ways other than working for wages. There are also some people who have such low living standards that welfare payments are sufficient to satisfy them.

Labor force participation rates go up or down depending upon a number of different variables. Changes in wages have both a substitution effect and an income effect on the amount of labor supplied. Clearly, higher wage rates, which mean a higher opportunity cost of not working, will attract people into the labor force and also keep other people from leaving the labor force. Lower wage rates, which mean a lower opportunity cost of not working, will often cause people to stay in school longer, retire earlier, stay at home to tend the garden, or stay at home to take care of the children. That is the substitution effect. However, the income effect is also functioning at the same time, but in the opposite direction. Participation rates are expected to have a negative response to changes in real income. When real income rises, people may want to have more leisure time and so will supply less labor. And when real income falls, people may be willing to supply more labor.

Cultural changes may also bring about increases or decreases in the labor force participation rate. For example, before World War II relatively few American women worked in factories, and it was customary for women who did work to quit when they married or became pregnant. But the needs for labor were so great during the war that women flocked to the factories. Working side by side with men, like "Rosie the Riveter," they convinced American society that they could handle what traditionally were "men's" jobs. Many families found that a second income in a household was a desirable thing. Today more than half of all working-age American women participate in the labor force.

A country's labor force participation rate is also affected by legislation. Laws prohibiting child labor or requiring attendance in school may decrease the labor force participation rate. By contrast, laws prohibiting forced early retirement and laws that are very strict about who may receive welfare payments tend to increase the labor force participation rate.

WORK PER YEAR, WEEK, OR DAY   The supply of labor is a function not only of how many people are available for work but also of how many hours per year, week, or day they are available for work. Before the American Civil War, most people worked twelve-hour days, six days a week, fifty-two weeks a year.[3] Vacations, holidays, a five- or even four-day workweek, and seven- to eight-hour workdays are relatively recent. As real wages increased, it took fewer hours of work to earn enough money to buy the necessities of life, so that some money was left over for luxuries. With the higher real wage, leisure time became not only more expensive but also more valuable. What good is it to earn enough to buy a sailboat, a sports car, and a house with a swimming pool, if one doesn't have time to sail, drive, or swim?

This point is a further application of the income effect and substitution effect. An increase in wages—the price of labor—has a tendency both to increase the number of hours people are willing to work (the substitution effect) and to decrease the number of hours they are willing to work (the income effect). Because the substitution effect of a wage increase makes leisure time relatively more expensive, it makes people more willing to give up some leisure time in order to get the additional goods and services they can afford with a higher income. But the income effect of a wage increase works in the opposite direction. It makes people richer, causing them to buy more of what they want, and that includes leisure time. What the net result will be is not easy to predict. People often respond positively—that is, they are willing to work more hours—when they are given

3. Harold F. Williamson, *The Growth of the American Economy* (New York: Prentice-Hall, 1951), p. 659.

a chance to receive time-and-a-half or double-time pay for overtime. However, over the longer run, more leisure has been chosen and less labor has been supplied as wages have increased. In the very long run, productivity increases enable everyone to work fewer hours while simultaneously receiving higher real income.

WORKING AGE So far we have used the term "working age" as though it had a fixed definition. It does not. The legal, socially accepted, or typical working age varies greatly from country to country and from time to time within the same country. Even though it is common today to see very young children working in the rural areas of developing countries, most industrial countries have strict laws that forbid young children to work. However, during the nineteenth century, particularly in the textile industries of England and America, young children worked long hours in sweatshops. Not until the 1930s were laws passed in the United States to prohibit child labor.[4]

The lower age limit for workers is also very much influenced by the society's attitudes about education, as reflected in its laws. The amount of taxpayer-supported public education affects how many years most people go to school. "Free" or largely subsidized higher education gives people a strong incentive to withhold their labor until about age twenty-two (or older if they pursue graduate education).

The supply of labor also depends upon the upper limit of the working age. Even though there is no legal upper limit, employers may set a mandatory retirement age at 70 or higher.[5] However, incentives for early or late retirement may be provided by firms or by the government.

For example, in the United States the retirement pension provided by the Social Security Act of 1935 can be claimed by a retired person at age 65 or a scaled-down version at age 62. From age 65 (or 62) until age 70, the Social Security recipient may earn only a small sum of money each year before having to pay back his or her Social Security benefits in the form of a 50 percent tax on "excess" earnings.[6]

SUPPLY FOR ALL USES OF ENTREPRENEURSHIP Much of our discussion about labor also applies to entrepreneurship. Of course, people may be willing and able to participate in the labor force, yet not willing and able to be entrepreneurs. Many do not like to take risks. Nor does everyone have the education, training, and other qualities to be able to visualize needs and take the necessary steps to initiate the process by which they will be met.

The laws, educational systems, and cultures in some countries offer more encouragement to entrepreneurs than in other countries. Just how the entrepreneurial "spirit" is best achieved and cultivated is not easy to determine and goes well beyond the subject matter of this book.[7]

The business ventures of many entrepreneurs have a short life span. In general, small firms fail at a higher rate than larger businesses.[8] One study found that about one-half of the new businesses that were founded or acquired during the late 1940s and early 1950s were "disposed of" within two years, one-third lasted as long as four years, and only one-fifth were still in operation after ten years.[9] According to another study for the years 1959 to 1962, the number of U.S. businesses increased by about 172,000, because

---

4. The Walsh-Healey Act of 1936 and the Fair Labor Standards Act of 1938 established a minimum age of 16 for general employment and 18 for employment in hazardous occupations. For certain occupations, where work is performed outside of school hours, the minimum age was established at 14.

5. Since the Age Discrimination in Employment Act was amended in 1978, employers may not force a person to retire before the age of 70.

6. A person may earn $5,760 if under age 65 and $7,800 if between the ages of 65 and 70 in 1986. There is no limit on property or pension income.

7. See Douglass C. North, *Structure and Change in Economic History* (New York: Norton, 1981).

8. A. B. Cochran, "Small Business Mortality Rates: A Review of the Literature," *Journal of Small Business Management*, October 1981, p. 57.

9. Betty C. Churchill, "Age and Life Expectancy of Business Firms," *Survey of Current Business*, December 1955, pp. 15, 16.

1,291,000 new businesses were started and 1,119,000 businesses failed.[10] There are many reasons for the rapid turnover and instability of entrepreneurs' business ventures. Unexpectedly poor business conditions causing low sales and high inventories are often cited to explain the rash of business failures during recessions and depressions. But Dun and Bradstreet, the leading source of information on business failures in the United States, stresses managerial incompetence and lack of experience as the major reasons for business failure.

The quantity supplied of entrepreneurs is believed to be positively related to the returns expected by would-be entrepreneurs. The higher the expected profit, the more likely it is that a person will become an entrepreneur and the greater the quantity supplied of this resource will be. As you have learned from your study of market types in Part VIII, firms are more likely to make a high and lasting profit in less-competitive rather than more-competitive markets. It follows then that the more monopoly control a potential entrepreneur expects to gain, the more likely it is that he or she will become an entrepreneur. In other words, entrepreneurs will be more attracted to oligopolistic and monopolistic industries than to those that approach monopolistic competition or pure competition.

For this reason, government policies in the areas of patents, taxation, and antitrust can influence the supply of entrepreneurs. Remember from Chapter 26 that a patent is a temporary (seventeen years in the United States) government-enforced actual monopoly that may be given to inventors or to companies that purchase the rights of inventors. The easier it is to get patents, the longer they run, and the harder it is to infringe upon them, the greater will be the supply of entrepreneurs. Also, low corporate income tax rates, generous deductions for business expenses, and favorable ways of figuring the depreciation of capital result in higher net profits and so should attract more entrepreneurs. Of course, antitrust law and enforcement is a two-way street. On the one hand, the less strict a country's antitrust laws

10. Cochran, *op. cit.*, pp. 56, 57.

(see Chapter 34) and the less vigorous their enforcement, the freer companies will be to pursue monopoly control and presumably the greater the supply of entrepreneurs will be. On the other hand, the stricter the antitrust laws and the better they are enforced, the easier it may be for entrepreneurs to enter industries and to compete on a fair basis.

SUPPLY FOR ALL USES OF NATURAL RESOURCES At first blush, natural resources seem to be fixed or unchanging. In the early nineteenth century, the well-respected British economist David Ricardo defined land as the "original and indestructible power of the soil." Indeed, there are some naturally renewable and therefore "indestructible" resources. The water in a stream fed by melting snow from a mountain may be used over and over again. However, most natural resources are at least to some extent "exhaustible" and will not easily or quickly renew themselves. Once crude oil, natural gas, or iron ore is taken out of the ground, there is that much less left for future production. The soil can be depleted or "farmed out," when farmers do not follow proper soil-maintenance practices. Waterways will no longer be productive if waste products are dumped into them.

If the price or rent of these resources is so low that it doesn't pay to maintain them, their supply may be allowed to dwindle. On the other hand, the supply of natural resources will be increased if their prices or rents are high enough to make it pay. Extensive exploration for crude oil, natural gas, or iron ore may lead to discoveries that increase the supply. In recent years the response to OPEC has included important new discoveries of oil in Alaska, the North Sea, and the Yucatán Peninsula in Mexico and of natural gas in Siberia. Certain natural resources may be replaced by others. Advances in technological knowledge can also change the amount of usable natural resources. For example, in the early 1950s, when the rich red ore of the Mesabi iron range in northeastern Minnesota and the upper peninsula of Michigan was nearly used up, new techniques were discovered that allowed the economical mining of a lower-grade ore called taconite. Once again a thriving iron ore industry was created in that part of the country.

In a sense, land can also be increased. That is, it can be reclaimed from under water, and deserts can be irrigated. Northwestern University has built a library on land that once lay under Lake Michigan. In the southwestern United States and in many parts of Israel, desert land has been made fertile through irrigation. In a new section of Belgrade, Yugoslavia, swamps have been drained to allow the building of huge apartment complexes and shopping areas.[11]

You can see, then, that the supply of natural resources responds to rent just as the supply of labor responds to wages and the supply of entrepreneurs responds to profit. With few exceptions, the higher the rent of natural resources, the higher the quantity supplied, and vice versa.

One important exception, however, should be noted. If a natural resource is defined in terms of a certain location, supply cannot be increased beyond its natural limitation. For example, no more street-level land on the northeast corner of State and Randolph streets in Chicago can be created. No matter how high the rent is, that precisely defined natural resource's supply is fixed. So over any price range at which its supply cannot be increased, its supply is perfectly inelastic, and its supply curve appears as a vertical straight line.

SUPPLY FOR ALL USES OF CAPITAL Recall that capital is divided between capital goods and capital skills, called human capital. The stock of capital goods is the quantity of factory buildings, tools, and equipment that exists at a particular time. In the production process, this stock of capital is continuously being reduced. That is, it is used up or depreciated when it is producing consumer goods or other capital goods. But at the same time, it is usual to produce capital goods to replace the ones that are used up and possibly to increase the stock of capital goods. Whether and to what degree capital goods are added or

drawn down depends on the return or expected return to capital, which is called an interest payment.

Since capital goods are themselves outputs produced by firms, the quantity supplied responds to price in the same way as other outputs. More will be supplied at a high price than at a low price, other things being equal. In considering the supply of capital for all uses, the choice is between using resources to produce capital goods or using them to produce consumption goods. In this context, the price of capital takes the form of an interest payment. When the interest payment for capital is high relative to the price of consumer goods, firms will use more resources to produce capital goods and less to produce consumption goods.

Human capital may be treated in much the same way as capital goods. However, it is more complicated because it is mixed with labor. The return to the labor–human capital package is a mixture of wages and interest. How much of your economics professor's paycheck is a return for his or her sweat, blood, and tears expended in teaching you the subject, and how much is a return for the many years of education and training in which he or she invested?

The supply of human capital depends on the return or expected return to human capital. The supply of human capital is positively related to that return. At higher returns from an education, we expect more people to go to school, and vice versa.

Supply for Specific Uses

As you may remember, we separated our discussion of the supply of resources into the supply for all uses and the supply for specific uses. The second is a subset of the first, so that everything we explained about the supply for all uses also applies to the supply for a specific use. Other things being the same, the greater the supply is for all uses, the greater will be the supply for each specific use, and likewise, the lower the supply is for all uses, the lower will be the supply for any specific use.

---

11. These are, of course, examples of resource packages. Capital, entrepreneurship, and labor are embodied in this additional land.

However, as we have already pointed out, the supply response to a change in the price of a resource defined in terms of a specific use is greater than when that resource is defined for all uses. In the case of resource supply for all uses, a higher price has to attract a greater total quantity of that resource. However, in the case of resource supply for a specific use, no more of that resource needs to be attracted, since it need only switch from one use to another. As we said, it may take a 10 percent wage hike to increase the quantity supplied of nurses by 5 percent; but a 10 percent wage increase for only those nurses working in hospitals is likely to swell the quantity supplied of hospital nurses by much more than 5 percent, since nurses working in doctors' offices, schools, factories, and nursing homes will want to take advantage of the relatively higher wage.

Resources have many different uses. If all uses of a certain resource are equally attractive to the owners of that resource, they will seek out the use that offers the highest price. In this case, all owners of that resource would be paid the same price. If, for some reason, there was a slight increase in the price for one use, much more would be supplied for that use and correspondingly less for other uses. This would mean that bids being made for the other uses would have to be higher, so that the price would once again be the same for all uses.

Actually, not all uses are equally attractive to owners of resources. Most nurses find it more pleasant to work in a doctor's office than in a hospital. This is probably the reason why hospital nurses earn higher wages than nurses in doctors' offices do. Similarly, real wages for certain labor resources vary according to the climate, the scenery, the environmental pollution, the cultural and recreational amenities, and the population density of a place.

Price Elasticity of Resource Supply

Recall from our discussion of supply in Chapter 24 that the concept of price elasticity of supply relates the percentage change in the quantity of something that is supplied to the percentage change in the price that brought about the change:

$$\frac{\text{percentage change in quantity supplied of X}}{\text{percentage change in price of X}}$$

In that earlier discussion, X was some output such as shoes or hamburgers. Now that we are discussing inputs for specific uses, X may be the nurses working in doctors' offices or land for growing wheat or die presses used to produce lawn mowers.

There are important differences in the price elasticities of supply for different resources. Some resources are very *mobile*—that is, they can easily change from one activity to another—and so may have high price elasticities of supply for any specific use. Others are relatively immobile, and so may have much lower elasticities. Unskilled labor is generally more mobile than skilled labor, which is more specialized. Flat, fertile land in the midwestern United States is much more mobile, in the sense that it can be used for many more different purposes, than the sharply sloped and rocky land in Albania. The rocky land might be productive only for raising goats, whereas the flat, fertile land may be suited to many different agricultural uses. For example, a 2 percent increase in the expected price of wheat may cause so many farmers to switch their planting from corn, barley, or soybeans to wheat that 20 percent more wheat is produced (price elasticity of supply equals 10). A drill press may be quite mobile, as it can be used to drill holes in many different metal products, but a die press used to stamp out lawn-mower parts is more specialized and less easily shifted to another use. It would therefore take a great decrease in its earnings (interest payments) to cause its owner to convert it to another use.

As with all applications of the elasticity concept, the time variable is very important. Nearly all resources are quite inelastic when measured over a very short period of time and become much more elastic over a longer period of time. A farmer isn't likely to switch from corn to wheat after the corn is already planted and before it is harvested, but at the next planting the change is easily made. Likewise, it takes time for people to learn about job opportunities in other parts of a country, and it takes even more time to make the move. If a new skill is required, it takes time to train or retrain. Sometimes the change is made in the next generation. For example, a farmer may see great opportunities in engineering or computer programming, but often the best he or she can do is support a child's education so that the child can later work as an engineer or computer programmer.

THE DEMAND FOR RESOURCES

As you learned in Chapter 21, consumer demand for a certain product depends on how much satisfaction consumers expect to receive from that product as compared with other products that they could buy for the same price. If we substitute the word *profit* for the word *satisfaction*, the statement also applies to business firm demand for resources. In this context the statement now reads: Business firm demand for a certain resource depends on how much profit business firms expect to receive from that resource as compared with other resources they could acquire for the same price.

Just changing that one word, and also the economic context, amounts to a very important change in the statement's meaning. Consumers demand goods and services because they like them—because they taste good, sound good, look good, or feel good. That is *not* the case with business firms. They are not likely to demand a worker's services simply because he or she is a nice person. Generally they will not demand a certain machine because of its exquisite design or beautiful shining metal. Nor will they usually demand a piece of land just because of its scenic beauty. These characteristics are not important unless they contribute to the reason why they will demand or not demand the resource: the firm's expected profit. Certainly, if a company is hiring a salesperson, it will prefer a "nice" person because he or she is expected to sell better. Similarly, the exquisitely designed machine may perform better, and the scenic piece of land may be just what is required for a resort hotel. But, a bouncer for a bar should be intimidating, a very

ugly machine may outperform all others, and the best farmland is often flat and dull. As has been our assumption in all of the economic theory of the firm, which you studied earlier, firms are in business to maximize their profit. Resources, whether human or nonhuman, are simply inputs needed to produce the outputs that business firms believe they can sell most profitably.

Derived Demand

The recognition that business firms do not demand resources as ends in themselves is expressed in the concept of derived demand. The demand for a resource is a **derived demand** because it is derived from the demand for the products that this resource helps to produce. The demand for automobile workers depends on the demand for automobiles, and the demand for buggy-whip makers depends on the demand for buggy whips. In the early twentieth century, when automobiles began to replace horse-drawn buggies, more automobile workers and fewer buggy-whip makers were demanded.

Important lessons can be learned from this simple concept. Derived demand tells labor that it doesn't matter how "skillful" people are in some abstract sense. What matters is that they are skilled at performing particular tasks that are important inputs to the production of those goods or services for which there is great demand. In the late 1970s and the first half of the 1980s, college students who majored in accounting, engineering, or computer science and otherwise prepared themselves for these careers found good jobs when they graduated. Other equally capable students who majored in sociology, history, or English found fewer jobs in their chosen fields. There was little demand for their labor because there was little demand for the services they were trained to produce.

Another lesson learned through the understanding of derived demand involved agricultural land values in early nineteenth-century England. The concept of derived demand, which tells us that the demand for land depends upon the demand for the goods and services produced on it, was not well understood at that time. Most people blamed the high price of wheat in England on the high rent that had to be paid for land. However, the leading British economist, David Ricardo, disagreed with many of his contemporaries. He argued that the high price for the use of land to grow wheat on was a result of the high price of wheat. England had a quite inelastic supply of rural land, so that rents on this land were largely determined by the demand for land on which crops might be grown or sheep grazed. Since growing wheat was very profitable at prevailing prices, farmers who wanted more wheat land would bid up the price (rent) for the use of land.

Price Elasticity of Resource Demand

At this point in your economics course, you will not be surprised to learn that the quantity demanded for specific resources is negatively related to their prices. For example, more automobile workers are demanded at lower wage rates for automobile workers, and fewer are demanded when their wage rates are higher. Why is this so? Remember that the demand for automobile workers is a derived demand and that automobile firms are not interested in hiring these workers as an end in themselves. The answer lies in a series of relationships. Since automobile workers' wages are a large part of the total cost of producing automobiles, lower wages paid to automobile workers will result in much lower production costs for automobile firms. If there is enough competition in the automobile industry, the lower cost will be passed on to consumers in the form of lower automobile prices. Since the quantity demanded for automobiles is negatively related to the price of automobiles, more automobiles will be demanded. The greater quantity demanded for automobiles means greater quantity demanded for automobile workers.

We call this response the **price elasticity of resource demand**—meaning the degree of responsiveness of the quantity demanded of a resource to a change in its price. The strength of the response depends upon a number of factors as shown in our automobile workers example.

First, the larger the proportion of the total production cost that is accounted for by a certain resource, the more price elastic is the demand for that resource. So if automobile workers' wages account for 50 percent of the total cost of producing automobiles, and their wages go down by 20 percent, the total cost decreases by 10 percent. But if, instead, workers' wages account for only 25 percent of the total cost, then a 20 percent decline in wages causes total cost to decrease by only 5 percent.

Second, the greater the price elasticity of demand of the final product (in this case, the automobile), the more price elastic is the demand for that resource. If the demand for automobiles is unitary elastic, a 10 percent decrease in the price of automobiles will be matched by a 10 percent increase in sales, which might mean a 10 percent rise in the demand for automobile workers. But if, instead, the price elasticity of demand of automobiles is 2, the same 10 percent decrease in the price of automobiles brings about a 20 percent rise in sales and presumably a 20 percent increase in the demand for automobile workers.

Third, the more competition there is in an industry, the more likely it is that changes in resource prices (costs) will be passed on to consumers, and so the more price elastic will be the demand for the resources used by the firms in that industry. If the automobile industry were a monopoly, most of the decrease in the wages of automobile workers might be retained by the monopolist in the form of higher profit. But if the industry were fairly competitive, most of the wage decrease would be passed on in the form of lower prices to consumers.

Finally, the price elasticity of resource demand depends upon how easy or difficult it is to substitute one resource for another. The easier it is for a firm to respond to a rise in the price of a resource by substituting other resources for it and the easier it is for a firm to respond to a decrease in the price of a resource by substituting it for other resources, the more price elastic the demand for the resource. For example, in recent years the price elasticity of demand for certain automobile workers has increased because of the development of robots that can perform their tasks.

Resource Demand and Marginal Productivity

As you know, the demand for resources is a derived demand. Of course, business firms demand resources in order to produce goods and services that they can sell at a profit. Since companies are assumed to be in business to earn as much profit as they can, we want to find out just how much of any resource a firm will demand. In answering this question, we use much the same reasoning that we used in Chapter 24 when we showed how much output a firm will produce. This answer depends on two variables: (1) the contribution that a resource makes to the value of the product it helps to produce and (2) the cost of that resource.

The contribution that a resource makes to the value of output is actually very hard to determine. As we noted earlier, there is much interdependence among resources in production. "Packages" of resources produce firms' outputs. But in order to present the logic of the theory of resource demand in a fairly simple way, we shall assume that we are able to add or subtract units of particular resources and evaluate their precise contributions to production one at a time.

The other variable used in predicting a firm's demand for a resource—the cost of the resource—may also be complicated. Firms often find that by buying more or less of a resource they can affect the price that they have to pay for it. But again to simplify our explanation, we shall assume that resources are sold in a pure competition setting, so that their prices will not change, no matter how little or how much a firm buys.

Given these assumptions about the contribution of a resource to a firm's production and the price at which that firm buys the resource, we can predict how much of that resource the firm will demand. The theory of resource demand is based on the logic that a firm will want to keep on buying additional units of a resource as long as it will add more to its revenue than to its cost. The extra cost to the firm is the price that it has to pay for another unit of the resource or factor of production. We call this the **marginal factor cost (MFC).** The extra revenue to the firm is the

amount of money it receives from selling the additional quantity of output that one more unit of the resource input (all other resources remaining the same) allow it to produce. This is called the **marginal revenue product (MRP).**[12] As long as a company's MRP is greater than its MFC, with regard to any specific resource, it will continue to demand more units of that resource. It will stop demanding more units of the resource when its MFC is greater than its MRP. Therefore, a firm will be in equilibrium with regard to any specific resource when its MFC is equal to its MRP.

Let us review this conclusion by using a hypothetical case. Suppose that a building products firm, the Buildem Company, produces a building material called Corterboard and that Corterboard is made by combining a number of different resources, including a certain natural resource called pertadium. Our problem is to predict how many units of pertadium the Buildem Company will demand per day. As before, we assume that we can separate "packages" of resources so that pertadium is not tied to other resources and that the Buildem Company buys pertadium in a purely competitive market so that it faces the same pertadium price no matter how little or how much it buys.[13] Let us also make the simplifying assumption that Buildem is operating in a purely competitive product market so that it does not have to lower its price for Corterboard in order to sell more of it.[14] Finally, since we are interested only in the demand for pertadium, we are keeping all the other resources that Buildem uses to produce Corterboard at a constant level. This means that diminishing returns (decreasing marginal product) will set in and that the marginal

12. Note that the terms *marginal factor cost* (MFC) and *marginal revenue product* (MRP) are variants of the terms *marginal cost* (MC) and *marginal revenue* (MR), which are used to express similar logic about the quantity of output that a firm wishes to produce and sell.

13. The assumption about the purely competitive market will be relaxed in the next chapter when we show the case of labor employed in a monopsonistic labor market.

14. This assumption will also be relaxed in the next chapter when we show the case of labor helping to produce a product that is sold in a monopolistic market.

TABLE 29-2 Derivation of Marginal Revenue Product of Pertadium for the Buildem Company, Which Produces Corterboard

(1) Quantity of Pertadium Used in Production (per day)	(2) Total Product (quantity of Corterboard produced per day)	(3) Marginal Physical Product (additional quantity of Corterboard produced per day)	(4) Price per Unit of Corterboard (in dollars)	(5) Total Revenue (dollar receipts from Corterboard per day)	(6) Marginal Revenue Product (additional dollar receipts from Corterboard per day)
0	0		$10	$ 0	
		30			$300
1	30		10	300	
		35			350
2	65		10	650	
		30			300
3	95		10	950	
		26			260
4	121		10	1,210	
		23			230
5	144		10	1,440	
		20			200
6	164		10	1,640	

revenue product will at some point have to diminish.[15]

Table 29-2 provides the data needed for deriving Buildem's marginal revenue product when it uses different amounts of pertadium. To derive MRP, we follow two steps. First, we calculate the marginal product, or more precisely, the **marginal physical product (MPP)**—meaning the additional output produced by an extra unit of the variable resource. Second, we multiply the MPP by the price of the product. For example, using the first unit of pertadium causes total product (the quantity of Corterboard that is produced each day) to increase from zero to 30 units, so that the MPP will be 30. Multiplying the MPP of 30 by the $10 price of Corterboard gives us MRP of $300. Note that increasing returns to pertadium occur when a second unit is added (the MPP rises from 30 to 35, and the MRP rises from $300 to $350). After

that point, diminishing returns set in, so that additional units of pertadium bring decreasing MPP and MRP.

Another way to calculate MRP is first to determine total revenue, as we have done in column 5 of Table 29-2. Then for each additional unit of the variable input, MRP is figured by subtracting the previous total revenue from the new one. For example, notice that in Table 29-2, by adding a fourth unit of pertadium we increase total revenue from $950 to $1,210, so that MRP is $260 ($1,210 − $950 = $260).

Given the information provided in Table 29-2, we need only know the price that Buildem must pay for pertadium to determine its demand for this input. Table 29-3 provides that additional information. It repeats columns 1 and 6 from Table 29-2 and adds three columns showing three different prices of pertadium. We follow the profit-maximizing logic that a firm will demand a resource up to the point where its MRP equals

15. See Chapter 23, especially pp. 437–439.

its *MFC*. In this way, we can predict that Buildem will demand a bit more than 6 units when pertadium is at a price of $190 per unit, just over 5 units at a price of $220 per unit, and between 3 and 4 units when pertadium costs $270 per unit. This is shown in Figure 29-1. We have drawn Buildem's *MRP* curve for pertadium by plotting amounts from column 2 of Table 29-3 and then joining the plotted points. The negatively sloping part of the *MRP* curve is Buildem's demand curve for pertadium. (Each possible price of pertadium is Buildem's *MFC* at that price, and it will demand that quantity where its *MFC* equals its *MRP*.) Also shown in the figure are *MFC* curves at the three different prices of pertadium—$190, $220, and $270—taken from columns 3, 4, and 5 of Table 29-3. Where each of these *MFC* curves intersects the *MRP* curve is Buildem's demand at that price—a little more than 6 units at $190, a bit more than 5 units at $220, and between 3 and 4 units at $270.

TABLE 29-3   Marginal Revenue Product and Marginal Factor Cost of Pertadium for the Buildem Company at Three Alternative Prices of Pertadium

(1) Quantity of Pertadium Used in Production (per day)	(2) Marginal Revenue Product (additional dollar receipts from Corterboard per day)	(3) (4) (5) Marginal Factor Cost (additional dollar cost for additional units of pertadium) When Price of Pertadium Is:		
		$190	$220	$270
0				
	$300	$190	$220	$270
1				
	350	190	220	270
2				
	300	190	220	270
3				
	260	190	220	270
4				
	230	190	220	270
5				
	200	190	220	270
6				

FIGURE 29-1   Three Alternative Demand Levels for Pertadium by the Buildem Company

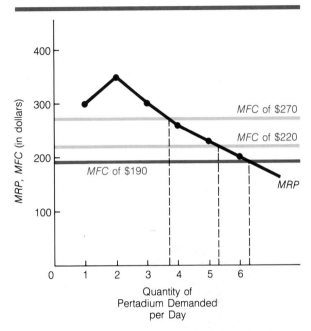

Pictured here is the marginal-revenue-product (*MRP*) curve for the natural resource pertadium used by the Buildem Company to produce Corterboard. It is plotted from column 2 in Table 29-3. Also shown are the three alternative marginal-factor-cost (*MFC*) curves plotted from columns 3, 4, and 5 in Table 29-3. Buildem's equilibrium level of demand is where its marginal revenue product (*MRP*) equals its appropriate marginal factor cost (*MFC*)—somewhat more than 6 units at the price of $190, slightly more than 5 units at the price of $220, and between 3 and 4 units at the price of $270.

THE INTERACTION OF SUPPLY AND DEMAND IN A RESOURCE MARKET

We have separately introduced you to the supply of resources and to the demand for resources. You are now ready to learn how they interact to determine equilibrium price and quantity of resources in a market. Our explanation of resource supply led us to expect positively sloped supply curves, and our explanation of the demand for resources led us to expect negatively sloped demand curves, so that we are on familiar ground. The interaction between supply and demand in resource markets is much the same as the interaction between supply and demand in product markets. Figure 29-2 pictures a supply curve and a demand curve for a resource called X. The supply curve pictures the total supply of X, and the demand curve is the sum of all the individual firms' demand curves for X. It doesn't matter whether X is a certain kind of skilled labor, agricultural entrepreneurs in a certain part of the United States, a certain natural resource like pertadium, or some sort of capital equipment. If the curves in Figure 29-2 reflect the market supply and demand functions for resource X, equilibrium takes place at price P, where Q is supplied and Q is demanded.

Transfer Earnings and Economic Earnings

The equilibrium earnings of a resource may be thought of as being composed of transfer earnings and economic earnings.[16] **Transfer earnings** are the part of the earnings of a resource that is equal to the earnings that this resource could command in the next-best use to which it can be put.[17] For example, the earnings of a certain piece of land that is presently being used as a site for a factory complex might be $1 million per year. Its next-best use might be as a wheat farm, in which it could earn only $50,000 per year. The $50,000 are the transfer earnings of this piece of land. Transfer earnings may also be thought of as that part of the earnings of a resource which it must earn to keep it from being transferred to its next-best use. In our example, if for some reason the earnings of the land as a factory site were to fall below

16. Because this analysis grew out of an early nineteenth-century concern about land values, much of the literature uses the term *economic rent* instead of *economic earnings*. Since we are applying this term, not just to land or other natural resources, but to all resources, the more neutral term *economic earnings* will be used.

17. Do not confuse transfer "earnings" with transfer "payments." *Transfer payments* are defined as payments that are *not* made in exchange for currently provided goods or services.

FIGURE 29-2 The Market Supply of and the Market Demand for Resource X

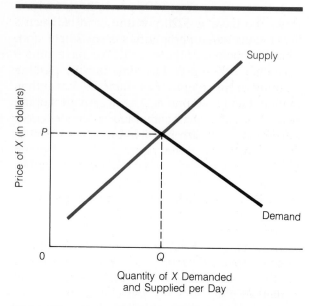

Quantity of X Demanded
and Supplied per Day

Pictured here are a supply curve and a demand curve, drawn in the usual fashion, for a resource called X. Equilibrium takes place at price P, where the quantity supplied (Q) is equal to the quantity demanded (Q).

$50,000 per year, the use of that piece of land would be switched to wheat farming.

The second part of the earnings of a resource is called economic earnings. **Economic earnings** are the part of the earnings of a resource that is not needed to keep that resource at its present use. In a sense, it is a surplus. It is the total earnings of a resource minus its transfer earnings. It represents that part of the earnings of a resource which is over and above what it would earn in its next-best use. In our case, where the earnings of a piece of land were $1 million per year and the transfer earnings were $50,000 per year, economic earnings are $950,000 per year.

Just as a piece of land generally has a next-best use in production, so do people have a next-best use for their production efforts. For example, a college professor who is employed at $32,000 a year may find that her next-best employment possibility is as a sales representative earning $28,000 a year. Her transfer earnings are $28,000, and her economic earnings are $4,000. If all other variables surrounding these two jobs—including relative satisfaction received, working conditions, and fringe benefits—were equal and held constant, the woman in our example would change jobs only if her teaching salary were cut by more than $4,000 a year.

Dramatic examples of persons receiving a huge amount of economic earnings can be found among athletes and entertainers. A very large part of the salaries of big-time athletes, actors, actresses, and musical groups consists of economic earnings. A seven-foot center on a major professional basketball team may earn $1 million a year. His transfer earnings might be the $20,000 a year he could earn as a medical technician, for which he trained during college. His economic earnings are $980,000 a year. Of course, the demand for his services is a derived demand. It is only because there is great competition among basketball club owners for the services of the few available seven-foot basketball players who are able to spark fans' interest and bring in large television and gate revenue that the athlete in our example is able to attract his high salary.

The breakdown of a resource's earnings into transfer earnings and economic earnings has important implications for resource allocation. The greater transfer earnings are in relation to economic earnings, the more likely it is that a resource will be transferred to another use. The lower the proportion of transfer earnings is to economic earnings, the less likely it is that a resource will be transferred to another use. You may understand this idea better after studying three different cases: two extremes and one case in between.

CASE I: ALL ECONOMIC EARNINGS   When a resource has only a single use, its transfer earnings are zero, and the price of the resource is made up entirely of economic earnings. Panel (a) of Figure 29-3 pictures such a case. Shown are a supply curve and a demand curve for land on a certain mountain in Vermont. The land is used as a ski slope and cannot be economically used for anything else. The mountain is in a fixed location, and we assume that a usable ski slope requires exactly these 800 acres. Its supply is perfectly inelastic. The demand for skiing on that mountain will determine its price, $100 an acre

in this case. Transfer earnings are zero, and so the whole payment for the 800 acres—$80,000, represented by the blue shaded area—is economic earnings. If the demand curve shifted down, the price would be lowered, but no land would be transferred to another use. If the demand curve shifted up, the price would be raised, but there would be no increase in supply.

CASE II: ALL TRANSFER EARNINGS   When a resource is put to a use for which it commands a price just barely above what it can command for its next-best use, its economic earnings are almost zero. Such a case is shown in panel (b) of Figure 29-3. You will recognize this case as the exact opposite of the previous one. In panel (a) the supply curve is a vertical straight line, whereas in this case it is a horizontal straight line. This might be a case of farmland used to produce beans. At $100 an acre, almost unlimited amounts of farmland are available to grow beans. The supply is virtually infinitely elastic. If the price were lowered by as little as a penny an acre, all 800 acres would switch over to their next-best use—say, the growing of peas. Thus, practically the whole payment for the 800 acres ($80,000, represented by the gray shaded area) is transfer earnings.

CASE III: MIX OF TRANSFER EARNINGS AND ECONOMIC EARNINGS   When a resource has more than a single use, and when a slightly lower price will not cause all of it to switch to its next-best use, its earnings are a mix of transfer earnings and economic earnings. This is a common situation. Panel (c) in Figure 29-3 pictures such a case, where the supply of a resource for a particular use is neither fixed nor infinitely responsive to changes in price. Here the supply curve is positively sloped. This might be a case of farmland used to produce corn. As in the other two panels, the payment for the 800 acres is $80,000, but this time it is made up partly of transfer earnings (the gray shaded area below the supply curve) and partly of economic earnings (the blue shaded area above the supply curve). If the demand curve shifts down ever so slightly, so that the price is lowered by a very small amount, one acre (the eight-hundredth acre) would be transferred to

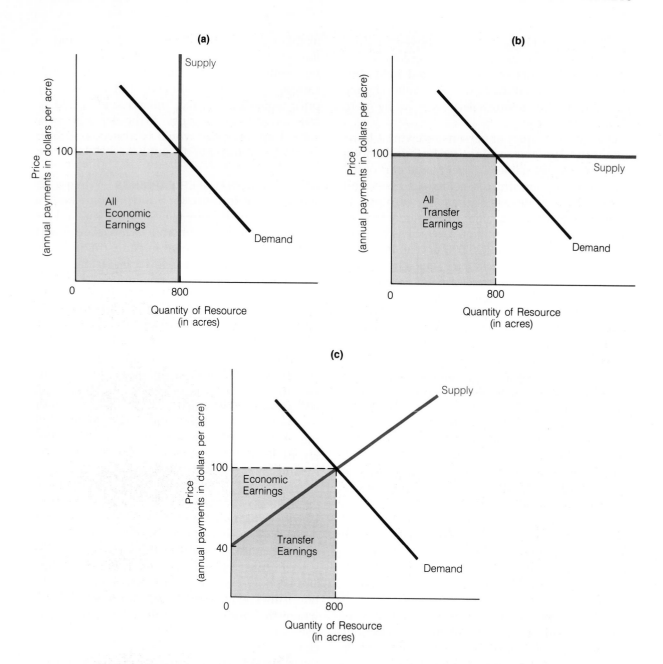

(a)

(b)

(c)

another use such as growing wheat or soybeans. At successively lower prices, more and more of this land would switch out of corn production and into other uses. However, some acreage will remain in corn until the price falls to just below $40 an acre. At prices below $40, all 800 acres will have been transferred out of corn into other uses. (This change took place at a price just below $100 in case II, shown in panel (b).)

Taxing Economic Earnings

By now you probably realize that the concept of economic earnings explained in this chapter has already been dealt with in this book. Recall that the concept of economic profit was first introduced in Chapter 24 and used in later chapters dealing with different market structures. Economic profit is just one kind of economic earn-

◀ FIGURE 29-3   Three Alternative Cases: All Economic Earnings, All Transfer Earnings, and a Mix of Economic Earnings and Transfer Earnings

Pictured here are three alternative cases showing different breakdowns of earnings paid to owners of resources. The shaded blue areas are economic earnings and the shaded gray areas are transfer earnings. Panel (a) shows the extreme case in which the supply curve of the resource is vertical. The resource is in limited supply and has only a single use. Transfer earnings are zero, and the entire earnings (800 acres at $100 per acre) are economic earnings. Panel (b) shows the opposite extreme case, in which the supply curve of the resource is horizontal. Its supply is virtually unlimited, and its next-best use commands a price that is almost as high as for its present use. Economic earnings are shown to be zero and the entire earnings (800 acres at $100 per acre) are transfer earnings. Panel (c) illustrates the usual case, in which the supply curve of the resource is positively sloped. The resource has more than a single use. A slightly lower price will cause the marginal acre to switch to its next-best use. Its earnings are a mix of transfer earnings and economic earnings.

ings—the one that entrepreneurs may receive. In addition, economic earnings may take the form of economic wages to labor, economic rent to natural resources, and economic interest payments to capital.

What do all these economic earnings have in common? They are all payments for the use of resources that are above what has to be paid to their owners in order to keep them in their present use. In Chapters 25 and 27 we praised the long-run equilibrium solutions of pure competition and monopolistic competition, in part, because only normal profit (not economic profit) is earned. Yet later on we recognized that oligopolistic and monopolistic firms might spend some or all of their economic profit on socially desirable things such as research and development of new products and processes. What about the other resources? Will the seven-foot basketball player in our example spend his economic wage of $980,000 a year in a socially desirable manner? Will owners of capital and natural resources spend their economic interest and rent payments in socially desirable ways? The answer to all of these questions has to be "maybe." We really don't know. All that our theory tells us is that if the owners of resources do not receive economic earnings, the allocation of resources will remain the same.

Henry George, an American social reformer in the late nineteenth century, understood this principle. In fact, he was nearly elected the mayor of New York City in 1886 on this issue alone. He proposed that all existing taxes be abolished and that they be replaced by a single tax on the economic earnings of urban land (but not buildings or improvements on the land). George believed that economic earnings on natural resources and particularly land were probably greater than for any other resource. He argued that a tax on economic rent is the best tax to impose for two reasons. The first was that rents go up because of population increases and not because of the services performed by landowners. Second, the tax would not cause landowners to shift the use of their land. He believed that there would be no need for any other taxes to meet the expenditures of government.

Whatever we may think of Henry George's theory, landowners are not the only ones who benefit from economic earnings. Taxes on land are of course commonplace in the United States, as well as in most other countries, today. But there is little justification for placing the whole tax burden on landowners while letting the owners of the other resources go without paying any taxes on their economic earnings.

SUMMARY

1. In the study of input markets we separate resources or factors of production into four categories: (a) labor, which includes all forms of human work efforts except entrepreneurship and which receives wages as payment; (b) entrepreneurship, which visualizes needs and takes the necessary actions to initiate the process by which they will be met and which receives profit as payment; (c) natural resources, which are "gifts of nature" and which receive rent as payment; and (d) capital, which is made up of goods and skills used to further production and which receives interest payments.

2. Resources are actually not as easy to separate as the four-part classification implies. Production usually calls for certain combinations of resources or "resource packages." Capital is embodied in most usable resources.

3. The supply of resources focuses, not on the amount of resources in existence, but rather on the quantity that is offered at various prices. Normally there is a positive relationship between the price of a resource and the quantity of it that is supplied. The supply of a resource defined in terms of a specific use is generally more price elastic than is the supply for all uses of a resource.

4. The supply for all uses of labor depends upon (a) population size, (b) age distribution, (c) labor force participation rate, (d) hours worked, and (e) working age. All of these factors are, in turn, more or less influenced by laws and customs.

5. The supply for all uses of entrepreneurship is to some degree dependent on the same variables that influence the supply of labor. However, some countries encourage entrepreneurship more than others do. The quantity supplied of entrepreneurship is influenced by expected profit, which is related to a country's patent, taxation, and antitrust policies.

6. Except for those natural resources that are defined in terms of particular locations, the supply for all uses of natural resources varies just as supplies of the other resource categories do. Many natural resources will not renew themselves. Others will, if properly cared for. At low rents there is a tendency for the quantity supplied to dwindle. At high rents natural resources are cared for, exploration is encouraged, and technology is put to work to find new uses for known natural resources.

7. The supply of capital is divided between capital goods and human capital. Since capital goods are themselves outputs of firms, the quantity supplied is expected to be greater at a high price than at a lower price, other things being equal. The supply for all uses of human capital is more complicated because human capital can-

not be divorced from labor. The supply of the labor–human capital package depends upon all the variables that influence labor plus those that influence society, firms, or individuals to invest in education and training. Higher expected earnings (interest payments) are expected to increase the quantity of human capital supplied.

8. Resources have many alternative uses. If owners of a resource find all uses for that resource equally attractive, use will be determined by price alone, and all owners of that resource will receive the same price. But, in fact, owners of resources do not find all uses equally attractive.

9. The price elasticity of supply of a resource depends upon its mobility and the time it takes to switch from one use to another. The less specialized a resource, the more mobile it is and the greater its price elasticity of supply will be. The more time that is allowed for a resource to switch from one use to another in response to a price change, the more elastic its supply will be.

10. Consumers demand mixes of products that allow them to use their limited incomes to maximize their satisfaction. In contrast, because firms are profit maximizers, they demand mixes of resources that let them produce their chosen outputs at the lowest possible cost. It follows, then, that the demand for resources is a derived demand—the demand for a resource is derived from the demand for the products that this resource helps to produce.

11. The price elasticity of demand for a resource is positively related to: (a) the proportion of the total cost of producing a product that is accounted for by that resource; (b) the price elasticity of demand for the product that it helps to produce; (c) the amount of competition in the product's industry; and (d) how easy it is to substitute it for other resources and to substitute other resources for it.

12. The quantity of a resource that a firm demands depends upon the contribution made by that resource to the value of the firm's output and upon the cost that the firm must pay for that resource. A firm will want to continue to buy additional units of a certain resource as long as they will add more to its revenue (marginal revenue product, *MRP*) than to its cost (marginal factor cost, *MFC*). A firm is in equilibrium in its purchasing of a resource when its marginal revenue product is equal to its marginal factor cost.

13. The interaction between resource supply and demand is much the same as the interaction between product supply and demand. Equilibrium price and equilibrium quantity are found where a positively sloped supply curve intersects a negatively sloped demand curve.

14. The earnings of a resource may be divided into two parts: transfer earnings and economic earnings. Transfer earnings are what a resource can earn in its next-best use, and economic earnings are the rest.

15. In the extreme case where a resource has only a single use, its earnings are entirely economic since its transfer earnings are zero. In such a case, the supply curve of the resource is vertical. In the opposite extreme case where a resource has more than a single use and it earns an amount just barely above what it can earn in its next-best use, its economic earnings are almost zero, and practically all of its earnings are transfer earnings. In such a case, the supply curve of the resource for that specific use is horizontal. A slightly lower price causes all of the resource to switch to its next-best use.

16. In the normal case, where a resource has more than a single use but where a slightly lower price will not cause all of it to switch to its next-best use, its earnings are a mix of transfer earnings and economic earnings. In such a case, the supply curve of the resource is positively sloped. At lower prices some, but not all, of the resource would switch to its next-best use.

17. Resource allocation does not change according to the amount of economic earnings that owners of resources receive. For that reason some people have found economic earnings to be an excellent target for taxation.

DISCUSSION QUESTIONS

1. Earlier in the book we separated resources into three broad categories: labor, natural resources, and capital. In this chapter we separated entrepreneurship out of the labor category. How is entrepreneurship different from labor?

2. Why is it more realistic to discuss inputs in terms of "resource packages," rather than in terms of individual resources?

3. The functional distribution of income in the United States during the past fifty years, indicates a substantial increase in the labor share as shown by the percentage of total national income accounted for by the "compensation of employees." How would you explain this change?

4. We expect the quantity supplied of resources to respond to the price of resources just as the quantity supplied of output responds to the price of output. However, it makes a great deal of difference whether we are referring to the response for all uses of a resource or for just one specific use of that resource. Explain this difference in general terms and then give an example for each of the resource categories.

5. What is the relationship between the "mobility" of resource use and the price elasticity of supply of resources? Give an example of a case in which you would expect the supply curve to be highly elastic and one in which you would expect it to be quite inelastic.

6. How does the concept of "derived demand" help you to analyze the demand for resources? How can you use the concept of derived demand to help you to determine what to major and minor in at your college or university?

7. Why is a firm said to be in equilibrium with regard to any specific resource that it uses in production when marginal factor cost is equal to marginal revenue product?

8. Carefully define each of the following concepts and explain how they relate to each other: (1) the earnings of a parcel of land, (2) the transfer earnings of that parcel, and (3) the economic earnings of that parcel. Give a numerical example to illustrate the relationships involved.

9. Larry says to Linda, "The price of wheat is so high because the price of farmland is so high." Linda says to Larry, "The price of farmland to grow wheat on is so high because the price of wheat is so high." Who is right? Discuss.

10. What makes it particularly appealing from an economic theory point of view to tax at least some of the economic wages of a rock star? The economic interest payment for a capital good? The economic rent for some natural resource? The economic profit of an entrepreneur?

30 *Labor, Wages, and Collective Bargaining*

PREVIEW In the last chapter we introduced you in a fairly general way to all of the input markets. Here we focus on just one—the labor markets. As you may remember, labor accounts for more than three-quarters of U.S. national income, by far the most of any of the resources.

We begin with the supply and demand for labor. After reviewing the analysis that was presented in Chapter 29 as it pertains to labor, we extend it beyond pure competition. We compare the case of a firm that hires workers in a purely competitive labor market and sells its output in a purely competitive product market with the case of a firm that hires workers in a purely competitive labor market but sells its output in a monopolistic product market. We then turn to monopsonistic labor markets, in which individual firms hire a large enough percentage of workers to influence their wages. The case of a firm that is a monopsonist in the labor market and sells its output in a purely competitive product market is compared with the case of a firm that is a monopsonist in the labor market but sells its output in a monopolistic product market.

To help you understand the part that labor unions and collective bargaining play in our economy, we present a few highlights from the history of the labor movement in the United States. We show how hard it was in the early days for the unions to get started because the laws reflected a strong resentment of unions by the general public. During the Great Depression of the 1930s many of these negative attitudes were turned around, though some persist even to the present time. The important events that gave rise to American unionism, the major labor laws passed by Congress, and some recent sta-

tistics on American organized labor are outlined here. We also discuss the main issues in collective bargaining—the conditions of employment and the relationship between union and management—as well as the process of collective bargaining and its possible results.

The last two parts of the chapter deal with how unions and government can and do affect workers' wages and general welfare. Having studied earlier the theory of wage rates in the absence of unions and government, you will learn here how much influence these two important forces have on the welfare of workers.

We first ask what unions can do to raise the wages of their members when they are working in a purely competitive labor market. Three possible answers are studied: (1) restricting the supply of labor, (2) bargaining for a higher-than-equilibrium wage, and (3) raising the demand for labor. Then we ask the same question for a union facing employers who have enough control in the labor market to be able to influence the wage that they pay (monopsonistic employers).

Next we turn to the part that the government plays through (1) the laws that strengthen or weaken unions, (2) tax policies, and (3) the direct setting of a minimum wage. We look at the effects of a minimum wage under conditions of a purely competitive labor market and of a monopsonistic labor market.

LABOR SUPPLY AND DEMAND

In the last chapter you learned about marginal productivity theory. We explained why a profit-maximizing company is expected to demand the amount of a resource that equates its marginal revenue product (*MRP*) with its marginal factor cost (*MFC*).

With this important background in mind, we are now ready to apply the theory to labor markets. In Chapter 29 we limited our attention to purely competitive product and resource markets, but here we move on to study monopolistic and monopsonistic cases as well. As you learned in Part VIII, a monopolistic product market is one in which individual companies can use their control over market supply to influence the price of the product. A **monopsonistic resource market** is one in which individual companies can use their control over the purchase of a resource to influence the resource price. Just as the companies that are monopolistic in product markets (monopolistic competition, oligopoly, or monopoly) face negatively sloped demand curves for their outputs, the companies that are monopsonistic in resource markets (monopsonistic competition, oligopsony, or monopsony) face positively sloped supply curves for their inputs.

Hiring in a Purely Competitive Labor Market

Let us quickly review from the last chapter the case of a company that is a pure competitor in both resource and product markets. Then we can show how much difference it makes when that company is a monopolist in its product market.

Our hypothetical case will deal with the bagel industry. We shall suppose it to be first purely competitive and later monopolistic. The variable labor resource in our case will be people who know how to prepare dough, boil, and bake the bagels. Let us turn our attention to a single company within the bagel industry, which we shall call the Big O Bagel Company.

SELLING IN A PURELY COMPETITIVE BAGEL MAR-KET Table 30-1 presents the data for the Big O Bagel Company when it is assumed to be a purely competitive seller in the bagel market and a purely competitive employer of bagel makers in the labor

market. No matter how many or how few bagels Big O produces, it is able to sell them at $2.00 a dozen. Similarly, no matter how many bagel makers Big O hires, it is able to hire them at $125 a day. Remember that marginal revenue product (*MRP*) is found by either multiplying marginal physical product (*MPP*) by the price (in pure competition) or subtracting the total revenue without the additional resource unit from the total revenue with the additional resource unit. Also recall that marginal factor cost (*MFC*) is equal to the wage (in pure competition) or to the change in total cost spent on that resource when one more unit of the resource is hired.

Figure 30-1 pictures the Big O Bagel Company's *MRP* and *MFC* curves taken from columns 6 and 9 in Table 30-1. The quantity of bagel makers demanded by Big O is shown at the intersection of its *MFC* curve and its *MRP* curve. In this case the wage is $125 a day. So it pays for Big O to hire the eighth bagel maker (*MRP* is $150, which is greater than *MFC*, which is $125), but not the ninth (*MRP* is $100, which is less than *MFC*, which is $125). The *MRP* curve is Big O's demand curve for bagel makers. The quantity demanded is found in the same way for all other wage rates.

SELLING IN A MONOPOLISTIC BAGEL MARKET In this case, Big O is again a pure competitor in the market for bagel makers, but this time it is a monopolistic seller in the bagel industry. Table 30-2 presents new data for the Big O Bagel Company. Except for columns 4, 5, and 6, it is the same as Table 30-1. As a monopolistic seller in the bagel market, Big O can now change the equilibrium price of bagels by changing the quantity of bagels that it produces and sells. Column 4 shows that Big O could still sell bagels at $2.00 a dozen if it hired 8 bagel makers and produced 1,450 dozen bagels a day. But now that Big O is a monopolistic seller of bagels, it must estimate the change in the price of bagels that would result from a change in its level of output. These price changes are also shown in column 4. Column 5 shows the total revenue corresponding to the different number of bagel makers that Big O might hire and column 6 shows the marginal revenue product for each successive bagel maker.

TABLE 30-1 Marginal Revenue Product and Marginal Factor Cost for the Big O Bagel Company: The Case of Pure Competition in Both the Bagel and Bagel Maker Markets

(1)	(2)	(3)	(4)	(5)	(6)	(7)	(8)	(9)
Quantity of Bagel Makers (per day)	Total Product (in dozens of bagels per day)	Marginal Physical Product (in dozens of bagels per day)	Price of Bagels (dollars per dozen)	Total Revenue (dollars)	Marginal Revenue Product (dollars)	Wage of Bagel Makers (dollars per day)	Total Cost of Bagel Makers (dollars per day)	Marginal Factor Cost (dollars)
3	800		$2.00	$1,600		$125	$ 375	
		200			$400			$125
4	1,000		2.00	2,000		125	500	
		150			300			125
5	1,150		2.00	2,300		125	625	
		125			250			125
6	1,275		2.00	2,550		125	750	
		100			200			125
7	1,375		2.00	2,750		125	875	
		75			150			125
8	1,450		2.00	2,900		125	1,000	
		50			100			125
9	1,500		2.00	3,000		125	1,125	
		25			50			125
10	1,525		2.00	3,050		125	1,250	

FIGURE 30-1   Big O Bagel Company's Marginal-Revenue-Product and Marginal-Factor-Cost Curves When the Market for Bagel Makers and for Bagels Is Purely Competitive

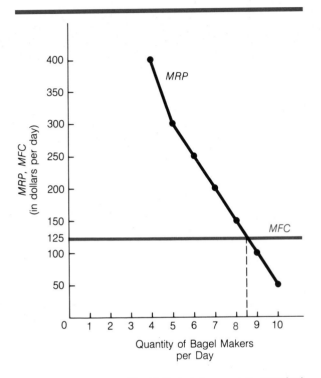

Shown here are the Big O Bagel Company's marginal-revenue-product (*MRP*) and marginal-factor-cost (*MFC*) curves plotted from columns 6 and 9 in Table 30-1. Big O is assumed to hire bagel makers in a purely competitive labor market and to sell bagels in a purely competitive product market. It can hire all the bagel makers it wishes at $125 per day. It will want to hire 8 bagel makers because its *MRP* exceeds its *MFC* when it hires 8, but its *MFC* exceeds its *MRP* when it hires 9.

We see that Big O's marginal revenue product from bagel makers is $400 a day for the fourth bagel maker, but that the marginal revenue product from bagel makers drops more rapidly when Big O is a monopolistic seller than when it is a purely competitive seller. This is because both the marginal physical product and the price of bagels drop as output increases for the firm that has monopoly power in the product market. For a firm that is a purely competitive seller, only

declining marginal physical product contributes to the decline in the marginal revenue product of an input.

Figure 30-2 pictures the Big O Bagel Company's *MRP* curve taken from column 6 in Table 30-2 and its *MFC* curve taken from column 9. In this figure the *MRP* curve reflects the monopolistic bagel market and so is steeper than *MRP* in the purely competitive case shown in Figure 30-1. In Figure 30-2 the *MRP* curve intersects the *MFC* curve at a point somewhere between 6 and 7 workers. It pays for Big O to hire the sixth bagel maker (*MRP* is $160, which is greater than *MFC*, which is $125), but not the seventh (*MRP* is $82.50, which is less than *MFC*, which is $125). The quantity demanded is found in the same way for all other wage rates. Thus, the *MRP* curve is Big O's demand curve for bagel makers.

In which of the two bagel markets are bagel makers better off? If you were a bagel maker, would you prefer the bagel industry to be monopolistic or purely competitive? You would recognize that, while the work and wages ($125 a day) are the same, your chances of getting a job are better in the competitive industry. That is, Big O hires 8 bagel makers when the bagel market is purely competitive and only 6 when it is monopolistic. This restriction in hiring is a reflection of the monopolistic firm's output restriction, which we studied in Chapter 26.[1]

LABOR SUPPLY OF AN INDIVIDUAL   You have seen how, under certain conditions, we can derive an individual firm's demand curve for a certain type of worker. Let us now switch to the supply side and see how we can derive a supply curve for this type of labor. Table 30-3 provides information concerning the supply of labor offered by an individual named Nancy. Nancy is willing to supply different amounts of her labor according to the wage rate paid. At $25 a day she is willing

1. We realize that the market for bagel-making labor could not actually be purely competitive if there were only one employer of bagel makers. But our illustration is important anyway, since it shows the effect of monopoly in the product market, without any additional complication from monopsonistic elements in the labor market.

TABLE 30-2 Marginal Revenue Product and Marginal Factor Cost for the Big O Bagel Company: The Case of a Monopolistic Bagel Market and a Purely Competitive Bagel Maker Market

(1)	(2)	(3)	(4)	(5)	(6)	(7)	(8)	(9)
Quantity of Bagel Makers (per day)	Total Product (in dozens of bagels per day)	Marginal Physical Product (in dozens of bagels per day)	Price of Bagels (dollars per dozen)	Total Revenue (dollars)	Marginal Revenue Product (dollars)	Wage of Bagel Makers (dollars per day)	Total Cost for Bagel Makers (dollars per day)	Marginal Factor Cost (dollars)
3	800		$2.50	$2,000.00		$125	$ 375	
		200			$400.00			$125
4	1,000		2.40	2,400.00		125	500	
		150			245.00			125
5	1,150		2.30	2,645.00		125	625	
		125			160.00			125
6	1,275		2.20	2,805.00		125	750	
		100			82.50			125
7	1,375		2.10	2,887.50		125	875	
		75			12.50			125
8	1,450		2.00	2,900.00		125	1,000	
		50			−50.00			125
9	1,500		1.90	2,850.00		125	1,125	
		25			−105.00			125
10	1,525		1.80	2,745.00		125	1,250	

FIGURE 30-2 Big O Bagel Company's Marginal-Revenue-Product and Marginal-Factor-Cost Curves When the Market for Bagel Makers Is Purely Competitive and the Market for Bagels Is Monopolistic

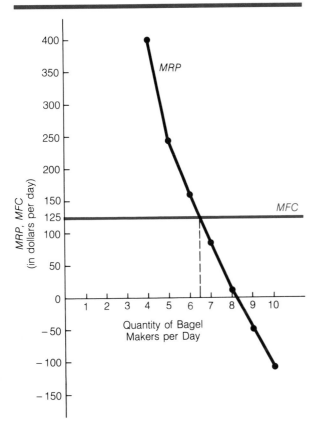

Shown here are the Big O Bagel Company's marginal-revenue-product (*MRP*) and marginal-factor-cost (*MFC*) curves plotted from columns 6 and 9 in Table 30-2. Big O is assumed to hire bagel makers in a purely competitive labor market and to sell bagels in a monopolistic product market. It can hire all the bagel makers it wishes at $125 per day. It will want to hire 6 bagel makers because its *MRP* exceeds its *MFC* when it hires 6, but its *MFC* exceeds its *MRP* when it hires 7.

to work for only 100 days a year, but at $175 a day she is willing to work three times as many days. At this point in your study of economics, you will not be surprised to find a positive supply relationship—the higher the wage rate, the greater the supply of labor, and vice versa. However, you may be a bit surprised to find that Nancy is

not willing to work more days when the wage rate is $200 a day than when it is $175 a day and that she is actually willing to supply less of her labor at even higher wage rates. Why? The reason involves the tradeoff between work and leisure, which we introduced in the last chapter. At higher wage rates Nancy's leisure time becomes more expensive, but also more valuable. The substitution effect of a higher wage rate has a tendency to increase the number of hours that she is willing to work, since her leisure time becomes relatively more expensive in terms of the goods and services that she gives up if she chooses leisure. On the other hand, the income effect of the wage increase causes her to demand more leisure. At wage rates from $25 to $175 a day, the substitution effect outweighs the income effect. Between the wage rates of $175 and $200 a day, the substitution effect and income effect exactly compensate for each other. At wage rates higher than that, the income effect outweighs the substitution effect. Compare Nancy's situation when the wage rate is $250 a day instead of $200 a day. At $250 a day she chooses to work 30 days less, yet she earns $7,500 more ($67,500 − $60,000). Had she chosen to work 300 days, she would have earned $75,000. However, the extra 30 days of leisure were more important to Nancy than the goods and services

TABLE 30-3 Nancy's Supply of Labor and Her Annual Income

Wage Rate (per day)	Supply of Labor (number of days per year)	Annual Income
$ 25	100	$ 2,500
50	170	8,500
75	190	14,250
100	240	24,000
125	270	33,750
150	290	43,500
175	300	52,500
200	300	60,000
225	290	65,250
250	270	67,500

FIGURE 30-3 Nancy's Supply of Labor

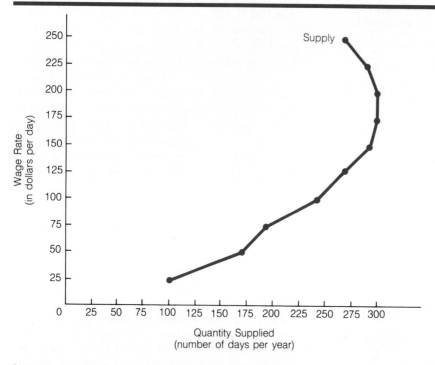

Shown here is the supply-of-labor curve for Nancy. She is willing to supply more days of labor at higher and higher wage rates up to the wage rate of $175 per day. At a wage rate of $200 per day she is willing to supply the same amount of her labor as she was at $175 per day. At still higher wage rates her supply curve bends back or displays a negative slope. She will supply less and less of her labor at higher and higher wage rates in this range.

she could have bought with the extra $7,500 ($75,000 − $67,500 = $7,500) she would have earned from working the additional 30 days.

Nancy's supply curve of labor is pictured in Figure 30-3. Notice that its slope is positive at wage rates up to $175 a day, vertical between $175 and $200, and negative or "backward-bending" at wage rates above $200 a day.

MARKET DEMAND AND MARKET SUPPLY You have seen that an individual firm's demand curve for labor in a purely competitive labor market is its *MRP* curve. Let us derive the market-demand curve for labor now by adding together the *MRP* curves of all the firms that demand this type of labor. Figure 30-4 shows the market-demand curve for bagel makers in our hypothetical ex-

ample. It is based on the assumption that the bagel industry is made up of a large number of bagel firms similar to the one in Figure 30-1.

Deriving the market-supply curve of bagel makers follows a somewhat different route. We have examined Nancy's supply curve of labor. If we were to add together the supply curves of all the people in an economy, we could derive a labor-supply curve for that economy. It would look something like Nancy's, but the backward-bending feature would probably disappear. This is because some people will experience the backward-bending (income) effect sooner than Nancy and some will experience it later.

Moreover, analyzing Nancy's labor-supply curve does not tell us whether Nancy will work as a bagel maker, or as a bricklayer, or as a schoolteacher. Similarly, the labor-supply curve for the economy or the labor market in general does not tell us how many workers will be offering their services as bagel makers or as bricklayers or as schoolteachers. Given enough time to learn skills, Nancy will offer to work in whatever job offers the highest wage rate, assuming that other aspects of the jobs are alike. If bagel-making wage rates rise in relation to other wage rates, she and thousands of others will offer their services as bagel makers. If the relative wage of bagel makers falls, she and many other workers will give up bagel making and turn to the jobs that are now more attractive. Figure 30-5 shows a supply curve for bagel makers that reflects this reasoning. If the wage rate for bagel makers is $125 a day, 5,000 people will offer their services as bagel makers. If the wage rate is $200 a day, over 6,000 bagel makers will be supplied, and so on.

FIGURE 30-4 Market-Demand Curve for Bagel Makers

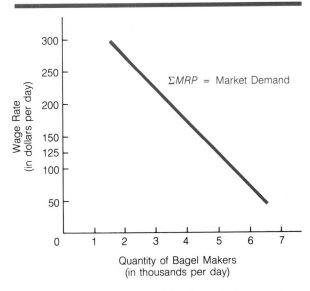

Shown here is the market-demand curve for bagel makers for our hypothetical purely competitive bagel industry. "Σ" is a summation sign, which indicates here that the market-demand curve for bagel makers is merely the addition of all the individual bagel firms' marginal-revenue-product (*MRP*) curves with regard to bagel makers.

FIGURE 30-5 Market-Supply Curve for Bagel Makers

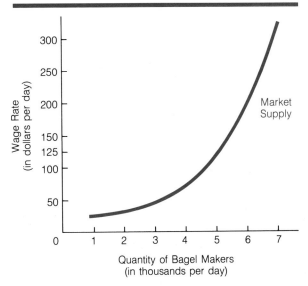

Shown here is the market-supply curve for bagel makers relating to our hypothetical bagel industry. As the wage rate for bagel makers rises in relation to the wage rates for other occupations, more and more people will offer their services as bagel makers. At a wage rate of $125 a day, 5,000 people will offer their services as bagel makers. At a wage rate of $200 a day, over 6,000 bagel makers will be supplied per day, and so on.

MARKET EQUILIBRIUM We are now ready to put demand and supply together and in this way to find the equilibrium wage rate and the equilibrium quantity. In panel (a) of Figure 30-6 we have redrawn the two market curves from Figures 30-4 and 30-5. The quantity demanded for bagel makers in this market is equal to the quantity supplied of bagel makers in this market when 5,000 bagel makers are hired at $125 a day. Since the market for bagel makers is assumed to be purely competitive, each bagel firm accepts the equilibrium wage for bagel makers as given and faces a horizontal supply curve. In panel (b) of Figure 30-6 we once again show the Big O Bagel Company. As shown in Figure 30-1, Big O will hire 8 bagel makers since its *MRP* is greater than the $125 wage rate (its *MFC*) up to that point, but its *MRP* from a ninth bagel maker is less than $125.

TABLE 30-4 Marginal Revenue Product and Marginal Factor Cost for the Big O Bagel Company: The Case of a Monopolistic Bagel Market and a Monopsonistic Bagel Maker Market

(1) Quantity of Bagel Makers (per day)	(2) Total Product (in dozens of bagels per day)	(3) Marginal Physical Product (in dozens of bagels per day)	(4) Price of Bagels (dollars per dozen)	(5) Total Revenue (dollars)	(6) Marginal Revenue Product (dollars)	(7) Wage of Bagel Makers (dollars per day)	(8) Total Cost for Bagel Makers (dollars per day)	(9) Marginal Factor Cost (dollars)
3	800		$2.50	$2,000.00		$ 95	$ 285	
		200			$400.00			$135
4	1,000		2.40	2,400.00		105	420	
		150			245.00			155
5	1,150		2.30	2,645.00		115	575	
		125			160.00			175
6	1,275		2.20	2,805.00		125	750	
		100			82.50			195
7	1,375		2.10	2,887.50		135	945	
		75			12.50			215
8	1,450		2.00	2,900.00		145	1,160	
		50			−50.00			235
9	1,500		1.90	2,850.00		155	1,395	
		25			−105.00			255
10	1,525		1.80	2,745.00		165	1,650	

FIGURE 30-6   Equilibrium Wage and Quantity of Bagel Makers When Hiring in a Purely Competitive Labor Market

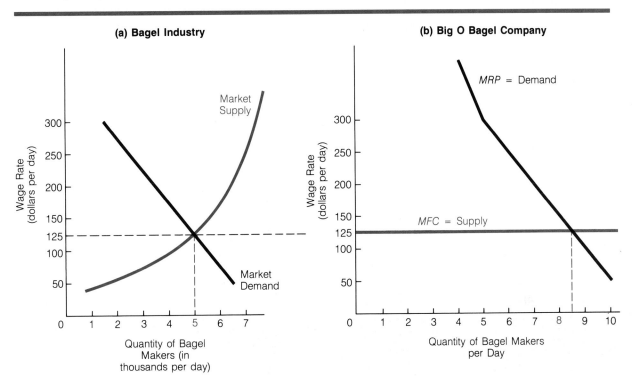

(a) Bagel Industry

(b) Big O Bagel Company

Panel (a) shows the market-demand curve for bagel makers and the market-supply curve for bagel makers, which were drawn separately in Figures 30-4 and 30-5. The equilibrium wage rate for bagel makers in the bagel industry is $125 per day, and the number of bagel makers that will be hired is 5,000.

Panel (b) shows one of the many bagel firms in the bagel industry: the Big O Bagel Company. It accepts the industry wage as the "going" wage at which it can hire as many bagel makers as it wishes. It will want to hire 8 bagel makers, since its MRP exceeds its MFC when it hires 8 and its MFC exceeds its MRP when it hires more than 8.

Hiring in a Monopsonistic Labor Market

Our discussion of the supply of labor and the demand for labor has assumed that workers are hired in a purely competitive labor market. Market supply and demand determined the equilibrium market wage, which was accepted as given by each company. Since there were so many companies employing the same kind of worker, the number of workers hired by each individual company was assumed to have no effect on the wage rate of those workers. We now abandon this assumption and go on to see what difference

it makes when individual firms have some monopsonistic control. Recall from earlier in the chapter that a monopsonistic market is made up of firms that each hire a large enough percentage of workers to influence the wage rate. Any one of them will bid up the wage rate when it hires more workers and cause the wage rate to fall when it hires fewer. Now, if Big O wishes to hire more bagel makers, it must raise the wage rate in order to attract them. In other words, it faces a positively sloped supply curve.

Table 30-4 repeats columns 1 through 6 from Table 30-2, showing that Big O sells bagels in a monopolistic market, but reflects in columns 7,

FIGURE 30-7 Supply-of-Bagel-Makers Curve and Marginal-Factor-Cost Curve of Big O Bagel Company in a Monopsonistic Bagel Maker Market

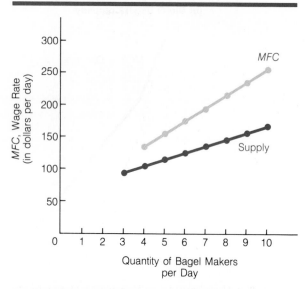

Shown here is the supply curve of bagel makers (plotted from column 7 in Table 30-4) that the hypothetical Big O Bagel Company faces in a monopsonistic labor market. Sloping above it is Big O's marginal-factor-cost curve (*MFC*) plotted from column 9 in Table 30-4. Big O's *MFC* is higher than the wage it must pay to the marginal worker because it must pay a higher wage not only to the marginal worker, but to all the workers who are already employed by Big O.

8, and 9 that Big O is hiring bagel makers in a monopsonistic market. Column 7 shows that Big O must offer a higher and higher wage rate in order to attract more and more bagel makers or can pay a lower wage rate if it hires fewer bagel makers. For example, Big O is able to hire 6 bagel makers at $125 a day, but if it wishes to hire 7, each must be paid $135 a day. Big O cannot get away with paying $125 to the first 6 workers and paying $135 only to the seventh worker, since each of the 6 workers receiving $125 a day would have good reason to quit and become the marginal worker who is paid $135 a day. Columns 8 and 9 in Table 30-4 show that Big O's total cost for 7 bagel makers is $945 and that this is $195 more than it has to pay for 6 workers. The *MFC* of $195 is made up of the extra $135 paid to the seventh

bagel maker plus the extra $10 paid to each of the first 6 workers ($135 + 6($10) = $195). As you can see, then, in a monopsonistic labor market the extra cost of hiring an additional worker (*MFC*) is greater than the wage that he or she receives. This is shown in Figure 30-7. Here the supply curve of bagel makers (the varying quantity of bagel makers' labor that is forthcoming at different wage rates) that is faced by Big O is drawn from column 7 in Table 30-4. With it is drawn Big O's *MFC* curve from column 9 of the table.

EQUILIBRIUM Having explained the *MFC* curve in a monopsonistic labor market, we are ready to determine the equilibrium quantity of labor that will be hired in such markets. The rule that we follow is the same as the one that we used in our discussion of competitive labor markets: a profit-maximizing firm will continue to hire more workers as long as its *MRP* exceeds its *MFC*.

Figure 30-8 pictures two equilibrium solutions. In both cases Big O is hiring bagel makers in a monopsonistic market. However, panel (a) assumes that Big O sells its bagels in a purely competitive market and panel (b) pictures the case where Big O sells its bagels in a monopolistic market. Panel (a) repeats the supply and *MFC* curves from Figure 30-7 (taken from columns 7 and 9 in Table 30-4) and adds the *MRP* curve from Figure 30-1 (taken from column 6 in Table 30-1). The equilibrium quantity of bagel makers is 7. As you can see, *MRP* exceeds *MFC* for 7 workers, but not for 8 workers. The diagram also shows the equilibrium wage rate that Big O must pay in order to attract 7 bagel makers a day. This point is read off the supply curve, which tells us that 7 bagel makers are willing to work at a wage rate of $135 a day. In a monopsonistic labor market, *MFC* is higher than the wage rate, since the additional cost to a firm of hiring another worker is not only the higher wage paid to that worker but also the wage increase that has to be paid to all the workers who are already employed by the firm.

Panel (b) in Figure 30-8 combines the same supply and *MFC* curves with Big O's *MRP* curve from Figure 30-2 (taken from column 6 in Table

FIGURE 30-8   Equilibrium Wage and Quantity of Bagel Makers When Hiring in a Monopsonistic Labor Market

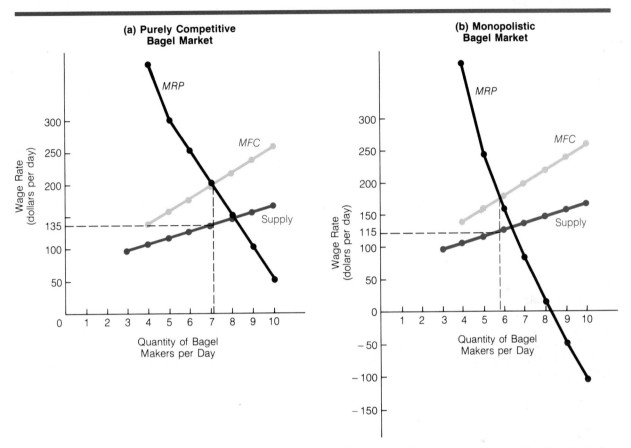

Both diagrams show the equilibrium wage and quantity of workers hired in a monopsonistic labor market. In panel (a) the firm is selling its output in a purely competitive product market, and in panel (b) the firm is selling its output in a monopolistic product market. In both diagrams the

equilibrium quantity of workers is determined by where the firm's *MFC* equals its *MRP*, and the equilibrium wage rate is found on the supply curve, which shows how high a wage rate must be paid to attract that number of workers.

30-2 and Table 30-4). The only difference between the two diagrams in Figure 30-8 is that *MRP* drops more quickly in panel (b), because of the monopolistic character of the bagel market. In such a market the equilibrium quantity of bagel makers and the equilibrium wage rate will be lower. Because *MFC* intersects *MRP* somewhere between 5 and 6 workers, it will pay for Big O to hire 5 workers, but not 6. The supply curve tells us that Big O can hire 5 bagel makers per day for a wage rate of $115.

EQUILIBRIUM WAGE AND MARGINAL REVENUE PRODUCT   You have probably noticed from our example that workers in a monopsonistic labor market receive a wage rate that is lower than their *MRP* but that workers in a purely competitive labor market are paid a wage rate equal to their *MRP*. This difference will always be found because *MFC* is equal to the equilibrium wage rate in a purely competitive labor market whereas it is above the equilibrium wage rate in a monopsonistic labor market.

LABOR UNIONS AND COLLECTIVE BARGAINING

In our example of bagel makers, we have assumed that workers compete among themselves in offering their services. In fact, this is not always the case. When labor unions bargain collectively for groups of workers, competition among workers is limited.

Labor unions are organizations whose major goals are to improve the wage rates and working conditions of their members. **Collective bargaining** is the approach used by labor unions to negotiate with employers or their representatives.

Labor unions in the United States had a hard time at the beginning. Many people resented them as intruders that undermined the legitimate rights of firms and threatened the free-enterprise system. Even today some people view unions as monopolistic organizations that benefit their members at the expense of the rest of society. Others go so far as to argue that labor unions don't even benefit their own membership on the whole. Many, however, view unions as a positive social force. They find unions to be the only reasonable way in which most wage and salary workers are able to increase their share of the economic pie. Without unions, they argue, workers would be powerless in relation to their (monopsonistic) employers. Feelings run high on both sides of the union issue, and unfortunately objectivity often takes a back seat.

Highlights in the History of the Labor Movement

The union concept goes back at least as far as the medieval craft guilds of twelfth-century England. Our brief history, however, will deal only with the labor movement in the United States. We shall divide this history into three parts: (1) before the American Federation of Labor, (2) from the 1880s to the Great Depression, and (3) since World War II.

BEFORE THE AMERICAN FEDERATION OF LABOR In colonial America, industry was largely in the handicraft stage. Master craftsmen, journeymen, and their apprentices carried on many trades such as carpentry, blacksmithing, milling, tanning, shoemaking, and bricklaying. They set up guilds, which at first were generally charitable and mutual-aid societies, but after a time many of them began to take part in certain activities that we now associate with unions. They often formed political action groups, working to rid themselves of unfavorable laws passed by colonial legislatures. Later on, they became more interested in internal craft matters, such as the use of apprentices and the level and structure of wage scales. For example, the Carpenters Society of Philadelphia, started in 1724, set up a secret wage scale for its members. Journeymen hatters, coopers, printers, and shoemakers also carried on wage negotiations.

After the American Revolution these organizations began to take on an even stronger resemblance to modern unions. The first wage earners to go on strike were the journeymen printers in Philadelphia in 1786. Then in 1799, the journeymen shoemakers in Philadelphia went on strike for nine weeks to oppose the cutting of their wages. However, these early unions faced many problems. They were challenged as illegal conspirators by employer associations and unfriendly courts. During recessions it was difficult for them to maintain membership. For these reasons, among others, most survived only a few years.

Before the 1820s, unions were almost exclusively of the craft type. **Craft unions** are organizations representing certain kinds of skilled workers such as carpenters, typographers, and plumbers. By the middle 1820s, the less-skilled workers in America's factories began to organize in industrial unions. **Industrial unions** represent all the workers in an industry, such as mine workers or clothing workers.

Union gains were largely wiped out by the recession of the late 1820s, and frustrated workers turned to political action—that is, they formed the first American labor parties. During the early to middle 1830s unionism began to revive, and on the eve of the 1837 panic union membership had reached 300,000, nearly half of all people employed in manufacturing. However, most of these unions were not able to survive the long depression that lasted until 1843.

During the 1840s workers made a great attempt to escape from the hardships of industrialization. Many joined so-called "utopias" of communal working and living, inspired by such leaders as Robert Owen and Charles Fourier. However, these experiments failed. They were based on a desire to return to the "good old days" of preindustrial society, but the forward movement of the Industrial Revolution was much too powerful to be put in reverse.

When economic conditions improved, local unions again emerged, and by the 1850s the first national ones were formed. The National Typographical Union was established in 1852. Then followed the hat finishers, stonecutters, iron molders, cigar makers, and locomotive engineers.

The Civil War brought the worst inflation and labor shortages that the country had ever experienced, but both actually helped the unions. The first federation of national unions was attempted by the National Labor Union in 1866. A more successful federation, the Noble Order of the Knights of Labor, followed in 1869. The Knights of Labor, which was a secret society in its early days, admitted all types and grades of labor except for lawyers, bankers, and saloon-keepers. During the hard times of the 1870s, the unions had few successes. But for the first time they were not generally wiped out, as had been the case in earlier depressions. By 1886 the Knights of Labor claimed 730,000 members, but then declined rapidly because of some unsuccessful strikes, loose organization, and a strong new competitor, the American Federation of Labor.

FROM THE 1880s TO THE GREAT DEPRESSION

The American Federation of Labor (AF of L) was formed by trade unionists who were unhappy with the Knights of Labor. Seceding from the Knights in 1881, they organized the AF of L in 1886. Under the leadership of two cigar makers,

Samuel Gompers and Adolf Strasser, the AF of L ushered in a new kind of unionism. These leaders decided, after many years' experience, that direct participation in politics and grandiose attempts to reform the whole economic system should be abandoned. Instead, they practiced **business unionism,** emphasizing that American trade unions must rely upon their economic power to achieve their goals of higher real wages and better working conditions. During its first dozen years the AF of L grew slowly but steadily and then at the turn of the century took a great leap forward. By 1904 its membership had grown to about 1.7 million, which accounted for about 80 percent of all union membership.

The conservative business unionism approach of the AF of L was not to everybody's taste. In 1905 eastern socialist labor groups joined with some militant western metal-mining and logging unions to form the Industrial Workers of the World (IWW). This radical union, with its revolutionary goals and violent tactics, received a great deal of notoriety, but actually never attracted more than about 70,000 members. By the eve of World War I, the IWW had lost most of its influence.

During World War I, unions began to grow once again, particularly the craft unions that represented workers in the war-related industries, such as the shipbuilding, machinery, and the garment trades. Union membership doubled from about 2.5 million in 1914 to 5 million in 1920.

The Roaring Twenties, a time of great industrial prosperity in the United States, were not a roaring success for unions. In fact, many workers who had joined during the war decided to drop out. A number of unpopular strikes gave unions a bad press. Taking advantage of this atmosphere, employer groups, backed by courts that were unfriendly to the unions, intensified their campaigns against the unions. But probably the most important reason for the decline of unions during this period was the AF of L's continued emphasis on craft unionism at a time when the mechanization of factories gave semiskilled workers much greater importance in American industry. By

1929, union membership had dropped to about 3.6 million.

The Great Depression of the 1930s was a time of economic chaos for most Americans. Workers were no exception. But along with the suffering during the Great Depression came a change in attitudes that was to benefit unions for many years to come. One observer later wrote,

For the first time in our history a national administration was to make the welfare of industrial workers a direct concern of the government and act on the principle that only organized labor could deal on equal terms with organized capital in bringing about a proper balance between those two rival forces in a capitalistic society.[2]

The first clear evidence of a more favorable union climate came with the passage of the **Norris-LaGuardia Act** of 1932. Before this Act, unions had often been frustrated by the unfriendly treatment they received from the courts. Employers found it very easy to get restraining orders, called injunctions, from the courts to keep workers from starting a union, striking, or picketing. The courts also enforced the so-called **yellow dog-contract**—an agreement that a worker will not join a union—which was often made a condition of employment. The Norris-LaGuardia Act made a blanket statement that workers should have full freedom of association and self-organization. It also specifically limited the courts' power to issue injunctions in labor disputes and made the yellow-dog contract unenforceable.

Three years later, Congress passed an even stronger law favoring unions. The **Wagner-Connery Act** of 1935, more formally called the National Labor Relations Act, is often referred to as the "Magna Carta of labor." Through this Act it became U.S. public policy to encourage "the practice and procedure of collective bargaining." Congress outlined several unfair labor practices by employers and set up the National Labor Relations Board to prevent these practices. Among other things, employers could no longer keep

2. Foster D. Dulles, *Labor in America: A History* (New York: Crowell, 1955), p. 264.

workers from starting a union, or discriminate against union members, or refuse to bargain collectively with duly elected worker representatives. For the first time it became possible for workers to organize into unions and to bargain collectively without getting into trouble with the law.

The year 1935 was also the year that an internal union conflict over craft versus industrial unionism came to a head. The AF of L served the craft unions and was controlled by them. However, the greatest opportunities for union organizing were to be found among semiskilled workers in the newer mass-production industries such as steel, aluminum, electrical equipment, and automobiles. In 1935 several national unions connected with the AF of L formed a Committee for Industrial Organization to promote industrial unionism. Driven out of the AF of L in 1938, they formed a rival federation, the **Congress of Industrial Organizations (CIO).** The CIO, which was led by John L. Lewis, the head of the United Mine Workers, was very successful and became a powerful competitor of the AF of L.

SINCE WORLD WAR II   Union membership had tripled from 1933 to the eve of World War II, when it reached about 9 million. By the end of the war in 1945 union membership had climbed to about 14 million. Among the reasons for this growth were the wartime labor shortages, rises in the cost of living, and a friendly government attitude toward unions as expressed by the War Labor Board's generous granting of fringe benefits.

THE TAFT-HARTLEY ACT   At the same time, however, unions declined somewhat in public favor. It was felt that some unions abused their newly gained power. And when an epidemic of strikes broke out just after the war, there was a growing popular demand for restraints on union power. As a result, the **Taft-Hartley Act,** more formally called the Labor-Management Relations Act, was passed in 1947. This law retains the key provisions of the Wagner-Connery Act, but added some unfair labor practices by unions. For example, unions are forbidden to interfere with the organization of employers, to refuse to bargain with employer representatives, or to enter into closed shop bargaining arrangements. (The **closed shop** arrangement requires a person to be a member of the union before he or she can be hired.) The Act also has a provision that temporarily prevents workers from striking. That is, the president of the United States is given the power to order an eighty-day "cooling off" period when it is judged that a dispute "imperils the national health or safety." In addition, the Act outlaws secondary boycotts and strikes, jurisdictional strikes, and featherbedding. A **secondary boycott or strike** is a boycott or a strike against an employer other than the one with which the union has a dispute. A **jurisdictional strike** is a strike concerning which union shall represent a given group of workers. **Featherbedding** is the practice of forcing an employer to pay for services that workers do not actually perform.

The rate of union growth slowed considerably after 1947, but one should not jump to the conclusion that this slowdown was necessarily due to the Taft-Hartley Act. In fact, even though the Taft-Hartley Act was often denounced by union leaders as a "slave labor act," it did not have a strong negative impact on organized labor. For example, while closed shops were outlawed, **union shops** (which allow employers to hire nonunion employees but require that they join the union within thirty days) remained legal.[3] Also, featherbedding has been interpreted so narrowly by the courts that very few contracts have been canceled because they call for "unnecessary" work to be performed.

MERGER OF THE AF OF L AND CIO   In 1955 the AF of L and the CIO merged. Over the years since the CIO was driven out of the AF of L in 1938, the AF of L itself had become much broader-based, with a large industrial union membership. Also, the struggle for the leadership of the merged federation was eased because the presidents of

both the AF of L and the CIO had died in 1953.[4] The merger did not give rise to a great "labor monopoly" as some had feared. After all, the AFL-CIO is a federation of separate national unions. Its main functions are lobbying, public relations, and research.

PROBLEMS WITH CORRUPTION   Soon after the merger, the AFL-CIO was faced with a major problem—corruption and racketeering in some of its member unions. The best known of these was the Teamsters Union, though several others such as the Bakers, United Textile Workers, the Operating Engineers, and the Laundry Workers were also involved. For a year and a half, a committee of the U.S. Senate, chaired by Senator John L. McClellan, investigated and held public hearings on union corruption. Even though the AFL-CIO expelled the Teamsters as well as several other unions (which together had more than 1.5 million members), public outrage was great enough to cause Congress to pass the **Landrum-Griffin Act,** officially called the Labor-Management Reporting and Disclosure Act, in 1959. This Act contains a detailed set of rules governing the relationship between union governments and their members. Besides offering a "bill of rights" for every union member, it sets forth rules for holding union elections, places limits on the control by national unions over local unions, and sets up strict penalties for any union official who is found guilty of mishandling union funds.

THE CIVIL RIGHTS ACT   In the early 1960s many unions became interested in the issue of racial discrimination. A number of the more industrial unions that had a large proportion of black members were strongly committed to the goal of racial equality. Along with the other civil rights groups, they worked hard to get the **Civil Rights Act** passed in 1964. Title VII of that Act prohibits discrimination in hiring, firing, or promotions

3. However, states that pass so-called "right-to-work" laws can outlaw union shops. About 40 percent of the states have chosen to enact such laws.

4. President William Green of the AF of L and President Philip Murray of the CIO both died in November 1953. George Meany of the Plumbers' Union became president of the AFL-CIO and remained in that position until 1979.

TABLE 30-5   Changes in the U.S. Population and Civilian Labor Force, 1960–1984

	1960	1965	1970	1975	1980	1984
	(millions of people)					
1. Total population	181	194	205	216	228	237
2. Noninstitutional population, 16 years of age and older	119	128	139	155	169	178
3. Civilian labor force	70	74	83	94	107	114
4. Union membership	18	19	21	22	22	17
	(percentages)					
5. Percentage of males in civilian labor force	84	82	80	78	77	76
6. Percentage of females in civilian labor force	38	39	43	46	52	54
7. Percentage of white males in civilian labor force	83	81	80	79	78	77
8. Percentage of black and other nonwhite males in civilian labor force	83	80	77	71	71	71
9. Percentage of white females in civilian labor force	37	38	43	46	51	53
10. Percentage of black and other nonwhite females in civilian labor force	48	49	50	49	53	55

Source: Statistics from the U.S. Department of Commerce, U.S. Bureau of the Census, *Statistical Abstract of the United States: 1981 and 1986;* and the U.S. Department of Labor, Bureau of Labor Statistics.

based on race, color, religion, sex, or national origin.

The Civil Rights Act carried a strong message, but its effects have been hard to measure. Lines 5 through 10 in Table 30-5 present labor force participation rates for certain classes of workers over the years 1960 to 1984. Whether any of these changes were affected by the Civil Rights Act and, if so, to what extent, is not known. What is quite clear from these numbers is that the proportion of males of all races in the labor force has fallen while the proportion of females of all races participating in the labor force has risen.

CHANGES IN UNION MEMBERSHIP   Union membership increased during the 1960s, held fairly constant during the 1970s, and fell dramatically in the early 1980s. Line 4 in Table 30-5 shows the

totals. As a percentage of the noninstitutional population, sixteen years of age and older (line 2 of Table 30-5), union membership has actually fallen from 15.1 percent in 1960 to 9.6 percent in 1984. The concentration of union membership is shown in Table 30-6, which lists 1983 membership figures for thirty-five large American unions.

A dramatic development in unions since the early 1960s is the falling percentage of private employees who are union members and the rising percentage of government employees who belong to unions. One explanation is that the greatest growth in private employment during this period was in jobs and regions of the country that have generally attracted the fewest union members, while the greatest declines were in jobs and regions that are more likely to organize. For example, young people, women, and white-collar

TABLE 30-6 Membership in Large U.S. Unions, 1983 (in thousands of people)

Union	Membership	Union	Membership
Teamsters	1,616	Paperworkers	234
Food & Commercial	1,203	Musicians	219
Auto Workers	1,026	Government (AFGE)	218
State, County (AFSCME)	955	United Transportation	205
Electrical	869	Letter Carriers	203
Steelworkers	694	Electrical	172
Carpenters	678	Firefighters	172
Service Employees	644	Iron Workers	169
Communications	578	Boilermakers	159
Machinists	540	Police	150
Laborers	461	Nurses	149
Teachers (AFT)	457	Painters	146
Engineers	436	Retail, Wholesale	143
Hotel & Restaurant	344	Transit	142
Plumbers	329	Bakery	142
Garment, Ladies	303	Sheetmetal	141
Clothing & Textile	251	Rubber	129
Postal Workers	226		

Source: Union Sourcebook, U.S. 1985, Leo Troy, Neil Sheflin, Industrial Relations Data Information Services, pp. 3–16.

workers became a larger percentage of the labor force, but blue-collar males decreased in relative importance. Many jobs were lost in the automobile and steel industries, which are highly unionized. Also, the industrial states of New York, New Jersey, Pennsylvania, Ohio, Michigan, and Illinois, where unionism made its greatest early gains, grew more slowly than the states in the southern and southwestern United States.

Before 1960 relatively few people who were working for the federal, state, or local governments were unionized. Only the state of Wisconsin allowed bargaining by public employees. But in 1962 President John Kennedy issued an executive order stating that federal employees have the right to organize and bargain collectively. This executive order was strengthened by another one issued by President Richard Nixon in 1969. Not only did these executive orders pave the way for large-scale unionization at the federal level, but they also led to more unionization among state and local government workers. Many profes-

sional public employees joined together in "associations" rather than "unions." But while there may be some philosophical differences, association activities are hard to distinguish from union activities. A case in point is the National Education Association, which had 1.7 million members in 1984. Lloyd Reynolds, a well-known labor economist, recently wrote: "If we include bargaining associations which function much like unions,... then about half of all federal employees are organized, as are 40 percent of state employees and 55 percent of local government employees."[5] Though public employees got a late start in American unionism, they are now about twice as heavily unionized as employees in the private sector.

CONFRONTATION AND COOPERATION IN THE 1980s Organized labor's bargaining clout has been seriously eroded in the 1980s. Union leaders

5. Lloyd G. Reynolds, *Labor Economics and Labor Relations*, 8th ed. (Englewood Cliffs, N.J.: Prentice-Hall, 1982), p. 337.

are struggling to halt the draining away of their rank and file and are surrendering on many fronts to employer demands for concessions. General wage concessions are sometimes won by companies that threaten plant shutdowns or moves to the less-unionized Sunbelt or to foreign countries. Some firms have even gone so far as to file for bankruptcy in order to void labor contracts.

One compromise solution that has developed takes the form of two-tier contracts that place new hires on a lower pay scale than previously hired workers. Contracts of this type have been agreed upon in the U.S. Postal Service and in the food wholesaling, food retailing, trucking, aerospace, and airlines industries. Unions claim that these concessions have had a devastating effect on worker morale.

Confrontation has appeared alongside a movement toward greater cooperation in relations between unions and employers. Worker concern about job security and income maintenance and employer realization that high productivity depends on satisfied workers with good attitudes about job performance have spawned a revolution of labor-management partnership. Following the Japanese model, this frequently involves profit sharing, long-term job security, bonuses linked to productivity increases, and the surrender by workers of hard-won systems of rigid work rules and job classifications. The most outstanding example thus far is the 1985 United Auto Workers (UAW) agreement with General Motors Corporation for the $5 billion Saturn project, which is to start producing small cars in 1989. Consensus is required for action. UAW representatives will sit in on planning and operating committees. Work teams will operate without foremen. Workers will participate in job assignment and be salaried, just like management, rather than paid by the hour. Under the agreement, wages will be about 80 percent of UAW scale, but workers will receive bonuses based on performance as measured by productivity and profitability.

Collective Bargaining

The goal of collective bargaining is to find terms satisfactory to both employees and management on many important issues. Once agreed upon, these terms are carefully set down in the form of a labor contract.

ISSUES IN COLLECTIVE BARGAINING The issues in collective bargaining fall into two very broad categories: (1) the conditions of employment and (2) the relationship between the union and management.

The conditions of employment include wage rates, fringe benefits, work standards, and job security. Among the wage issues are the basic rate for each job category and the pay steps for advancing within each category. **Fringe benefits** are forms of compensation other than wages, such as pensions, life insurance, health plans, severance pay, as well as paid vacations, holidays, birthdays, and even coffee breaks and cleanup time. **Work standards** specify the amount of work to be performed. For example, they state the size of the crew to be employed to do a standard job or the number of units to be handled on an assembly line. Finally, **job security** has to do with the conditions for job continuance and the handling of grievances. Generally, job continuance is determined by **seniority rules.** For example, the worker who has been on the job the longest is the last to be laid off and the first to be called back when the firm hires again.

Union and management must also agree on their own relationship over the life of the contract. They have to decide how to define the **bargaining unit,** which identifies the workers for whom the union is bargaining and so to whom the labor contract applies. They must also agree upon the privileges given to **shop stewards,** who are workers elected to represent the union on the job. For example, stewards may be allowed to confer with workers and supervisors during working hours. Union and management may also agree upon the checkoff of union dues. The **checkoff** is a form of union security that calls for the employer to deduct or withhold union dues from workers' paychecks and to pay those dues directly to the union. In many cases, labor contracts have provisions for **arbitration,** a procedure for settling union–management differences by having a neutral outside party make a decision that will be binding on both sides. Finally, the union and management must agree on when the contract begins and ends and how it may be renewed.

THE BARGAINING PROCESS AND SOME POSSIBLE RESULTS

In general, the union wants the bargaining process to lead to as favorable a "benefits package" of wages, fringes, and working conditions as possible, consistent with the firm's being able to remain in business at its existing scale. Likewise, management wants as low a "cost package" of wages, fringes, and expenses related to working conditions as possible, consistent with being able to attract a sufficient number of workers. Somewhere between these two positions, a settlement will eventually take place.

In the bargaining process the union and management each want the other to think that a settlement cannot be reached unless the other gives in to most of its demands. So each side must put on a great show of strength. For example, the union may reveal a large strike fund, and management may build up its inventory of finished goods. Each side tries to learn how far the other will really go before giving in, while concealing its own position.

At some point both parties usually will give up their extreme positions and reach a compromise. If negotiations break down, the employer may begin a lockout or, more commonly, the union may call a strike. A **lockout** is a work stoppage in which the company closes the plant to its workers. As you know, a **strike** is a stoppage in which the workers refuse to work. The strike is the ultimate weapon of a union. It is often supported by other weapons such as picketing and boycotts. **Picketing** refers to the parading of striking workers before the entrance to their plant or other work place in the hope of convincing other workers, customers, or suppliers not to enter. A **boycott** is an attempt to block the distribution and sale of the employer's products. It can be only a refusal by striking workers themselves to buy the products, but it may include a request that others also refuse to buy from the firm.

The longer a strike or a lockout continues, the easier it generally becomes to reach an agreement. Even though tensions may rise, over time both parties suffer more and more. As the union's strike fund dwindles and the company's losses grow, a compromise solution begins to look better and better.

THE IMPACT OF UNIONS ON WAGE RATES

As you learned earlier, a union's major goal is to improve the working conditions of its members. Management and unions usually recognize that there are important tradeoffs among different types of working conditions, such as wage rates, fringe benefits, work standards, and job security. Sometimes management will prefer to offer a more generous future pension instead of a higher present wage rate. Or it may be willing to hire larger work crews for certain jobs instead of paying a higher wage rate. Or it may even be willing to trade off some control over its work force for a lower wage rate. Since most changes in working conditions cost the employer something and may be translated into an equivalent amount of wages, our discussion will use wage rates to cover all working conditions.

Do unions have an impact on the level of wage rates? All the evidence at hand points to an answer of "yes," but it is hard to tell just how much impact they have. Although in the years 1983, 1984, and 1985 union wage hikes have trailed nonunion pay gains, we know that the average wage in unionized industries is from 15 to 20 percent higher than the average wage in nonunionized industries. But these figures may overstate the impact of unions because these industries also hire workers with a higher-than-average skill level. On the other hand, nonunion workers may be paid higher wages as a direct result of union successes. Sometimes nonunion workers are given higher wages in order to keep out the union. When unions are successful in raising wages, some nonunion employers who are afraid to lose valuable employees will match those wage increases.

How do unions go about raising wage rates? We shall answer this question, assuming first that a union faces a purely competitive labor market. Later we shall assume that firms are monopsonistic buyers of labor.

FIGURE 30-9   Equilibrium Wage Rate and Quantity of Workers Hired in a Purely Competitive Labor Market: The Case of No Union

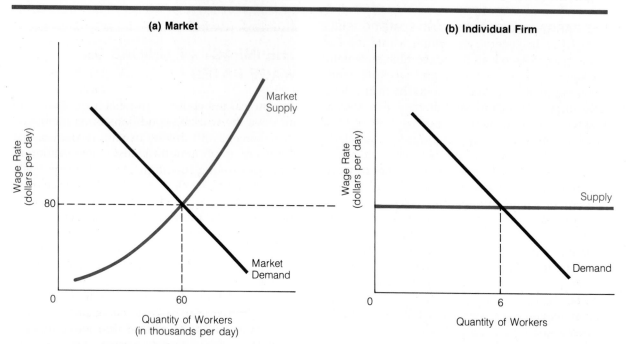

Shown here are market and individual firm diagrams for nonunionized workers who are hired in a purely competitive labor market. The intersection of the market-supply and market-demand curves determines the equilibrium quantity of workers (60,000) and the equilibrium wage rate ($80 a day). Each of the many firms, such as the one pictured in panel (b), accepts the equilibrium wage rate so that it faces a horizontal supply curve at $80. It hires workers to the point where its demand curve (*MRP*) intersects its supply curve (*MFC*), at 6 workers.

Bargaining in a Purely Competitive Labor Market

As you learned earlier, we describe a labor market as purely competitive when the individual firms in an industry made up of a large number of firms have no influence on the wage rate. Each firm faces a horizontal supply curve of labor and hires the number of workers shown by the point where its demand curve for these workers intersects that horizontal supply curve. Figure 30-9 shows such a case. (It is much like our hypothetical bagel-makers case shown in Figure 30-6.) In panel (a) are shown the market-supply and market-demand curves for a certain kind of worker. The equilibrium wage rate is $80 a day, and the equilibrium number of workers employed is 60,000.

Panel (b) shows the supply and demand curves for one of the many companies that hire this kind of worker. The negatively sloped demand curve is that firm's *MRP* curve. The supply curve facing the company is horizontal, since it hires only a very small percentage of the total number of these workers and so has no influence on their wage rate. At the equilibrium wage rate of $80 a day, this company will hire six workers.

Under these conditions, what can a union do to raise wage rates? There are three approaches. First, it may raise the equilibrium wage rate by shifting the market-supply curve to the left. Second, it may bargain for a wage rate above the competitive market equilibrium wage rate. Third, it may raise the equilibrium wage rate by shifting the market-demand curve to the right.

RESTRICTING THE SUPPLY OF LABOR A union can raise the equilibrium wage rate of its workers by restricting their supply—that is, by shifting the market-supply curve to the left. Craft unions have often used this approach. They have in the past tried to force companies to hire only union members. By restricting the number of people who can join their unions, they gain a great deal of control over the supply. Among their methods are high initiation fees, long periods of apprenticeship, and limits on the size of the union. Restricting supply may also be helpful for industrial unions. Both craft and industrial unions pressure employers for shorter workdays or workweeks, early retirement, and longer vacations. They pressure Congress for stricter child labor, mandatory retirement, and immigration laws. All of these methods aim at reducing the supply of workers. In other words, raising the age below which a child is not allowed to work, lowering the age above which a person may be forced to retire, and keeping foreigners from entering the country all reduce the supply of labor.

In recent years unions, or associations of workers in certain occupations that act like unions, have stepped up their efforts to have states pass laws requiring a license or certificate in order to practice their trade. Licensing and certification standards are generally determined by state boards, which are customarily packed with members of the occupations with which they deal. All states require licenses for doctors, dentists, lawyers, and teachers. But many states also require certification for auto mechanics, plumbers, barbers, beauticians, dog trainers, and hundreds of other occupations. What do the practitioners of all these occupations have in common? They all have a desire to control their supply in order to bring about and maintain higher wage rates. Each time a state board raises the standards—for the stated purpose of protecting the public from frauds and cheats—it lowers the supply of workers and raises their equilibrium wage rate.

Figure 30-10 pictures a union's successful effort in restricting supply and in this way raising the equilibrium wage rate paid to its members. As you can see, the original equilibrium is a market wage rate of $80 a day, total employment of 60,000 workers, and employment of 6 workers by the individual firm shown. This is the same as the no-union case pictured in Figure 30-9. However, in Figure 30-10 the monopoly power of the union is used to cause the market-supply curve to shift to the left. The equilibrium market wage rate is then raised to $120 a day and the employment in the market reduced to 42,000 workers. The individual firm that hired 6 workers at $80 a day now hires only 4 workers at $120 a day. Most likely, the workers who are still employed are very pleased with the union's effort, which raised their wage rate by 50 percent. However, the 18,000 persons who would be working in this occupation if the union had not become involved are probably worse off.

ABOVE-EQUILIBRIUM WAGE AGREEMENT A second approach that a union may take to raise the wage rate of its members is to bargain for a higher-than-competitive market equilibrium wage rate. The effect of a higher-than-competitive wage agreement is shown in Figure 30-11. The equilibrium solution is the same as in the no-union case pictured in Figure 30-9 and the original equilibrium in the case shown in Figure 30-10. This is a market wage rate of $80 a day, total employment of 60,000 workers, and employment of 6 workers by the individual firm shown. But this time the monopoly power of the union is used to bargain for a higher wage rate. In the case shown in Figure 30-11, collective bargaining ends up with a union contract that sets a wage rate of $100 a day. Thus, 50,000 workers will be employed in the industry and 5 workers by the individual firm shown. As before, each company hires only that quantity of workers at which its *MRP* (shown as its demand curve) equals its *MFC* (shown as its supply curve).

Industrial unions are more likely to use this approach than are craft unions. A union representing workers in an industry that hires mostly unskilled and semiskilled workers cannot easily restrict its membership. Moreover, industrial unions know that if some companies in their industry are not unionized and so pay lower wage rates and in turn charge lower prices for what they produce, the unionized companies will

FIGURE 30-10   Equilibrium Wage Rate and Quantity of Workers Hired in a Purely Competitive Labor Market: The Case of a Union Restricting Supply

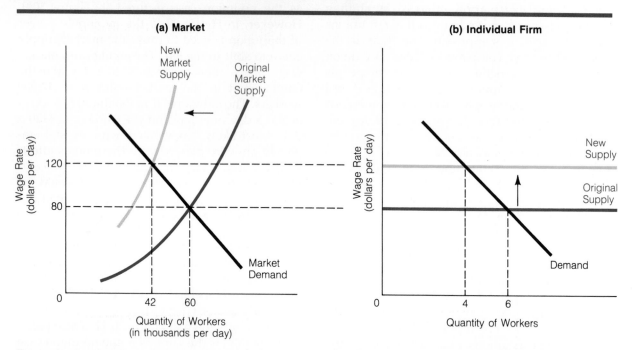

The market for a particular type of worker is shown to be in equilibrium where the original market-supply curve intersects the market-demand curve—60,000 workers are hired at a wage rate of $80. Panel (b) shows one of the many firms hiring workers in this purely competitive labor market. It is in equilibrium when it hires 6 workers at the $80 market wage rate.

The diagrams show the result of a successful union effort to raise wages by restricting the supply of workers. Supply restriction is shown by the leftward shift of the market-supply curve. The new market-supply curve intersects the market-demand curve at a lower equilibrium quantity of workers (42,000) and at a higher equilibrium wage rate ($120). The horizontal supply curve faced by the firm pictured in panel (b) shifts up to the new equilibrium wage rate of $120 so that it now intersects the firm's demand curve at only 4 workers.

---

suffer lower sales and hire fewer workers. The nonunionized firms will sell more and, since many of the workers are not skilled, will most likely have little trouble finding suitable nonunion workers. Even when industrial unions have been able to unionize nearly all of the domestic firms in an industry, there is still the threat of being undercut by foreign firms that pay lower wage rates to their workers. For example, this is one of the reasons why so many American unionized steel workers have been unemployed in the 1980s. Japanese firms paying as much as one-third less in hourly wages have been very successful in selling their lower-priced products in the United States.

RAISING THE DEMAND FOR LABOR   The demand for labor is a derived demand. When a union is able to increase the demand for the products that its workers produce, the union can shift the demand curve for its workers to the right. Figure 30-12 shows such a case. The original equilibrium is the same as Figures 30-9, 30-10, and 30-11, with a market wage rate of $80 a day, total employment of 60,000 workers, and employment of 6 workers by the individual firm shown. The union causes the demand curve for its workers to shift to the right, so that the new market equilibrium wage rate becomes $140 a day. (Its new *MRP* or demand curve then intersects its new *MFC* or supply curve at 8 workers.)

FIGURE 30-11 Wage Rate and Quantity of Workers Hired in a Purely Competitive Labor Market: The Case of Setting an Above-Equilibrium Wage Agreement

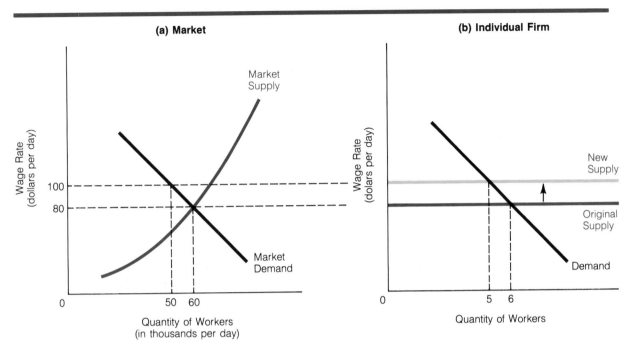

The market for a particular type of worker is shown to be in equilibrium where the market-supply curve intersects the market-demand curve—60,000 workers are hired at a wage rate of $80. Shown in panel (b) is one of the many firms hiring workers in this purely competitive labor market. It is in equilibrium when it hires 6 workers at the $80 market wage rate.

The diagrams show the result of higher wage rates achieved through bargaining. In this case the union is able to raise the wage rate to $100, but at the cost of 10,000 jobs (from 60,000 to 50,000). The horizontal supply curve faced by the firm pictured in panel (b) shifts up to the new equilibrium wage rate of $100, so that it now intersects the firm's demand curve at 5 workers.

In contrast to the first two approaches that we have described, this one, if successful, allows the union to "have its cake and eat it too." We recognized that restricting the supply of workers and getting an agreement on a higher wage rate enables a union to achieve a higher wage rate, but at a cost of unemployment for some of its workers. (The case shown in Figure 30-10 had 18,000 workers lose their jobs, and the case shown in Figure 30-11 reduced employment by 10,000.) Shifting the demand curve for labor to the right raises the wage rate while at the same time increasing employment.

How can unions raise the demand for union workers? Unions have followed four general approaches. First, they may try to raise the produc-

tivity of the union workers. Second, they may help in selling the product. Third, they may try to decrease competition from non-union-made goods. Last, they may try to raise the union-labor component in production.

To the extent that unions are able to influence the sort of technology and resource mix that companies use in producing their goods, unions can affect the companies' productivity. A lower unit cost of production is generally reflected in lower product prices, which increase the amount of product demanded (a downward movement along the product-demand curve) and, in turn, the amount of labor demanded.

A second approach that unions may take is to try to get their members to buy union-made goods

FIGURE 30-12   Equilibrium Wage Rate and Quantity of Workers Hired in a Purely Competitive Labor Market: The Case of a Union Raising Demand

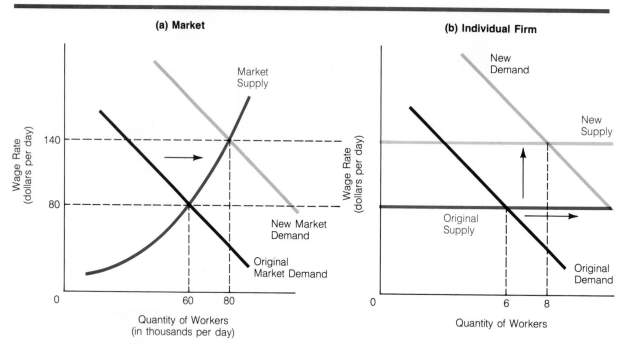

(a) Market

(b) Individual Firm

The market for a particular type of worker is shown to be in equilibrium where the original market-demand curve intersects the market-supply curve—60,000 workers are hired at a wage rate of $80. Shown in panel (b) is one of the many firms hiring workers in this purely competitive labor market. It is in equilibrium when it hires 6 workers at the $80 market wage rate.

The diagrams show the result of a successful union effort to raise the wage rate by raising the demand for its

members. The increase in the demand for these workers is shown by the shift to the right of the market-demand curve. The new market-demand curve intersects the market-supply curve at a higher equilibrium quantity of workers (80,000) and at a higher equilibrium wage rate ($140). The horizontal supply curve faced by the firm pictured in panel (b) shifts up to the new equilibrium wage rate of $140, so that it now intersects the firm's new demand curve at 8 workers.

and to ask family and friends to do the same. The union label that shows a product is union-made is sometimes used in such a program. In a few cases, unions will go even further. The International Ladies Garment Workers Union actually gave financial aid to employers so that they could do much more advertising of their union-made goods. The aim of this approach is to shift the product-demand curve to the right.

A third approach that unions may take is to try to stop or reduce nonunion or foreign competition. In recent years American unions have led the way in trying to get import quotas, voluntary compliance pacts, better enforcement

of antidumping laws, and higher tariffs. Such attempts have been very important in the steel, auto, electronics, and textile industries. This approach tries to shift the product-demand curve to the right or at least to keep the curve from shifting to the left.

Finally, unions may follow the most direct route of forcing companies to use more union workers in their production. This may take the form of featherbedding,[6] such as the requirement for a fireman on every diesel train, a standby surgeon for each operation, and a typographer to set type

6. Recall the definition on page 611.

that won't be used. Of course, because featherbedding raises the cost of production, it will be
self-defeating in the long run.

Bargaining in a Monopsonistic Labor Market

Unions are monopolistic sellers of labor. So far
we have assumed that they face firms that are
pure competitors in their labor markets. We now
relax that assumption to see what happens when
a union bargains with monopsonistic buyers of
labor. In such cases *both* the union and the firm
or firms with which it bargains have monopoly
power and so can influence the wage rate. The
extreme case in which a union represents all of
the workers in an industry and in which only a
single firm hires these workers is called **bilateral
monopoly.** This might be the case of a union
representing workers in a one-company town.
Workers have to move into the town if they are
hired by the company and move away from the
town if they lose their jobs. More common,
however, are cases in which unions face a few
firms that have monopsonistic power. Examples
are auto firms in the Detroit area, steel firms in
the Gary, Indiana, area, and aerospace firms in
the Houston area.

As you learned earlier, a monopsonistic firm
faces a positively sloped market-supply curve of
labor, and its marginal-factor-cost (MFC) curve
lies above this supply curve. Figure 30-13 shows
such a case. You may find that it looks familiar,
since the diagram is much like the ones in Figure
30-8. The demand curve for labor is the monopsonistic firm's *MRP* curve. The firm would like
to hire 7,000 workers, since this is where its *MFC*
curve intersects its *MRP* curve. It would like to
pay them a wage rate of $44, since the supply
curve indicates that 7,000 workers could not be
hired at a lower wage than that. However, the
union (the monopolistic seller of these workers)
will probably argue for a much higher wage rate.
It will recognize, of course, that there is a tradeoff
between the number of members that will be
employed and the wage rate that they will receive.
It might, for example, desire to have no fewer

FIGURE 30-13 Union-Management Bargaining in a Monopsonistic Labor Market

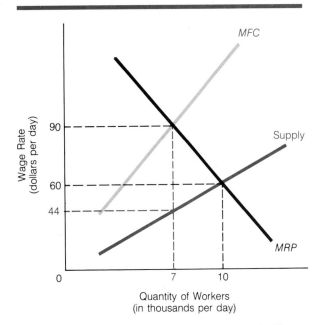

Shown here is a diagram much like the ones in Figure
30-8, where the firm is a monopsonist in the labor market.
In the absence of a union, 7,000 workers would be hired
(where *MFC* = *MRP*) at a wage rate of $44. Here we
suppose that a union represents these workers. It will
probably argue for a much higher wage rate. It might, for
example, argue for $90, which according to the demand
or *MRP* curve is the highest wage at which 7,000 workers
would be hired. Without knowing about the relative power
and bargaining skills of the union and management, it is
not possible to determine just where they will settle. One
possible settlement—at the competitive level—is shown at
$60, where 10,000 workers are hired.

than 7,000 members employed and therefore
argue for a wage of $90. At wage rates higher
than $90, the firm's demand curve (*MRP*) indi-
cates that it would not be willing to hire as many
as 7,000 workers.

This is as far as economic theory takes us.
Without knowing about the relative power of the
union and management, their respective bargaining skills, and the policies that they adopt, we
cannot predict just where the wage settlement
will take place. Our model suggests that the

supply curve will have a horizontal segment at whichever wage rate actually is determined and that this will determine the number of workers who will be employed. For example, as shown in Figure 30-13, if they settle at the competitive wage of $60 a day, 10,000 workers will be hired. Another kind of result will be described later in connection with the setting of a minimum wage rate.

THE EFFECT OF GOVERNMENT ON WAGE RATES

Wage rates and the quantity of workers employed are not determined only by labor and management. Government often also plays an important part. In our short history of the American labor movement, we described some of the labor laws that greatly strengthened union power as well as some that held union power in check.

Taxing Employees and Employers

Whenever the government levies a tax either on employees or on employers, it affects wage rates and employment. An added tax on employees' wages effectively decreases their disposable income. This has a substitution effect in that it discourages them from working as much as before and encourages them to buy more leisure time. It also has an income effect, which works in the opposite direction. If, as is very likely, the substitution effect outweighs the income effect, the result is an increase in before-tax wage rates and a decrease in employment.

A tax on employers is even more likely to decrease the number of workers who will be employed. A tax on employers that raises their marginal factor cost of hiring workers causes them to want to hire fewer workers. Given a firm's MRP for certain workers, fewer will be hired when the firm's MFC shifts upward. For example, if government raises the payroll tax (Social Security contribution by employers), it raises the cost of hiring workers, causing firms to hire fewer

people. In such a case it is hard to say whether wages were increased or not. Employers pay more for labor, but employees who keep their jobs may or may not receive more. If a higher payroll tax means higher Social Security benefits for workers, then we may say that wages have increased.

Setting Minimum Wage Rates

Finally, the government can affect wage rates and employment by setting a lower limit on the wage rate that firms are allowed to pay. This is called a **minimum wage.** Massachusetts set a minimum wage for women and children in 1912. The first federal minimum wage law in the United States, the Davis-Bacon Act of 1931, applied only to workers on federal construction projects. It was not until the Fair Labor Standards Act of 1938 that wider coverage was provided. It set the minimum wage at 25 cents an hour for millions of workers. Since then coverage has been widely extended, and the federal minimum wage has been increased to $3.35 an hour.

Minimum wage legislation does not affect all industries and all labor markets equally. Obviously it affects only those industries and labor markets in which workers could otherwise be hired below the minimum wage. If workers in an industry earn between $5.50 and $24.50 an hour, a $3.35-an-hour minimum wage has no direct effect on them. However, if workers in an industry are paid less than the minimum wage, they will probably be affected.

COMPETITIVE LABOR MARKETS   Firms in industries affected by minimum wage laws are generally in fairly competitive labor markets. Examples are found in much of retailing and especially in fast-food retailing industries. The workers are often teenagers and part-time help. Thus the competitive model is usually the most appropriate one to use in analyzing the effects of a minimum wage. Repeated in Figure 30-14 is the competitive-labor-market diagram that we have used several times before. We begin with an equilibrium wage of $2.00 an hour, at which 100,000 workers are

FIGURE 30-14 The Imposition of a Minimum Wage in a Purely Competitive Labor Market

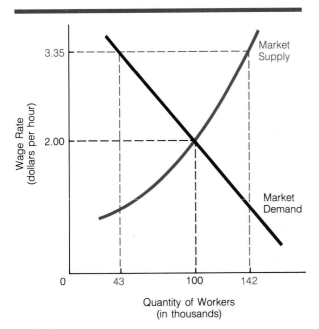

Shown here are a market-demand curve and a market-supply curve in a purely competitive labor market. In the absence of any government intervention 100,000 workers are hired at $2 an hour. When a minimum wage is imposed at $3.35 an hour, only 43,000 workers are hired, so that 57,000 workers who would otherwise have been employed in this market are not. Moreover, 42,000 additional workers who were not willing to work in this market at a $2 wage rate are willing to work at $3.35 an hour.

demanded and supplied. When a minimum wage is set at $3.35 an hour, some "bittersweet" results can be seen. It sweetens the wage rate for 43,000 workers from $2.00 to $3.35 an hour. Forty-three thousand workers (not necessarily the same people who held the jobs originally) will be demanded at $3.35 an hour. However, the bitter result of unemployment falls on the 57,000 workers who were demanded at a wage rate of $2.00, but are no longer demanded at $3.35 an hour. Furthermore, Figure 30-14 shows that an additional 42,000 workers who were not willing to work at $2.00 an hour are willing to work at $3.35 an hour. So the excess supply of labor created by

the minimum wage is shown as 99,000 workers—the 57,000 who would have worked at $2.00 an hour plus the 42,000 who have been persuaded to offer their labor at $3.35 an hour.

MONOPSONISTIC LABOR MARKETS Even though low-wage labor markets are generally competitive, an interesting exception to the conclusion that a minimum wage reduces employment is found in the rare case of a low-wage monopsonistic labor market. Figure 30-15 repeats the monopsonistic-labor-market diagram that we have used several times earlier. Equilibrium occurs where the monopsonistic firm's *MFC* curve intersects its *MRP* curve. A wage of $2.00 an hour is paid to 7,000 workers. Now suppose that a minimum wage is set at $3.35 an hour. The minimum wage causes the monopsonistic firm to face a horizontal supply (and *MFC*) curve for the quantity of labor willing to work at the minimum wage—10,000 workers in our example. To attract more than 10,000 workers, the firm must, as before, pay higher wages. The supply curve is therefore kinked at that point. (In Figure 30-15, where the minimum wage has been set at $3.35 an hour, we have drawn the supply curve as a blue continuous line.) Over the range of employment for which the supply curve is horizontal, so is the *MFC* curve, but when the supply curve resumes its upward slope, the *MFC* curve does the same. At 10,000 workers there is a discontinuity. Up to that level of employment the *MFC* curve is the horizontal part of the supply curve, but afterward it is that part of the former *MFC* curve that we have drawn in blue.

Given a minimum wage of $3.35 an hour, what is the equilibrium level of employment? The answer is determined as before—where *MFC* is equal to *MRP*. Figure 30-15 shows that *MRP* is greater than *MFC* (the horizontal line drawn in blue) for all employment levels below 10,000 and that *MRP* is less than *MFC* (the positively sloped part of the former *MFC* curve drawn in blue) for all employment levels above 10,000. Thus, the equilibrium level of employment in this market is 10,000 workers.

Had the minimum wage been set at a little higher level, say at $3.50 or $4.00 an hour,

FIGURE 30-15   **The Imposition of a Minimum Wage in a Monopsonistic Labor Market**

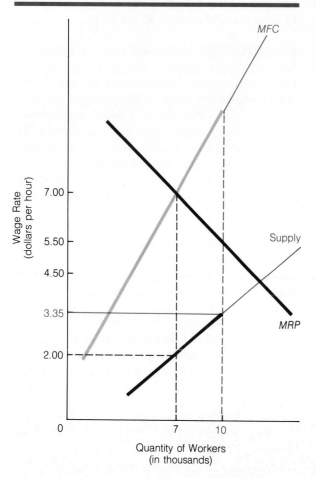

Shown here is the case in which a firm is a monopsonist in the labor market. In the absence of a union and of government intervention, 7,000 workers are hired at $2 an hour. When a minimum wage is set at $3.35 an hour, not only is the wage rate increased, but more workers are hired. The minimum wage causes the monopsonistic firm to face a horizontal supply curve (drawn in blue) for the 10,000 workers willing to work for the minimum wage. Additional workers are attracted according to the remainder of the supply curve (drawn in blue). When the supply curve is horizontal, it also represents the firm's *MFC*. But for the range of employment greater than 10,000, *MFC* is the segment of the former *MFC* curve that is drawn in blue.

The equilibrium level of employment in this case is 10,000 workers. The firm's *MRP* is greater than its *MFC* for all levels of employment below 10,000 and its *MFC* is greater than its *MRP* for all employment levels greater than 10,000.

equilibrium employment would be even higher. The largest number of workers are employed when the minimum wage is set at the level where supply intersects demand (*MRP*). At minimum wage levels higher than that, say at $5.50 or $6.00 an hour, the equilibrium level of employment is lower again. Finally, if it were set at $7.00 an hour, the same number of workers would be hired as when no minimum wage was set and the equilibrium wage rate was $2.00 an hour.

Policy makers are intrigued by this economic analysis. What can be better than creating higher wage rates that also bring about higher levels of employment? That scenario is surely better than the competitive one, in which jobs must be traded off for higher wage rates. Unions entering monopsonistic markets may be able to raise *both* wage rates and employment. But for governments legislating minimum wage laws the problem is that low-wage labor markets (those in which the minimum wage is greater than the equilibrium wage) are generally competitive and not monopsonistic. Studies have found that minimum wage laws do raise wage rates at the expense of some jobs.[7]

WAGE DIFFERENTIALS

Up to this point in our discussion we have explained the general theory of wage determination. You have learned that, in any particular labor market, an equilibrium wage rate is determined by the interaction of the forces of supply and demand. But that general proposition does not deal specifically with a great many variables that operate to produce wage differentials. We read in our newspapers that certain actors, athletes, and chief executive officers of giant corporations receive annual salaries in the range of $1 million or more, while the help-wanted ads in those same newspapers offer a baker's helper

7. Two very telling studies are: John Peterson, "Employment Effects of Minimum Wage Laws, 1938 to 1950," *Journal of Political Economy,* October 1957, pp. 412–430; and Finis Welch, "The Rising Impact of the Minimum Wage," *Regulation,* November/December 1978, pp. 28–37.

TABLE 30-7 Average Weekly Earnings in Selected U.S. Industries, December 1985

Industry	Average Weekly Earnings
Motor vehicles	625
Petroleum and coal	623
Primary metals	504
Chemicals	504
Fabricated metals	420
Food	354
Lumber and wood	333
Furniture and fixtures	306
Textile mill products	283
Apparel	216

Source: *Employment and Earnings*, U.S. Department of Labor, Bureau of Labor Statistics, February 1986, Table C-2, pp. 88–103.

$8,800 a year and a fast-food clerk $6,700 a year. So as not to dwell on extreme cases, Table 30-7 presents the average weekly earnings of workers in ten major U.S. industries in December 1985. A quick glance reveals that the wage differentials are quite great.

What explains these wage differentials? The answer to this question may be separated into three parts: (1) the qualifications of the workers, (2) the desirability of the job, and (3) the institutions that surround the labor market.

Worker Qualifications

Workers are not all alike. They have different abilities to get a job done. In the sense of having a higher marginal product, some workers are more "productive" than others because of innate characteristics. Some people are born with greater intelligence than others. If they have sufficient money to spend on education and enough motivation, they can become nuclear physicists, neurosurgeons, or high-level computer programmers. Others are born with superior physical characteristics that make them particularly productive in certain occupations. The seven-foot-four-inch basketball player, the big, strong foot-ball player, the small, agile jockey, the jet fighter pilot with perfect vision, and the exceptionally attractive model are all examples. Yet others are born with special talents that, with proper training and motivation, allow them to become successful painters, dancers, singers, or concert pianists.

The productiveness of workers may also depend on their socioeconomic background. The child who grows up in a home where education and good work habits are highly valued and where he or she has good role models is likely to develop the kind of personal characteristics that are appreciated in the work place.

Finally, how productive a worker will be depends greatly on his or her education and training. Intellect alone will not enable one to become a neurosurgeon or even a college professor. It takes an investment in human capital, which not everyone is willing or able to make. Since human capital comes from capital investment, we shall postpone our discussion of this important subject until the next chapter.

These differences in worker qualifications are part of the reason for wage differentials. Workers with desirable qualifications usually will receive higher wage rates than workers who do not have them.

Job Desirability

All jobs are not equally desirable. Even though people have different tastes and preferences for jobs, some jobs are generally considered to be more attractive than others. Most people prefer a clean job to one that is dirty. Most prefer a quiet office to a noisy factory. Safe working conditions are preferred to a dangerous work setting. Most people would rather have a challenging job with a varied pace than a boring job with a fixed pace of work. Finally, people generally have preferences about where they will work. Some parts of the country have a favorable climate or offer a relatively low cost of living, and most people would rather not have to commute.

If there were no wage differentials among jobs, most people would apply for the desirable jobs and few for the unattractive jobs. However, in a free market, employers who are swamped with applications for desirable jobs offer lower wage rates, and employers who can't fill their relatively undesirable jobs offer higher rates. In other words, people who accept unattractive jobs are paid a "compensating wage differential." This helps to explain the relatively high wage rates paid to coal miners, construction workers on high-rise projects, and oil drillers in northern Alaska. It also helps one to understand the 1,500 commercial deep-sea divers in the United States who "are exposed to the dangers of drowning, the rigors of construction work with cumbersome gear, a lonely and hostile work environment, . . . who earn $20,000 to $45,000 per year, or about 20 percent to 130 percent more than the average high-school graduate."[8]

Labor Market Institutions

Each labor market is surrounded by somewhat different institutions. None is perfectly free. But the sources of imperfection differ from one labor market to another. We have already discussed unions, governments, and monopsonistic employers as sources of imperfection. A union that is able to limit entry into its ranks and thereby restrict the supply of labor is able to raise wage rates for its members. Similarly, a government that sets a minimum wage for some workers or requires a license for workers to practice a craft, such as auto mechanics or hairdressing, restricts supply and raises wage rates for the affected workers. Monopsonistic employers can reduce both wage rates and employment below competitive levels.

The lack of geographic labor mobility is another source of market imperfection. For similar jobs, the wage rate may be higher in one part of the country than in another. People are often reluctant to move very far away for an only slightly better-paying job. Most reason that it doesn't pay to leave house and home and neighbors for 50

8. Ronald G. Ehrenberg and Robert S. Smith, *Modern Labor Economics: Theory and Public Policy* (Glenview, Illinois: Scott, Foresman and Company, 1982), p. 205.

cents or a dollar more an hour. Anyway, in a year or two that wage might be lowered or the job itself lost. Furthermore, those workers who might be willing to relocate for higher-paying jobs often don't know that these jobs exist. Of course, such information is often available and if workers have the initiative to search for it, they may be able to find it. In 1982, when the industrial midwestern United States was hit very hard by recession, Texas newspapers full of help-wanted ads were readily available at newsstands in Michigan and Ohio. However, that was an extreme situation. Usually workers employed in one part of the country have limited information about jobs and wage rates in faraway places.

Finally, most labor markets suffer from some discrimination, which shows up as wage differentials. Labor market *discrimination* means that different economic opportunities are offered to persons on the basis of their personal characteristics (especially their race or sex). The Civil Rights Act of 1964 declared it illegal for firms to discriminate in hiring or promoting persons on the basis of race, religion, sex, age, or national origin and created the Equal Employment Opportunities Commission (EEOC) to oversee compliance with the law. Through court orders the EEOC can force employers to compensate workers who have been held back or underpaid because of discrimination. Also, under the law, employers are not allowed to end wage discrimination by lowering the pay of those employees who have not suffered from discrimination. Even though the United States has laws against discrimination, it is often practiced in subtle ways that are hard to detect. The actual numbers seem to indicate that enforcement is not completely effective. It is clear that some part of the wage differentials that continue to exist between whites and blacks, between whites and other minorities, and between men and women are due to discrimination. In Chapter 33 we shall present some further data.

SUMMARY

1. Economists study the supply and demand for labor under different sets of conditions. Companies may hire workers in competitive or monopsonistic labor markets, and they may sell their output in competitive or monopolistic product markets. An individual company in a purely competitive product market cannot affect the price of the goods or services that it sells, nor can an individual company in a purely competitive labor market affect the wage rate that it pays to its workers. However, an individual company that is a monopolist in the product market does affect the price of the goods or services that it sells, and an individual company that is a monopsonist in the labor market affects the wage rate that it pays.

2. A company that hires workers in a purely competitive labor market faces a horizontal supply and *MFC* curve. It will want to hire more workers if it sells its goods or services competitively than if it is a monopolist in the product market. This is the case because in a monopolistic product market a company's *MRP* curve is steeper than in a purely competitive one and so will intersect its *MFC* curve at a lower level of employment.

3. An individual worker's supply curve of labor is expected to be positively sloped at most, but not necessarily all, wage rates. At very high wage rates it may "bend back" or become negative as the worker's income effect outweighs his or her substitution effect.

4. A market-supply curve of labor slopes upward because as the wage rate for that particular occupation rises in relation to the wage rates for other occupations, more and more people will offer their services for that occupation. A market-demand curve for labor is derived by aggregating all of the individual firms' *MRP* curves. The equilibrium wage rate and quantity of workers employed in a labor market is identified by the intersection of the market-supply curve with the market-demand curve. In a purely competitive labor market, that wage rate will be accepted as the going wage and each individual firm will be able to hire as many or as few workers as it wishes to hire at that wage.

5. Individual firms that are monopsonists in the labor market face positively sloped supply curves of labor. This means that in order to attract more workers, they have to pay higher wages. Their

MFC of hiring an additional worker is, however, higher than the wage paid to that additional worker, since all of the workers hired earlier must also be paid the higher wage rate. As in competitive labor markets, the equilibrium number of workers that a monopsonist will hire is found at the point where the monopsonist's *MFC* curve intersects its *MRP* curve. But, whereas for a purely competitive employer, *MFC* is equal to the equilibrium wage rate, for a monopsonistic employer, *MFC* is above the equilibrium wage rate.

6. Labor unions are collective organizations whose primary goals are to improve the wages and working conditions of their employee members. It was difficult for them to become established in the United States. At first many people resented them and considered them a threat to the American free-enterprise system.

7. Before the formation of the AF of L in 1886, American unions were fairly local and were often involved in political actions. In a sense, they were on a roller coaster, doing well during prosperous times, but being all but wiped out during recessions. With the founding of the AF of L came the beginning of business unionism.

8. It was not until the Great Depression of the 1930s that public opinion swung over to support the union cause. This change of heart led to the passage of two important pro-union laws, the Norris-LaGuardia Act and the Wagner-Connery Act. After World War II, Congress passed a somewhat compensating pro-employer labor law, called the Taft-Hartley Act.

9. An internal union struggle between craft unions, representing particular types of skilled workers and industrial unions, representing all the workers in an industry, had been festering during the first three decades of the twentieth century. This struggle came to a head in 1938 when the AF of L expelled the CIO from its ranks. It was not until 1955 that the two finally merged.

10. The problem of corruption and racketeering in some unions led to the passage of the Landrum-Griffin Act in 1959. The problem of racial discrimination was a major concern of many unions in the early 1960s. Unions supported the efforts to pass the Civil Rights Act of 1964.

11. Union membership increased during the 1960s, held fairly constant during the 1970s, and fell dramatically in the early 1980s. The 1960s and 1970s saw a great change in the composition of union membership. The percentage of private firm employees who were union members declined, whereas the percentage of public employees who were unionized rose.

12. Collective bargaining is the approach used by labor unions to negotiate with employers or their representatives. The issues in collective bargaining fall into two broad categories: (a) the conditions of employment, such as wage issues, fringe benefits, and work standards, and (b) the relationship between the union and management. The process of collective bargaining often calls for a great show of strength on both sides. The ultimate weapon of a union is the strike, which may be supplemented by picketing and boycotts.

13. Unions of course have an impact on wage rates. Just how much they are able to raise wage rates is difficult to determine. When bargaining takes place in purely competitive labor markets, unions may achieve higher wage rates through restricting the supply of labor, bargaining for an above-equilibrium wage rate, or raising the demand for labor. When bargaining takes place in a monopsonistic labor market, we cannot predict just how high the equilibrium wage rate will be. The relative power of the union and management along with the policies that they follow will dictate the result of the bargaining.

14. Government also has an impact on wage rates. Labor laws have strengthened unions and in turn have tended to raise wages. Whenever the government increases or decreases taxes that employees or employers must pay, it has an effect on both employment and wage rates.

15. Government affects some wage rates when it sets a minimum wage, or a lower limit on the wage rate that firms are allowed to pay. Generally, firms in industries affected by minimum-wage legislation are in fairly competitive labor markets, so that although the legislation increases the wage rates of some low-wage employees, it also reduces employment. In monopsonistic labor markets, the result of a minimum wage may be not only to increase the wage rate of low-wage employ-

ees but also to bring about a higher level of employment.

16. The general proposition that an equilibrium wage rate in a labor market is determined by the interaction of the forces of supply and demand hides a great many variables that operate to produce wage differentials. These variables may be placed in three categories: (a) the qualifications of the workers, (b) the desirability of the job, and (c) the institutions that surround the labor market. In most cases, workers who possess desirable qualifications will receive higher wages than workers who do not possess them. Workers who accept undesirable jobs are usually paid a compensating wage differential. Labor market institutions that stem from union action, government action, geographic labor immobility, and discrimination affect the degree of imperfection in a labor market and, in turn, wage rates.

DISCUSSION QUESTIONS

1. How is a firm's demand curve for labor affected by whether it sells its output in a purely competitive product market or in a monopolistic product market? Assuming that the firm hires workers in a purely competitive labor market, explain how the number of workers hired will depend on the type of product market in which the firm sells its output.

2. Explain why an individual worker's supply-of-labor curve may be backward-bending. In terms of the relationship between the substitution effect and the income effect, explain what is occurring when an individual worker's supply curve for labor is:

    a. positively sloped

    b. a vertical straight line

    c. negatively sloped

3. Distinguish between a purely competitive labor market and a monopsonistic labor market. Why is it that the marginal-factor-cost curve for labor is equal to the supply curve of labor for a firm that is a pure competitor in the labor market whereas this marginal-factor-cost curve lies above the supply curve for a firm that is a monopsonist in the labor market?

4. What role did each of the following play in the development of the labor movement in the United States?
  a. guilds
  b. Knights of Labor
  c. American Federation of Labor
  d. Industrial Workers of the World
  e. Congress of Industrial Organizations
5. Briefly discuss each of the four major pieces of labor legislation enacted in the United States during the years 1932 through 1959.
6. Briefly identify each of the following:
  a. yellow-dog contract
  b. business unionism
  c. craft unions
  d. jurisdictional strike
  e. a closed shop
  f. featherbedding
  g. industrial unions
  h. a union shop
  i. a lockout
7. "Labor unions made a lot of sense during the nineteenth century and the first few decades of the twentieth century, but they seem to have outlived their usefulness." Do you agree or disagree? Why?
8. Given the case of a purely competitive labor market, discuss the three approaches that a union may take to raise the wage rates of its members. Putting yourself in the place of each of the following persons, tell which approach you would prefer and why you would prefer it:
  a. a top-level official of this union
  b. a working member of this union who has substantial seniority
  c. a working member of this union who was recently hired
9. Without looking at Figure 30-14, draw a diagram showing what happens when a government imposes a minimum wage in a purely competitive labor market. Turn to Figure 30-14 to see if you have it right. What are the pros and cons of government taking such an action?
10. Discuss the most important explanations for the existence of wage differentials. Discuss five different actions that a government could take to decrease wage differentials.

31 Capital, Interest, and Investment

PREVIEW In Chapter 29 we introduced you to the different kinds of resources and also to the theory of marginal productivity, which explains why companies demand certain amounts of these resources. Chapter 30 applied that theory to labor resources. In this chapter we apply it to capital resources—both physical capital and human capital. In analyzing capital resources, we must take account of a number of variables that usually do not concern us when we study the use of other types of resources. They stem from the fact that capital generally lasts a long time and is expected to bring a return for many years after it is created.

We begin by reviewing the characteristics of capital resources. In explaining why they are created, we present the idea of "roundabout" production of consumer goods. We also explain what determines the amount of new capital created during any particular time period. Economists refer to the creation of new capital as "investment," and we analyze what is called the "investment decision."

The investment decision relates the cost of capital to the return that is expected to be generated from the use of capital. Since the return to capital often takes place over a long period of time, a rational investment decision calls for figuring the present value of future receipts, through a process known as discounting. Discounting recognizes the opportunity cost of the invested funds and also the risks and uncertainties inherent in investment decisions. In explaining a discounting formula, we give an example that shows how a company may find the present value of its future investment returns. Since investment returns must be discounted by using a specific interest rate, we then describe how interest rates are determined in a free market for loanable funds.

In the last part of the chapter, we compare investment decisions that involve physical capital with those that involve human capital. Human capital is different from physical capital because skills cannot be separated from the persons who possess them, and because human beings can no longer be bought and sold as slaves. Also, the returns to physical capital are mostly monetary, whereas psychic returns and consumption value are important in human capital investment decisions.

We separate the returns from human capital investment into private returns and social returns. Even though persons and companies invest in human capital in order to gain private returns, there may also be social returns. Similarly, governments invest in human capital to gain social benefits, but in doing so, they offer many private benefits as well.

Finally, we present some findings from studies done by economists who have tried to measure private and social rates of return from investing in education.

PHYSICAL CAPITAL

Recall from Chapters 4 and 29 that capital is used by business firms as an input—together with labor (including entrepreneurship) and natural resources—for the production of consumer goods and services or other capital goods. **Physical capital** such as factory buildings, machines, and equipment make it possible for companies to produce more efficiently than they can without them. Textile firms use mechanical looms, for example, because a worker can produce much more cloth with such a machine than he or she can produce by hand-weaving. Even when the cost of producing the loom is counted, cloth is still produced at a far lower cost with the loom than without it.

Physical capital is also used by governments. Such *social capital* helps to produce the many goods and services that governments provide. Some obvious examples are government office buildings, courthouses, school buildings, and roads.

Roundabout Production

The use of capital in production was first described as **roundabout production** by the Austrian economist Eugen von Böhm-Bawerk (1851–1914). He suggested that firms have a choice between using labor and natural resources for the direct production of consumer goods and using these resources first to produce capital, which in turn is used to produce consumer goods. Choosing roundabout production means that some resources are diverted from the direct production of consumer goods. At first, some amount of consumer goods must be given up in order to produce capital goods. But once the capital goods are available for the production of consumer goods, the greater efficiency that they offer may compensate for the initial reduction in consumer goods. In a successful business, the expanded production that is gained through the use of capital can finance the replacement of the capital goods as they wear out and may justify adding even more capital as more and more consumer goods are being produced. And in fact, the record of the so-called "industrial revolution" of the past two hundred years shows that roundabout production works.

The Investment Decision

Capital goods are created by purposeful human effort. They are produced with the use of other resources. To create capital, there must be a conscious decision on the part of a business firm. When a company decides to provide money for

the resources that are needed to create new capital, it has made an investment decision. The **investment decision**—whether to provide for the creation of new capital and, if so, how much—is much like the decisions that business firms make with regard to other resources. The marginal revenue product (*MRP*)–marginal factor cost (*MFC*) principle presented in Chapter 29 and applied to the labor resource in Chapter 30 governs the investment decision as well. For example, a company that manufactures shoes must decide how many shoe-making machines to use. For each added machine, the company must determine how many more pairs of shoes will be produced each year and how much more revenue will be received from shoe sales, assuming no change in any other inputs by the company. This additional revenue is the marginal revenue product from the added machine. Following the principle of diminishing marginal productivity, we expect the marginal revenue product to grow smaller as more machines are added.

Marginal factor cost is the addition to total costs that comes from adding one more machine. The company is expected to keep adding more machines as long as the marginal revenue product from an additional machine is greater than its marginal factor cost. Productivity theory predicts that when the marginal revenue product has fallen and becomes equal to the marginal factor cost, investment in more machines will stop.

THE RISKS AND UNCERTAINTY OF INVEST-MENT The theory behind the investment decision is the same as for decisions about other business inputs. However, there are certain points that are especially important in their application to investment. Three major problems faced in the investment decision are (1) the time problem, (2) the obsolescence problem, and (3) the derived-demand problem.

THE TIME PROBLEM Investment decisions usually must be made quite a while before receiving all or a major part of the return from that investment. Labor is paid after its work is performed, and raw materials are paid for after they are delivered. However, capital goods usually must be purchased before they are used in production.

For this reason, there is a time lag between the time the investment decision is made and when the new equipment actually starts operating on the production line. Also, capital goods tend to be rather durable. Factory buildings, blast furnaces, auto body presses, tractors, computers, and mechanical looms are produced and bought with the expectation that they will last for a fairly long time. These considerations combine to make time an especially important element in the investment decision. During all of the time that a firm has invested its funds but has received only part of its return on that investment, it suffers an opportunity cost. For example, a company that decides to expand its capacity by building a new factory will not receive any return from it for the years it takes to construct the building and ready it for production. Once in production, the payoff will not come all at once but may be spread over a period of fifty years. The opportunity cost of having these funds tied up in its new factory instead of in, say, stocks, bonds, or the bank must not be forgotten.

THE OBSOLESCENCE PROBLEM The term **obsolescence** means that something becomes no longer useful or economically suited for its intended purpose, even though it may still be in good working order. Since capital goods are usually expected to last for many years, one cannot be sure that they will not become obsolete at some point. For example, a computer that a firm plans to use for twenty years or more may actually become obsolete after only two years because a new generation of much more efficient computers is invented and readied for commercial use.

THE DERIVED-DEMAND PROBLEM A third problem in the investment decision arises from the fact that the demand for capital goods depends on the demand for the end products that these capital goods help to produce. That is, the demand for capital goods is a **derived demand.** For this reason, the expected return from an investment is linked to a firm's expectations about the price of its end products. Since the expected return from an investment extends over a long period of time, there is plenty of opportunity for the price of its end product to change. If the price of the end product is lower than expected, the firm may have a much lower than expected return from the investment. For example, the expected return from a machine used in the manufacture of video cassettes depends on the price of video cassettes. If more companies decide to produce video cassettes, or if the demand for them declines, their price will fall, and the expected return from the investment in the video cassette-making machine will have been too high.

DISCOUNTING FUTURE RETURNS The time, obsolescence, and derived-demand problems help explain why investment decisions involve more risk and uncertainty than do most decisions about other production inputs. Economists attempt to handle these problems through the process of discounting.

Recall from the last chapter that when economists predict the amount of labor that a firm will hire, their approach is to compare that firm's marginal revenue product from labor with its marginal factor cost for labor. In the simplest explanation of that process, time is not taken into account. It is assumed that the extra revenue contributed by an added worker flows into the firm during the same time period as the worker is paid for his or her labor. But time is an important element in the investment decision and must not be ignored. When making an investment decision, a firm must figure the present value of the marginal revenue product that flows to it over a period of time. Then this present value is compared with the marginal factor cost, most or all of which is incurred at the start of the process.

Present value is the value at the present time of a sum of money to be received in the future. To get a clearer understanding of present value, imagine that someone offers you a very pleasant choice. You may choose between receiving $1,000 right now or an iron-clad guarantee that $1,000 will be paid to you one year from today. Which would you choose? If your answer is that you would take the $1,000 right now, you are making the economically correct choice. The $1,000 paid to you now is worth more than the assurance that $1,000 will be paid to you in one year. Why is that so? Because money can earn money. By merely placing the $1,000 in your neighborhood commercial bank or savings and loan association, you may very well receive $1,060 one year from now (assuming that you are paid a 6 percent annual rate of interest). In that case, a rephrasing of our original question would be as follows: "Would you prefer $1,000 to be paid to you one year from now or $1,060 to be paid to you one year from now?" When the question is put this way, the answer is even more obvious than before. A certain sum of money received now has greater value than that same sum of money to be received in the future. Turning this sentence around and using the economist's language we can say, "The present value of a certain sum of money to be received in the future is less than the value of that same sum of money were it received now." The difference between the two values is determined by how far in the future the money will be received and by the interest rate used to discount the future payment. The rules that govern these relationships are as follows:

1. At any given interest rate, the further into the future a sum of money will be received, the lower is its present value.
2. The higher the interest rate used to discount the future payment, the lower is the present value of that future payment.

Discounting is the process of calculating the present value of payments that are to be received in the future. To begin with the simplest case, let us suppose that the payment will be made one year from now. The formula is as follows:

$$PV = \frac{X}{1 + i}$$

Here PV is the present value, X is the payment to be received in one year, and i is the annual rate of interest that could be earned on alternative uses of money that face the same amount of risk. This is so because in one year $PV(1 + i) = X$. For example, if the appropriate rate of interest is 8 percent and $1,000 is the payment to be received in one year, the present value is $925.93.

$$PV = \frac{\$1,000}{1.08} = \$925.93$$

And this is the same as $925.93 (1.08) = $1,000.

We use a slightly more complicated formula to derive the discounted present value of a sum of money that is to be received further into the future.

$$PV = \frac{X}{(1 + i)^t}$$

Here t is the number of years between the present time and the time that the payment will be received.

The t in the above formula reflects the fact that interest usually is compoundable. This means that each year after the first year, interest is earned not only on the principal amount of money but also on the interest paid earlier. So if $100.00 is placed in a savings bank at 5 percent interest, it will be worth $110.25 after two years. The $110.25 is made up of the original $100.00 placed in the bank, $5.00 interest earned on the $100.00 during the first year, $5.00 interest earned on the $100.00 during the second year, and $0.25 interest earned during the second year on the $5.00 interest earned during the first year.

To see the importance of compounding, let us calculate the present value of $1,000 that is received after four years rather than after only one year. At 8 percent interest, the PV of $1,000 in four years is as follows:

$$PV = \frac{\$1,000}{(1.08)^4} = \frac{\$1,000}{(1.08)(1.08)(1.08)(1.08)}$$

$$= \frac{\$1,000}{1.3605} = \$735.02$$

This example may be read as follows: At 8 percent interest, $735.02 would have to be "invested" today in order to receive $1,000.00 four years from today. Another way of reading it, which is more relevant to our discussion, is this: At 8 percent interest, $1,000 to be received four years from today is presently worth $735.02.

At lower rates of interest the present value is higher. At 4 percent interest, for example, the *PV* of $1,000.00 in four years is $854.80. Similarly, the further away the payment date, the lower is the *PV*. For example, at 4 percent interest, the *PV* of $1,000.00 in twelve years is $624.60

The discounting formula allows us to take care of the opportunity cost part of the problem that arises because the investment decision deals with returns that extend over a period of time. The obsolescence and end-product-price problems are more difficult to handle. In the discounting formula, higher discount rates should be used for investments that involve greater amounts of risk and uncertainty, and lower rates should be used for investments that are less risky and uncertain. But no simple formula can deal with these problems; that is, none can tell us what the probability of obsolescence or change in future end-product price actually is. Success in making investment decisions requires wisdom, experience, and a generous helping of luck. In some ways, investment decision making is an art as well as a science.

CAPITAL COSTS AND RETURNS For a firm to make an investment decision, such as whether or not to purchase a particular machine, both the marginal factor cost (*MFC*) of that machine and the marginal revenue product (*MRP*) expected from it must be calculated.

The *MFC* of capital is very easy to determine. It is merely the price of a capital good at the time of its purchase. The difficult problem is to estimate the *MRP* (the return to capital) in a way that is comparable. Two requirements must be kept in mind. First, the *MRP* that is to be counted must be net of all operating costs. For a machine, the *MRP* would be the value that it adds to what it receives as input minus the cost of labor required to operate it, the cost of energy to run it, and the cost incurred for maintenance. Second, as we have explained, the firm must discount future returns to their present values.

Suppose that a business firm is trying to decide whether to invest in a certain machine. The firm knows that its *MFC* for this machine is $35,000. Furthermore, it estimates that its *MRP* (net of all operating costs) from this machine will be $40,000

received in an income stream of $10,000 per year for four years.[1] Should the firm make this investment? To find the answer, let us calculate the present value of the *MRP* (the $40,000 income stream). If the appropriate interest rate to use for discounting the *MRP* were 2 percent, the following calculation would provide an answer of "yes."

$$PV = \frac{\$10,000}{1.02} + \frac{\$10,000}{(1.02)^2} + \frac{\$10,000}{(1.02)^3} + \frac{\$10,000}{(1.02)^4}$$

$$= \frac{\$10,000}{1.02} + \frac{\$10,000}{1.0404} + \frac{\$10,000}{1.0612} + \frac{\$10,000}{1.0824}$$

$$= \$9,803.92 + \$9,611.69 + \$9,423.29$$

$$+ \$9,238.73 = \$38,077.63$$

The present value of the *MRP* from the machine is $38,077.63, which exceeds the cost of the machine (*MFC*), which is $35,000.

If, however, the correct interest rate to use for discounting the *MRP* in this case were 8 percent, the firm would be expected to give a clear-cut answer of "no." As the following calculation shows, the present value of the *MRP* would be $33,121.29, which is less than the *MFC* of the machine ($35,000).

$$PV = \frac{\$10,000}{1.08} + \frac{\$10,000}{(1.08)^2} + \frac{\$10,000}{(1.08)^3} + \frac{\$10,000}{(1.08)^4}$$

$$= \frac{\$10,000}{1.08} + \frac{\$10,000}{1.1664} + \frac{\$10,000}{1.2597} + \frac{\$10,000}{1.3605}$$

$$= \$9,259.26 + \$8,573.39 + \$7,938.40$$

$$+ \$7,350.24 = \$33,121.29$$

Here we can see clearly why successful investment decision making calls for skill, experience, and good luck. Estimating the amount of risk and uncertainty in a given investment project is a very important part of the investment decision. Underestimating the amount of risk and for this reason using too low a discount rate will cause a company to make investments that turn out to

---

1. We have chosen an unrealistically short income stream in our example in order to save on space.

be unprofitable. On the other hand, overestimating risk and using too high a discount rate will cause the company to turn down investment opportunities that would have been profitable.

INTEREST-RATE DETERMINATION

Now that you understand the important part that the interest rate plays in investment decision making, we must look deeper to discover what determines interest rates in the economy. To start this analysis, it is helpful to recognize that, in economic theorizing, the interest rate is like the wage rate paid to hire labor or the rental rate paid to obtain the use of natural resources. Just as wages pay for the use of someone's time and skill, and just as rent pays for the use of someone's natural resources, interest pays for the use of someone's money. Also, just as wage rates are determined in a labor market or rent rates are determined in a natural resource market, interest rates are determined in a **loanable funds market.** This market consists of arrangements and procedures to carry out transactions between people who want to borrow money and people who want to lend money.

Figure 31-1 pictures supply and demand in a loanable funds market. On the horizontal axis are quantities of money demanded and supplied for loans (called **loanable funds**). On the vertical axis are rates of interest, which act as prices in bringing equilibrium between quantities of loanable funds demanded and supplied. The supply curve shows how lenders respond to interest-rate changes (if other things remain unchanged). The demand curve shows how borrowers respond to interest-rate changes (if other things remain unchanged). In this case, the equilibrium rate of interest, which balances the quantity demanded and the quantity supplied, is 8 percent. If the lending and borrowing in this loanable funds market involve risks that are the same as those faced by the company making the investment decision in our previous case, then the company will decide *not* to buy the machine.

FIGURE 31-1 Market for Loanable Funds

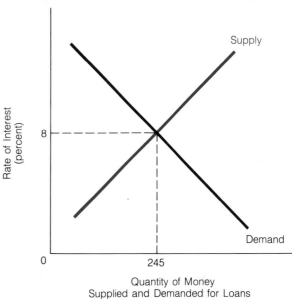

Quantity of Money
Supplied and Demanded for Loans
(in thousands of dollars)

Shown here are the supply and demand curves for loanable funds. The curves show that at higher rates of interest more loanable funds will be supplied and less will be demanded and at lower rates of interest less loanable funds will be supplied and more will be demanded. In the case shown the equilibrium rate of interest is 8 percent, at which $245,000 is supplied and demanded.

The Investment Demand for Loanable Funds

The $35,000 machine in the earlier example is just one of many capital goods that might be bought by that company or by other companies in the economy. We have already shown that investment in this machine would be profitable at an interest rate of 2 percent and that it would not be profitable at an interest rate of 8 percent. From this, we can reason that there is some interest rate, higher than 2 percent but lower than 8 percent, at which the company would just break even from investing in this machine. In other words, there is some interest rate where the present value of the future net income from the machine (*MRP*) is exactly equal to the $35,000

635

FIGURE 31-2   Investment Demand for Loanable Funds

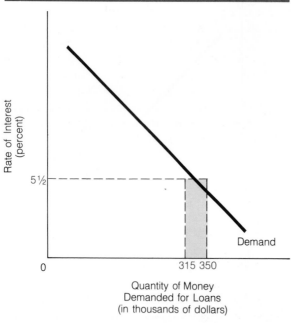

This graph shows the investment-demand curve for loanable funds. The shaded area represents the annual interest payment at a 5½ percent rate of interest for the $35,000 machine under consideration for investment by the firm in our example. Its 5½ percent breakeven interest rate (rate of return) determines its position along the demand curve compared with other potential investments. Investments that break even at higher rates of interest make up the demand for investment loans at higher rates of interest. Those that break even at lower rates of interest make up the demand at lower rates of interest.

cost of the machine (*MFC*). By trial and error, we estimate that this *breakeven interest rate* is 5½ percent.

Figure 31-2 repeats the demand curve from Figure 31-1 and shows where the machine in our example fits into the picture. As shown by the shaded area, this machine involves the money between $315,000 and $350,000 along the horizontal axis of this figure. If the interest rate were 5½ percent, this investment would have been exactly at the margin of profitable undertakings.

The demand curve for investment loans in Figure 31-2 combines the demand for the machine in our case with the demands for many other possible investments. Those investments that promise to pay off at a higher rate (have a higher breakeven interest rate) are located to the left of our machine along higher reaches of the demand curve. Those that pay off at a lower rate (have a lower breakeven interest rate) are located to the right along the lower reaches of the demand curve. Thus, the investment-demand curve for loanable funds shows a range of many possible investments, arranged in descending order of their expected returns.

As you learned in Chapter 5, a demand curve may *shift* because of a change in some variable other than the one shown on the vertical axis of a graph. Shifts in the investment demand for loanable funds can come from a change in any variable other than the interest rate. You were introduced to some of these other variables when we discussed business expectations about the likelihood of obsolescence for the machine or the likelihood that the price of the end product would rise or fall. We know that all these matters involve risk and uncertainty, but the borrower nevertheless must make his or her best estimate. When the best estimates about these matters change, the investment-demand curve for loanable funds shifts. Changes that promise greater returns shift the curve to the right and changes that promise smaller returns shift the curve to the left.

Other Demands for Loanable Funds

In this chapter, we have been most interested in investments made by business firms for such production inputs as machinery and equipment. We have noted, however, that there are other demands for loanable funds. Households sometimes want to borrow money to finance consumption purchases. This happens when members of households want to have consumption goods and services now and do not want to wait until they have saved enough money to buy them. If the desire for present consumption is strong enough, the household may be willing to pay the interest needed in order to buy now and save later.

Governments are responsible for another component of the demand for loanable funds. Like households, governments may also want to buy more today than can be financed from their current income (tax receipts). This means that there is a budget deficit. When this happens, governments enter the market as demanders for loanable funds.

The household and the government demands for loanable funds are also expected to be inversely related to the rate of interest. In other words, as the interest rate goes up, the quantity demanded for loans goes down, and vice versa. For this reason, the combined demand curve for all sources (firms, households, and governments) will have a negative slope. Shifts in household and government demand for loanable funds can arise from many non-interest-rate variables. For example, if households become more optimistic about the future, their demand for loans may increase, since they expect to have no trouble in repaying the loans. Government demand for loanable funds, on the other hand, would be expected to shift to the right if the economy goes into recession and government receives less money in taxes.

The Supply of Loanable Funds

What about the supply side of the loanable funds market? Here we must focus on households, firms, and governments that are saving, rather than spending, money. They are receiving more income than they wish to spend today. Their preferences between purchasing things today and postponing purchases until sometime in the future are just the opposite of the preferences of those on the demand side of this market. We are quite sure that this supply curve will slope upward to the right, as we have shown in the earlier figures. At low interest rates, these potential lenders are not nearly as eager to make loans as they are at high rates of interest.

The supply curve for loanable funds can shift in response to changes in any variable other than the interest rate. Much depends on the outlook and attitudes of the people who are lenders or potential lenders. If their attitudes change so that they want to use their wealth today and not postpone using it until later (that is, if their time preference changes in favor of more present consumption), the supply curve will shift to the left and interest rates will rise, if other things remain unchanged. Of course, if their time preference changes in the other direction, the supply curve will shift to the right and interest rates will fall, if other things remain unchanged. In the first half of the 1980s, an important part of the supply of loanable funds came from foreigners who found returns better in the U.S. loanable funds market than in the loanable funds markets in their home countries.

In Figure 31-1 the demand and supply for loanable funds are in equilibrium at $245,000 a year when the interest rate is 8 percent. At lower interest rates, more would be demanded than supplied, pushing the interest rate upward. At higher interest rates, more would be supplied than demanded, pushing interest rates down. The equilibrium interest rate itself may move up or down because of shifts in the demand curve, or the supply curve, or both.

Many Different Interest Rates

In beginning this section on interest-rate determination, we said that the interest rate is like the wage rate paid to hire labor or the rental rate paid to obtain the use of natural resources. Now we must add that, just as there are different wage rates for different kinds of labor and different rental rates for different kinds and locations of natural resources, so also are there different interest rates for different kinds of loans. The main reason for interest-rate differences is that some loans involve more risk than others. A higher interest rate will be charged on high-risk loans than on low-risk loans because the lenders insist on receiving enough interest from loans that are paid off to make up for the losses they will suffer on loans that are not paid off. At any given time, there are different kinds of loans involving many different degrees of risk. So it is not surprising that many different interest rates exist, all at the same time.

HUMAN CAPITAL

In Chapter 4, when we first presented the kinds of resources or factors of production, you learned that the skills that people use in combination with their labor effort are a kind of capital, called human capital. **Human capital** is that part of the productive power of individuals that has been developed through earlier expenditures for education, job training, and health care. The term recognizes that the capital concept can be applied to human beings as well as to physical capital. Economists speak of "investing in people" just as they do of "investing in machines."

Human beings have different degrees of productive capability. Just how good a "producer" a person is will depend on several important variables. One is how intelligent a person is. People are born with different kinds and degrees of intellectual ability, which can have an effect on their productive capability. Another variable is a person's socioeconomic background. The value system within which a person grows up affects his or her outlook on life including the attitude toward work. How productive a person is will also depend on his or her physical and mental health and the type and amount of education and on-the-job training he or she has received.

Investing in human capital—making people healthier, better educated, and more highly trained—may be thought of as capital creation. As with all capital creation, this form of investment uses the resources of the economy. Achieving a healthier population takes medical facilities, the services of physicians and other medical personnel, nutritious food, and healthful living and working conditions. To educate people requires school buildings, trained teachers, books,

and time for people to attend classes and to study. Developing job skills takes instructors and time away from the routine work tasks. Whether or not to allocate these scarce resources to human improvement, and if so, to what extent, is the human capital investment decision.

The Human Capital Investment Decision

The economic theory of the investment decision pertaining to human capital is like that involving physical capital. That is, investment in human capital is predicted to take place when the expected return from an investment exceeds its cost. However, there are some added complications, which differ depending on who is making the human capital investment decision. Business firms, for example, are expected to be most interested in the contribution that the investment will make to profits. That is, they are looking for monetary returns. Individuals, however, are expected to take into account more than the expected monetary returns when they decide whether or not to invest in their own or someone else's education. They will most likely consider that decision as involving not only investment but also consumption. Returns to investment in human capital by government also entail more than the monetary returns. A government may invest in its citizens' education in order to help them become better-informed voters or to bring about a more equal distribution of income.

Since the kinds of returns to investment in human capital differ so much, we shall treat individuals, firms, and governments separately.

INDIVIDUALS INVESTING IN HUMAN CAPITAL You, and probably your parents (or other benefactors), are investing in your higher education. How did you and they make that decision? Most likely in a more casual way than we describe in this chapter. It may have been taken for granted that you would go to college. But why? Why does it "obviously" pay to make this investment in you? In economic language, the answer is based on the results that are obtained from comparing the costs of this investment with the expected return from it.

COSTS OF THE INVESTMENT As in the case of physical capital, the cost is somewhat easier to identify and measure than is the return. For example, you may figure that the out-of-pocket cost to you and your family of a four-year college education is $12,000 tuition, $6,000 for added living expenses away from home, and $2,000 for books and supplies. To this total you might add $60,000 in lost wages—the difference between what you might earn if you were not going to college and what you expect to earn at part-time summer jobs while attending college. The total cost comes to $80,000.

RETURNS FROM THE INVESTMENT The estimates of the returns call for more guessing. You may discuss the present and expected salary ranges in the field of your choice with counselors, placement officers, and friends of the family whom you trust, and on that basis estimate your differential income stream for the years of your working life. You may estimate, for example, that your monetary income will be $8,000 a year higher with a college degree than without one and that your expected working life after college is thirty years. Your $80,000 cost is incurred during your college years. However, your monetary return from the college education is not the whole $240,000 (30 × $8,000 = $240,000) of additional salary, but only the present value of that additional income stream. Using the present-value formula presented earlier in this chapter, we would have to discount each $8,000 annual return by an appropriate interest rate over the number of years between college graduation and the time when you expect to receive it. The sum of the thirty separate present-value calculations would yield the present value of the entire monetary return from your college education. If, let us say, you choose 8 percent as the appropriate rate of interest by which to discount, then the present value of the $240,000 monetary return is $90,048.[2]

2. To save time, use a present-value table. These are found in the back of most basic mathematics books.

So the present value of your monetary return is more than $10,000 higher than your cost. On that basis alone, you and your family may decide to invest in your college education.

Let us now suppose that the present value of your monetary return from investing in your college education were below your cost. This could be the case when you estimate a lower monetary return, a shorter working career, or use a higher interest rate by which to discount the return. For example, had you estimated that your income would only be $7,000 a year higher with a college degree than without one, the present value of your income stream over thirty years at 8 percent interest would be $78,792. Similarly, if the appropriate interest rate to discount the return were 10 percent, the present value of $8,000 a year over thirty years would be $75,416. Does that mean that you would not attend college? Only you can answer that question. Possibly you and your family would still decide to invest in your college education. In that case, you and they may be expecting more than just a monetary return.

Economists refer to the nonmonetary returns from investing in human capital as **psychic returns.** Psychic returns from investing in your college education might come to you in the form of a higher social position, a better-educated marriage partner, pleasing your family, self-satisfaction, or the opportunity to obtain more enjoyable work in a more desirable location. Some of these returns may come to your parents in the form of pride in a son or a daughter with a college education and in knowing that they had a part in making that possible.

Besides the monetary and psychic returns that we have discussed so far, an individual's decision to invest in his or her own human capital may be in part a *consumption* decision. Most students consider the college years to be fun and therefore worth paying for. You may be less sure of that right before an important exam, but most students agree that going to school "beats working."

It is very difficult to separate the investment and consumption components in an individual's human capital investment–consumption decisions. It is also difficult to translate psychic returns into monetary returns. But there is little doubt that consumption and psychic returns are important considerations. A high school graduate may want very much to become an accountant and to associate with people who have attended college. He or she may also expect the college years to be enjoyable ones. Such a person will probably spend the money for a college education even if the present value of the monetary return is below the cost of going to college.

FIRMS INVESTING IN HUMAN CAPITAL Individuals are not the only ones to invest in human capital. Firms may invest in human capital as a strategy for gaining higher profits. Sometimes firms provide their employees with free medical checkups, nutritious lunches, and various kinds of safety equipment. These expenditures may be fringe benefits and part of total employee compensation (along with wages), but they may also be profitable investments in the firms' employees. Similarly, firms that offer training programs for their employees probably do so partly because they believe that such investments in human capital will be profitable to themselves. For example, the present value of the return from an investment of $1,000,000 in a training program for young managers may be significantly greater than $1,000,000. The return will depend on how much more productive the managers become as a result of the training that they receive and also on how long the trainees decide to remain with the company.

The fact that employees can leave their employer is unique to the human capital investment decision. When a firm invests in physical capital, it has a clear property right to the machine or building. Since firms do not have a property right in people—slavery being illegal—a firm cannot be sure that an employee trained at company expense will not soon resign. In fact, the U.S. labor force is quite mobile. Employees frequently "job hop" to improve themselves. For this reason, U.S. firms are generally reluctant to invest very much in human capital.

By contrast, in Japan it is common for workers to be employed by the same firm for their entire working lives. It follows, then, that Japanese companies are much more willing to invest in human capital than are American companies.

In the United States, human capital investment by employers is found to a more limited extent. As an investment it is most justified in fields such as professional sports and the armed forces, where courts have been willing to uphold certain work contracts. In some professional sports leagues, players are not permitted to change employment from one team to another for a specified number of years. The military offers specialized training only to persons who are willing to sign up for a certain number of years.

GOVERNMENT INVESTING IN HUMAN CAPITAL So far we have dealt only with private investment in human capital—private individuals and business firms seeking private returns. But, governments may also invest in human capital. Public investment in human capital is aimed at providing returns that benefit society as a whole.

There is a good deal of overlapping between government and private decisions. On the one hand, government investments can bring about both private and social returns. On the other hand, private decisions also can bring about both kinds of return. For example, a private investment in education not only offers a higher earning potential to those persons receiving the education but also produces better-informed citizens. An expansion of the frontiers of knowledge that is financed privately can increase both an individual's income and the well-being of the society as a whole. In a similar way, public investment results not only in social returns but also in private returns, such as higher earning potential for those citizens who are direct recipients of government-sponsored training programs or education grants.

In most countries the government is an important investor in human capital. The justification for this investment is that the social returns are substantial. Better-informed citizens are very important for the satisfactory functioning of a democratic country. The society as a whole depends on educated people to carry on the research and development leading to the discovery of the new products and new processes that raise the nation's standard of living. How productive people are and how much they earn affects a society's distribution of income and even its unemployment rate. Serious underinvestment in human capital might occur if the investment decision were left entirely to the private sector. To understand this point, suppose for a moment that education in the United States were not supported by the government. Would nearly all children attend primary school? Would the vast majority complete high school, and about half attend college? Would our citizens' health suffer if we had no programs for food stamps, subsidized housing, hot school lunches, and driver education? It is not easy to answer such questions in a precise way. But to the extent that the returns to investment in human beings are social rather than private, economists predict that the free market acting alone would devote fewer of our resources to such human capital investments.

Some Findings on the Returns from Education

Several economists have studied the economics of human capital and have tried to calculate the costs and monetary returns, both private and public. These studies have generally been limited to investment in formal education. For example, the 1979 Nobel Prize winner Theodore W. Schultz, a pioneer in this field, calculated that in 1949 the social rate of return on an investment in a grade school education was about 35 percent.[3] Another economist, Gary S. Becker, calculated that the private rates of return from a high school education were 16 percent in 1939, 20 percent in 1949, 25 percent in 1956, and 28 percent in 1958. He found private rates of return from investing in a college education to be much lower but still very high in relation to rates of return possible from other forms of investment. Specifically, he calculated that the private rate of return from investing in a college education ranged from 12 percent to 15 percent for the years 1939 to 1961.[4] The lowest calculated rates of return have been for investment in graduate studies. Orley Ashenfelter and Joseph D. Mooney found that in 1960 private returns to investing in an M.A. degree were under 8 percent and that returns to the Ph.D. degree ranged between 7 percent and 11 percent.[5]

Data from the 1960s by G. Hanoch, showing private monetary rates of return to formal education, are summarized in Table 31-1.[6] Notice that completing the eighth year of schooling (the last

TABLE 31-1 Estimated Rates of Return to Investment in Human Capital: Private Rates of Monetary Return to Investment in Additional Years of Formal Schooling

Additional Year of Schooling	Private Rate of Monetary Return (percent)
8th	22
9th	16
10th	16
11th	16
12th	16
13th	7
14th	7
15th	7
16th	12
17th or more	7

Source: G. Hanoch, "An Economic Analysis of Earnings and Schooling," The Journal of Human Resources 2, 1967, pp. 310–329 (data reprinted by permission of The University of Wisconsin Press); summarized by John T. Addison and W. Stanley Siebert, The Market for Labor: An Analytical Treatment (Santa Monica, California: Goodyear Publishing Co., 1979), p. 158.

3. Theodore W. Schultz, The Economic Value of Education (New York: Columbia University Press, 1963).

4. Gary S. Becker, Human Capital, 2nd ed. (New York: National Bureau of Economic Research, 1975).

5. Orley Ashenfelter and Joseph D. Mooney, "Graduate Education, Ability, and Earnings," Review of Economics and Statistics, February 1968, Vol. 50, pp. 78–86.

6. G. Hanoch, "An Economic Analysis of Earnings and Schooling," Journal of Human Resources, 2, 1967, pp. 310–329.

year of junior high school) provides a private monetary return of 22 percent, the twelfth year of schooling (the last year of high school) provides a 16 percent return, the sixteenth year of schooling (the last year of college) provides a 12 percent return, and the seventeenth or higher year (master's, doctoral, or professional school) provides a private monetary return of 7 percent.

Some more recent findings indicate that the private rate of return to higher education in the United States has dropped sharply. Comparing the years 1969 and 1974, Richard B. Freeman found that the average real income of college graduates dropped, while the average real income of high school graduates increased.[7] (However, college graduates still earned about one-third more than high school graduates.) Recent updates by Freeman show that this trend has been reversed. He finds modest improvement in the relative earnings of college graduates since the mid-1970s.[8] Furthermore, Freeman predicts that "sometime in the 1980s the market will indeed rebound for graduates, as the falling supply of new college workers . . . affects market conditions."[9]

If you are concerned about the possibly lower rate of return for a college education, there are several things to remember. First, this lower return from education may be a temporary situation brought on by the postwar "baby boom," which swelled the supply of college graduates without creating a comparable increase in the demand for their skills. Second, these data refer to all college degrees, whereas the returns differ greatly depending upon a student's major. There is no market for college-educated workers, but rather there are many markets, each for a different type of college-educated specialist. In recent years degrees in computer science, engineering, chem-

istry, and mathematics have offered much higher monetary returns than degrees in the humanities and social sciences such as philosophy, history, and sociology. Finally, remember that these data completely neglect psychic returns and the consumption value of attending college.

SUMMARY

1. Capital is a resource or factor of production used in combination with other resources to produce consumer goods and services or other capital goods. Capital may be either physical capital, such as factory buildings and machines, or human capital, such as education and training.

2. The use of capital in production is sometimes described as "roundabout production." That term recognizes that producers often have a choice between using labor and natural resources directly to produce consumer goods and services or first using these noncapital resources to produce capital, which is in turn used to produce the consumer products. Long-term efficiency is often increased by following the roundabout production method.

3. The creation of capital is called investment. Whether to provide for the creation of new capital, and if so, how much, is called the investment decision. Because a business firm will invest in order to make a profit, it is expected to invest up to the point where marginal revenue product of capital is equal to its marginal factor cost.

4. When making the investment decision, firms face problems related to the fact that the cost of capital is usually incurred well before the returns to capital are received. Capital is durable and generally provides returns in the form of an income stream over a considerable period of time. Not only do firms suffer an opportunity cost (the time problem), but they also must contend with the risks and uncertainties of obsolescence and the possible decrease in end-product prices (the derived-demand problem).

5. Discounting is the method used to determine the present value of returns that will be received

7. Richard B. Freeman, *The Overeducated American* (New York: Academic Press, 1976).

8. Richard B. Freeman and Wiley McCarthy, "The Overeducated American in the 1980s," Report to the National Commission on Student Financial Assistance, Washington, D.C., August 1982.

9. Ibid., p. 23.

in the future. Future returns from capital goods must be discounted to their present values to make the marginal revenue product of capital comparable to its marginal factor cost, most or all of which is incurred at the time the investment is made. Only the present value (*PV*) of the marginal revenue product should be used to compare with the cost.

6. The concept of present value recognizes that the value of a certain sum of money to be received in the future is less than the value of that same sum of money if it were received now. At any particular interest rate, the further into the future that a sum of money will be received, the lower is its present value. The higher the interest rate used to discount the future payment, the lower is the present value of that future payment.

7. An interest rate is payment for the use of someone's money. Interest rates are determined in markets for loanable funds. The equilibrium rate of interest is the interest rate at which the quantity demanded of loanable funds is just equal to the quantity that lenders are willing to supply. If a firm finds that its breakeven interest rate for a particular investment is below the equilibrium market rate, then it will not undertake this investment.

8. The demand for loanable funds comes from business firms, households, and governments. Business firms seek profits through investment. Because households want to buy consumer goods, they are often willing to pay the interest that will enable them to buy them now rather than later. Governments may also want to spend more than they can finance from their current tax receipts. The demand curve for loanable funds is expected to be negatively sloped, since high interest rates will discourage borrowing and low interest rates will encourage borrowing.

9. The supply of loanable funds comes from savers. At times, business firms, households, and governments don't want to spend all of their income right away. The supply curve for loanable funds is expected to be positively sloped, since high interest rates will usually encourage saving and lending and low interest rates will usually discourage saving and lending.

10. Human capital is that part of the productive power of individuals that has been developed through earlier expenditures for education, job training, and health care. How good a "producer" a person is will depend partly on the amount that has been invested in him or her. Whether or not to allocate scarce resources to human capital, and if so, in what amount, comprises the human capital investment decision.

11. Individuals invest in human capital for both monetary and psychic returns. They may also consider an investment in something like higher education to be partly consumption. Therefore, in analyzing an individual's "human capital investment decision," all three returns—monetary, psychic, and consumption—must be weighed against his or her cost.

12. Firms invest in human capital in order to gain higher profit. They do not have a property right in people as they do in physical capital. Therefore, in countries like the United States, where labor is quite mobile, firms are more reluctant to invest in training their employees than in a country like Japan, where employees are more likely to remain with the same firm.

13. Governments invest in human capital in order to benefit society as a whole. Their aim may be to have better-informed citizens or to expand the frontiers of knowledge. But just as private investment in human capital yields some social returns, government investment in human capital results in some private returns.

DISCUSSION QUESTIONS

1. What is meant by roundabout production? Under what circumstances would roundabout production add to an economy's efficiency? Give an example of roundabout production.

2. An investment decision by a firm involves three major problems:

    a. the time problem
    b. the obsolescence problem
    c. the derived-demand problem

Briefly explain the nature of each of these three problems.

3. When calculating the return to capital, why should a firm use the present-value technique?

4. Explain the relationship between the present value of the return to an investment and:

    a. the discount rate

    b. the number of years between the present and the time that the return will be received

    c. the number of payments of a given size that constitute the return in the form of an income stream

5. Would you expect a firm to invest in a certain machine under the following conditions?

    a. The cost of the machine is $10,000.

    b. Using a 5 percent discount rate, the present value of the firm's net return from this machine is $12,000.

    c. Using an 11 percent discount rate, the present value of the firm's net return from this machine is $9,300.

    d. The equilibrium rate of interest in the relevant loanable funds market is 12 percent.

Why or why not?

6. Distinguish between physical capital and human capital. Give three examples of each. Discuss the differences and the similarities in analyzing a possible investment in physical versus human capital.

7. John learns that it will cost him $50,000 in out-of-pocket expenses and $50,000 in forgone income to attend a professional school. He estimates that the degree he will attain will add $5,000 per year to his income for twenty-five years. The relevant rate of interest is 8 percent. Suppose that John is having some difficulty in deciding whether or not to attend the school and that he comes to you for advice. Carefully analyze his situation for him. (What questions would you ask him? What answers would you give him?)

8. Explain the reasons why business firms are usually more hesitant to invest in human capital than in physical capital?

9. Distinguish between private returns and social returns to investment in human capital. Give two examples of each. Is it correct to assume that investment in human capital by individuals and business firms will yield only private returns and that government investment in human capital will yield only social returns? Explain.

A Real Threat to the Labor Movement?

Two features of many contemporary market economies, decidedly including the American one, have been declines in the proportion of the employed labor force enrolled in labor unions and declines in the political clout of organized labor. The two declines are by no means unrelated, but their joint significance is in dispute. Do they indicate a long-term decline in the organized labor movement? Or are they simply a temporary halt in a long march onward and upward to what Sumner Slichter has called a "laboristic" economy? And how, if at all, may we expect the labor movement to respond to them?

"All power corrupts, and absolute power corrupts absolutely." Lord Acton, in making this statement, was speaking of political power—the rise and fall of empires and dynasties. Applying it to industrial relations, it is easy, and not 100 percent wrong, to claim that just as "the bosses" abused their power in the bad old preunion days, the unions have become too strong and are being punished by "the rest of us" for their sins. But this is far from a sufficient explanation. What, for example, is an "abuse" and what is a "sin"?

Everyone favors fairness and equity in industrial relations, but few agree on what fairness and equity are. Divine inspiration seems to be required to prove one's own views correct. What are, after all, the specific rights and duties of: (1) employers (including public agencies); (2) workers (blue-collar and white-collar, including supervisors); (3) consumers (including taxpayers), who buy, or at least pay for, the goods and services produced; and perhaps also (4) unemployed or underemployed outsiders desirous of competing for the better jobs currently held by others?

At one extreme we find slavery and the extreme forms of scientific management, which critics see as reducing the worker to an ox, a mule, or an animated robot, fed just enough to keep him or her alive and breeding. At another extreme we find proposals to replace the whole hierarchical scheme of "bosses" giving orders to "wage slaves" with teams of well-paid workers, "equal partners in planning," dividing up and executing the tasks of the workplace. Those proposals are attacked as featherbedding, with employers, consumers, and taxpayers reduced to the role of "cash cows" supporting the operation in style and making do with whatever it deigns to turn out. Most of us have views somewhere between these extremes.

Many students agree that trade unionism arose or at least revived[1] early in the nineteenth century among manual (blue-collar) workers, mainly skilled. Unions arose among workers in relatively large-scale plants by the standards of those days, and in labor markets closer to monopsony (in this case "employers' monopsony") than to pure competition.

Workers were poor and could move only at great economic and psychological cost from place to place or from trade to trade. (The American "wild frontier," for example, was not a viable alternative for the typical Philadelphia cordwainer (shoemaker) or New England mill hand.) The ordinary worker was in no position to bargain individually with the one or two employers of his particular skill in his particular town, especially when workers could be blacklisted for any kind of militance. As late as 1892, a bloody steel strike that broke a struggling union began with a unilateral order by Henry Clay Frick, superintendent of the Carnegie Steel workers at Homestead near Pittsburgh, reducing the standard daily wage from $1.50 to $1.00. This was not an unusual exercise of employer monopsony power in depressed periods.

To counteract employer monopsony (rather than exercising much monopoly power on their own), unions

---

1. "Revived" to whatever extent the moribund medieval guilds can be viewed as embryonic unions. But the typical guild seems to have been an association of "masters" who were proprietors of small businesses and employers of labor. Their "journeymen" (workers) and "apprentices" (trainees) were second-class citizens in guild organizations when they were admitted at all.

arose in Britain and northern Europe, with the United States generally lagging behind until the New Deal labor legislation of the 1930s.[2] This was especially true in the mass-production industries like steel and automobiles. By the late 1940s, however, the United States too was becoming a "laboristic" economy, thanks both to this legislation and to the high levels of employment and labor scarcity during and after World War II. From being "exploited" victims of employer monopsony, American workers in many industries were becoming something very much like monopolies,[3] using unions as their bargaining agents much as the oil-exporting countries would later use OPEC.

Given this additional power, many union members became labor aristocrats. Many trade unions became organs of labor aristocracy. Many processes of collective bargaining between labor and management became collusive bargaining, raising wages and prices more or less simultaneously against the unorganized consumer or taxpayer.

Union labor aristocracies were of two types, the old and the new. The old labor aristocracy of the craft unions was based on the possession of skills, safeguarded by limiting the numbers of young people and other outsiders admitted to apprenticeship and on-the-job training; in short, through control of the training process. The new labor aristocracy of the industrial unions was based on the monopoly or cartel status of the employing firm or industry, which within wide limits was supposedly able to pass wage and other concessions forward to the consuming or taxpaying public with little or no loss in employment opportunities for union members.

In this context, collusive bargaining is a collective-bargaining process in which it is tacitly taken for granted by both sides that the gains of organized labor will be paid for mainly by raising prices to consumers and not "out of profits." There remain problems of estimating the "swag" from price increases and its distribution between labor and management. These problems may create

2. Two pieces of New Deal legislation were the Norris–La Guardia Act and the National Labor Relations Act.

3. "How can a union be a monopolist? It is basically a political organization, and it does not sell labor." Technically true, but political organizations, even governments, can be monopolists on the side. A trade union can act as the business agent of a cartel of workers who ostensibly sell their own labor time. Similarly, during the heyday of the OPEC cartel, it did not sell oil but acted as a business agent for a group of oil-exporting countries.

sufficiently acrimonious debates to inspire long and bitter strikes and to conceal from the general public the collusive nature of the basic process.

For the union members the wage gains from union collective bargaining are probably less than is generally believed. Labor monopolies are less than perfect, and labor markets are usually "contestable." For the United States, the gains are estimated by H.G. Lewis at 10 to 15 percent of what wages might have been in the absence of unionism; the differential falls in boom periods and rises in recessions. But the public's image of the differential seems to be substantially higher; in any event, it was enough to arouse opposition in many quarters.

The politics of antiunion backlash was the demotion of organized labor from a special status as representing "the public" to the ordinary position of "just another special interest group." In situations of endemic inflation, the initial economic result of this political demotion can be seen in macroeconomic, and above all in monetary, policy. Wage and price increases were no longer necessarily ratified or validated by fiscal and monetary expansion. Without such ratification or validation, the wage and price increases, when obtained at all, led increasingly to unemployment. The unemployment was concentrated not on the senior members of the union aristocracy but on the younger members and would-be members, and likewise on the nonunion workers "protected" by minimum wages, unemployment benefits, and relief. As early as the 1950s it was noted that the peaks of recession unemployment were rising in each minor recession, while the troughs were falling in each recovery. A decade later, the term "stagflation" had come into general usage to describe such conditions.

Technical change and the international spread of heavy industrialization made matters worse for the blue-collar unions, both craft and industrial. In this connection technical change means first automation and later robotization—the substitution of machinery and white-collar labor for blue-collar labor in industry and the substitution of services for manufacturing in employment. (By 1960, the majority of nonagricultural American workers were in the tertiary or service industries.) We cannot tell to what extent these changes were spontaneous and to what extent they were induced by the deliberate concentration of research and development (R&D) expenditures in directions that would weaken union power.

On the international front, one low-wage, weak-union, developing country (LDC) after another moved into

Aftermath of the Homestead, Pennsylvania, strike

competition. The LDCs were aided and abetted by multinational corporations fighting home-country unions with long-range artillery after the failure of short-range weapons in one strike after another. (Why build the new plant or put the new machines in Pittsburgh or Liverpool when Faroffistan wages were lower and Faroffistan workers more "reasonable"?) First the export market, then the domestic market of one industry after another was contested, sometimes even vanishing under a flood of imports.

Something similar was also happening domestically. Industry was moving from high-wage, strong-union regions to lower-wage, weaker-union ones.[4] In the United States, the move was from the "snow belt" or "rust belt"

4. One litmus test for union weakness is the presence and effective enforcement of local "right-to-work" laws, so-called, which ban closed and union shops. (Unions have constantly tried and thus far failed to secure national legislation outlawing right-to-work laws.) A second test: can local police control illegal violence against nonstrikers, strikebreakers, suppliers, and customers of struck plants?

Union worker campaigning for steel import quotas

domestic front, the protectionist strategy calls for intensified campaigning both nationally and locally against right-to-work laws, and for broadening the effective limits of both picketing and boycotts.

2. White-Collarization Opening existing industrial unions to white-collar employees is less important than the creation or expansion of white-collar unions.[5] Such white-collar organizations have been in recent years the most rapidly growing unions in the United States; their growth has partially offset the declines in the traditional blue-collar sectors. (White-collar unions have been strongest among public employees, including teachers and hospital workers. In the Netherlands, they have also spread to the armed services.) It remains to be seen in each country to what extent the blue- and the white-collar interests can cooperate in framing policy either within or between unions, despite a certain tradition of mutual distrust.

3. Conciliation "When the Devil is sick, the Devil a saint would be." In labor relations, a conciliatory strategy for the sick union is the acceptance of cuts in real wages (less often in nominal wages) as preferable to unemployment. Another conciliatory strategy is cooperation with management in modifying work rules, increasing job flexibility, raising productivity, and improving product quality, often in exchange for employment guarantees and management support for union protectionism. Tiering—providing job opportunities and union membership for inexperienced outsiders employed at less than the standard union wage rate—has been a common American feature of this approach. It is quite conceivable that the conciliatory approach anticipates abuse by employers of their restored powers and prerogatives. Such abuse would promote a union comeback in the next period of high employment.[6]

5. Early nineteenth-century white-collar workers seemed to have seen their interests more as rising out of their class (into the management) than as rising within their class. This difference is much less important today; the so-called "white-collar differential" in pay and social status has been largely limited to the highest ranks.

6. But the courts have in some American states forestalled certain employer abuses, and unintentionally weakened the chances of union revival, by limiting management's legal right to hire and fire. When, in recruiting employees, a company has claimed that it does not dismiss workers without cause, such claims are being interpreted as implied offers, so that acceptance by the worker (in accepting employment) establishes an enforceable labor contract. This is still a minority view, however.

(the mid-Atlantic and north central states) to the "sun belt" of south central, southwestern, and Pacific coast states.

The union movement has been divided in its reaction to these developments, and these divisions have made organized labor appear more lethargic than the facts justify. Four of the more important reactions have been:

1. Protectionism Protectionism is the use of labor's still-substantial political power to turn the clock back. This may be done either through a labor party as in Britain or through labor influence in a national party like the American Democrats. This strength is used to secure or tighten tariffs, quotas, or outright bans on imports, particularly imports from low-wage or weak-union countries. In the European Community (EC) another protectionist goal is subsidy for exports. On the American

4. Radicalization   This term covers a large number of drastic measures to insulate workers and their unions from the market forces of the 1980s. The line between protectionism and radicalism is difficult to draw even subjectively, and more difficult to defend objectively.

The most common American union strategy that might be called radical is the demand for restrictions on plant closing and migration. A frequent entering wedge, hardly radical in itself, is the demand that workers be given notice substantially in advance before a plant closes or moves. This demand can be expected to escalate into severance pay for workers left behind, along with compensation to communities whose tax bases are eroded by plant relocation. The British national coal strike of 1984–1985 was fought (and lost) on a more clearly radical version of the same demand. The National Union of Mineworkers (NUM), under the leadership of Arthur Scargill, proposed to safeguard jobs even for future generations by a requirement that no coal pit be closed for "merely" economic reasons until its coal has been extracted.

Another marginally radical union strategy for recession is the shorter work week with no loss in pay (except as overtime may be reduced). Even West German co-determination (*Mitbestimmung*), with workers electing half the boards of directors, could not avoid a nationwide strike in 1985 on this issue in the automobile plants and other metal trades. It ended in a partial victory for the metal-workers.

In Sweden, where no firm may invest outside the country without the consent of the Swedish work force, the unions have demanded and won the Meidner plan to secure a greater voice in management. Under this scheme, a portion of the profits of large corporations must be set aside to buy stock in the company. When bought, the stock is to be held and voted not by individual workers but by their unions (and by civil servants). Dividends go to union treasuries. The union managerial role is expected to increase steadily over time.

Incomes policy proposals are not radical in themselves. In fact, union support for such policies is only lukewarm because they include wage-control features along with dividend and price controls. But exceptions to these generalizations come when the incomes policy or "social contract" involves a substantial rise in the wage share of the national income. An extreme example was the initial incomes policy of President Allende in Chile. It called for a 40 percent wage increase with no price increases—no collusive bargains here! It also forbade reductions in employment, on penalty of "intervention" in management by worker representatives or by the government itself. More generally, incomes policies may include provisions that, when a firm cannot avoid losses under the control regime, it must give workers the first refusal for its assets, before going out of business or selling out to another private capitalist.

Hampering radical or revolutionary strategies, however, is surely the fear of the typical transformation that the union itself undergoes under the typical socialist planned economy. Unions become agencies of government and party, with the functions of increasing productivity and transmitting the party line to the workers insofar as it affects their industry or trade. The Solidarity movement in Poland—and its suppression—constitutes a failed uprising of independent unionism against such a regime.

It should be clear that the situation of the 1970s and 1980s constitutes a real threat to trade unionism as previously established. What is not at all clear is how the labor movement will meet this threat and whether the current setback will have any long-term effect.

X *Applied Microeconomics*

- Government and Taxation
- Poverty and Income Distribution
- Government Antitrust and Regulation Policy
- International Microeconomics: Free Trade Versus Protection
- Agriculture, Food, and Hunger
- Natural Resources and the Environment

X. Applied Microeconomics

32 *Government and Taxation*

PREVIEW This is the first of a group of chapters on applied microeconomics. Their purpose is to explain how the tools of microeconomic analysis, which you have just studied, can help in understanding certain real-world situations and in solving some of the problems that face contemporary societies.

We begin with a chapter on government and taxation. As you learned in Chapter 2, government is one of the "actors on the economic stage." We start this chapter with an analysis of why government is needed for efficient resource use in a market-capitalist economic system. Then we explain the theory of public choice, which explores how the tools of economics can help in understanding how voters in a democracy try to tell the government what they want it to do. This includes a theory about how responsibilities might be divided between the national, state, and local levels of government in a federal system such as that in the United States. Then we give a brief description of government expenditures in the United States.

The remainder of the chapter examines the major revenue sources of governments in the United States—the individual income tax, Social Security taxes, the corporation income tax, sales and excise taxes, motor fuels taxes, and property taxes. We focus on using microeconomic tools of analysis to understand the effects of these taxes.

This chapter does not cover the macroeconomic aspects of government—activities relating to the control of business cycles, inflation, macroeconomic unemployment, and economic growth—which are considered in depth in macroeconomics.

MARKET SUPPORT AND MARKET FAILURE

In a market-capitalist economy, an important responsibility of government is to help ensure an economic environment that is suitable for the functioning of markets. For example, governments are expected to provide a legal system for the protection of property and the enforcement of contracts. The market system will function much more effectively when people can enter into contracts and be assured that they actually will be carried out. Along the same line is government's responsibility to help protect private property. Business firms are much more willing to invest in capital goods such as factory buildings and machines when they have a high probability of keeping their property safe from theft and destruction.

In addition to "market-support" activities such as those noted above, governments also are expected to play an active role in situations of **market failure,** that is, when markets fail to respond adequately to the demands of consumers. In this chapter, we will study market failures that arise because of externality and collective consumption characteristics of goods and services. A later chapter, Chapter 34, examines failures that can be traced to the structure of markets themselves.

FIGURE 32-1 Negative Externalities and Market Failure

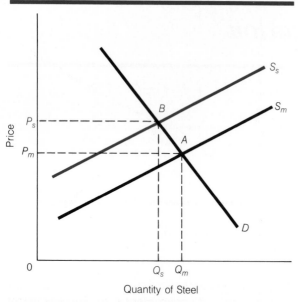

Quantity of Steel

The demand curve, *D*, represents the behavior of purchasers of steel. The market-supply curve S_m represents the behavior of the suppliers. Only private costs are reflected in this curve. The social-supply curve, S_s, reflects both private costs and external costs (negative externalities). External costs are represented by the vertical distance between S_m and S_s. At equilibrium point *A*, the market provides an inefficiently large quantity (Q_m). The socially efficient equilibrium is at *B*, with quantity Q_s and price P_s.

Externalities

An **externality** is an economic effect (either beneficial or harmful) experienced by a person who had no control, through the market system, over the action that led to the effect. For example, suppose a person contracts lung cancer from breathing smoke and fumes from the smokestacks of a steel mill. Suppose this person does not work at the steel mill and that his or her purchases of steel or steel-made products are an insignificant part of the mill's total demand. Since the victim had no power through the market system to influence the production methods used or to force the mill to stop the discharge of the harmful smoke and fumes, the lung cancer is a negative

(harmful) external effect of the operation of the mill. The effect is called "external" because it is outside the control mechanism of the market system.

Some externalities are positive (beneficial). For example, education (especially elementary and secondary education) is generally believed to provide benefits to the whole community as well as benefits to the children who attend school and to their families. Voters will be better informed, productivity will be higher, literature and the arts will advance, and so on. If schools were financed entirely by tuition payments, families would demand education service primarily for the private enjoyment and benefit of the family itself. These benefits would be internal to the market system of providing education services. Any benefits to others in the community would be external benefits, since others in the community would not be effective demanders of education services.

Externalities and Misallocation of Resources

Figure 32-1 illustrates market failure in the case of a good or service that generates negative externalities. Our earlier illustration of a negative externality was lung cancer caused by smoke from the smokestack of a steel mill. Steel production is shown on the horizontal axis of Figure 32-1 because the production of this product may generate these negative externalities. As you know from your study of microeconomics, the demand curve, *D*, illustrates how the quantity demanded depends on price. This curve represents the behavior of purchasers and reflects the benefits they expect to receive from consuming steel. The market-supply curve, S_m in Figure 32-1, illustrates how the quantity of steel offered for sale depends on its price. As you learned in microeconomics, the supply curve represents the behavior of those supplying the good or service. In this market, the equilibrium price is P_m and the quantity demanded and supplied is Q_m.

If negative external effects are generated by this good or service, some costs are being experienced by people not represented by either the market-demand curve or the market-supply curve. In other words, when negative externalities are generated, the market fails to record some costs associated with this product. Since costs normally are represented by the supply curve, we can say that the presence of negative externalities means that the market-supply curve, S_m, is too far to the right. A supply curve representing both the costs incurred by suppliers and also the costs experienced by those who suffer from externalities would lie to the left of supply curve S_m. The social-supply curve, S_s in Figure 32-1, is constructed to represent the full **social costs** of the good or service. These social costs include both the costs incurred by the producers of the good or service (called **private costs**) and also the **external costs,** that is, the costs experienced by those suffering negative externalities. For each successive unit of the good or service, the amount of external cost is represented by the vertical distance between the S_s curve and the S_m curve.

In negative externality situations, market failure results in the market providing an inefficiently large quantity of the good or service. This failure arises because the producers and consumers of the good or service (steel in our illustration) do not have to pay some of the costs of the product, in this case, the suffering from cancer and the costs of treating it. If all the social costs were recognized by the market, the equilibrium price and quantity would be P_s and Q_s, as indicated in Figure 32-1 by the intersection at point B of the demand curve, D, with the social-supply curve, S_s. By comparing this socially efficient equilibrium with the equilibrium shown by the market-demand curve and the market-supply curve, we can observe how market failure leads to a misallocation of resources. Unless some correction is applied, the market solution will result in too low a price to consumers (P_m) and too large a quantity demanded and supplied (Q_m). We may state it as a general rule that market failure takes the form of an excessive quantity produced and consumed when harmful externalities exist and no corrective action is taken.

Positive (beneficial) externalities also lead to market failure and resource misallocation. In this situation, the market failure takes the form of an

FIGURE 32-2   Positive Externalities and Market Failure

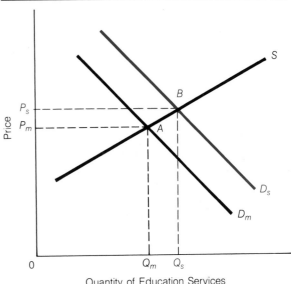

Quantity of Education Services

The supply curve, S, represents the behavior of suppliers of education services. The demand curve D_m represents the behavior of purchasers. Only private benefits are reflected in this curve. The social-demand curve, D_s, reflects both private benefits and external benefits (positive externalities). External benefits are represented by the vertical distance between D_m and D_s. At equilibrium point A, the market provides an inefficiently small quantity (Q_m). The socially efficient equilibrium is at B, with quantity Q_s and price P_s.

inefficiently small quantity being demanded and supplied. Figure 32-2 illustrates market failure through positive externalities such as those generated by elementary and secondary education. In this figure, the supply curve, S, represents the costs of supplying education services while the market-demand curve D_m represents the willingness to pay for these services as recorded by market transactions. In other words, the market-demand curve D_m represents only the willingness of families to purchase education services for their own children. This market-demand curve reflects only the **private benefits** and fails to include the **external benefits** received by others in the community. In terms of the microeconomic tools of analysis, the market-demand curve, D_m, is located too far to the left on the graph. The social-demand curve, D_s in Figure 32-2, includes both the private benefits and the external benefits of education services. It is located to the right of the market-demand curve, D_m. The vertical distance between the market-demand curve (D_m) and the social-demand curve (D_s) shows the amount of external benefit for each successive unit of education services. The socially efficient quantity is Q_s, as indicated by the intersection between the supply curve (S) and the social-demand curve (D_s). By comparing this socially efficient equilibrium with the market equilibrium, it is clear that the market failure that arises from positive externalities takes the form of a price to consumers (P_m) that is too high and a quantity demanded and supplied (Q_m) that is too small.

Government Corrections for Negative Externalities

The economic way of thinking that you have developed from your study of microeconomics suggests that market failures due to externalities can be corrected by making market-demand and market-supply curves reflect the full social costs and benefits of the goods or services being demanded and supplied. In the case of negative externalities, as illustrated in Figure 32-1, the effort to correct the market failure would take the form of shifting the market-supply curve (S_m) to the left until it matches the social-supply curve (S_s). After this correction was made, the market would provide the socially efficient quantity of the good or service. Resources would be efficiently allocated.

Governments have many powers that enable them to cause shifts in market-supply curves. For example, to correct for negative externalities from smoke and fumes coming from chimneys and smokestacks, government regulations might require the installation of filters or scrubbers that remove harmful materials from the emissions. To correct for negative externalities coming from automobile emissions, government may require cars to be equipped with exhaust systems that

remove or deactivate harmful substances. The costs of these filters, scrubbers, and exhaust systems would have to be paid initially by those who operate the chimneys or smokestacks and by those who manufacture autos and auto exhaust systems. This would shift the market-supply curve to the left. In this way, these costs would be passed on to the consumers who purchase products produced in factories and to motorists who purchase cars equipped with the improved exhaust systems. So, appropriate use of government's regulatory powers could bring the desired shift in the market-supply curve and could correct for market failure due to negative externalities.

Taxation is another government power that can be used to correct for market failure due to negative externalities. For example, a tax could be imposed on smoke and fumes coming from chimneys and smokestacks or on automobile emissions that are believed to cause negative external effects. The tax would have to be paid by the persons responsible for the harmful emissions—the firms or households operating the chimneys or smokestacks or the motorists operating the automobiles. Microeconomic analysis leads to the conclusion that these people would quickly start looking for ways to save taxes by reducing the amount of the taxable (i.e., harmful) substances coming from their chimneys, smokestacks, autos, etc. In other words, government need not require specific filters, scrubbers, or auto exhaust systems. Instead, it could count on the self-interest (economic rationality) of firms and households to discover and install effective devices on their own initiative and at their own expense.

Would the government raise much money from a tax designed to correct for market failures? The answer is that the government would not collect much money from the tax if the tax actually did its job of persuading people to stop doing the things that generated negative externalities. As better and better filters, scrubbers, and auto exhaust systems are invented and installed, less and less of the harmful substances will be generated and the tax will yield less and less money for the government. In other words, the purpose of the tax is not to raise money for the government but to persuade people to change their behavior and thereby avoid the tax. The main advantage of the tax approach over the regulatory approach is that the tax provides incentives that encourage people to discover better and less expensive ways to reduce the quantities of the substance being taxed.

Government Corrections for Positive Externalities

In the case of positive externalities, as illustrated in Figure 32-2, a remedy for market failure is to shift the market-demand curve (D_m) to the right until it matches the social-demand curve (D_s). Government might, for example, require all families to purchase some specified quantity of educational services for their children. If this requirement were enforced, the market-demand curve in Figure 32-2 could be shifted to the right and if the requirements involved exactly the services needed to match the external benefits, the market-demand curve (D_m) would shift to correspond with the social-demand curve (D_s) and the market no longer would fail to provide the socially efficient quantity of educational service. The efficient quantity (Q_s) would be demanded and supplied at price P_s.

A system of mandatory purchases, such as that described above, undoubtedly would run into difficulty because some consumers would not have the money to pay for the services they would be required to purchase. Moreover, why should any of the recipients of the private benefits, whether they are rich or poor, be required to pay for the benefits enjoyed by the external beneficiaries? Instead, the external beneficiaries—the community in general in the education illustration—should pay for services that generate the external benefits if we follow the ethical notion that people who benefit should pay for what they get. Therefore, government programs to correct for market failures caused by external benefits are likely to pay a **subsidy** to encourage the desired increase in production and consumption. A subsidy is a payment by someone other than the buyer that helps to cover the cost of a good

or service. It may be used either along with or entirely separate from mandatory purchase requirements.

In our education example, the government might give to each child a certificate (sometimes called a "voucher") redeemable at an approved school to help pay the tuition bill for required education services. The money to finance the certificates would come from taxpayers so that the community in general, which receives the external benefits, would pay its share of the cost of the service. The market failure would be corrected and the socially efficient quantity of education service would be demanded and supplied.

Subsidies Paid Directly to Suppliers

The number of firms that supply a good or a service usually is much smaller than the number of people who purchase it. Therefore, for goods and services generating beneficial externalities, it often is easier for the government to provide a subsidy through suppliers than to pay it to the purchasers. This typically is the case in education, where elementary and secondary schools are financed and operated by local and state governments. Figure 32-3 illustrates how subsidies paid to suppliers can correct for market failures related to beneficial externalities. In this figure, in the absence of government subsidy, the market demand is D_m and the market supply is S_m. At equilibrium (point A), the market provides an inefficiently small quantity of the good or service (Q_m).

In order to correct for the market failure, the government pays to the supplier a subsidy that covers part of the cost of supplying the good or service, thus shifting the market-supply curve to the right to S_s. The amount of the subsidy, per unit of the good or service, is shown by the vertical distance between the supply curves S_m and S_s. If the subsidy has been correctly calculated, this distance corresponds to the value of the external benefits enjoyed by the community. After the shift of the supply curve, equilibrium is at point B and the socially efficient quantity (Q_s) of the good or service is supplied. Consumers

FIGURE 32-3   Subsidy Paid to Suppliers

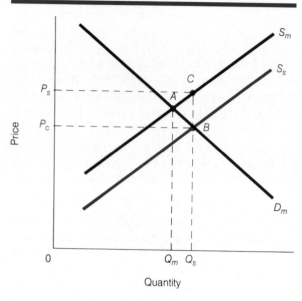

Market equilibrium is at *A*, where the market-demand curve, D_m, intersects the market-supply curve, S_m. Quantity Q_m would be demanded and supplied. A subsidy paid to suppliers shifts the supply curve to the right to S_s. The new equilibrium is at *B*, with the socially efficient quantity, Q_s, demanded and supplied. At this equilibrium, consumers pay price P_c and suppliers receive price P_s. The amount of the subsidy for the marginal unit of the good or service is shown by the distance from *B* to *C*.

pay price P_c, indicated by point *B* on the demand curve, but suppliers receive price P_s, indicated by point *C* on the presubsidy supply curve. Thus, suppliers receive the price needed to call forth the socially efficient quantity of the good or service. Only the part of this price that corresponds to marginal private benefit is paid by private consumers. The part that corresponds to marginal external benefit is paid by the government with money collected from taxpayers.

The actual system of education finance in the United States does not match the theoretical models explained above. In practice, public elementary and secondary schools in the United States do not charge any tuition at all—the subsidy from the government pays all of the costs of

supplying education services. Thus, the subsidies pay for some services that would have been financed privately if the government had not entered the picture. The schools themselves are operated by the government. A more extensive analysis of the economics of education would extend beyond the subject of beneficial externalities that we are considering here.

COLLECTIVE GOODS AND SERVICES

Collective goods and services are those that are consumed by the community as a group (i.e., "collectively"). Two characteristics of these goods and services—their qualities of nonrivalry and nonexcludability—explain why markets fail to provide them in efficient quantities. We shall examine these qualities below. Taken together, they provide another economic explanation for market failure and for government spending and taxation as necessary for the efficient functioning of a market-capitalist economic system.

Nonexclusion and Free Riders

One characteristic of a collective good or service is **nonexcludability,** which means that, once it has been produced, it is either not possible or extremely expensive to deny any person in the community the opportunity to consume it. For example, once weapons have been produced and service men and women have been hired to operate them, defense protection cannot be provided to one person in a community while being denied to another member of that community. All must be protected together, as a group. If New York City is protected from enemy attack, all the people in that city are protected. This is the meaning of the nonexcludability feature of a collective good or service.

Nonexcludability clearly distinguishes collective goods and services from private goods and services, which have excludability as a hallmark characteristic. Common exclusion devices include checkout counters, ticket takers, shoplifting alarm systems, bars on windows, locks on doors, and so on. Without exclusion devices, business firms would not be able to collect money in exchange for the goods and services that they supply. Without money from sales, these firms would have no incentive to engage in business and would not be able to finance the production of goods and services. In short, the market system will not provide goods and services unless exclusion devices operate.

For collective goods and services, the absence of exclusion devices opens the door to the **free-rider problem.** A person is a free rider if he or she obtains a good or service at the expense of others. When exclusion devices are not available, many people will refuse (or understate their willingness) to pay for a good or service because they hope that they will be able to obtain it without charge after others have paid for it. According to the free-rider logic, for example, you will refuse to pay for defense services, or understate your willingness to pay for them, hoping that others will come up with enough money to pay for the service, after which you will receive its benefits without paying or without paying your full share.

The seriousness of the free-rider problem depends on the number of people in the group that collectively consumes the good or service. The problem is not serious for small groups, such as the family. In small groups, people recognize that their own refusal to pay may mean that the good or service will not be provided at all. Knowing this, it is likely that all members will pay more or less their fair share. But in large groups, where formal governments operate, each person feels that his or her own payment has little effect on whether or not the good or service actually will be provided. Thus, the tendency to be a free rider becomes very widespread, perhaps almost universal. Because of nonexcludability and free riding, an efficient quantity of collective goods and services is not likely to be provided through a voluntary payment system such as the market, even when benefits clearly exceed costs.

As you probably have guessed, taxation is a cure for the free-rider problem. Taxes are not voluntary, unless you consider fines and imprisonment to be reasonable alternatives. By forcing people to pay, taxes make it impossible to have a free ride and enable governments to finance goods and services that people want and are willing to pay for, but which they could not obtain adequately through the voluntary payments procedures of the market system.

Nonrivalry in Consumption

There is **nonrival consumption** of a good or service if one person can benefit from it without causing any significant reduction in the benefits that others receive from it. The clearest example of a service that is nonrival in consumption is national defense. The fact that you are benefited by this service does not increase or decrease the benefit that others receive from it. If you die or move away, the benefit that others receive from national defense is not increased, nor does an increase in the population significantly reduce their benefit. Of course, all persons may not benefit equally or feel that the protection is equally valuable, but that does not change the fact that consumption of the service is nonrival.

The nonrival characteristic of a collective good or service is important in the economics of government because it means that people need not object to having their tax money pooled or combined to pay for the good or service. For example, if each of the 235 million people in the United States felt that he or she received $1,000 worth of benefit from the defense system, the government could collect this amount of tax from each person and spend $235 billion for defense. It could pool each person's payment of $1,000 into a common fund to finance national defense services. Unfortunately, calculating the efficient quantity of a collective good to provide is not as simple as this illustration implies. But the nonrival characteristic determines that funds can be pooled, no matter how tax payments themselves have been distributed.

PUBLIC CHOICE

So far we have explored the economic analysis of why markets fail to produce an efficient quantity of certain goods and services and why taxation and spending may enable governments to correct for these market failures. Now we can examine the question of how governments make decisions on these matters. This is the study of public choice. **Public choice** is an area of study that combines economics and political science in an effort to understand how decisions are made in group situations. It is an important, exciting, and relatively new field of study. Since our focus is on the U.S. economy, we will examine public choice analysis as it applies economic concepts to decision making in a democracy with free and frequent elections. As you can easily imagine, different public choice models apply in different governmental systems.

Taxation and Voting

In democratic public choice models, a key role of taxation is to provide information to voters about how the costs of government services will be shared among citizens. For example, suppose that a proposal is made that the government should provide a new missile defense system such as the Star Wars system proposed by the Reagan administration. According to public choice analysis, in a democracy each voter should be able to estimate how much he or she would have to pay in order to finance this new system. For example, if the government were financed entirely by an individual income tax and if the government proposed to finance the new missile system with a 1 percentage point increase in the tax rate, each citizen should be able to figure his or her share of the cost of the proposed system. If your taxable income were $30,000, you would have a tax increase of $300 if the system were installed. If your taxable income were $40,000, your share would be $400, and so on.

In the public choice model, the second step in democratic decision making is to give the citizens an opportunity to vote on whether or not the missile system should be provided. Each voter is expected to estimate the benefit he or she would get from the proposed system, to compare this benefit against his or her share of its cost, and to vote accordingly. If benefits exceed costs, they will vote "yes." They will vote "no" if their cost exceeds their estimate of benefit. In other words, voters are expected to vote according to their self-interest. In this approach, government is the servant of the people, providing those goods and services that citizens want and are willing to pay for.

The illustration above is a very simplified explanation of the basic idea of taxing and voting in public choice theory. Because we are offering only an overview of public choice theory, we will just note some of the many additional factors that go into this decision-making process. For example, is a simple majority vote really enough to make sure that the missile system is worth its cost, or would a two-thirds vote be better? Is the individual income tax the best way to divide costs among citizens, or would it be better to use some other tax, such as a sales tax or a property tax, which might come closer to matching the different amounts of benefit received by different citizens? These are important questions in the study of public choice.

The view that voters are motivated by self-interest illustrates the **benefits-received principle** of taxation, which says that the amount of tax that a person should pay for the marginal unit of a good or service should equal the money equivalent of the benefit that he or she expects to receive from it. It is quite different from the **ability-to-pay principle** of taxation, which says that higher tax rates should be paid by those who can afford to pay more, even if their benefit is equal to or less than the benefits received by others. The ability-to-pay approach often is used to support **progressive taxation,** that is, taxation designed to redistribute after-tax incomes in the direction of greater equality. Both the benefits-received and the ability-to-pay principles are normative statements about how the tax liabilities of different individuals *should* be determined. However, much of the research of public choice economists points toward benefits received as a positive statement about voter behavior.

Elected Officials

Public choice theory offers economic models to explain the behavior of elected officials. According to these models, the candidate for elective office assembles a package of proposals that he or she hopes will appeal to the voters. Candidates who do a good job of sensing the desires of the voters and of designing proposals to cater to these desires will be the ones who win elections and hold office. In this sense, political candidates have certain similarities to business entrepreneurs. The successful political entrepreneurs win elective offices. This means, however, that instead of choosing one item at a time as they usually can in a market, citizens need to vote for and appear to back the whole set of positions associated with some candidate for office, even though they differ from the candidate on some of these positions. All of us who have voted have experienced this frustration. Seldom is there a candidate who offers exactly the set of views that we favor. Therefore, messages from citizens to government are less than perfectly transmitted. Additional problems arise from the rather short time horizons that are forced on elected officials because they must seek re-election every few years. These officials are encouraged to take a biased view of government programs when the timing of benefits is different from the timing of costs. Since benefits help them to win votes and costs make them lose votes, the elected official favors programs that offer quick benefits but put off the tax costs.

Once elected, the officeholder starts working and planning for the next election. In part, this means trying to carry out the promises made to the voters in the past election. This may involve trading a vote on one issue in exchange for the vote of another officeholder on an issue that is more important to the candidate's re-election. Vote-trading and compromises, which are important in public choice theory, have obvious economic overtones.

It is generally recognized that people are more careful about spending their own money than they are about spending someone else's money. Undoubtedly this problem exists in large corporations as well as in governments. But governments not only spend someone else's money; they spend it through appropriations out of a "general fund." One of the theories of public choice economics is that general fund spending is often both unwise and excessive.

The potential waste and excessive spending under the general fund system is illustrated by the following hypothetical case. Suppose that the people in your congressional district develop a proposal that asks for $235 million of federal money to build a flood-control dam in your district. A program of this size will help a lot of people in your district, and your local representative will make every effort to pass the legislation. Since $235 million amounts to an average of only one dollar from each citizen of the country, most voters and taxpayers who pay into the general fund may not even notice the proposal, much less organize any campaign against it. Moreover, if your local representative is enterprising, he or she may promise to vote for harbor improvements or urban renewal projects for other districts if their representatives will vote for your flood-control measure. The net effect of all this political activity is that many local-interest projects may be undertaken that are wasteful or inefficient. Local benefits may exceed local costs, but only because most of the cost is borne by people elsewhere in the country and the amounts that these outsiders pay are so small for each individual that no effective political opposition is organized. Therefore, for many of these programs the total benefits are less than the total costs.

A similar public choice model provides an economic explanation of the power of special-interest groups as follows. Some government actions affect millions of people, but have so little effect on each individual that no one takes time off to go to Washington or the state capitol and lobby for or against the action. On the other hand, other government actions may affect only a few people, but if each of these individuals faces large gain or loss, most of them will appear at the capitol to influence the result. Because of this political fact of life, the influence of lobbies and pressure groups on government decisions is out of proportion to the overall importance of their positions or the number of people involved.

Bureaucracies and Budgets

Government bureaus and agencies provide another important dimension of public choice theory. They are composed of people employed by the government to implement existing legislation and to collect information related to possible new legislation. Typically, these bureaus and agencies are keyed to particular interest groups. The best known are the government departments, such as the Department of Agriculture, for the interests of farmers, the Department of Labor for workers, the Department of Commerce for business, and so on.

In public choice theory, government bureaucracies also are perceived as motivated by self-interest. Individuals working in these bureaucracies seek higher pay, security, prestige, and power. In each bureau and agency, these self-interest goals translate into an agency goal of obtaining as much money as possible from the Congress. Thus, the theory suggests that, in the government budget process, vigorous rivalries develop among agencies and bureaus. In order to get as much as it can, each agency or bureau is always looking for new programs and ideas, and is always trying to persuade voters and officeholders of the merits of agency proposals. They generate a strong pressure for ever larger budgets and ever more government spending.

BENEFIT-COST ANALYSIS Benefit-cost analysis is a procedure used by government agencies to decide whether or not a proposed project should be undertaken. As its name implies, the procedure involves estimating the money equivalent

of the benefits of the project and comparing these benefit estimates with the costs of providing the good or service. The cost estimates are similar to calculations done by business firms in making the investment decision. Also, since benefits usually are realized long after most costs have been incurred, discounting procedures must be used.[1] But, because of the nonrival and nonexcludable features of collective goods, benefit-cost analysis by government agencies faces problems that are different from those faced by business firms. Since prices cannot be charged, it is especially difficult to obtain reliable estimates of the willingness of benefit receivers to pay for the proposed services. Nevertheless, good benefit-cost analysis can help government agencies forecast whether legislators and voters will support their proposed projects. Therefore, benefit-cost analysis plays an important role when an agency prepares its proposals to present to the Congress.

THE BUDGET PROCESS Actual spending decisions are made through the budget process. Initial budget requests are prepared by the government departments (Agriculture, Defense, Interior, Education, and so on) and are assembled by the Office of Management and Budget into the official budget document that is presented by the president to the Congress in January or February each year. Congressional committees then consider separate parts of this budget request and make recommendations to the houses of Congress for action. During the spring and summer the Congress passes some dozen or fifteen appropriations bills, which, taken together, constitute the government's official budget. Tax legislation is separate from expenditure legislation. Even though the basic tax laws are not enacted anew for each budget year, a considerable amount of congressional action is usually taking place about proposals to alter tax rates or particular features of the tax laws.

A bias in the direction of deficit spending has been apparent for a long time to both public

---

1. For an explanation of the investment decision and discounting, see Chapter 31.

choice economists and to the general public. The basic source of the bias probably lies with the voters themselves, who give less support to legislators who raise taxes than they give to legislators who raise expenditures. Over the years, many attempts have been made to devise a budget process to counteract this bias toward deficits. In the 1960s, for example, Congress attempted to discipline itself through the **Planning-Programming Budget System (PPBS),** which required agencies to specify the different programs that they wished to carry out and to plan expenditure needs for several years in advance. In the 1970s, budget reform required the Congress to set spending targets for itself early in its deliberations and then to see that actual appropriations came close to the targets. However, not a single one of these measures has succeeded in preventing budget deficits.

The **Gramm-Rudman-Hollings Act,** passed in 1985, is the most recent, and in some ways the most radical, experiment in reforming the budget process in order to bring about balanced budgets. The Act establishes year-by-year deficit-reduction targets, culminating in a zero deficit for the 1991 fiscal year. The timetable for deficit reduction is shown in Table 32-1. Each year, estimates are to be made of the amount of revenue that will be raised by the tax system and of the amount of expenditure that would take place under prevailing legislation. If these estimates reveal impending deficits that are too large, a process is set in motion that, following guidelines established by the law, results in automatic expenditure reductions. According to the Gramm-Rudman-Hollings guidelines, the automatic expenditure reductions would be divided equally between defense and nondefense categories of expenditure. Within each of these categories, the programs vulnerable to reductions would be cut by equal percentage amounts.

Two features of the Gramm-Rudman-Hollings plan are particularly controversial. The first is that the law specifically exempts certain programs from the automatic expenditure-cutting process. These include such politically sensitive areas as Social Security, veterans' compensation and pensions, interest on the national debt, Aid for

TABLE 32-1   Timetable for Deficit Reduction Under the Gramm-Rudman-Hollings Act

Fiscal Year	Maximum Deficit (billions of dollars)
1986	$172
1987	144
1988	108
1989	72
1990	36
1991	0

Source: Office of Management and Budget, as published by Tax Foundation, Inc., *Tax Features,* Vol. 30, No. 1 (January 1986), p. 1.

Families with Dependent Children (AFDC), food stamps, and Medicaid. Cuts in these programs are not to be made automatically, although they can, of course, be cut (or increased) through the usual budgetary processes. The exemption of these programs from the automatic expenditure-cutting process increases the percentage cut required from the programs not thus exempted.

The second controversial aspect of Gramm-Rudman-Hollings arises because the Act delegates to nonelected agencies several important parts of the expenditure-reduction process. Estimates of impending deficits, and therefore the determination of the total amounts of the automatic expenditure cuts, are to be made by the Office of Management and Budget (in the executive branch of the government) and by the Congressional Budget Office (in the legislative branch). The specific reductions for individual agencies and departments are to be determined by the Comptroller General. Is it a violation of the Constitution for the Congress to delegate these powers to nonelected officials? This question will pose the first legal test of the Gramm-Rudman-Hollings Act. The answer may have been determined by the time you read this. But even if the Act is held to be constitutional, there will remain the question of whether Congress itself will follow its procedures or whether it will amend or repeal the law.

The Federal System

Another branch of public choice theory focuses on relationships among different levels of government. The United States has a **federal system** of government, that is, one formed through the consolidation of several previously separate states. The U.S. federal government has powers that are either specified or implied in the Constitution, while other governmental powers are not specified in the Constitution, but are instead reserved to the separate states that make up the federal union, or to their local governments, which have powers delegated to them by their state governments or constitutions. Thus, the United States has a multilevel system of government decision making—federal, state, and local.

In the part of public choice theory called **fiscal federalism,** the importance of a multilevel system of government lies in the opportunities that it offers for dividing up the responsibilities of government, placing each in the hands of the level that is able to do the job best. For example, responsibilities for police and fire protection are placed at the local level. Highways and higher education responsibilities are mainly at the state level, while national defense is a responsibility of the federal government. The theories of externalities and collective goods and services, which you studied earlier, provide models for how these governmental activities may be shared. The key idea is to assign each service responsibility to the level of government that comes closest to matching the geographic area over which collective benefits or external effects are important. For example, local governments are expected to do the best job with police and fire protection because the area of collective consumption is local and because local citizens have the most at stake in these operations. They can be counted on to see that effective service is provided at lowest possible cost. Similarly, national defense, which generates collective benefits nationwide, can be handled best by the federal government. When the areas of benefit do not exactly match the areas of government jurisdiction, intergovernmental cooperation is needed. Often, areas of responsibility shift as public demands change.

GOVERNMENT EXPENDITURES

Government expenditures in the United States, combining all levels of government from your local school district all the way up to the federal government in Washington, amounted to $5,407 per person in 1984. If you have a father and a mother and one brother or sister, government expenditure amounted to $21,628 for your family of four that year.

There are two basic categories of government expenditure. Some, called transfer payments, simply pass money to citizens. Other expenditures purchase goods and services for the use of the government itself. The difference between these types of expenditure merits a closer look.

Transfer Payments

Figure 32-4 pictures government expenditures in the United States for 1984. Look first at the shaded area at the bottom of the chart, which shows transfer payments. **Transfer payments** are payments that are not in exchange for any good produced or service rendered during the year in question. They include Social Security benefits, other retirement payments, unemployment insurance, and welfare payments. Interest on the public debt is another large expenditure recorded as transfer payment. Altogether, transfer payments amount to more than 40 percent of total government expenditures. Your own family may receive some of the money. These payments, which are often called "entitlements," have grown greatly in recent years.

Among the different levels of government in the United States, the federal government is responsible for most of the transfer payments. About 80 percent of all transfers come directly from the federal government, and much of the rest, though administered by state and local government, is actually financed through grants from the federal government. State and local governments have some freedom to design their own transfer payment programs, but most of the

FIGURE 32-4 Expenditures by National, State, and Local Governments in the United States, 1984 (percentage of total expenditures)

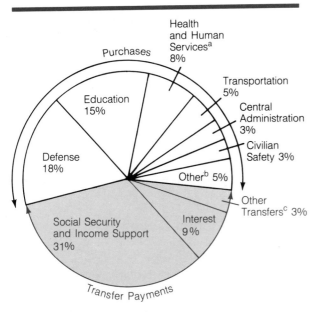

Over 40 percent of the total expenditures of governments in the United States are transfer payments, under which people receive money from the government without rendering service to the government that year. Nearly 60 percent of annual expenditures are for purchases of goods and services, directly generating demand for goods and services produced in the economy. This chart shows the breakdown of government expenditures by function.

a. Health and human services include goods and services purchases for veterans, health and hospital services, and housing and community services.
b. Other goods and services purchases include energy, natural resources, recreation, space, development and regulation, postal services, labor training, and agriculture.
c. Other transfer payments include international payments and miscellaneous unallocatable expenditures.
Source: Survey of Current Business, March 1986, Table 3-14.

direction is set by laws passed in Washington.

The purpose of most transfer payments is to redistribute spending power among individuals. For example, Social Security benefits transfer spending power from people who are currently working and paying Social Security taxes to others who are retired and receive Social Security benefit checks. Welfare payments generally transfer spending power from higher-income people to lower-income people.

Government Purchases

Now look at the top portion of Figure 32-4, which shows government purchases of goods and services. This part is especially important in the study of how government can influence aggregate demand in the economy. When government purchases are increased, jobs are created in the industries producing the goods and services desired by the government; when government purchases are decreased, jobs are lost.

Education and national defense are the two largest functional areas for government purchases of goods and services. They are also good illustrations of how, under a federal system, different functions are assigned to different levels of government. Defense is entirely funded by the federal government. Most of the funds for education come from state and local governments even though some federal government money is sent as grants to help the states, cities, and school districts to finance education.

The other government purchases are scattered over a wide variety of functions, and financial responsibility is often shared by national, state, and local governments. Under a complicated system of **grants-in-aid,** money from a larger government, such as the federal government or a state government, is handed over to a smaller government, such as a state or local one. Some of these grants are "conditional," meaning that the smaller government can receive the money only if it spends it according to rules set down by the granting government. Other grants-in-aid, such as revenue sharing, are "unconditional," so the receiving government can use the money any way it wants. The grant-in-aid system has expanded greatly in the United States since the 1930s.

An important fact about government expenditures that does not show up in Figure 32-4 is that state and local governments spend much more on currently produced goods and services than the federal government does. The major state

FIGURE 32-5 Receipts of National, State, and Local Governments in the United States, 1984 (percentage of total receipts)

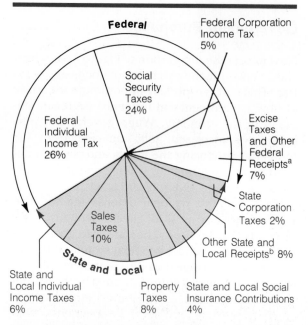

The federal government collects nearly two-thirds of total government receipts (as shown in the upper part of the circle), and state and local governments collect somewhat over one-third (as shown in the lower part). Individual income taxes and Social Security taxes are both assessed on individual earnings and total more than half of total government receipts. Some federal receipts are sent as grants-in-aid to state and local governments. Though they are not specifically shown on this chart, they amount to about 8 percent of total government receipts.

---

a. Other federal receipts include estate and gift taxes, customs duties, and miscellaneous receipts.
b. Other state and local receipts include fees and charges for services and miscellaneous nontax receipts.
Source: Survey of Current Business, March 1986, Tables 3-1, 3-2, and 3-3.

and local spending areas are education, health and human services, transportation, civilian safety, and housing. Even though federal grants help in many of these areas, state and local purchases would exceed federal purchases even if grant-in-aid funding were counted as federal purchases. Fiscal federalism theories suggest that grants-in-aid are useful when no single government has complete responsibility for a service.

GOVERNMENT RECEIPTS

The major sources of government receipts in the United States are shown in Figure 32-5. Again the circle is divided into two main parts. This time the bottom part, over one-third of the total, shows revenue collected by state and local governments. The top part of the circle shows revenue sources of the federal government. Even though the federal government collects almost two-thirds of the total, some of the money is turned back to the states and localities under grant-in-aid programs.

Individual Income Taxes

A careful look at Figure 32-5 shows that the individual income tax is the largest revenue producer in the system and that it is used by state and local governments as well as by the federal government. In 1984 the federal individual income tax accounted for about 26 percent of all government receipts, and state and local income taxes added another 6 percent. The United States relies more heavily on income taxes than most other countries do.

TAX BRACKETS AND PROGRESSION To understand how the United States individual income tax is applied, it is helpful to think of a person's income as consisting of successive layers, starting from zero and moving upward. The first layer of income is free of tax as a **personal exemption.** By 1989, each taxpayer will be entitled to a personal exemption of $2,000 for himself or herself plus $2,000 for each dependent.

The second layer of income is also tax free. This layer consists of expenditures that are allowed as **personal deductions** such as extraordinary medical expenses, charitable contributions, certain interest payments, certain state and local taxes, and casualty losses. For some taxpayers, these deductions are replaced by an allowance called the **standard deduction,** which is a deduction that applies if people choose not to itemize the specific personal deduction amounts.

TABLE 32-2   U.S. Individual Income Tax Rate Schedules for Single Taxpayers: Tax Reform Act of 1986 and the Previous Law

Previous Law			1986 Law		
Income Bracket[a]	Pay Base Tax of	Plus This Percentage of Amount Over Lower Bracket	Income Bracket[a]	Pay Base Tax of	Plus This Percentage of Amount Over Lower Bracket
2,610	0	11	$ 0	$ 0	15%
3,860	138	12	17,850	2,678	28
5,000	274	14			
7,390	609	15			
9,660	949	16			
12,270	1,367	18			
14,660	1,797	20			
17,050	2,275	23			
20,680	3,110	26			
26,710	4,678	30			
32,730	6,484	34			
38,750	8,531	38			
47,160	11,727	42			
62,850	18,316	48			
92,970	32,774	50			

a. Income bracket figures are net of the standard deduction under the 1986 rate structure but are gross of the comparable allowance under the previous law. Comparisons are for the 1987 tax year, indexed according to inflation estimates of the Congressional Budget Office.

With the third layer of income, the taxpayer enters the **tax brackets** established by the tax law. Table 32-2 compares, for 1987 incomes, the two-bracket system adopted in 1986 with the fifteen brackets used under the previous law. Under the Tax Reform Act of 1986, income in the first tax bracket is taxed at a rate of 15 percent. Income in the second bracket is taxed at 28 percent. Using the tax-rate schedule in Table 32-2, a person with income (after exemptions and deductions) of $30,000 would have a total tax liability of $6,080. This is $17,850 taxed at 15 percent ($2,678 of tax) plus $12,150 taxed at 28 percent ($3,402 of tax).

The system of exemptions, deductions, and tax brackets makes income taxation a very flexible instrument for government policy. Deductions can tailor the tax to suit special circumstances (such as extraordinary medical expenses) and can encourage certain private expenditures (such as charitable contributions). At the same time, the personal exemptions and tax-rate brackets make it possible for the tax to be **progressive,** meaning that persons with higher incomes pay a higher percentage of their income in tax than do persons with lower incomes. Progression is achieved because each higher layer of income pays a higher tax rate. The **marginal tax rate** for each taxpayer is the rate applicable to the next dollar of income received by that individual.

Unfortunately, the features that give the income tax its flexibility—exemptions, deductions, and rate brackets—have also generated serious problems for the tax. The flexibility offered by exemptions and deductions has encouraged special-interest provisions that lower taxes for some while forcing tax rates up for most taxpayers.

Each special exemption or deduction may make sense in itself, but their cumulative effect makes the tax extremely complicated and raises questions about its basic fairness. In the Tax Reform Act of 1986, Congress eliminated or reduced many special provisions and lowered tax rates substantially.

INDEXING THE INCOME TAX During the 1970s, many taxpayers experienced **bracket creep** as inflation pushed them into higher and higher tax-rate brackets. This happened because the dollar amount of their income, along with their cost of living, went up with the inflation. As they moved into higher brackets in the income tax, taxpayers faced higher and higher marginal tax rates, even when they were not better off in real terms. The net result of bracket creep was that average tax rates increased throughout the economy. Inflation was yielding a tax revenue bonus for the federal government without any new legislation to authorize the increase.

To put a stop to bracket creep, indexing was built into the federal individual income tax starting in 1985. **Indexing** is a system that automatically makes adjustments for changes in the general price level. For example, since prices increased by 4.1 percent during 1984, the personal exemption was increased from $1,000 in 1984 to $1,040 for 1985, an increase of 4 percent. In addition, each tax bracket was widened and limits on allowable deductions were increased by 4 percent. Indexing was continued in the 1986 law so that bracket creep caused by inflation would not be a serious problem.[2] A taxpayer would not move into a higher bracket unless his or her income increased proportionately more than the general price level.

TAX SIMPLIFICATION AND THE "FLAT TAX" As noted above, the flexibility of the income tax has

encouraged Congress to grant many special allowances to help particular interest groups or to promote politically popular causes. Income set aside for retirement can be "sheltered" from taxation, employer payments for employee health insurance are excluded from taxation, and so on. Over the years, increasing amounts of money flowed into these favored areas and off the tax rolls, reducing the **tax base,** which is the amount of income actually subjected to the tax. As a result, in order to maintain government revenues, tax-rate increases were enacted or rate reductions were smaller.

The Tax Reform Act of 1986 was the result of a concerted effort to reverse this erosion of the tax base. By eliminating many special deductions and exclusions, tax rates could be reduced while maintaining revenue neutrality—that is, not changing total tax revenue. In addition, the 1986 legislation reduced the number of tax-rate brackets to only two. In this respect, the ultimate simplification would be a **flat tax,** which would have only one tax-rate bracket.

In the years preceding the 1986 tax reform, flat-tax and tax-simplification proposals had been offered by each major political party—the Bradley-Gephart proposal by Democrats and the Kemp-Kasten proposal by Republicans—and the U.S. Treasury had offered several proposals. In the view of most taxpayers, tax simplification was long overdue. Moreover, it was argued that lower tax rates would increase incentives to produce and to invest. Proposals included limiting personal deductions for interest payments and for state and local taxes, taxing employer-paid fringe benefits such as health insurance and retirement programs, and taxing transfer payments such as unemployment compensation. As you can easily imagine, these tax-base increases faced resistance from powerful groups of voters. The final legislation reflected compromise on many of these

---

2. Inflation still causes some problems in taxing business profits and gains and losses on sales of assets. This is because indexing has not been applied to determining the costs of assets. Without such an adjustment, the dollar amount of gain on the sale of an asset overstates the real (price-level-adjusted) amount of that gain.

3. A flat-rate tax would still be progressive if personal exemptions were retained. Since the exemption would be a larger fraction of a low income than of a high income, the average tax rate on total income would be higher for high-income persons than for low-income persons.

proposals and produced a tax law that continues to be extremely complicated.

Social Security Taxes

Social Security taxes are the second largest revenue producer for government in the United States. Because there are two Social Security taxes, one of which is almost completely hidden from the taxpayer, many people do not realize how much money is actually paid. One of the Social Security taxes is taken directly out of the worker's paycheck. Most taxpayers are aware of this tax. For 1986, this tax was 7.15 percent of pay up to total pay of $42,000 each year (with no tax on pay over this amount). The second tax, of an equal amount, is paid by the employer, so that the total tax rate is 14.3 percent on pay covered by the law. Many people are not aware of this tax.

The Social Security taxes have no deductions for individual circumstances and the only exemption is for pay in excess of $42,000 a year. Therefore, among persons who receive less than $42,000 a year, it is a **proportional tax,** that is, the average tax rate is the same regardless of the amount of income. But average tax rates go down for people who receive more than $42,000 a year, since no tax is paid on amounts over this maximum. Therefore, considering the entire range of individual incomes, the Social Security tax is a **regressive tax,** that is, the average rate of tax is lower for those with high income than it is for those with lower income.

The money collected from Social Security taxes goes into a special trust fund that is used to pay benefits to retired people and others entitled to receive benefits under the law. In other words, Social Security benefits are part of the transfer payments component of government expenditure. However, amounts received in benefits are not exactly proportional to the amounts paid in taxes. Instead, the benefit system is tilted to favor low-income persons.

LABOR MARKET EFFECTS Your knowledge of microeconomics can help you recognize some of the economic effects of the Social Security system.

FIGURE 32-6   Payroll Tax and the Demand for Labor

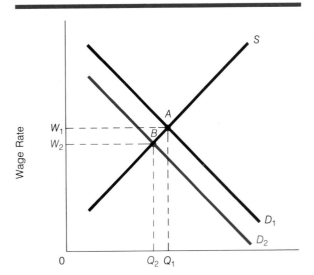

The supply curve, S, shows the quantities of labor supplied at various wage rates. The demand curve, D_1, shows quantities demanded at various wage rates if there is no tax on the payroll of the employer. A payroll tax, such as is imposed for Social Security, shifts the demand curve for labor to D_2. At the new equilibrium, B, the wage rate is lower and less labor is demanded and supplied than at the original equilibrium at A.

Since the employer pays tax on labor inputs but not on machinery inputs, the tax raises the relative cost of labor and encourages firms to substitute machines in place of workers in the production process. This is illustrated in Figure 32-6. In this figure, the horizontal axis shows quantities of labor demanded and supplied and the vertical axis shows market wage rates that might be agreed to between workers and employers. The supply curve S shows the amounts of labor that will be offered at various possible wage rates and the demand curve D_1 shows the quantities that would be demanded by employers if they did not have to pay the Social Security payroll tax. Equilibrium would be at A, with wage rate W_1 and Q_1 quantity of labor demanded and supplied. If the tax causes firms to use machines instead of labor, the payroll tax shifts the demand curve to the left, to D_2, and equilibrium will move to B, with wage rate W_2 and Q_2 quantity of labor demanded and supplied. Other things being equal, the wage rate will be lower and the quantity of labor demanded and supplied will be less because of this payroll tax. This is especially likely for unskilled workers, who are most likely to be displaced by machines.

The economic effect of the part of the tax that is taken out of the worker's paycheck is more difficult to analyze because much depends on whether workers believe that this tax payment (and the matching employer payment) is buying retirement income that would otherwise not be received. Let us assume that the supply curve in Figure 32-6 is based on workers believing that Social Security tax payments lead to higher retirement income. As long as workers hold this belief, equilibrium will be as described above. But if workers come to believe that the tax payments have no effect on the amount of retirement income they will receive, the amount of labor they will be willing to offer at any given market wage rate will be smaller and the supply curve will shift to the left. Market wage rates would move up from W_2 and employment would be less than Q_2.

EFFECTS ON SAVING   Another exercise in microeconomics arises from the benefit side of Social Security. Since government insurance is a substitute for private insurance, covered individuals may buy less retirement insurance from private insurance companies. Thus, voluntary saving for retirement is displaced, to some extent, by the Social Security system. This leads to one of the most controversial aspects of Social Security. Private insurance companies must, by law, build up reserves to guarantee the future payment of benefits. The companies loan these reserve funds to business firms to finance investment in machines and other forms of capital. But the Social Security system is not required to build up such reserves. Instead, today's tax receipts are used to pay benefits to today's retirees, with little or no money left over. By reducing the supply of loanable funds, the Social Security system may raise interest rates and reduce the equilibrium quantity

of investment in the economy. This could lead to a slower rate of economic growth for the economy.

Corporation Income Tax

The corporation income tax is another powerful revenue producer for government, though the amounts collected are much smaller than individual income and Social Security taxes. Like the individual income tax, the corporation income tax is used by both the federal government and state governments, with the federal government getting more money from the tax than state and local governments do.

Corporation income taxes are based on the net income (accounting profits) of corporations. The Tax Reform Act of 1986 set the highest bracket rate for the federal tax at 34 percent, but the brackets are so small that most corporate income falls in the highest bracket. For this reason, the federal government has a large stake in the profitability of U.S. corporations. The revenue that the federal government collects from the corporation income tax fluctuates greatly between good times and bad times, because corporate profits themselves fluctuate so much. Also, corporations are quick to react to changes that the government may make in defining income subject to the tax. For example, changes in ways of figuring depreciation or in credits allowed for investments can have powerful effects on the behavior of corporations.

Economists are not sure exactly who bears the major burden of corporation income taxes. To see why this is so, think back to your study of market types. Suppose that an income tax is imposed on a corporation that operates in a purely competitive market. At long-run equilibrium, this firm will have some accounting profit and some tax liability, but it will have zero economic profit. Therefore, the tax will force the firm out of business unless it can engage in **tax shifting** by transferring the burden of the tax either forward in the form of higher prices to consumers or backward in the form of lower wages for labor or lower prices for other inputs. Whether the tax can be shifted forward to consumers depends on whether competing firms also are subject to the tax and on whether there are good substitutes for the product. Similarly, whether or not labor and other resource suppliers can be forced to accept lower prices depends on conditions in their factor (resource) markets. If the firm is to stay in business, the tax will have to be shifted. The tax may be shifted partly forward and partly backward. Since individual firms and markets differ greatly from one another, it is not possible to make a general statement about who will bear the burden of the tax.

If the corporation is an actual monopoly or an oligopoly, microeconomic analysis suggests that it may receive some economic profit in the long run. In this situation, some of the tax may be paid from the economic profit. The owners of the corporation (the shareholders) might bear some of the burden of the tax through lower dividends and lower stock values. But there still may be forward shifting to consumers and backward shifting to labor and other resource suppliers. The part that is borne by shareholders may have a progressive effect, since most (but not all) corporate shares are owned by high-income people, but the part passed to consumers and the part passed to resource suppliers may have regressive effects.

Sales Taxes and Excise Taxes

A **sales tax** is imposed on the sale of a product. An **excise tax** may be imposed on either the sale or the manufacture of a product. Their economic effects are much the same. States and some local governments have general sales taxes, which apply across the board to most sales, as well as selective sales taxes on particular products, such as gasoline, cigarettes, and alcoholic beverages. The federal government imposes excise taxes on gasoline, motor oil, and a number of other products. Consumers are likely to pay higher prices for products that are subject to sales or excise taxes. That is, some of the burden of these taxes is shifted to consumers. However, some of the tax may be passed back to workers as well as the other owners of resources used to produce the

FIGURE 32-7 Effects of an Excise Tax

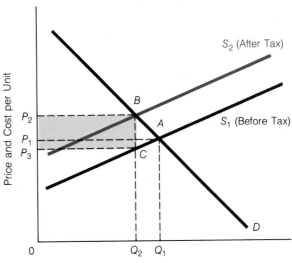

The supply curve for this product is S_1 when no tax is imposed on its manufacture. Equilibrium is at A, with quantity Q_1 demanded and supplied at price P_1. An excise tax is shown as an added cost of supplying the product. After the tax, the supply curve is S_2, and equilibrium is at B, with price P_2 and quantity Q_2. P_3 is the amount received per unit by suppliers after the tax is imposed. The shaded area shows tax revenue collected by the government, since the vertical dimension of this rectangle, BC, shows the amount of tax per unit, and the horizontal dimension shows the number of units on which the tax is collected. The triangular area ABC shows excess burden—that is, the net gain from those units of the product that were produced when there was no tax but that are not produced after the tax is imposed.

product. A simple supply-and-demand exercise shows how this can happen.

Figure 32-7 shows the demand curve for a product and two supply curves, one (S_1) showing supply without a tax and the other (S_2) showing supply after an excise tax is imposed. Without the tax, the equilibrium is at A, with quantity Q_1 demanded and supplied at price P_1. The tax is put into the model as an added cost of supplying the product. Thus, the supply curve is shifted upward by the amount of the tax, and the new supply curve is S_2. The new equilibrium is at B, with quantity Q_2 and price P_2. Because the price has risen from P_1 to P_2, consumers bear some of the burden of the tax. But the price increase is less than the full amount of the tax per unit, which is shown as the vertical distance from B to C. The per unit amount received by suppliers is P_3, which is less than they received before the tax was imposed. Therefore, part of the burden of the tax falls on people other than consumers of the product. Since the quantity of the product supplied has fallen because of the tax, some labor and other resources have been forced to accept lower wages or change jobs (or both), and some firms may have gone out of business. These workers, business people, and resource owners bear some of the burden of the tax if they cannot find new jobs that pay as well as the ones lost because of the tax.

EXCESS BURDEN   There is also an **excess burden** from this type of tax. That is, the total burden is greater in value than the amount of money collected by the government from the tax. The money collected by the government is shown by the shaded rectangle in Figure 32-7. The vertical dimension of this rectangle (BC) is the amount of tax collected per unit of the product, and the horizontal dimension shows the number of units on which the tax is collected. The excess burden is shown by the triangle ABC. This triangle shows net gains from units of the product that were produced when there was no tax, but which are not produced after the tax is imposed. Net gains existed because the amounts that consumers were willing and able to pay (shown by the demand curve) were greater than the amounts that suppliers needed to receive to persuade them to supply the product (shown by the supply curve).

A sales tax has much the same effect as an excise tax. By imposing a sales tax, the government requires purchasers to pay more when they purchase a taxed product. At equilibrium under a sales tax, consumers pay more per unit of the product than they did before the tax and less will be purchased, other things being equal. Suppliers receive less per unit than before the tax. Thus, some burden would be imposed on consumers and some would be shifted to suppliers of re-

sources used in producing the taxed goods and services.

PRICE ELASTICITY EFFECTS   The economic analysis of excise and sales taxes offers a convenient review of your understanding of the concept of price elasticity. For example, if the demand for the taxed good or service is price inelastic over the range of its price increase due to the tax, the total amount of money spent by purchasers will be greater after the tax than it was before the tax. The supply shift caused by the tax will bring a large price increase but little reduction in the quantity demanded. Most of the tax burden will be borne by consumers and little will be shifted back to suppliers of resources.

This is illustrated in panel (a) of Figure 32-8. The supply curve shifts from S to S_1 because of the tax. As a result, the equilibrium price rises from \$1.00 to \$1.50 and the equilibrium quantity falls from 50,000 to 40,000 per day. The proportionate change in quantity demanded is less than the proportionate change in the price. The coefficient of price elasticity is -0.556.[4] The total amount spent by purchasers increases from \$50,000 to \$60,000 a day.

On the other hand, if demand is price elastic over the price range involved, the supply-curve shift will bring a smaller price increase to consumers and there will be a larger reduction in the equilibrium quantity demanded and supplied. This is shown in panel (b) of Figure 32-8. In this panel, the two supply curves are identical to those in panel (a); that is, the original supply curve and the amount of the tax per unit of the product are the same. However, because demand is price elastic, the equilibrium quantity falls all the way to 30,000 units per day and the price rises only to \$1.20. The proportionate change in quantity is larger than the proportionate change in the price. Price elasticity of demand is -2.75.

---

4. The formula for calculating price elasticity of demand is

$$E_D = \frac{\dfrac{Q_{D_2} - Q_{D_1}}{Q_{D_1} + Q_{D_2}}}{\dfrac{P_2 - P_1}{P_1 + P_2}}$$

FIGURE 32-8   Price Elasticity of Demand and the Effect of an Excise Tax

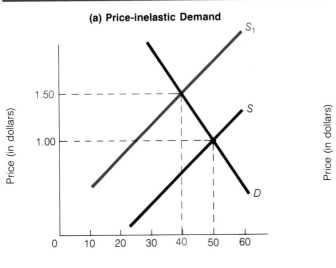

(a) Price-inelastic Demand

(b) Price-elastic Demand

Quantity (thousands per day)

Quantity (thousands per day)

In each panel, supply curve S represents the relationship between price and quantity supplied in the absence of an excise tax. Equilibrium exists where price is $1.00 and quantity is 50,000. Purchasers spend $50,000 a day for the good or service. In each of these panels, supply curve S_1 shows amounts offered for sale at various possible prices after an excise tax is imposed. The amount of the tax is the same in each panel. In panel (a), the demand curve D is price inelastic over this price range. After the tax, equilibrium is at a price of $1.50 and a quantity of 40,000 units a day. Purchasers spend $60,000 a day. In panel (b), the demand curve D is price elastic over this price range. After the tax, equilibrium is at a price of $1.20 and a quantity of 30,000 units a day. Purchasers spend $36,000 a day.

The total amount spent by purchasers falls from $50,000 to $36,000 a day. Consumers will spend less for this good or service after the tax than they did before and most of the burden of the tax will fall on resource owners rather than on consumers. Also, the government will collect less tax if demand is price elastic than if it is price inelastic, other things being equal. Therefore, economic analysis leads us to expect that both government and resource owners will prefer to have sales and excise taxes placed on goods and services for which demand is price inelastic. Taxes on cigarettes and alcoholic beverages, for example, are powerful revenue raisers and do relatively little to reduce quantities produced and consumed. These taxes do more to raise revenue than they do to reduce consumption.

Motor Fuels Taxes

The motor fuels tax ("gas tax") is a selective sales tax that is especially interesting because the money collected is put into a special fund and used to construct and maintain highways. This adds a new dimension to microeconomic analysis because highways are complementary in consumption with motor fuels. The tax will shift the supply curve for motor fuels to the left, but the new or better highways will shift the demand curve for motor fuels to the right. It is quite possible that the shift of the demand curve for motor fuels could more than make up for the reduction in the quantity demanded caused by the tax. More gasoline may be sold with the tax than would have been sold without it!

When motor fuel tax money is used for highway construction and maintenance, it is good microeconomic logic to see the government as a supplier of highway services and to see the motor fuels tax as a **user charge,** that is, as a price that the government charges to cover the costs of this service. Actually, highways are just one of many semicommercial activities carried on by government. Parking meters collect user charges for parking services, the postal service sells stamps for delivering mail, water departments charge fees for water service, and so on. For highway finance, the gasoline pump becomes a device (like a highway tollbooth) to collect a price for the use of the highway.

Property Taxes

A **property tax** is a tax that is imposed on the market value of property (mainly land and buildings) and collected annually from the owners of the taxed properties. In the United States, most property taxes are collected by local governments. They are especially important for school districts.

The system for collecting property taxes is different from the system used for income, profits, sales, or excise taxes, where some kind of transaction must take place before any tax is due. Property taxes are collected each year, whether or not there has been any transaction involving the property. An assessor estimates how much the property would sell for if an actual transaction were to take place, and this value is multiplied by the tax rate to determine the amount of tax to be paid. The payment is made by the person or business that holds legal title to the property. If the tax is not paid, the property may be taken by the government and sold for the amount of the taxes.

Another unique feature of the property tax is that the tax rate (often called **millage**—one mil being one-tenth of 1 percent) is set after, rather than before, the government's spending budget is determined. Government expenditure is determined and then the tax rate is set to bring in exactly the amount of money needed. This differs from the procedure for most taxes, where tax rates are set first and actual collections determine how much money will be available to spend. Public choice economists sometimes contend that the property tax gives citizens more control over local governments than they have over state and national governments that do not depend on the property tax.

PROPERTY TAXES AND HOUSING Property taxes offer many opportunities to apply microeconomic tools of analysis. For example, consider how the tax may affect the market for housing or the markets for factories or office buildings. If the tax is considered part of the cost of supplying housing, or factories, or office buildings, increases in the tax will shift the supply curves to the left. Other things being equal, this will result in higher prices for houses, factories, or office buildings compared with the prices of other things that are not taxed under the property tax. The higher relative prices will, economists predict, reduce the quantity of housing, factories, or office buildings compared with the quantities of goods and services not subject to the tax.

PROPERTY TAXES AND EDUCATION The largest use of property-tax revenues is to finance elementary and secondary schools. Because school districts involve relatively small geographic areas, it often happens that the property value per pupil is much greater in some school districts than in others. This, in turn, means that, in order to provide equal educational services per pupil, the low-property-value district would have to charge a higher tax rate ("millage") than the high-property-value school district. Alternatively, the low-property-value school district may simply spend less money per pupil, which may mean that pupils in these districts will be less well educated than pupils in high-property-value districts.

To apply microeconomic analysis to this situation, go back to the concepts of externalities and collective goods that you studied earlier in this chapter. The services of schools have important external and collective aspects, since students from one district often meet and work with people from other school districts. These externality and collective-consumption features, plus ethical considerations of human rights and income redistribution, have led states to set up grant-in-aid systems under which money from the state or the federal government is used to even out the services rendered by different school districts.

SUMMARY

1. Microeconomic analysis suggests that, in a market-capitalist system, government may be able to improve resource allocation by providing market-support services and by correcting for market failures, such as those that arise from externalities.

2. Markets provide excessive quantities of goods or services that generate negative externalities. Positive externalities cause markets to provide quantities that are less than the socially efficient quantity. Government may correct negative-externality market failure by shifting the supply curve to the left through regulations or through taxes. Government may correct positive-externality market failure by shifting the demand curve to the right through regulations or through subsidies to purchasers. However, it usually is easier to provide subsidies to suppliers, thereby shifting the supply curve to the right to correct for positive-externality market failure.

3. Because of nonexcludability, markets encounter the free-rider problem and fail to provide efficient quantities of goods and services that are consumed collectively. Government can overcome the free-rider problem by imposing taxes to finance collective goods and services. Because of nonrivalry in consumption, tax money can be pooled into a common fund to finance the provision of a collective good or service.

4. Public choice theory applies economic concepts to decision making in group situations. Taxpayers, voters, elected officials, and government employees are assumed to base their actions on self-interest. Taxation is based on benefits-received rather than on ability-to-pay principles. Government agencies use benefit-cost analysis in designing programs. Fiscal federalism studies the assignment of responsibilities to different levels of government in a multilevel system of government.

5. Government expenditures include both transfer payments, which distribute money to citizens, and purchases of goods and services, which are part of aggregate demand in the economy. About 57 percent of government expenditures are for purchases and 43 percent are for transfers.

6. About 62 percent of government receipts are from taxes imposed by the federal government and about 38 percent from taxes imposed by state and local governments. Through grants-in-aid, money collected by one level of government may be used to pay for goods and services provided by another level of government.

7. Individual income taxes are the largest source of government revenue in the United States. Through personal exemptions and tax-rate brackets, individual income taxes are progressive. Marginal tax rates are higher as income rises. Indexing has been installed in income taxes to prevent inflation from causing bracket creep. The Tax Reform Act of 1986 eliminated or reduced many deductions and exclusions so that tax rates could be lowered. However, the tax is still very complicated. Flat-tax proposals advocate having only one tax bracket and only one tax rate.

8. Two taxes are used to finance Social Security—one on the worker's pay and one on the employer's payroll. Microeconomic analysis indicates that the payroll tax reduces the demand for labor and lowers employment and wage rates. The Social Security system may reduce saving if it leads workers to reduce private saving to finance retirement.

9. Corporation income taxes are imposed on the accounting profits of corporations. These taxes may be shifted forward to consumers or backward to labor and other suppliers of resources. Dividends and other returns to stockholders also may be reduced by the tax. The actual burden of these taxes is uncertain.

10. Sales and excise taxes also may be shifted. Price-inelastic demand tends to place more burden on purchasers of the good or service, whereas price-elastic demand tends to place more of the burden on resource owners. Government collects more revenue if demand is price inelastic than if it is price elastic, other things being equal. Excess burden will arise from these taxes if reduced

quantities involve units of the good or service on which benefits exceeded costs.

11. Motor fuels taxes may be classed as user charges when the money collected from the tax is used to finance construction and maintenance of highways. A user charge is similar to a price charged for a good or service.

12. Property taxes are annual taxes on the value of property, mainly land and buildings. They tend to reduce the supply and increase the market price of housing. Property taxes are used mainly by local governments and are especially important in financing elementary and secondary education.

DISCUSSION QUESTIONS

1. Do you believe that cigarette smoking results in negative externalities? Are taxes on cigarettes an effective means of reducing such externalities? What use do you believe should be made of the money that the government collects from taxes on cigarettes? Draw a graph to illustrate how negative externalities lead to market failure.

2. Do you believe that especially good students generate positive externalities in your college or university? If so, construct a graph to illustrate the market for good students and explain how merit scholarships can improve resource allocation. Should tuition for ordinary students be increased to finance merit scholarships?

3. Explain how the free-rider problem may affect the amount of money raised by fund-raising activities (such as the United Way) in your local community. In what sense do the services financed by these contributions produce nonrival consumption benefits?

4. Discuss how benefit-cost analysis might be applied in deciding whether or not to obtain a college education. For which benefits is discounting likely to be important in your calculations? What are the major costs?

5. Explain the difference between transfer payments and government purchases. Which is part of aggregate demand? Why is the other part not part of aggregate demand? Name the three leading areas of government purchases. Check Figure 32-4 to make sure you are correct.

6. What is the difference between personal exemptions and personal deductions in the individual income tax? Considering the bracket system of tax rates, explain why an individual's marginal tax rate is expected to be higher than his or her average tax rate if the system is progressive.

7. Distinguish between the two taxes used to finance Social Security. Why does the payroll tax lower both employment and market wage rates? Explain how the Social Security tax system is regressive. Compare this with how a flat-rate income tax with personal exemptions would be progressive.

8. Illustrate graphically how an excise tax on a good or service may be shifted partly to consumers and partly to resource owners. How does price elasticity of demand influence these shifts? With a second graph, illustrate how price elasticity of supply affects forward and backward shifting.

9. Illustrate graphically how a property tax on houses can be expected to change the equilibrium price and quantity of housing, other things being equal. What features should be added to this graph if the money collected from the property tax is used to finance a fire station located four blocks away?

33 *Poverty and Income Distribution*

PREVIEW This chapter is about poverty and income inequality—problems that arise because the economy neither insures the whole population against poverty nor provides an income distribution that everyone considers fair and just. It also outlines some of the measures that may help to solve these problems.

First we deal with poverty. After discussing poverty concepts and statistical poverty lines, we describe the incidence of poverty among different groups in the population. Then we consider some of the methods for dealing with it. Particular attention is paid to what critics call the "welfare mess" and to proposals for negative income taxes and their impact on the labor supply.

In the second part of the chapter, we turn to the subject of income distribution and its inequality. We discuss the statistical problems of measuring income inequality and the weaknesses of published figures—such as their omission of nonmoney incomes from home-grown food or subsidized housing. We shall be especially interested in the *personal* income distribution—that is, the distribution among individuals by income size groups or brackets—but we shall also review the *functional* distribution, as between labor income and property income. In looking at the history of the personal income distribution in the United States, we find that its connection with the functional distribution is surprisingly imprecise.

Finally we examine the question of whether the measured degree of income inequality constitutes *maldistribution*, that is, an unacceptable amount of equality or inequality. We present some arguments that it does and some that it doesn't. The chapter ends by considering several methods of redistributing income.

POVERTY

"For ye have the poor always with you," said Jesus (Matthew xxvi:2), and Abraham Lincoln asserted that "God must love the poor—he made so many of them." Both Jesus and Lincoln left to lesser successors the jobs of deciding who was poor, who was not, and why.

Before considering some alternative poverty concepts, let us distinguish between poverty and income distribution. Even though poverty and income distribution are related matters, they are different and separate. For example, poverty exists when the real income or living standard of some members of the society is lower than is considered acceptable in that society. Income distribution, on the other hand, simply refers to income equality or inequality, the latter meaning that some people have a different amount of real income than others. Income inequality can exist without anyone's income being below the poverty level. However, in some countries today, complete equality would mean that *all* would be living in poverty, at least according to the standards of most other parts of the world.

Poverty Concepts and Poverty Lines

Over the years, four poverty concepts or criteria have arisen. We shall call them the amenity,

TABLE 33-1 1983 U.S. Poverty Lines by Family Size, Age, and Number of Children (in thousands of dollars)

	Number of Related Children Under 18									
Size of Family Unit	**0**	**1**	**2**	**3**	**4**	**5**	**6**	**7**	**8+**	**Weighted Average**
One person	5.1									5.1
Under 65	5.2									5.2
65 and over	4.8									4.8
Two persons	6.5									6.5
Householder under 65	6.7	6.7	6.9							6.7
Householder 65 or over	6.0	6.0	6.8							6.0
Three persons	7.8	8.0	8.0							7.9
Four persons	10.3	10.4	10.1	10.1						10.2
Five persons	12.4	12.6	12.2	11.9	11.7					12.0
Six persons	14.2	14.3	14.0	13.8	13.3	13.1				13.6
Seven persons	16.4	16.5	16.1	15.9	15.4	14.9	14.3			15.5
Eight persons	18.3	18.5	18.2	17.9	17.5	16.9	16.4	16.2		17.2
Nine persons or more	22.1	22.2	21.9	21.6	21.2	20.7	20.1	20.0	19.2	20.3

Source: Bureau of the Census, *Current Population Reports*, Series P-64, No. 147 (1985), Table A-2.

proportionality, budgetary, and public-opinion criteria. The *amenity* criterion is the most optimistic in its implications. An amenity is a component of some "decent" level of consumption, such as a certain calorie level in a person's diet, a certain number of square feet of living space per person in a family, or the availability of inside plumbing or running hot water. A person or a family is regarded as living in poverty if it has less than a certain level of such key amenities. This concept of poverty is optimistic because, under its terms, it is conceivable that poverty could be completely eliminated. By the amenity standards of the middle and late nineteenth century, poverty has today been almost eliminated in both Western Europe and North America, but not in the Third World countries where a great majority of the world's population lives.

The *proportionality* criterion is the most pessimistic in its implications. According to this concept, people in the lowest-income 10 (or 15, or 20) percent of the population generally feel psychologically alienated, or separated, from society and believe they are victims of discrimination or unfairly treated, whatever their income levels happen to be. "One feels poor with only a Rolls-Royce and a private plane when the neighbors own spaceships." By this criterion, there is no solution for the poverty problem short of something close to absolute equality of income and wealth.

The *budgetary* criterion is the most widely used in practice. The first step in developing this is to determine the cost of a set of standard food budgets providing nutritive diets for families of different sizes, ages, and environments (rural, urban, and so on). As applied in the United States, this food budget is multiplied by 3, since surveys suggest that poor American workers spend about one-third of their income on food.

TABLE 33-2   U.S. Poverty Profiles by Family Status, Family Type, Age, and Race, for Selected Years, 1959–1983

	Percentage of Population Below Poverty Level						
	Age 65 and over	Householders	Related Children Under 17	Other Family Members	All Family Members	Unrelated Individuals	Total
All races							
1959	35.2	18.5	26.9	15.9	15.8	46.1	22.4
1967	29.5	11.4	16.3	9.0	10.9	38.1	14.2
1975	15.3	9.7	16.8	6.4	12.5	25.1	12.3
1983	14.0	12.3	21.7	8.8	20.8	23.4	15.2
White							
1959	33.1	15.2	20.6	13.3	16.5	44.1	18.1
1967	27.7	9.0	11.3	7.2	9.2	36.5	11.0
1975	13.4	7.7	12.5	5.2	8.3	22.7	9.7
1983	12.0	9.7	16.9	6.8	10.7	20.9	12.1
Black							
1959	62.5	48.1	65.5	44.1	54.9	57.0	55.1
1967	53.3	33.9	47.4	27.1	38.4	49.3	39.3
1975	31.3	27.1	41.4	16.9	30.1	42.1	31.3
1983	35.7	32.4	46.3	23.7	34.7	40.8	35.7
Hispanic							
1973	24.9	19.8	27.8	12.6	21.5	12.6	21.9
1978	23.2	20.4	27.2	12.3	20.9	12.3	21.6
1983	23.1	26.1	37.8	17.0	27.8	17.0	28.4

Note: Data for Hispanics were not recorded separately until 1973.

Source: Bureau of the Census, *Current Population Reports*, Series P-64, No. 147 (1985), Table 1, p. 5.

When the basic food budgets are multiplied by 3, the result is a series of **poverty lines,** or income levels below which poverty is said to exist. In lower-income countries, the multiplier in computing poverty lines should be less than 3, since more than one-third of workers' income is spent on food.

The *public opinion* (or survey research) criterion is the most recent concept of poverty. Under this system, a sample of people are asked how much income a family of standard size (usually four including two small children) needs to ''get by'' (whatever that means) in a particular city. It is interesting that the answers seem to cluster in a range between 45 and 50 percent of the average

family income for the area where the survey is made.

POVERTY PROFILES IN THE UNITED STATES
Table 33-1 shows official poverty lines for the United States for 1983. Tables 33-2 and 33-3 show profiles of American poverty as measured by these official poverty lines. Table 33-2 covers the 24-year period from 1959 to 1983 and Table 33-3 provides detailed information for 1983. Several patterns emerge from these tables. Some popular notions are confirmed, but others are not.

1. Poverty, according to the official definition, has *not* been eliminated. Some 15 percent of the

TABLE 33-3 Characteristics of U.S. Poverty Population, 1983

Characteristic	Percentage of Population Below Poverty Line
Age	
Below 15	23.0
15–24	12.6
25–44	11.9
45–54	9.1
55–59	10.4
60–64	11.5
65 and over	14.1
Related children under 18	
In families	21.7
In unrelated subfamilies	61.2
All related children	22.1
City size	
In metropolitan areas	13.8
Central cities	19.8
Outside central cities	9.6
Outside metropolitan areas	18.3
Region	
Northeast	13.4
Midwest	14.6
South	17.2
West	14.7
Family type	
Married-couple family	2.6
Male householder, no wife present	13.0
Female householder, no husband present	36.0
All families	12.3
Unrelated individuals	
Male	19.9
Female	26.2
Total	23.4

Source: Bureau of the Census, *Current Population Reports*, Series P-64, No. 147 (1985), p. 2.

U.S. population lives below the poverty line. This poverty ratio fell quite steadily during the War on Poverty of the Kennedy and Johnson administrations, but has risen again since 1975.

2. Poverty is *not* exclusively a minority problem even though the poverty ratio for blacks and Hispanics is considerably higher than the white ratio.

3. Poverty is *not* entirely an urban problem. The central-city ratios are higher than the rural ones, but the "urban outside central cities" (suburban?) ratio is nearly 10 percent, and the ratio outside metropolitan areas is higher than the metropolitan ratio.

4. Poverty is *not* concentrated either in the Northeast "snowbelt" or the Southern "Appalachia." The "golden west" ratio is almost the same as the Midwest one, and higher than the Northeastern one.

5. Over time, the most marked alleviation of poverty (a falling poverty ratio) has been among the elderly (65 and over). The highest ratios are now among children (under 15), with young adults (15 to 24) in second place.

6. Poverty has "a female face," meaning that poverty ratios are especially high for female family heads (no husband present) and for single women outside families.

7. The highest single figure in the tables is for children under 18 living outside conventional families in what are called "unrelated subfamilies"—foster homes, orphanages, reformatories, hospitals, communes, etc.

All of these estimates, however, are criticized as too high because they are based entirely on money income, neglecting entirely any income in kind—from an owned home, a garden, food stamps, Medicaid, public housing. Several studies suggest that allowing for these omissions would cut the census estimates (of percentages below the poverty line) by one-half or three-quarters.[1]

1. Milton and Rose Friedman, *Free to Choose* (New York: Harcourt Brace Jovanovich, 1980), p. 108. The studies that the Friedmans mention are summarized in Martin Anderson, *Welfare* (Stanford, Calif.: Hoover Institution Press, 1978), Chapter 1.

THE ISLANDS AND THE CASES What sorts of Americans are most likely to be classified as living in poverty for part or all of their lifetimes? In his book *The Affluent Society*, J. K. Galbraith asserts that there are "islands" of poverty—economic backwaters with poor schools and poor opportunities for acquiring marketable skills. People who live their early lives in these areas are more likely to be poor. Among these areas are mountain Appalachia and the rural South, as well as black and Hispanic ghettos of the so-called "inner cities."[2] Also, there is "case" poverty, which relates to particular individuals and to characteristics that appear to be associated with poverty. Here are eight categories of such cases:

1. Nonwhites (especially blacks and Indians).
2. The young (under 20) and the elderly (over 65) living alone. However, poverty among the elderly is most likely to be exaggerated by official statistics since many low-income elderly people own their homes and cultivate small vegetable gardens.
3. Those handicapped by reason of present or recent-past deficiency, injury, or illness, either physical or psychological.
4. The unemployed and the intermittently employed.
5. Members of households headed by women—widows, divorcees, or unmarried mothers—who are employable only as unskilled laborers.
6. Those with less than a high school education, or the functionally illiterate in the English language.
7. Those with records of criminal behavior or prolonged unemployment.
8. Victims of racial, religious, and sexual discrimination. (These include many people in classes 1–7 above.)

These possible handicaps are cumulative. That is, combinations of them help explain why the incidence of poverty for, say, nonwhite single persons is greater than for either all nonwhites or for all single persons.

Antipoverty Policies

In rich countries, the poor become objects of either private charity (aid from friends and relatives or organizations such as churches and settlement houses) or public charity (generally called welfare or relief). In poor countries, they turn mainly to begging or worse. In all countries, the life expectancies of the poor are lower than those of the nonpoor of the same ages.

U.S. WELFARE PROGRAMS In the United States, much of the expansion of public welfare programs followed the publication, in 1962, of Michael Harrington's *The Other America*.[3] This book became the *Uncle Tom's Cabin* of antipoverty policy and the inspiration for the Johnson administration's War on Poverty. Among the major welfare programs are Aid for Families with Dependent Children (AFDC), food stamps (which allow people to buy food below market prices), subsidies for rent and medical care, and a guaranteed minimum Social Security payment for low-income persons who may not have qualified for that amount of benefit under the regular Social Security rules.

Of course, Social Security is not primarily an antipoverty program. The great majority of people receiving Social Security payments have qualified by reason of age, disability, or the death of a parent or spouse. They have incomes above the poverty line and have contributed to the cost of their benefits through taxes paid while they were employed.

Public assistance programs in the United States are both expensive and controversial. The "welfare mess" view points out that there is a great deal of cheating by recipients as well as harshness in the administration of welfare, and that administrative costs are high. If the whole welfare appropriation could go directly to the poor, the welfare family of four would be receiving an income above the U.S. median. The programs also have been described as "regulating the poor."

---

2. J. K. Galbraith, *The Affluent Society* (Boston: Houghton Mifflin Company, 1958).

3. Michael Harrington, *The Other America* (Baltimore: Penguin Books, 1962).

This point of view asserts that welfare programs expand when the poor threaten to revolt and then systematically dehumanize the recipients when the threat dies down.[4] A more supportive view of these programs is the following:

There may be great inefficiencies in our welfare programs, the level of fraud may be very high, the quality of management may be terrible, the programs may overlap, inequities may abound, and the financial incentive to work may be virtually nonexistent. But if we judge by two basic criteria—the completeness of coverage for those who really need help and the adequacy of the help they do receive—the picture changes dramatically. Judged by these standards, our welfare system has been a brilliant success.[5]

WELFARE REFORM Proposals for welfare reform abound on both the political left and right. Many persons have proposed ideas that combine the following three ingredients of welfare reform: (1) adequate payments to the poor, (2) greater motivation for the poor to exchange welfare payments for the wages of low-paying jobs, and (3) lower administrative costs, even though this means throwing many social workers, accountants, lawyers, and others out of work. In this imperfect world, however, welfare reformers also must pay attention to the political effects of their proposals. They must take care that their proposals will neither lower the living standards of any important group of present welfare clients nor reduce the political power of the "welfare constituency" of any member of Congress or other legislator who must depend on that group for votes in the next election. Violations of these rules have torpedoed many a nobly intentioned proposal.

Negative Income Tax

Under a **negative income tax,** persons who receive less than a specified amount of income receive payments from the government (a "negative tax"), and persons who receive more than that amount

of income pay money to the government (a "positive tax"). Thus, the idea of a negative income tax is really an extension of existing progressive income taxation.

Several widely discussed reform suggestions fit under the general heading of negative income taxes. We shall describe the simplest of these, presented by Milton Friedman.[6] Friedman would like to replace the whole public welfare system (including AFDC, food stamps, Medicaid, rent subsidies, and the welfare part of Social Security) with a single welfare payment in money, equal to half of the difference between a family's income and its personal exemptions under the federal income tax. These exemptions would be increased from their present level so that an amount equal to half of them would constitute a generous poverty line.

We shall illustrate the negative income tax with the help of Figure 33-1. The horizontal axis shows the family's income *before* these taxes. For simplicity, we shall call this income the family's earnings. The vertical axis is a family's income *after* income taxes, both positive and negative. The 45-degree line from the origin of the graph shows combinations where earnings are exactly equal to income after taxes. That is, it illustrates the relationship that would exist if there were no income taxes, either positive or negative. In Figure 33-1 we shall illustrate a system in which the poverty line is $8,000, personal exemptions under the income tax amount to $16,000, and in which, following Friedman, the negative tax takes up half of the difference between the family's earnings and its exemptions under the income tax. This means that the rate of negative tax is 50 percent.[7]

Let us begin with a family that has no earnings at all. This family would receive a negative tax payment from the government in the amount of $8,000, just equal to the poverty line. Such a situation is shown as point *A* in Figure 33-1. Now suppose that some members of this family get

4. Richard Cloward and Frances Fox Piven, *Regulating the Poor* (New York: Random House, 1971).

5. Martin Anderson, *op. cit.,* running quote from p. 135.

6. Milton Friedman, *Capitalism and Freedom* (Chicago: The University of Chicago Press, 1962).

7. Today's higher price level would require higher figures than in Friedman's illustration.

jobs and that their earnings amount to $6,000. The 50 percent negative tax rate in our illustration says that the government check would be reduced by half of these earnings, or by $3,000. Now the family receives only $5,000 in negative tax. But when this amount is added to their $6,000 earnings, they have a total of $11,000, as shown at point B in Figure 33-1.

Next we illustrate what is called the *breakeven point* in a negative income tax, that is, the situation in which the family neither receives a check from the government nor pays any tax to the government. Suppose the family's earnings rise to $16,000. When half of this amount is subtracted from the basic government check of $8,000, the government check is wiped out, and the family receives nothing in negative tax from the government. This breakeven point is shown at C in Figure 33-1. Following Friedman's system, personal exemptions under the income tax would amount to $16,000 to make this system operational. Of course, if the family earned more than $16,000, it would become a payer of positive taxes along the line from C to D in Figure 33-1. We have drawn the line CD somewhat steeper than the line ABC because we assume that the tax rate for positive income taxes would be something less than 50 percent.

INCENTIVE EFFECTS One of the basic appeals of the negative income tax is that a family will always have a higher after-tax money income from working than it will from not working. In our illustration, the family would retain 50 cents from every dollar earned by working. Although this tax rate is high compared with those now imposed on most incomes above the breakeven point, the negative income tax may provide more incentive to work than the present welfare system does. Under present regulations, if enforced strictly, every dollar (above a tiny minimum) earned from working would be deducted from the family's welfare check, and the family would retain none of its income from work. For this reason, the system very likely discourages people from working.

A number of costly experiments have been carried out in attempts to measure the incentive

FIGURE 33-1   Negative Income Tax

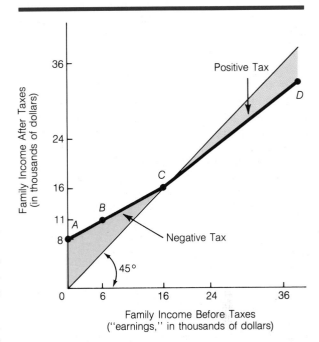

If this family had no earnings at all, it would receive a government check (negative income tax payment) for $8,000, which would place it at the poverty line, so that the family's income after taxes would be at point A. With a 50 percent negative tax rate, if the family earned $6,000 for working, its negative tax payment check would be reduced by half of these earnings ($3,000), and the family's after-tax income would be $11,000 ($6,000 earnings plus a $5,000 negative tax receipt). This situation is shown at point B. The breakeven point is at C, where the family earns $16,000 and receives no transfer payment. With earnings above $16,000, the family pays positive taxes, so that its after-tax income follows line CD. The 45-degree line shows combinations where there are no negative and no positive income taxes.

effects of the negative income tax. Negative income tax payments have actually been given to samples of families drawn from the "working poor"—that is, those slightly above present poverty lines—in the hope of determining the effects of the system on labor force participation. Unfortunately, the results are not very clear because the subjects received their payments only for short periods and not as a way of life. The results suggest, however, that not many principal bread-winners would quit work or reduce their working hours if a negative income tax plan were available. However, quite a few secondary workers in multiple-earner families (mainly wives and teenagers) would reduce the number of hours they work in order to care for children or get further education and training. This may of course be socially desirable in the long run at the same time that it acts as a short-run disincentive to work.

CONFLICTS AMONG OBJECTIVES As you may have observed already, there are three key features in a negative income tax system: (1) the poverty line or guaranteed minimum after-tax income, (2) the rate of negative tax, and (3) the breakeven income level. Because each of these features reflects a different policy objective in the system, conflicts arise among them. The poverty line represents the goal of eliminating poverty. The rate of negative tax reflects the work incentive feature of the system, with greater work incentives presumably coming from lower tax rates. Finally, the location of the breakeven point greatly influences the overall cost of the program. This cost increases rapidly as the breakeven level rises, since each upward move takes people out of the positive tax-paying group and adds them to the negative tax-receiving group. The resulting problems can easily be imagined. For example, lowering the rate of negative tax to offer stronger work incentives must either lower the poverty line or raise the breakeven level or do both things at the same time.[8] Or, an attempt to lower the cost of the program by lowering the breakeven level would require either a lower poverty line or a higher rate of negative tax. Raising the poverty line would increase the cost of the program unless the rate of negative tax were also raised, possibly damaging work incentives.

ADMINISTRATIVE AND POLITICAL PROBLEMS A negative income tax can also lead to certain administrative and political problems. Administrative problems arise in handling income from the short-term jobs that many poor people keep getting and losing. It is also alleged that the poor themselves would rather deal with social workers than with revenue agents. A major political problem is that many individual families would lose by a change from the present welfare system to a negative income tax, even if welfare recipients would gain in the aggregate. Among the possible losers are those who do little or no work and whose current welfare entitlements (food stamps, rent subsidies, and so on) are large, as indeed they are in many cities with high living costs. A change in political balances could arise if these people reacted to a negative income tax by moving back to the lower-cost small towns and rural areas from which many of them originally came. Any such dispersion of the "welfare vote" would surely lower the political power of welfare clients as a group and of legislators who depend largely on their votes.

INEQUALITY

As we said earlier, poverty and inequality are related but quite different things. We turn now to an examination of inequality. What are the facts about income inequality? Why does it arise? What can or should be done about it?

The Distribution of Income

Economists have always been interested in the distributions of income and wealth. There are many ways of organizing information on these matters, such as by countries at various stages of development, by sex, by race, by occupation, by region, and so on. But by far the most commonly considered distributions are the **functional** (between labor, property, and other sources of income) and **personal income distributions** (by income brackets or size classifications). These two are closely related. Because you studied the func-

---

8. The rate of negative tax is equal to the poverty line or guaranteed minimum income divided by the breakeven income level, provided a flat-rate tax is used.

tional distribution of income earlier in the book,[9] we shall simply review it briefly and then go on to discuss personal distribution.

FUNCTIONAL INCOME DISTRIBUTION In Part IX we explained how factor markets help to determine how the various factors of production will be combined to produce the goods and services demanded in the economy. A functional distribution of income for the United States was presented in Table 29-1.[10] There you learned that wages and fringe benefits amount to more than three-fourths of the total national income and that a part of proprietors' income in fact is also labor income. The remaining types of income—rental income, corporate profits, and interest—are property incomes and amount to less than one-fourth of the total. Table 29-1 showed that the labor share has grown over the past half-century and that the property income share has decreased.

PERSONAL INCOME DISTRIBUTION When we examine the personal distribution of income, we want to know about the individual people who provide the factors of production, whose shares of national income are shown in the functional distribution.

The two parts of Table 33-4 show two different ways of describing the personal income distribution of American households. (A household may be either a family or a single individual.) Personal income includes transfer payments—public and private pensions, relief payments, unemployment compensation, and so on. It excludes nonmoney income, capital gains, and the undistributed profits of corporations. In part (a), the arrangement is by income brackets in 1983 dollars and shows the effects of both the rapid real income growth from 1967 to 1975 and the slowdown from 1975 to 1983. In part (b), the arrangement is by quintiles (fifths) of equal numbers of households for 1983 plus a display showing the top 5 percent—the top one-fourth of the

9. See Chapter 2, especially Table 2-2.
10. See page 577.

top quintile. In the last column of this table, we can find the lowest income included in each income quintile.

In the lowest quintile are the poor and the near-poor. The second is mainly unskilled labor, both white-collar and blue-collar, sometimes called the working poor. The third (middle) quintile is mainly semiskilled labor (the assembly-line workers). In the fourth quintile are skilled labor and the lower "middle class" (clerical workers). The fifth (top) quintile includes both the upper middle class and the truly rich. Most tuition-paying college and university students do not think of themselves as rich, but in fact come from families mainly in the fifth or upper-fourth quintiles of the income distribution.

RELATIONS BETWEEN FUNCTIONAL AND PERSONAL DISTRIBUTIONS The functional distribution of income by type and the personal distribution of income by size classes are of course related. Most "workers," who receive most of their incomes from wages and salaries, are poorer than most "capitalists," whose income is derived mainly from property and profits. It is natural to suppose that any increase in the labor share of the functional distribution also increases the equality of the personal distribution.

This is not, however, always true, especially when the level of *total* income changes at the same time. During the Great Depression of the 1930s, the labor share seems to have risen, but measured equality declined. The main reason why this happened was that the distribution of labor income itself became more unequal, depending on how the individual worker families were affected by unemployment and underemployment. Another reason was that profit income was distributed more equally, with fewer big windfall gains—and more big windfall losses—than during the "roaring" 1920s.

Measuring Inequality

Of the many possible ways to measure inequality, we consider only two—the Gini ratio, used in

TABLE 33-4 Personal Income Distribution of Households in the United States

(a) By Income-Size Brackets in 1983 Dollars (Selected Years)

Income-Size Class (thousands of 1983 dollars)	Percentage of Households		
	1967	1975	1983
Under 5	10.3	8.1	9.2
5–9.99	12.1	13.8	13.7
10–14.99	11.1	12.3	13.0
15–24.99	26.4	23.2	22.8
25–49.99	33.1	33.6	31.0
50 and over	6.9	9.0	10.3
Total	100.0	100.0	100.0
Median income ($)	$21,315	$21,843	$20,885

(b) By Income Quintiles (1983)

Income Quintile	Aggregate Household Income (in billions of dollars)	Percentage of Total	Lowest Income in Group (in thousands of dollars)
First (lowest)	85.4	3.94	—
Second	214.9	9.91	8.8
Third	356.0	16.41	16.5
Fourth	535.2	24.67	25.4
Fifth (highest)	978.0	45.08	38.4
(Top 5 percent)	(307.7)	(16.95)	(62.9)
Total	2,169.5	100.0	

Sources: (a) *Statistical Abstract of the United States,* 105th ed. (1985) Table 734, p. 442. (b) Bureau of the Census, *Current Population Reports,* Series P-60, No. 146 (1985), Tables 2 and 5, pp. 8 and 18.

most countries of North America and Western Europe, and the quantile ratio, used in many socialist countries.

THE LORENZ CURVE AND THE GINI RATIO The Lorenz curve and the Gini ratio are ways of illustrating and measuring income inequality. A **Lorenz curve** is an illustration of inequality that is constructed by plotting the percentage of total income received by successive percentages of the population, starting from the lowest-income per-

sons and proceeding cumulatively upward. A Lorenz curve is shown in Figure 33-2. In this figure, the vertical axis shows the cumulative percentage of total income, and the horizontal axis shows the cumulative percentage of families. The curve itself is constructed by using the numbers in the middle column of Table 33-4(b). The lowest 20 percent of the households got 3.94 percent of the total income. This is plotted as point *a* in Figure 33-2. The lowest 40 percent of the families (the first and second quintiles combined) received 13.85 percent of the total income (3.94 + 9.91 = 13.85). This is plotted at point *b*. The bottom 60 percent of the families got 30.26 percent of the total income (3.94 + 9.91 + 16.41 = 30.26), which is plotted at point *c*, and so on. The curve drawn to connect the plotted points is called a Lorenz curve. If income were distributed with perfect equality, the Lorenz curve would be a straight line from one corner of the diagram to the other. This is called the "line of equality" in Figure 33-2. If income is not distributed with perfect equality, the Lorenz curve will lie below this perfect equality line, and an area of inequality will exist between the Lorenz curve and the line of equality. This is the shaded area in Figure 33-2.

The **Gini ratio** is a measure of inequality computed by dividing the area of inequality shown by a Lorenz curve by the whole right-triangle area (shown as *0AB*) in the Lorenz-curve diagram. If incomes are distributed with perfect equality, the Gini ratio is zero, because the area of inequality is zero. If incomes are distributed with perfect inequality, with all going to only one family, the ratio will be 1.00, since the area of inequality will be the same as the entire right triangle *0AB*.[11]

We estimate that the Gini ratio was about .35 for the United States in 1983 and considerably lower (under .30) in many other countries on both sides of the so-called Iron Curtain. A study by Williamson and Lindert estimates that the Gini ratio was low in colonial America (outside the South) but that it rose steadily because of expanding black slavery and unrestricted immigration.[12] They estimate, however, that the ratio has been falling since about 1929. Since 1945, the income share of the lowest quintile has been rising and that of the highest has been falling, with income shares of the three middle quintiles

11. The Gini ratio is sometimes called the concentration ratio, and the Lorenz curve is sometimes called the Gini curve. The original research to develop these concepts was done independently by the American statistician Max Lorenz and the Italian statistician Corrado Gini in the first decade of the twentieth century.

12. Jeffrey Williamson and Peter Lindert, *American Inequality* (New York: Academic Press, 1980).

FIGURE 33-2 Lorenz Curve, Family Personal Income in the United States, 1983

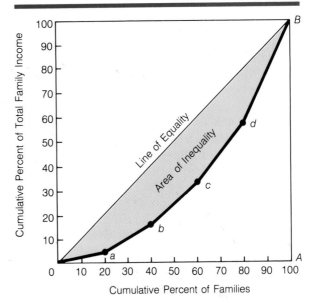

Point *a* shows the percentage of total income received by the lowest 20 percent of the families. Point *b* shows the percentage received by the lowest 40 percent of the families, and so on. The curved line connecting these plotted points is a Lorenz curve. The "line of equality" shows how the curve would look if incomes were distributed with perfect equality. The shaded area is the area of inequality. The Gini ratio is computed by dividing the area of inequality by the entire right-triangular area *0AB* of the lower right-hand half of the figure.

The figure is based on the data in Table 33-4(b).

remaining nearly constant. Williamson and Lindert do not explain these trends by changes in the functional distribution of income between labor and property. They claim the key factor is within the labor share, with a rise and then a fall in skilled labor wages in relation to unskilled labor wages. Their figures fit quite well with a theory about the distributional effects of economic development—that inequality increases in the early stages of development, but decreases later as physical capital accumulates and human capital becomes the key to further economic progress.

Economic statisticians have pointed out a number of flaws in the Gini ratio as a measure of inequality. One criticism is that these ratios may be affected by changes in the population itself. Because both young and elderly people on the average have lower incomes than prime-age workers, changes in the age pattern of the population will change the Gini ratio. Similarly, blacks and other minorities receive on the average lower wages than whites, so that changes in the racial mix may alter the ratio. For the United States, a Gini ratio designed to adjust for changes in variables such as age and race would probably show a stronger trend toward equality than is shown by the unadjusted ratio.[13]

Another criticism is that the statistics used to compute the ratio for the United States do not include government transfers in kind such as food stamps, subsidized housing, or subsidized medical care. These transfers rose during the 1970s and probably furthered the movement toward equality.

QUANTILE RATIOS Socialist countries do not use Lorenz curves and Gini ratios to measure inequality of income. Instead, they use a **quantile ratio,** which compares the percentage of total income received by the *highest k* percent of the population with the percentage of total income received by the *lowest k* percent. With the numbers from Table 33-4(b), we can illustrate this method as follows, where $k = 20$ and we are dealing with *quintile* ratios:

$$\frac{\text{percentage of income received by the highest 20 percent}}{\text{percentage of income received by the lowest 20 percent}} = \frac{45.08}{3.94} = 11.44$$

So for the United States in 1983, the quintile ratio was 11.44. A higher ratio would suggest more inequality, and a lower one would suggest less inequality. Changes among the middle-income ranges are ignored by this method. In practice,

socialist countries generally compute these ratios by comparing top and bottom tenths (deciles) or even top and bottom twentieths (semideciles) of the population, focusing even more on the extremes of the distribution and producing even higher ratios. One criticism of the socialist countries' distribution statistics is that they tend to compare wage rates rather than family incomes. In this way they hide two important sources of inequality: multiple-job holdings by individual workers and multiple-wage earning within households.

Why Inequality?

What are the major causes of inequality? A full answer to this question would require a long discussion of genetics, social conditions, and educational factors. Because our aim here is to give only a general understanding of why inequality persists, we shall simply list some of the major causes.

1. Genetic endowments Some people are born with either better or worse bodies, minds, and nervous systems than other people. Environmental factors cannot be counted on to cancel out such differences. More often, perhaps, they reinforce them, as when bright students go on to college and less-bright ones drop out of high school.

2. Environmental endowments Better or worse conditions and more or fewer facilities for health, safety, education, training, and socialization explain some income inequality. However, the child of rich, talented, and intelligent parents, brought up by a succession of expensive governesses, step-parents, tutors, and private schools under a cloud of unrealistic expectations, may get as poor a start in life as most children growing up in the slums.

3. Inheritances Wealth can be inherited. So can opportunities for education, training, and entry to meaningful jobs and professions—not to mention membership in exclusive trade unions, country clubs, and college Greek-letter organizations. Some studies suggest that education, not wealth,

13. Morton Paglin, "The Measurement and Trend of Inequality: A Basic Revision,"*American Economic Review,* Vol. 65, No. 5 (September 1975), pp. 598–609.

TABLE 33-5   Median Money Income of U.S. Households, by Racial Origin of Householders, for Selected Years, 1967–1983

| Year | Median Income (thousands of 1983 dollars) | | | | Ratios | |
	All Households	White	Black	Hispanic	Black/White	Hispanic/White
1967	21.3	22.2	12.9	—	0.58	—
1975	21.8	22.8	13.7	16.4	0.60	0.72
1983	20.9	21.9	12.4	15.9	0.57	0.73

Note: "Hispanics" are persons of all races who consider their first or native language to be Spanish. The term includes persons of all degrees of English-language fluency.

Source: Statistical Abstract of the United States, 105th ed. (1985), Table 743, p. 446.

is the most important mechanism of inheritance. Financial bequests are less closely correlated with heirs' economic status than are the number of years of education provided by parents.[14]

4. Discrimination   Inheritance can be a negative quantity. Just as some people inherit property and opportunity, others "inherit" the "wrong" race, sex, religion, or language. It is difficult to choose one's own parents. In the next section of the chapter, we shall have more to say about discrimination.

5. Economic change   Consider the workers on a Detroit assembly line. They "had it made" in the second, or possibly even the first, quintile of the personal income distribution in the late 1960s. Twenty-five years later, the demands for these workers' skills or human capital had been cut by three main factors: (1) automation and robotization, which have substituted machinery for the workers' skills within the factory; (2) OPEC, which for a decade reduced demand for automobiles, and especially for the heavy cars that the workers had been specially trained to make; (3) foreign competition, as more and more Asian workers acquired the same skills as American workers had, and in some cases more relevant ones.

14. John Brittain, *The Inheritance of Economic Status* (Washington, D.C.: The Brookings Institution, 1978).

6. Luck   There are elements of "pure blind luck" in every one of the above categories. But luck also enters in other ways as well. What if Shakespeare had never learned to read or write? And what if some super-Einstein capable of unifying all physics had not died at Auschwitz, Hiroshima, Stalingrad, Vietnam, or wherever he or she did die?

Discrimination and Inequality

Discrimination means that different economic opportunities are offered to persons on the basis of personal characteristics unrelated to the jobs themselves. The causes that we have just listed tell us that some inequality would exist even if there were no discrimination on such bases as race, sex, religion, or ethnic background. But the inequality that would exist in the absence of discrimination would not be strongly associated with sex, race, religion, and so on. However, it is clear that discrimination does exist. Data on incomes clearly reveal differences that are difficult to explain by the personal factors listed in the section above. Table 33-5 compares median annual incomes for white, black, and Spanish-origin households in the United States in 1967, 1975, and 1983. The incomes of black and Spanish-origin households are significantly less than those of white households. There is no clear evidence that the substantial differences are falling over time. Persistent differences of this size are strong evidence that discrimination is a cause of inequality.

The two panels of Table 33-6 compare incomes of households headed by males and females in 1983. "Headed by" means "who the principal income receiver was." Panel (a) shows that the annual income of the "female" households was significantly less than that of "male" households for all marital categories except possibly the frequently multiple-income families listed as "married, spouse present."

It is frequently maintained that much of the explanation for the significant and doubtless discriminatory inequality shown in Table 33-6(a) is the near-exclusion of women from high-paying and more prestigious occupations, and the concentration of female workers in a "pink ghetto" of "women's jobs"—nursing, social work, teaching, clerical and secretarial occupations, domestic service, and so on. This may be true, as argued by the feminist agitation for **comparable worth** in the pay scales for these jobs,[15] but it is not the whole story of the "gender gap" in income.

Panel (b) of Table 33-6 shows median annual earnings in 1983 for a number of generally high-ranking or high-prestige occupational categories. Only year-round, full-time employees' wages and salaries are compared. Although female/male ratios are generally larger than those of panel (a), female earnings were less than male earnings in each of these occupations. It is possible, of course, that these differences will shrink as women have

more time to work their way up to higher-paying levels in these occupations, but one cannot avoid the conclusion that discrimination (past and present) partly explains the inequality.

As you learned earlier, the economic case against discrimination is strong. Discrimination is not a rational policy for a profit-maximizing firm. Not only is discrimination ethically unfair to individuals, who deserve to be treated on their own merits, but it is wasteful not to make the best possible use of their resources in the economy.

Maldistribution

Maldistribution means excessive inequality or equality of personal income or wealth. Generally it implies that too much inequality exists. However, supply-side economics suggests that maldistribution can mean too much equality—with too little reward for hard work, risk-bearing, saving, and investment in physical and human capital. In these matters, equity and equality need not always move in the same direction.

Maldistribution may be individual, economic, or ethical. We shall consider each in turn.

INDIVIDUAL MALDISTRIBUTION Individual maldistribution means dissatisfaction about the particular people at the upper and lower ends of the income or wealth distribution. It may indeed be true, for example, that "good guys (and gals) finish last" in business. As Jonathan Swift said, "Mankind may judge what Heaven thinks of riches by observing those upon whom it has been pleased to bestow them."

ECONOMIC MALDISTRIBUTION Economic maldistribution theories raise the possibility that the market economic system may operate less well under some distributions than under others. One of the best known of these theories comes from John A. Hobson (1858–1940), an English economist whose doctrines influenced many, ranging from Lenin to Roosevelt, and whom Keynes recognized as a predecessor. Hobson believed that business depressions were caused by under-

---

15. Comparable worth means the basing of pay in different occupations largely on these occupations' scores on "scientific" point systems weighing, for example, the arduousness of the jobs, their education and experience requirements, and so on. The scores provide comparisons, independent of labor markets, between the "worth" of doctors (predominantly male) and nurses (predominantly female), or of truck drivers (male) and typists (female). Such systems are well designed to create and maintain labor shortages or unemployment, but are practiced in other connections when, for example, a Civil Service Commission or personnel office rates a job as Grade 5 or Grade 10, or when colleges pay teachers of chemistry and Romance languages on the same scale based on rank, age, and years in grade.

TABLE 33-6 Male-Female Money Income Comparisons, United States, 1983

(a) By Family-Status Categories

Category	Male (in thousands of dollars)	Female (in thousands of dollars)	Female/Male Ratio (percent)
All households	$25.5	$11.7	45.8
Married, spouse present	27.4	26.4	96.3
Married, spouse absent	15.8	8.9	56.3
Widowed	11.7	8.8	75.2
Divorced	20.6	13.5	65.5
Single, never married	17.4	13.3	76.4

(b) Median Incomes for Year-Round Full-Time Workers, in Selected Occupational Groups

Category	Male (in thousands of dollars)	Female (in thousands of dollars)	Female/Male Ratio (percent)
Administrators and officials, public sector	$29.7	$20.1	67.7
Administrators and officials, private sector	32.7	18.5	56.6
Engineers, architects, and surveyors	32.9	26.4	80.2
Natural scientists and mathematicians	31.4	25.7	81.8
Health diagnosing occupations	56.1	*	n.a.
Health assessment and treatment occupations	24.6	20.4	82.9
Technologists and technicians other than health	25.1	18.4	73.3
Lawyers and judges	47.4	*	n.a.
Teachers, post-secondary school	30.5	22.3	73.1
Teachers, all other	22.6	18.5	81.9

Note: The symbol (*) means that the sample was so small (in the opinion of census statisticians) that the results, if published, might be deceptive.

Sources: (a) Statistical Abstract of the United States, 105th ed. (1985), Table 736, p. 443; (b) Bureau of the Census, Current Population Reports, Series P-60, No. 146 (1985), Table 51, pp. 181, 185.

consumption (too little spending on consumer goods) and that this problem could be solved by redistributing income from the rich to the poor. However, the macroeconomics of Keynes says that government's taxing and spending policies and its control over banks and money can stabilize the economy and thus do the job that Hobson assigned to income redistribution. For this reason, interest in economic maldistribution has declined.

ETHICAL MALDISTRIBUTION Ethical maldistribution means that the income or wealth distribution does not correspond to some standard based on what is believed to be just or fair. Consider, for example, the doctrine of "justice is fairness," outlined by John Rawls, which concludes that complete equality is the best distribution.[16] Essentially, Rawls asks what sort of income distribution would be chosen by a person who had absolutely no idea what position he or she would occupy in it. Rawls supposes that if

16. John Rawls, A Theory of Justice (Cambridge, Mass.: Belknap Press of Harvard University Press, 1971).

we had no knowledge of the consequences of our own talents and circumstances, we would all choose equality in order to avoid the risk of poverty. In this construct, it is a person's *relative* income position that counts. It matters only whether you are better or worse off than those around you. It does not matter what the absolute size of your income is, as long as it is above the starvation level. In developing his theory, however, Rawls grants a case for some inequality. A higher income might be ethically justified for some person (presumably an inventor or innovator) who, in exchange for extra income for himself or herself, improves the absolute position of what Rawls calls "the poorest of the poor."

An entirely different ethical argument, this one presented by Robert Nozick, says that what matters in income distribution is the process by which it developed into whatever it is, rather than that end-state itself.[17] He argues that the present distribution is fair, no matter how nearly equal or unequal it may be, if the following conditions have been met: (1) An "original" distribution of abilities and property must have been fair, or at least no one can specify precisely to whom it was unfair and to what extent and who today represents those wronged by the unfairness. (2) All subsequent transactions must have been carried out without force or fraud.

To understand this argument better, consider the following story. Adams and Baker are about equal in income and wealth. By his own free choice, Adams saves and invests, leaving his son, Adams, Jr., a substantial income-yielding property and a degree from a college or university. In contrast, Baker, by his own free choice, enjoys the easy life and leaves his son, Baker, Jr., nothing at all. According to Nozick, the resulting distribution between Adams, Jr., and Baker, Jr., is entirely fair, no matter how unequal it is, because it resulted from the free choices of Adams, Sr., and Baker, Sr., without any force or fraud involved.

In the real world, you may wonder whether either condition 1 or condition 2 has been satis-

fied. Nevertheless, there is substance to Nozick's line of argument.

Another ethical argument is related quite directly to microeconomic analysis. John Bates Clark (1847–1938) was a leading American economist and one of the fathers of marginal analysis. Clark argued that, in an ethical sense, one deserves the marginal product of his or her labor and capital. Therefore, he said, whatever distribution results from the unrestricted operation of the marginal productivity principle is a correct one.

Again, objections arise. Is the owner of physical capital (machines and equipment) to be considered productive because his or her capital is? Does it matter whether this capital was inherited or accumulated by this person himself or herself? Or consider the income earned because of a professional education (human capital). Does it matter whether the education was financed by government or by gifts from alumni or educational foundations? Also consider the case of slavery. Southern masters often rented skilled and reliable slaves to other plantations and even to urban factories, collecting for themselves part or all of the wages paid the slaves.[18] Who was productive in these cases—the slave or the master? All of these objections relate to the institutions of private property in one form or another. But, as you already know, wages may not be equal to marginal revenue product in monopsonistic labor markets.

A COMPROMISE POSITION Since none of the maldistribution arguments that we have offered is entirely convincing, the door is open to compromise. Lester Thurow, a contemporary economist teaching at the Massachusetts Institute of Technology, has made the following suggestion: ". . . our general equity goal should be . . . a distribution of incomes for everyone that is no more unequal than that which now exists for the earnings of fully employed white males."[19] Thurow does not try to defend this proposition in

17. Robert Nozick, *Anarchy, State, and Utopia* (New York: Basic Books, 1974).

18. Robert Fogel and Stanley Engerman, *Time on the Cross* (Boston: Little, Brown, 1974).

19. Lester Thurow, *Zero-Sum Society* (New York: Penguin Books, 1981), p. 201.

TABLE 33-7 Thurow's Proposed Personal Income Distribution and Actual U.S. Distribution

Quintile	Percent of Total Income	
	Actual (1983)	Thurow's Proposal[a]
Fifth (highest)	45.1	36.7
Fourth	24.7	23.5
Third (middle)	16.4	18.2
Second	9.9	13.9
First (lowest)	3.9	7.7

a. Percentage distribution of earnings of fully employed white males, United States, 1977.

Source: U.S. Bureau of the Census, *Current Population Reports, Consumer Income 1977*, Series P-60, no. 118 (March 1979), p. 228; and Table 33-4(b).

ethical or operational terms but simply asserts that it would be better than the existing distribution or other suggestions.

Table 33-7 compares the Thurow distribution with the 1983 distribution, taken from Table 33-4(b). As you can see, his proposed distribution is closer to equality than the existing one for total income in the United States.

THE PARABLE OF THE BAMBOO FLUTE Before leaving the subject of maldistribution, we present the "parable of the bamboo flute," devised by the Indian economist Amartya Kumar Sen.[20] Suppose that only one bamboo flute exists and that it is to be given to only one of four persons, each of whom believes he or she deserves it. Table 33-8 describes these persons and their claims to the flute. One claims it because he or she made it, another because he or she has the most musical talent, a third because he or she is the poorest or has the greatest need, and a fourth because he or she will practice most. Which person should have the flute? In real life, there may also be a fifth claimant—the one who offers enough money

20. "Ethical Issues in Income Distribution," in A. K. Sen, *Resources, Values, and Development* (Oxford: Blackwell, 1984), p. 290f.

to buy the claims of the others. (Sen finds no ethical merit in mere economic demand.)

To make the parable more interesting to students, we have added to Table 33-8 a parallel list of claims relating to medical school admissions. Suppose there is one last vacancy in next year's entering class. Should it go to the one who studied the hardest as a premedical student, the one with the highest aptitude for medicine, the one who has obtained education so far under the most severe handicaps, or the one who will be most industrious as a medical student? Or, we might add, should it go to the one who can pay the most tuition?

REDISTRIBUTION METHODS

With the extension of democratic institutions, spokespersons for the poor have entered the political mainstream of the leading market-economy countries. In this section, we shall discuss redistribution methods in an equalizing direction. We begin with some familiar reformist measures and close with a brief note on more radical and socialist ones.

Progressive Taxation

Progressive taxation means that taxes take a larger percentage of income from those with high incomes than from those with low incomes. In individual income taxation, this is attempted through both substantial personal exemptions and increasingly higher tax rates as income rises. It has long been the standard means of redistributing income.

However, increasing doubt surrounds the effectiveness and wisdom of this instrument as it has evolved in practice. Over the years, more and more loopholes, preferences, and shelters have been built into the tax laws, greatly reducing their actual progressivity. The great expansion of the underground economy, caused partly by the desire to avoid taxes, also reduces its effectiveness. As measured by Gini ratios such as those

TABLE 33-8 The Parable of the Bamboo Flute

	Basis of Claim	
Claimant	Bamboo Flute	Medical School Admission
A	Made the flute	Studied hardest as premedical student
B	Most musical talent	Highest aptitude for medicine
C	Poorest claimant: greatest need	Has obtained education under most severe handicaps
D	Will practice flute most assiduously	Will be most industrious medical student

described earlier in this chapter, income after tax in the United States is only slightly more equal than income before tax.

Regressive Expenditures

Government social welfare expenditures are planned to provide goods and services that the poor could not otherwise purchase in private markets. Beginning with relief for the poor and elementary education for all, they have spread to higher education, social insurance, health care, and housing. These have become more powerful means of redistribution than the individual income tax. However, their net equalizing effect is reduced when higher-income people take advantage of these programs. It is often argued, for example, that state universities, when financed largely by sales taxes, are aimed at educating middle- and upper-class youth at the expense of taxpayers poorer than the students' families.

Price Fixing and Rationing

Minimum wages, food stamps, floors under farm prices, and ceilings on retail prices receive some support from people who hope that they will redistribute income. However, as equalizing devices, all look better on paper than they eventually become in practice. Minimum wage laws, for example, raise the wages of those poor workers who remain employed, but they reduce the num-

ber employed, at least in private profit-seeking businesses. They do nothing for those unable to find work at legal minimum wages. Similarly, farm price supports do little for the poorest farmers, who are for the most part subsistence farmers with only tiny cash crops to sell at any price. Also, retail price ceilings, with or without rationing, do not guarantee that goods will be available at the legal prices, even to honor minimum rations. An extreme case occurred in Japan under American occupation in 1945–1946. Extraordinary honesty and professional pride induced a Tokyo judge to limit his food to what he or his family could buy at controlled prices. He soon died of starvation or acute malnutrition.

Socialization of Wealth

Under socialist systems, most physical capital is taken over by the government or, if left in private hands, is taxed almost 100 percent ("socialization of the flow"). Much of the sentiment that favors these measures comes from a belief in the equalizing effects that they are expected to have. Both income and wealth appear to be more evenly distributed in socialist countries than in capitalist ones, but in no case does the distribution approach anything like complete equality. Even though government is expected to use a large part of the income from capital for investments to promote economic growth, it is not clear that socialist economies expand their production possibilities any faster than, or even as fast as, capitalist economies. Thus, even if greater equality is achieved, there may be slower improvement in the real standards of living. Whether the poor are actually better off under socialism remains an open question. Moreover, equalization of income is not necessarily the primary goal in socialist systems. We should not forget that Soviet dictator Josef Stalin considered egalitarianism to be a "petty bourgeois heresy" and favored substantial inequality of Soviet wages and incomes.[21]

Since Stalin's death in 1953, there has been some retreat from his hard-line anti-egalitarian position. The Soviet distribution of *labor* income remains unequal, but we must remember that the distribution of total income in capitalist countries is less equal than that of labor income alone. Also, we judge the Soviet distribution from published data on wage rates alone, not on family earnings. We can only guess at the distributional effects of multiple-job holding by individual Soviet citizens, and of multiple-wage-earner families in Soviet society. We believe that they result in greater inequality, because they do so in capitalist countries, but we cannot be certain.

SUMMARY

1. The problems of poverty and inequality are related but not the same. Inequality can exist without anyone being poor according to most definitions.

2. Poverty lines are estimated by four principal criteria: amenities, proportionality, budgetary, and public opinion. The results and implications differ. The budgetary criterion is the one most widely used.

3. Compared with the general population, families and single individuals below the poverty line are more likely to be nonwhite, to be very young, to be physically or mentally handicapped, to have had little formal education or training, to have records of criminal conduct or mental illness, to have no regular employment, to be members of households headed by females, or to have been

reared in economic backwaters. In general, the more of these handicaps that apply, the more likely is the family or individual concerned to be poor.

4. Antipoverty policies received great attention in the United States starting in the 1960s. Major programs include Aid for Families with Dependent Children, food stamps, subsidies for housing and medical care, and guaranteed minimum Social Security payments. These programs are controversial because of abuse, high costs, and adverse effects on work incentives.

5. Negative income tax proposals are among the reform suggestions for antipoverty programs. Three key elements in negative income taxes are a guaranteed minimum income to fight poverty, a rate of negative tax designed to preserve work incentives, and a breakeven income level that strongly influences the overall cost of the program. Conflicts exist among these elements. Besides these problems, there are political and administrative difficulties that might arise from negative income taxation.

6. Economists are interested in both the functional and the personal distributions of income, though there are many other ways of measuring inequality that apply to particular areas of study. The functional distribution is by income types, and the personal distribution is by income-size classes.

7. In the functional distribution, labor income amounts to over 75 percent of American national income and property income amounts to less than 25 percent. In the personal distribution, over 40 percent of personal income goes to the top fifth of recipients, and less than 5 percent goes to the bottom fifth.

8. Inequality of the personal income distribution is commonly measured in America and Western Europe by Gini ratios, based on Lorenz curves. In Eastern Europe, it is commonly measured by quantile ratios.

9. Changes in American inequality over time seem to depend more on the difference between the wages of skilled and unskilled labor than on the size of the labor share of total income.

10. There are many factors that may explain the continued existence of income inequality. Among

21. Abram Bergson, *The Structure of Soviet Wages* (Cambridge, Mass.: Harvard University Press, 1944), pp. 177–179.

these are genetic endowments, environmental endowments, inheritances, discrimination, and pure blind luck.

11. Several varieties of maldistribution can be identified, including individual maldistribution, economic maldistribution, and ethical maldistribution. There are many theories about whether particular income distributions are ethically justified.

12. Among the instruments for redistributing income, progressive taxation and regressive government expenditures are the most widely practiced in the United States. Price fixing and rationing are sometimes suggested as redistributional devices, though they typically fail in practice to accomplish this objective. Socialization of wealth sometimes is advocated as a redistributive measure, but this may have adverse effects on real income growth and is not necessarily a major aim in socialist systems.

DISCUSSION QUESTIONS

1. Explain the differences between the problems of poverty and maldistribution. Can either problem persist after the other is satisfactorily solved?

2. Explain the difference between "island" and "case" poverty in Galbraith's usage. Which variant do you think is more important in your community? In the United States as a whole?

3. What is the published poverty line? How well do you think it distinguishes the poor from the nonpoor? What if the American poverty line were applied to the population of Bangladesh or Haiti?

4. Developmental and child psychologists think the American standard of living leads to child neglect by forcing potentially poor parents to work full time to stay out of poverty. How important a social problem do you think this is?

5. Professor Robert J. Lampman (University of Wisconsin) distinguishes *income* poverty from other sorts of poverty, and from poverty in general. What other varieties of poverty might he have in mind?

6. Would a negative income tax be preferable to the present American "welfare mess"? Defend your answer.

7. Compare the Gini ratio and the quantile ratio as measures of income inequality. Which do you think is preferable? Defend your answer.

8. Dintinguish "ethical" from "economic" maldistribution. Is "bad ethics" necessarily "bad economics" or vice versa?

9. It has often been proposed to replace or supplement the federal income tax by a consumption tax (which excludes certain sorts of saving from the tax base). How would such a change affect the redistributive effectiveness of the tax system?

10. Compare the "fairness" concepts of Rawls, Nozick, and Thurow.

11. Many working-class married women have worked outside the home for a long time. With the rise of the women's movement, more middle-class and upper-class married women have also joined the labor force. What are the consequences of this change on the measured distribution of family income? (In your answer, assume that most married couples come from roughly similar income classes.)

12. As this is written, the American minimum wage is $3.35 per hour. It has been estimated that the productivity of the lower 10 percent of the labor force (with measured IQ under 85) does not justify employment at this wage rate. How do you think this problem should be handled? What is the distributional effect of doing nothing about it?

34 *Government Antitrust and Regulation Policy*

PREVIEW Competition in fairly free markets and government regulation in markets without competition can both work. Both can provide good results for society in terms of large levels of desired output at low prices. Consumer welfare is threatened, however, when companies find ways to limit competition and gain substantial monopoly control in markets where we depend on competition. Consumer welfare is also endangered when the government fails to regulate a market that is without competition or when it regulates it very poorly. It follows, then, that government has an important part to play in making sure that there is enough competition in those markets where competition is desirable and that regulation takes place and is effective in those markets where monopoly is desirable. This dual role of government is the subject of this chapter. In the first half we explain antitrust policy, and in the second half we deal with the regulation of certain actual monopolies.

In this chapter we examine the three major pieces of U.S. antitrust legislation—the Sherman Antitrust Act of 1890, the Clayton Act of 1914, and the Federal Trade Commission Act of 1914. Together they can be used to promote competition to almost any extent that is desired by the government.

We also trace the changing U.S. antitrust philosophy over the past one hundred years. By referring to a number of landmark court cases, we show how our antitrust laws have been used and interpreted. The discussion will be broken down into three parts: (1) monopolization, (2) mergers, and (3) price fixing.

We end the first half of the chapter with a discussion of international cartels, using the case of the Organization of Petroleum Exporting Countries (OPEC).

The second half of this chapter recognizes that competition may not be the best answer for all industries. Here we review the concept of natural monopoly and explain why the government sometimes gives certain companies public utility status.

Government regulation takes place on both the national and the state level. We mention some of the better-known federal regulatory commissions that are responsible for regulating certain industries. We also explain the theory of rate regulation.

During the eighty years following the establishment of the Interstate Commerce Commission in 1887, regulation in the United States continuously increased. By the mid-1970s the American public became concerned about the spread of regulation into a number of industries that seemed not to need it. We look at some of the problems of unneeded regulation and some of the efforts that have been made to reverse the trend. Deregulation, at first only a catchword, has to some degree become a reality.

ANTITRUST POLICY

The United States and many other industrialized countries of the Western world have long depended upon competition to provide the discipline that is needed for efficient allocation of scarce resources. When firms find ways to limit competition in such an environment, public welfare is in danger. Companies may restrict competition within their industries through certain practices such as agreements to limit output in order to be able to charge very high prices. Collusion among companies always aims at lessening or eliminating competition in their industry and at earning higher profits. Simply put, companies have a strong profit incentive to lessen or eliminate competition among themselves. In this way they act like monopolists. It stands to reason that this sort of behavior is more likely to occur in oligopolies, where there are "few" firms, than in industries that more closely resemble pure competition or monopolistic competition and which are made up of "many" companies. Also, oligopolies with rather high levels of economic concentration and with high entry barriers are more likely to act in a collusive way than are oligopolies with lower levels of economic concentration and with low barriers to entry.

For this reason, governments in the United States and other countries are on their guard against the dangers of anticompetitive practices. The government policy that deals with this threat to the public interest is called **antitrust policy.** It includes all of the executive, legislative, and judicial actions that aim at maintaining or restoring competition in markets where it is needed. Government may act directly to keep companies from colluding or from interfering with competition in other ways. Government may also use its antitrust powers indirectly by encouraging competitive market structures. For example, it may not allow a merger of two large firms in an industry that is already highly concentrated.

U.S. Antitrust Statutes

The policy in the United States has generally been to protect and foster competition. However, there are certain exceptions such as public utility pricing, which we explain later in this chapter, and some price freezes during times of war and rising inflation. The major laws that prohibit the restriction of competition are the Sherman Antitrust Act, the Clayton Act (including the Robinson-Patman Act and the Celler-Kefauver Antimerger Amendment), and the Federal Trade Commission Act (including the Wheeler-Lea Amendment).

THE SHERMAN ANTITRUST ACT During the quarter-century after the Civil War, big business in the United States was getting bigger, and many small businesses were driven out in the process. The public was very upset about these changes because they appeared to bring high prices for consumers and high income to giant firms. Some companies were able to eliminate competition almost completely by forming a **trust**—a device used by supposedly competing firms that allowed a central board of trustees to vote all of their stock. During the 1880s and 1890s, for example, John D. Rockefeller organized more than forty oil companies into the Standard Oil Trust, which nearly monopolized the whole crude and refined oil market in the United States.

In answer to what became a public clamor to do something about this "monopolization," both state and federal legislatures enacted antitrust laws. The U.S. Congress passed the first federal antitrust law, the **Sherman Antitrust Act,** in 1890. This law has two main parts. The first prohibits "every contract, combination in the form of a trust or otherwise, or conspiracy" that limits competition, and prescribes the penalties of imprisonment and/or fines for violators. The second part of the law prohibits monopolization or attempts to monopolize, again specifying the penalties for violators. Moreover, people or firms injured by a violation of the Sherman Act are allowed to sue for damages, and if successful, will be awarded an amount three times the actual damages suffered.

It soon became clear, however, that several problems had to be solved. One was that the Sherman Act was poorly enforced during its very early years. In fact, the government lost its cases against the whiskey and sugar trusts in the early 1890s. Besides the poor handling of cases, there was no government agency responsible for enforcing the Act. Therefore, at the urging of President Theodore Roosevelt, the Antitrust Division of the Department of Justice was created in 1903. Then in 1914 the Federal Trade Commission Act added a second enforcement agency—the Federal Trade Commission. Another major problem was that the language of the Sherman Act was too general and failed to state clearly just what practices were anticompetitive. The solution to this definition problem was the passage of the Clayton Act of 1914.

THE CLAYTON ACT The well-publicized Standard Oil and American Tobacco cases of 1911 directed public attention to certain restrictive practices. The **Clayton Act** was passed in 1914 to deal with four types of potentially anticompetitive business practices. These are: (1) price discrimination, (2) mergers, (3) exclusive dealing and tying arrangements, and (4) interlocking directorates.

PRICE DISCRIMINATION The practice of price discrimination by firms that have monopoly control was discussed at some length in Chapter 26 (see pp. 519–524). Recall that price discrimination is defined as a price differential that is not justified by a difference in cost to the seller. Section 2 of the Clayton Act prohibits such price discrimination when it "substantially lessens competition or tends to create a monopoly." The Act makes it illegal for a firm to try to drive out competitors in one of its geographic markets by charging a lower price to its customers in that market than in its other geographic markets.

It turned out that the language used in Section 2 still left some big loopholes. In fact, in the twenty-two years from 1914 to 1936 only eight price-discrimination cases (after all appeals) were decided in favor of the government.[1] Also, the retailing sector in the United States was rapidly changing during the 1920s and 1930s. Chain stores such as the A&P were replacing small independent retail stores. These independents and their supporters cried "foul" and argued that the large chain stores were winning in the competition against their smaller rivals mainly because they were able to get discriminatory price concessions from suppliers. Though the best explanation for the chains' success was actually their greater efficiency, the public outcry was politically powerful enough to cause Congress to amend Section 2. In 1936 the **Robinson-Patman Act** changed the language of Section 2 so that during the next thirty-five years over a thousand price-discrimination cases were decided in favor of the government.[2]

The Robinson-Patman Act is certainly the most controversial of all U.S. antitrust laws. Though in some cases it limits unfair pricing practices and so aids competition, in many other cases it simply protects competitors (keeps inefficient companies in business) and does not increase competition.

MERGERS We discussed merger, or the acquisition of one firm by another, in Chapter 28 (see pp. 556–560). There we explained that whether or not a certain merger has anticompetitive effects depends on the kind of merger and the conditions in the industry involved. Section 7 of the Clayton Act prohibited a company from acquiring the stock of another company if the deal would result in much less competition between *those two firms*. For this reason, it applied only to horizontal mergers. Vertical and conglomerate mergers were not covered by the Act. Also, since it dealt only with merger by stock acquisition, mergers in which a company acquired the assets of another company escaped the clutches of the Act. No wonder that more vertical and conglomerate mergers took place and that the horizontal mergers that did occur were completed through asset acquisition. It was not until 1950 that these loopholes were closed.

In 1950 Section 7 of the Clayton Act was amended by the **Celler-Kefauver Antimerger Amendment.** This new law covered asset acquisitions and eliminated the wording that made the Act applicable only to horizontal mergers. The Supreme Court has interpreted the Amendment as covering vertical mergers.[3] However, the Court has never heard a case in which it could offer a clear statement on the inclusion of conglomerate mergers. During the early 1970s several very promising conglomerate merger cases, including

1. F. M. Scherer, *Industrial Market Structure and Economic Performance*, 2nd ed. (Chicago: Rand McNally, 1980), p. 572.

2. Ibid.

3. Brown Shoe Co. v. U.S., 370 U.S. 294 (1962).

three by International Telephone & Telegraph, were headed for the Supreme Court, but they were settled out of court between the companies and the Department of Justice under the Nixon administration. It is quite strange that we do not even know whether conglomerate mergers—the most numerous and important of all mergers— are covered by merger-control laws passed as long ago as 1950. Some legislators and antitrust practitioners have called for new legislation to deal directly with conglomerate mergers. Others believe that the 1950 Amendment is sufficient.

EXCLUSIVE DEALING AND TYING ARRANGE- MENTS   Section 3 of the Clayton Act prohibits exclusive dealing and tying arrangements that substantially lessen competition or tend to create a monopoly. An **exclusive dealing arrangement** exists when a firm obtains the product of a certain supplier on the condition that it will not buy the products of competing suppliers. Often the buying firm that enters into such an agreement will receive in return the exclusive right to handle the seller's product in a particular market. For example, an exclusive dealing arrangement may be entered into between an auto manufacturer and a local auto dealership. The agreement may be that only cars produced by that manufacturer will be sold by the dealer and that the manufacturer will not sell its cars to any other dealers in that town. If many wholesale or retail companies are bound in this way, potential competitors for sales to these distributors will be severely hampered. In such cases, if these agreements are found to lessen competition substantially, they are illegal.

Tying arrangements are more often found to be illegal than are exclusive dealings. A **tying arrangement** is one that forces a firm to buy certain products along with certain other products. For example, the International Salt Company owned patents on two important salt-handling machines. One machine dissolved rock salt, and the other injected salt tablets into canned products during the canning process. Firms leasing these machines were required to purchase all the rock salt and salt tablets used in the machines from International Salt Company. In 1947 the Supreme

Court ruled that International Salt Company had violated the Clayton Act by preventing other firms from competing for the sale of salt to firms using International's machines.[4]

INTERLOCKING DIRECTORATES   Section 8 of the Clayton Act prohibits certain **interlocking directorates.** This term refers to a person serving on the boards of directors of two or more competing firms. The reasoning behind this provision was that such a person would be in a good position to restrict competition among the firms in which he or she had a policy-making role. Such "direct" cases of interlocking directorates are fairly easy to spot, and once the government decided to enforce Section 8 vigorously in the late 1960s, most were quickly eliminated. However, so-called "indirect" interlocking directorates seem to be outside the scope of the Clayton Act. These cases occur when directors of a firm—generally a bank— are placed on the boards of directors of various competing companies that do business with the firm (bank). For example, suppose that two directors, Mr. Pea and Mr. Pod, of the Wholesome National Bank serve on other boards of directors as well. Mr. Pea is on the board of ABC Computers and Mr. Pod is on the board of XYZ Computers. Since both ABC and XYZ do business with Wholesome National Bank, it is likely that when Mr. Pea and Mr. Pod get together at the bank, they discuss more than just bank business. They might even see to it that ABC and XYZ have a good, wholesome relationship.

THE FEDERAL TRADE COMMISSION ACT   The **Federal Trade Commission Act** was passed in 1914, the same year as the Clayton Act. It added a blanket statement outlawing "unfair methods of competition" to the illegal practices that had been listed in the Clayton Act. Among these unfair methods are corporate spying, boycotts, and bribing the employees of potential customers in order to get their business. The courts interpreted "unfair methods of competition" to refer only to the relationship among companies, and

4. International Salt Company v. U.S., 322 U.S. 392 (1947).

not to the relationship between firms and consumers. To fill this gap, the **Wheeler-Lea Amendment** to the Act was passed in 1938. It covered "unfair or deceptive acts or practices" aimed at the consumer. These include false advertising claims and deceptive packaging.

Possibly the most important provision of the Federal Trade Commission Act was its creation of the **Federal Trade Commission (FTC)** to enforce the law. The FTC supplemented the Antitrust Division of the Justice Department, as a second federal government antitrust agency. Its duty is to investigate and prosecute cases of unfair competition.

Antitrust Philosophy

How have these important U.S. antitrust laws been used and interpreted over the years? In answering this question, we shall discuss monopolization, mergers, and price fixing.

MONOPOLIZATION   Recall that Section 2 of the Sherman Antitrust Act prohibits monopolization and attempts to monopolize. What does that mean? Does the Act outlaw all cases of monopoly control (significant market power), or is it reserved only for those cases where a company abuses its monopoly control? The first answer to this question came from the Supreme Court in the 1911 Standard Oil case.[5] The Rockefeller brothers had gained a 90 percent market share of the important kerosene and lubricating oil markets of that time. They gained this control over a period of thirty or forty years, during which they acquired a large number of competing firms and engaged in **predatory price cutting** (price cutting aimed at forcing competitors out of business). The Supreme Court found Standard Oil guilty of violating Section 2 of the Sherman Act. However, the Court very clearly stated that it did so not just because of its "monopoly position," but rather because of Standard Oil's intention to become a monopoly and its unreasonable prac-

5. U.S. v. Standard Oil Co. of New Jersey, 221 U.S. 1 (1911).

tices in limiting competition. This focus on intent and conduct became known as the "rule of reason." The **rule of reason** means that substantial monopoly control alone is not against the law but that the intent to gain that control and the abuse of it make it illegal. In the same year the Supreme Court found the American Tobacco Company also guilty of violating Section 2 of the Sherman Act, again stating its "rule of reason" philosophy.[6] The Court held that the company's guilt was based on its hundreds of horizontal acquisitions and its unreasonable business practices such as predatory pricing and preventing competitors from dealing with suppliers.

Although the Standard Oil and American Tobacco cases were decided in favor of the government and both trusts were later broken up,[7] in 1920 the Supreme Court invoked the "rule of reason" to find the huge and powerful U.S. Steel (now USX Corporation) trust not guilty of violating Section 2 of the Sherman Act.[8] U.S. Steel clearly controlled prices during that period, but it did not undercut competitors to try to drive them out of business. The Supreme Court ruled that mere size and the possession of monopoly power are not offenses. Only when companies use their size and power to harm competitors are they in violation of the Sherman Act.

The "rule of reason" guided the Court for another twenty-five years after the U.S. Steel decision. It was not until the Alcoa case of 1945 that the Supreme Court reversed itself. Alcoa, like U.S. Steel, had a huge market share but had not abused it. The findings in the case reinterpreted Section 2 of the Sherman Act, saying that it did not condone "good" trusts and condemn "bad" ones, but rather that it forbade all trusts. Size alone became an offense because the possession of power could not be separated from the

6. U.S. v. American Tobacco Co., 221 U.S. 106 (1911).

7. Standard Oil was separated into thirty-three geographically determined subsidiaries, which later became Exxon, Standard Oil of California, Standard Oil of Indiana, Mobil Oil, and Standard Oil of Ohio. American Tobacco was separated into sixteen parts, including American Tobacco, Liggett & Myers, P. Lorillard, Reynolds, and a new American Tobacco.

8. U.S. v. U.S. Steel Corp., 251 U.S. 4–17 (1920).

abuse of that power. Alcoa's market share of 90 percent was "enough to constitute a monopoly."[9] The judge added that "it is doubtful whether 60 or 64 percent would be enough" and that "certainly 33 percent is not [enough]."[10]

The Alcoa decision was upheld by the Supreme Court in several important cases in the late 1940s and early 1950s.[11] In one of these cases involving the motion picture industry, Justice William O. Douglas stated that "monopoly power, whether lawfully or unlawfully acquired, may itself constitute an evil and stand condemned under Section 2 even though it remains unexercised."[12] The rule of reason was found to be unreasonable.

By the mid-1950s some backtracking took place. In a case concerning the monopolization of the cellophane market, Du Pont was found not guilty on the basis of the Supreme Court's willingness to accept a broad definition of what constituted the packaging materials market.[13] A number of cases that involved firms having a fairly large amount of monopoly control were initiated in the 1960s and 1970s, but these were resolved out of court or were thrown out of court altogether. Important cases that were settled out of court affected such firms as Eastman Kodak, RCA, AT&T, United Fruit, and General Motors. A case involving IBM that had been in court since 1969 was finally thrown out in 1982.

It is too soon to conclude that American antitrust philosophy has come full circle, with a return to a "rule of reason." What we can say, however, is that the view that "big is bad" is at least temporarily out of fashion.

MERGERS Closely related to monopolization is the practice of merger. It is the most common way for companies to gain monopoly control. As

you know, Section 7 of the 1914 Clayton Act and the 1950 Celler-Kefauver Amendment of that Act prohibit mergers that substantially lessen competition or tend to create a monopoly. How has this part of the law been interpreted by the courts? What has been the governing antitrust philosophy with regard to merger?

As we said earlier, the power of antitrust authorities was greatly increased by the passage of the Celler-Kefauver Antimerger Amendment in 1950. From 1950 to 1965 the Justice Department and the Federal Trade Commission initiated more than twice as many antimerger complaints as they had during the thirty-six-year life of the original Section 7 of the Clayton Act.[14] Furthermore, the government won many of these cases. In an important 1958 horizontal merger case, Bethlehem Steel Company, the nation's second-largest steel producer, was prevented from acquiring Youngstown Sheet & Tube Company, the sixth-largest steel firm.[15] In 1962 the Supreme Court ruled in favor of the government in a case that involved both a horizontal and a vertical merger. The Brown Shoe Company, which was primarily a manufacturer of shoes, acquired the G. R. Kinney Company, which also manufactured shoes, but was mainly in the retail shoe business. Although the two firms together accounted for only 4½ percent of shoe production in the United States and Kinney's market share at retail was only about 1½ percent, the Supreme Court did not allow the merger.[16] This decision was strengthened by a 1966 Supreme Court decision that ruled against the acquisition of Shopping Bag Food Stores by Von's Grocery Company. Von's accounted for less than 5 percent of the retail food market in the Los Angeles area, and the Shopping Bag Food Stores held less than a 3 percent share of the same market.[17] These and other 1960s cases made it clear that horizontal and vertical mergers of companies with as little

9. U.S. v. Aluminum Co. of America, 148 F. 2d 416 (1945).
10. Ibid.
11. These include the American Tobacco case of 1946, the Griffith Amusement Company case of 1948, the A&P case of 1949, and the United Shoe Machinery case of 1953.
12. U.S. v. Griffith Amusement Co., 334 U.S. 100 (1948).
13. U.S. v. E. I. du Pont de Nemours and Co., 351 U.S. 377 (1956).

14. F. M. Scherer, *Industrial Market Structure and Economic Performance*, 2nd ed. (Chicago: Rand, McNally, 1980), p. 548.
15. U.S. v. Bethlehem Steel Corp., 168 F. Supp. 576 (1958).
16. Brown Shoe Co. v. U.S., 370 U.S. 294 (1962).
17. U.S. v. Von's Grocery Co., 384 U.S. 270 (1966).

as 5 to 10 percent of the market share would be challenged and probably denied by the courts.

But what about conglomerate mergers? In Chapter 28 we showed that these accounted for more than three-quarters of all the mergers in the 1960s and 1970s. Earlier in this chapter we complained that no clear statement on the legal status of conglomerates has ever been issued by the Supreme Court. Many so-called conglomerate merger cases did reach the Supreme Court during the 1960s, and most rulings went in favor of the government. However, the rulings were not that conglomerate mergers were illegal, but rather that the mergers in question contained anticompetitive horizontal or vertical aspects or, in other words, that they were not conglomerate enough. As the Court became more conservative in the mid-1970s, chances decreased for a precedent-setting case refusing to allow a conglomerate merger merely on the grounds that the acquiring firm would become too large and powerful.

In early 1979, the Justice Department, the Federal Trade Commission, and certain members of Congress led by Senator Edward Kennedy tried to secure new legislation aimed directly at preventing large firms from becoming even larger through conglomerate mergers. One bill would have prohibited almost any merger between companies whose combined sales were $2 billion or more. Another would have required that mergers between companies where each had sales of $2.5 billion could take place only if the acquiring firm at the same time rid itself of an equal amount of business.[18] None of these bills was passed by Congress, and by the time President Reagan was elected to his first term in 1980, the "big is bad" philosophy had all but disappeared from Washington, D.C.

The first half of the 1980s were characterized by a much more friendly attitude toward merger. The concern has turned directly toward how a certain merger can be expected to affect efficiency and thus prices for consumers. Some predominantly horizontal mergers in highly concentrated

18. *The Wall Street Journal,* January 29, 1978, and January 17, 1979.

markets are still questioned, but vertical and conglomerate mergers are allowed to go through unchallenged. In 1981 Mobil, an oil company with $60 billion in sales, tried to acquire Conoco, another oil company with sales of $18 billion, and Marathon Oil Company with $8 billion in sales. In both cases, the Antitrust Division of the Justice Department announced that if the mergers went through, it would look into their effects on competition. In the meantime, du Pont acquired Conoco (a vertical merger), and U.S. Steel acquired Marathon (a conglomerate merger), both with the blessings of the Justice Department. But in 1984 the green light was given for Mobil to acquire Superior Oil, Texaco to acquire Getty, and Standard Oil of California (now Chevron) to acquire Gulf Oil. All three mergers contained a mixture of conglomerate, vertical, and horizontal aspects. In 1984 and 1985 mergers involving huge household brand-name firms were allowed to take place—Esmark by Beatrice Foods, Nabisco Foods by R. J. Reynolds, Carnation by Nestlé, General Foods by Philip Morris, and Richardson-Vicks by Procter & Gamble. At this writing General Electric Corporation is acquiring RCA for about $6.5 billion. Assuming that the terms will not change, this 1986 conglomerate and horizontal merger will be the largest non–oil industry acquisition ever made.

In 1982 the U.S. Department of Justice issued "Merger Guidelines" to update those that had been in effect since the late 1960s. The guidelines were further refined in 1984. The unifying theme of the new guidelines is that mergers generally play an important, positive role in the American economy, but that they should not be permitted in those cases where they create or enhance significant market power. The focus is on the postmerger concentration level of affected markets, as measured by the Herfindahl-Hirschman Index (HHI) of market concentration discussed in Chapter 28. Recall that the HHI is calculated by summing the squares of the individual market shares of all the firms in a market. A monopoly would have an HHI of 10,000 (100 × 100). The Department of Justice characterizes an industry with an HHI of below 1,000 as "unconcentrated," an HHI of between 1,000 and 1,800 as "moderately concentrated," and an HHI of over 1,800 as "highly concentrated."

PRICE FIXING The most steady and consistent part of the American antitrust policy has been with regard to price fixing. Agreements among competing firms to establish specific prices and to restrict output in order to maintain those prices have been prohibited in the United States ever since the passage of Section 1 of the Sherman Antitrust Act in 1890.

EARLY PRICE-FIXING CASES A precedent-setting case was decided by the Supreme Court in 1897. It involved a formal price (rate) agreement among eighteen western railroads that had engaged earlier in very damaging price wars.[19] The Court ruled that collusive agreements among competing firms to restrict output and fix prices was illegal *per se* (that is, illegal in any case, rather than just illegal in that particular case). That direct evidence of price fixing is enough to determine illegality was repeated by the Supreme Court in the 1927 Trenton Potteries case.[20] Remember that by this time the Court had adopted the "rule of reason" in monopolization cases, and there was concern that this rule might also be applied to price fixing. However, it was not. Even though the price-fixing arrangement in this case was weak and possibly "reasonable," the Court again stated its *per se* illegality decision. Reasonable or not, price fixing is against the law. With the exception of one Great Depression case in 1933,[21] the Supreme Court's blanket condemnation of price fixing has been consistent.

THE GREAT ELECTRICAL CONSPIRACY In spite of the Supreme Court's consistent action with regard to price fixing, each year many firms in many different industries are found guilty of this illegal practice. An outstanding case of price fixing

19. U.S. v. Trans-Missouri Freight Association, 166 U.S. 290 (1897).
20. U.S. v. Trenton Potteries Co., 273 U.S. 392 (1927).
21. Appalachian Coals, Inc. v. U.S., 288 U.S. 344 (1933).

in a highly concentrated industry is the "great electrical conspiracy" of the 1950s.

The case involved twenty-nine firms, including the two giants of the heavy electrical equipment industry—General Electric and Westinghouse. For a period of about seven years, the top electrical equipment executives from these companies met in hotel rooms, private homes, and resorts to fix prices, to share sales, and to rig bids on contracts involving some $7 billion worth of heavy electrical equipment. This practice began in the early 1950s, when the postwar demand had slackened and the industry had a great deal of excess capacity. The firms first resorted to price cutting to make use of their capacity and to sell their equipment, but this caused their profits to fall sharply. Getting together to discuss their mutual problems, they saw price fixing and market sharing as very tempting solutions. Clever ways of cutting down the number of meetings were worked out, such as "phase of the moon" pricing. This meant bidding high or low according to the moon's fullness.

The conspiracy did not come to light until a newspaper reporter noticed that several high bidders quoted exactly the same prices for transformers to be sold to the Tennessee Valley Authority. Before it was all over, seven executives were jailed, and fines totaling close to $2 million were levied. Hundreds of millions of dollars in damages have since been paid by the firms.

The Cartel

Price fixing may be practiced in a more formal setting than that described in the "great electrical conspiracy." A collusive arrangement among sellers that affects the level of their joint output and thus the price that they charge is called a **cartel**. Cartels depend upon companies' willingness to give up their independence in making their own decisions. For example, a group of companies that jointly controls all or most of the output of steel may decide that it pays for them to act together to limit their joint output so that they can sell it at a higher price. If, instead, each firm acted on its own, the whole industry's output would be much greater and the price much lower.

NATIONAL AND INTERNATIONAL CARTELS

Many people have never heard of any cartel except OPEC (Organization of Petroleum Exporting Countries). Actually, cartels are not rare, nor are they a new development. In the 1890s the sale of coal in the Ruhr Valley of Germany was conducted under a cartel known as GEORG. It allocated orders among different coal companies when the demand was low and rationed supply among buyers when the demand was high. In this way it effectively shut out all price rivalry. In the United States, certain agricultural producers' cooperatives operate as cartels.

International cartels for steel, copper, wire and cable, tiles, silica, vacuum cleaners, and phonograph records have been operating for many years in several Western European countries. For example, in 1953 Switzerland was found to be taking part in over 130 national and international cartels.[22]

THE INSTABILITY OF CARTELS

By joining a cartel, firms agree to reduce their output and to raise their price. Each firm is given a quota for production and sales that is lower than its sales volume before the cartel was formed. Once the members have all agreed to such changes, however, it will pay for any one firm in the cartel to break the rules set forth by the cartel. For example, a single firm may have been given a quota representing 10 percent of the total output that a cartel agrees to produce. The company will find it profitable to secretly produce and sell a little more than that amount. If it were to produce 10 percent more than its allotted output, only 1 percent would be added to the total output of the cartel. Such a small increase would not drive down the price very much. Because the company in our example would be selling 10 percent more output at a price that would be only slightly lower, it could earn a much higher profit. Of

course, the success of the company that cheats will depend upon how willing all other firms in the cartel are to abide by their quotas. If other firms in the cartel also produce more than their allotted quotas, the supply will rise enough to cause a large drop in price and finally to break up the cartel.

By its very nature, then, a cartel is unstable. If each firm in a cartel acts to maximize its own profit, the goals of the cartel cannot be met. Most successful cartels have been subject to the discipline of outside agencies, generally governments.

THE OPEC CARTEL

The cartel that has aroused the most attention in recent years is the international cartel known as OPEC (Organization of Petroleum Exporting Countries). It was formed in 1960 but was not very effective until the early 1970s. Among OPEC's members are Algeria, Ecuador, Gabon, Indonesia, Iran, Iraq, Kuwait, Libya, Nigeria, Qatar, Saudi Arabia, the United Arab Emirates, and Venezuela. In January 1971 the standard crude oil known as "Saudi Arabian Light" was selling for $1.10 a barrel. Two years later it was selling for $1.62. In October 1973 its price had gone up to $3.15 a barrel, and by January 1974 it sold for $7.11. In September 1975 the price of this crude oil was $11.50 a barrel, an increase of more than 1,000 percent in less than five years. For the next three years the price of OPEC crude oil increased only moderately, but in 1978 it once again took off, reaching $32 a barrel by early 1980 and $34 by mid-1982.

How can these dramatic price increases be explained? World inflation, a decrease in the excess capacity of crude oil in the United States and Canada, wars and revolutions in the Middle East, and a rising demand for petroleum products partly explain some of the increases. However, by far the most important part of the explanation is the ability of the OPEC cartel to restrict supply. Before the Yom Kippur war between some of the Arab states and Israel in 1973, the cartel was fairly ineffective. In fact, some members refused to abide by the quotas assigned to them. After the war a new unity emerged among the Arab states, allowing them to restrict effectively the supply of

22. Corwin D. Edwards, *Cartelization in Western Europe* (Washington, D.C.: U.S. Department of State), June 1964, p. 3.

crude oil. The fact that the arrangement worked so well for each of the members of the cartel further strengthened their determination. The Iranian revolution in 1978 reduced that country's previously large output to a trickle and brought a new wave of large price increases. Then came the war between Iran and Iraq, which further decreased supply and presented a new opportunity for increases in price.

What many economists had been predicting since the mid-1970s finally occurred in the 1980s. OPEC's monopoly prices reduced consumption, caused non-OPEC production to increase, and triggered cheating by OPEC members. World oil consumption decreased by almost 20 percent from 1979 to 1985 as consumers found ways to conserve oil and to use other fuels that were relatively cheaper. During that time period OPEC cut its production almost in half in an attempt to prop up prices. But that was not sufficient, since nonmembers of OPEC increased their combined production by at least one-third. Mexico tripled its output, Great Britain and Norway boosted North Sea output by about 60 percent, and other countries such as Angola, China, Colombia, Egypt, India, Malaysia, and the Soviet Union added new production as well. In 1973 OPEC accounted for 56 percent of world oil production, but in 1985 the same thirteen OPEC countries accounted for only about 30 percent. In 1983, for the first time in its history, OPEC reduced its official price from $34 to $29 per barrel. In January 1985 the price was further reduced to $28, but by that time the official OPEC price was no longer very important since at least 75 percent of its own members' oil sold at free-market prices.

Cheating has been a fact of life for OPEC from the start, but the progressively greater excess capacity that its members experienced increased the temptation. From the mid-1970s to the mid-1980s, when countries such as Nigeria, Ecuador, and Iran increased their production above their quotas, pleas for OPEC unity and Saudi Arabia's willingness to reduce its output below its quota, kept prices from plummeting. In December 1985 OPEC announced that it would no longer attempt to prop up oil prices by restricting its production. In other words, it had collapsed. At the time of

this writing in early 1986, we can imagine that either nonmembers of OPEC will join with OPEC in an enlarged cartel arrangement (formal or informal) or oil prices will fall considerably below the current official $28 level. Free market crude oil was transacted at prices in the range of $11 to $15 per barrel in the spring of 1986.

REGULATION POLICY

The philosophy that underlies antitrust policy is that competitive markets serve society better than do markets that are substantially monopolized. This philosophy agrees with the economic theories of competition and monopoly presented in earlier chapters. However, as we have said in discussing actual monopoly (see pages 506–507), there are some important exceptions. In order to stimulate research, most governments offer temporary legal monopolies in the form of patents. They also accept so-called natural monopolies on the grounds that in certain markets it is not efficient to have more than a single firm.

In government-enforced monopoly, there arises the question of whether or not the government should regulate the monopolies that it has created. For patent monopolies, government regulation makes little sense since the temporary monopoly granted by a patent is itself the incentive designed to stimulate research. Government regulation that would keep a patent holder from taking advantage of the monopoly position would not be helpful. Where patents are not involved, however, the case for government regulation is much stronger. If, indeed, the hope of gaining greater efficiency leads the government to put a company in a monopoly position in a market, government regulation may be in keeping with that goal. The reason for regulating a monopoly is that if government gives monopoly status to a firm, it must also guard against abuse of that monopoly power.

Nearly all American businesses are regulated by the government in some way. It is important, however, to point out the difference between social regulation and monopoly regulation. Most firms are subject to **social regulation,** such as environmental protection rules, food and drug rules, truth-in-packaging rules, and occupational health and safety rules. A much smaller number of companies, however, are subject to **monopoly regulation,** which covers a firm's level of output, its price, and the scope of its production. Firms in such fields as transportation, utilities (electric power and natural gas), and communications are sometimes granted a monopoly by government and then become subject to monopoly regulation. Such industries are called **regulated industries,** and they are governed not only by social regulation but also by monopoly regulation.

Natural Monopoly

A common reason why government grants a firm a monopoly position is that it is a natural monopoly. As you learned in Chapter 26, a **natural monopoly** refers to a market in which a single seller is required for efficient production. Cost conditions are such that it doesn't pay for more than one company to operate in such a market. Economies of scale—or the decrease in long-run average total cost as the level of output rises— are so important, relative to the limited demand in such markets, that only a single firm can take full advantage of them.

In most industries the minimum size at which a firm can be efficient is much smaller than the total demand in the market. For example, the market demand in the U.S. women's and misses' dresses industry can support thousands of efficient firms. Each firm's long-run average-total-cost curve may look like the one drawn in panel (a) of Figure 34-1. It shows that a firm in an industry such as women's and misses' dresses reaches minimum optimal scale at 100 units a day, while the market demand at the prices being charged is far greater—maybe 7,000 times that much. (Such a market is able to support 7,000 efficient firms.) However, in some industries the minimum size at which a firm can be efficient is much larger than the total quantity demanded in the market at the price being charged. An example might be a company running an electric trans-

mission system. Panel (b) in Figure 34-1 pictures the long-run average-total-cost curve for such a firm. It shows minimum efficient scale at 500 million units, while at the price being charged the total market demand is only 200 million units. (At no price sufficient to cover long-run average total cost would the quantity demanded be high enough to come even close to the minimum efficient scale of 500 million units.) In this way the firm is seen to be a natural monopolist since only a single seller is required for efficient production. If two or more electric transmission firms shared this market, each would have a much higher long-run average total cost than if it were a monopoly. In our example a single firm has an average total cost of 4.2 cents, but if two equal-sized firms shared the market, each would have an average total cost of 6.3 cents. Furthermore, if two or more electric transmission firms shared this market, competition among them would most likely bring about a monopoly anyway. If the market is shared unequally, the largest of the firms—the one that benefits the most from economies of scale—is able to charge a price lower than the average total cost of its somewhat smaller rival or rivals. After a while, all but the largest firm will be forced to exit, and the industry will become a monopoly. If, instead, the market is equally shared, so that no one firm has an advantage over another, we would still expect only one firm to survive. This is because marginal cost is below declining average total cost. In a competitive situation the market price is expected to be bid down to a level just above marginal cost, which will not be high enough to cover average total cost. If so, firms have an economic loss, and one by one they will leave the industry. The company that can hold out the longest will be the surviving monopolist.

Government Intervention

Should government intervene in markets that are natural monopolies? Many economists believe that it should. In its role of protecting the public interest, the government might be able to prevent some of the problems often associated with

FIGURE 34-1   Long-Run Average Total Cost: A Normal Industry and a Natural Monopoly

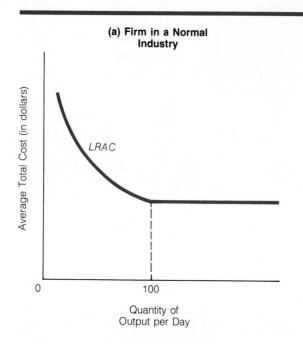

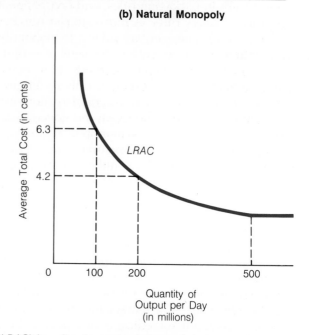

Panel (a) shows a long-run average-total-cost curve (*LRAC*) for a firm in an industry in which the minimum efficient scale is 100 units per day. This is one of a very large number of efficient firms that this industry is able to support since the market demand at the price being charged is far greater than 100 (700,000 units per day in the example on page 707).

Panel (b) shows a long-run average-total-cost curve

(*LRAC*) for a firm in a natural monopoly industry. Minimum optimal scale is 500 million units per day, but the total market demand at the price being charged is only 200 million units per day. This industry must be composed of a single firm in order to be efficient. A single firm has an average total cost of 4.2 cents. If, instead, two equal-sized firms shared the market, each would have an average total cost of 6.3 cents.

natural monopolies. First, if firms were to compete actively, much waste of economic resources would take place. For example, four electric transmission firms might each lay a transmission line when one would be enough. Second, as already explained, severe price competition among the firms would eventually drive out all but one firm. Consumers would then suffer from the restricted output and high prices of an unregulated monopolist. Third, firms might anticipate ruinous competition and so enter into a collusive agreement to avoid price competition. The result would be a waste of resources stemming from unnecessary duplication of facilities along with restricted output and high monopoly prices. Finally,

firms may not enter such industries at all. They may expect that collusion will fail and that they will only be involved in ruinous competition. If companies avoid such industries altogether, consumers would be without some essential services.

For these reasons the government often tries to recognize the industry as a natural monopoly before firms begin operation and the undesirable results occur. Sometimes the government itself will go into such a business, but more often it will give a special status to a private firm.

PUBLIC ENTERPRISE   On the federal, state, and local level, government may decide to provide a **public enterprise** (a government monopoly).

Among the many such enterprises run by the federal government are the U.S. Postal Service, the Tennessee Valley Authority (TVA), which provides electric power for residents in that region of the country, and Amtrak, which operates railroads in some parts of the United States. State governments generally monopolize lotteries, ports, and parks. Some states go even further. Nebraska, for example, is the only provider of electricity in the state. Finally, local governments often operate public enterprises for such utilities as water, sewage disposal, garbage disposal, some forms of transit, and such social services as libraries, museums, zoos, and cemeteries.

REGULATED PUBLIC UTILITIES More often in the United States, however, government chooses to regulate privately owned companies rather than to go into business itself. Certain firms are given **public utility** status. This means that the government provides them with monopoly positions in their own markets—presumably because it has recognized those markets to be natural monopolies. Even if a certain market is not really a natural monopoly, the company that is chosen to become a public utility is given an exclusive franchise and is subjected to government regulation at all times. Whether this turns out to be in the public interest will depend upon whether or not the market really is a natural monopoly and, if it is, whether or not it is regulated well enough.

Regulatory Commissions

Both state and federal governments regulate public utilities through regulatory commissions. Most of the states regulate local electric, gas, and telephone service, as well as railroad, bus, and trucking service. Some of the states also regulate water, sewage, pipelines, warehouses, taxis, and cable television. State public utility commissions are generally made up of three to seven commissioners who set policy and from forty to a thousand engineers, lawyers, accountants, and economists who act as support staff.

On the federal level there are many regulatory bodies. These have authority over interstate mar-

kets. The best-known ones are the Interstate Commerce Commission (ICC), the Federal Communications Commission (FCC), and the Federal Energy Regulatory Commission (FERC). These commissions have from five to seven members and staffs of about eight hundred to two thousand people.

Regulation

Regulatory commissions become involved in almost all parts of a regulated company's business. However, the most important of their duties have to do with pricing or the setting of rates. They are interested in the level and the structure of these rates.

THE LEVEL OF RATES When the government assures certain firms of a monopoly position, it has a duty to protect society from any harmful actions of the monopoly. But what rate level should regulated firms be allowed to charge? What return on invested capital should they be allowed to earn? In the language of regulators, the general answer is "a fair return on a fairly valued rate base." What this answer means in the language of economists is "normal profit on replacement cost of capital." **Normal profit,** you will recall, is the opportunity cost of a firm—the minimum amount that it must earn in its industry in order for it to remain in this business. **Replacement cost** refers to the method of determining the value of capital (the rate base) by estimating what it would cost to replace it.[23] Earning a normal profit on replacement cost of capital means that consumers will continue to receive the services provided by these firms, yet the minimum amount

23. Other methods of determining the value of capital are "original cost," which uses the amount that the firm originally paid for its capital minus depreciation, and "reproduction cost," which uses what it would cost the firm to literally replace its present capital. Economists find "replacement cost" to be the fairest valuation of a firm's rate base because inflation causes "original cost" to be unrealistically low and technological change causes "reproduction cost" to be unrealistically high. Replacement cost allows for the fact that technological change may force the firm to replace its equipment with different (more productive, new-generation) equipment.

of resources needed for supplying these services will be used. It also means that regulated firms will have no difficulty in attracting further resources for necessary replacement and expansion, since the regulated firms are earning a rate of return that is equal to what they have to pay to borrow funds in financial markets.

One problem connected with rate regulation is that it may discourage cost efficiency. If commissions use a cost-plus-normal-profit formula, firms have no incentive to use lowest-cost methods, and their higher operating costs plus a normal profit will just be passed on to consumers. Regulatory commissions are aware of this problem and have tried to offer incentives to keep costs down. Also firms can sometimes gain a temporary benefit from cost cutting through **regulatory lag.** This term refers to the length of time it takes a regulatory commission to bring about a rate change that reflects a regulated company's change in average total cost. Regulatory lag works against the firms when average total costs are rising. During periods of high inflation, regulatory lag can place a heavy burden on public utilities. For example, during the double-digit inflation period of the late 1970s and early 1980s a number of states were so concerned about regulatory lag that they eliminated it by adopting rules that provided for automatic pass-through of higher utility-firm costs to consumers in the form of higher rates.

The economic theory of the rate regulation of a natural monopoly is illustrated by the three different cases shown in Figure 34-2. Panel (a) shows an unregulated monopolist in a natural monopoly market. The company maximizes its profit (where its marginal-cost curve, MC, intersects its marginal-revenue curve, MR, from below) when it produces 22 units a day and sells them for $8 a unit. Notice that the price of $8 is well above the firm's marginal cost of $3. The loss of consumer welfare that stems from monopoly pricing was discussed in Chapter 26. In this case, some consumers who are willing to pay a price greater than marginal cost are denied the use of the product. The firm earns economic profit of $2.20 a unit, or $48.40 a day ($8.00 − $5.80 = $2.20; $2.20 × 22 = $48.40).

Panel (b) in Figure 34-2 shows the same firm, but under very different conditions. In this case the firm is regulated. Furthermore, the regulatory commission requires the firm to act like a pure competitor—that is, to equate its price to its marginal cost. The reasoning behind this policy is that it provides the social optimum as it avoids restriction of output and monopoly pricing. Indeed, it does. This firm in our example produces 48 units a day (where its marginal-cost curve intersects its demand curve) and charges a price of $3.50. However, you will notice a problem. Since average total cost is falling, marginal cost is below it. This means that the firm will suffer an economic loss. In our example, average total cost is $4.90 while average revenue is $3.50, so that the firm has an economic loss of $1.40 a unit, or $67.20 a day ($1.40 × 48 = $67.20). Here we see the regulatory dilemma. Unless the government gives the firm a subsidy equal to the economic loss—so that it will earn a normal profit— the firm will eventually leave the industry.[24] When this happens, the consumer will not receive the product, and welfare will be diminished.

Panel (c) shows the same firm under still different conditions. It is regulated as in the previous case, but this time the regulatory commission recognizes the regulatory dilemma—that without a government subsidy, marginal-cost pricing would cause the firm to exit—and so it requires the company to set its price equal to average total cost. This ensures a normal profit—the fair return that regulatory commissions seek to provide. The firm in panel (c) of Figure 34-2 produces 38 units a day (where its average-total-cost curve intersects its demand curve) and charges a price of $5.20. Since a normal profit is always included in average total cost, charging a price equal to average total cost allows the company to earn a normal profit. This case offers a solution that deviates from the

---

24. In order not to clutter the diagram, we have not included the firm's average-variable-cost curve. If we had, we could see whether or not the firm will shut down in the short run. It will shut down if its average variable cost is above $3.50. If its average variable cost is below $3.50, it will continue to produce in the short run. In either case, it will exit in the long run.

FIGURE 34-2 **Alternative Pricing by a Natural Monopolist**

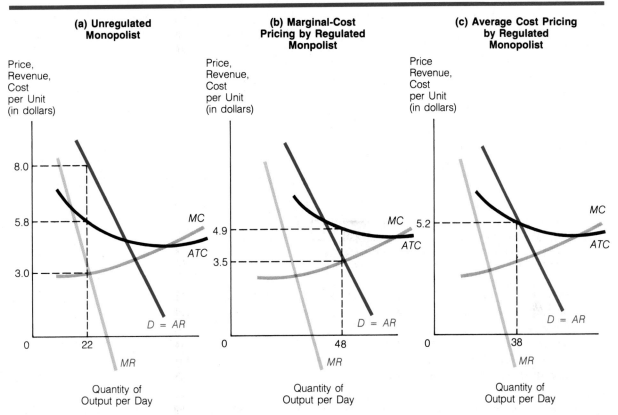

Shown are the demand or average-revenue (*D = AR*), marginal-revenue (*MR*), marginal-cost (*MC*), and average-total-cost (*ATC*) curves for a firm in a natural monopoly market under three different conditions. Panel (a) shows this firm's equilibrium position (a level of output of 22 units and a price of $8.00) when it is not regulated. Panel (b) shows this firm's equilibrium position (a level of output of 48 units and a price of $3.50) when it is required by a regulatory commission to set its price equal to its marginal cost. Panel (c) shows this firm's equilibrium position (a level of output of 38 units and a price of $5.20) when it is required to set its price equal to its average total cost.

The case shown in panel (c) provides the firm with only normal profit, whereas the firm earns economic profit of $2.20 per unit of output ($8.00 − $5.80) in the case shown in panel (a) and economic loss of $1.40 per unit of output ($4.90 − $3.50) in the middle case.

social optimum, but in the absence of a government subsidy is a more sensible solution than either of the two other cases. The firm is not allowed to take advantage of its monopolistic position by earning an economic profit as was true in our case of the unregulated monopolist. Nor is the company regulated to the point of an economic loss (leading to exit) as in our case of the firm that had to equate its price to its marginal

cost. Regulatory commissions aim at setting rates that generate average revenue equal to firms' average total costs. Of course, the question still remains as to whether or not this solution is better than a government-subsidized social optimum solution.

THE RATE STRUCTURE Regulatory commissions are interested in more than just the level of rates

711

set by firms. They are also interested in the **rate structure,** which refers to the variation in rates that are charged according to such variables as customer classification, quantity purchased, and time of delivery. Price differentials based upon any of these criteria may or may not reflect the difference in the cost of providing the product. Remember from Chapter 26 (page 520) that a price differential that is not based on the difference in cost is price discrimination. Since public utilities are monopolists, they can sometimes keep different classes of customers separate, and often face different elasticities of demand among customer classes. These industries are likely areas for price discrimination to take place.

For example, if a home user of electricity requires more costly services than does a business customer, the rate differential will be discriminatory if the rate paid by the residential user is either greater or smaller than the difference in unit cost. At the same time, the greater use of electricity by business customers may justify certain lower unit rates. The actual rate differences may or may not be discriminatory. Rate differentials may also be justified by the time of day or week or year that the electricity is demanded. For example, an electric utility firm must build up its capacity so it can supply enough electricity at the peak level of demand, as on the hottest days of the summer when air conditioners are on at full blast. Customers who use electricity mostly during off-peak times, when there is excess capacity in the system, can be served at a relatively low cost. Higher rates should be paid by peak-load users to finance the otherwise unneeded capacity. Most regulatory commissions encourage price differentials, but try to avoid price discrimination. They want prices to reflect costs so that greater efficiency may be gained.

Deregulation

Regulation has been a part of U.S. economic policy for a hundred years. An 1887 landmark court case, Munn v. Illinois, set the general precedent that monopolies can be regulated to protect the public interest. Soon afterward the

ICC was created to regulate railroads. After the turn of the century, regulation began to spread, but it became fully established only in the mid-1930s. For the next quarter of a century, regulation was little questioned. It was the way to control an ever-increasing number of American industries. Besides the traditional regulated industries such as railroads, telephone and telegraph service, and electric power, regulation also covered trucking, airlines, natural gas, television broadcasting, cable television, taxis, and others.

During the 1960s some economists suggested that certain regulated industries that had been natural monopolies when they were first regulated had over the years attracted actual and potential competition and should therefore be deregulated. For example, the wider use of trucks and more superhighways to drive them on meant actual and potential competition for railroads. A more recent example where technological change altered the status of an industry is long-distance telephone service. This industry was a natural monopoly when telephone lines had to be laid, but no longer is a natural monopoly because of the introduction of modern microwave transmission.

In the early 1980s several economists suggested that even if a market is a natural monopoly, it may still not be a good candidate for regulation.[25] They say that in **contestable markets** (markets that are very easy to enter and leave) potential competition will keep a monopolist from charging high prices. For example, it may be efficient for only a single airline to provide passenger service between two specific cities. Yet this monopoly firm need not be regulated if other airlines have access to this market (route). If the airline flying between these two cities charges a monopoly price, another airline can easily enter this route and be successful by offering somewhat lower prices.

Those who favor deregulation also point to economic studies showing that many public utilities invest in too much capital equipment in order to broaden their rate base. Others show that regulation has prevented new competitors and the

25. William J. Baumol, John C. Panzar, and Robert D. Willig, *Contestable Markets and the Theory of Industry Structure* (San Diego: Harcourt Brace Jovanovich, 1982).

introduction of new technologies, both of which would lead to better service and lower prices.

In the 1970s more voices joined the call for deregulation. Inflation, rising energy prices, and environmental protection issues all touched upon the performance of regulated industries. And perhaps just as important, economic education had spread the word that competition was a good thing. When deregulation was proposed, the regulated firms and their employees cried "foul." The public was shocked to learn that those who opposed deregulation the most were the regulated firms themselves. Contrary to what it had been led to believe, the public began to realize that the regulated firms were not shackled in chains by the commissions, but instead had to some degree captured their regulators. Many had developed a cozy relationship in which firms were all but guaranteed the "good life"—a good return on their investment and no trouble from competitors or would-be competitors.[26]

The first serious political rumblings in favor of deregulation were heard during the Nixon administration in the early 1970s. These views were picked up by President Ford in the mid-1970s, and this time attention was directed specifically at the airline and trucking industries. In 1977 President Carter continued the effort, which finally led to the Airline Deregulation Act of 1978 and the Motor Carrier Act of 1980. The Airline Deregulation Act called for a gradual decrease of the control of routes and fares by the Civil Aeronautics Board (CAB) ending in its elimination in late 1984. New airlines have entered the industry, and established airlines have entered new routes. Air fares have been substantially reduced, and fewer empty seats are flying in the sky. One exception is the international portion of the airline industry, which had not been deregulated—as of late 1985 about five hundred ex-CAB personnel were busy regulating international routes and fares from their offices in the Department of Transportation.

The Motor Carrier Act diminished the regulatory powers of the Interstate Commerce Commission (ICC), which had been regulating almost every aspect of trucking since 1935. As a result, the first half of the 1980s witnessed the entry of thousands of new trucking firms, improved services (such as guaranteed delivery time), and substantially lower prices.

Deregulation has also occurred in other industries, including the railroad, taxicab, bus, petroleum, natural gas, telecommunications, broadcasting, cable TV, stockbrokerage, and banking industries. Deregulation has been in various degrees and has accomplished uneven results. It has brought massive restructuring in the railroad industry. The clearest success of deregulation in telecommunications has been in the equipment segment of that industry. Relatively little regulation is left in the broadcasting and cable TV industries. Some taxicab markets, such as Boston and New York City, are still highly regulated. Others, such as San Diego and Kansas City, have begun to deregulate. Deregulation in the stockbrokerage industry has significantly lowered the average price paid to make a stock market transaction. Finally, banking deregulation has eliminated interest-rate ceilings and has blurred the difference among the functions of varying financial institutions such as commercial banks, savings and loan associations, and credit unions.

SUMMARY

1. The firms in an oligopolistic industry, more so than firms in a purely competitive or a monopolistically competitive industry, are susceptible to collusion aimed at lessening or eliminating competition among them so that each can earn a higher profit. The government policy that deals with this threat to the public interest is called antitrust policy. It includes all government action aimed at maintaining or restoring competition.

---

26. A few examples follow. A trucking firm was required to have a "certificate of public convenience and necessity" issrued by the ICC in order to be able to haul certain goods over a particular interstate route. An airline had to be certified by the Civil Aeronautics Board (CAB) in order to fly passengers between two cities. In order to broadcast on the radio or on television, a license has to be obtained from the FCC. Before a new gas pipeline can be run, the FERC must approve it. Driving a taxi in some large cities requires a license in the form of a medallion.

2. In reaction to a large amount of monopolization during the quarter of a century after the Civil War, the first federal antitrust law, the Sherman Antitrust Act, was passed in 1890. It prohibited the restriction of competition, monopolization, and attempts to monopolize.

3. In order to be more specific about firms' actions that are likely to restrict competition, Congress passed the Clayton Act in 1914. It dealt with four types of potentially anticompetitive business practices: (a) price discrimination, (b) mergers, (c) exclusive dealing and tying arrangements, and (d) interlocking directorates. Two of the sections of the Act were beefed up in later amendments—the price-discrimination section in the Robinson-Patman Act of 1936 and the merger section in the Celler-Kefauver Antimerger Amendment of 1950.

4. The third major piece of antitrust legislation, the Federal Trade Commission Act, was also passed in 1914. It prohibited unfair methods of competition among firms, and after the Wheeler-Lea Amendment in 1938, it also covered unfair and deceptive practices toward consumers. In addition, the Act set up a second enforcement agency. The Federal Trade Commission was added to the already established (1903) Antitrust Division of the Justice Department.

5. The Sherman Antitrust Act prohibited monopolization or attempts to monopolize, but it was left to the courts to interpret just what that meant. From the time of the Standard Oil case in 1911 until the Alcoa case in 1945, the Supreme Court adopted a "rule of reason," which focused on intent and conduct rather than on the presence or absence of substantial monopoly control. The Alcoa case and several others that followed in the late 1940s and early 1950s overturned the "rule of reason" and made monopolization itself illegal. Since then some backtracking toward a "rule of reason" has occurred.

6. Mergers that substantially lessen competition are illegal under the Clayton Act, but because of certain loopholes the Act had limited power until the Celler-Kefauver Antimerger Amendment in 1950. During the 1950s and 1960s the government impressively won a number of horizontal and vertical merger cases. However, the Supreme Court was not given a good opportunity to make a definitive statement regarding conglomerate merger. Attempts in the 1970s to pass new legislation that would prevent huge firms from making acquisitions failed. In the first half of the 1980s the "big is bad" philosophy was pretty well discarded, and acquisitions by huge firms of other huge firms were given the government's blessings.

7. Ever since the passage of the Sherman Antitrust Act in 1890, the courts have ruled that price fixing—the agreement among competing firms to restrict output in order to maintain high prices—is illegal. Despite the "rule of reason," the Supreme Court's blanket condemnation of price fixing has been consistent.

8. A cartel is a collusive arrangement among sellers to fix output and prices. Cartels are inherently unstable. It pays for individual members to cheat because they can sell additional output at monopoly prices. However, when cheating becomes widespread, the level of industry output increases so much that monopoly prices can no longer be maintained. The best-known cartel is OPEC. For the decade beginning with 1973 it was quite successful in restricting the supply of crude oil and raising its price. Since that time the combination of lower demand, lower market share, and cheating by various OPEC members has seriously eroded OPEC's ability to control the world oil market.

9. Some industries, called "regulated industries," are granted monopoly status by the government. In return they are regulated so that they are not able to take advantage of their monopoly power. Such "monopoly regulation" is in addition to the usual "social regulation," to which most firms are subject.

10. Most regulated industries are diagnosed as natural monopolies. A natural monopoly is a market in which a single seller is required for efficient production. Economies of scale are so great in relation to the quantity demanded in the market that only one firm can take full advantage of them. If more than one firm operated in a natural monopoly market, price competition among them would cause all but the strongest firm to leave the market.

11. The government attempts to recognize an industry as a natural monopoly before firms begin operation and ruinous competition takes place. In such instances the government may establish a public enterprise, but more likely it will grant a private firm public utility status and then regulate it. Regulation takes place by both state and federal regulatory commissions. The three most prominent federal regulatory commissions are the ICC, FCC, and FERC.

12. Regulatory commissions concern themselves mainly with the prices that public utilities charge. They regulate both the level of rates and the structure of rates. They seek to set a rate level that gives public utility firms a fair return on a fairly valued rate base. This is usually interpreted as normal profit on the replacement cost of a firm's capital. Regarding the structure of rates, firms have an incentive to charge different rates according to the class of customer, the quantity purchased, and the time of delivery. Regulatory commissions encourage price differentials based on cost differences, but try to prevent price discrimination.

13. Until the 1960s few economists and government officials questioned the appropriateness of regulation. But in the 1960s and more so in the 1970s, suggestions to deregulate were frequently heard. Because of technological change, some industries no longer were natural monopolies. Some natural monopoly industries were recognized to be contestable markets, in which regulation actually prevented new firms from entering and offering better service and lower prices. The public also became more disenchanted with regulation because of high prices and a greater recognition that regulated firms had in many cases captured their regulators. Recently various degrees of deregulation have occurred in many public utility industries, the outstanding example being the domestic airline industry.

DISCUSSION QUESTIONS

1. List and briefly describe each of the most important U.S. antitrust laws.

2. In retrospect, how reasonable was the U.S. Supreme Court's "rule of reason"?

3. What is meant by a cartel? Cartels are said to be very unstable. Why is that so? Why, in your opinion, did the cartel known as OPEC remain relatively stable over most of the 1970s and early 1980s?

4. Suppose that you were hired to manage a cartel made up of the copper-producing companies of the world. How would you manage the cartel? What rules would you set and how would you justify them to your members?

5. What are the characteristics that enable economists to single out industries as "natural monopolies"? Give two examples of industries that are probably natural monopolies. Give one example of a regulated industry that is probably not a natural monopoly.

6. "Regulatory agencies are doing consumers a disservice when they compel natural monopolies to equate price to average total cost rather than to marginal cost." Do you agree or disagree? Explain.

7. "Government is really very inconsistent; the United States has a whole lot of antitrust laws designed to combat monopolization but at the same time it gives some firms an exclusive right to operate an entire industry." Do you agree or disagree? Explain.

8. Once government recognizes an industry to be a natural monopoly, it has a choice between providing a public enterprise or conferring public utility status on a private firm. Suppose that you were in a government position that called for you to make a recommendation on this matter. What would you recommend and why?

9. Under what condition does the theory of contestable markets argue against government regulation of natural monopoly industries?

35 *International Microeconomics: Free Trade Versus Protection*

PREVIEW The choice of free trade versus protection has been a key policy issue for generations and centuries. In the past, it was a conflict between market and planning principles. Those who favored free trade believed that competition among trading countries would lead to greater economic efficiency. Those favoring protection felt that a certain amount of protection of domestic industries from the effects of trade with other countries was necessary for effective economic planning.

We begin with a simple case of a freely traded standardized product in a freely competitive world. We discuss gains and losses in both importing and exporting countries from trade in such a product. Then we turn to a second question: Which goods will a country export when free trade is opened up, and which goods will it import? This leads to the classical idea of "comparative advantage," and the various reasons or explanations for its existence. One explanation is based on differences in productive efficiency, and another on differences in "endowments" of resources or factors of production.

Next we examine the gains from trade between two or among several countries and the effects of trade on wages and interest rates in the trading countries. You will see that free trade has much the same effect as free immigration or free movement of capital in equalizing wages and interest rates between countries. This is called "factor price equalization."

So much for free trade. Next we define *protection* and consider some of protection's many forms: tariffs, export duties, quotas, antidumping duties, and administrative protection, including an important distinction between *nominal* and *effective* rates of protection. We present a number of arguments for protection. Some of these are economic, relating to such questions as "cheap foreign labor" and helping "infant industries." Others are non-economic, such as those related to national defense and the dangers of boycott or blockade. These formal defenses of protection, however, may have little to do with its wide popularity. Many economists believe that its popularity is due largely to the activities of "intense minorities," otherwise known as "special interests."

The last major subject that we cover is international negotiation. Trade treaties are discussed first and then customs unions and free trade areas, which can be viewed as attempted compromises between free trade and protection.

GAINS AND LOSSES FROM TRADE

The basic principles of international trade are among the best established in the whole field of economics. Economic arguments for free trade were prominent in the writings of the classical economists of England in the eighteenth and nineteenth centuries and fitted in well with the trading interests of an island nation.

The basic case for free international trade is an extension of the case for free trade among individuals. For individuals, the freedom to engage in trade makes it feasible for each person to specialize in the tasks for which he or she is relatively well suited. As each person specializes, production goes up and the fruits of the greater output can be traded with others who, likewise, have specialized in the things they do relatively well. In other words, trading opens the door to specialization, specialization increases productivity, and higher productivity raises real living standards.

International free trade arguments simply observe that these same principles hold when the two parties to an exchange are of different nationalities. Even though most actual international trade is carried on between individuals or firms in one country and individuals or firms in another, it is usual to speak of countries trading with one another. Then it is noted that, just as individuals differ from one another in talent and endowments, countries differ in climate, soil conditions, the size and skill of their labor forces, the availability of capital, and so on. Thus, the theory readily shows that free international trade can raise the per capita real income in all trading countries.[1] Once the advantages of free international trade have been demonstrated, debate then usually centers on the following two questions. First, given the level of aggregate input and output, which goods should a country produce for itself and which ones should it produce for export? And second, what other goods, if any, would it be cheaper to import?

Unfortunately, for those who favor internationalism, even though free trade may raise the measured real production and income per capita in all trading countries, it is not true that all persons who are affected gain from such trade. For example, when a country increases its exports, domestic consumers of the exported goods face higher prices for those goods, and their living standards may go down. In the same way, when a country increases its imports, domestic producers of goods that compete against these imports may lose. These facts of life must be recognized in understanding the conflict between free trade and protection.

1. The principles governing trade and payments between American states are the same as those between countries. If U.S. prosperity is attributed largely to its being the world's most important free trade area, why not extend the same principle to whole continents, to the capitalist world, or to the world as a whole?

Trade in a Single Commodity

We begin by describing the effects of trade in one commodity, such as wheat, which is produced in two countries. To keep our analysis simple, we shall consider trade between the United States and "the rest of the world," as if the rest of the world were all one country. Actually, the United States trades with many separate countries, involving many different situations.

Figure 35-1 shows the market for wheat in each of these two "countries." We use the same scale on the vertical (price) axis of both graphs. This means either that the two countries use the same currency or that their currencies exchange in a fixed ratio to each other.[2] In each graph, the demand curve D_1 shows only demand from domestic purchasers, and the supply curve S_1 shows only the supply from domestic suppliers. In the absence of trade, wheat sells for P_1 per bushel in the United States and for P_2 in the rest of the world. These prices differ from each other because the two countries differ in their demands for wheat and in their endowments of resources used in producing it. Without trade, wheat would be more expensive in the rest of the world than in the United States.

We can illustrate the results of opening up trade between these countries by using the concepts of excess demand and excess supply. **Excess demand** is the amount by which the quantity demanded exceeds the quantity supplied at any specified price. In the absence of trade, excess demand would be zero in each country at the price at which domestic demand, D_1, intersects domestic supply, S_1. But a positive amount of excess demand would exist at any lower price. **Excess supply** is the amount by which the quantity supplied exceeds the quantity demanded at any specified price. In the absence of trade, excess supply would be zero at the price where the domestic demand and supply curves intersect, but would be positive at any higher price.

In Figure 35-1, the United States will export wheat because the U.S. price is lower than the

2. The determination of exchange rates between currencies is explained in Chapter 18.

FIGURE 35-1   Trade in a Single Commodity

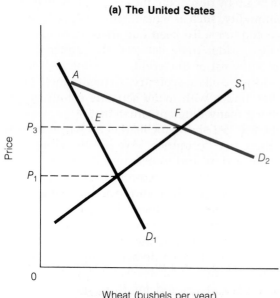

(a) The United States

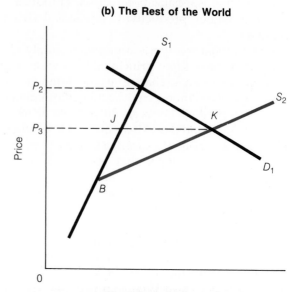

(b) The Rest of the World

Panel (a) represents the wheat market in the United States and panel (b) represents the wheat market in the rest of the world, treated as one country. In each panel, D_1 and S_1 represent demand and supply before there is any international trading in wheat. Excess supply exists in the United States at prices above P_1. In panel (b), the U.S. excess supply at each price is added to the domestic supply in the rest of the world to generate the supply curve S_2 for the rest of the world.

In the rest of the world, excess demand exists at any price below P_2. In panel (a), this excess demand at each price is added to domestic demand in the United States, generating the demand curve D_2. Equilibrium international trading occurs (ignoring shipping costs) at price P_3, with quantity EF exported by the United States and quantity JK (which is equal to EF) imported by the rest of the world. At equilibrium, there remains neither excess demand nor excess supply in either country.

price in the rest of the world. For an exporting country, the effect of trade is to add at each price the excess demand of other countries to its own domestic demand. The demand curve D_2 in the U.S. panel of Figure 35-1 shows the result of adding, at each price, excess demand from the rest of the world to the domestic demand D_1 in the United States. Point A corresponds to the pretrade price for wheat in the rest of the world, so that excess demand is zero. The horizontal distance between the pretrade demand curve (D_1) and the demand curve (D_2) in the United States is the same as the horizontal distance between S_1 and D_1 in the rest of the world at prices below P_2. At equilibrium the quantity exported by the United States (distance EF) is the same as the

quantity imported by the rest of the world (JK).

The parallel situation for the rest of the world is illustrated by the supply curve S_2 in panel (b) of Figure 35-1. Point B corresponds to the price at which there is no excess supply in the United States. But at higher prices, excess supply exists in the United States, measured by the horizontal distance between its domestic demand and supply curves. The supply curve S_2 for the rest of the world is drawn by adding, at each price, excess supply from the United States to the domestic supply curve (S_1) of the rest of the world. At equilibrium, the quantity imported by the rest of the world (JK) is equal to the excess supply in the United States (EF). In Figure 35-1, the new equilibrium price is P_3. We show it as

FIGURE 35-2   Gains and Losses from Trade in a Single Commodity

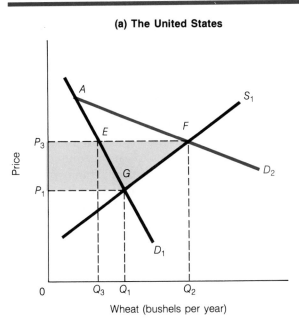

(a) The United States

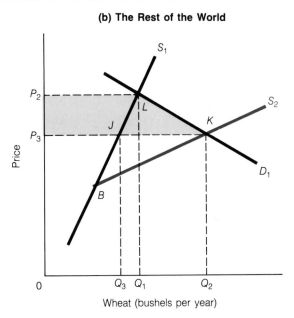

(b) The Rest of the World

The demand and supply curves on these graphs are the same as those on the graphs in Figure 35-1. In the United States, export of wheat causes the price to rise to P_3 and the quantity supplied to increase to Q_2. Producers' gain is represented by the shaded area in this panel. But U.S. wheat consumers pay a higher price (P_3) and consume fewer bushels (Q_3). The consumer loss is that part of the shaded area to the left of the demand curve (D_1). The net gain in the United States is the triangular area EFG.

In the rest of the world, importing causes the price to fall to P_3 and consumers increase their purchases to Q_2 bushels per year. Their gain is shown by the shaded area in panel (b). Wheat suppliers in the importing country lose because they sell less wheat at a lower price. Their losses are represented by that part of the shaded area to the left of the supply curve (S_1). The net gain from trading for the importing country is the triangular area JKL.

the same in both panels because we ignore the cost of shipping wheat between the countries. In practice, of course, the price in the importing country would be higher than the price in the exporting country by the amount of such shipping costs, and the quantity exchanged would be less than illustrated in Figure 35-1.

Gains and Losses to Producers and Consumers

To analyze the gains and losses to producers and consumers from trade, we shall use Figure 35-2, which reproduces Figure 35-1, but adds further information. Let us first examine what happens

in the exporting country (the United States). Before international trade, Q_1 wheat was sold at price P_1. After equilibrium is reached in international trade, Q_2 bushels of wheat per year are sold at price P_3. Total gain to wheat producers in the United States is shown by the shaded area in panel (a). For all outputs up to Q_2, their prices have risen more than their costs, which are represented by the supply curve. U.S. consumers lose, however. Before international trade, they consumed Q_1 bushels of wheat and paid price P_1, but after equilibrium is reached in international trade, they consume only Q_3 bushels per year and pay price P_3. The higher price, P_3, that they pay for the quantity that they purchase, Q_3, is clearly a loss to consumers. They also lose the consumers' surplus (the benefit that consumers gain from being able to buy a good at a uniform price lower than what they would be willing to pay for it) on the quantity of wheat between Q_1 and Q_3. Thus, the consumers' loss is represented by the part of the shaded area that lies to the left of the demand curve (D_1). The total of producers' gain is greater than the total consumers' loss in the exporting country by the area of the triangle EFG in the U.S. panel of Figure 35-2. This shows the presumed net gain from export trade.

Panel (b) traces a similar argument for the rest of the world. Before international trade, consumers purchased Q_1 bushels of wheat per year and paid price P_2. After equilibrium is reached in international trade, these consumers purchase Q_2 bushels per year at price P_3. The combination of more wheat and the lower price expands their consumers' surplus by the amount represented by the shaded area in the rest-of-the-world panel. But wheat producers in the importing country lose from international trade. Before such trade, they sold Q_1 bushels at price P_2, but international trade causes both the price and the quantity that they sell to fall. Their loss is that part of the shaded area to the left of the supply curve S_1. But the gain to consumers in the importing country is greater than the loss to producers by the triangular area JKL in panel (b).

Our analysis has demonstrated that both the exporting country and the importing country gain from free international trade. It does not necessarily follow, however, that the gains are evenly divided. The country that experiences the greatest price change for the traded commodity will gain more than the country that experiences a lesser change in price. From this fact, we can reason that small countries may gain more from international trade than do large countries, which tend to dominate world trade and whose domestic prices may not change as much as a result of trade. This view is contrary to a popular one that the economic giants gain most from trade.

Other Economic Effects

Per capita real income gain, however, is not the whole story, because a gain to the country as a whole may still imply a loss to some and perhaps even to a majority of the country's citizens. Consider, for example, the cheap machine-made textiles exported to China from the West (primarily from England) in the half-century before World War I. The consumer gain to China, which economic theory suggests outweighed the loss to producers, went chiefly to those urban people (skilled workers, middle and upper classes) who bought them. The producers' loss was borne chiefly by poor peasants who had in the past spun and woven textiles to earn second incomes in the agricultural slack season. China was then an 80 percent peasant economy. So more individual Chinese lost than gained from the textile imports, and the distributional effects were in the direction of greater inequality. Moreover, the loss of a dollar of income probably meant more (in terms of utility, or anticipated satisfaction) to a rural peasant than to an urban white-collar worker. From this point of view, China may well have lost by the textile trade. As you can see, the presumption of net gains from trade is not a conclusive argument that trade is desirable.

Another point is that not all products are traded between countries. Some, like real estate, are physically tied to one place. The more common problem, however, is that transportation costs are so high in relation to the prices of some goods that they are not exported or imported. Can producers and consumers of nontraded goods be left out when we try to assess the gains and losses from trade? The answer is "no," if these nontraded goods are complementary to or substitutes for either imports or exports in either production or consumption.[3] For example, consider the case of a Latin American country that exports a cash crop (such as coffee, sugar, or bananas) raised on land that might have been used for domestic food production (such as beans,

3. Two goods are substitutes in production if they both use the same specialized inputs. Examples are corn and soybeans, which require the same type of land and climate. Two goods are complementary in production when they are joint products of a single production process, such as beef and hides, or when one is a raw material or an intermediate product in the making of another, as fish and fishing boats. Substitution and complementarity in consumption have been discussed in Chapter 22.

rice, or other vegetables). In this case, producers of domestic food will lose from trade, because of the higher prices and rents they must pay for land and labor. The consumers of domestic food will also lose, because the price of domestic food will rise. Antitrade feeling results when the producers and/or consumers of domestic food are "the poor" and the majority of the population.

Another example is the importing of rice cookers into the United States. Invented in Japan, these cookers increased the American demand for American rice, by making it easier to cook and reducing the risk of cooking failures. (In this example, American rice plays the role of a nontraded good, though in fact much of it is exported.) Rice is complementary to rice cookers in consumption. The import of rice cookers, by raising the demand for rice, might be expected to raise its price—a good thing for rice producers but not for rice consumers.[4]

COMPARATIVE ADVANTAGE

India and Western Europe were almost completely cut off from each other for more than 500 years after the decline of the Western Roman Empire. This period was the so-called Dark Ages. But despite high transportation costs and high risks, a trickle and then a stream of trade developed during and after the Crusades. What determined which goods would move in each direction? Similarly, what goods did Japan export and import when she was forced to open her doors to trade after 250 years of semi-isolation under the Tokugawa Shoguns?

Economists try to answer such questions by using the theories of comparative advantage. Here is the argument. When there is no trade or when it is restricted, a country will normally have a set of relative prices that is different from the set that exists in the rest of the world. For example, the price of apples may be twice the price of potatoes in one country, but may be three times

4. In fact, however, American agricultural policy both supported the domestic price of American rice above the world level and prevented the rice cooker from raising it further.

the price of potatoes in the rest of the world. This is so because countries normally will have different combinations of resource endowments or will have developed special skills in different things. A good whose pretrade price or restricted-trade price is relatively lower in a country than in the rest of the world is likely to be exported by that country. On the other hand, a commodity whose pretrade or restricted-trade price is relatively higher in a country than in the rest of the world will likely be imported by that country. This is the well-known principle of **comparative advantage.**

The following illustration, which comes from the English economist David Ricardo (1772–1823), is the classic demonstration of the principle of comparative advantage. Assume that one unit of English cloth requires 100 hours of English labor and that one unit of Portuguese wine requires 80 hours of Portuguese labor. Assume also that 120 hours of English labor would have been needed to produce a unit of wine in England. If, at equilibrium, one unit of cloth is exchanged for one unit of wine in international trade, England gains the product of 20 hours of labor by importing wine from Portugal in exchange for cloth. Ricardo does not tell us how many hours of Portuguese labor would be required to produce a unit of cloth. But any figure above 80 would give Portugal a gain from trade. If we suppose the figure to be 90, we would have the following costs for the two countries.

Country	Labor Cost per Unit Traded (in hours)	
	Cloth	Wine
England	100	120
Portugal	90	80

In terms of labor cost, Portugal has an absolute advantage in both cloth and wine since she can produce either one with less labor than would be required in England. Relative prices, however, would be 5:6 (100:120) in England and 9:8 (90:80) in Portugal. Cloth is relatively cheaper in England and wine is relatively cheaper in Portugal, giving England a comparative advantage in cloth and Portugal in wine. England would gain the product of 20 hours of English labor through trade and Portugal would gain the product of 10 hours of Portuguese labor. One partner's gain does not mean a loss to the other. However, one partner's gain may be larger than the other's. For example, were a unit of cloth in Portugal to cost 81 hours of Portuguese labor, the Portuguese gain would have been very small. Were a unit of wine in England to cost 101 hours of English labor, the major gain from trade would have gone to Portugal.

Another way to look at Ricardo's case is that Portugal is one-third better than England in wine production ($^{40}/_{120} = \frac{1}{3}$), but only one-tenth better in cloth production ($^{10}/_{100} = \frac{1}{10}$). Therefore, once we grant the existence of gains from trade, it is more rational for England to export cloth and Portugal to export wine than for them to do the opposite.

A later explanation of comparative advantage came from two Swedish economists, Eli Heckscher (1879–1952) and Bertil Ohlin (1899–1979). They explained comparative advantage as being due to differences between countries in their "endowments" of productive inputs, which affect the pretrade prices of goods traded. The United States, for example, has accumulated a great deal of capital equipment, but its labor has remained relatively scarce. This means that American real interest rates have been generally low, but American real wage rates generally high. For this reason, according to this theory, the United States should export capital-intensive goods and import labor-intensive ones, while the trade of Mexico or Guatemala should follow the opposite course.

Of course, there are complications and modifications. Countries produce many goods that can be traded. Comparative advantage cannot tell us exactly where the lines will be drawn between the potential exports, nontraded goods, and potential imports. Demand or supply may be so price inelastic that relative prices may change (and comparative advantage with them) when trade is freed. And trade may itself affect tastes and techniques so much and so permanently that the pretrade relative prices become entirely obsolete. But even with these and other qualifications, comparative advantage remains important in explaining trade patterns.

Comparative Advantage and Choosing a Career

A simple example of comparative advantage, outside the realm of international economics, is in students' choices of college majors and careers. Most economics teachers have had "star" students ask them about possible careers as economists. It is clear from their classroom performances that they have *absolute* advantages in economics. **Absolute advantage** simply means being more proficient than others in doing a given thing. However, *comparative* advantage is another matter. For all the economics teacher knows, the star student may be even more outstanding in history or mathematics, or even better suited to a career in law or medicine or engineering or journalism. So all the teacher can do for students is to estimate the size and the meaning of their *absolute* advantages in economics, while advising them to estimate for themselves their *comparative* advantages in various fields before making up their minds.[5]

It is equally rational for a mediocre student to choose a major or a career in some field where his or her performance, while below average, is still better than in any other subject in terms of class ranking. Such a student's absolute disadvantage might be the least in economics, giving him or her a comparative advantage in that field as large or larger than that of the class's star student.

The Dynamics of Comparative Advantage

So far, we have presented comparative advantage as something static. That is, we might say, "A country *has* a comparative advantage in agriculture." To do so, however, is misleading in the light of economic history. As a country develops, its comparative advantages generally shift away

5. Of course, the relative incomes to be expected in different fields of endeavor are important too. One might hesitate to advise a student to become a tramp, a bum, or a hobo, however great that student's comparative advantage might be in such occupations.

from farming and handicrafts, first toward light industry and then toward heavy industry and later to service industries. These changes take place because land becomes more scarce, industrial capital accumulates, and labor increases in skill. In some cases, the process is only partial, as in Denmark or Iowa, which are developed areas that remain largely agricultural. In other cases, the process is nearly complete, as in the Ruhr Valley of West Germany or the "silicon valley" of California.

An especially interesting aspect of changes in comparative advantage over time is called the **product cycle.** At first, the comparative advantage in producing steel or automobiles is in developed high-wage countries that export to lower-wage developing ones. As the developing countries learn the manufacturing processes, and as these processes themselves become less skill-intensive, the less developed countries can first reduce their imports and then take up exporting on their own. After a time, the comparative advantage has shifted to newly industrialized developing countries, which come to dominate the world market. If the older developed country's import-competing industries survive, they do so largely because they are protected. The following "cycle" takes place in the developed country's industry. At first it is purely domestic. Next it becomes more and more of an export industry. Then, as lower-wage countries take over, it becomes more and more an import-competing industry.

Some countries fear that comparative advantage dynamics eventually will completely eliminate their exports of goods. Countries in such a position would pay for imports only by earnings on their earlier foreign investments. No country has yet reached this extreme point, but it has been suggested that countries such as Britain and the United States are potential candidates.

FACTOR PRICE EQUALIZATION

Up to this point, we have explained that, except for transportation costs, freedom of trade equalizes the prices of traded goods and services across

frontiers. However, what about the prices of nontraded inputs, such as wage rates for labor and interest rates for capital? The **factor price equalization theorem** states that free trade of goods and services across countries not only equalizes output prices but also input (or resource or factor of production) prices.

To illustrate this theorem, let us consider two countries (Mexico and the United States), two commodities (cars and textiles), and two inputs (labor and machinery). Cars and textiles are freely traded between the two countries. However, there is no migration of labor or trade in machinery between them, and in the short run neither the stock of labor nor the stock of machines in either country changes. We further assume that the quality of labor and of machines is identical between the two countries.

Suppose that, before trade, the price of textiles in relation to the price of cars is higher in the United States than in Mexico and that the price of cars in relation to the price of textiles is higher in Mexico than in the United States. Comparative advantage predicts that the United States will export cars, which cost relatively less to produce than textiles, and that Mexico will export textiles, which cost relatively less to produce than cars. If the textile industry is labor intensive, its expansion in Mexico will cause Mexican wage rates to rise in real terms and also in relation to interest rates in Mexico. In the United States, where the capital-intensive auto industry is expanding because of the export of cars, the realignment of industry causes the return to machines (interest rates) to rise both in real terms and in relation to wages. The real wage of Mexican workers should come closer to the real wage of American workers and would ultimately equal the American real wage if the volume of trade in textiles were large enough. Similarly, interest rates (the return to investments in machinery) in the United States should rise both in real terms and in relation to the U.S. wage rate as the American auto industry expands. These interest rates will come closer to real interest rates in Mexico and would ultimately equal the Mexican real interest rates if the volume of trade were large enough. Thus, trade tends to equalize input prices, even when these inputs themselves were not traded.

In the real world, this theorem operates only as a general tendency. Free trade does tend to draw input prices closer together, but without leading to full factor price equality.[6] In practice, wages vary more than interest rates between countries, since capital moves more freely than labor migrates. However, even in its weakened real-world form, the factor price equalization theorem helps to explain why opposition often arises to free trade between countries with widely differing real wage and interest rates.

PROTECTION

The term **protection** makes most people think at once of **tariffs** (taxes on imports) and **quotas** (limitations on the quantity of imports) used to protect domestic import-competing industries. These are indeed cases of protection, but there are many others. An important one is **administrative protection,** which bans imports or subjects them to burdensome, costly, and time-consuming inspection often for reasons of safety or health. The American ban on fresh beef from Argentina, for example, was imposed at a time when many Argentine cattle suffered from contagious hoof-and-mouth disease. An export industry may also be protected by an export bounty (reward) or a

---

6. Why doesn't the equalizing process go all the way to bring about complete uniformity? Or to put the matter differently, what further conditions beyond freedom of trade are needed for our theorem to hold literally? Here are seven such conditions.

   1. Conditions are stationary, with fixed amounts of each input in each country.
   2. Transportation costs can be ignored.
   3. Specialization is incomplete. Each country continues to produce some of each traded good under free trade.
   4. Knowledge is uniform. Each country has access to the same set of production techniques, the same "book of blueprints."
   5. Production takes place in both countries under purely competitive and increasing-cost conditions.
   6. There are no factor-intensity "crossovers." If farming, let us say, is more labor-intensive than manufacturing when wages are low and interest is high, it will remain so even when wages are high and interest is low.
   7. The number of separate outputs equals the number of inputs.

subsidy.[7] Or an import-competing industry may receive its own protection in bounty or subsidy form, in an effort to meet world prices. (An American example is shipbuilding.)

Of the many examples of protection, we shall note only two. During the nineteenth and twentieth centuries, British duties on exporting wool were protective—for the rising British textile industry, to which the duties ensured cheap wool as raw material.[8] The OPEC countries collected large export duties on crude oil, which were intended to raise money and also to gain time for these countries to develop their agricultural and industrial economies before their oil resources were used up. (These policies became progressively less effective over the long term as non-OPEC countries increased their production and as oil-importing countries developed substitutes for petroleum products and otherwise economized on their use.) This is a form of protection for an economy as a whole rather than for any *specific* industry.

Nominal versus Effective Protection

The **nominal protection** given for an industry is simply the rate of the tariff imposed on the importation of foreign supplies of the industry's product. **Effective protection** involves two further variables. The first is whether protection also is given to goods that are raw materials or intermediate goods used in producing the protected good. Suppose that we want to estimate effective protection for the textile industry. If cotton is a

---

7. If an industry that produces only for the domestic market is subsidized, bountied, or tax-relieved, it is not being protected in the international economic sense. But what of an industry that sells part of its output at home and part as exports? This is an important question in U.S.–Japanese economic relations because Japan uses general or production subsidies, without special favors for exports. The United States feels free to impose counterbalancing duties on goods benefiting from *specific* export subsidies, but what is the status of *production* subsidies, such as the Japanese, that extend also to domestic sales?

8. The U.S. Constitution (Article I, Section 9) bans export duties. This provision was a concession to Southern agricultural interests. It is not clear whether this provision can also be extended to cover export bounties (negative export duties).

raw material or intermediate good for the textile industry, and if cotton also is protected from foreign competition by a tariff, the effective protection for the textile industry is reduced. The reason is that the protection for cotton raises its price and so also raises the cost of producing the textiles. Foreign textile producers, who can buy cotton at lower (world) prices may be able to move into the "protected" market in spite of the tariff on imported textiles.

The second variable in estimating effective protection centers on the value added (mainly the profits earned and wages paid) by the protected industry. Owners and workers in protected industries are interested in how much protection they get as a percentage of their own earnings, that is, of the value added. Suppose that for every $100 of textiles produced, $50 is paid out for raw materials and other intermediate goods and that $50 goes for wages and profits. If there is no tariff on raw materials or intermediate goods but the tariff on textiles allows the price of textiles to rise to $110, the tariff has raised wages and profits by 20 percent, that is, by $10 from the original $50. Effective protection will almost always be greater than nominal protection, unless raw materials and intermediate goods are given substantial protection at the same time.[9]

Disguised Forms of Protection

Besides these forms of more or less open protection, there are also three forms of hidden or disguised protection: (1) voluntary export restrictions, (2) orderly marketing agreements, and (3) the trigger price mechanism. Since World War II they have gained in popularity as substitutes for

open protection in countries that, like the United States, have pressed other countries for greater freedom of trade.

Voluntary export restrictions are usually bilateral (between just two countries)[10] and seldom completely voluntary. Under such provisions an exporting country agrees to lower its exports to an importing country to a certain level or in accordance with a certain formula. For example, the United States has put pressure on Japan first to reduce and then not to increase too rapidly her exports of cars and trucks to the United States. **Orderly marketing agreements** try to prevent "disorderly" price cutting in importing countries and are generally multilateral. That is to say, several exporting countries and/or several importing countries are usually involved. In most cases, the agreement is carried out under the threat of protective duties or quotas by one or more of the importing countries. A **trigger-price mechanism** need involve no agreement at all. An importing country, like the United States in the case of steel products, acting alone, may announce one or more "trigger prices" for different types of steel. Any imports below these prices are considered to be **dumping** (a sale below what authorities consider average total cost plus a fair mark-up) and subject to special "antidumping" duties.[11]

Economic Arguments for Protection

"Free trade wins all the arguments, but protection wins all the votes." There is a great deal of truth in this statement. The historical record reveals

---

9. An equation for estimating effective protection is as follows. Let t_x be the tariff rate on imports that compete with an industry's output (such as textiles). Let t_y be the tariff rate on raw materials and intermediate goods (such as cotton), and let q be the share that raw materials and intermediate goods contribute to the value of final output. Then we have

$$T = \frac{t_x - q t_y}{1 - q}$$

where T is the rate of effective protection.

10. We usually treat the European Community (EC) as a single country.

11. The traditional international economic meaning of *dumping* has been the sale of some product abroad at a price lower than its domestic price (plus transportation costs). Dumping was regarded as a predatory tactic, designed to drive competitors out of business and then to exploit consumers. For this reason, countries impose antidumping duties, which are not usually considered strictly protective.

However, as goods have become less standardized and marketing tactics more complex, the term *dumping* has been redefined in the United States to mean any sale below what the American authorities consider "average total cost plus a fair mark-up," regardless of price in the exporting country.

the political effectiveness of "intense minorities" and "special interests."

Steel companies, their workers, and whole "steel communities" like Pittsburgh, Gary, and Birmingham *care* about that import-competing industry's prosperity, because steel is their livelihood. Steel consumers all over the United States may well lose more, in total, from steel protection than the steel industry gains. But each individual consumer's loss is minor, and consumers are spread over a wide area.

But over and above these political arguments, there are sound economic ones, which we should not forget. We shall briefly describe several of these arguments.

THE INFANT INDUSTRY ARGUMENT   Perhaps the most important of the economic cases that favor protection is the **infant industry** argument, sometimes referred to as "learning-by-doing." We have already pointed out that comparative advantage is generally not a static but a changing concept. Why not speed up the changes if they seem desirable, or slow them down if they seem harmful?

The desire to speed up a change and the willingness to accept a loss in the present for the sake of the future were the base of the infant industry argument for protection, which Alexander Hamilton outlined in his *Report on Manufactures* during the late eighteenth century. The reason why American manufacturers were less efficient than their British or European counterparts, Hamilton believed, was that they lacked experience and on-the-job training. For this reason, Hamilton urged the country to protect American manufacturers temporarily while they were gaining experience. Then the next generation would be better off, particularly if manufacturing demanded higher skills and paid better wages than agriculture did.

Sometimes we hear this argument in exaggerated form, to the effect that the latecomer's disadvantage simply *cannot* be overcome at all without some measure of protection. To see that this argument is often wrong, we might look at Japan in the last third of the nineteenth century. Manufacturing developed very rapidly, even though Japan had been forbidden, by "unequal

treaties" with Western powers, from imposing tariffs on foreign goods at rates higher than 5 percent. Or consider a case of free trade within the United States—the southward migration of the cotton textile industry. Under free trade, comparative advantage in textiles shifted from New England to the South. However, it might have shifted earlier had the Confederacy won the Civil War and imposed tariffs on the New England textiles. One can compare the infant industry argument to a request for a loan at zero interest from today's consumers, who pay higher prices, to tomorrow's workers and consumers, who may, as a result, have higher incomes.

Since there are senile as well as infant industries, there is also a "senile industry" argument for protection. It is quite different from the infant industry argument, however. Consumers are asked to pay more for certain goods to keep specialized workers in dying industries employed and off the relief rolls. This is an act of charity—which also saves taxes.

THE HIGH WAGES ARGUMENT   The *high wages* or "cheap foreign labor" argument for protection is very popular in high-wage countries. A high-wage country tries to limit imports of a low-wage country's goods to check or slow down the working of the factor price equalization theorem, to raise real wages, and perhaps also to make income distribution in the high-wage country more nearly equal. Most workers in a high-wage country feel that it is "unfair" that they should have to compete with goods from low-wage countries. American textile workers, for example, complain about competition from Taiwan and South Korea. Workers in Taiwan or South Korea might complain about unfair competition between people and the "cheap American machinery," which replaces labor in America. Essentially, the cheap foreign labor argument is an outright rejection of the theory of comparative advantage. Less developed countries rightfully complain that this form of protection impedes their development.

THE TERMS OF TRADE ARGUMENT   A country's **terms of trade** are measured by an average of its export prices divided by an average of its import prices. The terms of trade improve when the average price of the country's exports rises or the average price of its imports falls, both being computed net of tariffs. Higher terms of trade with a given trade volume are considered beneficial. However, a rise in the terms of trade may not be favorable if the trade volume decreases. Lower terms of trade, similarly, are considered disadvantageous unless the trade volume rises.

Terms of trade arguments for protection make use of any monopoly or monopsony (buyers' monopoly) power that a country may have to drive up its own terms of trade ratio and to drive down the terms of trade ratio of its trading partners. If a country has monopsony power, it can impose a tariff that would raise the price of an imported good to consumers and lead them to reduce the quantity demanded. The foreign producers then face the uncomfortable choice of either (a) lowering their prices to cancel the effect of the tariff or (b) accepting a lower volume of sales, which may mean unemployment and hardship. Countries that depend on the monopsonist's market often will lower their price, and part of the tariff is actually shifted to the resource owners in the producing country. A country with monopoly power can accomplish the same result by imposing export duties, as OPEC tried to do. These duties are borne mostly by customers in consuming countries.

THE HOME MARKET ARGUMENT   In the nineteenth century, the protectionist *American System of Political Economy* had two major parts. One was the Hamilton infant industry argument, stated above, which was addressed mainly to urban people. The other part, addressed to farmers, was the "home market" argument associated with Henry Clay, the "great compromiser" who would "rather be right than be President."[12] Clay's view was that some farm income should be sacrificed in favor of greater stability and certainty. The more U.S. agriculture remained dependent on the European market for its exported staples (cotton, corn, tobacco, and wheat), the more subject it would remain to disruption from European warfare, revolution, and depression—and

12. It is quite a feat in any field to be at once a great compromiser and always right!

also from European protection. Tariffs on European manufactured goods would reduce farm sales to Europe, but these tariffs would bring prosperity to American manufacturing and expand the home market for U.S. farm products. Farm prices would remain high and uncertainty would be reduced. The general idea involved is *risk aversion,* or at least a preference for one bundle of risks over another. It remains important even though Henry Clay's "American System" has been largely forgotten.

THE CAPITAL-ATTRACTION OR TARIFF FACTORY ARGUMENT   The capital-attraction or **tariff factory** argument states that, if a country's market is important, tariffs and quotas set to keep out foreign goods will induce foreign capitalists to invest in that country and employ that country's labor in order to avoid the tariff. Canada has applied this approach effectively against the United States. American visitors to Canada may be surprised at the number of "American" brand names attached to products of "XYZ Company, Canada," with headquarters in Toronto, as distinguished from "XYZ Company" itself, with headquarters in New York. During the 1950s and the early 1960s, the European Community (EC) caused many American firms to establish European branches not only by setting up high Community-wide tariffs against U.S. goods but also by eliminating tariffs between member countries. This last change meant that a single American tariff factory in, say, Belgium, could service the whole EC. Thus there would no longer be any need to set up separate factories in each member country, a costly and often uneconomical procedure.

THE RETALIATION OR BARGAINING ARGUMENT   The *retaliation* or *bargaining* argument for protection, like the infant industry one, involves "time preference." A retaliatory tariff or quota has the same harmful short-run welfare effects as any other tariff or quota. But, according to this argument for protection, in the long run it may cause foreigners to lower their duties or ease their quotas against one's exports. The historical record, however, suggests that retaliatory tariffs seem rather to lead to further retaliation and feed on themselves, growing more and more restrictive over time. Interest groups that gain from the retaliatory tariff gain strength the longer it remains effective. As time passes, it becomes increasingly difficult to oppose the political strength of these groups.

MACROECONOMIC ARGUMENTS We may lump together a number of economic arguments for protection that aim at relieving macroeconomic ills. For example, if a country has widespread unemployment, a tariff may be used to keep foreign goods out in order to open up more jobs for that country's own people. Or if the government's budget is in deficit, an argument can be made that tariffs should be used to raise revenue, rather than lowering public spending or taxing the people directly. Or if a country's total value of imports is exceeding the total value of its exports so that it is running a balance of payments deficit, tariffs may be used to reduce these imports and the deficit.[13]

Political Arguments for Protection

The political arguments for protection have been even more effective than the economic ones. Some of these are described below.

THE NATIONAL DEFENSE ARGUMENT The national defense argument was persuasive for Adam Smith himself. In a famous passage from *The Wealth of Nations,* defending the Navigation Acts[14] against which the Thirteen Colonies were then protesting, Smith admitted that "defense is of much more importance than opulence." So he

joined the chorus in favor of protecting potential defense industries.

The aim of the British Navigation Acts was to maintain ships and sailors for the Royal Navy. In the same way, Imperial German tariffs on grain were justified by the argument that country boys from the farm made better soldiers than city boys from the factory. However, the most common national defense arguments today are based on the need for tariffs and quotas on the importation of such "defense goods" as steel and ships. The country, it is said, should not become dependent on unreliable foreign sources for important defense needs.

THE "CRITICAL MINIMUM" ARGUMENT Allied to the national defense argument is protection aimed at supporting a *critical minimum* of production in some basic industry. An example today is from Japan, which imports a larger proportion of its staple foods (rice and wheat) than any other country in recorded history—larger even than Great Britain, which suffered under German submarine blockades in two world wars. It is therefore necessary for Japan—so runs the argument—with its dense population and its small post-1945 "maritime self-defense force," to protect its agriculture from low-price American and other import competition. At the very least, it must keep its dependence on foreign food from increasing any further.

THE PREDATORY FOREIGNER ARGUMENT The *predatory foreigner* argument assumes that foreign suppliers have hostile intentions. According to this argument, it is especially dangerous to let one's country become dependent on unfriendly countries, which may cut off one's supplies of some critical commodity for political reasons or form cartels and raise prices. Even previously friendly countries can become hostile. If the United States had listened to free traders and become completely dependent on imported oil, the Arab boycott of 1973–1974 would have caused even more harm than it did. The United States is fortunate, or so runs the argument, to have protected its high-cost domestic oil industry during the years before the boycott.

---

13. Macroeconomic arguments for tariffs and quotas are discussed more fully in Chapter 18.

14. During the seventeenth and eighteenth centuries these Acts limited British and colonial coastwise trade, as well as trade between Britain and its colonies, to British and colonial ships with British and colonial crews. They also prohibited import trade in ships other than those of Britain, its colonies, and the exporting country—a move aimed at French and Dutch competition in the "carrying trade" between third countries. Present American law bans only coastwise trade to foreign shipping, but requires that the bulk of American aid goods be carried in American ships.

SPECIAL INTERESTS The most effective way of getting protection, year in and year out, has been *intense minority* or *special interest* pressure. The beneficiaries of protection, however few they may be, put their hearts and their money into their cause. They also tend to be concentrated in particular areas. On the other hand, the injuries from protection are spread too thinly, both geographically and economically, for the victims to be mobilized year after year for commodity after commodity.

COMMERCIAL TREATIES, FREE TRADE AREAS, AND CUSTOMS UNIONS

Trade between countries is governed by commercial treaties and other forms of international negotiation. We shall outline some of the important principles of these treaties, including those that involve customs unions and free trade areas.

Commercial Treaties

A **commercial treaty** is an agreement between countries dealing with economic and trade relations. Since World War II, most such treaties have been reasonably reciprocal. For example, under a treaty, the rights and duties of American citizens in Yugoslavia would be much the same as those of Yugoslav citizens in America, with certain allowances for such facts as America being a capitalist and Yugoslavia a socialist country.

However, many, if not most, nineteenth-century commercial treaties between more developed countries (MDCs) and less developed countries (LDCs) were very unequal. Some gave Westerners in LDCs what was called "extraterritorial" rights to civil and criminal trial under MDC law in MDC courts attached to MDC embassies or consulates, without giving the same rights to Turks (or Persians or Chinese) living in the West. One reason for such laws was the practice of some LDC legal systems of getting evidence from peo-

ple by torture and imposing "cruel and unusual punishment" for minor offenses. Other provisions of unequal treaties gave Westerners rights to seize LDC customs receipts for payment of debts owed to MDC governments, restricted LDC rights to put tariffs on MDC goods, set aside areas in LDC cities where only MDC citizens could live, and so on. In all these cases, there were no reciprocal rights for LDCs. None of these unequal treaties survived World War II.

Commercial treaties are generally in force for a term of years, after which either party may reject the treaty and perhaps propose a new one more favorable to its interests. But even while the treaty is in force, the legal standing of its provisions varies between countries. No U.S. Congress can bind those that follow it. In fact, many Congresses have felt free to amend or to make laws in violation of commercial treaties that earlier Congresses had approved. For this reason, many countries feel that the United States is not a very reliable partner for a commercial treaty.

Free Trade Areas and Customs Unions

Commercial treaties may raise the degree of economic integration among the contracting parties, rather than simply legalizing and regulating the existing situation. Recent economic integrations have taken the forms of free trade areas and customs unions. In both cases, trade between the members is made free, either immediately or after periods of adjustment, by one or more commercial treaties. Differences exist, however, in how they deal with outsiders.

In the **free trade area,**[15] there are no tariffs or other trade restrictions for member countries, but each member country has its own set of tariffs, quotas, and so forth, for nonmember countries.

---

15. A free trade area should be distinguished from a *free port*. In a free port like Hong Kong or Singapore, there is a special restricted area where raw materials or goods in process are landed duty free, processed further by local labor and materials, and then re-exported without entering the general Hong Kong or Singapore market.

In the **customs union,** there is also free trade for members, but a common tariff, generally based on an average of the member countries' previous tariffs, which nonmembers must face. (Each country, however, may keep its separate quota arrangements.) So an American exporter faces different tariffs in Norway and Sweden, both members of the European Free Trade Association (EFTA), but the same tariff in France and West Germany, both members of the European Community (a customs union).

Today the most important experiment in economic integration is the European Community (EC). It developed in the 1950s from a number of multilateral agreements about (a) the division of Marshall Plan aid from the United States for rebuilding after World War II and (b) the reorganization of European production of such commodities as coal, steel, and atomic energy. Its founders and supporters, including many Americans, hoped that it might become a strong economic and financial community with a common circulating currency, and a political community as well. Another early hope, especially in the United States, was that the EC would be satisfied with a low common tariff, and that countries like the United States, Canada, and several former British dominions would join with it economically. In this way, the EC would not be simply a Western European power but would become a non-Communist world economic power as well.

These things have not happened. The low-tariff British refused to join unless allowed to continue to import cheap food from the dominions. Representatives of high-cost European agriculture would not make this concession. Without the British, the EC became a high-tariff organization, especially after the strongly nationalist General Charles de Gaulle took power in France and a "farm bloc" of French and German agricultural interests gained political power. It has remained a high-tariff organization even after Great Britain, Ireland, and several other countries later joined.

Because the free trade area and customs union appear to be movements away from economic nationalism and protectionism, they seem to be steps toward freedom of trade. We might expect many internationalists and free-trade economists to welcome them wholeheartedly as steps in what they believe to be the right direction. In fact, their enthusiasm has been lukewarm at best. How can this be?

The problem is that a free trade area, a customs union, or any other experiment in partial economic integration has a dual effect on trade. Within the free trade area or the customs union itself, it *creates* trade between the individual member countries, which might not have developed if each country had kept its own tariff wall. At the same time, the free trade area or customs union *diverts* trade from nonmember to member countries, and in this case is usually a step away from freedom of trade.

If a highly isolationist self-sufficient country like North Korea today were to join a free trade area or customs union, the trade-creation effect would dominate the trade-diversion effect. If a free trade country like pre-1914 Britain were to join the same free trade area or customs union, the trade-diversion effect would dominate.

An example of trade diversion might be American automobiles in Denmark. Before Denmark joined the EC, U.S. automobiles competed there on equal terms with automobiles from Britain, France, Germany, and Italy. (Denmark itself has no automobile industry.) After Denmark joined the EC, competition for the Danish automobile market shifted favorably to Denmark's new EC partners, and away from outsiders like the United States and Japan. This move was against freedom of trade, even though Ford and General Motors continued to sell in Denmark the products of their European subsidiaries.

ITO and GATT

After World War II, the "free world" members of the United Nations proposed that the world economy return to freer and less-discriminatory trade than had prevailed in the 1930s and that a new international code of conduct be set up to regulate quotas and other forms of nontariff protection. Their representatives drew up a charter for an **International Trade Organization (ITO)**. The proposed charter, however, included a number of safeguards and escape clauses, which the U.S. Senate considered discriminatory against the United States. The Senate refused to ratify the proposed charter, and the ITO never came into being.

To replace the aborted ITO, a number of countries, mainly the industrial countries of North America and Western Europe, framed a less-formal **General Agreement on Tariffs and Trade (GATT)**. GATT established its own bureaucracy, and representatives of GATT countries have held several "rounds" of meetings. It seeks to carry out gradually and by stages what ITO hoped to accomplish more quickly. GATT, however, has become something of an exclusive club for the wealthier nations, in the view of many LDCs. These countries, preferring a New International Economic Order (NIEO) to trade liberalization, have refused to join or cooperate with GATT. But within the so-called First World GATT remains an active and often successful organization.

THE SHIFTING U.S. TRADE POSITION

The U.S. balance of trade, which had been positive since the depression of the 1890s, went into reverse about 1970. For 1985, the trade deficit was around $150 billion, approximately one-fifth with Canada and one-third with Japan—America's most important trading partners. For 1984, the U.S. trade deficit was $108 billion. Table 35-1 shows the wide range of products involved in that year. For nonfarm products (especially in skilled and high-wage industries), deficits reflect primarily rises in imports. In agriculture, the primary cause has been a decline in exports. The change also involves a large number of America's trading partners. This is shown in the data in Table 35-2.

The combined effect of these changes has produced consternation in the United States. The situation has been called "the export of the good

TABLE 35-1   U.S. Balance of Trade by Product, 1984

Billions of Dollars	Products
Over 15	Cereals and grains
10 to 15	(none)
5 to 10	Aircraft equipment and space-craft
0 to 5	Coal; professional scientific and engineering equipment; construction and engineering equipment; organic chemicals; medical and pharmaceutical products
0 to −5	Telecommunications; paper and board products
−5 to −10	Footwear; nonferrous metals; consumer electronics
−10 to −15	Iron and steel; clothing and textiles
−15 to −20	(none)
−20 to −25	(none)
−25 to −30	Automobiles and trucks
−50 to −55	Petroleum and Petroleum products

(The "Positive" bracket spans Over 15 through 0 to 5; the "Negative" bracket spans 0 to −5 through −50 to −55.)

Source: "Why America Cannot Pay Its Way," *Economist* (London), July 13, 1985, from U.S. Department of Commerce and International Trade Administration.

jobs" and turning the nation into "an economy of hamburger stands." It has been blamed on "unfair" tactics overseas, especially on export subsidies, administrative protection, and market closures. All of these have occurred in and are practiced by the United States as well. Nonetheless, the shift has given rise in America to demands for increased and tighter trade restrictions, not only through higher tariffs but also through a "new protectionism" of quotas and administrative protection devices that cannot be overcome by foreign costs.

TABLE 35-2   Changes in U.S. Balance of Trade with Selected Countries, 1983–1984

Change from 1983 to 1984 (billions of dollars)		Country	1984 Balance (billions of dollars)
Increase	1–2	Mexico	−6.3
		USSR	2.7
	0–1	Australia	1.9
		Chile	−0.1
Decrease	0–1	(none)	
	1–2	Hong Kong	−5.8
	2–3	Italy	−4.1
		S. Korea	−4.0
	3–4	Brazil	−5.6
	4–5	Taiwan	−11.1
	5–6	West Germany	−8.7
	6–7	Canada	−20.4
	15 and over	Japan	−36.8

Source: "Why America Cannot Pay Its Way," *Economist* (London), July 13, 1985, from U.S. Department of Commerce and International Trade Administration.

The shift has not been entirely a result of an allegedly overvalued dollar brought on by budget deficits and anti-inflation monetary policies, high interest rates and a rise in the foreign exchange value of the dollar. Nor should it be ascribed to the OPEC cartel and the oil shocks of the 1970s. Both of these macroeconomic factors—the dear dollar and the aggregate supply shock—played significant roles in the history of the American trade balance. However, as Table 35-3 shows, the decline in the American trade balance was already underway at the time of the first oil shock (1973–1974), and it continued through the period of the "dollar glut" and the "undervalued" dollar of the Carter administration (1977–1980).

The Passing of the "Dollar-Shortage" Era

A full history of the U.S. trade balance must go back to the end of World War II and to the half-generation (1945 to 1966 approximately) that followed. During that period, North America (the United States and Canada) was the paramount source of both agricultural and manufactured goods for the entire world outside the Soviet bloc,[16] which, after 1949, included China. Because of America's dominant position, these twenty-one years, particularly the first ten, were times of "dollar shortage"—since foreign countries had little to exchange for American goods. The leading American firms in a number of industries and American growers of a number of farm products found themselves in a position to obtain higher profits from their monopoly control. In turn, these high returns were reflected in the wages of specialized labor in those industries, the prices of agricultural land, and even in the sizes of welfare programs in the public sector.

Roughly midway in what was described as America's "soaring sixties," foreign recovery, accelerated by American aid, gradually brought this euphoric period to a close. The special demands and inflationary financing of the Vietnam War postponed public consciousness of this development, which emerged as something of a shock when hostilities died down in the early 1970s. Hindsight makes it clear that many segments of the American economy have been unwilling or politically unable to adapt to the new situation by appropriate or sufficient combinations of lower real wage rates, lower profit margins, lower tax burdens, higher productivity growth rates, and improved product quality. The net result of this refusal or inability is called declining American international "competitiveness." It is blamed on labor (by business), on management (by labor),

16. Under the Marshall Plan in 1947, the United States offered to extend economic assistance to Soviet bloc countries. But the Soviet Union rejected the American offer and required its allies to do likewise—even after Czechoslovakia and Poland had already accepted. This rejection was due to Stalin's fear that economic dependency upon the United States would lead to economic and political subordination.

**TABLE 35-3   U.S. Balance of Trade in Selected Years, 1960–1983
(in billions of dollars)**

Year	Exports	Imports	Balance
1960	$ 19.6	$ 14.8	$ 4.9
1962	20.8	16.3	4.5
1964	25.5	18.7	6.8
1966	29.3	25.5	3.8
1968	33.6	33.0	0.6
1970	42.5	39.9	2.6
1972	49.4	55.8	− 6.4
1973	71.8	87.9	− 16.1
1975	113.8	118.0	− 4.2
1977	131.9	176.6	− 44.7
1979	222.2	249.2	− 27.0
1981	287.7	310.3	− 22.6
1983	256.0	312.0	− 56.0

Note: The 1960–1972 figures refer to "merchandise trade"; the 1973–1983 figures include both goods and services, while excluding "goods under military grant" and "income from foreign (or U.S.) assets."

Source: Richard E. Caves and Ronald W. Jones, *World Trade and Payments: An Introduction,* 4th ed. Tables 15.1 and 15.2. Copyright © 1985 by Richard E. Caves and Ronald W. Jones. Reprinted by permission of Little, Brown and Company.

on government waste (by taxpayers), and so on. No group has been willing to accept any substantial share of the blame. The universal path of least resistance has been to blame the foreigner—particularly the Asian foreigner—and to push for bigger and better protection, while leaving unquestioned the comfortable, if outmoded, relics of the dollar-shortage period.

Changing Factor Endowments

An additional element in the new U.S. trade position has arisen from changes in rival countries' factor endowments, especially their endowments of human capital. The American view of Oriental labor remained, for entirely too long, that of illiterate coolies producing, with little mechanical aid, bottom-quality merchandise for the bottom fourth of the world's income distribution, while subsisting on "a fishhead and a handful of rice a day." However incorrect this picture might already have become before World War II, it became much more inaccurate thereafter. Oriental labor acquired training and skills,

Oriental skilled labor endowments increased, and Oriental wage rates became a larger fraction of American wage rates. Now it paid Oriental employers to increase labor productivity with better and newer machines of various kinds. In short, Asian labor could enter advanced industries formerly thought to be reserved for the West in general and for America in particular.

An Accelerated Product Cycle

Another element in the changing U.S. trade position has been an acceleration of the product cycle. We have already mentioned this cycle by which an economic innovation in a high-wage country moves by stages from a domestic industry in that country to an export industry and then to an export industry in some lower-wage country with the product imported into the country where the innovation originally took place. The automobile, radio, television, and computer industries in the United States are examples of this. We did not inquire then how long such a product cycle might take.

For the mass-produced automobile, forty years seem to have been required for the Ford Model T and its American successors (Chevrolet, Plymouth, and later Ford models) to be threatened seriously in their home market. When the threat came, it was initially from relatively high-wage European companies—Volkswagen of Germany, Renault of France, Fiat of Italy, and Austin and Morris of Great Britain. An additional ten to fifteen years were required for Japanese competitors to enter the American domestic market to any serious extent. But the product cycle took much less time (only five or ten years) for the television set (first black and white and then color), the computer (whether hand-held, mainframe, or personal), the video-cassette recorder, the air conditioner and heat pump, or the recreational vehicle and motorcycle developments of the automobile itself. Pity the American television set or computer manufacturer counting on a full generation's profits on its technological lead before foreign competitors would invade not only its export market but even its domestic market!

The acceleration of the product cycle by the up-market moves of competitors in lower-wage countries is an economic aspect of the more general phenomenon popularized by the sociologist Alvin Toffler as *Future Shock*—except that the shocks are not future ones, but present and recent-past ones. The moral is that one cannot safely rest on one's laurels as many traditional American export industries have sought to do. Together, the passing of the "dollar-shortage" era, changing factor endowments, and the accelerated product cycle surely have been more important causes of the change in America's international trade position than the popular "dirty tricks," "subsidies," or "market closure" explanations so often given.

SUMMARY

1. Trade makes it feasible for people to specialize in jobs for which they have special talents. Specialization increases productivity. Therefore trade can play a role in raising real production and income.

2. Because countries differ from one another in resources and special talents, trade between countries can be shown, under competitive conditions, to benefit both the exporting country and the importing country.

3. Nevertheless, particular groups lose from trade. Consumers of exportable goods lose from export trade under competitive conditions. Producers of importable or import-competing goods lose from import trade under the same conditions. Producers and/or consumers of nontraded goods may also lose from trade if the particular nontraded goods they produce or consume are complementary to or competitive with imports or exports in consumption or in production.

4. A country is said to have a comparative advantage in the production of one good and a comparative disadvantage in the production of another good if its pretrade or restricted-trade relative price of the first good is lower, and its relative price of the second good is higher, than those of its actual or potential trading partners or in "the rest of the world."

5. Comparative advantages and disadvantages, when they exist, may be due to a number of different causes. The classical (Ricardian) theory stresses differences in productivity for different goods and services. The later Heckscher-Ohlin theory puts the most stress on differences in "factor endowments," meaning supplies of the several productive inputs.

6. Comparative advantage is not a static concept, but varies over time. The so-called product cycle is a case in point, as applied to advanced industrial products.

7. Under free trade, countries tend to export those goods in which they have a substantial comparative advantage and import those in which they have a substantial comparative disadvantage. The resulting specialization is usually incomplete, however, with much surviving production of "importables" or import-competing goods in all countries.

8. Free trade also tends to equalize input resource prices between trading countries in the same manner as migration.

9. Free trade tends to optimize production and real per capita income both in the world as a

whole and in each participating country. Conversely, protection tends to involve a dead-weight loss.

10. We cannot define protection rigorously. However, it includes a wide variety of aids to a country's import-competing goods and to its exports. It extends well beyond the traditional import tariffs and quotas to a wide range of bounties, tax preferences, and types of administrative protection.

11. The effective rate of protection is usually different from the nominal rate. The effective rate takes account of the protection given to the raw materials and components that go into a product in addition to the nominal rate on the product itself. Protection given to raw materials lessens the effect on that given to final products.

12. Among economic arguments for protection, the most effective have been the infant industry (learning-by-doing) and the high-wage (cheap foreign labor) arguments. Others have been: the terms of trade argument; avoidance of risks by developing the home market; the attraction of foreign capital, and sometimes also of skilled labor, to "tariff factories"; the response or bargaining reaction to foreign protection; and the solution of problems connected with the country's employment level, payments balance, or government budget.

13. Among the political (and social) arguments for protection are: the national defense argument; the critical minimum of basic goods argument; resistance to possible predatory activities by foreign interests; and, most important, the political influence of "intense minorities," otherwise known as "special interests."

14. Commercial treaties regulate trade and commerce among nations. Multinational treaties can be used to form free trade areas and customs unions, which are important means of economic integration. They differ mainly in that the members of a free trade area retain their separate tariffs against nonmember countries, while a customs union has a common tariff structure.

15. The European Community is the most important move toward economic integration today. It is a customs union. There is also a European Free Trade Association.

16. Free trade areas and customs unions both create and divert trade. The trade-creation effects are welcomed by internationalists as moves toward greater freedom of trade; the trade-diversion effects work in the opposite direction.

17. After World War II, a proposed International Trade Organization (ITO), affiliated with the United Nations, never came into being because of United States opposition. The various First World countries, however, are seeking to reduce the general level of tariff and nontariff protection among themselves, using for this purpose a General Agreement on Tariffs and Trade (GATT).

18. After a long period of positive balances, the U.S. balance of trade has been increasingly negative since about 1970. America's reduced international competitiveness is attributed to an inability or unwillingness to adjust to increased productivity in the rest of the world. Factor endowments in foreign countries have improved and the product cycle has accelerated.

DISCUSSION QUESTIONS

1. To remedy famine and malnutrition in poor countries, it has been suggested that they raise "food first" and consume it locally, rather than raising cash crops for export (tobacco, coffee, cotton, rubber, etc.). Can such suggestions be reconciled with the theory of comparative advantage?

2. Students often complain that many good teachers prefer to do their own research, leaving the teaching to ineffective teachers. To meet this complaint, one college president suggested that students grade their teachers, and that teachers graded lowest by the students be assigned exclusively to research. Would this suggestion make "comparative advantage" sense?

3. The theory of factor price equalization has not been borne out by historical experience. Why do you think this is so, and does the experience invalidate the theory?

4. What do you think is meant by the term "dumping"? Do you think antidumping duties are justified? What about duties against goods whose production has been subsidized? What

about duties against goods whose export has been subsidized?

5. Should high-wage domestic industries be protected from the products of lower-wage foreign labor? Should labor-intensive industries be protected from the products of automated or robotized foreign plants, which use less labor or none at all?

6. Do you think most American industries enjoy higher or lower effective protection than is suggested by nominal tariff rates? Explain.

7. Why has protection shifted away from tariffs to quotas, to voluntary export agreements, orderly marketing arrangements, and other forms of administrative protection?

8. Can you find examples of "product cycles" in the histories of such American industries as shoes, steel, or automobiles? Explain.

9. What is the difference between a customs union and a free trade area? How would you characterize the arrangements between the fifty American states?

10. It is generally agreed that American prosperity has been enhanced by the regional specialization permitted by the absence of interstate tariffs and other forms of protection. Should this result be applied to the world as a whole?

11. Why has the American "industrial crisis of the 1980s" developed? Is it a real crisis? What, if anything, should be done about it?

36 *Agriculture, Food, and Hunger*

PREVIEW When peasants are slaves, or serfs, or peons, what they claim to want is freedom. But when free peasants must rent their land from the lord of the manor or the absentee landlord in the city, or when they are hired hands on a plantation or a collective farm, what they say they want is a farm of their own. Therefore, readers of ancient and medieval agricultural history might think that the farmers' complaints would be muted in countries such as the United States which are dominated by the tradition of family farming. But this has not been the case. Agricultural unrest has been a recurring theme in American life. Indeed, most countries have had farm problems of one kind or another at various times in their histories. We will discuss the economics that surrounds these problems.

The first part of this chapter focuses on the problems faced by American farmers and their reactions to these problems. Their reactions have included the economic one of leaving the farm for other occupations and the political one of agitating for government help in controlling prices and quantities in the markets for major farm products. They also have formed cooperatives in efforts to help themselves.

The second part of the chapter examines the government programs that have arisen in the United States as a result of farm political action. These include price support programs and controls on the amount that farmers can produce. We take a look at how subsidies for farm output offer an alternative to the present system of price controls.

The last part of the chapter addresses the fear of increasing food shortages and malnutrition, if not real famine, as world population grows. Except for a few agricultural giants like the United States and Canada, the danger of shortages and hunger for most of the world has been increasing as soil is depleted and as what has been farm land is diverted to nonagricultural uses. We discuss several proposed solutions for this problem. The proposals include further increases in agricultural productivity per acre and per worker, falling rates of population growth mainly through lower birthrates, and shifting agricultural output to staple foods like grain and vegetables and away from luxury foods like meat and sugar or nonfood products like tobacco and flowers. We close with a discussion of the Food First proposals for resolving world food problems.

AMERICAN FARMERS AND FARM PROBLEMS

American agriculture is the envy of most of the world. Fertile soil, advanced technology, and highly skilled farmers produce outputs per hour of labor that were undreamed of only a generation or two ago. Nonetheless, the "farm problem" continues. To understand more clearly why the farm problem has been a recurring theme in American life, we begin by noting a few highlights of American agricultural history. We follow this overview by exploring the farmers' complaints and some of the responses farmers have made to their problems.

Historical Patterns and Highlights

Our brief review of the role of agriculture in U.S. history begins with a farmers' rebellion not long after the country won its independence. Then, as background for the rest of the chapter, we trace the events and the protests that followed the Civil War and the two world wars.

THE WHISKEY REBELLION Before the building of canals or turnpikes, the cost of transportation meant that grain could not be marketed profitably by the farmers of western Pennsylvania. But the high value and small bulk of whiskey was a different matter. To sell their grain on the Atlantic seaboard, it was first distilled into whiskey. Thus, whiskey was an important farm crop in western Pennsylvania in the years shortly after the American revolution. During Washington's administration, the new federal government imposed a tax on distilled liquor. When serious attempts were made to collect the tax, the farmers rebelled. President Washington feared that the rebellion might become a real revolution and threaten the new government. He raised a force of 13,000 soldiers and put down the rebellion with a large show of force.

POPULISM The Civil War was financed by inflationary means. The country abandoned the gold standard and printed paper money—"greenbacks" that were not convertible into gold. Both prices and nominal interest rates rose, and in both the North and the South, farmers were encouraged to clear land, enlarge their farms, and expand production. To finance this expansion, farmers borrowed money secured by mortgages on their homes and land. After the war ended in 1865, deflationary policies were adopted by the government, and both farm prices and nominal interest rates fell. Farmers who had borrowed money during and right after the war found that interest charges and principal repayments at the old high rates were too high in terms of bushels of wheat or pounds of other produce at the new lower prices. Moreover, they were competing against farmers who had borrowed money later and were paying lower interest rates.

During the recessions that followed financial panics in 1873, 1890, and 1893, many farmers could not keep up their payments and lost their lands and homes. The resulting protest movement, called **Populism,** swept both the West and the South. It was the basis for two political parties, the People's Party and the Greenback Party, which wanted the government to increase the money supply by printing more greenbacks. The populist movement provided substantial support for William Jennings Bryan in his almost successful run for the presidency in 1896. About the same time, however, gold was discovered in the Yukon and in South Africa, and a new method of extracting precious metals from low-grade ore was found. Under the gold standard, which had been re-established in 1879, this new supply of gold brought an increase in farm prices and eased the plight of the farmer. The rise in farm prices is credited with killing Populism as a major political force and bringing on a "golden age of agriculture" during the years just before World War I.

WAR PROSPERITY AND POSTWAR RECESSION The story was similar after both World War I and World War II. During and right after each war, farmers were encouraged by patriotism and high farm prices to borrow money and expand production. But after each war, when normal peacetime conditions returned to the countries that were devastated by the war, "overproduction" from American farmers hastened a fall in world prices for farm products. In the 1930s, the Roosevelt New Deal caused farm prices to increase again. However, these were years of drought, soil erosion, the Dust Bowl, and the "tractoring off" of tenant farmers by landlords who wanted to substitute machinery for labor. In the late 1930s, the great migration of the "Okies" and the "Arkies" to California seems to have been due more to tractoring off than to either dust-bowl drought conditions or foreclosures on farm mortgages. After World War II, the Roosevelt program remained in effect, but farmers called for more and more support to keep up with postwar advances in both agricultural productivity and urban incomes.

The U.S. experience can be paralleled to some extent in other agricultural-exporting countries like Canada, Australia, and Argentina. But agricultural problems are different in countries and regions like the African Sahel (the southern edge of the Sahara Desert). Malnutrition and famine are serious problems because their agricultural productivity is low and because they do not have friendly or dependable sources for the import of basic foodstuffs.

The Farmers' Complaints

Why are so many farmers so sure that the economic cards are stacked against them, even when they own their own land? Basically, there are two types of complaints—one about the market structures in which farmers buy and sell and the other about the inelasticity of demand for farm products.

COMPETITORS IN A MONOPOLISTIC WORLD In economists' language, the farmers' most common complaint is that they have been pure competitors at the mercy of monopolistic sellers and monopsonistic buyers. Individual farmers see themselves as pure competitors or price takers in the markets for the goods they buy, including such inputs as agricultural machinery, fertilizers, insecticides, and credit. In addition, they see themselves as price takers in selling their output at harvest time. On the other hand, those who sell inputs to farms and buy farm products seem to be either local monopolists or agents of national monopolies. For these reasons, farmers believe they are exploited.

The list of alleged exploiters is a long one and varies from time to time and from place to place. It has included the following:

1. Local money lenders, such as bankers or other suppliers of credit. Rural towns are small, and small farmers have no access to larger market areas. For this reason, collusion between local money lenders is often easy to maintain, and farmers get little benefit from competition in the world outside.

2. Railroad or trucking companies, which transport farm goods to market.
3. Local grain elevators, warehouses, or other storage companies that hold farm goods for shipment.
4. Processing plants (flour mills, cotton gins, canneries, or creameries), which may be owned by a national or regional chain or a nationwide conglomerate.
5. Local agricultural implement dealers, who may be agents of national companies.
6. Local general stores or specialized merchants who sell seeds and fertilizers, fencing materials, work clothes, bagging, and even staple foods in the off-season. These too may be local monopolies or owned by a national or regional chain.
7. Speculators on the commodity exchanges in Chicago and elsewhere who allegedly push the prices of the farmers' crops down just at harvest time when they have to sell it.

Regarding farm land, there are complaints on both sides of the market. Partly because of demand for nonfarm purposes like housing and partly because of demand by nonfarmers for investments and inflation hedges, the price of farm acreage is "too high" in relation to crop prices. A young couple may be unable to establish a family farm of economic size unless they have inherited such a farm. But at the same time, land prices are "too low" to justify the property, capital gains, and estate taxes levied on farm owners and their heirs. Moreover, farm land is a very nonliquid asset and must often be sold at a sacrifice in an emergency (by both the land-rich and the land-poor) to raise cash for the payment of debts or taxes or to permit the farmer to retire quickly under pressure of age or ill health.

INELASTICITY OF DEMAND The second set of farmers' complaints usually is more impersonal. It centers around the low price and income elasticities of demand for most basic farm products. The low *price* elasticity of demand for a farm product such as the whole American output of red winter wheat means that, in a free market, a large crop often brings farmers less income than a small crop. This is true even though the price elasticity of demand for the output of any individual farm is almost infinite.[1]

The low *income* elasticity of demand for a farm product means that, as consumers' per capita income rises, the percentage that they spend for this product falls. This applies not only to particular crops but to food products as a whole. It causes farm incomes to lag behind nonfarm incomes and has prompted migration from the farm to the cities and to nonfarm occupations. The tendency for the percentage of a family's budget spent for food to decline as income rises sometimes is called **Engels' Law.**

Some specialized and large-scale farmers, like the citrus and raisin growers of the South and Southwest, have been able to take advantage of the low price elasticity of demand for their crops and keep their incomes high without government aid. To do this, they form organizations to "manage" their outputs—that is, to reduce output and sometimes to destroy "surpluses." But for major crops with more producers, there have been enough rugged individualists and free riders to break down such cartel arrangements despite urgings to "raise less corn and more Hell."

The Farmers' Responses

Farmers have reacted to unfavorable conditions in several ways. As individuals, they, and more importantly their children, have reacted both by supplementing farm income with income from nonfarm employment and by leaving the farm for nonfarm jobs in rural areas or by moving to the cities. They also have reacted by forming farm organizations and by striving, either directly or by political means, to change the rules of the economic game in their own favor, both within and beyond the limits of the ordinary market system.

AGRICULTURAL FUNDAMENTALISM When an economic group feels systematically disadvantaged, it usually tries to prove that its interest is also the interest of the whole country. Farmers

are no exception. The special doctrine that supports their claims has been called **agricultural fundamentalism.** The argument is that, since food is necessary to life, farmers should be at least as well off as any other group. Moreover, not only is farm produce fundamental in itself, but the agricultural countryside is the main market for the manufactured products of the city. The agricultural fundamentalists say that business depressions are "farm led and farm fed" because when farm income falls below a certain proportion of nonfarm national income, the farmers cannot purchase the products of the cities. From the failure of farm purchasing power comes urban overproduction and depression, say the agricultural fundamentalists. The Great Depression of the 1930s was often cited as a case in point because agriculture had been in a depressed state for several years before the Wall Street crash of 1929.

Agricultural fundamentalism has declined in the United States as the farm market has become less important as an outlet for the sale of manufactured goods. As part A of Table 36-1 shows, at the turn of the century, nonfarm production in the United States was a little over three times as great as farm production. But part B of the table shows that, by 1985, nonfarm production was about 48 times as great. This decline in the relative importance of farm production is reflected in the smaller proportion of Americans now living on farms, a trend that we shall examine next.

FARMERS LEAVE THE FARM Quantitatively speaking, the farmer's most important reaction has been to leave the farm—as one might expect from conventional economic theory. As is shown in Table 36-2, over 30 percent of all U.S. households were farm households in 1910, but the farm household percentage had fallen to only 2.1 percent in 1984. During World War II, farmers left the farm to take defense jobs; many never returned to farming. In peacetime, they often sell their farms when they retire and go to live in town. Sometimes, of course, landlords who wish to increase the size of their own farms force their tenant farmers off the land, or mortgage holders evict farmers who cannot meet mortgage payments. Forcing farmers off the land to allow landlords to increase the size of their farms is

---

1. See Chapter 22 for an explanation of price and income elasticity of demand.

TABLE 36-1   U.S. Farm and Nonfarm Production, 1897–1985

A. Gross Domestic Private Product (in billions of dollars, 1929 prices)

Years	Farm Product	Nonfarm Product	Nonfarm/Farm Product Ratio
1897–1901 (average)	8.4	27.4	3.26
1902–1906 (average)	8.9	36.3	4.08
1907–1911 (average)	9.2	43.7	4.75
1912–1916 (average)	10.1	49.8	4.93
1917–1921 (average)	9.7	57.3	5.90
1924	9.7	74.3	7.66
1929	10.7	88.6	8.28

B. Gross Domestic Business Product (in billions of dollars, current prices)

Year	Farm Product	Nonfarm Product	Nonfarm/Farm Product Ratio
1929	9.7	84.8	8.74
1939	6.3	73.0	11.59
1949	18.8	213.3	11.35
1959	19.0	417.9	21.99
1969	25.2	798.8	31.70
1979	71.8	2,054.5	28.61
1980	65.5	2,236.4	34.14
1981	79.8	2,498.9	31.31
1982	77.0	2,581.3	33.52
1983	60.8	2,802.0	46.09
1984	80.2	3,124.4	38.96
1985	69.2	3,322.0	48.01

Note: Private product (A) excludes only government agencies, whereas business product (B) excludes also nonprofit agencies such as private hospitals and universities.

Sources: (A) Ben J. Wattenberg, ed., *Statistical History of the United States,* Bureau of the Census, Series F 125–129; (B) *Economic Report of the President, 1986,* Table B-8, p. 262.

parallel, in some respects, to the "enclosure movements" in the late Middle Ages when sheep and cattle raising, which required little labor per acre, were substituted for grain farming, which required much more. In the 1950s, the development of the mechanical cotton picker displaced the sharecropper from much of the cotton-growing South.

POLITICAL PRESSURE BY FARMERS Because farmers tend to be law-abiding property owners whose farms are scattered over wide areas, they have not been able to organize as successfully as

many other groups. Farm organizations also have been less likely to strike or to take similar forms of direct action than have labor unions.[2] Instead

2. Exceptions to this generalization are not hard to find, particularly when farmers live close together in villages or small farms. The "Farmers' Holiday" movement of the 1930s, for example, stopped farm trucks and dumped milk on the roads. During the same period, farmers disrupted foreclosure sales of farms, permitting the mortgagor to buy his or her mortgaged farm free and clear for a fraction of its value by keeping outsiders from bidding on the property. Similiar disruptions of farm sales occurred again on a smaller but increasing scale in the 1980s.

TABLE 36-2 U.S. Farmers Leave the Farm, 1910–1984 (households in millions)

Year	Total Households	Farm Households	Nonfarm Households	Percentage of Farm Households
1910	20.2	6.2	14.0	30.7
1920	24.5	6.8	17.7	27.8
1930	30.0	6.7	23.3	22.3
1940	35.2	7.2	28.0	20.5
1950	43.6	6.3	37.3	14.4
1960	52.8	4.1	48.7	7.8
1970	62.9	2.7	60.2	4.3
1980	79.1	1.9	77.2	2.4
1984	85.4	1.8	83.6	2.1

Sources: Ben J. Wattenberg, ed., *Statistical History of the United States,* Bureau of the Census, Series A 350–352. Data for 1980 are from *Statistical Abstract of the United States, 1981,* Table 64, p. 45. Data for 1984 are from *Farm Population of the United States 1984,* Bureau of the Census, Series P-27, No. 58, December, 1985.

they have depended on their voting power, which is a much smaller share of the total than in the past. They use this power to lower the prices and improve the quality of the things they buy, but their main effort has been to try to raise and maintain the prices of the crops they sell.

FARMERS' COOPERATIVES As Benjamin Franklin said, "God helps those who help themselves." Accordingly, in addition to giving up farming and seeking aid from Washington, farmers have tried to help themselves by organizing cooperatives to give themselves the market power required to counteract their several "exploiters." These co-ops, as they are called, have been of two general types, *producers' co-ops* and *marketing co-ops;* some co-ops combine both functions. Producers' co-ops concentrate on bulk buying of farm equipment and supplies. While they ordinarily sell at market prices, the profits are distributed to farmers in proportion to their purchases, and increase their incomes. Several types of farmers may belong to one producers' co-op. Marketing co-ops concentrate on bulk sales of particular products and are usually limited in the range of products they sell. The most powerful ones have attained some degree of monopoly control in dealing with wholesalers and chain stores in dairy

products, citrus fruits, and dried fruit. They have formed powerful organizations, which operate stores, grain elevators, and processing plants.

Both types of co-op aim at securing part or all of "the middleman's profit" for farmers themselves, and both have had difficulties in hiring and retaining good managers. Both types have also been active politically. Some, dominated by the richer owners of the larger farms, have been conservative. Others have turned collectivist and sought public ownership of banks, railroads, and public utilities. The left-wing collectivist cooperative movement reached its peak in the Non-Partisan League of North Dakota, the Farmer-Labor Party of Minnesota, and the Progressive Labor Party of Wisconsin during and shortly after World War I.

GOVERNMENT AGRICULTURAL PROGRAMS

When people speak of the American "farm program" without further specification, they usually mean the programs for six basic commodities (wheat, corn, rice, cotton, tobacco, and peanuts) and major storable commodities such as oats,

TABLE 36-3 U.S. Farm Population, Employment, and Acreage, 1933–1985

| Year | Farm Population | | Farm Employment (millions) | Farm Acreage (millions) |
	Millions	Percentage of U.S. Total		
1933	32.4	25.8	12.7	340
1940	30.5	23.1	11.0	341
1945	24.4	17.5	10.0	354
1950	23.0	15.2	9.9	345
1955	19.1	11.5	8.4	340
1960	15.6	8.7	7.1	324
1965	12.4	6.4	5.6	298
1970	9.7	4.7	4.5	293
1975	8.9	4.1	4.3	336
1980	7.2	3.2	3.7	352
1985[a]	5.4	2.2	3.4	347

a. Data for 1985 are preliminary.

Source: Economic Report of the President, 1986, Table B-95, p. 362.

hay, milk, wool, and soybeans. Altogether, these amount to 14 out of a total of 116 farm products on which the U.S. Department of Agriculture keeps records, and they are raised by approximately one-third of the country's 2.3 million farmers.

The primary purpose of these programs has been to close the gap between the income of the average farmer and that of the average city dweller. In 1983, the national average family income was $28,638 while the average net income per farm family was $22,953. Because of the larger size of farm families, the per capita income of the farm population was even further below the national average.[3]

A second purpose of American farm programs has been to preserve family farming as a way of life for a substantial fraction of the American people. Until the time of the Civil War, an absolute majority of the American population lived on farms. The percentage was 44 in the first Census Bureau official estimate in 1880, and 26 at the time of the first government price support programs in 1933. The government programs have not prevented further declines in the farm population, as shown in Table 36-3, but they may have slowed them down.[4]

It may seem strange for farmers to combat reductions in the number of their own competitors. The paradox is explained partly by a widespread belief in the innate naturalness and superiority of rural over urban and suburban living, and partly by the desire to maintain farmers' traditional political clout at all levels of government. In addition, farmers seldom regard their

3. U.S. Bureau of the Census, jointly with U.S. Department of Agriculture, Current Population Reports, Series P-27, No. 58, Farm Population of the United States: 1984, U.S. Government Printing Office, Washington, D.C., 1985, Table 13, p. 15. Comparisons between agricultural and nonagricultural incomes are treacherous for at least three reasons: (1) there are wide variations around the average in each group, (2) approximately seven-eighths of the "farm families" in the United States (concentrated in the lower income brackets) receive less than half of their incomes from farming, and (3) farm families typically are larger than nonfarm families.

4. The actual decline may be larger than the numbers indicate because the opportunity to shelter other income from taxation by "tax losses" on "farm operations" keeps a certain number of individuals registered as living on "farms" that are such in name only.

neighbors as competitors—a sentiment that rarely extends to farmers in other regions, let alone to farmers in foreign countries. The noncompetitor attitude stems from the realization that all of the farmers in one township or county can exercise only infinitesimal influence over farm product prices and that nobody is lowering anyone else's income by raising his own output.

The American system, or rather systems, of farm price supports and income supplements has developed over a half-century, starting as a temporary program in 1933, part of the initial Roosevelt New Deal. It has since spread, with modifications, to other countries including the European Community (EC) and Japan. It has been characterized, somewhat unfairly, as "The government shows you how to grow two ears of corn where one grew before and then pays you not to harvest either one."

The programs have become an important, and perhaps basically immovable, aspect of the American economy, resulting from generations of political compromise among farmers, taxpayers, and consumer interest groups. We should not be surprised to find separate programs for different farm products and to find them imperfectly consistent with each other. After all, the buyers of such farm products as cotton, wheat, and tobacco are business firms rather than final consumers. Moreover, in the case of feed grains, farmers producing meat, eggs, or dairy products purchase the products of other farmers.

Farm Parity

Parity means equality or equivalence. In general, **farm parity** refers to the relationship between the purchasing power or real incomes of farmers compared with the purchasing power or real incomes of others in the economy. If farmers had the same purchasing power or real income as others in the economy, they would have 100 percent of parity.

In government farm programs, the parity concept is applied to the prices of individual farm products. For example, the **parity price** of wheat of a standard grade is the price that bears the same relation to some index of the farm produc-

tion costs that it did in some past period. In these programs, the time period chosen as a reference or base in calculating parity prices usually has been a time of special prosperity for farmers, such as the "golden age of agriculture" in the years before World War I. However, farm prices usually are not supported at 100 percent of parity. Government programs simply prevent prices of supported farm products from falling below some politically determined relationship (percent of parity) to the prices of goods and services that farmers buy. Nothing prevents the market prices of these products from rising above 100 percent of parity in periods of high demand or low supply.

Market Prices, Support Prices, and Target Prices

To understand the price control aspects of the programs for major crops, it is helpful to identify three different prices for each product. These are (1) the **market price,** which is the price that would prevail in the absence of the government programs and which would involve only negligible surpluses resulting from speculation on "higher prices next year," (2) the **support price,** which is the price at which government agencies buy and store crop surpluses that accumulate at these higher prices,[5] and (3) the **target price,** which is still higher than the support price and which is the basis for calculating "deficiency payments" to farmers, as will be explained shortly. The target price system did not exist in America until 1973, but had been used earlier in Japan and in the European Community.

Figure 36-1 illustrates the three-tier system of prices for a crop covered by these government programs. The horizontal axis shows quantities of the crop (wheat, for example) demanded and supplied. The vertical axis shows price per bushel. The market price for this crop (P_m) is indicated by the intersection of the demand curve (D) and

---

5. Sometimes the government holdings of crops are called **buffer stocks** or an **ever-normal granary** being kept as reserves against periods of bad weather or other disasters at home or abroad. However, these stocks often have been larger than necessary for these purposes.

the supply curve (*S*) at point *E*. At this price, the market is cleared and there is no surplus or unsold output. The quantity demanded and supplied is Q_1 and total farm receipts from this crop are represented by the rectangle $0P_mEQ_1$. If Congress decides that this is not enough to attract or hold the farm vote, it may decide to raise the price to a higher and more attractive percentage of parity. Accordingly, Congress may decide to provide a support price of P_s.

The support price (P_s) is implemented by the government through a system of **no-recourse loans.** Under the no-recourse loan system, farmers borrow money from a government agency and, as collateral for the loan, pledge their crop evaluated at the support price (P_s). If, at harvest time, the market price were higher than the support price, the farmer would sell the crop in the market, repay the government loan, and keep the difference. However, if the market price is below the support price (as shown in Figure 36-1), the farmer will turn over the crop to the government in repayment of the loan and the government must bear any resulting loss. The no-recourse feature of the loan means that the government cannot require the farmer to do more than turn over the crop.

At the support price P_s in Figure 36-1, quantity Q_2 will be demanded in the market, but quantity Q_3 will be supplied, leaving an unsold or "surplus" quantity of Q_2Q_3, shown by the horizontal distance from point *A* (on the demand curve at price P_s) to point *B* (on the supply curve at price P_s). This surplus is purchased, stored, and held off the market, mainly by government agencies but partly by individual farmers and other speculators. Some of it is given away in aid programs or sold under such programs at prices below the world price, which we suppose is close to the market price of P_m.

Under the support price system, the total receipts of farmers are represented by the rectangle $0P_sBQ_3$, which is considerably greater than the amount received at the equilibrium market price. Of these higher farm receipts, purchasers in the market (i.e., consumers) pay the amount represented by the rectangle $0P_sAQ_2$, and the government (i.e., taxpayers) pay the amount represented by the rectangle Q_2ABQ_3. If the demand curve is

FIGURE 36-1   Market Price, Support Price, and Target Price for a Farm Crop

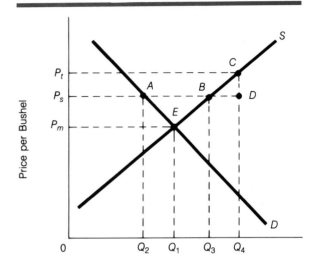

Quantity (millions of bushels)

In the absence of government price and production controls, the market would clear at the equilibrium point *E*, with market price P_m and quantity Q_1 demanded and supplied. If the price is supported at P_s, quantity supplied will be Q_3, as indicated by point *B* on the supply curve, but consumers will purchase only quantity Q_2, as indicated by point *A* on the demand curve. Government must purchase quantity Q_2Q_3. At a target price of P_t, farmers will supply quantity Q_4. Consumers will again buy quantity Q_2 at the support price of P_s. The government will buy the remainder, quantity Q_2Q_4, at the support price, P_s. Farmers will receive deficiency payments in the amount of $P_t - P_s$ per unit of output. Total deficiency payments are represented by the area of the rectangle P_sP_tCD.

price inelastic over the price range from P_m to P_s, which is usually the case, consumers' payments for this crop will be greater than before (even though they are buying less) so that they contribute to the farmers' gains. But most of the increase in farm receipts is paid by taxpayers. Taxpayers may recoup some money from sales of the surplus (as noted above) but they also have to pay for storing the crop after it has been transferred to the government.

The price support system that we described above prevailed for the forty years from 1933 to 1973, with some departures during the years of

U.S. participation in World War II (1941–1945) and its immediate aftermath. But the farmers eventually wanted more. Partly because of consumer resistance to higher food prices and partly because of problems in storing large quantities of surplus crops, the government responded to the new farm demands with the target price system rather than with higher support prices.

Under the target price system, for each crop in the program, the government selects a price, such as P_t in Figure 36-1, which is above the support price. At this price, farmers will supply quantity Q_4, as shown by point C on the supply curve for this crop. Since the support price remains unchanged at P_s, the quantity purchased by consumers is unchanged at Q_2 and the entire increase in output (from Q_3 to Q_4) is purchased by the government along with the previously purchased quantity of Q_2Q_3.

The distinctive feature about the target price system is that the farmer receives a **deficiency payment** directly from the government for each bushel produced and sold. The deficiency payment is equal to the difference between the target price and the support price so that, in Figure 36-1, the total of deficiency payments received by farmers is represented by the rectangle P_sP_tCD. Thus, the target pricing system means no additional cost to consumers but a substantial increase in cost to taxpayers, who finance not only the deficiency payments but also the purchase and storage of the increases in crop surpluses generated by the target price. The addition of the target price feature accounts for much of the rise in the cost of government farm programs since 1973. In 1985, Congress reduced support levels to increase the competitiveness of U.S. farm exports, but kept target prices unchanged.

Production Controls

To reduce the cost to taxpayers (and also to reduce soil erosion), many American farm programs include production controls. These may be voluntary, as in "soil bank" programs, with payments for participants in exchange for removing acreage from production, or they may be com-

FIGURE 36-2 Production Controls Combined with Support and Target Prices

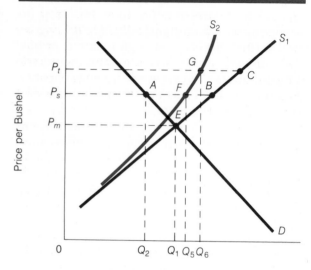

Quantity (millions of bushels)

The demand curve, D, and the prices P_m, P_s, and P_t are the same as in Figure 36-1. The supply curve from Figure 36-1 appears here as supply curve S_1. Production controls shift the supply curve to the left, from S_1 to S_2. They reduce the quantity purchased by the government under a price-support-only program to quantity Q_2Q_5, as indicated by point F on supply curve S_2. They reduce the quantity purchased by the government under the support-plus-target-price system to Q_2Q_6, as indicated by point G on supply curve S_2.

pulsory, as in the case of tobacco. In the tobacco program, each farmer proposing to grow this crop must first receive or purchase an allotment for the number of acres he or she may plant. It is illegal to grow tobacco, even for the farmer's own use, on acres not covered by an allotment. The right to grow tobacco on an acre of land was based, originally, on the use of land for tobacco-growing in 1933, but these rights could be sold apart from the land and transferred to other land owned by the buyer, provided that this land was in the same county. In tobacco-growing states today, rights to grow tobacco are worth more than the raw land without such rights. Once possessed of the right to grow tobacco on a given acre, the farmer may increase its yield and raise its quality to whatever extent that he of she considers worthwhile by piling on more labor, machinery, fertilizer, pesticide, and so on. As a result, tobacco production has decreased less than originally anticipated.

Figure 36-2 illustrates how a production-control program operates along with price support and target price programs. The demand curve (D), and the three prices $(P_m, P_s,$ and $P_t)$ are the same as in Figure 36-1. The supply curve from Figure 36-1 has been relabeled as supply curve S_1 in Figure 36-2. In addition, there is a new supply curve (S_2) that shows the results of the production-control program. The production-control program shifts the supply curve to the left. This reduces surpluses and government purchases under a price-support-only program to the quantity Q_2Q_5, as shown by point F on the new supply curve. Under the system involving both price supports and target prices, the supply shift reduces the surplus purchased by the government to Q_2Q_6, as shown by point G. This saves money for taxpayers, although they still must finance the payments that are made, under voluntary programs, to induce farmers to remove land from production. As long as the support price, P_s, is above the market price that would exist without controls (P_m), the cost to consumers is not affected by the production controls.

Costs and Benefits

Over the half-century since their inception in 1933, the American farm price and income support systems are estimated to have cost taxpayers some $130 billion. Even adjusting for inflation, it now costs thirty times what it did in the era of Franklin Roosevelt. In the 1930s, the cost was less than a penny per dollar of farm income. The mid-1980s figure is about 43 cents. And were the system to be dismantled, the Department of Agriculture estimates that American farm income would fall by some 40 percent.

Table 36-4 shows that U.S. government expenditure on farm programs totaled $16.2 billion for the year 1985. In addition, $18 billion was

TABLE 36-4   U.S. Government Expenditure on Farm Programs, Fiscal Year 1985 (billions of dollars)

Program	Cost
Payments to cut production	1.6
Purchase and storage of surpluses	3.3
No-recourse loans	4.4
Deficiency payments under target price systems	5.8
Research and development in agriculture	1.1
Total	16.2

Source: U.S. Department of Agriculture, reproduced by Mike Meyers et al., "Propping up the Farm," *Minneapolis Star and Tribune*, August 11, 1985.

spent to maintain or increase consumer demand for farm products. The largest domestic programs for "supplementary purchases of farm products" were for food stamps and school lunches. In addition, there were various international forms of food aid financed by U.S. taxpayers. The primary beneficiaries of this aid were poor and near-poor victims of unemployment, poverty, crop failures, or famine. But farmers in America were also beneficiaries.

In view of the great expansion of benefits, one may well wonder why so many people continue to leave the farm. The answer is not difficult. The key statistics can be seen in Table 36-5, which shows the distribution of farm support payments for 1985. Over 70 percent of the farms received only 11.2 percent of the direct government support payments. In contrast, 66.5 percent of the payments went to only 14.5 percent of the farms. The farmers who have been abandoning agriculture have been overwhelmingly those with small farms. They have little to sell.

In another group are those who have been producing unsupported crops, primarily fruits, vegetables, and other garden truck. Since payments under most government programs are based mainly on farm marketings, most gains go to the larger farms with large capital investments in land, machinery, and equipment. The operators of these farms rarely consider changing their occupation. True, there is a cap of $50,000 per

TABLE 36-5 Farm Support Payments and Numbers of Farms, by Farm Size Class, 1985

Farm Size (annual sales in thousands of dollars)	Percent of Farms	Percent of Direct Government Support Payments
Under 40	70.4	11.2
40–100	15.2	22.2
100–250	9.9	35.4
250–500	3.3	18.7
500 and over	1.3	12.4

Source: *Economic Report of the President, 1986*, Table 4-1, p. 132.

year in target-price deficiency payments to a single farm, but this can be avoided by subdividing properties among family members.

The evaluation of farm programs and of proposals to expand or contract them varies from time to time and from place to place. Farming communities naturally feel differently about them than do nonfarming communities. The analysis provided here can be usefully supplemented by intensive studies for particular crops and for smaller areas.[6]

For eight important commodities, the Council of Economic Advisers (CEA) has assembled and prepared estimates of gains and losses from farm programs as of the mid-1980s. We reproduce the CEA results as Table 36-6. In every case, the losses to consumers and/or taxpayers exceed the gains to producers. When the beneficiaries of a policy (here, the farmers) gain less than the rest of society loses (here, consumers and taxpayers), economists speak of a "dead-weight loss."

The CEA goes on to present two proposals to reduce the losses to consumers and taxpayers, while maintaining benefits to farmers at present levels. Their basic idea is to break the link between benefits and production by freezing benefits per

acre, or by basing them on past rather than on future production. This reform is intended to reduce farmers' incentives to overproduction, while permitting prices to fall to free-market levels. Students with special interests in agricultural economics can profit by considering these proposals further.

International Involvements

Other countries have farm programs of their own, all different from the American ones. Some, like the Common Agricultural Policy of the European Community (EC) are extremely complex, because of the desire to preserve "equity" among farmers in the different member countries. Because the agricultural exports of different countries compete on the world market and therefore sometimes influence each other's internal markets, trade conflicts are common even between political allies. Thus the major U.S. agricultural customer is Japan—which completely bans the import of rice and puts import restrictions on beef and citrus products. (Other Japanese rules discriminate by season; cherries, for example, are banned until July 1 of each year, to aid the earlier marketing of the domestic crop.) American-Canadian agricultural trade disagreements have centered on grains, potatoes, dairy products, and sugar.

In recent years, the main American agricultural-trade conflicts have been with the European Com-

6. A model study for Minnesota appeared in a Minneapolis newspaper and was attacked vigorously by representatives of farm organizations in the Minnesota countryside! See Mike Meyers et al., "Propping up the Farm," *Minneapolis Star and Tribune*, August 11–12, 1985.

TABLE 36-6 Losses and Gains from Farm Income Support Programs (annual costs in billions of dollars)

Commodity	Consumer Loss	Taxpayer Cost	Producer Gain	Total Loss
Sugar	2.5 to 2.9		1.6 to 1.8	0.9 to 1.1
Milk	1.7 to 3.7	1.9	1.8 to 3.9	1.7 to 1.8
Wheat	0.1	3.2	2.1	1.2
Corn	0.5 to 0.6	3.0 to 4.1	2.1 to 2.5	1.5 to 2.1
Cotton		1.5	1.1	0.4
Rice	0.09	0.71	0.58	0.22
Peanuts	0.184		0.180	0.004
Oranges[a]	0.047 to 0.059		0.026 to 0.043	0.016 to 0.021
Total	5.12 to 7.63	10.31 to 11.41	9.49 to 12.20	5.94 to 6.85

a. California and Arizona navel oranges.

Source: Economic Report of the President, 1986, Table 4-4, p. 156.

munity. Because EC production controls must be allocated between and among so many countries in widely differing agricultural circumstances—some high-cost and some low-cost, some net exporters and other net importers—such controls are fewer than in the United States. Production goes flat out, and surpluses are proportionately much larger—"butter mountains," "wine lakes," and so on. The costs of accumulating and maintaining these mountains and lakes must also be allocated among member governments and their taxpayers. The temptation is greater than in the United States both to exclude competitive imports "unfairly" and to engage in export subsidies that force down world prices. (The United States claims it avoids export subsidies and takes world prices as given.) In 1985–1986 the EC restricted imports of American grain and canned fruit. U.S. retaliations included penalties on the import of Italian *pasta* (allegedly made from export-subsidized wheat). This sort of sniping is nothing new, and it seems certain to continue.

THE FARM DEBT PROBLEM

If you turn back to Table 36-3, you will see that U.S. farm acreage rose from 298 million in 1965 to 347 million in 1985. This is a 16½ percent

increase, almost one-sixth. The bulk of this increase occurred in the 1970s, set off by a great expansion of U.S. agricultural exports to the Third World and the USSR. The expansion was encouraged by the U.S. government, which expected export demand to continue growing and hoped to avoid rises in domestic food prices. Encouragement took the form not only of propaganda but of easy credit in the inflation following the first oil shock (1973).

Farmers rushed to mortgage their land and houses, using the money to bring more land into cultivation (as shown in Table 36-3). They also bought farm buildings, farm machinery, and livestock to increase their production per acre. When the export boom in fact subsided—partly because rival exporters also increased their outputs, and partly because the exchange value of the U.S. dollar rose in international markets—many of these borrowing farmers found themselves overextended and could not meet their obligations. Having followed the government "line" in getting into debt, resentful farmers naturally expected the government to bail them out after its forecasts had turned sour—which is to say, after farm prices turned down.

Making matters worse for the farm debtors, the end of the export boom coincided with a shift to disinflation (falling inflation rates) in domestic monetary policy. This hurt farmers by decreasing the market value of the real-estate collateral for their loans. Land prices fell because so much of the demand for rural real estate had been for an inflation hedge related only indirectly to real agricultural productivity.

Total farm debt in 1985 was estimated at $210 billion—more than the international debts of Brazil and Mexico combined at that time. The seriousness of the problem to the debtor farmers was summarized by the Council of Economic Advisers as follows:

A succinct indicator of U.S. agriculture's financial problem is its debt/asset ratio. This ratio fell in the early 1970s, but in 1974 [it] again started to rise. In the 1980s [it] jumped to levels unseen since the Great Depression. A major reason was the erosion of land and machinery values. Land values fell an average of 19 percent between 1981 and 1985.

Financial problems are concentrated in the regions with the largest land-value declines; i.e., the Corn Belt, the Lake States, and the Northern Plains. Roughly 60 percent of farms classified as financially distressed by the U.S. Department of Agriculture (USDA) was in these regions; a farm is considered financially distressed if its debt/asset ratio exceeds 40 percent and it cannot generate enough cash income to pay its bills. About 12½ percent of all farms were in this category on January 1, 1985.[7]

In terms of farm size (as measured by crop value), financial distress is concentrated in the $40,000 to $250,000 categories. These medium-large farms account for 25 percent of the total number, produce 41 percent of gross farm income, and include 51 percent of the financially distressed farms, as shown in Table 36-7. The smaller farms were in most cases unwilling or unable to overborrow; the largest ones were more nearly able to finance their debt burdens.

Under these circumstances it is natural to argue that any reform in the existing price support systems would endanger those farmers who are under the greatest financial stress—those in danger of being forced off the farm entirely or reduced to tenancy status on the farms they now own. But the present support systems are not well adapted to meeting the debt crisis, since the

7. Running quotation from *Economic Report of the President, 1986*, pp. 132–133.

TABLE 36-7 Financially Distressed Farms by Sales Class, January 1985

Farm Sales Class (in thousands of dollars)	Percentage of Farms in Financial Distress
Less than 10	15
10–20	9
20–40	15
40–100	29
100–250	22
250–500	7
Over 500	3

Source: *Economic Report of the President, 1986*, Chart 4-1, p. 134.

largest support payments go to the farms that produce the most. As Table 36-7 shows, these are in a less difficult position than somewhat smaller farms. Another way of looking at the situation is that farms in financial distress (as defined by USDA) receive only 24 percent of direct government payments. Of these, the most distressed receive slightly less than half (11 percent). The great bulk of government payments go to American farms that are not in a distressed position.

THE AMERICAN AGRICULTURAL FUTURE

Farming in America has long been the butt of economic humor. Because land values have often been rising while farm incomes are low, it has been said that "farming is a way to live poor and die rich" or that farming is "a losing proposition financed by the profits from land speculation." Conventional views about the future of American agriculture include the following extensions of historical trends: (1) that the number of farms and farmers will continue to fall, (2) that the average size of farms will continue to rise, (3) that the proportion of farm families who rent part or all of their land from others will continue to rise, and (4) that the average measured income of farmers will continue to lag behind the measured income of nonfarmers. All of these conventional views may be correct, but they are often misinterpreted. Many demographic, technical, and economic factors work to modify them. For example, the average price of farm land, which rose quite steadily for the generation after World War II, fell during the first half of the 1980s.

Misinterpreting Trends

Lower relative farm incomes need not mean lower relative incomes for families living on farms, because the multiple-earner family has come to the country. The farm husband, or wife, or young adult child, or semiretired parent can now commute for part-time or full-time work off the farm, as factory and office jobs move away from urban centers. More than most other kinds of work, farming can become and is becoming a part-time or part-family business, and farm families remain larger than nonfarm families.

Larger farms, higher land prices (if the 1945–1980 trend resumes), and more farm tenancy need not doom the family farm, lead to "corporate farming," or turn the farmer into a peasant. It is true that corporate farms and farm management companies are no longer novelties and will remain with us. This trend will become even stronger if nonfarmers continue to use investment in farm land as a hedge against inflation and if the "urban sprawl" of growing suburbs raises the price of land near cities. But there is little reason to expect corporate farming and farm management companies to replace the family farm. What is more likely is that the representative head of the farm family will be both wealthier and more highly trained than his or her parents or grandparents were. As to farm tenancy, many tenant farmers are young people in the process of buying some or all of the land they work, and many farm landlords are retired farmers.

Demographic, Technological, and Economic Factors

In the generation following the end of World War II, the so-called "population explosion," espe-

cially in developing countries, sharply raised world demand for American grains and other farm products. It is hard to predict how fast world population will grow in the future and to what extent that growth will mean increases in the commercial demand for American farm products. Since so many of these countries and people are poor, much of their demand has, in the past, been met on a relief rather than a commercial basis.

Technological advances in grain production (such as the Green Revolution, which we shall discuss later in this chapter) may continue to raise the capability of the growing populations in tropical and semitropical countries to feed themselves or even to export grain in competition with American farmers. Other technological revolutions, from the cotton picker to oleomargarine and the "square tomato," may affect other crops. An example is the hydroponic raising of vegetables on chemicals and water (without soil). This technology has been known for at least a generation but is not yet economically feasible.

Finally, the amount of freedom present in international trade will affect the size of the market for U.S. farm products. But here the picture depends on which farm crop we are talking about. On the one hand, Soviet purchases of American grain are important. So American farmers objected strongly to the export limitation imposed in protest against the Soviet invasion of Afghanistan in 1979. On the other hand, freer trade would hurt American dairy farmers, potato farmers, producers of cane and beet sugar, and cattle ranchers. It would mean that more Canadian dairy products and potatoes, more Latin American and Philippine sugar, and more Argentine and Australian meat and wool would be supplied to the American market causing downward pressure on the prices of these products.

FOOD AND POVERTY

For the rest of this chapter, we move from the American to the world economy and from relative prosperity to threatening poverty. To mark this change, our section heading is part of the title of

TABLE 36-8 World Population Estimates and Forecasts for the Twentieth Century

World population, 1900	1,620 million
World population, 1980	4,374 million
World population, 2000	6,260 million
Annual increase rate, 1900–1980	1.25 percent
Annual increase rate, 1980–2000	1.81 percent
Annual increase rate, 1900–2000	1.36 percent

Source: David Barrett, ed., *World Christian Encyclopedia* (Nairobi, Kenya: Oxford University Press, 1982). Used by permission.

a pessimistic study of the world food problem by the Indian economist Radha Prasad Sinha.[8]

We have never had, and still do not have, any accurate count of world population, let alone an accurate forecast of its future course. (Imagine sending census takers into the middle of the Sahara Desert or into the Amazon jungles or up the Himalayas!) But reasonable estimates, such as those presented in Table 36-8, suggest that world population has increased rapidly so far in the twentieth century and that it is expected to increase still more rapidly in the remaining years before 2000. It is now estimated that the increase in world population during the first 80 years of this century was some 70 percent greater than all the previous increase from the beginning of the human race to the year 1900. In other words, world population in 1980 was 2.7 times greater than in 1900. Despite the apparent spread of various forms of birth control, the world population growth rate seems to be accelerating, thanks mainly to falling infant mortality rates and adult death rates from communicable and epidemic diseases. These bald figures, estimates, and forecasts raise very important questions. How can all these people be fed? What will happen if they are not fed? The major contemporary danger is concentrated in the twenty-odd countries of sub-Saharan Africa, particularly those of East Africa.

In his famous *Essay on Population*, which appeared in 1798, the British economist Thomas

Malthus predicted that limitations on the food supply would operate to limit population growth. He wrote of "positive checks," such as war, famine, and pestilence, as placing natural limits on population growth. Indeed, it does appear that such checks may have slowed the growth of world population, at least until the start of this century.

Even though economics has been called the "dismal science," most economists refuse to accept the grim forecast that world population growth must lead to world famine. We shall describe four scenarios offering hope that famine can be prevented.

Agricultural Technology

One scenario points to continuing or accelerated advances in agricultural productivity—in other words, technological "fixes" of many kinds, large and small, which Julian Simon and other writers trace largely to population growth itself.[9] Simon believes that the more people there are, the greater is the long-term likelihood of technological innovations and advances, even in the absence of higher education in any formal sense. So far, these advances have kept total food production per person rising steadily in spite of the twentieth-century population explosion. Some of the technological fixes may be new products, from chemical "food pills" to edible algae or bacteria. More likely are better methods of growing present crops or improving varieties of our present crops. More multiple cropping or better blight resistance, for example, could lead to larger farm yields, and new means of controlling weather, rodents, and insects during harvests or in storage could lead to smaller losses.

The Green Revolution

To date, the most ambitious technological fix to make the desert blossom like the farms of Iowa

8. Radha Prasad Sinha, *Food and Poverty: The Political Economy of Confrontation* (London: Croom Helm, 1976).

9. Julian Simon, *The Ultimate Resource* (Princeton, N.J.: Princeton University Press, 1981).

has been called the **Green Revolution.** This consisted of the development and propagation of high-yielding dwarf and hybrid varieties of both wheat and rice. Though it has not yet fulfilled the high hopes generated for it in the 1960s, it may not yet have received a fair test.

The new varieties of crops are greatly dependent on modern inputs, mainly chemical fertilizers and pesticides. These in turn are feasible only in areas with both assured water supplies and little danger of flooding. Even in such areas, there is concern about the possible environmental effects of these chemicals in the long run. Also, successfully raising the new crops calls for increases in agricultural credit, which in many less developed countries is available at reasonable rates only to the large farms.

"As a result," says Professor Sinha with reference to Indian conditions, "the main advantage of the new technology accrued to the rich farmers or to regions which already had adequate factor endowments. . . . Undoubtedly, it was the large and medium farmers who were the main beneficiaries of the 'Green Revolution' in India. Some of these farms bought tractors and other agricultural machinery, which may have had some labour-displacing effect."[10]

To put matters more bluntly, the Green Revolution had the unintended side effect of turning many small farmers and tenants into landless laborers, since they could not obtain the credit they needed to use the new techniques and therefore sold their rights to their richer neighbors. Some, indeed, seem to have left the land entirely, or been driven from it like the Okies and Arkies in *The Grapes of Wrath.*

Family Planning

Drastic reductions in world birthrates offer another possible way to solve the problems of food and poverty. In addressing the United Nations on October 4, 1965, Pope Paul VI said, "You must strive to multiply bread so that it suffices for the tables of mankind." After calling for this multi-

plication of bread, the Pope restated the traditional view of the Roman Catholic Church, opposing any "artificial control of birth, which would be irrational, in order to diminish the number of guests at the banquet of life." So far, much of the world seems to be following his advice. However, resistance to family planning is due only in part to the influence of Catholicism and other natalist religions. Certain social and economic considerations also play an important part.

In poor countries with traditionally high infant mortality rates, poor educational systems, and few facilities for the care of needy older people, children are their parents' social security; the more, the better. Children can work from early ages, either for their own families or for outside employers. There is little or no opportunity for a tradeoff between having many "low-quality" (unskilled, uneducated, and undernourished) children and fewer "higher-quality" (skilled, educated, and healthy) ones. Supporting these economic facts of life are social attitudes. A man who has fathered more children is believed to be sexually superior to a man who has fathered fewer children, and a woman who has borne more children is similarly thought to be superior to a woman who has borne fewer children.

But when economic growth does take place, birthrates soon fall, whether or not the people adhere to natalist religions or philosophies. The demographic records of the Western world, of Japan, and more recently of Taiwan and South Korea, show that both birthrates and (with a lag) population growth rates generally fall as medical and public health techniques improve and as per capita income rises, especially when modernization also includes mass education and social security institutions. The People's Republic of China is another, much larger example, but the Chinese government has used unusually harsh methods—the so-called "one-child policy"—to bring this about. The lag in the population figures is due to the rising life expectancy of adults and the gradual aging of the population as a whole. However, doubt remains as to whether economic growth will in fact take place in enough less developed countries to lower the population growth

10. Sinha, op. cit., p. 32.

TABLE 36-9   Average Energy and Protein Supply, by Region

Region	Energy (calories per person per day)	Protein (grams per person per day)
World	2,480	69.0
Developed countries	3,150	96.4
(North America)	(3,320)	(105.2)
(Western Europe)	(3,130)	(93.7)
Developing countries	2,200	57.4
(Latin America)	(2,530)	(65.0)
(Africa)	(2,190)	(58.4)
(Far East)	(2,080)	(50.7)

Source: Radha Prasad Sinha, *Food and Poverty: The Political Economy of Confrontation* (London: Croom Helm, 1976), Table 2. Used with permission.

rates in time to keep the Third World malnutrition rate from rising as rapidly as the pessimists fear.

Income Redistribution

A middle-class American today consumes nearly twice as many nutrients per day as the average person in a less developed country. Average energy and protein supplies are shown in Table 36-9. Redistribution of income would mean that less land would be used for raising luxury foods, particularly meat, and nonfood "crops" like flowers and tobacco, lawns, and golf courses. More land would be used for raising grains, vegetables, fruit, eggs, and dairy products.

Food First is the title of a book by two American writers, Frances Moore Lappé and Joseph Collins.[11] This book calls for both income redistribution and a restructuring of productive activity in the direction of food for the world's poor. It makes the following main arguments:

1. A concentration of land use and agricultural production on a basically vegetarian diet along

with eggs, dairy products, and some fish, would allow "Spaceship Earth" to support 10 billion people free from famine and major malnutrition. This number would be more than twice the present world population.

2. Given the present international distributions of income and wealth, neither technological fixes nor population restriction will prevent a future wave of malnutrition for the world's poor.

3. The redistribution needed for a "Food First" policy can come about only after a major revolution or similar confrontation between rich and poor people and between rich and poor nations. (The Sinha study comes to similar conclusions.)

Certain clear but insoluble normative questions are raised in connection with any Food First program. One might ask, for example, how important the goal of alleviating hunger among the world's poor is, compared with the prospective living standards of the world's rich and middle classes.[12] Also, one may ask about the effect (perhaps positive) on consumers, both rich and poor, of shifting land to the Food First system

11. Frances Moore Lappé and Joseph Collins, *Food First: Beyond the Myth of Scarcity* (New York: Ballantine Books, 1979).

12. During World War II, Secretary of Agriculture Henry A. Wallace was ridiculed for "globaloney" and "milk for Hottentots" even though his food-sharing proposals were mild compared with those in the Food First program.

and having less of certain industrial products, like rubber and wool, which are now produced on these lands. Remember that the consumer does not live by bread alone.

However, the three Food First propositions are stated in a positive rather than a normative way. For the sake of discussion, let us assume that the first and the third are true—that many more people could be supported at a poor person's living level than at a rich person's living level (given the amount and quality of the world's agricultural land) and that a major redistribution would require confrontation if not actual revolution. The second statement, however, needs further explanation. Why can't technological fixes and lower birthrates solve food problems and bring down real food prices as readily as redistribution and Food First?

In answering this question, the main point is that both technical fixes and lower birth rates act slowly and differentially. That is, they benefit some people much more immediately and completely than they benefit the mass of the population. As you may recall, higher- and middle-income Indian farmers benefited more immediately than the rest of the Indian people in the Green Revolution case. This may mean that beneficiary groups will react by enlarging and improving their diets in the direction of the diets presently followed by high-income people and high-income countries. That is, they will eat more meat, fish, eggs, and sugar. As the ill-fated Marie Antoinette suggested, they may eat cake, pie, or pastry instead of bread, rice, or potatoes. They will also consume more coffee, tea, cola, tobacco, and alcohol. Not that there is anything immoral about luxuries, but their production may shift land at the margin away from the staples eaten by the poor. These marginal substitution processes may be so rapid and strong as to outweigh the expected effects of technical fixes and lower population growth rates themselves on the diets of the remaining poor. The poor may become a somewhat smaller proportion of the population and they may become fewer in number, but their misery, alienation, and susceptibility to violence would be no less.

SUMMARY

1. Farm discontent is a recurring theme in U.S. history. An especially widespread protest movement, called Populism, arose during the period between the American Civil War and the turn of the century.

2. Part of the farmers' dissatisfaction arises from the belief that they must sell their produce for what it will bring on competitive markets, while the prices of many goods and services that farmers buy are monopolized, cartelized, or otherwise controlled by nonfarm people.

3. Among the "exploiters" cited by farmers and their protest movements have been the suppliers of credit (bankers), the railroads and truck lines, the operators of grain elevators and other storage facilities, the sellers of agricultural implements and fertilizer, and general merchants in rural towns.

4. Another set of problems for farmers arises from the price and income inelasticities of demand for their products. Price inelasticity means that large crops may mean low income. Income inelasticity means that the quantity of farm products demanded does not keep up with other products when consumers' incomes rise.

5. Farmers also complain that farm land prices are too high to permit a young person to establish a family farm early in life, and at the same time that these prices are too low to justify the property and estate taxes on farm owners and their families.

6. One response from farmers has been agricultural fundamentalism, the doctrine that, since food is essential to life, farmers should be at least as well off as others in the population. Depressions are allegedly "farm led and farm fed."

7. Farmers have reacted to their grievances, and to technological changes that made them more acute, by leaving the farm, by political agitation, and by forming farmers' cooperatives.

8. The principal benefit gained by political agitation in the United States is a system of farm price supports, based on a concept of parity for farm prices and incomes. The price support system uses the device of the no-recourse loan to permit farmers to hold crops off the market while awaiting higher prices, without market risk if prices fall.

9. The American price support system usually involves government purchase of surpluses or buffer stocks and raises prices and gross incomes of farmers at the expense of both consumers and taxpayers. When price supports are combined with production restrictions, the burden on taxpayers is less than it would otherwise be.

10. Under the target price system, farmers are compensated at taxpayer expense by the receipt of deficiency payments per unit of farm output.

11. It is estimated that the cost of U.S. farm income support programs to consumers and taxpayers far exceeds the gains to producers.

12. Government farm support programs result in conflict with other countries when these programs lower the prices of products exchanged in international trade.

13. Indebtedness of U.S. farmers reached unprecedentedly high levels in the 1980s because of declines in farm exports and farm real estate values. Farm income support programs were poorly suited to meeting this problem.

14. The future of American agriculture depends on a variety of demographic, technological, and economic factors. Much depends on the freedom of international trade and on population trends in the world.

15. The accelerating rate of world population growth could bring severe suffering. At the same time, the planet could support a much larger population than the present one if agricultural land were shifted from its present uses to the growing of staple foods.

16. The main remedies proposed for the threat of world malnutrition have been continued or accelerated technological improvements in agriculture, declining population growth, and the redistribution of world income and wealth. The Green Revolution in the production of wheat and rice has been an outstanding technological development in world agriculture.

17. Many countries, including both developed countries and newly industrializing ones, have in fact lowered their reproduction and population growth rates.

18. Living standards have risen in many countries. Because these higher standards have placed a burden on world agricultural facilities, the world's poor are no better off today than they were in the past, and the threat of major famines remains.

19. If worldwide income and wealth redistribution reduced malnutrition and the threat of famine in the world, it could be at the expense of a considerable decline in the living standards of people who are not poor. Therefore, any significant redistribution or equalization of world income and wealth might require revolution or similar confrontation.

DISCUSSION QUESTIONS

1. What was "Populism"? Briefly describe how government monetary policies played a role in this movement. Why have farmers often prospered during wartimes but suffered hard times after the war was over?

2. Explain how both price and income inelasticities of demand for farm products have caused problems for farmers. How does price inelasticity of demand play a role in making government price support programs attractive for farmers? How do consumers fare under these programs?

3. Discuss the belief that American recessions and depressions are "farm led and farm fed."

4. Farm prices are systematically lower at harvest time than six or eight months later, other things being equal. Does the differential indicate exploitation of farmers by speculators on the commodity exchanges? Explain your answer.

5. Explain how the target price system differs from the procedures under price support plans.

6. Do you believe that farmers facing a debt crisis in the 1980s are entitled to help from the government? Why or why not? In what way are existing farm income support programs poorly suited to helping farmers facing the debt crisis?

7. In your opinion, is the world facing a major food crisis? Why or why not?

8. Church, campus, and other socially conscious groups stage campaigns during which participants either fast or limit themselves to the diets

of Asian or African peasants. Money saved by this frugality is sent to poor countries for food purchases. What good, if any, do you think is done by these campaigns?

9. It is forecasted that meat will become a much less important element in our diets during future years. What is the argument in back of such forecasts? Do you agree?

10. Should controls be enacted to limit the use of farm land for housing, factories, or other nonagricultural uses? Defend your answer.

11. Should American agriculture shift from non-food cash crops to a Food First policy? Why or why not? Should Mexican agriculture make this shift? Why or why not?

37 *Natural Resources and the Environment*

PREVIEW Your training in microeconomics can be helpful in understanding many issues relating to the conservation of natural resources and care of the environment. This chapter considers three such issues—the conservation of exhaustible resources such as petroleum or mineral deposits, the management of renewable resources such as wildlife or forests, and the protection of the environment from excessive pollution.

The first section of the chapter, on exhaustible resources, shows how the market system contains certain built-in features that control the depletion of these resources. It shows how production costs and interest rates help determine how rapidly known deposits of these resources are used. It also explains how markets fail to control the use of these resources efficiently and thus invite intervention by government.

The second part of the chapter focuses on renewable resources, such as wildlife and trees in the forest. Microeconomic analysis provides useful guidelines for the efficient use and propagation of these resources. It also explains how treating these resources as common property can result in an inefficiently small amount for future generations.

The last section of the chapter applies economic analysis to the relationship between the quality of the environment and the disposal of waste generated by production and consumption. It explains how pricing mechanisms can be used to prevent excessive generation and dumping of waste. It also notes some of the problems that arise in using these pricing mechanisms and discusses how government controls may be used or misused in regulating environmental quality.

EXHAUSTIBLE NATURAL RESOURCES

Exhaustible natural resources are those for which, at any given time, a fixed stock exists. What was used by past generations is not available today and what is used today will not be available to future generations. Crude petroleum is an exhaustible natural resource. The petroleum that exists today is the result of eons of time in the earth's evolution, during which the earth received energy from the sun and various forms of life grew, died, and decayed. In this sense, even now oil pools and new coalfields are being formed. Realistically, however, the time required for these changes to take place is so great that the process is irrelevant from the human point of view. For the people living today, or even for all of humanity, past, present, and, presumably, future, the stock of exhaustible natural resources cannot be increased.

Exhaustible natural resources should be clearly distinguished from **nonexhaustible natural resources,** such as energy from the sun, from winds, or from tides. Since the earth receives a continuing flow of these resources from the sun and from gravitational forces, there is no conservation problem. The economic questions for exhaustible resources are fundamentally different from those for nonexhaustible resources. For exhaustible resources, the overriding economic question is how rapidly the existing stock of these resources should be used.

In the market system, there are certain mechanisms that regulate the rate at which exhaustible resources are used. This should not be surprising if you remember that the rate of use, per unit of time, is the variable that customarily appears on the horizontal axis of supply and demand graphs. The very first graph that you studied (Figure 3-2 in Chapter 3) showed, on the horizontal axis, the number of hours that coal miners worked *per week*. That is a rate of use per unit of time. In Chapter 5 you studied the quantity of jeans demanded and supplied *per year*, and so on. These flows per unit of time are an easy starting place for our study of conservation. Figure 37-1 shows supply and demand for an exhaustible natural resource. Moving to the right along the horizontal axis means that the rate of use is increased and that less of the resource remains for future generations. Moving to the left along this axis means that the rate of use is decreased, leaving more for future generations. As you know, these moves along the quantity axis take place because of shifts in demand and/or supply curves, which change the equilibrium point identified by their intersection. The supply curve shows the willingness of resource owners to extract the resource from its natural state and offer it for sale. For this reason, we are especially interested in forces that can shift the supply curve.

Shifting the Supply Curve

In Figure 37-1, supply curve S_1 shows how the quantity extracted from the earth and offered for sale depends on the market price of the natural resource. Extracting and selling the resource is more profitable at higher prices than at lower prices, other things being equal. Therefore, economic analysis leads us to expect that firms will respond to higher prices by increasing the rate of extraction of the resource.

As you have learned from your study of microeconomics, the supply curve may shift when

FIGURE 37-1   Shifting the Supply Curve of an Exhaustible Natural Resource

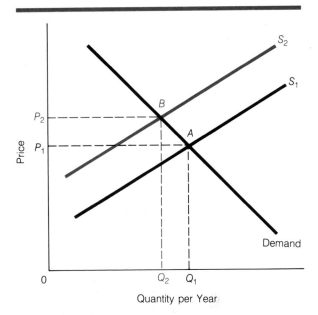

Supply curve S_1 reflects the cost of extracting a resource when easily accessible deposits are being used. Equilibrium is at A, with price P_1 and quantity Q_1. When easily accessible deposits of the resource have been used up, so that supply must come from more expensive sources, the supply curve shifts to S_2. Equilibrium is now at B, with price P_2 and quantity Q_2. As more and more of the relatively accessible deposits of the resource are used up, supply continues to shift to the left, and, other things being equal, equilibrium quantities extracted decrease.

the *ceteris paribus* assumption is relaxed and some variable other than the price of the product or resource changes. In analyzing the supply of an exhaustible natural resource, the accessibility of deposits of the resource is a very important variable that can cause a shift of the supply curve. In terms of accessibility, firms engaged in mining coal or iron ore or in pumping crude oil usually start by extracting the deposits that are the easiest to get, since, at any given price, extracting and selling them generally brings the largest profit. In fact, if a firm holds title to a deposit that is difficult or costly to extract, it may simply be unprofitable to extract and sell the coal or oil in competition with supplies from firms that are using deposits that are easier and cheaper to extract. In such cases, the going price in the market will not be high enough to cover the costs of extracting the less-accessible deposit. So these deposits will not be brought to the market until the more-accessible ones have been used up or until new technologies lower the cost of extraction.

As easily accessible deposits of a resource are exhausted and supply must come from more expensive sources, the market-supply curve will shift to the left. Figure 37-1 shows what happens in this case. The supply curve S_1 reflects the costs of extracting the resource when easily accessible deposits are being used. It slopes upward because, even with easily available deposits, suppliers are willing to offer more at higher prices than at lower prices. While easily accessible deposits are available, equilibrium is at point A, with price P_1 and quantity Q_1 demanded and supplied per year. But when the easily accessible deposits have been used up, so that supply must come from more costly sources, the supply curve shifts to S_2 and equilibrium is at point B, with price P_2 and quantity Q_2 demanded and supplied each year. As more and more of the relatively accessible deposits of the resource are used up, other things being equal, the supply curve shifts still farther to the left. The price climbs and the amount of the resource that is used each year falls. The market system of conservation is acting to prevent sudden shortages or exhaustion of the resource.

The accessibility of deposits of an exhaustible natural resource is not the only variable that can shift the supply curve in Figure 37-1. Changes in the technology of extracting the resource can have powerful effects on the location of the curve. Technological advances that lower costs of extraction shift the supply curve to the right. In this case, the price to consumers may not rise as the more accessible deposits are used up. The rate of use of the resource may not decrease. It is possible that the effect of technological advances in extracting the resource can exceed the price-increasing tendency of the exhaustion of easily accessible deposits. Therefore, we should not conclude that

the market price of an exhaustible resource will necessarily increase just because the more accessible deposits have been used up. Sometimes, advances in technology lead to the discovery of previously unknown deposits of the resource itself. This also can shift the supply curve to the right and lower the price of the resource.

The Mystery of "Proven Reserves"

Over the years, a great deal of confusion has arisen from published statistics on the amounts of "proven reserves" that exist for such exhaustible natural resources as oil, natural gas, iron ore, and coal. These statistics report the number of barrels of oil, or tons of coal, or cubic feet of natural gas that are known to remain. Confusion has arisen because the amount remaining often appears to *increase* at the same time that increasing amounts are extracted and used. To have more of the resource available when the rate of use rises seems to contradict the whole idea that resources are exhaustible. Fortunately, your understanding of economics can help you unravel this apparent contradiction.

The search for deposits of exhaustible resources is a more or less continuous process. Exploration companies are looking for new deposits at the same time that production companies are drawing down deposits already known. However, the expected future price of the resource greatly influences the explorations that are undertaken. If the price of the resource is expected to rise, searches become more frequent and more intensive, since discoveries promise to be more profitable. Firms will be willing to spend more on exploration and on extraction of both old and new deposits. For example, at any given time, petroleum geologists know of many areas where oil is likely to be found. They also know that the cost of extracting the oil from many of these places would make production unprofitable. For this reason, they do not go to the expense of actually proving the presence of these deposits. But as price rises are predicted, it pays to explore and prove the existence of these previously suspected deposits. In this way, "proven reserves" may indeed increase at the same time that current production rises.

Geologists who estimate the total quantities of various natural resources find that impressively large amounts of most of them exist in small or inaccessible quantities scattered here and there throughout the world. It is not likely that we shall literally "run out" of any of them. However, for economic reasons, we may stop using some of them as their cost rises in relation to the cost of alternative resources.

The Importance of Price Elasticity of Demand

It is easy to see from Figure 37-1 that the price elasticity of demand plays an important part in the market's method of conserving exhaustible natural resources. Shifting the supply curve to the left brings a much greater reduction in annual equilibrium quantities if the demand is elastic than if it is inelastic over that range. This is the case because an elastic demand generally means that there are good substitutes, so that consumers switch to them as the price of the exhaustible resource rises. Conservation is easier and quicker when good substitutes are available than when they are not. Indeed, the whole problem of resource conservation melts away if good substitutes can easily be found.

Our story cannot end, of course, with the confusing statement that conservation is both easier and less critical when demand is price elastic than when it is price inelastic. One of the most appealing features of the method that the market system uses to conserve resources comes from the likelihood that price elasticity itself increases as time passes. As you learned in Chapter 22, if only a very short time period is considered, consumers have little opportunity to discover substitute goods or services and to adjust their lifestyles to make use of these substitutes. Demand for an item that is presently being used may be quite price inelastic. But as time passes and consumers keep searching for ways to avoid

the higher price of an increasingly scarce natural resource, new products are developed to take the place of those that have become more expensive and people change their lifestyles so they can use these new substitutes. The demand curve becomes more price elastic as time passes, and the market system's conservation process becomes more and more effective.

The response of the American consumer to rising prices of oil during the 1970s is an excellent example of how the passage of time affects price elasticity of demand. At first, after oil prices shot upward in 1973–1974 and again in 1979, consumers could only make small adjustments in their earlier patterns of consumption. Vacation trips could be shortened and home heating temperatures could be reduced (and more sweaters worn), but these measures offered relatively little opportunity to reduce the amount of oil demanded. But as time passed, consumers were able to change their lifestyles by joining car pools, taking fewer drives in the country, and so on. Also, small cars that use less gasoline per mile were introduced, better insulation was put into homes, and a host of energy-saving devices were developed to help consumers use less oil. The price elasticity of demand for oil was much greater when viewed over a five- or ten-year period than when viewed over a one-year period.

The Interest Rate and Conservation

The rate of interest has an important effect on the conservation of exhaustible natural resources. In our study of the role of interest rates, we shall first see how they are related to the price of exhaustible natural resources and then we shall see how they provide a connection between conservation and other values in the economy.

HOW INTEREST RATES AFFECT NATURAL RE-SOURCE PRICES To understand the role of interest rates on the price of exhaustible natural resources, imagine that you own an oil well, that you know exactly how much oil is in the ground and that you expect the cost of extracting the oil to be a constant fraction of its selling price. All you need to do is decide how much of the oil to extract this year and how much to leave for future years. Here is how the rate of interest affects your decision.

Suppose that the present price of the oil allows you to earn $10 a barrel profit after all costs of extraction have been paid. If the present rate of interest on securities of equivalent risk is 10 percent, you could extract a barrel of the oil, receive $10, and buy securities that would provide $11 one year from now. In other words, you could invest (in the financial sense) the $10 at 10 percent interest and realize $11 one year from now ($10 × 1.1 = $11). Is it a wise move for you to extract the oil today? The answer depends on what the price of the oil turns out to be one year from now. If the price one year from now yields a profit of $12 a barrel, leaving a $10 barrel in the ground would earn a return of 20 percent ($12/$10 = 1.2, that is, a gain in one year of $2 on an initial sum of $10 is a 20 percent gain). Your best choice would be to leave the oil in the ground. On the other hand, if the profit on the oil one year from now is only $10.50, your return per barrel left in the ground will be only 5 percent ($10.50/$10.00 = 1.05, that is, a $0.50 gain on an initial sum of $10.00 is a gain of 5 percent). In this case, your best move is to extract the oil and buy securities. Only if the profit one year from now is $11 a barrel are you exactly on the margin of whether or not to extract the resource.

The economic aspects of this little exercise arise from the effects that your decision has on the present and future prices of the resource. If you and thousands of others like you decide to leave the resource in the ground (as in the case of the $12 expected future profit), the supply curve for the resource in the *current* market will shift to the left and the current price will rise to yield more than $10 profit per barrel. At the same time, the increased likelihood that a greater amount of the resource will be extracted one year from now will shift the supply curve in the *future* market to the right and lower the expected future price so that the expected future profit will be less than $12. Thus, the decision to leave the resource in the

ground will tend to lower the rate of return from this strategy to less than the original 20 percent. The reasoning applies equally well in reverse. If you and thousands like you decide to go ahead and extract the resource and sell it in *today's* market (as in the case of the $10.50 expected future profit), the current price will fall to yield less than $10 profit, and the expected future profit will rise above $10.50. The rate of return from keeping the resource in the ground will rise above 5 percent.

As suppliers and potential suppliers routinely make calculations like these, an equilibrium will arise in which the year-to-year rate of increase in the price of the resource will approximate the rate of interest on alternative investments that are exposed to the same degree of risk. If this rate of interest is 10 percent, the resource price will rise at a rate of about 10 percent a year, other things being equal. The spread between present and future prices will be greater if the interest rate is higher and will be smaller if the rate of interest is lower, if other things remain unchanged. In effect, the expected future price of the resource, discounted to its present value with the appropriate interest rate, fixes a **reservation price**—that is, a price below which the resource will be reserved for future use by its owner.

CONSERVATION AND OTHER ECONOMIC VALUES The exercise that we have just carried out leads to some interesting ideas about the relationship between interest rates, conservation, and other values in the economy. To help you understand these relationships, we must review some of the key principles about interest rates that we presented earlier.

When you studied interest rates in Chapter 31, you learned that there are two major forces operating on them. One is the willingness of people to put off immediate consumption in exchange for greater future consumption, called "time preference." The other is the ability of machines and other capital equipment to raise output through roundabout methods of production, called "the productivity of capital." Those ideas are presented here in Figure 37-2. The

FIGURE 37-2 Supply and Demand for Loanable Funds

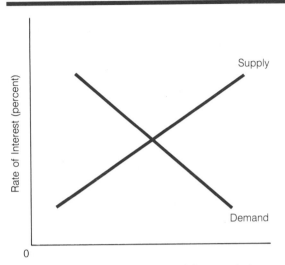

In the market for loanable funds, the supply curve incorporates the time preferences of suppliers of these funds. Under any given set of time preferences, higher interest rates call forth a larger flow of loanable funds, other things being equal. When time preferences change, the supply curve shifts. The demand curve incorporates the productivity of capital. Under given productivity conditions, the quantity demanded is greater at lower interest rates than at high interest rates. When the productivity of capital changes, the demand curve shifts. The interaction between suppliers and demanders of loanable funds tends to establish an equilibrium rate of interest.

supply curve incorporates the time preferences of suppliers of money for loans. Under any given set of time preferences, higher interest rates call forth a larger flow of funds to be loaned. When time preferences change, the supply curve shifts. The demand curve incorporates the productivity of capital. Under given productivity conditions, the quantity of loanable funds demanded will be greater at low interest rates than at high interest rates, other things being equal. When the productivity of capital changes, the demand curve shifts. The interaction between suppliers and

demanders of loanable funds tends to establish an equilibrium rate of interest that balances the quantity demanded with the quantity supplied.

FALLING INTEREST RATES To see how interest rates relate conservation of exhaustible natural resources to other economic values, suppose that something happens to change the time preferences of potential suppliers of loanable funds. To be specific, suppose that their time preferences change so that current consumption becomes less important and consumption in the future becomes more important. This might happen, for example, if war or the fear of war decreases, making people feel safer in planning for the future. This change in time preference would shift the supply curve in Figure 37-2 to the right and would bring a drop in interest rates, if other things remain unchanged.

As you learned earlier, lower interest rates narrow the spread between the present prices of exhaustible natural resources and their future prices. In this case, the narrowing takes place because resource owners find that the percentage return on other uses (financial investments) for their wealth has become less attractive. With less incentive to obtain funds for other uses, less of the resource is extracted, reducing the supply in the current market and raising its price.[1] In this way, the market responds to a shift in time preferences. When the preference for future consumption rises in relation to current consumption, interest rates fall and the rate of extraction of exhaustible natural resources also goes down. Thus, the pattern of use of the resource is consistent with time preference.

RISING INTEREST RATES Let us next take a case where interest rates rise because of a shift in the demand for loanable funds. Suppose there is a

1. We assume that the demand curve for the resource does not shift or at least that any shift in it will be quite small. We do so because the suppliers of loanable funds, whose time preferences have changed, are only a part of the total group of consumers of this resource and because this resource is only one of many items for current production.

technological breakthrough that increases the productivity of machines and equipment. In order to finance the construction of these machines, firms borrow money—that is, they demand loanable funds. The demand curve for loanable funds shifts to the right and interest rates rise. Our analysis of how interest rates affect the rate of extraction of exhaustible natural resources says that the spread between today's resource price and tomorrow's resource price will widen. This change takes place in the following way. With higher returns for alternative uses of their wealth, resource owners raise the rate at which they extract the resource in order to obtain the funds to take advantage of these new opportunities. The supply curve of the resource shifts to the right, and if other things remain unchanged, its current price falls, bringing a rise in the quantity demanded to match the rise in current extraction. The higher interest rate has encouraged more rapid use of the resource.[2]

These exercises show how rising and falling interest rates are signals of changes in preferences for present and future consumption and of changes in the productivity of machines and equipment. In this way, the price system integrates resource use rates with other aspects of the economic system. We do not mean to suggest, however, that high or low interest rates are either good or bad or that conservation of exhaustible resources is necessarily good or bad. Nor do we imply that the welfare of one generation of people is necessarily more or less important than that of another generation. We are simply showing you that the price system, when working smoothly, helps to answer the question of how rapidly these resources will be used.

How Markets May Fail

Why do markets sometimes fail to regulate the use of exhaustible natural resources as neatly as was implied in the model we just presented? We shall give several reasons why they may fail. We shall also explain how government regulations and monopoly can influence conservation. All of these observations suggest that markets, in practice, may not work quite so "perfectly" (or smoothly) as we assumed in our earlier discussion.

GOVERNMENT INFLUENCES ON INTEREST RATES
In discussing interest-rate determination, we noted only time preferences and the productivity of capital as forces that can shift the supply and demand for loanable funds. There are, however, other forces that can shift these curves. Government tax policies about funds saved for retirement, for example, can encourage saving and shift the supply curve to the right or can discourage saving and shift it to the left. In a similar way, tax policies giving investment credits or favorable depreciation allowances to companies can affect the profitability of machines and equipment and shift the demand curve for funds to be loaned. In macroeconomics it is agreed that government budget deficits and surpluses and central bank policies also can raise or lower real interest rates, at least in the short run. Interest rates may also be raised or lowered by changes in the desire to hold cash and to speculate on future price changes. For these and other reasons, one cannot be sure that owners of resources dance to an interest-rate tune that will always lead to the "right" rate of extraction for exhaustible natural resources.

MONOPOLY AND CONSERVATION   Both our cost-of-extraction and our interest-rate models for exhaustible natural resource extraction assumed a competitive market. In fact, many deposits of exhaustible resources are owned by companies that have some monopoly control. Also, much of the demand for these resources comes from firms that are monopolistic. Economic theory is quite clear that monopolistic firms generally hold down

---

2. Of course, interest is also one of the costs of extracting the natural resource, since machines are used in these operations. This will moderate, but probably not eliminate, the changes just described. Also, it is important to distinguish this microeconomic exercise from macroeconomic models showing that higher interest rates reduce the volume of economic activity. This reduction does not take place in our model because it started with a technological breakthrough that increased demand for machines used in production.

output in order to get higher prices and earn larger profits. Producing less means using fewer exhaustible natural resources and other raw materials. For this reason, monopolistic firms may, in fact, aid conservation. The case of OPEC is well known. In trying to maximize profits, OPEC attempts to limit the number of barrels of oil that are pumped.

Of course, OPEC is not the first or the only monopolistic organization in the exhaustible natural resource area. High levels of concentration exist in other parts of the petroleum industry as well. As it happened, however, this monopolistic situation may have speeded up rather than slowed down the extraction of oil. Major discoveries of oil in the Middle East and North Africa in the 1950s put a downward pressure on oil prices that threatened the profitability of oil companies depending mainly on higher-cost fields in the United States. These companies reacted by obtaining government restrictions on the amount of oil that could be imported into the United States and tax concessions (such as very generous depletion allowances) that amounted to a large subsidy for extracting oil from wells in the United States. The result was that market prices for oil remained relatively low, consumption was high, and auto makers, highway builders, and many others enjoyed prosperous times. But U.S. deposits of crude oil were pumped down at a rapid rate. For this reason, we must conclude that monopoly may promote conservation, but that much depends on the specific case, on the policies of the firms themselves, and on what protection and tax breaks they are able to get from government.

Nonmarket Systems and Conservation

Since the market system does not necessarily result in the best possible rate of use for exhaustible natural resources, other conservation arrangements can be considered. We have already noted how import restrictions in the 1950s and 1960s hastened the use of oil deposits in the United States while helping to conserve those

located in foreign areas. Now we shall take a look at several other government policies that have had an important impact on the rate of extraction of exhaustible natural resources in the United States.

PREFERENTIAL TAX TREATMENT Several features of U.S. income taxation encourage the exploration for and the extraction of exhaustible natural resources. Depletion allowances are the best known of these features. Under depletion allowances, part of the value of a resource that is removed from the earth is not counted as income to the owner of that resource. The reasoning behind this tax-free extraction is that the taxpayer already owns the oil or other resource that is in the ground, so that extracting and selling it does not really amount to any net improvement in his or her economic condition; that is, no income is received. In this sense, the allowance is like a deduction for the depreciation (wearing out) of a machine used in production. Actual income should be recognized only after the owner has gotten back all of his or her initial investment in the resource.

The details of depletion allowances are complicated. For our brief discussion, we shall note only two points. First, the value that can be recovered tax-free is not, in fact, limited to the taxpayer's original investment in the resource. Therefore, finding and extracting exhaustible natural resources may be more profitable, after tax, than other economic undertakings. Second, the taxpayer can cash in on this extra advantage only by actually extracting the resource. The combination tends to speed up the discovery and extraction of resources eligible for depletion allowances.

A related tax feature that hastens exploration and extraction is a provision that allows an immediate tax deduction for the expenses of unsuccessful explorations, such as dry holes in oil exploration. The combination of an immediate tax deduction for unsuccessful searches plus overdeduction for the cost of successful searches has greatly speeded up the use of these resources in the United States.

FIGURE 37-3   Regulated Natural Gas Prices Below Market Equilibrium

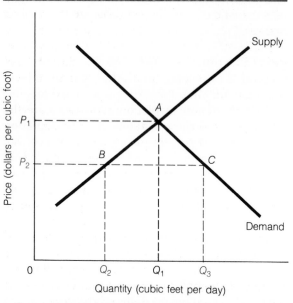

Without regulation, the interaction of supply and demand would result in equilibrium at A, with price P_1 and quantity Q_1. If the regulated price is below this equilibrium, as at P_2, natural gas suppliers reduce the quantity supplied, moving along the supply curve from A to B, and consumers increase the quantity demanded, moving along the demand curve from A to C. A shortage of natural gas appears, as illustrated by the horizontal distance from B to C. Actual production and consumption are at Q_2. Price controls can reduce usage of natural gas.

PRICE CONTROLS   Price controls are generally associated with wartime and with the fight against inflation. However, price controls in energy resources markets have been used fairly often in the United States in times of peace as well. These controls have influenced the conservation of energy resources.

PRICE CONTROLS ON NATURAL GAS   Price controls in the natural gas market became effective after the Supreme Court ruled in 1954 that regulation of natural gas prices paid by households and companies in consuming areas called for the regulation of the prices of gas in the natural gas fields themselves. It had long been recognized

that public utility companies selling gas in consumer areas were natural monopolies subject to regulation.[3] Also, as they developed, pipeline companies carrying gas from production areas were seen as natural monopolies. In the gas-producing areas, however, there are often many companies, since gas production is not a natural monopoly. But, in most cases, only one pipeline company serves a given production area and can have monopsonistic influence over price. For this reason, the Supreme Court ruled that the Federal Power Commission (later the Federal Energy Regulatory Commission) should fix natural gas prices at the well itself in order to protect consumers at the other end of the line.

Once regulation was in effect, natural gas prices were held below the equilibrium price that otherwise would have prevailed. The results of below-equilibrium prices are well known. As pictured in Figure 37-3, without regulation the interaction of supply and demand would result in equilibrium at A with price P_1 and quantity Q_1. If the regulated price is set below this equilibrium, say, at P_2, natural gas suppliers lower the quantity of gas supplied (a movement along the supply curve from A to B), and consumers raise the quantity demanded (a movement along the supply curve from A to C). As these responses take place, a shortage of natural gas appears, as shown by the distance from B to C. Part of the shortage comes from the greater quantity demanded, and part comes from the lower quantity supplied.

Actual U.S. experience with natural gas price controls has generally followed this simple economic model. However, because of the nature of the industry the consequences were slow to appear. Exploration and discovery of new gas reserves slowed down and the drawing down of proven reserves set the stage for shortages. In the early 1970s, the relative price of natural gas went even lower after the OPEC embargo and the large price rises for oil. Many consuming industries switched from oil to gas. Others switched to natural gas from coal because of the environmental restrictions on coal burning. In the winter of 1976–1977, serious natural gas shortages threat-

3. See Chapter 34 for a discussion of monopoly regulation.

ened and gas was unavailable in some areas for some users.

Regulators were, of course, aware of the economic problems. Even before the emergencies of the winter of 1976–1977, prices of natural gas from certain sources were allowed to rise in order to provide incentives to explore for new gas reserves. Low prices were continued for gas from "old" wells (those in operation before January 1, 1973), but higher prices were allowed for gas from "new" wells (those drilled or completed after that date). In response to these higher prices, the number of new gas wells completed rose rapidly. Legislation in 1978 set down a schedule for ending all price controls on newly developed gas resources.

Our brief survey of natural gas price controls suggests that regulatory measures may have had an impact on the rate of extraction of this exhaustible natural resource. However, many additional relationships would have to be examined before a conclusion could be reached. For example, government subsidies in the form of income tax depletion allowances (noted above in relation to oil production) may have speeded up the use (or the "burning off") of the natural gas resource. Moreover, oil and natural gas often are found in the same areas and in the same exploration and drilling operations. This close production relationship between natural gas and oil suggests that restrictions on imports of petroleum may have increased the extraction of natural gas from domestic fields. It is not clear, therefore, whether actual regulation, combined with the other events of the period, resulted in much net conservation of gas in the United States.

PRICE CONTROLS ON OIL The story of price controls on oil is slightly different from the one about price controls on natural gas, though the economics of the two is alike. Except for wartime, price controls on oil did not come in the United States until the crisis of the OPEC embargo in 1973 and the rapid increases in oil prices that followed. As the price of imported oil rose, huge profits were expected from the discovery and extraction of oil in the United States. The government faced a policy dilemma. Even though policy

makers were eager for larger supplies of domestic oil, they did not want the owners of existing oil reserves to reap what they believed would be excessive profits. Price controls were imposed and, as in the natural gas case, a higher price was allowed for oil from "new" wells than was allowed for oil from "old" wells. Neither of these prices, however, was allowed to reach the level of the imported oil.

With oil from different sources (new domestic, old domestic, and imported) commanding different prices, a very complicated situation arose. Since oil from U.S. sources was priced below imported oil, one might have expected the quantity demanded from foreign sources to fall. However, this expectation was upset by a system of **entitlements,** certificates that refiners were required to obtain in order to purchase domestic oil at low controlled prices. In an attempt to make the multiple-price system fair among refineries, those that bought low-priced domestic oil had to purchase entitlements to bring their costs up. On the other hand, refineries that bought high-priced imported oil received entitlements, which they could sell to lower their cost of crude oil. The aim was to have all refineries pay the same average price for crude oil. Several results followed. Even though foreign oil was no longer more costly for the refineries than domestic oil, the domestic oil producers still received prices below the world (and the expected domestic) price for oil. For this reason, they had an incentive to postpone production. Imports increased. At the same time, petroleum products were priced to consumers according to average total cost rather than marginal cost, which was the price of imported oil. From an economic efficiency point of view, prices to consumers were too low, and consumption was too high.

As in the case of natural gas controls, price controls over oil tended to keep U.S. prices at the well below market equilibrium levels and to slow down the extraction of oil. They may have contributed to some conservation, but caused great uncertainty, confusion, and frustration.

In the face of high payments to foreign producers and complaints from domestic producers, President Carter, in 1980, launched a program to remove price controls on crude oil. President Reagan speeded up the decontrol process. With controls removed, domestic oil production increased. Oil production also increased from discoveries in Mexico, the North Sea, and Alaska. Oil shortages were replaced by downward pressures on price. In 1985, the OPEC cartel proved unable to continue its restrictions on oil production and the price of crude oil fell dramatically.

RENEWABLE RESOURCES

Renewable resources are different from exhaustible resources. As noted earlier, wildlife such as migratory birds, wild game, whales, and fish in the oceans are renewable natural resources. Similarly, forests can renew themselves. Under normal conditions, nature can replace these resources rather quickly. From the economist's point of view, the problem is to work with nature to maintain adequate reproduction and restoration of these resources.

Environmental Constraints

We humans generally regard ourselves as one of the more successful species of animal life on the earth. Our numbers have risen greatly over the years, claiming ever-widening rule over other species. As human activities spread more widely over the earth, the space left undisturbed for other species contracts. Foraging areas for wild animals become smaller. Breeding areas for migratory birds are taken over by humans or so fouled by unwanted by-products of human consumption that they are no longer able to maintain the bird population. Marshlands are drained for farms or homes. River estuaries are contaminated or changed so much by sedimentation or the needs of commerce that they are not suited for fish spawning. Even the oceans, covering two-thirds of the earth's surface, feel the impact of human activity as oil spills and other pollutants contaminate the water.

Our claims on nature are a constraint or limit on the supply of fish, birds, and wild game and other renewable natural resources. Have we spread our influence too far and reduced the supply of renewable natural resources too much? Even by our very egocentric calculation, using only our own values, the answer is probably "yes." Externalities, which you studied in Chapter 32, provide the main basis for this conclusion. When we consider expanding our human domain by draining a swamp or building a housing development or drilling an oil well or damming a stream, benefits in most cases are clearly recognized because property rights to these benefits have been established. Farmers will gain from draining the swamp. Developers will gain from the land they build on. Oil companies will make profits from the new oil wells. Electric utilities, irrigation projects, or recreational entrepreneurs will gain from damming the stream. On the other hand, many costs of the expansion may be unrecognized. Who is poorer when the quantity of wild game decreases? Who will speak for the migratory birds whose breeding grounds are gone? Who are the hunters that are denied the game or the fishermen who are denied the fish? In many cases, the costs of human intrusion, though real, are widely scattered and not clearly recognized.

When costs and/or benefits are not recognized, externalities and market failures arise. As you recall from Chapter 32, negative externalities exist when costs are imposed on persons whose interests are not reflected in the market. In all likelihood, this is the case when swamps are drained for farmland or development projects, when oil wells are drilled, when streams are dammed, and so on. Thus, microeconomic analysis leads us to suspect that too many swamps may be drained, that too many oil wells may be drilled, and that too many streams may be dammed, since some of the costs of these enterprises probably are not reflected in market-supply curves.

For renewable natural resources, market failure arises, in part at least, because no one has property rights to the wildlife that will be destroyed when extensions of human habitation shrink the habitat of the wildlife. If clear property rights existed, markets would more fully reflect the costs of actions that lead to reductions in wildlife living areas. Unfortunately, behind the problem of fixing authority over resources lie the even more basic problems of defining and measuring those resources. For example, is the oxygen content of the water in a flowing stream a separate kind of property? Are we able to identify and measure it so that rights over its use can be exercised by government or private individuals? What about the salt content of water in fish breeding areas or the water level in the Everglades? Can property rights be identified and enforced for whales in the ocean? Or for a certain kind of whale?

The economist's way of thinking suggests that efficiency in the extent of human intrusion in nature's domain is not likely to be achieved when the gains on one side of the bargain are clearly recognized by specific property rights, but the costs on the other side are vague and not imposed on anyone in particular. Laser beams, sonar, computers, and satellites can expand our ability to identify and measure things in nature and so can help set the stage for wise decisions about the balance between our development projects and those of nature. But the problems and conflicts are serious and progress is likely to be slow.

Harvesting Constraints

The second economic problem for conserving renewable resources is control over harvesting— that is, control of the number of fish, birds, deer, or other wildlife that can be taken each year for human use. In this matter, the size of the parent population is a key variable. If the yearly catch is so great that it lowers the parent population, the species may be on its way to extinction. Let us look at the problem first from the biological point of view and then from the economic point of view.

SUSTAINABLE ANNUAL YIELD   The biological aspect of the harvesting of a renewable natural resource is pictured in Figure 37-4. Shown on the

FIGURE 37-4   The Sustainable-Annual-Yield Curve

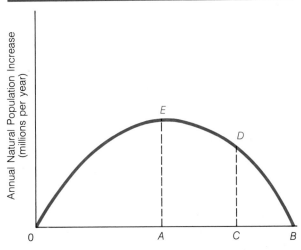

The sustainable-annual-yield curve shows the quantity of a renewable natural resource that could be harvested each year for an indefinite period. At the origin of the graph, there is zero population. The species does not exist. Moving to the right along the horizontal axis, births exceed deaths and the population increases. At A, births exceed deaths by a maximum amount, and the quantity that could be harvested annually (AE) is at a maximum. As population exceeds A, environmental constraints raise the death rate so that births exceed deaths by less than before. At B, the death rate equals the reproduction rate. At any given population, such as A or C, humans could harvest the natural annual increase, which is shown by AE and CD, without upsetting the stability of the population at that level.

horizontal axis is the population of some renewable natural resource, such as fish, deer, or wild geese. Shown on the vertical axis is the annual natural increase in this population. The graph tells a story of what happens when the habitat for the species is fixed in terms of land and water area, rainfall, temperature, and so forth. The only relationship that we show is between the size of the population and its own natural annual increase, with all other variables fixed.

At the origin of the graph, there is no population and no annual natural increase. The species does not exist! To the right of the origin, there is some parent population, and reproduction takes place. As we move to the right along the horizontal axis, there are more births than deaths, so the population rises. At population *A*, births exceed deaths by the greatest possible amount, and the annual population increase is at a maximum, as shown by the peak of the curve. As population exceeds quantity *A*, the environmental constraints become effective—crowding becomes worse, the food supply becomes less abundant, and the death rate rises so that births exceed deaths by less than before. This lowers the annual natural population increase, and the curve slopes downward. At population *B*, the environmental constraint has increased the death rate until it matches the reproduction rate and the annual natural population increase is zero. The population has reached a natural equilibrium.

Suppose that we or some other predator enters the picture and begins to kill off the population. How many fish, birds, deer, or other members of the population can be taken and still leave a large enough parent population to sustain the species? The answer is shown by the sustainable-annual-yield curve. Consider, for example, the annual population increase at population *C*, as shown by the vertical line from *C* on the horizontal axis to *D* on the sustainable-annual-yield curve. This number of fish or deer or wild geese could be harvested every year and the population would remain stable at *C*. The easiest way to understand this idea is to imagine that we harvest from the parent population after their offspring for the year have been born. In the year ahead, the offspring replace their parents and the species carries on with the stable population.[4]

Figure 37-4 suggests several interesting features about harvesting nature's renewable resources. One is that, moving to the left from point *B*, harvesting can increase all the way up to the yearly amount of *AE* without endangering the

species itself. In a sense, harvesting reduces crowding and other environmental pressures on the species and permits a larger annual natural population increase. But a conservation problem arises from annual harvesting greater than *AE* because this will lower the parent population and cause a smaller natural population increase in the next reproduction cycle. If excessive harvesting continues, the population may be driven to zero and the species to extinction. Clearly, efficient conservation requires that the population be maintained at *A* and that harvesting not be allowed to exceed the quantity represented by the vertical distance *AE*, the maximum sustainable annual yield.

ECONOMICS AND HARVEST CONTROL The economic aspects of harvest control do not focus just on preventing the extinction of a species of wild animal, bird, or fish. In fact, because the cost of finding and harvesting is likely to rise as the resource population declines, harvesting alone might not by itself lead to the extinction of the species. From an economic point of view, the aim of harvest control should be to prevent any entry into the "danger zone" where the population of the species is less than *A* (in Figure 37-4). The next step is to work out practical ways of moving toward this result.

COMMON PROPERTY One way that does *not* work well is the system of **common property**, under which everyone has a legal right to harvest the resource. The problem is that no one has an incentive to limit his or her harvest on the basis of what that harvest may do to future supplies of the resource. Instead, each individual reasons that his or her harvesting will not make any difference, first because it is a very small part of the total, and second because if they do not catch the fish or shoot the bird, someone else will and the resource will be depleted anyway. In this variation of the free-rider problem, each individual harvests without effective constraint. People behave in much the same way when they litter parks and roadsides with bottle caps and empty containers. As you can see, the common property

---

4. Wildlife management specialists know that much depends on when hunting and fishing are allowed and on which members of the population are actually taken. Distinctions are made between male and female members of the species and their ages. Different guidelines apply for different species.

system opens the way for people to impose the costs of their consumption on others. In other words, it is a variety of the externalities problem.

PROPERTY RIGHTS AND RESERVATION PRICES

Property rights provide owners with an incentive to take account of the effects that present use will have on future production. Property owners build the future into their current supply decisions by means of **reservation prices,** as explained earlier in connection with decisions about whether or not to extract exhaustible natural resources. The reservation price is the present value of the future production that would be sacrificed if the resource were harvested today. To apply the reservation-price concept to decisions about harvesting renewable natural resources, the owner first estimates the changes in future harvests that would take place as a consequence of current harvesting. Will current harvesting reduce future harvests (that is, put the population of the resource in the left-hand part of the sustainable-yield curve)? If so, the owner estimates the profit that would be lost if this future production were sacrificed, at whatever prices and production costs he or she expects will prevail in the future. Next, this future profit is discounted to determine its present value, using whatever interest rate the owners believe to be correct in view of the amount of risk involved. This discounted amount is the reservation price of the resource. It becomes part of the cost of harvesting the resource. In this way, the reservation price provides an operational recognition of future interests and a guide for conservation.

Examples of the property rights system of harvest control exist in many areas. Foresters know how long trees should be allowed to grow for maximum yield and oystermen make similar calculations before harvesting oysters. Perhaps modern technology will lead to new kinds of property rights and new ways of applying economic principles to the conservation of renewable natural resources.

GOVERNMENT REGULATION As you learned in Chapter 32, the existence of externalities is one

of the reasons for government intervention in the economy. When externalities arise from common property in renewable natural resources, government may step in and place limits on common property rights. Hunting and fishing may be restricted to certain times of the year, licenses may be required, and limits may be placed on the number of fish or birds or animals each person can take. Many governments have programs of this sort, which, in effect, raise the cost that a person must bear in order to harvest some of the resource. These costs (both money cost and time-and-convenience costs) reduce the quantity harvested. Ideally, this quantity could be brought in line with the maximum sustainable yield.[5]

Difficulties for government regulation arise when the habitat of a renewable resource extends across the borders of several states or countries. Sometimes agreements between governments can be reached, such as migratory bird agreements between states in the United States and among the United States, Canada, and Mexico. More serious problems arise when resources are found in areas where no government has jurisdiction, such as the oceans, the atmosphere, or outer space. Many governments have extended their territorial waters outward from the old twelve-mile limit to two hundred or more miles. These extensions, often taken without consulting other countries, can increase international tensions. Even so, they fail to solve the problems for resources farther out in the oceans. Establishing government jurisdictions in the atmosphere and outer space pose similar difficulties. These problems are not new, of course. Over the centuries, as population has grown and new technologies have developed, countries have time and again faced such challenges. Sometimes they have led to wars and conflict. Can we hope that international cooperation will result in better-reasoned solutions in the future?

---

5. You may find it interesting that governments sometimes offer cash payments (bounties) to encourage people to increase their hunting of species that are increasing too rapidly and making inroads on farm crops or other, more desired, species of game. This is just the reverse of the system of requiring licenses and paying fees for hunting.

THE ENVIRONMENT

In this section, we shall examine how the techniques of economic analysis can help in understanding some important aspects of humanity's relationship with the environment. We deal specifically with pollution that may arise from the dumping of waste materials into the environment. In this analysis, a key idea is to recognize that nature's ability to recycle many waste materials is a natural resource that should be utilized efficiently.

The Laws of Conservation of Energy and Matter

Until the space age, it was generally believed that what goes up must come down. A similar law (with similar space age exception) applies to the unwanted by-products of human occupation of the earth. The law of the conservation of matter states that the mass of waste material is approximately equal to the mass of raw materials used in production. This means that production and consumption simply rearrange materials to put them into forms that provide the services desired by humans. There is no change in the mass of these materials themselves, and at some point all that is used becomes waste. In a parallel way, the law of the conservation of energy suggests that humans can redirect but cannot destroy the energy that the earth receives or has received from the sun.

Two important ideas that follow from the laws of conservation of matter and energy should be emphasized in our study of environmental pollution. First, any action that increases the mass of material taken out of the earth or the amount of energy diverted from its usual path always increases the amount of waste that must finally be put back into the earth or its atmosphere. On this basis, one can argue that economic growth and higher living standards should discourage increases in material goods and should, instead,

stress increases in services and other nonmaterial satisfactions.

The second message from these laws is that waste treatment cannot reduce the mass or the energy aspects of waste. Instead, waste treatment can only move the waste to more acceptable places or process it into more acceptable forms before putting it back into the earth or the atmosphere. Therefore, two questions require attention in analyzing the environmental impact of the unwanted by-products of human activity. The first is "How much waste should be generated?" The second is "What are the most acceptable forms and locations for waste?" Are they the forms and locations that cause the least trouble for people today? Are they the ones that will yield the best environment for our children and grandchildren?

The Efficient Quantity of Waste

Figure 37-5 illustrates an economic model that will help to analyze the question of the efficient quantity of waste that should be generated and disposed of in the environment. To use this graph, think of "Mother Nature" as providing waste disposal services—a dumping ground for the unwanted by-products of human consumption. The horizontal axis of the graph shows the quantities of this service demanded and supplied, the tons or cubic yards of waste discharged into the environment. The vertical axis shows the price and the cost of this service. The cost represents the dollar equivalent of the damages and disruptions that come from waste disposal.

The demand curve on this graph shows the quantities of waste disposal service demanded at various prices. To understand this curve, we must recognize that wastes are unwanted by-products generated in the production and consumption of goods.[6] How much we are willing to pay for the disposal of unwanted by-products depends on

6. Unlike goods, the production and consumption of services usually do not generate unwanted by-products of the sort that involve waste disposal problems.

FIGURE 37-5   The Efficient Quantity of Waste Disposal Service

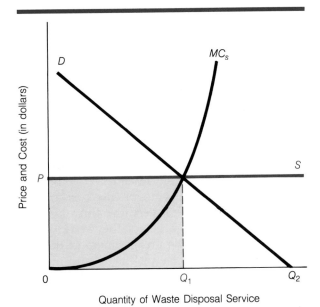

Quantity of Waste Disposal Service

Wastes are unwanted by-products from the production and/or consumption of goods. The demand curve, D, is derived from the demand for goods that generate the waste. Consumers will be willing to pay a high price to dispose of waste generated by final goods that they value highly and a low price to dispose of waste from final goods of low value. The MC_s curve illustrates the marginal cost to society that arises when waste disposal disrupts nature's existing ecological systems. The efficient quantity of waste disposal service is Q_1, identified by the intersection of the demand curve for waste disposal service with the MC_s curve. If nature supplies waste disposal services at zero price, the equilibrium quantity will be Q_2. An effluent charge of P per unit would result in the supply curve S and equilibrium at the efficient quantity of waste disposal service, Q_1.

how much we value the good that comes along with this by-product. For goods that we value very highly, we are willing to pay a large amount for disposal of the wastes generated. The willingness to pay for disposal of these wastes is represented along the upper-left part of the demand curve for waste disposal service. We are willing to pay less for disposal of the unwanted by-products of goods that are themselves less valu-

able to us. Therefore, the willingness to pay for their disposal appears farther down along the demand curve for Mother Nature's waste disposal service. We can view nature's waste disposal service as a natural resource and the demand for this resource as being like the demand for other resources. Thus, the demand for nature's waste disposal service is a **derived demand,** much as the demands for other resources or factors of production are derived demands (see Chapter 29).

COST OF WASTE DISPOSAL   Now look at the curve in Figure 37-5 labeled MC_s, which represents the marginal cost to society of disposing of waste. The first part of this curve lies along the horizontal axis itself, meaning that marginal cost is zero over this range of waste disposal service. This reflects the assumption that a certain volume of waste can be handled without damage to nature's existing ecological system. Within this range, humans disposing of unwanted by-products of their consumption are in the same class as squirrels disposing of acorn shells. Nature has come to terms with this volume of waste, and the process that takes care of the waste is viewed as "natural."

As the volume of waste (per year, for example) increases beyond this zero-marginal-cost range, nature's ecological systems are changed. Water from certain sources or air in certain areas may become dangerous to the health of existing life, possibly even yours. The change in the ecology harms some life forms, and we record this harm as a social cost of nature's waste disposal service. In Figure 37-5 the MC_s curve becomes steeper and steeper as the volume of waste each year increases. This is because it appears that ecological disruption has more than a simple arithmetic relation to the volume of waste. That is, the more waste generated per unit of time, the higher is the cost of disposing of each additional unit of waste.

BALANCING COST AND BENEFIT   All waste must be disposed of through nature's waste disposal service. In Figure 37-5, the efficient volume of waste is shown by the intersection of the demand curve and the MC_s curve. The efficient quantity is Q_1. Each unit of waste disposal service up to this point generates benefits (as shown by the demand curve) that are greater than its cost (as shown by the MC_s curve). On the other hand, a volume of waste disposal service in excess of Q_1 is inefficient because the costs from these units are greater than their benefits.

Although some people are uncomfortable with the idea that any volume of waste that changes nature's established ecological systems can be called efficient or optimal, the concept of an efficient quantity of waste and an efficient amount of environmental degradation is clear. Difficulties arise only in the practical application of the concept, most often in determining the location of the MC_s curve. If we underestimate the effects of wastes and place the MC_s curve too low or too far to the right, our model will justify too much use of nature's waste disposal service. On the other hand, if we overestimate the effects, the MC_s curve will be too high, and society will not make full use of available natural resources.

THE SUPPLY OF NATURE'S WASTE DISPOSAL SERVICE The MC_s curve in Figure 37-5 is *not* a supply curve. A supply curve, as you know, shows the quantities of a good or service that will be offered at various possible prices. Economists say that the quantity supplied depends on the price. But nature is not in a position to charge a price for the use of her waste disposal service. Instead, her service is given at zero price to anyone who chooses to use it. In terms of Figure 37-5, if nature supplies waste disposal service at zero price, the supply curve is on the horizontal axis of the graph, and the equilibrium quantity of nature's waste disposal service is Q_2, where the demand curve meets the horizontal axis. The economic model indicates that an inefficiently large amount of waste will be generated and dumped if the price for nature's disposal service is zero.

Since Q_2 is greater than the efficient quantity, Q_1, social policy for efficient resource use may try to find a way to lower the volume of waste. Economic analysis suggests that one way to do so is to charge a price to those who use nature's

disposal system. As the price rises from Mother Nature's zero offering, the intersection of the supply and demand curves will move upward along the demand curve. The efficient quantity would be generated if the price were P, resulting in the supply curve shown in the figure and an equilibrium quantity of Q_1.

EXCESS WASTE AS AN EXTERNALITIES PROBLEM It is easy to see how the dumping of excessive waste into nature's disposal system can be explained as market failure coming from negative externalities.[7] For example, consider the nonreturnable soft-drink container. If you throw it along the roadside, your private cost for disposing of the container is very low. But you know that your private cost is not the whole story. Others must suffer the unsightliness of the discarded container or else pick it up and dispose of it properly. Thus, the social cost of disposing of the unreturnable container includes both your effort in throwing it away and the discomfort and exertion of others in dealing with it later. The costs imposed on others are external costs or negative externalities.

As you learned in Chapter 32, the market-supply curve is located too far to the right when negative externalities exist. This is precisely the situation that was illustrated in Figure 37-5. When nature charges a zero price for waste disposal, virtually all of the costs of each act of waste generation and disposal are imposed on some person other than the one generating the waste. Moreover, people often reason that their own small amount of waste is insignificant compared with the total amount generated. Since the environment will be polluted in any event, they conclude that their small amount of waste will not make any perceptible difference. In other words, the individual not only sees little private cost from dumping but also sees that little will be gained by not adding his or her bit to the total. With nature's service at zero price, economists predict that waste generation will greatly exceed the socially efficient quantity.

7. Negative externalities were discussed in Chapter 32.

Pricing to Internalize Externalities

In Figure 37-5, the price P can represent an **effluent charge** or price for the use of nature's waste disposal service.[8] A firm might be required, for example, to pay a specific amount for each cubic yard of refuse deposited in a land fill, for each gallon of sewage sent to a disposal system, and so on. When this price is charged, the supply curve S in Figure 37-5 becomes effective and the efficient amount of waste would be generated.

ADVANTAGES OF EFFLUENT CHARGES The main advantage of effluent charges is that they put self-interest to work to reduce the generation of wastes. The reason why this charge is so effective is that, in a competitive system, consumers themselves end up paying the charges imposed on the unwanted by-products of goods that they consume. Wastes that are generated in manufacturing processes will be paid for at first by the firms that produce these goods, but then the costs will be passed on to consumers in higher prices. For the leftovers from consumption, such as empty cartons and garbage, consumers pay the effluent charge directly to the local waste disposal service.

Self-interest provides powerful incentives to reduce waste in the least-costly (and least-wasteful) way. For example, firms that discover new production processes or new products that generate less waste will be able to sell at a lower price and gain customers and profits at the expense of firms that have not found ways to reduce waste. Also, consumers have an incentive to use fewer disposable containers when they must pay the local garbage service to dispose of them. Probably the greatest reduction in waste comes through the change in the product mix, as consumers change their consumption patterns to goods that cause less waste.

An interesting aspect of effluent charges is that the revenue collected from these charges may be more than enough to cover the costs of waste

8. An *effluent* is "something that flows out . . . an outflow of a sewer, storage tank, irrigation canal or other channel." *The American Heritage Dictionary of the English Language, New College Edition.* © 1976 by Houghton Mifflin Company.

disposal and the cost of administering the charge itself. If all disposers of waste pay price P, the money paid in effluent charges is represented by the shaded area in Figure 37-5. Since the total social cost of disposing of these wastes is only the part of this area lying beneath the MC_s curve, surplus money would be available to use for other purposes. In other words, providing efficient use of natural resources could generate a surplus and add to the financial power of the public sector. The meaning of this model, then, is not so different from the meaning of Henry George's idea of a single tax on land values (see Chapter 29). In fact, there is plenty of precedent for gaining public sector revenue from natural resources. In oil- and gas-rich areas, governments that have retained title to mineral rights enjoy abundant revenue.

PROBLEMS WITH EFFLUENT CHARGES The greatest technical problem with effluent charges is discovering the actual location of the MC_s curve in Figure 37-5. Our model greatly oversimplified this task. For example, we implied that there is only one sort of waste and only one MC_s curve that must be estimated when, in fact, there are many different kinds of waste and many different MC_s curves. Solid waste is not the same as chemical waste or the disposal of heat. Waste released into the air from a smokestack, your cigarette, or your car is not the same as waste dumped into the ocean, lakes, or flowing streams or buried in the ground. Effective action against one kind of waste or one method of waste disposal may simply lead to a shift to some other kind of waste or method of disposal. If the second type or method is more harmful than the first, effective action may do more harm than good. A great deal of information and analysis is needed to plan a wholly constructive program of effluent charges.

To identify the efficient quantity of nature's waste disposal service, we must also discover the location of the demand curve for these services. There are several ways this might be done. If we use a trial-and-error approach, a series of different prices might be charged, eventually leading to some knowledge of the demand curve. Another method is to advertise for bids for waste disposal permits. The bids could be arranged from the highest to the lowest, and the demand curve could be constructed by adding up the cumulative total amount of waste disposal service requested, starting from the top down. If the cost curve had already been estimated, the equilibrium quantity could be determined and the bids accepted, from the highest down, until the efficient quantity had been authorized. This method would allow the government to operate like a discriminating monopolist (see Chapter 26) and gain revenue corresponding to the whole area under the demand curve up to quantity Q_1 in Figure 37-5.

Textbook exercises such as this, however, cannot solve a remaining, and perhaps the key, problem with effluent charges. This is the problem of enforcement. Under a waste disposal permit or effluent charge system, dumping waste without a permit or without paying the charge would be illegal. To carry out the program effectively would require fines and penalties as well as allocation of other resources for detecting, apprehending, and prosecuting those who break the law. All of these things are expensive and are upsetting to many Americans, who cherish the image of the frontier, where nature's services could be treated as free goods.

Government Standards

As an alternative to effluent charges, the government may establish rules governing methods of production, the ingredients in products, and waste treatment procedures in order to control various types of waste. For example, government regulations may prohibit the use of certain chemicals, or require filters on smokestacks, or specify that all autos be equipped with emission-control devices. Even though these standards and controls do not raise any money for the government, they usually are more appealing than effluent charges, which are thought of as taxes by the public and their representatives. Moreover, laws setting standards enable elected officials to point to specific and supposedly constructive actions that have been taken. The requirements will raise the price of the product to the consumer almost as

certainly as a tax on that product would. But a tax that would bring about an equal reduction in the quantity of that product is almost certain to be more unpopular than standards and controls.

Although government standards and controls are a politically popular approach to problems of waste disposal and environmental pollution, economic analysis brings to light some serious shortcomings in them. Standards and controls tend to freeze methods of production or of waste disposal into the technology specified in the laws. Two separate problems arise. The first is the problem of too much uniformity. Production methods that are the best for large firms may not be the best for small firms, and methods that are the best for firms in one part of the country may not be the best for those in another part of the country. Requiring all to use the same technology means that some companies must use less than the best technology for their particular size and situation. For example, air quality problems in the Los Angeles basin are different from those at the "four corners," where New Mexico, Arizona, Colorado, and Utah come together. Applying the same standards to both areas can prevent the full use of natural resources. An especially glaring case of too much uniformity arises when all the businesses in an area (along a given river system, for example) are required to lower their waste discharges by the same percentage. Since marginal cost for this reduction may be much more for some than for others, the costs of cleaning the river are much too high for the amount of cleaning accomplished. Moreover, those who had reduced emissions before the law was passed are penalized for their socially constructive action.

The second problem with standards and controls is that they may slow the search for better methods of waste treatment or for new production methods that cause less waste. This problem is probably more serious than the uniformity problem because new products and techniques for production and waste treatment probably offer the most promising routes to reducing harmful externalities. As noted above, effluent charges offer profit incentives for companies to find better methods. Those that succeed will be able to lower the charges that they have to pay and in this way raise their net profits. To most economists, the incentive effect is the strongest argument for effluent charges as well as the greatest weakness of standards and controls.

Subsidies for Waste Treatment

During the 1960s and 1970s, many cities and towns built new sewage treatment plants, partly with federal money and partly with local money. The local money for these facilities usually was raised by selling bonds, which would be paid off from charges collected from the households and firms that would dispose of sewage through the facility. Thus, the local funding illustrated the use of effluent charges. The federal money was a subsidy paid by taxpayers.

From the perspective of economic analysis, there is a fundamental difference between subsidies for waste treatment on the one hand and effluent charges and government standards on the other. Both effluent charges and government standards raise the price of goods that generate waste, thus activating economic incentives to encourage consumers and firms to reduce the amount of waste generated. But subsidies for waste treatment operate in the opposite direction. They lower the cost of producing goods that generate waste and lower the price to consumers. Thus, subsidies for waste treatment tend to *increase* the total amount of waste actually generated. When taxpayers pay part of the bill for waste treatment, the private cost to producers and consumers of goods that generate waste are reduced and the quantity demanded rises. For this reason, economists are critical of this procedure.

Much of the appeal of waste treatment subsidies is political rather than economic. Government spending programs that concentrate benefits in local areas but spread tax costs in small amounts over millions of taxpayers are attractive vehicles for legislative vote trading.[9] For citizens of the district on the receiving end, benefits are far greater than tax costs. Even though many people realize that their taxes also pay for thousands of

9. See Chapter 32 for a discussion of vote trading.

projects in other districts, most are not willing to drop out of the game, fearing that their own project will simply be carried out in some other district. Partly because of this political fact of life, too much money may have been spent on waste treatment facilities. Of course, the idea of treating waste before it is released into the environment is quite sound, since this treatment can lower the social costs of waste. The problem with treatment subsidies is not with the facilities, as such, but with the financing method, which increases the quantity of waste itself.

SUMMARY

1. Customary supply and demand graphs show how rapidly a good is being consumed. For exhaustible natural resources, conservation takes place when the quantity on the horizontal axis moves to the left. Conservation can be achieved by shifting the supply curve on such a graph to the left.

2. The cost of extracting a resource is one of the forces affecting the location of the supply curve. Easily accessible deposits, with low extraction costs, are generally used first. So, other things being unchanged, as more and more of the resource is used, the supply curve for an exhaustible resource tends to shift to the left and encourages conservation.

3. The conservation effect of shifting the supply curve to the left is greater when the price elasticity of demand for the resource is high, and it is smaller when price elasticity is low. Since price elasticity of demand is usually greater as the length of time increases, conservation effects of supply-curve shifts increase with the passage of time.

4. As exhaustible natural resource prices rise, it pays firms and individuals to search more vigorously for new deposits of the resource. For this reason, "proven reserves" often increase as prices rise.

5. Low interest rates encourage the conservation of exhaustible natural resources, and high interest rates discourage conservation, other things being equal. This is so because high interest rates mean, for resource owners, that alternative uses of their wealth are more attractive than leaving that wealth in its natural state as a resource.

6. Because interest rates reflect time preferences and the productivity of capital goods, they provide a connection between resource conservation and other aspects of an economic system. Conservation of exhaustible natural resources is just one aspect of the many different choices between the present and the future.

7. Interest rates may fail to provide appropriate guidelines for conservation. Central bank policies, government budget surpluses or deficits, and tax policies relating to saving and investing all can influence the real interest rate in the economy.

8. Monopoly power exists in some natural resource markets. Since monopolistic firms tend to restrict output in order to increase profits, they may help to conserve exhaustible natural resources. However, much depends on the specific circumstances and policies followed by these monopolistic enterprises.

9. Government tax policies and price controls can affect the conservation of exhaustible natural resources. U.S. preferential tax treatment for natural resource extraction may have speeded up the use of some resources. However, price controls on natural gas and on oil may have slowed down the use of these resources.

10. For renewable resources, conservation calls for attention to the economic factors that determine the environmental conditions for the reproduction and growth of such resources. Because property rights are not clearly defined in some areas, human activities may have reduced renewable resource habitats too much and worked against the conservation of these resources.

11. Conservation of renewable resources also may require some limitations on the annual harvesting of these resources. The sustainable-annual-yield curve shows the quantities that may be harvested without causing a change in the population of the species. To conserve the species, harvesting should not be allowed to exceed the maximum sustainable yield.

12. The common property system sometimes fails to ensure that harvesting of renewable resources does not exceed the maximum sustainable yield. Government regulations may be used to limit harvesting in common property areas. Extending the scope of private property rights is another way to control harvesting. The concept of a reservation price shows how property rights build future interests into present decisions about resource use.

13. The laws of the conservation of energy and matter suggest that waste treatment cannot reduce the total amount of waste but can change the forms and locations of waste dispositions.

14. The demand for nature's waste disposal services is derived from the demand for the goods and services that produce the waste. Waste disposal generates social costs through its disruption of natural ecological systems. In economic terms, the efficient quantity of nature's waste disposal service is achieved when the value of the marginal unit of waste disposal service, as indicated by the demand curve, is equal to the social cost of that unit.

15. Waste disposal charges (effluent charges) can make up for nature's inability to charge a price as a condition for disposing of waste. Correct effluent charges can establish a supply curve and bring about the efficient quantity of waste disposal service.

16. Externality problems arise in waste disposal because property rights are not well established or enforced for waste disposal into the air, streams, and large bodies of water. Government can improve the efficiency of waste disposal by exercising property rights in areas where private property rights are not established.

17. Effluent charges lead to price rises to producers and consumers for goods and services that generate harmful externalities. In this way they provide incentives for consumers to switch to other goods and services and for producers to find methods of production that cause less waste. These are attractive features of effluent charges. Developing reliable estimates of the actual demand and costs of waste is the main problem with these charges.

18. Standards and controls are a means of limiting waste by specifying product characteristics and methods of production and waste treatment. These methods of controlling the volume of waste are attractive politically. However, economists are critical of standards and controls because they tend to freeze production and treatment methods into current technologies and to offer little incentive for developing better technologies.

19. Subsidies for waste treatment are criticized by economists because they tend to lower costs to producers and prices to consumers of goods that generate waste and in this way tend to increase the total volume of waste.

DISCUSSION QUESTIONS

1. Why is the supply curve for an exhaustible natural resource expected to shift to the left as more and more of the stock of that resource is used up? How can technological changes slow down or even reverse this shift?

2. "The market's method of conserving exhaustible natural resources operates more effectively when demand is price elastic than when it is price inelastic and more effectively when long time periods are considered than when short time periods are considered." Explain and illustrate with graphs.

3. "Proven reserves of crude oil always go up when the price of oil rises and go down when the price falls. This proves that these numbers have no basis in fact but are simply made up by oil companies for propaganda purposes." Do you agree or disagree? Explain.

4. If you owned an oil well and had to decide whether to pump oil or to cap the well, how would the interest rate influence your decision? Use the interest-rate connection to illustrate what would tend to happen to the extraction rate of exhaustible natural resources if people change their time preferences toward more current consumption.

5. Construct a supply and demand graph to illustrate a regulated price for energy set below the free-market equilibrium price. Compare your graph with Figure 37-3. Will this regulated price increase or decrease the rate at which deposits of the natural resource are used? Explain.

6. The "entitlements" oil-pricing system in the United States in the 1970s led to oil being priced to consumers below its actual marginal cost and increased both consumption and oil imports. How

might a refinery operate at its profit-maximizing output and still sell at a price below the actual marginal cost? How did the system lead to increased imports?

7. How has the difficulty of establishing property rights tended to reduce the habitat of renewable resources such as wild game below the economically efficient level? Explain how this problem involves the concept of externalities. Does government have a role to play?

8. Construct a graph of the sustainable-yield curve for a renewable natural resource. Compare your graph with Figure 37-4. How does this help explain why the threat of extinction appears quite suddenly, even though harvesting has increased for many years with no apparent problem?

9. Explain how a reservation price operates to limit the current harvesting of a renewable resource. How is this similar to the way interest rates influence extraction of nonrenewable resources? Why does a common property system fail to install the reservation-price constraint on current harvesting?

10. Explain how the demand for waste disposal service is a derived demand stemming from the demand for goods that satisfy wants. Construct a graph illustrating the economically efficient quantity of waste disposal. Why will this efficient quantity usually not be obtained unless effluent charges are established?

11. It is sometimes argued that it is a waste of time to make firms pay for the waste they deposit in nature or for the environmental damage caused by their production processes because they simply pass the cost on to the people who buy their product and then continue to pollute as before. Do you agree or disagree with this position? Why or why not?

12. Excessive uniformity and failure to use the profit motive effectively are weaknesses of the standards and controls approach to limiting harmful externalities. Explain the basis for each of these criticisms.

13. What is the economist's basic criticism of government subsidies that help pay the costs of waste treatment facilities? Does it follow that economists believe that waste treatment facilities are not useful? Why or why not?

The Deregulation Movement

Like "Free Silver," "Back to Normalcy," and "Get the Country Moving Again," "Deregulation" has become an economic slogan. Economists, with their "irrational passion for dispassionate rationality," think such economic slogans should be examined with some care, to see what they do or do not imply, before one jumps on the bandwagon to favor the movement, or on the counter-bandwagon to oppose it.

Beyond Price Controls

Were you to ask the man or woman on the street what he or she thinks deregulation means, the most likely answer would stress the reduction or elimination of controls on prices, wages, and interest rates, in other words, the phasing out or repeal of fixed electric and taxicab rates, farm prices, minimum wages, usury laws setting minimum rates for small loans, banking laws setting maximum rates for bank deposits, and so on. And these are certainly an important part of the deregulation picture—but only a small part. They do not come near exhausting the field.

Only by a few random examples can we indicate the vast network of regulations that constitute the institutional "rules of the economic game" in all countries. They may be based on legislation, administrative orders, or judicial decrees. Or their basis may be administrative "guidance" (*gyosei shido* in Japanese, meaning advice from the capital to do or not to do thus and so, often with veiled threats of unspecified penalties if the advice is disregarded too frequently). The penumbra of vagueness recalls some nonsense verse by Edward Lear:

I sent a message to the fish.
I told them "This is what I wish."
The little fishes of the sea
Then sent an answer back to me.
The little fishes' answer was,
"We cannot do it, Sir, because—."
I wrote to them again to say,
"It would be better to obey."

and so on at some length, punctuated in the real world by judgments, appeals, and legal fees.

The content of regulatory orders and restrictions—*positive* and *negative* regulations, if you wish—may cover a wide range of business and economic practices, as for example:

1. *Who may engage* in a particular activity, usually as a seller but sometimes as a buyer, can be regulated. An attorney at law, a securities dealer, the operator of a gambling casino must, in most states, be a person of "good moral character" without "undesirable" associates, whatever these terms may mean. So must the purchaser of a handgun, although buyers and sellers of most other goods and services are permitted ordinary human frailties. And in some communities, access to skilled-labor and white-collar jobs outside certain "ghettoes" has had and sometimes still has racial, sexual, or religious limitations. (Consider the American South, not only during slavery but also for a century afterwards, or *apartheid* in South Africa. Consider the restrictions against Jews in Nazi Germany, against Chinese in Southeast Asia, and against all "Asians," but chiefly persons from the Indian subcontinent, in Black Africa.) Many of these are "nativist" restrictions to increase the natives' low shares of good jobs. And one may consider immigration restrictions, including the American ones, as attempts to keep "foreigners" from competing in any economic activity whatever throughout the restricting country.

2. Then we have the associated issues of *licensure* and *credentialism*. One may not, in any American state, practice medicine or dentistry without a license from that state, or from some other jurisdiction to which that state grants reciprocity. And one may not obtain such a license without proper credentials or education and experience—completing accredited courses of classroom instruction and technical training, passing technical examinations, completing "internship" or "residence" under the supervision of accredited practitioners. Nor can one, in many European countries, engage in specified branches of wholesale or retail trade without a "certificate of convenience and necessity" stating that this particular branch is not overcrowded where the applicant proposes to engage in it. (In America, such regulation is largely limited to banking and public utilities, including the ownership and operation of taxicabs.) In New Zealand, the newcomer must also gain trade-union approval of his or her "manning" policies—enough union workers must be hired, union wages paid, and union rules observed—before the new enterprise is permitted to open its doors.

And the entrepreneur or entrepreneurs may be required, in addition, to have certain amounts of their own capital invested in a business, to post bonds against its failure, or to be approved by some approved agency that assures one's customers or clients against such failure. Banking is again a standard example, at least if the bank is to be a corporation with limited liability.

3. *Definition* of particular business activities imposes restrictions. What advice may a druggist, even a licensed pharmacist, give customers without being charged with the "unlicensed practice of medicine"? What assistance in tax-law interpretation may a licensed tax consultant, a certified public accountant, a notary public, or a legal secretary provide (for a fee) without being charged with the "unlicensed practice of law"? What is a non-bank bank, and what may a non-bank bank do that your common or garden variety bank cannot do? What is the fine line between barbering, beauty culture, and cosmetic surgery? (Figaro, the Barber of Seville in Beaumarchais' nineteenth-century comedy and Rossini's nineteenth-century opera, would land in jail in twentieth-century America.)

Positive regulation may also specify what a business must *include*. A public utility, of course, must in principle serve all customers equally and may not pick and choose its clientele. In some cities, including San Francisco, a builder of office buildings or luxury housing projects must simultaneously erect a certain amount of low-cost housing nearby. Prior to its dissolution, the American Telephone and Telegraph Company (AT&T) was required to divert part of the profits of its near-monopolistic long-distance telephone network into subsidized low rates for local telephone subscribers. Japanese petroleum refineries may gouge motorists who buy their gasoline, but must subsidize the homeowners who buy their kerosene for home heating. Indeed, a standard argument against deregulation—for limiting competition with such regulated monopolies as the Post Office—is precisely that

the competitor will "cream off" such profitable services as intracity first-class mail, while leaving "rural free delivery" to the official public corporation. And although airline deregulation has not eliminated air service from as many small and middle-sized communities as had been forecast, many of these places have found themselves cut back from ordinary transport planes to the small, less comfortable "puddle-jumpers" used by the commuter airlines.

4. As stated above, *enforcement of the rules* of various business "games" is the special province of regulatory agencies. Their rules cluster in the areas of safety and health (including pollution and hazardous waste), quality control (including testing of product content and performance), imports and exports (tariffs, quotas, administrative protection), patents and copyrights, and labor relations (including mediation and arbitration of labor disputes). If protests are loud and long enough, any entrepreneur planning a large-scale project or a large-scale expansion of an existing plant may be required to submit and defend an "environmental impact statement" before obtaining the requisite building permits to go ahead.

It should be noted that such rules are by no means all oppressive to all firms and industries subject to regulation. The typical pattern, rather, hurts some business firms (or workers, or consumers) while aiding others. It is to my advantage, for example, that the firm that competes with me is delayed by environmental impact troubles in expanding its plant or building a new one. A tariff, or an import quota, or a nit-picking and time-consuming inspection procedure aids domestic producers of import-competing products at the expense of importers and domestic consumers—including other business firms when the import is a raw material or an intermediate product. Many countries, especially developing countries, also impose export requirements, principally on final products, and especially on foreign firms or importers of foreign raw materials and intermediate products. Although these requirements hamper these firms themselves (and likewise their domestic customers), they aid other firms that supply the domestic raw materials.

Market Failure: The Rationale of Regulation

What is the rationale of this near-impenetrable maze of regulations? It can be summed up in the statement that

Love Canal neighborhood built at toxic waste site

unregulated markets have "failed," or if they have not been tried, that they probably would fail. This may mean that such markets have broken down or would break down, by reason of some technical instability. More commonly—almost always, in practice—it means only that free markets have worked or would work less than optimally (from the viewpoint of the critics, at least). Regulation, of course, is expected to do better—as indeed it surely would in any event, if the regulators were all-wise, all-seeing, omnipotent, and benevolent gods.

The most important types of market failure for our present purposes are probably associated with monopoly (and monopsony), with ignorance, with externalities, and with the dependence of the "bottom line" of economic outcomes upon the "top line" of the initial distributions of income and wealth.

Monopoly (and monopsony) speak for themselves. Let us simply note that public utility regulations and antitrust laws are types of regulations aimed at overcoming and counteracting monopolistic activities.

Ignorance—of what a good contains, how it has been made, what it is good for, and the possible side effects and dangers arising from its use—is a pervasive problem, especially when the ultimate consumer is unwarned and unwary. One need not be a "foul fiend" to take advantage of another person's ignorance. No manufacturer of refrigerators, for example, wanted children to suffocate by locking themselves in (discarded) refrigerators. Nor would any child, playing hide and seek, choose to hide in an abandoned refrigerator if he or she had any idea of the dangers of being locked in. Neither the companies who developed and manufactured the tranquilizer thalidomide nor the physicians who prescribed it for their patients had any idea that, if taken by expectant mothers, it would somehow and sometimes lead to birth defects in newborn babies. But children did suffocate in discarded refrigerators, "thalidomide babies" were born in several countries, and regulation was demanded by public outcry, to see that "it doesn't happen again."

The problems of toxic and hazardous wastes in chemical dumps illustrate market failure on externality grounds, with ignorance present at the same time. A chemical company closes or moves, selling to a city or a developer land on or under which it has previously disposed of wastes, of whose toxicity the business office may or may not have been informed by its chemists or chemical engineers. The site becomes a residential area, usually for working-class people. Five, ten, or twenty years later the industrial history may have been forgotten, but the residents become aware of an abnormally high incidence of various cancers, birth defects, etc. Or perhaps the wells that they have dug become contaminated and the water is condemned as unfit for human consumption. Regulation is enacted to force such companies to clean up toxic wastes before moving, quitting business, or selling their land for other reasons. (We call this an externality case because transactions between the chemical company and the purchasers of its property result in substantial damage to third parties, the residents of the affected area.)

The market has been called a system of "dollar votes." Compared with a hypothetical egalitarian system with income and wealth both divided equally, the market produces more "goods for the rich" and fewer "goods for the poor." "Who gets what" is determined, quite considerably, by the prior distributions of income and wealth. This statement applies not only to luxuries and "the finer things of life," but also to goods like housing, education, health, and old age security, which help the poor to rise and assume the roles of investors and entrepreneurs. So we have modified the pure market economy with such regulations as compulsory public education, social insurance, rent controls, and requirements that landlords up-grade substandard housing. These are all aspects of the so-called welfare state. With the benefits of the welfare state has also come more detailed regulation, first and foremost of initial

eligibility for benefits, but also enforcement of such conditions as may be imposed to compute benefits or maintain eligibility for them. For many years the principal American relief program, AFDC (Aid to Families with Dependent Children) was burdened with a "man in the house" rule, under which the female heads of such families were spied upon to make sure they were not being supported by their "missing" husbands or by boyfriends. The purpose of the regulations is to minimize the disadvantages of being or becoming poor, while at the same time minimizing both cost to the public treasury and disincentives to work. Other programs, such as rural electrification, try to minimize the disadvantages of living so "far from the madding crowd" that services would be unbearably costly unless they were public, with accompanying regulations to control abuse.

Although, as we have said, regulation is not price and wage control, such controls are important aspects of regulation. They fit into the total regulation picture at this distributional point, to the extent that their stated objectives are to raise the poor person's wage or the farm price of the poor farmer's crops, while lowering the poor person's cost of food (as by food stamps), or housing (as by rent controls), or borrowing money (as by usury laws).

The Rationale of Deregulation

Countering the above outline of the rationale of regulation, the case against "excessive" regulation is based on two main points. In the first place, regulation requires regulators, who are not all-knowing, benevolent gods. Administrative discretion can seldom, if ever, be avoided and is sometimes abused, by malice, misinformation, corruption, or some combination of the three. (As Nikita Khrushchev allegedly said, "There may be neutral countries, but there are no neutral men.") And in the second place, regulation is costly, both in money and in time. And, of course, one must add the costs borne by the taxpayers who finance the regulatory agencies to the cost borne by individuals and business firms being regulated, either in complying with the regulations or seeking to avoid them by migration or litigation.

No more than other laws can economic regulations be enforced 100 percent. Since they are enforced only selectively, decisions must be made about the distribution of surveillance efforts over potential or suspected

A result of deregulation—new airline with lower fares

violators. This fact opens the door to political influence—practical immunity for some and "enemies' lists" for others. Bias, harassment and nit-picking by antibusiness or antiemployer activists are complained of in the case of prolabor or proconsumer regulations. At the opposite extreme, we have observed regulatory agencies "captured" by the industries or individuals they were established to regulate. They become agencies to protect that industry, or at least the established firms of that industry, against interlopers, new techniques, or competitive industries. In the United States, the Interstate Commerce Commission (ICC) became a standard example of such development as it extended its regulations to trucking in order to protect the railroads and railway labor from competition from the newer form of land transport.

Regulation has tended also, on balance, toward caution and delay in sanctioning technical progress, when there is any hint of danger or of injury to established interests. We have mentioned the thalidomide case as prompting tighter regulation of the pharmaceutical industry. To prevent such cases—called by statisticians Type II errors[1]—the Food and Drug Administration (FDA) requires an elaborate routine of testing and retesting,

1. In statistical terminology, it is a Type I error to call an observed difference significant when it is actually the result of random sampling variance. On the other hand, it is a Type II error to ascribe a deviation to sampling error when it is in fact significant—such as a side effect in the pharmaceutical case we are discussing. Tradeoffs are involved between the two sorts of error, because reduction of the probability of a Type I error raises the probability of a Type II error, and vice versa.

even for substances already regarded as safe and effective overseas. The result has been a certain number of Type I errors, which of course never make the news headlines. Not only are American patients denied remedies available abroad, but American pharmaceutical companies claim to find it unprofitable to invest in innovative research when products cannot be marketed prior to costly and time-consuming testing and retesting. Another example, this time from banking, deals with the introduction and use of automatic teller machines by the more enterprising banks. In some jurisdictions this has been delayed until poorer or less enterprising competitors can "afford" the new machines. A third example is Sunday closing for small (Mom and Pop) retail establishments. These laws are enforced less to encourage church attendance than to protect employment for unionized retail clerks, whose collective bargains require Sunday closing and whose employers are concerned with competition from small family stores that remain open seven days a week.

How Far Deregulation?

Although all anarchists are deregulators, few deregulators are either anarchists or thoroughgoing libertarians. Their ideal society is not "the jungle." Neither, incidentally, do the deregulators represent "big business" against "small business" (or "labor" or "consumers" or "the general public"). Both the deregulation movement and its opposition are more complex than that.

For one example, it is not proposed to repeal the laws against force and fraud. It will surely remain illegal to have one's competitor murdered or to burn down his or her establishment. Or let us suppose the practice of medicine deregulated to the point where a high-school dropout, having picked up some rudiments of medical practice as an enlisted soldier in the Army Medical Corps, might practice as a civilian physician after military discharge. It would still remain illegal (fraudulent) for such a physician to claim the standard medical education and training that he or she does not possess. (It would also be legal for medical societies to refuse him or her admission, and for hospitals to exclude such "physicians" from their facilities.)

Most deregulation is not a matter of "all or none." It is usually a slow process of removing a few regulations or restrictions at a time, or reducing appropriations for

enforcing regulations and restrictions a little at a time, and observing who seems to be helped and who seems to be injured, before proceeding further. There may even be reversals along the way ("two steps forward, one step back") when freedoms are abused, new problems recognized, and particular regulations accordingly restored despite a general deregulatory trend.

The main purposes of deregulation are to increase competition and to open up businesses and professions to the newcomer, the outsider, the new process, and, yes, the "chiseler" and the "inferior" substitute (Brand X or no brand name at all). Deregulation is also designed to break down artificial and functionless walls separating one occupation or business from another, in the interest of interindustry and interproduct competition. The key arguments here are the opening up of closed markets, accelerating processes of technical change and "creative destruction," and eliminating convenient refuges from competition. Obvious losers are business "establishments," entrenched managements, and their associated labor aristocracies, both white- and blue-collar. Along with more liveliness and fun for the risk-preferrer, deregulation will breed strain, headaches, ulcers, alcoholism, and heart attacks among the risk-averters. For that matter, these may also occur among some consumers who have become used to one firm in each branch of business and report themselves unpleasantly "confused" by too many new alternatives.

General Principles?

There is as yet no general answer to problems of deregulation, and there may never be one. You will find yourself making up your own mind on each case on its own merits as you see it. It would not, for example, be unreasonable to favor a larger (or possibly smaller) measure of professional licensing for surgeons than for barbers, nurses, schoolteachers, auto mechanics, or taxi drivers. It would not be unreasonable to retain environmental impact statements for new projects concentrating on pollution problems, but not on the protection of endangered species or the provision of new housing for persons displaced by the project under consideration. To put the matter differently, deregulation is a field in which strict logic and strict analogy play smaller roles than they do in many branches of either theoretical or applied economics.

Comparing American society of the early twentieth century (before 1914) with its contemporary, Hohenzollern Germany, it used to be said that in America everything was permitted unless explicitly prohibited, but in Germany everything was *streng verboten* (strictly forbidden) unless explicitly permitted. What the deregulation movement proposes to accomplish, and what it may already have accomplished to some degree, is to turn the American clock back, restoring late twentieth-century American society to something like its pristine model and reversing an "irresistible" trend toward something like an Imperial German one. Or in terms of burdens of proof, the deregulation movement aims at, and may already have accomplished, a shift of this burden from the regulated to the regulators, giving the private person or firm, rather than Mr. "Pass-Another-Law" or Ms. "Set-Up-Another Commission," the benefit of the doubt in more of the numerous complex cases where the probable results of both the free market and public controls fall far short of heart's desire.

XI *Comparative Economic Systems*

- Comparative Economic Systems — More Planning or Less?
- Radical Economics

38 *Comparative Economic Systems— More Planning or Less?*

PREVIEW As you learned earlier, societies manage their scarcity problems in different ways. In today's world, the most important of these are the impersonal *market* and deliberate *planning* by the public authorities, though in some places *traditional* economies survive.

You also know that no existing economy is *pure* and that all are *mixed.* The United States is primarily, but by no means exclusively, a market economy, since about 30 percent of the American gross national product now passes through the public sector and need not "meet the test of the market." Similarly, the Soviet Union is primarily but not exclusively a planned economy, since much of its agricultural output is raised and marketed by peasants from their private plots.

The question raised in this chapter is a normative one. Should we favor using "more planning" or "less planning" by public agencies in our economy? In other words, should we shift our economic "mix" toward greater reliance on public planning, greater reliance on the market, or leave it alone?

We begin by reviewing our criteria for judging economic systems. Next we discuss the relationship of planning to freedom and power, and distinguish between planning, collectivism, and the welfare state. Even though these three kinds of institutions are often found together, a country may have any one or two without the rest. Then, turning specifically to planning, we introduce several general planning types.

At this point, we discuss first the Soviet Union as a representative of collectivist (also socialist) planning, and then Japan and Sweden as two widely different examples of economic planning under capitalism. As examples of socialist collectivism that is combined with a largely market economy, we turn to the countries of Yugoslavia and China.

To illustrate some of the problems raised by the Russian experience in particular, we return to theory for the last part of the chapter. One theory that we present is the market socialist model of Oskar Lange and A. P. Lerner. The other is the forecast of Ludwig von Mises and Friedrich von Hayek that planning is incompatible with freedom and will lead eventually to what Hayek calls "serfdom."

SOCIAL GOALS

We take as given the goals suggested in Chapter 1, but not their relative importance. These goals are as follows:

1. High *present* standards of living
2. High growth rates, leading to high *prospective* standards of living
3. Equitable distribution of income and wealth
4. Security of the standard of living against short-term downward shocks from recessions and depressions, and also against long-term shocks from resource exhaustion and technological change
5. Compatibility of economic institutions with personal liberty and civil rights
6. Compatibility of economic institutions with physical and mental health

Even with agreement on these goals, the question of "more planning or less?" arouses violent and sometimes irrational emotions. Two stories illustrate this point.

The first story is about Hassan, an Egyptian student of one of the authors, who was describing the wonders that the Aswan Dam, built in the late 1950s, would bring to his country. The teacher recalled that the British, during their period of rule over Egypt, had also built an Aswan Dam and placed high hopes upon it, with disappointing results. "But, Professor," said Hassan politely, "you don't understand. This Aswan Dam is *planned!*" Hassan knew that the British dam was also planned—engineering projects always are! He meant that the Egyptian dam was part of a comprehensive national plan for Egypt, whereas the British dam had been an isolated project. Confidence like Hassan's that a plan will work just because it *is* a plan is what we call "magic wand" planning. Much of the appeal of some of the more grandiose kinds of planning is of the magic-wand sort.

The second story is about a Polish friend of one of the authors. When the Nazis invaded Poland in 1939, this man fled to the Soviet Union. The U.S.S.R., then allied with the Nazis, sent him to a remote part of Siberia. There, after the Nazis had invaded the U.S.S.R., a peasant asked him if the Nazis were as bad as he had been told. The Polish refugee assured the Siberian peasant that the Nazis were indeed bad people who committed atrocities, but the peasant was not satisfied. "Do the Nazis have collective farms in Germany?" he asked. (Collective farms are the basis for Soviet agricultural planning.)

"No, there are no collective farms in Germany."

"Well, then, the Nazis cannot be so bad as you say," concluded the peasant.

PLANNING, FREEDOM, AND POWER

When economists speak of planned economies, the planning they have in mind is done by legislators, experts, and civil servants. But in any case, every individual, to some extent, plans for

himself or herself. Every family plans for itself. Every organization—be it a corporation, a university, a club, or a government bureau—plans for itself. In economics **planning** means an institutional arrangement in which some individual or organization in a public position plans for another individual or organization, who or which has little say about the plan and whose economic freedom is restricted by the planning decision.

The relation between freedom and planning is by no means a simple matter. When I plan for myself today, my freedom is restricted by whatever long-term plans I may have made earlier. For example, I cannot buy a new car or take a trip to Europe because I carried out last year's plan to buy a house, and "my mortgage payments are killing me." Families and organizations present even more problems than individuals. Students have lost their best friends because their parents decided to move from one neighborhood to another, or from the Snow Belt to the Sun Belt. Workers have lost their jobs when their employer's home office decided to close their factory or office. Retailers have gone bankrupt when major suppliers or customers closed down or moved away—or when competitors opened up shop across the street. When City Hall, the State Capitol, or "Washington" carries out some plan we dislike, and which limits our economic freedom in some way, are we hurt any less because we can still vote for legislators who promise to change or repeal the plan, or because we can "vote with our feet" by moving to some other place? One point should be clear: public planning, when carried out through laws and regulations, may be either more or less restrictive of freedom than private planning, when carried out through market forces.

Freedom should be distinguished from *power.* You are quite free to visit the moon, or Mars for that matter, but are powerless to exercise that freedom unless you are an astronaut, a cosmonaut, or a flying-saucerite from outer space. You have the power to abuse small children or drive while drunk, but your freedom does not extend to such illegal activities. Planners, too, often do not have the power to carry out plans they are free to make. The controversial architect and city planner Frank Lloyd Wright said that one American city "needs another fire" and that another should be "torn down and started over," but no urban planner has the power to burn or tear down any city.

Freedom-versus-power problems arise whenever the protection of someone's freedom interferes with someone else's planning power, or whenever the protection or enhancement of someone's planning power interferes with someone else's freedom. Yet a more basic freedom-power problem is this one: Can a person be said to have freedom at all, when either natural forces or the actions of others—including their economic plans—deprive him or her of the power to exercise it effectively? Is your freedom of speech worth anything if you do not own a newspaper or a television station, have no pulpit or professorship, and cannot otherwise persuade people to listen to you? What is it worth to be free to air your views if you are shunned by your customers or lose your job because of them, even when you fear neither legal prosecution nor mob violence? And if your freedom of speech cannot be translated into the power to influence others, how much better off are you than someone else who must follow the "party line," keep his or her mouth shut, or else face "re-education" in prison, labor camp, or mental hospital?

PLANNING, COLLECTIVISM, AND THE WELFARE STATE

We have already suggested that planning is related to both freedom and power. Now we consider how it is related to collectivism and to the so-called welfare state.

In **collectivist economies,** land and physical capital instruments such as buildings and machinery are largely or completely owned by collective agencies, not by private individuals or business firms. Most, but not all, planned economies are in fact collectivist, and most of them are socialistic. In **socialistic economies** these col-

FIGURE 38-1 Types of Economic Systems

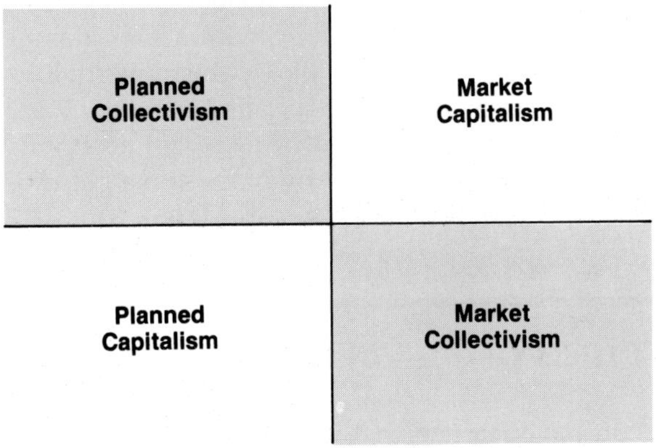

| Planned Collectivism | Market Capitalism |
| Planned Capitalism | Market Collectivism |

Planned economies are indicated to the left of the center line, and market economies to the right. Collectivist economies are shaded, and capitalist economies unshaded. Most collectivist economies are in fact socialistic.

lective agencies are governmental.[1] On the other hand, most but not all market economies are **capitalistic.** In these economies, physical capital instruments are owned largely by private individuals or business firms. Aside from traditional economies, there are four distinct types of economic systems, as pictured in Figure 38-1. In this figure, planned economies are shown to the left of the center line and market economies to the right. Collectivist (usually socialist) economies are shaded, and the capitalist ones unshaded.

Just as many people confuse planning with socialism or communism, and the market with capitalism, they also associate planning with the welfare state, and the market with something less compassionate.

A **welfare state** is an economy that places an especially high value on our goals 3 and 4 among the objectives of the economy. The "equity" of its income and wealth distributions is a matter of

1. A **communist** is a socialist who believes that socialism on a world scale will lead to an economy of abundance, and who accepts violence, revolution, and dictatorship as a means to that end.

first importance. "Equity," moreover, is treated as including a relatively high poverty line or "safety net," below which no person or family need remain for long, along with a high degree of distributional equality above this poverty line. Either a capitalist or a socialist economy, and likewise either a planned or a market economy, may be a welfare state. Any of these may also be something other than a welfare state.

TYPES OF PLANNING

You have learned that not all markets are alike. Monopoly, for example, is different from competition. In the same way, planning systems are not all alike. In the next few paragraphs we outline several of the major types of planning.

Imperative Planning

The most rigorous form of planning is **imperative planning.** It is imperative in that, to quote Josef Stalin, "A plan is a command." Failure to reach an important plan target is a criminal offense. In extreme cases those who fail may be punished by imprisonment or even death, as sometimes happened in Stalin's Russia. Imperative planning goes beyond the aggregate economy to include the "fine structure" of the economy as a whole and also of a country's regions.

Indicative Planning

A milder form of planning is **indicative planning.** It operates mainly by convincing plan participants that following the plan will help them economically, though in some cases they are threatened with the denial of privileges (or even with penalties) for not following "administrative guidance." Most peacetime capitalist planning is of this kind. Indicative planning is generally also *consensual*, meaning that the planning authority includes representatives of various interest groups as well as civil servants and planning technicians.

Among the groups represented may be some or all of the following: the financial community, the military, organized business, organized labor, organized agriculture, organized taxpayers, organized consumers, and spokespersons from the different regions of the country.

Public Sector Planning

Public sector planning covers only the public sector. The many different organs of central and local government, while producing a small percentage of the total national income and product, often dominate the economy's "commanding heights," or key industries, in mixed systems. To treat them as a single enterprise, therefore, goes a long way toward controlling the whole economy. However, it is also hard to do so, because of jealousy between different branches of the government—between "national defense" and "social services," between the central and local governments, and between the more and less advanced parts of the country. The private sector is also affected by public sector planning because private companies sell to or buy from public agencies, and because the plan gives the public sector priority over strategic and especially over imported resources. This kind of planning has been used most widely in India.

Macroeconomic Planning

Macroeconomic planning is less ambitious than any of the three kinds of planning covered so far. Planned or target quantities generally include standard aggregate measures such as gross national product, the division between consumption, investment, and government sectors, the supplies of money and credit, the government surplus or deficit, international balances, and interest rates. The fine structure of the aggregates is left to the market.

Macroeconomic planning generally includes the simple forecasting or projection of present policies or the results of certain changes that have been proposed. This is technically not planning at all.

Indeed, it is sometimes done entirely by computer simulation, with little aid from human hands or brains. It often precedes real planning, but is treated as planning by the mass media.

Magic Wand Planning

We have already noted **"magic wand" planning.** A magic wand plan is built around a collection of projects and/or an appealing slogan. The projects or the slogan are expected to produce all kinds of good things by some unspecified processes, including the mystical power of the word *planning*. One example is the "fourth national plan" proposed for Japan in Herman Kahn's *Japanese Challenge*. This plan proposed to produce an industrialized environmentalist utopia, called "the machine in the garden." Another is the Humphrey-Hawkins bill in the United States. In its original form, it called for targets of low inflation and low unemployment to be reached in 1983, but indicated only in the vaguest language how this was to be done.

In the next few parts of this chapter, we shall present case studies of actual economies illustrating planned collectivism, planned capitalism, and one form of market socialism. (Most of this book has assumed a market-capitalist economy, and so we see no need to illustrate such an economy again here.)

A PLANNED COLLECTIVIST ECONOMY: THE SOVIET UNION

We begin with the Soviet model of imperative planning. Its vision of the economy is a huge factory, producing not only the country's final products, or consumer goods, but also its own intermediate products. As his model for Russia, Vladimir Lenin (1870–1924) may have used the Ford works in and around Detroit, which were the industrial marvels of his time. Ford produced not only automobiles, trucks, and tractors, but also many of their parts, and raw materials like

coal and steel. Another vision was one that the Soviets shared with many other hostile critics of capitalism: that business administration can be reduced to the clerical routine of "office management," if the firm only had the information that a plan could provide and if it need not be concerned with competition. In this way, Lenin hoped that a national plan, maximizing welfare for the whole society much as a business firm plans to maximize profits, could be made simple and clear enough so that the average worker, without formal training in economics or statistics, could understand it and criticize it intelligently.

Stalin and the Growth of Gosplan

The Russian revolutions of 1917 were followed by civil war, foreign intervention, and famine. With all these troubles, the planning process floundered over the years from 1917 to 1928. After Lenin died in 1924, the "Soviet" planning model developed under the leadership of Josef Stalin (1880–1953). This model was both imperative and highly centralized in a single agency, called **Gosplan,** which has since grown to huge proportions. Gosplan is subdivided along both industrial and regional lines, with consultation extending down to and up from the individual factory. That is, the manager of a factory or a collective farm is informed of his or her role in the plan: what outputs should be produced, and what inputs should be used to produce them. The manager may suggest changes, but final authority rests with Gosplan in Moscow.

The plans are usually but not necessarily for five-year periods. The actual length of time is a practical compromise. Shorter periods may not allow completion of many planned projects, and could overtax Gosplan facilities. Longer periods might result in many plants being out of date by the time they were built.

Every part of the plan must be coordinated with other parts, since in economics nearly everything depends on nearly everything else. Every output has to be expanded as fast as its inputs, and no faster than its own demand. To coordinate the parts of the plan, the Soviets have used two

TABLE 38-1 **An Input-Output Table (in dollars)**

Supplying Industry	Using Industry				
	Agriculture and Fisheries (1)	Food and Kindred Products (2)	Tobacco Manufactures (3)	Textile Mill Products (4)	Apparel (5)
(1) Agriculture and Fisheries	.2609	.4041	.2941	.2139	.0015
(2) Food and Kindred Products	.0572	.1319	.0055	.0062	.0007
(3) Tobacco Manufactures	0	0	.3110	0	0
(4) Textile Mill Products	.0015	0	0	.1341	.2955
(5) Apparel	.0011	.0055	0	0	.1494

This is a portion of the American input-output table for 1947, published by the Bureau of Labor Statistics and condensed in Robert Dorfman's book, *The Price System* (Englewood Cliffs, N.J.: Prentice-Hall, 1964); used with permission.

We focus our attention on the number .2955, shown in blue. It says that to produce a dollar's worth of its own output, a using industry (apparel) bought $.2955 worth of products from a supplying industry (textiles).

For a complete input-output table, each column and each row would add up to 1.00 (one dollar), since "industries" can be included for "households," "foreign trade," or any other source or use of output.

specialized techniques—materials balancing and input-output analysis.

MATERIALS BALANCING The simpler of the two seems to be **materials balancing.** For every one of the thousands of final and intermediate products, potential supplies and demands are estimated for each year of the plan, allowing for both domestic production and international trade. The problem with this method is the difficulty of tracing the results of changes from the last plan, of technological progress, or of economic growth. For example, how much will a rise in the output of heavy trucks, including their engines and tires and fuel, eventually increase the demand for coal? And by how much will these trucks increase the supply of coal?

INPUT-OUTPUT ANALYSIS To solve problems of this last sort, **input-output analysis** was developed (outside the U.S.S.R.) by the Russian-born Nobel Prize–winning economist Wassily Leontief (1906–   ).

Input-output analysis is based on matrix algebra, which is studied in more advanced economics as well as mathematics courses. We can illustrate the basic features of the process with the help of Table 38-1, which is part of an input-output table. The first step in setting up the system is to divide the economy into separate industries for which data can be collected. The table illustrates five such industries—agriculture and fisheries, food and kindred products, tobacco manufactures, textile mill products, and apparel. Each of these industries is listed twice in the table, once as a supplying industry at the left end of a row, and again as a using industry at the head of a column in the table. In the body of the table, each number shows the value of goods from a supplying industry that is used to produce a dollar's worth of goods from a using industry. For example, the blue number in the table tells us that $.2955 worth (or 29.55 cents' worth) of supplies from the textile mill products industry is used by the apparel industry for each dollar's worth of apparel produced. In the complete system, the whole column for the apparel industry would add up to 1.00 (one dollar). Similarly, the whole row of values for the textile mill products industry would add up to 1.00, since all of its output supplied will be used somewhere in the economy. One of the "industries" is "households," so that consumption is recognized. Another "industry" can be foreign trade, to account for exports and imports, and so on.

For the planning specialists at Gosplan, the problem is to estimate accurately what the actual input-output relationships are for the economy. If their estimates do not correspond to what happens in the actual execution of the plan, shortages and surpluses will develop, and the goals of the plan will not be met. As you can easily imagine, the method becomes unwieldy when the classification of the outputs and inputs approaches the fineness of materials balancing. One needs not only to have enough steel for rails but also to have it in the form of rails as distinguished from girders, stainless steel, or armor plate. Nevertheless, progress in planning has been marked by a rise in the relative importance of input-output techniques.

Problems of Soviet Planning

Far from being clear enough for Lenin's "ordinary worker" to understand, Soviet planning is a highly complex system that has not always worked very well. Before the day of the computer, Soviet writers feared "drowning in an ocean of paper" by the year 1980, in the effort to record, digest, and apply the information needed in forming and revising plans. Even though the computer has provided a breathing space, the danger of "drowning in computer output" remains for the planners.

In practice, the key problems of Soviet planning can be reduced to three. The first is disappointingly low productivity, particularly for labor on collective farms. (Peasants do much better, it appears, on their private plots.) Second, since planning is done in terms of physical quantities or weights of goods, quality is often skimped or products are too heavy for use, particularly toward the ends of planning periods. Third, the plans are too rigid. They do not allow for unavoidable shortfalls, so that they have seldom, if ever, been carried out in full. For this reason, the

plans include a **leading links** system. This means that when the whole plan cannot be carried out, certain leading links are completed in full, and the rest of the plan is postponed in part until the next planning period. The leading links are generally military hardware and capital goods; the postponements are generally in consumption goods. This is why each successive plan promised Western European living standards to the Soviet citizen, and why the promises have remained unfulfilled. However, the conditions of the Russian economy and the Russian consumer were so poor under the Czarist regime[2] that to the Soviet citizen these deficiencies of Soviet planning seem minor when compared with the advances made over prerevolutionary Russia, and with the conditions of most LDCs of the present world.

Soviet Planning Since Stalin

Stalin died in 1953. Under his successors, Soviet-style planning has become less severe. The change is more marked in the Soviet-bloc countries of Eastern Europe than in the U.S.S.R. itself. The principal reforms, sometimes lumped together as **Libermanism** from the name of an early advocate, are as follows:

1. A wider scope for an unplanned, private, but usually noncapitalistic[3] "dual economy" alongside the planned socialist one.

But the process of this "reform" in the U.S.S.R. has been uneven. Among the successors of Stalin, only Nikita Kruschchev advocated it—in a lukewarm fashion. It was resisted by both the (Communist) Party and the planning bureaucracy,

2. Some economic historians, notably Alexander Gerschenkron, have argued that Czarist Russia was making rapid progress during the 1890–1913 generation, so that continuation of the 1890–1913 trend would have equaled actual Soviet performance had Czar Nicholas II and his ministers avoided the disastrous World War I. But this is all conjecture.

3. How can a private economy be noncapitalistic? It can be noncapitalistic only if the "firms" are family firms or workers' cooperatives, and do not employ more than a specific number of people in the production of goods. (Employment of people for wages or fees as servants, doctors, lawyers, etc., is also legal in socialist states because no salable goods are produced.)

fearing for their own power and prestige and ideologically opposed to taking the capitalist road. After Kruschchev's fall in 1964, the reform movement lapsed almost completely. There is talk of revival under the present leader, Mikhail S. Gorbachev, but as of this writing (mid-1986), Gorbachev's reform effort has stressed less controversial matters like reduced corruption and inertia among the bureaucracy and alcoholism among the peasants and workers.

2. More "slack" in the plans themselves, so that a bad harvest, an earthquake, or a power failure does not force extensive plan revision.

3. More leeway for plant managers on the input side of their plans. If the planned targets are met at the planned prices, if minimum wages are paid, and if the state receives all the economic earnings from the land and capital that the firm uses, the "firm" may make a "profit." If it does so, some part of the profit may be kept by the managers for sharing with the work force, for improving housing and other facilities, or even for the manager's own use.

To show how this newer style of planning works, let us take the example of a Hungarian bakery, run by a family or by a producers' cooperative. The bakery receives a planned allotment of flour and must produce a planned amount of bread to be sold at planned prices. But it may also buy additional flour on the open market, and sell bread, cake, and pastry to private customers for whatever prices the market will bear, just like an American bakery. (Hungary has moved further away from Stalinist planning than have other Eastern European countries.)

Under the Chinese variant of a planned economy propounded by Mao Zedong (Mao Tse-tung, 1892–1976), not only the peasantry but some urban people lived and worked in **communes.** Rural communes were large collective farms. Each commune, particularly in the countryside, strove for self-sufficiency and drew up its own plan to produce and consume a wide variety of agricultural and manufactured goods. It then presented to the authorities, first in the provincial capital and finally in Beijing (Peking), only a list of its expected surpluses and deficits (production mi-

nus consumption). The planning authorities acted as a clearinghouse for these communal plans, representing the government, the foreign trade sector, and the rest of China—especially the urban sector, which was less thoroughly organized into communes. They tried to match up the surpluses and deficits (the demands and supplies of each major commodity) as well as possible but with minimal changes in relative prices.

PLANNING UNDER CAPITALISM: JAPAN AND SWEDEN

Business people and procapitalists desire planning chiefly under one or more of four sets of conditions: (1) a serious or prolonged depression; (2) a major war, including both its preparation and its aftermath; (3) a widespread desire to speed up economic growth beyond what the market has provided; (4) a desire to ensure that political power will be held by moderates more dedicated to planning than to socialization. (By going along with a limited amount of planning, one perhaps can avoid the socialization of one's business and have a voice in the planning process.)

The United States has not been immune to the desire for planning. A planning "boom," led by business people along with academics, was a feature of the Great Depression of the 1930s. One of the most widely discussed plans was outlined by Gerard Swope, then president of General Electric. The National Recovery Administration was a 1933 New Deal experiment that reflected the planning philosophy but accomplished little and was finally ruled unconstitutional by the Supreme Court. During the Great Stagflation of the 1970s, the desire for planning revived in the form of the Humphrey-Hawkins bill, which we have already mentioned. Calling for the reduction of both unemployment and inflation, it made the government the employer of last resort. (It was passed by Congress only in weakened form after Senator Hubert Humphrey's death as a tribute to his memory. In its weakened form, as we have said, it mandated nothing even though it expressed fond hopes.)

Because large-scale "capitalist planning" has had little success in the United States, we draw our examples from overseas. The Japanese plan, our first example, was inspired by the desire to move beyond mere recovery to rapid growth after the disaster of World War II. Carried out under conservative governments, it featured the doubling of the GNP in less than a decade. The Swedish plan, our next example, arose under the long rule of the Social Democratic Party, partly as a defense against nationalization of the private sector. Because the two systems turned out so differently, we describe both. Other countries that we might have cited are France, the Netherlands, Norway, and India.

Japan, Incorporated

The Japanese economy is often called "Japan, Incorporated," by those who charge that all other interest groups, perhaps including even the government, are subordinated to big business. However, one government department, the notorious MITI (Ministry of International Trade and Industry), has attracted worldwide attention. Its notoriety is based on the charge that the whole economy is run by its bureaucracy. How can both these charges be true at once? Is Japan run by big bureaucracy or by big business?

Both sets of charges are exaggerations. Japan's long-range plans are purely indicative. They are drawn up, not in MITI, but in the Economic Planning Agency, which is connected with the Finance Ministry. It receives information from other government departments (including MITI), from business firms and their organizations, from agricultural organizations and their government representatives, and from the Ministry of Agriculture and Forestry. Workers and consumers, however, are mainly "on the outside looking in."

INDICATIVE PLANNING MECHANISMS How does Japan's indicative planning work? First of all, the government approves and assists projects within these plans. As long as they operate within the plan, it also protects the larger Japanese companies against failure, forced cutbacks, or "excessive

competition,"[4] especially from other countries and from Japanese branches of foreign companies. For companies planning ambitious expansion programs aimed at increasing their shares of Japanese and world markets, there may also be "administrative guidance" against such recklessness. This guidance has no legal force but does bring the veiled threat of unspecified government displeasure (selective enforcement of tax or antimonopoly laws, unfavorable consideration in government purchases, and so on.) In some firms and on some issues, guidance has the force of unwritten law. Other firms, on the other hand, ignore it entirely.

PRODUCTIVITY Another feature of the Japanese economy is its high and rising labor productivity. Even though the government plan allows for this high productivity, the planning for it is done only by individual companies, with the cooperation of the educational system, both public and private. Many male workers (but fewer females) are hired with the expectation that they will never be fired or laid off, but will be kept on until retirement or until the company goes out of business. For this reason, it pays the employer to invest heavily and continuously in their on-the-job training and retraining. Neither workers nor their unions[5] object to technological progress. At the same time, "dead wood"—defined as people hard to train or to promote—is reduced by careful selection and training programs. The most successful companies limit their search to high-level graduates of "good" high schools and universities.[6] They investigate and interview even the brightest and most promising applicants in order to weed

4. This term covers *any* competition that threatens to force any leading Japanese firm to cut its price, or profit margin, or scale of operations for the Japanese market.

5. Japanese unions are enterprise and not craft unions. This means that a worker can be retrained in a different craft—a welder as a machinist, for example—without jurisdictional disputes between separate union locals.

6. Entrance examinations are required for Japanese high schools and universities, both public and private. A "good" high school or university is one whose entrance examinations are difficult, and which can reject a high percentage of applicants on academic grounds.

out troublemakers, deviants, militants, or even simple nonconformists. The successful candidates are then subjected to a period of "basic training," observation, and "socialization" by the company before they are accepted as permanent employees. Young men and women who do not make the grade may find work in less good firms, in a succession of temporary jobs, or in family businesses. As a result, unemployment has been a serious problem only for young people who have "dropped out" for a while, or for older workers whose employers have gone out of business.

REACTION TO JAPAN'S SUCCESS   The outstanding success of the Japanese economy and the high rate of measured Japanese growth since the end of the Korean War (1953) have inspired great interest in the West. At the same time, they have caused great envy and resentment, expressed in the form of restrictions on the export trade that Japan needs in order to buy both its food and nearly all of its industrial raw materials. Such restrictions have been strongest in the countries of the European Community. As anti-Japanese protectionism has spread to the United States and the Third World, Japan's economy, its capitalism, and its indicative planning are all being severely tested. Japan remains a fragile economy, dependent on the goodwill of its suppliers and its customers.

Sweden's Welfare State

Sweden is famous for its welfare-state institutions. The Social Democratic Party has dominated Swedish politics since the Great Depression, and Sweden has had a flourishing consumer cooperative movement for many years. For these reasons, many non-Swedes believe Sweden to be a socialist country. It is not. The Swedish mixed economy remains largely capitalist, with certain features that are called "laboristic." That is, even though capital and land are privately owned, employees as well as stockholders must be represented on the boards of directors of large Swedish corporations, and corporate decisions are "co-determined" by labor and capital.[7] Swedish companies must share their profits with workers and are allowed to establish foreign branches or export capital to existing branches only with the consent of their workers in Sweden.

ELEMENTS OF SWEDISH PLANNING   Most of Sweden's plans are indicative and short term. In a changing world, and particularly in a small country like Sweden, dependent on both foreign imports and foreign markets, it seems impractical to draw up comprehensive five-year plans. One-year plans are the standard practice. However, there are some long-term public works and housing projects as well.

A Swedish corporation does not have to pay corporate income tax on the part of its profits that it places in a special investment reserve. As a rule, funds in this reserve cannot be invested free of tax during boom periods when labor is in short supply, but can be invested tax free whenever unemployment exists or is threatened. Moreover, these investment reserves can be invested tax free only in those parts of Sweden where there is underemployment and surplus labor—often in the cold northern half of the country. If the United States were to follow this Swedish policy, the government would be guiding capital to the Snow Belt by offering tax privileges, rather than letting Snow Belt workers find their own way to the Sun Belt, where investment has been concentrated in recent years.

Swedish planning is also *consensual*. That is to say, the indicative plan targets must be accepted by representatives of large and small business, labor, agriculture, finance, the public sector, and so on. Such major macroeconomic variables as the growth rates of money, credit, employment, labor productivity, and wage and price levels must also be agreed upon. The same is true of changes in taxes and spending, as well as the means of financing deficits and surpluses. Even changes in imports, exports, capital movements,

---

7. This co-determination system is not peculiar to Sweden. It is most highly developed in West Germany, and is common in Northern Europe.

and the balance of payments position must be approved by consensus.

PROBLEMS OF SWEDISH PLANNING Two basic problems have developed in connection with Swedish planning, and have given the economy an inflationary twist. The first has to do with forecasts. It is nearly always easier to reach a planning consensus under optimistic "first-best" assumptions, which let every interest group have most of what it wants, than under more cautious assumptions, whose results would disappoint some or all of the bargainers. For example, the forecast of a sharp rise in labor productivity plus ideal weather on the farms will permit larger wage increases, smaller price rises, and a more positive trade balance than will more realistic forecasts. In fact, "first-best" assumptions are very seldom justified. There may be droughts and floods, strikes and absenteeism,[8] oil shocks and foreign wars, tax evasions and welfare frauds. The public deficit, the volume of credit, and the money supply are the variables with most "give" when the first-best combination of circumstances does not come about, so that the inflation is generally greater than expected.

In mentioning strikes, we have already hinted at the second problem. Suppose that a general wage rise of 5 percent is accepted by the representative of the national labor federation. Further suppose that this rise keeps all wage differentials in place, in percentage terms. The problem is that no representative of any pressure group can speak for all the subgroups within it, particularly in the case of labor. It has happened that the workers with less skill or education or the workers in jobs hiring mainly the young, the elderly, or the female worker may demand that the traditional differentials be ended or reduced. However, if these demands are met and the differentials are reduced, the skilled workers and male family heads may press for the return of their advantage on grounds of custom, usage, and equity. This kind of whipsaw movement raises wages all around. The next step is a price rise. If consumers are not willing to pay higher prices, the government meets the resulting unemployment with unplanned transfer payments or unplanned public-service jobs financed by unplanned money and credit expansion along with higher-than-planned inflation rates, and so on.

THE MEIDNER PLAN The planned Swedish economy has remained largely capitalistic, but some elements of the socialist-dominated trade union movement and the Social Democratic Party propose to turn it sharply in a collectivist direction. The labor economist Rudolf Meidner is author of a nonviolent but revolutionary proposal for bringing this change about.

The basic Meidner plan is simple. Corporate income taxation of large companies is increased. The revenues from the increased tax rates go to the trade unions.[9] The unions use these revenues to buy shares in Swedish corporations on the stock exchange. With this process repeated every year, the unions eventually own enough stock to control all the larger corporations of Sweden.[10] This result would be technically **syndicalist,** with the economy controlled by trade unions rather than by the government as under socialism. It is ordinarily called socialism, however.

The main arguments against the Meidner plan are the power it gives the trade-union leadership and the fear that union-controlled firms would try to maximize wage rates and employment, which might lead to featherbedding and low productivity. Such union-controlled companies may eventually need subsidies to keep going, may oppose labor-saving technological changes, and may fail in international competition with

---

8. Swedish companies and unions have led the way in devising ingenious systems of job sharing and job rotation, aimed at motivating workers and reducing high absenteeism rates on Mondays and Fridays particularly. So far, these systems have not been notably successful.

9. *Not* to individual workers! Socialists fear that profit-sharing will turn workers into petty capitalists, and oppose it.

10. Were American unions to control pension funds, invest these funds in corporate stock, and vote that stock at stockholders' meetings, the United States too might become a country of "pension-fund socialism" (actually syndicalism).

capitalist business. In addition, private saving is likely to fall, in which case investment would presumably be financed by still higher taxes, or by inflation.

To forestall such problems, the Meidner plan, at least the mild version adopted in 1984, shares control over the "workingman's funds" between union leaders and civil servants, the latter representing the interests of the nonunion public. Also, control is decentralized regionally, rather than being centralized in Stockholm.

MARKETS UNDER SOCIALISM: YUGOSLAVIA AND CHINA

The Yugoslav Case

Karl Marx's attempt to control the International Workingmen's Association (First International) was opposed by **anarchists.** Anarchists propose to abolish all forms of government compulsion. For example, they believe that compulsory collection of taxes is a form of robbery. Instead, they would like to have people join and contribute to small voluntary associations, which they could leave at any time, either to join some other group or to form new ones. These associations could themselves combine voluntarily to manage larger projects. The anarchists accused Marx and his followers of planning to substitute bureaucratic control for capitalistic ownership of the means of production. Such a change, they thought, was likely to make matters worse rather than to help the people.

Marshal Josip Broz Tito of Yugoslavia (1892–1980) was a Marxist and a communist, not an anarchist. Even while rebelling in 1948 against the spread of Soviet Stalinism to his own country, he kept his strong government under Yugoslav Communist Party control. For the Yugoslav economy, however, Tito and his advisers downgraded central planning, substituting a system of workers' self-management that has attracted a great deal of attention.

THE ROLE OF WORKERS' COLLECTIVES Yugoslavia is a socialist state where land and capital goods are publicly owned. However, many of these resources are leased to and operated by groups of workers at rentals set by the state. These workers' collectives or cooperatives decide their own inputs and outputs as well as their own membership of workers with various skills. They elect their own managers and set their own prices for the goods they produce. If they make any profits after taxes are paid, they may distribute them among their members as they wish (subject to the requirement that minimum "wages" be paid), or they may use them for such purposes as housing or environmental improvements. To a certain extent, they may even act as a bank and lend surplus funds to other groups.

THE ROLE OF THE CENTRAL AUTHORITIES Plenty is left for the central economic authorities of Yugoslavia to do, as well as for the authorities of the six republics that make up the country. They must enforce minimum income levels for participants in the cooperative firms. The authorities also make sure that new or younger people in these firms have equal shares in management and are not simply disguised employees of the older workers. They must judge the creditworthiness of the firms' requests for continued and expanded rentals of land and capital, and keep them from wasting these resources. When a new firm is either being set up "from scratch" or separating from an old one, the authorities must judge whether it should receive land and capital at all.

Macroeconomic planning includes the goal of bringing the six Yugoslav republics closer together. The two northernmost republics, Croatia and Slovenia, were under Austro-Hungarian rule for several centuries. They are economically ahead of the other four republics, Bosnia-Herzegovina, Macedonia, Montenegro, and Serbia, which were then under the Turks. Central government policy aims at reducing the economic gaps between and among these two groups. To do so is difficult, however, since the republics have different languages, religions, and cultures.

WEAKNESSES OF THE YUGOSLAV SYSTEM Like all other economic systems, the Yugoslav system has developed certain weaknesses in practice. We shall note six of them:

1. Labor-managed firms are sometimes run by a small minority of "labor aristocrats," usually skilled or white-collar workers, while the other members remain passive most of the time.

2. The Yugoslav Communist Party has feared the creation, within the labor-managed firms, of an economic base for opposition political movements like the Polish Solidarity movement of 1980–1981. The Party has therefore encouraged its individual-enterprise "cells" to interfere in in-plant elections so as to win managements supportive of government policies. In such attempts, it has allegedly had the strong-arm support of the local and national police forces.

3. Once in place and flourishing, the more established Yugoslav firms have been able to use a good deal of political influence and monopolistic power to delay and limit the progress of rival firms and the opening up of Yugoslavia to foreign competition.

4. The labor-managed firm of the Yugoslav sort can be looked on as maximizing net income *per worker* rather than its total net income or profit. This puts the Yugoslav firm under pressure to use more capital and less labor than would a private company in a similar case. This is unfortunate in a country like Yugoslavia, which is capital-poor and labor-rich.[11]

5. Partly for the same reason—too much capital per worker—Yugoslavia seldom attains high employment in practice. To find jobs, Yugoslav workers have left the country in large numbers and become "guest workers" in other European countries.

6. The inflation rate in Yugoslavia has been one of Europe's highest. Nominal interest rates have been held down, and credit has been offered at

these rates to new and rising labor-managed firms.[12]

The Chinese Case

Mao Zedong, "Great Helmsman" of Chinese Communism and author of a *Little Red Book* containing cryptic answers to all social problems, died in 1976. Chairman Mao's death set off a struggle between the so-called "Gang of Four," headed by his widow and faithful to his doctrines, and the so-called "Capitalist Roaders," headed by Deng Xiaoping (Deng-Hsiao-ping, 1904–   ), which proposed various "revisionist" reforms.

With almost no bloodshed, the capitalist-roaders won, and Premier Deng proceeded with "four modernizations" of China's agriculture, economy, technology, and national defense. Progress since 1977 has been marked in the countryside—less so in the cities. To the foreign observer, the most interesting points include these four.

1. Drastic modification—which some call abolition—of Mao's communes. The state still owns all agricultural land, but now leases plots to individual families, which are no longer compelled to join collective farms or communes (although a great majority have chosen to remain members).

2. Breaking Mao's "iron rice bowl." Under Mao, full employment meant, in practice, the assignment of workers by batches of 50,000 or more to organizations that might or might not have any use for them. Also, managers and supervisors could not dismiss individual workers, so that laziness and absenteeism were prevalent. The worker's "rice bowl" (his or her income) was

---

11. Maximizing company income per worker also leads to "wrong" reactions to product price changes—raising output when prices fall, and vice versa. This results from microeconomic considerations too advanced for this book.

12. The theory is that if more credit to a firm is matched by an equal increase in that firm's output, the credit expansion is not inflationary.

This argument is fallacious. Insofar as the firm increases its output only by bidding labor and materials away from other firms after obtaining more credit, there is an output increase for the community only if that firm is more efficient than other firms. Also, even if the economy increases its output, the new money will circulate more rapidly than the new goods, so that the net long-run effect will be inflationary.

"iron," meaning it could not be broken or the worker dismissed. Workers are still assigned in batches and wages remain fixed, to the great disgust of foreign concerns used to "cherry-picking" individual workers by paying wages above the market level.

While full employment is still officially enforced, many young high school graduates spend months or even years waiting for their "work assignments." (Nobody is expected to look for a job in China.) To keep these people busy and out of trouble, they may be herded into "collectives," given some machinery and a little training, and let loose on society without wages or benefit guarantees. Some of the collectives, and their members, have been highly successful. Most, however, have not.

3. The one-child family. To reduce both present consumption and future "assignment problems," the Deng regime has imposed a stringent one-child policy on Chinese urban families. (Minority races are exempted and pressure to conform seems to be looser in rural areas.) Families with two or more children are discriminated against in various ways, such as access to education and medical care. The program is allegedly voluntary, but there are many reports of compulsory abortion. Also, in a society that has traditionally undervalued its female members, the one-child family has led to neglect and even infanticides of sickly, defective, and girl babies to give the family another chance for a "good" (i.e., healthy male) child. The rigor of this policy is expected to be relaxed. It was adopted as a short-run expedient when the population of China ran to over a billion people.

4. Special economic zones. In a number of areas, many of them close to Hong Kong, foreign companies have been invited to set up shop and earn profits much as they would in a capitalist country. (Legal details are difficult to specify, however, since Communist China has neither a commercial code nor a governing body of case law.) The areas are expected to do two things: offer Chinese workers training in high technology, and process both imported and Chinese raw materials for export. Initial reports indicate that production is mostly low-tech, that it is aimed at the Chinese internal market, and that the zones themselves threaten to become foci of "dangerous thoughts," "capitalist decadence," and other forms of sacrilege to the memory of the Great Helmsman.

"Special economic zones" have, at various times, been established in many Third World countries as aids to the country's international trade and financial position. A special financial zone has even been proposed for the United States, where participants might enjoy the protection of American law without the handicaps of American taxes and financial regulations. But nowhere else were "special economic zones" to play so large a part in the twentieth-century economic development of their host country.

Aside from these features, Chinese socialism appears less different from the post-Stalinist Soviet variety—or from the Hungarian one—than is believed generally. Were China a smaller country instead of possessing nearly a quarter of the world's population—or were China still a Soviet ally or satellite in the political realm—Premier Deng's experiments would deserve less intensive attention than they are receiving.

THE THEORY OF MARKET SOCIALISM

Market socialism is an adaptation of the microeconomics of pure competition to a socialist system. Oskar Lange (1904–1965), born and educated in Poland, and Abba Lerner (1904–1982), born in Bessarabia and educated in Britain, were both socialists. After meeting in Britain in the 1930s, the two men continued their friendship in the United States.[13] Their views are not in complete agreement but the term "market socialism" applies equally well to the work of either man.

13. Lange, then a political refugee, later became Polish Ambassador to the United States, Polish delegate to the United Nations, and finally Vice-President of Communist Poland after World War II—after disavowing many of the views that will concern us here.

How the System Works

The Lange-Lerner theory of market socialism reacts strongly against both the weakened capitalism of the Great Depression and the tough Stalinist planning methods of arbitrary pricing, imperative production quotas, and consumer rationing. Under the Lange-Lerner system, prices would be set by public authorities, but they would be changed when necessary to maintain approximate equilibrium between supply and demand for most products. Managers of firms would be civil servants, who need not depend on capitalists or on workers or on consumers. They would be required to operate industrial plants or large farms so as to keep the marginal cost of output about equal to output price at all times. Similarly, they would be required to keep the marginal revenue product of each input equal to the input price at all times. In the short run, profits would go to the state, with losses subsidized by the state (unless it was decided to shut the business down). In the long run, it was hoped that changes in the number and/or size of firms would reduce both profits and losses almost to zero.

So far, this theory is just like that of pure competition, but with fuller and more reliable information available to both buyers and sellers of all goods and services. However, since the economy would be a socialist one, there would be no landlords and capitalists to claim the returns from land and capital, which would go instead to the state. The state would accept these returns in place of taxes and carry on the usual government activities including subsidies to businesses suffering losses. Whenever possible, the state would distribute what would otherwise be property income equally to all the people as a social dividend—so much for each person or for each family. If socialism could also sharply lower military spending, the social dividend would be far greater than transfer payments in any capitalist welfare state!

Of course, if the socialization process were undertaken within the rule of law, the socialist state would have a huge debt for buying the capitalists' properties. This burden might be ex-

pected to keep the social dividend very low over its first few generations.

Planning for the proportion of national income to be saved and invested would be left in the hands of a central planning agency. The agency could raise the investment rate, and most likely the rate of growth as well, by imposing higher taxes or lowering social dividend distributions, and using the extra funds for investment. Private saving and dissaving would be entirely legal, but at zero or very low rates of interest to keep a capitalist class from springing up.[14] Private investment in single-family housing would also be legal, with gains from resale or speculation taxed at high rates for the same reason: to keep capitalism from returning.

Criticisms of the Theory

Many questions about technique and procedure have been raised in criticism of the Lange-Lerner scheme of market socialism. How, in real life, would managers be chosen and assigned? What if they followed the rules but were lacking in "human relations" skills? How could one decide after the fact whether the rules had been followed without turning half the population into accountants, statisticians, or computer technologists?

Suppose, however, that it was determined that a manager had failed to equate marginal cost to output price, or marginal revenue product to input price. The problems would not be over. Was the differential avoidable, or had there been unforeseeable problems like machine breakdowns, worker illness, or delays in delivery of raw materials or parts? If the differential appeared both large and avoidable, was it a misdemeanor or a crime? Was it just an honest mistake, or was it unlawful speculation that prices might change

14. At minimal interest rates, the demand for personal consumption loans (dissaving) might well exceed the supply (saving), creating a black market in consumer credit. As a control on such a market, loan contracts between private individuals could be made unenforceable at interest rates above the legal limit.

in the course of production? Was it an attempt to influence future prices by creating shortages or surpluses, after the fashion of a monopolistic firm or the member of a cartel?

Let us consider a hypothetical case from Lange-Lernerland. Sourpuss Smith and Jovial Jones are plant managers in Podunk. They are also rival candidates for promotion to a larger and more important plant in Megalopolis. Sourpuss Smith, a lightning calculator, has followed all the rules to the letter and the last decimal place. In doing so, he has come to be regarded as a holy terror by his subordinates. Morale and productivity in the Smith plant are low, and it is plagued by high labor turnover. Jovial Jones, on the other hand, plays fast and loose with the rules, some of which he is not smart enough to apply accurately. He hires "too many" workers, puts them into wage brackets that are "too high," turns out "too much" product, and fails to maximize returns. But productivity in the Jones plant is the pride of Podunk, so that costs are correspondingly low. Which manager should get the Megalopolis promotion?

This answer is easy by business standards under the rules of the capitalist game: Jones goes onward and upward to Megalopolis, and Smith goes back to Podunk or perhaps to a cost accountant's job. But it is not clear that this will happen under the Lange-Lerner rules.

From a socialist point of view, a more important social or philosophical question is raised by the whole process of market socialism, and by the Lange-Lerner variety in particular. Among other things, socialism aims at fostering the new socialist men and women, who subordinate their personal interests to the interest of the society as they have been taught to see them. Such persons demand fewer economic rewards, especially consumer goods and leisure time, than they would have demanded as individualists, and also supply more and better labor services. The Lange-Lerner men and women, however, remain essentially individualists in socialist clothing. To maximize their own utility, they demand what they want when they want it. They supply labor according to their own labor-leisure choices and are subject to dismissal if the value of their marginal revenue product falls below their wage rate. Such "selfish"

individualism, relying on "economic" as against "moral" incentives, makes market socialism suspect in socialist eyes, particularly in the eyes of the advocates of socialist central planning.

AUSTRIAN THEORY: PLANNING AS THE ROAD TO SERFDOM

Many writers take strong stands against planning, whether the planning is socialist or capitalist. They claim that pricing and resource allocation in a planned economy must be arbitrary and dictatorial, unless the planners adopt the international prices of the remaining market-economy countries. These writers argue that the processes of setting and enforcing arbitrary prices and wages lead to an increasingly serious loss of individual freedoms.

Three economists are well known for their views on this question—Friedrich von Hayek (1899–   ), Ludwig von Mises (1881–1973), and Joseph Schumpeter (1883–1950).[15] All three were born and educated in Austria, and their views are called "Austrian." None of the three ever lived under communist rule. However, it is interesting to note that many refugees from socialist or communist countries share the Austrian view of planning.

The Growth of Controls Under Planning

Four points, all made by Hayek, explain why he thinks planning leads to "serfdom." The first is that partial planning or control tends to grow in its extent and rigor, in order to keep people from dodging its rules. For example, one might ask: Why not simply control prices and wages in

15. Schumpeter, unlike both Mises and Hayek, saw socialism and planning as inevitable consequences, like death and taxes, of capitalism and of the "treason" of intellectuals who have lost social status to business people. Schumpeter's vision of the socialist planned economy was also less grim than Hayek's serfdom or Mises' "planned chaos."

"essential" industries and jobs in order to check inflation and leave the rest of the economy free? The answer is that if the uncontrolled sectors are free to pay higher wages and make higher profits, labor and capital will move, unless restricted, away from essential to nonessential activities—from making work shirts to making sports shirts. One might also ask how civil liberties could be preserved while preventing capital from being taken out of the country where most of "the rich" distrust the economic plan. Hayek believes that people are clever about arranging "capital flights" by mail, by telephone, and by foreign travel, in underpriced exports, overpriced imports, and other fictitious deals. For this reason, mail and telephone censorship, as well as passport controls over people on "watch lists," would be essential to the enforcement of capital controls.

Arbitrary or Corrupt Bureaucracy

The second point that Hayek stresses is that, however detailed and comprehensive a plan may be, it cannot cover all the special cases that later arise under it. So a great deal of leeway must be left to administrative (bureaucratic) judgment. For example, if a Soviet citizen wants to repair or enlarge his or her house in a city where building materials are in short supply, the citizen must obtain two permits if the work is to be legally done. The person must convince one government official that his or her needs are great enough to obtain certain building materials. Once the materials are received, another official (possibly located at the other end of the city) must be convinced that he or she *has* these materials, and that they are adequate for the project. Such procedures allow plenty of opportunity for arbitrariness, which is our problem here, and also for corruption.

Propaganda and Suppression

According to Hayek's third point, morale is so important to the success of the plan that critics are often silenced. Official propaganda will of course sing the plan's praises and advertise its successes. The temptation is very great to suppress and punish any who spread pessimistic rumors about the plan and its feasibility, who forecast its failure in whole or in part, or who want the present plan scrapped in favor of another one—or in favor of the market. Under Soviet and Eastern European conditions, critics blame the plan's concentration on the "leading links" of heavy industry and military hardware for shortages of consumer goods and civilian housing. It is rare, however, for such critics to be allowed open expression of their views, let alone access to the public, since the plan regulates the supply of paper, the programs of the schools, and the broadcast media, as well as the economy. Nevertheless, the misdeeds of particular incompetent, tyrannical, or corrupt bureaucrats or administrators are often exposed in official publications, and punished in official courts.

The Power Seekers

Finally, "the worst get on top," Hayek claims. This fourth and last point means that the would-be dictator, the corrupt grafter, and the envious or vindictive person is most likely to seek work in carrying out the daily and minor details of running and enforcing the plan. Such people are also very likely to call for extending the plan's authority over the remaining unplanned sectors of the economy.

Criticism of the Theory

Many criticisms of the Austrian theory have been voiced. The simplest is the claim that the benefits of planning are worth its costs, and that the critics of planning are reactionaries who are destined for "the dust-bin of history." This approach is most effective where the market economy is associated with recent-past colonialism, backwardness, or dependency, and where there has been no experience with successful liberal democracy. In more advanced countries, however, it is argued that existing liberal or democratic traditions will be strong enough to keep the citizens from traveling the road to serfdom despite the problems Hayek sees. Furthermore, as in Sweden, dependence on foreign trade with countries that have market economies will limit the spread and the impact of arbitrary planning. One can even rely on institutions based on merit, such as schools, colleges, and civil service examinations, to lower the likelihood that the worst will get on top.

Perhaps the most effective anti-Austrian argument is that serfdom does not have to be the end of the road. One can gain comfort from the experience of the U.S.S.R., Poland, Hungary, and Yugoslavia in backing away from the extremes of Stalinism after Stalin's death in 1953; and from the experience of the Chinese People's Republic in reversing the Maoist "cultural revolution" after Mao Zedong's death in 1976.

SUMMARY

1. The controversy between advocates of market and planned economic systems is a heated one, even though all existing economies are mixed systems. The distinction between the two types of system is a useful one.

2. Every person or organization plans for itself. However, we speak of an economy as being planned only when a central planning body (public, private, or mixed) makes plans that dominate those of the individual persons, firms, or industries that make up the economy.

3. A market economy is more likely to be capitalist than is a planned one. However, a planned economy is more likely to be collectivist than an unplanned one.

4. Planning and collectivism are not the same thing, any more than capitalism and a market system are the same. Furthermore, neither planning nor collectivism should be confused with the welfare state. Any economic system that places high value on a high poverty line and on lowering inequality in the distribution of income and wealth may be called a welfare state.

5. Planning is of different sorts. We distinguish imperative, indicative, public sector, macroeco-

nomic, and magic-wand planning. We do not consider statistical projections of past trends to be plans at all, unless they are combined with measures to see that these trends continue.

6. The Soviet Union is the most important example of imperative planning under socialist collectivism. Planning is highly centralized in a single agency called Gosplan. Among the techniques of Soviet planning are materials balancing and input-output analysis. An important modification of the Soviet planning model is found in the People's Republic of China, which is a more decentralized system.

7. The United States has a large public sector and so has more public sector planning than is generally realized. Proposals for more comprehensive planning in the United States were made during the years of the Great Depression (for example, the National Recovery Administration), during both World Wars, and more recently in the original Humphrey-Hawkins bill.

8. Japan and Sweden are widely differing examples of economic planning within a capitalist framework. In the Japanese case, sometimes called "Japan, Inc.," the principal planners come from big business, agriculture, and the public bureaucracy. In Sweden, labor also participates in the planning, and the government is dominated by the Social Democratic Party.

9. Yugoslavia is a socialist country with a substantial degree of workers' management supplementing or even replacing its central plan.

10. China, under the leadership of Deng Xiaoping, has moved ever further from the Soviet planning model. Agricultural collectivization is now voluntary. The "iron rice bowl" variety of full employment is in the process of being eliminated. Foreign techniques and management methods are permitted to foreign firms in special economic zones. Prices and wages, however, remain fixed and the government continues to own land and capital goods.

11. The Lange-Lerner scheme of market socialism attempts to combine the advantages of market and planned economies in a somewhat utopian socialist model.

12. A number of writers, chiefly Austrian, hold that planning, once undertaken under either capitalism or socialism, tends to increase in both importance and arbitrariness over time. They expect planning to end in a servile state, which Hayek has called "serfdom," with few individual freedoms and civil rights remaining. Some writers of the "Austrian school" believe that there is little hope of preserving the market economy and avoiding "serfdom," but others are more optimistic.

DISCUSSION QUESTIONS

1. Jonathan Swift (1667–1745) is best known as the author of *Gulliver's Travels,* and is considered the greatest satirist in the English language. His works include a *Modest Proposal for Preventing the Children of Poor People from Being a Burden to Their Parents or the Country.* (They are to be fattened, and then sold for food to the rich.)

Suppose that one were to believe seriously— as Swift did not—in exporting fattened babies from overpopulated poor countries for food in rich countries as part of a development plan for the poor countries. Should such a person be allowed to propagate his or her "outrageous" opinions? Suppose that this person were an organic chemist; should he or she be permitted to teach organic chemistry? If his or her specialty were development economics, what would your answer be? Suppose that this person were already teaching development economics before being converted to cannibalism, should he or she be forbidden to continue teaching in this field? Finally, are your answers to the four preceding parts of this question logically consistent with each other?

2. The Swedish economist Knut Wicksell was prosecuted and imprisoned, at the turn of the century, for propagating certain radical ideas, including contraception and the disestablishment of the state church. (One of his major works,

Interest and Prices, was finished in prison.) When his jail term was over, Wicksell returned to his teaching at the University of Lund. Some years later, the American economist Scott Nearing, a socialist and pacifist, advocated strict neutrality in World War I and opposed "preparedness." He was not prosecuted, but his contract (at the University of Pennsylvania) was not renewed, and he could obtain no other teaching post. Which system, the Swedish or the American, impinged more harshly on freedom of expression? Explain.

3. Distinguish between collectivism, socialism, and communism.

4. Can a market-capitalist economy also be a welfare state? Explain.

5. Briefly distinguish between imperative planning, indicative planning, public sector planning, and macroeconomic planning. Which, if any, of these are used in the United States?

6. Distinguish between materials balancing and input-output analysis as tools for economic planning.

7. Why, in your opinion, has the People's Republic of China shifted to a less completely planned economy since the death of Chairman Mao Zedong? (In your answer, consider primarily economic reasons for the change.)

8. Market-socialism proposals, such as those of Lange and Lerner, are usually proposed for societies in which all production processes are already known. How would an innovation (a new product or process) be introduced under market socialism? (In your answer, assume that there are no other economies from which to copy.)

9. Describe the important features of the Japanese economic system that have contributed to Japanese economic growth. Do you believe that similar arrangements would be workable and desirable for the United States?

10. Briefly summarize the Meidner plan. Do you believe that it is a feasible alternative to socialist revolution? Explain.

39 *Radical Economics*

PREVIEW This chapter goes beyond economics as usually conceived. It deals with questions that political scientists, sociologists, or psychologists handle more fully and expertly than economists do. We begin by discussing the dissatisfactions that many people (not only radicals) feel with market-capitalist institutions as they exist in North America. Rather than arguing about the justice of this indictment, we go on to outline the social theory that is used by the radical Left in advocating the overthrow of capitalism. Marxian economics is a very important part of this theory. As further "background," we note certain characteristics that distinguish the radical from the reformist critic of market-capitalism.

In the second half of the chapter, we look at contemporary radical movements, primarily but not only on the political Left. First we take up the so-called New Left, which has itself become divided into a number of groups—some socialist, some anarchist, and some syndicalist. Then we consider the radical Right, which may be descended from what is called Social Darwinism—the doctrine of "survival of the fittest" among social groups and institutions.

INDICTMENTS OF CAPITALISM

In the eyes of its critics, capitalism is "the root of all (social) evil." To many people, some of the indictments seem far-fetched, or related to industrialization under any economic system. Nevertheless, we offer a sweeping picture of the indictment, to show the scope and intensity of radical views. At the beginning of the book, we singled out six criteria for judging economic systems, and for preferring one system to another.[1] In none of these does market-capitalism represent any utopian ideal.

With discontent about every point, we single out three criteria among our six, since they seem to have caused the greatest amount and intensity of discontent. These are:

1. The alleged maldistribution of income and wealth, both within and between individual countries.
2. The alleged insecurity of the standard of living already achieved against downward pressure, both short-run and long-run.
3. The alleged incompatibility of the system with full mental health.

Maldistribution

It is no secret that the distribution of income is unequal both within and between individual countries, that people at the bottom of the income and wealth distributions are living in poverty, that "it takes money to make money," and that in many fields of economic activity "nice guys finish last." For the great majority of the world's population, upward mobility within the world economy is blocked, except by rules and on terms set by those already at the top. A low-wage country's rise to affluence may be blocked if it

1. See Chapter 1.

can no longer use the cheapness of its labor as a competitive advantage because the access of its goods to affluent markets is blocked by protectionism. When its workers cannot migrate to high-wage areas, the country's rise is limited to methods more acceptable to those who are already affluent. One route may be receiving aid on terms set by the givers. Others may include a more restrictive population policy, or more reliance than the low-wage country desires on unskilled hand labor in agriculture and mining.

Within a country like the United States, the question is the *terms* on which blacks or other minorities can rise. When black people's chances of becoming wealthy depend largely, as is alleged, on following white people's rules, the economically successful blacks are not, to put it mildly, objects of admiration within the black community itself. For this reason, their chances of advancement are much less in fact than they are in the statistics.[2]

To some extent, inequality is based on prejudice—racial, sexual, religious, linguistic, and so forth. Capitalism and the capitalists are blamed for fostering such prejudices to keep workers or farmers disunited, reducing both their economic and their political power. When blacks came north or were brought north during and after World War I to break strikes or to forestall them, one result was an outbreak of race riots, and another was a weakening of organized labor. When a multinational corporation holds down wages in several countries at once by threatening major shifts of its operations from one country to another, critics of capitalism blame such action for any prejudice and hostility between the countries and between their populations, which those threats provoke, whether intentionally or otherwise.

Insecurity

Under capitalism, mass living standards are supposedly under constant pressure, both from the short-term shocks associated with business-cycle

declines and from the long-run shocks associated with chronic inflation, technological change, pollution, resource exhaustion, warfare, and so on. "Hoovervilles," which were shantytowns for the unemployed in flood plains and city dumps, are among the best-remembered pictures of the Great American Depression of the 1930s. A half-century later, the corresponding pictures are "rust bowls" of obsolete factories.

On the individual level, there are different kinds of threats to the living standards of certain people, especially the aged or otherwise immobile. One such threat is currency inflation, a device to which capitalism has often turned for recovery from recessions and depressions. Capitalism is also blamed for technical change, symbolized by automation and robotization, which throws some people out of work at the same time that it provides opportunities for others. Pollution is a third living standard threat blamed on capitalism and population growth. Pollution has turned fields and forests into lunar landscapes, and rivers and streams into open sewers. Also, its health effects may become apparent only after many years, often in the form of cancer. A fourth threat is resource exhaustion, which turns prosperous lumbering, mining, and oil-well communities into ghost towns, and fertile farmland into desert. And finally, there is war, the supreme pollutant, now associated with genocide, nuclear holocaust, and the possible extermination of humanity.

In all of these cases, capitalism is blamed for failure either to prevent the catastrophes or to provide adequate "safety nets" to those who are injured. In every case, market-capitalism and the urge for short-term profits are blamed for causing or at least accelerating the catastrophe and for allowing too little time for adjustments to be made.

Alienation

The characteristic psychological ailment of capitalism—and also of any other social system in which one or another social class or group dominates or exploits the rest of the society—is called **alienation.** This ailment is most serious among the victimized classes, races, or other social groups.

2. Anthropologists speak of "cultural rape" when members of one culture are either forced or bribed to conform to the mores and standards of another and quite different culture.

However, a "guilty conscience" can also lead to alienation in the upper classes.

When one feels always hostile or indifferent to someone or something that people in one's society generally consider attractive, one is said to be "alienated" from that person or thing. Alienation may appear in many different forms. The victim may actively hate himself or herself, or be bored to the point of disgust, not with "the real me," but with the self as "processed" by advertising, propaganda, television, or the school system. Or one's feelings of alienation may focus on a "dull" or "commonplace" family, a "meaningless" or "dehumanizing" job, a "hopeless" future, a "drab" community, a society "rotten to the core."

The sufferer from alienation may just become sleepy, lazy, and vaguely depressed. In more acute cases, he or she may take refuge in overeating or starving, in overconsumption or oversaving, in drink or drugs or sex, in "dropping out" of mainstream society, or even in suicide. Alienation may also lead to violent or criminal behavior, even to terrorism and mass murder.[3]

While admitting or even insisting that criminal behavior be punished, critics of capitalism believe that an exploitative society is, in the last analysis, responsible for the actions of those whom it alienates. They protest against "blaming the victim," meaning the criminal, whom they see as being hurt by the society.

Here is a single extreme case:

CAMBRIDGE—A former Polaroid Corp. engineer who attacked his wife and child with an ice pick won a $1.9 million out-of-court settlement from Polaroid, claiming that the company was negligent in treating the depression that led to his assault.

Lawrence L. Okerblom, Jr., his wife and son, will receive the money in monthly payments for at least 25 years. Most of the money will go to the son, who was brain-damaged and lost much of his vision in the attack.

After attacking his family, Mr. Okerblom tried to kill himself. The family split up after the incident.

In the suit filed in 1974, Mr. Okerblom said that a Polaroid doctor and counselor were negligent in treating his anxiety. Mr. Okerblom was in a "psychotic state" because he feared Polaroid was about to fire him, his lawyer said. The Polaroid doctor and counselor didn't take Mr. Okerblom's symptoms seriously and didn't prescribe the proper treatment, the attorney said. Polaroid officials weren't available for comment.[4]

Both the "insecurity" and the "alienation" aspects of this case are obvious and interrelated. There is, of course, also a "maldistribution" aspect. Do you think the settlement was unreasonably high or low, given the circumstances? Was Polaroid exploiting Mr. Okerblom, or was Mr. Okerblom exploiting Polaroid? If similar cases had arisen among lower-ranking blue-collar workers, do you think they would have been handled in the same way?

SOME MARXIAN PROPOSITIONS

In North America leftist critics of market capitalism may not think of themselves as Marxists, and have never read much of Marx's writings. Nevertheless, they have almost certainly been influenced indirectly by some of Marx's ideas.

Karl Marx (1818–1883), a German philosopher and economist of Jewish descent, lived the last thirty-five years of his life as a refugee in London. He was both capitalism's greatest critic and socialism's greatest prophet. He may also have been the greatest overall secular (nonreligious) social scientist who has yet lived. He made important contributions not only to economics but to the other social sciences as well, including history and philosophy.

It is an injustice to Marx, and likewise to his great co-worker Friedrich Engels (1820–1895), to compress their whole system into a small set of propositions, which is all we can do here. These propositions are eight in number. While we have

---

3. The Jonestown colony of Guyana had both an alienated leader and an alienated population when it exploded in 1978. Many leaders and members of the Nazi Party were alienated both by the Germany of the Weimar Republic, which followed World War I, and the whole "Jazz Age" civilization of the 1920s.

4. Abridged from *The Wall Street Journal*, March 10, 1983. Reprinted by permission of *The Wall Street Journal*, copyright © Dow Jones & Company, Inc. 1983. All rights reserved.

tried to ensure that they are distilled accurately from the writings of Marx and Engels, none is a direct quotation.

1. Natural science and technology have advanced to the point where, in a well-run world, all basic goods and services can be made free to all, the economy of abundance can be realized, and the profession of economist can become obsolete.[5]

2. The history of past societies has shown that nearly all surplus production, above some minimal subsistence level, has been appropriated by the social class that owns strategic inputs or factors of production. At successive stages of history, these strategic inputs have been raw physical labor (in slave societies), farmland and mines (in feudal societies), and industrial plant and equipment (in capitalist societies). At every stage, membership in the ruling class has been largely hereditary.

3. The exclusion of the main body of a society from the bulk of that society's economic surplus is called **exploitation.** Because of their exploitation and their resentment of it, members of exploited classes often become alienated from the society, from their work, from each other, and even from themselves. That alienation leads to crime and other ills, which societies blame on the victims of alienation rather than on the exploiting institutions that have brought about the alienation.

4. The governmental, educational, religious, and other noneconomic institutions of society generally support and legalize the interests of its ruling class. At the same time, they seek to suppress the hostilities of the exploited and the alienated. Examples are "pie in the sky when you die" religion, relief systems that "regulate the poor," judicial systems too costly for the average person, representative governments with voters' choices limited to candidates who supply or attract large-scale campaign financing, and so on. The list is long and scandals under each head are, to the

Marxist, more than just scandals. Rather, they are the way the system works.

5. What is important in history is the record of conflict between one exploiting class and its successor, or between the exploiters and the exploited. This is the meaning of the Marxist statement that "history is the record of class struggles." As in proposition 4, certain excesses and outrages on both sides are more than scandals. They are the way the system has worked, with war and violent revolution as integral parts of the whole process.

6. Whereas Adam Smith called the market-capitalist economy "the obvious and simple system of natural liberty," Marxists think of it as just another exploitative regime. True, it has accomplished great things—which Marx and Engels took great pains to recognize in their *Communist Manifesto* of 1848—but it harbors within itself class conflicts and "contradictions," which will lead ultimately to its collapse. The *economic* aspects of Marxism enter into the demonstration of this proposition. We shall outline them in the next part of this chapter.

7. The revolution that overthrows capitalism will involve the whole exploited underclass, the workers or **proletariat.** When the proletariat comes to power, it will own the means of production through a government that it controls. This is the regime of socialism, in which there will be no class left to be exploited because all the means of production will be owned by society as a whole.[6]

8. In a relatively few years after the firm establishment of socialism in the major countries of the world, there will emerge a **New Socialist Man and Woman.** Such persons will willingly work harder and more skillfully than anyone in the past. As Leon Trotsky (1879–1940) put it, the average man or woman will rise to the level of "an Aristotle, a Hegel, or a Marx." At the same time, the New Socialist Man or Woman will demand less from society in terms of wealth or

---

5. In the late twentieth century this seems an extravagant conclusion to have drawn a century earlier. But Marx and Engels were both greatly impressed by the technical achievements of the Industrial Revolution in England, then in full swing—as well as with its seamy side, which inspired much of their anticapitalism.

6. But *ownership* need not be *control,* and anti-Marxists see Marxian socialism as a regime controlled by a "new class" of military and civilian bureaucrats and administrators, with the rest of society exploited much as the proletariat is exploited under capitalism.

the consumption of luxuries. A few generations will be enough to bring on the economy of abundance and to overcome scarcity. With no scarcity or class conflict, the repressive political state can and will wither away.

Marxian Economics: The Statics

Marxian economics is most easily explained in macroeconomic terms, though Marx himself set it out microeconomically. We shall begin with the statics of how the capitalist economy operates and then go to the dynamics of how it changes through time. Remember that Marx was analyzing market-capitalism as he saw it. (Marxian economic analysis deals with capitalism and not with socialism.)

The macroeconomic formulation of Marx's theory uses W to represent the national income, evaluated in hours of labor. This W is divided into three parts, also expressed in labor hours. These are constant capital (C), variable capital (V), and surplus value (S). Therefore,

$$W = C + V + S$$

CONSTANT CAPITAL Of total labor input (W per period), **constant capital** (C) is the number of labor hours embodied in (used to produce) raw materials and in the depreciation of machinery and other long-lived capital goods. Marxian constant capital is not the same as the "fixed capital" of conventional accounting.

VARIABLE CAPITAL Nor is V the "variable capital" of conventional accounting. **Variable capital** represents hours of direct labor—mainly blue-collar labor, but also the "productive" portions

of white-collar labor[7]—but not all those hours! Suppose that you work a 40-hour week on an assembly line but that your week's wages will buy only 30 hours of others' labor as embodied in food, clothing, and other consumption goods. In that case, your 40 hours of labor will represent only 30 hours of variable capital, the Marxian V.

SURPLUS VALUE But what of the other 10 hours of your labor? Marx does not forget them, but calls them "surplus" labor. The value of the surplus labor is retained by the employer. Out of it is paid all kinds of property income—interest, rent, and profits—and also the "unproductive" portion of white-collar labor (including, for example, doctors, lawyers, soldiers, bureaucrats, and teachers as predominantly present or potential members, dependents, or hangers-on of the capitalist class). Surplus labor is, in the case of your work on the assembly line, your personal contribution to total **surplus value** or S.

How large is this surplus value, in relation to the total of variable capital? In this microeconomic case, it is $^{10}\!/_{30}$ or $\frac{1}{3}$. In an aggregate economy with $C = 5,000$, $V = 3,000$, $S = 1,000$, W would equal their sum, or 9,000, and the ratio $S\!/_V$ would again equal $\frac{1}{3}$. In many of the numerical illustrations in his *Capital*, Marx himself sets this ratio equal to one. However, Marxists believe that in the United States today it is actually above one and tending to rise over time, at least in periods of prosperity.

The ratio $S\!/_V$ or S' is called the **rate of surplus value,** or sometimes the **exploitation rate.** It represents the contribution of each hour of variable capital to the total of social surplus value. It is important in Marxian economic analysis, as you will see.

PROFIT The Marxian concept of profit comprises all surplus value, including the wages and salaries of unproductive labor. This concept of profit is clearly more inclusive than the "net income" of either conventional economics or conventional accounting.

To compute a rate of profit, which Marx calls P', we divide total surplus value S by total capital, defined as $C + V$. The result is: $P' = S\!/_{(C+V)}$.

7. The distinction between "productive" and "unproductive" labor is very difficult in all economic theories that, like the Marxian, make such a distinction. For an elaborate explanation of the issues from a Marxian viewpoint and with careful attention to Marx's own statements, see David Laibman, "Unproductive Labor: Critique of a Concept," in William L. Rowe, editor, *Studies in Labor Theory and Practice* (Minneapolis: Marxist International Press, 1982).

If we divide both numerator and denominator of this expression by variable capital V, the numerator becomes, by definition, the exploitation rate $^S/_V$, which Marx called S'. In the denominator, dividing by V gives us $^C/_V + {}^V/_V$ or $^C/_V + 1$. Marx used the term **organic composition of capital** for the ratio between constant capital (raw materials plus depreciation) and variable capital (direct labor, as described above). Calling this ratio k, Marx's formula for profit becomes

$$P' = \frac{S'}{1 + k}$$

In terms of our figures for an aggregate economy if $C = 5,000$, $V = 3,000$, and $S = 1,000$, the organic composition of capital k becomes $^{5,000}/_{3,000}$ or $^5/_3$, and the exploitation rate S' is $^1/_3$. This makes the profit rate equal to

$$P' = \frac{1/3}{1 + 5/3} = \frac{1/3}{3/3 + 5/3} = \frac{1}{8}$$

Marxian Economics: The Dynamics

Then Marx goes on to investigate "the laws of motion of capitalism." Therefore, the main purpose of all his apparatus was dynamic. As he moves from economic statics to economic dynamics, Marx uses the last equation. He argues that the organic composition of capital k (like the static capital-labor ratio) tends to rise over time. It rises because, in the absence of war or of natural catastrophe, the capital stock generally grows at a faster rate than does the labor force or employment, and also because innovations tend to be motivated to save direct labor costs more than to save capital costs. That is, they are more likely to be labor-saving than capital-saving.[8] As capitalism progresses and capital is accumulated, the

8. Notions of class warfare are not required to explain the tendency of innovations to be labor-saving rather than capital-saving. A sufficient explanation is that labor costs (primarily payrolls) are a larger part of production costs than are capital charges, so that a 1 percent saving of labor costs is worth more than a 1 percent saving of capital charges. In contemporary North America, a 1 percent saving of labor cost is worth approximately as much as a 2.5 percent saving of capital charges.

rising trend of k means that the profit rate P' must fall, that the exploitation rate S' must rise, or most commonly both.

FALLING RATE OF PROFIT At some point, however, either of the above developments will be disastrous for capitalism. If the rate of profit falls below a certain level, capitalists will no longer find it worthwhile to invest much more than the amount needed to replace fixed capital as it wears out. Marx thought that capitalists would not raise their consumption very much but would try to hoard money, real estate, "collectibles," or other goods not currently being produced. In this way, they would in turn lower the equilibrium level of national output and raise the unemployment rate. Increasing unemployment is one form of what Marxists call the "increasing misery" of the working class, which they see as the consequence of capitalism as it matures.

Marx predicted long-term stagnation for capitalism, with short business-cycle booms and long business-cycle depressions and with a rising rate of measured unemployment. In Marxian literature this is called a **liquidity crisis.** If wages were raised in relation to prices to maintain mass purchasing power, the liquidity crisis would only be intensified, since the rate of profit would fall even lower. Falling-rate-of-profit arguments are used by Marxists against liberal reformers and trade unionists who propose to save capitalism by income-redistribution measures.

TENDENCY TO OVERPRODUCTION Suppose that capitalists form cartels to keep profit rates up or even raise them, in spite of the rising organic composition of the capital. Marxists answer that such moves cause prices to rise in relation to wages and cause the exploitation rate S' to rise, and that the capitalists will not find buyers for the goods produced. As the exploitation rate rises, a falling proportion of the labor force is needed to produce the output that the masses can still buy. Again there is rising unemployment and increasing misery, even though the profit rate remains high. Such a development is called a **realization crisis.** This argument is used by Marxists to answer the conservatives who would call for "self-government in business," as well as for wage cutting, union busting, and similar cures for business recessions and depressions.

In closing this section, we make three final points. First, Marx's *Capital* is about capitalism, and it has little to say about how a socialist system would manage the problems that capitalism allegedly mismanages. Second, Marx's labor theory of value builds upon the classical theories of Smith and Ricardo and does not deal with demand and utility as determinants of value. Finally, the Marxian analysis leaves no major role for government fiscal or monetary policy. In Marx's day, these instruments most likely played too small a part for them to make much difference. Could they today offer a way out of the Marxian dynamic-economic dilemma?

ARE YOU A RADICAL?

In the dictionary, the term **radical** is defined as extreme, sweeping, or revolutionary. However, yesterday's radical ideas may be today's moderate, conservative, or reactionary ones, and today's radical ideas may be tomorrow's moderate, conservative, or reactionary ones. And what is true over time is equally true over space. The Soviet "conservative" is a Stalinist.

The conventional connotation of *radical* is unfavorable, at least in the United States. Its associations are with mob violence, terrorism, bomb-throwing, and assassination. What is overlooked is that radical ideas have sometimes been correct in the past and may be so again. Within the radical movement itself, on the other hand, the connotation of the term is favorable. Anything less than radicalism is cowardly, pussyfooting, compromise with "the Establishment" or with "the Great Satan." What the movement overlooks is that radical ideas can be and have been wrong. Neither radicalism nor its alternatives can insure anyone against making stupid mistakes.

Radicalism, including radical economics, may be of the political Left or the political Right. In the contest of planning versus the market, the radical Left generally, but not always, calls for giant steps toward a purely planned economy,

and the New Right proposes equally giant steps toward a purely market one.

It is a long way from Karl Marx developing "the law of motion of capitalism" in the British Museum to the campus radical howling down some visiting speaker who he or she has been told is "reactionary." Marx himself, by the way, warned his audience that he was not a Marxist!

Here is a set of seven questions. If you answer "Yes" to most or all of them, you probably qualify as a true believer "under the radical sign."

1. Are you sure that piecemeal reforms (monetarism or fiscalism, demand side or supply side, more deregulation or less, freer trade or more protection) are like "rearranging of deck chairs on the *Titanic*"—too marginal to carry out the "radical restructuring" that society needs?
2. If some combination of such reforms (as in the last paragraph) were indeed massive enough and well enough thought out to do much good, would you oppose the reforms all the more? Do you want to see "the system" overthrown *rather than* improved, even when improvement is possible?
3. Do you believe "the Revolution" must take place very soon—in your own generation—if world war or world pollution or some similar catastrophe is to be avoided?
4. Do you favor mass demonstrations and "direct action,"[9] distrusting the electoral process and representative government because the electoral process is too slow, too heedless of intense-minority opinion, too easily thwarted by judges or bureaucrats, or "all of the above"?
5. Is the present system so bad that there is no real danger that its overthrow would lead to something worse? Is there no danger of jumping from the frying pan into the fire?
6. Do you have no clear idea of what the new system that would succeed the present one might look like, beyond such general ideas as "a planned society" or "public ownership of the means of production" or "more equality"? Are you willing to leave the everyday details to be worked out "in the course of the struggle"?

---

9. "Direct action" may range from individual kidnappings and assassinations to mass revolts and revolutions, which turn violent if resisted.

7. Do you believe the intellectual support for your position has already been worked out well enough by one or more great intellectual leaders to allow you to accept it as given, so that you can depend on nonrational ways of knowing—such as faith, intuition, song lyrics, or the authority of the leadership group of your particular movement?

THE NEW LEFT

In most countries the main body of radical economists has been affiliated with the so-called **New Left.** However, most supporters of the New Left are neither economists nor radicals as we have described radicalism. A question then arises: If Marx and Engels may be taken to represent the Old Left at its best, why do we need a New Left?

In the first place, Marx's theories were not accepted by all the political Left of Marx's own day. Marxists struggled continually both with reformists and with anarchists for control of the First International—the International Workingmen's Association of which Marx was a founder and which was the center of his political activism for the last dozen years of his life. Today we would call the reformists liberals or social democrats.[10] We shall discuss the anarchists later in this chapter.

In the second place, within fifteen years after Marx's death, Marxists began to differ among themselves with increasing vehemence.[11]

In the third place, and most importantly, the victories of European fascism in the period between the two world wars were blamed on disagreement and disunity among members of the political Left. The story was especially tragic in Germany, where the Social Democratic Party had been both strong and well organized, but had been unable to form any common front with the Communist Party to check the rise of Hitler and his National Socialists (Nazis). The Social Democratic Party collapsed after Hitler came to power in 1933.

The New Left hopes to avoid a similar fate by playing down intellectual hair-splitting and by maintaining a united front. The American New Left grew out of the conviction of both liberals and radicals that the "McCarthyism" of the 1950s was a real fascist threat, which the country had been lucky to avoid. Next came the formation of a university-based (not labor-based) organization called Students for a Democratic Society (SDS) at Port Huron, Michigan, in 1962. In the SDS "Port Huron Statement," doctrinal differences both economic and political were papered over with evangelical language. However, the SDS was overcome by some of these same differences—in particular, the role of violence—and broke up in 1968–1969.

SDS was founded before the upsurge of the civil rights movement and any extensive military involvement in Indo-China. These issues became the focal points for agitation against the entire capitalist civilization, including the capitalist economy. As the civil rights movement and the Vietnam War retired from the front page, student interest shifted from reform or revolution to qualifying for good jobs in the world much as it was. The SDS, the New Left, and the racial and campus riots all retreated into ancient history, sometimes tinged with nostalgia. (Something similar happened in other countries, where direct involvement with American civil rights and Vietnam problems had been minimal but where pervasive anti-Americanism had become part and parcel of the political left.)

Since 1970, there have been a number of efforts to revive the New Left coalition of the late 1960s, but around other issues. Some candidates for a unifying issue have been ecology and environmentalism, nuclear war, feminism, South African *apartheid*, and American policy in Central America. As of 1986, none of these issues had succeeded.

---

10. In most of the nineteenth century the term *liberal* meant a doctrinaire disciple of free enterprise and *laissez-faire*. Now it means an advocate of various economic and social reforms attached to a framework that includes private ownership of most of society's capital goods. A *social democrat* differs from a liberal in advocating public ownership of the means of production. But, like a liberal, the social democrat proposes to achieve change entirely by nonviolent means centering on free elections.

11. We discuss the evolution of Marxian ideas "from Karl Marx to the New Left" in the essay that concludes this part of the book.

Nevertheless, the "ancient history" label is premature for the New Left.

Branches of the New Left

The New Left is not and never has been an exclusively radical movement. It has always had and continues to have a liberal and reformist following. Its radical vanguard, however, has been divided between anarchists, socialists, and syndicalists, who get along together well at some times, badly at others. All three are **collectivist**, since they all oppose individual or private ownership of the means of production. All of them want capital goods—including consumers' goods held in inventories—to be owned "collectively." But they mean quite different things by collective ownership. It may be helpful to classify the New Left radicals further into five groups. There seem to be two quite distinct anarchist groups, two different socialist (or communist) groups, and a single embryonic syndicalist group.

Anarchists, who fear the state as much as they fear the capitalist class, want control of capital goods to be by purely voluntary associations, which people may enter by negotiation and leave more or less as they please. These groups would have no power to levy taxes or to impose compulsory penalties on members except to suspend or expel them from membership.

ANARCHISM I What we shall call *Anarchism I* includes variations of the counterculture. Its common feature is withdrawal from organized society into independent communes, whose members now and then go forth with food, medical aid, and political propaganda for people in the slums. These groups attempt to show the larger society the error of its ways. They hope that such demonstrations will lead to the reorganization of society as a network of larger communes.

Some communes are rural, with strong back-to-the-land, ecological, or primitivistic flavors, like the *kibbutzim* in Israel. Others are urban, sometimes using violent guerrilla tactics. They may center on economic, sexual, or psychedelic experimentation, religious revivalism, occultism, or simply "living cheap." More than any other

radicals, these people often feel that economic issues are irrelevant. So, while most radicals call for massive redistribution of income and wealth, these folks would most likely accept these views:

Distribution is irrelevant because income is irrelevant. There is already too much consumption of the wrong kind: soul-less, artificial "satisfaction" encouraged by advertising, which robs people of their freedom, makes them empty and unhappy. Property is theft, and 'income distribution' fits in with it. We ought to abandon the whole rotten production and consumption structure of industrialism. We ought to live in communes, be directly supplied with simple, natural goods, and arrange distribution in direct consultation with one another.[12]

Terrorism and parasitism are among the charges that have been made against this radical group. However, those who believe in violence as a way of life are a rather small fraction. Most prefer to provoke the Establishment, by ridicule or violence, into dropping its liberal front and showing its true colors, which they consider repressive. Neither should they be considered parasites. Many traffic and barter with "straight" society, selling farm products and handicrafts to earn money for what they need to buy. Parasitism is dependence on handouts from parents, friends, passers-by, and the government relief system. This aspect of communal living also obviously exists, but only as an offshoot.

ANARCHISM II This group works within society but only to destroy it, either by violence (terror) or by ridicule.

In the United States of the late 1960s, the favorite weapon was ridicule, in the grand tradition of Till Eulenspiegel, Voltaire, and Bernard Shaw. Their "revolution" would be a day or week of merry pranks—fraternity initiations on a grand scale. It is hard to believe that their manifestos were meant to do more than shock

the doctors, the lawyers, the business executives,
they're all made of ticky-tacky,
and they all look the same[13]

12. Jan Pen, *Income Distribution: Facts, Theories, Policies* (London: Allen Lane, 1971), p. 293.
13. Extract from the song "Little Boxes." Words and music by Malvine Reynolds. Used by permission. All rights reserved.

into serious thought about social issues. Their high priest, Abbie Hoffman, produced for the 1968 Democratic Party convention held in Chicago the best known of these manifestos. Planks 7 and 8 dealt with economic matters:

7. The abolition of money, the abolition of pay housing, pay medicine, pay transportation, pay food, pay education, pay clothing, pay medical help, and pay toilets.
8. A society which works for and actively promotes the concept of full unemployment. A society in which people are free from the drudgery of work. Adoption of the concept "Let the machines do it."

"Machines" were to produce everything we need, and repair each other in their spare time, whatever damages they may have suffered in the Revolution. The people, meanwhile, would dance and sing, write poetry, make love, and heighten their awareness through "body chemistry."[14]

New Left anarchists have subsequently stopped playing games and turned to terroristic violence. The Baeder-Meinhof gang in West Germany and the Red Brigades in Italy seem to be examples of terrorism with an anarchist accent. (The American Weathermen, the violent offshoot of the SDS, were, however, Trotskyist rather than anarchist.) It is in general a great, though common, mistake to associate terrorism exclusively with anarchism, socialism, or any other form of radicalism, Old or New, Left or Right. Terrorism is a set of violent tactics that, when used by others than the uniformed armed forces and the police, is aimed at some sort of social change and is denounced by worldwide public opinion. But the American Ku Klux Klan, the Nazi Gestapo, the Irish Republican Army (IRA), the extremist factions of the Palestine Liberation Organization, and the shadowy overseas agencies of the Khaddafi government of Libya, are none of them either anarchist or primarily leftist in orientation. They aim at such diverse goals as white supremacy, anti-communism, a united Ireland, and the elimination of Israel from the Middle East. Some profess leftist sympathies and others profess anti-leftist ones, but the particular cause seems unrelated to the

tactics. Terrorism, in short, is not an economic category.

Socialists are both more numerous and more important than the anarchists within the New Left. Their tradition is also more rational and less emotional, as indicated by the importance attached to Marxian analysis. Socialists (and communists)[15] see ownership of land and capital by the political state and its agencies (themselves controlled by a political party representing the working class) as the only feasible short-run alternative to capitalism. When the world turns socialist, it may be sensible to speak of the eventual "withering away" of political states. At the present time, say the socialists, such talk is a harmful diversion.

SOCIALISM I What we shall call *Socialism I* embodies a neo-Stalinist approach, which its enemies call "Red Fascism." The economy is to be planned on scientific principles, and planning is to be largely imperative—the Plan plus a machine gun or a firing squad. Dissent, including economic dissent, is tolerated only "repressively," if at all, meaning that the dissenters may let off steam harmlessly, short of action. Monopoly of the formal means of propaganda is imposed and reinforced if necessary by compulsory study and by criticism and self-criticism sessions. In such group therapy, orthodoxy is drummed into the

15. Communists go beyond socialists in three main ways, more political than economic.
  1. They believe more firmly than other socialists that an economy of abundance would shortly follow the establishment of socialism on a world scale. In this way, they are closer to the teachings of Marx.
  2. Orthodox communists (or Marxist-Leninists) accept violence as a necessary aspect of revolution, especially in less developed countries. They propose not only to use it in self-defense, but also to take the offensive when the time is right. As a result, they want their political party to be limited to activists, and to be disciplined tightly like a military organization.
  3. Orthodox communists also see a need for a dictatorship of the proletariat (and its "vanguard party") for a long period after the socialist revolution—again, especially in less developed countries.
  They do not believe that any existing economy has actually gone beyond socialism to communism, though Mao Zedong hoped to attain communism for China in a "Great Leap Forward," which ended in failure in 1958–1962.

14. "Free" [Abbie Hoffman], *Revolution for the Hell of It* (New York: Dial Press, 1968).

members, who are expected to apply it to current practical problems. No one is allowed to remain silent, or to hide dissent behind a mask of ignorance. "I don't know" is not an escape hatch.

"Liberty," Lenin is supposed to have said, "is a commodity so precious that it must be rationed." Under the neo-Stalinists, civil rights are subordinated to the dictates of planning. The rule of law normally remains in effect, but the content of the law is shifted in favor of the state and against defendants in such "details" as the presumption of innocence, protection against self-incrimination, free choice of defense lawyer, double jeopardy, and the statutes of limitation.

SOCIALISM II

The camp we call *Socialism II* is often referred to as "Marxist humanism." Its inspiration comes from the younger Marx of the 1830s and 1840s, who was more concerned with "human values" and less with "class struggles" than he was later on. Socialism II is less authoritarian than Socialism I, and seems less concerned with orthodoxy. However, the government monopoly of formal education and propaganda is as strong as under Socialism I. In practice, Socialism II may lead to the substitution of mob rule for bureaucracy, as in the Chinese Cultural Revolution of Mao Zedong's last decade (1966–1975).

Among the leading economic doctrines of Socialism II are the following: (1) there should be equality of income and wealth; (2) a wider range of goods and services should be made available completely free of charge; (3) "material incentives" should be replaced by "moral incentives" for economic activity; (4) there should be an end to the hierarchy and alienation of modern industrial society.

Isn't it likely that Socialism II would degenerate in practice to Socialism I? Without doubting the sincerity of Marxist humanists, one may indeed wonder if a society can go from the status quo to Marxist humanism without a longer or shorter period of "proletarian dictatorship." There is also the danger that a ruling bureaucracy under Socialism I would not permit the peaceful transition to Socialism II. One may also wonder if the degree of ideological control needed to make the New Socialist Man and Woman out of ordinary people

can be combined with the Bill of Rights quite as easily as Socialism II followers expect or hope.

SYNDICALISM

Syndicalists favor the separate ownership of each productive facility (which may be a single workshop, a factory, or a large industrial complex) by its own workers, who would elect representatives to a weak state, which would referee disputes between groups of workers and coordinate their economic plans. *Syndicalism* is an almost-forgotten word today. But California's "anti-Red" laws of World War I were anti-*syndicalist* rather than anti-*communist*, and a well-known economist chose the title "Reflections on Syndicalism" for his attack on the New Deal for strengthening the organized labor movement.[16]

Syndicalism is a system of economic and political rule by syndicates—a *syndicate* being another name for a guild or trade union. The syndicates are themselves above the law. Thus syndicalism could mean replacing Congress by a national assembly made up of trade unions. At one time, the Industrial Workers of the World (IWW) embodied the syndicalist threat in the United States.

An interesting feature of syndicalism is its strategy of the general strike rather than political revolution as the weapon of social change. Syndicalists hope not only to win strikes but also to prevent the workers' gains from being passed on to consumers in price rises. Starting with individual companies, syndicalism would spread to the whole economy as local strikes grew into general strikes, and as the issues turned from the purely economic to the openly political. The process of winning strikes, repeated over and over again, would both bring the value of the owners' equity down to zero and paralyze the economy. The unions could then buy out their employers for little or nothing.

It goes without saying that unions would be free to break all contracts and would not be subject to any lawsuits. Also, laws against striking or using the strike weapon for political ends would be ignored.

16. Henry C. Simons, *Economic Policy for a Free Society* (Chicago: University of Chicago Press, 1948), Chapter 6.

Many proposals and activities, not necessarily radical, have syndicalist implications. For example, in support for public employees' and welfare recipients' rights to strike and bargain collectively, the "syndicalist" feature is that their bargains are considered sacred. Elected legislatures may not refuse funding to carry them out. A case on the local level is a teachers' union (not consciously syndicalist) bargaining for higher pay and smaller classes, and in this way using the strike weapon to force hikes in property tax rates, which the people through their elected representatives may have refused. In other words, the elective machinery of government is downgraded in relation to bargaining by employee unions, in terms of control of the taxpayer's dollar. If the legislature is limited to backing up the results of collective bargaining, the government's "power of the purse" is weakened.

Earlier versions of syndicalism were built around economic *blitzkrieg* or lightning warfare. All workers were to lay down their tools at the same time, and that would be enough to paralyze the economy immediately. It was hoped that such a general strike might be spontaneous, so that the capitalists would be taken by surprise. There have in fact been general strikes. Some of them have succeeded, but the successful ones have been a part of or a trigger for political revolution, not substitutes for it.

THE NEW RIGHT

From the New Left, we turn to the **New Right.** More than the New Left, it changes in character from one country to another. Moreover, it lacks any towering figure who corresponds to Karl Marx. The New Right is composed of people disgusted with things as they have become, but should not be confused with conservatism. Neither should it be confused with fascism, for its majority is composed of people bitterly opposed to authoritarian regimes. In the United States at least, the incidence of radicalism as we have defined it is less in the New Right than in the New Left. However, the truly radical New Right

is a collection of paramilitary cells, which stage shoot-outs and bust-ups with people they call "commies" or racially inferior or which plot guerrilla warfare to follow nuclear attacks or communist takeovers. The Ku Klux Klan and the Survivalists, respectively, exemplify these two strains.

Three intertwined branches compose the American New Right. Only one of these, on which we concentrate our attention, is primarily economic. The other two branches are ethical and political. The ethical-religious branch wants the recognition of absolute ethics and morality. The political branch is strongly anti-Soviet, fearing Soviet plots for world domination and empire.

The Market Economy New Right

The market economy New Right glories in being reactionary, and proposes a return to the old-time religion of *laissez-faire*. On the macroeconomic side, it also calls for restoring the gold standard, the annually balanced budget, and sometimes Say's Identity (aided by downward wage flexibility) to ensure high employment. The New Right's god is Adam Smith, whose faith in free enterprise was much less fervent than their own.

The market economy New Right can be subdivided into those for and those against trust-busting and similar controls. The **trust-busters** see a "decline of competition," which they would like to reverse. They fear that control by a big-business oligarchy will restrict output and employment, raise prices, and stifle the opportunity for new businesses to enter the prosperous mainstream of the American economy. Another of their fears is that a growing proportion of the people are being pushed into a relatively poor competitive segment of the economy.

The **laissez-faire** New Right is less impressed by the threat of economic segmentation into tightly knit oligopoly and competitive sectors. It depends not on antitrust laws or other controls but on technical change, which Joseph Schumpeter called "creative destruction," to overcome any tendencies toward segmentation. This group points, for example, to the displacement of the railroad "octopus" of the late nineteenth century by trucks, buses, planes, and automobiles less than fifty years later. It also points to a "product cycle" in international trade that leads to more foreign competition for companies like General Motors and Ford in automobiles, or like U.S. Steel and Bethlehem Steel in the steel industry. To these people, monopoly and tightly knit oligopoly may indeed be diseases, uncomfortable where they strike and while they last, but more like the common cold than cancer. They believe that the struggle to gain and hold on to market positions in oligopolistic industries spurs both invention and innovation.

The two groups within the economic New Right agree in general that the economy would do better with less regulation and greater reliance on law and equity. But how much less regulation? Less in what fields of economic activity? Which regulations should be lightened or scrapped first? We find disagreement on the specifics.

Similar disagreement on specifics plagues the New Right case against progressive taxation of income and wealth. But there is nearly unanimous New Right support for the view that such taxes be cut, that they should be simplified, and that their degree of progression should be reduced—possibly to zero.

The Libertarian Movement

The most radical branch of the economic New Right in its thinking, although decidedly not in its political tactics—is the **Libertarian** movement. There is no gospel common to all libertarians. Radical libertarians are like anarchists in their fear of the state as an engine of tyranny. However, they depart from collectivist anarchism by supporting private ownership of the means of production. Libertarians offer many proposals for changes in the rules of the economic game, intended to allow the market to govern and reduce the state (and therefore social planning) to zero. Money, defense, protection, streets, sewers, and the framing and administration of law would all be left to private firms and associations. Any

person or voluntary group could found a new firm, or buy an existing one in any field (including the practice of law or medicine) without any formal certification of training or competence. All taxes would be replaced by payments for services and by voluntary dues to cooperative associations. People could move freely from place to place and from association to association, but no association would be forced to accept any particular new member or partner.

Objectivism and Social Darwinism

Objectivism is the belief that each person's most objective view of "the good" is his or her knowledge of what is in his or her own (subjective) best interest. Another objectivist argument is that "altruism," "the general good," and "social equity" in practice are often self-interest arguments of various other people, who usually do not turn out to be in any way admirable. In the words of objectivist leader Ayn Rand (1905–1982), objectivism is "rational selfishness."[17]

To those who call themselves objectivists, the world and the economy are so interrelated that the Darwinian principle of "survival of the fittest" should include survival of those who perform the best in the free market.

The ideas of Rand and her followers are a revival of a philosophy called **Social Darwinism,** associated particularly with the English sociologist and philosopher Herbert Spencer (1820–1903). Social Darwinists believe that the survival and prosperity of individuals, families, nations, and races are determined, like those of animal species, by their biological and psychological fitness in

---

17. Ayn Rand was Russian-born, and was (like Karl Marx) a philosopher by training. Disgusted with Soviet Russia after the Revolution, she emigrated to America in 1926. She became a Hollywood screen writer, and later wrote a series of novels or "tracts for the times." Her ideas are expressed most clearly in the novel *Atlas Shrugged*, which deals with the disastrous things that would happen to society if the few superior individuals should all decide, like ordinary workers, to go on strike. Of her nonfiction works, a collection called *Capitalism: The Unknown Ideal* is the most explicitly economic. In it there is much that could pass as libertarian doctrine, but never a hint of anarchism.

perpetual struggle against each other and against the environment. It is dangerous in the long run for any family, nation, or race to thwart this struggle for survival, either by placing restrictions on its fittest members or by giving special aid to the least fit. It is not that "the fittest" are above the law, but if enforcement of the laws must be bent in any direction, it is better for society's future if the favored party is the superior person.

SUMMARY

1. Opposition to the capitalist-market economy, when it transcends envy and "me-for-dictator" ambition, centers on three problems: (a) inequality of the distributions of income and wealth; (b) insecurity of the standard of living against downward shocks, both cyclical and long-term; and (c) incompatibility with physical and mental health. The major problem is psychological alienation. Alienation takes many forms, and explains many forms of social pathology, ranging from boredom to violent crime.

2. Marxism is an integrated, unified system of social philosophy, including both economic statics and economic dynamics, and culminating in certain "laws of motion of capitalism."

3. While admitting the accomplishments of the Industrial Revolution, Marxian economics uses a strict labor theory of value to develop certain "contradictions of capitalism." In its Marxian form this theory develops ideas about the exploitation of the worker and the receipt of surplus value by the capitalist class.

4. In the economic dynamics of Marx's theories, the contradictions of capitalism lead to "increasing misery" and to the eventual downfall of capitalism, either because a falling rate of profit leads to a *liquidity* crisis or because a tendency toward overproduction leads to a *realization* crisis.

5. Marxian analysis leaves no important role for monetary and fiscal policy. Also, the labor theory of value does not deal with demand and utility as determinants of value.

6. Radicalism may be radical either because of what it proposes to accomplish, as in "a radical restructuring of society," or because of the tactics that it considers legitimate to accomplish these ends, which sometimes include illegality, violence, dictatorship, and the disregard of public opinion by a tightly organized political party.

7. Marxian theories are major influences upon critics of market-capitalism, including those critics who do not consider themselves Marxists and who do not know Marxian literature well.

8. The American New Left arose in the early 1960s as a search for unity on the political Left. Disunity of the Old Left was blamed for the rise of fascism in the period between World War I and World War II and McCarthyism in the 1950s. It is not an exclusively radical movement, but its leadership is for the most part radical. It has lost importance since 1970, but keeps trying for revival using new issues in domestic and foreign policy.

9. The radical groups within the New Left are all *collectivist*. They favor collective ownership of the means of production. Subdivisions are *anarchist*, *socialist*, and *syndicalist*.

10. The anarchist wing of the New Left can be subdivided into the "counterculture," which withdraws from the mainstream of society into communes, and the revolutionary wing, which proposes tearing down institutions and then possibly starting over.

11. Socialists favor state ownership of the means of production. The socialist wing of the New Left can be subdivided into neo-Stalinist imperative planners and "Marxist humanists," who emphasize equality, mass participation in decision making, and moral (rather than material) incentives.

12. Syndicalists favor ownership by trade unions of the workers. They believe that unions can bring down capitalism by winning strikes. Unions would be immune from lawsuits and could break all contracts.

13. The economic New Right concentrates on achieving *laissez-faire*; the ethical-religious New Right, on re-establishing the old-time religion and morality, and the political New Right on thwarting alleged communist conspiracies to dominate the world. These three groups overlap to some extent, and only the first is relevant to our study of economics. It includes both libertarians and objectivists.

14. Libertarians are, ideologically speaking, the most radical branch of the economic New Right. They favor complete reliance on the free capitalist market, and hope for the demise of the political state. They are distinguished from collectivist anarchists by their beliefs in private enterprise and private property.

15. Objectivists believe that our most nearly objective knowledge of the "good" and the "just" is our knowledge of what is good for ourselves. We should follow this knowledge rather than the urgings of ethical altruism, which is often a cover for dishonesty.

16. Objectivists are impressed with the contribution to society of the few superior individuals. They fear that human evolution toward some ideal will be sidetracked if such people are restricted or if inferiors are helped to survive and reproduce. To this extent objectivists are Social Darwinists, applying the principle of "survival of the fittest" to social as well as biological relations.

17. Terrorism is a set of violent tactics, which can be used by partisans of a great variety of political, religious, racial, economic, or social positions, but it is not itself a category of economic thought. It is a great mistake to associate terrorism exclusively with any economic philosophy—radical or conservative, old or new, Right or Left.

DISCUSSION QUESTIONS

1. Do you believe that the inequalities in the American distributions of income and wealth constitute "maldistribution"? Explain why or why not.

2. Does the market-capitalist economy make adequate provision for a future in which the relative prices of natural resources and energy are both high and rising steadily? Would a socialist economy do better? Explain.

3. Is alienation the root cause of social pathology, as Karl Marx believed, or are those who engage in pathological behavior responsible for their own actions? Explain your answers.

4. What is meant by the Marxist "economic interpretation of history," "contradictions of capitalism," and "principle of increasing misery"?

5. Karl Marx states in the first chapter of *Capital* what he considers the chief theoretical problem of competitive capitalism. A capitalist buys labor power, raw materials, and intermediate goods at their values. He also sells his final product at its value, and still makes a profit. But where does this profit come from, and why has not competition eliminated it?

Marx then goes on to answer his own questions at some length. What, do you think, is the nature of Marx's solution?

6. Do you think that Marx would be satisfied with the economic performance of the contemporary United States? The contemporary Soviet Union? Contemporary Cuba or China? Explain why or why not in each case.

7. Distinguish between: (a) the Marxist and conventional concepts of profit and (b) the breakdowns of capital into "fixed and variable" (conventional) or "constant and variable" (Marxian).

8. Do you have an economic explanation for the relative decline of the American New Left after the end of the Vietnam War? Explain what economic circumstances, if any, might cause its revival.

9. To what extent is it reasonable to associate terrorism with the New Left or with any particular wing of the New Left, or with the New Left in general?

10. Distinguish libertarianism from both anarchism and objectivism.

11. What is Social Darwinism? How does it differ from ordinary (biological) Darwinism? Is it a racist doctrine? Explain why or why not.

From Karl Marx to the New Left

A prominent slogan of the New Left in the 1960s and early 1970s was "Marx, Mao, and Marcuse!" To this trio we add Lenin, whose importance is reflected in the fact that today Communist parties call themselves Marxist-*Leninist,* and not merely Marxist. Here we shall give a thumbnail sketch of the contributions of Lenin, Mao, Marcuse, and several other left-wing economists and social philosophers during the period between the deaths of Marx and Engels (late nineteenth century) and the rise of the American New Left, which we date from the SDS "Port Huron Statement" of 1962. Our account does not pretend to be a connected history of socialist thought.

Marx died in 1883. Engels, who lived until 1895, edited the last two volumes of Marx's *Capital.* At the same time, however, Engels's revolutionary zeal seemed to wane both with the passing of Marx and the failure of the Revolution to arrive "on schedule"[1] in any of the advanced countries of Europe and North America, where the evolution of capitalism had gone the furthest toward its expected downfall. In spite of several serious economic depressions in the 1870s and 1890s, the socialist revolution seemed much more remote when Engels died than it had seemed in the 1848 "year of revolution," when he and Marx had written their *Communist Manifesto.*

Marx's Followers

The first split in the Marxist ranks came in 1899, sixteen years after Marx's death and only four years after that of Engels. It came within the German Social Democratic Party, then mainly Marxist and also the world's leading socialist party. The arch-heretic was Eduard Bernstein (1850–1932), who had been Engels's secretary. Bernstein wrote a book best known under its English title of *Evolutionary Socialism.* Bernstein's main points were the following:

1. Capitalism was *not* collapsing from internal contradictions. The middle class was *not* dying out, workers' living standards were *not* falling, and large-scale agriculture was *not* replacing either the American family farm or its European equivalents.

2. Capitalism would not collapse, and therefore socialism must prove its own superiority and "fitness" in free competition in the marketplace of ideas.

3. Accordingly, socialists should stress reformist electoral and parliamentary paths, and give up the idea of violent revolution in the republics and constitutional monarchies of Europe and America.

Bernstein was answered by Karl Kautsky (1854–1938), "the Socialist Pope" and Engels's successor as editor of Marx's unpublished manuscripts. The German party, and other European Social Democratic parties,[2] officially accepted Kautsky's "orthodox" answer to Bernstein's economic heresies, but then quietly began to follow Bernstein's recommendations on political tactics.[3] For this reason, social democracy is regarded today as reformist rather than revolutionary.

The then much weaker and less important Russian Social Democratic Party, operating largely underground and in exile, faced the same conflict. Its Menshevik (minority) faction favored positions close to Bernstein's.

---

1. Marx and Engels never drew up a timetable for the Revolution. They apparently expected it for 1848 or shortly thereafter. When it failed to occur, they wisely refrained from "rescheduling" it. But surely they would be disappointed to find capitalism still controlling major industrial countries in the late twentieth century.

2. The American Socialist Party was never a Marxist party, though many of its individual leaders were Marxists.

3. The test came with the outbreak of World War I in 1914. The Social Democratic Party, demonstrating its patriotism, voted to support war credits (war loans). Kautsky went along with this decision. Social Democratic parties in other countries on both sides also expressed patriotic solidarity with their capitalist governments, though the pre-1914 party line had been to resist and sabotage international warfare and transform it into socialist revolution.

Karl Marx

Its Bolshevik (majority) faction, which would later be led by Vladimir Ilich Lenin (1870–1924), also known as Nikolai Lenin, went beyond Kautsky in the vigor of its denunciations. In view of the later world leadership of the Russian party and of Lenin's remarkable success in combining theoretical and practical leadership, we move on to discuss the "Leninist" component of Marxism-Leninism.

Lenin

Lenin's major contributions to world socialism—as distinguished from his contributions to specifically Russian problems—are three in number, two of them ideological and the third tactical.

1. Lenin more than any other single Marxist writer is responsible for the "internationalization" of the argument in Marx's *Capital*.[4] Lenin's explanation of capitalist survival was imperialism, the export of capital and capitalist domination to the less developed countries of the world. This extension kept the organic composition of capital—the k term in Marxian equations—low, thereby avoiding both the falling rate of profit and the "increasing misery" of at least the organized labor aristocracy of the capitalist countries. Lenin called such workers the "pampered palace slaves" of capitalism. But imperialism, with or without colonial rule, was not a permanent cure for capitalism's contradictions. On the one hand, it led to imperialist war between rival capitalist powers, for example, World War I. On the other hand, it led to warfare with the natives of the countries being "imperialized." In either form of warfare, the masses in the capitalist countries must be armed and could be turned against their capitalist exploiters. "The road to London and Paris," Lenin once said, "runs through Peking and Calcutta."

2. It followed for Lenin that the worldwide socialist revolution against capitalist rule need not begin in those lands where capitalism had gone the furthest. It might just as well begin with a war of liberation in some colonial backwater, and spread from there. In fact, it might just as well begin in Czarist Russia, where misery and oppression were particularly bad, even though Russia was, economically speaking, only a backward outpost of European capitalism, and even though Russian capitalism was not well developed.

3. In a backward country like Russia, the workers were not ready for revolutionary activity "on their own." Marxists believed that trade unions could easily be sidetracked into "economism"—that is, concentrating on economic demands for small groups of labor aristocrats "within the system" and ignoring the need to overthrow the system as a whole. What was needed was a revolutionary "vanguard party" to represent the workers' true interests. Such a vanguard party must, Lenin felt, be revolutionary. It must not only be an elite group, unfettered by bourgeois law and morals, but must include an underground core organized in military fashion. This underground party must be prepared to seize full power in the revolutionary

4. A number of Marxist writers made important contributions to this "internationalization" process, summarized in Anthony Brewer, *Marxist Theories of Imperialism* (London: Routledge and Kegan Paul, 1980). Chapter 2 deals explicitly with Lenin's *Imperialism, the Highest Stage of Capitalism*.

struggle, with no need for alliances with liberals and other reformists. Membership in the vanguard party should be limited to loyal activists who make the Revolution the main object of their lives. Also, once the vanguard party has seized power, it should hold on to its "proletarian dictatorship" until socialism is firmly established once and for all, ignoring the forms and machinery of electoral democracy. Of course, for Russia today, the vanguard party is the Communist Party.[5]

Luxemburg

A middle position in these conflicts, both in Germany and Russia, was held by Rosa Luxemburg (1870–1919). Born in Poland, "Red Rosa" spoke German and Russian as well as Polish, and was active in the revolutionary Marxist politics of all three countries.[6] Her views have come to be respected since her death even more than during her rather short life.

Luxemburg too had a theory of imperialism. But whereas Lenin stressed the export of capital to prop up the domestic rate of profit and prevent *liquidity* crises, Luxemburg stressed the dumping of consumer goods in the less developed countries, when they could not be sold domestically at profitable prices. In terms of Marxist theory, the Luxemburg approach concentrates on avoiding *realization* crises by imperialist expansion.

Luxemburg was no Bernstein disciple or Menshevik reformist. Neither was she an "orthodox" follower of "Pope" Kautsky. She broke with him over the "war credits" issue in 1914, just as Lenin broke with the "patriotic" Mensheviks in Russia. Also, like Lenin, Luxemburg favored an activist, paramilitary vanguard party, ready to seize power in revolutionary struggles without waiting for the election returns. Unlike Lenin, however, she was always suspicious of party dictatorship. She took the "democracy" of the Social Democratic Party

Vladimir Ilich Lenin

label seriously in its conventional sense, which calls for the rule "of" and "by" the people as well as "for" them. Though welcoming the Bolshevik seizure of power in Russia in November 1917, she opposed the reign of terror by which the Bolsheviks held on to their power in the following years, beginning when they dissolved a constitutional convention in January 1918. These aspects of her thinking are highly respected by the "Marxist humanist" wing of the New Left.

From Lenin to Stalin

Lenin died in 1924. In the Soviet Union his death signaled a long struggle for power among the subordinate Bolshevik leaders, ending in the dictatorship of Josef Stalin (1880–1953) and the execution of most of Stalin's rivals. This struggle too had important economic implications.

---

5. After the two Russian Revolutions of 1917, the Bolshevik wing of the former Social Democratic Party called itself the Communist Party. The Menshevik wing continued to call itself the Social Democratic Party, but was largely liquidated in the Red Terror and Russian Civil War of 1918–1920.

6. She was assassinated in Berlin while under arrest as a leader of the "Spartacist" revolt. This was an attempt to duplicate in Germany the success of the Bolsheviks in Russia, in the chaos that followed the German defeat in World War I and the abdication of the last Hohenzollern Kaiser, Wilhelm II.

Faced with domestic economic disorganization and a major famine after the end of the Russian Civil War, Lenin had modified his extremism[7] and accepted a "New Economic Policy" for the Soviet Union. Under this policy, private enterprise was allowed in small-scale industry, light industry, and agriculture, while heavy industry and finance remained in state hands. In the midst of economic revival, an agricultural crisis developed. Russia had lost perhaps 20 million people during World War I, the 1917 revolutions, and the Civil War. Because of the rapid industrialization of the New Economic Policy, many workers left the farms for jobs in the cities.[8] Farm prices began to rise, lowering workers' real wages and hampering industrialization by lowering the urban-rural income differential. But the pace of industrialization had to be maintained, both to prevent any future capitalist "encirclement" or economic "squeeze" and to provide an industrial working class that would support continued socialization. To the Marxist, the peasant was essentially a small capitalist, interested mainly in owning land and profiting by its produce. What was to be done?

In this crisis, the Communist Right Wing (later called *Right Deviation*) was led by an economist, Nikolai Bukharin (1888–1938).[9] Bukharin considered the rising trend of agricultural prices as only temporary, since he expected the higher farm prices would lead to more farm production. He saw no need to abandon the New Economic Policy or to put direct pressure upon the peasants. The Left Wing (later called *Left Deviation*) was led by Leon Trotsky (1879–1940), whose lieutenant in economic matters was Yevgeny Preobrazhensky (1886–1937). Trotsky's position is not easy to understand. On the one hand, he favored the use of "persuasion" on the peasants to squeeze out more production at con-trolled prices while making them consume less and save more. But he also favored bringing the peasants into collective farms, along with their private holdings of land, machinery, farm animals, stored grain, and so on.

In the power struggle, Stalin at first sided with Bukharin against Trotsky and Preobrazhensky. Since that time, "Trotskyism" has remained a label attached in the Soviet Union to almost any Left deviation from the current party line. At the same time, Trotskyism became a flag under which dissidents from Stalinism rallied outside the Soviet sphere of influence.[10] Trotsky himself was sent to Siberia, exiled, and later murdered in Mexico. With Trotsky out of the way, Stalin adopted and intensified what had been the Left Wing economic platform. The New Economic Policy was followed by the Five Year Plans. The peasants were collectivized on harsher terms than had been recommended by the Left Wing. A quarter-century of Stalin's dictatorship ended only with his death in 1953.

Mao Zedong and Communist China

Our scene now shifts to China. To the historian of economic thought, the most important innovation of Mao Zedong (1894–1976) was his basing of the Chinese Communist revolution on discontented peasant farmers (for the most part tenants of richer farmers or absentee landlords), rather than on urban workers (the Marxian proletariat). In the late 1920s and early 1930s, urban-based attempts at revolution in China had failed despite Soviet support and advice, and the Soviets had been lukewarm in their backing of Chairman Mao's successful leadership in the late 1940s.[11]

Then, ten years after expelling the previous Chinese government to the island of Taiwan, Mao first led a "Great Leap Forward" (1958–1962) and then a "Great Cultural Revolution" (1966–1976). The Great Leap was intended to achieve the Communist goal of an economy

7. Lenin's "extremism," shared by other Bolshevik economists at the time of the Bolshevik Revolution, had been based on an oversimplified planning system modeled after a concept of the country as "one big factory" and intuitively understandable to the average worker. Such a plan would, it was hoped, permit the Soviet Union to operate on a barter system, dispensing with the "bourgeois" social contrivance of money.

8. Technically, this drain of workers from the farms was largely a return flow. Urban workers and demobilized soldiers had gone to the country (where the food was) during the Civil War and the famine that followed it. With greater availability of food in the cities by the middle 1920s, many of these people were simply returning there.

9. Bukharin was the model for the hero "Rubashov" in Arthur Koestler's *Darkness at Noon*.

10. Trotsky lives on in literature as "Emmanuel Goldstein" in George Orwell's *Nineteen Eighty-Four*.

11. The Soviets have generally looked with disfavor on Communist Party leaders in other countries who have assumed leadership positions without receiving their training in Russia and without the blessings of the Soviet leadership when other leaders having these advantages were available. Mao Zedong is the most important example.

of abundance through largely decentralized communes, combining agricultural and industrial production in "rural cities." The Cultural Revolution aimed at substituting moral incentives for material ones, at equalizing income and wealth, and at preventing the rise of any bureaucratic "New Class" of white-collar elite workers within the Communist Party, the government, or the People's Liberation Army.

Both of these innovations are now judged as failures. The Great Leap Forward, which planned to take over from the Soviet Union the world leadership of the communist movement, led instead to a near-famine in China and to a breakdown in the shaky alliance between the two leading Marxist countries. Such breakdowns were not dreamed of in Marx's philosophy. The Cultural Revolution degenerated into chaos and mob rule, which required military intervention to restore order and revive the economy. Before its failure, however, the Cultural Revolution had attracted worldwide New Left support for its "participatory democracy," its attacks on the Chinese bureaucracy, and as an egalitarian alternative to the Soviet system.[12]

Marcuse and the New Left

Our account continues with Herbert Marcuse, the final member of the trio "Marx, Mao, and Marcuse." Marcuse (1898–1981) was a German sociologist of the so-called Frankfurt school. For much of his early life he was an academic, respected for his scholarship, but quite unknown to the general public. And before his death he had already been almost forgotten. But after fleeing to America to escape Hitler, he enjoyed more than a decade of fame, both in his native Europe and his adopted America, as a darling of the New Left. The slogan "Marx, Mao, and Marcuse" meant what it said. Marcuse was, for the time being, classed with Marx and Mao, despite the handicap of a difficult literary style.

Marcuse's main contributions were four in number. They ranged from his treatment of demand in economics to theories in the fields of sociology, psychology, and philosophy, with which Marcuse was more at home.

---

12. Strangely enough, Mao Zedong found Stalinism less reprehensible than the somewhat milder regimes that were in power between Stalin's passing and his own death twenty-three years later.

---

1. There has always been a libertine "free love" tradition in the political Left, which has had to exist along with the rival puritanical tradition, which equates sexual experimentation with "capitalist decadence." In *Eros and Civilization,* Marcuse combined ideas of Karl Marx and Sigmund Freud, and argued that true socialism means freedom for the human spirit. Such freedom, he said, must include sexual freedom—the liberation from "middle-class morality." This was what some members of the Left wanted to hear, and they welcomed it with enthusiasm.

2. "Work is a four-letter word," according to the hippies, and Marcuse "proved" it was quite unnecessary. In *One-Dimensional Man,* Marcuse argued that if we could only restrain our demands, we should easily be able to produce all we want by voluntary work, and could have the economy of abundance the minute after the Revolution. Also, we would be just as well off as we are now. Consumption—more goods, newer goods, new models, more *de luxe* frills—is simply narcotic and does *not* give more satisfaction. Marcuse argued that we are alienated from our society, as Marx had said, but we still expect fancier and more numerous consumer goods to cure our alienation, even though they have never done so in the past. So we become one-dimensional people—consumers of goods. It is better to forget about consumption and standards of living and to give up the rat race in favor of the natural life of play and song and love, all "on the cheap."

3. Marcuse said that the working class is hopelessly narcotized by consumerism and by advertising. It cannot be trusted to overthrow the system. Who then can overthrow it? Marcuse's answer is the student youth, not yet quite overcome by the pressure to consume, and possibly still able to resist the lure of one-dimensional "consumer fascism." As for allies, there are the underclasses at home and abroad—racial minorities, Third World peoples, domestic drifters, dropouts, junkies, hippies, migrants, even criminals—whom Marx himself had scorned as *lumpenproletariat* (bums). The youth and the students, not the blue-collar working stiffs, will be the vanguard of the new society.

4. Nor did Marcuse believe in the need to tolerate the opposition. After all, he argued, Mussolini's Fascists and Hitler's Nazis got their start because of misplaced tolerance. They should not have been tolerated at all, but put down at once. Furthermore, today's Establishment

827

uses toleration mainly to allow opponents to "let off steam" ineffectually. This tolerance simply conceals the repressive nature of society, which becomes apparent whenever the opposition becomes a real danger to "things as they are" or to the interests of the capitalist class. Such is the message of Marcuse's *Critique of Pure Tolerance*.

All this was heady stuff for student radicals, who were used to being patted on the head or told to go home and grow up. It went over big in the 1960s and the early 1970s. In fact, Marcuse's message was never refuted. Instead, the job market tightened after the Vietnam War, placing a greater value on "a smile and a shoeshine" and making potential troublemakers "think twice."[13] So the New Left and its heroes fell from fashion into nostalgia, with Marcuse a principal victim. Will New Left ideas and New Left tactics return to favor in the next period of high employment and labor shortage? We do not know, and we dare not forecast.

13. Unlike the situation of the Great Depression, unemployment was not a severe problem for the white students with the proper credentials and "nothing against them." Employers could and did engage in political discrimination. If the situation had deteriorated further, with no jobs for anyone, discrimination would have again been meaningless.

Glossary

A

ability-to-pay principle a guide for taxation that advocates that tax liability should be a larger fraction of income (or wealth) for high-income (or high-wealth) receivers than for low-income (or low-wealth) receivers.

absolute advantage being more proficient than one's trading partner in some branch of production.

absolute amount of cost difference (entry barrier) the difference in average total costs existing between established firms in an industry and potential entrants.

absolute full employment a situation in which all firms in an economy are operating at capacity and only seasonal, frictional, and structural unemployment exist.

accelerating inflation a situation in which the rate of inflation is increasing; if the acceleration is unexpected, money illusion and wage-cost lags continue to affect employment decisions, and unemployment remains below its natural rate.

accelerator effect the effect that a change in the rate of expansion or contraction in the economy has on the absolute volume of production and income in capital goods industries.

accommodation an action by monetary authorities shifting the money-supply curve so that shifts in the demand-for-money curve do not cause changes in the rate of interest; sometimes called *validation.*

accord, the an agreement reached in 1951 between the Federal Reserve System and the U.S. Treasury under which the Fed was freed from a wartime commitment to support the price of government securities.

acquisition See *merger.*

actual monopoly a real-world form of monopoly; a market in which there is a single seller, sellers in other markets may offer fairly good substitutes, potential competition cannot be ruled out, and the government protection that an actual monopoly may enjoy is not secure, as it may be taken away or altered.

adaptive expectations the view that the price level in the coming time period will be the same as the current price level.

administrative protection a general term covering forms of protection other than tariffs and quotas on imports and subsidies to import-competing goods.

aggregate demand the total value of goods and services demanded in an economy, measured at some specified price level.

aggregate-demand curve a graphic illustration of the relationship between a change in the price level and the quantity of real national income and product demanded.

aggregate economic concentration the share of economic activity undertaken by the largest firms in a region of the world, in an economy, or in some major sector beyond traditional industry lines.

aggregate supply the total value of all goods and services supplied in an economy, measured at some specified price level.

aggregate-supply curve a graphic illustration of the relationship between the price level and the quantity of real national income and product supplied.

agricultural fundamentalism the doctrine or argument that since food is a necessity and since the countryside is the main market for the manufactured products of the city, farm revenue cannot fall below a certain percentage of national income or GNP without bringing on a depression.

alienation a psychological ailment expressed in the feeling of hostility or indifference to someone or something in one's society that is generally considered attractive to others in that society.

allocation function the function or role of government involving influence upon the kinds and quantities of different goods and services produced in the economy.

American Federation of Labor (AF of L) a federation of national unions established in 1886 to practice business unionism and merged with the CIO in 1955 to form the AF of L–CIO.

anarchist one who opposes all forms of government compulsion and favors a society organized on the basis of voluntary associations, which individuals can leave at any time.

antitrust policy the course of action (by the government) aimed at maintaining or restoring competition in markets.

appreciation (in foreign exchange rates) an increase in the foreign exchange value of a nation's money.

arbitrage the purchase of a product in one market for the purpose of immediately reselling it in another market in order to take advantage of a price difference.

arbitration a procedure for settling union-management disputes by having a neutral outside party make a decision that is binding on both sides.

area of inequality the space between a Lorenz curve and the diagonal line of perfect equality on a Lorenz curve diagram.

assets valuable items that are owned; balance sheet entries recording the values of items that are owned.

assumption a statement that is accepted as being true in order to set forth the limits of the variables in a theory.

automatic (or built-in) stabilizers provisions of tax and spending laws that work automatically to moderate expansions and contractions of the economy.

automatic transfer service (*ATS*) a procedure through which balances can be changed automatically from one account to another in a financial institution.

autonomous consumption expenditure the amount of planned consumption expenditure that is independent of the level of disposable personal income.

average fixed cost (*AFC*) the total fixed cost of a firm divided by the quantity level of its output in that period. It is also the difference between a firm's average total cost and its average variable cost.

average product the total product that a firm produces in a given period divided by the quantity of a variable input that it uses to produce it.

average revenue the total revenue of a firm in a given period divided by the quantity level of products that it sells in that period.

average total cost (*ATC*) the total cost of a firm in a given period divided by the quantity level of its output in that period.

average variable cost (*AVC*) the total variable cost of a firm in a given period divided by the quantity level of its output in that period. A firm's average variable cost plus its average fixed cost equals its average total cost.

B

balanced-budget multiplier a change in the equilibrium level of national income and product divided by the size of the (equal) changes in government purchases and net taxes that brought it about.

balance of payments account a record of transactions affecting the international demand and supply for a nation's money.

balance of trade the amount by which the value of a country's exports of goods exceeds the value of its imports of goods. It may be negative.

balance on current account the balance of payments account entry showing the extent to which credit items exceed debit items in a country's international transactions in goods, services, and unilateral transfers.

balance sheet an accounting report on the condition of a business firm or other organization as of the close of business on a particular date.

bank charter a document issued by a state or the federal government granting permission to engage in banking and specifying the terms and conditions of such permission.

bank examiner a government agent who investigates the condition and operation of a bank.

bank note   paper currency issued by a bank.

bankruptcy   a legal concept indicating a state of insolvency—of being unable to repay creditors.

bargaining unit   the workers for whom a particular union is bargaining and to whom a particular labor contract applies.

barometric firm price leadership   a condition in an oligopolistic industry in which one firm's price changes are followed by other firms in that industry because they respect the price leader and see its changes as being "correct" responses to market conditions.

barter   the exchange of one good or service for another without the use of money as a medium of exchange.

base period   the time period chosen as the reference period in constructing an index number.

basic balance of payments   the international balance of payments concept that adds a country's long-term private capital imports and subtracts that country's long-term private capital exports from its balance on current account.

basic human needs   amounts of food, clothing, shelter, education, health care, and access to public decision making considered to be necessary as a minimum before attention should be directed to conventional economic growth; a point of view that development is taking place only when a steadily falling percentage of the people of a country lacks good food, clean water, decent shelter, basic health care, elementary education, and a means of presenting their views to their government.

basing-point system   an industry agreement calling for each firm, no matter where it is located, to charge the same delivered price for a product.

beneficial externalities   See *externalities*.

benefit-cost analysis   a procedure for the systematic evaluation of the economic merits of a proposed undertaking.

benefit-received principle (of taxation)   a guide for taxation that advocates that the tax payment made by an individual or a firm should be related to the value of goods and services provided by the government to the taxpayer.

bilateral monopoly   a market situation in which a monopolist seller faces a monopsonist buyer.

black market   an illegal market in which goods or services are sold above a legally set maximum price. See also *ceiling price*.

Board of Governors (of the Federal Reserve System)   seven people, appointed by the President of the United States to establish policy for and supervise the operation of the Federal Reserve System.

bond   a certificate of indebtedness promising to repay a principal sum and interest on specified dates.

boycott   refusal to engage in trade with another country or firm in specific goods of that country or firm; in labor-management relations, an attempt by employees (or a union) to block the distribution and sale of an employer's product.

bracket creep   the effect that inflation has of pushing taxpayers into higher tax rate brackets and increasing the proportion of income payable under progressive income tax systems that are not indexed.

break-even point   in macroeconomics, the level of disposable personal income at which planned consumption expenditure equals disposable personal income and planned saving is zero; in microeconomics, a level of output at which a firm's total revenue is equal to its total cost.

Bretton Woods system   the rules and institutions established at Bretton Woods, New Hampshire, in 1944, to regulate the international economic system. The principal Bretton Woods institutions are the World Bank and the International Monetary Fund.

budget deficit   See *deficit*.

budget line   in the indifference analysis theory of consumer behavior, a line showing the combinations of goods and/or services measured on the axes that can be purchased by an individual who has a particular income and who faces particular prices for these goods and/or services.

buffer stocks   government holdings of farm products kept as reserves against periods of bad weather or other disasters to ensure an adequate supply. An "ever-normal granary" is a buffer stock of a basic grain such as wheat or rice.

building cycle   See *Kuznets cycle*.

built-in stabilizers   See *automatic stabilizers*.

bullionism   a seventeenth- and eighteenth-century school of economic thought that emphasized the accumulation of treasure.

burden (of a tax) a reduction in real income resulting from a tax.

business cycles expansions and contractions in the volume of aggregate economic activity that alternate with some regularity in an economy. Referred to as business "fluctuations" by those who wish to imply less regularity.

business unionism a union philosophy that relies on economic power to achieve goals of higher real wages and better working conditions.

buyer response bias the effect on the consumer price index of its failure to recognize that consumer buying patterns respond to changes in relative prices.

C

capital (or capital resources) a factor of production or resource that is composed of goods and skills that are used as inputs for production. Unlike the other resources, it must first be produced itself before it is available for use in further production. See also *human capital*.

capital account in balance of payments accounts, the record of international transactions in securities, long- and short-term loans, and deposits in financial institutions.

capital consumption allowance the national income accounting estimate of the value of capital goods (production equipment) used up in producing other goods. It is subtracted from gross national product to obtain net national product.

capital gain (or loss) the gain (or loss) from a change in the market value of an asset that takes place while it is owned by a given individual.

capital goods See *physical capital*.

capital resources See *capital*.

capitalist system an economic system in which most physical instruments of production are owned by private individuals and business firms.

capital/output ratio the value of capital used in production divided by the value of output produced per time period.

capital requirement (entry barrier) the minimum amount of money needed to acquire the capital goods necessary for a new firm to compete adequately with the established firms in an industry.

capital resources See *capital; physical capital*.

capital skills See *human capital*.

cartel an organization that coordinates and limits the outputs of producers for the purpose of raising the price of the product and the profits of the producers.

ceiling price a maximum price at which a product can legally be sold. A meaningful ceiling price is set below the equilibrium price that would otherwise be established in that market.

Celler-Kefauver Antimerger Amendment a 1950 amendment to the Clayton Act, which added coverage of asset acquisitions and eliminated the wording that made the Act applicable only to horizontal mergers.

ceteris paribus a Latin phrase meaning "other things being equal," used in economic theorizing to hold constant all variables but those being considered.

checkable accounts See *transactions accounts*.

checkoff a form of union security that calls for the employer to deduct union dues from workers' paychecks and to pay those dues directly to the union.

circular flow model a diagram illustrating the macroeconomic functioning of an economy as a system in which funds that flow from business firms to households constitute the national income and flows from households to business firms through various channels make up the national product.

Civil Rights Act a law passed by the U.S. Congress in 1964. Title VII prohibits discrimination in hiring, firing, or promotions based on race, color, religion, sex, or national origin.

civilian employment rate the number of civilians employed as a percent of the total civilian noninstitutional population age 16 years and over.

civilian labor force the noninstitutional civilian population age 16 and over who are willing and able to work and who are either employed or actively seeking employment.

civilian labor force participation rate the percentage of the civilian noninstitutional population age 16 or older that is working or looking for work.

civilian unemployment rate the percentage of the civilian labor force that is unemployed according to official statistics.

classical economics the school of economic thought, based on the ideas of Adam Smith (1723–1790), David

Ricardo (1771–1823), and their successors, which was prominent in the first half of the nineteenth century.

Clayton Act a law passed by the U.S. Congress in 1914 to control anticompetitive price discrimination, mergers, exclusive dealing and tying arrangements, and interlocking directorates. It also excluded trade union activities from the scope of the antitrust laws.

closed economy a country that severely restricts trade across its borders.

closed shop a form of union security arrangement requiring that a person must be a member of a certain union before he or she can be hired. It is illegal under the Taft-Hartley Act of 1947.

collective bargaining the approach used by labor unions to negotiate with employers or their representatives.

collective goods and services goods and services which, by their nature, must be consumed in common by all people in an area.

collectivist system an economic system in which land and physical instruments of production are owned by collective agencies, such as the government or labor organizations, not by private individuals or business firms.

collusion (or collusive agreement) an agreement among buyers, sellers, and/or outsiders upon a particular course of action. Firms may collude to gain monopoly control in order to achieve high economic profit. See also *price fixing*.

commercial bank a financial institution that provides a wide range of services including checking accounts.

commercial treaty an agreement between countries dealing with economic and trade relations.

commission a charge made by a stockbroker for services rendered in carrying out a transaction.

Common Market a term generally used in reference to the European Community, which is a customs union of nations in Europe.

common property a legal arrangement that gives everyone equal rights to particular resources.

commune a cooperative farm or other collectively organized unit.

communist a socialist who believes that after a few generations of near-worldwide socialism, socialist economies will reach a stage of communism where most or all important goods will be free and scarcity will have been eliminated. Violence, revolution, and dictatorship are accepted means to that end.

comparable worth basing pay in different occupations on scores or point systems weighing, for example, the arduousness of the work, education requirements, and so on.

comparative advantage a principle of international trade that explains which commodities a given country is likely to import and export.

competition used in two different senses in economics: (1) rivalry among sellers or buyers; striving among a number of rivals in a contest aimed at purchasing or selling a particular product; (2) the market structure resulting from pure competition.

competitive depreciation a situation in which countries contest with each other in trying to increase exports and reduce imports by lowering the foreign exchange value of their monies.

complements (or complementary goods) products that are used in conjunction with each other such as automobiles and gasoline or cameras and film.

concentration ratio a measure that expresses the percentage share of some key variable such as sales or assets accounted for by the largest firms. See also *economic concentration*.

concessional loan credit extended on terms that are more favorable to the borrower than are available in loanable funds markets; typically, long-term development loans to LDCs at interest rates well below international market rates.

condition of entry the "extent to which established sellers can persistently raise their prices above a competitive level without attracting new firms to enter the industry" (Bain, *Barriers to New Competition*).

conglomerate merger the acquisition by a firm of another firm engaged in a different industry.

Congress of Industrial Organizations (CIO) a federation of national industrial unions established in 1938 and merged with the AF of L in 1955.

conspicuous consumption the use of certain goods and services to display the owner's wealth and to gain prestige and the envy of others.

constant capital a Marxian concept describing the labor hours embodied in raw materials and in the depreciation of machinery and other long-lived capital goods.

constant dollars   dollars adjusted by an index number to base year purchasing power.

constant returns to scale   long-run returns when an increase in the level of output of a firm is exactly proportionate to the increase in that firm's inputs.

consumer equilibrium   the condition existing when an individual has made all purchases and finds that the marginal utility per dollar spent for each good or service is the same. Maximum possible utility and satisfaction are realized. *Consumer equilibrium* (or *consumer equilibrium rule* in the theory of indifference analysis): the condition achieved when an individual consumes the combination of goods and services indicated at the point where his or her budget line is tangent to one of his or her indifference curves.

consumer price index (CPI)   an index number representing a weighted average of the prices of all goods and services purchased by representative families in an economy; often called the cost-of-living index, used to measure changes in the cost of purchasing a group of basic consumer goods and services.

consumer rationality   See *rational consumer.*

consumer sovereignty   a condition in which the consumer is free to determine the mix of goods and services that he or she will purchase, subject only to income limitations and prices to be paid.

consumers' surplus   the difference between the amount that a consumer pays for purchases of a product and the total utility obtained from these products by that consumer; the benefit that consumers gain from being able to buy many units of a good or service at the price they are willing to pay for the last unit consumed.

consumption   expenditure by households and individuals on goods and services; household use of goods and services.

consumption function   the relationship between the level of disposable personal income and the amount of planned expenditures by households on currently produced consumer goods and services.

contestable markets   markets that are very easy to enter and leave. Such markets may be actual monopolies, but the ease of potential entry makes them poor candidates for government regulation.

contractionary gap   a situation in which the predicted

equilibrium level of national income and product in the economy is lower than the target level.

contraction phase   the portion of a business cycle or fluctuation in which the volume of economic activity in an economy is steadily falling.

controls   See *price controls.*

corporation   a business firm chartered by the government and established as a legal person separate from its owners and managers; a common feature is limited liability for individual shareholders.

corporation income tax   a tax based on the net income of corporations.

corrective tax   a tax on a particular good or service imposed for the purpose of correcting for resource misallocations due to harmful externalities.

cost   See *opportunity cost.*

cost of living adjustment (COLA)   a provision in a labor contract specifying automatic changes in wage rates based on changes in an index number of prices.

cost of living index   See *consumer price index.*

cost-plus pricing principle   a rule of thumb practiced in some industries in which firms determine their selling price by adding a uniform percentage to certain elements of average total cost.

cost-push inflation   a rise in the price level due to a leftward shift in the short-run aggregate-supply curve.

Council of Economic Advisers   three persons appointed by the President under the authority of the Employment Act of 1946, whose job is to conduct research and to advise the President on economic policy.

countertrade   a fancy name for barter.

craft union   a union representing a particular type of skilled worker such as carpenters, typographers, or plumbers.

credit   an amount of money loaned; also, a positive accounting entry.

cross demand   the relationship between the price of one product and the quantity demanded of another product.

cross elasticity of demand   the relationship of the percentage change in the quantity demanded of a product and the percentage change in the price of a different product.

crowding out the reduction in planned investment that takes place when real interest rates rise because of government borrowing to finance budget deficits.

currency paper money usually issued by a government or central bank and given legal tender status.

current dollars dollars with purchasing power based on the price level prevailing at the time when a purchase is made or income is received.

customs union a form of economic integration among a group of countries that establishes a common tariff against nonmembers.

cycles See *business cycles.*

cyclical unemployment joblessness that arises because there are not enough job openings at current wage rates for all those qualified to fill them. See also *macroeconomic unemployment.*

D

debit a negative entry in an accounting system.

debt renegotiation changing the terms of existing loans, usually by extending or "stretching out" repayment dates without increases in nominal interest rates.

decelerating inflation a situation in which the rate of inflation is falling. See *disinflation.*

decision-making lag the time required to debate alternative remedies for economic problems and to choose among them.

deficiency payment In U.S. farm programs, a payment to a farmer from the government equal to the difference between the target price and the support range for quantities sold by the farmer.

deficit a state of budget imbalance in which expenditures exceed receipts; in balance of payments accounting, a condition in which negative or debit entries exceed positive or credit entries.

deflation a sustained decrease in the general level of prices, usually measured by the rate of change in some index number.

demand the willingness and ability to buy at certain prices. See also *individual consumer demand, market demand, quantity demanded.*

demand curve graph of a demand schedule; a curve illustrating the quantities of a good or service that are demanded at various possible prices.

demand deposits funds placed with a financial institution under terms that require the institution to pay out upon the demand of the depositor. A type of checkable account or transaction account.

demand for money the quantity of the monetary unit desired to be held as cash balances. See *precautionary, speculative,* and *transactions demands for money.*

demand-for-money curve the relationship between the rate of interest and the quantity of money demanded.

demand schedule a table showing the relationship between different prices of a good or service and the quantity demanded of that good or service at each of these prices.

demand-side economics an approach to macroeconomic analysis that emphasizes the aggregate-demand curve and includes both Keynesian and monetarist positions.

dependencia (theory of underdevelopment) the theory that countries with an early advantage in military technology used this power to impose domination over other countries and to prevent them from developing by taking their resources, denying them technological knowledge, and shifting the terms of trade against them.

dependent variable a variable that depends upon some other variable or variables in a functional relationship.

depletion allowance a provision of income taxation permitting resource owners to deduct from taxable income part of the value of resources that are extracted from the earth.

deposit-contraction process the sequence of events through which a withdrawal of funds from the banking system leads to a contraction of the total amount of checkable account balances.

deposit-expansion factor the ratio between the amount of a change in total checkable account balances and the amount of a new deposit that caused that change. The factor is estimated to be approximately equal to the reciprocal of the reserve ratio.

deposit-expansion process the sequence of events through which a new deposit in the banking system leads to an increase in the amount of checkable account balances.

deposit insurance insurance issued by the Federal Deposit Insurance Corporation or other agencies to protect depositors from loss in the event of the failure of a financial institution.

depository institutions institutions that accept deposits of funds from customers.

Depository Institutions Deregulation and Monetary Control Act of 1980 legislation that, among other things, required the elimination, over a six-year period, of upper limits on interest rates payable on deposits in depository institutions. See also *Monetary Control Act of 1980*.

depreciation the decline in the market value of a capital good as it wears out or becomes old-fashioned and out-of-date. In foreign exchange theory, a decline in the foreign exchange value of a nation's money.

depression severe contraction phase of a business cycle involving high rates of unemployment and a decline in national income.

deregulation the repeal of monopoly regulation.

derived demand a demand for a resource or factor of production that arises because of the demand for a product that it helps to produce.

desired excess reserves excess reserves maintained by banks to enable them to respond easily to unanticipated withdrawals or requests for loans.

devaluation the lowering of the foreign exchange value of a currency by reducing the amount of gold that will be exchanged for it.

diminishing marginal utility the assumption in the theory of utility analysis that during some specified time period an individual's added satisfaction diminishes as he or she purchases additional units of the same good or service.

diminishing returns decreases in marginal product that eventually set in when a variable input is successively added to one or more fixed inputs.

direct relationship (or positive relationship) a relationship in which the dependent and independent variables change in the same direction.

direct transmission mechanism the means whereby changes in the money supply affect the equilibrium level of national income and product through planned consumption expenditure with no necessary change in interest rates.

dirty float a situation in which official exchange rates among currencies are not fixed but governments intervene in exchange markets from time to time to influence foreign exchange rates.

discounting the practice of purchasing securities or promissory notes for less than their maturity values; a procedure through which a Federal Reserve Bank makes loans to member banks; also, the process of calculating the present value of payments to be received in the future.

discount rate the rate of interest used in determining the price that will be paid when securities or promises to pay are purchased by a Federal Reserve Bank from a member bank.

discouraged workers people who have stopped searching for work because they believe there is little chance of finding a job; they are not counted in official measurements of the labor force.

discrimination the practice of treating persons differently on the basis of their personal characteristics, as in offering different economic opportunities on the basis of sex, race, or ethnic origin. See also *price discrimination*.

diseconomies of scale long-run returns resulting when an increase in the output level of a firm is less than proportionate to the increase in that firm's inputs; also called decreasing returns or increasing long-run average total cost.

disequilibrium a state in which opposing forces are not in balance, so that there is a tendency for change to take place.

disinflation a reduction in the rate of increase in the price level; a lowering of the rate of inflation.

disintermediation the widespread withdrawal of funds from financial institutions that may occur when the limits on interest rates payable by these institutions are lower than rates of return that can be obtained elsewhere.

disinvestment a reduction in the stock of capital goods or inventories.

dismal science the label attached to economics in the nineteenth century because of forecasts of subsistence wages and diminishing returns.

displacement effect a change in one component of

planned expenditure that arises because of and offsets an opposite change in some other component.

disposable personal income (DPI) the amount of personal income that remains after personal taxes and certain nontax items are subtracted. It is the amount available to households for either saving or consumption spending.

dissaving negative saving; financing current consumption by borrowing or by drawing from past savings.

distribution function the function or role of government involving changes in the amount of income or wealth inequality among people in the society.

dividends distributions of money or additional stock from a corporation to its shareholders.

division of labor labor specialization; the assignment of tasks among workers.

do-it-yourself production production without exchange, such as growing food in a family garden plot; often not included in official measures of national income and product.

dominant firm price leadership a condition in an oligopolistic industry where one firm is so powerful that other firms follow the price that it sets.

dumping the sale of some product abroad at an unfairly low price, as measured against its domestic price.

duopoly an oligopoly made up of two firms.

E

easy entry the absence of entry barriers in an industry.

econometrics an aspect of economics that combines theory, mathematics, and statistics to analyze economic questions.

economic concentration the control of a particular economic activity in terms of the number or percentage of firms in an industry, in a sector of the economy, in an entire economy, or in a region of the world.

economic development economic growth plus other changes that are judged to constitute progress or to make life better; progress in some sense that makes life better in an economy or society and brings gains in welfare for the people.

economic dualism a situation that frequently arises in developing countries in which a relatively modern and prosperous economy, often urban, exists while most of the country, especially the rural areas, continues in age-old patterns of poverty.

economic earnings (also economic rent) the part of the earnings of a resource that is not required to keep that resource at its present use.

economic efficiency the lowest dollar cost of inputs that a firm requires to produce a certain amount of output.

economic growth increasing per capita real output in an economy.

economic loss an amount of accounting profit or loss that is less than normal profit.

economic maldistribution a division of income and wealth among individuals and groups that has an undesirable effect on the operation of the economic system.

economic profit an amount of accounting profit that is greater than normal profit.

economic rationality an assumption made in many economic theories that people can and will take actions that will make them better off or will prevent them from becoming worse off.

economic rent See *economic earnings*.

economics the social science concerned with using or administering scarce resources so as to attain the greatest or maximum fulfillment of society's wants; a method rather than a doctrine, an apparatus of the mind, a technique of thinking that helps its possessor to draw correct conclusions.

economic systems the combinations of institutions that different societies have developed to deal with economic problems.

economic theory See *model, theory*.

economies of scale long-run returns occurring when an increase in the output level of a firm is more than proportionate to the increase in that firm's inputs; also called increasing returns to scale or decreasing long-run average total cost.

effective full employment the level of employment that exists when an economy is in long-run macroeconomic equilibrium. See also *natural rate of unemployment*.

effective protection the tariff rate on a product, reduced by the tariffs on raw materials and intermediate products that go into it, with the result expressed as a percentage of the value added by the producers of that product.

efficiency   See *economic efficiency, technical efficiency*.

effluent charge   a price that is charged for depositing waste in the earth or its atmosphere.

elastic demand   a condition existing whenever the percentage response in the quantity demanded is greater than the percentage change in the price that caused it.

elasticity   a measure that relates the percentage change in quantity to the percentage change in price or income that caused it.

elasticity coefficient   the numerical value of elasticity.

elasticity of demand   See *cross elasticity of demand, income elasticity of demand, price elasticity of demand*.

elasticity of supply   See *price elasticity of supply*.

elastic supply   a condition existing whenever the percentage response in the quantity supplied is greater than the percentage change in the price that caused it.

Employment Act of 1946   landmark legislation through which the U.S. government announced its goals and established procedures to promote maximum employment, production, and purchasing power.

employment rate   See *civilian employment rate*.

Engels' Law   the tendency for the percentage of a family's budget spent for food to decline as its income rises.

enterpriser (or entrepreneur)   one of the factors of production or resources employed in production; a person who visualizes needs and takes the necessary action to initiate or change the process by which they will be met or the products used to meet them.

entitlements   certificates used in the United States during the 1970s authorizing the purchase of oil from domestic producers at controlled prices, which were lower than the prices of oil from other sources; government transfer payments, the amount of which has been connected to events or circumstances in such a way that the recipients understand that the payment is assured once these conditions are met.

entrepreneur   See *enterpriser*.

entry   the act of coming into an industry by a new firm which adds capacity to that industry.

entry barriers   See *absolute amount of cost difference entry barrier, capital requirement entry barrier, minimum optimal scale effect entry barrier, product differentiation entry barrier*.

equation of exchange   the statement that the quantity of money in the economy multiplied by the number of times the average dollar is used each year to purchase newly produced final products must be equal to the quantity of these final products multiplied by their average price. The equation is $MV = PQ$.

equilibrium   a state of balance in which the forces for change within a system offset each other so that there is no net tendency for change.

equilibrium price   a price that equates the quantity demanded with the quantity supplied in a market.

equilibrium quantity   a quantity of a good, service, or resource that equates the quantity supplied and the quantity demanded at a particular price in a market. The quantity supplied and demanded in a market when the equilibrium price prevails.

equity   fairness, justice; also, ownership share in a corporation.

ethical maldistribution   lack of correspondence between the actual income or wealth distribution and some standard of what is considered just or fair. See also *maldistribution*.

Eurocurrency   deposits of one nation's money in banks of a different nation, which provide reserves for loans and which are free from regulations.

European Community (EC)   a customs union among a number of nations in Europe.

European Currency Unit (ECU)   the monetary unit of the European Currency Union; a money of account that does not exist in a physical sense; a weighted average of the value of the monies of member countries.

ever-normal granary   See *buffer stocks*.

ex ante   identifying a viewpoint of planned or anticipated activity as distinguished from an *ex post* viewpoint, relating to past activity.

excess burden (of a tax)   the amount by which the burden or economic loss caused by a tax exceeds the amount of money received by the government from the tax.

excess demand   the amount by which the quantity

demanded of a good, service, or resource exceeds the quantity supplied at any specified price.

excess reserves official reserves over and above the reserve requirement.

excess supply the amount by which the quantity supplied of a good, service, or resource exceeds the quantity demanded at any specified price.

exchange controls restrictions on the purchase or sale of foreign exchange, such as requiring licenses to engage in this trade and/or applying different exchange rates to different transactions.

exchange value (of a currency) See *foreign exchange value.*

excise tax a tax imposed on the manufacture or sale of a product.

exclusive dealing arrangement an agreement that gives a firm the exclusive opportunity to obtain a product from a supplier within a specified geographic area, usually on the condition that it will not buy the products of competing suppliers.

exhaustible natural resources a gift of nature usable in production, the supply of which could be eliminated by human use.

exit a firm leaving an industry as a result of its inability to earn at least normal profit in the long run. See also *normal profit.*

expansionary gap a situation in which the predicted equilibrium level of national income and product in an economy is higher than the target level.

expansion phase the portion of a business cycle or fluctuation in which the volume of business activity in an economy is steadily increasing.

experience variables variables that oligopolists take into account in addition to consumer demand and cost variables. Examples include the previous reactions by rival firms to price changes in the industry, personality traits of key managers of rival firms, and the political consequences of the rivals' reactions.

explicit costs money payments by firms for the use of inputs to production.

exploitation restriction of some members of a society to an inferior income or welfare position; a wage rate that is less than the marginal revenue product.

exploitation rate (or rate of surplus value) a ratio representing the proportion of each hour of labor contributed to surplus value in Marxian economics.

exporting unemployment efforts to create jobs in the domestic economy by expanding exports and reducing imports, usually by trade restrictions and manipulation of foreign exchange rates.

exports goods and services sold to foreigners.

ex post identifying past actions, as distinguished from an *ex ante* viewpoint, which deals with planned or anticipated events.

external benefit a benefit experienced by someone not a party to a transaction; a benefit experienced by one receiving a beneficial or positive externality.

external cost a cost experienced by someone not a party to a transaction; a cost experienced by one suffering a negative externality.

external growth See *merger.*

externalities costs or benefits from the consumption or production of a good or service affecting people other than the buyer and seller of the good or service.

F

factor price equilization theorem a proposition stating that free trade tends to equalize input prices among trading countries.

factors of production (or resources) inputs to production that are used to create goods and services (labor, entrepreneurship, capital, natural resources).

fallacy of composition the false notion that what is true for one part is necessarily true for the whole, or vice versa.

farm parity the relationship between the purchasing power or real income of farmers compared with the purchasing power or real income of others in the economy.

favorable balance (of trade) a positive, credit, or surplus balance in a country's international transactions in merchandise.

featherbedding the practice of forcing an employer to pay for services that workers do not actually perform.

Federal Deposit Insurance Corporation (FDIC) a U.S. government agency that insures deposits in certain financial institutions.

federal funds member banks' official reserve deposits with a Federal Reserve Bank.

GLOSSARY

federal funds rate the rate of interest charged when federal funds (reserve deposits at the Federal Reserve Bank) are loaned by one bank to another.

Federal Open Market Committee (FOMC) twelve people, including the seven members of the Board of Governors of the Federal Reserve System, who are responsible for directing the buying and selling of securities for the system.

Federal Reserve Banks the twelve district banks that together constitute the Federal Reserve System.

Federal Reserve Note currency issued by Federal Reserve Banks.

Federal Reserve System twelve district Federal Reserve Banks under the direction of policies set by its Board of Governors, appointed by the President of the United States, and fulfilling the functions of a central bank.

federal system a governmental structure formed through the consolidation of several previously separate states.

Federal Trade Commission (FTC) a federal agency established in 1914 which enforces legislation aimed at deterring unfair methods of competition and restraint of trade.

Federal Trade Commission Act a law passed by the U.S. Congress in 1914 to prohibit unfair methods of competition among firms, and establish the Federal Trade Commission.

financial markets the organized interaction of buyers and sellers of financial assets.

fine tuning an approach to macroeconomic policy that calls for frequent adjustments in government spending, taxing, open market operations, and so forth, aimed at holding the economy near some target level of national income and product, employment, price level, foreign exchange rates, and interest rates.

firm a business that combines factors of production or resources—natural resources, capital, labor, and entrepreneurship—to produce certain goods or services.

First World the more-developed countries of Western Europe and North America plus Australia, Japan, and New Zealand.

fiscal related to the taxing and spending operations of a government.

fiscal federalism a system under which financing responsibilities are shared among different levels of government; the study of ways to allocate financial responsibilities among different levels of government.

fiscal instruments taxing and spending devices used to influence the performance of the economy. Examples are tax rates and government purchases.

fixed cost See *total fixed cost.*

fixed exchange rate the exchange value at which a nation's currency is held through government buying and/or selling of official reserves in the foreign exchange market, or through the operation of a metallic standard.

flat tax a tax without any graduation of rates; a tax with a single rate applicable to all amounts of the tax base.

flexible exchange rates See *free exchange rates.*

floating exchange rates See *free exchange rates.*

floor price (or support price) a minimum price at which a product may legally be sold. A meaningful floor price is set above the equilibrium price that would otherwise be established in that market.

fluctuations See *business cycles.*

foreign aid a unilateral transfer from one nation to another, usually as an encouragement to economic development.

foreign exchange the money of other countries.

foreign exchange markets markets in which the monies of different countries are bought and sold.

foreign exchange value the price of one nation's monetary unit in terms of the monetary units of another country or group of countries, or a weighted average of such monetary units.

45-degree line a straight line drawn at a 45-degree angle from the origin of a diagram, such as the Keynesian cross.

Fourth World those Third World countries that are the "poorest of the poor."

fractional reserves See *partial reserves.*

free enterprise freedom of opportunity to pursue any business venture; no legal restrictions to entry.

free (or floating or flexible) exchange rates foreign exchange rates that can move up or down in response to shifts in demand and supply arising from international trading and investment and that are not purposefully influenced by governmental action.

free market a market in which the economic forces of demand and supply have the full opportunity to alter the price.

free rider problem the fact that people usually will not voluntarily pay for a good or service if they believe that they can consume it without paying.

free trade area a form of economic integration among a group of countries that allows each member to maintain its own set of tariffs, quotas, etc., against nonmembers.

frictional unemployment joblessness that arises because time is required to change from one job to another.

fringe benefit a form of worker compensation other than wages, such as a pension, life insurance, health plan, vacation, and holidays.

full employment See *absolute full employment* and *effective full employment.*

Full Employment and Balanced Growth Act (1978) See *Humphrey-Hawkins Act.*

full-employment balanced-budget (rule) a policy guideline under which Congress would decide on the amount of government purchases that voters would want at effective full employment, and would set tax rates and transfer payment systems so that net taxes would balance government purchases at effective full employment. Neither the tax rates nor programs would be changed because of business cycle conditions. Automatic stabilizers would moderate economic fluctuations.

function the way in which one variable depends on some other variable or variables.

functional distribution of income the division of income between different types of production inputs, such as labor and property.

G

game theory an approach to analyzing competition in an oligopoly market that likens economic behavior to a game of cards (like poker) or chess, and even to war.

Garn–St. Germaine Depository Institutions Act (1982)

provided aid for depository institutions in distress and expanded the lending authority of thrift institutions.

General Agreement on Tariffs and Trade (GATT) an agreement, mainly between the industrial countries of North America, Western Europe, and Japan for the gradual liberalization of world trade.

general equilibrium analysis a method of analysis that takes into account all the different effects related to the specific variables that are being studied.

general fund a budget category denoting a source of financing available for a variety of expenditures.

generalized (macroeconomic) protection attempts by a country to deal with its international balance of payments problems by imposing a flat overall tax on all imports or by imposing restrictions on the export of capital.

general price level an average of all prices in the economy.

geographic market extension conglomerate merger the acquisition by a firm of another firm engaged in the same activity, existing on the same level, but serving a different geographic market.

Gini ratio a measure of income inequality computed by dividing the area between a Lorenz curve and the line of equality by the entire area under the line of equality on a Lorenz curve diagram. See also *Lorenz curve.*

Glass-Steagall Act (1932) legislation affecting the banking industry and permitting Federal Reserve Banks to use government securities as backing for Federal Reserve Notes.

gold standard a monetary system featuring a constant price of gold in units of a country's currency; for example, a system in which the monetary authorities of a country promise to exchange a specified amount of gold per unit of the country's currency.

good a tangible product that is considered desirable or "good" by those who own it or could acquire it.

Gosplan the central planning agency of the Soviet Union.

government purchases currently produced goods and services bought by government.

Gramm-Rudman-Hollings Act legislation passed by the U.S. Congress in 1985 establishing deficit reduction targets and procedures to reach these targets.

GLOSSARY

grants-in-aid money given by a superior government, such as the federal or a state government, to a subordinate government, such as a state or local government.

Great Depression the period of severe unemployment, falling price level, and economic stagnation extending through the decade following the stock market crash of 1929.

greenbacks originally, inconvertible currency issued by the U.S. Treasury during the Civil War; sometimes used in reference to any U.S. currency.

Green Revolution the development and propagation of high-yielding dwarf and hybrid varieties of wheat and rice, which led to high hopes in the 1960s for alleviating world hunger.

Gresham's Law the statement that the base (less valuable) money will always drive the dear (more valuable) money out of circulation and into hoards.

gross national product (GNP) the total of all spending—by consumers, business firms, governments, and (net) foreigners—to purchase currently produced goods and services.

growthmanship an overemphasis on measured economic growth.

guilds predecessors of modern unions; charitable and mutual-aid societies made up of workers in certain crafts who after a time took on certain activities that we now associate with unions, but including master craftsmen who employed journeymen and apprentices.

H

Herfindahl-Hirschman Index (HHI) a measure of market economic concentration derived by summing the squares of the individual market shares of all the firms in a market.

horizontal merger the acquisition by a firm of another firm engaged in the same activity, existing on the same level, and serving the same geographic market.

household a group living together and pooling major expenses in the same dwelling unit. Usually, members are related by blood, marriage, or adoption.

human capital (or capital skills) the portion of the productive power of individuals that has been developed through expenditures for education, job training, and health care.

Humphrey-Hawkins Act legislation, passed by the U.S. Congress in 1978, establishing goals in terms of price stability and low unemployment, but providing no enforcement mechanism.

hyperdeflation a situation in which the pessimism generated by unemployment and falling prices induces a leftward shift in the aggregate-demand curve, so that a recession feeds on itself, becomes worse, and is not alleviated by falling prices.

hyperinflation a situation in which the price level is rising rapidly, causing an increase in the velocity of circulation of money, and usually culminating in the breakdown of the monetary system.

I

identity an equation whose two sides are equal by definition.

immature creditor the international trade and finance situation of a country in the stage of its economic development in which its current balance is positive and its capital balance negative. Its exports of capital exceed return flows to it from investments abroad.

immature debtor the international trade and finance situation of a country in an early stage of its economic development in which its current balance is negative and its capital balance is positive.

imperative planning a rigorous form of planning under which failure to reach an important plan target may be treated as a criminal offense.

implementation lag the time required for programs to take effect, after they have been decided upon.

implicit costs costs incurred by firms for which no money payment is made, usually because the firms are using resources which they own themselves.

implicit price deflator for GNP an index number used to compare GNP measured in current dollars with the amount that would have been needed to purchase the same goods at the prices existing in some base year.

imports goods and services and resources purchased from foreign suppliers.

income the amount of money or its equivalent received in exchange for services rendered, or as net receipts over costs of a firm.

income effect the effect that a change in a person's real income (resulting from a change in the price of a good or service that the person buys) has on the quantity that this person demands of that good or service.

income demand the relation between the quantity demanded for a product and the income level of consumers or potential consumers of that product.

income elasticity of demand the relationship between the percentage change in the quantity demanded of a product and the percentage change in the consumer's income.

incomes policy an application of wage and price controls in a coordinated attempt to reach a set of macroeconomic goals.

income statement (or profit and loss statement) an accounting report of the operations of a business firm over some specified period of time.

inconvertible currency a currency that cannot be used in international trading by a country's citizens without a special license.

increasing returns, short run gains in marginal product that often occur over low levels of output when a variable input is successively added to one or more fixed inputs.

increasing returns to scale See *economies of scale.*

increasing total utility the assumption in utility analysis theory that during some specified time period an individual's total satisfaction increases as he or she consumes additional units of the same good or service.

independent variable the variable on which another variable depends in a functional relationship.

indexing a system that automatically builds an inflation or deflation adjustment into agreements for wage rates, savings accounts, taxes, interest rates, bond values, and other contracts in an economy.

index number a number that expresses a particular value in relation to some other value that has been specified as a base or reference value.

indicative planning a form of planning that operates primarily by convincing participants of a plan's economic benefits to them.

indifference curve analysis a theory of consumer behavior that expresses consumers' tastes in curves based on the ranking of combinations of goods and/or services in order of preference, but avoids the notion of measurable utility.

indifference curve a curve representing different combinations of goods and/or services that satisfy a consumer equally well.

indifference map a number of indifference curves representing an individual's preferences.

indirect business taxes in national income accounting, taxes imposed on the production or sale of goods and services; excise, sales, and property taxes.

individual consumer demand the amount of a good or service that an individual consumer wants and is able to purchase at a particular moment at each possible price that might be charged for that good or service.

individual firm supply the amount of a good or service that an individual business firm is willing and able to sell at a particular moment at each possible price that it might receive for that good or service.

individual maldistribution an unsatisfactory situation in respect to the particular people at the upper and lower ends of the income or wealth distribution.

induced expenditure in Keynesian analysis, a change in the volume of planned consumption, investment, government purchases, exports, or imports caused by a change in level of national income and illustrated as a movement along the $C + I + G + X - Im$ curve.

industrial union a union representing all the workers in an industry, such as auto workers, mine workers, or clothing workers.

industry a group of competing firms.

inelastic demand a condition existing whenever the percentage response in quantity demanded is less than the percentage change in the price that caused it.

inelastic supply a condition existing whenever the percentage response in the quantity supplied is less than the percentage change in the price that caused it.

infant industry (argument for protection) a proposal for temporarily protecting a country's new industries to give them time to catch up with more efficient foreign industries.

inferior good or service a good or service for which there is a negative relationship between quantity demanded and income level.

infinitely elastic See *perfectly elastic.*

infinitely elastic supply a condition existing when a price change causes an infinite response in the quantity supplied.

inflation a significant and sustained increase in the general level of prices, usually measured by the rate of change in some price index number.

inflationary expectations anticipations that the price level will rise in the near future.

inflation rate the rate of change in the index number that has been selected for measuring the general price level.

infrastructure See *social overhead capital.*

injections expenditures for currently produced goods and services except those for domestic consumption.

injunction a court order enjoining or prohibiting a person or firm from following a specific course of action.

innovation the development of an invention from the original discovery to a practical use.

innovator one who brings an invention out of the laboratory, makes it practical, and applies it to actual production.

input-output analysis a technique, developed by Wassily Leontief, that uses matrix algebra to solve production planning problems, including the relation between economic sectors.

inputs (or factors of production or resources) the labor, entrepreneurship, natural resources, and capital that are used in production.

interdependence a small enough number of firms in an industry to require that each considers its rivals' reactions to any action that it is thinking of taking; the most important characteristic of an oligopoly industry.

interest (or interest payment) the return or payment to capital in production.

interest rate the annual interest payment expressed as a percentage of the amount loaned.

interest rate parity a condition in international capital account transactions when the domestic money rate of return would be the same as the foreign money rate of return after conversion to domestic money.

interlocking directorates the potentially anticompetitive practice of having the same person serve on the boards of directors of two or more competing firms.

intermediate product an output which itself becomes an input in further production.

internal growth the growth of a firm through building from within as contrasted to acquiring other firms.

international fundamentalism an explanation for the Great Depression asserting that the U.S. economy was not able to support prosperity throughout the world and that recession elsewhere spread to the United States.

International Monetary Fund (IMF) an organization established in 1944 for the purpose of stabilizing exchange rates in international trade; a pool of gold and foreign exchange from which loans can be made to help countries stabilize foreign exchange rates. See also *Bretton Woods system.*

International Trade Organization (ITO) an organization proposed by "free world" members of the United Nations aimed at making world trade freer and less discriminatory. Never went into operation.

invention discovery of a new product or process.

inventor one who discovers or devises a new or improved process or product.

inventory stocks of unsold goods and resources.

inventory cycle See *Kitchin cycle.*

inverse relationship (or negative relationship) a relationship in which the dependent and independent variables change in opposite directions.

investment the creation of capital; in national income accounting, the purchase of currently produced capital goods and additions to inventories.

investment decision a decision as to whether to provide for the creation of new capital and, if so, how much.

investment income receipts from capital goods or from securities, usually in the form of dividends or interest.

iron law of wages the doctrine that population growth will push wages down to the subsistence level.

isocost line a line showing the combinations of inputs that a firm can buy for a given cost outlay.

isoquant same quantity; a curve (derived from a firm's production function) that shows all of the technically efficient combinations of inputs for producing a particular quantity of output.

isoquant map a number of isoquants (each for a different quantity of output that a firm might produce).

J

job security   in collective bargaining agreements, conditions for hiring, job continuance, and the handling of grievances.

Joint Economic Committee   a committee of the Congress established under the Employment Act of 1946 to conduct research and advise the Congress on economic policy.

Juglar cycle   a business fluctuation that has a period of some seven to ten years and that has been a prominent feature in economic history.

jurisdictional strike   a strike concerning which union shall represent a given group of workers.

K

Keynes effect   the relationship between the price level and the quantity of real national income and product demanded that arises because of an induced change in real rates of interest.

Keynesian   a person who accepts the teachings of John Maynard Keynes. One who believes that government purchases and tax collections are key instruments of macroeconomic policy.

Keynesian cross   graphic representation of a relationship between the flow of planned expenditure and the level of national income and product.

Keynesian economics   the school of economic thought based on the work of John Maynard Keynes (1883–1946), particularly *The General Theory of Employment, Interest and Money* (1936).

Keynesian-monetarist debate   an extended discussion among macroeconomists concerning the best demand-side instruments to use in carrying out macroeconomic policy.

Keynesian theory   the systematic body of knowledge associated with the work of the British economist John Maynard Keynes.

Keynesian transmission mechanism   the means whereby changes in the real money supply affect the equilibrium level of national income and product through changes in interest rates and planned investment expenditure.

kinked demand curve   a curve (characteristic of some oligopolistic industries) made up of two demand segments divided at the existing price, with the segment at lower prices less elastic than the segment at higher prices.

Kitchin cycle   a business cycle that has a length of some three to five years and that is believed to be connected with the alternate buildup and depletion of business inventories; sometimes called the *inventory cycle.*

Kondratieff cycle   a long wave or cycle of economic activity that has a length of 30 to 50 years and is sometimes thought to be associated with major technological innovations.

Knights of Labor, Noble Order of   one of the first national federations of unions in the United States. Established in 1869, it was the forerunner of the AF of L.

Kuznets cycle   a business cycle that lasts between 15 and 25 years and appears based on the construction and replacement of buildings and transportation facilities; also called the *building cycle.*

L

labor   the resource or factor of production that includes most forms of human activity directed toward production.

labor force   See *civilian labor force.*

Labor-Management Relations Act   See *Taft-Hartley Act.*

Labor-Management Reporting and Disclosure Act   See *Landrum-Griffin Act.*

labor mobility   the degree to which workers will move to available jobs or more attractive jobs.

labor resources   See *labor.*

labor union (or trade union)   a labor organization whose immediate objective is to improve the wage rates and the working conditions of its members.

Laffer curve   a curve representing a relationship between average tax rates and the amount of government net tax revenue collected, and suggesting that tax revenues will rise as average tax rates rise, but only up to a point. Beyond that point, higher tax rates will result in lower tax revenues.

laissez-faire   a policy position favoring the market economy and opposing interference in the economy by the government.

land the ground or the earth that makes up a large portion of the factor of production or resource called natural resources.

Landrum-Griffin Act (or Labor-Management Reporting and Disclosure Act) an act passed by the U.S. Congress in 1959 that set forth rules governing the relationship between union governments and their members.

Lange-Lerner theory a socialist plan that attempts to retain the advantages of competitive market economies.

leading links (system) a policy followed in Soviet planning that calls for the fulfillment of production plans for goods that the government considers most important even at the expense of other parts of the plan.

leakages uses of funds that take them out of the consumption path of the circular flow, such as net taxes, savings, or imports.

legal reserves See *official reserves*.

legal tender currency that, when offered in payment of an obligation, precludes the creditor from denying that payment was offered and from collecting further interest on the debt.

lender of last resort a responsibility of Federal Reserve Banks to make loans to member banks facing crisis situations.

less developed countries (LDCs) nations with levels of per capita income far below those in the industrialized or modern countries.

liabilities claims that outsiders have for payments from a business firm—usually the value of such claims as reported on a balance sheet.

Libermanism a policy position favoring a number of reforms aimed at introducing market-style decisions into Soviet-style planning.

libertarian one who fears government control of the economy, supports private ownership of the means of production and, in extreme cases, private control of money, defense, police protection, streets, sewers, and law-making and administration.

limited liability a characteristic of the corporate form of business that limits the responsibility of stockholders for losses suffered by the business.

limited life a condition in which a business firm does not continue to exist after the death or withdrawal of a proprietor or a partner.

linear relationship a relationship which, when plotted on a graph, will appear as a straight-line curve.

liquidity the ease with which an asset can be used in exchange or converted into a form that can be used in exchange.

liquidity crisis in Marxian terms, the long-term stagnation that results as capitalism matures. It is caused by the fall of the profit rate to a level that discourages investment and encourages hoarding.

liquidity trap a situation in which increases in the supply of money are absorbed into cash balances and do not lower the rate of interest or increase investment.

L (money supply concept) the M3 money supply plus U.S. Savings Bonds, some relatively liquid U.S. government securities, payment promises by large corporations, etc.

loanable funds money demanded and supplied for loans.

loanable funds market the arrangements and procedures for carrying out transactions between people who want to borrow money and people who want to lend money.

lockout a work stoppage in which the employer closes the plant to its workers.

locomotive theory the view that a large country, by expanding its economy and letting its inflation rate rise, can and should stimulate economic expansion in other countries.

long run in microeconomics, a period of time long enough to permit all changes that a firm wants to make within the limits of its existing production function; in macroeconomics, a period of time long enough to eliminate money illusion and wage-cost lags from price level changes.

long-run aggregate-supply curve the graphed representation of the relationship between changes in the price level and changes in the quantity of real national income and product supplied that arises as long as there is no change in physical production capability but when enough time has passed for people to eliminate wage-cost lag and money illusion.

long-run average total cost (*LRAC*) the long-run total cost of a firm divided by the quantity level of its output.

long-run consumption function the relationship between disposable personal income and planned consumption expenditure when the level of disposable personal income has existed for a long enough period of time for consumers to adjust to it.

long-run marginal cost (LRMC) the addition to a firm's long-run total cost when it produces one more unit of output.

long-run total cost (LRTC) the total cost of producing a certain level of output when a firm is able to vary all of its inputs.

Lorenz curve a curve that illustrates income inequality by plotting the cumulative percentage of total income received by successive percentages of the population, starting from the lowest-income persons and proceeding cumulatively upward. See also *Gini ratio.*

lower turning point the point in a business cycle when a contraction phase ends and an expansion phase begins.

M

macro-dot a combination of the real rate of interest and the volume of real national income and product such that the flow of planned expenditure exactly matches real production in an economy and the demand for the country's stock of money is equal to its supply.

macroeconomic equilibrium the situation in which the real national income and product demanded at a given price level is equal to the real national income and product supplied at that price level; the condition existing at the intersection of an aggregate-demand curve and an aggregate-supply curve.

macroeconomic planning planning that includes target quantities only for macroeconomic measures (national income and product; the division between consumption, investment, and government sectors; the supplies of money and credit; the government surplus or deficit; international balances; and interest rates) but not the composition of the aggregates.

macroeconomic protection See *generalized protection.*

macroeconomics the branch of economics that focuses on aggregate or grand total economic activity. Unemployment and inflation are major problems considered in macroeconomics.

macroeconomic unemployment unemployment that exists throughout the whole economy or affects many parts of the economy at the same time and is not related to particular decisions about what or how to produce. See also *cyclical unemployment.*

"magic wand" planning a plan built around a collection of projects and/or an attractive slogan, which promises good things but does not specify adequately any processes for achieving them.

maldistribution excessive inequality or equality of personal income or wealth. See also *economic maldistribution, ethical maldistribution,* and *individual maldistribution.*

Malthusian theory of population the proposition that population increases according to a geometric progression until stabilized by death rates, which rise because of inadequate food supplies.

marginal additional or incremental.

marginal analysis a method used by economists for predicting or evaluating outcomes that is based on the last unit added or the next unit to be added.

marginal benefit the additional advantage gained when one more unit of a good or service is consumed.

marginal cost (MC) the addition to total cost when one more unit of output is produced.

marginal factor cost (MFC) the extra cost that a firm incurs for an additional unit of a resource or factor of production.

marginal physical product (MPP) the additional output that a firm can produce by using one more unit of a resource or factor of production.

marginal product, short run the amount of extra output that results from the addition of one more unit of a variable input to one or more fixed inputs.

marginal propensity to consume (MPC) the fraction or percentage of a change in disposable personal income that appears as a change in planned consumption expenditure.

marginal propensity to save (MPS) the fraction or percentage of a change in disposable personal income that appears as a change in planned saving.

marginal revenue (MR) the extra revenue that a firm receives when it sells one more unit of output.

marginal revenue product (MRP) change in the total revenue of a firm resulting from the sale of the additional quantity of output that one more unit of a resource allows it to produce.

marginal tax rate the rate of income tax that applies to additional income received by an individual; the percentage of an additional dollar of income that would be payable in income tax.

marginal utility the additional utility gained from one more unit of a good or service.

margin requirements rules set down by the Federal Reserve Board specifying the minimum portion of the price of stock purchased that must be paid by the purchaser (not borrowed from the stockbroker).

market the organized action between potential buyers (market demand) and potential sellers (market supply) that permits trade.

market demand the sum of all the individual consumers' quantities demanded at particular prices for a particular product in a particular geographic area over some period of time.

market economic concentration the share of economic activity undertaken by the largest firms in a particular market or industry. See also *Herfindahl-Hirschman Index*.

market economy an economic system built around the unrestricted exchange of goods, services and resources.

market failure a market outcome judged to be inadequate or unacceptable in relation to some goal of the society.

market price the equilibrium price that tends to be established by the interaction of demand and supply for a specified product.

market socialism an adaptation of the microeconomics of pure competition to a socialist system.

market supply the sum of all of the individual firms' quantities supplied at particular prices of a particular good or service in a particular geographic area over some period of time.

materials balancing a planning technique that requires estimating potential supplies of and demands for each of a number of final and intermediate products taken separately.

mature creditor the international economic situation of a country in an advanced stage of its economic development, in which its current balance is negative and its capital balance is positive. Returns from previous investment abroad are greater than current capital exports (net of repayments).

mature debtor the international trade and finance situation of a country in an intermediate stage of economic development, in which its current balance is positive and its capital balance is negative. The return flow of capital to foreigners (repayment of past debts) exceeds net capital inflows from them.

mechanism (basis for classifying economic systems) procedures used for making economic decisions—for example, markets, planning, and tradition.

medium of exchange a function of money that enables people to trade with one another more easily, since they do not need to match their specific wants with those of other people.

member bank a commercial bank that is a member of the Federal Reserve System.

mercantilism an eighteenth-century school of economic thought that emphasized the achievement of economic power as a basis for military power. It emphasized high population and employment, low interest rates, accumulation of money, and strict regulation of trade, particularly international trade.

merger (or external growth or acquisition) the acquisition of one firm by another firm which adds to the acquiring firm's productive capacity.

microeconomics the branch of economics that focuses on the behavior of individual decision makers such as consumers, workers, business firms, and governments, assuming the major macroeconomic variables to be given. It focuses on how their behaviors affect the types of goods and services produced, the methods of production, and the distribution of income in the economy.

microeconomic unemployment unemployment that can be traced to decisions about what to produce or how to produce. It includes seasonal, frictional, and structural unemployment.

millage the rate of tax applied under a property tax, with one mil equal to one-tenth of one percent.

minimum optimal scale effect (entry barrier) the effect on the price of the product of an industry that results from adding the volume of output that a new firm of minimum optimal scale would supply if it enters that industry.

minimum wage   a wage rate set by government as the lowest that firms are allowed to pay.

mixed economy   an economic system combining significant elements of both planning and market modes of organization.

mobility   See *labor mobility.*

model   a formal statement of a theory.

modern monetarism   the school of economic thought which holds that, in the long run, changes in the money supply influence the general price level but do not significantly affect the level of real national income and product.

monetarism   the belief that the nominal money supply is usually more closely related to nominal national income and product than are nominal government expenditures and nominal investment expenditures.

monetarist   a person who believes that control of the money supply is an important element in macroeconomic policy.

monetary base   the total of bank reserves and coins and currency in circulation in the economy.

Monetary Control Act of 1980   legislation that broadened the authority of the Board of Governors of the Federal Reserve System, including the authority to set required reserve ratios for all institutions offering checking account services. The full name of the legislation is the Depository Institutions Deregulation and Monetary Control Act of 1980.

monetary growth rule   a policy guideline under which the money supply is increased at a constant rate without regard to cyclical fluctuations in the economy. The rate of money supply increase is to be approximately equal to the long-term growth trend in real productive capacity of the economy.

monetary instruments   controls over financial markets and intermediaries used to influence the performance of the economy. The principal monetary instruments are reserve requirements, open market operations, and discount rates.

monetary policy   a plan or a course of action governing the use of monetary instruments in an economy.

monetized debt   financial obligations that provide reserves to support money, as when loans provide a step in the expansion of bank deposits.

monetizing a public debt   supporting the price of public debt instruments by monetary expansion if necessary.

money   anything that is generally accepted in an economy as a medium of exchange, a unit of account, a store of purchasing power, and a standard for deferred payment.

money illusion   the belief that nominal values are the same as real values; a belief that changes in nominal values brought on by a price-level change are also changes in real values.

money income   receipts measured in terms of the monetary unit and not adjusted for changes in the price level.

money market   the interaction of the demand-for-money and the supply-of-money for use as a financial asset.

money multiplier   the ratio between the amount of money (such as M1) in the economy and the size of the monetary base.

money supply (stock of money)   the total quantity of money existing in an economy at a particular time (See *L, M1, M2,* and *M3* money supply concepts).

money supply curve   the graphic representation of the relationship between the real rate of interest and the total quantity of money existing in an economy.

M1 (money supply concept)   a money supply concept widely used by economists, consisting of coins and currency, demand deposits, and other checkable account balances.

M2 (money supply concept)   the M1 money supply plus savings accounts, small time deposits, short-term repurchase agreements, money market mutual funds, and Eurodollars.

M3 (money supply concept)   the M2 money supply plus fairly long-term repurchase agreements, large time deposits, and certain other assets.

monopolistic competition   a market structure with a large number of sellers, some product differentiation, and fairly easy entry and exit.

monopoly   a market in which there is only a single seller. See also *actual monopoly, pure monopoly.*

monopoly control (or monopoly power)   the degree of control or power that a firm has over the price of the product it sells. Varying degrees are possessed by all but purely competitive firms.

monopoly regulation   rules and laws that apply to firms granted monopoly status by the government and that involve the firm's level of output, its prices, and the scope of its production.

monopsonistic resource market (monopsony, oligopsony, monopsonistic competition)   a market in which individual firms have some control over the quantity demanded of a resource and thus can influence the resource price.

monopsony   a market in which there is only a single buyer.

moral suasion   attempts by government and Federal Reserve System officials to persuade banks and others in the economy to cooperate with their policy views or actions.

movement along a demand (supply) curve   a change from one point on a demand (supply) curve to another point on the same curve due to a change in the price of the product.

multinational (or transnational) corporation   a corporation that has its headquarters in one country and carries on important business operations in several countries, including the home country.

multiplier   the ratio of the change in the equilibrium level of national income and product to the change in planned expenditure that caused equilibrium to change. It is estimated to be equal to $1/(1 - MPC)$ when no changes are induced in net taxes or in expenditure streams other than consumption.

N

national banks   commercial banks whose charters are issued by the federal government.

national income (NI)   in national income accounting, the total amount earned by owners of resources used in producing goods and services during the accounting period.

national income gap   the difference between the target level of national income and the level that is predicted to prevail if the government undertakes no new action to change that level.

National Industrial Recovery Act (NIRA)   legislation enacted in 1933 containing a variety of emergency programs designed to help the economy recover from the Great Depression. Major portions of the act were ruled unconstitutional.

National Labor Relations Act   See *Wagner-Connery Act*.

national product   in national income accounting, the value of all goods and services produced in the economy during a given year, measured in terms of the prices prevailing at the time of production. See also *gross national product* and *net national product*.

natural monopoly   an industry in which only a single seller is required for efficient production.

natural rate of unemployment   the rate of measured unemployment that is estimated to prevail in long-run macroeconomic equilibrium.

natural resource   one of the factors of production or resources; a gift of nature that can be used in production, such as unimproved land or minerals in the ground.

near money   forms of wealth such as U.S. Savings Bonds, relatively liquid U.S. government securities, payment promises by large corporations, and so on, which can, with some delay, be converted into more liquid wealth forms, which would be counted as money.

negative income tax   a tax under which persons receiving less than a specified amount of income would also receive payments from the government.

negative relationship   See *inverse relationship*.

negative returns, short run   a decrease in total product (negative marginal product) that may occur after a great deal of a variable input has successively been added to one or more fixed inputs.

negative slope   an inverse relationship between variables, as shown on a graph.

negative taxes   transfer payments from the government.

negotiable order of withdrawal account (NOW)   a type of checkable account provided by savings and loan associations.

neoclassical economics   the school of economic thought based on the work of Alfred Marshall (1842–1924) and others, which dominated non-Marxian economic thought in the late nineteenth and early twentieth centuries.

neocolonialism   domination by a more developed

country over a less developed country, carried out without a military presence of the more developed country, and without any formal colonial relationship.

neo-Keynesians followers of Keynes who have added refinements and extensions to his work, particularly along the lines of incomes policies.

net exports the entry in the U.S. national income and product accounts showing the excess of exports over imports of currently produced goods and services. It may be negative.

net national product (NNP) in national income accounting, the value of all currently produced goods and services (GNP) minus an estimated capital consumption (depreciation) allowance.

net taxes the total amount of taxes paid minus transfer payments from the government.

net worth the difference between the amount of total assets and the amount of total liabilities as reported on a balance sheet.

New Deal a name used to refer to the economic programs of the first two administrations of President Franklin Roosevelt (1933–1941).

New International Economic Order (NIEO) a pattern of international economic relations proposed by less developed countries as a replacement for the existing arrangements of international trade and aid; a set of demands from less developed countries for a restructuring of economic relations between developed and less developed countries.

New Left contemporary radical groups that generally call for major steps away from a market economy.

New Right contemporary radical groups that generally call for major steps toward a purely market economy.

New Socialist Man or Woman a person, expected to emerge after socialism is firmly established, who will work harder than anyone in the past and will demand less in terms of wealth and luxurious consumption.

nominal protection the statutory rate of a tariff on a product.

nominal value value that is stated or measured in terms of some monetary unit and that has not been adjusted for changes in the general price level.

nominal wage rate the amount of money a worker receives per hour (or other time unit) of work.

nonexcludability the characteristic of public goods and services that makes it impossible to prevent someone from consuming them, once they have been provided for others.

nonexhaustible natural resources gifts of nature usable in production, the supply of which cannot be eliminated by human use.

nonlinear relationship a relationship in which equal changes in the independent variable do not bring about proportional responses in the dependent variable. When plotted on a graph, it will not appear as a straight line.

nonprice competition competition among firms by such nonprice means as advertising and product changes.

nonrenewable resources inputs for production that, once used, cannot be regenerated by natural processes within a time span that is relevant from the point of view of humans.

nonrival consumption consumption of a good or service by one person that does not prevent another person from consuming it.

no-recourse loan a government loan that a farmer may obtain on a crop at some percentage of its parity or target price, and on which the government has no recourse against the debtor except the crop itself.

normal good or service a good or service for which there is a positive relationship between the income level and the quantity demanded.

normal profit the return to enterprise that is necessary for a firm to receive in order for it to be willing to continue its operation in the long run.

normative economics an approach to economics that is subjective and expresses an opinion or preference.

Norris-LaGuardia Act pro-union act passed by the U.S. Congress in 1932.

O

objectivism the belief that each person's most objective view of the "good" is knowledge of what is in his or her own best interest.

obsolescence the process of becoming no longer useful or economically feasible for some intended purpose.

official reserves vault cash and deposits in Federal

Reserve and other banks that are approved by the Federal Reserve System as meeting requirements.

official settlements balance   the international balance of payments concept that combines all the entries in the capital account with all the entries in the current account and shows the net effect of all transactions except those in official government reserves.

oligopolistic coordination   practices in oligopoly industries by which firms coordinate their output levels and pricing decisions. Practices include collusive agreement, price leadership, and rules of thumb.

oligopoly   a sellers' market structure made up of a few interdependent firms.

oligopsony   a market in which there are few buyers so that individual buyers can influence the price.

OPEC (Organization of Petroleum Exporting Countries)   international petroleum cartel.

open economy   a country that allows relatively unrestricted trade across its borders.

open market operations   the buying and selling of government securities in the open market by the Federal Reserve System.

opportunity cost   the true cost of choosing one alternative over another; that which is given up when a choice is made.

orderly marketing agreement   an agreement among countries aimed at preventing price cutting in importing countries.

organic composition of capital   the ratio between Marxian constant capital (raw materials plus depreciation) and variable capital (direct labor).

origin   the point of intersection of the horizontal and vertical axes of a graph.

other things being equal   See *ceteris paribus*.

outputs   the economic goods and services that business firms produce for sale to consumers, other business firms, and governments.

overemployment   working more hours than desired at a given wage rate.

owners' equity   See *net worth*.

ownership (basis for classifying economic systems)   the entities such as individuals, firms, collectives, or governments that are permitted to hold legal title to natural resources and capital goods.

P

paper gold   See *special drawing rights*.

paradox of value   the fact that things with the greatest value in use frequently have relatively little value in exchange, and vice versa.

parity price (of a farm product)   a price of an agricultural product that gives it a purchasing power, with respect to prices farmers pay, equivalent to what its price provided in some past period.

partial equilibrium analysis   a method of analysis that deals with the effects of some disturbance on one set of economic variables, assuming that all other variables are unaffected.

partial (or fractional) reserves   the characteristic of modern banking operation under which the bank keeps less cash and immediately available funds on hand than the total of its obligations to depositors.

participation rate   See *civilian labor force participation rate*.

partnership   a business firm created through an agreement in which two or more people share financial and managerial responsibilities as well as profits and losses.

patent   a right of temporary limited monopoly over a new product or process granted to its inventor or to a firm that purchases the right from the inventor.

payments equilibrium   in a balance of payments account, any situation in which a country's balance on current account is matched by an equal but opposite balance on its capital account.

PCE deflator   an index number of prices for goods and services included in the personal consumption expenditures component of gross national product.

perfect competition   a purely competitive market with the added feature that buyers and sellers have complete and continuous knowledge of all bids and offers in the market and the mobility to take immediate action on the basis of that knowledge.

perfectly elastic   a condition existing when a price change causes an unlimited change in quantity.

perfectly inelastic demand   a condition existing when a price change causes no change in the quantity demanded.

perfectly inelastic supply   a condition existing when a price change causes no change in the quantity supplied.

permanent income hypothesis the proposition that the level of a household's planned consumption expenditure is based on what it believes to be its long-run or "permanent" level of income.

perpendicular a straight line drawn from a point on a graph to form a right angle with the horizontal axis, the vertical axis, or some other line on the graph.

personal deduction in individual income taxation, an allowance for certain expenditures that may be subtracted from income in determining the tax base.

personal exemption in individual income taxation, a portion of a person's income that is free of tax.

personal income (PI) the national income accounting concept equal to national income plus receipts not earned and minus earnings not received.

personal income distribution the division of income among individuals classified according to income size.

Phillips curve a relationship between an economy's unemployment rate and its inflation rate suggesting that trade-offs exist between these two rates such that policy makers can choose a preferred combination from among those that constitute the curve.

physical capital (or capital goods) resources or factors of production such as factory buildings, tools, and equipment that enable business firms to produce more efficiently.

physiocrats an eighteenth-century school of economic thought contending that economies operate according to certain natural laws and that government interference was useless and wasteful.

picketing the parading of striking workers before the entrance to their work place in the hope of convincing other workers, customers, or supplies not to enter.

Pigou effect the relationship between the price level and the quantity of real national income and product demanded that arises because of the effect of price-level change on the value of wealth holdings.

planned consumption in Keynesian analysis, the amount of expenditure on currently produced consumption goods and services that households intend to carry out in the time period under study.

planned economy an economic system that is directed by government.

planned investment in Keynesian analysis, the amount of expenditure on currently produced capital goods and inventories that firms intend to carry out in the time period under study.

planned saving in Keynesian analysis, the amount of current disposable personal income that households intend to withhold from expenditure on consumption.

planning the directing of economic activity through prearranged priorities, and procedures, sometimes enforced by sanctions.

Planning-Programming Budget System (PPBS) a budgeting procedure that requires agencies to specify the programs they wish to carry out and to plan expenditure needs several years in advance.

plant a factory or other production facility in a particular geographic location that belongs to a firm, which may operate only this one plant or a number of different plants.

political economy the economic analysis of public policy questions.

populism a protest movement in the United States during the last decades of the nineteenth century that expressed farm dissatisfaction with the prices farmers paid and the prices they received, with interest and repayment requirements on farm loans, and with deflationary monetary policies.

positive economics the aspect of the discipline dealing with objective facts (what is) rather than value judgments and opinions (what ought to be).

positive relationship See *direct relationship.*

positive slope a direct relationship between variables, as shown in a graph.

post-Keynesians economists who use Keynesian and neo-Keynesian models, but emphasize institutional features of the economy, such as monopoly power and price rigidity, and often advocate incomes policy.

potential entry the likelihood that one or more firms will enter an industry or market.

poverty living at a standard or level below that considered adequate by the society.

poverty line an income level below which poverty is said to exist.

Prebisch thesis that the international economy has developed in a way that is unfair to agricultural and raw material producers because the producers of these goods are not able to restrict output and raise prices, as can be done by producers of manufactured goods.

precautionary demand for money a desire to hold money in order to be prepared for unexpected changes in the pattern of receipts or expenditures.

predatory price cutting reduction in price aimed at forcing competitors out of business.

present value the discounted value at the present time of a sum of money to be received in the future. See also *discounting*.

present value formula the equation that illustrates the determination of the present value of an asset by the relation between the expected income flow and the rate of interest: PV = expected annual income flow/ the rate of interest.

price the exchange value of a product or resource.

price controls the setting of maximum or minimum prices by the government. See also *ceiling price, floor price*.

price differential a difference between the prices charged to different buyers by a firm for the same product at the same time.

price discrimination the practice of charging a price differential that is not justified by a difference in cost to the seller.

price-earnings ratio the ratio between the price of a share of a firm's stock and the firm's earnings per share.

price elasticity of demand the degree of responsiveness of the quantity demanded of a good, service, or resource to a change in its price.

price elasticity of resource demand the degree of responsiveness of the quantity demanded of a resource to a change in its price.

price elasticity of supply the degree of responsiveness of the quantity supplied of a good, service, or resource to a change in its price.

price fixing agreement among the firms in an industry to establish specific prices. See also *collusion*.

price leadership a practice by firms in some oligopoly industries that coordinates their pricing behavior, where one or more firms announce a price change and other firms in the industry quickly follow it.

price leadership to avoid competition a practice in an oligopolistic industry based on voluntarily following the price changes of significant firms in that industry in order to avoid price competition harmful to industry profits.

price level the average of all prices in the economy.

price maker a firm with sufficient control to be able to affect the price it can charge (or pay) by the level of output it chooses to produce (or the level of input it chooses to buy). See also *price searcher*.

price rigidity a tendency for prices to be sticky or rigid in oligopoly industries because of the interdependence among firms and their fear of being misinterpreted by rivals.

price searcher a firm that is able to choose the price for its product, but because it lacks perfect information, it must search for its profit-maximizing price.

price-specie flow the process of adjustment that the gold standard offered for countries with international balance of payments problems; the flow of gold to settle international payments imbalances and the resulting change in the price levels of trading partners.

price supports (in agriculture) government-operated programs that make sure the prices farmers receive for certain crops do not fall below specified levels. See also *floor price, parity (price)*.

price taker a firm that accepts prices set by the market as given and cannot influence them by changing its own sales or purchases. Characteristic of pure competition.

primitive economy an economic system, usually traditional, that uses technologies significantly less advanced than those used elsewhere.

private benefit benefits that accrue to individuals and firms as distinguished from benefits that accrue to the society as a whole.

private cost the value of opportunities forgone by individuals and firms directly involved in the production and consumption of a good or service. It does not include external cost.

private returns benefits that accrue to certain individuals or firms as contrasted to society as a whole.

private sector the part of an economy directed by the decisions of individuals and firms.

producer price index a measure of the level of prices paid for inputs, expressed in terms of base year prices. See also *consumer price index*.

product the output of a firm; either goods or services or both.

product cycle a principle that explains changes over time among countries in their comparative advantage in producing a given product.

product differentiation changes in basically similar products in order to create some differences among them in the eyes of consumers.

product differentiation (entry barrier) an entry barrier determined by the extent to which established firms can differentiate their relatively well-known products from those of a newcomer.

product extension conglomerate merger the acquisition of a firm in an allied industry—one whose product is functionally associated with that of the acquirer.

production the transformation of inputs into outputs by firms.

production controls, agricultural legislation requiring farmers to limit their output of a supported crop.

production function the relationship between a business firm's physical inputs and outputs at a given level of technological development.

production possibilities boundary a curve that represents all of the alternative maximum combinations that can be produced during a given period of time with a given stock of resources and technological knowledge.

production possibility a concept describing the maximum quantity of goods and services that can be produced with a given stock of resources and technological knowledge during any given period of time.

productivity the amount of output produced by a unit of resource input during a given span of time.

profit the return to the entrepreneurial resource or factor of production; also the difference between a firm's total revenue and total cost.

profit and loss statement See *income statement*.

profit maximization an assumption made in the theory of the firm that a firm will seek to produce a level of output and charge a price so that its total revenue exceeds its total cost by the greatest possible amount. A consequence is that its marginal cost equals its marginal revenue.

progressive tax a tax under which the percentage of income paid in tax increases as the amount of the taxpayer's total income increases.

proletariat a term used by Karl Marx to refer to the working class, which would come to power after the socialist revolution.

propensity to consume the inclination of households to spend a predicted portion of disposable personal income on goods and services for current consumption.

propensity to save the inclination of households to desist from spending a predicted portion of disposable personal income for consumption goods and services.

property rights the rights enjoyed by a property owner by reason of his or her ownership.

property tax a tax imposed on the estimated value of specified types of property, typically land and buildings.

proportional tax a tax under which the percentage of income paid in tax is the same without regard to the size of the taxpayer's income.

proprietorship a business firm owned and managed by one person.

prosperity a condition of an economy existing when living standards are relatively high and unemployment is relatively low; also, the expansion phase of a business cycle.

protection a system of tariffs and other measures aimed at defending a country's industries from foreign competition in its home market.

protectionism a policy position favoring aid to import-competing industries by tariffs, subsidies, quotas, other restrictions on imports, and sometimes also aid to export industries by direct or hidden subsidies.

proven reserves estimates of the amount of a natural resource that remains available for economically feasible extraction.

psychic returns nonmonetary returns such as prestige, excitement, and other personal feelings of satisfaction and enjoyment.

public choice an area of study that combines economics and political science ideas to gain a better understanding of how governments actually operate.

public enterprise a government commercial undertaking such as the U.S. Postal Service or Amtrak on the federal level; state lotteries or parks; local sewage disposal or libraries.

public goods and services goods and services supplied either wholly or in large part through government because externality, nonrivalry, and nonexcludability features are so important that provision through market processes is seriously deficient.

public sector the part of an economy directed by government.

public sector planning planning that covers only the public sector of the economy.

public utility a private firm that has been granted a monopoly position in its own market by the government and is regulated by the government.

pump-priming temporary injections of government money in an effort to build up business confidence and to raise planned investment; an economic policy model of the mid-1930s.

purchasing power of the dollar the reciprocal of the index number for the consumer price index, or the goods and services that a dollar will buy in a given year compared to what it would buy in the base year.

purchasing power parity a condition prevailing when the quantity of internationally traded goods and services that can be bought with a unit of a nation's money is the same in international trade as at home.

pure competition a type of market structure with a large number of sellers, a standardized product, no artificial restrictions on price or quantity, and easy entry and exit into and out of the industry, so that each firm is a price taker.

pure monopoly a market structure in which there is only a single seller, no acceptable substitutes are available for the product offered for sale, and no entry into the market is possible.

pyramiding of reserves the arrangement, in effect before the Federal Reserve System was established in 1913, under which reserves of country banks were held as deposits in city banks, which held their reserves in still larger banks in major cities (reserve cities).

Q

quadrant one of four sections of a graph formed by the intersection of horizontal and vertical axes. Each axis usually represents a variable with both positive and negative values.

quality bias the effect on a price index number of the failure to recognize that the quality of goods and services changes over time.

quantile ratio the percentage or fraction determined by dividing the percentage of total income received by the highest k percentage of the population with the percentage of the total received by the lowest k percentage. (k is a fraction. Commonly chosen values are .05, .10, and .20.)

quantity demanded the amount demanded per time period of a good, service, or resource at a certain price. See also *demand, individual consumer demand, market demand*.

quantity supplied the amount supplied per time period of a good, service, or resource at a certain price. See also *individual firm supply, market supply, supply*.

quantity theory of money the proposition, based on the equation of exchange, that changes in the quantity of money provide a useful way of predicting changes in nominal GNP.

quota a limitation on the quantity of imports.

R

radical extreme, sweeping, or revolutionary; a person whose beliefs are radical.

rate of return the proceeds or receipts from an undertaking expressed as a percentage of the amount put into it.

rate of surplus value See *exploitation rate*.

rate structure (for a public utility) pattern of prices charged according to such criteria as customer classification, quantity purchased, and time of delivery.

rational consumer a consumer who attempts to maximize his or her satisfaction in the selection of goods and services.

rational entrepreneur (business firm decision maker) a person who seeks to maximize profit and minimize loss over a certain period.

rational expectations the theory that, after sufficient experience with inflationary consequences of increases in aggregate demand, people will adjust their price-level expectations quickly when expansionary monetary or fiscal actions are taken, so that such actions have little effect on real output in the economy.

rationality See *economic rationality*.

rationing any method of restricting the demand for a good or a service. Government may formally invoke a system of rationing in order to deal "fairly" with what would otherwise be an excess demand situation.

Reaganomics the package of economic policy positions arising from the groups backing the Reagan administrations: anti-inflationists, anti-high-taxers, anti-high-interest-rate advocates, and those who favored more defense spending.

real balances wealth holdings adjusted for changes in the price level.

real balances theory the proposition that changes in the price level affect aggregate demand through changes in the real value of assets.

real income the quantity of goods and services that can be purchased with the money received by a household; receipts adjusted for changes in the price level.

realization crisis in Marxian terms, the stage of capitalism where the profit rate remains high but less than full-employment output can be bought by workers and other consumers.

real values values stated or measured in terms of goods and services; numerical values that have been adjusted for price-level changes by applying an index number or deflator.

real wage rates wage rates adjusted for changes in the price level.

recession the contraction phase of a business cycle; a period of a relatively low volume of production and income in an economy.

recognition lag the time required for economists to recognize that there is trouble in the economy, to diagnose the trouble, and to prescribe remedies.

recovery the early part of the expansion phase of a business cycle; the phase immediately following the lower turning point of a business cycle.

reflation a rise in the price level toward a level that prevailed earlier.

regressive tax a tax under which the percentage of income paid in tax decreases as the amount of a taxpayer's total income increases.

regulated industries (or regulated firms) industries or firms whose prices (and sometimes other operations) are subject to monopoly regulation.

regulation See *monopoly regulation, social regulation.*

regulatory commissions federal and state agencies that regulate firms that have been given public utility status.

regulatory lag the length of time that it takes for a regulated firm's changes in costs to be reflected in rate changes.

relative price the market value of a good or service compared to the market value of certain other goods and services.

relatively pure conglomerate merger the acquisition by a firm of a firm whose activities have only remote relationships to those of the acquirer.

renewable resources inputs to production that, under normal conditions, can be replaced through natural processes.

rent the return or payment for the use of natural resources in production.

replacement cost the value of a firm's capital estimated by what it would cost to replace it.

required reserves See *reserve requirement.*

reservation price a price below which a resource will be held for future use or sale by its owner.

reserve ratio the total official (government-approved) reserves held by a bank divided by the amount of checking account liabilities of that bank.

reserve requirement the amount of official reserves that a bank must, by law, maintain in order to avoid legal penalties.

reserves vault cash and deposits with the Federal Reserve Bank, which may be used by a bank to fulfill official reserve requirements.

resource package a combination of two or more of the factors of production or resources necessary for production.

resources See *factors of production.*

revenue See *total revenue.*

revenue sharing a system under which revenues collected by a superior government are transferred to subordinate governments in a federal system.

risk the probability that a harm or loss will be suffered.

rivalry competition among sellers or among buyers.

GLOSSARY

Robinson-Patman Act   a 1936 amendment to the Clayton Act, which strengthened the government's control over price discrimination.

roundabout production   the diversion of resources from the direct production of consumer goods to the production of capital goods, which are then used in further production.

rule of reason   a guiding principle adopted by the Supreme Court in 1911 that focused on intent and conduct rather than the presence or absence of substantial monopoly control.

rules of thumb   conventions developed as a means of coordinating decisions among firms in an oligopoly industry.

run on a bank   a situation in which many of a bank's depositors want to withdraw their deposits at the same time, and immediately.

S

sales tax   a tax imposed on the sale of a product.

satisfice   to seek satisfactory profit rather than maximum profit.

saving   devoting a portion of disposable personal income to a use other than consumption expenditure.

saving function   the statement of a relationship between the level of disposable personal income and the volume of planned saving.

Say's Identity   the proposition that supply creates its own demand at any given price level.

scaling   the marks and numbers that indicate units of measure of the variables on the horizontal and vertical axes of a graph.

scarcity   the circumstance in which the supply of something would not be sufficient to satisfy the demand for it if it were provided "free of charge."

seasonal unemployment   joblessness that arises because some occupations require workers during only part of each year.

SDRs   See *special drawing rights.*

secondary boycott (or strike)   a boycott (or strike) by a union against an employer other than the one with which the union has a dispute.

Second World   European communist countries regardless of their economic levels.

self-liquidating loans   extensions of credit that are to be repaid from charges collected for goods or services financed by the credit.

seniority rule   the requirement that the worker who has been on the job the longest shall receive preferential treatment in respect to layoff, rehiring, and other conditions of employment.

services   intangible products.

shares of stock   securities that represent ownership rights in a corporation.

Sherman Antitrust Act   a law passed by the U.S. Congress in 1890 prohibiting the restriction of competition, monopolization, and attempts to monopolize.

shift of a demand (supply) curve   a displacement of an entire demand (supply) curve to the right or left showing a change in demand (supply).

shop steward   a worker elected to represent the union on the job.

shortage   a disequilibrium market situation that results in excess demand.

short run   the period of time during which at least one of a firm's inputs cannot be varied; a period of time not long enough for entry into an industry or exit from an industry to take place.

short-run aggregate-supply curve   the relationship between the price level and the quantity of real national product supplied. There are no changes in production capability, and behavior is based on the belief that changes in nominal wages and profits are also changes in real wages and profits. (The curve incorporates behavior based on money illusion.)

short-run consumption function   the relationship between disposable personal income and planned consumption expenditure during a limited time period after changes in disposable personal income.

shutdown decision   the prediction in the theory of the firm that in the short run a firm will cease producing if its revenue is insufficient to at least cover its variable cost.

skill   See *technological know-how.*

slope   the change in the variable read on the vertical axis of a graph divided by the associated change in the variable read on the horizontal axis of that graph.

social cost   the total value of opportunities forgone

because of the production and consumption of a product. It includes both private cost and external cost.

Social Darwinism the belief that the survival and prosperity of individuals, families, nations, and races are determined, like those of animal species, by their biological and psychological fitness in the struggle not only against each other but also against the environment.

socialist system an economic system in which land and physical instruments of production are largely or completely owned by the state.

social overhead capital facilities such as roads, harbors, schools, and public health installations that provide public sector services needed by a society; also known as infrastructure.

social regulation rules and laws that protect the public against potentially harmful practices by business firms. Examples are environmental protection, food and drug, truth-in-packaging, and occupational health and safety rules.

social returns benefits that accrue to society as a whole as contrasted to individuals or firms.

Social Security Act (1935) legislation establishing a compulsory system of retirement and survivors' benefits financed by taxes from employers and employees. The system has since expanded to include certain disability, hospital, and medical care benefits.

special drawing rights (SDRs) or paper gold credit entries on the books of the International Monetary Fund given to particular countries, which can, in turn, use them to meet their international obligations.

speculation taking action based on expectations of future changes in market values.

speculative demand for money a desire to hold money arising because of an expectation that the market values of nonmoney assets are going to fall in the future, or that interest rates will rise in the future.

stabilization function the function or role of government involving the direction of the aggregate economy in order to prevent serious depressions or inflations and to maintain high levels of employment and a reasonable rate of economic growth.

stable equilibrium a state of balance that tends to restore itself after disturbances.

stages of production (short-run theory of the firm) the division of a firm's input-output relationships into three categories when a firm adds successive units of a variable input to one or more fixed inputs. In Stage I average product increases. In Stage II average product decreases, but marginal product remains positive. In Stage III total product also decreases, and marginal product is negative.

stagflation a prolonged combination of inflation, substantial unemployment, and sluggish growth.

standard deduction in individual income taxation, an amount that can be subtracted from income provided that the taxpayer does not itemize personal deductions.

Standard Industrial Classification (SIC) system a classification system, used by the U.S. Bureau of the Census, that divides the outputs of firms into industry and product groupings.

standard for deferred payment a function of money used to specify amounts to be exchanged at some future date.

standardized product the product of different firms that is so much alike that customers do not prefer one seller's product over another's. Sometimes called a homogeneous product.

standard of living the well-being of people, usually expressed in terms of current income or consumption per person of real goods and services.

standards and controls rules governing such characteristics of goods as methods of production or methods of waste disposal.

statistical discrepancy in national income and product accounting, the difference between the estimate of national income and the estimate of net national product after allowing for indirect business taxes and subsidies.

stock a fixed quantity, such as the stock of money; also, a certificate denoting an ownership share in a corporation.

stockbroker an individual or a firm which carries out transactions in corporate securities (stocks and bonds) on behalf of their buyers and sellers.

stock exchange an organization through which transactions in corporate stocks may be carried out.

store of purchasing power a function of money that enables people who have money to save some of it for use at a later time.

strike a work stoppage in which employees refuse to work until certain conditions are met.

structural unemployment joblessness that arises when changes take place in production methods (how to produce) or in the types of goods and services produced (what to produce).

subsidy a grant or gift, often from a government, designed to give aid to and provide incentives for the recipient.

substitutes (substitute goods or services) goods or services that may be used instead of one another, such as beer and ale or pastel blue shirts and pastel green shirts.

substitution effect the effect that a change in relative prices of substitute goods or services (resulting from a change in the price of a good or service) has on the quantity that a person demands of that good or service.

supply the willingness and ability to offer for sale at certain prices. See also *individual firm supply, market supply, quantity supplied.*

supply curve graph of a supply schedule.

supply schedule a table showing different prices of a good or service and the quantity supplied of that good or service at each price.

supply shock an independent or exogenous event that shifts both the short-run and long-run aggregate-supply curves for an economy.

supply-side economics the approach to economics that is concerned with the forces that can shift the short-run and long-run aggregate-supply curves of an economy.

support price See *floor price.*

surplus the excess supply that stems from a disequilibrium situation; in budgets, the excess of receipts over expenditures for the budget period.

surplus value a Marxian concept describing the value of labor that the employer retains to pay interest, rent, dividends, profits, and the unproductive portion of white-collar labor.

sustainable annual yield the quantity of a renewable natural resource that can be harvested each year consistent with maintaining a stable population of that resource.

syndicalism the ownership of individual capital facilities (such as workshops, factories, or industrial complexes) by their own workers, who would elect representatives to a weak government, which would act as a referee in disputes and as an economic plan coordinator.

T

Taft-Hartley Act (or Labor-Management Relations Act) pro-management act passed by the U.S. Congress in 1947.

target level of national income and product the level of national income and product that policy makers believe to be most desirable in terms of its effects on employment, prices, economic growth, and other goals of the economy.

target price a price for an American-grown farm product set by the U.S. Secretary of Agriculture under the Agriculture and Consumer Protection Act of 1973. Farmers who qualify under the terms of the legislation receive payments from the government if they sell their crop for less than the target price.

tariff a tax on imports.

tariff factory a plant set up by a foreign firm in order to avoid a tariff imposed by the country in which the plant is located.

tax a payment to government required by law.

tax base the amount of income or value on which tax liability is calculated.

tax brackets in individual income taxation, the layers or portions of income subject to different tax rates.

tax-change multiplier the ratio between a change in the level of equilibrium national income and product and the change in net tax collections that brought it about.

tax shifting transferring the burden of a tax to some person or group other than the one making the actual payment to government.

technical efficiency the least amount of inputs, measured in physical terms, required to produce a certain amount of output.

technological know-how the ability to combine resources in producing goods and services.

technological progress an advance in knowledge of the industrial arts and/or improved techniques of organizing production.

terms of trade the ratio of an index number of the

prices of the goods and services that a country exports to an index number of the prices of the goods and services that it imports.

theory a systematically organized body of knowledge that can be applied in a fairly wide range of circumstances and that provides a set of rules or assumptions for analyzing information and studying relationships.

Third World all countries not classified as in the First World or the Second World; characteristically, the less developed countries.

time deposit funds placed in a financial institution under terms that allow the institution to delay repayment for some period.

time lag the amount of time it takes for a change in an economic variable to have an effect.

total cost (*TC*) the sum of total fixed costs and total variable costs; explicit and implicit costs that a firm incurs in production.

total fixed cost (*TFC*) short-run costs of a firm that do not vary with the quantity level of output that the firm produces.

total planned expenditure the sum of planned consumption expenditure, planned investment expenditure, government purchases, and exports minus imports.

total product the total quantity of output produced by a firm during a period of time.

total revenue the total income or receipts during a period of time that a business firm receives from selling its product.

total utility See *utility*.

total variable cost (*TVC*) the sum of those costs of a firm that vary with the quantity level of output that the firm produces. (In the long run, all costs are variable.)

tradeoff an exchange of one thing for another; especially, the quantity of one good or service that must be given up to gain a certain quantity of another good or service.

traditional economy an economic system in which decisions are made primarily on the basis of past practice.

transactions accounts deposits in financial institutions that provide the depositor with checking-account privileges; also called *checkable accounts*.

transactions demand for money the desire to hold some wealth in the form of money because money is convenient for day-to-day buying and selling of goods and services.

transfer earnings the part of the earnings of a resource that is equal to the earnings that this resource could command in the next-best use to which it could be put.

transfer payments payments, such as Social Security benefits, unemployment compensation, or welfare, that are not compensation for any service rendered or product sold during the current accounting period.

transmission mechanism the means whereby changes in the money supply affect the level of national income and product. See *Keynesian transmission mechanism* and *direct transmission mechanism*.

transnational corporation See *multinational corporation*.

Treasury Bills a short-term debt instrument issued by the U.S. Treasury.

trigger-price mechanism a method of protection whereby an importing country unilaterally announces one or more prices, below which all sales are considered to be below cost and subject to antidumping duties.

trust a legal device through which supposedly competing firms allow a central board of trustees to vote all of their stock.

trust-buster an advocate of the market economy who fears control by big-business oligarchy and believes that the decline in competition should be reversed.

turning point in business cycle measurement, the change from expansion to contraction or from contraction to expansion in the volume of economic activity.

tying arrangement a scheme that forces a firm to buy certain products along with certain other products.

U

uncertainty the condition of not knowing the probability of the outcome of an event.

underemployment working fewer hours than desired at a given wage rate; working at a job that does not utilize all of the skill and training that the worker possesses.

underground economy income and production, both criminal and otherwise, that are not reported in official statistics, often because people want to evade regulations, union rules, or taxes.

undistributed profits tax a tax on the portion of corporation net income not distributed as dividend payments to stockholders.

unemployment in official statistics, a condition in which a person who desires and is able to work at the going wage rate is not able to find a job; in economic theory, a condition in which a person is spending more time for leisure than desired and less time for wage earning than desired at the going wage rate.

unemployment rate See *civilian unemployment rate.*

unfair labor practices practices by employers and by unions made illegal in the Wagner-Connery Act and the Taft-Hartley Act.

unfavorable balance (of trade) a negative, debit, or deficit balance in a country's international transactions in merchandise.

unilateral transfer in balance of payments accounting, a current account entry recording amounts of funds transmitted not in exchange for goods and services, such as gifts, donations, or foreign aid.

union (labor union/trade union) an organization of workers for the purpose of collective bargaining.

union shop a form of union security arrangement that allows employers to hire nonunion employees but requires that they join the union soon after employment.

unitary elasticity a condition existing where the percentage response in quantity is exactly equal to the percentage change in the price that caused it.

unit of account a function of money that enables people to measure the values of different items.

unlimited liability an obligation that is not restricted or confined to a specified amount. For example, a proprietor's or a partner's responsibility for the obligations of a firm is not restricted to the amount of his or her financial investment in the firm.

unlimited life a condition in which the continued existence of a business firm is not restricted to the period of participation of any owner or manager.

unstable equilibrium a state of balance that has no tendency to restore itself if upset.

upper turning point the point in a business cycle when an expansion phase ends and a contraction phase begins.

user charge a price that government charges for services that it renders.

util a unit of anticipated satisfaction used to express an individual consumer's degree of pleasure derived from a unit of a product.

utility a measure or expression of an individual consumer's anticipated satisfaction to be derived from goods and services.

utility analysis a theory of consumer behavior based on assumptions of consumer rationality, the measurability of utility, decreasing marginal utility, increasing total utility, limited income, and knowledge of prices.

V

validation See *accommodation.*

value added the increase in the value of a good in each stage of its production; the difference between the value of materials that a firm buys and the value of what it sells.

value in exchange the transaction price of a good, service, or resource.

value in use the total utility that is gained from a product.

value of output a method of measuring national income and product that makes no attempt to avoid double counting.

variable a quantity that can assume any of a set of values.

variable capital a Marxian concept of direct labor hours—not hours actually spent at work, but hours used to produce goods consumed by workers.

variable cost See *total variable cost.*

velocity (of circulation of money) the number of times a year, on the average, that a dollar of the money supply is spent in the purchase of currently produced goods and services. Velocity is usually measured by dividing the GNP by some measure of the money supply, such as M1.

vertical merger the acquisition by a firm of a firm that operates on a different level of a particular business activity, such as one that is a supplier or a customer of the acquirer.

very long run the period of time long enough so that a new technology can be introduced and the production function itself can be altered.

voluntary export restriction reduction of exports to a certain level or in accordance with a certain formula, undertaken by an exporting country.

W

wage and price controls restrictions imposed by law on wage rates and prices.

wage and price guidelines suggested and voluntary constraints on changes in wage rates and prices.

wage-cost lag theory the proposition that changes in costs of production and wage rates lag behind changes in the general price level.

wage differentials differences in wage rates usually due to different qualifications of workers, desirability of the job, and the institutions of the labor market.

wage rate the payment to labor per unit of time worked.

wages the return or payment to labor in production.

Wagner-Connery Act (or National Labor Relations Act) a pro-union act passed by the U.S. Congress in 1935. It proposed to guarantee rights of collective bargaining, outlawed various employer labor practices as unfair, and set up a National Labor Relations Board as its enforcement mechanism.

wealth an accumulation of assets.

welfare the state of well-being or the quality of life; also, a term applied to government transfer payments designed to alleviate poverty.

welfare loss triangle a graphic representation of the amount of economic well-being that is lost to consumers because a product is produced and sold by a monopolist instead of by purely competitive firms.

welfare state an economic regime that places an especially high value on the equity of income and wealth distributions and on the provision of a floor or "safety net" below which income should not fall.

Wheeler-Lea Amendment a 1938 amendment to the Federal Trade Commission Act that outlaws unfair or deceptive acts or practices aimed at the consumer.

worker's self-management a system of production, most notably in Yugoslavia, in which workers' collectives operate and manage firms with capital leased from the state.

work standards criteria determining the amount of work to be performed, such as the size of a work crew for a job or the number of units to be handled on an assembly line during a certain period of time.

X

X-inefficiency waste of inputs due to a lack of motivation by management, which results in poor cost control; often displayed by monopolists.

Y

yellow-dog contract an agreement that a worker will not join a union, which was often made a condition of employment before the Norris-LaGuardia Act of 1932.

Index

Burns, Arthur, 248
Business conditions, planned investment and, 165–166
Business cycles, 92, 183–195, 184
  cumulative phases of, 186–187
  expansion and contraction phases of, 184–185
  historical record of, 185–187
  Marxian theory of, 190
  measuring, 185
  patterns in, 186–187
  Schumpeter's theory of, 190–191
  simple theory of, 186–190
  turning points of, 188–190
  see also Great Depression
Business firm(s), 23–28
  accounting for, 25–28
  decision to cease production by, 470–471
  demand and revenue for, 487–488
  human capital investment by, 640
  individual supply decisions of, 71–75
  interdependence among, 537
  interest paid to, 124
  investment decisions of, 631–635
  partnership, 23–24
  production possibilities for, 58
  productivity decisions of, 453–454
  profitability of, 490–493
  proprietorship, 23
  in pure competition, 486–493
  rational, 462–463
  stock market and, 25
  supply and cost for, 488–489
  see also Corporation(s); Entrepreneur(s); Production
Business firm choice, 433–455
  decision-making time spans and, 437
  long-run production and, 446–453
  production and, 433–536
  short-run costs and, 441–446
  short-run production and, 437–441
  very long-run production and, 453–454
  see also Decision making
Business fluctuations, see Business cycles
Business goals, 462–463
Business taxes, in national product, 122
Business unionism, 609. See also Unions
Buyer-response bias, in CPI, 108–109

CAB, see Civil Aeronautics Board
Canada, tariffs of, 352
Capital, 46, 576
  constant, 812

human, 53, 576, 583, 638–642. See also Labor
organic composition of, 813
physical, 630–635
productivity of, 762–763
resource supply for all uses of, 583
social, 631
social overhead, 366
variable, 812
Capital-attraction argument for protection, 727
Capital consumption allowance, 122
  natural disasters and, 127
Capital costs, returns and, 634–635
Capital-export restrictions, 352
Capital formation, in Japan, 391
Capital gains and losses, 206
Capital goods, 576, 630–35. See also Capital resources
Capitalism, 10, 12, 791, 808–810
  advertising and, 529
  alienation under, 809–810
  income distribution in, 13, 808–809
  insecurity under, 809
  Marx's views on, 190
  "penny," 12
  planning under, 796–800
Capital movements, LDCs and, 381–384
Capital/output ratio, 368
Capital requirement entry barrier, 563
Capital resources, 52, 54–55
Carlson, Chester, 453
Carlyle, Thomas, 86, 402
Cartel(s), 704, 704–706
  favored by LDCs, 380
  instability of, 705
  national and international, 705
  see also Organization of Petroleum Exporting Countries
Carter, Jimmy
  balance of payments under, 353
  balance of trade under, 732
  defeat of, 114
  deregulation under, 713
  expansionary policy under, 248
  interest rates under, 147
  price controls removed under, 767–768
"Case" poverty, 681
Cash, on bank's balance sheet, 227
Castro, Fidel, 383
Causation, mistaken, 47
CEA, see Council of Economic Advisers
Ceiling price, 79. See also Wage and price controls

Celler-Kefauver Antitrust Amendment, 699–700, 702
Central bank, 235–236. See also Federal Reserve System
Certification, labor supply restriction and, 617
Ceteris paribus, 36
  individual consumer demand and, 67–70
  individual firm supply and, 71–72
Chain stores, 699
Chamberlin, Edward, 527–528
Cheating, in OPEC, 706
Checking account balances, see Demand deposits
Checkoff, 614
Chiang Kai-shek, 392n
Chicago School, 270
Child labor laws, labor supply and, 580, 581
China
  Communist Party in, 826–827
  economic development of, 363
  economy of, 31, 796
  family planning in, 753
  GNP of, 119n
  human rights in, 14
  modernization of, 381n
  planning in, 796, 801–802
  revolution in, 826–827
  textile imports and, 720
Choice
  public, 660–664
  scarcity and, 55
  see also Business firm choice; Consumer choice
Chow, Gregory C., 431
Churchill, Betty C., 581n
CIO, see Congress of Industrial Organizations
Circular flow, 130–143
  consumption only, 130–131, 132 (fig.)
  equilibrium and disequilibrium in whole economy and, 141–142
  with financial markets, government, and foreign markets, 131–138, 133 (fig.)
  key position of financial markets in, 138–140
  leakages and injections and, 142–143
  macroeconomic equilibrium and, 131
Circulation, velocity of, 253–255
Civil Aeronautics Board (CAB), 713
Civilian employment rate, 102, 102–103
Civilian labor force, 96

Economic systems, 8, 8–14, 789–806
  evaluating, 12–14
  mechanism basis of, 10–12
  ownership basis of, 10, 12
Economic theory, 34–38
  assumptions and, 36
  economic rationality and, 36–38
  policy and, 324–325
  testing, 35–36
Economic welfare, 127
Economies of scale, 447, 447–448
  causes of, 449–450
  natural monopolies and, 707
  in oligopoly, 543
Economist, 34
Economy(ies)
  closed, 31
  market, 10–11
  planned, *see* Planning
  production possibilities for, 58
  traditional, 12
  see also Capitalism; Collectivist econ-
    omy; Socialism
ECU, *see* European Currency Unit
Edgeworth, F.Y., 479, 480
Education
  government spending for, 665
  property taxes and, 674–675
  returns from, 641–642
Edwards, Corwin D., 705n
EEOC, *see* Equal Employment Oppor-
    tunities Commission
Effective full employment, 289
Effective protection, 724, 724–725
Efficiency, 60, 434–436
  economic, 436
  technical, 434–436
Effluent, 775n
Effluent charge, 775
  advantages of, 775
  problems with, 775–776
EFTA, *see* European Free Trade Associ-
    ation
Ehrenberg, Ronald G., 626n
Eisner, Robert, 148
Elastic demand, 424
Elasticity
  cross elasticity of demand, 428–430
  of demand, advertising and, 530–531
  income elasticity of demand, 430–431
  perfect, 424
  price discrimination and, 520–522
  price elasticity of resource demand,
    586
  price elasticity of resource supply,
    584–585
  unitary, 424

see also Price elasticity of demand;
  Price elasticity of supply
Elasticity coefficient, 423–424
Elected officials, public choice and,
  661–662
Elzinga, K.G., 431
Employee compensation, *see* Compen-
  sation; Wage(s)
Employment: full, 156–157
  absolute, 281
  effective, 289
  neoclassical theory of, 156–157
  see also Unemployment
Employment Act of 1946, 297
Employment rate, 102–103, 103 (fig.)
Energy resources, price controls and,
  766–768
Engels, Friedrich, 810, 811
Engels' Law, 740
Engerman, Stanley, 692n
English classical system, 86
Enterprisers, 52. *See also* Entrepre-
  neur(s)
Entitlements, 767. *See also* Transfer
  payments
Entrepreneur(s), 52, 576
  rational, 37
Entrepreneurship, resource supply for
  all uses of, 581–582
Entry, 561. *See also* Market entry
Environment, 772–777
  efficient quantity of waste and, 772–
    774
  government standards and, 776–777
  income inequality and, 688
  laws of conservation of energy and
    matter and, 772
  pricing to internalize externalities
    and, 774–775
  relations with, 126–127
  renewable resources and, 768–769
  social, 401
  subsidies for waste treatment and,
    777
Equal Employment Opportunities
  Commission (EEOC), 626
Equation of exchange, 252–253, 480
Equilibrium, 45, 45–46, 131
  in balance of payments, 357–358
  changing, 177–178
  consumer, 404–406, 415–417
  desirability of, 142
  foreign exchange rates and, 338–339
  at full employment, 156–157
  Keynesian and neoclassical views of,
    172–173

between leakages and injections,
  142–143
long-run, 492–493, 535
macroeconomic, 83, 131, 283
in money market, 260–261
in monopsonistic labor market, 606–
  607
output and price at, in monopoly,
  511–512
partial versus general, 46
in purely competitive labor market,
  603
short-run, 490–492, 533–535
stable and unstable, 45–46
wage and marginal revenue product
  at, 607
wages above, 617–618
in whole economy, 141–142
see also Disequilibrium
Equilibrium foreign exchange rates,
  338–339
Equilibrium method of market manipulation, 79
Equilibrium national income, 168–172
  leakage-and-injection method for,
    171–172
  total-planned-expenditure method
    for, 169–171
Equilibrium price, 77, 77–78
Equilibrium quantity, 77, 77–78
Equity, as criterion for evaluating economic systems, 13
Error(s)
  in international accounts, 347
  pervasive, 48
  Type I and Type II, 784–785
Ethical maldistribution, 691, 691–692
Eulenspiegel, Till, 816
Eurocurrencies, 344
Eurodollars, in money supply, 223
Europe
  credentialism in, 780–781
  gold inflation in, 149
  during Great Depression, 246
  inflation in, 114
  mercantilism in, 364–365
European Community (EC), 344, 648,
  730
  farm program of, 748
  U.S. agricultural trade conflicts with,
    748–749
European Free Trade Association
  (EFTA), 730
European Currency Unit (ECU), 344
Ever-normal granary, 744n
Ex ante plans, 134
Excess burden, 672, 672–673

Households (*Continued*)
  income distribution and, 685–686
  loanable funds and, 636–637
Housing, property taxes and, 674
Houthakker, H.S., 426
Hughes, John J., 431
Human capital, 53, 576, 638, 638–642
  investment decision and, 638–641
  returns from education and, 641–642
  supply of, 583
  see also Labor
Human rights, as criterion for evaluating economic systems, 14
Humphrey, Hubert, 796
Humphrey-Hawkins Act of 1978, 297, 796
Hungary, economy of, 10
"Hyperbola, rectangular," 424
Hyperdeflation, 284
Hyperinflation, 114, 286

Icahn, Carl, 559
ICC, *see* Interstate Commerce Commission
Identity, 135
Ignorance, as rationale for regulation, 782–783
Ikeda, Hayato, 392
IMF, *see* International Monetary Fund
Immature creditor, 348–349
Immature debtor, 348
Immigration
  labor supply and, 579
  regulation of, 780
Imperative planning, 792
Imperialism, economic development and, 364
Implementation lag, 303
Implicit costs, 441, 441–442
Implicit price deflator for GNP, 106–107
Import(s)
  in circular flow model, 137–138
  in Keynesian model, 167–168
  national income accounts and, 119, 122
  unions and, 620
  see also Balance of payments; International trade
Income
  discretionary, 124
  disposable, personal (DPI), 162–163
  family, median, 20–21
  money, 21
  national, 20, 162–164, 197–198
  nonmoney, 21
  per capita, international comparisons of, 360, 362

permanent, 161
price elasticity of demand and, 426
of proprietors, 123
real, 69
rental, 123
shift of demand curve and, 70–71
sources of, 20
of Third World, 363
unreported, 125–126
uses of, 22
utility analysis and, 403
see also National income; National income accounting
Income demand, 430
Income distribution, 684–695
  under capitalism, 808–809
  as criterion for evaluating economic systems, 13
  discrimination and, 689–690
  economic growth and, 371–372
  farmers and, 743
  functional, 577–578, 684, 685
  as function of government, 29–30
  Great Depression and, 192
  market demand and, 420
  measuring inequality and, 685–688
  personal, 684–685
  reasons for inequality in, 688–689
  redistribution and, 693–695, 754–755
  see also Maldistribution
Income effect, 69, 399
  monopoly and, 507
  taxes and, 622
  of wage changes, 580
Income elasticity of demand, 430, 430–431
Income redistribution, 693–695, 754–755
Incomes policy, 146–147, 318
  unions and, 649
Income statement, 28, 28 (table)
Income tax(es)
  brackets and progression and, 666–668
  corporate, 670–671
  indexing, 668
  individual, 666–669
  negative, 682–684
  simplification and "flat tax" and, 668–669
  supply-side economists' views on, 331
  Swedish, 798–799
  see also Tax(es)
Inconvertible currency, 340n
Increasing returns, 439

Increasing total utility, 402, 402–403
Independent variable, 39
Index(es), to measure economic development, 8
Indexing, 317, 316–317, 668
  of income tax, 668
Index numbers, 104, 104–110
  in measuring business cycles, 185
  special-purpose, 110–111
Indicative planning, 792
  in Japan, 797–798
Indifference curve(s), 412, 413 (fig.), 413–414
  relationships among, 412–413
  shape of, 413–414
Indifference curve analysis, 412, 412–418
  behavioral predictions and, 418
  budget line in, 414–415
  consumer equilibrium and, 415–417
  demand curve derivation and, 417–418
  indifference curve and map in, 412–414
Indirect business taxes, in national product, 120 (table), 122
Individual
  human capital investments by, 638–639
  labor supply of, 599, 601–602
  opportunity cost and, 56–57
Individual consumer demand, 66, 66–71
  changes in quantity demanded and changes in demand and, 69–71
  demand schedule and curve and, 67–68
  slope of demand curve and, 68–69
Individual firm supply, 71, 71–75
Individual maldistribution, 690
Induced expenditure, 180–184
Industrial unions, 608
Industrial Workers of the World (IWW), 609, 818
Industry(ies)
  classification of, 553–555
  redeployment of, 380–381
Inelastic demand, 424
Inequality, *see* Income distribution
Infant industry argument, 726
Inferior products, 71n, 431
Infinite elasticity, 424
Inflation, 5, 82, 104, 104–114, 146–151
  accelerating, 316
  balance of payments and, 350–351
  biases overstating in CPI, 108
  biases understating in CPI, 110

Italy, military imperialism of, 343
ITO, *see* International Trade Organization
IWW, *see* Industrial Workers of the World

Jacobs, Irwin, 559
Japan
  aggregate economic concentration in, 550
  agricultural policy of, 748
  dumping by, 521
  economic development of, 389–391, 393–395
  economic growth of, 366
  economy of, 10, 13
  mercantilism of, 393
  military imperialism of, 343
  noninflationary finance in, 147
  planning in, 797–798
  productivity in, 797–798
  protectionism of, 393–394
  reconstruction of, 389, 391–393
  tariffs levied against, 335–336
Jevons, William Stanley, 399, 479
Job desirability, wage differentials and, 625–626
Job security, 614
Job training programs, 98–99
Johnson, Harry G., 371, 372n
Johnson, Lyndon B., 328
  budget deficit under, 137
  refusal to discontinue War on Poverty, 329
  rising inflation under, 306
Joint Economic Committee, 297
Jones & Laughlin case, 193
Juglar cycle, 186
Jureen, Lars, 429, 431
Jurisdictional strike, 611

Kahn, Herman, 793
Kautsky, Karl, 823, 825
Kendrick, John W., 367–368
Kennedy, Edward, 703
Kennedy, John F., 328, 329
  1960 campaign of, 304
  unions under, 613
Keynes, John Maynard, 3–4, 30, 92, 155–156, 214, 323, 328
  development of theory of, 368–369
  economic misfortune predicted by, 245n
  influence on New Deal, 193n
  on power of ideas, 294
  suppressed inflation and deflation and, 147

Keynes, John Neville, 155
Keynes effect, 277
Keynesian cross, 160 (fig.), 160–161
Keynesian economists, 214, 298n
Keynesian-monetarist debate, 297–298, 297–304
  independence of Federal Reserve and, 301–303
  rules versus discretion and, 303–304
  strength of monetary instruments and, 298–301
Keynesian theory, 92, 155–174
  antidepression implications of, 295–297
  causes of Great Depression and, 191–192
  contractionary and expansionary gaps and, 198–201
  of economic growth, 368–369
  equilibrium national income and, 168–172
  government purchases and, 166–167
  imports and exports and, 167–168
  monetarist and supply-side viewpoints compared with, 323–325
  neoclassical economics and, 155–157
  neoclassical view of equilibrium contrasted with, 172–173
  planned consumption expenditure and, 157–164
  planned investment expenditure and, 164–166
  see also Fiscal instruments; *see also* Monetary policy
Keynesian transmission mechanism, 262
"Keynes's Law," 328
Khomeini, Ruhallah, 12
Kinked demand curve, 539, 539 (fig.), 539–540
Kinney, G.R. Company, 702
Kitchin cycle, 186
Klein, Lawrence, 329, 330
Knights of Labor, 609
Koestler, Arthur, 826n
Kondratieff cycle, 186–187
Korea
  economic development of, 381n
  U.S. aid to, 382
Kottke, Frank J., 555n
Krushchev, Nikita, 12, 783, 795
Kuhn, Thomas, 480
Kuznets, Simon, 118
  on economic growth and income distribution, 371–372
Kuznets cycle, 186

L money supply, 222–223
Labor, 576, 596–628
  "black," 126
  combination with other resources, 53–54
  exploitation of, 364
  foreign, protection of, 726
  Japan and, 391, 392
  lack of international mobility of, 724
  market supply of, 602–603
  quantity and quality of, 53
  resource supply for all uses of, 579–581
  see also Union(s); Wage(s)
Labor demand, 94–95, 596–607, 618–621
  hiring in monopsonistic labor market and, 604–607
  hiring in purely competitive labor market and, 597–603
  market, 602–603
Labor force
  civilian, 96
  discouraged workers and, 96
  population trends and, 19
  see also Unemployment
Labor force participation rate, 21
  Civil Rights Act and, 612
  labor supply and, 579–580
Labor-Management Relations Act of 1947, *see* Taft-Hartley Act of 1947
Labor-Management Reporting and Disclosure Act of 1959, *see* Landrum-Griffin Act of 1959
Labor market
  competitive, 622–623
  discrimination and, 626
  monopsonistic, 623–624
  purely competitive, 597–603
  Social Security taxes and, 669–670
  unemployment in, 94–95
Labor market institutions, wage differentials and, 626
Labor movement, *see* Union(s)
Labor resources, 52, 52–54
Labor supply, 93 (fig.), 93–94, 579–581, 596–607
  age distribution and, 579
  baby boom and, 104
  hiring in monopsonistic labor market and, 604–607
  hiring in purely competitive labor market and, 597–603
  of individual, 599, 601–602
  labor force participation rate and, 579–580
  population size and, 579
  restricting, 617

Mature creditor, 349
Mature debtor, 348
MC, *see* Marginal cost
MDCs, *see* More developed countries
Means, Gardner, 552
Meany, George, 611n
Measure of economic welfare (MEW), 127
Mechanism basis, of economic systems, 10–12
Medium of exchange function of money, 218, 218–219
Meidner, Rudolf, 799
Meidner plan, 649, 799–800
Mellon, Andrew W., depression policies of, 192
Menger, Karl, 399, 479
Mental health, as criterion for evaluating economic systems, 14
Mercantilism, 91
  balance of payments and, 349
  Japanese, 393
  underdevelopment and, 365
Merger(s), 556, 556–560
  antitrust statutes and, 699–700
  concentration and competition and, 560
  conglomerate, 556–557, 560, 699–700, 703–704
  geographic market extension conglomerate, 556–557
  horizontal, 556, 560, 699
  motives for, 558–560
  product extension conglomerate, 556
  vertical, 556, 560, 699–700
Merger movements, 557–558
MEW, *see* Measure of economic welfare
Mexico
  economic growth of, 366
  gold inflation following conquest of, 149
Meyers, Mike, 748n
MFC, *see* Marginal factor cost
Microeconomics, 4, 4–5
Microeconomic unemployment, 5–6
Migration
  of farmers, 740–741
  restrictions on, 649
Mill, John Stuart, 87, 478n
  on economic growth, 370
Millage, 674
Minimum optimal scale effect entry barrier, 564, 564–565
Minimum wage, 622
Minimum wage rates, 622–624
  in competitive labor markets, 622–623

in monopsonistic labor market, 623–624
Ministry of International Trade and Industry (MITI), 395, 797
Minorities
  discrimination and, 689–690
  income distribution among, 13
  labor market discrimination and, 626
  poverty among, 679–681
  unemployment rates of, 100–101
  unions and, 611–612
Mises, Ludwig von, 804
Mishan, Ezra, on economic growth, 370
Mistaken causation, 47
MITI, *see* Ministry of International Trade and Industry
MNC, *see* Multinational corporation(s)
Mobil Oil Corporation, 557, 703
Model, 34
Monetarism, 252–268, 330–331
  of Friedman, 271
  Keynesian and supply-side viewpoints compared with, 323–325
  non-Friedman, 272
  see also Keynesian-monetarist debate; Quantity theory of money
Monetary accommodation, to supply shocks, 146
Monetary base, 244
Monetary Control Act of 1980, 240–241
Monetary growth rule, 304
Monetary instruments, 201, 239–244
  discount rate as, 242–243
  effects on real national income and product, 262
  expansionary, 248
  feedback to demand-for-money curve and, 262–264
  historical record of use of, 245–249
  without inflation, 261–264
  with inflation, 264–266
  inflationary expectations and, 264, 266
  interest rate changes and, 266
  interest rate limitations as, 243–244
  margin requirements as, 243
  monetary base and, 244
  money multiplier and, 244–245
  moral suasion and, 244
  open market operations as, 241–242
  reserve requirements as, 239–241
  strength of, 298–301
  transmission mechanisms and, 262
  see also Federal Reserve System
Monetary policy
  accommodation as, 301–303

as balance of payments solution, 351–352
  contractionary, 341
  discretionary, 330–331
  expansionary, 341
  foreign exchange rates and, 341
  monetarists' views on, 330–331
  supply shocks and, 313
  see also Bank(s); Keynesian-monetarist debate; Money
"Monetized debt," 222. *See also* Glass-Steagall Act
Money, 220, 217–223
  backing for, 148–149
  checking account balances as, 221–222
  coins as, 220
  commodity, 148
  currency as, 221
  defined, 220–222
  demand for, 258–260, 298–299, 300–301
  full-bodied, 148
  M1 measure of, 223
  M2, M3, and L measures of, 223
  medium of exchange function of, 218–219
  near, 223
  precautionary demand for, 259
  quantity theory of, 252–255, 480
  shifting demand for, 259–260
  speculative demand for, 258–259
  standard for deferred payment function of, 219–220
  store of purchasing power function of, 219
  transactions demand for, 259
  unit of account function of, 219
  velocity of, 253–255
Money-demand curve, *see* Demand-for-money curve
Money illusion theory, 280–281
  changes and, 282
  inflationary expectations and, 314–317
Money market, 257, 257–258
  demand for money in, 258–260
  equilibrium in, 260–261
  supply of money in, 260
Money market mutual funds, in money supply, 223
Money multiplier, 244, 244–245
Money supply, 222 (fig.), 222–223, 227–232
  controlling, 232
  deposit-contraction process and, 230–231

Selected Data for 100 Countries* (in ascending order of 1984 income per capita)

	Population (millions) Mid-1984	Average Annual Growth of Labor Force (percent) 1965–73	1973–84	Percentage of Labor Force in Agriculture 1965	1980	GNP per capita Dollars 1984	Average Annual Growth (percent) 1965–84[a]	Average Annual Rate of Inflation (percent) 1965–73	1973–84[b]
Low-income economies	2,389.5	2.3 w	2.2 w	78 w	70 w	260 w	2.8 w	1.6 w	5.9 w
China and India	1,778.3	2.3 w	1.8 w	—	70 w	290 w	3.3 w	1.0 w	4.0 w
Other low-income	611.2	2.0 w	3.8 w	78 w	71 w	190 w	0.9 w	4.6 w	14.9 w
Sub-Saharan Africa	257.7	2.2 w	2.2 w	86 w	79 w	210 w	−0.1 w	4.1 w	20.1 w
Ethiopia	42.2	2.2	2.2	86	80	110	0.4	1.8	4.4
Bangladesh	98.1	2.3	2.6	84	75	130	0.6	7.3	9.9
Mali	7.3	2.2	1.9	90	86	140	1.1	7.6	10.4
Zaire	29.7	1.9	2.3	82	72	140	−1.6	18.7	48.2
Burkina Faso	6.6	1.6	1.4	89	87	160	1.2	2.6	10.6
Nepal	16.1	1.6	2.3	94	93	160	0.2	5.8	8.1
Burma	36.1	1.3	1.3	64	53	180	2.3	2.8	6.0
Malawi	6.8	2.3	2.5	92	83	180	1.7	4.5	9.4
Niger	6.2	2.1	2.8	95	91	190	−1.3	4.0	11.5
Tanzania	21.5	2.6	2.6	92	86	210	0.6	3.2	11.5
Uganda	15.0	3.1	2.2	91	86	230	2.9	5.6	64.5
India	749.2	1.8	2.1	73	70	260	1.6	6.3	7.8
Madagascar	9.9	1.9	2.0	—	88	260	−1.6	4.1	14.4
Rwanda	5.8	2.7	2.8	94	93	280	2.3	7.7	10.5
China	1,029.2	2.6	1.6	—	69	310	4.5	−0.9	1.8
Kenya	19.6	3.3	2.8	86	81	310	2.1	2.3	10.8
Guinea	5.9	1.2	1.2	87	81	330	1.1	3.0	4.5
Ghana	12.3	1.4	1.5	61	56	350	−1.9	8.1	52.2
Sri Lanka	15.9	2.0	2.1	56	53	360	2.9	5.1	14.9
Sudan	21.3	2.8	2.4	82	71	360	1.2	7.2	19.3
Pakistan	92.4	2.3	3.3	60	55	380	2.5	4.8	10.8
Senegal	6.4	1.7	2.2	83	81	380	−0.5	3.0	9.0
Middle-income economies	1,187.6	2.2 w	2.6 w	57 w	44 w	1,250 w	3.1 w	5.5 w	38.0 w
Oil exporters	556.1	2.2 w	2.6 w	61 w	49 w	1,000 w	3.3 w	4.9 w	21.6 w
Oil importers	631.5	2.1 w	2.6 w	53 w	40 w	1,460 w	3.1 w	5.7 w	44.5 w
Sub-Saharan Africa	148.4	2.0 w	2.3 w	75 w	69 w	680 w	2.4 w	4.9 w	12.2 w
Lower middle-income	691.1	2.1 w	2.5 w	66 w	56 w	740 w	3.0 w	5.6 w	20.6 w
Liberia	2.1	2.1	3.6	79	74	470	0.5	1.5	6.7
Zambia	6.4	2.3	2.1	79	73	470	−1.3	5.8	10.4
Bolivia	6.2	1.8	2.5	54	46	540	0.2	7.5	54.5
Indonesia	158.9	1.9	2.3	71	57	540	4.9	63.0	17.4
Yemen Arab Rep.	7.8	1.0	2.1	79	69	550	5.9	—	12.6
Cote d'Ivoire	9.9	4.2	3.9	81	65	610	0.2	4.1	11.7
Philippines	53.4	2.1	3.1	58	52	660	2.6	8.8	12.9
Morocco	21.4	1.8	2.6	62	46	670	2.8	2.0	8.3
Honduras	4.2	2.4	3.3	68	61	700	0.5	2.9	8.6
El Salvador	5.4	3.2	2.9	59	56	710	−0.6	1.6	11.3
Papua New Guinea	3.4	1.9	2.0	87	76	710	0.6	6.6	6.8
Egypt, Arab Rep.	45.9	2.1	2.5	55	46	720	4.3	2.6	13.1
Nigeria	96.5	1.7	2.0	72	68	730	2.8	10.3	13.0
Zimbabwe	8.1	2.7	1.5	79	53	760	1.5	1.1	11.4
Cameroon	9.9	1.9	1.8	87	70	800	2.9	5.8	12.8
Nicaragua	3.2	3.0	3.2	57	47	860	−1.5	3.4	17.2
Thailand	50.0	2.4	3.0	82	70	860	4.2	2.5	8.2
Dominican Rep.	6.1	2.7	3.3	59	46	970	3.2	2.7	9.0
Peru	18.2	2.4	2.9	50	40	1,000	−0.1	10.1	56.7
Ecuador	9.1	3.1	2.9	55	39	1,150	3.8	6.2	17.8
Jamaica	2.2	0.7	2.3	37	33	1,150	−0.4	5.9	16.6
Guatemala	7.7	2.7	2.8	64	57	1,160	2.0	1.9	9.4
Turkey	48.4	1.8	2.0	75	58	1,160	2.9	10.5	42.4
Costa Rica	2.5	3.7	3.8	47	31	1,190	1.6	4.7	24.1
Paraguay	3.3	2.5	3.3	55	49	1,240	4.4	4.3	12.9
Tunisia	7.0	1.3	2.9	49	35	1,270	4.4	3.3	9.9
Colombia	28.4	3.1	2.8	45	34	1,390	3.0	10.8	23.8